HUMAN RESOURCE MANAGEMENT
FOUNDATIONS OF PERSONNEL

. . . .

FIFTH EDITION

HUMAN RESOURCE MANAGEMENT
FOUNDATIONS OF PERSONNEL

· · · · · · ·

JOHN M. IVANCEVICH

CULLEN PROFESSOR OF ORGANIZATIONAL
BEHAVIOR AND MANAGEMENT

UNIVERSITY OF HOUSTON

IRWIN

HOMEWOOD, IL 60430
BOSTON, MA 02116

Sponsoring editor: *Kurt Strand*
Developmental editor: *Laura Hurst Spell*
Project editor: *Lynn Basler*
Production manager: *Carma W. Fazio*
Designer: *Kay Fulton*
Art manager: *Kim Meriwether*
Cover & part illustrations: *Cathie Bleck*
Compositor: *Better Graphics, Inc.*
Typeface: *10/12 Berling*
Printer: *Von Hoffmann Press*

Library of Congress Cataloging-in-Publication Data

Ivancevich, John M.
   Human resource management : foundations of personnel / John M.
Ivancevich. — 5th ed.
     p.   cm.
   Rev. ed. of: Foundations of personnel. 4th ed. 1989.
   Includes bibliographical references and indexes.
   ISBN 0-256-09166-8
   1. Personnel management. 2. Personnel management — Case studies.
I. Ivancevich, John M. Foundations of personnel. II. Title.
HF5549.I88 1992
   658.3 — dc20   91–29571

Printed in the United States of America
1 2 3 4 5 6 7 8 9 0 VH 8 7 6 5 4 3 2 1

PREFACE

. . . .

The first edition of this text was published a decade ago. Bill Glueck was the author of the first edition, which was entitled *Foundations of Personnel*. It was Bill's belief that many faculty members wanted an uncluttered, straightforward, practically oriented text to use in their personnel courses. He provided a text that appealed to both instructors and students, and this accomplishment is a tribute to his ability to communicate his knowledge in a clear, intelligible way.

Students and faculty identify readability as a key strength of this book. It was never intended to be an encyclopedia or a compendium of human resource management tools, laws, or ideas. Instead, the intent was to provide a book that instructors and students could learn from, and which would stimulate their own ideas and keep them up to date on human resource management thinking and practice.

Bill's untimely passing prevented his further development and refinement of the text through the four revised editions. However, this edition, as will all future editions, incorporates many of Bill Glueck's ideas, orientation, and basic text structure in its examination of human resource management (HRM). His original crafting of a high-quality and teachable text remains noticeable in this fifth edition.

Human resource management is a necessary activity in all organizations. Its focal point is *people*. People are the lifeblood of organizations. Without them, there is no need for HRM systems, programs, or procedures. Because HRM activities involve people, they have to be finely tuned and properly implemented in order to achieve desired outcomes. The uniqueness of HRM lies in its emphasis on people in work settings and its concern for the well-being and comfort of the human resources in an organization. This edition focuses on people who work directly in HRM as specialists and those who, as employees (e.g., engineers, clerks, typists, machinists, chemists, teachers, nurses), are influenced by it.

In order to make the book interesting, scholarly, and practical, a number of pedagogical procedures were adopted:

1. Each chapter begins with a brief list of behavioral learning objectives, key terms that will be covered, and an outline of the chapter.

2. Each chapter is introduced by a Career Challenge, a short situation which emphasizes applied HRM techniques and issues. At various points in the chapter and at its conclusion, the situation is further developed.

3. Most chapters include the diagnostic model that serves as the integrative framework of this book.

4. In most chapters, the role played by a HR manager, specialist, or operating manager is described.

5. Most chapters include a Professional Profile. These real-life personal viewpoints of HRM managers or specialists answer the question: "What does someone actually working in the HRM field do?"

6. Most chapters conclude with recommendations for the most effective use of HRM in seven kinds of organizations, which differ on the basis of size (number of employees), complexity of products or services, and degree to which products or services change over time.

7. Each chapter summary provides students with

a handy, concise reference to the chapter's main points.

8. Cases and experiential exercises at the end of various chapters reflect HRM issues, concerns, and problems faced in organizations such as Supreme Textile Corporation; Goldman, Sachs & Co.; Southland Corporation; Eckel Industries; Dunkin' Donuts; Domino's Pizza; Alief Casting Corporation; and Toyota. The realism offered by the cases and exercises illustrates the vital role played by HRM in organizations of all sizes.

9. A list of key terms with page references is provided at the end of each chapter and a comprehensive glossary of key terms appears at the end of the book.

THE PARTS AND APPENDIXES

The fifth edition consists of six parts. Part One, Introduction to Human Resource Management and the Environment, contains four chapters. Chapter 1 defines the role or HRM in organizations. Chapter 2 provides the integrative model that is used throughout the book. Chapter 3 is a comprehensive treatment of equal employment opportunity laws and programs. Chapter 4 is a new chapter on international HRM issues, concerns, and practices.

Part Two, Analysis, Planning, and Staffing, contains four chapters, including Chapter 5: human resources planning, Chapter 6: job analysis and design, Chapter 7: recruitment, and Chapter 8: selection.

Part Three examines performance evaluation and compensation. Chapter 9 covers performance evaluation. Chapter 10 provides an overview of compensation. Chapter 11 discusses compensation methods and policies of personnel. Chapter 12 describes employee benefits and services.

Part Four, Training and Development for Better Performance, contains four chapters. Chapter 13 discusses orientation and training. Management and organizational development are covered in Chapter 14. Career planning and development is presented in Chapter 15. Discipline and the difficult employee are covered in Chapter 16.

Part Five, Labor Relations, includes Chapter 17 on labor unions and Chapter 18 on union organizing and collective bargaining.

Part Six, Employee Safety, Health, Work Life, and Evaluation, includes three chapters. Chapter 19 covers employee safety and health. Chapter 20 covers work schedules and the quality of work life. Chapter 21 discusses procedures for evaluating the HRM function.

Three main appendixes were added to the last edition and are retained in the fifth edition. Appendix A — Measuring the Human Resource Activities — was originally prepared by Jac Fitz-enz, Ph.D., president of the Saratoga Institute. This appendix spells out the reasons why measurement is important and how a measurement system for the HRM unit can be developed and styled.

Appendix B — Sources of Human Resource Management Information: Where to Find Facts and Figures — was originally prepared by Paul N. Keaton of the University of Wisconsin, LaCrosse, and has been updated for this edition. This appendix provides valuable sources of information that are useful in HRM.

Appendix C — Career Planning — was prepared by the author of the text. It examines the important steps involved in career planning that each person must accept responsibility for and initiate at the appropriate time. Each reader of the book must become actively involved in his or her own career plan.

NEW AND STRENGTHENED FEATURES

The dynamic changes in human resource management required some alteration, deletion, and expansion of material presented in the previous edition. Instructor and student comments were reviewed and carefully considered in the course of the revision. In addition, numerous human resource experts in organizations have been interviewed in the past decade. These endeavors resulted in some new features which add to Bill Glueck's original ideas and views about HRM:

- Coverage of the expanded role of HRM in strategic planning and implementation. The integration of HRM practices and strategy are spelled out.
- Discussion of cultural diversity, workforce skill requirements, and international competitiveness.
- An examination of organization culture and its impact on human resources.
- A look at President Bush's veto of the Civil Rights Act of 1990.

- Coverage of the Americans with Disabilities Act (ADA) and its intentions.
- An entire chapter is devoted to international HRM issues, concepts, and applications.
- Expanded and updated coverage of human resource information systems (HRIS).
- New material on multimethod job analysis.
- Lessons acquired from Japanese management practices that have impacted American job design procedures.
- More extensive coverage of the use of computer data bases as recruitment tools.
- A discussion on the problems of selecting expatriate managers for overseas assignments.
- Updated discussion of the legal aspects of performance evaluation.
- Expanded coverage of MBO as a viable motivational and performance evaluation method.
- The coverage on comparable worth has been extensively expanded.
- Specific and up-to-date examples of a variety of pay strategies.
- New material on eldercare, women and social security, housing and relocation help, and SEP-IRAs for small business pensions.
- Clearer explanation of training needs assessment and its importance.
- Discussion of learning objectives and how humanist, congnitivist, and behaviorist techniques view learning.
- Expanded discussion of careers and career advancement.
- Updated discussion of random drug testing and AIDS in the workplace.
- New discussion on foreign unions and unions in multinational corporations.
- Suggestions for new union leadership strategies are presented.
- Updated and expanded coverage of health care strategies and the smoke-free workplace.
- New discussion of employee-centered work redesign strategies.

Each of these new or modified features was designed to (1) stimulate student interest in HRM as a field of study and as a set of programs and procedures that influence people within organizations; (2) clearly illustrate that HRM is a dynamic, chang-

ing field; (3) show by example that what is being discussed has both a theoretical rationale (often a research base) and offers practical useful applications in the "real world" — the organization; and (4) provide instructors with material, statistics, and illustrations that can help make the classroom experience more exciting. In essence, the third edition was written for students and instructors alike.

A complete set of instructor's resource materials is available with this text. These materials include an instructor's manual with test bank, Irwin's Computerized Testing Software (a computerized version of the test bank), color acetates, and a lecture resource manual. Jean Hanebury carefully updated and revised the materials to help the instructor. In keeping with the times, a great many new international examples were added to the lecture resource manual.

Contributions of Two Special Colleagues

The importance of sharing ideas, debating issues, and comparing notes is what makes revision work on any text satisfying. In preparing this addition, two colleagues played a special role. Jim Phillips, Associate Professor of Management at the University of Houston, and Jean Hanebury, Assistant Professor of Management at Salisbury State University, prepared chapter material, reviewed suggestions, read galley and page proofs, and were involved in the development of the fifth edition. Their contributions made the revision work more pleasant, thorough, and rewarding for the author. Jim and Jean did an outstanding job of updating, modifying, and expanding the text. The result of this entire fifth edition effort is an even better product for the instructor and students.

ACKNOWLEDGMENTS

The fifth edition in its final form incorporated the efforts of numerous people. Special thanks are due to the following HRM managers and specialists who willingly provided ideas, information, and data:

David A. Allen
Internal Revenue Service
Gary Alston
Chief Financial Officer/Executive Vice President
The Temporary Connection

Paul J. Beddia
Vice President/Human Resources
Lincoln Electric

Betty Bessler
Vice President of Human Resources
Mary Kay Cosmetics, Inc.

Roger Blakeney
Director/Center for Executive Development
College of Business Administration
University of Houston

Lasha Dagg
British Columbia Telephone Company

R. William Flock
Senior Vice President of Human Resources
Jerrico

Jan T. Gillespie
Vice President Human Resources
Randall's Food Markets, Inc.

Mary Kale
Manager of Compensation
Bethlehem Steel Corporation

Timothy Mooney
Vice President, Eastern Region
Development Dimensions International

David M. Nicol
President
HCS Technology, Inc.

John L. Quigley, Jr.
Vice President for Human Resources
Dr Pepper/Seven Up, Inc.

Donna Seckar
Director, Career Services
Cabrini College

G. Dean Smith
Director, Industrial Relations
Dresser Industries, Inc.

Beverly Tarulli
BellSouth Corporation

R. Gary Thomas
Forest City Technologies, Inc.

Kenneth W. Tynes
Manager — Professional Employment
Cessna Aircraft Company

Gregory Watts, APM
Personnel Director
Chicago Switch Inc., a division of
Illinois Tool Works, Inc.

Helpful comments were provided for each edition by outstanding reviewers, many of whose ideas and recommendations were used. Their promptness, tactfulness, and knowledge about HRM were certainly appreciated. The lead reviewers for the fifth edition were:

Carol Anselm, *The University of Michigan-Flint*
Francis E. Bray, Jr., *Widener University*
Steve Byrd, *Southeast Missouri State University*
Joseph H. Culver, *University of Texas at Austin*
D. James Day, *Shawnee State University*
Richard L. Drury, *George Mason University*
Nina Gupta, *University of Arkansas*
Jean M. Hanebury, *Salisbury State University*
Martin F. Hanifin, *Prairie State College*
Coy A. Jones, *Memphis State University*
John Kohls, *Gonzaga University*
Edwin C. Leonard, *Indiana University-Purdue University at Fort Wayne*
John A. Lust, *Illinois State University*
Robert L. McGinty, *Eastern Washington University*
Robert C. Roth, *City University*
Kathryn J. Ready, *University of Minnesota*
Ted H. Shore, *Kennesaw State College*
Clyde A. Voris, *University of Cincinnati*
James M. Wilson, *University of Texas-Pan American*

My team of word processing, administrative detail, and special data base experts were Ginger Roberts, Jacque Franco, Dana Comer, and Eric Meimoun. Without the effort, input, and quality of work provided by my team, the work on this revision would be incomplete and would not have been done in a timely fashion. These four colleagues helped me make deadlines and juggle a schedule that is difficult to even put on a calendar.

Finally, I want to dedicate this fifth edition, like all of my other editions, to the memory of Bill Glueck. Bill was a hard worker whose contributions have endured long beyond his passing. The continued success of *Human Resource Management* was made possible only because he took the necessary pioneering step of developing an idea and converting it into an educationally sound text.

John M. Ivancevich

CONTENTS IN BRIEF

· · · · · · ·

CONTENTS

· · · · · · ·

PART

```
┌─┐
 2
└─┘
```

ANALYSIS, PLANNING, AND STAFFING 142

PART

┌─┐
│ 3 │
└─┘

PERFORMANCE EVALUATION
AND COMPENSATION   290

PART

┌ ┐
   4
└ ┘

TRAINING AND DEVELOPMENT FOR BETTER PERFORMANCE   472

PART

⌐5⌐

LABOR RELATIONS   618

HUMAN RESOURCE MANAGEMENT
FOUNDATIONS OF PERSONNEL

. . . .

INTRODUCTION TO HUMAN RESOURCE MANAGEMENT AND THE ENVIRONMENT

· · · · · · ·

Human resource management (HRM) is the effective management of people at work. HRM examines what can or should be done to make people both more productive and more satisfied with their working life.

This book has been written for all those interested in people working within organizations. Its goal is to help develop more effective managers and staff specialists who work directly with the human resources of organizations. This function is called *personnel*, *employee relations*, or *human resource management*. In this book, however, the term *human resource management* will be used.

Part 1 consists of four chapters. Chapter 1, Human Resource Management, introduces the reader to HRM and careers in HRM. The diagnostic approach to HRM is introduced in Chapter 2, A Diagnostic Approach to Human Resource Management. Chapter 2 also reviews behavioral science perspectives on people and how a knowledge of these can be used to influence employee effectiveness at work. In addition, the chapter discusses the ways managers use knowledge of environmental factors — the work setting, government regulations, and union requirements — to influence the performance of people at work. Chapter 3, The Law and Human Resource Management, describes the influences of the legal environment on HRM. A number of major laws and regulations are discussed in this chapter, as well as throughout the book. Chapter 4 introduces the notion of international human resource management. The "global enterprise" and the interdependence of nations have become a reality. Global markets, mass markets, and market freedom have fostered an international interest in managing human resources. Chapter 4 discusses the management of human resources in this new era of globalization.

1

HUMAN RESOURCE MANAGEMENT

· · · · · · ·

LEARNING OBJECTIVES

After studying this chapter, you should be able to:

· · ·

Define the term *human resource management*

· · ·

Describe the strategic importance of human resource management activities performed in organizations

· · ·

Explain what career opportunities are available in the HRM area

· · ·

Discuss the role that specialists and operating managers play in performing human resource management activities

· · ·

List three of the main objectives pursued by HRM units in organizations

CAREER CHALLENGE

*D*on Brokop has, over the past nine years, proved himself to be an outstanding shift supervisor at the Melody Machine Products Corp. plant in South Chicago. He has worked every shift, likes people, and recently was the winner of the Outstanding Plant Manager award. Don is now 34 years old and is beginning to look closely at his career plans. He believes that he needs to gain some experience in jobs other than production.

Last week a position opened at the plant for an assistant director of human resources. At first, Don gave no thought to the position; but later he asked his boss, Marty Fogestrom, about it. Marty encouraged Don to think his plans through and to consider whether he wanted to work in the human resource management area.

Don talked with plant colleagues about the new position, looked over the want ads in the *Chicago Tribune*, read *The Wall Street Journal*, and found a number of interesting news items concerning human resource management. He found that many different careers existed in the human resource management field. He realized that he had not really understood the job being done by Melody's department of human resources. What struck him the most was that issues, problems, and challenges concerning people are what human resources are about.

Here are a few of the news items that caught his eye:[1]

- As companies move toward the "New Europe" of 1992, many new HRM opportunities will emerge in Europe and the United States. The "Euro-Human Resource" manager will have job opportunities if he or she can speak English and one or two European languages, has international experience, is skilled in the human resource area, and is creative. Jobs in New York, Paris, Brussels, and in many other locations will be open for the Euro-Human Resource expert.
- Health insurance costs for medical treatment for AIDS are skyrocketing. Human resource specialists are searching for ways to keep up with these spiraling costs. Some businesses, because of the expense, are switching to medical programs that exclude AIDS from coverage. U.S. companies do not yet know how to deal with this serious personal issue and its costs.
- Training U.S. managers to work harder on quality is an important human resources responsibility. Every year millions of managers are trained to understand quality control, statistical control procedures, empowerment of the employees, the role of self-improvement in quality control, and the relationship between price, cost, and quality.
- Workplace literacy is a cause célèbre of human resource specialists. These specialists are now charged with finding methods and procedures for improving the literacy of workers. Waiting for educators to solve the problem of 28 million Americans who are illiterate is not a viable solution. Human resource managers must develop training, exercises, and procedures to address the literacy problem of the U.S. work force.
- Benchmarking, or the comparison of a business function, like human resource management, across units or companies, is a performance evaluation procedure. How does the human resource area at Xerox function in comparison to Apple Computer? Or how does our human resource department compare with our financial administration unit? Human resource managers are being asked to develop benchmark assessment instruments and techniques.
- The HR (human resource) department at the Spring Hill, Tennessee, General Motors Saturn plant has helped create a harmonious team of engineers, managers, and production workers. It is teamwork that had to be created to produce a high-performing, excellent quality car to compete with such fierce competitors as Toyota and Honda.
- Since over 60 percent of U.S. mothers work outside the home today and over half of them have children under a year old, child care is a top-priority issue for human resource managers.

(continued on next page)

CAREER CHALLENGE
(*continued*)

However, it should be noted that child care is not a new concern. The first child-care center opened in New York City on May 23, 1827.

- More lawsuits are being filed by employees than ever before. Work-related fears, distress, and safety are at the top of the list in employee-against-employer lawsuits. HR departments are being asked by management to develop methods, procedures, rules, and programs to slow down this flood of lawsuits. Not only in the United States, but across the world, sexual harassment is a major human resource management and personal concern. For years in Japan, posters of scantily clad women decorated male-dominated corporate and government offices. Male bosses would pat their secretaries on the shoulders or bottom. Male workers would regularly crack lewd jokes. A citizen's group called "Sexual Harassment in the Workplace Network" has been formed to demand that sexual harassment be stopped. Shoichiro Irmajiri, formerly the president of Honda America Manufacturing, says he learned valuable lessons in the United States about how to combat sexual harassment. He has brought new thinking and procedures to Japan to help Honda develop a grievance policy to give Japanese women a way to air complaints.

Don thought about his recent conversations, his career plans, the news stories, and the challenges of moving from production to human resource management. He thought his experience in supervisory management would be helpful if he were fortunate enough to land the job, but he wondered if he was qualified for this kind of job. He was confident and considered his college education and experience invaluable. He wanted new challenges. Then he learned through the grapevine that the job was his if he wanted to make the move. (If you were Don, would you be likely to make this kind of career shift? Don's decision will be presented at the end of this chapter.)

P eople; human resources; making organizations more aware of human resources; being in the people business — these words and thoughts are common in our modern society. Today bromides and panaceas for solving people problems are being replaced by a total, professional approach to **human resource management.** Don Brokop is considering the challenges associated with this new wave of professional treatment and concern for people within organizations. Organizations are definitely in the people business — Don certainly saw this after only a quick review of a few news stories.

This book will focus on people in organizational settings. The entire book will be concerned with the employees of organizations — the clerks, technicians, supervisors, managers, and executives. Large, medium, and small organizations, such as IBM, Weaver Production, Fiesta Supermarket, Procter & Gamble, Victoreen, Medco, Greensway Pharmacies, Tenneco, and TRW Systems, understand clearly that to grow, prosper, and remain healthy, they must optimize the return on investment of all resources — financial and human.

When an organization is really concerned about people, its total philosophy, climate, and tone will reflect this belief. In this book, HRM is used to describe the function that is concerned with people — the employees. Human resource management is the function performed in organizations that facilitates the most effective use of people (employees) to achieve organizational and individual goals.

Terms such as *personnel, human resource management, industrial relations,* and *employee development* are used by different individuals to describe the unit, department, or group concerned about people. The term *human resource management* is now widely used, though many people still refer to a *personnel department.* In order to be up-to-date, the more modern term, *human resource management* will be used throughout the book. It is a term that reflects the increased concern both society and organizations have for people. Today employees — the human resource — demand more of their jobs and respond favorably to management activities that give them greater control of their lives.

Human resource management consists of numerous activities, including:

- Equal employment opportunity compliance.
- Job analysis.
- Human resource planning.
- Employee recruitment, selection, and orientation.
- Performance evaluation and compensation.
- Training and development.
- Labor relations.
- Safety, health, and quality of work life.

These activities are topics of the various chapters in this book. They also appear as elements in the diagnostic model of the HRM function that is used throughout the text. (This model is described in Chapter 2.)

The following three things should be stressed about HRM at the outset:

1. *It is action oriented* — Effective HRM focuses on action rather than on record-keeping, written procedure, or rules. Certainly, HRM uses rules, records, and policies, but it stresses action. HRM emphasizes the solution of employment problems to help achieve organizational objectives and facilitate employee development and satisfaction.

2. *It is individual oriented* — Whenever possible, HRM treats each employee as an *individual* and offers services and programs to meet the individual's needs. McDonald's, the fast-food chain, has gone so far as to give its chief personnel executive the title of vice president of individuality.

3. *It is worldwide oriented* — HRM is not only an American function or activity; it is being practiced efficiently and continuously in Mexico, Poland, and Hong Kong. Many organizations around the world treat people fairly, with respect, and with sensitivity. Thus, HRM practices in Brazil can be reviewed by U.S. practitioners to determine if there may be some principles that can be applied or modified to work in the United States.

4. *It is future oriented* — Effective HRM is concerned with helping an organization achieve its objectives in the future by providing for competent, well-motivated employees. Thus, human resources need to be incorporated into an organization's long-term strategies.

A BRIEF HISTORY OF HUMAN RESOURCE MANAGEMENT

The history of HRM can be traced to England, where masons, carpenters, leather workers, and other craftspeople organized themselves into guilds. They used their unity to improve their work conditions.[2] These guilds became the forerunners of trade unions.

The field further developed with the arrival of the Industrial Revolution in the latter part of the 18th century, which laid the basis for a new and complex industrial society. In simple terms, the Industrial Revolution began with the substitution of steam power and machinery for time-consuming hand labor. Working conditions, social patterns, and the division of labor were significantly altered. A new kind of employee, a boss, who wasn't necessarily the owner as had usually been the case in the past, became a power broker in the new factory system. With these changes also came a widening gap between workers and owners.

The drastic changes in technology, the growth of organizations, the rise of unions, and government concern and intervention concerning working people resulted in the development of personnel departments. There is no specific date assigned to the appearance of the first personnel department, but around the 1920s more and more organizations seemed to take note of and do something about the conflict between employees and management.[3] Early personnel administrators were called *welfare secretaries*. Their job was to bridge the gap between management and operator (worker); in other words, they were to speak to workers in their own language and then recommend to management what had to be done to get the best results from employees.

The early history of personnel still obscures the importance of the HRM function to management. Until the 1960s, the personnel function was considered to be concerned only with blue-collar or operating employees. It was viewed as a record-keeping unit that handed out 25-year tenure pins and coordinated the annual company picnic. Peter Drucker, a respected management scholar and consultant, made a statement about personnel management that reflected its blue-collar orientation. Drucker stated that the job of personnel was "partly a file clerk's job, partly a housekeeping job, partly a social worker's job, and partly fire fighting, heading off union trouble."[4]

The HRM function today is concerned with much more than simple filing, housekeeping, and record-keeping.[5] When HRM strategies are integrated within the organization, HRM plays a major role in clarifying the firm's human resource problems and develops solutions to them. It is oriented toward action, the individual, worldwide interdependence, and the future. Today it would be difficult to imagine any organization achieving and sustaining effectiveness without efficient HRM programs and activities. The strategic importance of HRM to the survival of an organization will become clearer as we move into the book.

For years the HRM function had not been linked to the corporate profit margin or what is referred to as the *bottom line*. The role of HRM in the firm's strategic plan and overall strategy was usually couched in fuzzy terms and abstractions. HRM was merely a tag-along unit with people-oriented plans, but was not a major part of the planning and strategic thinking process. Today, because of the recognition of the crucial importance of people, HRM is increasingly becoming a major player in developing strategic plans.[6] Organizational plans and strategies and human resource plans and strategies are inextricably linked. The HRM strategies must reflect clearly the organization's strategy with regard to people, profit, and overall effectiveness. The human resource manager is expected to play a crucial role in improving the skills of employees and the firm's profitability. In essence, HRM is now viewed as a "profit center" and not simply a "cost center."

The strategic importance of HRM means that as a "profit center" a number of key concepts must be applied. Some of these concepts are:

- Analyzing and solving problems from a profit-oriented, not just a service-oriented, point of view.
- Assessing and interpreting expenses or benefits of such HRM issues as productivity, salaries and benefits, recruitment, training, absenteeism, overseas relocation, layoffs, meetings, and attitude surveys.
- Using planning models that include realistic, challenging, specific, and meaningful goals.
- Preparing reports on HRM solutions to problems encountered by the firm.
- Training the human resources staff and emphasizing the strategic importance of HRM and the importance of making contributions to the firm's profits.

The increased strategic importance of HRM means that human resource specialists must show that they make contributions to the goals and mission of the firm.[7] The actions, language, and performance of the HRM function must be measured, precisely communicated, and evaluated. The new strategic positioning of HRM means that accountability must be taken seriously.

ORGANIZATIONAL EFFECTIVENESS

HRM activities play a major role in ensuring that an organization will survive and prosper. Organizational effectiveness or the lack of it is described in this book in terms of such criteria and components as performance, legal compliance, employee satisfaction, absenteeism, turnover, scrap rates, grievance rates, and accident rates. In order for a firm to survive and prosper, and earn a profit, reasonable goals in each of these components must be achieved.[8] In most organizations, effectiveness is measured by the balance of such complementary characteristics as reaching goals, employing the skills and abilities of employees efficiently, and ensuring the influx and retention of well-trained and motivated employees.

Around the world, managers recognize that human resources deserve attention because they are a significant factor in top-management strategic decisions that guide the organization's future operations. Three crucial elements are needed for firms to be effective: mission and strategy, organizational structure, and HRM.[9] However, it is important to remember that people do the work and create the ideas that allow the organization to survive. Even the most capital-intensive, well-structured organizations need people to run them.

People limit or enhance the strengths and weaknesses of an organization. Current changes in the environment are often related to changes in human resources, such as shifts in the composition, education, and work attitudes of employees. The HRM function should provide for or respond to these changes.

One problem top management has in making strategic planning decisions regarding people is that all other resources are evaluated in terms of money, and at present, in most organizations, people are not. There has been a push toward human resource accounting, which would place dollar values on the human assets of organizations.[10] Professional sports teams, such as the New York Yankees, Boston

Celtics, and Washington Redskins, place a dollar value on athletes. They then depreciate these values over the course of time.

If the **objectives** of HRM are to be accomplished, top managers will have to treat the human resources of the organization as the *key* to effectiveness. To do this — to accomplish the important objectives of HRM — management must regard the development of superior human resources as an essential competitive requirement that needs careful planning, hard work, and evaluation.

OBJECTIVES OF THE HRM FUNCTION

The contributions HRM makes to organizational effectiveness include the following:

- Helping the organization reach its goals.
- Employing the skills and abilities of the work force efficiently.
- Providing the organization with well-trained and well-motivated employees.
- Increasing to the fullest the employee's job satisfaction and self-actualization.
- Developing and maintaining a quality of work life that makes employment in the organization desirable.
- Communicating HRM policies to all employees.
- Helping to maintain ethical policies and behavior.
- Managing change to the mutual advantage of individuals, groups, the enterprise, and the public.

Helping the Organization Reach Its Goals

Bruce R. Elly, vice president of personnel at Pfizer, Inc., expresses the role of the HRM function this way:

The HR function is a very key portion of the organization today. That message is coming across consistently in surveys of CEOs. So far, the emphasis has been on doing things right. The real jump in effectiveness will come when the focus is first placed on doing the right things. I can't imagine how a HR functions without thoroughly knowing the business issues of its organization. Every business issue has HR implications.[11]

Employing the Skills and Abilities of the Work Force Efficiently

Clyde Benedict, the chief personnel officer for Integon Corporation, stated this purpose somewhat differently. He said the purpose is "to make people's strengths productive, and to benefit customers, stockholders, and employees. I believe this is the purpose Walt Disney had in mind when he said his greatest accomplishment was to build the Disney organization with its own people."

Providing the Organization with Well-Trained and Well-Motivated Employees

This is an effectiveness measure for HRM. David Babcock, chairman of the board and chief executive officer of the May Company, phrases this purpose as "building and protecting the most valuable asset of the enterprise: people." Andrew Grove is the president of Intel, a high-technology company, who considers training and motivation to be extremely important for accomplishing performance objectives. He stated:

> The single most important task of a manager is to elicit peak performance from his subordinates. So if two things limit high output, a manager has two ways to tackle the issue: through training and motivation. . . . How does a manager motivate his subordinates? For most of us, the word implies doing something to another person. But I don't think that can happen, because motivation has to come from within somebody. Accordingly, all a manager can do is create an environment in which motivated people can flourish.[12]

So HRM's effectiveness measure — its chief effectiveness measure, anyway — is to provide the right people at the right phase of performing a job, at the right time for the organization.

Increasing to the Fullest the Employees' Job Satisfaction and Self-Actualization

Thus far, the emphasis has been on the organization's needs. But unlike computers or cash balances, employees have feelings of their own. For employees to be productive, they must feel that the job is right for their abilities and that they are being treated equitably. For many employees, the job is a major source of personal identity. Most of us spend the majority of our waking hours at work and getting to and from work. Thus, our identity is tied closely to our job.

Satisfied employees are not *automatically* more productive. However, unsatisfied employees do tend to quit more often, to be absent more frequently, and to produce lower-quality work than satisfied workers. Nevertheless, both satisfied and dissatisfied employees may perform equally in quantitative terms, such as processing the same number of insurance claims per hour.

Developing and Maintaining a Quality of Work Life That Makes Employment in the Organization a Desirable Personal and Social Situation

This purpose is closely related to the previous one. Quality of work life is a somewhat general concept, referring to several aspects of the job experience. These include such factors as management and supervisory style, freedom and autonomy to make decisions on the job, satisfactory physical surroundings, job safety, satisfactory working hours, and meaningful tasks. Basically, a sound quality of work life (QWL) program assumes that a job and the work environment should be structured to meet as many of the worker's needs as possible.

Jac Fitz-enz, president of Saratoga Institute, believes that U.S. business has done a good job of dealing with many organizational inefficiencies, such as poor productivity, spiraling benefits costs, and poor quality.[13] He believes that people need to have a stake in their work and that employees will respond when employers pay attention to their personal needs and their work situations. He cites the example of Tandem Computers, which builds a strong bond between the development of a good QWL and the retention of employees. He states that, at Tandem, "the critical difference seems to be trust. . . . Technology and trust have turned Tandem into a miniversion of the global village." Tandem has paid attention to the personal and social situation of each employee, and, as a consequence, it has one of the lowest turnover rates in the Silicon Valley.

Community HRM Policies to All Employees

Chuck Kelly, director of a human resources of a small manufacturing firm, expressed this objective as follows: "We can't afford to not communicate our programs, policies, and procedures fully. There are effectiveness, personal development, and legal reasons why everyone in the firm has to be HRM knowledgeable. Communicating HRM programs just does not happen; a manager has to work at it constantly." HRM's responsibility is "to communicate in the fullest possible sense both in tapping ideas, opinions, and feelings of customers, noncustomers, regulators, and other external publics, as well as in understanding the views of internal human resources. The other facet of this responsibility is communicating managerial decisions to relevant publics in their own language."

Closely related to communication within the organization is representation of the organization to those outside: trade unions and local, state, and federal government bodies that pass laws and issue regulations affecting HRM. The HRM department must also communicate effectively with other top-management people (e.g., marketing, production, research and development) to illustrate what it can offer these areas in the form of support, counsel, and techniques, and increase its contribution to the overall strategic mission and goals of the organization.

Helping to Maintain Ethical Policies and Behavior

Managers throughout the world stress the importance of visionary leadership. The 21st-century chief executive officer must be a leader who inspires managers to achieve ambitious goals. However, a study of 1,500 senior managers in 20 nations conducted by Korn/Ferry and the Columbia University Graduate School of Business emphasized the importance of vision as well as ethics.[14] The study found that the ideal CEO in the year 2000 must be above reproach because impeccable ethical standards are indispensable to a firm's success and credibility.

Survival, growth, and profit are each very important and necessary goals of organizations. However, addressing ethical abuses is an important responsibility of HRM and every business manager. Self-interest and profits at any cost are not acceptable goals for HR specialists. Mary Parker Follette, a management writer and scholar, captured what the HRM area needs to accomplish when she stated that we need leaders who "do not conceive their tasks as that of fulfilling purpose, but as also that of finding ever larger purposes to fulfill and more fundamental values to be reached."[15]

Managing Change to the Mutual Advantage of Individuals, Groups, the Organization, and the Public

In the past decade, there has been rapid, turbulent, and often strained development in the relationship between employers and employees. New trends and changes have occurred in telecommuting, paternity leave, QWL programs, spouse-relocation assistance, gain-sharing, benefit cost-sharing, union-management negotiations, testing, and many other HRM areas of interest. Nearly all of these trends and changes can be traced to the emergence of new lifestyles and an aging population.[16] What these changes mean to HR managers is that new, flexible approaches must be initiated and used effectively without jeopardizing the survival of the organization. HRM managers must cope with trends and changes, while still contributing to the organization. Jerry Holder, senior vice president for Marion Laboratories, makes a crucial point about HR managers when he says: "Those who fail to measure up will suffer the same fate as technical staff who become obsolete — downgrades, reassignment, and even replacement."[17]

Robert B. Kurtz, chairman of Manufacturing Studies Group, in the following statement called specific attention to the need for managing change:

> Relatively few domestic manufacturers have devised effective responses to ensure success in the new manufacturing environment. . . . Without changes in corporate culture, organizational structure, and human resource management, new technologies will not produce the results needed for competitive manufacturing. These changes are far more difficult than plugging in a new machine — they require creative thinking, new attitudes and a willingness to embrace change.[18]

These are the most significant and widely accepted HRM objectives. There are, of course, other objectives and different ways of stating them. But these can serve as guidelines for the HRM function in organizations. Effective HR departments set specific, measurable objectives to be accomplished within specified time limits. Chapter 21 shows how this is done. Other chapters discuss cost/benefit analyses to determine whether measurable objectives have been met.

WHO PERFORMS HRM ACTIVITIES

Certain facts are known about the professional in HRM work. In 1990, there were over 450,000 people employed in HR work in the United States. About 60 percent of them work in the private sector, 30 percent in the public sector, and the remaining 10 percent in the third sector (health, education, the arts, libraries, voluntary organizations, and so on). There has been about a 5 percent growth in HRM positions each year since 1970.[19]

Delegation of HRM duties has changed over time. In most organizations two groups perform HRM activities: HR managers/specialists and operating managers. Operating managers (supervisors, department heads, vice presidents) are involved in HRM activities since they are responsible for effective utilization of *all* the resources at their disposal. The human resource is a very special kind of resource. If it is improperly managed, effectiveness declines more quickly than with other resources. And in all but the most capital-intensive organizations, the people investment has more effect on organizational effectiveness than resources such as money, materials, and equipment.

Therefore, operating managers spend considerable time managing people. In the same way an operating manager is personally responsible if a machine breaks down and production drops, he or she must see to the training, performance, and satisfaction of employees. Research indicates that a large part of an operating manager's day is spent in unscheduled and scheduled meetings, telephone conversations, and solving problems that directly impact people. The manager, through constant contact with many different people, attempts to solve problems, reach decisions, and prevent future difficulties.[20]

Smaller organizations usually have no HR unit, so the operating managers have many HRM responsibilities, such as scheduling work, recruitment and selection, and compensating people. As the organization increases in size, the operating manager's work is divided up, and some of it becomes specialized. HRM is one such specialized function. Usually the manager of a unit first assigns an assistant to coordinate certain HRM matters. HR specialists are employed in organizations with about 100–150 employees, and an HR department is typically created when the number of employees reaches 200–500, depending on the nature of the organization.

The Interaction of Operating and HR Managers

With two sets of employees (operating managers and HR specialists) making HRM decisions, there can be conflict.[21] Conflict occurs because operating and HR managers sometimes differ on who has authority for what decisions, or there may be other differences between operating and HR managers. They have different orientations, called *line* and *staff*, which have different objectives. A *staff* person/manager/specialist typically supports the primary functions such as marketing and production by providing advice, counsel, and information. The picture of organizational life portrayed by a textbook assumes that the staff does not wield direct authority over the line manager. *Line* managers have the authority to make final decisions concerning their operations. However, the specific distinction between line and staff is not as clear-cut in organizations. More often than not, members of the HR unit have much to say about various programs and activities. Consider recruitment and selection practices and the crucial role played by HR specialists. Line managers are generally not familiar with the legal requirements concerning recruitment and selection. Therefore, they welcome the HR experts' involvement and direct decision-making authority in final decisions.

The conflict between HR employees and operating managers is most pressing when the decisions must be joint efforts on such issues as discipline, physical working conditions, termination, transfer, promotion, and employment planning. Research indicates that operating managers and HR specialists differ on how much authority personnel should have over job design, labor relations, organization planning, and certain rewards, such as bonuses and promotions.[22]

One way to minimize the conflict between operating managers and HR employees is to show the operating manager that it is beneficial to use HRM techniques and programs. Daniel Ewing of Boston Gas Company urges HR managers to involve operating managers in the design of human resource systems. "It's amazing how their attitudes change when they are asked to help create a system — that will serve them," he said, then added jokingly, "You start talking to them about their problems, and you can't shut them up."[23]

John W. O'Brien of Digital Equipment Corporation (DEC) also believes that working together can reduce unproductive conflict between operating managers and HR employees. He said that at DEC, "They determine what human resources will be required to attain their objectives, taking environmental factors in consideration."[24]

Another way to work out actual or potential conflicts of this type so that the employee is not caught in the middle is to try to assign the responsibility for some HRM decisions exclusively to operating managers and others exclusively to HR specialists. Some observers feel that this is what is happening, and HRM is gaining more power at the expense of the operating managers.[25]

Another approach is to train both sets of managers in how to get along and how to make better joint decisions. This training is more effective if the organization has a career pattern that rotates its managers through both operating and staff positions, such as those in HRM. This rotation helps each group understand the other's problems.

The Role of the HR Manager or Specialist

When an organization creates specialized positions for the HRM function, the primary responsibility for accomplishing the HRM objectives described earlier in the chapter is assigned to the HR managers. But the chief executive is still responsible for the accomplishment of HRM objectives. At all levels in the organization, HR and operating executives must work together to help achieve objectives. The chief HR executive promotes the HRM function within the organization to employees and operating executives both.

The ideal HR executive understands the objectives and activities of HRM. He or she has had some experience as an operating manager, as well as experience in HRM. The ideal HR manager has superior interpersonal skills and is creative. It is vital that operating management perceives the HR manager as a manager first, interested in achieving organizational goals, and as a specialist adviser in HR matters second. This makes the HR executive a member of the management team and gives the function a better chance to be effective.

HRM's Place in Management

How important is HRM in the top-management hierarchy? In the past, HRM clearly was not very important. As in Drucker's statement, personnel, as it was called, was "work suitable for a file clerk." This view has changed. Articles have proclaimed that HRM is the fast track to the top and HRM directors are the new corporate heroes.[26] In fact, HRM is advancing rapidly as a vital force in top management. At some firms, such as RCA, United Parcel Service, and Brown and Williamson Tobacco, the top HR executive is on the board of directors.

What appears to be occurring in an increasing number of firms is recognition that the HR department has a responsibility to be a proactive, integral component of management and the strategic planning process.[27] This new emphasis does not replace the competence required in counseling, consulting, industrial relations, or managerial control systems. Instead, it is an orientation that states that HR department must do more than simply sit and listen when strategic management plans are nurtured and developed. The department must determine a strategic direction for its own activities that will make it a proactive arm of the management team. To accomplish this new role, HRM must ascertain specific organizational needs for the use of its competence, evaluate the use and satisfaction among other departments, and educate management and employees about the availability and use of HRM department services. The long-range goal of any HRM strategic plan must be to build on the firm's strengths.[28]

As HR executives play an increasingly dominant role at the organization's strategic planning table they must educate the members of other departments or units about the human resource implications of various decisions.[29] Thus, the HR executive must be familiar with other aspects of the organization — investments, advertising, marketing, production control, computer utilization, research, and development.

HR DEPARTMENT OPERATIONS

Both the makeup and procedures of HR departments have changed over time. HR units vary by size and sector, but most organizations keep them small. One study found that in the largest headquarters unit there were 150 people.[30]

The number of HR specialists in relation to the number of operating employees, or the *personnel ratio*, varies in different industries. According to one study, the national average is 1 HR specialist per 200 employees. Some industries — construction, agriculture, retail and wholesale trade, and services — have fewer personnel specialists than the average. Others — public utilities, durable goods manufacturing, banking, insurance, and government — have an above-average ratio.

Clarifying Meaningful HRM Objectives

The objectives of an organization or department are the ends it seeks to achieve — its reason for existence. Eight objectives of the HRM function have already been pointed out, but most of these objectives were stated in very general terms.

To help the organization achieve these objectives, more specific statements are developed in larger, most middle-sized, and some smaller organizations. For example, suppose that one of a number of HRM objectives is: To increase our employees' job satisfaction with advancement opportunities.

How can this objective be achieved? First, management must measure employee satisfaction with advancement opportunities. Management could design an attitude survey to ask employees how satisfied they are with facets of their jobs. The key issue is to determine the degree of job satisfaction associated with advancement opportunities. Next, the organization could use the survey information to develop plans to correct any deficiencies in advancement opportunity satisfaction. These plans are called *policies* and *procedures/rules*. Exhibit 1–1, which illustrates the relationship between the objectives, policies, and rules, indicates that objectives are the most general factor. For example, job satisfaction for employees is an objective. An organization makes an objective more specific by developing policies.

HRM Policy

A **policy** is a general guide to decision making. Policies are developed for past problem areas or for potential problem areas that management considers important enough to warrant policy development. Policies free managers from having to make decisions in areas in which they have less competence or on matters with which they do not wish to become involved. Policies ensure some consistency in behavior and allow managers to concentrate on decisions in which they have the most experience and knowledge.

After the broadest policies are developed, some organizations develop **procedures** and *rules*. These are more specific plans that limit the choices of managers and employees, as Exhibit 1–1 shows. Procedures and rules are developed for the same reason as policies.

HRM Procedure

A *procedure* or *rule* is a specific direction to action. It tells a manager how to do a particular activity. In large organizations, procedures are collected and put into manuals, usually called *standard operating procedures (SOPs)*.

EXHIBIT 1-1   Relationship among Objectives, Policies, and Rules

---

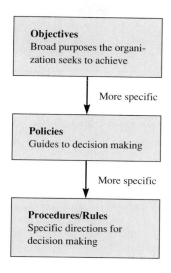

Organizations must be careful to have consistent decision making that flows from a well-developed, but not excessive, set of policies and procedures. Some organizations, in effect, eliminate managerial initiative by trying to develop policies and procedures for everything. Procedures should be developed only for the most vital areas.

Organization of the HR Department

In most organizations, the chief HR executive reports to the top manager; in the larger firms, perhaps to an executive vice president. Exhibit 1–2 shows the way HRM is organized in a large insurance business. The vice president of human resources has responsibility and authority for all HRM activities within the firm. Specific attention is given to the insurance firm's employee relations organization and job duties in Exhibit 1–3. Notice the wide range of HRM activities carried out in this unit. The activities range from developing attitude surveys to preparing a report on the number of maternity leaves taken. In some other organizations, HRM is divided into two departments, personnel and labor relations.

In medium-sized (500 to 5,000 employees) and smaller (under 500 employees) organizations, HRM and other functions, such as public relations, may be part of a single department.

Thirty percent of all HR managers work for local, state, and federal governments. Exhibit 1–4 is an example of HR organization within the structure of a typical state government. The legislature and the governor set policy for departments, subject to review by the courts, and then appoint an HR commission that is headed by an HR officer. This central HR unit is a policymaking body that serves a policy, advisory,

EXHIBIT 1-2   Organization of Large Insurance Company

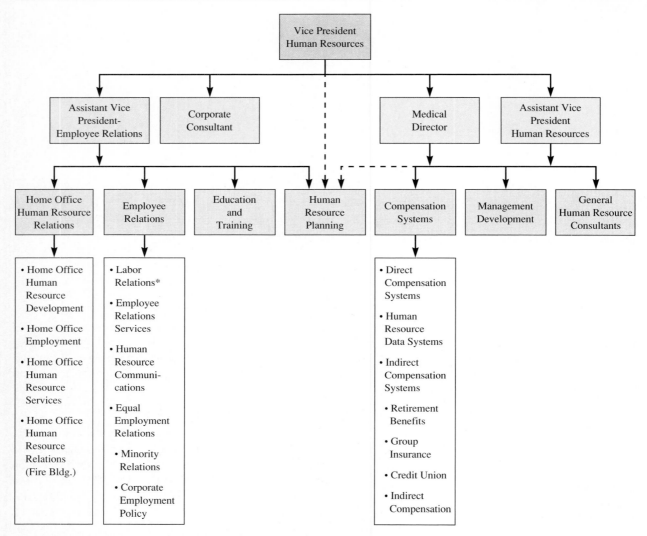

* Manager of function is also assigned general human resource consultant responsibilities.

and regulatory purpose similar to that of the home-office HR unit of a business. At the federal government level, this personnel commission is called the U.S. Civil Service Commission.

In nonprofit organizations, such as hospitals and universities, HRM typically is a unit in the business office, as shown in Exhibit 1–5. More will be said about differences in HRM work in these three settings in Chapter 2. HR specialists are

EXHIBIT 1-3   The Organization of the Insurance Company's Employee Relations Division

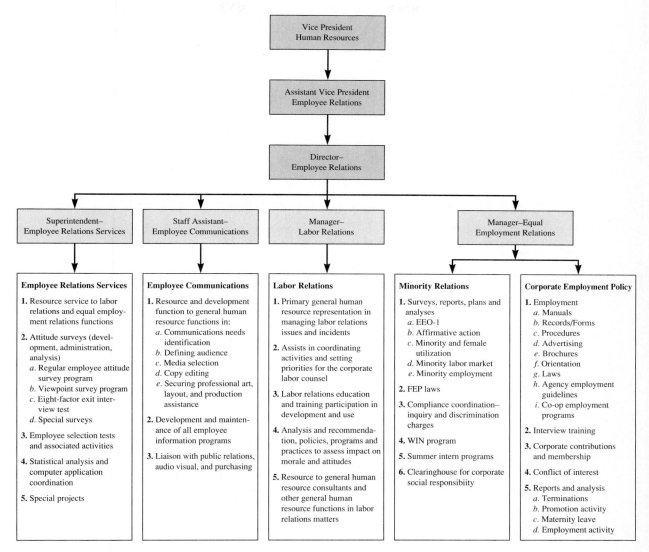

Note: Manager of function is also assigned general human resource management consultant responsibilities.

usually located at the headquarters of an organization, but larger organizations may divide the HRM function. Usually the largest group is at headquarters, but HR advisers may be stationed at unit and divisional levels. In this case, the headquarters unit consists of specialists or experts on certain topics and advisers to top management, while the unit-level HR people are generalists who serve as advisers to operating managers at their level.

EXHIBIT 1-4   State Government Structure

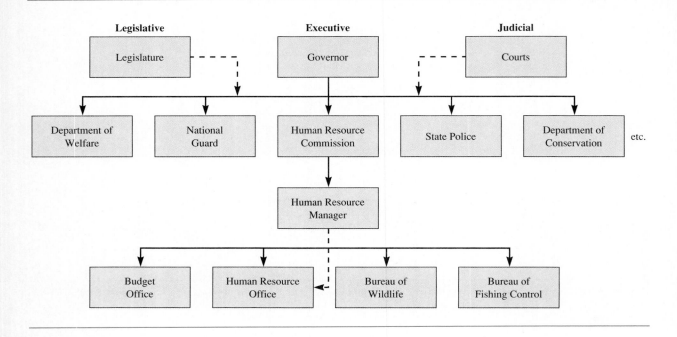

PLAN OF THE BOOK

This book is designed to show how HR departments work, to discuss the importance of HR activities in organizations of any size, and to describe the challenges that exist for HR department employees. The chapters (and many of the sections) begin with an HRM in Action vignette, an example from a real organization that describes an HRM problem or issue. Solving the problem or issue is an HRM activity. This activity is explained, and then the type of HRM staff who performs this activity is discussed. The role of top management in the activity and the interrelationship between operating and HR managers are described and analyzed.

In each chapter (or group of chapters), the development of the activity is analyzed. Some HRM activities are quite well established, while others are just emerging. The activity being considered is assigned to one of four stages through which HRM activities seem to evolve (see Exhibit 1–6). The activity's stage can be assessed by examining the literature on the topic.

It is most likely that the HRM activities of career pathing, two-tier compensation, outplacement, drug testing, and preventive health are in Stage I. Stage II includes systematic evaluation of the total HRM function and formal orientation. Typical activities in Stage III are performance evaluation and informal management development. Stage IV functions include many employment and compensation activities.

EXHIBIT 1-5   Organization of a County Hospital

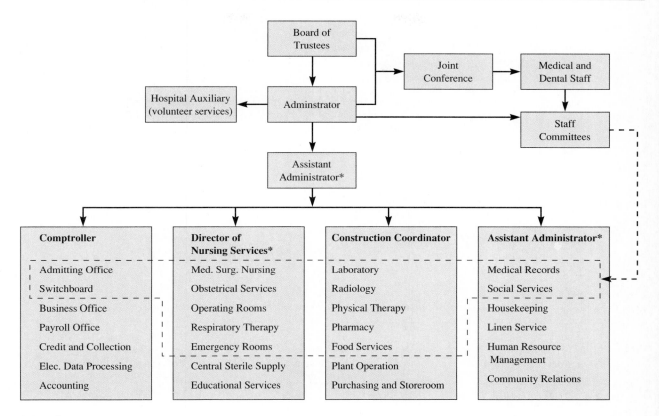

* Area directors

This chart reflects the "line" responsibility and authority in the hospital organization. It should be understood, however, that a great part of the work of the hospital is accomplished through informal interaction between the identified services and functions. These "functional" working relationships are encouraged. Where there is a difference in understanding or when changes in procedure are required, the line organization should be carefully observed.

Each chapter also includes a diagnostic analysis of the activity being discussed. It is assumed that HRM activities are affected by many different factors, such as the types of people employed, organized labor, and government. The solution of HRM problems depends on consideration of all these factors. The diagnostic theme will be thoroughly examined in Chapter 2.

For each HRM activity, suggestions are given for the techniques, tools, and approaches available to solve the problem, with an evaluation of when each tool is most useful and tips on how to use it well. When feasible, the various HRM activities are evaluated with a cost/benefit approach. Since HRM must compete

EXHIBIT 1-6   Stages of Development of an HRM Activity

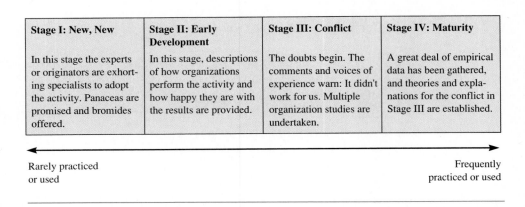

Stage I: New, New	Stage II: Early Development	Stage III: Conflict	Stage IV: Maturity
In this stage the experts or originators are exhorting specialists to adopt the activity. Panaceas are promised and bromides offered.	In this stage, descriptions of how organizations perform the activity and how happy they are with the results are provided.	The doubts begin. The comments and voices of experience warn: It didn't work for us. Multiple organization studies are undertaken.	A great deal of empirical data has been gathered, and theories and explanations for the conflict in Stage III are established.

Rarely practiced
or used

Frequently
practiced or used

EXHIBIT 1-7   The Organization of *Human Resource Management/Foundations of Personnel*

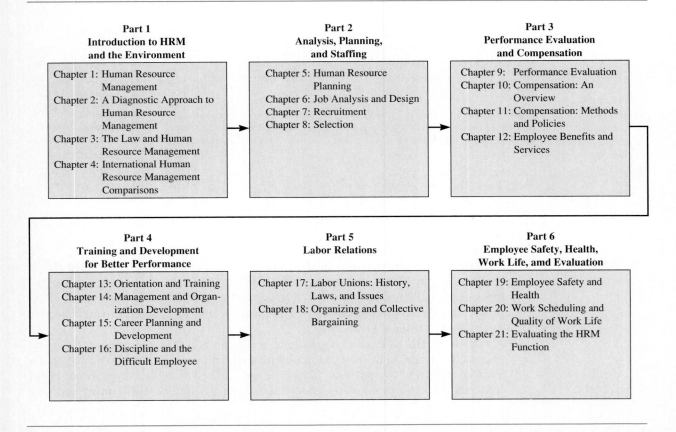

Part 1
Introduction to HRM
and the Environment

Chapter 1: Human Resource Management
Chapter 2: A Diagnostic Approach to Human Resource Management
Chapter 3: The Law and Human Resource Management
Chapter 4: International Human Resource Management Comparisons

Part 2
Analysis, Planning,
and Staffing

Chapter 5: Human Resource Planning
Chapter 6: Job Analysis and Design
Chapter 7: Recruitment
Chapter 8: Selection

Part 3
Performance Evaluation
and Compensation

Chapter 9: Performance Evaluation
Chapter 10: Compensation: An Overview
Chapter 11: Compensation: Methods and Policies
Chapter 12: Employee Benefits and Services

Part 4
Training and Development
for Better Performance

Chapter 13: Orientation and Training
Chapter 14: Management and Organization Development
Chapter 15: Career Planning and Development
Chapter 16: Discipline and the Difficult Employee

Part 5
Labor Relations

Chapter 17: Labor Unions: History, Laws, and Issues
Chapter 18: Organizing and Collective Bargaining

Part 6
Employee Safety, Health,
Work Life, amd Evaluation

Chapter 19: Employee Safety and Health
Chapter 20: Work Scheduling and Quality of Work Life
Chapter 21: Evaluating the HRM Function

EXHIBIT 1-8   Seven Model Organizations in Which Various HRM Practices
Might Be Used

---

1. Large size, low complexity, high stability.
   Examples: Social security agencies, copper smelter, tuberculosis hospital.
2. Medium size, low complexity, high stability.
   Examples: Running and sport shoe manufacturer, Department of Commerce, state of Indiana.
3. Small size, low complexity, high stability.
   Examples: Wooden pencil manufacturer, small insect exterminator.
4. Medium size, moderate complexity, moderate stability.
   Examples: Food manufacturer, Memphis city welfare agency.
5. Large size, high complexity, low stability.
   Examples: Mattel Toy Corporation, innovative community general hospital.
6. Medium size, high complexity, low stability.
   Examples: Fashion clothing manufacturer, innovative multipurpose hospital.
7. Small size, high complexity, low stability.
   Examples: Solar energy producer, computer manufacturer, elite psychiatric hospital, small media conglomerate.

---

with requests for other resources (machinery, advertising, buildings, and so on), the expenditures and investments in the organization's people must be justified in cost/benefit terms.

The chapter summary sections review the major points in each chapter. The organization of the book's chapters is presented in Exhibit 1–7. The 6 parts and 21 chapters cover HRM activities that need to be performed to achieve acceptable levels of organization effectiveness and employee development.

The recommendations for applications of the activity are presented as suggestions for use in various types of organizations. Since HRM functions are not performed the same way in all organizations, recommendations are given for the most effective way to handle each problem in seven model organizations which are defined in Exhibit 1–8. These organizations differ systematically by size (number of employees), complexity of the technology needed to produce products or services (equipment, resources, expertise), and stability or volatility (degree to which the organization's products or services change over time). If you match your organization (where you have worked or want to work) with one of these models, you can get an idea of how the HR challenge would be handled there.

To conclude this introductory section, the career histories and job descriptions of two HR leaders are given below.

PROFESSIONAL PROFILE

Donna Seckar
Cabrini College

Biography

Donna Seckar has been employed as director of career services at Cabrini College, Radnor, PA, for the past 10 years. She was graduated from Gettysburg College with a B.A. in psychology. She holds an M.Ed. from the University of Cincinnati in guidance and counseling.

Career Placement: A Viewpoint   College and university career services (sometimes known as "career planning and placement") professionals work with human resources professionals to achieve mutually beneficial goals. The college professional can assist in the matching of graduates and alumni to job vacancies.

The best-known method by which college and university offices can assist employers is by facilitating on-campus recruiting. Additionally, job openings can be posted and/or listed in newsletters that some offices produce. Newsletters often go to alumni requesting these publications as well as to current students. Databases such as kiNexus and Connexion are also becoming a part of the campus placement service. Employer information can also be made available to students in the the career services library. Many institutions, both individually and as consortia, sponsor career/job fairs that enable employers to present information and meet potential job candidates. In many cases colleges and universities also coordinate internships and cooperative education programs. Finally, summer and part-time openings are posted by most career services offices.

The working relationship between college and university career services professionals and human resources professionals can be enhanced in several ways. One of the main roles of the career services professional is to counsel students as they are involved in their career searches. The more the professional knows about the employer's needs, the better the counselor can suggest appropriate matches to the student and explain potential career opportunities. A brief visit or telephone call by the human resources professional can be a good beginning. Well-defined job descriptions, including requirements and job responsibilities, are extremely beneficial. An ongoing relationship with a particular human resources representative in a company enables the counselor to call that person with questions and to facilitate recruiting of candidates. A visit to the employer can enhance the college representative's understanding of the corporation. Additionally, active involvement by both college and employer representatives in regional associations such as the Middle Atlantic Placement Association can be a route for productive exchange.

PROFESSIONAL PROFILE

Biography

R. William "Bill" Flock is senior vice president, human resources for Long John Silver's, Inc., Lexington, Kentucky. He was graduated from Ohio State University with a Bachelor of Science in commerce and administration.

Mr. Flock's experience has been gained through positions in manufacturing, consulting, and multi-unit food service. Early in his career, he held positions in compensation, recruiting, and organization development with the Mead Corporation. He served as director of employee relations for the Multigraphics Division of AM International and as director of corporate organization and management development. Mr. Flock entered the multi-unit food service industry with Ponderosa, Inc. While there, he held the positions of vice president, training and development and vice president, human resources. Before joining Long John Silver's, Inc., he provided human resource consulting services to both private and publicly held corporations.

Job Description As senior vice president, human resources, Bill Flock is responsible for developing and directing his corporation's strategic human resource policy. Through a professional staff reporting to him, tactical plans and programs in the areas of staffing, compensation and benefits, compliance, training and development, and communications are carried out to support Long John Silver's strategies.

The Human Resource Executive as a Strategist: A Viewpoint Today's human resource executive must provide his or her corporation with the strategic lead-

R. William Flock
Long John Silver's, Inc.

ership necessary to address the critical work force issues facing U.S. businesses in this decade and the next. He or she must grasp and deal with the marketing, financial, and operational implications of the nation's societal problems — a diminishing workforce, illiteracy, substandard education, women and minorities in the work force, drugs, and an aging population. In addition, today's human resource executive must take a leadership position in the transformation of our country's economic base from manufacturing to information technology. While it is important that he or she know the technical aspects of traditional human resource functions such as staffing, compensation and benefits, training, affirmative action, and labor relations, a technical focus at the executive level is not enough to ensure that his or her corporation will be able to successfully compete in the years ahead. In short, the human resource executive must be a strategist; he or she must be every bit the business leader expected of the marketing, manufacturing, and financial executive.

CAREER CHALLENGE
(*concluded*)

Don Brokop is ready to make an important career decision. He now understands the role that human resource management plays at Melody. He can see that HRM is important not only to his firm, but also to society. The people business is the job of all managers in all organizations. Don has decided to accept the assistant director position and to really become involved on a full-time basis with HRM activities.

The activities that Don will learn about firsthand are what this book is about. As you learn more about HRM, think about Don Brokop and how he stepped from the operating level of management into the HR role in the Melody plant. His on-the-job training will be invaluable in his personal growth and development. However, Don will also have to supplement this first-hand experience with reading and self-learning. Your job now is to dig into the type of reading and self-learning that Don will use to make himself a more successful HRM practitioner.

There are, of course, other decisions that could be made in this situation. Don's decision is not the only one to make. What would you have decided if you were Don?

SUMMARY

This chapter (and all others in the text) concludes with a list of statements summarizing the most important concepts covered in the chapter. You can use this list to review your understanding of the HRM process and the HR manager's job.

In your introduction to this field, HRM has been defined as the function, in all organizations, that facilitates the most effective utilization of human resources to achieve both the objectives of the organization and the employees. It has described some of the characteristics of today's HR managers and a number of approaches to the organization and operation of HR units. It concludes with a brief description of how the material in this book is organized and the devices we have used to present it. A special appendix to the chapter describes typical careers in HRM, suggest ways HR specialists can achieve greater professionalism, and briefly describes accreditation procedures.

To summarize the major points covered in this chapter:

1. HRM is action, future, and worldwide oriented and focuses on satisfying the needs of individuals at work.
2. HRM is a necessary function. Effectively performed, it can make the crucial difference between successful and unsuccessful organizations.
3. One of the challenges faced in HRM is that many decisions require input from both operating managers and HR specialists.
4. This dual purpose can lead to conflict, or it can result in more-effective HRM decisions.

HRM is one of the most challenging and exciting functions in an organization. This book has been written to help you face these challenges more effectively.

KEY TERMS

QUESTIONS FOR REVIEW AND DISCUSSION

1. Why is the HR department playing a more significant role in organizational strategic planning processes today than it did 20 years ago?
2. Why is it correct to conclude that all managers are involved in the human resource management function?
3. What type of HRM jobs are available at the entry level for college graduates?
4. Would managing human resources be as important in Mexico as it is in the United States? Why?
5. Why has the HRM function increased in stature and influence in many organizations?
6. Do accreditation procedures make the HRM field professional? In other words, are lawyers, doctors, and HRM managers professional?
7. What difficulties does an HR executive face in assessing the contribution of his or her area to the company profit margin?
8. Peter Drucker seems to be incorrect when he states that work in HRM is nothing more than the work of a file clerk. What has happened in the world of work to make this statement false?
9. Why is it necessary for the HRM area to clearly communicate human resource policies?
10. Why should even very small firms (with 10 to 100 employees) be concerned about HRM?

NOTES

[1] These news items are a sample of those that appear daily in the press and in periodicals. For more information, see John Hillkirk (October 15, 1990), "On Mission to Revamp Workplace," *USA Today*, p. 4B; (September–October 1990) "Child Day Care an Old Issue," *Heritage*, p. 53; Amy Dockser Marcus (July 11, 1990), "Fearful of Future, Plaintiffs Are Suing Firms for What Hasn't Happened Yet," *The Wall Street Journal*, pp. B1 and B4; Kathryn Graven (March 21, 1990), "Sex Harassment at the Office Stirs Up Japan," *The Wall Street Journal*, pp. B1 and B5; and Doron P. Levin (January 23, 1990), "G.M. Saturn Plant Makes Friends," *New York Times*, p. C1.

[2] Henry S. Gilbertson (1950), *Personnel Policies and Unionism* (Boston: Ginn and Co.), p. 17.

[3] Henry Eilbert (Autumn 1959), "The Development of Personnel Management in the United States," *Business History Review*, pp. 345–64.

[4] Fred K. Foulkes (March–April 1975), "The Expanding Role of the Personnel Function," *Harvard Business Review*, pp. 71–72.

[5] Randall S. Schuler (Spring 1987), "Personnel and Human Resource Management Choices and Organizational Strategy," *Human Resource Planning*, pp. 1–17.

[6] George F. Kimmerling (June 1989), "The Future of HRD," *Training and Development Journal*, pp. 46–55.

7 Randall S. Schuler (August 1990), ''Repositioning the Human Resource Function: Transformation or Demise?'' *Academy of Management Executive*, pp. 49–60.

8 Robert Howard (September–October 1990), ''Values Make the Company: An Interview with Robert Haus,'' *Harvard Business Review*, pp. 132–144.

9 Peter M. Senge (1990), *The Fifth Discipline* (New York: Doubleday).

10 Jac Fitz-enz (1984), *How to Measure Human Resources Management* (New York: McGraw-Hill).

11 Thomasino Rendero (August 1990), ''HR Panel Takes a Look Ahead,'' *Personnel*, p. 24.

12 Andrew S. Grove (1983), *High Output Management* (New York: Random House), p. 158.

13 Jac Fitz-enz (August 1990), ''Getting and Keeping Good Employees,'' *Personnel*, p. 28.

14 Robert LePage (May–June 1990), ''The Global Executive of the Twenty-First Century,'' *The Journal of European Business*, pp. 62–64.

15 Terence R. Mitchell and William G. Scott (August 1990), '' America's Problems and Needed Reforms: Confronting the Ethic of Personal Advantage,'' *Academy of Management Executive*, pp. 23–35. Quoted in L. M. Lane (May 1986), ''Karl Weick's Organizing: The Problem of Purpose and the Search for Excellence,'' *Administration and Society*, pp. 132–133.

16 John K. Ortman (June 1984), ''Human Resources 1984: The State of the Profession,'' *Personnel Administrator*, pp. 35–48.

17 Ibid., p. 40.

18 Jeffrey J.. Hallett (May 1987), ''Worklife Visions,'' *Personnel Administrator*, p. 62.

19 These are estimates based on data obtained from the Occupational Outlook Handbook: 1987–1989 (Washington, D.C.: U.S. Department of Labor, 1990).

20 Henry Mintzberg (1980), *The Nature of Management Work* (Englewood Cliffs, N.J.: Prentice Hall), p. 52.

21 Barry D. Leskin (December 1986), ''Two Different Worlds,'' *Personnel Administrator*, pp. 58–60.

22 T. F. Cawsey (January-February 1980), ''Why Line Managers Don't Listen to Their Personnel Department,'' *Personnel*, p. 4.

23 (June 1984), ''How the Human Resources Function Contributes to Corporate Goals,'' *Management Review*, p. 31.

24 Ibid., pp. 31–32.

25 Wickham Skinner (September–October 1981), ''Big Hat, No Cattle: Managing Human Resources,'' *Harvard Business Review*, p. 107.

26 M. Beer, B. Spector, P. R. Lawrence, D. Q. Mills, and R. Walton (1984), *Managing Human Assets* (New York: Free Press).

27 Janet R. Andrews (June 1986), ''Is There a Crisis in the Personnel Department's Identity?'' *Personnel Journal*, pp. 86–93.

28 (October 1990), ''A Solid Strategy Helps Companies' Growth,'' *Business Life*, p. 10.

29 George G. Gordon (April 1987), ''Getting in Step,'' *Personnel Administrator*, pp. 45–48, 134.

30 David Babcock and John Boyd (1978), ''PAIR Department Policy and Organization,'' in *PAIR Policy and Program Management*, ed. Dale Yoder and Herbert Heneman, Jr. (Washington, D.C.: Bureau of National Affairs).

31 Thomas J. Bergmann and M. John Close (April 1984), ''Preparing for Entry Level Human Resource Management Positions,'' *Personnel Administrator*, pp. 95–98.

APPLICATION CASE 1–1 · · · · · The Human Resource Manager and Managing Multiple Responsibilities

At 7:30 A.M. on Monday, Sam Lennox, human resource manager of the Lakeview plant of Supreme Textile Corporation, pulled out of the driveway of his suburban home and headed for work. It was a beautiful day; the sun was shining in a bright blue sky, and a cool breeze was blowing. The plant was about nine miles away, and the 15-minute ride gave Sam an opportunity to think about business problems without interruption.

Supreme Textile Corporation owned and operated five plants: one yarn-spinning operation, two knitting plants, and two apparel-making operations. Supreme enjoyed a national reputation for quality products, specializing in men's sports shirts. Corporate headquarters was located in Twin-Cities adjacent to two of the plant operations. The Hillsville, Eastern, and Lakeview plants were 100–200 miles distant. Each employed 70–100 people. About 250 employees were located in Twin-Cities.

Sam had started with Supreme's Eastern plant after college. He progressed rapidly through several staff positions. He then served two years as a night foreman. He became known for his ability to organize a "smooth team," never having a grievance procedure brought against him. While his productivity figures were not outstanding, he was given credit by many people in the company for being the person who prevented the union from successfully organizing the Eastern plant. As a result he was promoted to assistant personnel manager.

Sam's progress was noted by Glen Johnson, corporate vice president of personnel. Glen transferred Sam to the Lakeview plant, which was having some personnel problems, as a special staff assistant. Six months later he was made personnel manager when the incumbent suddenly resigned. Sam had been able to work out most of the problems and was beginning to think about how to put together a first-rate personnel program.

Sam was in fine spirits as his car picked up speed, and the hum of the tires on the newly paved highway faded into the backgound. He said to himself, "This is the day I'm really going to get things done."

He began to run through the day's work, first one project, then another, trying to establish priorities. After a few minutes, he decided that the management by objectives (MBO) program was probably the most important. He frowned for a moment as he recalled that, on Friday, Glen Johnson had asked him if he had given the project any further thought. He had been meaning to get to work on this idea for over three months, but something else always seemed to crop up. "I haven't had much time to sit down and really work it out," he said to himself. "I'd better hit this one today for sure." With that, he began to break down the objectives, procedures, and installation steps. "It's about time," he told himself. "This idea should have been followed up long ago." Sam remembered that he and Johnson had discussed it over a year ago when they had both attended a seminar on MBO. They had agreed it was a good idea, and when Sam moved to the Lakeview plant it was decided to try to install it here. They both realized it would be met with resistance by some of the plant managers.

A blast from a passing horn startled him, but his thoughts quickly returned to other projects he was determined to get underway. He started to think about ideas he had for supervisory training programs. He also needed to simplify the employee record system. The present system not only was awkward, but key information was often lacking. There were also a number of carryover and nagging employee grievance problems. Some of this involved weak supervisors, some poor working conditions, and some just poor communication and morale. There were a few other projects he couldn't recall offhand, but he could tend to them after lunch, if not before. "Yes, sir," he said to himself, "this is the day to really get rolling."

Sam's thoughts were interrupted as he pulled into the parking lot. He knew something was wrong as Al Noren, the stockroom foreman, met him by the loading dock. "A great morning, Al," Sam greeted him cheerfully.

"Not so good, Sam; my new man isn't in this morning," Al growled.

"Have you heard from him?" asked Sam.

"No, I haven't," replied Al.

* This case was prepared by Jack D. Ferner, Lecturer in Management, Babcock Graduate School of Management, Wake Forest University, Winston-Salem, N.C.

Sam frowned as he commented, "These stock handlers assume you take it for granted that if they're not here, they're not here, and they don't have to call in and verify it. Better call him."

Al hesitated for a moment before replying. "Okay, Sam, but can you find me a man? I have two cars to unload today."

As Sam turned to leave, he called, "I'll call you in half an hour, Al," and headed for his office.

When he walked into the personnel office, there were several plant employees huddled around his secretary, Terry. They were complaining that there was an error in their paychecks. After checking their files and calling payroll twice, he found an automatic pay increase had not been picked up properly. He finally got everyone settled down.

He sat down at his desk, which was opposite Terry's and two other clerks. One of the clerks brought him a big pile of mail. He asked her to get him some office supplies and started to open the mail. The phone rang; it was the plant manager asking him about finding a new secretary. As Sam hung on the phone listening to all the problems the "old man" had with secretaries, he thought, "Fussbudget." He started to call a couple of foremen to see if they had someone to fill in for Al in the stockroom when he was interrupted by one of his clerks asking him to check over several termination reports. He was trying to decide whether any of these represented trouble spots when the phone rang again. Glen Johnson was on the other end. With an obvious edge in his voice, he asked, "I've heard rumblings about some of the grievances we can't seem to solve. What about it?" Sam responded that he hadn't had time, but would. There followed a series of questions. The conversation ended with, "Sam, you really need to get after those problems." Sam sighed. Terry was at his desk asking him to approve a couple of rate changes.

Several job applicants came into the office as a result of want ads the company had run over the weekend. There was a buzz as the applications and interviews progressed. Sam started to help out. Sam was talking with one applicant when Cecil Hardy came in. Cecil was the plant engineer, who liked to stop by to chat and have a cup of coffee. He was approaching retirement and today wanted to talk about the company's pension benefits. He also described in detail a round of golf he had played Sunday afternoon. Sam had played a lot when he

was in school and enjoyed an occasional game with Cecil.

It was suddenly 10:45 and time to go to a staff meeting. They were going to discuss something about quality control, and Sam wasn't awfully interested, but the plant manager wanted all the department heads at staff meetings. "They always drag on so long, and we get off on things that don't seem real important to all of us," Sam reflected as he headed toward the conference room.

Sam went to lunch with a friend who owned a plastics fabrication business. He called an hour ahead to say he wanted to discuss a major medical package that had been proposed by an insurance company. They drove across town to a new restaurant.

When Sam returned at about 2 P.M. the office was busy again with job applicants. He suddenly remembered the replacement stock clerk. "Too late now," he mused. He sat down and began to assemble the files relating to the grievances. The production superintendent called to discuss his need for several production people. He wanted experienced people and wasn't happy with some of the prospects Sam's department had sent him. Sam took a break to get a soft drink from the storage room. He noticed some of the confidential employee files had been pulled out and not returned. As he straightened them out he thought, "I wonder who did this?"

Sam returned to his desk to find a Boy Scout troop selling advertisements in a program for a rally they were putting on. This was one of the odd tasks Sam had been assigned by the plant manager. As the afternoon wore on, Sam became increasingly irritated at not being able to make much progress with the grievances. "Trouble is, I'm not sure what should be done about the Sally Foster and Curt Davis cases."

At 4:45 the personnel manager at the Eastern plant called to ask about some employee matters Sam had handled when he was there. When he finished, it was 5:30 and he was the only one left in the office. Sam was tired. He put on his coat and headed toward the parking lot. He also ran into Al Noren who was also heading for his car. "Thanks for the stock clerk," Al grumbled as he drove off.

With both eyes on the traffic, Sam reviewed the day he had just completed. "Busy?" he asked himself. "Too much so—but did I accomplish anything?'' His mind raced over the day's activities. *Yes* and *no* seemed to be the answer. ''There was the usual routine, the same as any other day. The personnel function kept going, and we must have hired several new people. Any creative or special project work done?'' Sam grimaced as he reluctantly answered, ''No.''

With a feeling of guilt, he probed further. ''Am I a manager? I'm paid like one, respected like one, and have a responsible assignment with the necessary authority to carry it out. Yet, one of the greatest values a company derives from a manager is his creative thinking and accomplishments. You need some time for thinking. Today was like most other days; I did little, if any, creative work. The projects that I so enthusiastically planned to work on this morning are exactly as they were last week. What's more, I have no guarantee that tomorrow will bring me any closer to their completion. There must be an answer.''

Sam continued, ''Night work? Yes, occasionally. This is understood. But I've been doing too much of this lately. I owe my wife and family some of my time. When you come down to it, they are the people for whom I'm really working. If I am forced to spend much more time away from them, I'm not meeting my own personal objectives. What about church work? Should I eliminate that? I spend a lot of time on it, but I feel I owe God some time, too. Besides, I believe I'm making a worthwhile contribution. Perhaps I can squeeze a little time from my fraternal activities. But where does recreation fit in?''

Sam groped for the solution. By this time, he had turned off the highway onto the side street leading to his home — the problem still uppermost in his mind. ''I guess I really don't know the answer,'' he told himself as he pulled into his driveway. ''This morning, everything seemed so simple, but now. . . .'' His son ran toward the car, calling out, ''Mommy, Daddy's home.''

Discussion Questions

1. Human resource management consists of numerous activities. What areas were illustrated by Sam's schedule on this particular day?
2. List the areas of ineffective management and time robbers that are affecting Sam.
3. Discuss Sam's career progress. Is he now promotable?

CAREERS IN HRM

· · · · · · ·

This appendix discusses what a HR career is like, describes some typical personnel specialists' positions, suggests ways HR specialists can achieve greater professionalism, and briefly describes accreditation procedures.

HR Careers

Let us begin this section by discussing what current HR professionals are like. When this edition was published in 1992, about 68 percent of HRM managers were male. Female HR managers were usually found in medium-sized and smaller organizations. Most HR managers have college degrees. Those who attended college in recent years usually majored in business, economics, or psychology. Their experience has been primarily in HR work, especially the younger managers.

One study of the 300 largest employing firms in the United States was conducted to determine the key skills and backgrounds organizations are looking for in staffing entry-level positions in HR units.[31] The HR managers were asked to order their choice of academic preparations for those interested in entry level positions. They ranked business administration first, followed in order by social sciences and humanities, and science and education tied for fourth and fifth positions.

HR specialists have been moving toward greater specialization, if not actual professionalism. College training includes courses such as HRM, compensation administration, HRM problems, labor law and legislation, and collective bargaining. Those who want to become more specialized can join associations, such as the American Society for Human Resource Management, previously called the American Society for Personnel Administrators (ASPA), attend meetings, read professional journals, or seek accreditation. There are 33,500 members of the Society for Human Resource Management, and more than 390 local chapters.[1]

HR specialists generally are paid comparably to other graduates of business schools at the supervisory and middle-management levels. At top-management levels, they sometimes are paid slightly less than operating vice presidents. Current average salaries of HR specialists and executives are presented in Exhibit 1A–1. The career ladder opportunities in various HR positions are also shown in the exhibit. For example, a junior training specialist's average salary is $28,600. Working up the career ladder in this area could result in a training manager position with an average salary of $55,300.

An HR professional can enter the field through different types of positions. One way is to become an HR manager for a small unit of a large organization. Remember Don Brokop at the beginning of this chapter? This is what he would be doing if he accepted the Melody Machine Products plant position. When a person enters the small unit of a large organization, he or she implements headquarter's HRM policies at that level and works with local operating managers to help achieve unit goals, as well as personnel objectives. The other route is to become a specialized HR professional. Typically, this position is found in a large organization, and the duties are associated with a single HRM function — interviewing, recruiting, compensation, labor relations, or training and development.

As positions open up, the HR professional can usually move up in the hierarchy. Or the specialist at a large organization can move to a smaller organization as the chief HR executive. Typically, a person with a college degree and HRM training can move up the career ladder without much difficulty if he or she is willing to work hard.

Three HRM area job descriptions are provided for review in Exhibit 1A–2. The job descriptions capture some of the activities of the person performing the job.

Career Development for the HR Professional

The HR specialist can advance his or her knowledge of the field by reading specialized journals. Appendix B at the end of the book provides information on trade, professional, and scholarly journals and literature that can provide relevant HRM information, data, and statistics.

Accreditation

One move to increase the professionalism of HR executives is the Society of Human Resource Management Accreditation Program. SHRM has set up an Accreditation Institute to offer HR executives the opportunity to be accredited as specialists (in a functional area such as employment, placement and HR planning, training and development, compensation and benefits, health, safety and security, employee and labor relations, and personnel research), or generalists (multiple specialties). Specialists can qualify as accredited HR specialists (accredited human resource specialist) or the more advanced accredited HR diplomates (accredited human resource diplomate). Accreditation requires passing three-hour examinations developed by the Psychological Corporation of New York. Tests are given by SHRM in these HRM activity areas:

- Employment, placement, and personnel planning.
- Training and development.
- Compensation and benefits.
- Health and safety.
- Employee and labor relations.
- Personnel research.

The American Society for Training and Development is comprised of over 22,000 members who are concerned with the training and development of human resources.[2] The ASTD professional development committee is working to identify the competencies needed to master training and development activities.

The International Association for Personnel Women (IAPW) was founded in 1950. Its purpose is to expand and improve the professionalism of women in HRM. Its approximately 2,000 members are generalists and specialists working in various industries.[3]

---

[1] Thomas J. Bergmann and M. John Close (April 1984), "Preparing for Entry Level Human Resource Management Positions," *Personnel Administrator*, pp. 95–98.
[2] Ibid.
[3] Ibid.

EXHIBIT 1A-1   Salaries in Human Resource Management

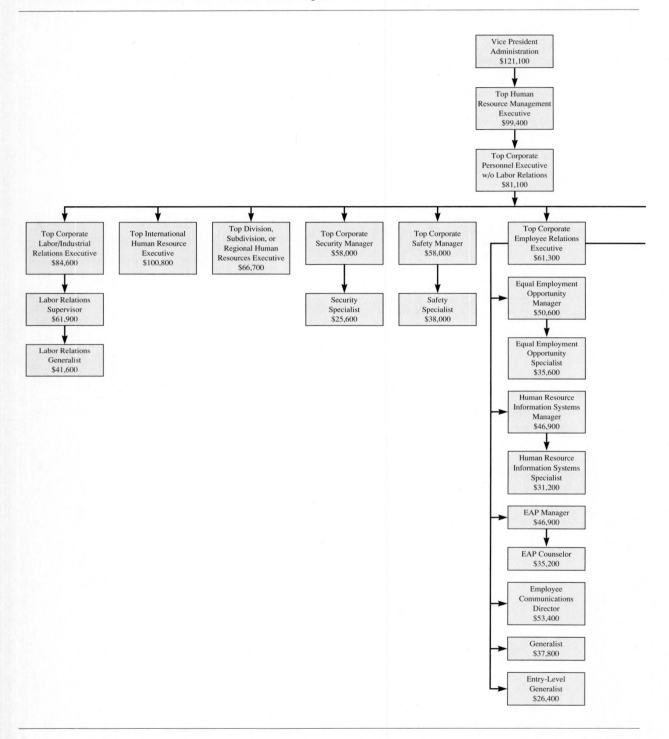

EXHIBIT 1A-1   *(continued)*

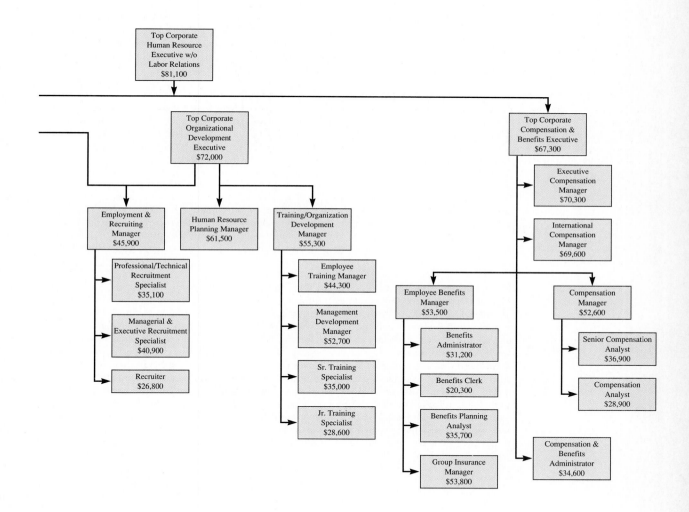

EXHIBIT 1A-2   Three HRM-Related Job Descriptions

Manager Personnel (profess. & kin.)

Plans and carries out policies relating to all phases of personnel activity: Recruits, interviews, and selects employees to fill vacant positions. Plans and conducts new employee orientation to foster positive attitude toward company goals. Keeps record of insurance coverage, pension plan, and personnel transactions, such as hires, promotions, transfers, and terminations. Investigates accidents and prepares reports for insurance carrier. Conducts wage survey within labor market to determine competitive wage rate. Prepares budget of personnel operations. Meets with shop stewards and supervisors to resolve grievances. Writes separation notices for employees separating with cause and conducts exit interviews to determine reasons behind separations. Prepares reports and recommends procedures to reduce absenteeism and turnover. Contracts with outside suppliers to provide employee services such as canteen, transportation, or relocation service. May keep record of hired employee characteristics for governmental reporting purposes. May negotiate collective bargaining agreement with Business Representative, Labor Union (profess. & kin.).

Training Representative (education)

Prepares and conducts training programs for employees of industrial, commercial, service, or governmental establishment. Confers with management to gain knowledge of identified work situation requiring preventive or remedial training for employees. Formulates teaching outline in conformance with selected instructional methods, utilizing knowledge of specified training needs and effectiveness of such training methods as individual coaching, group instruction, lectures, demonstrations, conferences, meetings, and workshops. Selects or develops teaching aids, such as training handbooks, demonstration models, multimedia visual aids, and reference works. Conducts general or specialized training sessions covering specified areas, such as those concerned with new employees' orientation, specific on-the-job training, apprenticeship programs, sales techniques, health and safety practices, public relations, refresher training, promotional development, upgrading, retiring displaced workers, leadership development, and other such adaptations to changes in policies, procedures, regulations, and technologies. Tests trainees to measure their learning progress and to evaluate effectiveness of training presentations.

Manager Compensation (profess. & kin.) wage and salary administrator

Manages compensation program in establishment: Directs development and application of techniques of job analysis, job descriptions, evaluations, grading, and pricing in order to determine and record job factors and to determine and convert relative job worth into monetary values to be administered according to pay-scale guidelines and policy formulated by Director, Industrial Relations (profess. & kin.). Analyzes company compensation policies, government regulations concerning payment of minimum wages and overtime pay, prevailing rates in similar organizations and industries, and agreements with labor unions, in order to comply with legal requirements and to establish competitive rates designed to attract, retain, and motivate employees. Recommends compensation adjustments according to findings, utilizing knowledge of prevailing rates of straight-time pay, types of wage incentive systems, and special compensation programs for professional, technical, sales, supervisory, managerial, and executive personnel. Approves merit increases permitted within budgetary limits and according to pay policies. Duties may also include administration of employee benefits program [Manager, Benefits (profess, & kin.)].

Source: From the *Dictionary of Occupational Titles* (1977), 4th ed. (Washington, D.C.: U.S. Department of Labor), pp. 97–100.

2

A DIAGNOSTIC APPROACH
TO HUMAN RESOURCE MANAGEMENT

· · · · · · ·

LEARNING OBJECTIVES

───◦───

After studying this chapter, you should be able to:

· · ·

Describe how a diagnostic HRM model can be used to examine people problems

· · ·

Explain the difference between external and internal environmental forces that affect HRM problems

· · ·

Discuss the role that HRM can play in accomplishing the organization's strategic plan

· · ·

Identify how HRM activities contribute to a firm's productivity

CAREER CHALLENGE

Martha Winston is the newly appointed manager of the National Pancake House in Ft. Lauderdale, Florida, which is known for its beach area. Officially, the restaurant is known as unit 827. National is a large chain. Martha believes that if she does a good job of managing 827 she has an excellent chance to be promoted at National. She is also thinking about opening her own restaurant someday.

Martha entered National's management training program after completing college at a small liberal arts school that is well known in her part of the country. The focus of the training program was technical. Martha learned all about the equipment of a typical National restaurant. She also learned about National's finance and accounting system, theft control, and advertising. She was taught a great deal about National's goals for the firm and for Unit 827. The topics included sales goals, financial return goals, cleanliness goals, customer service goals, and so on.

She has been at 827 three weeks now and is adjusting pretty well. She is not reaching all the goals National set up for her yet, but she feels she will do so in time. She often wishes the training program had taught her more about the people part of the success equation. Her college courses were not much help to her on this either.

This problem was on her mind as she sat in her office one morning staring at her paperwork over a cup of coffee. She was thinking of the two cooks on duty, Lenny and Harry. Lenny Melvina is about 24. He's been with National as a cook for almost six years. He finished high school locally. It's the only job he's ever had. He arrives on time, works hard, and leaves on time. He's never absent except for perhaps one day a year for illness.

Everyone likes Lenny: the other help, his managers, the customers. It's easy to see why. He does his job well and in a friendly manner. For example, today Martha watched Lenny deal with a customer. National has a policy that second helpings are free. A girl, about 13, came up to Lenny and asked for seconds. He asked her in a friendly manner how many more pan-cakes she wanted. She said: "Oh, I don't know, one or two."

Instead of having her wait at the serving line, he suggested that she be seated and said he'd bring her the pancakes. He delivered a plate with three pancakes on it that looked like this:

The customer and her family were very pleased with his effort to please her and give them a little joke too. They told Martha they'd come back again.

The other cook is Harry Bennis. Harry is about 19. He didn't finish high school. He's worked at National for two years. Harry is tolerated rather than liked. Most of his coworkers tend to ignore him. He rarely says anything beyond the minimum to coworkers, bosses, and customers. He is often late or absent. In about 1 case in 10, his food is sent back. He's not surly, but not too pleasant either. He's not bad enough to fire, but not good enough to be pleased with.

Martha wonders why there are these differences in Lenny and Harry, and what, if anything, she can do about it. It affects her now because she must hire a cook. Business at 827 has been growing faster than usual, even for this busy season. So the staff needs to be expanded to include at least one new cook. Martha wondered how she can be sure to choose a person like Lenny, not another Harry.

It's also raise time. She doesn't have enough money to give everyone a raise. And, to hire a new cook *(continued on next page)*

CAREER CHALLENGE
(*continued*)

she may have to pay close to what she pays Lenny, because few cooks are out of work at present. Yet company policy says she must pay senior people like Lenny more. And, already if things weren't complicated enough, the pay must be above the government minimum wage.

Many of the employees at 827 told Martha they wanted more pay because the job wasn't too pleasant: The stove was hot, and they had to deal with the public. What should she do?

To help her make an intelligent, effective decision, she went to visit a friend, Amy Adams, who had majored in human resource management at university.

Amy spent an afternoon with Martha explaining how to deal with the the four personnel problems Martha faced (employee satisfaction, performance, selection, and pay) by understanding how three sets of factors affects HRM and organizational effectiveness.

These are:

- People.
- The internal and external environment of the organization.
- The organization, task, work group, and leadership.

Think about how Martha must diagnose the present situation and work with people at the restaurant.

A DIAGNOSTIC HRM MODEL

When you're experiencing pain and must see a physician, you are typically asked a number of questions. Where do you hurt? When did the pain start? What does the pain feel like — is it sharp or dull? The doctor examines you and may also run a number of tests. What the doctor is doing is diagnosing the problem. He or she is performing a diagnosis by examination and observation.

The problem faced by Martha at National Pancake House could also be examined through a systematic diagnosis. A human resource management *diagnostic model* might be of help to her. A diagnostic model in HRM is a framework that can be used to help managers focus on a set of relevant factors. The model is a map that aids a person in seeing the whole picture or parts of the picture. The three factors that Martha was concerned about (people, the internal and external environment, and the organization itself) would be included as parts of any HRM diagnostic model.

Exhibit 2–1 presents the diagnostic model that will be used throughout the book. The model emphasizes some of the major external and internal environmental influences that directly and/or indirectly affect the match between HRM activities and people.

By studying the diagnostic model, you should see that in order to work with people effectively a number of HRM activities must be efficiently practiced. For example, to encourage individuals to use their abilities, it may not be sufficient to have only a properly analyzed job. A sound performance evaluation, equitable benefits and services, and an attractive work schedule may also be needed. HRM activities are all related to each other and have a combined effect on people. It is

EXHIBIT 2-1   A Diagnostic Model for Human Resource Management

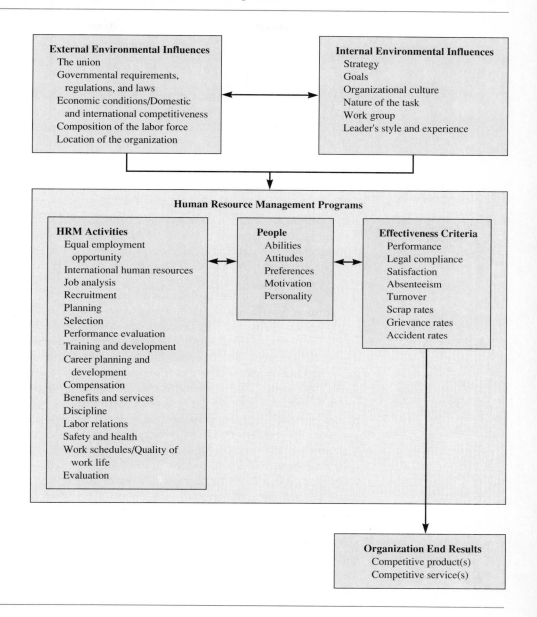

because of this effect on people and, ultimately, on effectiveness criteria that the HRM function is now recognized as an important part of organizational management. The objectives of the HRM functions must be accomplished in order for an organization to remain competitive and to survive in the environment.

Each area of the diagnostic model is important in achieving the eight HRM objectives presented in Chapter 1. Again, it should be pointed out that a significant reason for the eventual success of any HRM activity is that the organization's employees are the best qualified and are performing jobs that suit their needs, skills, and abilities. The matching of people and activities to accomplish desirable goals is made easier by using a diagnostic map. Of course, the map shown in Exhibit 2–1 can't include every important environmental influence, HRM activity, or effectiveness criterion. Instead, it is designed to provide an orderly and manageable picture of how HRM diagnosis should proceed.

HOW TO USE THE HRM DIAGNOSTIC MODEL

The diagnostic model is a way of providing a map of the important factors affecting HRM. The model tells you that three sets of factors—external, internal, and people—influence the HRM activities used by an organization.

It is reasonable to conclude that managers who must make HRM decisions are more effective if they think about the three sets of factors influencing HRM activities and effectiveness before they make a decision. Chapters 3–20 tell you *how* each of these factors affects a specific HRM decision.

Managers concerned with the HRM function, activities, and role in strategy development and implementation need some kind of model to guide the way. First, they need to analyze the HRM problem—or the person with a problem—by looking at all the data at hand. Then they decide which causes are operating and how the problem can be solved. They do not give up if the most probable cause does not seem to be operating. Rather, they proceed down the list of causes until the underlying source of the problem is found.

Suppose, for example, that a manager notices from the weekly production reports that productivity in the department has been declining over the past few weeks. There could be a number of reasons for this decline. Perhaps the equipment in the department has become defective and is not working properly, or the materials and supplies have been of a comparatively lower quality. Or the cause might be the employees: Perhaps some of the more highly skilled employees have been promoted, transferred to other departments, or have quit, and their replacements lack the necessary skills and experience to perform the work effectively. Or perhaps the problem is one of poor employee morale.

In investigating the problem, the manager using a diagnostic framework may find that turnover in the department has been quite high, that absenteeism has been increasing, and that there have been more complaints and grievances of late. All of these are symptoms of low employee satisfaction and detract from the organization's effectiveness. If the manager concludes that the most likely cause of poor production in the department is the low satisfaction of employees, a solution for this problem will be sought. The manager may consider such solutions as providing better working conditions, increasing pay and other financial benefits, improving communication between supervisor and employees, redesigning the jobs to make them more interesting and challenging, or modifying the manager's own leadership style. If after treating the morale problem productivity is still low, the manager will turn to the next most probable cause of the problem and continue down the list of causes until the right one is found and corrected.

EXTERNAL ENVIRONMENTAL FORCES

Exhibit 2–1 is intended to show that an HRM program in an organization does not operate in a vacuum. It is influenced by and influences the external (outside the organization) and the internal (inside the organization) environments. On the one hand, **external environmental influences**—such as government laws and regulations, union procedures and requirements, economic conditions and the labor force — have a significant impact on HRM programs. On the other hand, the HRM program of a firm must operate within guidelines, limits of available resources, and competencies produced by the organization. HRM is one important function among other internal functions, including finance, accounting, research and development, marketing, and production. The interaction of these internal programs sets the tone of the entire organizational system.

At the National Pancake House, Martha's HRM problems are aggravated by external environmental factors. Remember that Martha is faced with a tight labor market and government wage legislation. Let's look at some external environmental factors.

The Union

The presence of a union directly affects most aspects of HRM — recruiting, selection, performance evaluation, promotion, compensation, and benefits, among others. These effects will be discussed later in the book. Chapters 17 and 18 focus directly on relations with labor unions.

Unions differ just as people differ. There are cooperative unions and combative unions, just as there are sensitive organizations and socially irresponsible organizations. Those familiar with union history are aware of the kind of toughness a James Hoffa or a John L. Lewis can bring to the employment scene. The union leadership of the Air Line Pilots Association; State, Local, and Municipal Workers; Baseball Players Association; and others is not so well known, because they have different bargaining styles and philosophies.

At one time, unions were concentrated in a few sectors of the economy, such as mining and manufacturing, and were influential in only a few sections of the United States, primarily the highly industrialized areas. But the fastest growing sectors for unions in the United States are in the public and third sectors. It is no longer useful to think of the unionized employee as a blue-collar factory worker. Engineers, nurses, teachers, secretaries, salespersons, college professors, professional football players, and even physicians belong to unions. In sum, unions often play a significant role in HRM programs.[1]

Government Law and Regulations

Another powerful, external environmental influence is government law and regulations, which affects many organizations directly. Federal regulations influence HRM activities, policies, and programs. When an organization makes hiring, promotion, performance evaluation, layoff, and discipline decisions, it must weigh the impact of government regulations.

The government regulates and influences aspects of HRM more directly than others. A few of the major areas of legislation and regulation include:

Equal employment opportunity and human rights legislation, which affects recruiting, selection, evaluation, and promotion directly, and employment planning, orientation, career planning, training and development indirectly.

Employment of illegal aliens.

Sex, age, and handicap discrimination.

Compensation regulation, which affects pay, hours of work, unemployment, and similar conditions.

Benefits regulation, which affects pension and retirement.

Workers' compensation and safety laws, which affect health and safety.

Labor relations laws and regulations, which affect the conduct of collective bargaining.

Privacy laws.

Government regulation is increasing substantially. In 1940 the U.S. Department of Labor administered 18 regulatory programs; in 1990 it administered over 140.[2] And that's just *one* government agency affecting managers and the activities of the HR department.

John Dunlop lists a number of the problems government regulation imposes on management.[3] All of these make the operating and HR managers' job more difficult:

- Regulation encourages simplistic thinking on complicated issues. Small enterprises are treated like large ones. Different industries are regulated the same.
- Designing and administering regulations is an incredibly complex task, leading to very slow decision making.
- Regulation does not encourage mutual accommodation but rather leads to complicated legal maneuvering.
- Many regulations are out of date and serve little social purpose, yet they are not eliminated.
- There is increasing evidence of regulatory overlap and contradictions among different regulatory agencies.

To cope with increasing governmental control, management has tried to influence the passage of relevant legislation and the way it is administered. Managements have sued to determine the constitutionality of many of the laws. When such efforts fail to influence the process as management prefers, it has learned to adapt its HRM policies.

In sum, there are almost no HRM decisions that remain unaffected by government. In what ways and to what degree government affects the HRM function will be discussed in each chapter, beginning with Chapter 3.

Economic Conditions

Three aspects of economic conditions affect HRM programs: productivity, the nature of competitiveness, and the nature of the labor market.

Productivity   Data, empirical evidence, and general opinion indicate that the productivity of employees is an important part of a nation's general economic condition. Managers are concerned with productivity because they feel it is a representative indicator of the overall efficiency of an organization. **Productivity** is defined as:

Output of goods and services per unit of input of resources used in a production process.[4]

Inputs, as applied in productiviy measurement, are expressions of the physical amount or the dollar amount of several elements used in producing a good or a service, including labor, capital, materials, fuel, and energy.

Before productivity can be effectively managed and improved, it must be measured. This can be done by isolating the outputs — division by division, department by department, work team by work team, individual by individual, or even product line by product line. Next, the costs that went into producing the output must be determined, including labor costs (salaries, bonuses, fringes), heating, lighting, and capital costs.[5] Then, using the previous year as a baseline period, the manager must compare the current year's figures with those of the previous year. Some period of comparison is needed to make necessary adjustments. While productivity improvement is a worthy goal, managers should, before they rush into changes, lay the groundwork for measuring and monitoring productivity.

The industrial world's productivity growth passed through three major cycles during the past century.[6]

1. A slow cycle for eight decades (1870–1950), averaging about 1.7 percent a year.
2. Unprecedented growth during the two post–World War II decades, with such rates as Japan's 7.9 percent a year.
3. Although the productivity rate in the United States was virtually zero (no growth) from 1978 through 1982, there are some signs of slow growth.

Averaged over the economy as a whole, for each unit of input the United States still produces more output than any other nation.[7]

Why, then, is there reason for concern? First, U.S. growth in productivity is not as fast as in Japan and Germany, for example. Second, in some areas of industrial performance that are not as easily measured as productivity, there are concerns. In such areas as product development, product quality, service to customers, and loyalty of human resources, U.S. companies are beginning to be viewed as lagging behind. For example, an advertisement by Buick brags about having the best American car quality ranking in the world. Buick is rated fifth behind four foreign manufacturers.

Can the United States turn around the slow-productivity saga? What has happened to the creativity, inventiveness, work ethic, and loyalty of the skilled work force? Are the human resources in organizations letting the United States down? Apparently, Japanese plants in Kentucky, Indiana, and Tennessee find nothing wrong with the productivity of their U.S. workers. Americans, in plants set up and run by Japanese managers (such as the General Motors–Toyota NUMMI plant in California), are as productive as any Japanese workers. The failure to properly manage human resources — not intrinsic values and work ethic — appears to explain the difference in productivity between U.S. workers and those from Japan, Germany, Mexico, or any other nation.[8]

Some suggested solutions for enhancing productivity growth include the reduction of government controls, more favorable income tax incentives to invest in new plants and equipment, and the reindustrialization of the entire business/industrial complex (such as plants and equipment). These suggested solutions have both proponents and opponents.[9] For example, there are many citizens who believe that reducing or eliminating legislative controls will have an adverse effect on the quality of life and society for decades to come. Toxic waste, radiation, air pollution, and other forms of destruction must be carefully controlled. In reality, the HR executive or specialist has little control over the environmental pollution problem. Certainly, he or she is concerned, but has little power to initiate policies or programs in this area.

On the other hand, the HR staff can influence productivity by the sound application of HRM programs. There are specific activities and practices that can improve individual performance and, consequently, organizational productivity. For example, recruitment and selection techniques can be used to attract and hire the best performers. Motivational and compensation techniques can be used to retain employees and improve job performance. Training and development can be used to improve job performance. Training and development can be used to improve skill and competency deficiencies that, in turn, increase performance.

A study conducted by McKersie and Klein showed how the productivity problem is linked to a firm's HRM policies and programs.[10] Corporate staff personnel and operating employees were asked to identify restraints to productivity growth. Interviews and questionnaires were used to collect the data. Operating employees identified as major productivity restraints such factors as worker resistance to change, poor motivation, government regulations, and ineffective work rules. The productivity improvement programs most widely mentioned and used were training programs, employee involvement (e.g., quality circles and labor-management committees), and relating pay directly to performance.

A number of procedures to overcome restraints to productivity improvement were suggested by Charles Kepner of Kepner-Tregoe, Inc., and they included: commitment to improve productivity, teaching employees at all levels how to be effective problem solvers, leaders who encourage followers to use their problem-solving skills, and rewards for successful problem solving.[11]

Productivity problems will not be solved without concern for the HRM function and the activities it performs. Every HRM activity covered in the diagnostic model (Exhibit 2–1) can affect productivity. Thus, productivity pressure from the external environment directly and indirectly affects an organization's HRM program.

The Nature of Competitiveness
At the macroeconomic level, the term *competitiveness* is defined as:

> The degree to which a nation can, under free and fair market conditions, produce goods and services that meet the test of international markets while simultaneously maintaining or expanding the real incomes of its citizens.[12]

The word *organization* can be substituted for *nation*, and the word *employees* can be substituted for the word *citizens*. This would yield a definition of *organization* (not national) *competitiveness*.

At the organizational level, competitiveness is a serious issue.[13] How efficiently do the workers produce the product? How good is the quality of the services or goods provided? Can employees handle the new technology and produce the product at lower costs? Does the firm have the human resources needed to increase the size of the manufacturing facility to handle global demand? Will the push to work harder and faster result in higher turnover, absenteeism, and number of defects?

The HR specialist is important in answering these competitiveness-related questions. The competition for a Seattle machine shop may be found in Hong Kong, New York, or across town. It is not that important where the competition is coming from. Understanding the importance of competitive forces and their impact on HRM programs and end results is the reason why the nature of competitiveness must be evaluated regularly.

The Nature of the Labor Market
The labor market directly affects HRM programs. When there are more workers than jobs, employers find recruiting costs minimal. Employees apply readily, and selection is less difficult; the employer may

be able to choose from five or more qualified applicants for each position. Work attitudes tend to be work-ethic oriented. Martha Winston, in the opening Career Challenge, has significant staffing problems at the National Pancake House because this is not the case. When the work ethic predominates in employees attitudes, output increases and performance evaluation can be a motivating experience. A surplus of labor can also reduce employee pressures for compensation and benefit increases. Disciplinary problems, absenteeism, and turnover are likely to decrease, and equal employment opportunity goals may be easier to fill.

The Hudson Institute, a nonprofit research organization in Indianapolis, Indiana, provided a report, *Workforce 2000: Work and Workers for the 21st Century*.[14] This comprehensive analysis of workers and jobs in the year 2000 identified four key trends that will shape the last decade of the 20th century:

- The American economy will grow at a relatively healthy pace.
- U.S. manufacturing will be a much smaller share of the economy in the year 2000 than it is today.
- The workforce will grow slowly, becoming older, more female, and more disadvantaged.
- The new jobs in service industries will demand much higher skill levels.

As labor market issues are presented, review these four trends. They appear to be on target and can help HR managers prepare for the future.

The employer must be aware of several labor markets, trends, and changing demographics. The primary concern is the local labor market, from which most blue- and white-collar employees are drawn. Managerial, professional, and technical employees may be recruited from a regional, or even a national, market.

It is possible that the local labor market is different from the regional or national markets. For example, in January 1991 the national employment rate was about 7 percent, but in Laredo, Texas, 12.6 percent of the workers were unemployed.[15] Recruiting blue-collar workers in Laredo is three or four times easier than in Austin, Texas.

Even though the national and local labor markets differ significantly, there will still be some exchange between them. Thus, if Laredo's unemployment rate stays consistently high, those among the unemployed who are younger, have knowledge of jobs elsewhere, and have the money and motivation to move will do so. This movement tends to increase the labor supply in areas with shortages. There also are international labor markets. Illegal aliens who come to the United States to seek work change the labor market balance. It was estimated that there were over 2 million illegal aliens working in the United States in 1990.[16]

In addition to labor markets defined by geographic boundaries are markets defined by skill, sex, and age considerations. If you are seeking an accountant, a general labor market surplus is not much help if accountants remain scarce. The supply of labor with a particular skill is related to many factors: the number of persons of work age; the attractiveness of the job in pay, benefits, and psychological rewards; the availability of training institutes; and so on.

With regard to age, the Hudson Institute states that because of the aging of the baby-boom generation (those born between 1946 and 1961) the U.S population will become, on average, much older.[17] The median age of the population will reach 36 by the year 2000. Where will the new, young workers come from? This becomes a serious HRM question as the population becomes six years older, on average, than any other time in U.S. history.

To summarize, the HRM function is affected fundamentally by the nature of the labor market, not only in the organization's location in the region, but also in the nation and the world. Also, the specific markets for the kinds of employees the enterprise seeks will affect that function.

The Work Sector of the Organization   The diagnostic model presented in Exhibit 2–1 does not take into consideration the work sector in which the organization is located. This was done so that the model could remain relatively uncluttered.

About 60 percent of professional HR specialists work in the *private sector*, consisting of businesses owned by individuals, families, and stockholders, while 30 percent of all HR employees in the United States work in the *public sector*, which is that part of the economy owned and operated by the government. Many economists define other institutions in society that are neither government nor profit oriented as the *third sector*. Examples of these institutions are museums, symphony orchestras, private schools and colleges, not-for-profit hospitals and nursing homes, and voluntary organizations such as churches and social clubs. About 10 percent of HR specialists and employees work in the third sector.

In general, private- and third-sector HRM is structured similarly. Hospitals have different internal organization problems than most businesses, though. For example, the presence of three hierarchies — physicians, administrators, and the board of trustees (representing the public) — can lead to conflicts. Pressures from third-party payees such as Blue Cross or Medicare can lead to other conflicts. Hospitals employ professional groups that zealously guard their "rights," which also leads to conflict. Structurally, HRM work in the private and third sectors is similar, but because of organizational differences jobs in the HRM function vary.

HRM in the public sector is *fundamentally different* from the other two sectors because it varies *structurally*. And the public manager faces a different world. In fact, a manager who moves from the private or third sector to the public sector will find the HRM role much more complicated. HRM in the public sector generally is much more laden with direct outside pressures. Politicians, the general public, pressure groups, and reporters influence the HR manager much more than in a private business or in the third sector.

For example, most public managers must deal with a central personnel bureau such as the Civil Service Commission. A special problem faced by these managers has always been political appointments. Formerly, politicians always saw to it that their party workers were rewarded with government jobs between elections; this is usually called the "spoils systems." In an attempt to ensure that public jobs are assigned on the basis of merit rather than political pull, the Civil Service Commission and equivalent central personnel bureaus were established to set personnel policies governing public employment. Civil service standardized examinations are now required as part of the selection process of many public-sector jobs. This system was intended to establish merit as the criterion for public employment, but it also increases the system's rigidity and entrenches bureaucracy.

The differences among public-, private-, and third-sector HRM activities are largely in the structure of the HRM function and the environment of the public manager's job. The HRM function does vary by sector, and these differences will be discussed where they are significant.

Composition of the Labor Force

In 1990 the U.S. population was approximately 252 million and the labor force comprised about 115 million persons. There are about 65 million men and 50 million women in the 1990 workforce of the United States.[18] By 1995 about 130 million persons will be in the labor force. Female employment participation is now 54 percent and growing. The highest employee proportion is about 60 percent of women 45–54, and only 9 percent of women over 65. From 1947 to 1975, the female population increased 52 percent, but the percentage of women working increased 123 percent.

The U.S. labor force is now composed of more single and fewer married persons. One third of all workers are single, and 90 percent of the recent growth in the labor force has been in unmarried workers.

More participation in the labor force has become possible as the life span of the population has lengthened. In the United States, men live about 72 years, and women live about 78 years.

The percentage of the labor force employed by manufacturing, construction, mining, and agriculture has stabilized or declined.[19] It is estimated that by the year 2000 two times as many persons will be employed in service industries, such as transportation, utilities, trade, financial, general services, and government, as in the stabilized industries. As far as type of workers is concerned, by the year 2000 it is predicted that farm workers will represent about 2 to 3 percent; service workers, about 16 percent; blue-collar workers (skilled, semiskilled, and unskilled operating-level employees—assembly-line worker, steelworker), 31 percent; and the rest—over 50 percent—will be white-collar workers (professional and technical, clerical, sales, and managers). Blue-collar workers, especially unskilled workers, are declining in relative importance.

Women   In 1990 about 47 percent of the full-time U.S. work force consisted of women. The number of married women in the labor force has increased 230 percent since 1947, while the number of male married employees has increased by only 30 percent.

Although women are supposed to have equal job opportunities, it is difficult to argue with the facts of discrimination against women in the workplace. Women today typically hold the lower-status, low-paying jobs. There are some signs, however, that by the year 2000 more women will be found in professional jobs: college teachers, lawyers, physicians, and accountants. Women are increasing in numbers of professional jobs that require advanced education. For example, 45 percent of the recipients of accounting degrees and 42 percent of business school majors are women.

Minorities   The situation for racial and ethnic minorities in the United States is similar to that for women. Large numbers of minority people, such as Hispanics, blacks, and Native Americans, are employed in low-skill, low-paying jobs, and few are in high-status, high-paying jobs.

Historically, the most recent immigrant groups took the lowest level jobs offered. This was true of the Irish, Polish, Yugoslavs, and Jews. One difference between the immigrant groups and other minorities like blacks, Hispanics, and Native Americans is that the minority groups were living in the United States long before the immigrants arrived. Native Americans have been in the United States before the time of "discovery," as were many of the Hispanics in the Southwest, and blacks since the mid-1700s. They have not advanced to the degree that the immigrants have, however. Native Americans were kept on reservations, and Hispanics remained in the areas that once belonged to the Mexican Republic (except for the Cuban and Puerto Rican immigrants, who came much later). Most blacks worked in southern agriculture until relatively recently. These minorities represent about 13 percent of the U.S. population. They have been less educated than the majority, although recent programs have attempted to improve this situation.

Nonwhites will comprise 29 percent of the net additions to the labor force between 1985 and the year 2000. Projections in Exhibit 2–2 indicate that the nonwhite share of the labor force will increase from 11.1 percent in 1970 to 15.5 percent in the year 2000.

It is likely that the number of legal and illegal immigrants coming to the United States will be significant. The Immigration Reform and Control Act of 1987, which imposes sanctions against employers of illegal aliens, may reduce the economic attraction. However, without vigorous enforcement, there is likely to be an increase in legal and illegal immigrants. It is predicted that immigration (including the children of immigrants) will add about 9.5 million to the U.S. population in the 1990s. Illegal immigration at a rate of about 750,000 per year will mean another 7.5 million immigrants joining the population.

One concern with immigration is the impact on the job prospects of native minorities. However, the results of one statistical analysis of 247 metropolitan areas concluded that black unemployment rates do not increase with a rise in the population of Mexican immigrants in a local labor market.[20]

The Older Employee   About 21 percent of the labor force currently is between the ages of 40 and 70. The over 40-year-old portion of the labor force is protected by law because some employers hold negative stereotypes about older workers.[21]

Probably one of the most difficult employment problems today is the older employee who loses a job through no personal fault. In some cases, employers assume that because a person is older he or she is less qualified to work and less able to adapt to changes. Also, benefit plans (which may amount to one third of base compensation) are set up in such a way that it costs more to employ older people (the cost of insurance premiums is higher for older people).

An important fact to remember is that each person ages at a different rate. As we grow older, we lose some of our faculties. But this process is ongoing: Rarely is a swimmer better than in his or her midteens, for example. The key, then, is to match employees with jobs. Older workers may be less efficient on some jobs requiring quick physical response rates. But speed or response is more important for a race driver or airline pilot than for a stock analyst or social worker.

EXHIBIT 2-2   Nonwhites Are a Growing Share of the American Work Force (numbers in millions)

	1970	1985	2000
Working-age population (16+)	137.1	184.1	213.7
Nonwhite share	10.9%	13.6%	15.7%
Labor force	82.8	115.5	140.4
Nonwhite share	11.1%	13.1%	15.5%
Labor force increase (over previous period)		32.7	25.0
Nonwhite share		18.4%	29.0%

Source: William B. Johnston and Arnold H. Packer (1987), *Workforce 2000: Work and Workers for the 21st Century* (Indianapolis: Hudson Institute), p. 89.

Most studies indicate that even for jobs requiring physical work employees over 45 do not have more accidents than younger employees. Older employees also have the same or lower rates of absenteeism — at least until age 55. The worst accident rate observed in one study was for employees under 35 years old.[22] When total performance is considered (including factors such as speed, accuracy, judgment, loyalty), the older employee has been found to be at least as effective as the younger one.

Handicapped Workers

Handicapped Workers   The Americans with Disability Act of 1990 (ADA) will have far-reaching effects on HRM for many years (see Chapter 3 for a more complete discussion). The ADA is designed to prevent discrimination against persons with physical or mental disabilities. Approximately 43 million Americans have one or more physical or mental disabilities. Studies of the approximately 10 million employed handicapped persons indicate that they are of all age groups, of both sexes, and in many occupations.[23] About 56 percent have been disabled by disease, 30 percent by accident, and 14 percent from birth. In the latter category, the largest group of people do not have the use of limbs or have back problems. The next largest number are amputees and blind (or partially blind) employees.

The ADA is patterned after the Federal Rehabilitation Act of 1973, which defines a handicapped person as anyone who:

1. Has a physical or mental impairment that substantially limits one or more major life activities.
2. Has a record of such an impairment.
3. Is regarded as having such an impairment.

Major life activities include communication, ambulation, self-care, socialization, education, transportation, and employment.

Many handicapped persons have had difficulty finding employment of any kind because employers and fellow workers believe that they could not do the job or would cause an excessive number of accidents. However, few people use all their faculties on a job, and there are many jobs for those who do not have all their faculties. When the handicapped are properly matched to jobs, studies show that two thirds of the physically handicapped produce at the same rate as nonhandicapped workers, 24 percent perform at higher levels, and only 10 percent perform at a lower rate. Absenteeism and turnover are normally lower for the handicapped for two reasons — the handicapped have had their abilities matched to their jobs better, and most handicapped workers seem better adjusted to working and have more favorable attitudes toward work. Thus, they are better motivated to do a good job. Studies indicate that handicapped persons have fewer accidents than nonhandicapped persons.[24]

Of course, some handicapped people are physically or psychologically unable to work. Some who are marginally employable can work in training jobs at sheltered organizations such as Goodwill Industries. But for those who are handicapped and able to work, it is most important that they be treated like other workers. They will respond better to fair treatment than to paternalism.

Veterans

Veterans   Veterans are former servicemen and women released from active duty by the military. They are not easily recognized as special employees by employers, but they do have to readjust to civilian life. The government has attempted to ease reentry to civilian life by Vietnam veterans, for whom there are several programs.

About one fourth of all returning veterans have resumed their interrupted educational careers. But the great majority have entered the civilian labor market, many seeking their first full-time jobs. As of January 1, 1981, there were 545,000 Vietnam veterans aged 20–34 unemployed in this country. The overall unemployment rate for veterans was 8.9 percent while the average unemployment rate was 7.7 percent. Among 20–24-year-olds, the veterans' unemployment rate was 18 percent.[25]

Congress has provided specific reentry adjustments for veterans, usually referred to as *reemployment rights*. In addition to providing for reemployment, Congress has enacted laws making it easier for veterans to enter the federal career service. These include a preference system of points added to test scores for veterans, the Veterans Readjustment Appointment, waivers of physical requirements, the restriction of certain jobs to veterans, preference for retention in case of reduction of force, and other similar procedures. The Veterans' Administration also assists veterans who are seeking employment through job marts and apprenticeship training programs. Priority for referral to appropriate training programs and job openings is given to eligible veterans, with first consideration to the disabled veteran. Other federal benefits have also become available to veterans operating their own businesses from the Small Business Administration. Similarly, unemployment compensation for veterans provides a weekly income for a limited period of time, varying with state laws.[26]

Geographic Location of the Organization

The location of the organization influences the kinds of people it hires and the HRM activities it conducts. A hospital, plant, university, or government bureau located in a rural area confronts different conditions than one located in an urban area. For example, the work force in a rural area might be more willing to accept a bureaucratic organization style. Recruiting and selection in rural areas will be different in that there may be fewer applicants. Yet the organization may find a larger proportion of hirable workers ingrained with the work ethic. It may be harder to schedule overtime if workers are supplementing farm incomes with an eight-hour shift at a factory. There may be fewer minority "problems," but it also may be difficult to recruit professional/technical personnel, who have shown a preference to work near continuing education and cultural opportunities. While pay may be lower in rural areas, so is the cost of living.

An urban location might be advantageous for recruiting and holding professional workers. Urban locations provide a bigger labor force but generally call for higher wages. The late shifts may be a problem here, too, but for different reasons. Workers may not feel safe at night in the parking lots or going home.

Geographic location, therefore, influences the kinds of workers available to staff the organization. The location or setting is extremely significant for companies operating in other countries. The employees may speak a different language, practice different religions, have different work attitudes, and so on. Let's consider some of the major differences between home-based and multinational organizations.

Educational Factors   Examples include the number of skilled employees available, attitudes toward education, and literacy level. Educational deficiencies in some

countries can lead to a scarcity of qualified employees, as well as a lack of educational facilities to upgrade potential employees.

Behavioral Factors
Societies differ in factors such as attitudes toward wealth, the desirability of profits, managerial role, and authority.

Legal-Political Factors
Laws and political structures differ and can encourage or discourage private enterprises. Nations also differ in degree of political stability. Some countries are very nationalistic in their business practices (even xenophobic). Such countries can require local ownership of organizations or, if they are so inclined, expropriate foreign concerns.

Economic Factors
Economies differ in basic structure, inflation rate, ownership constraints, and the like. The nations of the world can be divided into three economic categories: fully developed, developing, and less developed. The fully developed nations include the United States, Canada, Australia, Japan, and most European countries (the United Kingdom, Germany, France, Belgium, Luxembourg, the Netherlands, Switzerland, Italy, Sweden, Denmark, Norway, Finland). In these countries, managers will find fewer differences in educational, behavioral, economic, and legal-political factors than they are likely to encounter in developing or less developed countries.

The developing nations are those that are well along in economic development but cannot yet be said to be fully developed. Examples include Brazil, Mexico, Argentina, Venezuela, Spain, Nigeria, Saudi Arabia, India, and Eastern Europe.

Third-World nations — the less developed countries — are the most difficult to work in because of significant constraints in all four factors. The remaining 90 or so countries in the world are in this group. A sample list would include Ethiopia, Bolivia, and Pakistan.

To be successful abroad, HR managers must learn all they can about the countries in which they will be working. There are many sources of this kind of information. Knowledge of differences among nations in educational, behavioral, legal-political, and economic factors is essential for managerial success abroad. It is equally important (and more difficult) for the enterprise to obtain managers with proper attitudes toward other countries and their cultures. A manager with the wrong set of attitudes may try to transfer North American ways of doing things directly to the host country, without considering the constraints in these four factors. The more significant the differences, the more likely they are to cause problems for the unperceptive manager.

Effective managers who work abroad must adapt their HRM practices to conditions in the host country and learn to understand the new culture. A whole new field is developing for human resource planning in multinational organizations. There are significant challenges in such HRM activities. Just as the tools of management science do not work on very unstable problems, leadership styles and HRM activities that work for educated, achievement-oriented employees may not do so for uneducated nonachievers.

In sum, the physical location of the organization (rural or urban, at home or abroad) can have a significant impact on how HRM programs are used and which activities are conducted. The manager using a diagnostic orientation will be better able to closely examine, consider, and understand the complexities involved with physical location differences.

INTERNAL ENVIRONMENTAL INFLUENCES

The **internal environmental influences** listed in Exhibit 2–1 (goals, organization style, nature of the task, work group, and leader's style and experience) involve characteristics and factors that are found within the organization. Let's examine how each of these influences affects the HRM program.

Goals

The goals of organizations differ within and among departments. All departments probably have goals that include employee satisfaction, survival, and adaptability to change. The differences arise in the *importance* the decision makers place on the different goals. In some organizations, profit is of such major importance that other goals such as increased employee satisfaction are not well developed. In these organizations where profits take precedent, HRM goals involving the human resources are paid only minimal attention. The result of such negligence is typically problems in the effectiveness area of the diagnostic model (e.g., high absenteeism, performance decrements, high grievance rates). In other organizations, HRM-related goals are highly regarded by decision makers. Thus, how much the HRM function is valued and how it is implemented are affected by these goals.

Organization Culture

Organization culture refers to a system of shared meaning held by members that distinguishes the organization from other organizations.[27] The essence of a firm's culture is emitted from the firm's way of doing business, the manner in which it treats customers and employees, the extent of autonomy or freedom that exists in the departments or offices, and the degree of loyalty expressed by employees about the firm. Organization culture represents the perceptions held by the organization's employees. Is there a sense of shared value? Is there a common value system held by employees? These are the kinds of questions asked to arrive at a picture of the firm's culture.

There is no one "best" culture for the development of human resources. What culture exists in McDonald's is different than the one found at KFC. There is also the issue of strong and weak culture. A firm with values being shared by a large majority of the employees is said to have a strong culture. Japanese companies like Sony, Honda, and Toyota are often cited as firms with strong cultures. IBM, 3M, and Merck are examples of firms with strong cultures in the United States.

Culture can have an impact on the behavior, productivity, and expectations of employees. It provides a benchmark of the standards of performance among employees. For example, it can provide clear guidelines on attendance, punctuality, concern about quality, and customer service.

Preston Trucking is a firm that had little value sharing among management and labor (represented by the Teamsters and International Longshoremen's Association).[28] After bickering and a lack of cooperation for years, Teamsters now sing praises about working for Preston. Why? One reason is that Preston's management created a family feeling, a sense of sharing, a new culture. Managers were trained and expected to treat every employee with respect. Managers were to be fair, firm, and positive in correcting performance problems. They were also expected to reward and recognize good performance. The consequence of management's dedication to its people has been the creation of a feeling at Preston Trucking that human resources are the most important asset of the firm. The organization culture at Preston has made a difference in performance, loyalty, and commitment. Preston Trucking has used organization culture to improve the relationships between management and labor.

Nature of the Task

Many experts believe that the task to be performed is one of the two most vital factors affecting HRM. They describe HRM as the effective matching of the nature of the task with the nature of the employee performing the task.[29]

There are perhaps unlimited similarities and differences among jobs that attract or repel workers and influence the meaning of work for them. Some of the most significant are:

Degree of Physical Exertion Required   Contrast the job of ditch digger with that of a computer programmer. In general, most people prefer work involving minimal amounts of physical exertion. Some companies, like IBM, believe that working with the mind is better for curing productivity problems than working with the back. Exhibit 2–3 captures some of IBM's thinking on this matter.

Degree of Environmental Unpleasantness   Contrast the environment of a coal miner with that of a bank teller. People generally prefer physically pleasant and safe conditions.

Physical Location of Work   Some jobs require outside work; others, inside. Contrast the job of a telephone craftsperson during the winter in Minnesota with that of a disc jockey. Some jobs require the employee to stay in one place. Others permit moving about. Contrast the job of an employee on an assembly line with that of a traveling sales representative. There are individual differences in preference for physical location.

Time Dimension of Work   Some jobs require short periods of intense effort, others long hours of less taxing work. In some jobs the work is continuous; in others, intermittent.

Human Interaction on the Job   Some jobs require frequent interaction with others. Contrast the position of a radar operator in an isolated location who rarely sees anyone else with that of a receptionist in a busy city hall.

Degree of Variety in the Task   The amount of freedom and responsibility a person has on the job determines the degree of *autonomy* provided for in the work. Contrast the autonomy of a college professor with that of an assembly-line worker.

Task Identity   The degree of wholeness in a job — the feeling of completing a whole job as opposed to contributing to only a portion of a job — is its *task identity*. Contrast the job of an auto assembler with that of a tax accountant.

Task Differences and Job Design   Because jobs are not created by nature, engineers and specialists can create jobs with varying attention to the characteristics

EXHIBIT 2-3

WORKING SMARTER VS. WORKING HARDER.

Japan's productivity keeps improving.
Germany's too.
"So America's going to have to work harder," people say.
But that's not enough anymore.
We also have to work *smarter.*
America's productivity problem isn't caused by lazy workers. It's partly caused by lazy factories, lazy tools, and lazy methods which dilute the efforts of hard-working people.
Working smarter can help change that.
Today, thousands of IBM customers are working smarter by using computers, word processors, and electronic office machines. Insurance companies, retailers, banks, farmers, aerospace companies have all become more productive by making *information* work harder.
In world trade, productivity is a key to success. And America has long been the most productive country on earth.
We can stay that way by working smarter. **IBM**

described here. There are a number of approaches to those aspects of job design that affect variety, autonomy, task identity, and similar job factors. These approaches will be covered in Chapter 6.

How do these task factors affect HRM decisions? They obviously affect recruiting and selection, since employees will probably be more satisfied and productive if their preferences are met. As was mentioned, few jobs match all preferences exactly — there are not too many of them. With jobs that are difficult, dirty, or in smoky or hot environments, the manager must provide additional incentives (more pay, shorter hours, or priority in vacations) because few people prefer such jobs. Or the manager may try to find employees who can handle the conditions better.

Work Group

Groups play a major role in the life of an individual. You probably belong to family, friendship, and student groups. Once a person joins an organization, his or her experiences are largely influenced by a work group.

A **work group** consists of two or more people who consider themselves a group, who are interdependent with one another for the accomplishment of a purpose, and who communicate and interact with one another on a more or less continuous basis. In many cases (but not always), they work next to each other.

An effective group is one whose:

- Members function and act as a team.
- Members participate fully in group discussion.
- Group goals are clearly developed.
- Resources are adequate to accomplish group goals.
- Members furnish many useful suggestions leading to goal achievement.

Most effective work groups are small (research indicates that 7 to 14 members is a good range), and their members have eye contact and work closely together. Effective groups also generally have stability of membership, and their members have similar backgrounds. Their membership is composed of persons who depend on the group to satisfy their needs.[30] An effective work group will help achieve the goals of the organization. Thus, it is in the manager's interest to make the groups effective. It is also in the interest of employees, because effective groups serve their members' social needs.

Although the effective group supports management and the organization's goals, it can also work against them. This is usually the case when the group perceives the organization's goals as being in conflict with its own. If the work group is effective and works with management, the manager's job is easier, and objectives are more likely to be achieved. If the group is working against the manager, an effort must be made to change the group's norms and behavior by the use of the manager's leadership, discipline, and reward powers, or by the transfer of some group members.

Work groups are directly related to the success of HRM activities. If the work group opposes HRM programs, it can ruin them. Examples of programs that can be successes or failures depending on work-group support or resistance include incentive compensation, profit sharing, safety, and labor relations. Operational and HR managers who desire success in such programs should at least consider permitting work-group participation in designing and implementing HRM.

Leader's Style and Experience

The experience and leadership style of the operating manager or leader directly affects HRM activities because many, if not most, programs must be implemented at the work-unit level. Thus, the operating manager-leader is a crucial link in the HRM function.

Leaders must orchestrate the distinctive skills, experiences, personalities, and motives of individuals. Leaders also must facilitate the intragroup interactions that occur within work groups. In his or her role, a leader provides direction, encouragement, and authority to evoke desired employee behaviors.[31] In addition, leaders reinforce desirable behavior so that it is sustained and enhanced. The leader is an important source of knowledge about the tasks, the organization, and the HRM policies, programs, and goals. The experience and operating style of a leader will influence which HRM programs are communicated, implemented, and effective.

Strategic HRM: An Important Key to Success

There is now little disagreement with the position that the HRM function is a vital contributor to the organization's mission. As indicated in Chapter 1, HR managers are becoming more involved in the establishment of the strategy formulation and implementation in the organization. A **strategy** indicates what an organization's key executives hope to accomplish in the long run.[32] There is also an intermediate and a short-term strategy position in any organization. Exhibit 2–4 presents the three levels of strategy — strategic, managerial, and operational — as they apply to five specific HRM activities.

The efforts to formulate and implement sound HRM strategies at the three levels presented in Exhibit 2–4 are designed to achieve desirable end results such as competitive products and/or services. In other words, sound strategies are intended to result in growth, profits, and survival. One study of corporations with publicly recognized accomplishments showed that these recognized productivity leaders act by emphasizing the importance of HRM in strategic decision making.[33] The study compared the practices of productivity leaders and comparison firms from *Fortune* 500 corporations. Five practices differentiated the leaders from the comparison firms.

- Leaders define the HRM role in terms of the function's participation in business decisions and in the implementation of business strategies.
- Leaders focus the current resources devoted to the HRM function on important problems before they add new programs or seek additional resources.
- Leaders' HR staffs initiate programs and communication with line managers.
- Leaders' line management share the responsibility for HRM programs.
- Leaders' corporate staffs share responsibility for human resource policy formulation and program administration across organizational levels.

The study clearly showed that the HRM function is a major force in developing the strategic thrust in the successful firms. In contrast, in the comparison companies, the HRM function was not in the mainstream of developing organizational strategies.

Strategic planning by an organization leads to informed, purposeful actions. By articulating a clear common vision of what the organization exists for, now and in the future, a strategic plan provides direction and a cornerstone for making impor-

EXHIBIT 2-4   Human Resource Activities by Level

Level	Employee Selection/ Placement	Rewards (Pay and Benefits)	Appraisal	Development	Career Planning
Strategic (long-term)	Specify the characteristics of people needed to run business over long term Alter internal and external systems to reflect future	Determine how work force will be rewarded over the long term based on potential world conditions Link to long-term business strategy	Determine what should be valued in long term Develop means to appraise future dimensions Make early identification of potential	Plan developmental experiences for people running future business Set up systems with flexibility necessary to adjust to change	Develop long-term system to manage individual and organizational needs for both flexibility and stability Link to business strategy
Managerial (medium-term)	Make longitudinal validation of selection criteria Develop recruitment marketing plan Develop new markets	Set up five-year compensation plans for individuals Set up cafeteria benefits packages	Set up validated systems that relate current conditions and future potential Set up assessment centers for development	Establish general management development program Provide for organizational development Foster self-development	Identify career paths Provide career development services Match individual with organization
Operational (short-term)	Make staffing plans Make recruitment plans Set up day-to-day monitoring systems	Administer wage and salary program Administer benefits packages	Set up annual or less-frequent appraisal system Set up day-to-day control systems	Provide for specific job-skill training Provide on-the-job training	Fit individuals to specific jobs Plan next career move

tant HRM decisions. The planning process when applied to HRM activities expands awareness of possibilities, identifies strengths and weaknesses, reveals opportunities, and points to the need to evaluate the probable impact of internal and external forces.

A well-designed organizational strategic plan permits the HR department to be better prepared to cope and deal with changes in both the internal and external environments presented in Exhibit 2–1. The idea of incorporating HRM activities and plans into the organization's strategic plan to cope with changes is not new. Each organization can adopt a specific form of strategy that best fits its goals, environments, resources, and people. Gerstein and Reisman have identified five corporate strategies and the employee characteristics that fit each strategy. Exhibit 2–5 presents some HRM activities that represent a "best fit" for each strategy. The matching of an organization's strategic plan, employee characteristics, and HRM activities is important for achieving desirable organizational end results — competitive products and competitive services.

The days of viewing the personnel or HRM area as only a highly specialized and technical staff activity are over. Human resources are vitally important to the firm's success, and the HRM function must be involved in all aspects of an organization's operation. The end results of having competitive products and/or services means that employees must be performing at an optimal level so that the overall strategy and goals can be achieved. The HR unit must make everyday contributions to the

EXHIBIT 2-5   HRM Practices and Organizational Strategy

Strategy Type	Needed Employee Characteristics	HRM Practice Choices
Entrepreneurial Projects with high financial risk are undertaken, minimal policies and procedures are in place, resources are insufficient to satisfy all customer demands, and multiple priorities must be satisfied. The focus here is on the short run and getting the operation off the ground.	To varying degrees, employees need to be innovative, cooperative, longer-term oriented, risk taking, and willing to assume responsibility. It is critical that key employees remain.	a. Employee selection/placement—seek out risk takers; high need for achievement people. b. Rewards—competitive, external equity, and employee-preference-based when possible. c. Appraisal—results-based; not too rigid. d. Development—informal, mentor-oriented. e. Career planning—focus on interest of employees and matching jobs with personal interests.
Dynamic Growth Strategy Risk taking on projects is more modest. The constant dilemma is between doing current work aand building support for the future. Policies and procedures are starting to be written, as the need is for more control and structure for an ever-expanding operation.	Employees need to have high organizational identification, be flexible to change, have a high task orientation, and work in close cooperation with others.	a. Employee selection/placement—seek out flexible and loyal individuals. b. Rewards—internal and external equity, high recognition-based program. c. Criteria-based. d. Development—emphasis on QWL programs, participation. e. Career planning—present opportunities, multiple career paths.
Contract Profit Rationalization Strategy The focus is on maintaining existing profit levels. Modest cost-cutting efforts and employee terminations may be occurring. Control systems and structure are well developed along with an extensive set of policies and procedures.	The focus is on quality and efficiency, the short term, and results with a relatively low level of risk and a minimal level of organizational identification.	a. Employee selection-placement—very selective, some outplacement. b. Rewards—merit-based, seniority, internal equity. c. Appraisal—specific, results-oriented, carefully reviewed. d. Development—emphasis on task competence, developing experts in narrow area. e. Career planning—narrow, few opportunities and paths available.
Liquidation/Divestiture Strategy The focus involves selling off assets, cutting further losses, and reducing the work force as much as possible. Little or no thought is given to trying to save the operation, as declining profits are likely to continue.	Employees need a short-term narrow orientation, low organizational commitment, a low need to remain, and a limited focus on high quality.	a. Employee selection/placement—not likely because of cutbacks. b. Rewards—merit-based, few perks, no incentives. c. Appraisal—rigid, formally conducted, management-based criteria. d. Development—limited, based on task-competence. e. Career planning—those with required skills will have opportunities.
Turnaround Strategy The focus is to save the operation. Although cost-cutting efforts and employee reductions are made, they are short-term programs for long-run survival. Worker morale may be somewhat depressed.	Employees need to be open to change, have a high task orientation, have a longer-term focus, and engage in some nonrepetitive behavior.	a. Employee selection/placement—need multitalented individuals. b. Rewards—incentive systems, merit reviews, and employee participation. c. Appraisal—results-oriented, encourage participation. d. Development—increased opportunities, carefully select participants. e. Career planning—multiple career paths, encourage participation.

Source: R. S. Schuler (1987), "Personnel and Human Resource Management Choices and Organizational Strategy," in *Readings in Personnel and Human Resource Management*, 3d ed., ed. R. S. Schuler, S. A. Youngblood, and V. Huber (St. Paul: West Publishing).

organization. Thus, the HRM programs must be comprehensive, adaptable with the organization's culture, and responsive to employee needs. This means that management creativity and action must be exerted to match an organization's overall strategy with its HRM programs, activities, and talents.

PEOPLE AND THE HRM DIAGNOSTIC MODEL

People, the employees — the human resource element — are the most important concern in the diagnostic model. Simply putting together HRM activities without paying attention to employee characteristics would be ill-advised. The most carefully designed and implemented HRM activity may backfire because adjustments for individual differences were not built into the program. In the Career Challenge earlier in the chapter, Martha is attempting to understand why Lenny and Harry behave differently on the job at the National Pancake House. She will discover that people differ in many characteristics. Lenny and Harry differ in their abilities, attitudes, and preferences. They also have different styles, intellectual capacities, and ways of doing the job.

Abilities of Employees

Some employee differences affecting HRM programs are due to differences in abilities. Abilities can be classified by mechanical, motor coordination, mental, or creative skills. According to many psychologists, some abilities are caused by genetic factors that are rarely subject to change through training. Examples of these differences are finger dexterity and response time. Other abilities, such as interpersonal skills and leadership, are much more easily subject to change. People learn abilities at home, at school, and at work; their present inventories of abilities are, at least partly, a consequence of this past learning.

Because people differ in abilities, the extent to which they can be trained in a specific skill varies. In most cases, an aptitude can be developed into an ability by training and experience. But in other cases, it's more sensible to place people with certain abilities in jobs requiring those abilities. Not everyone will have all the abilities necessary to do every job, and a manager does not always have the time or money needed to train people who do not have them.

The importance of a manager's understanding of employee ability differences is emphasized by the example of Harry at National Pancake. Does he lack the abilities to do the job? If it appears that Harry's problem is in fact ability, Martha would have at least two options. One is training, whereby Harry's aptitudes would be developed into the ability needed for the job. The other is placement, whereby Harry could be transferred to another job, such as busboy or cashier.

Do you think Harry's problem is an ability problem?

Employee Attitudes and Preferences

How an individual thinks, feels, and behaves toward work and the place of work is his or her life forms one important attitude. An **attitude** is a characteristic and usually long-lasting way of thinking, feeling, and behaving toward an object, idea, person, or group of persons. A *preference* is a type of attitude that evaluates an object, idea, or person in a positive or negative way.

People are motivated by powerful emotional forces, and work provides an opportunity for the expression of both aggressive and pleasure-seeking drives.

Besides offering a way to channel energy, work also provides the person with income, a justification for existence, and the opportunity to achieve self-esteem and self-worth. The amount of energy directed toward work is related to the amount directed to family, interpersonal relations, and recreation.

What kinds of attitudes about work do Lenny and Harry have?

How can an awareness of work attitudes and preferences help managers understand workers and improve their effectiveness? Many HRM programs (job enlargement, compensation, leadership, and participation programs) are designed to create a more favorable individual attitude toward work. The assumption is that a positive attitude will result in higher-quality performance and increased production. Recall, however, that performance is also influenced by learning, perception, abilities, and motivation.

Motivation of Employees

Work motivation is concerned with those attitudes that channel a person's behavior toward work and away from recreation or other life activity areas. The motivation to work is likely to change as other life activities change. **Motivation** is that set of attitudes that predisposes a person to act in a specific goal-directed way. Motivation is thus an inner state that energizes, channels, and sustains human behavior to achieve goals.

A number of theories have attempted to explain work motivation. The theories differ in their assumptions about how rational people are and about the degree to which the conscious and the unconscious mind directs behavior. All of these theories have received some research support, but none has been overwhelmingly substantiated. At the moment, attention is focused on the importance of individual motivation in achieving organizational and individual goals.

How will the knowledge of employee motivation help a person be a more effective manager of people? As with work attitudes, a manager who can determine what the work motivations of the employees are will make more effective HRM decisions. For employees who appear to be work oriented and motivated toward working hard, incentive compensation systems will likely lead to higher productivity and higher-quality work. Those who are consciously motivated to do a better job benefit from performance evaluation techniques such as management by objectives. Managers who can determine or predict which employees are motivated can create the work environment that will most optimally sustain the motivation.

The determination of a person's state of motivation is undoubtedly very difficult. Remember, motivation is *within* a person, and a manager must infer the individual's motivational level from his or her behavior. The manager uses his or her understanding of individual motivation to select the best possible HRM program.

Personality of Employees

Each employee has a unique personality. Because of this, it is highly unlikely that a single set of HRM activities or leadership approaches will be equally successful for *all* employees. **Personality** is the characteristic way a person thinks and behaves in adjusting to his or her environment. It includes the person's traits, values, motives, genetic blueprints, attitudes, emotional reactivity, abilities, self-image, and intelligence. It also includes the person's visible behavior patterns.

PROFESSIONAL PROFILE

Biography

David A. Allen is the personnel officer for the Philadelphia District of the Internal Revenue Service. He is
a 1972 graduate of St. Lawrence University, where he
earned a BA in history. He enjoys family activities and
is involved with his two daughters in various sporting
endeavors, serving as both soccer and softball coach.
He is also an active member of his church.

Allen joined the IRS directly out of college, working as a temporary taxpayer service representative. He
also was a tax auditor before becoming a successful
candidate for the Resources Management Intern program. He has worked in the personnel disciplines of
employment and labor relations and gained experience in a staff management position in the regional
IRS office before returning to his first love, line operations. He has been involved with developing the IRS
Flexible Workplace pilot and a rating schedule for the
Internal Revenue Agent occupation.

Job Description   Dave serves as the top technical
personnel authority in the district, responsible for developing and recommending procedures and programs
to enable the personnel management function to best
serve and support district management and employees. This includes planning recruitment, administering
internal promotion activity, processing the full range
of personnel payroll actions, delivering employee benefit programs, providing labor relations services, and
overseeing employee relations activity.

Challenges and Opportunities Facing the Government: A Viewpoint   Many challenges face the federal
sector in the years ahead. Our greatest task is attracting and retaining a top-quality workforce. We must
overcome many obstacles, including generally low
starting salaries, limited benefits, and poor public image. To overcome these hurdles, we must emphasize
our strengths and work to become a model employer.
To this end, the IRS has taken steps to test a flexible
workplace program and has encouraged the establishment of child-care and physical wellness facilities.

We have also been a leader in the federal sector in
the quality improvement movement, looking to make
quality an integral part of our "corporate culture."
This, in turn, has caused us to concentrate even more
on the necessity for exceptional customer service. Our
customers are diverse and have varying demands.

David A. Allen
Philadelphia District of the Internal
Revenue Service

The challenge constantly before us is to remember
that people with payroll problems, managers with
position management issues, or union officials with
concerns are not interruptions to our work but the
reason for our jobs.

The IRS has a long way to go in the computerized
area. Our hardware and software do not even meet
our basic needs. Compounding this problem is the
lack of skilled computer people available to support
applications development. Since we are not competitive in the marketplace, we often have to "grow
our own." However, once they are trained and fully
functional, they are often lured away by much better
financial packages offered in the private sector. Thus,
we are in a constant recruitment and training mode.
Hiring of people with disabilities has been one way we
have successfully found quality employees.

We must also look to the future to anticipate, as
best we can, the problems we will encounter there.
Work force 2000 issues, such as an aging work force
and low-skilled entry-level employees, are very real
right now. Strategies must be implemented now to
deal with these issues. We must start now to develop a
workplace where people want to remain.

The challenges facing a human resources professional in the federal sector today call for imagination and flexibility in responding within the limits
prescribed by law and regulation. We must surmount
the obstacles to remain a vital entity in the years
ahead.

The content of this profile is the opinion of the writer and does not
necessarily represent the position of the Internal Revenue Service.

CAREER CHALLENGE
(*concluded*)

Martha picked up her cup of coffee and thought: "Amy helped me a lot. But it is my job to figure out what to do." She wonders what factors could cause the differences between Lenny and Harry. It could be personality differences. Lenny is an outgoing person, and Harry tends to be introverted. There are some difficulties in abilities. Lenny is more agile. He uses his hands well. Harry seems a bit clumsier. And Lenny is more experienced — he's been on the job four more years than Harry.

Lenny and Harry have the same leader and work group. They do the same task at the same time. The environment is the same. These couldn't cause the differences.

This narrows the option down to motivation and attitude differences. Was there a good match of interests and abilities with the job? Martha decided to discuss the issues formally with Harry. Later that day, she invited Harry to have a chat with her.

Martha Harry, this is the first chance I've had to chat with you for very long. How do you like it at National by now?

Harry It's O.K. It's a job.

Martha Is there anything we can do to make it better than just a job for you?

Harry Not really. Jobs are jobs. They're all the same.

Martha All of them? Did you ever have a dream about what you wanted to do?

Harry Sure. I've always wanted to be a disc jockey, but I hated school. So I quit. Then I got married and I'm locked in. I can't go back to school and make it.

Martha I didn't know you wanted to go back to school. I'm sure you could go to night school.

Harry I might be ready for that now.

Martha If I can help by scheduling you differently, let me know. Everyone should get all the schooling they can. And who knows? You could go on to be assistant manager here — or even a disc jockey.

After talking with Martha, Harry did go back to school. His work improved, as did his willingness to be friendlier with coworkers and customers. Martha's chats became more frequent with all the employees, including Harry. Harry did graduate from high school and now is an assistant manager for National. He's very happy in his job.

What about Lenny? He's chief cook at 827. He's had several opportunities to become assistant manager, but he loves his work and has refused to be transferred. As Lenny put it, "I've found my niche. I do my job, then go to the beach. No worries. And I get to talk to lots of nice people."

What about the new cook? The pay issues had to be settled first. Martha contacted the home office, emphasizing that business had been steadily increasing at 827. When she told them that she needed more money to hire an extra cook to handle the increased business, they gave her more, but not enough to completely satisfy everyone.

Instead of hiding this fact from the rest of her employees, Martha explained the situation and asked them for their suggestions. Their solution was to help her recruit a cook with some experience, but one who would not demand so high a salary that their raises would be eliminated. All of the employees asked their friends for leads to fill the vacancy. Martha called guidance counselors at schools and the state employment service.

Within a week, Martha had hired Dan, a friend of Harry's. Lenny, Harry, and all the other employees liked him very much, and he worked out well as the third cook. Besides that, employee satisfaction improved all around. Not only could Martha pay Dan what he expected as a beginning wage, but all the other employees got a slight increase in pay, too.

Behavioral scientists have found that:

1. The employee, as a person, is both rational and intuitive-emotional in makeup and behavior. Therefore, his or her choices and behavior are a consequence of rational (conscious) and emotional (unconscious) influences. Choices are occasionally entirely influenced by one or the other, but most behavior is influenced by both.
2. A person acts in response to internal inclinations and choices and environmental influences.
3. Each person is unique and acts and thinks in a certain way because of:
   . The personality the person develops.
   . The abilities the person has or learns.
   . The attitudes and preferences the person has or develops.
   . The motives the person has or develops.

This section has touched briefly on some relevant concepts from the behavioral sciences that will be developed further in later chapters. Theory and research indicate that the nature of the employee has a great influence on HRM decisions. The effective manager realizes that the employee's nature is a crucial variable in HRM activities and organizational effectiveness. The implications of this knowledge of human behavior for the various HRM activities will become more obvious as we move into the book.

Now, after learning about the diagnostic model, let's find out what happened at National Pancake House 827. The conclusion of this chapter's Career Challenge will show you how Martha worked on the problem and solved the mystery of Harry's behavior.

SUMMARY

The main objective of this chapter has been to introduce you to the diagnostic model of HRM. The model will serve as the framework for observing, analyzing, and solving HRM problems. The chapter also briefly reviews some concepts from the behavioral sciences to show you how they apply to HRM decisions. It further examines two other aspects of the environment of the HRM function: the physical location of the organization in a labor market and the work sector in which it is located. This book has been written with the assumption that HRM programs are more likely to be effective if the manager or specialist follows a diagnostic approach.

To summarize the major points covered in this chapter:

1. A sound HRM program can contribute to organizational effectiveness.
2. The diagnostic approach suggests that before you choose an HRM program you should examine the nature of the employees, the external and internal environmental influences on the organization, and organizational factors. These factors act as moderating variables in HRM decisions, and HRM activities are influenced by them.
3. Various factors in the external environment, such as unionization of employees, government regulations, and competitive pressure, also exert strong influences on the HRM function.

4. Understanding the characteristics and composition of the labor force is important when designing an HRM program.

5. HRM has become a strategic area and is now recognized as important in creating and implementing the overall strategies of a firm.

6. The work sector in which the organization is operating — public, private, or third — determines the complexity, strategic importance, and power of the HRM function.

7. Organization factors, including goals, organization culture, the nature of the task, makeup of the work group, and leader's style and experience, must be taken into account to maximize the effectiveness of the HRM function.

8. An attitude is a characteristic and usually is a long-lasting way of thinking, feeling, and behaving. A preference is a type of attitude that evaluates an object, idea, or person in a positive or negative way.

KEY TERMS

external environmental influences	42	personality	62
		productivity	44
internal environmental influences	54	strategy	58
		work group	57
motivation	62		

QUESTIONS FOR REVIEW AND DISCUSSION

1. How is the work of HR specialists similar to that of physicians who must conduct a diagnosis before treating a patient?

2. Visit an organization to observe rituals, behaviors, dress codes, and interactions that help identify the firm's culture. Report your observations to the class and instructor.

3. Why is it important for an HR department to be respected by other units when an organization is developing its strategic plan?

4. How can an HR department make daily contributions to the goals of an organization?

5. Why must external environmental forces be considered when designing an HRM program?

6. What is your opinion about immigration to the United States? Why have you developed this opinion? Since almost everyone you meet has immigrant roots, what should the United States do regarding illegal immigrants?

7. What effectiveness criteria are used to examine the success of an HRM program?

8. Small firms, like large enterprises, must engage in developing clearly stated strategic plans? Why?

9. Someone stated that, "If unemployment in the national and local labor markets differs, there will be a natural movement of people between the markets." What did she mean by this statement?

10. What did you like about Martha's leadership style at National Pancake House 827?

NOTES

[1] E. Herman, Alfred Kuhn, and Ronald L. Seeber (1987), *Collective Bargaining and Labor Relations* (Englewood Cliffs, N.J.: Prentice-Hall), pp. 1–27.

[2] (February 1988), U.S. Department of Labor Office of Information and Public Affairs, Telephone Communication.

[3] John Dunlop (February 1976), "The Limits of Legal Compulsion," *Labor Law Journal*, pp. 69–70.

[4] Arthur S. Herman (April 1987), "Productivity Gains Continued in Many Industries during 1985," *Monthly Labor Review*, p. 48.

[5] Michael B. Packer (March 1983), "Measuring the Intangible in Productivity," *Technology Review*, pp. 48–57.

[6] (February 13, 1984), "The Reward of Productivity," *Business Week*, pp. 92–96; and Elliott S. Grossman (1980), "Total Factor Productivity Dynamics," in *Productivity Perspectives* (Houston: American Productivity Center), pp. 2–10.

[7] Michael L. Dertouzos, Richard K. Lester, and Robert M. Solow (1989), *Made In America* (Cambridge, MA: The MIT Press), p. 26.

[8] Anne V. Corey (Spring 1991), "Ensuring Strength in Each Country: A Challenge for Corporate Headquarters Global Human Resource Executives," *Human Resource Planning*, pp. 1–8.

[9] Rosabath Mose Kanter (May–June 1991), "Transcending Business Boundaries: 12,000 World Managers View Change," *Harvard Business Review*, pp. 151–64.

[10] Robert B. McKersie and Janice A. Klein (Winter 1983–84), "Productivity: The Industrial Relations Connection," *National Productivity Review*, pp. 26–35.

[11] (1983), "Productivity," *Personnel Management Policies and Practices* (Englewood Cliffs, N.J.: Prentice-Hall), pp. 23, 71–72.

[12] (1985), Global Competition: *The New Reality*, Vol. II, Report of the President's Commission on Industrial Competitiveness (Washington, D.C.: U.S. Government Printing Office), p. 6.

[13] Betsy D. Gelb, Mary Jane Saxton, George M. Zinkhan, and Nancy D. Albers (January–February 1991), "Competitive Intelligence: Insights From Executives," *Business Horizons*, pp. 43–47.

[14] William B. Johnston and Arnold H. Packer (1987), *Workforce 2000: Work and Workers for the 21st Century* (Indianapolis: Hudson Institute).

[15] Texas Employment Commission, Economic Analysis & Research (Labor Market Information), Telephone Communication, March 25, 1991.

[16] Marilyn Loden and Judy B. Rosener, *Workforce v America*, Homewood, IL: Business One Irwin, 1991, p. 7 and *What Lies Ahead*, Alexandria, VA: United Way of America, 1989, p. 15.

[17] Chris Telly (March 1991), "Reasons for the Continuing Growth of Part-Time Employment," *Monthly Labor Review*, pp. 10–18.

[18] (January 1991), *Monthly Labor Review*, p. 82.

[19] Steven E. Hangen and Joseph R. Neisenheimer II (February 1991), "U.S. Labor Market Weakened in 1990," *Monthly Labor Review*, February 1991, pp. 3–16.

[20] Johnston and Packer, *Workforce 2000*, pp. 93–94.

[21] (1989), *What Lies Ahead: Countdown to the 21st Century* (Alexandria, VA: United Way Strategic Institute), pp. 17–18.

[22] Sydney P. Freedberg (October 13, 1987), "Forced Exits? Companies Confront Wave of Age Discrimination Suits," *The Wall Street Journal*, p. 33, and H. Kahne et al. (January 1957), "Don't Take the Older Workers for Granted," *Harvard Business Review*, pp. 90–94.

[23] Paul E. Pryzant (September 1990), "New Disabilities Act to Have Big Impact on Business," *Buttler & Bincon Report*, pp. 1–5.

24 R. B. Nathanson (May–June 1977), "The Disabled Employee: Separating Myth from Fact," *Harvard Business Review*, pp. 6–8.

25 Bureau of National Affairs (May 21, 1981), *Fair Employment Practices — Summary of Latest Developments* (Washington, D.C., 1981).

26 Ibid.

27 Edgar H. Schein (1985), *Organizational Culture and Leadership* (San Francisco: Jossey-Bass), p. 168.

28 Robert Levering (1988), *A Great Place to Work* (New York: Random House), pp. 139–161.

29 Sak Onkvist and John Shaw (January–February 1991), "Myopic Management: The Hollow Strength of American Competitiveness," *Business Horizons*, pp. 13–19.

30 James L. Gibson, John M. Ivancevich, and James H. Donnelly, Jr. (1991), *Organizations: Behavior, Structure, Processes* (Homewood, IL: Irwin), p. 268.

31 John W. Gardner (Spring 1987), "The Tasks of Leadership," *New Management*, pp. 9–14.

32 Lee Dyer (Fall 1983), "Bringing Human Resources into the Strategy Formulation Process," *Human Resource Management*, pp. 257–71.

33 Kenneth F. Misa and Timothy Stein (October 1983), "Strategic HRM and the Bottom Line," *Personnel Administrator*, pp. 27–30.

EXERCISE 2–1   Dissecting the Diagnostic Model and Its Application
· · · · ·

Objective   The objective of this exercise is to have students examine in detail the main diagnostic model used in this book (Exhibit 2–1).

SET UP THE EXERCISE

1. Each student is to individually examine the various parts of Exhibit 2–1. Note the three main parts of HRM programs — activities, people, and effectiveness criteria.

2. Set up groups of four students each. Each student is to take a hypothetical organization type — a large manufacturing firm, a medium-sized community hospital (350 beds), a government agency such as the Equal Employment Opportunity Commission, and a small mom-and-pop department store that employes 10 full-time and 15 part-time employees.

3. Each student is to develop an analysis of the type of environmental influences, and of the HRM activities, people characteristics, criteria, and results that pertain to their organization type. Thus, each group will have four separate analyses to prepare. The analyses should use Exhibit 2–1 as the diagnostic model for putting together the analyses.

4. Students will bring their analyses to a group meeting for discussion and to compare similarities and differences.
   a. What are the criteria used in the different organizations?
   b. What are the end result factors?
   c. What environmental forces are important for the various organizations?

A Learning Note

This exercise will require individual and group work. It should show that the diagnostic model (Exhibit 2–1) can be applied to large, medium-sized, and small organizations.

APPLICATION CASE 2–1   Towers Perrin and Hudson Institute Study — HR Executives
. . . . .

Towers Perrin and Hudson Institute joined together in 1990 to conduct a survey of HR executives. What the survey data reveal most clearly is that the workplace of the future is, to a great extent, already here. Indeed, just three years after publication of the Hudson Institute study — and popularization of the phrase *Workforce 2000* — it may be more apt to talk of *Workforce Today*, because many of the employers in the survey group are already struggling with the implications of recruiting and managing a work force composed less and less of white American males.

Among the survey's key findings are:

- *The survey companies are literally in the midst of a sea change.* The average survey company's work force is already just about one-half female. Minorities now compose up to 20 percent of the work force at just under 60 percent of the survey companies and more than 26 percent of employees at almost a quarter of the survey group.

- *Most of the companies are aware of and concerned about their demographic destiny.* As might be expected, given the shifting racial and ethnic mix of employees at many of the survey companies, cultural diversity is the paramount worry for most organizations, with just under three quarters of the respondents noting some level of management focus on the hiring and promotion of minority employees.

    Almost as prevalent is concern about the special needs of female employees, expressed by 68 percent of respondents. On the other hand, relatively few companies are concerned about the aging of their work force — even though age 40-plus employees make up about 35 percent of the work force, on average, at the survey companies.

    The implications of competing in a seller's market for talent is also a key concern. Sixty-five percent of the respondents note that their senior management is concerned about impending shortfalls in the labor pool. For 36 percent, that level of concern is strong enough — even today — to shape management decisions and corporate strategy.

    But worries about finding individuals to fill available jobs apparently have not yet sparked

an equal level of concern about prospective workers' abilities to perform effectively on the job. Compared with the 65 percent reporting management concern about labor shortages, 42 percent of the survey respondents cite some level of management concern about a gap between the skills employees possess and those required to get the job done.

More telling, perhaps, 46 percent were either unable or unwilling to answer the question on management concern about skills mismatches. This high percentage of nonrespondents (more than three times that for any of the other questions relating to management concern about Workforce 2000 issues) may be indicative of just how unknown this particular territory remains for many companies. Their unfamiliarity with the issue appears great enough to discourage many from making any sort of determination about current or looming skills gaps.

- *Many companies are acting on their concerns — formulating new approaches to recruitment, for instance, and exploring different ways to structure the workday or week. But traditional solutions still largely hold sway.* The most prevalent approach to helping employees learn and improve skills, for instance, is tuition reimbursement, used by 78 percent of the survey companies. Just 8 percent, by contrast, undertake remedial training, although another 9 percent are piloting a remedial education program and 14 percent are planning to adopt one.

- *Recognizing where the problems lie doesn't necessarily lead to targeted solutions.* The most common reason for rejecting potential job candidates is inadequate writing or verbal skills. Yet training — either before employment or on the job — doesn't yet appear to be a priority at many companies, if measured by monetary outlays. Two thirds of the group spend less than $2,000 a year on any kind of training for entry-level new hires and many companies spend nothing at all.

- *New approaches to staffing and managing the "new" work force appear to be a function of top-management support and need.* Support from the top seems to count strongly in giving human resource professionals the wherewithal to expand their efforts and, perhaps, experiment with leading-edge programs as well. For example:

1. Among organizations where concern about labor shortages is reflected in strategic plans, 42 percent recruit nontraditional workers (e.g., the handicapped or elderly) and 51 percent apply a marketing approach to hiring. By contrast, among those that have not yet translated concerns into specific plans, just 16 percent recruit from nontraditional sources and 35 percent "market" to prospective candidates.

2. Remedial education programs are more common at those companies whose strategic plans take into account skills gaps than at those that have not yet planned how to address skill mismatches. Thirty-eight percent of the former provide remedial training, compared with 16 percent of the latter.

Need plays a large role in sparking creative problem solving, too. Companies that recruit heavily, for example, are more prone than others to move beyond conventional solutions. Those recruiting more than 300 entry-level workers a year are twice as likely to recruit outside their local area, build partnerships with educational institutions, and use part-time workers than are companies recruiting less than 75 entry-level workers annually. Similarly, companies with a relatively large percentage of its work force over age 40 are more likely to use retirees as consultants and for special projects than are companies with a smaller percentage of age 40-plus workers.

Discussion Questions

1. What role are demographics likely to play in the future success or failure of organizations?
2. What conclusions about the challenges facing HRM have you reached?
3. What indicators in the survey results indicate that strategic HRM decision making must become the rule rather than the exception in organizations?

3

EQUAL EMPLOYMENT OPPORTUNITY: LEGAL ASPECTS OF HUMAN RESOURCE MANAGEMENT

· · · · · · ·

LEARNING OBJECTIVES

After studying this chapter, you should be able to:

· · ·

Determine three major reasons why equal employment opportunity (EEO) programs have evolved

· · ·

Describe two major criteria used to determine EEO and affirmative action compliance or noncompliance

· · ·

Explain what is meant by the term *discrimination*

· · ·

List the enforcement agencies that are responsible for administering Title VII of the Civil Rights Act, Executive Order 11246, and the Americans with Disabilities Act

· · ·

Outline how an organization can implement an affirmative action program

CAREER CHALLENGE

*H*ugo Gerbold, the director of human resource management at Reliable Insurance, is sitting in his office, thinking. The problem is equal employment opportunity. Reliable is a middle-sized company in the Midwest that specializes in homeowners', auto, and, to a lesser extent, life and health insurance. As is typical of firms of this type, the top-management team members are all white, in their 60s, and have been with the firm all their careers. The work force is mainly composed of:

Salespersons — 98 percent white males, the rest white females and black males.

Underwriters — 98 percent white males, 2 percent white females.

Claims agents — 90 percent white males, 8 percent white females, 2 percent black males.

Clerical staff — 90 percent white females, 10 percent black females.

Other administrative personnel: Computer programmers, marketing staff, security, etc. — 95 percent white males, 5 percent white females.

Reliable is located in an area where at least 35 percent of the labor force is black.

Hugo knows many firms just like Reliable have been fined back-pay differentials and ordered to set up affirmative action plans. At a recent conference, Reliable's lawyers devoted much time to discussing the laws and recent cases. This had prompted Hugo to visit the company president, Gregory Inness.

Gregory, 64 years old and a lawyer by training, did not give Hugo much hope that things were going to change at Reliable with regard to equal employment opportunities.

It is a few days after this meeting. Hugo has just received a call from a professor at one of the local universities. The professor had encouraged Osanna Kenley to apply at Reliable for a management trainee position that had been advertised. She had been discouraged by the HRM department because, they said, she was a liberal arts major. She'd also been told there were no positions. In fact, the company had just hired a white male for a trainee position. Somehow she'd found out about this.

The professor informed Hugo that Osanna is going to file a complaint against the firm with the Equal Employment Opportunity Commission (EEOC). He suggests Hugo talk with her before she goes to the EEOC. In fact, she is on her way over to see Hugo right now.

Hugo and Osanna have a pleasant talk, but it is clear that she means to open up Reliable to all applicants, even if she personally does not get a job there. He arranges to see Gregory right after Osanna leaves.

Hugo Gregory, remember how I was just talking about equal employment opportunities? Well, we may have a case on our hands. And remember the insurance company that just paid out $15 million in back pay and had to hire their fair share of minorities as a result?

Gregory Well, maybe we should hire this young woman. That ought to take care of the problem, won't it?

Hugo No, it won't. We'd better get going on an EEO program now. Hugo then explains the legal details of recent court cases on affirmative action.

INTRODUCTION

The impact of law on the HRM function is indicative of the development of laws governing all business and societal activities. Around 1970, people began to want to be legally protected from every problem. Patients sued doctors, consumers sued manufacturers of faulty products, children even began to sue parents for not being supportive and nurturing. In 1960, there were about 59,000 civil suits filed in U.S. district courts. By 1990, this figure had increased to over 211,000, an increase of over 250 percent, in a period when the population increased by only 27 percent.[1]

Although suits by consumers against manufacturers of defective products account for a large proportion of the increased litigation, suits by employees or job candidates against employers are increasing rapidly.[2] Therefore, it is in the best interest of the organization for the HR executives to develop policies and procedures that comply with the law. The best way to begin studying the relationship between HRM functions and the law is to devote time and attention to equal employment opportunity (EEO). No other regulatory area has so thoroughly affected HRM as EEO. EEO has implications for almost every activity in HRM: hiring, recruiting, training, terminating, compensating, evaluating, planning, disciplining, and collective bargaining.[3] **Equal employment opportunity (EEO) programs** are implemented by employers to prevent employment discrimination in the workplace or to take remedial action to offset past employment discrimination.

EEO cuts across every HRM activity, and this means that HR officials and managers in every function of the organization are involved. Top managers must get involved in EEO issues and programs to make sure that the organization is in compliance with the law, to avoid fines, and to establish a discrimination-free workplace. Operating managers must assist by changing their attitudes about protected-category employees and by helping all employees to adjust to the changes EEO is bringing to the workplace.

Exhibit 3–1 highlights the key factors in the HRM diagnostic model that affect equal employment opportunities. Some of these were noted in the introduction union requirements, goals of the organization, and HRM activities involved. Others are discussed later in the chapter: societal values, preferences of workers as reflected in economic status of minorities and women, and government regulations. Knowledge of these factors can contribute to an understanding of why EEO developed and how it operates. To be effective, HR managers must pay close attention to EEO in designing HRM activities, policies, and programs.

HOW DID EEO EMERGE?

The three main factors that led to the development of EEO were: (1) changes in societal values; (2) the economic status of women and minorities; and (3) the emerging role of government regulation. The first two are briefly discussed in this section; information on the third factor is discussed in detail in the next section.

Societal Values and EEO

Throughout history, Western society has accepted the principle that people should be rewarded according to the worth of their contributions. When the United States became a nation, that principle was embodied in the American dream: the idea that any individual, through hard work, could advance from the most humble origins to the highest station, according to the worth of her or his contributions. In the United

EXHIBIT 3-1   Factors Affecting Equal Employment Opportunity Programs

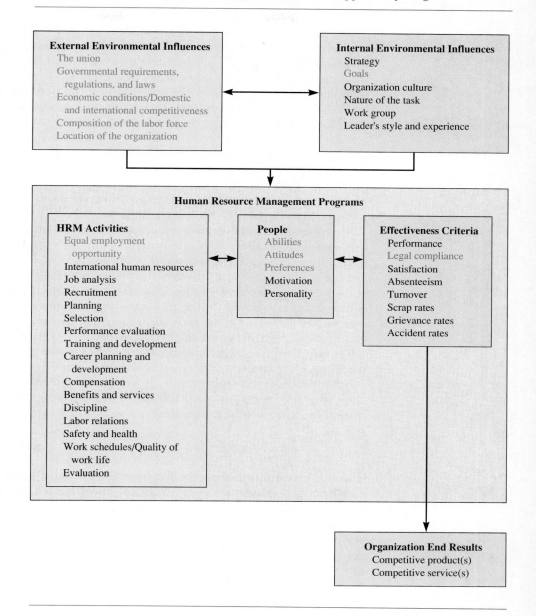

States, success did not depend on being born into a privileged family; equal opportunity was everyone's birthright. To this day, the American dream, with its emphasis on merit rather than privilege, is widely accepted by the public.

Another value that has encouraged equal opportunity is the profit motive. Nondiscrimination makes good business sense. If a company limits opportunities to white males, it cuts itself off from the vast reservoir of human talent comprised of women and minorities. Moreover, it adds to such societal problems as poverty, crime, high taxes, and civic disorder, which also hurt the business community.

Until the early 1960s, it was not unusual for many people, while believing in the American dream of rewards based on merit, to also believe that blacks (and other minorities) had their "place" — a place largely cut off from the rewards that the majority received. This apparent contradiction in beliefs was the U.S. dilemma as observed even in the 1940s by the distinguished Swedish economist, Gunnar Myrdal, in his studies of U.S. race relations for the Carnegie Corporation. Blacks were often excluded from schools, public accommodations, jobs, and voting; and economic realities for blacks belied the ideals of the American dream.[4]

The differences between American ideals and American realities lent special significance to the civil rights conflict of the 1960s. The conflict began in Montgomery, Alabama, on December 1, 1955, when Rosa Parks, a black department store worker in her 50s, was arrested for refusing to give up her bus seat to a white man. Out of that single act of protest emerged a previously unthinkable act — a bus boycott by blacks. At the center of the boycott was a loosely knit group called the Montgomery Improvement Association, which chose as its leader a new young minister in town, Dr. Martin Luther King, Jr.

Then came years of demonstrations, marches, and confrontations with the police that captured headlines throughout most of the early 1960s. Television accounts included scenes of civil rights demonstrators being attacked with cattle prods, dogs, and fire hoses. These events shocked the public into recognition that civil rights was a serious social problem in the United States. Gradually, overt discrimination declined and recognition of the problems faced by minorities grew. The business community shared in this attitude change, voluntarily supporting such EEO-related efforts as the National Alliance of Businessmen.

As the U.S. Congress turned its attention to civil rights, laws were passed prohibiting discrimination in education, voting, public accommodations, and the administration of federal programs, as well as discrimination in employment. The civil rights movement was instrumental in raising congressional concern and stimulating the passage of this legislation.

Economic Status of Minorities: Before 1964

Undeniable economic inequality helped focus national attention on employment as a specific area of discrimination. Unemployment figures for blacks were twice as high as for whites, and higher still among nonwhite youth. While blacks accounted for only 10 percent of the labor force, they represented 20 percent of total unemployment and nearly 30 percent of *long-term* unemployment. Moreover, in 1961, only one half of black men worked steadily at full-time jobs, while two thirds of white men did so. Blacks were three times as likely as whites to work less than full time. Similar statistical differences existed for other minorities, such as Hispanics and Native Americans.[5]

When they did find work, minorities were relegated to lower-status jobs, and consequently their income was far below that of whites. Minorities such as blacks were over three times as likely as whites to be unskilled laborers. Whites were over three times as likely as blacks to be in professional or managerial positions. While only 9 percent of black men were skilled craftsworkers, 20 percent of white men were. In the tobacco, paper, and trucking industries, blacks were ordinarily segregated into less desirable lines of progression or sections of the company. In the building trades, they were concentrated in the lower-paying "trowel trades," such as plastering and bricklaying. Some unions excluded blacks entirely, and others organized separate locals for them.

The inequalities are especially striking in the income comparisons between blacks and whites. In 1962, the average family income for blacks was $3,000, compared with nearly $6,000 for whites. More importantly, the relative position of blacks had been worsening during the preceding 10 years. While black family income was only 52 percent of white family income in 1962, it was 57 percent of white family income in 1952. These inequalities could not be attributed entirely to differences in educational level between blacks and whites. The average income of a black high school graduate was lower than the average income of a white elementary school graduate.[6]

The Government

There is no need to develop a detailed analysis to convince you that the government is playing an increasing role in all phases of life. According to some estimates, government expenditures on federal regulation have increased from $750 million in 1970 to over $4 billion in 1987.[7] But this is only a small fraction of the total cost of regulation. The public spends billions of dollars to comply with regulations.

In organizations, much of the compliance burden has been directed to the HR department. The growth of equal employment opportunity has given employees specific rights in their relationship with their employers. Employee rights were not widely publicized or seen as front-page news prior to the early 1970s.

THE 1964 CIVIL RIGHTS ACT AND TITLE VII

Today, there are many laws and executive orders (issued by presidents, which have the force and effect of laws enacted by Congress) prohibiting employment discrimination. Since it would be impossible to discuss all of them in a single chapter, this chapter will primarily focus on **Title VII** of the **1964 Civil Rights Act** and a few of the presidential executive orders. Considerable understanding of the entire legal framework can be gained by examining how these regulations operate.

Title VII: A Major Part of Civil Rights Guarantees

Employers, unions, employment agencies, and joint labor-management committees controlling apprenticeship or training programs are prohibited from discriminating on the basis of race, color, religion, sex, or national origin by Title VII of the 1964 Civil Rights Act. Other laws protect the aged, the handicapped, and special classes of veterans.[8] Title VII prohibits discrimination with regard to any employment condition, including hiring, firing, promotion, transfer, compensation, and admission to training programs. The Equal Employment Opportunity Act of 1972 amended Title VII by strengthening its enforcement and expanding its coverage to include employees of state and local governments and of educational institutions, as well as private employment of more than 15 persons. However, Native American tribes and private membership clubs are not covered, and religious organizations are allowed to discriminate on the basis of religion in some cases. Federal government employees are also covered by Title VII, but enforcement is carried out by the Civil Service Commission with procedures that are unique to federal employees.

The EEO coverage of government employees is noteworthy. While discrimination has been illegal in government employment since the end of the spoils system and the advent of open competitive examinations in the public service, race and sex inequalities have persisted in public service. The "merit system" in government employment has had a mixed record. Some of its features have held back minorities over the years. With the 1972 amendments to Title VII, public administrators found themselves subject to the the same sorts of EEO burdens that managers in private enterprise had shouldered since the passage of Title VII in 1964.

One clause of Title VII permits employers to discriminate based on sex, religion, or national origin if these attributes are a "bona fide occupational qualification" (BFOQ). This seems like a loophole, but it is a small one indeed. For instance, courts have said that the clause does not allow an employer to discriminate against women simply because they feel that the work is "inappropriate" for them or because customers might object. A good example of this reasoning was the decision in *Diaz v. Pan American Airways* that an airline could not limit its employment of flight attendants to women. Pan American Airways was challenged in court by a male applicant. The airline pointed to section 708(e) of Title VII and claimed that sex was a bona fide occupational qualification for the position of flight attendant. As evidence, the airline offered the following:

- Passenger preference: Surveys showed that passengers preferred women to men as flight attendants.
- Psychological needs: A clinical psychologist testified that women, simply because they were women, could provide comfort and reassurance to passengers better than men could.
- Feasibility: An industrial psychologist testified that sex was the best practical screen device to use in determining whom to hire for the position.

At the time, the idea of a male flight attendant was unusual, but that was not a legal justification for Pan American's refusal to hire Diaz in that position.[9]

When *is* sex a bona fide occupational qualification? One obvious but unusual situation is when one sex is by definition unequipped to do the work — as in the case of a wet nurse. Another is when the position demands one sex for believability — as in the case of a fashion model. A third instance is when one sex is required for a position in order to satisfy basic social mores about modesty — as in the case of a locker room attendant.

Executive Order 11246 was issued by President Lyndon B. Johnson in 1965, superseding President John F. Kennedy's Executive Order 10925. Employment discrimination by federal government contractors, subcontractors, and federally assisted construction contracts is prohibited. While Executive Order 11246 prohibits the same actions as Title VII does, it carries the additional requirement that contractors must develop a written plan of affirmative action and establish numerical integration goals and timetables to achieve equal opportunity. The affirmative action planning requirement is discussed in greater detail later in this chapter.

Virtually every state also has some form of equal employment law. In 41 states, plus the District of Columbia and Puerto Rico, there are comprehensive "fair employment" laws similar in operation to Title VII. In fact, some of these state laws antedate Title VII. If a state's law is strong enough, charges of discrimination brought under Title VII are turned over by the federal government to the state fair employment practices agency, which has the first chance at investigating it.

Discrimination: A Legal Definition

All the laws discussed above are designed to eliminate *discrimination*. Would you believe the laws never defined it? It's true; the courts have had to do this when they have interpreted the laws. The courts arrive at definitions by looking at the history behind a statute, examining the *Congressional Record* to gain insight into the social problems Congress hoped it would solve. Then they define terms like *discrimination* in a way to help solve these problems. For Title VII, the history of the civil rights conflict clearly identifies the problems: economic inequality and the denial of employment opportunities to blacks and other minorities.

The courts have defined discrimination in three different ways since the first days of federal involvement in employment practices.[10] Initially, during World War II, discrimination was defined as *prejudiced treatment:* harmful actions motivated by personal animosity toward the group of which the target person was a member. However, that definition was ineffective as a means of solving the problem of economic inequality, because it is difficult to prove harmful motives, and that made it difficult to take action against many employment practices that perpetuated inequality.

Then the courts redefined discrimination to mean *unequal treatment*. Under this definition, a practice was unlawful if it applied different standards or different treatment to different groups of employees or applicants. This definition outlawed the practice of keeping minorities in less desirable departments (different treatment), and it also outlawed the practice of rejecting women applicants with preschool-aged children (different standards). The employer was allowed to impose any requirements, so long as they were imposed *on all groups alike*.

To enable Title VII to solve the social problems that Congress wanted it to, the U.S. Supreme Court arrived at the third definition of employment discrimination: *unequal impact*. In the case of *Griggs v. Duke Power Co.*, the Court struck down employment tests and educational requirements that screened out a greater proportion of blacks than whites.[11] These practices were prohibited because they had the *consequence* of excluding blacks disproportionately, *and* because they were not *related* to the jobs in question. The practices were apparently not motivated by prejudice against blacks. And they certainly were applied equally: both whites and blacks had to pass the requirements. But they did have an adverse impact on blacks. Today both unequal treatment and unequal impact are considered discrimination.

By way of a summary, the determination for EEO and affirmative action compliance or noncompliance can theoretically be reduced to two criteria. In question form, the criteria are:

1. Does an emloyment practice have unequal or adverse impact on the groups covered by the law? (Racial, color, sex, religious, or national origin groups.)
2. Is that practice job related or otherwise necessary to the organization?

A practice is prohibited *only* if the answers to *both* questions are unfavorable. Even practices that are unnecessary and irrelevant to the job are legal if they have equal impact on the groups covered by the law. This means that employers do not have to validate tests or follow the employee selection regulations if their tests do not exclude one group disproportionately.

This two-question approach does have some exceptions, and getting a straight answer to the second question is especially difficult because of the stringent guidelines that employers must follow. Nevertheless, the two questions are a good place to begin in understanding EEO and affirmative action. It is important to remember that new cases are constantly being decided, and guidelines are undergoing important changes. Therefore, EEO programs are in a period of total uncertainty. Nevertheless, these two basic questions remain as underlying principles through all the changes.

The Discrimination Case Process

In a discrimination case, a person alleges that he or she is being, or has been, discriminated against due to an unlawful employment practice. The person filing the suit is called the *plaintiff*. The person or organization against whom the charge of discrimination is made is called the *defendant*. The plaintiff must demonstrate that a prima facie (evidence exists) violation has occurred by gathering evidence showing that the employment practice has had an adverse impact.[12] The **adverse impact** criterion refers to the total employment process that results in a significantly higher percentage of a protected group in the available population being rejected for employment, placement, or promotion.

This means that the minority applicant for a job would have to show that the HRM activity (e.g., testing, promotion, selection) had an adverse impact on his or her minority group. For example, a plaintiff might demonstrate that out of 50 black and 50 white applicants for a job who completed a test, no blacks were hired while 15 whites were placed on the job. This would be evidence of adverse impact, and a prima facie violation of Title VII would be established.

Those in HRM use what is called the **4/5ths rule** for judging adverse impact. This rule notes that discrimination typically occurs if the selection rate for a protected group is less than 80 percent of the selection rate for a majority group. Thus, if 20 out of 100 white applicants are selected (20 percent), at least 16 percent (4/5ths or 80 percent of 20) of minority applicants (e.g., black or Hispanic) should be selected to avoid being accused of adverse impact. It should be pointed out that adverse impact need not be considered for groups that constitute less than 2 percent of the relevant labor force.

Once adverse impact has been demonstrated, the burden of proof shifts to the defendant. The defendant must demonstrate that the testing or selection activity at issue is job related or has some business necessity. If the defendant cannot demonstrate the job relatedness of the testing activity, the judgment will probably be awarded to the plaintiff.

The "shifting burden of proof" model is applied in most suits in which there is a claim of employment discrimination. Exhibit 3–2 presents the model graphically.

EXHIBIT 3-2   Shifting Burden of Proof Model

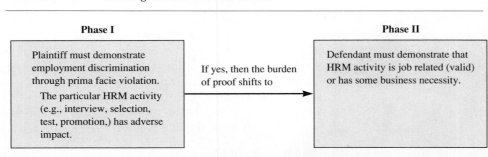

Phase I		Phase II
Plaintiff must demonstrate employment discrimination through prima facie violation. The particular HRM activity (e.g., interview, selection, test, promotion,) has adverse impact.	If yes, then the burden of proof shifts to →	Defendant must demonstrate that HRM activity is job related (valid) or has some business necessity.

This model and adverse impact and job-relatedness criteria are important in understanding most court judgments.

Other Federal Laws

There are a number of federal laws that are related to EEO and Title VII. These include the Age Discrimination Act of 1967, as amended in 1978, the Equal Pay Act of 1963, the **Rehabilitation Act of 1973,** and the Vietnam Era Veteran's Readjustment Assistance Act of 1974. Exhibit 3–3 briefly presents important sections of the

---

EXHIBIT 3-3   Major Equal Employment Opportunity Laws and Regulations

---

Civil Rights Act of 1964, as amended by the Equal Employment Opportunity Act of 1972

Sec. 703(a)   It shall be an unlawful employment practice for an employer (1) to fail or refuse to hire or to discharge any individual, or otherwise to discriminate against any individual with respect to his compensation, terms, conditions, or privileges of employment, because of such individual's race, color, religion, sex, or national origin; or (2) to limit, segregate, or classify his employees or applicants for employment in any way which would deprive or tend to deprive any individual of employment opportunities or otherwise adversely affect his status as an employee, because of such individual's race, color, religion, sex, or national origin.

Age Discrimination in Employment Act of 1967, as amended in 1978

Sec. 4(a)   It shall be unlawful for an employer (1) to fail or refuse to hire or to discharge any individual or otherwise discriminate against any individual with respect to his compensation, terms, conditions, or privileges of employment, because of such an individual's age.

Equal Pay Act of 1963

Sec. 3(d)(1)   No employer having employees subject to any provisions of this section shall discriminate, within any establishment in which such employees are employed, between employees on the basis of sex by paying wages to employees in such establishment at a rate less than the rate at which he pays wages to employees of the opposite sex in such establishment for equal work on jobs the performance of which requires equal skill, effort, and responsibility, and which are performed under similar working conditions, except where such payment is made pursuant to (i) a seniority system; (ii) a merit system; (iii) a system which measures earnings by quantity or quality of production; or (iv) a differential based on any other factor other than sex. . . .

Rehabilitation Act of 1973

Sec. 503(a)   Any contract in excess of $2,500 entered into by any federal department or agency for the procurement of personal property and non-personal services (including construction) for the United States shall contain a provision requiring that, in employing persons to carry out such contract the party contracting with the United States shall take affirmative action to employ and advance in employment qualified handicapped individuals. . . .

Vietnam Era Veterans' Readjustment Assistance Act of 1974

Sec. 2012(a)   Any contract in the amount of $10,000 or more entered into by any department or agency for the procurement of personal property and non-personal services (including construction) for the United States, shall contain a provision requiring that the party contracting with the United States shall take affirmative action to employ and advance in employment qualified special disabled veterans and veterans of the Vietnam era.

Executive Order 11246 (1965), as amended by Executive Order 11375 (1967) and Executive Order 12086 (1978)

Sec. 202(1)   The contractor will not discriminate against any employee or applicant for employment because of race, color, religion, sex, or national origin.

Civil Rights Act of 1964, as amended by the Equal Employment Opportunity Act of 1972 and these other relevant EEO laws.

The total impact of the type of laws and regulations presented in Exhibit 3–3 are made clear by the example in Exhibit 3–4 — that a plaintiff could lose her claim in 11 different forums, yet still end up winning a judgment from the employer in the 12th.[13]

President Bush vetoed the Civil Rights Act of 1990. He considered the act a "quota bill," which the president considered unacceptable. There were, however, a number of items in the act that may eventually be included in future bills the president of the United States will be asked to sign.[14] For example, the act extended to women and religious minorities legal remedies now restricted to blacks in the Civil Rights Act of 1964. The legislation also would permit for the first time compensating and punitive damages — not just job reinstatement — for intentional discrimination. The emphasis on this feature of the bill is to introduce a financial disincentive for intentional discrimination in the workplace. The act would also allow individuals to challenge hiring and promotion decisions that result in discrimination even if it's unintentional. These civil rights issues are likely to be closely examined again when future civil rights legislation is considered.

AFFIRMATIVE ACTION

In 1967, Executive Order 11246 was amended to conform with Title VII by including sex. The basic theory of all executive orders is that it is a privilege to do business with the federal government and, therefore, to continue doing such business, certain conditions must be followed. The condition imposed by 11246 is that a contractor or subcontractor cannot discriminate in employment because of race, sex, creed, color, or national origin.

Many employers took Executive Order 11246 more seriously than Title VII, probably because under Title VII a charge had to be filed and a long period of contestation resulted, while under 11246 the firm complied or lost its contracts with the government request.[15] One response to equal opportunity laws and executive orders such as 11246 is the development of affirmative action plans (AAP).

There are a number of important differences between equal opportunity and affirmative action that need to be noted by HR experts and managers. For example,

- Equal opportunity is a legal obligation; affirmative action is voluntary.
- Equal opportunity is neutral with respect to protected characteristics; affirmative action gives preference to individuals, based on protected characteristics.
- Equal opportunity is prohibitory; affirmative action is promotional in the sense of preferring members of protected groups.
- Equal opportunity is a permanent obligation; affirmative action, by its nature, is a temporary remedy.[16]

Affirmative action is defined as "those actions appropriate to overcome the effects of past or present practices, policies, or other barriers to equal employment opportunity."[17] The most controversial interpretation of affirmative action is that it grants special treatment to some individuals. It suggests that affirmative action gives preferential treatment in hiring, recruitment, promotion, termination, and development to groups that have been discriminated against.

The legality of preferential treatment depends in part on whether the affirmative action is involuntary (court ordered) or voluntary (not court ordered). When an employer violates the law, an affirmative action plan may be required. Any employer having a contract with the federal government of at least $50,000 and employing at least 50 people must put their AAP in writing. Although not all employers are required to have an AAP, some have elected to develop them as an indication of being a socially responsible business. By having an AAP, the organization is suggesting to the public and the courts that it is attempting to deal with discrimination.

Affirmative Action Guidelines

The regulation that suggests the format and parts of AAPs is Revised Order No. 4, issued by the Office of Federal Contract Compliance Programs, a subdivision of the U.S. Department of Labor. Three main planning steps are presented in Revised Order No. 4.

1. *Perform a Utilization Analysis* — This analysis compares employment of women and minorities in the employer's work force with the availability of women and minorities in the labor market. The analysis will show the percentage of the employer's work force that belongs to the group in question (e.g., Hispanic) and the percentage of the available labor supply that belongs to that group (e.g., Hispanic). If there is a smaller percentage in the work force than in the labor supply, then the group is said to be "underutilized."

2. *Goals and Timetables* — This step specifies the percentage of a job group (one or a group of jobs having similar content wage rates and opportunities) to be filled by women or minorities and the date by which that percentage is to be attained. Goals and timetables are required for all job groups in which underutilization is found.

3. *Action Steps* — These are steps that can be taken by employers to reduce underutilization and achieve their goals. Steps mentioned include publicizing the firm's AAP, both inside and outside the firm, communicating top management's support for the program, removing any barriers to employment, validating job specification and selection methods, and auditing the entire affirmative action program.

Affirmative action does not demand that underutilization be correct, but that a good faith effort be made by the organization to increase the number of women and minorities in certain job groups. It appears that in order for AAPs to have a chance to succeed they must be written down and they must be vigorously supported and communicated by top management. Without top-management support, it is difficult to show that there is a good faith effort being exerted to deal with discrimination.

Despite lingering controversy, AAPs are found in many organizations. It is likely, no matter which way the courts rule, that affirmative action will remain a part of HRM programs. Almost on a daily basis, there is a critic, supporter, court order, or legal analyst making statements about affirmative action. Since 1986, Supreme Court decisions have established three rules that govern court-ordered affirmative action.

EXHIBIT 3-4   The Wide Reach of the Law

A minority female with a heart murmur who is over 40 and working in New York City for an employer who is a government contractor can precipitate legal or administrative action, or both, against that employer in 12 different forums because of alleged discrimination. Theoretically, she could lose in 11 forums, yet still receive relief from the employer in the 12th.

She could accuse the employer of discrimination on the basis of race or sex under Title VII.,[4] thereby precipitating "enforcement" either by EEOC or herself. In any event, she would precipitate an investigation by such a charge.

She could accuse the employer of discrimination on the basis of age, under the Age Discrimination in Employment Act of 1967,[5] and thereby precipitate court enforcement action by EEOC or herself. At a minimum, this would cause an attempted conciliation by EEOC.

She could file a lawsuit in federal court on the basis of race discrimination under the Civil Rights Act of 1866, 42 U.S.C. *1981.

She could file a claim of discrimination under the Equal Pay Act of 1963,[6] and thereby precipitate court enforcement action by either EEOC or herself. At a minimum, this charge would trigger an investigation.

She could file a claim of discrimination based upon her status as "handicapped"[7] and precipitate court enforcement action by the U.S. Department of Justice or herself[8] under the Rehabilitation Act of 1973. The same charge could also precipitate sanctions against the employer under the Rehabilitation Act of 1973, and the rules and regulations issued pursuant to that law.[9] Thus, this charge would trigger an investigation that could lead to an administrative hearing and, alternatively, federal court proceeding[10] — as two possible forums.

By filing a charge of discrimination with OFCCP claiming race or sex discrimination in violation of Executive Order 11246,[11] she could precipitate sanctions against the employer because the employer is a government contractor. At a minimum, this charge would trigger an investigation, and it could precipitate an administrative hearing or a federal court action by the federal government[12] — again, two possible forums.

She could file a charge of discrimination on the basis of race, sex, disability, or age with the New York State Division of Human Rights and thereby precipitate an investigation.[13] She can either go to court directly herself, or await the administrative proceedings and then appeal an adverse determination to court. The New York statute offers her two distinct forums.[14]

She can file a charge of discrimination based on age, sex, race, or disability with the New York City Commission on Human Rights and thereby precipitate an investigation and an administrative determination, with court review.[15]

---

[4] 42 U.S.C. **2000e et seq.
[5] 29 U.S.C. **621 et seq. (now enforced by EEOC).
[6] 29 U.S.C. *206(d) (now enforced by EEOC).
[7] U.S.C. *701.
[8] In Carmi v. St. Louis Sewer District, 20 FEP Cases 162 (E.D.Mo.1979), the court recognized the individual's right of action, but ruled against the plaintiff on the merits. Carmi discusses the cases which have split on the issue of whether there is an independent right of action available to a private party under the Rehabilitation Act.
[9] 41 C.F.R. *60–741.
[10] See Davis v. Bucher, 451 F.Supp.791 (E.D.Pa.1978).
[11] 3 C.F.R. *339.
[12] See United States v. New Orleans Public Services, Inc., 553 F.2d 459 (5th Cir.1977), vacated and remanded, 436 U.S. 942 (1978).
[13] N.Y. Exec. Law **290–301 (McKinney 1972); 3 Empl. Prac. Guide (CCH) **26000 et seq.
[14] Under Section 291 of the New York State Human Rights Law, the opportunity to obtain employment without discrimination because of age, race, creed, color, national origin, sex, or marital status was recognized and declared to be a civil right. As such, it is enforceable by direct court action. Additionally, a complainant may follow the procedures outlined in Section 297, which leads to administrative action and possible court review.
[15] The New York City Commission on Human Rights and its powers are described in the Administrative Code of the City of New York, **B1–1.0 et seq. Commissions such as the New York City Commission are allowed to exist pursuant to the General Municipal Law, Article 12–D, **239 et seq. That law, apparently, did not grant to cities full hearing and court enforcement powers. See General Municipal Law, *239–R. However, in interpreting the law, the New York Court of Appeals has ruled that the New York City Commission on Human Rights does have jurisdiction to decide a controversy raised by a discrimination claim. See Maloff v. City Commission on Human Rights, 38 N.Y.2d.563, 379 N.Y.S.2d 788 (1975).

Source: Kenneth J. McCulloch, Selecting Employees Safely Under the Law, © 1981, pp. 7–8. Reprinted by permission of Prentice-Hall, Inc., Englewood Cliffs, New Jersey.

EXHIBIT 3-4   *(concluded)*

She can file a charge of discrimination based on age, sex, race, or disability under the Mayor's Executive Order, thereby precipitating sanctions against the employer because the employer is a city contractor. At a minimum, this charge would lead to another investigation.

If the woman were a disabled veteran, she could file a charge of discrimination with OFCCP on that basis, thereby precipitating possible sanctions against the employer because it is a government contractor and, possibly, court action initiated by either the Department of Justice or herself, or an administrative hearing.[16]

If the woman were covered by a collective bargaining agreement, she could precipitate an arbitration if there were a nondiscrimination clause in the agreement, or a lawsuit, under the Labor-Management Relations Act, against the union and the employer.[17]

If the employer were a New York State defense contractor, a charge of discrimination on the basis of race could lead to investigation and criminal conviction of a misdemeanor.[18]

[16] The possibility of a court enforcement proceeding by the Department of Justice is indicated by 41 C.F.R. *60–250.28(b). The possibility of an administrative hearing is indicated by 41 C.F.R. *60–250–29 and 41 C.F.R. *60–250.26(g) (3). The possibility of an independent right of action for an individual claiming to be aggrieved by a violation of the Vietnam Era Readjustment Act of 1974 is enhanced by the Supreme Court's decision in *University of California Board of Regents v. Bakke*, 438 U.S. 265 (1978), 17 EPD (CCH) #8402 (June 28, 1978).
[17] 29 U.S.C. **141 *et seq.*
[18] See N.Y. Civ. Rights Law **44, 44a (McKinney 1976); 3 Empl. Prac. Guide (CCH) #26,105.

---

1. Courts may order affirmative action as a remedy for past or present discrimination.
2. The victims of past or present discrimination do not have to be identified before the court may order such relief.
3. In situations where parties themselves may agree to affirmative action beyond what may be required by law, the court may order such relief by issuing a consent decree.[18]

Affirmative action plans must be carefully implemented if they are to have a beneficial impact. The Supreme Court decision in *Santa Clara County Transportation Agency v. Johnson* (1987), a suit brought by a white male who charged that he was more qualified for a promotion than a female, indicates that a poorly presented and implemented affirmative action plan is no excuse.[19] Poor affirmative action plans will be judged by the courts to be as inadequate as having no plan at all.

AT&T's Affirmative Action Program for Women — Outside Crafts

Of all employers in the United States, probably none has received more attention for its affirmative action program than the American Telephone and Telegraph Company.[20] AT&T was involved in the largest back-pay settlement in the history of equal employment. As part of that settlement, the company was required to make significant strides in increasing employment opportunities for women and minorities. The program that resulted from the settlement exemplifies some of the more advanced EEO efforts in U.S. industry.

The scope of AT&T's affirmative action program is so vast that it is impractical to focus on more than a small segment here. We will discuss one particularly interesting segment of AT&T's program — its provisions for increasing the employment of women in outside-crafts positions: the various line workers, telephone installers, and repair workers whose work is mostly done outdoors.

The steps outlined below are an integral part of affirmative action for any job at any company.

Step 1: Analyzing Underrepresentation and Availability

AT&T found a problem simply by examining the sex composition of their job classes: There were almost no women in outside-crafts positions. But how great was the extent of underrepresentation? Many organizations find the answer to this question in the statistics compiled for affirmative action plans by state labor departments, which show the number of women and minorities in each of 10 or 20 broad occupational groups. Others use the overall population figures compiled by the U.S. Census. Both sets of data are readily available from the appropriate government agencies. In addition, some larger firms are investing in sophisticated labor market studies to arrive at a more accurate estimate of availability. Of course any set of statistics is open to criticism. Many employers strive to collect statistics that put them in the best light. While some may argue that such a strategy is manipulative, it often does succeed in reducing enforcement pressures. Employers are likely to continue using it until such time as there emerges a generally accepted statistical definition of availability.

Step 2: Goal Setting

Once the statistics are agreed upon, the organization sets goals to help achieve greater minority representation in the job in question. The EEO goals have to be realistic, and they have to be attainable without discriminating against those in the majority. Nevertheless, while good availability statistics help make goals realistic, there is no way to be sure that goals will not discriminate in reverse, unless the means by which the company seeks to attain them are carefully planned.

Step 3: Specifying How Goals Are to Be Attained

If the means to goal attainment are to be nondiscriminatory against white males, management should find out the causes of underrepresentation of women and minorities in the company's work force. Otherwise, it will now know what discriminatory employment practices must be changed in order to increase representation without preferential treatment of women and minorities. For example, the underrepresentation of women in a certain job class may be caused by a company's reputation for being rough on women or by a policy that unnecessarily schedules work shifts so that women workers cannot meet family responsibilities. If management knows the cause, it can attempt to increase the representation of women by working on its public image and by exploring the possibility of retiming the shifts. But if management doesn't know it, it may attempt to increase the representation of women by lowering the requirements for women applying from the outside, or by granting transfers to women employees while refusing to grant them to more qualified male employees. This would not only increase the risk of discrimination charges from white males, it would also contribute to morale problems and foster resentment against women in the company.

At AT&T, 24 reverse discrimination cases eventually went to court. In one case, the union claimed that reverse discrimination resulted because of promotion policies favoring qualified women and minorities. A district court and an appeals court ruled against the union and supported preferential treatment and quotas. The courts reasoned that such treatment was justified to correct the abuses of past discrimination.

The AT&T case illustrates that even a large company (at the time of the initial court case, AT&T employed 980,000 employees) can take specific action to alleviate discrimination. AT&T took these steps:

- It tried to change the image of outside-crafts employees from male to neutral by advertising, public relations, and relationships with guidance counselors.
- It redesigned the jobs so that women could perform them more easily.
- It provided detailed information to the Department of Labor on the status of the AAP. The information provided exceeds what is ordinarily required by federal rules.[21]

IMPORTANT COURT DECISIONS

Knowledge about the law and affirmative action is important to the HR manager. However, the court's interpretation of the laws and regulations must also be followed. Numerous court cases involving employment discrimination have become public record.[22] There are, however, a few cases that have been widely publicized and used as important precedent-setting cases involving the law and HRM.

Griggs v. Duke Power (1971)

Willie Griggs was an applicant for a job as a coal handler at the Duke Power Company.[23] Duke required coal handlers to be high school graduates and receive a satisfactory score on two aptitude tests. Griggs claimed that these requirements were unfairly discriminatory in that they were not related to job success. Thus, they resulted in a disproportionate number of blacks being disqualified.

Duke Power Company lost this suit. Supreme Court Chief Justice Burger ruled that (1) discrimination need not be overt; (2) the employment practice must be shown to be job-related; and (3) the burden of proof is on the employer to show that the hiring standard is job related.

Perhaps the most important aspect of the *Griggs* decision was the emphasis on the consequences of an employment practice in addition to the examination of the intent involved. It opened the door for giving serious consideration to what the actual consequence of a practice was. The use of statistical methods in reviewing consequences became accepted.

Albermarle Paper Company v. J. Moody (1975)

The *Albermarle* case is important because the courts provided details on how an employer should go about validating a test; that is, how an employer must prove that the test predicts on-the-job performance.

Albermarle had required applicants for employment to pass various tests. The court found that the Albermarle tests were not validated for all jobs for which people were recruited.[24] This court decision indicated that tests or other screening tools that had the effect of screening out a disproportionate number of minorities or women (that is, those tests that had an adverse impact) had to be validated properly. The test had to validly predict performance.

Washington v. David (1976)

The *Washington v. Davis* case involved a metropolitan police department (Washington, D.C.) that had been using a test for the selection of police recruits. Between 1968 and 1971, 57 percent of the blacks failed the exam compared to 13 percent of whites. The police department demonstrated that the test score was related to examinations given during the police recruits' 17-week training course.[25]

The Supreme Court ruled that the city of Washington, D.C., did not discriminate unfairly against minority police recruits because the test was job related. The decision was a departure from previous court decisions. The implication was that a job-related test is not illegal simply because a large percentage of minorities do not successfully pass it. This decision provided test users with hope that testing could still be used as a screening device.[26]

Bakke v. University of California (1978)

The central issue of the now-famous *reverse discrimination* case involving Allan Bakke (a white male) was the legality of the admission policy of the University of California at Davis Medical School. The Davis system set aside 16 of 100 places in its entering classes for "disadvantaged" applicants who were members of racial minority groups. Competitors for these places were evaluated on the basis of lower-than-normal standards. Thus, Bakke sued the university under the Equal Protection Clause of the 14th Amendment. The suit claimed that Bakke could compete for only 84 of the 100 places, while minorities could compete for all 100. All individuals were therefore not treated equally.

Justice Lewis Powell, writing the key opinion, concluded that the Davis racial quota system was not acceptable because it disregarded Bakke's rights to equal protection under the law. However, the Court also stated that AAPs in general are permissible, as long as they consider applicants on an individual basis and do not set aside a rigid number of places.[27]

The *Bakke* case indicated that HRM selection decisions must be made on an individual, case-by-case basis. Certainly race can be a key factor in an applicant's favor, but the final decision must be made on the basis of a combination of factors.

Weber v. Kaiser (1979)

Brian Weber, a laboratory analyst at a Kaiser Aluminum plant in Louisiana, brought suit under the Title VII of the 1964 Civil Rights Act. He had been bypassed for a crafts-retraining program in which the company and the union jointly agreed to reserve 50 percent of the available training places for blacks.[28]

The company and the union were faced with a dilemma. Eliminating the affirmative action training plan would risk suits by minority employees. However, to retain the plan would run the risk of a reverse discrimination charges by white employees. As discussed earlier, affirmative action goes beyond equal employment opportunity. It is a systematic plan that specifies goals, time tables, and audit procedures for an employer to make an extra effort to hire, promote, and train those in a protected minority. Kaiser's affirmative action plan focused on giving preference to blacks in the crafts-retraining program.

On June 27, 1979, the U.S. Supreme Court ruled that employers can give preference to minorities and women in hiring and promoting for "traditionally segregated job categories." Thus, where there has been a societal history of purposeful exclusion of blacks from the job category, resulting in a disparity between the proportion of blacks in the labor force and the proportion of blacks who hold jobs in the category, preference can be given. The Court also noted that the Kaiser plan was a "temporary measure" to eliminate a racial imbalance in a job category.[29] This decision definitely put pressure on employers to establish AAPs.

Fire Fighters Local Union 1784 v. Stotts (1984)

The *Weber* decision did not guarantee that all affirmative action programs would be approved. The Supreme Court ruled in *Fire Fighters Local Union 1784 v. Stotts* that a bona fide seniority system cannot be overridden in a layoff situation to protect an affirmative action program.[30] The City of Memphis, Tennessee, had a budget deficit and decided to lay off some employees. The city believed that the most equitable procedure would be to use a last-hired, first-fired seniority system. The union and the city went to court on behalf of nonminority employees. Stotts appealed the layoff sequence asking for an order forbidding the layoff of any black employee. The union and city last-hired, first-fired plan ultimately prevailed. Both the district court and the appeals court ruled in favor of Stotts, but the Supreme Court overturned the ruling. In ruling for the minority, Justice White stated that, "Title VII does not permit the ordering of racial quotas in business or unions."[31]

Wards Cove Packing Co. v. Antonio (1989)

A case that may have far-reaching effects is *Wards Cove Packing Co. v. Antonio*.[32] Wards Cove operated two salmon canneries in which there were both cannery and noncannery jobs. Generally, the cannery jobs were unskilled positions held by nonwhites (Filipinos and Alaskan natives) and the noncannery jobs were skilled positions filled mostly by whites. A group of nonwhite cannery workers brought a class action suit alleging that the company's hiring and promotion practices violated Title VII.

Statistics showed a high percentage of nonwhite workers in cannery jobs and a low percentage of nonwhite workers in noncannery jobs. The Supreme Court ruled that this was an improper comparison. It stated the the proper comparison is between the racial composition of workers in the jobs at issue, not the racial composition of the qualified persons in the labor market. If it turns out that any statistical disparities in the work force are due to a shortage of qualified minorities, then the employer's selection methods cannot be said to have had a disparate impact on nonwhites. This reasoning assumes the reasons for a shortage of qualified candidates is not the fault of the employer.

The *Wards Cove* decision has the potential to be of immense potential to employers. It relieves employers of a burden of proof that the Court itself said was almost impossible to meet. Also, the decision means that employers will not be found in violation of Title VII merely because there are racial imbalances in their work forces. The decision is a rejection of the use of racial quotas to comply with Title VII.

These seven cases are landmarks in discrimination law. They have provided prospective plaintiffs and defendants with insight into the Supreme Court's view of discriminatory practices. Exhibit 3–5 gives a concise summary of these seven landmark cases and the outstanding feature(s) of each Supreme Court decision.

EXHIBIT 3-5   Seven Precedent-Setting Supreme Court Decisions

Case	Outstanding Feature(s) of Court's Ruling
Griggs v. Duke Power (1971)	If adverse impact is established, defendant must demonstrate that selection practice is valid.
Albermarle v. Moody (1975)	Validation is not proven unless test can predict job success.
Washington v. Davis (1976)	If a test is job related, it is not illegal simply because a greater percentage of minorities do not successfully pass it.
Bakke v. University of California (1978)	Reverse discrimination is not allowed; however, race can be used as a factor in selection decisions.
Weber v. Kaiser (1979)	Employers can give preference to minorities and women in hiring and promoting for "traditionally segregated job categories."
Fire Fighters Local Union 1784 *v. Stotts* (1984)	A bona fide seniority system cannot be overridden in a layoff situation to protect minority employees with less seniority.
Wards Cove Packing Co. v. Antonio (1989)	Relieves employers of burden of proof it there are racial imbalances in their work forces.

ENFORCING THE LAWS

Most employment discrimination laws provide for enforcement agencies that issue the regulations that affect HR administrators most directly. Exhibit 3–6 provides an overview of the complex agency scene, showing some of the principal laws, the agencies that enforce them, and the guidelines issued by these agencies. The units of government *most* responsible for enforcing the regulations considered here are the **U.S. Equal Employment Opportunity Commission (EEOC)** and the federal courts, which enforce Title VII; and the Office of Federal Contract Compliance Programs (OFCCP), which enforces Executive Order 11246.

Equal Employment Opportunity Commission

Title VII originally gave EEOC the rather limited powers of resolving charges of discrimination and interpreting the meaning of Title VII. Later, in 1972, Congress gave EEOC the power to bring lawsuits against employers in the federal courts, but the agency still does not have the power to issue directly enforceable orders, as many other federal agencies have. Thus, EEOC cannot order an employer to discontinue a discriminatory practice, nor can it direct an employer to give back pay to victims of discrimination. However, the EEOC has won these issues in out-of-court settlements, and it has made effective use of the limited powers it does have.

EEOC has the power to:

Require employers to report employment statistics. Typically, they do so by completing a form called EEO–1 each year (see Exhibit 3–7).

Process charges of discrimination, as follows:

- The preinvestigation division interviews the complainants.
- The investigation division collects facts from all parties concerned.

EXHIBIT 3-6   Partial Summary of Major Employment Discrimination Laws and Orders, Enforcement Agencies, and Regulations

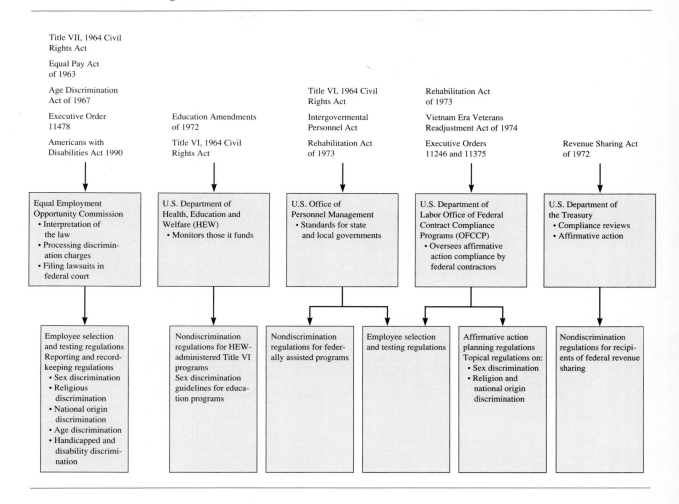

- If there seems to be substance to the charge, the EEOC tries to work out an out-of-court settlement through conciliation.
- If conciliation fails, the EEOC can sue the employer.

Is the EEOC Effective?   In its fiscal year 1990, the EEOC handled approximately 640 lawsuits. Job bias complaints received by the EEOC during this same period totaled 62,135.[33] When the EEOC sought to clear away some of the backlog, its employee union complained this was a speedup and forced employees to violate the law in processing the cases and charges too hastily. Each year, the agency tries to deal with the backlog by requesting sharp increases in its budget. As a result of the backlog, charges can take years to be investigated. During that time, records get lost and memories fade, making it hard for investigators to determine how justifiable the original charge was. Besides that problem, critics claim that investigations are often not conducted competently enough to uncover all the information that is available, which leads to selective enforcement of the law.

EXHIBIT 3-7 EEO–1 Form

Standard Form 100
(Rev. 5-84)

O.M.B. No. 3046-0007
EXPIRES 5/31/86
100-212

Joint Reporting
Committee

- Equal Employment
  Opportunity Com-
  mission
- Office of Federal
  Contract Compli-
  ance Programs (Labor)

EQUAL EMPLOYMENT OPPORTUNITY
EMPLOYER INFORMATION REPORT EEO–1

SAMPLE

Section A — TYPE OF REPORT
Refer to instructions for number and types of reports to be filed.

1. Indicate by marking in the appropriate box the type of reporting unit for which this copy of the form is submitted (MARK ONLY ONE BOX).

   (1) ☐ Single-establishment Employer Report

   Multi-establishment Employer:
   (2) ☐ Consolidated Report (Required)
   (3) ☐ Headquarters Unit Report (Required)
   (4) ☐ Individual Establishment Report (submit one for each establishment with 50 or more employees)
   (5) ☐ Special Report

2. Total number of reports being filed by this Company (Answer on Consolidated Report only) _____

Section B — COMPANY IDENTIFICATION (To be answered by all employers)

1. Parent Company

   a. Name of parent company (owns or controls establishment in item 2) omit if same as label

   Name of receiving office   Address (Number and street)

   City or town   County   State   Zip Code
                                                                   b. Employer Identification No.

2. Establishment for which this report is filed. (Omit if same as label)

   a. Name of establishment

   Address (Number and street)   City or town   County   State   Zip Code

   b. Employer Identification No.   (Omit if same as label)

Section C — EMPLOYERS WHO ARE REQUIRED TO FILE (To be answered by all employers)

☐ Yes ☐ No 1. Does the entire company have at least 100 employees in th payroll period for which you are reporting?

☐ Yes ☐ No 2. Is your compnay affiliated through common ownership and/or centralized management with other entities in an enterprise with a total ewmployment of 100 or more?

☐ Yes ☐ No 3. Does the company or any of its establishments (a) have 50 or more employees AND (b) is not exempt as provided by 41 CFR 60-1.5, and either (1) is a prime government contrator or first-tier subcontractor, and has a contract, subcontract, or purchase order amounting to $50,000 or more, or (2) serves as a depository of Government funds in any amount or is a financial institution which is an issuing and paying agent for U.S. Savings Bonds and Savings Notes?

If the response to question C–3 is yes, please enter your Dun and Bradstreet identification number (if you have one): ☐☐☐☐☐☐☐☐☐

☐ Yes ☐ No 4. Does the company receive financial assistance from the small Business Administration (SBA)?

NOTE: If the answer is yes to questions 1, 2, or 3, complete the entire form, otherwise skip to Section G.

NSN 7540–00–180–6384

EXHIBIT 3-7   *(concluded)*

SF 100 Page 2

Section D — EMPLOYMENT DATA

Employment at this establishment—Report all permanent full-time or part-time employees including apprentices and on-the-job trainees unless specifically excluded as set forth in the instructions. Enter the appropriate figures on all lines and in all columns. Blank spaces will be considered as zeros.

JOB CATAGORIES		OVERALL TOTALS (SUM OF COL. B THRU K) A	MALE					FEMALE				
			WHITE (NOT OF HISPANIC ORIGIN) B	BLACK (NOT OF HISPANIC ORIGIN) C	HISPANIC D	ASIAN OR PACIFIC ISLANDER E	AMERICAN INDIAN OR ALASKAN NATIVE F	WHITE (NOT OF HISPANIC ORIGIN) G	BLACK (NOT OF HISPANIC ORIGIN) H	HISPANIC I	ASIAN OR PACIFIC ISLANDER J	AMERICAN INDIAN OR ALASKAN NATIVE K
Officials and Managers	1											
Professionals	2											
Technicians	3											
Sales Workers	4											
Office and Clerical	5											
Craft Workers (Skilled)	6											
Operatives (Semi-Skilled)	7											
Laborers (Unskilled)	8											
Service Workers	9											
TOTAL	10											
Total employment reported in previous EEO-1 report	11											

(The trainees below should also be included in the figures for the appropriate occupational categories above)

Formal On-the-job trainess	White collar	12											
	Production	13											

NOTE: Omit questions 1 and 2 on the Consolidated Report.

1. Date(s) of payroll period used:

2. Does this establishment employ apprentices?
   1. ☐ Yes   2. ☐ No

Section E—ESTABLISHMENT INFORMATION (Omit on the Consolidated Report)

1. Is the location of the establishment the same as that reported last year?
   1. ☐ Yes   2. ☐ No   3. ☐ No report last year

2. Is the major business activity at this establishment the same as that reported last year?
   1. ☐ Yes   2. ☐ No   3. ☐ No report last year

OFFICE USE ONLY

3. What is the major activity of this establishment? (Be specific, I.e., manufacturing steel castings, retail grocer, wholesale plumbing supplies, title insurance, etc. Include the specific type of product or type of service provided, as well as the principal business or industrial activity.)

Section F—REMARKS

Use this item to give any identification data appearing on last report which differs from that given above, explani major changes in composition or reporting units and other pertinent information.

Section G—CERTIFICATION (See INstrucitons G)

Check one   1   All reports are accurate and were prepared I naccordance with the instructions (check on consolidated only)

2   This report is accurate and was prepared in accordance with the instructions.

Name of Certifying Official	Title	Signature	Date
Name of person to contact regarding this report (Type of print)	Address (Number and street)		
Title	City and State	Zip code	Telephone Area Code	Number	Extension

The result of these problems is that only a very small percentage of charges ever get resolved by the EEOC or the courts. Consequently, civil rights advocates are not happy with the agency, and, of course, many employers are less than enthusiastic about it (or any regulatory agency, for that matter).[34] In spite of this, the EEOC has made legal history. It provides individuals and groups with a government contact point to voice their complaints.

Office of Federal Contract Compliance Programs

The OFCCP was originally established to enforce Executive Order 11246. Note it also enforces laws covering employment of veterans and the handicapped. OFCCP has the power to remove a federal contractor's privileges of doing business with the government, but it seldom exercises that power.

Is the OFCCP Effective?   Some data have indicated few positive effects on employment gains for black males; fewer gains for white males; zero or negative effect for other minorities and women; and zero effects on wage and occupational gains for all minority groups. Some experts doubt that the OFCCP can alter employment distributions of minorities.[35]

One reason for the limited success of the OFCCP is the need to delegate its compliance review authority to 13 other agencies. It is no surprise, therefore, that contractors complain of conflicting agency regulations. Moreover, the 13 agencies are principally in business for some reason other than equal employment. For instance, the Department of Defense had an EEO operation housed in the bureau that was principally responsible for making sure that defense contracting was carried out well, with the right goods and services delivered at the right time. Undue concern with EEO, however, could be seen as impeding contract fulfillment. Thus, EEO was not an overriding concern in some of these agencies. President Carter in 1978 consolidated theses compliance functions, as shown in Exhibit 3–6.

The Courts

Besides federal and state agencies, the courts are constantly interpreting the laws, and rulings sometimes conflict. Appellate courts then reconcile any conflicts. All the employment discrimination laws provide for court enforcement, often as a last resort if agency enforcement fails. With regard to Title VII, the federal courts are frequently involved in two ways: settling disputes between the EEOC and employers over such things as access to company records, and deciding the merits of discrimination charges when out-of-court conciliation efforts fail. The possible legal routes for complaints against an employer's HRM activities are presented in Exhibit 3–8.

Legal maneuvering often makes the court enforcement picture confusing, largely because every step of the process can be appealed. And with three parties involved—the EEOC, the plaintiff, and the defendant—appeals are commonplace. All these possibilities for trial, appeal, retrial, and even appeal of the retrial can cause several years' delay before an issue is settled. When that delay is added to the EEOC's charge-processing delay, the result is discouraging to the parties involved.

Once a final court decision is reached in a Title VII case, it can provide drastic remedies: back pay, hiring quotas, reinstatement of employees, immediate promotion of employees, abolition of testing programs, creation of special recruitment or training programs. In a class action suit against George Power Company that sought back pay and jobs for black employees and applicants, the court ordered the

EXHIBIT 3-8   Legal Courses for Complaints against an Employer's HRM Policies

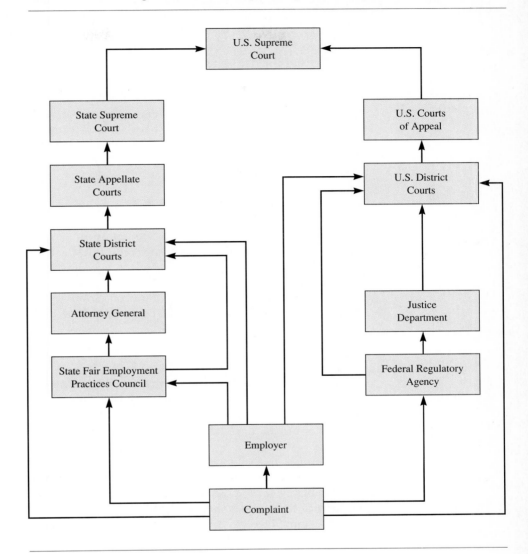

company to set aside $1.75 million for back pay and another $388,925 for other purposes. Moreover, the court imposed numerical goals and timetables for black employment in various job classes. If Georgia Power failed to meet the goals, then the court order provided for mandatory hiring ratios: One black was to be hired for each white until the goal percentages were reached. Other courts have ordered companies to give employees seniority credit for the time they have been discriminatorily denied employment.[36]

Many court orders are not so drastic, however. Much depends, of course, on the facts surrounding the case. One important factor is whether the employer is making any voluntary efforts to comply with employment discrimination laws. If the company shows evidence of successfully pursuing an AAP, the court may decide to impose less stringent measures. This situation is discussed further in the section on costs and benefits of AAPs later in this chapter.

OFCCP has the power to order an employer to:

Survey the labor market and determine the availability of minorities.

Prepare an affirmative action plan to show the jobs minorities are underrepresented in.

Set goals and timetables for making the work force representative of the labor market.

Audit the affirmative action plan to see if the goals are being met.

If the investigator decides that the contractor is not in compliance with Executive Order 11246, he or she may have a "show cause" order issued against the contractor. This order triggers a lengthy sequence of administrative decisions and appeals, which can culminate in the contractor being debarred from government contract work.

VARIOUS GROUPS AND EEO

As already mentioned, EEO permeates most HRM activities. It can require changes in employment planning, recruiting, selecting, evaluating, career planning, training, and other activities. Rather than discuss each HRM activity, this section focuses on some special features of EEO programs for various groups. In future chapters, the law as it pertains to a specific HRM activity will be discussed.

Women

In many companies, EEO for women is more a matter of career design than job design. Women often find themselves locked into their positions with no career path upward; this situation is especially true for clerical positions. Typists and secretaries usually have little likelihood of promotion to supervisory or managerial positions.

Sometimes the solution to that problem involves training or job rotation for clerical workers. Management training can give them the specific skills they need to assume higher-level positions, and job rotation can give them the breadth of experience they need to become effective managers. In other cases, the problem is that the employees of the organization, women included, are unaware of the promotion and transfer opportunities it offers. Larger companies often establish very thorough and elaborate systems to inform employees of job openings in the company. Among other things, these systems may include individual career counseling for employees, which helps identify promising talent at the same time it keeps employees informed.

A second problem area for women involves insurance and leaves for pregnancy. Prior to the **Pregnancy Discrimination Act of 1978,** women could be forced to resign or take a leave of absence because of pregnancy. Furthermore, employers did not have to provide disability or medical coverage, even when coverage was provided for other disabilities and medical problems. The Pregnancy Discrimination amendment to the 1964 Civil Rights Act now prevents this form of discrimination against women. The act makes it an unfair employment practice to discriminate on the basis of pregnancy, childbirth, or related medical conditions in hiring, promotion, suspension, discharge, or in any other term of employment. The act prohibits an employer from failing to pay medical and hospital costs for childbirth to the same extent that it pays for medical and hospital costs for other conditions.[37]

An interesting court ruling was issued in 1984 involving women returning to work after maternity leave. The U.S. District Court in Los Angeles ruled that a 1978 California law guaranteeing a job following childbirth is unconstitutional. It was judged to discriminate against men and, therefore, was a violation of Title VII.[38] Lillian Garland was a receptionist at California Federal Savings and Loan Association when she took maternity leave. After eight weeks, she returned and found that her position had been filled.[39] No other jobs were available at that time, she was advised. Under the California law, firms were told they must offer the same or equivalent jobs to women returning from maternity leave, regardless of what was being offered other workers. If a man was out of work for an operation and a company refused to rehire him, that was allowed under the state law. However, every woman was owed a job-secure leave of up to four months if disabled by childbirth.

The judge in the case ruled that California law was in direct conflict with Title VII. Pregnancy had to be treated like any other disability. Receiving special treatment meant that females had different rights than males, which is illegal according to the federal law. A study of maternity and paternity leave policies among the 1,500 largest industrial, financial, and service companies showed that only 38 percent of the companies guaranteed women their same jobs back after a disability leave for childbirth. Another 43 percent provided a comparable job, and 6 percent more gave returning mothers some job. Thirteen percent made no promise of any job.[40]

May an employer terminate an employee because she has an abortion? The Pregnancy Discrimination Act states that nothing shall "require an employer to pay for health insurance benefits for abortion, except where the life of the mother would be endangered if the fetus were carried to term or except where medical complications have arisen from an abortion." However, it says nothing about whether an employer may terminate an employee for having an abortion.

In *Doe v. First National Bank*, the court held that it is conceivable to read the law as providing that an employer who bases an employment-related decision on an individual's choice to have an abortion is engaging in sex discrimination.[41] The court in this decision never actually stated that the Pregnancy Discrimination Act forbids discharge because of having an abortion. The court decided that Doe was dismissed because of poor performance and that she had failed to establish a prima facie case that she was dismissed because she had an abortion.

A third problem area involved sexual harassment on the job. **Sexual harassment** is unwelcome sexual attention that causes the victim distress and results in an inability on the part of the victim to effectively perform his or her job.[42] Women facing sexual harassment are often subjected to mental anxiety, humiliation, reprimand, or loss of job or promotion. According to a federal government survey of federal employees, 42 percent of the female and 15 percent of the male respondents reported that they had experienced sexual harassment in the previous two years.[43]

In order for a woman to recover on a claim of sexual harassment under Title VII of the Civil Rights Act, she must allege and establish that submission to the sexual suggestion constituted a term or condition of employment. A course of action cannot arise from an isolated incident or a mere flirtation.

An analysis of court decisions provides insight into the various types of sexual harassment cases being argued. One type of sexual harassment is sexual favors being exchanged for employment opportunities. In order for this type of activity to be considered sexual harassment under Title VII, it must be shown that job opportunities would be denied if sexual favors were refused.

Another type of sexual harassment is referred to as *environmental sexual harass-ment*. This is where no job opportunities are involved, just unwanted attention by someone of the opposite sex. The comments or innuendos of a sexual nature, physical contact, or other overt acts that convey a message that going further would be desirable fall in this category. This type of harassment is considered a violation by some courts because the employees contend that it interferes with work perform-ance or makes work unpleasant.

The existence of sexual harassment is often difficult to determine because con-sent is not known until after the act is committed.[44] Any degree of consent would make the conduct a normal consequence of one sex being attracted to another.

The court also looks at the employer's knowledge of the conduct. In a leading case in the area of employer knowledge, a worker subjected a female coworker to verbal sexual advances, made sexually derogatory remarks, and on one occasion physically grabbed her while she was bending over. The female complained to her supervisors, who did nothing to stop the harassment. The company was found liable under the Minnesota discrimination law because an employee complained and it took no action.[45]

In another leading sexual harassment case, *Bundy v. Jackson*, Title VII was used as the basis for a discrimination claim. Sandra Bundy, a vocational rehabilitation specialist, in 1972 received and rejected sexual propositions by a fellow employee. The accused employee eventually became director of the agency that employed Bundy. After being passed over for promotion for alleged inadequacy of work performance, Bundy filed an informal complaint with the EEO officer and a formal complaint with the department. The director failed to investigate the complaints. However, two and a half years later, Bundy received a promotion. She filed a complaint in the district court. The court concluded that Bundy was not entitled to relief because sexual harassment did not constitute discrimination within the mean-ing of Title VII. The District of Columbia Circuit Court of Appeals in 1983 reversed the earlier ruling.[46]

In a precedent-setting decision, the EEOC in 1984 found a restaurant owner responsible for the sexual harassment of an employee by customers, since the owner had it within his power to take corrective action, but failed to do so.[47] A waitress had complained to the owner about four male customers — friends of the owner — but the owner ignored her complaints. The customers made loud jokes and com-ments of a sexual nature about the waitress. When she tried to take their order, one man made grabbing gestures toward her and then grabbed and pinched her. The owner claimed he had spoken to the men, but no apology was forthcoming. The waitress refused to serve the men again, and the owner said he might not be able to continue her employment.

After the waitress said an attorney had advised her to have a witness present if her job was to be discussed, she was fired. The EEOC found that "evidence corrobo-rates the plaintiff's allegation that she was harassed." No previous EEOC decision had addressed the issue of an employer's responsibility for the sexual harassment of an employee by a nonemployee.

Sexual harassment suits need not result in liability for an employer.[48] What the employer needs to do is to establish a policy and communicate it to all employees. Second, there is a need to establish an easy-to-use grievance procedure. Alleged victims must feel free to use such a system without fear of retribution (such as being given more difficult job assignments, laid off, or unfairly bypassed for promotion). Third, violators of sexual harassment guidelines need to be promptly and fairly disciplined for their conduct. Finally, managers and other employees must be educated on what constitutes sexual harassment. Company newspapers, harassment notices placed on bulletin boards, and training programs may all prove beneficial in improving employees' awareness of what constitutes sexual harassment.[49]

In June 1986, the United States Supreme Court, in the first sexual harassment case to reach it, issued a significant decision in *Meritor Savings Bank, FSB v. Vinson* (1986).[50] The case firmly established the principle of employer liability for sexual harassment of employees under Title VII of the Civil Rights Act of 1964, while simultaneously limiting the extent of that liability. In this case, the plaintiff, a female assistant bank manager, claimed that her supervisor, a male vice president, made repeated sexual advances, resulting in sexual intercourse "some 40 or so times" over several years. The vice president and the bank denied the plaintiff's allegations. The court ruled in favor of the plaintiff because of the hostile environment she worked in and also suggested that the existence of an effective grievance procedure could insulate an employer from liability for sexual harassment.[51]

This ruling implies that employers must perform specific corrective actions that halt sexual harassment once they have learned of a violation. At a minimum, if an employer's investigation reveals that sexual harassment did occur, immediate imposition of counseling or progressive discipline should be initiated. It is important not only that a specific program exists, but also that the program function efficiently.

Older Employees

Age discrimination has been called the "third wave" and a "sleeper" in equal employment opportunity.[52] The **Age Discrimination Employment Act of 1967** and the amendments of 1978 and 1986 protect workers between the ages of 40 and 70 from job discrimination. In the past, the enforcement agencies did not press too hard on discrimination against older persons, but recent actions suggest this will no longer be true. The law prevents employers from replacing their staffs with younger workers, whether the purpose is to give the company a more youthful image or to save money in the pension program. The October 7, 1986, amendment eliminates a 70-year-old age cap for most private-sector employees. While age requirements are illegal in most jobs, the law does not cover all of them. For example, Greyhound was allowed to refuse bus driver jobs to applicants over age 40 with the justification that aging brings on slow reaction times, which can adversely affect safety.[53] Greyhound claimed that physical changes that begin around age 35 have an adverse effect on driving skills. Chronological age was used as an indicator of the physical changes.

Voluntary retirement has emerged as a major issue in age discrimination cases: Older employees allege that they were virtually forced to accept early retirement under threat of being dismissed, and younger employees claim they were discriminated against by not being offered the option. For example, in *Henn v. National Geographic Society*, the firm had been experiencing a decline in advertising, so it decided to reduce the number of employees. National Geographic offered an early retirement plan to every salesperson over 55 and gave them two months to consider the offer.[54] The plan included:

• One year's salary as severance.
• Retirement benefits calculated as if the retiree had retired at 65.
• Medical coverage for life.
• Supplemental life insurance coverage.

Of the 15 eligible salespersons, 12 accepted the offer. All 12 who accepted the offer did in fact receive the promised benefits, but four of them nevertheless sued

National Geographic for violating the Age Discrimination Employment Act. The court ruled in favor of National Geographic and stated that retirement is not itself a prima facie case of age discrimination.

A number of barriers face older workers in many organizations. Some are a matter of company economics, others a matter of management attitudes and stereotyping.[55] The economic reasons include the added expense of funding pensions for older workers and the increased premiums necessary for health and life insurance benefit plans. The attitude problems are more difficult to pin down. Perhaps some managers feel that older workers lose their faculties, making them less effective on the job. There are, however, advantages to hiring older workers: lower turnover, greater consciousness of safety matters, longer work experience, more maturity, and more loyalty to the enterprise.[56]

McDonald's actively recruits older workers. The firm decided to permit older workers to proceed at their own pace, provide them with experts they can consult with, and then get out of their way and let them work.[57] McDonald's is very satisfied with their older workers' productivity, attendance, and attitudes.

Racial and Ethnic Minorities

The laws prohibit discrimination against a person because of race, color, and national origin. The specifically protected minorities are blacks, Hispanics, Native Americans, Asian-Pacific Islanders, and Alaskan natives. These groups historically have had higher unemployment and underemployment and have held the lowest level jobs.

While every ethnic and racial minority is unique, one problem facing them all is adverse HRM policies. Examples of such practices are numerous. Height and weight requirements, which have an adverse impact on Asian Americans and Hispanic Americans, were, until recently, commonplace among police departments in the United States. Seniority and experience requirements based on time in a department tend to lock in blacks who move out of segregated departments. They find themselves at the bottom of the seniority lists in their new departments, even though they have had many years with the company. Vague, subjective performance evaluations by supervisors are so subject to bias that many minority group members find they cannot attain high enough ratings to get promotions or merit pay increases. All these practices, along with others, are prime targets for change in the EEO program.

As in the case of sexual harassment, complaints of racial harassment must be carefully reviewed. If harassment is found to exist, the company must immediately correct the situation. In *Hunter v. Allis-Chalmers Corp.*, *Engine Division*, a supervisor was found guilty under Title VII. He failed to protect the plaintiff, a black, from racial harassment and for having fired him when he filed a harassment complaint. The plaintiff was awarded $25,000 for the indignity and stress suffered and also $25,000 in punitive damages. He was also awarded back pay.[58]

Religious Minorities

The EEO-type laws prohibit discrimination in employment based on religious preference, but there have been few cases thus far charging that employers have discriminated against religious groups in employment and promotion. This is surprising given the reality that certain employers have had a policy of limited or no hiring of persons who are Jewish, Orthodox Christian, or Roman Catholic, at least for the managerial class. Roman Catholics, for example, are seriously underrepresented in managerial and professional groups in the United States.[59]

The focus of religious discrimination cases has been on hours of work and working conditions. The cases largely concern employers telling employees to work on days or at times that conflict with their religious beliefs — at regular times or on overtime. For example, employees who are Orthodox Jews, Seventh Day Adventists, or Worldwide Church of God members cannot work from sunset Friday through sundown Saturday.

One religious discrimination case involved Trans World Airlines and an employee, Larry G. Hardison. Mr. Hardison was a member of the Worldwide Church of God.[60] His seniority enabled him to avoid Saturday work; however, when he asked to be transferred to another department, his low seniority in the new unit required him to work on Saturday. The employer permitted the union to seek a work-scheduling change for Hardison, but the union refused to change seniority provisions to accommodate Mr. Hardison's religious requirements.

The Supreme Court upheld the employer's discharge of Hardison for refusing to work on Saturdays. The Court reasoned that the employer would have to incur overtime costs to replace Hardison on Saturday, which constituted an undue hardship. Although this ruling may appear to be unsympathetic to religious minorities, some observers believe that the First Amendment of the Constitution supersedes discrimination laws from mandating an employer's accommodation to a person's religion.

In another interesting case, a Jewish employee requested time off to observe Rosh Hashanah and Yom Kippur. She met with no resistance from her employer, a city housing authority. The employer gave her the time off.[61] However, the employer's policy stated that, "Excused absence for (religious observance) may be charged against personal leave, vacation leave, or compensatory leave." That is, the employee had to charge the time off to one of the leave categories, or she could take the days off without pay.

The employee filed suit. The New York State court that heard the case ruled that the employer did make accommodations by giving the employee time off. Thus, the employee could be forced to charge the days she took off to leave if she wanted to be paid for them.[62]

Physically and Mentally Handicapped Workers

The **Americans with Disabilities Act** (ADA) was passed by Congress in 1990. The ADA is a comprehensive, antidiscrimination law aimed at integrating the disabled into the work force. The ADA prohibits all employers, including privately owned businesses and local government, from discriminating against disabled employees or job applicants when making employment decisions.[63] Instead, employers now must provide "reasonable accommodations" to disabled employees and job applicants so long as doing so doesn't inflict "undue hardship" on the business. Under the ADA, "reasonable accommodations" may include making existing facilities readily accessible, modifying work schedules, job restructuring, reassignment to vacant positions, acquiring or modifying equipment, providing readers or interpreters, or adjusting or modifying examinations.

The ADA is patterned after Section 504 of the Rehabilitation Act of 1973. A person with a disability is someone who has a physical or mental impairment that substantially limits that person in some major life activity, has a record of such impairment, or is regarded as having such an impairment.

The EEOC enforces the employment requirements of the ADA. This will be a large enforcement job, since 43 million Americans have some sort of disability.[64] The ADA adopts all of the enforcement powers and remedies set forth in the Civil Rights Act of 1964, which can include hiring or reinstatement, with or without back pay, and reasonable attorneys' fees. Remedies include injunctive relief to order the alteration of facilities, monetary damages, and civil penalties.[65] Businesses need not worry about legal suits or going to court if they prepare themselves for compliance. It is important for businesses to identify trouble spots, such as hard-to-reach public areas, and find help to have them fixed. By January 1992, businesses will have to be ready to serve disabled people as they do all other customers. By January 1993, any new building must have complete access for people with disabilities.

The ADA protects individuals who have Acquired Immune Deficiency Syndrome (AIDS) or the AIDS virus against discrimination (more details on AIDS in the workplace will be provided in Chapter 19). This forces employers to hire or keep employed otherwise qualified individuals infected with AIDS or the AIDS virus. While the ADA does not protect an individual who is currently engaging in illegal drug use, a former drug abuser who has been rehabilitated successfully and is no longer using drugs is protected by the ADA.

Veterans

The Vietnam Era Veterans Readjustment Act of 1974 requires federal contractors to take affirmative action for the employment of disabled veterans and veterans of the Vietnam conflict. This act imposes fewer obligations than the other employment discrimination laws. No numerical goals are required, but the organization must show it makes special efforts to recruit them. In determining a veteran's qualifications, the employer cannot consider any part of the military record that is not directly relevant to the specific qualifications of the job in question.

White Males

If you are a white male, you are by now probably thinking: Women and minorities are getting a better chance for employment and promotion than they used to. But what does this do for me? Will I get a job? Will I get promoted to a better job? Or is reverse discrimination likely in my future? This concern is natural. The *Bakke v. University of California* and the *Weber v. Kaiser* cases show the concern of white males about reverse discrimination. These cases will continue to have a significant impact on EEO programs. Title VII prohibits discrimination based on race and sex, and that includes discrimination against white males. The laws that were originally passed to give better opportunities to women and minorities are now being interpreted as protecting the rights of the majority as well.

The obligations of the organization to white males are the same as its obligations to other groups: It must not discriminate for or against any race, sex, religion, or minority group. This presents a problem for employers with numerical affirmative action goals. How are goals to be attained without favoring the disadvantaged groups? The answer is to seek *other* means for satisfying goals that do not in turn discriminate against the advantaged groups. For example, employers would undertake more intensive recruiting efforts for women and minorities, as well as eliminating those employment practices that inhibit their hiring and promotion.

Employers should *never* set numerical goals so high that they can be attained *only*

CAREER CHALLENGE
(*concluded*)

Hugo Gerbold has just returned from his discussion with Gregory Inness, company president. Gregory seemed impressed with Hugo's presentation. But he still doubts that more women and minorities would "fit in" at Reliable. Hugo had pointed out that the EEOC and the courts wouldn't think much of this reasoning. He wondered if Gregory would take the next step in instituting an EEO plan at Reliable Insurance.

Hugo decided to be ready, just in case. He prepared an EEO program designed to focus on the areas where he felt Reliable was in the worst shape. He prepared a list of current employees, primarily in the clerical ranks, who could be promoted to underwriters and claims agents. These promotions could increase female representation in better jobs fairly quickly. They would require training, but it could be done.

To get minorities represented fairly in all categories would require special recruiting efforts. Hugo prepared a plan to increase Reliable's recruiting efforts in all categories of employment. The plan was drawn up to protect the position of current white male employees and applicants. In no case would a person be hired with fewer qualifications than white male applicants.

Luckily, Reliable was growing and was hiring more people as it expanded. Attrition would also open positions in most lower-level managerial, professional, and sales positions.

After spending quite a bit of time on development of the plan, Hugo waited. When he didn't hear from Gregory, he made an appointment to see the president.

Hugo Gregory, you recall we discussed the EEO issue. We hired Osanna, but that's as far as our effort went. I've prepared an EEO . . . .

Gregory Hugo, after we discussed it, I checked with the rest of the management. We feel we're OK as is. We don't want to upset our local work force with an EEO plan. Now, about the pay plan for next year . . . .

And that was that. Hugo took his EEO plan and placed it in a folder in his desk drawer.

Six months later, another female employee, Dot Greene, filed a complaint. The EEOC came to investigate, and the investigation indicated that Reliable had not taken the necessary steps to eliminate job discrimination. The company was instructed to develop an EEO plan to correct the problem.

---

through reverse discrimination. If the goals are already too high, action should be taken to lower them. The courts are increasingly saying that employers cannot use their numerical affirmative action goals as an excuse to discriminate against white males.

At present, there appear to be problems in interpreting these rules. For example, the New York Bell Division of AT&T promoted a woman rather than a white male who had greater seniority and better performance evaluation ratings. The judge ruled that the company should have promoted the woman to meet its EEO goals, but the male was discriminated against. The judge ordered the promotion to go through but also ordered the company to pay the white male $100,000 in damages.[66]

The courts themselves may still impose goals that discriminate against white males. But federal agencies may not impose such goals on employers, and employers may not impose them on themselves.

The conclusion that emerges is that employment discrimination laws were passed for the benefit of those groups that have historically been the victims of discrimination; nevertheless, these laws do not allow the employer to bestow such benefits voluntarily by depriving white males of their rights.

COST/BENEFIT ANALYSIS OF EEO PROGRAMS

The cost of an EEO plan can be calculated for an employer. It includes the added expense of recruitment, special training programs, test validation, job-posting systems, equipment redesign, and whatever other programs the organization includes in its plan. The calculation also must include an added cost for the preparation of reports. The HR manager or specialist may have to compute these costs and justify the expense of such a plan to higher management by citing the benefits to be derived.

Unfortunately, the benefits are difficult to compute. Even if they can be computed, they may not outweigh the costs in the short run. Consequently, some top managers may tend to view EEO as a necessary evil, something that must be done because the government requires it, not because of any benefits to be derived by the organization. This consequence can do much to destroy the HR manager's position as the person responsible for the plan, because top-management attitudes are contagious. If higher management does not provide the necessary support and resources, then lower levels of management may be reluctant to cooperate.

Therefore, it is important for managers to be aware of the benefits of EEO programs, even if they are long-range ones that are difficult to quantify. One immediate benefit is that EEO increases the likelihood that the company will stay eligible for government contracts. Another benefit is an increase in the pool of eligible employees that results from providing opportunities to women and minorities. Then there is the obvious benefit of better public relations and increased goodwill among employees that comes from a properly administered EEO program.

One benefit that EEO does not provide is insulation from liability in discrimination lawsuits. While a good EEO plan may make employees more satisfied and less likely to file charges of discrimination, it provides no presumption of innocence if an employee does take a charge to court. For instance, one General Motors plant had a good record of hiring minorities, but that did not keep a court from finding that it was guilty of discrimination in promoting them.[67] Still, EEO programs can help an employer in court. Some courts have been less stringent when companies seem to be making progress with their AAPs. This alone may make the costs of EEO worth it.

SUMMARY

This chapter focused on EEO programs designed to eliminate bias in HRM programs. The role of EEO and the law as a significant force in shaping HRM policies and programs is now an accepted fact in society. The law, executive orders, and the courts' interpretations will continue to have an influence on every phase of HRM programs and activities. This influence will become clearer as specific HRM activities are discussed in Chapters 4–21. This chapter provides only the general theme of the importance of the law in HRM. The remaining chapters will at times spell out specifically how the law impacts HRM.

To summarize the major points covered in this chapter:

1. Equal employment opportunity is one of the most significant activities in the HRM function today.
2. The three main influences on the development of EEO were:
   a. Changes in societal values.
   b. The economic status of women and minorities.
   c. The emerging role of government regulation.
3. Laws prohibiting employment discrimination that were discussed in this chapter are:
   a. Title VII of the 1964 Civil Rights Act.
   b. Executive Order 11246.
   c. The Vocational Rehabilitation Act.
   d. The Age Discrimination Act.
   e. Pregnancy Discrimination Act.
4. Three different definitions of discrimination have been arrived at by the courts over the years:
   a. Prejudiced treatment.
   b. Unequal treatment.
   c. Unequal impact.
5. The criterion for EEO and affirmative action compliance can theoretically be reduced to two questions:
   a. Does an employment practice have unequal or adverse impact on the groups covered by the law (race, color, sex, religious, or national origin groups)?
   b. Is that practice job related or otherwise necessary to the organization?
6. The government units *most* responsible for enforcing EEO regulations are:
   a. U.S. Equal Employment Opportunity Commission (EEOC) — Title VII.
   b. Office of Federal Contract Compliance Programs (OFCCP) — Executive Order 11246.
7. Courts are constantly interpreting the laws governing EEO. Due to numerous appeals, an EEO complaint can take years before settlement is reached.
8. EEO planning can be used as a preventive action to reduce the likelihood of employment discrimination charges and ensure equal employment opportunities for applicants and employees.
9. There are special aspects of EEO planning for each of these groups:
   a. Women.
   b. Older employees.
   c. Racial and ethnic minorities.
   d. Physically and mentally handicapped workers.
   e. Veterans.
   f. White males.

Exhibit 3–9 on page 106 lists some recommendations for effective EEO programs using the model organization presented in Chapter 1 (Exhibit 1–8).

EXHIBIT 3-9 EEO Programs for Model Organizations

Type of Organization	Who is responsible for organization's EEO program?			How are women and minorities recruited in EEO program?			Other activities engaged in by organization to encourage EEO		
	Separate Department	Separate Program Director	Part of Manager's Job	State Employment Service	Liaison with Community Groups	Separate Offices, etc.	Longer Training Periods	Transportation to Work	Financial Counseling
1. Large size, low complexity, high stability	X		X	X	X	X	X	X	X
2. Medium size, low complexity, high stability		X	X	X	X	X	X		X
3. Small size, low complexity, high stability			X	X	X		X		
4. Medium size, moderate complexity, moderate stability		X	X	X	X	X	X		X
5. Large size, high complexity, low stability	X		X	X	X	X	X	X	X
6. Medium size, high complexity, low stability		X	X	X	X		X		X
7. Small size, high complexity, low stability			X	X			X		

KEY TERMS

QUESTIONS FOR REVIEW AND DISCUSSION

1. The ADA could be a very costly law for employers to comply with in terms of facilities. What could be some of the costs that employers must bear?
2. Why is it proposed that the *Wards Cove Packing Co.* case could have far-reaching effects?
3. What could be some of the psychological effects of being discriminated against because of race, sex, or age?
4. Examine the equal opportunity laws of another country, such as Mexico, Japan, or France. Are there such laws? Explain.
5. What can employers do to minimize their chance of litigation and being found negligent in sexual harassment matters?
6. Why is the *Griggs v. Duke Power Company* court decision considered a landmark case?
7. The EEOC suggests that every organization should have an affirmative action policy. Is this a good suggestion? Why?
8. What does *unequal treatment* mean in terms of discrimination?
9. What is meant by the term *bona fide occupational qualification* (BFOQ)?
10. Why are the *Bakke v. University of California* and *Weber v. Kaiser* rulings considered significant for the HRM area of an organization?

NOTES

[1] (1987), 1987 *Annual Report of Director of Administrative Office of U.S. Courts* (Washington, D.C.: U.S. Government Printing Office 1960, 1990); Census Bureau, Population Division.

[2] Kenneth Sovereign (1984), *Personnel Law* (Reston, Va: Reston Publishing), p. 22.

[3] For an excellent discussion of federal regulations applied to HRM see James Ledvinka (1982), *Federal Regulation of Personnel and Human Resource Management* (Boston: Kent), p. 21.

[4] Gunnar Myrdal (1944), *An American Dilemma: The Negro Problem and American Democracy* (New York: Harper & Row).

[5] Charles Silverman (1964), *Crisis in Black and White* (New York: Random House).

[6] St. Clair Drake (1966), "The Social and Economic Status of the Negro in the United States," in *The Negro American*, ed. Talcott Parsons and Kenneth B. Clark (Boston: Houghton Mifflin), pp. 3–46.

[7] The estimate was provided in discussion with an EEOC representative, Houston, Texas, office on June 30, 1987.

[8] For an excellent discussion and presentation of the federal laws regarding discrimination, see Lee Modjeska (1980), *Handling Employment Discrimination Cases* (Rochester, N.Y.: Lawyers Cooperative).

[9] *Diaz v. Pan American Airways*, 442 F. 2d 385.

[10] Alfred Blumrosen (November 1972), "Strangers in Paradise: *Griggs v. Duke Power Co.* and the Concept of Employment Discrimination," *Michigan Law Review*, pp. 59–110.

[11] Ibid.

[12] Richard D. Arvey (1979), *Fairness in Selecting Employees* (Reading, Mass.: Addison-Wesley Publishing), pp. 50–52.

[13] Kenneth J. McCulloch (1981), *Selecting Employees Safely under the Law* (Englewood Cliffs, N.J.: Prentice-Hall), pp. 7–8.

[14] Tim Smart (November 5, 1990), "After the Election, Civil Rights May Get a Fighting Chance," *Business Week*, p. 52.

[15] Sovereign, *Personnel Law*, p. 80.

[16] Gerald P. Panaro (1990), *Employment Law Manual* (Boston: Warren, Gorham, & Lamont), pp. 5–3.

[17] 29 CFR 1608. 1 C (1979).

[18] Dorothy P. Moore and Martha Haas (February 1990), "When Affirmative Action Clouds Management Bias in Selection and Promotion Decisions," *Academy of Management Executive*, pp. 84–90.

[19] Transportation Agency, Santa Clara City, CA (1987), 107 S. Ct. 1442.

[20] (January 15, 1979), "AT&T: In the Throes of Equal Employment," *Fortune*, pp. 44–57.

[21] (November 26, 1982), "AT&T Signs Accord to Review Hiring of Women, Minorities," *The Wall Street Journal*, p. 3.

[22] For an up-to-date summary of cases, awards, and remedies, see *Employment Practices*, published twice monthly by Commerce Clearing House, Inc., 4025 W. Petersen Avenue, Chicago, IL 60646.

[23] *Griggs v. Duke Power Co.*, 401 U.S. 424 (1971).

[24] James Ledvinka and Lyle Schoenfeldt (Spring 1978), "Legal Developments in Employment Testing: Albermarle and Beyond," *Personnel Psychology*, pp. 1–13.

[25] *Washington v. Davis*, 12 FEP 1473 (1976).

[26] Arvey, *Fairness in Selecting Employees*, p. 76.

[27] (June 29, 1978), "The Bakke Ruling," *The Wall Street Journal*, pp. 1, 17, and 18.

[28] Michael J. Phillips (August 1980), "Paradoxes of Equal Employment Opportunity: Voluntary Racial Preferences and the Weber Case," *Business Horizons*, pp. 41–47.

[29] Ibid.

[30] *Memphis Fire Department v. Stotts*, 82–206, U.S. Supreme Court (1984).

[31] Louis P. Britt, III (September 1984), "Affirmative Action: Is There Life after Stotts," *Personnel Administrator*.

[32] *Wards Cove Packing Co. v. Antonio* (1989). 49 Fair Employment Practices Cases 1519.

[33] Source: Based on telephone conversation on July 1, 1991, with a Washington, D.C., EEOC official who quoted from the EEOC news release, "Resolution of Job Bias Charges Up at EEOC in Fiscal Year 1990," dated February 15, 1991.

[34] Tony Marino (August 1984), "How the EEOC Is Reaching Out to Employees," *Nation's Business*, pp. 25–26

[35] (February 1988), "Increase in Affirmative Action Enforcement," *Personnel Journal*, p. 34.

[36] U.S. Supreme Court, *Teamsters Union*, U.S. 14 EPD, 7579 (1977).

[37] Richard Trotler, Susan Rawson Zacur, and Wallace Gatewood (February 1982), "The

Pregnancy Disability Amendment: What the Law Provides: Part 1," *Personnel Administrator*, pp. 47–54.

[38] (May 19, 1984), "Guaranteed Job Law," *Resource*, pp. 1–2.

[39] (July 30, 1984), "Maternity Leave Case Gives Birth to Bitter Debate," *Chicago Tribune*, p. 2.

[40] Ibid.

[41] *Doe v. First National Bank*, 668 F. Supp. 1110 (N.D. Ill. 1987).

[42] (January 14, 1986), "Sexual Harassment — Already a Major Concern May Become Even a Higher Priority," *Human Resources Management Ideas and Trends*, pp. 9–12.

[43] (June 30, 1988), "Workers Tell of Sexual Harassment," Vughun-Pilot, p. A12.

[44] Sovereign, *Personnel Law*, p. 146.

[45] *Continental Can Co. v. State of Minnesota*, 297 N.W. 241 (Minn. Sup. Ct. 1980).

[46] *Bundy v. Jackson*, 641 F. 2d 934 (D.C. Cir. 1981).

[47] (April 1984), "EEOC Finds Employer Liable for Harassing Act of Restaurant Customers," *Resource*, p. 3.

[48] Elizabeth C. Wesman (November 1983), "Shortage of Research Abets Sexual Harassment Confusion," *Personnel Administrator*, pp. 60–65.

[49] *Heelan v. Johns-Manville Corporation*, 451 F. Supp. 16 EPD No. 8330 (D.C. Colo. 1978); and Donna C. Ledgerwood and Sue Johnson-Dietz (April 1981), "Sexual Harassment: Implications for Employer Liability," *Monthly Labor Review*, pp. 45–47.

[50] *Meritor Savings Bank v. Vinson*, 91, L. Ed. 2d 49 (June 9, 1986).

[51] Jonathan S. Mount and Angel Gomez (December 1986), "Sexual Harassment: The Impact of *Meritor Savngs Bank v. Vinson* on Grievances and Arbitration Decisions," *The Arbitrator Journal*, pp. 4–29.

[52] Nicholas J. Beutrell (August 1983), "Managing the Older Worker," *Personnel Administrator*, p. 31.

[53] *Brennen v. Greyhound Lines, Inc.*, 9 F. Cas. 58 (1975).

[54] *Henn v. National Geographic Society* (1987), 819 F. 2d 824, cert. denied, 108 S. Ct. 454, 98 L. Ed. 2d 394 (1987).

[55] Jerome M. Rosow and Robert Zagar (October 1981), "Work in America Institute's Recommendations Grapple with the Future of the Older Workers," *Personnel Administrator*, pp. 47–54, 80.

[56] Constance Matthiessen (October–November 1990), "Bordering on Collapse," *Modern Maturity*, pp. 30–32, 38.

[57] Walter Kiechel, III (November 5, 1990), "How to Manage Older Workers," *Fortune*, pp. 183–86.

[58] *Hunter v. Allis-Chalmers Corp., Engine Div.*, 797 F. 2d 1417 (7th Dir. 1986).

[59] EEOC (1977), "Guidelines on Religious Discrimination."

[60] *Trans World Airlines, Inc. v. Hardison*, 432 U.S. 63 (1977).

[61] *State Division of Human Rights v. Rochester Housing Authority*, 446 N.Y.S.2d 736.

[62] (October 1983), "Time Off for Religious Observance: At Whose Expense?" *Fair Employment Practices*, p. 6.

[63] J. Freedley Hunsicker, Jr. (August 1990), "Ready or Not: The ADA," *Personnel Journal*, pp. 80–86.

[64] Bradford A. McKee (November 1990), "Planning for the Disabled," *Nation's Business*, pp. 24–26.

[65] Paul E. Pryzant (1990), "New Disabilities Act to Have Big Impact on Business," *Bulter & Business Report*, pp. 1–4.

[66] (January 18, 1978), Equal Opportunity Agreement, U.S. Department of Labor, Commerce Clearing House *Labor Law Reports*, No. 373, 1973.

[67] *Rowe v. General Motors Corp.*, 457 F. 2d 348, 5th Cir. (1972).

At a Goldman, Sachs & Co. office in Boston, some male employees allegedly pasted photos of bare-breasted women on company newsletters, next to biographies of new female employees (suggesting that the photos were pictures of the new staff members). Copies of the newsletters were circulated around the office. Sexist literature such as "The Smart Man's Creed or Why Beer is Better than Women" ("After you've had a beer, the bottle is still worth a dime.") was allegedly also distributed. Kristine Utley, a former Goldman sales associate has made these allegations in a suit charging that the environment at Goldman, Sachs & Co. constitutes sexual harassment. Fired for refusing a transfer to a New York Office, she is suing to gain reinstatement and damages and to eliminate the harassment.

Joanne Barbetta has filed a similar suit seeking damages for harassment caused by an environment that she asserted "was poisoning my system." Ms. Barbetta reports that during her tenure as a clerk at Chemlawn male employees circulated porno-graphic magazines and pinup posters. She viewed a slide presentation that included suggestive pictures (e.g., a nude woman) put there, said management, "to keep the guys awake," according to Barbetta. After these experiences and continual breast-grabbing shenanigans by a male employee, Ms. Barbetta quit.

Marie Regab, formerly an 18-year employee of Air France, has filed similar charges concerning the Washington office where she worked as a salesperson. She alleges that several characteristics of the office environment combined to create harassment including propositions by one of her bosses, circulation of *Playboy* and *Penthouse* magazines in the office, and open discussion of sexual activity by male employees. "It was sickening and an insult to women in the office," she claims. Ms. Regab was fired; she is suing to gain reinstatement, for $1.5 million in damages, and to eliminate the harassment in the office.

These three situations are examples of a growing number of suits being filed in courts by women who are charging that a sexist environment in the workplace constitutes sexual harassment and that their employers are therefore liable. Plaintiff actions in this area have been fueled by the U.S Supreme Court's ruling that sexist behavior that creates an "intimidating, hostile, or offensive working environment" is sexual harassment and violates Title VII of the 1964 Civil Rights Act.

The Court's ruling has spurred an increasing number of companies to act to prevent sexual harassment in the workplace and to deal with it effectively when the problem occurs. Other factors have triggered company action. Employers are realizing that the costs of harassment can be high in terms of lowered productivity, absenteeism, and turnover. One study of female employees in the federal government concluded that the government loses about $200 million each year to the effects of sexual harassment. Costs can also be high if an employee sues. Even if the plaintiff opts for an out-of-court settlement, the costs of these settlements are often in the six figures, and it's the company who pays. Companies are also realizing that sexual harassment is a very real issue in today's and tomorrow's workplace; from 20 to over 50 percent of working women have experienced sexual harassment (and so have at least 15 percent of male employees).

Thus, companies are tackling the issue; the more effective stategies developed so far contain four primary features:

1. *Training programs that educate employees concerning the meaning of sexual harassment and the behaviors that comprise a hostile and harassing workplace:* Training is especially important simply because men and women often differ in their perception of what constitutes harassment. Most training is in the form of seminars and workshops, often with films and videos.

Written by Kim Stewart and adapted from Joseph Pereira (February 10, 1988), "Women Allege Sexist Atmosphere in Offices Constitutes Harassment," *The Wall Street Journal*, p. 19; Cathy Trost (August 28, 1986), "With Problem More Visible, Firms Crack Down on Sexual Harassment," *The Wall Street Journal*, p. 19; Walter Kiechel III (September 14, 1987), "The High Cost of Sexual Harassment," *Fortune*, p. 147ff; and Marisa Manley (May 1987), "Dealing with Sexual Harassment," *Inc.*, p. 145ff.

Philip Morris USA conducts a mandatory training program for its field managers that includes viewing a video called "Shades of Gray." General Motors conducts an awareness seminar for employees and offers this benchmark for judging the appropriateness of office conduct: "Would you be embarrassed to see your remarks or behavior in the newspaper or described to your own family?"

Du Pont has developed one of the most comprehensive antiharassment programs in business (begun in 1981). Recently, the corporation added a $500,000-funded course on personal safety, rape, and harassment prevention primarily for its female employees (many of whom are moving into traditionally male jobs at Du Pont such as agricultural products sales). The course offers no-nonsense advice on how to handle a harasser. For example, if a male customer fondles a woman's knee, Du Pont advises that she "firmly remove his hand . . . and then say, 'Let's pretend this didn't happen.'" If she receives a verbal proposition, Du Pont advises that she say, "No, I wouldn't want our business relationship to be jeopardized in any way." About 1,600 employees have completed the course.

Like General Motors, Du Pont offers its employees a guideline for evaluating their behavior. Said a Du Pont spokesman, "We tell people: It's harassment when something starts bothering somebody."

Some other companies provide advice concerning how to handle harassment. One popular piece of advice: Document the incident as soon as possible by describing on paper what happened in full detail and talking to someone informally about the incident. A relatively mild case of harassment can be handled by talking to the harasser, explaining what he or she did, how it made you feel, and telling the harasser to stop. In a more serious situation, communicating these points via a certified letter sent to the harasser with the victim keeping a copy is often recommended (and reportedly proven to be quite effective).

2. *An internal complaint procedures:* Ideally, the procedure provides for fast action and confidentiality and ensures that the employee can report the problem to a manager who is not involved in the harassment. Some companies encourage employees to report a problem to their immediate supervisor but also designate an individual (often a woman) in the HR department as someone employees can speak with in cases where the immediate supervisor is involved in the problem. To ensure speedy action, some companies require that an investigation begin within 24 hours after the harassment complaint has been reported. The procedure also ideally stipulates how investigations will be conducted.

3. *Speedy, corrective action that solves the problem:* If the investigation supports the employee's claims, corrective action is quickly taken. Such action can range from simply talking to the harasser to discharge, depending on the severity of the offense. One federal agency requires offending employees to publicly apologize to the individuals they've harassed. Staffing changes also sometimes occur. One New York bank faced a problem of a highly talented male executive who generated much profit for the bank — and also several costly EEOC complaints from his secretaries. The bank solved the problem by assigning the executive an all-male secretarial staff. Corrective action is particularly important because it communicates to both potential offenders and victims that harassment will not be tolerated.

4. *A written and communicated antiharassment policy:* The written policy is documented and distributed to all employees. The policy contains a definition of harassment, the company's position prohibiting harassment, the grievance procedure, and penalties.

While a growing number of companies are implementing antiharassment policies, the courts have yet to establish a consistent record concerning the issue of "hostile environment" as illegal harassment. For example, a federal district court in Michigan dismissed a claim by Vivienne Rabidue that sexual posters and obscene language in her office at Osceola Refining Co. constituted illegal sexual harassment.

However, Joanne Barbetta has won the first round of her court battle with Chemlawn. The judge hearing her complaint rejected Chemlawn's motion to dismiss the suit; he has ordered Ms. Barbetta's case to trial. Chemlawn is expected to present a vigorous defense, asserting that the men involved in the newsletter incident have been disciplined and that the situations Ms. Barbetta cites occurring "over the course of two years fall far short" of creating a hostile, harassing environment.

Discussion Questions

1. Assume that you are an HR executive for a company that manufactures and sells agricultural products (for example, fertilizers and grain feeds). The company's work force of 1,200 employees is 70 percent male and 30 percent female. Drawing from this case and the chapter content, develop an antiharassment policy/program. What are the major challenges you see in implementing the policy?

2. Many experts assert that reported cases of sexual harassment comprise a small percentage of the total number of incidents that actually occur in the workplace. If their assertions are true, why do so many cases go unreported? How would your HRM policy on harassment address this situation?

3. As research indicates, people differ widely in their perceptions of sexual harassment. What is a harmless remark to one individual can be an annoying, even infuriating insult to another. In your view, what separates harmless conduct from harassing behavior? In the same vein, when does a sexist environment become a hostile, harassing one?

4

GLOBAL HUMAN RESOURCE MANAGEMENT

· · · · · · ·

LEARNING OBJECTIVES

After studying this chapter, you should be able to:

· · ·

Describe the trend toward globalization in business in the 1990s

· · ·

Discuss the role that culture plays in determining the effective use of human resource management practices in a global organization

· · ·

Identify critical HRM issues faced by multinational and global organizations when they conduct business in the international marketplace

CAREER CHALLENGE

Boswell Technologies is a computer software development firm located in Akron, Ohio. Michael Carl, vice president for human resources at Boswell Technologies, has just returned from San Benedetto, Italy. It seems that Boswell is soon going to become Boswell International. The company has just acquired a successful software firm located in San Benedetto. The purpose of the acquisition was to quickly allow Boswell to become a premier supplier of new and innovative computer software in Europe.

On his first day back in Ohio, Michael has been called into the office of the president of Boswell, David Randolf, to give David a status report.

David Well Mike? How soon can we get our American management team into place over there in Italy and phase out their current staff. I've heard how slow and inefficient Italian businesses are run and I don't want to waste time getting our company's policies in action. Maybe we can get a head start on the European competition with good old American know-how.

Michael It is not going to be that easy, Dave. I think it might be a mistake to send our people. The Italians have an excellent sense of how we should try to run operations in Europe. I am concerned that some of our HRM policies might not work as well in Europe.

David What do you mean, our HRM policies won't work. We've been very successful here in Ohio and have even been singled out for our training and compensation programs. Of course they will work. I do not care whether we are in Ohio or Rome; business is still business.

Michael If we do send some of our people, who should go?

David Mike, the international operation is our future. Let's send our best performers for a year or two to be sure we get the job done right the first time. Let's send them just as soon as possible, too. They have the skills and know-how. All they need is the chance.

Michael But what about the costs?

David Costs? We cannot be talking about that much money can we? Airline tickets, room and board? That should not run us more than a few thousand dollars for each person we send. The new markets we tap into will give us a quick pay back.

INTRODUCTION

Today's business environment is changing in many ways. One of the most noticeable is the move toward an international marketplace. Companies are becoming international enterprises through a variety of foreign investment strategies including importing/exporting, licensing, joint venture participation, and mergers and acquisitions of foreign-owned businesses.

The trend toward an international business environment has been supported by many recent social and political events. The world is waiting to see what will happen to the Soviet Union in coming years, especially given the failure of the August 1991 coup. The face of Europe also continues to be reshaped as members of the European Community prepare for a unified marketplace. Closer to home, the United States and Canada are now operating under new, open trade agreements and the same is occurring with Mexico. Thus, a vast portion of North America will soon be an open trade region. The sum of these social changes—barriers to international trade are disappearing in all parts of the world and organizations from many nations are prepared to capitalize on the new markets that will be created.

Regardless of how a company expands beyond the domestic business environment, most are faced with HRM challenges associated with managing employees from diverse backgrounds. Although an organization is faced with many problems when it decides to become international, the "people challenge" might, in fact, be the most difficult one faced by organizations. In a recent survey of top executives, HRM problems comprised 12 of the 60 issues that were identified as the most troublesome for organizations entering international business.[1] These 12 critical HRM issues are summarized in Exhibit 4–1. As the student will learn later in this chapter, effectively dealing with these issues requires a global human resource management perspective.

Global human resource management (GHRM) refers to the policies and practices related to managing people in an internationally oriented organization. Although GHRM includes the same functions as domestic HRM, there are many unique aspects to human resource management in the international organization.

EXHIBIT 4-1   HRM Problems for the International Corporation

Human Resource Issue	Percent Reporting This as a Major Problem:
Selecting/training local managers	70%
Companywide loyalty and motivation	70
Speak, understand local language/culture	66
Appraising managers' overseas performance	65
Planning systematic management succession	59
Hiring local sales personnel	57
Compensating local foreign managers	54
Hiring/training foreign technical employees	52
Selecting/training U.S. managers for overseas	48
Dealing with foreign unions/labor laws	44
Promoting/transferring foreign managers	42
Compensating U.S. managers on overseas assignment	42

Source: Spencer Hayden (August 1990), "Our Foreign Legions Are Faltering," *Personnel*, p. 42.

The purpose of this chapter is to make students aware of the unique character of GHRM and to provide a framework for understanding the effects of national, cultural, and global business differences on effective HRM practices.

THE DIAGNOSTIC MODEL AND GLOBAL HUMAN RESOURCE MANAGEMENT

The diagnostic model (see Exhibit 4–2) is helpful for understanding the critical HRM challenges that an organization faces when it has decided to become an international enterprise. The most significant aspects of the model for a global perspective have been highlighted.

As can be seen in the exhibit, the external environment is one of the most important influences on HRM activities for the international organization. This is due to the fact that each country in which the international organization operates will have its own laws, business customs, and work-force characteristics. In addition, the international organization must constantly be aware of the political climate of each country in which it is located. Changes that can affect the organization occur very rapidly. Just a couple of years ago, China was a popular location for U.S. investments and joint ventures. When the military put down the students' protests in Tienamen Square, foreign investments in the country suddenly became far more risky.

When using the diagnostic model, it should be understood that all of the HRM activities defined by the model must be engaged in by the global human resource manager. The specifics of these activities will be covered in detail in the chapters of this book. In addition to these, however, becoming a global company adds several new and unique activities that have been highlighted in Exhibit 4–2. This chapter will focus on these unique aspects; after finishing the text, you can return to this chapter to more clearly see how an organization goes about conducting the HRM aspects of its foreign operations.

There are many reasons that an organization might expand its operations beyond its domestic boundaries, but all are intended to help achieve the end results outlined in the diagnostic model: having competitive products and/or services. The specific reasons include a search for new or broader markets, the acquisition of new and more-efficient manufacturing technology, and the capitalization on a large, inexpensive labor force. Using labor costs as an example, Exhibit 4–3 shows how much less expensive it can be for a typical manufacturing operation if it locates some of its production outside of the United States.

One example of how U.S. firms are trying to use this large, relatively untapped source of inexpensive labor is the maquiladoras or "twin plants" just inside of Mexico along the border with the United States. The *maquiladoras* are Mexican assembly plants that are used by U.S. corporations for the routine aspects of the production process. They are sometimes called *twin plants* because many of the U.S. companies that use them also have a large operation such as research and development located just inside the U.S. border.[2]

The advantage of the maquiladoras is that they allow the U.S. companies to have routine assembly work done at a fraction of the cost of having it done in the United States. The popularity of this approach to production has resulted in growth of from 640 maquiladoras in 1980 to over 1,600 of them in 1991.[3]

Mexico is not the only popular area for U.S. firms to develop cooperative business relationships, nor is a search for less expensive labor the only driving force

EXHIBIT 4-2   The Diagnostic Model and Global HRM

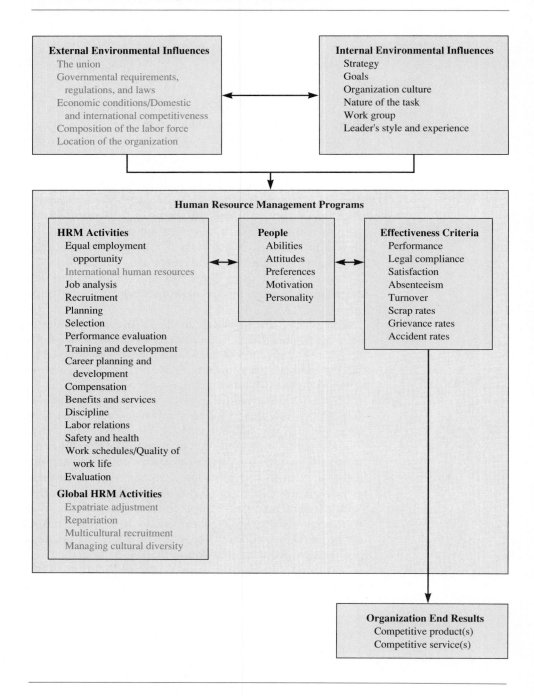

EXHIBIT 4-3   The Cost of Labor

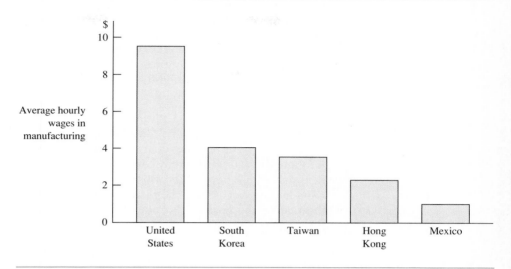

Source: Janet Lowe (July 1990), "Banking on Beans," *North American International Business*, p. 18.

behind such relationships. Between 1972 and 1986, there were 272 joint ventures with China involving U.S. firms. These represented financial commitments in excess of $1,000 billion.[4] Although the recent political unrest in China has increased the risk of investments, it is still seen as a future market of incredible potential.

Foreign investments in the United States have increased at the same remarkable rate as U.S. investments overseas. To develop a sense of how much other nations now invest directly in the United States, consider the extent of Japanese ownership in the United States. There are over 600 major manufacturing plants in the United States owned completely or partially by the Japanese alone. The total number of Japanese businesses with a stake in the United States exceeds 5,000. The manufacturing plants employ over 160,000 workers, and it is estimated that before the year 2000, this number may increase to over 800,000.[5]

Nowhere else is the trend toward globalization more evident than in the automobile industry. The distinction between "buying American" and "buying foreign" is no longer a battle of GM, Ford, and Chrysler versus the world. All of the big three automobile companies have numerous joint ventures with Japanese, Korean, and/or European automobile companies. For example, most Honda Accords sold in the United States are produced in Ohio; the Tracer is basically a Mazda-designed car that is assembled in Mexico for Lincoln-Mercury; the Geo Prism is essentially a Toyota Corolla produced in California.

The Cultural Nature of Global Human Resource Management

Most HR professionals no longer question whether there are important cultural differences between nations that might influence the effectiveness of HRM policies and practices. The real issue is understanding these differences and ensuring that HRM and the cultural orientation of workers are congruent with one another.

Several models of how **culture** influences work behavior exist. Perhaps the most recognized is Hofstede's "Theory of the Cultural Relativity of Organizational Practices."[6] Hofstede argues that national cultural differences are not changing much at all even though more-superficial work-related norms and values might be. As a result, he feels that national culture will continue to have strong effects on the effectiveness of various business practices.

According to Hofstede, cultures differ along at least four major dimensions. Differences in any of these dimensions might influence how effective HRM policies are. The four dimensions include:

Individualism/Collectivism. Cultures differ in terms of the relationship of a person to his or her "family." In some societies, the collective remains very strong throughout an individual's lifetime; people tend to think in terms of the group or extended family. In collectivistic societies, the group's achievement and well-being will be emphasized over the individual's. In contrast, individualistic societies place more emphasis on individual actions, accomplishments, and goals.

Power Distance. Cultures also vary in the ways that they view power relationships. Human inequality is almost inevitable, but cultures with high power distances emphasize these differences. For example, symbols of power and authority such as large offices, titles, and so on are usually found in a high power distance culture. In a low power distance culture, there is less emphasis on such displays. In German corporations, the concepts of codetermination and worker councils are common. Giving employees genuine input into important decisions is an organizational practice typical of low power distance cultures.

Uncertainty Avoidance. Another inevitability is not knowing what the future holds. High uncertainty avoidance cultures attempt to predict, control, and influence future events while low uncertainty avoidance cultures are more willing to take things day by day. To the extent that control reduces uncertainty, the rigid use of managerial control systems is more likely found in organizations within high uncertainty avoidance cultures.

Masculinity. The final dimension refers to the division of roles for males and females that a particular culture imposes. Masculine cultures have strict sex roles; feminine cultures have less well-defined ones. From an organizational perspective, masculine cultures might tend to be less supportive of efforts to integrate women into upper-level management than feminine cultures.

Virtually every aspect of HRM can be influenced by cultural differences. Therefore, these must be taken into consideration when an organization structures its HRM policies for overseas operations.

The Concept of "Fit" in Global Human Resource Management

When an organization structures its HRM policies for international operations, the way that it considers cultural differences should be through the concept of "fit." *Fit* refers to the degree that HRM policies are congruent with the strategic international plan of the organization and with the work-related values of the foreign culture.[7]

For an organization to be successful in the international marketplace, it must be concerned with this fit from both an internal and an external perspective. *Internal fit* is concerned with making sure that HRM policies facilitate the work values and motivations of employees. Policies must be structured in ways that allow headquarters and foreign subsidiaries to interact without sacrificing efficiency.

External fit, on the other hand, refers to the degree to which HRM matches the context in which the organization is operating. In this regard, HRM is critical to international operations because of its effects on cross-cultural interaction.[8] To be effective, the cultural and socioeconomic environments of the foreign subsidiary must be understood.[9]

Multinational and Global Corporations

Although the terms are often treated as the same, there are distinctions between a **multinational corporation** and a **global corporation** that have important HRM implications. A multinational corporation (MNC) might have operations in different nations but each is viewed as a relatively separate enterprise. Key personnel are usually from the company's home offices, and most decision making remains at corporate headquarters. Thus, although the MNC will largely be staffed by people from the nation in which a particular facility is found, managers from the home country of the corporation retain most authority.[10] The multinational corporation does not yet see its potential market as the world. Rather, it views each of its foreign operations as a specialized market for a particular product. In other words, each foreign subsidiary concentrates its efforts on the nation in which it is located.

In contrast to an MNC, the global corporation (GC) is structured so that national boundaries disappear; this leads to staffing practices in which the organization hires the best persons for jobs irrespective of their national origin. The global corporation sees the world as its labor source as well as its marketplace. Thus, the global corporation will locate an operation wherever it can accomplish its goals in the most cost-efficient way.[11] The true global corporation also believes in a world market for essentially similar products. Moreover, the national affiliation of an employee becomes rather unimportant. For example, Mars Inc.–Spain has an English general manager and a French finance manager, and the HRM director is Swiss.[12]

GHRM in the 1990s will be a challenging task for both an MNC and a GC. Many of the problems that the MNC and GC will face are the same; others are unique. Exhibit 4–4 illustrates the major focus of GHRM processes for these two different international perspectives.

Perhaps the most important GHRM task for the multinational corporation is managing the expatriate adjustment process. An **expatriate manager** is a manager from the corporation's home nation that is on a foreign assignment. The focus for the MNC will therefore be on the selection, training, appraisal, and compensation of the expatriate. Significant efforts will also be placed on career management as it relates to the expatriate's return to headquarters.

In contrast to the MNC, problems associated with differences in local recruiting methods and the problems associated with effectively managing cultural diversity are going to be the greatest challenges for the global corporation. Although the GC will still use expatriates for certain assignments, it staffs operations with persons from all over the world. As a result, it will have tremendous diversity in its workers and will also utilize local managers more often.

Since business seems to be moving toward global rather than multinational corporate structures, the warning offered by Peter F. Drucker cannot be ignored.[13]

We are reaching a point where there is going to be a revolt against the attempt to impose economics on culture. When I read of our Government asking the Japanese to

EXHIBIT 4-4   HRM Focus for Multinational and Global Corporations

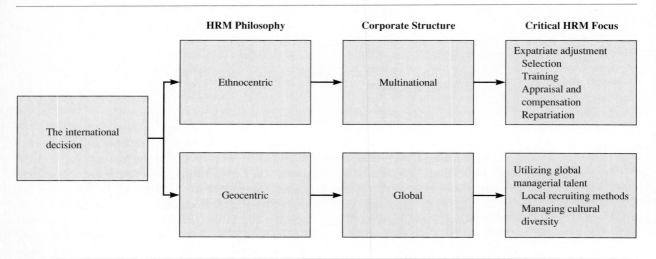

change their social order, I think this is hubris; it can't work and it's dangerous. Further, I think globalization, while irreversible, is going to run into very severe backlashes.

Thus, the real challenge for GHRM will be to capitalize on the diversity of a global work force without suppressing each nation's desire to maintain its own cultural heritage. Perhaps the biggest mistake unsuccessful global organizations make is to assume that there is ''one best way'' to structure HRM policies and practices. For example, as many as 120 critical differences between Japanese and U.S. workplace norms that might affect HRM policies have been identified. Many of these center around HRM policies related to feedback and performance evaluation methods, lines of authority, and information management.[14] Therefore, trying to apply HRM principles that work well in one work environment may not lead to the same degree of success in another.

Generally speaking, there are three sources of employees for an international assignment. For key managerial and technical positions, all three sources of workers are frequently used in international organizations. Which source is used the most depends, however, on the GHRM perspective of the company. The organization might choose to hire:

Host country nationals (HCN), who are workers from the local population. A worker from Riyadh employed by a U.S. firm operating in Saudi Arabia would be considered a host country national. Sometimes, they are referred to as a *local nationals*.

Parent country nationals (PCN), who are sent from the country in which the organization is headquartered. These persons are usually referred to as *expatriates*. A U.S. manager on assignment in Saudi Arabia is an expatriate or parent country national.

Third country nationals (TCN), who are from a country other than where the parent organization's headquarters or operations are located. If the U.S. firm employed a manager from Great Britain at their facilities in Saudi Arabia, he or she would be considered a third country national.

PROFESSIONAL PROFILE

Biography

Since 1986, David M. Nicol has been the President of HCS Technology, Inc. After receiving his bachelor's degree in economics, David obtained his M.B.A. from Arizona State University. Prior to being president of HCS, David had been a senior financial analyst for Hallmark Cards and a manager of analysis and reporting for Frito-Lay.

In his role as president of HCS, he was responsible for the U.S. operations of a Dutch conglomerate that included a holding company and three operating companies. David reported directly to a group managing director in Holland and had several Dutch expatriates reporting to him. Thus, he was truly "a man in the middle" from a cultural perspective.

Managing Cultural Diversity: A Viewpoint Although he had been very successful in a variety of jobs concerned only with domestic operations, David realized very quickly that working for a multinational corporation was an entirely new experience. He learned first-hand how much influence cultural differences can have on effective management. While there were obviously many adjustments that had to be made to his management style, David noticed that daily interactions were potentially even more frustrating than broad strategic differences in how business is conducted. "I found that in meetings with my management team, the expatriates would periodically shift

David M. Nicol
HCS Technology, Inc.

from speaking English to Dutch in front of me. It wasn't their way of talking behind my back as I originally assumed. Rather, it was their way of communicating with each other more efficiently—to facilitate interaction. But, suddenly not understanding conversations in the board room was unnerving."

Language is not the only barrier to managing cultural diversity, however. "Work values and HRM policies also differ. For example, work scheduling, vacation times, and how to motivate people are just a few things that really are affected by culture. I could never seem to get my Dutch managers to respond to deadlines the same way we do in the United States. It took a while to realize that their system wasn't wrong; it was just different. The only solution is to be flexible and adaptable."

If the company is an MNC, especially one that is in the early stages of becoming an international enterprise, it will probably take a relatively *ethnocentric* perspective by trying to use the HRM policies from the home country with at best minor adaptations to them. The new, ethnocentric multinational organization generally believes that all key personnel should be PCNs because it believes that its ways of doing things are superior to those of other cultures.

The tendency to be ethnocentric is a strong one for new and even for many well-established foreign organizations conducting business in the United States, especially the Japanese. Virtually every executive-level position in Japanese-owned businesses in the United States is occupied by a Japanese national. Only about 31 percent of the senior management positions in such firms are occupied by U.S. managers. More commonly, local nationals are used for specific functions such as a liaison, but Japanese organizations have a reputation for showing little regard for the career development of these persons. In contrast, foreign companies in Japan hire local Japanese managers for nearly 80 percent of their management needs.[15]

In contrast to the ethnocentric perspective, a mature MNC or a true global corporation will tend to have more of a *geocentric* orientation to HRM. It will begin seeing the world as its labor market and, therefore, will hire key personnel from wherever they are available. The geocentric organization will ignore national boundaries for staffing its overseas operations.

THE EXPATRIATE MANAGER IN THE MULTINATIONAL CORPORATION

As mentioned previously, managing the expatriate adjustment process is a primary focus of GHRM for the multinational corporation. Although many companies are expected to rely less and less on expatriates for staffing overseas operations,[16] parent country nationals continue to occupy a significant portion of key managerial and professional positions in most MNCs. Dow Chemical, for example, has approximately 1,000 expatriates on overseas assignments at any given time. Out of a staff of 125 at its Brazilian offices, Pectin International still employs about 25 expatriates.[17]

Based on recent surveys, selecting and training expatriates are two aspects of GHRM that many companies are not doing particularly well. Estimates of the failure rates for expatriate managers range anywhere from lows of 40 percent in Europe and Asia to as high as 70 percent for assignments in Third World countries.[18] In addition, estimates are that between 30 and 50 percent of the expatriates who remain on their overseas assignments are considered unsuccessful by the parent organization.[19]

At the same time that failure rates among expatriates are high, a study of *Fortune* 500 international HR managers indicated that slightly more than one third of their companies provided systematic cross-cultural orientation training for expatriates.[20] This suggests that reducing these failure rates will require an integrated program of expatriate selection and more-adequate training before they are sent overseas.

Selecting the Expatriate Manager

Exhibit 4–5 lists the factors that seem to be most commonly associated with expatriate success and failure. It is obvious from the list that selection for expatriate assignments will be an extremely complex and sensitive task. Many of the factors that are related to a successful expatriate assignment will be difficult to measure, and the managers' levels of success in domestic operations may have very little to do with their success overseas. One of the major reasons that expatriate failure rates are so high for many U.S. companies is that these companies continue to believe that a manager's domestic performance will always be related to his or her overseas performance. As a result, they frequently overemphasize technical competency and disregard more important factors when selecting the expatriate.[21]

As Exhibit 4–5 shows, the real keys to a successful expatriate choice are finding managers who are culturally flexible and adaptable, who have supportive family situations, and who are motivated to accept the overseas assignment. Other factors such as cultural familiarity and language fluency are also apparently more important than technical competency.

Staffing an international joint venture with expatriates can be challenging since the partners in the venture might disagree about the necessary qualifications for a manager. For example, a Japanese partner might be looking for a manager who is a real "team player" while a U.S. partner might be seeking a "highly aggressive, self-

EXHIBIT 4-5   Expatriate Manager Success and Failure

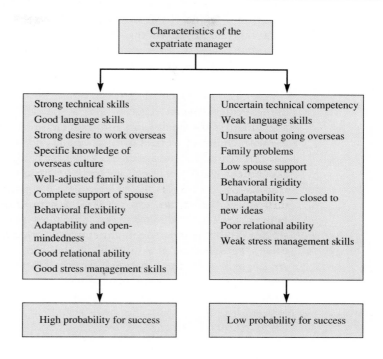

starter'' for the same position. Such disagreements are one of the reasons that joint ventures that use one of the partner's management philosophies rather than shared systems seem to work better.[22]

Motivation to accept an overseas assignment is also a factor in the expatriate's success. Without a strong commitment to completing the assignment, the expatriate's chances of success are small. The organization can help create this motivation in several ways. Compensation programs that are attractive to the expatriate can help. Perhaps more important, however, is creating a system where the overseas assignment is beneficial to the expatriate's long-term career objectives. One of the most commonly mentioned concerns of expatriates is that their position in the home offices may be jeopardized if they are away too long. That is, many expatriates believe that accepting a lengthy overseas assignment will derail any successful career path they had established in the domestic operations.

A recent Supreme Court ruling has added a potentially interesting twist to instilling expatriates with the motivation necessary for successfully completing their assignments. In *Equal Employment Opportunity Commission v. Arabian American Oil Co.* (1991), Chief Justice Rehnquist argued that:

> [the case] presents the issue whether Title VII applies extraterritorially to regulate the employment practices of United States employers who employ United States citizens abroad. The United States Court of Appeals for the Fifth Circuit held that it does not, and we agree with that conclusion.

Simply stated, the Supreme Court determined that equal employment opportunity protection afforded under Title VII (prohibiting discrimination on the basis of sex, race, religion, color, and national origin) may not extend to the typical expatriate manager's situation. Although any such decision cannot be overinterpreted since they address specific circumstances, the general notion of this ruling suggests that expatriates do not have the same degree of protection against discrimination as managers employed in the United States. This could potentially reduce many managers' interest in accepting such assignments.

The role of the expatriate's family should also never be underestimated when making decisions about overseas assignments. Research indicates that when the spouse becomes dissatisfied, it can significantly affect the expatriate's performance. Some evidence even suggests that a spouse's inability to adjust to the overseas assignment is the single most common factor in expatriate failures.[23] For an expatriate with children, worries over schooling and leisure activities can add to the stress associated with the assignment. Eventually, if these worries are not resolved, the assignment might end with an early return of the expatriate to his or her parent country.

Because the family can be such an important factor in expatriate manager failures, the temptation for many companies may be to only send managers who are single. While this practice might eliminate one problem, it could easily create many others. For example, it is quite likely that a greater proportion of men than women are single in certain occupational groups. If a company only selects single persons for desirable overseas assignments, it might have unintentionally discriminated against women.

Culture Shock and the Expatriate Manager

A trip to a foreign culture can cause tourists and expatriate managers alike to go through a predictable series of reactions to their unfamiliar surroundings. Exhibit 4–6 illustrates the cycle of these reactions. First, there is a period of fascination where all of the different aspects of the culture are viewed with interest and curiosity. This first reaction to a new culture is generally a positive experience.

EXHIBIT 4-6   The Culture Shock

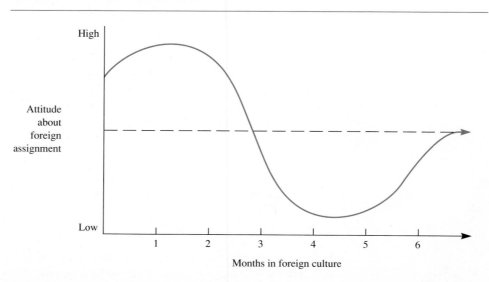

Months in foreign culture

Next, however, comes a period known as *culture shock. Culture shock* refers to the frustration and confusion that result from being constantly subjected to strange and unfamiliar cues about what to do and how to get it done.[24] Notice from the exhibit that culture shock does not typically occur during the earliest days of a trip overseas. Thus, while many expatriate managers' assignments begin very positively, their experiences often turn negative soon after.

The successful expatriate must cope effectively with culture shock. It is a period in which the manager may miss the familiar surroundings of the home offices. Simple, daily events can become sources of stress and dissatisfaction. For example, being denied access to a favorite snack food or leisure activity because they are unavailable in the host country may not seem like important issues. To the expatriate on a lengthy overseas assignment, they can become extremely frustrating.

The final stage of coping with a new culture is an adaptation stage. During this stage, the expatriate has made reasonable adjustments to the new culture and is able to deal effectively with it. Although this stage seldom returns the expatriate to the heights of excitement that he or she first experienced, a successful transition to a new culture does return the expatriate to manageable levels of a "normal" lifestyle.

Training the Expatriate Manager

Once the groundwork for a successful overseas assignment has been laid by choosing expatriates who have good chances of succeeding, the next step toward ensuring success is for the organization to properly train and prepare these managers for their upcoming assignments. As with selection, expatriate manager training programs need to focus on issues that are not typically dealt with in domestic training programs.

Intercultural training does seem to improve the chances for success on an overseas assignment.[25] There are, however, several different kinds of training to choose from. "Documentary" training and "Interpersonal" training methods are two of the major types. Documentary training involves relatively passive learning about another culture and its business practices; interpersonal approaches focus on intercultural role playing and self-awareness exercises. Both can be valuable forms of preparation for the expatriate manager.[26]

According to Tung,[27] there are two primary determinants of how much and what kind of training expatriate managers should receive. These are the level of contact with the host culture that the expatriate will encounter and the degree of dissimilarity between the home and host cultures. As either of these increases, the expatriate will require more in-depth training for the overseas assignment.

Exhibit 4–7 shows the content and structure of an integrated expatriate manager training program. It involves three different phases, and each phase has specific objectives for helping the expatriate to be successful.

Predeparture training includes the critical activities of preparing the expatriate for the overseas assignment. Its purpose is to reduce the amount of culture shock that the manager and his or her family encounters by familiarizing them with the host country. Among the most important predeparture activities are language training and cultural orientation training.

Self-awareness is an important aspect of successfully preparing for an international assignment. Assessment techniques such as the one shown in Exhibit 4–8 can be very helpful to the expatriate. Responding to these kinds of questions can help the manager to know just where he or she is most likely to encounter the ill effects of culture shock. This kind of advanced preparation can go a long way toward reducing the negative effects of being transplanted to a new culture.

EXHIBIT 4-7   Phases of an Expatriate Manager Training Program

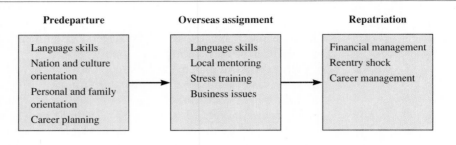

Adapted from Edward Dunbar and Allan Katcher (September 1990), ''Preparing Managers for Foreign Assignments,'' *Training and Development Journal*, p. 47.

EXHIBIT 4-8   Expatriate Self-Awareness: Being Prepared for Culture Shock

Prospective global managers should prepare satisfactory answers to the following questions before going on an overseas assignment:

1. How will living abroad affect me and my family?
2. What will my spouse do in terms of work and home life?
3. Are my children prepared for living abroad?
4. What assistance and support will be available to us?
5. What will happen to our home and other personal property while we are gone?
6. What arrangements can be made for family pets?
7. How will we handle health care while we are overseas?
8. Can we expect to encounter any anti-Americanism? What about the threat of terrorism?
9. What security measures should we take?
10. What kinds of recreational opportunities are available?
11. Will language barriers present problems for me?
12. What is the proper form of dress for various occasions?
13. How will we handle transportation at the overseas location?
14. What kinds of food can we expect to eat?

Adapted from Philip R. Harris and Robert T. Moran (1991), ''So You're Going Abroad Survey,'' in *Managing Cultural Differences*, 3rd ed. (Houston: Gulf Publishing).

The second phase of an expatriate manager training program occurs at the host country site. In other words, expatriate training does not stop just because the manager has his or her boarding pass in hand. As can be seen from Exhibit 4–7, language training continues to be a priority during this phase of training. In addition, mentoring relationships have proven to be very effective expatriate training tools. For many organizations that have several expatriates at the same overseas location, local support groups have developed to help the entire family of a newly arriving expatriate. Some organizations even make participation and leadership in such support groups a part of senior expatriates' jobs.[28]

Many experts suggest that one method for helping the expatriate manager to cope with a new culture is to get him or her involved with daily experiences as soon

---

EXHIBIT 4-9   How to Get in Step Quickly without Wasting Time (a checklist of things to do on arrival)

- Walk around, just like at home.
- Get to know the neighborhood.
- Learn how to get around on public transportation: taxis, buses, subways, trains, motorscooters, rickshaws.
- Do some shopping—even if you don't buy anything: salespeople are often extremely well informed, especially about the marketplace.
- Learn how to bargain if you're in a bazaar economy.
- Stop converting local currency into dollars; learn local values.
- Do the museums, especially the historical and cultural.
- Talk with everyone who will give you an ear, but especially with host country nationals.
- Sightseeing is good; guides rarely have reliable data.
- Talk to people standing in queues.
- Go to the university and talk with faculty and students.
- Accept as many social invitations as you can.
- Follow up on all contacts from home, even if they are from people you don't really care about back there, for everyone counts. Do the social contacts first, then the business when you're a better-informed guest.
- Read the local papers if in a language you understand, picking up on the issues of the day; informing yourself on the latest scandals shows you care about what's going on, but avoid talking about the political scandals.
- Establish your bank account.
- Locate the post office.
- Eat out at restaurants, outside the hotel; learn to read the menus; and learn the meaning of various dishes.
- Read signs on the street, above shops, on houses.
- Look for signs of national identity in symbols, signs, flags, etc.; learn political party signs.
- Listen to the radio in your spare time; watch television.
- Go to the movies, but avoid American flicks.
- Go to the theater, listen to the living local language.
- Attend musical and dance performances, concentrating on the indigenous music and dance.
- Identify the most popular sports and attend games.
- Go to religious services, even if it is not your faith.
- Keep a notebook or diary, and write in it biographical sketches of people you have talked with. Write down questions you think of afterwards that you want to ask someone else.
- Write letters home and ask them to ask you questions. Be sure they save your letters.
- Write down *only* positive statements or neutrals. Avoid negatives in anything written.
- Never talk negatively even when alone with your spouse.

Source: Henry Ferguson (1988), *Tomorrow's Global Executive* (Homewood, Ill.: Dow Jones-Irwin), p. 144.

as possible.[29] The suggestions presented in Exhibit 4–9 are intended to familiarize the expatriates with these daily experiences so they can begin concentrating on business within a reasonable period of time.

The final phase of an integrated expatriate training program occurs when the manager is preparing to return to the parent country. The process of being reintegrated into domestic operations is referred to as *repatriation*. And, although it may seem straightforward, repatriation can cause culture shock that is very similar to the shock that occurred when the expatriate originally went overseas. Some of the more critical issues that repatriation training must deal with are contained in Exhibit 4–7. These include the financial adjustments that must be made since the expatriate will frequently lose overseas living subsidies and salary premiums. Helping the manager to get back on career tracks is also important for repatriation.

Compensating the Expatriate Manager

One reason that many companies are trying to reduce their reliance on expatriate managers for staffing overseas operations is the cost associated with such assignments. Estimates are that a middle- to upper-level expatriate can cost an organization anywhere from $100,000 to $300,000 more each year in comparison to using a host country national manager.[30] Exhibit 4–10 is an excerpt from a recent recruitment ad for a public relations specialist for Saudi Aramco. It should help in giving an appreciation of the costs of using expatriates.

There are also many additional costs associated with expatriates that are not mentioned in this employment advertisement. It can be very expensive to relocate an expatriate and his or her family; usually these costs are incurred twice since most expatriates eventually return to the parent country.

The actual cost of living in many foreign settings is extremely high. For example, it can cost nearly four times as much for a family of four to live in Tokyo, Japan, than in Chicago, Illinois.[31] The expatriate's compensation will usually include a cost-of-living premium to offset these differences. These premiums might be further supplemented with a home maintenance allowance, a home furnishings allowance, assistance with maintaining or selling the expatriate's home before leaving for the overseas assignment, transportation differential allowances, educational allowances, and hardship premiums in difficult or hazardous environments.

When all of the costs associated with an expatriate are added together, a company is faced with spending as much as five times the manager's domestic salary to maintain him or her and the family overseas for just one year.[32] Exhibit 4–11 is an example of the different costs that would be incurred by a U.S. corporation conducting business in several European countries. It also shows how much less expensive it would be to use someone either from the host country or a third country national from another European nation.

EXHIBIT **4-10**   An Expatriate Manager Compensation Package

Public Relations Specialist

As a Saudi Aramco employee, you will receive a highly competitive base compensation package, as well as a substantial expatriate premium. Additional benefits include noncontributory group life insurance, company-matched savings, free medical care at Saudi Aramco's hospital and clinics, housing inside a company community, and extensive recreation facilities and activities. Your eligible children will be enrolled in company schools, comparable to U.S. private schools. There are up to 13 company holidays annually, and you will be eligible for 36 calendar days of vacation, with round-trip airfares to the U.S. or Canada for you and your family.

Source: Employment advertisement in the Sunday, March 31, 1991, *Houston Chronicle*.

EXHIBIT 4-11   Costs of Expatriate, Host, and Third Country National Managers

		Total Compensation Expenses							
		U.K. Third Country National*		Belgian Third Country National*		U.S. Foreign Service Employee at $30,000*		U.S. Foreign Service Employee at $45,000*	
Country of Operation	Local National	Married	Single	Married	Single	Married	Single	Married	Single
U.K.		—	—	$ 66,053	$57,143	$ 66,999	$52,599	$ 93,175	$ 76,161
	$20,916	—	—	78,458	66,039	89,113	63,900	117,039	89,383
Germany		$60,652	$51,282	87,492	78,170	$ 92,553	81,524	134,584	115,742
	35,860	73,968	57,141	103,373	87,035	114,895	92,882	158,678	129,021
Italy		42,510	28,517	74,518	$58,654	69,340	50,328	97,368	74,561
	24,305	56,042	34,430	90,635	67,378	91,834	61,724	121,612	87,878
Belgium		61,484	43,770	—	—	81,971	58,425	111,831	82,073
	53,020	74,864	49,445	—	—	104,189	69,752	135,799	95,321

* The figure on the first line in each column represent the employer's total first-year compensation costs per employee *excluding* relocation expenses. The figures shown on the second line include relocation expenses.
Source: Neil B. Krupp (July 1990), "Overseas Staffing for the New Europe," *Personnel*, p. 23.

HOST COUNTRY NATIONALS AND THE GLOBAL CORPORATION

When an organization adopts a global rather than a multinational orientation, it might still rely on expatriates for some of its management needs. But it will also make far greater use of host country nationals for filling key positions. As was seen in Exhibit 4–11, this can be much less expensive than using expatriates. However, many companies still have strong reservations about using HCNs. Some of the most frequently mentioned reasons for not using locals are (1) a concern that the locals will not adopt the parent company's culture and management system; (2) a concern over the level of commitment that locals may have to the organization; (3) a concern that HCNs may not have the expertise that expatriates have; and, (4) a concern over how effective communication will be between the host country and home offices.

Careful recruitment, selection, and training can reduce or eliminate many of the potential problems with using HCNs. Generally speaking, the organization should use the same strategy and criteria that it uses in the selection of expatriates.[33] It is also worth noting that some research indicates that HCN and expatriate managers have similar levels of organizational commitment.[34] And, despite important differences between cultures, there is also evidence that managers' specific work-related values are reasonably similar.[35] Thus, although HRM practices need to be culturally adapted, it appears that organizations can capitalize more on local management talent than they have in the past.

Another useful technique for becoming less dependent on expatriates is for organizations to have systematic mentoring programs to assist with the transition to host national management. Hewlett-Packard, for example, now has a Japanese president in Japan.[36] This individual worked closely with an expatriate for a one-year period to become familiar with the company's philosophy and culture.

As mentioned earlier, the Japanese are reluctant to use HCNs in key positions. They too, however, are beginning to change. Pilot Pen Corporation of America is a subsidiary of Japan's oldest and largest pen maker. Currently, the U.S. subsidiary is being headed up by an American, Ronald G. Shaw, who was hired away from Bic Pens several years ago. Since taking over the subsidiary, the host country president has dramatically improved the company's U.S. market share. According to Shaw, his familiarity with U.S. customs and culture can be credited with much of the turnaround success, and the Japanese parent company allowed him the freedom to run the company from his own perspective. He developed advertising campaigns aimed at the U.S. audience and implemented changes in HRM policies that the U.S. workers were more accustomed to, even though they were unfamiliar to the Japanese parent firm.[37]

When an organization recruits HCNs, it should not assume, however, that the same sources that it uses for domestic applicants will be effective. Its HRM policies will definitely have to be more flexible, and the organization will have to strive for a reasonable fit between these policies and cultural values. For example, it is not uncommon for the ties between foreign business and universities to be weaker than they are in the United States. Thus, university recruitment programs may be less effective than they are here.[38]

Several suggestions can improve the effectiveness of HCN recruiting efforts. Overall, the best advice is for the organization to follow the example of other companies doing business in a particular country. Try to use the same methods and sources as the host country organizations.[39] Specifically, a recruiting liaison can help with the details of the process. Recruitment ads should be written in ways that are consistent with local custom and jargon so there are no misunderstandings. In addition, so the company can get the best picture of an applicant's qualifications, HCNs should be allowed to use their native language during interviews.[40]

Global Corporate Boards of Directors

In spite of the movement toward global corporations in today's business world, the boards of directors of most major U.S. corporations have been slow to include non-U.S. members. In a survey of 589 U.S. corporations, only 24 percent of the manufacturing firms, 14 percent of the financial firms, and 9 percent of other nonfinancial firms had a global representative on their boards. And, while major Japanese corporations continue to share the United States' ethnocentrism on corporate boards, European companies are progressing more quickly. Nestlé, Unilever, Fiat, and Volvo all have global representation on their boards.[41]

SPECIAL RESPONSIBILITIES FOR GLOBAL HUMAN RESOURCE MANAGEMENT

The major functions performed by HRM are similar for domestic and global corporations. There are, however, a variety of services that the GHR department should be prepared to perform that are unique to international assignments and operations. The following list is compiled from services provided by Ferro for its expatriate managers.[42]

Tax and financial advice. Personal income tax preparation can become very complex for expatriates on extended overseas assignments. In addition, both

---

Optima Award for Excellence in HRM

Each year, *Personnel Journal* congratulates several corporations for their efforts in HRM by honoring them with an Optima Award. The Optima is **Personnel Journal's** "Oscar" for HRM.

The 1991 Optima award winner for excellence in Global Human Resource Management was the Whirlpool Corporation. In January 1989, Whirlpool acquired 53 percent ownership of N.V. Philips of the Netherlands to form Whirlpool International. With the acquisition of a majority ownership in Philips, Whirlpool suddenly found itself as a premier player in the international marketplace. To help the organization develop and maintain excellence at a global level, Whirlpool's HR group held a global leadership conference for 140 of its top executives. The purpose of the conference was to provide these leaders with the insights necessary for being an innovative, global corporation.

Congratulations to Whirlpool on a job well done.

Source: Diane Filipowski (January 1991), "Optima Awards," *Personnel Journal*, p. 52.

expatriation and repatriation frequently lead to abrupt changes in levels of income.

Housing and school assistance. Locating and securing both housing and schools can be difficult overseas. The public school systems in many countries differ tremendously from those in the United States. Desirable, affordable housing is also difficult to find.

Bank and personal records transfers. Establishing foreign bank accounts, handling currency exchanges in an equitable way, transferring medical records, finding acceptable medical facilities, and other essential document transfers are part of the GHRM function.

Language training. The importance of language skills has been emphasized in this chapter. The responsibility for seeing that programs are available rests with the GHR department.

Work and family adjustment assistance. Dual-career couples are more common than they used to be. These create special problems for attracting expatriates. GHRM in many corporations has work location assistance programs for spouses in addition to household assistance programs.

THE LEGAL AND ETHICAL CLIMATE OF GLOBAL HUMAN RESOURCE MANAGEMENT

When an organization decides to become an international enterprise, it will be confronted with new and potentially unique standards of legal and ethical conduct. International business is conducted in a maze of international trade agreements, parent country laws, and host country regulation of foreign enterprises. In addition, many decisions that might challenge an organization's normal standards of ethical conduct may be encountered. For example, environmental regulation is weaker in many countries around the world than it is in the United States. Since relaxed environmental controls can allow an organization to operate at lower cost, management philosophy about protecting the environment will inevitably have to be dealt with. Should the organization continue to meet or exceed U.S. standards or should it merely attempt to meet less-stringent foreign standards?

Other business practices that are considered unethical or illegal in the United States might be considered part of the normal conduct of business in other countries. "Gift giving" is a common practice in many parts of the world. Unfortunately, in situations where there is a conflict of interest, such gift giving can be considered bribery in the United States. The Congress of the United States was so concerned with this particular issue that it passed the Foreign Corrupt Practices Act of 1977 (FCPA).

The purpose of the FCPA was to make it illegal for employees of U.S. corporations to induce foreign officials, by offering monetary or other payments, to use their influence to gain an unfair competitive advantage for the organization. It does not prohibit, however, payments made to minor officials if the payments are intended to get the official to simply provide normal clerical services (e.g., processing paperwork at a customs office) in a more timely fashion. This kind of "greasing" is rather common in many countries, but such payments are probably not a violation of the FCPA since they do not have a corrupt intent. At the same time, many forms of payments that are not illegal in the host country might very well be considered violations.[43]

Doing business overseas can also create ethical dilemmas related to the sale or transfer of technology and knowledge. Corporations might also be faced with decisions about what kinds of business relationships should be established in foreign nations whose political or social values differ from those of the United States. Perhaps the most famous case where business, morality, and politics have clashed is in the divestiture of most U.S. corporations from South Africa because of that country's apartheid policies. Although there is government regulation that answers some of these ethical questions, many of the most important difficult decisions about how to conduct operations overseas will ultimately fall on the shoulders of the corporation.

The GHR department can play an important role in shaping the conduct of international business by providing predeparture training programs that cover the essentials of both the legal and ethical climates of the countries that expatriates are being assigned to. Ethics training programs, in general, are increasing in popularity and typically target key managerial personnel as their starting point. These programs focus on increasing the managers' awareness of the consequences of their decisions from both a legal and an ethical perspective.[44] The complexity of international business will probably cause an even greater emphasis on the issues addressed by ethics training programs in the coming years.

LABOR RELATIONS AND THE INTERNATIONAL CORPORATION

Both multinational and global corporations encounter a variety of labor relations issues that are different from purely domestic operations. There are many differences in the structure of unions and the influence that they have over an organization's operations worldwide. Coupled with these differences are labor laws that will be virtually unique to every nation in which an organization wishes to do business.

Differences in how much participation employees are entitled to in setting HRM policies is one critical area for the global human resource manager to understand. If an organization tries to impose policies and procedures on workers who are used to making HRM decisions along with management, then the imposed policies will be met with resistance. Thus, before establishing operations in a different country, one important task for the global HR manager is to research the local labor relations climate.

CAREER CHALLENGE
(*concluded*)

*A*fter reading this chapter, David now knows how difficult it can be to become an international corporation. He also knows that there are cultural differences among nations that influence how business is conducted and what HRM practices will work. Finally, he has a real sense of just how expensive it can be to send an expatriate manager overseas and how difficult it is to prepare someone to be successful in the overseas assignment.

In their next meeting, David told Michael that he had reconsidered and decided that more careful study of the situation should be done before making any final management team decisions. Both agreed, however, that one or two key people from Ohio would undoubtedly be assigned to the European operation at least long enough for a successful transition to occur.

David So, who should we send, Mike? There are several people who have the technical skills to do the job.

Michael We need to finish our assessments before I can give you an answer. At least we now know what characteristics to focus on. And please do not forget that you authorized money to establish the expatriate manager training program we talked about.

David Stop worrying, you've got the money. Just give me some expatriates who are prepared for the challenges ahead.

There are many examples of important differences in employee participation under the U.S. labor relations system and the labor relations systems in other countries. While it is beyond the scope of this chapter to outline all of these, several examples should help to reinforce the need for understanding local labor relations before an organization becomes an MNC or GC.

Employee codetermination is a legally guaranteed right in Germany. German law gives employees three different degrees of participation, depending on the issue in question. German worker councils merely have to be informed and consulted for most economic decisions. But they are allowed to participate in decisions such as dismissals, work procedures, and the design of the workplace. At an even greater level of involvement, worker councils have approval rights over decisions such as working hours, training programs, and safety regulations.[45.]

Labor relations in Korea's giant industrial firms, the *chaebol*, is an entirely different matter. The chaebol are Korea's enormous conglomerates such as Hyundai and Samsung. To understand their size, Samsung's sales were equal to 17.8 percent of Korea's entire gross national product in 1987. For a U.S. corporation to have comparable relative size, it would need to have sales that were 15 times greater than IBM's.

Labor relations in the chaebol are characterized by the philosophy of ruling with an iron fist. The chaebol control every aspect of the workers' lives including much of their nonworking time. For example, as recently as 1987, many Korean corporations dictated proper nonworking dress for women and acceptable hairstyles for men. At work, laborers were not given a work schedule but were expected to be available whenever they were needed and they were expected to work long overtime hours without notice.[46]

Government regulation of business is another area where the U.S. firm will encounter vastly different systems around the world. For example, in Singapore, there is a National Wages Council that sets guidelines for annual wage adjustments; work stoppages are nearly impossible because of governmental controls; and, there is legislation that regulates working conditions to a great extent.[47]

It should be obvious that there is no simple solution to the labor relations problems that MNCs and GCs are confronted with. Nor is there any simple solution for unions who must deal with these corporations. The response of labor has been to try to establish global organizations to represent labor. These International Trade Secretariats have yet to be very successful since MNCs tend to have considerable financial resources and readily available alternative sources of labor. At the same time, labor has made some progress in presenting its global reactions to MNCs and GCs. For example, as a unified Europe approaches, labor is getting prepared with its own organizations such as the European Trade Union Confederation. And the International Labor Organization adopted a code for labor relations policies in MNC dealings.[48]

SUMMARY

This chapter was designed to increase the student's awareness of the critical issues faced by organizations that conduct international business. Global human resource management is an important component of an organization's success in a global marketplace. For an organization to become a successful international enterprise, it must be sure that its HRM policies can accommodate a culturally diverse work force. As students proceed through the book and learn the details of HRM, including activities such as selection, training, appraisal, and compensation, they should become capable of adapting and then applying principles of domestic HRM to an international organization.

To summarize the major points covered in this chapter:

1. International business continues to grow at a remarkable rate. In the coming years, a majority of corporations will have internationalized to one degree or another.

2. Any attempt to become an international organization must include a systematic evaluation of how HRM will adapt to the diverse cultural backgrounds of employees.

3. There are basically three sources of employees for an international organization:
   a. Parent country nationals (PCNs).
   b. Host country nationals (HCNs).
   c. Third country nationals (TCNs).

4. An ethnocentric corporation tends to view its HRM policies as the best method for dealing with employees and, therefore, relies on PCNs to fill key managerial and technical positions in its overseas operations.

5. In contrast, a geocentric corporation ignores national boundaries in favor of managerial expertise when filling key positions in the organization.

6. Currently, expatriate manager failure rates are very high in many U.S. corporations. The major reasons for the high failure rates are:
   a. Selection processes that focus too much on technical skills and too little on cultural factors.
   b. A lack of systematic training for the overseas assignment.

7. Family adjustment plays a critical role in an expatriate manager's success overseas.

8. The cost of keeping an expatriate manager on an overseas assignment can be as much as $300,000 per year more than the cost of using a host country national for the same position.

9. An important part of an expatriate manager's training should be an overview of the legal and ethical issues that are likely to be encountered on the overseas assignment.

10. Labor unions have begun to form international organizations to negotiate with the growing number of multinational and global corporations. To date, these international unions have only met with limited success.

KEY TERMS

culture	120	global human resource	
expatriate manager	121	management	116
global corporation	121	multinational corporation	121

QUESTIONS FOR REVIEW AND DISCUSSION

1. What factors have led to the recent growth of international business?

2. What are the HRM differences between an ethnocentric and a geocentric organization? How do these influence staffing decisions for international assignments?

3. What kinds of characteristics are important when selecting an individual for an overseas assignment?

4. Discuss the role of predeparture training for expatriates. How can it improve success overseas?

5. What is culture shock? When does it occur? What can be done to reduce its negative effects?

6. What are the major issues that an organization should consider during repatriation?

7. Discuss the advantages and disadvantages of using PCNs and HCNs for filling key managerial and technical positions in an international organization.

8. What are the major costs associated with using expatriate managers overseas?

9. What is the Foreign Corrupt Practices Act of 1977? How can it affect HRM policies?

10. What are some of the major ethical issues faced by an organization that conducts business in the international marketplace.

NOTES

1 Spencer Hayden (August 1990), "Our Foreign Legions Are Faltering," *Personnel*, pp. 40–44.

2 Susan S. Jarvis (June 1990), "Preparing Employees to Work South of the Border," *Personnel*, pp. 59–63.

3 Janet Lowe (July 1990), "Banking on Beans," *International Business*, pp. 17–19.

4 National Council for U.S.-China Trade (March 1987), *U.S. Joint Ventures in China: A Progress Report* (Washington, D.C.: U.S. Foreign Commerical Service, International Trade Administration).

5 (October 1990), "East Meets West: An Interview with Clifford Clarke," *Training and Development Journal*, pp. 43–47.

6 Geert Hofstede (1984), *Culture's Consequences: International Differences in Work-Related Values* (Newbury Park, Calif.: Sage Publishing).

7 John Milliman, Mary Ann Von Glinow, and Maria Nathan (April 1991), "Organizational Life Cycles and Strategic International Human Resource Management in Multinational Companies: Implications for Congruence Theory," *Academy of Management Review*, pp. 318–39.

8 J. Stewart Black and Mark Mendenhall (January 1990), "Cross-Cultural Training Effectiveness: A Review and a Theoretical Framework for Future Research," *Academy of Management Review*, pp. 113–36.

9 John F. Milliman and Mary A. Von Glinow (1991), "Strategic International Human Resources: Prescriptions for MNC Success," in *Research in Personnel and Human Resources Management*, Supplement 2, ed. Kendrith Rowland (Greenwich, Conn.: JAI Press), pp. 21–35.

10 James H. Donnelly, Jr., James L. Gibson, and John M. Ivancevich (1990), *Fundamentals of Management*, 7th ed. (Homewood, Ill.: Irwin), p. 720.

11 Paul W. Beamish, J. Peter Killing, Donald J. LeCraw, and Harold Crookell (1991), *International Management: Text and Cases* (Homewood, Ill.: Irwin), pp. 94–104; and Preston Townley (January–February 1990), "Global Business in the Next Decade," *Across the Board*, pp. 13–19.

12 Barry Louis Rubin (January 1991), "Europeans Value Diversity," *HRMagazine*, pp. 38–41ff.

13 Peter F. Drucker, S. Dhanabalan, Saburo Okita, and Tore Browaldh (January–February 1990), "Tomorrow, and Tomorrow, and Tomorrow," *Across the Board*, p. 20.

14 "East Meets West," pp. 43–47.

15 Susan Moffat (December 3, 1990), "Should You Work for the Japanese?," *Fortune*, p. 107ff.

16 Nakiye Boyacigiller (1991), "The International Assignment Reconsidered," in *International Human Resource Management*, eds. Mark Mendenhall and Gary Oddou (Boston: PWS-Kent Publishing), pp. 148–55.

17 (January 1991), "A Global Community," in *Venture, A Shell Oil E & P Newsletter*, Bill Scrimpshire, ed. p. 3.

18 Rosalie Tung (1982), "Selecting and Training Procedures of U.S., European, and Japanese Multinationals," *California Management Review*, pp. 51–71; and R. L. Desatnick and M. L. Bennett (1978), *Human Resource Management in the Multinational Company* (New York: Nichols).

19 L. Copeland and L. Griggs (1985), *Going International* (New York: Random House).

20 Edward Dunbar and Allan Katcher (September 1990), "Preparing Managers for Foreign Assignments," *Training and Development Journal*, pp. 45–47.

21 J. Stewart Black, Mark Mendenhall, and Gary Oddou (April 1991), "Toward a Comprehensive Model of International Adjustment: An Integration of Multiple Theoretical Perspectives," *Academy of Management Review*, pp. 291–317.

[22] Oded Shenkar and Yoram Zeira (January 1990), ''International Joint Ventures: A Tough Test for HR,'' *Personnel*, pp. 26–31.

[23] J. Stewart Black and Gregory K. Stephens (December 1989), ''The Influence of the Spouse on American Expatriate Adjustment and Intent to Stay in Pacific Rim Overseas Assignments,'' *Journal of Management*, pp. 529–44.

[24] Nancy J. Adler (1991), *International Dimensions of Organizational Behavior*, 2nd ed. (Boston: PWS-Kent Publishing), p. 228.

[25] Black and Mendenhall, ''Cross-Cultural Training Effectiveness,'' pp. 113–36.

[26] P. Christopher Earley (December 1987), ''Intercultural Training for Managers: A Comparison of Documentary and Interpersonal Methods,'' *Academy of Management Journal*, pp. 685–98.

[27] Tung, ''Selecting and Training Procedures,'' pp. 57–71.

[28] Mark E. Mendenhall and Gary Oddou (September–October 1988), ''The Overseas Assignment: A Practical Look,'' *Business Horizons*, pp. 78–84.

[29] Henry Ferguson (1988), *Tomorrow's Global Executive* (Homewood, Ill.: Dow Jones-Irwin), pp. 141–43.

[30] Neil B. Krupp (July 1990), ''Overseas Staffing for the New Europe,'' *Personnel*, pp. 20–25.

[31] Peter Van Pelt and Natalia Wolniansky (July 1990), ''The High Cost of Expatriation,'' *Management Review*, pp. 40–41.

[32] Ibid., p. 40.

[33] Peter J. Dowling and Randall S. Schuler (1990), *International Dimensions of Human Resource Management* (Boston: PWS-Kent Publishing), pp. 66–70.

[34] Ugur Yavas, Mushtaq Luqmani, and Zahir Quraeshi (1990), ''Organizational Commitment, Job Satisfaction, Work Values: Saudi and Expatriate Managers,'' *Leadership and Organization Development Journal*, pp. 3–9.

[35] Dov Elizur, Ingwer Borg, Raymond Hunt, and Istvan Magyari Beck (January 1991), ''The Structure of Work Values: A Cross-Cultural Comparison,'' *Journal of Organizational Behavior*, pp. 21–38.

[36] ''East Meets West,'' pp. 43–47.

[37] Janet L. Cappiello (April 7, 1990), ''American Executive Clicks at Japanese Pen Operations,'' *The Houston Chronicle*, p. 2F.

[38] Dowling and Schuler, *International Dimensions*, p. 68.

[39] George M. Taoka and Don R. Beeman (1991), *International Business: Environments, Institutions, and Operations* (New York: Harper-Collins), pp. 518–19.

[40] Keith Allen (October 1989), ''Making the Right Choices in International Recruiting,'' *Personnel Management*, pp. 56–59.

[41] John Thackray (January–February 1990), ''Foreigners on Board?,'' *Across the Board*, pp. 11–12.

[42] Ellen Brandt (March 1991), ''Global HR,'' *Personnel Journal*, pp. 38–44.

[43] Michael Litka (1988), *International Dimensions of the Legal Environment of Business* (Boston: PWS-Kent Publishing), pp. 82–83.

[44] Susan J. Harrington (February 1991), ''What Corporate America Is Teaching about Ethics,'' *Academy of Management Executive*, pp. 21–30.

[45] Peter Conrad and Rudiger Pieper (1990), ''Human Resource Management in the Federal Republic of Germany,'' in *Human Resource Management: An International Comparison*, ed. Rudiger Pieper (Berlin: Walter de Gruyter), pp. 109–39.

[46] Robert P. Kearney (April 1991), ''Managing Mr. Kim,'' *Across the Board*, pp. 40–46.

[47] Dahlia Hackman and Brian H. Kleiner (1990), ''The Nature of Effective Management in Singapore,'' *Leadership and Organization Development Journal*, pp. 28–32.

[48] Dowling and Schuler, *International Dimensions*, pp. 147–50.

EXERCISE 4–1 Expatriate Manager Compensation

· · · · ·

Objective: This exercise will give students an understanding of the costs associated with using expatriate managers for overseas assignments.

SETTING UP THE EXERCISE

1. Divide the class into groups of three to five persons.
2. Each group will be assigned a different country and a different expatriate manager for use in the exercise by the instructor.
3. Each group's task will be to develop an expatriate manager compensation program for a particular overseas assignment.
4. Each group will need to do some outside library research in order to arrive at accurate estimates of the costs of compensating its expatriate.
5. After developing the programs, the groups should compare their results during class.

Expatriate Managers

1. John Jackson is the vice president for HRM for a major manufacturing organization, Polyplas, Inc. John has been with Polyplas for 12 years and his annual salary is $52,000. Headquarters for Polyplas are located in Denver, Colorado.

   John is married to Jean, who is a computer specialist for Polyplas. She earns $31,000. John and Jean own a home in suburban Denver, and they have a time-share condo in Winter Park. The Jacksons have three children, Ron, Mary, and Lisa. Ron is a junior in high school, Mary is a first grader, and Lisa is three months old. Since both parents work, Lisa is enrolled in a company-sponsored day-care facility located at Polyplas's headquarters.

2. Peter Watson is a senior financial analyst for New Trust Corporation, which is a financial services organization located in Phoenix, Arizona. Peter has been with New Trust for five years and earns $42,500 annually.

   Peter is single, and he has no immediate plans to marry although he has been dating another New Trust employee for the past two years. He lives in a rented home in Scottsdale. Peter is very active in the Phoenix chapter of the Society for the Prevention of Cruelty to Animals. He has two Great Danes of his own.

3. Danielle Coletta is a store manager for Les Fleurs, which is an international chain of exclusive boutiques specializing in teen fashion. The company is French owned and their headquarters are in Paris. It doesn't pay its managers a straight salary. Rather, they receive a salary that is equivalent to $15,000 plus a commission based on the store's sales. Currently, Danielle is managing a store in an exclusive suburb of Rome, Italy. The store has been very successful, and Danielle's commissions have averaged the equivalent of $10,000 for each of the past three years.

   Danielle is married to Sergio Coletta. Sergio is a teacher and also the assistant soccer coach at a school located in urban Rome. Between his teaching and coaching, Sergio makes the equivalent of $17,000 per year. The Colettas have no children but they do own their own home in the Rome area.

The Overseas Assignments

1. Polyplas has just built a fabrication plant outside of Mexico City. Although it plans on staffing the plant primarily with host country nationals, it wants the HRM program at the new plant to be like the one at their facilities in the United States. As a result, they are sending John Jackson to Mexico to get things up and running. John's assignment is expected to last three years.

2. New Trust Corporation has entered the financial services market in Europe, which is growing rapidly because of EC92. They are opening branch offices in London, Frankfurt, and Madrid. Peter will be responsible for all three of these branch offices, although he will be based in London. The assignment is expected to last one to two years, and Peter will be expected to visit the branches in Frankfurt and Madrid at least four times each year.

3. Les Fleurs has just opened a new store in Beverly Hills, California. Because she was so successful in the Rome store, the company is sending Danielle to California. She understands that she is being assigned to the Beverly Hills store for an undetermined period of time. All the company will tell her is that she will manage this store until it is a complete success.

A Learning Note

This exercise can also be used to highlight selection, training, and repatriation issues if time permits.

ANALYSIS, PLANNING, AND STAFFING

P art Two consists of four chapters. Chapter 5, Human Resource Planning (HRP) emphasizes the important role of planing in an organization's overall human resource strategy. In Chapter 6, Job Analysis and Design, methods for analyzing and describing jobs are discussed and critiqued. Numerous approaches to recruitment, as well as currently popular alternative to recruitment, are presented in Chapter 7, Recruitment. In Chapter 8, Selection, the various steps in the selection are presented and several alternative methods of selection are described.

HUMAN RESOURCE PLANNING

· · · · · · · ·

LEARNING OBJECTIVES

───⊖───

After studying this chapter, you should be able to:

· · ·

Discuss the importance of human resource planning in organizations of any size

· · ·

Describe how managers forecast demand for and analyze the supply of employees in the organization

· · ·

List four forecasting techniques that are used in human resource planning

· · ·

Define what is meant by the terms *skills inventory* and *replacement chart*

· · ·

Identify reasons why a computerized human resource planning system could be useful to an organization.

CAREER CHALLENGE

*W*hat do you mean we're going to lose the government contract?'' asked the company president, Ted Sloane.

"We're going to lose it," said the human resource management vice president, Anne Wilson. "We don't have trained personnel to meet the contract specifications. We have to furnish records to show that we have an adequate number of employees with the right technical qualifications who meet the government's equal employment opportunity goals. I don't have those kinds of records available at a moment's notice. You know I asked you to let me set up a human resource information system (HRIS). "Why didn't we get around to it?"

Ted didn't know what Anne had in mind. Everything he ever heard about computer systems suggested that they were expensive and complex. He wanted to learn more about HRISs.

E xperiences like Ted's are common, and, as the complexity of doing business increases due to foreign competition, they are probably going to become more common. Today, more than ever, success in business is dependent on being able to react quickly to opportunities that arise. To do so, it is important for organizations to take cognizance of the supply and demand for human resources and to be prepared in advance to deal with any surplus or shortage that may come about. This is the basic issue that is addressed in this chapter.

Human resource planning (HR planning) is both a process and a set of plans.[1] It is the process used by organizations for assessing the supply and demand for future human resources. In addition, an effective HR plan also provides the mechanisms that will be used to eliminate any gaps that may exist between supply and demand. Thus, HR planning is the process that is used to determine the numbers and types of employees to be recruited into the organization or phased out of it.

STRATEGIC AND HUMAN RESOURCE PLANNING

Exhibit 5–1 models the HR planning process. As the model indicates, HR planning goes hand in hand with an organization's strategic planning. **Strategic planning** refers to an organization's decision about what it wants to accomplish (its mission) and how it wants to go about accomplishing it.[2] Although HR planning is important for developing a strategic plan, it is perhaps even more critical to the implementation of that plan.[3] Thus, once the strategy is set, the HRM function must do its part to ensure the strategy's success, thereby helping the organization to achieve its objectives.

There are many roles for HRM in helping the organization to implement its strategic plan. For example, recruitment and selection are responsible for ensuring that the organization has the necessary kinds of skills available for accomplishing its objectives. Likewise, compensation will help the organization to maintain a competitive advantage by retaining high-quality employees. As a result, HRM policies must complement the strategic plan if it is going to be successful.

Reasons for Human Resource Planning

All organizations perform human resource planning, either formally or informally. The formal employment planning techniques are described in this chapter because informal methods are typically unsatisfactory for organizations requiring skilled human resources in a fast-changing labor market. It is important to point out that most organizations do more talking about formal employment planning than actual performance.[4] Therefore, personnel and employment planning as an HRM activity is in Stage II of development, or early development (see Exhibit 1–7).

The major reasons for formal employment planning are to achieve:

- More effective and efficient use of human resources.
- More satisfied and better-developed employees.
- More effective equal employment opportunity planning.

More Effective and Efficient Use of People at Work   Human resource planning should precede all other HRM activities. For example, how could you schedule recruiting if you did not know how many people you needed? How could you select effectively if you did not know the kinds of persons needed for job open-

EXHIBIT 5-1   The Human Resource Planning Process

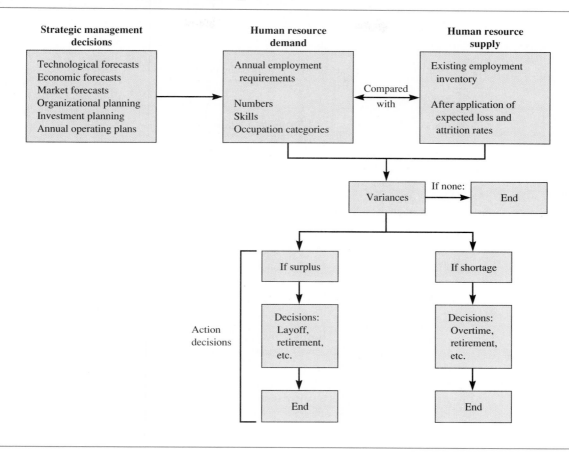

ings? Careful analysis of all HRM activities shows that their effectiveness and efficiency, which result in increased productivity, depend on human resource planning.

More Satisfied and Better-Developed Employees   Employees who work for organizations that use good human resource planning systems have a better chance to participate in planning their own careers and to share in training and development experiences. Thus, they are likely to feel their talents are important to the employer, and they have a better chance to utilize those talents. This situation often leads to greater employee satisfaction and its consequences: lower absenteeism, lower turnover, fewer accidents, and higher quality of work.

More Effective EEO Planning   As we pointed out in Chapter 3, the government has increased its demands for equal employment opportunities. Organizations are required to maintain complete records about the flow and utilization of minority applicants and workers. They must also be aware of the representation of minorities in the various departments and jobs in the company. Thus, government and internal utilization reports are much easier to complete if there is thorough HR planning.

EXHIBIT 5-2   Human Resource Activities Performed by HR
               and Operating Managers

Human Resource Planning Activities	Operating Manager (OM)	HR Manager
Strategic management decisions	Performed by OM with inputs from HRM	Provides information inputs for OM
Forecasting demands		Performed by HRM based on strategic management decisions
Job analysis	Provides information inputs for HRM	Performed by HRM with information inputs from OM
Analysis of supply of employees	Provides information inputs for HRM	Performed by HRM with information inputs from OM
Work scheduling decisions	Joint responsibility	Joint responsibility
Action decision: Analyzing the composition of the work force		Performed by HRM
Action decision: Shortage of employees	Provides information inputs for HRM	Performed by HRM with information inputs from OM
Action decision: Surplus of employees	Policy decisions by OM with inputs from HRM	Implementation decisions by HRM

In sum, effective human resource planning ensures that HRM activities and programs will be built on a foundation of good planning. Proper planning should cut down on the number of surprises that occur involving human resource availability, placement, and orientation. Not having the right person in the right place at a particular moment is a surprise and usually a problem. These kinds of surprises can be reduced through effective personnel and employment planning.

Who Performs the Planning?

Effectiveness in HRM activities requires the efforts and cooperation of HR managers and operating managers. The activities described in this chapter are outlined in Exhibit 5–2, which shows the kind of planning activities that are performed by operating and HR managers.

A DIAGNOSTIC APPROACH TO HUMAN RESOURCE PLANNING

Exhibit 5–3 highlights the factors in the diagnostic model that are crucial to planning. One of the most significant factors affecting planning involves the goals of the controlling interests in the organization. If planning and effective utilization of human resources are not a significant goal for the organization, employment planning will not be performed formally, or it will be done in a slipshod manner. If the goals of top management include stable growth, employment planning will be less important than if the goals include rapid expansion, diversification, or other factors with a significant impact on future employment needs.

Government policies are another important factor in planning. Requirements for equal employment opportunity and promotion call for more HR planning for women and other employees in minority groups and special categories. Other examples include the government's raising the age of mandatory retirement and the encouragement of hiring handicapped employees and veterans (see Chapter 3).

EXHIBIT 5-3   Factors Affecting Human Resource Planning and Effectiveness

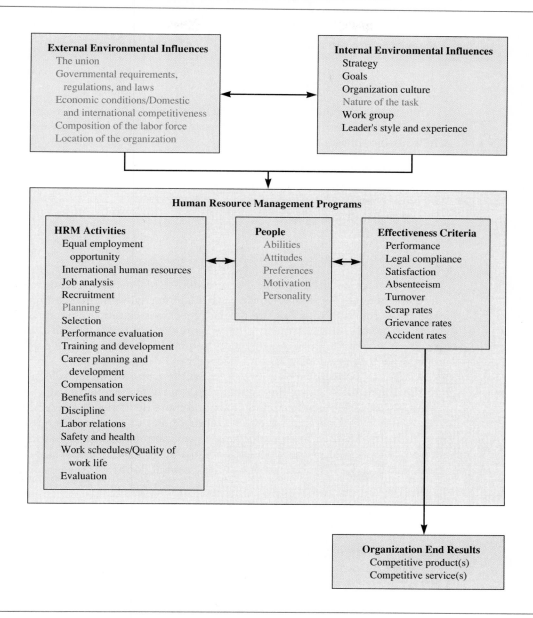

The conditions in the labor market also have a significant impact on the amount and type of employment planning done in an enterprise. For example, when there is 20 percent unemployment in, for instance, Laredo, Texas, an employer in that city could be more selective than another employer in Dallas, Texas, where there is a 5 percent rate of unemployment.

To a lesser extent than the government, unions may restrict the ability to hire and promote employees, so they, too, are a factor in planning. In discussing the planning activity, it is more realistic to take into consideration the important role played by the segments highlighted in Exhibit 5–3.

The types of people employed and the tasks they perform also determine the kind of planning necessary. Need for unskilled employees does not have to be planned two years ahead; but computer salespersons, for example, need years of training before coming on track. Planning for highly skilled employees usually requires more care and forecasting.

THE HR PLANNING PROCESS

While these and other factors influence the specifics of an HR plan, all effective HR planning shares certain features. It is generally agreed that HR planning involves four distinct phases or stages:[5]

- Situation analysis or environmental scanning.
- Forecasting human resource demands.
- Human resource supply analysis.
- Action plan development.

Situation Analysis and Environmental Scanning

The first stage of HR planning is where the HRM function and strategic planning initially interact. The strategic plan must adapt to environmental circumstances, and the HRM function is one of the primary mechanisms that an organization can use during the adaptation process.[6] For example, rapid technological changes in the environment can force an organization to quickly identify and hire employees with new skills that previously weren't needed by the organization.

Without an effective HR plan to support the recruitment and selection functions in the organization, it will be impossible to move fast enough to stay competitive. Thus, organizations are becoming more and more dependent on an ability to gather relevant information about their environment and to react to this information.

The problems associated with changing environments are greater today than ever before because success now depends on an ability to be a "global scanner." Global scanning is, in fact, considered one of the essential skills for managers of the 1990s.[7]

Forecasting Future Demand for Employees

The next phase of an effective HR planning process is estimating not only how many but what kinds of employees will be needed in the future. Forecasting yields these advanced estimates or calculations of the organization's staffing requirements. Although there are many quantitative tools to help with forecasting, it is a process that involves a great deal of human judgment. In addition, many successful HR planners also rely heavily on their "gut instincts" about future conditions. For example, planners at Unilever attribute much of their global successes to such instincts.[8]

Four forecasting techniques will be described here: three top-down techniques — expert estimate, trend projection, and modeling — and the bottom-up unit forecasting technique.

The Expert-Estimate Technique   The least sophisticated approach to employment planning — yet the one most frequently used — is for an "expert" to forecast the employment needs based on her or his own experience, intuition, and guess. The HR manager may do this by thinking about past employment levels and

questioning future needs. This method is an informal system. The expert-estimate technique can be more effective if the experts use the Delphi technique.

The Delphi technique is a set of procedures originally developed by the Rand Corporation in the late 1940s.[9] Its purpose is to obtain the most reliable consensus of opinion of a group of experts. The Delphi technique consists of intensive questioning of each expert, through a series of questionnaires, to obtain data that can be used to make "educated" forecasts. The procedures are designed to avoid direct meetings between the experts in order to maximize independent thinking.

A person who serves as intermediary in the questioning sends the questionnaires to the experts and asks them to give, for example, their best estimates of employment needs for the coming year. The intermediary prepares a summary of the results, calculating the average response and the most extreme answers. Then the experts are asked to estimate the number again. Usually, the questionnaires and responses tend to narrow down over these rounds. The average number is then used as the forecast.

A forecast by a single expert is the most frequently used approach to forecasting employment. It works well in small and middle-sized enterprises that are in stable environments. However, the Delphi technique improves these estimates in larger and more volatile organizations.

The Trend-Projection Technique   The second technique is to develop a forecast based on a past relationship between a factor related to employment and employment itself. For example, in many businesses, sales levels are related to employment needs. The planner can develop a table or graph showing past relationships between sales and employment. Exhibit 5–4 gives an example of a trend-projection forecast for a hypothetical company, Rugby Sporting Goods Company. Note that, as Rugby's sales increased, so did the firm's employment needs. But the increases were not linear. Suppose that in late 1988 Rugby instituted a productivity plan that led to a 3 percent increase in productivity per year. As Rugby forecasted employee needs, it adjusted them for expected productivity gains for 1992 and 1993.

Trend projection is a frequently used technique, though not as widely used as expert estimate or unit demand. Trend projections are an inexpensive way to forecast employment needs.

EXHIBIT 5-4   Sample Trend-Protection Employment Forecast for Rugby Sporting Goods Company

Year Actual Data	Sales	Employee Census	Employee Forecast Adjusted for Annual Productivity Rate Increase of 3 Percent
1988	$100,000,000	5,000	5,000
1989	120,000,000	6,000	5,825
1990	140,000,000	7,000	6,598
1991	160,000,000	8,000	7,321
Forecast	Sales Forecast	Employee Forecast	
1992	$180,000,000	9,000	7,996
1993	200,000,000	10,000	8,626

Modeling and Multiple-Predictive Techniques   The third top-down approach to prediction of demand uses the most sophisticated forecasting and modeling techniques. Trend projections are based on relating a single factor (such as sales) to employment. The more advanced approaches relate many factors to employment, such as sales, gross national product, and discretionary income. Or they mathematically model the organization and use simulations, utilizing such methods as Markov models and analytical formulations such as regression analysis. These are the most costly approaches to employment forecasting because of the cost of computer time and salaries of highly paid experts to design the models.

The use of the Markov chain analysis involves developing a matrix. This matrix shows the probability of an employee moving from one position to another or leaving the organization. A full treatment of HRM applications of Markov analysis is found in management science or operations management literature.[10]

Markov analysis begins with an analysis of staffing levels in various levels from one period to another time period. Suppose that professional nursing employees have shifted from hospitals I, II, and III in the Houston Medical Center complex. That is, they quit working in one hospital and went to work for another in the Medical Center (i.e., a complex of 11 hospitals in Houston that employs approximately 30,000 people). An HR specialist in hospital I is interested in analyzing the human resource shifts that are occurring between her hospital and hospitals II and III. Exhibit 5–5 illustrates the movement of nurses.

The HR specialists could next calculate transition probabilities for all three hospitals. That is, the probablility that a hospital will retain its nurses can be calculated. Exhibit 5–6 illustrates the transition probabilities for the retention of professional nurses.

The data in Exhibit 5–6 indicate that hospital I has a probability of .80 of retaining its nurses, while hospital II has a probability of .90 and Hospital III has a probability of .85. Both hospitals II and III have a higher probability of retaining their nursing staff. Therefore, the HR specialist in hospital I needs to study further the issue of why her hospital has a lower probability of retention. Is it because of some particular HRM program? Markov analysis can help identify the lower retention probability, but it does not suggest any particular solution to the potential problem.

EXHIBIT 5-5   Movement of Nurses during 1990

Hospital	1988 Level of Nurses	Gain	Loss	1989 Level of Nurses
I	200	60	40	220
II	500	40	50	490
III	300	35	45	290

EXHIBIT 5-6   Nurse Transition Probabilities

Hospital	1990	Nurses Lost	Nurses Retained	Probability of Retention
I	200	40	160	160/200 = .80
II	500	50	450	450/500 = .90
III	300	45	255	255/300 = .85

Regression analysis is a mathematical procedure that predicts the dependent variable on the basis of knowledge of factors known as *independent variables*.[11] When only one dependent and one independent variable are studied, the process is known as *simple linear regression*. When there is more than one independent variable being considered, the technique used is referred to as *multiple regression*.

Most uses of multiple regression emphasize prediction from two or more independent variables, X_i to a dependent variable, Y. For example, suppose an HR manager wants to predict how many manufacturing workers are needed. Assume that the manager is attempting to predict the number of workers (the dependent variable) by using sales, efficiency of the work force, and productivity per worker as the independent variables.

A simplified example of an application of regression analysis is presented in Exhibit 5–7. The number of lathe operators (the dependent variable) is predicted by the level of production. Data compiled by the organization for the years 1980 to

---

EXHIBIT 5-7   Regression Analysis Demand Forecast

Year (I)	Units of Production (000)(x)	Number of Lathe Operators (y)	$(x_i - \bar{x})$	$(x_i - \bar{x})^2$	$(y_i - \bar{y})$	$(x_i - \bar{x})(y_i - \bar{y})$
1980	11	21	−8	64	−8	64
1981	13	22	−6	36	−7	42
1982	14	23	−5	25	−6	30
1983	14	25	−5	25	−4	20
1984	17	28	−2	4	−1	2
1985	16	30	−3	9	1	−3
1986	19	32	0	0	3	0
1987	21	31	2	4	2	4
1988	20	32	1	1	3	3
1989	24	34	5	25	5	25
1990	28	34	9	81	5	45
1991	31	36	12	144	7	84

$\Sigma x_i = 228$
$\Sigma y_i = 348$
$\Sigma (x_i - \bar{x})^2 = 418$
$\Sigma (x_i - \bar{x})(y_i - \bar{y}) = 316$

$N = 12 \qquad \bar{x} = \dfrac{\Sigma x_i}{N} = 19 \qquad \bar{y} = \dfrac{\Sigma y_i}{N} = 29$

Simple regression formula:

$y = \alpha + Bx + \epsilon$

where

$$B = \frac{\Sigma[(x - \bar{x})(y - \bar{y})]}{\Sigma(x - \bar{x})^2} = \frac{316}{418} = .76$$

$\alpha = \bar{y} - B\bar{x} = 29 - (.76)(19) = 14.56$

ϵ is assumed equal to zero.

Forecast for the 1992 production goal of 40,000 units is:

$Y = 14.56 + (.76)(40) = 44.96 = 45$ lathe operators

Source: Formula adapted from R. S. Pindyck and D. L. Rubenfeld (1976), *Economic Models of Economic Forecasts* (New York: McGraw-Hill), pp. 11–16.

1992. In the example, management assumes that 40,000 units will be produced in 1992.

The discussion of the specific statistical notations and procedures presented in Exhibit 5–7 are beyond the scope of this book. More details on regression analysis can be found in most applied statistics books.[12]

The Unit-Demand Forecasting Technique

The unit (which can be an entire department, a project team, or some other group of employees) forecast is a bottom-up approach to forecasting demand. Headquarters sums these unit forecasts, and the result becomes the employment forecast. The unit manager analyzes the person-by-person, job-by-job needs in the present as well as the future. By analyzing present and future requirements of the job and the skills of the incumbents, this method focuses on quality of workers.

Usually, the manager will start with a list of the jobs in the unit by name. This list will also record the number of jobholders for each job. The manager evaluates both the numbers and skills of the present personnel. Consideration is given to the effects of expected losses through retirement, promotion, or other reasons. Whether the losses will require replacement and what the projected growth needs will be are questions the manager must answer and project into his or her calculations in determining net employment needs.

A manager's evaluation that is based on the present number of employees has two assumptions built into it: (1) that the best use has been made of the available personnel, and (2) that demand for the product or service of the unit will be the same for next year as for this. With regard to the first assumption, the manager can examine the job design and workload of each employee. The manager may also attempt to judge the productivity of the employees in the unit by comparing the cost per product or service produced with those of similar units in this organization and in others. Past productivity rates can be compared with present ones, after adjusting for changes in the job; or subjective evaluations can be made of the productivity of certain employees compared to others. In addition, it may be necessary to base employment needs on work force analysis, with adjustments for current data on absenteeism and turnover.

The unit analyzes its product or service demand by projecting trends. Using methods similar to the trend techniques for the organization, the unit determines if it may need more employees because of a change in product or service demand. Finally, the unit manager prepares an estimate of total employment needs and plans for how the unit can fulfill these needs.

In larger organizations, an HR executive at headquarters who is responsible for the employment demand forecast will improve the estimates by checking with the HR and operating managers in the field. If the units forecast their own needs, the HR executive would sum their estimates, then this becomes the forecast.

What happens if both the bottom-up and top-down approaches are used, and the forecasts conflict? In all probability, the manager reconciles the two totals by averaging them or examining more closely the major variances between the two. The Delphi technique could be used to do this. Thus, one or several forecast techniques can be used to produce a single employment forecast.

In the employment-demand forecasting aspect of human resource planning, the bottom-up or unit-forecasting method calls for each unit to determine the number of people needed to accomplish the unit's objectives. The basic building block of this forecast is the number of jobs to be filled. As will be seen in Chapter 6, job analysis becomes an essential component of successful use of these forecasting techniques. That is, job analysis will yield descriptions of the jobs in question as well as the ideal persons to fill those jobs. This information, in turn, can be used to study whether there are more effective ways to design the jobs, perhaps by reducing the number of people needed.

Typically, these four forecasting methods, which use statistics-based techniques and computers, are resisted by some managers.[13] They are resisted because:

. The forecasters and users of the data and information make the methods difficult to understand.
. Managers assume they require an understanding of advanced statistics.
. They are often irrelevant in terms of the overall corporate strategic plan.

As the simplified discussion of these four forecasting methods shows, however, these points of resistance can be minimized with the cooperation of the HR department. The statistical treatment of data ought to be left primarily to the HR experts who then have the responsibility of making sure that the operational managers receive timely summaries of the information most critical to their forecasting needs.[14] The ability of computers to deliver information quickly and efficiently has led many companies to adopt computerized human resource information systems (HRISs) as part of their HR planning process. These systems will be discussed in detail later in this chapter.

Analysis of the Supply of Current Employees

The third phase of HR planning is designed to answer the question, "How many and what kinds of employees do I currently have in terms of the skills and training necessary for the future?" It should be obvious that this phase of HR planning involves much more than simply counting the number of current employees in the organization.

The major tool used to assess the current supply of employees is the **skills inventory.** In some organizations, there will also be a separate inventory just for managers called a *management inventory.* Both of these serve the same purpose: to keep track of what kinds of skills, abilities, experiences, and training the employees currently have. By keeping track of these, the organization can quickly determine whether a particular skill is available when it is needed. For example, a change in strategy might create the need for more-aggressive marketing tactics. The skills inventory should be able to identify who in the organization has had prior experience or training in the techniques that the organization now feels will be needed. Skills inventories are therefore also useful in career planning, management development, and related activities. A *skills inventory* in its simplest form is a list of names, certain characteristics, and skills of the people working for the organization. It provides a way to acquire these data and makes them available where needed in an efficient manner.

For a small organization, it is relatively easy to know how many employees there are, what they do, and what they can do. A mom-and-pop grocery store may employ only the owners and may only have two part-time helpers to "plan" for. When they see that one part-time employee is going to graduate in June, they know they need to replace him or her. Sources of supply could include the owners own children, converting their other part-time helper into a full-time assistant, or the local school's employment office.

It is quite a different situation with a school system employing hundreds at numerous locations, or such mammoth organizations as Procter & Gamble and IBM.

These kinds of organizations must know how many full-time and peripheral employees they have working for them, and where. They must know what skills prospective employees would need to replace people who have quit, retired, or have been fired, or what skills current employees need to have in order to be relocated for new functions or more work.

Skills inventories vary greatly in their sophistication. Some are as simple as a file drawer containing index cards with relevant information typed on them. Others are tied into extremely expensive and complex computer databases. But, regardless of the technique used to maintain the skills inventory, its purpose is essentially the same.

Contents of the Skills Inventory   Once the decision has been made to create a skills inventory, the HR manager must determine what information will actually be contained in the system. The only data available to the organization for later use will be whatever has been designed into the system.

The list of data coded into skills inventories is almost endless, and it must be tailored to the needs of each organization. Some of the more common items include: name, employee number, present location, date of birth, date of employment, job classification or code, prior experience, history of work experience in the organization, specific skills and knowledge, education, field of education (formal education and courses taken since leaving school), knowledge of a foreign language, health, professional qualifications, publications, licenses, patents, hobbies, a supervisory evaluation of the employee's capabilities, and salary range. Items often omitted, but becoming increasingly important, are the employee's own stated career goals and objectives, including geographical preferences and intended retirement date.

The components of a skills inventory are shown in Exhibit 5–8. Note the main category headings: I. Data summarizing the employee's past; II. Data summarizing present skills' status; and III. Data that focuses on the future.

The data collected in a skills inventory are used to identify employees for specific job roles and assignments that will fulfill the organization's objectives, as well as individual career and job objectives.

Maintaining the Skills Inventory   While designing the system is the most difficult part of developing a skills inventory, planning for the gathering, maintaining, handling, and updating of data is also important. The two principal methods for gathering data are the interview and the questionnaire. Each method has unique costs and benefits. The questionnaire is faster and less expensive when many employees are involved, but inaccuracies often prevail. People often do not spend enough time on a questionnaire. There are those who contend, therefore, that the trained interviewer can complete the reports more quickly and accurately, a procedure which in the long run more than offsets the costs of the interviewer.

A procedure for keeping the files updated also must be planned. The procedure depends on the frequency of change and the uses of the data. For some organizations, an annual update is adequate. In others, where changes are made often and use is frequent, shorter update periods may be necessary. Some organizations make provisions for monthly updating of changeable data and annual checks for less changeable data. One method includes updating forms in payroll envelopes.

Finally, a decision whether to store the data manually or on the computer must be made. This decision is based on cost of the computer and frequency of use of the

---

EXHIBIT 5-8   Skills Inventory Components

I. Data summarizing the employee's past.
  A. Titles and brief job description highlights from positions held in the last two to five years.
    1. This organization.
    2. Previous organization(s).
  B. Critical skills needed or developed while in these positions.
    1. Manual.
    2. Cognitive.
    3. Creative.
  C. Educational achievements.
    1. High school: job-relevant classes.
    2. College.
      a. Major.
      b. Minor.
      c. Job-relevant courses.
  D. Significant special projects accomplished during the last three years.
    1. This organization.
    2. Previous organization(s).
II. Data summarizing present skills' status.
  A. Skill-related highlights: last three performance appraisals.

  B. Employee's perception of what is done well on present job, i.e., skill competencies, perceptions of how skills could be improved or augmented.
  C. Same data as II.B, from the employee's superior.
III. Data that focuses on the future.
  A. Personal career goals.
    1. One year.
    2. Three years.
    3. Identify specific positions and aspirations. Avoid global generalities, i.e., "higher up."
  B. The views of the individual's present superior(s) as to what he or she could be prepared to become. List specific positions.
  C. Specific training and development efforts the individual is motivated to undertake.
    1. On-the-job.
    2. Off-the-job.
    3. Classroom.
    4. Experiential.

Source: By permission of *Personnel Journal*, March 1987, p. 130.

data. The computer also provides the possibility of using comparative analyses of employment over a period of time.

Skills inventories are useful only if management uses the data in making significant decisions. Top-management support is necessary here. Before a manager uses the skills inventory as an aid in selection decisions, he or she must be trained to avoid system abuse. Examples of this are:

- Making requests simply on the basis that "it would be nice to know."
- Making requests for searches that are not backed up by bona fide requisitions that have been budgeted.
- Specifying too many characteristics for a desired employee so that no one fits all the characteristics.

As an example of the third type of abuse, consider the following request of a skills inventory system:

Wanted — A person with the following qualifications: B.S. in business, experience in finance and marketing, with at least two years with the company and willing to relocate overseas.

Assume that the organization has 1,000 employees. The chance of finding a person with all these characteristics is the product of the percent of probability in each category. Thus, if 20 percent of the 1,000 have a B.A. in business, 10 percent have experience in finance, 10 percent have experience in marketing, 70 percent have two years or more seniority, and 40 percent are willing to relocate overseas, the chance of finding such a person is $0.20 \times 0.10 \times 0.70 \times 0.40$, or 0.0056, or less than 1 chance in 1,000. Those who set requirements must recognize that being overly specific reduces the chance of finding any suitable employee.

Action Decisions in Human Resource Planning

After the HR planning system has analyzed both the supply of and demand for future workers, these two forecasts are compared to determine what, if any, action should be taken. Whenever there is a discrepancy between these two estimates, the organization needs to choose a course of action for eliminating the gap.

No matter how good the HR planning system is, an exact match between supply and demand forecasts is rare. Even when overall estimates are similar, there are frequently important gaps in certain subgroups. These data become inputs to facilitate decisions about training, promotion, demotion, and similar decisions. Exhibit 5–9 presents a supply and demand report for 1990–1994. For two years, there is no need to find and identify a new district manager. However, suppose that in 1993 the present district manager will retire. The firm has Bob Ratky available to fill the district manager vacancy. Thus, the variance would be zero for 1993. However, for the director of unit maintenance job, there is a different situation. In 1994, there is a need for a director and no one available inside the firm to fill the position. Also, in 1993, there is a vacancy and no one available. Thus, the firm would need to look outside the organization or train someone inside to fill these vacancies. The supply and demand chart will clearly illustrate to the HR specialist variance, shortage, and surplus circumstances.

EXHIBIT 5-9   Human Resource Supply and Demand Report

	Manpower Report						
	1991 Needs	Variance	1992 Needs	Variance	1993 Needs	Variance	1994 Needs	Variance
District manager	0	0	0	0	Ratky, Bob 1	0	0	0
Manufacturing superintendent	0	0	0	0	Tracey, Mark 1	0	0	0
Mechanic shop manager	0	0	1	1	0	0	0	0
Director of unit maintenance	1	1	0	0	1	1	Maria, Donna 0	1
Floor manager	0	0	Semoski, John 1	0	0	0	0	0
Safety engineer	0	0	Wittsell, Mark 1	0	0	0	0	0
Quality control supervisor	0	0	0	0	0	0	1	1

Source: © Adapted from Charles F. Russ, Jr., (1982), "Manpower Planning Systems: Part II," *Personnel Journal*, p. 122.

Action Decisions with a Shortage of Employees   When employment specialists comparing demand to supply find the supply of workers is less than the demand, several possibilities are open to the organization. If the shortage is small and employees are willing to work overtime, it can be filled with present employees. If there is a shortage of highly skilled employees, training and promotions of present employees, together with the recruitment of lower-skilled employees, are possibilities. This decision can also include recalling previously laid-off employees. Outside the organization, additional part-time or full-time employees can be hired, or some of the work can be contracted out to other organizations.

Action Decisions in Surplus Conditions   When comparison of employee demand and supply indicates a surplus, the alternative solutions include attrition, early retirements, demotions, layoffs, and terminations. Employee decisions in surplus conditions are some of the most difficult decisions managers must make, because the employees who are considered surplus are seldom responsible for the conditions leading to the surplus. A shortage of a raw material such as fuel, or a poorly designed or marketed product can cause an organization to have a surplus of employees.

As a first approach to deal with a surplus, most organizations avoid layoffs by such means as attrition, early retirement, and work creation. Many organizations can reduce their work force simply by not replacing those who retire or quit (attrition). Sometimes this approach is accelerated by encouraging employees close to retirement to leave early, but this approach can amount to layoffs of older employees if the organization is not careful.

Another variation of this approach is work sharing, which will be discussed in detail in Chapter 20. Instead of attempting to decide whom to lay off, the organization asks all employees to work fewer hours than normal and thus share the work. Many unions favor this approach. During recessions, many firms give the employees a say in how to deal with surplus conditions, and some groups of employees decide in favor of work sharing.

If there is a surplus of employees at higher levels in the organization, demotion can be used to reduce the work force. After World War II, as the U.S. Army reduced its size, it had too many higher-level officers to staff the number of positions left. As a result, many officers were demoted to the "permanent" rank, not the one they held in 1945. The numerous ways that an organization can handle demotion include:

- Lowering an employee's job status while maintaining or lowering salary.
- Maintaining an employee's status while lowering salary.
- Bypassing an employee with seniority when promoting.
- Moving an employee to a less desirable job.
- Maintaining an employee's formal status, but decreasing his or her span of control.
- Excluding an employee from a general salary increase.
- Inserting positions above an employee's position in the hierarchy.
- Moving an employee to a staff position.

Demotions are very difficult for employees to accept, and valued employees may leave because of them.[15]

In managing a surplus through layoffs, employers take the surplus employees off

EXHIBIT 5-10   Organization Size and Software Ranked in Top Five

Group	Organization Size (Full-Time Employees)	Percent of Organizations (N = 706)
1	Fewer than 500	38.0% (268)
2	500–2,000	32.7 (231)
3	2,000 or more	29.3 (207)

	Software Ranked in Top Five Size Groups (Full-Time Employees)					
	Group 1*		Group 2†		Group 3‡	
Computer Application for the Future	N	Percent	N	Percent	N	Percent
Job analysis	69	25.8	72	31.2	69	33.3
Automated applications	22	8.2	29	12.6	25	12.1
Work samples	10	3.7	2	0.9	5	2.4
Ability/aptitude tests	26	9.7	21	9.1	17	8.2
Vocational tests	8	3.0	11	4.8	5	2.4
Personality tests	10	3.7	6	2.6	6	2.9
EEO/AA records	128	47.8	122	52.8	98	47.3
Recruitment/tracking	103	38.4	111	48.1	90	43.5
Job previews	11	4.1	9	3.9	9	4.3
Person-job matching	45	16.8	35	15.2	50	24.2
Adaptive testing	10	3.7	7	3.0	10	4.8
Performance appraisal	91	34.0	83	35.9	67	32.4
In-basket techniques	4	1.5	4	1.7	5	2.4
Assessment centers	11	4.1	14	6.1	12	5.8
Training needs	43	16.0	35	15.2	38	18.4
Stress management	9	3.4	7	3.0	2	1.0
Career pathing	33	12.3	38	16.5	68	32.9
Outplacement counseling	5	1.9	5	2.2	7	3.4
Attitude questionnaires	39	14.6	42	18.2	29	14.0
Suggestion systems	10	3.7	7	3.0	5	2.4
Management information systems	159	59.3	151	65.4	125	60.4
Personnel inventories	162	60.4	141	61.0	113	54.6

* Fewer than 500 full-time employees; N = 268.
† 500 to 2,000 full-time employees; N = 231.
‡ 2,000 or more full-time employees; N = 207.
Source: David S. Zurakowski and William G. Harris (August 1984), "Software Applications in Human Resource Management," *Personnel Administrator*, p. 80.

the payroll temporarily to reduce the surplus. Some employers may feel more willing to accept this method because unemployment compensation plans are now available (see Chapter 11). If the layoff is likely to be semipermanent or permanent, it is in effect a termination and results usually in the payment of severance pay, as well as unemployment compensation.

How does a manager decide whom to lay off? Two criteria have been used: merit and seniority. In the past, the most senior employee was laid off last. A second approach now is to lay off those with lower merit ratings. Merit means that those who do the job the best are kept; those who perform poorly are laid off. If merit ratings are not precise, unions may fight their exclusive use as a reason for laying off particular employees.

HUMAN RESOURCE INFORMATION SYSTEMS

It should be obvious by now that the key to successful HR planning is information. All of the activities discussed in this chapter assume that the organization is able to collect, store, and evaluate large amounts of information about the internal and external environments. For many organizations, mechanical techniques for dealing with these large amounts of information are no longer adequate. Fortunately, there now exist very sophisticated computerized systems that allow organizations to successfully cope with these information demands.

A human resource information system (HRIS) is much more than a computerized skills inventory. An HRIS is an integrated approach to acquiring, storing, analyzing, and controlling the flow of information throughout an organization.[16] Highly developed HRISs can be useful in nearly all HRM functions. The system might contain an applicant tracking program, a skills inventory, a career planning program, and employee service programs such as an electronic bulletin board. Their applications are, therefore, almost endless. Exhibit 5–10 presents many of the potential uses of an HRIS along with survey results about the frequency of desired use.

As Exhibit 5–10 indicates, one of the most common anticipated uses for an HRIS is in recruitment and applicant tracking. IBM has such a system that they call IRIS (IBM Recruiting Information System). Employees complete a booklet periodically called a *data-pak*. They answer questions about age, experience, education, skills, and qualifications. When there is a need to fill a vacancy, a manager describes the position and what he or she is looking for in terms of individual qualifications. The manager's requirements are entered into the computer. The IRIS system is used to match available candidates for the position described by the manager. The manager then receives a computer listing of possible candidates.[17]

Many other successful HRISs are used to help organizations identify and track potential applicants for job openings. By using its applicant tracking program, along with supply and demand analysis, Bell Helicopter Company credits its HRIS with helping to secure a multibillion dollar government contract. The presence of an integrated HRIS convinced a Navy review team that Bell could acquire the necessary technical staff for meeting contract due dates by staying ahead of the supply and demand gap.[18] This capacity was viewed as critical for the Navy's project.

In contrast to these specialized HRISs, computer technology has also made it possible for organizations to integrate multiple HR needs into a single system. Apple Computer has installed an HRIS designed for a wide array of uses. Apple believes that many HRM decisions can be made more efficiently at the operational management level. Employees can also use the system to eliminate some of the demand on the HR professionals. For example, employees enroll themselves in benefits programs through the HRIS. Line managers can process traditional employee transactions such as pay increases, and they have access to an automated résumé screening program to help with recruitment and selection.[19]

In contrast to either Apple Computer's HRIS, which is designed to be used by every employee in the company, or to systems that serve a single function, a third kind of HRIS has been developed specifically for use by upper-level executives.

CAREER CHALLENGE

(*concluded*)

After reading this chapter, talking to friends from other firms, and examining some literature, Ted Sloane was not at all confused about HRISs. He called his vice president of human resource management, Anne Wilson, and said, "Anne, I want to thank you for calling my attention to how we could use and benefit from an HRIS. Without good forward planning, we are going to be in trouble with the law. Let's move ahead and set up an HRIS. By the way, are you familiar with the IBM IRIS system? It's a dandy."

These systems are sometimes referred to as **executive information systems (EISs).**[20] For example, after a corporate restructuring that eliminated several layers of management, Phillips Petroleum installed an EIS in order to cope with the increased span of control its managers were faced with. The company estimates that its system was able to save over $100 million by decentralizing decision making and delivering needed information directly to the managers.

A **replacement chart** is another forecasting tool that can be enhanced with an HRIS. A replacement chart is less sophisticated than an IRIS-type system, and it is used primarily with technical, professional, and managerial employees. It is a display of summary data about individuals currently in the organization. The replacement chart is a concise map that can be readily reviewed to pinpoint potential problem areas in terms of human resource planning.

Exhibit 5–11 presents a replacement chart that can be reviewed easily by Wiley Department Store managers. This chart provides information about individuals in the organization in terms of age, performance, and tenure. This type of information can be combined with more extensive background data on each of the individuals shown on the chart to make planning decisions.

Employee Privacy and HRIS

There is no question that HRISs have dramatically increased the effectiveness of HR planning. However, the introduction of these computer systems has not been without problems. One of the major concerns is that an HRIS makes it easier for someone in the organization to invade the privacy of other employees. The friendlier the system, the easier it can be for unauthorized access to personnel files to occur.[21]

Although it is impossible for an organization to guarantee that information about employees will not be seen or used inappropriately by unauthorized persons, there are several safeguards that can help to minimize the privacy risks of an HRIS. Exhibit 5–12 summarizes the steps that organizations should take to ensure that their HRIS is relatively secure and is used only for the purposes that it is intended.

EXHIBIT 5-11   Replacement Chart: Wiley Department Stores

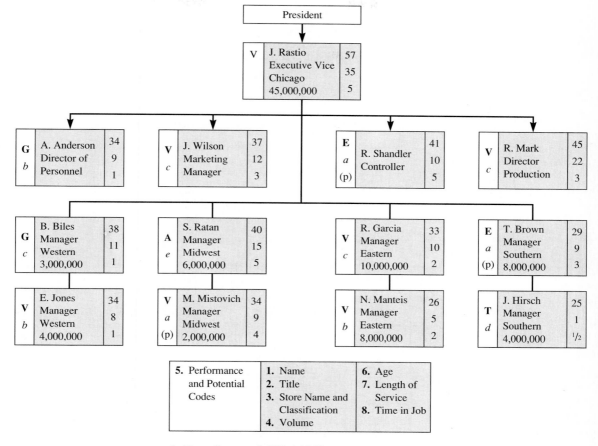

5. Performance and Potential Codes	1. Name 2. Title 3. Store Name and Classification 4. Volume	6. Age 7. Length of Service 8. Time in Job

1. Name–first name/middle initial/last name.
2. Title–example: Mgr.
3. Store name and classification.
4. Total sales volume in region.
5. Performance and potential codes (see below).
6. Age in years.
7. Length of service–number of years of unbroken service wtih company.
8. Time in job–number of years in current position.

Performance Code

E Excellent: Represents the top 10% of all executives in all catagories.

V Very good: Represents upper 25% in performance and generally indicates a high level of achievement of objectives.

G Good: Represents the level of performance expected from most of our experienced executives and indicates upper-middle level of performance.

A Adequate: Represents the minimum level of performance that is acceptable under usual circumstances.

U Unsatisfactory: Represents unsatisfactory level of performance and indicates that failure to improve will result in termination or change of position.

T Too new to rate:

Potential Code

a. Promotable now. One of two subdesignations must be made:
   (p) "up"–will indicate readiness for promotion to a higher level.
   (l) "lateral"–will indicate readiness for lateral promotion or transfer.

b. Promotable within two years or less.

c. Potentially promotable–time uncertain.

d. Potential good, but at present level only.

e. Potential and future is questionable.

EXHIBIT 5-12 Safeguarding Information Privacy in an HRIS

- Review information-gathering practices to determine best way to collect data.
- Limit the information you collect to what's relevant to a specific business decision.
- Inform employees about the types of information kept on file and how it is used.
- Let employees inspect and, if necessary, correct the information maintained on them.
- Keep sensitive information separate from other records.
- Limit the internal use of personal information to those activities where it is necessary.
- Disclose personal employee information to outsiders only after employee consent.

Source: Robert Stambaugh (February 1990), "Protecting Employee Data Privacy," *Computers in HR Management,* pp. 12–20.

EXHIBIT 5-13 Recommendations on Human Resource Planning for Model Organizations

Type of Organization	Analysis of Supply (Skills Inventory)		Method of Demand Analysis				Level Where Planning Is Analyzed		
	Manual	Computerized	Expert	Trend	Model/ Multiple	Unit	HQ	Unit	Both
1. Large size, low complexity, high stability		X			X	X	X		
2. Medium size, low complexity, high stability	X	X			X	X	X		
3. Small size, low complexity, high stability	X	X		X			X		
4. Medium size, moderate complexity, moderate stability	X			X		X		X	
5. Large size, high complexity, low stability		X		X		X			X
6. Medium size, high complexity, low stability	X	X		X		X		X	
7. Small size, high complexity, low stability	X	X	X					X	

SUMMARY

As with nearly all of the HRM activities to be discussed in this book, there is no one best method for conducting HR planning. How much planning is needed, which forecasting techniques will work best, and how far into the future these estimates should extend all differ from organization to organization. Exhibit 5–13 provides some recommendations about these issues for the model organizations.

Surveys do indicate, however, that many companies probably do not devote enough time and energy to the HR planning process. Others are not aware that many solutions exist to any gap that might exist between the supply and demand of labor.[22] Finally, organizations must begin to realize that an effective HR plan should work in partnership with a strategic plan. For this to happen, organizational goals must be clearly understood and effectively communicated to employees.[23]

To summarize the other major points covered in this chapter:

1. The major reasons for formal employment planning are to achieve:
   a. More effective and efficient use of human resources.
   b. More satisfied and better-developed employees.
   c. More effective equal opportunity planning.
2. The human resource planning process is a joint responsibility of HR and operating managers, with each performing specific functions in the process.
3. Four forecasting techniques used to determine work-force needs described in the chapter are: expert-estimate, trend-projection, modeling, and unit-forecasting techniques.
4. An important step in the planning process is to determine the availability of those presently employed by the organization who can fill projected vacancies. The skills inventory can serve this purpose.
5. Action decisions in an employee-shortage situation depend on the magnitude of the shortage: overtime, retraining of lower-skilled employees, hiring additional employees, and subcontracting some of the work.
6. A growing number of firms are now using computerized human resource information systems to help in the planning process. HRISs perform a number of functions, including applicant tracking, succession planning, maintaining skills inventories, and employee services.
7. Action decisions in surplus conditions include attrition, early retirement, demotions, layoffs, and terminations.
8. Organizations need to analyze the supply-demand match of employees in advance so they can take necessary steps to reschedule, recruit, or lay off employees. The organization should analyze work-force composition to determine whether it meets legal constraints.

Human resource planning can be an integral part of the HRM program. It is most directly related to recruitment, selection, training, and promotion. By matching employment supply and demand, the organization can know how many persons of what type it needs to fill positions from within (by promotion or training) and how many it must acquire from outside (by recruitment and selection).

Chapters 7 and 8 are devoted to recruitment and selection, in which employment needs are filled from outside the organization when personnel and employment planning decisions show this need.

KEY TERMS

QUESTIONS FOR REVIEW AND DISCUSSION

1. What is human resource planning? How does it relate to other human resource management activities?
2. What is an HRIS? What activities do they help organizations to perform?
3. How do replacement charts and applicant tracking systems help to improve
   HR planning decisions?
4. What factors would affect your choice of an HR planning system? What factors would influence your choice of forecasting methods?
5. What is an EIS? How does it differ from an HRIS? How is it similar?
6. Describe the contents of a skills inventory. How is this information used in
   HR planning?
7. What should be done to maintain the security of a computerized HRIS?
8. What kinds of action decisions are available to an organization when there is
   a surplus of labor? A labor shortage?
9. Why have many forecasting techniques been resisted or not used by managers?
10. Describe how operating managers and human resource managers can work
    together to make an HR planning system work.

NOTES

[1] Ronald C. Page and David M. Van De Voort (1989), "Job Analysis and HR Planning,"
in *Human Resource Planning, Employment, and Placement*, ed. Wayne F. Cascio
(Washington, D.C.: Bureau of National Affairs), pp. 34–72.

[2] Alan Scharf (January–February 1991), "Secrets of Strategic Planning: Responding to
the Opportunities of Tomorrow," *Industrial Management*, pp. 9–10.

[3] William E. Fulmer (1990), "Human Resource Management: The Right Hand of Strategy Implementation," *Human Resource Planning*, pp. 1–12.

[4] W. S. Wikstrom (1971), "Manpower Planning: Evolving Systems," Report no. 521,
(New York: The Conference Board).

[5] Page and Van De Voort, "Job Analysis and HR Planning," p. 62.

[6] John E. Butler, Gerald R. Ferris, and Nancy K. Napier (1991), *Strategy and Human Resources Management* (Cincinnati: South-Western Publishing).

[7] William H. Davidson (Winter 1991), "The Role of Global Scanning in Business Planning," *Organization Dynamics*, pp. 4–16.

[8] F. A. Maljers (April 1990), "Strategic Planning and Intuition in Unilever," *Long Range
Planning*, pp. 63–68.

[9] N. Dalkey (1969), *The Delphi Method: An Experimental Study of Group Opinion* (Santa
Monica, Calif.: Rand).

[10] Richard I. Levin and Charles A. Kirkpatrick (1980), *Quantitative Approaches to Management*, (New York: McGraw-Hill).

[11] A clear and concise discussion of regression analysis can be found in R. Dennis Middlemist, Michael A. Hitt, and Charles R. Green (1983), *Personnel Management* (Englewood Cliffs, N.J.: Prentice-Hall), pp. 112–115.

[12] Jacob Cohen and Patricia Cohen (1973), *Applied Multiple Regression/Correlation Analysis for the Behavioral Sciences* (Hillsdale, N.J.: Lawrence Erlbaum).

[13] John D. Gridley (May 1986), "Who Will Be Where When? Forecast the Easy Way," *Personnel Journal*, pp. 50–58.

[14] Alan Paller and Richard Laska (1990), *The EIS Book: Information Systems for Top Managers* (Homewood, Ill.: Dow Jones-Irwin), pp. 1–3.

[15] Bill Saporito (May 25, 1987), "Cutting Costs Without Cutting People," *Fortune*, pp. 26–32.

[16] Michael J. Kavanagh, Hal G. Gueutal, and Scott I. Tannenbaum (1990), *Human Resource Information Systems: Development and Application* (Boston: PWS-Kent), p. 29.

[17] Gary Dessler (1984), *Personnel Management* (Reston, Va.: Reston Publishing), p. 120.

[18] Jac Fitz-Enz (March 1990), "HR Forecasts That Will Benefit Your Bottom Line," *Computers in HR Management*, pp. 24–33.

[19] Kirk Anderson (March 1990), "Apple's HRIS Changes How HR Works," *Computers in HR Management*, pp. 14–23.

[20] Paller and Laska, *The EIS Book*, pp. 1–2.

[21] Robert Stambaugh (February 1990), "Protecting Employee Data Privacy," *Computers in HR Management*, pp. 12–20.

[22] David M. Reid (April 1990), "Where Planning Fails in Practice," *Long Range Planning*, pp. 85–93.

[23] Toyohiro Kono (August 1990), "Corporate Culture and Long Range Planning," *Long Range Planning*, pp. 9–19.

Computers are becoming a widely used tool for human resource planning. Southland Corporation, which owns and operates the 7-Eleven convenience food stores, is one company that has computerized aspects of its planning function. The company inputs results from the twice-yearly personnel evaluation of its management into a computer system. Southland regularly obtains computer analyses on the promotability of each manager and the impact of future promotions on job openings and staffing requirements. Southland also uses computers in establishing career development programs for its employees. The computer software identifies skills gaps for each employee and even suggests remedies (a special assignment, training, college course work).

Tenneco, Inc., a Houston-based international conglomerate, uses a $15,000 program called Executive Track to track its 800 executives. Each year the company uses the program to conduct an annual resource review, analyzing promotions, transfers, and performance of its executive corp and evaluating the probability and location of future executive openings. When an opening occurs in one of Tenneco's 11 divisions, Executive Track provides a written preliminary screening analysis that provides a list and summary of all employees who meet the stated qualifications for the position. Tenneco's HR department uses the analysis to prepare a written report for division management. The computer's preliminary analysis is provided in minutes; before computerization the task required hours to complete.

Executive Track also performs a "position blockage" analysis that identifies high performers who have not been promoted for at least two years because the jobs above them are filled.

HR departments that have computerized elements of their succession planning assert that computerization affords at least three advantages. Computerization makes succession planning more objective because the system evaluates all potential candidates for promotion using the same, specified criteria (a particular performance rating, number of years of experience, and so on). Politics or the old boy's network aren't a factor.

Second, computerization opens up succession planning in the organization because it can more easily evaluate a larger number of people as potential candidates to fill open positions. Consider that in companies the size of Tenneco, for example (100,000 employees), a computer can evaluate in a matter of seconds scores of employees (some of whom otherwise wouldn't be considered simply because of the hours required for the task).

Third, computerization provides sophisticated analysis for human resource planning. Many HR departments have used programs to conduct "if-then" scenarios concerning possible turnover in key positions. One executive asserts that computerization is very useful in contingency planning for what he calls "the truck problem — what you do if a guy is hit by a truck." Computer analysis can calculate and lay out the "domino effect" that vacancies in the upper levels of an organization can have on positions on lower levels when filled internally. Computer analysis can also uncover potential snags in human resource planning. For instance, one employee may emerge as clearly the most qualified candidate for one job; however, he or she could be the only qualified person for a critical position that will probably open a few months down the road. Well-designed computer programs catch potential pitfalls that are difficult to spot when manually reviewing stacks of personnel files.

However, computerized human resource planning has its critics. Some cite that computers tend to impersonalize planning and that relying too much on computer-provided analysis may produce poor decisions. However, one executive notes, "The computer doesn't make the decisions. People make the decisions. It's just a catcher of information."

Written by Kim Stewart and adapted from: William M. Bulkeley (September 18, 1985), "The Fast Track: Computers Help Firms Decide Whom to Promote," *The Wall Street Journal*, p. 33; (July 15, 1985), "Tenneco Tracks Its Executives," *Computer Decisions*, p. 98; and Richard B. Frantzreb (July 1986), "Microcomputer Software for Human Resources: A Directory," *Personnel Administrator*.

Discussion Questions

1. The case and chapter describe some uses of computers in human resource planning. In what other ways can computers be used in performing human resource planning tasks?

2. Some consultants assert that many CEOs aren't enthusiastic about using computers in succession planning. Why? As an HR manager, how could you deal with this problem?

3. Besides the issue of privacy and critics' concerns stated in this case, are there other shortcomings in computerizing elements of human resource planning? Explain.

6

JOB ANALYSIS AND DESIGN

· · · · · · · ·

LEARNING OBJECTIVES

After studying this chapter, you should be able to:

· · ·

Define what is meant by the terms *job analysis, job description,* and *job specification*

· · ·

Illustrate the uses that job analysis information can serve in an organization's HRM program

· · ·

Describe four methods used to collect job analysis information

· · ·

Interpret job codes and information found in the *Dictionary of Occupational Titles*

· · ·

List the five core job dimensions used in job enrichment programs

· · ·

Compare the strengths and weaknesses of the mechanistic and motivational approaches to job design

· · ·

Describe briefly current job design approaches in Europe and Japan

CAREER CHALLENGE

*T*im Huggins is the new director of human resources of Sprowl Manufacturing, a division of the MBTI corporation. Tim wanted to start a job analysis program immediately. Six weeks after he took over, job analysis questionnaires (six pages each) were given to employees. The results were puzzling. Responses from the operating employees (machinists, lift operators, technicians, draftspeople, and mechanics) were quite different from responses from their supervisors about these jobs.

The fact that supervisors viewed the jobs differently from those doing the work fueled Tim's desire to do a job analysis. He wanted to study and specifically define the jobs so that misunderstandings, arguments, and false expectations could be kept to a minimum.

The supervisors listed job duties as simple and routine. The operating employees disagreed and claimed that their jobs were complicated and constrained by limited resources. They complained that work areas were hot, stuffy, and uncomfortable. These disagreements soon became the basis for some open hostility between supervisors and workers. Finally, Nick Mannis, a machinist, confronted supervisor Rog Wilkes and threatened to punch him out over the "lies" Rog and other supervisors had concocted in the job analysis.

Tim was worried that the job analysis program was getting totally out of hand. He had to do something about it. Everyone was getting up in arms over a program Tim felt was necessary.

Should a manager like Tim, who knows a lot about HRM, but who was not trained in the specifics of job analysis, undertake this kind of program?

INTRODUCTION

Organizations have evolved because the overall mission and objectives of most institutions are too large for any single person to accomplish. Consequently, the organization must have a systematic way for determining which employees are expected to perform a particular function or task that must be accomplished. The cornerstone of the organization is, therefore, the set of jobs performed by its employees. These jobs, in turn, provide the mechanism for coordinating and linking the various activities of the organization that are necessary for success. As a result, studying and understanding jobs through the process known as **job analysis** is a vital part of any HRM program.

Job analysis provides answer to questions such as:[1]

How much time is taken to complete important tasks?

Which tasks are grouped together and are considered a job?

How can a job be designed or structured so that employee performance can be enhanced?

What kinds of behaviors are needed to perform the job?

What kind of person (traits and experience) is best suited for the job?

How can the information acquired by a job analysis be used in the development of HRM programs?

In this chapter, the contributions made by job analysis to an organization's HRM program and specific activities will become clearer. Furthermore, the careful planning needed and various general and specific techniques of a job analysis program will also be highlighted. Finally, the importance of job analysis in the design of jobs will be discussed. The chapter will show that job analysis is a necessary part of HRM and in many respects is the foundation upon which all other HRM activities must be constructed. It is this necessity that is pushing Tim in his drive to institute job analysis at Sprowl Manufacturing.

Job Analysis Vocabulary

Before discussing the specific process and techniques involved in job analysis, the language of job analysis should be learned. Although many of these terms are often used interchangeably by people who are unfamiliar with job analysis, the expert will use them more precisely in order to avoid confusion and misinterpretation. Precision in the use of these terms is, in fact, required by federal and state legislation. It is therefore important for the HR manager to use each of them in a way that is consistent with such legislation.

The following definitions are consistent with those provided by the U.S. Employment Service and the U.S. Office of Personnel Management.[2]

Job analysis. The process of gathering, analyzing, and synthesizing information about jobs.[3]

Job description. The principal product of a job analysis. It represents a written summary of the job as an identifiable organizational unit.

Job specification. A written explanation of the knowledge, skills, abilities, traits, and other characteristics (KSAOs) necessary for effective performance on a given job.

Tasks. Coordinated and aggregated series of work elements used to produce an output (e.g., a unit of production or service to a client).

Position. Consists of the responsibilities and duties performed by an individual. There are as many positions in an organization as there are employees.

Job. A group of positions that are similar in their duties, such as a computer programmer or compensation specialists.

Job family. A group of two or more jobs that have similar job duties.

THE STEPS IN JOB ANALYSIS

The job analysis process involves a number of steps, which have been outlined in Exhibit 6–1.[4] As it appears in the exhibit, the process assumes that the job analysis is being conducted in an ongoing organization; in other words, an organization that is already in operation as opposed to a new venture.

Step 1 provides a broad view of how each job fits into the total fabric of the organization. Organization charts and process charts (which will be discussed later) are used to complete Step 1. Step 2 encourages those involved to determine how the job analysis and job design information will be used. This step will be further explained in the next section. Since it is usually too costly and time consuming to analyze every job, a representative sample of jobs needs to be selected. In Step 3, attention is called to the selection of jobs that are to be analyzed.

Step 4 involves the use of acceptable job analysis techniques. The techniques are used to collect data on the characteristics of the job, the required behaviors, and the employee characteristics needed to perform the job. The information collected in Step 4 is then used in Step 5 to develop a job description. Next, in Step 6, a job specification is prepared.

EXHIBIT 6–1   Steps in the Job Analysis Process (1–6) and Its Relationship to HRM and Job Design

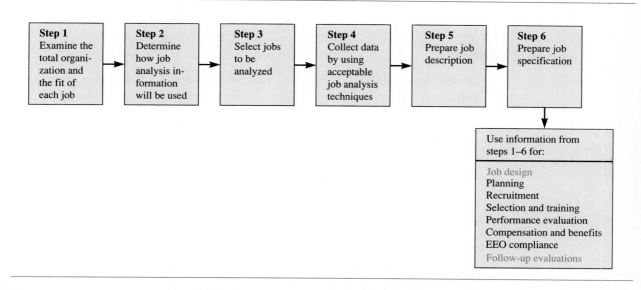

The knowledge and data collected in Steps 1–6 are then used as the foundation for virtually every other HRM activity. As shown in Exhibit 6–1, these include activities such as recruitment, selection, training, performance evaluation, and compensation. The information gathered during job analysis is essential to each of these.

As is also shown in the exhibit, the information gathered is used as inputs into job design and redesign, which is a specific use that will be discussed in detail later in this chapter. Job analysis provides information necessary for organizing work in ways that will allow employees to be both productive and satisfied. Finally, information from a job analyses can be used in an organization's follow-up evaluations of its job design efforts. At this step, it is important for an organization to evaluate its efforts and determine whether the goals of productivity and satisfaction are in fact being achieved.

Tim failed to explain these steps at Sprowl. He simply handed out questionnaires. Naturally, this resulted in concern among supervisors and operating employees. The people whose jobs were being analyzed and their supervisors simply were not informed of what Tim had in mind. Tim knew what job analysis was, but he was never actually trained in the "how to" specifics. Unfortunately, other people at Sprowl were not sure what job analysis was, because Tim failed to communicate what he had in mind.

THE USES OF JOB ANALYSIS

HR managers, specialists, and managers in general know that job analysis has many uses. Some of these individuals now believe that there is no longer even a choice about whether job analysis should be conducted. Administrative guidelines accompanying various civil rights/EEO laws and judicial recommendations are clear. The question has become how to conduct a legally defensible job analysis rather than whether to conduct such an analysis at all.[5] For example, the EEOC's *Uniform Guidelines on Employee Selection Procedures* states that:

There should be a job analysis which includes an analysis of the important work behaviors required for successful performance. . . . Any job analysis should focus on work behavior(s) and the tasks associated with them.[6]

Job analysis is also specifically linked to various laws including each of the following:[7]

- *Equal Pay Act (1963)* — In order for work to be considered the same, the jobs must involve equal skill, equal effort, and equal responsibility and be performed under similar working conditions in the same establishment. A job analysis can be used to show similarities or differences in skill, effort, responsibility, and working conditions to provide a rationale for compensation levels.

- *Fair Labor Standards Act (1938)* — Exempt employees do not have to be paid overtime pay. Typically, managers, technical workers, and professionals are considered exempt. Nonexempt employees are required to receive overtime pay for working in excess of 40 hours per week. Generally, blue-collar, clerical, and semiskilled workers are classified as nonexempt. The job analysis clarifies the category, exempt or nonexempt, of each employee.

- *Civil Rights Act (1964)* — A job description based on a properly conducted job analysis can provide support for preparing a defense against unfair discrimination charges. Not having job analysis data weakens the defense against discrimination charges. For example, stating that certain physical requirements (e.g., strength of stamina) are needed to perform a job without having determined their necessity through job analysis can subject the employer to discrimination charges.

- *Test Validation* — Landmark cases discussed in Chapter 3 such as *Griggs v. Duke Power Co.* (1970) and *Albermarle Paper Company v. J. Moody* (1975) established the legal need for job analysis in the validation of employee selection procedures. For example, the court held that Albermarle's test validation effort was inadequate because there had been "no analysis of the attributes of, or the particular skills needed in, the structured job group."[8]

The conclusion seems obvious. As long as equal employment opportunity laws exist in their present form, job analysis will have to be viewed as a mandatory activity for HRM. More important, the quality of an organization's job analysis procedures will be evaluated from a legal perspective. A good job analysis will have to provide the following if it is going to be viewed favorably by the courts:[9]

1. It should yield a thorough, clear job description.
2. The frequency and importance of task behaviors should be assessed.
3. It must allow for an accurate assessment of the knowledge, skills, abilities, and other characteristics (KSAOs) required by the job.
4. It must yield information about the relationship between job duties and these KSAOs. That is, it must clearly determine which KSAOs are important for each job duty.

In addition to helping organizations satisfy their legal requirements, job analysis is intricately tied to HRM programs and activities. It is used extensively in each of the following areas:

1. Preparation of *job descriptions*. A complete description contains a job summary, the job duties and responsibilities, and some indication of the working conditions.
2. Writing *job specifications*. The job specification describes the individual traits and characteristics required to perform the job well.
3. *Job Design*. Job analysis information is used to structure and modify the elements, duties, and tasks of specific jobs.
4. *Recruitment*. Job analysis information is useful when searching for the right person to fill the job. It helps recruiters to seek and find the type of people that will contribute to and be comfortable with the organization.
5. *Selection*. The final selection of the most qualified people requires information on what job duties and responsibilities need to be performed. This type of information is provided in the job description.
6. *Performance evaluation*. The evaluation of performance involves comparison of actual versus planned output. Job analysis is used to acquire an idea of acceptable levels of performance for a job.
7. *Training and development*. Job analysis information is used to design and implement training and development programs. The job description provides information on what skills and competencies are required to perform the job. Training and development work is then conducted to satisfy these skill and competency requirements.

PROFESSIONAL PROFILE

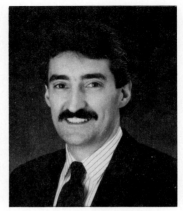

Timothy P. Mooney
Development Dimensions
International

Biography

Timothy P. Mooney is a regional vice president for Development Dimensions International (DDI), a Pittsburgh-based consulting company that specializes in assessment and training and development systems. After graduating from Butler University (Indianapolis, Indiana) with a B.A. in psychology, Tim earned an M.A. in industrial-organizational psychology from the University of Akron in 1979.

Tim started his career as a training supervisor for Clark Equipment Company, and joined DDI in 1980 as an assessment consultant. Since then he has served as the targeted selection product manager and the national accounts manager, and was promoted to regional vice president in 1989.

One of his proudest contributions to the field was being the project manager for the team that developed the world's first computer-based job analysis system, **Identifying Criteria for Success (ICS).**

Job Description   As a regional vice president, Tim is responsible for leading a team of more than 20 people to market, deliver, and provide customer service for DDI's consulting services in a seven-state area.

The regional vice president's time is divided among the following functions:

- Coaching and developing regional staff — 25%
- Sales and marketing — 30%
- Consulting — 5%
- Customer service — 10%
- Business planning — 5%
- Administration — 25%

Implementing Solutions for Current Business Situations: A Viewpoint   To be successful in today's highly competitive marketplace, organizations can no longer use a "hiring hall" approach in which people are hired on the basis of a strong back when they staff new operations. Just as they exercise great care in investing in the right location, equipment, and facilities design, they must be equally accurate in their human investments.

DDI has helped more than 65 organizations design and implement selection and training systems for greenfield startups and facility retrofits. As a project manager and project team member, Tim has been involved in the following activities for several startups:

- Conducting a **job analysis** to pinpoint the most important motivations and skills for success in each new job family.
- Designing a **selection system** to process large numbers of applicants (startups usually draw 50 to 100 applicants for every opening).
- **Identifying/developing selection instruments,** including motivation inventories, tests, and simulations, to assess candidates against special skill requirements in a team environment.
- **Training interviewers and assessors** to accurately and objectively evaluate candidates.

These projects have resulted in hiring a highly motivated work force with:

- Effective team skills.
- High ability to learn.
- Strong customer and quality orientation.

8. *Career planning and development*. The movement of individuals into and out of positions, jobs, and occupations is a common procedure in organizations. Job analysis provides clear and detailed information to those considering such a career movement.

9. *Compensation and Benefits*. Compensation is usually tied to a job's required skill, working conditions, and so on. Job analysis is used to compare and properly compensate jobs.

10. *Safety*. The safety of a job depends on proper layout, standards, equipment, and other physical conditions. What a job entails and the type of people needed also contribute information to establish safe procedures. This information is also provided by job analysis.

11. *Strategic Planning*. Organizations must adapt to the environment. This may require changing, eliminating, or combining jobs. Thus, job analysis information is necessary for meeting future needs in the structure of jobs and the kinds of people that will be needed to fill the jobs.

It should be obvious from this list that the potential uses of job analysis cover the entire domain of HRM activities. It is, in fact, difficult to imagine how an organization could effectively hire, train, appraise, compensate, or utilize its human resources without the kinds of information derived from job analysis. But the value of job analysis doesn't end with HRM. Managers involved in virtually all aspects of the organization's planning, organizing, controlling, and directing functions can and do also benefit from job analysis information.

WHO SHOULD CONDUCT THE JOB ANALYSIS

The steps spelled out in Exhibit 6–1 suggest that care and planning are important features of any job analysis effort. As the opening career challenge illustrates, Tim really didn't take the care and do the planning that he should have before starting the job analysis program — he started the program too abruptly.

Part of the planning that Tim should have engaged in involves choosing the persons who will actually conduct the analysis. If an organization only has an occasional need for job analysis information, it may hire a temporary job analyst from outside. Other organizations will have job analysis experts employed on a full-time basis. Still other organizations will use supervisors, job incumbents, or some combination of these to collect job analysis information. In any of these cases, training in the methods and procedures of good job analysis is essential. It is not a job for an amateur.

Regardless of who collects the information, the individuals should thoroughly understand people, jobs, and the total organizational system. They should also have considerable knowledge about how work is expected to flow within the organization.

At an even more general level, the job analyst needs to understand how HRM fits into the overall structure and mission of the organization. There is a growing acknowledgement of the need to match human resource activities with an organization's strategic planning.[10] Modern organizations must learn to adapt and be willing to change when necessary. The very nature of the jobs performed by employees might have to change as a part of this adaptation process. Thus, in many cases, job analysis should not be seen as a "snapshot" of the job but must also be able to predict what the job will look like in the future.[11] Therefore, the job analyst cannot just be knowledgeable about the current nature of the job. Strategic information about the organization's plan for the future is also essential.

Despite the importance of job analysis to an organization's effectiveness, some managers do not respect the work of the job analyst. The following statement presents an interesting message about job analysis:

> Although job analysis is an essential feature of almost every activity engaged in by industrial-organization psychologists, the subject is treated in textbooks in a manner which suggests that any fool can do it, and thus it is a task which can be delegated to the lowest level technician. This is quite contradictory to the position taken by Otis (1953) . . . , and is clearly at variance with the statements in the EEOC Selection Guidelines . . . . Job analysis for these purposes is not accomplished by rummaging around in an organization; it is accomplished by applying highly systematic and precise methods.[12]

SELECTING METHODS AND PROCEDURES: THE USE OF CHARTS

The job analyst has to select the best methods and procedures available to conduct the job analysis. However, even before this selection is made, an overview of the organization and jobs is required. An overview provides the job analyst with an informed picture of the total arrangement of departments, units, and jobs.

The Organization Chart

An organization chart presents the relationship among departments and units of the firm. The line functions (the individuals performing work duties) and staff functions (the advisers) are spelled out.

A typical organization chart for a manufacturing firm is presented in Exhibit 6–2. This chart shows the vertical levels in the organization and the various departments. It provides the job analyst with a general picture of what departments exist and the hierarchy and formal communication networks in the organization. Emphasis is placed on the word *general*. A chart shows the way the organization is *supposed* to be arranged. The actual arrangement of the organization and the flow of communication are often different from the plan on the chart. However, even a partial view aids in forming a broad conception of the organization.

Process Chart

A **process chart** such as the one shown in Exhibit 6–3 shows how a specific set of jobs are related to each other.[13] In the example, the focus is on the technician job, and the job analyst would, therefore, be interested in the flow of work to and from it. In particular, Exhibit 6–3 shows the flow of activities necessary to prepare the specs for the construction of an engineering prototype (model).

With the help of organization and process charts, the job analyst should be able to begin identifying which specific job analysis techniques will be most suitable. An analysis of a managerial position may, for instance, require using different procedures and sources of information than an analysis of a semiskilled labor position. In addition, the purpose and focus of the analysis will help to determine which data collection technique should be utilized. For example, if a job analysis is being conducted to aid in the redesign of work stations, the job analyst might use a different method than if the analysis is being conducted to determine whether a new method of employee selection should be implemented. Thus, organization charts,

EXHIBIT 6-2   Organization Chart (Sample)

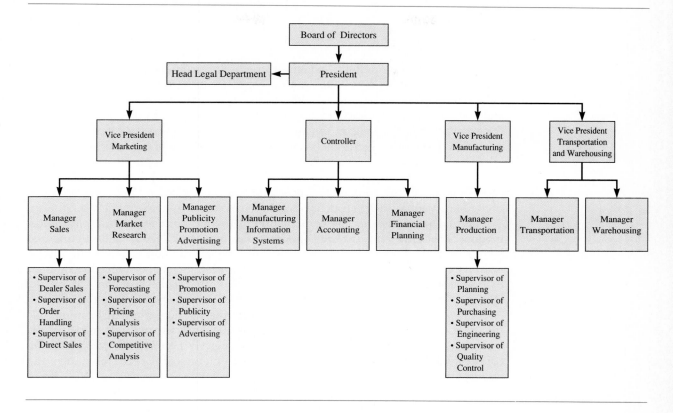

EXHIBIT 6-3   Process Chart of Job Relationships

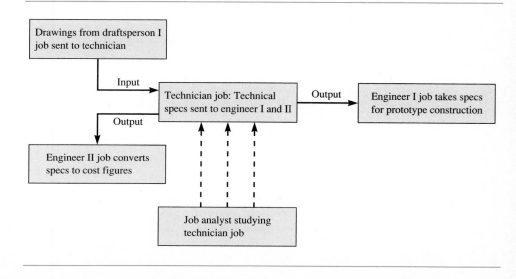

process charts, and other similar sources of preliminary information should be consulted before the actual job analysis is conducted.

JOB ANALYSIS: METHODS OF DATA COLLECTION

There are four basic methods, which can be used separately or in combination, of collecting job analysis data — observation, interview, questionnaires, and job incumbent diary/logs. In each of these methods, the information about the job is collected and then the job is studied in terms of tasks completed by the job incumbent (person presently working on the job). This type of job analysis is referred to as *job oriented*. On the other hand, a job can be analyzed in terms of behaviors or what the job incumbent does to perform the job (such as computing, coordinating, negotiating). This is referred to as *work-oriented* job analysis.[14] Both of these orientations are acceptable under the *Uniform Guidelines on Employee Selection Procedures* as long as they identify job duties and behaviors that are critical to performing the job.

The four methods — or any combination of them — must focus on critical information. Since time and cost are considerations, managers need to collect comparable, valid data. Consequently, some form of core information is needed no matter what data collection method is used.[15] A professional job analyst typically conducts extensive interviews with incumbents and supervisors, collects records about the job, and, if feasible, directly observes the job incumbents performing the job.[16]

A questionnaire called the **Job Analysis Information Format (JAIF)** can provide the basic core information for use with any job analysis method — observation, interview, questionnaire, or incumbent diary/logs. It permits the job analyst to collect job information that provides a thorough picture of the job, job duties, and requirements.

Job incumbents are asked to complete the JAIF. These answers (of course, some questions may not be answered or can't be answered because of a lack of job incumbent knowledge about the question) are then used to specifically structure the data collection technique that will eventually be implemented. Exhibit 6–4 presents a portion of one type of JAIF.

Differences among job incumbents should be considered during the analysis of JAIF information in addition to the actual job analysis. The job analyst should not assume that all incumbents or their supervisors will view a job in the same way. A safeguard against developing a distorted picture of a job is for the job analyst to collect information from a variety of incumbents. The job analyst should probably try to get information from males and females, older and younger workers, and high- and low-performing incumbents (the research is mixed about whether there will be differences between them in terms of their view of the job[17]). Finally, the job analyst should not assume that all incumbents and supervisors have the same amount of knowledge about a job. This is important because research indicates that too little knowledge about a job can lead to inaccurate job descriptions.[18]

Observation

Direct observation is used for jobs that require manual, standardized, and short–job-cycle activities. Jobs performed by an automobile assembly-line worker, an insurance company filing clerk, and an inventory stockroom employee are examples of these. The job analyst must observe a representative sample of individuals performing these jobs. Observation is usually not appropriate where the job involves

---

EXHIBIT 6-4

JOB ANALYSIS INFORMATION FORMAT

Your Job Title _____ *Code* _____ *Date* _____

Class Title _____ *Department* _____

Your Name _____ *Facility* _____

Supervisor's Title _____ *Prepared by* _____

Superior's Name _____ *Hours Worked* _____ AM _____ *to* AM _____
                                                                        PM   PM

---

1. What is the general purpose of your job?

2. What was your last job? If it was in another organization, please name it.

3. To what job would you normally expect to be promoted?

4. If you regularly supervise others, list them by name and job title.

5. If you supervise others, please check those activities that are part of your supervisory duties

   __ Hiring   __ Coaching   __ Promoting

   __ Orienting   __ Counseling   __ Compensating

   __ Training   __ Budgeting   __ Disciplining

   __ Scheduling   __ Directing   __ Terminating

   __ Developing   __ Measuring performance __ Other _____

6. How would you describe the successful completion and results of your work?

7. *Job Duties* — Please briefly describe *what* you do and, if possible, *how* you do it. Indicate those duties you consider to be most important and/or most difficult.

   a. *Daily duties* —

   b. *Periodic duties* — (Please indicate whether weekly, monthly, quarterly, etc.) —

   c. *Duties performed at irregular intervals* —

   d. How long have you been performing these duties?

   e. Are you now performing unnecessary duties? If yes, please describe.

   f. Should you be performing duties not now included in your job? If yes, please describe.

EXHIBIT 6-4   *(concluded)*

---

8. *Education.* Please check the blank that indicates the educational *requirements* for the job, not your *own* educational background.

    a. _____ No formal education required.

    b. _____ Less than high school diploma.

    c. _____ High school diploma or equivalent.

    d. _____ 2-year college certificate or equivalent.

    e. _____ 4-year college degree.

    f. _____ Education beyond undergraduate degree and/or professional license.

    List advanced degrees or specific professional license or certificate required.

    Please indicate the education you had when you were placed on this job.

9. *Experience.* Please check the amount needed to perform your job.

    a. __ None.

    b. __ Less than one month.

    c. __ One month to less than six months.

    d. __ Six months to one year.

    e. __ One to three years.

    f. __ Three to five years.

    g. __ Five to 10 years.

    h. __ Over 10 years.

    Please indicate the experience you had when you were placed on this job.

10. *Skill.* Please list any skills required in the performance of your job. (For example, amount of accuracy, alertness, precision in working with described tools, methods, systems, etc.)

    Please list skills you possessed when you were placed on this job.

11. *Equipment.* Does your work require the use of any equipment? Yes ___ No ___. If Yes, please list the equipment and check whether you use it rarely, occasionally, or frequently.

	Equipment	Rarely	Occasionally	Frequently
a.	_____	_____	_____	_____
b.	_____	_____	_____	_____
c.	_____	_____	_____	_____
d.	_____	_____	_____	_____

---

significant amounts of mental activity, such as the work of a research scientist, a lawyer, or a mathematician.

The use of the observation technique requires that the job analyst be trained to observe *relevant* job behaviors. In conducting an observation, the job analyst must remain as unobtrusive as possible. He or she must stay out of the way so that the work can be performed.

Interview

Interviewing job incumbents is often done in combination with observation. Interviews are probably the most widely used job analysis data collection technique. They permit the job analyst to talk face to face with job incumbents. The job incumbent can ask questions of the job analyst, and this interview serves as an opportunity for the analyst to explain how the job analysis knowledge and information will be used.

Interviews can be conducted with a single job incumbent, a group of individuals, or with a supervisor who is knowledgeable about the job. Usually a structured set of questions will be used in interviews so that answers from individuals or groups can be compared.

One major problem with interviewing is that inaccurate information may be collected. For example, if a job incumbent believes that the job analysis interview will be used to set the job's compensation amount, he or she may provide inaccurate information. Therefore, interviewing more than one person (job incumbents and supervisors), careful planning, good questions, and establishing rapport between the job analyst and interviewees are extremely important guidelines. Using these guidelines is time consuming, but their use improves the quality of information collected. Interview information can be further refined by use of observation and/or questionnaires.

Questionnaires

The use of questionnaires is usually the least costly method for collecting information. It is an effective way to collect a large amount of information in a short period of time. The JAIF presented in Exhibit 6–4 is a structured questionnaire. It includes specific questions about the job, job requirements, working conditions, and equipment. A less structured, more open-ended approach would be to ask job incumbents to "describe their job in their own terms." This open-ended format would permit job incumbents to use their own terms and ideas to describe the job.

The format and degree of structure that a questionnaire should have are debatable issues. Job analysts have their own personal preferences on this matter. There really is no best format for a questionnaire. However, here are a few hints that will make the questionnaire easier to use:

- Keep it as *short as possible* — people do not generally like to complete forms.
- *Explain* what the questionnaire is being used for — people want to know why it must be completed. Tim Huggins (in the Career Challenge in this chapter) failed to explain his job analysis questionnaire. Employees wanted to know why the questions were being asked and how their responses would be used.
- Keep it *simple* — do not try to impress people with technical language. Use the simplest language to make a point or ask a question.
- *Test* the questionnaire before using it — in order to improve the questionnaire, ask some job incumbents to complete it and to comment on its features. This test will permit the analyst to modify the format before using the questionnaire in final form.

Job Incumbent Diary/Log

The diary/log is a recording by job incumbents of job duties, frequency of the duties, and when the duties were accomplished. This technique requires the job incumbent to keep a diary/log on a daily basis. Unfortunately, most individuals are not disciplined enough to keep such a diary/log.

If a diary/log is kept up to date, it can provide good information about the job. Comparisons on a daily, weekly, or monthly basis can be made. This permits an examination of the routineness or nonroutineness of job duties. The diary/log is useful when attempting to analyze jobs that are difficult to observe, such as those performed by engineers, scientists, and senior executives.

Summary

Although any of these four basic methods can be used either alone or in combination, there is no general agreement about which methods of job analysis yield the best information. There is some evidence that the various methods are not interchangeable inasmuch as certain methods seem to be better suited to a given situation than others.[19]

In the absence of a strong theoretical reason why one method should be superior to another, most organizations make their choice depending on their current needs.[20] In other words, the choice of a job analysis method is determined by circumstances such as the purpose of the analysis and time and budget constraints.

Since these four basic methods seem to have different strengths and weaknesses, many organizations are turning to a **multimethod job analysis approach.**[21] In this approach, the job analyst first conducts interviews with incumbents and supervisors in conjunction with on-site observation. Next, a task survey based on expert judgments is constructed and administered. Finally, a statistical analysis of the task survey responses is conducted in order to assess their consistency and to identify any systematic variation in them. There might, for example, be variation in the descriptions provided by incumbents and supervisors, by incumbents at different geographic locations, or by members of different departments. Regardless, differences in how the job has been described need to be resolved so there is general agreement about its true nature.

Using a comprehensive process such as the multimethod job analysis approach will, of course, be relatively expensive and time consuming. However, it does offer one distinct advantage over any of the basic methods used alone: the quality of information derived from these more comprehensive approaches is strongly endorsed by the courts in cases that rely on job analysis information.[22]

JOB ANALYSIS: SPECIFIC QUANTITATIVE TECHNIQUES

The four job analysis methods of data collection just described were presented in general terms. They form the basis for construction of specific techniques that have gained popularity across many types of organizations. When they are used properly, these specific techniques can provide systematic and quantitative procedures that yield information about what job duties are being accomplished and what knowledge, skills, abilities, and other human characteristics (KSAOs) are needed to perform the job. Three of the more popular quantitative techniques are: functional job analysis, the position analysis questionnaire, and the management position description questionnaire.

Functional Job Analysis

Functional job analysis (FJA) was the result of a major research effort undertaken by the U.S. Training and Employment Service.[23] Its purpose was to help classify jobs that had been defined in the early editions of the *Dictionary of Occupational*

Titles (DOT).[24] FJA provides a description of a job in terms of data, people, and things. To do so, FJA assumes:

. To varying degrees, all jobs are concerned with data, people, and things.

. It is important to make a distinction between what gets done and what job incumbents do to get things done.

. Mental resources are used to describe data; interpersonal resources are used with people; physical resources are applied to things.

. Each function performed on a job draws on a range of worker talents and skills to perform job duties.

The range of activities used in FJA that are associated with data, people, and things appear in Exhibit 6–5. These activities are then used to describe more than 20,000 jobs in current editions of the DOT.

The DOT classifies jobs by means of a nine-digit code. If someone is interested in a general description of a job, the DOT serves as a good starting point. Exhibit 6–6 provides DOT descriptions of several jobs. The first three digits of any one of these listings (for example, meteorologist–025) specify the occupational code, title, and industry. The next three digits (062) designate the degree to which a job incumbent typically has responsibility and judgment over data, people, and things. The lower the numbers, the greater the responsibility and judgment. The final three digits (010) are used to classify the alphabetical order of the job titles within the occupational group having the same degree of responsibility and judgment.[25]

DOT descriptions help a job analyst to begin learning what is involved with a particular job. FJA can then be used to elaborate and more thoroughly describe the content of the job.

The FJA form of analyzing the job of a dough mixer appears in Exhibit 6–7. The dough mixer's activities in terms of data, people, and things are quantitatively rated 5, 6, and 2, respectively, in item 5. These ratings are based on the analyst's judgment concerning the activities presented in Exhibit 6–5. That is, a dough mixer must be able to copy data (5), speak effectively (6), and control (2) his or her work.

If the job analyst was examining the job of an executive secretary, the quantitative score might be 5, 6, 5 (copying, speaking-signaling, tending). On the other hand, a research scientist in a laboratory might be rated a 2, 0, 1.

One advantage of the FJA is that each job has a quantitative score. Thus, jobs can be arranged for compensation or other HRM purposes because jobs with similar

---

EXHIBIT 6-5   Activities to Be Rated: Data, People, and Things

Data		People		Things	
0	Synthesizing	0	Mentoring	0	Setting up
1	Coordinating	1	Negotiating	1	Precision working
2	Analyzing	2	Instructing	2	Operating/controlling
3	Compiling	3	Supervising	3	Driving/operating
4	Computing	4	Diverting	4	Manipulating
5	Copying	5	Persuading	5	Tending
6	Comparing	6	Speaking/signaling	6	Feeding/offbearing
		7	Serving	7	Handling
		8	Taking instructions/helping		

Source: Adapted from U.S. Department of Labor, Employment Service, Training and Development Administration (1972), *Handbook for Analyzing Jobs* (Washington, D.C.: U.S. Government Printing Office), p. 73.

EXHIBIT 6-6   DOT Descriptions of Jobs

025.062-010 METEOROLOGIST (profess. & kin.)

Analyzes and interprets meteorological data gathered by surface and upper-air stations, satellites, and radar to prepare reports and forecasts for public and other users: Studies and interprets synoptic reports, maps, photographs, and prognostic charts to predict long and short range weather conditions. Issues weather information to media and other users over teletype machine or telephone. Prepares special forecasts and briefings for those involved in air and sea transportation, agriculture, fire prevention, and air-pollution control. Issues hurricane and severe storm warnings. May direct forecasting services at weather station. May conduct basic or applied research in meteorology. May establish and staff observation stations.

166.117-014 MANAGER, EMPLOYEE WELFARE (profess. & kin.) employee-service officer; manager, welfare.

Directs welfare activities for employees of stores, factories, and other industrial and commercial establishments: Arranges for physical examinations, first aid, and other medical attention. Arranges for installation and operation of libraries, lunchrooms, recreational facilities, and educational courses. Organizes dances, entertainment, and outings. Insures that lighting is sufficient, sanitary facilities are adequate and in good order, and machinery safeguarded. May visit workers' homes to observe their housing and general living conditions and recommend improvements if necessary. May assist employees in the solution of personal problems, such as recommending day nurseries for their children and counseling them on personality frictions or emotional maladjustments.

184.117-022 IMPORT-EXPORT AGENT (any ind.) foreign agent.

Coordinates activities of international traffic division of import-export agency and negotiates settlements between foreign and domestic shippers: Plans and directs flow of air and surface traffic moving to overseas destinations. Supervises workers engaged in receiving and shipping freight, documentation, waybilling, assessing charges, and collecting fees for shipments. Negotiates with domestic customers, as intermediary for foreign customers, to resolve problems and arrive at mutual agreements. Negotiates with foreign shipping interests to contract for reciprocal freight-handling agreements. May examine invoices and shipping manifests for conformity to tariff and customs regulations. May contact customs officials to effect release of incoming freight and resolve customs delays. May prepare reports of transactions to facilitate billing of shippers and foreign carriers.

187.167-094 MANAGER, DUDE RANCH (amuse. & rec.)

Directs operation of dude ranch: Formulates policy on advertising, publicity, guest rates, and credit. Plans recreational and entertainment activities, such as camping, fishing, hunting, horseback riding, and dancing. Directs activities of DUDE WRANGLERS (amuse. & rec.). Directs preparation and maintenance of financial records. Directs other activities, such as breeding, raising, and showing horses, mules, and livestock.

732.684-106 SHAPER, BASEBALL GLOVE (sports equip.) steamer and shaper.

Forms pocket, opens fingers, and smooths seams to shape baseball gloves, using heated forms, mallets, and hammers: Pulls glove over heated hand-shaped form to open and stretch finger linings. Pounds fingers and palm of glove with rubber mallet and ball-shaped hammer to smooth seams and bulges, and form glove pocket. Removes glove from form, inserts hand into glove, and strikes glove pocket with fist while examining glove visually and tactually to ensure comfortable fit.

---

ratings are assumed to be similar. For example, all jobs with 5, 6, 2 or 2, 0, 1 scores could be grouped together and treated in much the same way.[26]

Position Analysis Questionnaire

A structured questionnaire for quantitatively assessing jobs was developed by researchers at Purdue University and is called the **position analysis questionnaire (PAQ)**.[27] The PAQ contains 194 items (11 of these are shown in Exhibit 6–8). Because the questionnaire requires considerable experience and a high level of reading comprehension to complete properly, it is often filled out by a trained job analyst. For each item, the job analyst must decide whether it applies to a particular

---

EXHIBIT 6-7   Sample of Result of Functional Job Analysis

U.S. Department of Labor
Manpower Administration
(USTES)

JOB ANALYSIS SCHEDULE

1. Established Job Title _____ DOUGH MIXER _____

2. Ind. Assign _____ (bake prod.) _____

3. SIC Code(s) and Titles(s) _____ 12051 Bread and other bakery products _____

---

4. JOB SUMMARY:

Operates mixing machine to mix ingredients for straight and sponge
(yeast) doughs according to established formulas, directs other workers in
fermentation of dough, and cuts dough into pieces with hand cutter.

---

5. WORK PERFORMED RATINGS:

	D	P	(T)
Worker Functions	Data	People	Things
	5	6	2

Work Field _____ Cooking, Food Preparing _____

---

6. WORKER TRAITS RATINGS: (To be filled in by analyst)
    Training time required
    Aptitudes
    Temperaments
    Interests
    Physical Demands
    Environment Conditions

---

job. For example, measuring devices (item 6) plays a very substantial role (5) for the
job being analyzed in Exhibit 6–8.

The 194 items contained on the PAQ are placed into six major sections:

1. *Information input*. Where and how does job incumbent get job information?
2. *Mental processes*. What reasoning, decision-making, and planning processes are
    used to perform the job?
3. *Work output*. What physical activities and tools are used to perform the job?
4. *Relationship with other people*. What relationships with others are required to
    perform the job?
5. *Job contacts*. In what physical and social context is the job performed?
6. *Other job characteristics*. What activities, conditions, or characteristics other
    than those described in Section 1–5 are relevant?

EXHIBIT 6-8   Portions of a Completed Page from the Position Analysis Questionnaire

INFORMATION INPUT

1   INFORMATION INPUT

1.1   Sources of Job Information

Rate each of the following items in terms of
the extent to which it is used by the worker as
a source of information in performing his job.

	Extent of Use (U)
NA	Does not apply
1	Nominal/very infrequent
2	Occasional
3	Moderate
4	Considerable
5	Very substantial

1.1.1   Visual Sources of Job Information

1 | 4   Written materials (books, reports, office notes, articles, job instructions, signs, etc.)

2 | 2   Quantitative materials (materials which deal with quantities or amounts, such as graphs, accounts, specifications, tables of numbers, etc.)

3 | 1   Pictorial materials (pictures or picturelike materials used as *sources* of information, for example, drawings, blueprints, diagrams, maps, tracings, photographic films, x-ray films, TV pictures, etc.)

4 | 1   Patterns/related devices (templates, stencils, patterns, etc., used as *sources* of information when *observed* during use; do *not* include here materials described in item 3 above)

5 | 2   Visual displays (dials, gauges, signal lights, radarscopes, speedometers, clocks, etc.)

6 | 5   Measuring devices (rulers, calipers, tire pressure gauges, scales, thickness gauges, pipettes, thermometers, protractors, etc., used to obtain visual information about physical measurements; do *not* include here devices described in item 5 above)

7 | 4   Mechanical devices (tools, equipment, machinery, and other mechanical devices which are *sources* of information when *observed* during use or operation)

8 | 3   Materials in process (parts, materials, objects, etc., which are *sources* of information when being modified, worked on, or otherwise processed, such as bread dough being mixed, workpiece being turned in a lathe, fabric being cut, shoe being resoled, etc.)

9 | 4   Materials *not* in process (parts, materials, objects, etc., not in the process of being changed or modified, which are *sources* of information when being inspected, handled, packaged, distributed, or selected, etc., such as items or materials in inventory, storage, or distribution channels, items being inspected, etc.)

10 | 3   Features of nature (landscapes, fields, geological samples, vegetation, cloud formations, and other features of nature which are observed or inspected to provide information)

11 | 2   Man-made features of environment (structures, buildings, dams, highways, bridges, docks, railroads, and other "man-made" or altered aspects of the indoor or outdoor environment which are *observed* or *inspected* to provide job information, do not consider equipment, machines, etc., that an individual uses in his work, as covered by item 7)

Note: This exhibits 11 of the "information input" questions or elements. Other PAQ pages contain questions regarding mental processes, work output, relationships with others, job context, and other job characteristics.
Source: *Position Analysis Questionnaire*, Occupational Research Center, Department of Psychological Sciences, Purdue University. Position Analysis Questionnaire, copyright 1979 by Purdue Research Foundation, West Lafayette, Indiana 47807. Reprinted by permission.

Computerized programs are available for scoring PAQ ratings on the basis of seven dimensions—decision making, communication, social responsibilities, performing skilled activities, being physically active, operating vehicles and/or equipment, and processing information. These scores permit the development of profiles for jobs analyzed and the comparison of jobs.

Like other job analysis techniques, the PAQ has advantages and disadvantages. One of its biggest advantages is that the PAQ has been widely used and researched.

The available evidence indicates that it can be an effective technique for a variety of intended purposes.[28] It is reliable in that there is little variance among job analysts' ratings of the same jobs. It seems to be an effective way of establishing differences in ability requirements for jobs.[29] And, it also seems to be valid in that jobs rated higher with the PAQ prove to be those that are being paid higher compensation rates.

A major problem with the PAQ is its length. It requires time and patience to complete. In addition, since no specific work activities are described, behavioral activities performed in jobs may distort actual task differences in the jobs. For example, the profiles for a typist, belly dancer, and male disco dancer may be quite similar since all involve fine motor movements.[30] There is also some research that suggests that the PAQ is only capable of measuring job stereotypes.[31] If this is true, then the PAQ may be providing little more than common knowledge about a job. That is, ratings on the PAQ might represent information that makes up the job analyst's stereotype about the work in question rather than actual differences among jobs.

Management Positions Description Questionnaire

Conducting a job analysis for managerial jobs offers a significant challenge to the analyst because of the disparity across positions, levels in the hierarchy, and type of industry (for example, industrial, medical, government). An attempt to systematically analyze managerial jobs was conducted at Control Data Corporation. The result of the work is the **management position description questionnaire (MPDQ).**[32]

The MPDQ is a checklist of 208 items related to the concerns and responsibilities of managers. It is designed to be a comprehensive description of managerial work, and it is intended for use across most industrial settings. The latest version of the MPDQ is classified into 15 sections. Items were grouped into sections in order to reduce the time it requires to complete and to help with the interpretation of responses.[33]

1. General information
2. Decision making
3. Planning and organizing
4. Administering
5. Controlling
6. Supervising
7. Consulting and innovating
8. Contacts
9. Coordinating
10. Representing
11. Monitoring business indicators
12. Overall ratings
13. Knowledge, skills, and abilities
14. Organization chart
15. Comments and reactions

Section 8 (Contacts) appears in Exhibit 6–9. To complete this section of the MPDQ, the managers must consider which kinds of persons they communicate

EXHIBIT 6-9   Rating Internal and External Contacts Using the Management Position
Description Questionnaire (MPDQ)

To achieve organizational goals, managers and consultants may be required to communicate with employees at many levels within the corporation and with influential people outside the corporation.

The purposes of these contacts may include such functions as:

• Informing
• Receiving information
• Influencing
• Promoting
• Selling
• Directing
• Coordinating
• Integrating
• Negotiating

DIRECTIONS:

Describe the nature of your contacts by completing the charts on the opposite page as follows:

STEP 1

Mark an "X" in the box to the left of the kinds of individuals that represent your major contacts internal and external to Control Data Corporation.

STEP 2

For each contact checked, print a number between 0 and 4 in each column to indicate how significant a part of your position that PURPOSE is. (Remember to consider both its *importance* in light of all other position activities and its *frequency* of occurrence.)

0-**Definitely not** a part of the position.
1-A **minor** part of the position.
2-A **moderate** part of the position.
3-A **substantial** part of the position.
4-A **crucial** and **most significant** part of the position.

STEP 3

If you have any other contacts please elaborate on their nature and purpose below.

226 _____

_____
_____
_____
_____
_____
_____
_____
_____
_____

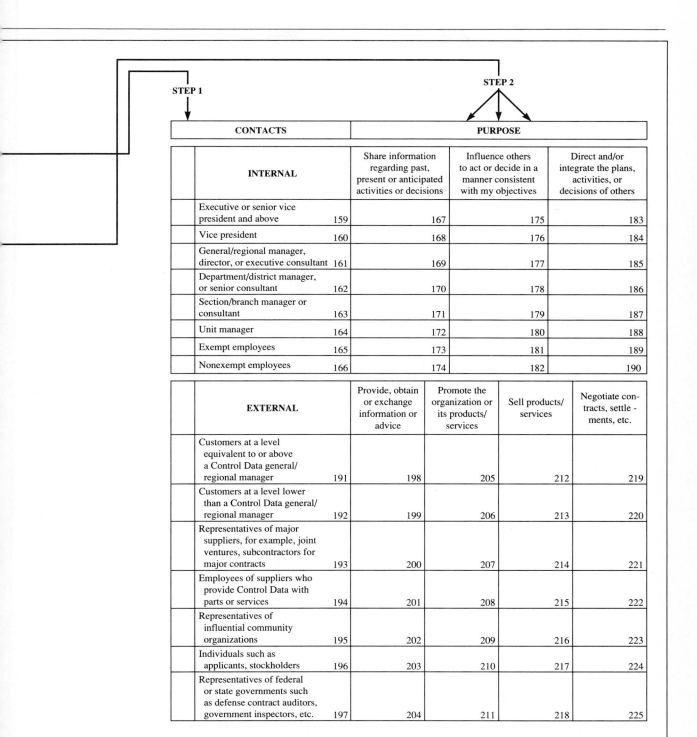

STEP 1

STEP 2

CONTACTS		PURPOSE		

INTERNAL		Share information regarding past, present or anticipated activities or decisions	Influence others to act or decide in a manner consistent with my objectives	Direct and/or integrate the plans, activities, or decisions of others
Executive or senior vice president and above	159	167	175	183
Vice president	160	168	176	184
General/regional manager, director, or executive consultant	161	169	177	185
Department/district manager, or senior consultant	162	170	178	186
Section/branch manager or consultant	163	171	179	187
Unit manager	164	172	180	188
Exempt employees	165	173	181	189
Nonexempt employees	166	174	182	190

EXTERNAL		Provide, obtain or exchange information or advice	Promote the organization or its products/ services	Sell products/ services	Negotiate contracts, settle-ments, etc.
Customers at a level equivalent to or above a Control Data general/ regional manager	191	198	205	212	219
Customers at a level lower than a Control Data general/ regional manager	192	199	206	213	220
Representatives of major suppliers, for example, joint ventures, subcontractors for major contracts	193	200	207	214	221
Employees of suppliers who provide Control Data with parts or services	194	201	208	215	222
Representatives of influential community organizations	195	202	209	216	223
Individuals such as applicants, stockholders	196	203	210	217	224
Representatives of federal or state governments such as defense contract auditors, government inspectors, etc.	197	204	211	218	225

with in order to do their job. These persons are both internal and external to the organization. For example, the executive vice president is an internal person while a customer is an external person. After the managers indicate which persons they communicate with, they must rate how important the various potential purposes of communication are with these persons. Thus, if sharing information with the executive vice president is *crucial* for a manager's job, then he or she would put an X under Step 1 in Exhibit 6–9 and a 4 in the rating box numbered "167" under Step 2.

Although FJA, the PAQ, and the MPDQ are all intended for use across a large number of jobs, many other quantitative job analysis methods are also receiving attention. A considerable amount of job analysis research is currently being conducted in Europe on alternative quantitative methods.[34] Many of these alternative methods are taking a microanalysis perspective on the problem of describing human work. For example, VERA (Verfahren zur Ermittlung von Regulationserfordernissen in der Arbeitstatigkeit)[35] represents a microanalytic approach that attempts to describe work in terms of sequences of subtasks. It is considered a microanalysis since each subtask is analyzed separately in terms of the technical processes utilized; tools, materials, and machines used; and the work units for which an employee is responsible.[36]

JOB DESCRIPTIONS AND JOB SPECIFICATIONS

As previously mentioned, the job description (see Exhibit 6–1) is one of the primary outputs provided by a systematic job analysis. It is a written description of what the job entails. While there is no standard format for a job description, almost all well-written ones will include information regarding:[37]

Job Title. A title of the job and other identifying information such as its wage and benefits classification.

Summary. A brief one- or two-sentence statement describing the purpose of the job and what outputs are expected from job incumbents.

Equipment. A clear statement of the tools, equipment, and information required for effectively performing the job.

Environment. A description of the working conditions of the job, the location of the job, and other relevant characteristics of the immediate work environment such as hazards and noise levels.

Activities. Includes a description of the job duties, responsibilities, and behaviors performed on the job. Also describes the social interactions associated with the work (for example, size of work group, amount of dependency in the work).

The job specification evolves from the job description. It addresses the question "What personal traits and experience are needed to perform the job effectively?" The job specification is especially useful for offering guidance for recruitment and selection. For example, suppose that you were looking for an HR professional to fill the position described in Exhibit 6–10. From the job specification, you would know that the successful applicant would have a college education and would already have at least six years of experience in HRM.

It is important to note that any trait or experience that is stated on the job specification should actually be required for effectively performing the job. That is,

---

EXHIBIT 6-10   Job Description of a Human Resource Manager

JOB TITLE: HUMAN   Department: HRM
          RESOURCE MANAGER   Date: Jan. 1, 1992

General Description of the Job

Performs responsible administrative work managing personnel activities of a large state agency or institution. Work involves responsibility for the planning and administration of an HRM program that
includes recruitment, examination, selection, evaluation, appointment, promotion, transfer, and recommended change of status of agency employees, and a system of communication for disseminating
necessary information to workers. Works under general supervision, exercising initiative and independent judgment in the performance of assigned tasks.

Job Activities

Participates in overall planning and policymaking to provide effective and uniform personnel services.
Communicates policy through organization levels by bulletin, meetings, and personal contact.
Interviews applicants, evaluates qualifications, classifies applications.
Recruits and screens applicants to fill vacancies and reviews applications of qualified persons.
Confers with supervisors on personnel matters, including placement problems, retention or release of
    probationary employees, transfers, demotions, and dismissals of permanent employees.
Supervises administration of tests.
Initiates personnel training activities and coordinates these activities with work of officials and super-
    visors.
Establishes effective service rating system, trains unit supervisors in making employee evaluations.
Maintains employee personnel files.
Supervises a group of employees directly and through subordinates.
Performs related work as assigned.

General Qualification Requirements
    Experience and Training
    Should have considerable experience in area of HRM administration. Six-year minimum.
Education
    Graduation from a four-year college or university, with major work in human resources, business
        administration, or industrial psychology.
Knowledge, Skills, and Abilities
    Considerable knowledge of principles and practices of HRM selection and assignment of personnel;
        job evaluation.
Responsibility
    Supervises a department of three HRM professionals, one clerk, and one secretary.

---

an organization must be able to show that the job specification actually describes
characteristics that are job related. This is especially true since federal and state
legislation has placed new emphasis on job descriptions and job specifications. For
example, if an organization is suspected of violating the Equal Pay Act, it will
conduct a compensation audit. The purpose of this analysis would be to determine if
the jobs in question are equal in terms of ability, effort, responsibility, and working
conditions.[38] Information about these factors should be contained in the job descriptions and job specifications. Therefore, they will be consulted to determine
compliance with the law.

   In addition, to the extent that job specifications (for example, height, weight,
educational requirements) are not essential for effective job performance, they may
be associated with indirect violations of Title VII of the 1964 Civil Rights Act.

Suppose for a moment that an organization has a minimum height requirement of 5 feet 10 inches for a job. Clearly, such a requirement might exclude a significant proportion of female applicants. If such a requirement cannot be shown to be essential for effective performance, then the organization might indeed have violated Title VII.

It is also clear that job analysis is considered a necessary process for developing legally defensible job descriptions. While there is no single job analysis process that will always be preferred by the courts, one absolutely essential ingredient seems to be direct consultation and input from people actually performing the job.[39] Thus, regardless of the method or methods of job analysis an HR manager chooses, job incumbents must be given ample opportunity to express their views of the work.

JOB DESIGN

Once a thorough job analysis has been conducted and there are high-quality job descriptions and job specifications available, an organization can use this information for designing or redesigning jobs. This information is very useful for structuring job elements, duties, and tasks in a manner that will help to achieve optimal performance and satisfaction.

There is, however, no one best way to design a job. Different situations call for different arrangements of job characteristics. In addition, approaches to job design place different emphasis on performance and satisfaction as desired outcomes. In other words, certain methods of job design are primarily interested in improving performance; others are more concerned with satisfaction. Thus, it is unlikely that any one approach will fully satisfy all of the goals of a manager. This means that the choice of job design will involve making trade-offs based on the more critical needs of the organization.[40]

Perspectives on the design of work can be classified into four major categories: the perceptual/motor approach, the biological approach, the mechanistic approach, and the motivational approach.[41] Both the perceptual/motor approach and the biological approach have their roots in human factors engineering. Their major focus is on the integration of human-machine systems. As such, they emphasize equipment design and the proper match between machines and operators.

The two remaining approaches more clearly highlight the potential trade-offs that must frequently be made by organizations when making job design decisions. They are also the two that have received the most attention in the management literature. The mechanistic approach is best exemplified by Taylor's scientific management and the motivational approach by job enrichment.

Scientific Management and the Mechanistic Approach

Job design was a central issue in F. W. Taylor's model of scientific management. His use of job design is an excellent example of the rational approach and shows how certain job design perspectives focus more heavily on productivity than on satisfaction. In 1911, he stated:

Perhaps the most prominent single element in modern scientific management is the task idea. The work of every workman is fully planned out by the management at least one day in advance, and each man received in most cases complete written instructions, describing in detail the task which he is to accomplish. . . . This task specifies not only what is to be done but how it is to be done and the exact time allowed for doing it.[42]

The work of Taylor and the principles of scientific management initiated a great deal of interest in systematically studying the structure of jobs. The emphasis was clearly on structuring jobs so that they were broken down into simple, repetitive tasks. Once learned, these tasks could be done quickly and efficiently.

Although the principles of scientific management were formally introduced in the early 1900s and many current job design methods criticize the use of repetitive task structure, many of the principles are still relevant today. Among these are recommendations stemming from Taylor's scientific management such as:

- Work should be scientifically studied (note: this is what job analysis attempts to do).
- Work should be arranged so that workers can be efficient.
- Employees selected for work should be matched to the demands of the job (note: job descriptions and job specifications used in recruitment and selection should achieve this).
- Employees should be trained to perform the job.
- Monetary compensation should be tied directly to performance and should be used to reward the performance of employees.

Many managers find the scientific management approach to job design appealing because these kinds of recommendations point toward increasing organizational performance. It is assumed that the specialization and routine nature of jobs designed according to scientific management principles will lead to higher levels of output and require minimal training before employees are able to master the work.

Despite the appeal of these potential advantages, research has found that repetitive, highly specialized work can lead to employee dissatisfaction.[43] Thus, the gains in efficiency that scientific management may offer can be offset by losses in satisfaction and higher levels of absenteeism and turnover.

Early strategies for overcoming some of the problems associated with jobs designed according to scientific management focused on job enlargement.[44] Job enlargement attempts to increase work satisfaction by giving employees a greater variety of things to do. The expansion of the work is, however, considered horizontal since the employees are not given more responsibility or authority in decision making. Rather, they are merely allowed to do a greater number of tasks. Thus, an enlarged job is not as specialized or routine as a job designed according to scientific management but it may not be any more meaningful.

Job Enrichment: A Motivational Approach to Job Design

In the past two decades, much work has been directed at changing jobs in more meaningful ways than job enlargement was able to do. Rather than simply increasing the variety of tasks performed by an employee, **job enrichment** tries to design jobs in ways that help incumbents satisfy their needs for growth, recognition, and responsibility. Thus, enrichment differs from enlargement since the job is expanded vertically; employees are given responsibility that might have previously been part of a supervisor's job.[45]

The notion of enhancing employees' need satisfaction as a way of designing jobs comes from Frederick Herzberg's two-factor theory of work motivation. His basic idea is that employees will be motivated by jobs that enhance their feelings of self-worth.[46]

EXHIBIT 6-11   The Job Characteristics Model of Work Motivation

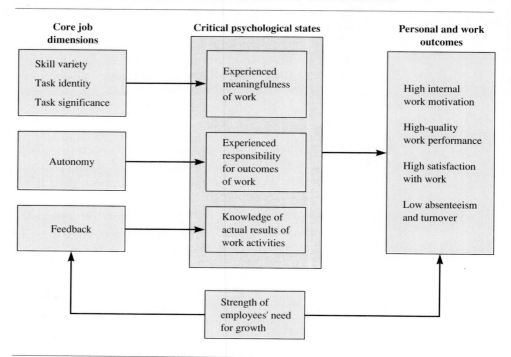

Source: Adapted from J. Richard Hackman and R. G. Oldham, (August 1976), "Motivation through the Design of Work: Test of a Theory," *Organizational Behavior and Human Performance*, p. 256.

Although there are many different approaches to job enrichment, the **job characteristics model** is one of the most widely publicized.[47] This model is depicted in Exhibit 6–11. It shows that for a job to lead to desired outcomes it must possess certain "core job dimensions." These include:

Skill variety. The degree to which the job requires a variety of different activities in carrying out the work, which involves the use of a number of an individual's skills and talents.

Task identity. The degree to which the job requires completion of a "whole" and identifiable piece of work — that is, doing a job from beginning to end with a visible outcome.

Task significance. The degree to which the job has a substantial impact on the lives or work of other people — whether in the immediate organization or in the external environment.

Autonomy. The degree to which the job provides substantial freedom, independence, and discretion to the individual in scheduling the work and in determining the procedures to be used in carrying it out.

Feedback. The degree to which carrying out the work activities required by the job results in the individual's obtaining direct and clear information about the effectiveness of his or her performance.

If these core dimensions are present in a job, they are expected to create three critical psychological states in job incumbents.[48] The key psychological states that are necessary for motivation and satisfaction are:

1. *Experienced meaningfulness.* The degree to which the job incumbent experiences work as important, valuable, and worthwhile.
2. *Experienced responsibility.* The extent to which the job incumbent feels personally responsible and accountable for the results of the work performed.
3. *Knowledge of results.* The understanding that a job incumbent receives about how effectively he or she is performing the job.

The more these three states are experienced, the more the job incumbent will feel internal work motivation. To the extent that these three states are important to the job incumbent, he or she will then be motivated to perform well and will be satisfied with the job.

As presented in Exhibit 6–11, three job dimensions — **skill variety, task identity,** and **task significance** all contribute to a sense of meaningfulness. **Autonomy** is directly related to feelings of responsibility. The more control job incumbents feel they have over their job, the more that they will feel responsible. **Feedback** is related to knowledge of results. For job incumbents to be internally motivated, they must have a sense of the quality of their performance. This sense comes from feedback.

The job characteristics model describes the relationships that are predicted to exist among four sets of factors — core job dimensions, psychological states, personal and work-related outcomes, and need strength. Since different people have different capabilities and needs, it is important to be aware of the potential for individual differences to moderate the linkages shown in Exhibit 6–11. If, for example, a person does not have a strong need for personal growth, then job enrichment will probably have less of an effect than for a person who values personal growth.

Work behavior and individual job incumbent feelings appear to be more positive where there is a fit between the job and the person. Exhibit 6–12 depicts the results of a match and a mismatch between an individual and the job.[49] The managerial implication of Exhibit 6–12 is that not all jobs should be designed to be high on the core job dimensions of job enrichment, and that the personal traits and characteristics of the persons holding the job must be considered. In other words, Exhibit 6–12 suggests that not all persons will respond positively to an enriched job.

It is also important for managers to realize that adding job enrichment might change the skill requirements for the job. Thus, not everyone will necessarily be able to perform the enriched job, especially without additional training. And, it may be necessary for the organization to adjust its compensation rates for the enriched job because of the higher skill levels required.[50]

Before any job enrichment effort is undertaken, at least two actions should be completed. First, the job in question needs to be thoroughly understood. It may be that enrichment isn't feasible because of costs or other technological constraints. Second, individual preferences about enriched work should be considered. Do the employees want the work to be enriched? It should be obvious that answers to questions related to both of these issues can be greatly facilitated with accurate job descriptions and job specifications.

EXHIBIT 6-12   Results of Match/Mismatch of Job and Employee

Degree of Job Enrichment	Intensity of Desire for Job Enrichment	
	High	**Low**
Enriched	"Match" 1. Performance quality is high. 2. Satisfaction is high. 3. Absenteeism and turnover are low.	"Mismatch" 1. Employee is overwhelmed and possibly confused. 2. Performance is poor. 3. Absenteeism and turnover are high.
Simple	"Mismatch" 1. Employees feel underutilized. 2. Job satisfaction is low. 3. Absenteeism and turnover are high.	"Match" 1. Employees can be motivated by pay incentives in the absence of intrinsic motivation. 2. Performance is high.

Job Enrichment in the United States

Numerous examples of job enrichment programs developed at organizations in the United States can be found. Most programs share characteristics, such as the programs that were implemented at Prudential Life Insurance and General Foods.

Prudential Life Insurance's Job Enrichment Program   The chief executive officer of Prudential decided that all jobs at Prudential should be made as interesting as possible. Each unit was charged with redesigning its own jobs with special attention to be paid to enrichment. The workers redesigned their jobs. The results were impressive:

. 57 percent of the units reported improvements in employee attitudes; only 4 percent indicated a deterioration.

. 31 percent of the units reported a decrease in turnover; only 5 percent reported an increase.

. 93 percent of the units indicated that the abilities of workers were being more fully utilized.[51]

General Foods' Topeka Plant Job Enrichment Program   When General Foods constructed a new plant to manufacture pet foods, it designed the plant so that concepts of job enrichment could be utilized in a variety of ways. Management systematically structured jobs so they would involve maximum variety, autonomy, and feedback.[52] The early results in the new plant were outstanding:

. Quality control improved.

. Turnover was down.

. Job attitudes were better than at other plants.

. Cost savings amounted to about $2 million per year.

These successes, however, began to fade about five or six years after the plant was built. One former employee noted:

Creating a system is different from maintaining it. There were pressures almost from the inception, and not because the system didn't work. The basic reason was power. We flexed in the face of corporate policy. People like stable states. This system has to be changing or it will die.

In fact, 70 workers ran the entire Topeka operation. The need for middle managers in the plant was eliminated. The result of the new plant arrangement was a power struggle of managers versus workers. Lyman Ketchum (the manager who had thought up the redesign experiment) was fired.

The Prudential experiment was a success, while the Topeka plant experiment with job enrichment resulted in mixed findings — some successes and some failures. These two cases illustrate that job enrichment, or any redesign strategy, is not always successful. Some of the common problems with job enrichment reported in the management and HRM literature include:

1. Technological constraints — the job simply can't be enriched because of machine constraints.
2. Costs — the costs of starting and sustaining job enrichment for tools, training, and consultants are often high.
3. Failure to recognize job incumbent preferences — not everyone wants an enriched job.
4. Mickey Mouse changes — changes in core dimensions are so minor that they have no impact.
5. Managerial and union resistance — managers are sometimes threatened by increased subordinate autonomy. The union also may feel threatened because it sees its power base shrinking.[53]

Job Design for the 1990s: The Global Challenge

Throughout Europe and Asia, the concept of job design is again being revolutionized. Many of the basic elements of scientific management have been replaced with an emphasis on worker autonomy, added decision-making responsibility, and skill variety. Although similar in nature, this new form of job design goes beyond traditional job enrichment programs. Work teams that are responsible for an entire assembly process are rapidly replacing the traditional assembly line for manufacturing everything from automobiles to jet engines for the world's most advanced aircraft. Equally important to this revolution is an acknowledgement that changes in the design of work at lower levels must be supported by changes in the basic structure of the organization itself.[54]

The focus on teamwork and autonomy is not, however, just for humanitarian reasons. Experts agree that the superiority of the Japanese automobile industry should not be attributed to technology or engineering but rather to the way that management structures the workplace and interacts with its employees. The same conclusions are being reached in Europe. For example, at the most technologically advanced automobile assembly line in Europe, Volvo was experiencing a 300 percent annual turnover rate. In response to this, the company opened a new manufacturing plant with no assembly lines and no repetitive work tasks. Instead, cars are built by teams of employees in small, self-contained areas called "workshops." According to Volvo officials, turnover has been dramatically reduced and profits are rising.[55]

Type of Organization	Has a Permanent Job Analysis Unit	Use of JAIF-Type Instrument	Formal Job Analysis Program	Observation Method Used	Interview Method Used	Questionnaire Method Used	Diary/Log Method Used
1. Large size, low complexity, high stability		X	X		X	X	
2. Medium size, low complexity, high stability		X	X		X	X	
3. Small size, low complexity, high stability		X	X		X	X	X
4. Medium size, moderate complexity, moderate stability	X	X	X	X	X	X	
5. Large size, high complexity, low stability	X	X	X	X	X	X	
6. Medium size, high complexity, low stability	X	X	X	X	X	X	
7. Small size, high complexity, low stability		X	X	X	X	X	X

CAREER CHALLENGE
(*concluded*)

What do you now think about Tim Huggins's job analysis process? Do you now see why some type of training in job analysis is required? Tim really lacked sufficient training, and this lack was clearly revealed as the process got out of hand. Using questionnaires requires preparation and careful initial steps. A trained job analyst knows that distribution of questionnaires without an explanation is bound to set off negative feelings. Tim failed to plan thoroughly what he wanted to do. He was a new boss, and this alone was threatening to many people. A new person has to establish rapport with employees before changing things. In the case of Sprowl Manufacturing, Tim's haste and poor preparation have now reached a boiling point. He needs to backtrack and slow down. Perhaps the distribution of memos, open discussions with informal leaders, and using the expertise of trained job analysts can improve the atmosphere at Sprowl.

What would you advise him to do about job analysis at this point?

General Motors was so impressed with the success of its foreign competition that the new Saturn assembly plant in Spring Hill, Tennessee, has duplicated many of the most important job design features used by Europe and Japan. Prior to construction of the plant, a team of Saturn workers visited 160 different corporations worldwide to see how their success had been achieved. Among these were competitors such as Volvo, Kawasaki, and Nissan. Most of the innovations that were adopted emphasize the team concept in job design.[56]

Job design is a process that influences the behavior and attitude of a job incumbent. The job is such an important foundation of any organization's effectiveness that it needs to be clearly understood and designed in a way that allows for both productivity and satisfaction. Any given job doesn't exist in a vacuum. They are dynamic and changing. Consequently, job analysis is an important technique that can capture and help to change the nature of jobs so that the best job design decisions can be made and implemented.

HR managers are involved in both job analysis and job design decisions. Exhibit 6–13 provides recommendations for the use of job analysis and job design for model organizations.

SUMMARY

This chapter has emphasized the major role that job analysis plays in HRM activities and programs. Each part of the diagnostic HRM model is in some way affected by job analysis. The job is the major building block of an organization. Therefore, it is essential that each characteristic of the job's presence in an organization is clearly understood.

To summarize the major points covered in this chapter:

1. There are six sequential steps in job analysis, starting with examining the total organization and fit of jobs and concluding with the preparation of a job specification (see Exhibit 6–1).

2. The uses of job analysis information seem endless. Strategic planning, recruitment, selection, training, compensation, and job design actions all benefit immensely from job analysis information.

3. Job analysis is not for amateurs to conduct. Training is required.

4. Before conducting a job analysis, organization and process charts should be consulted to acquire an overview of the organization.

5. Four general job analysis techniques can be used separately or in combination: observation, interviews, questionnaires, and job incumbent diary/logs.

6. The multimethod approach to job analysis uses a combination of these four general methods. It is a comprehensive approach and is currently viewed very favorably from a legal perspective.

7. Functional job analysis (FJA) is used to describe the nature of jobs, prepare job descriptions, and provide details on employee job specifications. The job is described in terms of data, people, and things.

8. The *Dictionary of Occupational Titles* is a listing of over 20,000 jobs on the basis of occupational code, title, industry.

9. The position analysis questionnaire (PAQ) is a 194-item structured instrument used to quantitatively assess jobs on the basis of decision making, communication/social responsibilities, performing skilled activities, being physically active, operating vehicles and/or equipment, and processing information.

10. The management position questionnaire (MPDQ) is a checklist of 208 items that assesses the concerns and responsibilities of managers.

11. Job design involves structuring job elements, duties, and tasks to achieve optimal performance and satisfaction.

12. Job design was a concern of F. W. Taylor, the famous industrial engineer and father of what is called *scientific management*.

13. Job enrichment involves designing jobs so that job incumbent needs for growth, recognition, and responsibility are satisfied.

14. There is no one best way to design jobs. An organization will be forced to make trade-offs based on its critical needs since some methods of job design are better able to address problems of productivity and others are better able to address problems of satisfaction.

KEY TERMS

autonomy	196	job characteristics model	196
feedback	196	job description	192
functional job analysis (FJA)	184	job enrichment	195
job	173	job family	173
job analysis	172	job specification	192
job analysis information format(JAIF)	180	management position description questionnaire (MPDQ)	189

QUESTIONS FOR REVIEW AND DISCUSSION

1. What are the six steps in the job analysis process?
2. Job analysis is often referred to as the "cornerstone" of HRM. Do you agree? Why?
3. How might job analysis be helpful to an organization that is being sued for sex discrimination in promotion?
4. What are the advantages of using the multimethod approach to job analysis?
5. What core information should be included in most job descriptions and job specifications?
6. Briefly describe four approaches to job design.
7. What are the strengths and weaknesses of the mechanistic and motivational approaches to job design? Which one is more focused on employee satisfaction?
8. Describe the major components of the job characteristics model of job enrichment.
9. Should all jobs be enriched? Why?
10. What characteristics of jobs and work are currently being emphasized by job design experts in Europe and Japan?

NOTES

1 Edward T. Cornelius (1988), "Practical Findings from Job Analysis Research," in *The Job Analysis Handbook for Business, Industry, and Government*, vol. 1, ed. Sidney Gael (New York: John Wiley & Sons), pp. 48–68.

2 Bureau of Intergovernmental Personnel Programs (1973), "Job Analysis: Developing and Documenting Data" (Washington, D.C.: U.S. Government Printing Office).

3 Jai Ghorpade (1988), *Job Analysis: A Handbook for the Human Resource Director* (Englewood Cliffs, N.J.: Prentice-Hall), p. 2.

4 Jai Ghorpade and Thomas J. Atchison (Summer 1980), "The Concept of Job Analysis: A Review and Some Suggestions," *Public Personnel Management Journal*, pp. 134–44; and Ronald A. Ash and Edward L. Levine (November–December 1980), "A Framework for Evaluating Job Analysis Methods," *Personnel*, pp. 53–59.

5 Mary G. Miner and John B. Miner (1979), *Uniform Guidelines on Employee Selection Procedures* (Washington, D.C.: The Bureau of National Affairs).

6 Section 14.C.2 of the EEOC's *Uniform Guidelines on Employee Selection Procedures*, 1978.

7 James W. Hunt (1984), *The Law of the Workplace* (Washington, D.C.: Bureau of National Affairs).

8 Duane E. Thompson and Toni A. Thompson (Winter 1982), "Court Standards for Job Analysis in Test Validation," *Personnel Psychology*, pp. 865–74.

9 Gerard P. Panaro (1990), *Employment Law Manual* (Boston: Warren, Gorham & Lamont), pp. 3.27–3.33.

10 John E. Butler, Gerald R. Ferris, and Nancy K. Napier (1991), *Strategy and Human Resources Management* (Cincinnati: South-Western Publishing).

11 Benjamin Schneider and A. M. Konz (Spring 1989), "Strategic Job Analysis," *Human Resource Management*, pp. 51–63.

12 Erich P. Prien (Summer 1977), "The Functions of Job Analysis in Content Validation," *Personnel Psychology*, pp. 167–74. The "Otis (1953)" reference in the quote is in J. L. Otis (1953), "Whose Criterion?" Presidential address to Division 14 of the American Psychological Association.

13 Richard L. Henderson (1989), *Compensation Management: Rewarding Performance*, 5th ed. (Englewood Cliffs, N.J.: Prentice-Hall), p. 100.

14 John G. Veres III, Toni S. Locklear, and Ronald R. Sims (1990), "Job Analysis in Practice: A Brief Review of the Role of Job Analysis in Human Resources Management," in *Human Resource Management: Perspectives and Issues*, 2nd ed., eds. Gerald R. Ferris, Kendrith M. Rowland, M. Ronald Buckley (Boston: Allyn & Bacon), pp. 86–89.

15 Henderson, *Compensation Management*, pp. 138–39.

16 L. Friedman and Robert J. Harvey (Winter 1986), "Can Recruiters with Reduced Job Description Information Provide Accurate Position Analysis Questionnaire (PAQ) Ratings?" *Personnel Psychology*, pp. 779–89.

17 Patrick R. Conley and Paul R. Sackett (August 1987), "Effects of Using High- versus Low-Performing Job Incumbents as Sources of Job Analysis Information," *Journal of Applied Psychology*, pp. 434–37; and Patrick M. Wright, Chris Anderson, Kari Tolzman, and Tom Helton (August 1990), "An Examination of the Relationship between Employee Performance and Job Analysis Ratings," in *Academy of Management Best Papers Proceedings*, eds. Lawrence Jauch and Jerry Wall (San Francisco: Academy of Management), pp. 299–303.

18 Robert J. Harvey and Susana R. Lozada-Larsen (August 1988), "Influence of Amount of Job Descriptive Information on Job Analysis Rating Accuracy," *Journal of Applied Psychology*, pp. 457–61.

19 Edward L. Levine, Ronald A. Ash, Hardy Hall, and Frank Sistrunk (June 1983), "Evaluation of Job Analysis Methods by Experienced Job Analysts," *Academy of Management Journal*, pp. 339–48.

20 Edward L. Levine, James N. Thomas, and Frank Sistruck (1988), "Selecting a Job Analysis Approach," in *The Job Analysis Handbook for Business, Industry, and Government*, vol. 1, ed. Sidney Gael (New York: John Wiley & Sons), pp. 339–52.

21 Schneider and Konz, "Strategic Job Analysis," pp. 53–54.

22 Veres, Locklear, and Sims, "Job Analysis in Practice," p. 92.

23 Sidney A. Fine (1988), "Functional Job Analysis," in *The Job Analysis Handbook for Business, Industry, and Government*, vol. 2, ed. Sidney Gael (New York: John Wiley & Sons), pp. 1019–35.

24 U.S. Department of Labor (1977), *Dictionary of Occupational Titles*, 4th ed. (Washington, D.C.: U.S. Government Printing Office).

25 Pamela S. Cain and Donald J. Treiman (June 1981), "The *Dictionary of Occupational Titles* as a source of Occupational Data," *American Sociological Review*, pp. 353–78.

26 Fine, "Functional Job Analysis," p. 1029.

27 Ernest J. McCormick, Paul R. Jeanneret, and Robert C. Mecham (August 1972), "A Study of Job Characteristics and Job Dimensions as Based on the Position Analysis Questionnaire (PAQ)," *Journal of Applied Psychology*, pp. 347–68; and Ernest J. McCormick, Paul R. Jeanneret, and Robert C. Mechan (1978), *User's Manual for the Position Analysis Questionnaire System II* (West Lafayette, Ind.: Purdue University Press).

28 Ernest J. McCormick, Angelo S. DeNisi, and James B. Shaw (February 1979), "Use of the Position Analysis Questionnaire for Establishing the Job Component Validity of Tests," *Journal of Applied Psychology*, pp. 51–56.

[29] Robert C. Carter and Robert J. Biersner (1987), "Job Requirements Derived from the Position Analysis Questionnaire and Validated Using Military Aptitude Test Scores," *Journal of Occupational Psychology*, pp. 311–21.

[30] Wayne F. Cascio (1989), *Managing Human Resources: Productivity, Quality of Work Life, Profits*, 2nd ed. (New York: McGraw-Hill), p. 129.

[31] Angelo S. DeNisi, Edwin T. Cornelius III, and Allyn G. Blencoe (May 1987), "Further Investigation of Common Knowledge Effects on Job Analysis Ratings," *Journal of Applied Psychology*, pp. 262–68; and Robert J. Harvey and Theodore L. Hayes (Summer 1986), "Monte Carlo Baselines for Interrater Reliability Correlations Using the Position Analysis Questionnaire, *Personnel Psychology*, pp. 345–57.

[32] Walter W. Tornow and Patrick R. Pinto (August 1976), "The Development of a Managerial Job Taxonomy: A System for Describing, Classifying, and Evaluating Executive Positions, *Journal of Applied Psychology*, pp. 410–18.

[33] Ronald C. Page (1988), "Management Position Description Questionnaire," in *The Job Analysis Handbook for Business, Industry, and Government*, vol. 2, ed. Sidney Gael (New York: John Wiley & Sons), pp. 860–79.

[34] K. Landau and Walter Rohmert (1989), *Recent Developments in Job Analysis* (London: Taylor and Francis).

[35] "Instrument to Identify Regulation Requirements in Industrial Work."

[36] W-G. Weber and R. Oesterreich (1989), "VERA Microanalysis: Applied to a Flexible Manufacturing System" in *Recent Developments in Job Analysis*, eds. K. Landau and W. Rohmert (London: Taylor and Francis), pp. 91–100.

[37] Ghorpade, *Job Analysis*, pp. 93–134.

[38] Philip C. Grant (February 1988), "What Use Is a Job Description?" *Personnel Journal*, pp. 44–53; and Frederick S. Hills and Thomas J. Bergmann (1987), "Conducting an 'Equal Pay for Equal Work' Audit," in *New Perspectives on Compensation*, eds. David B. Balkin and Luis R. Gomez-Mejia (Englewood Cliffs, N.J.: Prentice- Hall), pp. 80–89.

[39] Panaro, *Employment Law Manual*, p. 3.28.

[40] Michael A. Campion (August 1988), "Interdisciplinary Approaches to Job Design: A Constructive Replication with Extensions," *Journal of Applied Psychology*, pp. 467–81; and Michael A. Campion and Paul W. Thayer (Spring 1987), "Job Design: Approaches, Outcomes, and Trade-Offs," *Organizational Dynamics*, pp. 66–79.

[41] Michael A. Campion and Gina M. Sanborn (1991), "Job Design," in *Handbook of Industrial Engineering*, 2nd ed., ed. G. Salvendy (New York, John Wiley & Sons).

[42] Frederick W. Taylor (1911), *The Principles of Scientific Management* (New York: Harper & Row), p. 21.

[43] David A. Nadler, Richard L. Hackman, and Edward E. Lawler III (1979), *Managing Organizational Behavior* (Boston: Little, Brown), p. 79.

[44] Ricky W. Griffin (1982), *Task Design: An Integrative Approach* (Glenview, Ill.: Scott, Foresman), p. 21.

[45] Griffin, *Task Design*, pp. 31–34.

[46] Frederick Herzberg, B. Mausner, and B. Snyderman (1959), *The Motivation to Work* (New York: John Wiley & Sons).

[47] J. Richard Hackman (1976), "Work Design," in *Improving Life at Work*, eds. J. Richard Hackman and J. L. Suttle (Santa Monica, Calif.: Goodyear Publishing), pp. 96–162.

[48] J. Richard Hackman and Greg R. Oldham (August 1976), "Motivation through the Design of Work: Test of a Theory," *Organizational Behavior and Human Performance*, pp. 250–79; and J. Richard Hackman, Greg R. Oldham, R. Janson, and K. Purdy (Summer 1975), "A New Strategy for Job Enrichment," *California Management Review*, pp. 57–71.

[49] John P. Wanous (Summer 1976), "Who Wants Job Enrichment?" *S.A.M. Advanced Management Journal*, pp. 15–22.

50 Michael A. Campion and Chris J. Berger (Autumn 1990), "Conceptual Integration and Empirical Test of Job Design and Compensation Relationships," *Personnel Psychology*, pp. 525–54; and Michael A. Campion and Carol L. McClelland (April 1991), "Interdisciplinary Examination of the Costs and Benefits of Enlarged Jobs: A Job Design Quasi-Experiment," *Journal of Applied Psychology*, forthcoming.

51 James O'Toole (1981), *Making America Work* (New York: Continuum), pp. 67–68.

52 Richard E. Walton (Winter 1978), "Teaching an Old Dog New Tricks," *Wharton Magazine*, pp. 38–48.

53 M. Fein (Winter 1974), "Job Enrichment: A Revolution," *Sloan Management Review*, pp. 69–88; and Edwin A. Locke, D. Sirota, and A. D. Wolfson (December 1976), "An Experimental Case Study of the Successes and Failures of Job Enrichment in a Government Agency," *Journal of Applied Psychology*, pp. 701–11.

54 Bjorn Gustavsen and Lajos Hethy (1989), "New Forms of Work Organization: An Overview," in *New Forms of Work Organization in Europe*, eds. Peter Grootings, Bjorn Gustavsen, and Lajos Hethy (New Brunswick, N.J.: Transaction Publishers), pp. 1–27.

55 William E. Nothdurft (September 1990), "How to Produce Work-Ready Workers," *Across the Board*, pp. 47–52.

56 S. C. Gwynne (October 29, 1990), "The Right Stuff," *Time*, pp. 74–84.

EXERCISE 6–1   Conducting a Job Analysis

· · · · ·

Objective   This exercise is designed to permit students to become familiar with the U.S. Department of Labor method and form for conducting a functional job analysis.

SET UP THE EXERCISE

1. Reread the discussion of functional job analysis (FJA) in the chapter.

2. Secure a copy of the *Handbook for Analyzing Jobs* (U.S. Government: Department of Labor). Your school or local library will have a copy.

3. Set up groups of four or five students. After reading the *Handbook* on job analysis, your instructor will assign the following jobs — one to each group:

   A. Police officer   F. Prison warden
   B. Lathe operator   G. Military officer
   C. Computer programmer   H. Radio disc jockey
   D. Movie stunt artist   I. Tennis coach
   E. Airplane pilot   J. Operating room nurse

4. Complete the job analysis form for the assigned job. Meet with your group to discuss similarities and differences in the job analysis.

A Learning Note

This exercise will illustrate the difficulty in conducting a job analysis and in reaching a consensus among analysts.

1. ESTABLISH JOB TITLE _____

2. JOB SUMMARY:

3. WORK PERFORMED RATINGS

	D	P	T
Worker functions	Data	People	Things

    Work Field _____

4. WORKER TRAITS RATINGS

    GED   1 2 3 4 5 6 __ __ __ __ __ __ __ __ __

    SVP   1 2 3 4 5 6 7 8 9

    Aptitudes   G __ V __ N __ S __ P __ Q __ K __ F __ M __ E __ C __

    Temperaments D F I J M P R S T V

    Interests   1a 1b 2a 2b 3a 3b 4a 4b 5a 5b

    Phys. demands S L M H V 2 3 4 5 6

    Environ. cond. 1) B 2 3 4 5 6 7

5. GENERAL EDUCATION

    a. Elementary _____ High school _____ Courses _____

    b. College _____ Courses _____

6. VOCATIONAL PREPARATION

    a. College _____ Courses _____
        _____

    b. Vocational education _____ Courses _____
        _____

    c. Apprenticeship _____
        _____

    d. In-plant training _____
        _____

    e. On-the-job training _____

    f. Performance on other jobs _____

7. EXPERIENCE _____

8. ORIENTATION _____

9. LICENSES, etc. _____

10. RELATION TO OTHER JOBS AND WORKERS

    Promotion: From _____ To _____

    Transfers: From _____ To _____

    Supervision received _____

    Supervision given _____
    _____

11. MACHINES, TOOLS, EQUIPMENT, AND WORK AIDS

12. MATERIALS AND PRODUCTS

13. DESCRIPTION OF TASKS

14. DEFINITION OF TERMS

15. GENERAL COMMENTS

RECRUITMENT

· · · · · · ·

LEARNING OBJECTIVES

After studying this chapter, you should be able to:

· · ·

Discuss how to develop an effective recruiting program for an organization

· · ·

Describe the recruiting process: who does it, how they do it, and where they find recruits

· · ·

Define what is meant by a realistic job preview

· · ·

Identify typical flaws that college students find in recruiters

· · ·

Discuss different strategies that organizations might use to recruit blue-collar, white-collar, managerial, technical, and professional applicants

CAREER CHALLENGE

Clark Kirby is just entering the office of the vice president of human resource management, Lewis Yates. Clark has worked for Gunther Manufacturing for 10 years, in Los Angeles. After a short management training program, Clark spent almost two years as operating supervisor in a plant. After that, a position opened up in the HR department. Clark had majored in personnel at California State University at Los Angeles and wanted to try HRM work.

He moved up in the department headquarters in Chicago during the next seven years.

Gunther is a growing firm. For a middle-sized operation, it has one of the fastest growth records in the industry. Now, Gunther is opening up a new plant in the quickly expanding Tampa market.

Lewis has selected Clark to be the Tampa plant human resource manager. This was what Clark had been waiting for: a chance to be on his own and to show what he can do for Lewis, who has been very supportive of his career, and for Gunther. He was very excited as he entered Lewis's office.

Lewis greeted him with, "Well, Clark, I hope you realize how much we are counting on you in Tampa. Shortly you'll be meeting your new plant manager, Ed Humphrey. You'll be working for him, but responsible to me to see that Gunther's HRM policies are carried out.

"The plant will be staffed initially with the following employees. These are, in effect, your recruiting quotas:

Managers	38
Professional/technical	10
Clerical	44
Skilled employees	104
Semiskilled employees	400

Also note that you will receive a budget for maximum initial pay for this group shortly.

"You and Ed should work out the details. You are eligible to recruit some employees from the home office and other plants. But excessive raiding is not allowed. Remember, too, that Gunther has an equal employment opportunity problem. Wherever possible, try to hire qualified minorities and women to help us meet our goal.

"Your own HR office consists of yourself, one HR specialist to help you run the employment office, and one clerical employee. Good Luck!"

Clark quickly arranged for a meeting with Ed, his new boss. Ed is about 50 years old. He is a high school graduate who started with Gunther as a blue-collar employee when he was 18 years old. After 10 years in various blue-collar positions, Ed became a foreman. Eight years later he was selected as an assistant to the plant manager. After several years in this position, he was made one of the three assistant plant managers at one of Gunther's plants in Chicago. He held that position until being given the position of plant manager at the new Tampa plant.

After introductions, Clark and Ed talked.

Clark Here are the figures for employees that Lewis gave me. He also said we could recruit some people from Gunther, but not to raid beyond company policy. Also, Lewis said we needed to do an exceptional job recruiting minorities and women because we have an EEO problem.

Ed Let's get something straight right off. You work for me now, not Lewis. Here's a list of 20 managers I want to take with me. It's your job to convince them to come to Tampa with me. In cases where my help might persuade some to come along, call on me. But I'm very harassed now trying to get machinery ordered, the plant laid out, financing arranged, and so on. Call on me only when you must, you *understand*?

Oh, one more thing. That EEO * #/OX, you can forget that. The Tampa plant is going to be the most efficient in the company, or else! And if that means hiring the best workers and they all turn out to be white men, that's tough, you get me? Keep me posted on what's happening. Good to have you on board.

After some thought, Clark decided to use job posting as a method of attracting professional/technical and managerial employees at the Los Angeles office to the new plant in Tampa. He also made the personal contacts Ed asked for in recruiting managerial employ-
(continued on next page)

CAREER CHALLENGE

(continued)

ees, and the skills inventory was used to come up with more applicants. Clark contacted these also. He did not use job posting or the skills inventory for clerical, skilled, or semiskilled employees. He knew that, for Gunther, as with most organizations, these categories of employees rarely wish to move to another location. Most companies don't want to pay relocation costs for these categories of employment, either.

Clark went to Tampa and set up the employment office at the new location. He ran an ad in Tampa's afternoon paper and placed a job listing with a private employment agency for the HR specialist and clerk-typist for his office. Then he hired these two employees and set up the office to receive walk-ins. He provided application blanks and policy guidelines on when selection would proceed.

Clark listed the available positions with the U.S. Employment Service. He also contacted private agencies. He selected the private agencies after calling a number of HR managers in the Tampa area in similar businesses and who were also SHRM members. The HR specialist notified the high school, vocational-technical schools, and colleges of the positions. The schools selected included all the vocational-technical schools, the junior colleges, and the colleges in the Tampa area. Also, all high school guidance counseling departments were notified. Now Clark wonders what other media he ought to use to publicize the positions.

Clark found out quickly, as you will find in this chapter, that recruitment is a little more complicated than he originally thought.

*B*efore an organization can make a job offer, it must find people who want the job. This chapter describes effective ways to recruit the people needed to offset shortages in human resources that become apparent as a result of the human resource planning process. **Recruiting** is that set of activities an organization uses to attract job candidates who have the abilities and attitudes needed to help the organization achieve its objectives.

Job search is the set of activities a person undertakes to seek and find a position that will provide him or her with sustenance and other rewards. Recruiting is related directly to a number of HRM activities, as shown in Exhibit 7–1.

The average cost to recruit and relocate a new professional or managerial employee in most medium-sized or large companies is in the $30,000 to $40,000 range. Though most of the cost comes from a company's relocation policy provisions, a substantial portion comes from the recruitment budget. Depending on the job and the methods used to recruit applicants, recruitment charges can be in the neighborhood of 30 to 40 percent of the manager's expected salary. For certain executive positions that require the services of an executive search firm, the costs can even be higher. Thus, to recruit a $40,000-per-year manager, a company can expect recruitment expenses of about $16,000. These expenses include advertising costs, recruiter and candidate travel, agency search firm fees, and recruiter's salary and benefits.[1]

EXHIBIT 7-1   Recruiting and Other Human Resource Management Activities

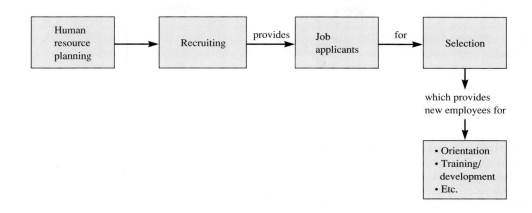

Despite the amount of money that organizations spend on recruiting, it is not a well-developed HRM function. During the 1990s, however, experts agree that recruitment will become a central focus for organizations. Some human resource managers believe that recruitment will, in fact, be the most important component of a successful integrated HRM system for many organizations.[2] This acknowledgement stems from the fact that there will be critical labor shortages in both skilled and unskilled areas during the coming years. A recent survey conducted by *Nation's Business* indicated that over 55 percent of the companies represented felt that the labor supply would be inadequate to fill their needs over the next five years.[3]

This increased competition for qualified workers is expected to enhance the importance of the recruiting function. Although there is going to be more competition to identify and attract qualified workers, organizations are also becoming increasingly concerned with the efficient use of resources. As a result, some people expect recruiting activities to be a primary target for organizational cost-cutting measures. This means that recruiters will have to become acquainted with new and more cost-effective ways of attracting qualified applicants.[4] These innovative recruiting approaches for the coming decade will be highlighted later in this chapter.

A DIAGNOSTIC APPROACH TO RECRUITMENT

Exhibit 7–2 examines how the recruiting process is affected by various factors in the environment. The recruiting process begins with an attempt to find employees with the abilities and attitudes desired by the organization and to match them with the tasks to be performed. Whether potential employees will respond to the recruiting effort depends on the attitudes they have developed toward those tasks and the organization on the basis of their past social and working experiences. Their perception of the task will also be affected by the work climate in the organization.

How difficult the recruiting job is depends on a number of factors: external influences such as government and union restrictions and the labor market, plus the employer's requirements and candidates' preferences. External factors are discussed in this section, and the important interaction of the organization as a recruiter and the employee as a recruit is examined in the next section.

Since Clark Kirby has just moved to Tampa, he will have to learn about the external influences in the new location. Each area of the country has its own unique

EXHIBIT 7-2   Factors Affecting Recruitment of Employees

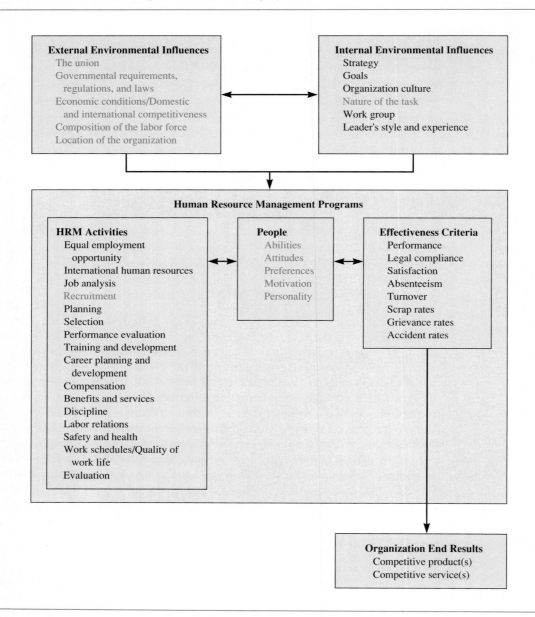

culture, problems, and situations that an HR manager must study and understand. Clark will be doing a lot of studying of his new location.

External Influences

Government and Union Restrictions
Government regulations prohibiting discrimination in hiring and employment have a direct impact on recruiting practices. As described in detail in Chapter 3, government agencies can and do review

---

EXHIBIT 7-3   Guidelines for Legal Recruitment

---

a. Post notices regarding the availability of a job.

b. Publish a list of qualifications necessary to fill the job. Distinguish between essential qualifications and desirable ones.

c. Do not rely only on word-of-mouth sources of recruits.

d. Use recruiting sources that will reach the greatest number of potential applicants in the job market.

e. Be wary of establishing qualifications that might directly or indirectly exclude members of protected groups.

f. Be sure the job qualifications are applied to every applicant in a consistent manner.

Adapted from: Gerard Panaro (1990), *Employment Law Manual* (Boston: Warren, Gorham, & Lamont), pp. 1–10.

the following information about recruiting to see if an organization has violated the law:

- The list of recruitment sources (such as employment agencies, civic organizations, schools) for each job category.
- Recruiting advertising.
- Estimates of the firm's employment needs for the coming year.
- Statistics on the number of applicants processed by category (sex, race, and so on) and by job category or level.
- Checklist to show what evidence was used to verify the legal right to work.

Although there is no guaranteed way to avoid legal entanglements associated with recruiting, Exhibit 7–3 provides some basic principles of sound recruiting practices.

Since recruiters are frequently the first personal contact that an applicant has with an organization, it is also very important for the recruiters to utilize effective interviewing skills. Exhibit 7–4 provides a guide to what recruiters can and cannot legally ask or do during a recruiting interview. Other personal characteristics recruiters need to be wary of, because they may discriminate or do not relate directly to performance, are birthplace; use of second names or aliases; religious affiliation; citizenship; membership in clubs, societies, and lodges; and social security numbers. In some states, it is illegal to ask about the type of military discharge and past police records. Many public organizations must be careful to follow state or local statutes on recruiting.

Obviously, these government restrictions affect who can be recruited, how, and where. In addition, some union contracts restrict recruiting to union hiring halls. This restriction does not apply to many employers; but where it does, the recruiting function is turned over to the union, at least for those employees who are unionized.

The **Immigration Reform and Control Act (IRCA) of 1986** has placed a major responsibility on employers in stopping the flow of illegal immigration to the United States. The employer — not the government — is the chief enforcer of the prohibition against the unauthorized recruitment and employment of foreign-born individuals.[5] Under the law's "employer sanctions" arrangement, all employers are required to screen every applicant's eligibility for lawful employment and maintain records demonstrating employment authorization.

The IRCA is a complex piece of legislation, but its basic features fit into four broad categories:

EXHIBIT 7-4   Do's and Don'ts in Recruiting Interviews: The Law

Subject	Can Do or Ask	Cannot Do or Ask
Sex	Notice appearance.	Make comments or notes unless sex is a bona fide occupational qualification.
Race	General distinguishing characteristics such as scars, etc., to be used for identification purposes.	Color of applicant's skin, eyes, hair, etc., or other direct or indirect questions indicating race of color.
Handicap	Are you able to carry out necessary job assignments and perform them well and in a safe manner?	What is the nature and/or severity of any handicaps you have?
Marital status	Ask status *after* hiring, for insurance purposes.	Are you married? Single? Divorced? Engaged? Are you living with anyone? Do you see your ex-spouse?
Children	Ask numbers and ages of children *after* hiring, for insurance purposes.	Do you have children at home? How old? Who cares for them? Do you plan to have more children?
Physical data	Explain manual labor, lifting, other requirements of the job. Show how it is performed. Require physical exam.	How tall are you? How heavy?
References	By whom were you referred for a position here?	Requiring the submission of a religious reference.
Criminal record	If security clearance is necessary, can be done prior to employment.	Have you ever been arrested, convicted, or spent time in jail?
Military status	Are you a veteran? Why not? Any job-related experience?	What type of discharge do you have? What branch did you serve in?
Age	Age *after* hiring. Are you over 18?	How old are you? Estimate age.
Housing	If you have no phone, how can we reach you?	Do you own your home? Do you rent? Do you live in an apartment or a house?

Source: Clifford M. Doen, Jr. (October 1980), "The Pre-Employment Inquiry Guide," *Personnel Journal*, pp. 825–29. Reprinted with permission of *Personnel Journal*, Costa Mesa, Calif., all rights reserved; and *Business Week* (May 26, 1975), p. 77. Also see Stephen Sahlein, (1982) *The Affirmative Action Handbook* (New York: Executive Enterprises Publishing).

1. The employer's duty not to recruit, hire, or continue to employ "unauthorized aliens."

2. The employer's duty to verify the identity and work authorization of every new employee.

3. The employer's duty not to discriminate on the basis of citizenship or natural origin.

4. The amnesty rights of certain illegal aliens who are eligible to achieve temporary or permanent resident status in the country.

The IRCA went into effect in May 1988, 18 months after the bill became law, to ensure a period of education among employers.[6] Initial penalties for employers who violate the IRCA entail a cease and desist order along with a fine from $250 to $2,000 for each unauthorized alien. Second violations result in a fine of between $2,000 and $5,000 per unauthorized alien. Third offenses lead to fines of $3,000 to $10,000 per unauthorized alien. A person or firm may be charged criminally for having a pattern of violations, with a maximum sentence of six months imprisonment and/or a $3,000 fine per violation.[7]

The IRCA and existing civil rights laws indicate that employers must avoid hiring illegal immigrants while not discriminating against prospective employees just because they look or sound foreign. This type of enforcement and nondiscrimination role is extremely difficult to perform effectively.[8] Every employee — white, black, Hispanic, Asian — recruited and hired must provide acceptable documentation of their status: a valid U.S. passport, unexpired Immigration Authorization Service, unexpired work permit, birth certificate, driver's license, social security card. In the first two months of the law's existence, 64 complaints were reported in New York alone and 350 complaints have been filed with California, Illinois, and Texas offices of the Mexican American Legal Defense and Education Fund.[9]

Even with the complexities and ambiguities of the IRCA, most major employers appear to be committed to abiding by the law. The IRCA created another formal step in the recruitment and selection process that puts a part of immigration control in the hands of employers.[10]

Labor Market Conditions

Another external environmental factor affecting recruiting is labor market conditions (these were described in some detail in Chapter 2). The labor market affects recruiting in the following ways: (1) If there is a surplus of labor at recruiting time, even informal attempts at recruiting will probably attract more than enough applicants, (2) when full employment is nearly reached in an area, skillful and prolonged recruiting may be necessary to attract any applicants that fulfill the expectations of the organization.

The employer can find out about the current employment picture in several ways. The federal Department of Labor issues employment reports, and state divisions of employment security and labor usually can provide information about specific types of employees. There are also sources of information on local employment conditions as they affect their members. Current college recruiting efforts are analyzed by the Conference Board, A. C. Nielsen, and the Endicott Report, which appears in *The Journal of College Placement*. Various personnel journals, the *Monthly Labor Review*, and *The Wall Street Journal* also regularly report on employment conditions.

Other sources provide summary data such as indexes of employment. One of the most interesting indexes is that of the Conference Board, which keeps track of help-wanted advertising in 52 major newspapers across the nation, using 1967 as a base year of 100. Local conditions are more important than national conditions, unless the employer is recruiting nationwide.

Composition of Labor Force and Location of Organization

The influence of HRM law on activities was noted in Chapter 3. As the number of legal requirements has increased, it has become important for an organization to analyze the composition of its work force. Such an analysis is done to determine whether the firm's employment practices are discriminatory.

The location of the organization and the relevant labor market will play a major role in the composition of the work force. That is, the number of black, Hispanic, Asian or Pacific Islander, Native American, or Alaskan native employees in the work force depends largely on the availability of these minority employees in the relevant labor market.

Therefore, government and union restrictions, labor market conditions, the makeup of the work force, and the location of the organization are external forces that affect each other. None of these forces is necessarily more important than any other force. Each of them must be considered in developing a sound recruitment plan that results in an effectively functioning organization.

INTERACTIONS OF THE RECRUIT AND THE ORGANIZATION

After considering how external factors such as government, unions, labor market conditions, composition of the work force, and location of the organization restrict the options of an organization to recruit (an applicant to be recruited), the next step in understanding the recruiting process is to consider the interaction of the applicants and the organization in recruiting.

In Exhibit 7–2 (the diagnostic model), the nature of the organization and the goals of the managers are highlighted, as is the nature of the task. The techniques used and sources of recruits vary with the job. As far as the applicants are concerned, their abilities, attitudes, and past work experience affect how they go about seeking a job.

The Organization's View of Recruiting

Several aspects affect recruiting from the organization's viewpoint: the recruiting requirements set, organization policies and procedures, and the organizational image.

Recruiting Requirements
The recruiting process necessarily begins with a detailed job description and job specification.[11] Without these, it is impossible for recruiters to determine how well any particular applicant fits the job. It should be made clear to the recruiter which requirements are absolutely essential and which ones are merely desirable. This can help the organization avoid having unrealistic expectations of potential employees: An employer might expect applicants who stand first in their class, are president of all extracurricular activities, have worked their way through school, have Johnny Carson's ability to charm, are good-looking, have 10 years' experience (at age 21), and are willing to work long hours for almost no money. Or, to meet federal requirements, they might specify a black woman, but one who is in the top 2 percent of her graduating class and has an undergraduate degree in engineering and an M.B.A.

Contrasted with this unrealistic approach, the effective organization examines the specifications that are absolutely necessary for the job. Then it uses these as its beginning expectations for recruits (see the section on job analysis, job description, and job specifications in Chapter 6).

Finding applicants who possess the needed skills for a job is the "science" of recruiting. There is another component to an effective recruitment program that some consider an "art" rather than a science.[12] Beyond determining whether an applicant has the skills needed for the job, recruitment in the coming years will also have to determine whether the applicant would function well within the culture and value system of the organization. This is becoming increasingly important, once again because of projected shortages in critical personnel.

Organization Policies and Practices
In some organizations, HRM policies and practices affect recruiting and who is recruited. One of the most important of these is promotion from within. For all practical purposes, this policy means that many organizations only recruit from outside the organization at the initial hiring level. They feel this is fair to present loyal employees and assures them a secure future and a fair chance at promotion, and most employees favor this approach. Some employers also feel this practice helps protect trade secrets. The techniques used for internal recruiting will be discussed later in this chapter.

Is promotion from within a good policy? Not always. An organization may become so stable that it is set in its ways. The business does not compete effectively, or the government bureau will not adjust to legislative requirements. In such cases, promotion from within may be detrimental and new employees from outside might be helpful.

Other policies can also affect recruiting. Certain organizations have always hired more than their fair share of the handicapped, veterans, or ex-convicts, for example, and they may look to these sources first. Others may be involved in nepotism to favor relatives. All these policies affect who is recruited.

Organizational Image   The image of the employer generally held by the public can also affect recruitment. All else being equal, it is easier for an organization with a positive corporate image to attract and retain employees than an organization with a negative image. Thus, for organizations such as Merck, Procter & Gamble, and 3M that consistently rank high on surveys such as those of *Fortune* magazine, the time and effort to recruit high-quality workers may be less than that of their less-fortunate competitors who rank poorly.[13]

As you can imagine, the good or bad, well-known or unknown images of these organizations will affect how they are viewed by job recruits. The organization's image is complex, but it is probably based on what the organization does and whether or not it is perceived as providing a good place to work. The larger the organization, the more likely it is to have a well-developed image. A firm that produces a product or service the potential employee knows about or uses is also more likely to have an image for the applicant. The probability is that a potential employee will have a clearer image of a chewing gum company than a manufacturer of subassemblies for a cyclotron.

The organization's image is also affected by its industry. These images change. In the past, petroleum had a positive image. The ecology movement has changed this universally good image. Petroleum organizations, such as Exxon, Shell, and Chevron, now actively advertise their positive contributions to society and try to improve their public images.

How does this image affect recruiting? Job applicants seldom can have interviews with all the organizations that have job openings of interest to them. Because there are time and energy limits to the job search, they do some preliminary screening. One of these screens is the image the applicants have of the organization, which can attract or repel them.

In sum, the ideal job specifications preferred by an organization may have to be adjusted to meet the realities of the labor market, government or union restrictions, the limitations of its policies and practices, and its image. If an inadequate number of quality people apply, the organization may have to adjust the job to fit the best applicant or increase its recruiting efforts.

The Potential Employee's View of Recruiting

Exhibit 7–2 highlighted several factors relevant to how a recruit looks for a job. The applicant has abilities, attitudes, and preferences based on past work experiences and influences by parents, teachers, and others. These factors affect recruits two ways: how they set their job preferences, and how they go about seeking a job. Understanding these is vital to effective recruiting organizations.

Preferences of Recruits for Organizations and Jobs

Just as organizations have ideal specifications for recruits, so do recruits have a set of preferences for a job. A student leaving college may want a job in San Diego because of its quality of life, paying $30,000 a year, and with little or no responsibility or supervision. This recruit is unlikely to get *all* his or her expectations fulfilled. The recruit also faces the limits of the labor market (whether there are a lot of job openings or very few), government and union restrictions, and the limits of organizational policies and practices. The recruit must anticipate compromises just as the organization does.

From the individual's point of view, organization choice is a two-step process. First, the individual makes an occupational choice — probably in high school or just after. Then she or he makes a choice of the organization to work for within the occupation chosen.

What factors affect the organization decision? A number of researchers have found that more-educated persons know the labor market better, have higher expectations of work, and find organizations that pay more and provide more stable employment. Although much of the research suggests that this decision is fairly rational, the more careful studies indicate that the decision is also influenced by unconscious processes, chance, and luck.

Some studies have indicated that the organizational choice tends to be correlated with single factors. For example, a recent survey of college students who were also employed indicated that 69 percent of them planned on changing jobs upon graduation. More important, there was a strong bias among these college students against smaller organizations. Most indicated a preference for larger, well-established firms.[14]

Job Search and Finding a Job: The Recruit

People who are successful at finding the "right job" tend to follow similar search processes. It is not always enough to simply be in the right place at the right time. The effective job searcher creates opportunities in a systematic way. Effective job search involves several steps including: self-assessment, information gathering and networking, targeting specific jobs, and successful self-presentation.[15]

The job search process begins with self-assessment. The purpose of self-assessments is for job searchers to recognize their career goals, their strengths and weaknesses, interests and values, and preferred life styles. This information is used later in the search process to help the applicant assess whether there is a fit with a particular job offer. This assessment is similar to what organizational recruiters will be doing, only from the perspective of the applicant.

Information gathering and networking are methods for generating lists of potential employers and jobs. Information sources include newspapers, trade publications, college recruitment offices, and organizational "insiders."

Many questions about possible employers and about the job searchers themselves must be answered before a list of alternatives can be generated.

Questions about Employers:

1. Do I have a size preference: small, medium, or large, or no certain size?
2. Do I have a sector preference (private, not for profit, public sector)?
3. What kinds of industries interest me? This question is usually based on interests in company products or services. Do I prefer mechanical objects or counseling people? This is a crucial question.
4. Have I checked to make sure that the sector or product or service has a good future and will lead to growth and opportunity?

Questions about Me:

1. How hard do I like to work?
2. Do I like to be my own boss, or would I rather work for someone else?
3. Do I like to work alone, with a few others, or with large groups?
4. Do I like work at an even pace or in bursts of energy?
5. Does location matter? Do I want to work near home? In warmer climates? In ski country? Am I willing to relocate?
6. How much money do I want? Am I willing to work for less money but in a more interesting job?
7. Do I like to work in one place or many? Indoors or outdoors?
8. How much variety do I want in work?

Once a list of prospective employers has been identified, the successful job searcher usually targets a limited number of the most desirable ones from the list. An organization can be contacted in a number of ways. One of the most common is to mail a résumé to the HR department. If an insider has been identified, the résumé can be directed to this person. Although it may be impossible to visit each organization being considered, personal contacts should be used whenever possible.

Self-presentation is very important at this phase of the job search process. One study of over 200 human resource managers who normally screen applicants for positions found that it is essential for cover letters accompanying résumés to be personally typed, no longer than one page, and truthful.[16] They should include these items, in order of importance:

1. Position you are seeking.
2. Specific job objectives.
3. Your career objectives.
4. Reason you are seeking employment.
5. An indication that you know something about the organization.

The same study found that preferred résumés were personally typed, no more than two pages in length, on high-quality paper, and so on. The most important items the managers surveyed in this study were looking for on a résumé were, in order: current address; past work experience; college major; job objectives and goals; date of availability for the job; career objectives; permanent address; tenure on previous jobs; colleges and universities attended; specific physical limitations; and job location requirements. Other items they preferred were, in order: overall health status; salary requirements; travel limitations; minor in college; grades in college major; military experience; years in which degrees were awarded; overall grade point average; membership in organizations; and awards and scholarships. A sample of a résumé is presented in Exhibit 1, in Appendix C at the end of the book.

Video résumés are now being used by job seekers. Individuals are paying up to $300 to put themselves and their qualifications on a video tape. Some consider such approaches a costly gimmick. However, some employers prefer video résumés mainly to screen from a large pool of recruits.[17]

Successful job seekers prepare for job interviews. They do their "homework" and learn as much about the company as possible. In addition, they use impression management tactics to their advantage. Although it is not a good idea to present an unrealistic picture of one's qualifications, interviewers are influenced by an applicant's behavior during the interview. Research indicates that interviewers make two kinds of judgments about applicants. A general impression of the applicant's suitability for employment is made on the basis of objective qualifications. But, job- or firm-specific judgments seem to be strongly influenced by the applicant's interpersonal skills, future goal orientations, and general appearance.[18]

WHO DOES THE RECRUITING

Clark Kirby's situation at Gunther illustrates that he is responsible for recruiting employees. This is an extremely important responsibility that will in the long run determine whether Gunther will be successful in the Tampa area. The roles of operating and HR managers in recruiting are shown in Exhibit 7–5.

Human resource planning gives operating managers the data needed to set recruiting quotas. Sometimes this process is formalized by authorizations. That is, a budget is prepared showing the maximum number of people to be recruited and the maximum salary that can be paid. Lewis gave these items to Clark at Gunther Manufacturing.

Who does the recruiting? In larger organizations, the HR department does it. The branch of the department with this responsibility is called the employment office or department. It is staffed by recruiters, interviewers, and clerical employees. This group also does the preliminary selection, as will be described in Chapter 8. Employment offices are specialized units that provide a place to which applicants can apply. They conduct the recruiting, both at the work site and away from it.

When applicants appear in person at the work site, the employment office serves a similar purpose. This initial meeting might be called the reception phase of employment. The applicant is greeted, supplied with an application blank, and perhaps given some information on present hiring conditions and the organization as a place of work. If the applicant is treated indifferently or rudely at this phase, he or she can form a lasting poor impression of the workplace.[19] The reception phase is a great deal like the initial contact a salesperson makes with a prospective customer.

All applicants are potential employees, as well as clients for the organization's services or products. Therefore, it is vital that those who greet and process applicants (in person or by phone) be well-trained in communication techniques and interpersonal skills. They should enjoy meeting the public and helping people in stressful conditions, because job seeking can be a difficult experience for many applicants.

In smaller organizations, multipurpose HR people do the recruiting, along with

---

EXHIBIT 7-5   The Roles of Operating and HR Managers in Recruitment

Recruiting Function	Operating Manager	Human Resource Manager
Set recruiting goals	Set by OM with advice of HRM	Advises OM on state of labor market
Decide on sources of recruits and recruiting policies	Policy decision, outside versus inside, set by OM with advice of HRM	Advises OM on status of possible inside recruits
Decide on methods of recruiting	OM advises HRM on methods of recruiting	HRM decides on recruiting methods with advice of OM
College recruiting	OM occasionally recruits at colleges	HRM normally recruits at colleges
Cost/benefit studies of recruiting	OM evaluates results of cost/benefit studies and decides accuracy	HRM performs cost/benefit studies

their other duties, or operating managers may take time to recruit and interview applicants.[20] Sometimes the organization puts together a recruiting committee of operating and HR managers.

The role of recruiter is very important. The recruiter is usually the first person from the organization that an applicant meets. Applicants' impressions about the organization are based to a large degree on their encounter with the recruiter.

METHODS OF RECRUITING

Once the organization has decided it needs additional or replacement employees, it is faced with the decision about how to generate the applications necessary for filling its labor needs. The organization can look to sources internal to the company and, if necessary, to sources external to the company. Most organizations have to use both internal and external sources for generating a sufficient number of applicants. Whenever there is an inadequate supply of labor and skills inside the organization, it must effectively "get its message across" to external candidates. It is here where the organization's choice of a particular method of recruitment can make all the difference in the success of the recruiting efforts.

Internal Recruiting

Organizations can make effective use of skills inventories for identifying internal applicants for job vacancies. It is difficult, however, for the HR manager to be aware of all current employees who might be interested in the vacancy. To help them with this problem, they use an approach called **job posting and bidding.**

In the past, job posting was little more than the use of bulletin boards and company publications for advertising job openings. Today, however, job posting has become one of the more innovative recruiting techniques being used by organizations. Many companies now see job posting as an integrated component of an effective career management system.

A model job posting program was implemented at National Semiconductor. Postings are computerized and easily accessible to employees. Computer software allows the employees to match an available job with their skills and experience. It then highlights where gaps exist so the employees know what is necessary if they wish to be competitive for a given job.[21]

Inside Moonlighting and Employees' Friends
If there is a labor shortage and it is short-term, or if a great amount of additional work is not necessary, the organization can use inside moonlighting. It could offer to pay bonuses of various types to people not on a time payroll. Overtime procedures are already developed for those on time payrolls.

Before going outside to recruit, many organizations ask present employees to encourage friends or relatives to apply. Some organizations even offer "finder's fees" in the form of monetary incentives for a successful referral. When used wisely, referrals of this kind can be a powerful recruiting technique. Organizations must be careful, however, not to accidentally violate equal employment laws while they are using employee referrals. For example, in *EEOC v. Detroit Edison* (1975),[22] the U.S. Court of Appeals, Sixth Circuit, found a history of racial discrimination that was related to recruitment. The court stated:

> The practice of relying on referrals by a predominantly white work force rather than seeking new employees in the marketplace for jobs was found to be discriminating.

This case suggests that employee referrals should be used cautiously, especially if the work force is already racially or culturally imbalanced. It also suggests that it might not be wise to rely exclusively on referrals but rather to use them as supplements to other kinds of recruiting activities.

External Recruiting

When an organization has exhausted its internal supply of applicants, it must turn to external sources to supplement its work force. Research indicates that walk-ins provide an important external source of applicants. As the labor shortages of the 1990s increase, however, organizations are becoming more proactive in their recruitment efforts.

A number of methods are available for external recruiting. Media advertising, employment databases, employment agencies and executive search firms, special-events recruiting, and summer internships are discussed here. There is also a separate section on college recruitment of potential managers and professionals.

Media Advertisements
Organizations advertise to acquire recruits. Various media are used, the most common of which are the daily newspaper help-wanted ads. Organizations also advertise for people in trade and professional publications. Other media used are billboards, subway and bus cards, radio, telephone, and television. Some job seekers do a reverse twist; they advertise for a situation wanted and reward anyone who tips them off about a job.

In developing a recruitment advertisement, a good place to begin is with the corporate image. General Mills used its Trix cereal logo to create instant recognition among M.B.A. graduates. The ad featured the Trix rabbit with the headlines: "It's Not Kid Stuff Anymore." The copy continued: "Now you're an MBA who's looking for a dynamic growth-directed career environment . . . . look to General Mills. Because it's not kid stuff anymore. It's your future."[23]

Simply using a corporate logo is not enough, however. Effective recruiting advertising is consistent with the overall corporate image. That is, the advertisement is seen as an extension of the company. Therefore, it must be representative of the values that the corporation is seeking in its employees. Apple Computer's advertising campaign has been very successful, in large part because it has achieved this congruence.[24]

An innovative way to attract nurses was used in an ad campaign for Children's Hospital Medical Center in Cincinnati. The ad appealed to nurses' sense of pride in themselves and their profession. The ad ran in the *Cincinnati Engineer* newspaper. The headlines, "Nurses are smart and they know how to make you feel better," "Nurses are there to make sure you don't get real scared," "Nurses are kind and they don't laugh when you cry," are written in a child's handwriting and combined with hand-drawn pictures of nurses and children.

Another innovative way to attract prospective employees with particular skills is the use of recorded want ads. Want ad recordings were used by 40 companies recruiting engineers and scientists at a New York City convention. At a special recruiting center, job hunters were able to pick up a telephone and hear a three-minute taped recruiting message that included a job description and company contact details.

Help-wanted ads must be carefully prepared. Media must be chosen, coded for media study, and impact analyzed afterwards. If the organization's name is not used and a box number is substituted, the impact may not be as great, but if the name is

EXHIBIT 7-6   A Questionable Want Ad

Is sex a bona fide occupational qualification for this job? Probably not under federal laws. You're in trouble.

Can you prove the age requirement is a business necessity? If you can't show that someone over age 40 can't do the job, you might be subject to a bias suit.

> **HELP WANTED**
>
> Telephone Sales
>
> Women, age 25-40, needed for telephone sales. Must have high school diploma and good credit rating. Call Mr. Smith at Acme Manufacturing Co. Inc., 555-3333.

Is this necessary for the successful performance of the job? Another strike against you.

Will your business suffer without this condition? Is a person's credit rating important when you're talking about his or her ability to sell by phone? Think again.

used, too many applicants may appear, and screening procedures for too many people can be costly. This is a difficult decision to make in preparing recruitment advertisements.

In addition, the ad must not violate EEO requirements by indicating preferences for a particular racial, religious, national origin, or sex group. The advertisement shown in Exhibit 7–6 is the type that will create trouble for a firm. Look at the questions that could be raised by this ad.

Computer Databases   In 1985, there were approximately 35 firms selling résumé databases. Today, that number has risen to over 159.[25] The reason for the dramatic increase is simple. Organizations can quickly and efficiently gain access to national samples of prospective applicants by using these databases.

Existing résumé databases can be classified into five different categories depending on who owns the database and how much public access there is to it. These categories include:

1. Databases maintained by executive search firms.
2. Those maintained by university alumni groups.
3. Those owned by private employment agencies.
4. Corporate job banks.
5. Databases open to the general public.[26]

Obviously, a résumé database that is operated by either an executive search firm or a private employment agency can only be used by clients. Organizations can, however, tap into a large pool of potential applicants by developing partnerships with government-affiliated job search services. For example, by using computer programs such as the automated job posting programs, organizations can now interface effectively with members of several state job services. A program used by Tracor Applied Sciences allows the organization to deal very effectively with the Maryland state job service. The success of the program is attributed to being able to create postings that contain information that parallels the information that employment counselors have access to. This dramatically reduces the difficulty of matching applicants to postings.

Another creative use of public databases is being used by UPS. Working through a United Way counseling agency, it was able to hire 1,500 people in 1988 alone.[27]

College and university alumni groups have also become very effective recruiting tools for organizations. It is estimated that over 200 universities now have alumni résumé databases; perhaps the largest is one run by an alumni group from Stanford University.

Employment Agencies and Executive Search Firms

Although similar in purpose, **employment agencies and executive search firms** differ in many important ways. Executive search firms tend to concentrate their efforts on higher-level managerial positions with salaries in excess of $50,000 while agencies deal primarily with middle-level management or below. Most executive search firms are on retainer, which means the organization pays them a fee whether or not their efforts are successful. In contrast, agencies are usually only paid when they have actually provided a new hire. Finally, executive search firms usually charge higher fees for their services. One of the reasons that organizations are willing to pay these higher fees is that executive search firms frequently engage in their recruiting efforts while maintaining the confidentiality of both the recruiting organization as well as the person being recruited.[28]

Special-Events Recruiting

When the supply of employees available is not large or when the organization is new or not well-known, some organizations have successfully used special events to attract potential employees. They may stage open houses, schedule headquarters visits, provide literature, and advertise these events in appropriate media. To attract professionals, organizations may have hospitality suites at professional meetings. Executives also make speeches at association meetings or schools to get the organization's image across. Ford Motor Company conducted symposia on college campuses and sponsored cultural events to attract attention to its qualifications as a good employer.

One of the most interesting approaches is to provide job fairs and native daughter and son days. A group of firms sponsors a meeting or exhibition at which each has a booth to publicize jobs available. Some experts claim recruiting costs have been cut 80 percent using these methods. They may be scheduled on holidays to reach college students home at that time or to give the presently employed a chance to look around. This technique is especially useful for smaller, less well-known employers. It appeals to job seekers who wish to locate in a particular area and those wanting to minimize travel and interview time. For example, a recent job fair held in Virginia was able to generate 4,000 job candidates in a little under four hours of operation.[29]

Summer Internships

Another approach to recruiting and getting specialized work done that has been tried by some organizations is to hire students during the summer as interns. This approach has been used by businesses (Sherwin-Williams Company, Chase Manhattan Bank, Standard Oil Company of Ohio, Kaiser Aluminum, First National City Bank), government agencies (City of New York), and hospitals. Students in accredited graduate hospital programs, for example, serve a summer period called a *preceptorship*.

There are a number of purposes for these programs. They allow organizations to get specific projects done, expose themselves to talented potential employees who may become their "recruiters" at school, and provide trial-run employment to determine if they want to hire particular people full-time. Interns also typically bring high levels of creative energy and new, fresh, and unbiased ideas to a job.[30]

From the student's point of view, the summer internship means a job with pay; some experiences in the world of work; a possible future job; a chance to use one's talents in a realistic environment; and in some cases, earning course credit hours. In a way, it is a short form of some co-op college work and study programs.

The organization usually provides supervision and a choice of projects to be done. Some of the projects the City of New York's college interns worked on during one summer were snow emergency planning, complaint handling, attitude survey of lower-level employees, and information dissemination.

There are costs to these programs, of course. Sometimes the interns take up a lot of supervisory time, and the work done is not always the best. But the major problem some organizations have encountered concerns the expectations of students. Some students expect everything to be perfect at work. When it is not, they get negative impressions about the organization they have worked for, assuming that it is less well-organized than others in the field. Such disillusioned students become *reverse recruiters*. This effect has caused some organizations to drop the programs. Others have done so when they found they were not able to recruit many interns.

College Recruiting   The gap that exists between the skills that organizations will need over the next several years and those currently possessed by potential employees is growing. Estimates are that three quarters of new candidates in the work force will only be qualified to perform about 40 percent of the available jobs.[31] In addition, the number of jobs requiring a college degree is also expected to rapidly increase. Unfortunately for the organization, college recruiting can be extremely difficult, time consuming, and expensive. But pressures from the external environment will continue to force organizations to be highly visible and active in this kind of recruiting.

The college recruiting process is similar in some ways to other recruiting. However, in college recruiting, the organization sends an employee, usually called a *recruiter*, to a campus to interview candidates and describe the organization to them. Coinciding with the visit, brochures and other literature about the organization are often distributed. The organization may also run ads to attract students or conduct seminars at which company executives talk about various facets of the organization.

In the typical procedure, those seeking employment register at the college placement service. This placement service is a labor market exchange providing opportunities for students and employers to meet and discuss potential hiring. During the recruiting season (from about mid-October to mid-March), candidates are advised of scheduled visits through student newspapers, mailings, bulletin boards, and so forth. At the placement service, they reserve preliminary interviews with employers they want to see and are given brochures and other literature about the firms. After the preliminary interviews and before leaving the campus, each recruiter invites the chosen candidates to make a site visit at a later date. Those lower on the list are told they are being considered and are called upon if students chosen first decide not to accept employment with the firm.

Students who are invited to the site are given more job information and meet appropriate potential supervisors and other executives. They are entertained and may be given a series of tests as well. The organization bears all expenses. If the organization desires to hire an individual, he or she is given an offer prior to leaving the site or shortly thereafter by mail or phone.[32] Some bargaining may take place on salary and benefits, depending on the current labor market. The candidate then decides whether to accept or reject the offer. The college recruiting process is modeled in Exhibit 7–7. As you can see, effective recruiting requires the attention of both human resource and operating executives.

As with other forms of recruiting, organizations are becoming more creative in their use of colleges and universities. Many of the changes are designed to reduce the overall recruiting costs while maintaining a strong applicant flow into the organization. The trend seems to be for an organization to develop a stronger, ongoing relationship with a relatively select number of schools. For example, Mobil used to actively recruit at approximately 200 universities; that number is now closer to 50. In return for the schools' cooperation, Mobil assists with career-related activities throughout the year. It does things like sponsoring career days and providing speakers for special events.[33]

The Effective College Recruiter   Various persons will influence the applicant during the job choice process: peers, family, spouse, friends, and professors. One of the most important influences remains, however, the recruiter. The recruiter is the filter and the matcher, the one who is actually seen by the applicants and is viewed as an extension of the organization. The recruiter is seen as a primary example of the kind of person the organization values and wants to attract in the future.

For these reasons, recruiters must be carefully chosen by the organization. Good recruiters convey an image and appearance that reflects favorably on the organization. They must be outgoing, self-motivated, and obviously good salespersons. In addition, however, good recruiters also possess well-developed interpersonal skills since part of their responsibility should be to determine why job offers are accepted or rejected by candidates. Finally, recruiters should be very familiar with the company they represent for at least two reasons. First, applicants want to discuss opportunities with someone they perceive to be knowledgeable about the company. Second, the recruiters need to be able to determine whether the applicant will fit into the value system of the organization.

Students prefer recruiters who have work experience in their specialties and have some personal knowledge of the university they are visiting. Students also have preferences for specific behavior during the recruiting interview. Characteristics in the recruiter they want most are: friendliness, knowledge, personal interest in the applicant, and truthfulness. Second, some applicants prefer enthusiastic and knowledgeable communicators.[34]

Major flaws students have found in typical recruiters are:

Lack of Interest in the Applicant. Students infer indifference if the recruiter's presentation is mechanical, bureaucratic, and programmed. One student reported, "The company might just as well have sent a tape recorder."

Lack of Enthusiasm. If the recruiter seems bored, students infer that he or she represents a dull and uninteresting company.

Stress or Too-Personal Interviews. Students resent too many personal questions about their social class, their parents, and so forth. They want to be evaluated for their own accomplishments. They, like most people, also unanimously reject stressful or sarcastic interviewing styles.

Time Allocation by Recruiters. The final criticism of recruiters has to do with how much time they talk and how much they let applicants talk or ask questions. From the point of view of the applicant, much of the recruiter's time is

EXHIBIT 7-7   The College Recruiting Process

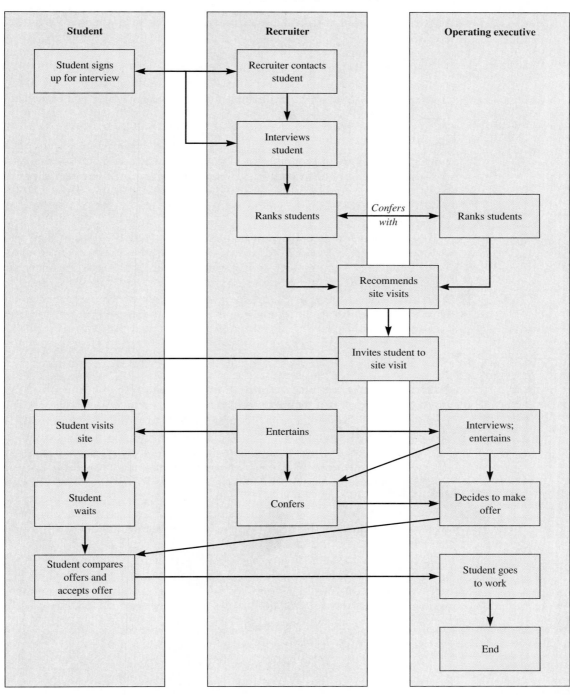

wasted with a long canned history of the company, number of employees, branches, products, assets, pension plans, and so forth. Many of the questions the recruiter asks applicants are answered on the application blank anyway.

A good recruiter is not going to guarantee success in filling positions, however. Although they can and do make a difference, applicants' job acceptance decisions are affected more by characteristics of the job and the organization than they are by particular characteristics of recruiters. Other research also suggests that recruiters may have very little positive influence on an applicant's job choice. Where they do make a difference is when the recruiters do not present themselves well. In this case, they can have a negative effect on applicants even when the job and organization are both appealing.[35]

College Recruitment in Japan   Major Japanese employers rely very heavily on university recruitment programs for identifying and attracting managerial talent. As a result, the amount of money that Japanese firms are spending on college recruitment is more pronounced than ever. Estimates are that major Japanese employers will spend up to 13 months and in excess of $50,000 to attract a single university graduate.[36]

Competition for desirable university graduates is at an all-time high in Japan. Although some of this is due to labor shortages, Japanese firms worsen matters by being unwilling to experiment with alternative sources of executive talent. For this reason, conditions are not likely to improve. For example, these firms still recruit men from a select few universities; they are not highly receptive to hiring managers from other countries; and women and minorities are rarely hired for executive positions.

REALISTIC JOB PREVIEW

It is important for recruiters to provide realistic expectations of the job. When they do so, there is significantly lower turnover of new employees, and the same number of people apply. Researchers have found that most recruiters give general, glowing descriptions of the company rather than a balanced or truthful presentation.

Research suggests that recruitment can be made more effective through the use of **realistic job previews** (RJPs).[37] A realistic job preview provides the prospective employee with pertinent information about the job without distortion or exaggeration. In traditional job previews, the job is presented as attractive, interesting, and stimulating. Some jobs are all of these things. However, most jobs have some unattractive features.[38] The RJP presents the full picture, warts and all, as suggested in Exhibit 7–8.

Exhibit 7–8 presents the typical consequences of traditional previews versus realistic previews. Studies conducted at Southern New England Telephone, Prudential Insurance Co., Texas Instruments, and the U.S. Military Academy have used and reported on the RJP.[39] The results indicated that:

Newly hired employees who received RJPs have a higher rate of job survival than those hired using traditional previews.

Employees hired after RJPs indicate higher satisfaction.

An RJP can "set" the job expectations of new employees at realistic levels.

RJPs do not reduce the flow of highly capable applicants.

EXHIBIT 7-8   Typical Consequences of Job Preview Procedures

Traditional Preview	**Realistic Preview**
Set initial job expectations too high ↓	Set job expectations realistically ↓
Job is typically viewed as attractive, stimulating, and challenging ↓	Job may or may not be attractive, depending on individual's needs ↓
High rate of job offer acceptance ↓	Some accept, some reject job offer ↓
Work experience disconfirms expectations ↓	Work experience confirms expectations ↓
Dissatisfaction and realization that job not matched to needs ↓	Satisfaction; needs matched to job ↓
Low job survival, dissatisfaction, frequent thoughts of quitting	High job survival, satisfaction, infrequent thoughts of quitting

Source: Adapted from John P. Wanous (July–August 1975), "Tell It Like It Is at Realistic Job Preview," *Personnel*, p. 54.

An analysis of 15 RJP experiments that involved over 5,000 subjects revealed that RJPs can be expected to result in an average 9 percent reduction in employee turnovers.[40] The analysis, however, suggested that the reduction was moderated by job complexity. In jobs lower in complexity, there was a smaller reduction in turnover than in jobs higher in complexity.

These findings suggest that RJPs can be used as an innoculation against disappointment with the realities of a job. At this stage of development, however, there is not conclusive evidence supporting the effectiveness of realistic job previews.[41] Although it seems clear that RJPs can have beneficial effects, at present there is still uncertainty as to why RJPs have the effects they do, and in what contexts they are likely to be the most effective.

ALTERNATIVES TO RECRUITMENT

An organization's human resource plan may suggest that additional or replacement employees are needed. However, because of the cost and permanency of recruiting individuals, an alternative to recruitment may be used.

Overtime

When a firm faces pressures to meet a production goal, it may mean that employees need to work overtime. By having employees work overtime, organizations avoid the costs of recruiting and having additional employees. Overtime can provide employees with additional income. However, there are potential problems with fatigue, increased accidents, and increased absenteeism.

On a limited and short-term basis, having some employees work overtime may be an alternative to recruitment. However, continuous overtime has often resulted in higher labor costs and reduced productivity.

PROFESSIONAL PROFILE

Gary Alston
The Temporary Connection

Biography

Gary Alston is executive vice president and chief financial officer for The Temporary Connection, which is a middle-sized temporary employment agency located in Houston, Texas. Gary is one of the cofounders of The Temporary Connection, which was established in 1984. Prior to his involvement with The Temporary Connection, Gary had been a Houston firefighter for 10 years, an experience that he claims was valuable for coping with the stress of being an entrepreneur.

Temporary Employment Agencies as a Valuable Recruiting Source for Companies of All Sizes: A Viewpoint The use of temporary employees surged during the late 1980s as companies recovered from the dramatic downsizing that occurred as a result of an economic slump in the early part of the decade. The fall 1990 issue of *P.R. Overview*, which is a newsletter published by the National Association of Temporary Services, estimates that over 1 million temporary positions are filled on a daily basis. Moreover, independent surveys indicate that nearly 100 percent of businesses in the United States make some use of temporary employees to help solve their labor demands. According to many experts, corporations are using temporary employees to help keep their human resources "leaner" while still maintaining the necessary flexibility to adapt to changing economic conditions.

Gary sees several distinct trends in the temporary employment business. "Corporations no longer view temporary employees as 'warm bodies' who are not expected to do much. The companies we deal with expect their temporaries to exhibit the same quality of work and commitment to the organization as they expect from full-time employees."

He also believes that this change has resulted in some of the growth of the temporary industry. "Companies now see us as a recruitment partner, an integral part of their overall human resource needs. Many of our clients actually have an HRM professional whose primary responsibility is to manage the company's temporary work force."

"To be successful and competitive in today's temporary employment industry, we need to develop long-lasting working relationships with companies. We don't stop at finding a temporary that has the skills needed by the company. Today, our clients demand much more; they want a temporary that 'fits' with their style and climate."

Historically, temporary employees were used primarily to fill basic clerical positions such as filing for short periods, usually during peak workload times. Beyond this traditional use, corporations now rely on temporaries as a supplemental work force available whenever the need arises. They are used for staffing during vacation periods, maternity leaves, illness, and, quite frequently, as additions to short-term project teams. "The current demand in the clerical area is for experienced word processors and workers with other kinds of computer skills."

The temporary employee is also changing. Although most still use temporary work as a solution to unemployment or as a way of "getting a foot in the door," Gary also has noticed that an increasing number of people see temporary employment as an interesting career path. He estimates that approximately 25 percent of the temporaries employed at The Temporary Connection are "career temps." The advantages these people see in not working full-time for one company are variety and unsurpassed flexibility in scheduling.

Employee Leasing

Employee leasing involves the payment of a fee to a leasing company that performs all the HRM recruiting, hiring, training, compensating, and evaluating.[42] The employee leasing firm is paid to provide a ready-made labor pool. Small and medium-size firms find advantages in the employee leasing arrangement because they do not have to become involved in HRM and other administrative activities. Employee leasing is similar to the temporary help arrangement, but under leasing the employees are not temporary.

Many leasing firms have employment areas they specialize in. One company, for example, specializes in supplying labor to the transportation industry — truck drivers, dock workers, maintenance personnel.[43]

Temporary Employment

One of the most noticeable effects of the downsizing epidemic of the 1980s and the labor shortages of the 1990s has been the rise in organizational use of temporary help. Historically, temporary employment agencies were only seen as sources of semi-skilled clerical help during peak work periods. The picture today is much different. Agencies such as The Temporary Connection (see Professional Profile) are now providing organizations with employees in areas ranging from clerical help to executives. Using temporary agencies is, in fact, seen as one of the more effective solutions to the labor shortages of the 1990s.[44]

The major advantages of "temporaries" include relatively low labor costs, an easily accessible source of experienced labor, and flexibility in responding to future changes in the demand for workers.[45] The cost advantage of using temporary help stems from the fact that the organization does not have to provide fringe benefits, training, or a compensation and career plan. The temporary can move in and out of the firm when the workload requires such movement. A disadvantage of hiring temporary help is that these individuals do not know the culture or workflow of the firm. This unfamiliarity detracts from the temporary's commitment to organizational and department goals.

COST/BENEFIT ANALYSIS OF RECRUITING

Many aspects of recruitment, such as the effectiveness of recruiters, can be evaluated. Organizations assign goals to recruiting by types of employees. For example, a goal for a recruiter might be to hire 350 unskilled and semiskilled employees, or 100 technicians, or 100 machinists, or 100 managerial employees per year. Then the organization can decide who are the best recruiters. They may be those who meet or exceed quotas and those whose recruits stay with the organization and are evaluated well by their superiors.

Sources of recruits can also be evaluated. In college recruiting, the organization can divide the number of job acceptances by the number of campus interviews to compute the cost per hire at each college. Then it drops from the list those campuses that are not productive.

The methods of recruiting can be evaluated by various means. Exhibit 7–9 compares the popularity of a number of these methods. The organization can calculate the cost of each method (such as advertising) and divide it by the benefits

EXHIBIT 7-9   Sources of Job Candidates by Job Type

	Office/ Clerical	Production/ Service	Professional/ Technical	Commissioned Sales	Managers/ Supervisors	All
Internal Sources						
a. Promotion from within	94%	86%	88%	75%	95%	99%
b. Employee referrals	87	83	78	76	64	91
c. Walk-in applicants	86	87	64	52	46	91
Advertising						
d. Newspapers	84	77	94	84	85	97
e. Journals/magazines	6	7	54	33	50	64
f. Radio/television	3	6	3	3	2	9
g. Direct mail	4	3	16	6	8	17
Employment Services						
h. U.S. Employment Service (USES)	19	20	11	7	7	22
i. State employment service	66	68	38	30	23	72
j. Private employment agencies	28	11	58	44	60	72
k. Search firms	1	Less than 1	36	26	63	67
l. Employee leasing firm	16	10	6	2	Less than 1	20
m. Computerized résumé service	0	0	4	0	2	4
n. Video interviewing service	0	Less than 1	1	0	1	2
Outside Referral Sources						
o. Local high schools/ trade schools	60	54	16	5	2	68
p. Technical/vocational institutes	48	51	47	5	8	77
q. Colleges/universities	24	15	81	38	45	86
r. Professional societies	4	1	5	19	37	55
s. Unions	1	10	1	0	1	10
t. Community agencies	33	32	20	16	10	39
Special Events						
u. Career conferences/ job fairs	20	16	44	19	19	52
v. Open house at your organization	10	8	17	8	7	22
Other	5	5	7	6	7	9
Number of respondents	245	221	237	96	243	245

Source: Reprinted with permission from The Bureau of National Affairs, Inc. (May 1988), "Recruiting and Selection Procedures" in Personnel Policies Forum, Survey No. 146, copyright © 1988, p. 7.

it yields (acceptances of offers). After the interviews, the organization can also examine how much accurate job information was provided during the recruitment process.

Another aspect of recruiting that can be evaluated is what is referred to as the *quality of hire*. This measure can provide management with an assessment of the quality of new employees being recruited and hired.[46] The quality-of-hire measure is calculated as follows:

$$QH = PR + HP + HR/N$$

CAREER CHALLENGE

(concluded)

Clark Kirby got prices of ads from all the Tampa papers, including suburban papers and ethnic papers. He also discussed the impact and readership of the papers with the human resource managers he'd befriended. On this basis, he chose the major Tampa afternoon paper, the leading black newspaper, the leading Hispanic paper, and a suburban paper in an area near the plant.

He also investigated the leading radio stations and selected the one that had the highest rating of the top three and the lowest commercial cost. He chose commuter times to run the radio ads. The advertising approach was innovative.

The pay and working conditions offered at the Tampa plant were competitive. After Clark's recruiting campaign, he had the following numbers of applicants:

Managerial positions	68
Professional/technical	10
Clerical	78
Skilled employees	110
Semiskilled employees	720

Clark notified Ed of the results. The job now was to select the best of the applicants. Clark knows that is no easy job. Effective selection/hiring is the subject of Chapter 8.

where

QH = quality of recruits hired
PR = average job performance ratings (20 items on scale) of new hirees (e.g., 4 on a 5-point scale or 20 items × 4)
HP = percent of new hirees promoted within one year (such as 35 percent)
HR = percent of hirees retained after one year (e.g., 85 percent)
N = number of indicators used

Therefore,

$$QH = 80 + 35 + 85/3$$
$$= \$200/3$$
$$= 66.6\%$$

The 66 percent quality of hire rate is a relative value. It will be up to management to determine whether this represents an excellent, good, fair, or poor level.

Some caution must be exercised with the quality-of-hire measure when evaluating the recruitment strategy. Performance ratings and promotion rates are all beyond the control of a recruiter. A good new employee can be driven away by few promotion opportunites, inequitable performance ratings, or job market conditions that have nothing to do with the effectiveness of the recruiter. Nevertheless, the quality-of-hire measure can provide some insight into the recruiter's ability to attract employees.

An additional tool available to the HR manager of the 1990s for assessing the value of recruiting efforts can be computerized through an applicant tracking system (ATS). Not only are these systems capable of producing fast, up-to-date job requisitions, they also narrow the applicant search process substantially over manual systems. In this way, an ATS can significantly reduce the cost per hired employee that an organization must invest in recruiting.

SUMMARY

This chapter has demonstrated the process whereby organizations recruit additional employees, suggested the importance of recruiting, and shown who recruits, where, and how.

To summarize the major points covered in this chapter:

1. Recruiting is the set of activities an organization uses to attract job candidates who have the abilities and attitudes needed to help the organization achieve its objectives.
2. External factors that affect the recruiting process include influences such as government and union restrictions, the state of the labor market, composition of the labor force, and the location of the organization. The passage of the Immigration Reform and Control Act of 1986 has placed a major responsibility on employers to stop the flow of illegal immigration to the United States.
3. Three factors affect recruiting from the organization's viewpoint: the recruiting requirements set, organization policies and procedures, and the organizational image.
4. Applicants' abilities, attitudes, and preferences, based on past work experiences and influences by parents, teachers, and others, affect them in two ways: how they set job preferences, and how they go about seeking a job.
5. In larger organizations, the HR department does the recruiting; in smaller organizations, multipurpose HR people or operating managers recruit and interview applicants.
6. Two sources of recruits could be used to fill needs for additional employees: present employees (internal) or those not presently affiliated with the organization (external).
   a. Internal sources can be tapped through the use of job posting and bidding; moonlighting by present employees; and seeking recommendations from present employees regarding friends who might fill vacancies.
   b. External sources include walk-ins, referrals from schools, and state employment offices.
7. Alternatives to recruiting personnel when work must be completed include overtime, temporary employees, and employee leasing.
8. Advertising, personal recruiting, computerized matching services, special-event recruiting, and summer internships are methods that can be used to recruit external applicants.
9. The criteria that characterize a successful college recruiter include:
   a. Showing a genuine interest in the applicant.
   b. Being enthusiastic.
   c. Employing a style that is neither too personal nor too stressful.
   d. Allotting enough time for applicants' comments and questions.

10. A better job of recruiting and matching employees to jobs will mean lower employee turnover and greater employee satisfaction and organizational effectiveness.

11. In larger organizations, recruiting functions are more extensively planned.

Likely approaches used on the seven model organizations specified in Exhibit 1–9 (Chapter 1) are summarized in Exhibit 7–10. It should be noted that several of the model organizations employ different categories of employees. For example, a small volatile hospital and a small volatile toy company employ different kinds of employees, and the sources of recruits used would vary in such organizations. Only a few of the aspects of recruitment have been summarized in this table.

KEY TERMS

employee leasing	231	job posting	221
employment agencies and		job search	210
executive search firms	224	realistic job preview	228
Immigration Reform and		recruiting	211
Control Act (IRCA) of 1986	213		

QUESTIONS FOR REVIEW AND DISCUSSION

1. What guidelines should be followed to make sure that recruitment advertising does not violate equal employment laws?

2. Give some do's and don'ts in recruiting interviews in terms of the legality of questions asked.

3. What role do job descriptions and job specifications play in an effective recruitment program?

4. Describe the components of an effective job search from the perspective of the applicant.

5. What has led to an increased use of temporary employees in organizations? What are the major advantages of using temporary employees?

6. What are the similarities and differences between traditional employment agencies and executive search firms?

7. Describe a realistic job preview. How can it be used to reduce turnover?

8. Computers have changed the way that organizations recruit. Discuss their use in an effective recruitment program.

9. What are the characteristics of an effective and an ineffective college recruiter?

10. When might an organization use overtime or employee leasing as alternatives to recruitment?

NOTES

[1] Margaret Magnus (February 1987), "Is Your Recruitment All It Can Be?" *Personnel Journal*, pp. 55–63.

[2] J. Scott Lord (1989), "External and Internal Recruitment," in *Human Resource Planning, Employment, and Placement*, ed. Wayne F. Cascio (Washington, D.C.: Bureau of National Affairs), pp. 73–102.

[3] "Labor Availability Survey Results" (February 1991), *Nation's Business*, p. 22.

EXHIBIT 7-10 Recommendation on Recruiting Practices for Model Organizations

Type of Organization	Employment Conditions Affect Recruiting		Importance of Image		Methods of Recruiting							
	Greatly	Little	Crucial	Not too Important	Employment Agencies	Newspaper Ads	Radio Commercials	Present Employees	Computer Databases	Special Events	College Recruiting	Summer Internships
1. Large size, low complexity, high stability	X			X	X	X	X		X		X	X
2. Medium size, low complexity, high stability		X		X	X	X		X	X		X	
3. Small size, low complexity, high stability	X		X			X	X	X		X		
4. Medium size, moderate complexity, moderate stability		X	X		X	X	X	X	X	X	X	
5. Large size, high complexity, low stability		X		X	X	X			X		X	X
6. Medium size, high complexity, low stability		X	X		X	X	X	X		X	X	
7. Small size, high complexity, low stability	X		X		X	X	X	X		X		X

[4] Rod Willis (May 1990), "Recruitment: Playing the Database Game," *Personnel*, pp. 25–29.

[5] Bruce D. May (March 1987), "Law Puts Immigration Control in Employer's Hands," *Personnel Journal*, pp. 106–11.

[6] David P. Berry and Jeff T. Appleman (March 1987), "Policing the Hiring of Foreign Workers: Employers Get the Job," *Personnel*, pp. 48–51.

[7] Philip R. Voluck (May 1987), "Recruiting, Interviewing, and Hiring: Staying within the Boundaries," *Personnel Administrator*, pp. 45–52.

[8] David S. Bradshaw (April 1987), "Immigration Reform: This One's for You," *Personnel Administrator*, pp. 37–40.

[9] Dianna Soles (June 5, 1987), "Double Bind: Employers Who Hire Illegals Risk Discrimination Charges," *The Wall Street Journal*, p. 8.

[10] Dianna Soles (May 1987), "Immigration Cops: New Law Puts Task of Enforcement on Employers," *The Wall Street Journal*, pp. 28–29.

[11] Lord, "External and Internal Recruitment," pp. 73–102.

[12] Willis, "Recruitment," pp. 25–29.

[13] Sarah Smith (January 29, 1990), "America's Most Admired Corporations," *Fortune*, pp. 58–66.

[14] Edward D. Bewayo (May 1990), "What College Recruits Expect of Employers," *Personnel*, pp. 30–34.

[15] David Bowman and R. Kweskin (1990), Q: *How Do I Find the Right Job* (New York: John Wiley & Sons).

[16] Hubert Feild and William Holley (March 1976), "Résumé Preparation: An Empirical Study of Personnel Managers' Perceptions," *Vocational Guidance Journal*, pp. 229–37.

[17] John Knowlton (June 22, 1987), "Smile for the Camera: Job Seekers Make More Use of Video Résumés," *The Wall Street Journal*, p. 25.

[18] Sara Rynes and Barry Gerhart (Spring 1990), "Interviewer Assessments of Applicant 'Fit': An Exploratory Investigation," *Personnel Psychology*, pp. 13–36.

[19] Dann L. Dennis (September 1984), "Are Recruitment Efforts Designed to Fail?" *Personnel Journal*, pp. 60–67.

[20] Barry M. Farrell (May 1986), "The Art and Science of Employment Interviews," *Personnel Journal*, pp. 91–94.

[21] Milan Moravec (September 1990), "Effective Job Posting Fills Dual Needs," *HRMagazine*, pp. 76–80.

[22] *EEOC v. Detroit Edison Company* (1975), U.S. Court of Appeals, Sixth Circuit (Cincinnati), 515 F. 2d. 301.

[23] Margaret Magnus (August 1986), "Recruitment Ad Vantages," *Personnel Journal*, pp. 58–79.

[24] Jennifer Koch (March 1990), "Recruitment: Apple Ads Target Intellect," *Personnel Journal*, pp. 107–114.

[25] Willis, "Recruitment," pp. 73–102.

[26] Ibid.

[27] Andrew Bargerstock (August 1990), "Low Cost Recruiting for Quality," *HRMagazine*, pp. 68–70.

[28] Lord, "External and Internal Recruitment," pp. 73–102.

[29] Bargerstock, "Low Cost Recruiting," pp. 68–70.

[30] Robert E. Hite (February 1986), "How to Hire Using College Internship Programs," *Personnel Journal*, pp. 110–12.

[31] Joan C. Szabo (February 1991), "Finding the Right Workers," *Nation's Business*, pp. 16–22.

[32] Thomas J. Bergman and M. Susan Taylor (May–June 1984), "College Recruitment: What Attracts Students to Organizations," *Personnel*, pp. 34–36.

[33] Philip Farish (1990), "Recruitment Sources," in *Human Resource Planning, Employment, and Placement*, ed. Wayne F. Cascio (Washington, D.C.: Bureau of National Affairs), pp. 103–34.

[34] John Boudreau and Sara Rynes (March 1987), "Giving It the Old College Try," *Personnel Administrator*, pp. 78–85.

[35] Therese Hoff Macan and Robert L. Dipboye (Winter 1990), "The Relationship of Interviewers' Preinterview Impressions to Selection and Recruitment Outcomes," *Personnel Psychology*, pp. 745–68.

[36] F. J. Logan (September 1990), "Executive Recruitment: Japanese Style," *Across the Board*, pp. 24–28.

[37] John P. Wanous (1975), "A Job Preview Makes Recruiting More Effective," *Harvard Business Review*, pp. 121–25.

[38] Larry Reibstein (June 10, 1987), "Crushed Hopes: When a New Job Proves to Be Something Different," *The Wall Street Journal*, p. 25.

[39] P. Popovich and John P. Wanous (October 1982), "The Realistic Job Preview as a Persuasive Communication," *Academy of Management Review*, pp. 570–78.

[40] G. M. McEvoy and Wayne F. Cascio (May 1985), "Strategies for Reducing Employee Turnover: A Meta-Analysis," *Journal of Applied Psychology*, pp. 342–53.

[41] Steven L. Premack and John P. Wanous (December 1985), "A Meta-Analysis of Realistic Job Preview Experiments," *Journal of Applied Psychology*, pp. 706–19; and James A. Breaugh (October 1983), "Realistic Job Previews: A Critical Appraisal and Future Research Directions," *Academy of Management Review*, pp. 612–19.

[42] Paul C. Driskell (October 1986), "A Manager's Checklist for Labor Leasing," *Personnel Journal*, pp. 108–12.

[43] Marion R. Selter (April 1986), "On the Plus Side of Employee Leasing," *Personnel Journal*, pp. 87–91.

[44] George S. Odiorne (July 1990), "Beating the 1990s' Labor Shortage," *Training*, pp. 32–35.

[45] Ibid.

[46] This measure was developed by Jac Fitz-enz (1984) in *How to Measure Human Resource Management* (New York: McGraw-Hill), pp. 86–87.

APPLICATION CASE 7–1   So Long to the Sunday Classifieds

. . . . .

In a time when many companies are cutting costs across their operations, a growing number of HR departments are changing the ways they recruit. Their goal: to boost recruiting efficiency (reducing recruiting costs per hire). Their means: innovative recruiting approaches that bring imagination and aggressiveness to a company's overall recruiting function. Innovations are occurring in several elements of the recruiting process. Here is a look at innovations in five areas.

Recruitment Advertising

An increasing number of companies are supplementing and even replacing the traditional classified ad approach to advertising with creative, clever, and eye-catching ads. These ads are essentially a company's résumé and cover letter, designed to send a unique and memorable message about the company to sought-after prospective applicants. Recently, *Personnel Journal* reviewed several hundred ads submitted by subscribers and reported some trends in this type of advertising. They include:

1. **Use of Employees in Ads**   Instead of the traditional testimonials, more company ads are spotlighting employees, talking about their skills, jobs, and accomplishments. For example, General Dynamics has run a series of ads that, by comparison to great inventors, compliments profiled employees and their colleagues. For example, one ad headline in the series proclaims, "We're looking for another Newton . . . And another Newman" (Howard Newman, one of General Dynamic's senior project engineers). The ad's text showcases Mr. Newman's accomplishments and long tenure with the company and then urges those interested and qualified to "join Howard in the pursuit of technology excellence and discovery, apply for a position with us. . . . Who knows? You might become the next Newman." In some other ads in the series,

General Dynamics has declared, "We're looking for another Edison. . . . And another Hardison" (electrical engineer Corrine Hardison), and another Da Vinci. Like many employee-spotlight ads developed by other companies, this series portrays the corporation as a place where very talented and dedicated people work and reach their potential.

2. **Promotion of Intangible Benefits**   In cases where a job is highly attractive and thus doesn't need promoting, employers have turned to emphasizing certain intangible benefits of the company such as advancement opportunities, employment security, creative freedom, and entrepreneurial opportunities. Lockheed Missile & Space Company has run a series of sports-related ads that promote company benefits. One such ad is entitled "Net Gain." Featuring a tennis racket and tennis balls in a partly closed briefcase, the text offers, "Along with a diverse and challenging project list, Lockheed Missile & Space Company makes a point of providing employees with truly comprehensive recreational programs and facilities." The St. Paul Medical Center has developed a series of one-word headline ads that promote certain themes such as "Commitment" (describing the center's commitment to patient care and employee career development) and "Balance" ("Between caring professionals . . . between tradition and technology . . . between performance and opportunity"). Washington University in St. Louis uses creative advertising to promote its flexible work schedules, and in one ad entitled, "Even you-know-who rested on the seventh day," the company published its nursing salaries.

3. **Point-of-Purchase Recruitment** A growing number of service companies with high turnover in low-skilled jobs are recruiting using point-of-purchase ads. For example, Pizza Hut places recruiting coupons on their carry-out boxes. Featuring a drawing of a large lead pencil, the ad suggests,

Written by Kim Stewart and adapted from: Bob Martin (August 1987), "Recruitment Ad Ventures," *Personnel Journal*, pp. 46–54; J. Scott Lord (November 1987), "Contract Recruiting Comes of Age," *Personnel Administrator*, pp. 49–53; Maury Hanigan (November 1987), "Campus Recruiters Upgrade Their Pitch," *Personnel Administrator*, pp. 55–58; and Margaret Magnus (February 1987), "Is Your Recruitment All It Can Be?" *Personnel Journal*, pp. 54–63.

"If you want a good job, get the lead out." The coupon provides a mini résumé form for prospective applicants who don't have résumés. The Quik Wok chinese food takeout chain uses bag-stuffers that picture a broken fortune cookie and proclaim "Not everyone will have the good fortune to work at Quik Wok." The stuffer describes job opportunities. The success of point-of-purchase ads has eliminated Quik Wok's use of classified ads. Other users have found the strategy to be a low-cost, highly efficient and flexible form of recruiting; when a new position needs to be filled, they simply distribute the bag stuffers.

Contract Recruiting

Companies in fast-growing industries are seeking the expertise of a relatively new type of external specialist: the contract recruiter. This specialist is contracted on a temporary basis to perform recruiting functions for different job openings. The recruiter screens résumés, conducts telephone and in-person interviews, coordinates campus recruiting, prepares and executes formal offers, and performs any number of contractual recruiting responsibilities. He or she is not affiliated with an employment agency and does not receive a commission or a percentage of the hiree's salary. Rather, the recruiter is self-employed and is paid at an hourly rate negotiated with the client company.

These self-employed specialists are becoming popular because they can provide several benefits to client companies. When a company is undergoing exceptionally fast growth with immediate hiring needs, a recruiter can be quickly brought in to handle the suddenly burdensome task. The recruiting is performed without hiring permanent (and later unnecessary) staff. For example, when GTE in Needham, Massachusettes, suddenly found itself with a Department of Defense contract requiring 1,200 professional employees to be hired in 16 months, GTE turned to 12 contract recruiters who became an instant employment department. They set up the system, completed the task, and then trained their replacements before departing 16 months later. Cosmetics manufacturer Helene Curtis, Inc., regularly calls on contract recruiters to help the company handle its 15 to 20 percent yearly growth. Recruiters can also serve as external, objective advisors to the company's human resource function.

Some contract recruiters develop expertise in certain employment fields (such as electrical engineering or computer software design). Companies with hiring needs in these areas benefit from the specialists' contacts and highly focused capabilities. Some companies hire the same recruiters time and again, finding that the subsequent knowledge of the company's recruiting needs and functions that the recruiter acquires helps to further reduce per-hire costs.

Campus Recruiting

With declining college enrollments and growing demand for recruits with college degrees, companies are finding that recruiting on college campuses has become very competitive. As a result, many are launching strategies to both boost their offer-acceptance rates and lower recruiting costs.

Rather than select recruits from the placement office's résumé file, some companies are identifying a number of students in their junior year and focusing efforts on these select recruits. More firms are establishing programs that educate professors more fully on the company's career opportunities for graduates. For example, Macy's brings professors to a showcase store where the educators spend a day observing trainees and meeting with managers. Other companies such as Citibank hire professors to lecture in the company's training programs. Organizations such as Texas Instruments also provide executives as guest lecturers at several universities. These actions are designed to enhance the professor's knowledge of the company, which hopefully is communicated to students, and to develop executives' relationships with certain schools.

Some companies are also refining their recruitment brochures. Rather than providing the traditional, very general brochure on the company, firms are now developing smaller, more individualized publications that provide information on particular jobs and departments and information on the respective community where a prospective applicant would work (for instance, information on cost of living, community recreation facilities). Invitation letters to a campus interview are being personalized, often explaining why the company is interested in that particular student. More companies are producing recruiting videos for show on campus. Companies are also paying more attention to the quality of their on-campus interviewers, providing their recruiters with communications skill training. And many firms are replacing the form rejection letter with one that is more tactful and considerate. Firms are mindful of the impact that a word-of-mouth reputation created by an inconsiderate, disinterested recruiter can have on a company's campus recruiting efforts.

Computer Databases

Computer databases are being developed as job and résumé data banks. For example, Job Stores, Inc., has developed a franchise chain of "stop and shop" employment centers located in high-traffic shopping malls. At any center, a job hunter can tap the Job Stores Network computer database by obtaining a computer printout on job openings in the local area and nationwide. The fee: $75 for 90 days' access to the network. Any company can list its job openings on the network at no charge. In seeking participation from businesses, Job Stores' franchisees focus on jobs in the $11,000–22,000 pay range, job openings that companies usually don't fill via employment agencies.

JobNet, another computer database network, allows job hunters to place their résumés in the network at no charge. Companies pay a fee for access to the database, which has over one million résumés of technical professionals on-line. A company can search the database by specifying any of a number of criteria, such as the résumé's recency. Career Technologies runs the network and obtains résumés via job fairs, advertising, and exclusive contracts with over 20 professional associations and societies.

Some college placement centers are also establishing computer databases to link students with prospective jobs. For example, the Career Connection Company, of State College, Pennsylvania, has established Job Search, a computer database of job information. The network provides job listings (up to 20 lines each provided by companies) and is available for all students.

Employee Referrals

Lastly, companies are adding pizzazz to the widely used employee referral/bounty system. A growing number of companies are aggressively promoting referral campaigns with special themes and prizes. Referral bonuses run the gamut from money and trips to time off and credit used to "buy" items from a special catalog. Many referral programs are periodically given a boost with new bonuses and new themes.

Discussion Questions

1. Assess the effectiveness of a recruitment advertising strategy that relies on imaginative, highly visual and eye-catching ads. What are the potential strengths and drawbacks of this approach to recruitment advertising?

2. What type of company (in what kind of industry) would most benefit from contract recruiters? What type would least benefit?

3. Suppose you are faced with the task of developing a college recruiting strategy for obtaining talented business school graduates with degrees in management information systems (developing and managing a company computer information network). Demand for these individuals is currently very high; supply is limited. Develop a recruiting strategy that addresses innovations discussed in the case and includes your own ideas.

8

SELECTION

· · · · · · ·

LEARNING OBJECTIVES

After studying this chapter, you should be able to:

· · ·

Define the steps in the selection process

· · ·

List what selection criteria are available and how they can be used to make selection more effective

· · ·

Describe how to use selection tools such as interviews and biodata more effectively

· · ·

Compare the different types of validity — content, construct, and criteria-related

· · ·

Illustrate the methods used to observe and evaluate the performance of individuals in an assessment center

CAREER CHALLENGE

Clark Kirby is satisfied. He and his assistants have recruited 986 applicants for the 596 positions Gunther will have at its Tampa plant. But before getting too satisfied, he realized that there is a big job ahead of him. Which 596 of the 986 should be hired? And who should do the hiring?

The HR specialist has done some preliminary screening. Most of the applicants have completed an application blank. But where does he go from here?

Clark called Ed Humphrey, the plant manager, and asked if he wanted to be involved in the hiring. Ed said that he only had time to choose his top management team. The rest is up to Clark. Ed reminded Clark that the company didn't want them to raid other plants. Raiding other plants for employees was simply against company policy. Clark said he knew that and would abide by company policy.

Clark is now faced with making 596 selection decisions. As this chapter will show, selection involves making many decisions. Selection is a vital and continuous process in an organization. Employee selection is important because the goals of the organization can only be accomplished if the right match is made between the person and the job.

S election is the process by which an organization chooses from a list of applicants the person or persons who best meet the selection criteria for the position available, considering current environmental conditions. Although this definition emphasizes the effectiveness aspect of selection, decisions about whom to hire must also be made efficiently and within the boundaries set forth in equal employment opportunity legislation. Thus, there are actually multiple goals associated with an organization's selection process.

At a basic level, all selection programs attempt to identify the applicants who have the highest chance of meeting or exceeding the organization's standards of performance. In this case, however, *performance* does not refer simply to quantity of output. It can also involve other objectives such as quality of output, absenteeism, theft, employee satisfaction, and career development. It is unlikely that any given selection process can effectively cope with all of these objectives. As a result, one of the initial tasks involved in developing and implementing an effective selection process is for the organization to identify which of these objectives is most important for its circumstances.

A DIAGNOSTIC APPROACH TO THE SELECTION PROCESS

As Clark Kirby sets out to hire 596 employees, he will follow a selection process influenced by many factors. These factors are highlighted in the diagnostic model in Exhibit 8–1. We'll begin by examining the factors in the internal and external environments.

Environmental Circumstances Influencing Selection

The Internal Environment The nature of the organization doing the selecting affects the process it uses. The private and third sectors use similar methods, but the public sector is different. Traditionally, selection in the public sector has been made on the basis of either political patronage or merit. The patronage system gives jobs to those who have worked to elect public officials. This was the only method used in the public sector until the civil service reforms of the late 1800s. In the private and third sectors, friendship with managers or employees can become a factor in the choice, but this is not the same thing as patronage. Pure "merit" selection (choice based on the employee's abilities and experience) is an ideal that systematic human resource selection tries to achieve but seldom does.

Other aspects of the organization that affect selection are the organization's size, complexity, and technological volatility. Systematic, reliable, and valid HRM selection techniques are sometimes costly to develop and use. When this is so, typically only large organizations can afford to use them. To justify the development of these techniques, there must be a sufficient number of jobs to fill and a pool of candidates to fill them. If the organization is complex and has a large number of jobs with only a few occupants, sophisticated selection techniques are not cost-effective. The extent to which size dictates the number of employees in each work group also affects the usefulness of the techniques. In sum, the size, complexity, technological volatility, and nature of the organization will determine which selection techniques are cost-effective for the organization.

Nature of the Labor Market The second circumstance affecting the selection process is the labor market within which the organization must function. A large supply of applicants can significantly complicate the selection decision since the

EXHIBIT 8-1   Factors Affecting Selection of Human Resources and Effectiveness

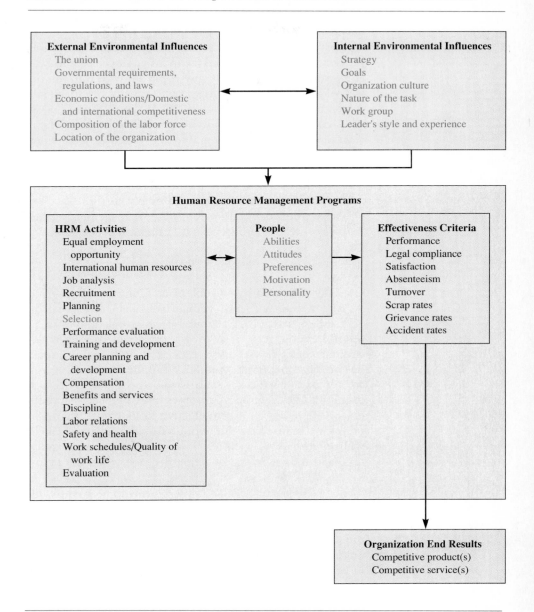

organization has many people from which to choose. When there are relatively few applicants, the decision can actually be quite simple. However, as we will see later, a limited supply of applicants can also reduce the overall effectiveness of selection decisions. The labor market for the organization is affected by the labor market in the country as a whole, the region, or the city in which the organization is located. It is further affected by the working conditions offered by the organization, the nature of the job itself, and the organization's public image.

To illustrate these effects, consider the circumstances under which hospital dieticians may be trying to hire dishwashers or food preparation helpers. The job can be unpleasant, and it is performed at unpopular hours (the breakfast crew might have to arrive at 5:30 A.M.). The workday can be long, the pay isn't good, and, frequently, there are no possibilities for promotion. For jobs like these, the selection process might be simple and inexpensive since there may be few applicants available at a given time. As a result, any applicant who walks in the door and is found to be free of a communicable disease will usually be hired. In such cases, there is little reason or opportunity to worry about the selection decision.

In contrast to the hospital dietician's situation, when the military is selecting candidates for flight training, it is confronted with an enormously complex selection decision. There are frequently an abundance of applicants, the job is difficult, the costs of failure are high, and the opportunities for advancement are numerous. These conditions will lead to a substantially more detailed selection decision, not to mention one that can become extremely costly.

Those who work in human resource management evaluate the effects of the labor market on selection decisions by using a *selection ratio*.

$$\text{Selection ratio} = \frac{\text{number of applicants hired}}{\text{total number of applicants}}$$

Consider Clark Kirby's problem at Gunther. The selection ratios are: managers 38/68, or about 1:2; professional/technical, 10/10, or 1:1; clerical, 44/78, or about 1:2; skilled, 104/110, or about 1:1; semiskilled, 400/720, or almost 1:2. When the selection ratio gets close to 1:1, it is called a *high selection ratio*. Under these circumstances, the selection process is short and unsophisticated, although it may not be effective. As the number of applicants increases relative to the number who are hired, the selection ratio is said to be *low*. With a lower selection ratio, for example, 1:2, the process becomes more detailed. A ratio of 1:2 also means that the organization can be more selective in its choice than when the ratio is 1:1. It is, therefore, more likely that employees who fit the organization's criteria for success will be hired. It is also likely, however, that the organization will have to invest more time and money in the selection decision when the ratio is 1:2.

Union Requirements

If the organization is wholly or partly unionized, union membership prior to or shortly after hiring is a factor in the selection decision. Sometimes, the union contract requires that seniority (experience at the job with the company) be the only criterion — or at least a major one — in selection. If the union has a hiring hall, the union makes the selection decision for the organization. In many ways, openly and subtly, a union can affect an organization's selection process.

Government Requirements

The fourth circumstance affecting selection is government. In the United States, governments have passed laws designed to guarantee equal employment opportunity and human rights. Some of the legal requirements were described in detail in Chapter 3.

Composition of the Labor Force

Organizations often attempt to hire a labor force that reflects the makeup of their clients or customers. Even if government requirements regarding equal employment did not exist, it would be advisable for an organization to examine the composition of the labor force to help meet the needs of clients or customers. For example, in predominantly Spanish-speaking sections in Denver, the police department attempted to hire some Spanish-speaking police officers. To do so, the Denver police department attempted to recruit and select police officers who could speak Spanish fluently. Unfortunately, the police department found a shortage of police recruits who could speak fluent Spanish.

Location of the Organization   The location of the organization also affects the selection process. Many high-technology firms have located their facilities in the Silicon Valley of California; Austin, Texas; and Boston, because of the abundant supply of job applicants. These regions of the country have attracted many skilled individuals who are properly trained to work for high-technology firms.

The Immediate Environment and Selection

You will note that the people factor is emphasized in Exhibit 8–1. This is not surprising since the basic organizational objective for its selection process is to obtain high-performing employees. Operating managers, functional subunits, or other controlling interests might, however, view this overall objective in somewhat different ways. In some departments, a high-performing employee may be someone who is rarely absent; in other departments, the key aspect of employees' overall performance may be their accident rates. Thus, while it is management's responsibility to set selection objectives, these will not always correlate perfectly with optimal levels of performance for all operating units.

At the core of an effective selection process is an identification of the abilities, skills, knowledge, and other personality characteristics necessary for performance. The goal of selection is, therefore, to match applicant characteristics to job requirements. Job analysis plays a crucial role in this matching process. Recall from Chapter 6 that the major by-products of a job analysis are a job description and a job specification. Up-to-date job specifications are essential for determining what kind of an applicant the organization should hire.

There is another aspect of the immediate environment, which is not shown in Exhibit 8–1, that influences the selection decisions — the amount of time available to make the selection decision. If there is adequate time, the organization may be able to use all the selection tools it normally uses. If there is an emergency, the selection decision may be shortened by dropping one or several of the steps in the selection process.

The selection activity is in Stage IV of development or maturity (see Exhibit 1–6, Chapter 1). It is well-developed, and many studies have been conducted that analyze the use of the various selection methods.

WHO MAKES SELECTION DECISIONS?

In smaller organizations with no HRM unit, the operating manager makes selection decisions. In medium-sized and larger organizations, both operating and HR managers are involved in selection decisions, as Exhibit 8–2 indicates.

Some organizations also give employees a voice in the selection choice. Applicants are interviewed by employees, who are then asked to express their preferences. This procedure is used in university departments where the faculty expresses its preferences on applicants, and at the Lincoln Electric Company in Cleveland, where the work group recruits and selects replacements or additions. Similarly, work groups at the revolutionary Saturn automobile plant in Spring Hill, Tennessee, are responsibility for selecting new workers for their groups, which are comprised of approximately 12 persons.[1]

EXHIBIT 8-2   The Role of Operating and HR Managers in Selection

Selection Function	Operating Manager (OM)	Human Resource Manager (HRM)
Choice of selection criteria	Selected by OM	Recommends and implements the selection criteria based on job specifications
Validation of criteria		Performed by HRM
Screening interview		Normally performed by HRM
Supervision of application/ biodata form		Normally by HR representative
Employment interview	OM and HRM	OM and HRM
Testing		Performed by HRM
Background/reference chart		Normally performed by HRM
Physical exam		Normally performed by HRM
Selection/decision	OM decides after considering HRM recommendation	Recommendation by HRM to OM

Generally, more-effective selection decisions are made when many people are involved in the decisions and when adequate information is furnished to those selecting the candidates. The operating manager and the work group should have more to say about the selection decision than the HR specialist.

SELECTION CRITERIA

If a selection program is to be successful, the employee characteristics stated in the job specification must accurately summarize what is necessary for effective performance on the job. This is where the role of job analysis in selection becomes most apparent since an accurate list of characteristics can only be generated after the organization has conducted a thorough job analysis. The criteria typically used by organizations for making selection decisions can be summarized in several broad categories: education, experience, physical characteristics, and other personal characteristics.

Basically, the characteristics listed in the job specification should describe current employees who have performed well in the position to be filled.[2] If this list of desired characteristics is too long, however, it may be impossible to find an applicant meeting all of the selection criteria. On the other hand, without a list of criteria, it is quite likely that many of the wrong kinds of persons will be hired. An effective selection process needs to find a compromise between these two extremes, using the most critical criteria for making the actual selection decisions.

Formal Education

An employer selecting from a pool of job applicants wants to find the person who has the right abilities and attitudes to be successful. These cognitive, motor, physical, and interpersonal attributes are present because of genetic predisposition and because they were learned in the home, at school, on the job, and so on. Most employers attempt to screen for abilities by specifying educational accomplishments.

PROFESSIONAL PROFILE

Biography

Dean Smith is director, industrial relations for Waukesha Engine Division, Dresser Industries, Inc., Waukesha, Wisconsin. He has been employed by Dresser Industries since 1965. His 1962 undergraduate degree is from the School of Industrial and Labor Relations at Cornell University, and he also holds an M.B.A. (1968) from the University of Southern California.

During his career with Dresser Industries, Mr. Smith has been assigned to eight different manufacturing and administrative locations, from Olean, New York, to Los Angeles, California. He has been a generalist with supervisory responsibility at each of these locations. Prior to 1965, Mr. Smith was a personnel administrator with a western New York manufacturer, Champion Products.

Job Description As director, industrial relations, Dean Smith is responsible for compensation and benefits, employee training and development, employee communications, labor relations, occupational health and safety, employment, and community relations. Excluding medical and security personnel, Mr. Smith supervises a staff of seven supervisory, professional, and clerical employees.

Key Current Human Resouce Issues: A Viewpoint A most challenging goal of a human resource generalist employed by an old-line (founded 1906) engine-manufacturing firm is to be an effective change agent for an organization where managerial and professional employees are particularly resistant to modifying how people and systems are managed, regardless of the degree of top-management support for the change desired. Non-supervisory employee and labor union resistance to change is relatively mild when compared to the tendency of managers and professionals to feel threatened.

Equally challenging are the purely economic issues of controlling health-care costs and introducing more flexibility in the employee benefits programs. These

G. Dean Smith
Dresser Industries, Inc.

two related issues will probably vex employers and society into the 21st century.

An enduring skill shortage will be the inadequate supply of scientific and engineering talent. In manufacturing, the scarcity of engineers is exacerbated by the problem that only one of eight college engineering students is a woman. Attracting women into the field of engineering would mitigate two key socio-economic problems; it would increase:

1. The pool of entry-level engineers.
2. The pay earned by female employees, whose average compensation still lags male employees partially because women too often train for occupations where the demand does *not* exceed the supply.

The successful employer in the 1990s will continue to encourage an increasingly heterogeneous work force in all occupations and organizational levels, but especially in those occupations requiring chronically scarce skills, for example, engineering. The growing cooperation between employers and educators should serve many mutually beneficial purposes, not the least of which will (or should) be to encourage women and minorities who are still in school to focus their training selections on the scarce skills. Of course, human resource professionals are uniquely qualified to represent their employers in these efforts to assist educators in performing their crucial societal mission.

Employers tend to specify as a criterion a specific amount (in years) of formal education and types of education. For the job of accountant, the employer may list as an educational criterion a bachelor's degree in accounting. The employer may even prefer that the degree be from certain institutions, that the grade point average be higher than some minimum, and that certain honors have been achieved. To be legal, educational standards such as these must be related to the performance of successful accountants at the firm. In addition, care must be exercised not to employ standards that are higher than is actually required by the job. All else being equal, an organization typically prefers more education to less and higher grades to lower ones. However, it must always be aware of the consequences of using unnecessarily high standards that might exclude too many minority group members from being hired.

Experience/Past Performance

Another useful criterion for selecting employees is experience and past performance. Many selection specialists believe that past performance on a similar job might be one of the best indicators of future performance. In addition, employers often consider experience to be a good indicator of ability and work-related attitudes. Their reasoning is that a prospective employee who has performed the job before and is applying for a similar job must like the work and be able to do the job well. Since loyalty to the job and the organization are both important and tenure with the company implies these, the tendency for many organizations is to hire from within before seeking applicants from outside the organization.

One way to measure experience within the organization is to provide each employee with a seniority rating, which indicates the length of time he or she has been employed in the organization. In the military, the date of rank is an equivalent seniority measure. Seniority can be measured in various ways: as total time worked for the firm, or time worked for the firm on a particular job or in a certain unit. If an organization has discriminated against minority group members, retroactive seniority can be awarded by the courts as part of the settlement of a case.[3]

Physical Characteristics

In the past, many employers consciously or unconsciously used physical characteristics (including how an applicant looked) as a selection criterion. Studies show that employers were more likely to hire and pay better wages to taller men, and airlines chose flight attendants and companies hired receptionists on the basis of beauty (or their definition of it). Many times, these practices discriminated against minority groups including ethnic groups, women, and handicapped persons. For this reason, the practice is now illegal unless it can be shown that a physical characteristic is directly related to work effectiveness. For example, visual acuity (eyesight) would be a physical characteristic that could be used to hire commercial airline pilots. It might not, however, be legal to use it for hiring a telephone reservations agent for an airline.

In a similar way, candidates for a job cannot be screened out by arbitrary height, weight, or similar requirements. These can be used as selection criteria when the job involves tasks that require these characteristics.

In recent years, another form of testing has made yet another kind of physical characteristic potentially usable in selection decisions. Today, genetic testing can identify a variety of inherited abnormalities. While rare, such testing has been used in the workplace although it is probably unwise to use such tests in selection. Many believe that genetic testing will be seen by the courts as a violation of the newly passed Americans with Disabilities Act of 1990.[4]

Personal Characteristics and Personality Type

The final criterion category is a catch-all that includes *personal characteristics* and *personality types*. Personal characteristics include marital status, sex, age, and so on. Some employers have, for example, preferred "stable" married employees over single ones because they have assumed that married persons have a lower turnover rate. On the other hand, other employers might seek out single persons for some jobs since a single person might be more likely to accept a transfer or a lengthy overseas assignment.

Age, too, has sometimes been used as a selection criterion. While it is illegal to discriminate against persons who are over the age of 40, there is no federal law that specifically addresses this issue for younger persons. In addition, minimum and maximum age restrictions for jobs can only be used if they are clearly job-related. Thus, age should be used as a selection criterion only after very careful thought and consideration.

Certain specific aptitudes and/or skills can also be considered part of this criterion category. Although education and past experience are often used as measures of ability, many organizations also try to assess whether applicants possess certain aptitudes. For example, a successful applicant for pilot training in the military does not need actual flying experience. Rather, the military uses spatial relations aptitude as one criterion for pilot selection.

Many employers also prefer to hire persons with certain personality types. Some jobs such as being a police officer may require extensive, systematic personality testing using a variety of standardized measures. Other jobs may require essentially no consideration of an applicant's personality. Many jobs fall between these extremes. For example, one particular aspect of personality such as being an outgoing person may be useful for salespersons, caseworkers, or others who work extensively with the public.

As with other personal characteristics, selection using one or more aspects of personality should always be based on whether it is really a necessary characteristic for high performance. Many personality measures run an even greater risk of being legally challenged as an invasion of privacy than other kinds of selection tools. Thus, the organization wishing to use personality as a selection criterion must be certain that successful and unsuccessful employees can be distinguished in terms of their personalities. Finally, it is probably unwise to use personality as a general criterion for screening out "undesirable" applicants since the same personality characteristic that leads to failure in one job might lead to success in another.[5]

RELIABILITY AND VALIDITY OF SELECTION CRITERIA

Once an organization has decided upon a set of selection criteria, a technique for assessing each of these must be chosen. The alternatives are numerous: application blanks and biodata forms, interviews, psychological tests of aptitude and personality, work sample tests of present skills, physical and medical testing, and previous experience checks through references. Regardless of the method chosen for collecting information about applicants, the organization must be certain that the information is both *reliable* and *valid*.

Reliability

The main goal of selection is to make accurate predictions about people. The organization wants to make its best guess about who will be a successful employee. In this way, the organization can avoid hiring the wrong persons for a job. In other words, the main purpose of selection is to make decisions about people. If these decisions are going to be correct, the techniques used for making them must yield reliable information.

Reliability refers to how stable or repeatable a measurement is over a variety of testing conditions.[6] As a simple example, imagine that you attempted to use a tape measure to determine a firefighter applicant's height in feet and inches. If you measured a single applicant three different times on the same day resulting in different measurements of 5 feet 10 inches, 6 feet 3 inches, and 6 feet, you would not know how tall the applicant actually was. The same is true for any other assessment technique used in personnel selection. If Dan scored a 70 on an employment test on Wednesday, and a 95 on Friday, it would not be possible to determine Dan's true ability. The test would be too unreliable to be used effectively.

Returning to our effort to determine how tall the firefighter applicant was, if the measurements varied from 6 feet to 6 feet 2 inches, you may not know exactly how tall he or she is, but you would have a reasonably good idea of his or her height. In contrast, imagine that the tape measure indicated that the applicant's height was 5 feet, 6 feet, and 6 feet 6 inches over your three attempts. In this case, you would have virtually no idea how tall he or she was. The point is that reliability is a matter of degree. If a measuring instrument is only somewhat unreliable, it can still be very useful; if it is too unreliable, then it becomes meaningless to try to use it.

The reliability of a selection tool can be judged in a variety of ways. In practice, one common way to assess reliability is to correlate the scores of applicants given the same test on two different occasions. This is called *test-retest reliability*. *Alternate-form reliability* is determined by correlating scores from two alternate forms of the same test. Most standardized academic achievement tests like the SAT or the GMAT have numerous forms, all of which are assumed to be reliable. An applicant's score should not vary much according to which form of the test they happen to take. When a measuring tool relies on the judgments of people (such as employment interview), reliability is often determined by using *interrater reliability*. This refers to the extent to which two or more interviewers' assessments are consistent with each other.

Validity

For a selection tool to be useful, it is not sufficient for it to be repeatable or stable. Both legally and organizationally, the measures that it yields must also be valid. There are many ways of assessing validity, but all of them focus on two issues. Validity addresses the questions of what a test measures and how well it has measured it.[7] In selection, the primary concern is whether the assessment technique results in accurate predictions about the future success or failure of an applicant.

To illustrate these two issues and the relationship between validity and reliability, let's return to our example of measuring the firefighter applicant's height. As noted previously, if it is too unreliable, then it will be impossible to determine his or her correct height. Even if the tape gives the same measurements (high reliability), it might still have very little accuracy (validity). For example, the tape measure may not have been calibrated properly at the factory where it was made (the manufacturer may have thought it was marking it in feet and inches when it was actually using centimeters). If so, it will still be almost impossible to accurately determine the applicant's height. Finally, this tape measure might be perfectly reliable and an accurate way to measure height, but, if you try to weigh applicants with it, it will yield totally useless information.

To summarize, for a measuring tool to be useful, it must be reliable, valid, and put to the use for which it was actually intended.

A detailed explanation of the various strategies for determining the validity of a selection tool can be found in the *Principles for the Validation and Use of Personnel Selection Procedures*.[8] The following, however, are brief descriptions of three types of validity that the HR specialist should be familiar with: (1) content, (2) construct, and (3) criterion-related.

Content Validity   The degree to which a test, interview, or performance evaluation measures the skill, knowledge, or ability to perform the job is called **content validity.** For example, employment tests used in the plumbing, brick-laying, and electrical construction trades are considered content valid when test content and job content correspond closely. Test and job content are directly observable, meaning that content validity is an appropriate type of validity.

An example of a content-valid test is a typing test for a secretarial position. Such a test can roughly replicate conditions on the job. The applicant can be given a typical sample of typing work under working conditions, and his or her performance on the sample can be evaluated. Assuming that the sample of typing work constitutes a random sample of typical work, the test is content valid. The typing test score is used to predict how successful a person will be in performing a job involving typing.[9] It is important to select a sample of work that closely resembles the type of work that will be done on the job.[10]

Content validity is not appropriate for more-abstract job behaviors, such as leadership potential, leadership style, or work ethic. When selection procedures involve the use of tests to measure leadership characteristics and/or personality, construct validity rather than content validity is appropriate.

Construct Validity   A *construct* is a trait; a test is *construct valid* when it measures a trait that is important for a job. **Construct validity** is defined as a demonstrated relationship between underlying traits or "hypothetical constructs" inferred from behavior and a set of test measures related to those constructs. Construct validity is not established with a simple study but only with the understanding that comes from a large body of empirical evidence.[11] To use an example, if leadership is important for performing the work of a project manager, a test that measures leadership is said to have construct validity. To prove construct validity, an employer has to prove that the test actually does measure the trait (leadership), and that the trait actually is necessary for the job. It is extremely difficult to prove construct validity.[12]

The Uniform Guidelines on Employee Selection Procedures which provide the standards used by federal EEO agencies, has established three stringent requirements to show construct validity.[13]

A job analysis must systematically define both the work behaviors involved in the job and the constructs that are believed to be important to job performance.

- The test must measure one of those constructs. In selecting a project manager, there must be evidence that the test validly measures leadership. For example, scores on the test might have correlated with leadership ratings given to other employees in other organizations upon previous administration of the test.
- The construct must be related to the performance of critical work behavior. For example, it must be shown that leadership ability is correlated with job performance for the position of project manager. That is, it is necessary that a criterion validity study between leadership and job performance be conducted, or that such data collected by another test user be used to support the claim of construct validity.

Criterion-Related Validity   The extent to which a selection technique can accurately predict one or more important elements of job behavior is referred to as **criterion-related validity.** Scores on a test or performance in some simulated exercise are correlated with measures of actual on-the-job performance. The test is called a *predictor* while the performance score is referred to as a *criterion*. Criteria relevant to personnel selection include measures such as quality or quantity of output, supervisory ratings, absenteeism, accidents, sales results, or whatever the organization deems most relevant. However, the choice of a criterion is at the very heart of determining whether a selection system is legal.[14] The organization must exercise care in choosing a measure that best reflects the actual contributions of employees to its effectiveness. Not all criteria can be predicted equally well from any particular type of selection tool.[15]

Two popularly used types of criterion-related validity are predictive and concurrent. *Predictive validity* is determined by using the scores obtained from a sample of applicants for a job. The steps in a predictive validity study for a given test are:

1. Administer the test to a large sample of applicants.
2. Select individuals for the job. It is actually preferable if the test whose validity is being measured is not used in the hiring decisions.
3. Wait an appropriate amount of time and then collect measures of job performance.
4. Assess the strength of the predictor-criterion relationship (typically by calculating a correlation coefficient).

Predictive validity is an important form of criterion-related validity, but it does have drawbacks. The employer must wait until it has hired a large number of people for whom it has predictor scores. It can also be time consuming because the employer must also wait until it can obtain meaningful measures of job performance on the people who were hired. For some jobs, the time it takes to determine who is a good employee can be long.

Concurrent validity is also used to determine whether a selection test can predict job performance. It differs from predictive validity in at least one important way. Concurrent validity is determined by using data obtained from the present work force. In concurrent validation, the first step is to administer the tests to present employees performing the job. At approximately the same time, performance measures for these employees are also collected. The test scores are then correlated with the performance measures. If the test is significantly related to performance, it would be a candidate for future use with applicants in the selection process.

The biggest advantage of concurrent validation is that it can be conducted relatively quickly. Therefore, it is usually less expensive than predictive validation. However, there are several potential problems associated with the use of concurrent validation. First, this method involves the use of experienced employees. If job experience is important in job performance, the results of such validation will be biased in favor of applicants with experience. Second, present employees often balk at completing tests. They are puzzled by the requests to take a battery of tests, and often will not provide honest or best answers. Therefore, the test scores may not be a true indicator of their skills and abilities. Third, there is a self-selection bias that can restrict the range of test scores. Among present employees, there is likely to be a restriction because the least skilled and able workers have been terminated, demoted, or transferred, and the most skilled and able have been placed in more responsible jobs. The restriction of range in test scores causes the correlation between test scores and performance ratings to be understated.

Despite these potential problems, concurrent validation can be an effective method for assessing the validity of certain kinds of selection tests.[16] However, it should not automatically be used as an alternative to predictive validation simply because it can be done more quickly. The organization should carefully analyze its circumstances before choosing which of the methods to use.

THE SELECTION PROCESS

All organizations make selection decisions, and most make them somewhat informally. The smaller the organization, the more likely it is to take an informal approach to selection decisions. Formal or systematic selection decisions were developed during World Wars I and II, when employee shortages brought tremendous placement problems and the military had to select and place large numbers of workers in many different jobs very quickly and efficiently.

In the past, selection was often thought to be an easy decision. The boss interviewed applicants, sized them up, and let his or her gut reaction guide the choice. Decisions were based on the subjective likes or dislikes of the boss. Selection tools were designed to aid this gut reaction. For most selection decisions, that is all the tools were intended to do; they were designed to increase the proportion of successful employees selected. Today, selection is viewed as more than simply relying on intuition.

The selection decision is usually perceived as a series of steps through which applicants pass. At each step, a few more applicants are screened out by the organization, or more applicants accept other job offers and drop from the applicant list. Exhibit 8–3 illustrates a typical series of steps for the selection process.

This series is not universally used; for example, government employers test at Step 3 instead of Step 4, as do some private- and third-sector employers. It is important to note that few organizations use all steps, for they can be time consuming and expensive; and several steps, such as 4, 5, and 6, may be performed concurrently or at about the same time. Generally speaking the more important the job, the more each step is likely to be used formally. Most organizations use the screening interview, application blank, and interview. Tests are used by a relatively small number of employers. Background and reference checks and physical exams are used for some jobs and not others. Exhibit 8–4 presents results of a study of 437 firms' procedures used to make selection (hiring and promotion) decisions.

Step 1: Preliminary Screening Interview

Different organizations can handle Step 1 in various ways — ineffectively or effectively. For some types of jobs, applicants are likely to walk into the employment office or job location. In these cases, an HR specialist or line manager usually spends

EXHIBIT 8-3   Typical Selection Decision When All Possible Steps Are Used (Private and Third Sectors)

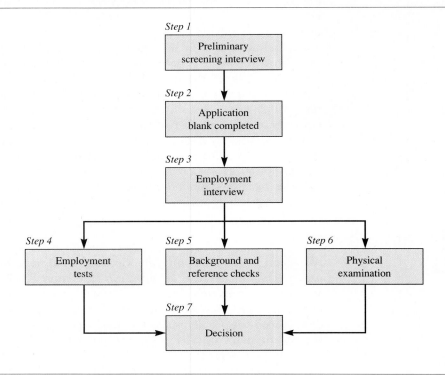

a few moments with applicants in what is called the *preliminary screening*. The organization develops some rough guidelines to be applied in order to reduce the time and expense of actual selection. These guidelines could specify, for example, minimum education or the number of words typed per minute. Only those who meet these criteria are deemed potential employees and are interviewed.

After applicants have been screened for these minimum qualifications, additional preliminary screening is often done through a brief personal interview in which the HR specialist or manager attempts to obtain key information and forms a general impression of the applicant. On the basis of the interviewer's judgments, successful applicants then move to the next step in the selection process, perhaps with the knowledge that the lack of an essential characteristic has lessened the chances of being seriously considered for the job. In smaller organizations, if the applicant appears to be a likely candidate for the position, the preliminary screening can proceed as an employment interview (Step 3).

The employer must be sure that the criteria used in this first step do not violate government antidiscrimination laws. The EEOC has a publication, *Affirmative Action and Equal Employment: A Guidebook for Employers*, which provides help on this issue (vol. 1, pp. 40–44). Copies can be found in any U.S. Government Printing Bookstore.

Step 1 is part of the reception portion of recruiting (see Chapter 7). The organization has the opportunity to make a good or bad impression on the applicant in this step.

EXHIBIT 8-4   Selection Procedures Used in Hiring and Promoting

	Percent of Companies ($n = 437$)	
	Procedures for Outside Applicants	Procedures for Candidates for Promotion
Reference/record check	97% (426)	67% (292)
Unstructured interview	81 (355)	70 (305)
Skill performance test/work sample	75 (329)	40 (176)
Medical examination	52 (229)	8 (34)
Structured interview	47 (206)	32 (142)
Investigation by outside agency	26 (112)	3 (14)
Job knowledge test	22 (94)	15 (64)
Mental ability test	20 (89)	10 (44)
Weighted application blank	11 (49)	7 (30)
Personality test	9 (39)	4 (18)
Assessment center	6 (28)	7 (30)
Physical abilities test	6 (27)	4 (16)
Polygraph test/written honesty test	6 (27)	1 (4)
Other	3 (13)	2 (9)

Source: Bureau of National Affairs (May 5, 1983), "Employee Selection Procedures," *Bulletin to Management*, ASPA-BNA Survey No. 45, p. 2. Reprinted by permission.

Step 2: Completion of Application Blank/Biodata Form

Applicants applying for a job with an organization almost always have to complete an application blank. Often, this is the very first part of the selection process; sometimes, it occurs after a very short initial screening interview. Application blanks are subject to the same legal restrictions as any other selection test. They must be job relevant and should avoid asking questions that might be discriminatory. Thus, items on an application blank should be kept to a minimum and should only ask for data that the enterprise's studies have indicated actually do predict performance. Exhibit 8–5 is an example of an application blank for the Dr. Pepper Company.

Essentially, those advocating the biodata approach argue that past behavior patterns are the best predictor of future behavior patterns. Thus, data should be gathered on a person's demographic and attitudinal characteristics and previous work experience in a form that lends itself to psychometric evaluation and interpretation. In constructing the biodata form, a variety of approaches can be used. According to experts, the form should be brief; the items should be stated in neutral or pleasant terms; the items should offer all possible answers or categories plus an "escape clause"; and numbered items should add to a scale.[17] It is argued that sequenced items are preferable to nonsequenced items, and select–one option items are better than multiple-choice items.

An important biodata substitute or supplement for the application blank is the *biographical information blank (BIB)*. The BIB usually has more items than an application blank and includes different kinds of items relating to such things as attitudes, health, and early life experiences. It uses the multiple-choice answer system. Instead of asking just about education, it might ask:

EXHIBIT 8-5

DR PEPPER COMPANY
APPLICATION FOR EMPLOYMENT

INTERVIEWER _____

INTERVIEWER _____

POSITION APPLIED FOR

PERSONAL DATA

FIRST NAME	MIDDLE NAME	LAST NAME	DATE

STREET ADDRESS	CITY AND STATE	ZIP CODE	SOCIAL SECURITY NUMBER

DATE OF BIRTH*	YES ☐ NO ☐	IF NO, RESIDENT CARD NUMBER	AREA CODE - TELEPHONE NUMBER

CAN YOU WORK REGULAR HOURS? YES ☐ NO ☐	CAN YOU WORK OVERTIME? YES ☐ NO ☐	DO YOU HAVE TRANSPORTATION TO YOUR JOB? NO ☐ YES ☐

DO YOU HAVE ANY FRIENDS OR RELATIVES WORKING HERE? IF YES, NAME AND LOCATION;   NO ☐   YES ☐

HAVE YOU EVER BEEN CONVICTED OF A CRIME OR REFUSED SURETY BOND? IF YES, GIVE DATE, PLACE, AND REASON: NO ☐   YES ☐

NAME AND ADDRESS OF PERSON TO BE NOTIFIED IN CASE OF EMERGENCY:	NAME	STREET ADDRESS	CITY AND STATE	TELEPHONE

PHYSICAL RECORD

PRESENT STATE OF HEALTH	*PHYSICAL HANDICAPS OR LIMITATIONS: IF YES DESCRIBE: NO ☐ YES ☐

DO YOU HAVE OR HAVE YOU HAD ANY ALLERGIES (INCLUDING ASTHMA)? NO ☐ YES ☐	DO YOU HAVE HISTORY OF NERVOUS CONDITION? IF YES, EXPLAIN: NO ☐ YES ☐
HAVE YOU HAD ANY OPERATION OR MAJOR ILLNESS IN LAST 5 YEARS? IF YES, EXPLAIN: NO ☐ YES ☐	HAVE YOU EVER HAD BACK TROUBLE OR INJURY? IF YES, EXPLAIN: NO ☐ YES ☐

HAVE YOU EVER RECEIVED WORKMAN'S COMPENSATION FOR ANY ACCIDENT OR DISABILITY? IF YES, EXPLAIN: NO ☐   YES ☐

EDUCATION

CIRCLE HIGHEST GRADE COMPLETED:		GRAMMER SCHOOL 1 2 3 4 5 6 7 8	HIGH SCHOOL 9 10 11 12	COLLEGE 1 2 3 4

HIGH SCHOOL NAME(S)	LOCATION(S)	DATES FROM	TO	GRADE AVERAGE	GRADUATE? YES ☐ NO ☐

COLLEGE NAME	LOCATION	FROM	TO	DEGREE/MAJOR	GRADUATE? YES ☐ NO ☐

OTHER SCHOOLING

U.S. MILITARY SERVICE

ARE YOU IN THE MILITARY RESERVE? NO ☐ YES ☐ STATUS: ACTIVE ☐ INACTIVE ☐	WERE YOU EVER IN THE SERVICE? NO ☐ YES ☐	DATE ENTERED	DATE DISCHARGED	RANK AT DISCHARGE

DO YOU RECEIVE A.V.A. PENSION CAUSED BY DISABILITY INCURRED DURING U.S. MILITARY SERVICE?   NO ☐   YES ☐   IF YES, STATE PERCENT OF BENEFIT, IF ANY:

SKILLS/SCHOOLS DURING SERVICE

OFFICE SKILLS   INDICATE THOSE SKILLS YOU HAVE

TYPEWRITER? NO ☐ YES ☐ SPEED	DICTAPHONE? NO ☐ YES ☐	ADDING MACHINE? NO ☐ YES ☐	CALCULATOR? NO ☐ YES ☐ WHAT TYPE?
DO YOU TAKE SHORTHAND? NO ☐ YES ☐ SPEED	BOOKKEEPING MACHINE? NO ☐ YES ☐ WHAT TYPE?		DATA PROCESSING? NO ☐ YES ☐ WHAT TYPE?

* ALL LEGAL REQUIREMENTS PERTAINING TO FAIR EMPLOYMENT PRACTICES ARE COMPLIED WITH BY DR. PEPPER CO. HENCE ITEMS COVERING INFORMATION WHICH IN YOUR STATE MAY NOT BE LEGALLY REQUIRED (INCLUDING ITEMS WITH ASTERISKS) SHOULD NOT BE COMPLETED. DR. PEPPER IS AN EQUAL OPPORTUNITY EMPLOYER.

EXHIBIT 8-5   *(concluded)*

PERSONAL DATA BEGIN WITH MOST RECENT POSITION AND WORK BACK, BEING SURE TO ACCOUNT FOR ANY TIME LAPSE, INCLUDE SUMMER AND PART TIME JOBS

DATES FROM / TO	NAME OF FIRM		JOB TITLE	REASON FOR LEAVING
	ADDRESS	TELEPHONE	SUPERVISORS NAME	
	CITY STATE	ZIP CODE	FULL TIME □ SALARY PART TIME □	
	GENERAL DUTIES			

DATES FROM / TO	NAME OF FIRM		JOB TITLE	REASON FOR LEAVING
	ADDRESS	TELEPHONE	SUPERVISORS NAME	
	CITY STATE	ZIP CODE	FULL TIME □ SALARY PART TIME □	
	GENERAL DUTIES			

DATES FROM / TO	NAME OF FIRM		JOB TITLE	REASON FOR LEAVING
	ADDRESS	TELEPHONE	SUPERVISORS NAME	
	CITY STATE	ZIP CODE	FULL TIME □ SALARY PART TIME □	
	GENERAL DUTIES			

DATES FROM / TO	NAME OF FIRM		JOB TITLE	REASON FOR LEAVING
	ADDRESS	TELEPHONE	SUPERVISORS NAME	
	CITY STATE	ZIP CODE	FULL TIME □ SALARY PART TIME □	
	GENERAL DUTIES			

DATES FROM / TO	NAME OF FIRM		JOB TITLE	REASON FOR LEAVING
	ADDRESS	TELEPHONE	SUPERVISORS NAME	
	CITY STATE	ZIP CODE	FULL TIME □ SALARY PART TIME □	
	GENERAL DUTIES			

ACCEPTABLE STARTING WAGE _____

DRIVING RECORD

DRIVER'S LICENSE NO. TYPE AND STATE ISSUED:	YEARS OF DRIVING EXPERIENCE:	INDICATE NUMBER OF VEHICLE ACCIDENTS INVOLVED IN LAST:
ARE THERE ANY RESTRICTIONS ON YOUR DRIVER'S LICENSE? NO□ YES□ COMMENT:		12 MONTHS _____ 5 YEARS _____ EXPLAIN
HAVE YOU EVER HAD YOUR DRIVER'S LICENSE SUSPENDED OR REVOKED? NO□ YES□ COMMENT:		MOVING TRAFFIC VIOLATOINS IN LAST: 12 MONTHS _____ 5 YEARS _____ COMMENT:

I CERTIFY THAT ALL OF THE FOREGOING STATEMENTS ARE TRUE AND CORRECT TO THE BEST OF MY ABILITY. I UNDERSTAND THAT MISREPRESENTATION OR ADMISSION OF FACTS IS CAUSE FOR DISMISSAL.
I AM WILLING TO TAKE PHYSICAL OR OTHER EXAMINATIONS WHEN REQUIRED. I UNDERSTAND THAT AN INVESTIGATIVE REPORT MAY BE MADE WHEREBY INFORMATION IS OBTAINED FROM THIRD PARTIES. THIS INQUIRY INCLUDES INFORMATION AS TO YOUR CHARACTER, GENERAL REPUTATION, PERSONAL CHARACTERISTICS, MODE OF LIVING, ETC. AND RELEASE OF SCHOOL AND OR COLLEGE TRANSCRIPTS.
YOU HAVE THE RIGHT TO MAKE A WRITTEN REQUEST WITHIN A REASONABLE PERIOD OF TIME FOR A COMPLETE DISCLOSURE OF ADDITIONAL INFORMATION CONCERNING THE MATURE AND SCOPE OF THE INVESTIGATION.

_____
SIGNATURE OF APPLICANT

DO NOT WRITE BELOW THIS LINE - FOR COMPANY USE ONLY

INTERVIEWER'S COMMENTS:

- -

MVR _____ DATE ORDERED _____ REF CHECK _____ PHYSICAL _____ DATE SENT _____ DATE & TIME OF RETURN _____

START DATE _____ LOCATION _____ DEPARTMENT _____ POSITION _____ WAGE _____

ITEM#CP 026 W/10-1 80 Qty

How old were you when you graduated from the 6th grade?

1. Younger than 10
2. 10–12
3. 13–14
4. 15–16

It also asks opinion questions, such as:

How do you feel about being transferred from this city by this company?

1. Would thoroughly enjoy a transfer.
2. Would like to experience a transfer.
3. Would accept a transfer.
4. Would reject a tranfer.

To use the BIB as a selection tool, the HR specialist correlates each item on the form with the selection criteria for job success. Those criteria that predict the best for a position are used to help select applicants for that position.

Another variety of biodata form is the **weighted application blank,** an application form designed to be scored as a systematic selection device. Weighted application blanks have been used for predicting success and turnover for office, manufacturing, hospital, and banking jobs.[18] The purpose of a weighted application blank is to relate the characteristics of applicants to success on the job. It has been estimated that it takes about 100 hours to develop a weighted blank for a job.

The typical approach is to divide present jobholders into two or three categories (in half, high or low; or in thirds, high, middle, or low), based on some success criterion such as performance as measured by production records, supervisor's evaluation, or high versus low turnover. Then, the characteristics of high and low performers are examined. For many characteristics for a particular organization and job, there may be no difference by age or education level, but there may be differences according to where applicants live and their years of experience, for example. A weight is assigned to the degree of differences: for no difference, 0; for some difference, ±1; for a big difference, ±2. Then these weights are totaled for all applicants, and the one with the highest positive score is hired, assuming that the score meets the minimum that past and currently successful employees have attained.

These predictive characteristics vary by job and occupation. For example, the age of the applicant is a good predictor for some jobs; for others, it is not. How predictive a characteristic is might also change over time. Weights need to be recomputed every several years or so, and, generally speaking, the weighted application blank must be validated for each job and organization. However, biodata forms can sometimes show validity across different jobs and organizations. This is most likely to occur when applicants or employees from several companies were used in the original development and keying of the items.[19]

Most researchers have found that biodata approaches are reliable and they often have high validity.[20] However, studies indicate that, although most organizations use application blanks, fewer than a third of the larger organizations have utilized weighted application blanks or other biodata approaches. Given the problems with tests, references, and other selection techniques, the percentage of organizations using biodata approaches is likely to increase.[21]

Step 3: Employment Interview

Without question, employment interviews are the most widely used selection tool. When used extensively by an organization, they can also be an expensive proposition. Consider the case of one large organization that spent approximately $100,000 to interview applicants for 150 jobs.[22] Thus, it is very important for HR specialists to understand this selection technique so it can be used to its fullest potential while avoiding many pitfalls associated with it.

Types of Interviews
There are a number of general types of employment interviews. Some organizations use more than one type to help them make a selection decision:

- Structured
- Semistructured
- Unstructured

While all employment interviews are alike in certain respects, each type is also unique in some way. All three include interaction between two or more parties, an applicant and one or more representatives (people serving on an interview panel hold what is called a *group interview*) of the potential employer, for a predetermined purpose. This purpose is consideration of an applicant for employment. Information is exchanged, usually through questions and answers. The main differences in employment interviews lie in the interviewer's approach to the process, and the type used depends both on the kind of information desired and the nature of the situation.

In the **structured employment interview,** the interviewer prepares a list of questions in advance and does not deviate from it. In many organizations, a standard form is used on which the interviewer notes the applicant's responses to the predetermined questions. Many of the questions asked in a structured interview are forced-choice in nature, and the interviewer need only indicate the applicant's response with a check mark on the form.

If the approach is highly structured, the interviewer may also follow a prearranged sequence of questions. In such an interview, the interviewer is often little more than a recorder of the interviewee's responses, and little training is required to conduct it. The structured approach is very restrictive, however. The information elicited is narrow, and there is little opportunity to adapt to the individual applicant. This approach is equally constraining to the applicant, who is unable to qualify or elaborate on answers to the questions. The Bureau of National Affair's survey found that 19 percent of the companies used a written interview form, while 26 percent employed a standard format for employment interviews.[23] Exhibit 8–6 is an example of a form used for a structured employment interview.

An interesting and effective variation of the structured interview is the *situational interview*.[24] It seeks to identify whether an applicant possesses relevant job knowledge and motivation much like other interviews. In addition, however, it asks the applicant to respond to hypothetical situations they might encounter on the job. Responses to these are then scored according to their appropriateness for that job.

In the *semistructured interview*, only the major questions to be asked are prepared in advance, though the interviewer may also prepare some probing questions in areas of inquiry. While this approach calls for greater interviewer preparation, it also

EXHIBIT 8-6   Structured Employment Interview Form — Executive Position

Date _____ 19 _____

SUMMARY

Rating [1] [2] [3] [4]   Comments: _____

In making final rating, be sure to consider not only what he applicant can do but also his/her stability, industry,

perseverance, loyalty, ability to get along with others, self-reliance, leadership, maturity, motivation, and domestic situation and health.

_____

_____

_____

Interviewer: _____   Job considered for: _____

Name _____   Date of birth _____   Phone No. _____

The age discrimination in the employment act and relevant FEP Acts prohibit discrimination with respect to individuals who are at least 40 but less than 65 years of age.

Present address _____   City _____   State _____   How long there? _____

Were you in the Armed Forces of the U.S.? Yes, branch _____   Dates _____ 19___ to _____ 19 _____

(Not to be asked in New Jersey)   _____ 19___ to _____ 19 _____

If not, why not? _____

Were you hospitalized in the service? _____

Are you drawing compensation? Yes_____ No_____

Are you employed now?   Yes ☐   No ☐ (If yes) How soon available? _____

What are relationships with present employer?

Why are you applying for this position? _____

Is his/her underlying reason a desire for prestige, security, or earnings?

WORK EXPERIENCE. Cover all positions. This information is very important. Interviewer should record last position first. Every month since leaving school should be accounted for. Experience in Armed Forces should be covered as a job (in New Jersey exclude military questions).

LAST OR PRESENT POSITION _____

Company _____   City _____   From _____ 19___ to _____ 19 _____

How was job obtained? _____   Whom did you know there? _____

Has applicant shown self-reliance in getting jobs?

Nature of work at start _____   Starting salary _____

Will applicant's previous experience be helpful on this job?

In what way did the job change? _____

Has applicant made good work progress?

Nature of work at leaving _____   Salary at leaving _____

How much responsibility has applicant had?   Any indication of ambition?

Superior _____   Title _____   What is he/she like? _____

Did applicant get along with superior?

How closely does (or did) he/she supervise you? _____   What authority do (or did) you have? _____

Number of people you supervised _____   What did they do? _____

Is applicant a leader?

Responsibility for policy formulation _____

Has applicant had management responsibility?

To what extent could you use initiative and judgment? _____

Did applicant actively seek responsibility?

allows for more flexibility than the structured approach. The interviewer is free to probe into those areas that seem to merit further investigation. With less structure, however, it is more difficult to replicate these interviews. This approach combines enough structure to facilitate the exchange of factual information with adequate freedom to develop insights.

The *unstructured interview* involves little preparation. The interviewer prepares a list of possible topics to be covered and sometimes does not even do that. The overriding advantage of the unstructured type is the freedom it allows the interviewer to adapt to the situation and to the changing stream of applicants. Spontaneity characterizes this approach, but, under the control of an untrained interviewer, digresssions, discontinuity, and eventual frustration for both parties may result.

While the unstructured approach lends itself to the counseling of individuals with problems, it is not limited to guidance. Students frequently encounter HR recruiters whose sole contribution, other than the opening and closing pleasantries, is ''Tell me about yourself.'' When used by a highly skilled interviewer, the unstructured interview can lead to significant insights that might enable the interviewer to make fine distinctions among applicants. However, as used by most employment interviewers, that is not the case, and it is seldom appropriate for an employment interviewer to relinquish control to such an extent.

Some interviewers try to induce stress into the employment interview process. For example, the interviewer may ask questions in a hostile tone or deliberately interrupt the interviewee. It is assumed that stressful situations will show how a person really reacts under pressure. Generally speaking, creating stress in the interview is dysfunctional to the selection process. However, introducing stress is still used when interviewing individuals for high-pressure jobs such as police work, emergency care centers, and fire fighting.[25]

Interviewing Errors   Despite its extensive use, there are many questions about the reliability and validity of the interview.[26] To a large extent, whether an interview can be useful in the selection process depends on how it is conducted and by whom. Recent studies indicate that some interviewers show considerable validity in their recommendations while others do not. In addition, interviewers differ substantially in terms of the kinds of information they use to arrive at their judgments about applicants.[27] It is also important to be aware of several errors that are frequently committed by even the best of interviewers.[28]

First-Impression Errors   There is a tendency for interviewers to make up their minds early in the interview process. The first few minutes are critical for determining who will be judged suitable for a job even when additional important information is exchanged later in the interview.

Contrast Errors   A contrast error has occurred when an interviewer is overly influenced for or against an applicant by the interviews of previous applicants. For example, if a qualified applicant follows an exceptional applicant, his or her qualifications tend to pale in comparison. The result can be that the qualified applicant's evaluation may be lower that it should be. This situation is unfortunate since the qualified candidate may be rejected because of the contrast error.

Similar-to-Me Errors   Other research indicates that, all else being equal, interviewers tend to give higher ratings to applicants that they perceive to be similar to themselves. These similarities might be in terms of seemingly unimportant issues such as hobbies, area of town lived in, or favorite foods. Even more dangerous is the case where a similar-to-me error has occurred because of an applicant's sex or race.

Misinterpretation of Nonverbal Cues   Interviewers sometimes use nonverbal behavior information while formulating their judgments about applicants. That is, how the person looks, sits in the chair, or maintains eye contact may be the major factors used in rating the applicant. The problem is that paying too much attention to this kind of nonverbal behavior can result in bypassing competent applicants.

Sex and Attractiveness   Another potential problem that some interviewers encounter is relying on an applicant's sex or physical attractiveness for making judgments about their suitability. The effects, however, are not always constant. That is, one study found that whether attractiveness was a help or a hindrance to applicants depended on the sex of the applicant and the nature of the job being filled. Attractiveness was a major advantage for male applicants seeking managerial jobs.[29] However, attractiveness tended to work against a woman interviewing for a managerial job.

Interviewer's Knowledge of Job   Another interview problem involves the interviewer's lack of knowledge about the job. An interviewer that is not clear about a job's responsibilities often has difficulty providing a good impression to the applicant about the organization. This impression by an applicant can play a role in his or her final decision about accepting a position.

These and other interview errors must be understood so that they can be avoided. Interviewers often make errors in interviewing because they do not understand the errors and they are not formally trained to conduct interviews. A trained interviewer is likely to make fewer errors because he or she understands potential errors, has learned how to ask questions effectively, is able to establish a positive relationship with applicants, and has systematically organized the interview. These are characteristics of effective interviewing that would be stressed in interview training programs.

Following is a concise summary of some key points to follow when conducting an interview:

1. Work at listening to what and how the applicant communicates with you. Unlike hearing, listening is an active process and requires concentration. Many interviewers plan their next question when they should be listening to the applicant's present response.

2. Be aware of the applicant's nonverbal cues as well as the verbal message. In attempting to get as complete a picture of the applicant as possible, you must not ignore what some consider the most meaningful type of communication, body language.

3. Remain aware of the job requirements throughout the interview. No one is immune to the halo effect, which gives undue weight to one characteristic. You must constantly keep the requirements of the job in mind. Sometimes, an applicant possesses some personal mannerism or trait that so attracts or repels the interviewer that the decision is made mostly on the strength of that characteristic, which may be completely irrelevant to the requirements of the job in question.

4. Maintain a balance between open and overly structured questions. Too many of the former make the interview a meandering conversation; while too many of the latter turn the interview into an interrogation.

5. Wait until you have all of the necessary information before making a decision. Some interviewees start more slowly than others, and what may appear to be disinterest may later prove to have been an initial reserve that dissipates after a few minutes. *Don't evaluate on the basis of a first impression.*

6. Do not ask questions that violate equal employment opportunity laws and regulations (see list in Chapter 3). Focus the interview on the variables identified as crucial criteria for selection.

An overall evaluation of the interview as a selection technique is not easy to give. Early reviews of its effectiveness were very pessimistic. More recently, however, there has been some reason for increased optimism about its validity.[30] As more and more research focuses on the process of interviewing, hopefully, HR specialists will continue to refine and improve its use. At the very least, experts now understand that as the structure of the interview increases so does its validity, and, perhaps more important, interviewing is a skill that can be learned and apparently improved with training.

Step 4: Employment Tests

A technique that some organizations use to aid their selection decisions is the employment test. An employment test is a mechanism (either a paper-and-pencil test or a simulation exercise) that attempts to measure certain characteristics of individuals. These characteristics range from motor coordination aptitudes, such as manual dexterity, to intelligence to personality.

It can be very expensive to develop a test to measure these kinds of characteristics. For this reason alone, many employers purchase existing tests from a variety of sources. There are literally hundreds of published tests from which to choose with some of the more useful tests costing as little as $1 per applicant to purchase. Anyone interested in selecting a test for use in personnel selection can begin with the *Mental Measurements Yearbook*,[31] which summarizes many of the tests and includes a brief evaluation of their effectiveness.

Regardless of whether an organization develops its own test or purchases an existing one, there are additional costs associated with using them in selection. Any of these devices should be validated before it is actually used to make hiring decisions. Validation studies are also expensive if they are conducted properly. An organization can very quickly spend $50,000 or more to conduct a validation study for a single occupational grouping.[32] The validation process becomes even more expensive if questions of discrimination arise. In such instances, the organization is expected to validate its selection devices separately for majority and minority group members.

Despite the potentially staggering costs associated with employment tests, many of them can more than pay for themselves through increased efficiency in selection. However, because they can be expensive to use, an organization should carefully decide which tests will help them hire the best applicants possible. In other words, care should be taken to only use tests that are job-related.

There are various kinds of tests. Job sample performance tests, simulations of performance, paper-and-pencil tests, personality and temperament inventories, and others are discussed below.

Job Sample Performance Tests

Job Sample Performance Tests   A job sample performance test is an experience that involves actually doing a sample of the work the job involves in a controlled situation. Examples of performance tests include:

1. A programming test for computer operators.
2. Employees running a miniature punchpress.
3. A standard driving course as a performance test for forklift operators.
4. The auditions used by symphony orchestras for hiring purposes. For example, when symphony orchestras select new musicians, the selection panel listens to them play the same piece of music with the same instrument. The applicants are hidden behind a screen at the time.
5. A tool dexterity test for machine operators.
6. Standardized typing tests. The applicants are asked to type some work. Their speed and accuracy are then computed.

Variations of these performance tests exist in many organizations. The applicants are asked to run the machines they would run if they got the job, and quality and quantity of output are recorded.

Job sample tests tend to have the highest validities and reliabilities of all tests because they systematically measure behavior directly related to the job. This is not surprising. Imagine that you are an artist who is applying for graduate study in art. You typically must take the Graduate Record Exam, a paper-and-pencil test designed to measure verbal and mathematical "ability." You also must present 12 paintings, drawings, and watercolors (a portfolio) to the art department. Which of these selection devices appears likely to be the more reliable and valid measure of your painting ability? Or recall that when you applied for your driver's license, you took two tests: a paper-and-pencil test, and, when you drove the car, a performance test. Which better tested your driving ability: the paper-and-pencil test, or that tension-filled drive with the observer who rated your driving ability? A similar principle applies to job selection. Which would be a better predictor of the forklift operator's job performance: the standardized test, in which the applicant drives the truck down and around piles of goods, or a paper-and-pencil test of driving knowledge, intelligence, or whatever?

Reliability and validity figures for all the standardized tests discussed here are available from the test developers. Many are reviewed in regular summaries, such as the *Annual Review of Psychology*.

Performance Simulations

Performance Simulations   A performance simulation is a non-paper-and-pencil experience designed to determine abilities related to job performance. For example, suppose job analysis indicates that successful job occupants of a specific job require highly developed mechanical or clerical abilities. A number of simulations are available to measure these abilities. The simulation is not the actual performance of part of the job, but it comes close to that through simulation. You may have learned to drive by performing first on simulation machines; it was not the same as on-the-street driving, but it was closer than reading about it or observing other drivers.

There are many of these simulation tests. Here are some:

Revised Minnesota Paper Form Board Test

Revised Minnesota Paper Form Board Test   Exhibit 8–7 is an excerpt from the MPFB, which is a test of space visualization. It is used for various jobs. For example, to be a draftsperson requires the ability to see things in their relation to

EXHIBIT 8-7   Excerpt from Revised Minnesota Paper Form Board Test

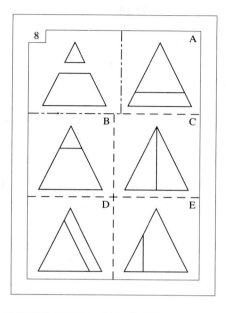

EXHIBIT 8-8   O'Connor Finger and Tweezer Dexterity Test Equipment

space. The applicant must select the item (A–E) that best represents what a group of shapes will look like when assembled.

Psychomotor Ability Simulations   There are a number of tests that measure such psychomotor abilities as choice reaction time, speed of limb movement, and finger dexterity. One of these is the O'Connor Finger and Tweezer Dexterity Test (see Exhibit 8–8). The person being tested picks up pins with the tweezer and row by row inserts them in the holes across the board, or inserts the pins with the hand normally used. These tests are used for positions with high manual requirements for success, such as assemblers of radio or TV components and watches.

Clerical Abilities   Exhibit 8–9 is the first page of the Minnesota Clerical Test. It is a typical test for clerical abilities. This simulation requires the applicants to check numbers and names, skills frequently used in clerical tasks.

Paper-and-Pencil Tests

In the third group of tests are paper-and-pencil tests, designed to measure general intelligence and aptitudes.[33] Many employers assume that mental abilities are an important component of performance for many jobs. Intelligence and mental ability tests attempt to sample intellectual mental development or skills.

Some examples of paper-and-pencil tests are:

Otis Quick Scoring Mental Ability Test   This test samples several intellectual functions, including vocabulary, arithmetic skills, reasoning, and perception, totaling them to one score. It includes items such as the following:

---

a.   Which one of the five things below is soft?
  (1) glass (2) stone (3) cotton (4) iron (5) ice
b.   A robin is a kind of:
  (6) plant (7) bird (8) worm (9) fish (10) flower
c.   Which one of the five numbers below is larger than 55?
  (11) 53 (12) 48 (13) 29 (14) 57 (15) 16

Wechsler Adult Intelligence Scale   The Wechsler is a comprehensive paper-and-pencil test of 14 sections grouped into two scores. The verbal score includes general information, arithmetic, similarities, vocabulary, and other items. The performance score includes picture completion, picture arrangement, object assembly, and similar items.

Wonderlic Personnel Test   The Wonderlic is a shortened form of the Otis test. It uses a variety of perceptual, verbal, and arithmetical items that provide a total score. (Other well-known tests include the Differential Aptitude Test, the SRA Primary Mental Abilities Test, and multiple aptitude tests.)

The above three tests are administered to individuals and are paper-and-pencil tests similar to those taken in school.

California Test of Mental Maturity (adult level)   This is a test of mental ability administered to groups and scored by machine. Scores are developed from a series of short tests on spatial relationships, verbal concepts, logic and reasoning, numerical reasoning, memory, and others. The scores are converted to IQ equivalents, and profiles are developed for analyzing performance.

The reliability and validity of paper-and-pencil tests have been studied extensively. In general, they are not as reliable as performance tests or other selection devices, such as biodata forms or structured interviews.

EXHIBIT 8-9

MINNESOTA CLERICAL TEST
(formerly the Minnesota Vocational Test for Clerical Workers)
by Dorothy M. Andrew, Donald G. Patterson, and Howard P. Longstaff

Name _____   Name _____

TEST 1–Number Comparison   TEST 2–Name Comparison

Number Right _____   Number Right _____
Number Wrong _____   Number Wrong _____
Score = R – W _____   Score = R – W _____
Percentile Rating _____   Percentile Rating _____
Norms Used _____   Norms Used _____

INSTRUCTIONS

On the inside pages there are two tests. One of the tests consists of pairs of names and the other of pairs of numbers. If the two names or the two numbers of a pair are exactly the same make a check mark (√) on the line between them: if they are different, make no mark on that line. When the examiner says "Stop!" draw a line under the last pair at which you have looked.

Samples done correctly of pairs of NUMBERS

79542___79524
1234567_√_1234567

SAMPLES done correctly of pairs of NAMES

John C. Linder___John C. Lender
Investors Syndicate_√_Investors Syndicate

This is a test for speed and accuracy. Work as fast as you can without making mistakes. Do not turn this page until you are told to begin.

Personality Inventories and Temperament Tests   The least reliable of the employment tests are those instruments that attempt to measure a person's personality or temperament. The most frequently used inventory is the Minnesota Multiphasic Personality Inventory. Other paper-and-pencil inventories are the California Psychological Inventory, the Minnesota Counseling Inventory, the Manifest Anxiety Scale, and the Edwards Personal Preference Schedule.

A more optimistic picture of the value of personality inventories comes from efforts to specifically construct a measure for a particular job. That is, some of the disappointing results previously obtained with personality inventories in selection could be attributed to a mismatch between the test and the situation in which it was being used.[34] When personality tests are specially constructed to measure work-related characteristics such as achievement and dependability, they can show good validities.[35]

A different approach, not as direct as the self-reporting inventory, utilizes projective techniques to present vague stimuli, the reactions to which provide data on which psychologists base their assessment and interpretation of a personality. The stimuli are purposely vague in order to reach the unconscious aspects of the personality. Many techniques are used. The most common are the Rorschach Inkblot Test and the Thematic Apperception Test.

The Rorschach Inkblot Test was first described in 1921. The test involves 10 cards, on each of which is printed a bilateral symmetrical inkblot similar to that illustrated in Exhibit 8–10.[36] The person responding is asked to tell what he or she sees in the inkblot. The examiner keeps a verbatim record of the responses, the time taken to make the responses, emotional expressions, and other incidental behavior. Then, a trained interpreter analyzes the data set and reaches conclusions about the personality patterns of the person being examined.

The Polygraph and Honesty Tests   Another method currently used by some employers to test employees is the polygraph, sometimes erroneously called a *lie detector*. The polygraph is an instrument that records changes in breathing, blood pressure, pulse, and skin response associated with sweating of palms, and then plots these reactions on paper. The person being tested with a polygraph attached is asked a series of questions. Some are neutral, to achieve a normal response, others stressful, to indicate a response made under pressure. Thus, the applicant may be asked: "Is your name Smith?" Then, "Have you ever stolen from an employer?"

Although originally developed for police work, the polygraph had become an extremely popular selection tool by the mid-1980s. It has been estimated that, prior to 1988, nearly 2 million polygraph tests had been administered each year by private employers in the United States.[37] This popularity was understandable since on-the-job crime has increased tremendously; it is estimated that dishonest employees cost employers about $65 billion per year in theft and other acts of dishonesty.[38] Since a polygraph will only cost about $25, it seems like a small investment to help reduce workplace dishonesty.

In recent years, objections to the use of the polygraph in personnel selection have been raised. There are concerns that it is an invasion of an applicant's privacy and that its use can lead to self-incrimination, which would be a violation of the Fifth Amendment to the Constitution. Above all, however, the most serious question concerning the polygraph became one of whether it was, in fact, a reliable and valid method for predicting on-the-job dishonesty.

EXHIBIT 8-10   An Inkblot of the Type Employed in the Rorschach Technique

These concerns became serious enough that the U.S. government passed the *Employee Polygraph Protection Act* of 1988. This legislation has made it illegal for most private organizations to use the polygraph as a selection device. Government agencies and certain Department of Defense and Department of Energy contractors are exempted from the act. In addition, private employers whose business involves security and controlled substances are also allowed to continue using the polygraph. Finally, it is still legal to use the polygraph as a part of an on-going investigation of employee dishonesty as long as the individual employee's rights are safeguarded.[39]

Organizations searching for an alternative to the polygraph are increasingly turning to paper-and-pencil tests of honesty. Estimates are that 5,000 to 6,000 firms in the United States now use these during screening.[40] Several kinds of honesty tests exist ranging from direct assessment technique tests (straightforward questions about integrity) to more indirect methods that infer dishonesty from other characteristics.

The test results from a reliable honesty test are only one aspect of information gathered about the job applicant.[41] Other performance tests, previous work experience, reference checks, and previous employer recommendations should also be carefully screened. Because of the problems and costs of employee theft, espionage, and dissatisfaction, it is likely that honesty tests will continue to be used as part of the selection process in the future.

Employment Testing and the Law   Perhaps the first event signaling the involvement of the courts in employment testing was the *Myart* v. *Motorola* (1964) case.[42] In 1963, Leon Myart, a black man, was refused a job as a "television phaser and analyzer" at one of Motorola's plants because his score on a five-minute intelligence test was not high enough, although he had previous job-related experience. Myart filed a complaint charging that he had been racially discriminated against in his denial of the job. At the hearing, an examiner for the Illinois Commission ruled that: (1) Myart should be offered a job; (2) the test should no longer be used; and (3) every new test developed in its place should take into account environmental factors contributing to cultural deprivation. Although this ruling was eventually overturned for lack of evidence by the Illinois State Supreme Court, it set the precedent to hear employment testing complaints in the courts.

The National Research Council's 19-member Committee on Ability Testing prepared two books that examine employment testing and the law.[43] Among the conclusions reached by the committee were these:

- No alternative to a standardized test has been found that is equally informative, equally adequate technically, and also economically and politically viable.
- Validation of tests is important, but it should be recognized that it is an expensive and time-consuming process.
- Standarized tests do not necessarily discriminate against minorities, but employers should not rely on them solely to make selection decisions.
- Tests have been used to bring about increased government involvement in the selection process of organizations.

These conclusions and the content of the books suggest that valid and reliable tests do not alone ensure EEO compliance, but remain accurate predictors of job performance and a force against discrimination in employment. However, no test is infallible or immune from legal repudiation.[44]

Employment testing will undoubtedly remain a part of many organizational selection programs. In the years to come, however, more and more emphasis is going to be on the organization's responsibility to see that they are used properly.[45] Thus, it is advisable for an organization to choose selection tests carefully, to examine the reliability and validity of the tests used, to validate the tests used, and to be certain that the persons in charge of the selection program are fully qualified in the use of tests.

Step 5: Reference Checks and Recommendations

If you have ever applied for a job, at some point you were asked to provide a list of references of past supervisors and others. In general, you picked people who could evaluate you effectively and fairly for your new employer — people who know and express your good and bad points equally.

For years, as part of the selection process, applicants have been required to submit references or recommendation letters.[46] These indicate past behavior and how well the applicant did at her or his job. Studies indicate that this has been a common practice for white-collar jobs.

For a letter of recommendation to be useful, it must meet certain conditions:

The writer must know the applicant's performance level and be competent to assess it.

The writer must communicate the evaluation effectively to the potential employer.

The writer must be truthful.

If the applicant chooses the references, the first two conditions may not be met. With regard to the third, many people are reluctant to put in writing what they really think of the applicant, since he or she may see it. As a result, the person writing the reference either glosses over shortcomings or over-emphasizes the applicant's good points. Because of these and other shortcomings, studies of the validity of written references have not been comforting to those using them in selection.

Kessler and Gibbs propose a method for potentially improving the validity of letters of reference as a selection tool.[47] In their approach, letters of reference are required only for jobs that have had job analysis performed to develop job specifications (see Chapter 6). A panel of judges (three to six persons) familiar with the job ranks the specifications for relative importance. Then, a reference letter is drafted, asking the respondent to rate the applicant on the job specifications, which are listed randomly. A sample of such a reference letter is shown in Exhibit 8–11. The references must be familiar with the applicant's past employment. The rankings of the panel and the references are correlated, and the greater the correlation, the more likely it is that the applicant will be hired.

Congress has passed the Privacy Act of 1974 and the Buckley amendment.[48] These allow applicants to view letters of reference in their files. The laws apply to public-sector employees and students. But private- and third-sector employers are afraid that the laws will soon apply to them, so many of them will now give out only minimal data: dates of employment, job title, and so on. If this becomes a common practice, reference letters may not be very useful.

When there is a need to verify biodata, a more acceptable alternative for a letter might be a phone call to the applicant's previous supervisors to cross-check opinions or to probe further on doubtful points.[49] Most studies indicate that few employers feel written references alone are a reliable source of data. A majority of organiza-

---

EXHIBIT 8-11   Sample Reference Letter for Applicant for Employment Interviewer
Positions

Dear_____

_____ is applying for a position with our company and has supplied your name
as a reference. We would appreciate it if you would take a few moments to give us your opinions
about him.

   Listed below is a series of items that may describe skills, abilities, knowledge, or personal characteristics of the applicant to a greater or lesser degree. Will you please look at this list and rank them
from most to least like the applicant by placing the appropriate letter in the space below. If you do
not have an opinion about a specific item, skip it and rank what you can, beginning with Space 1.

   A.   Has the ability to develop scheduled and nonscheduled interview formats for various jobs.
   B.   Can conduct an interview using the nondirective approach.
   C.   Has a neat appearance (clothes clean, in good condition).
   D.   Makes checks to see if people understand his meaning when he speaks to them.
   E.   Checks to see if he understands people when they speak to him.

      1.   _____ (Most characteristic of the applicant)
      2.   _____
      3.   _____
      4.   _____
      5.   _____ (Least characteristic of the applicant)

Now, on the rating scale below, please indicate with a check in the appropriate space the degree to
which the applicant possesses the last ranked skill, ability, knowledge or personal characteristic. If he
is very high in the characteristic, give a rating of 5; if he is very low, give him a rating of 1. Place
your check in between the two extremes if you consider that a more appropriate rating.

Very low |___|___|___|___|___| Very high
           1   2   3   4   5

Comments about the applicant:

Source: Clemm C. Kessler III and Georgia J. Gibbs (January–February 1975), "Getting the Most from Application
Blanks and References," *Personnel*, pp. 53–62. Reprinted by permission of AMACOM, a division of American Management Associations. All rights reserved.

tions combine telephone checks, written letters of reference, and data obtained
from the employment interview. Items checked most frequently are previous employment and educational background (in that order).

   Although little data on phone references are available, phone calls appear to be
very useful to find out how the applicant performed on previous jobs. This can be
the most relevant information for predicting future work behavior. Reference
checks should be conducted for the most crucial jobs at any time. Costs of these
checks vary from a few cents for a few quick telephone calls to several hundred
dollars for a thorough field investigation.

STEP 6: PHYSICAL EXAMINATIONS

Some organizations require that those most likely to be selected for a position
complete a medical questionnaire or take a physical examination. The reasons for
such a requirement include:

   In case of later workers' compensation claims, physical condition at the time of
   hiring should be known.

. It is important to prevent the hiring of those with serious communicable diseases. This is especially so in hospitals, but it applies to other organizations as well.

. It may be necessary to determine whether the applicant is physically capable of performing the job in question.

These purposes can be served by the completion of a medical questionnaire, a physical examination, or a work physiology analysis. Chase has discussed the latter technique, which is neither a physical examination nor a psycho-motor test.[50] Commonly used for the selection of manual workers who will be doing hard labor, it attempts to determine, by physiological indexes (heart rate and oxygen consumption), the true fatigue engendered by the work. Fatigue is analyzed through simulated job performance. First the analyst measures applicants and obtains baseline information on these indexes while they are seated. Then, data are gathered while they are working. The data are analyzed and the workers are ranked; those with the lowest heart rate and oxygen consumption should be hired (all other factors being equal).

Physical examinations have *not* been shown to be very reliable as a predictor of future medical problems.[51] This is at least partially so because of the state of the art of medicine. Different physicians emphasize different factors in the exam, based on their training and specialties. There is some evidence that correlating the presence of certain past medical problems (as learned from the completion of a medical questionnaire) can be as reliable as a physical exam performed by a physician and is probably less costly.

When the Americans with Disabilities Act of 1990 goes into effect in 1992, employers' rights to require medical exams prior to making job offers will be severely restricted. In addition, it will be a clear violation of the act to make an employment decision on the basis of either a real or a perceived disability. As a result, after 1992, nearly all medical exams given will have to occur after an initial job offer has been made.

Acquired immune deficiency syndrome (AIDS) has reached epidemic proportions. Fear and reality are often confused when this devastating illness is discussed. Despite the fears that AIDS invokes, it appears that few employers have resorted to AIDS testing as a condition of employment. Estimates are that less than 2 percent of firms routinely test for the disease.[52] Once the Americans with Disabilities Act becomes effective, this number will probably decrease since it provides broader legal protection to individuals with AIDS than is currently available.

Drug Testing   Perhaps no other selection practice elicits more of an emotional response than **drug testing.** Much of the rationale for the continued increase in the use of preemployment drug testing comes from statistics such as the following:

. 6 million Americans regularly use cocaine (900 died from cocaine abuse in 1986).

. 22 million Americans use marijuana at least once a month.

. Approximately 5 million adults are dependent on drug use as a way of life.[53]

These statistics, employer concerns about productivity and safety, and government-initiated publicity have encouraged a growing number of firms to require all job applicants to pass a urinalysis test for cocaine and marijuana. In general, approximately 15 percent of those tested are eliminated from the selection process because of testing results.[54]

Research now indicates that one half to two thirds of the large companies surveyed use some form of drug testing to help curb the problems that drug abuse can cause at the workplace.[55] Some evidence indicates that there are wide differences in applicants' opinions about organizations that routinely test for drug abuse.[56] Not surprisingly, the most negative attitudes are held by those who admit to having used illegal drugs.[57]

In a study of 5,000 applicants for the U.S. Postal Service, the potential value of preemployment drug testing was clearly demonstrated. Applicants who had tested positive for drug use had a 59 percent higher absenteeism rate and a 47 percent higher involuntary turnover rate than applicants who had not tested positive.[58]

The legality and reliability of drug testing are, however, being seriously questioned. The most serious challenges to its use are based on the Fourth Amendment stricture against unreasonable search and seizure. The Supreme Court of the United States has, however, ruled in at least two cases that drug-testing programs in federal agencies did not violate employees' constitutional rights. Thus, it is likely that drug-testing programs in private organizations will also stand legal challenges as long as good faith efforts to guard employees' rights are maintained.[59]

When employers conduct drug testing through procedures such as urinalysis, they should still be aware of the questionable reliability of these testing methods. There is a propensity for delivering false positives (indicating the presence of drugs when in reality there is none) as often as one third of the time.[60] Reports indicate that false positives occur because test results do not distinguish between Advil and marijuana, Contac and amphetamines, and tonic water and heroin. The National Institute of Drug Abuse issued some words of caution about drug-testing reliability. They stated that, until there is a widely accepted accreditation system or routine proficiency evaluation, the booming "diagnostics industry" will remain highly competitive. The race to be the swiftest with results may not necessarily mean that the results will be the most reliable.[61]

Chemists from the Centers for Disease Control mailed a number of urine samples that either had been spiked with known chemical substances such as cocaine and barbiturates or were blank to 13 drug-testing laboratories. The results were dramatic. The laboratory results contained a large proportion of false negatives and false positives in 66 percent of the reports.[62] Thus, quality control is important in any drug-testing program for job applicants or present employees.

To avoid legal entanglements, morale problems, and public image difficulties, employers need to:

1. Inform all job applicants of the organization's drug-testing screening program.
2. Establish a high-quality control testing procedure with a reliable testing laboratory.
3. Perform any drug tests in a professional, non-threatening manner.
4. Keep all drug test results confidential.

SELECTION OF MANAGERS

The process of selecting managers and the tools used vary with the type of employee being hired. The preceding section focused on blue-, gray-, and white-collar employees, but the general process is similar for the managerial employee.

Before a manager is hired, the job is studied. Then, the criteria for hiring are selected, based on the characteristics of effective managers in the organization at present and likely future needs. *Each* organization must do this, since the managerial task differs by level, function, industry, and in other ways. Studies of successful managers across these groups have concluded that many (not all) successful executives have intelligence, drive, good judgment, and managerial skills. Most studies avoid real-world problems like these: Candidate A scores high on intelligence and motivation, low on verbal skills, and moderate on hard work. Candidate B scores moderate on intelligence, high on motivation, moderate on verbal skills, and high on hard work. Both have good success records. Which one would you choose? The trade-offs must be assessed for particular jobs and particular organizations.

One recruiter stated:

I've read the studies about high intelligence, test scores, and so on in managerial selection. But I've found I've got to look at the job. For example, our most successful *sales managers* are those who grew up on a farm where they learned to work hard on their own. They went to the nearest state college (all they could afford) and majored in business. They got good to better-than-average grades. They might have done better gradewise if they hadn't had to work their way through school. Our best *accounting managers*, however, did not have that background.

The message is that these studies can indicate the likely predictors of success *in general*, but executive success must be analyzed in each organization. Each of the factors mentioned must be correlated with success measured several ways to see which works for the organization. However, the focus of selection must be on *behavior*, not just on scores on tests or general impressions.

Once the criteria of managerial success are known, the selection tools to be used are chosen. In general, tests are not frequently used in managerial selection. Reference checks have been a major source of data on managerial applicants, but the legal problems with this tool also apply for executives. Biodata analysis is a major tool used for managerial selection. It has been stated that, "Very often, a carefully developed typical behavior inventory based on biographical information has proved to be the single best predictor of future job behavior. . . . biographic information has proved particularly useful for assessing managerial effectiveness."[63]

The most frequently used selection tool for managers is the interview. More often than not, it is used in conjunction with the other methods. But if only one method is used by an organization, it is likely to be the personal interview.

Studies indicate that more successful managers are hired using judgments derived in employment interviews than decisions based on test scores. This is no doubt so, because these judgments can be based on factorially complex behavior, and typical executive performance is behaviorally complex. The interview is likely to continue to be the most-used selection method because organizations want to hire managers they feel they can trust and feel comfortable with.

ASSESSMENT CENTERS

An assessment center is not a building or a place. *Assessment centers* are designed to provide a view of individuals performing critical work behaviors.[64] The assessees are asked to complete a series of evaluative tests, exercises, and feedback sessions. The popularity of the assessment center can be attributed to its capacity for increasing an organization's ability to select employees who will perform successfully in management positions. The assessment center was first used by the German military in World War II. The Office of Strategic Services (OSS) in the United States began to use it in the mid-1940s. American Telephone and Telegraph Company (AT&T) in the 1950s introduced assessment centers to the business world. Since 1956, AT&T has used assessment centers to evaluate more than 200,000 employees.[65]

The object of an assessment center is to use a wide array of methods including several interviews, work samples and simulations, and many kinds of paper-and-pencil tests of abilities and attitudes.[66] Exhibit 8–12 presents briefly a typical two-and-a-half day assessment center schedule.

Most assessment centers are similar in a number of areas:

1. Groups of approximately 12 individuals are evaluated. Individual and group activities are observed and evaluated.

2. Multiple methods of assessment are used — interviewing, objective testing, projective testing, games, role plays, and other methods.

3. Assessors doing the evaluation are usually a panel of line managers from the organization. They can, however, be consultants or outsiders trained to conduct assessments.

4. Assessment centers are relevant to the job and have higher appeal because of this relevance.

As a result of assessees' participating as part of a group and as individuals, completing exercises, interviews, and tests, the assessors have a large volume of data on each individual. Individuals are evaluated on a number of dimensions, such as

---

EXHIBIT 8-12   Assessment Center Schedule (2½ Days)

Day 1	Day 2	Day 3
A. Orientation of approximately 12 ratees.	A. Individual decision-making exercise — Ratees are asked to make a decision about some problem that must be solved. (*Raters* observe fact-finding skill, understanding of problem-solving procedures, and risk-taking propensity.)	A. Individual case analysis and presentation. (*Raters* observe problem-solving ability, method of preparation, ability to handle questions, and communication skills.)
B. Break up into groups of four or six to play management simulation game. (*Raters* observe: planning ability, problem-solving skill, interaction skills, communication ability.)		B. Evaluation of other ratees. (Peer evaluations.)
C. Psychological testing — Measure verbal and numerical skills.	B. In-basket exercise. (*Raters* observe decision making under stress, organizing ability, memory, and ability to delegate.)	
D. Interview with raters. (*Raters* discuss goals, motivation, and career plans.)	C. Role play of performance evaluation interview. (*Raters* observe empathy, ability to react, counseling skills, and how information is used.)	
E. Small group discussion of case incidents. (*Raters* observe confidence, persuasiveness, decision-making flexibility.)	D. Group problem solving. (*Raters* observe leadership ability and ability to work in a group.)	

organization and planning ability, decision-making decisiveness, flexibility, resistance to stress, poise, and personal styles.

The rater judgments are consolidated and developed into a final report. Each assessee's performance in the center can be described if the organization wants this type of report. Portions of the individual reports are fed back to each assessee, usually by one or more members of the assessment team.

Because it is an integrated attempt to measure a variety of characteristics of managers, the assessment center report permits the organization to make a number of human resource determinations as:

1. The qualifications of individuals for particular positions.
2. The promotability of individuals.
3. How individuals function in a group.
4. The type of training and development needed to improve behaviors of individuals.
5. How good assessors are in observing, evaluating, and reporting on the performance of others (assessees).

Overall, the results of research on assessment centers have indicated that they are a valid way to select managers. The initial work at AT&T indicated that assessment centers can predict future success with some accuracy.[67] Since this original work, many other reports on assessment centers have yielded similar conclusions.[68]

In spite of the general support for assessment centers that has been found, they are not without disadvantages. Generally speaking, they are a relatively expensive managerial selection technique and are, therefore, not going to be a reasonable alternative for many smaller organizations. Moreover, there are circumstances in which less costly and less administratively complicated techniques are just as effective in managerial selection.[69] Therefore, they are frequently not the technique of choice even for organizations that have the resources to utilize them.

Selecting Managers for an Overseas Assignment: The Expatriate Manager Challenge

Multinational corporations continue to rely on expatriate managers for conducting operations overseas. Unfortunately, the failure rates among expatriates are very high and the costs of such failures can be staggering. Thus, organizations with operations overseas are becoming increasingly concerned with selecting managers with a greater likelihood of success on such an assignment.

A variety of special problems face the organization attempting to select an expatriate manager. Research indicates that technical skills alone are no guarantee of success. Rather, organizations need to select someone who is interested in the overseas assignment and is flexible enough to successfully adapt to a new culture. The ability to adapt is perhaps the best predictor of success.[70] Expatriate managers should not be marginal domestic performers, and only those whose careers can benefit from an overseas assignment ought to be selected.[71]

One final consideration that complicates matters for the organization is the need to actively involve the potential candidate's family in the selection decision. On extended assignments, the family frequently accompanies the expatriate manager.

Thus, their ability to cope with the overseas environment is also important to consider. It may be tempting, therefore, to only select expatriate managers who are single. The problem is that an organization risks violating EEO legislation if it selects on the basis of characteristics such as marital status.

COST/BENEFIT ANALYSIS FOR THE SELECTION DECISION

Once an organization has made a commitment to investigate what types of selection devices it will use, it must attempt to evaluate whether its efforts are worthwhile. Ultimately, a large part of the answer to this question involves the utility of the selection process. **Utility** refers to the degree to which a selection system's use improves the quality of the individuals being selected by the organization.[72]

Utility has two related components *Statistical utility* is the extent to which a selection technique allows an organization to better predict who will be successful. *Organizational utility* , which is dependent, in part, on statistical utility, is a matter of costs and benefits. In other words, answering the question of whether the selection system should be developed and used is ultimately an issue of whether it saves the organization more money than it costs.

Generally speaking, an analysis of the costs versus benefits of selection requires estimates of the direct and indirect costs associated with the selection system. Direct costs are things such as the price of the tests, the salary paid to an interviewer, or the equipment used in a work sample test. Indirect costs include changes in public image associated with implementing procedures such as drug testing.

The organization must also estimate how much money it is able to save by hiring more qualified employees using the selection system. These savings can come from improved outcomes such as higher levels of quality or quantity of output, reduced absenteeism, lower accident rates, or less turnover.

Not only can the overall selection system be evaluated in this way, each component can also undergo a cost/benefit analysis. For example, the six steps to selection that were outlined in this chapter represent a series of hurdles that the successful applicant must overcome. At each step, it is hoped that the least qualified candidates are identified and eliminated from further consideration.

Method	Cost
1. Preliminary screening	Negligible
2. Application blank/biodata	Negligible
3. Employment interview	Time used × Cost per hour
4. Employment tests	$5–$1,000
5. Background and reference checks	$100
6. Physical examination	$100
7. Decision	

Steps 1, 2, and 3 will probably be used in most cases. The number of interviews conducted at step 3 might vary depending on the job. Steps 4 and 5 are the ones that are most questionable and probably will be the subject of the closest cost/benefit analysis. Step 6 has become less appropriate because of restrictions on the use of physical exams. Generally speaking, however, the greater the number of sources of data used in the selection decision, the more likely it is that the final decision will be a good decision.

CAREER CHALLENGE

What did Clark Kirby do? He didn't have the resources or time to hire all 596. Besides, he believed that operating managers should participate in decisions. So his strategy was to hire the managers first. Then, he had the managers help screen and hire the clerical and semiskilled employees.

As far as selection objectives were concerned, Clark accepted the home office's objectives. These were to hire those employees who were most likely to be effective and satisfied. He accepted the job specifications for the most similar positions he could find in the Chicago plant. These specifications listed minimum requirements in education and experience for managers and professional/technical employees. For clerical employees, the emphasis was on minimum experience, plus performance simulation test scores. For skilled employees, the job specifications included minimum experience and test scores on performance simulation tests. The same criteria were used for semiskilled employees.

Clark decided that, because of time pressures and the nature of the job differences, he would use the following selection process.

Managers: screening interview, application blank, interview, reference check.

Professional/technical: screening interview, application blank, interview, reference check.

Clerical: screening interview, application blank, interview, tests.

Skilled: screening interview, application blank, tests, and interviews for marginal applicants.

Semiskilled: screening interview, application blank, tests, and interviews for marginal applicants

Clark and Ed hired the managers. Clark himself hired the professionals. While these groups were being hired an HR specialist administered the tests to the clerical employees and supervised the reference-checking process on the managers and professionals. The HR specialist hired the clerical employees. But the managers and professionals were involved in hiring the clerical personnel to be under their direct supervision.

Then Clark and the HR specialist administered the tests to skilled and semiskilled employees. Clark hired the clearly well-qualified semiskilled employees, except in marginal cases. Candidates received a review and were interviewed by the managers to whom they would report. A similar process was used to hire the semiskilled employees. Since there were few choices among professional/technical and skilled employees, it was more efficient not to involve the new managers, too.

Several problems developed. Clark and Ed had no trouble agreeing on 20 managerial candidates. But in 18 additional cases, Clark felt he had found better candidates. Ed wanted more Chicago people that he knew. Lewis, reflecting the position of Chicago managers, objected. Clark found many more-qualified minority and female managerial candidates than Ed wanted to accept. They compromised. Ed gave up half his choices to Clark, and Clark did likewise.

There were also problems in the skilled professional categories. These people generally wanted more pay than the budget called for. And the last 20 percent hired were somewhat below minimum specifications. Clark appealed for a bigger budget, given these conditions. The home office gave him half of what he needed. He had to generate the other half by paying less for the bottom 20 percent of the semiskilled and clerical employees. Clark alerted Ed to the probable competence problem. He promised Ed that he'd begin developing a list of qualified applicants in these categories in case they were needed.

In sum, Clark hired the people needed within the adjusted budget, on time, and generally with the required specifications. He was able to make a contribution to equal employment opportunity objectives by hiring somewhat more minorities and women than the total population, less than he could have and less than Lewis wanted, but more than Ed wanted. All were qualified. No reverse discrimination took place.

One final note about selection and a cost/benefit analysis of it — the way that an organization hires employees is directly tied to other human resource programs. Perhaps the most important linkage is with training. There are many trade-off decisions between selection and training that must also be made. At the very least, the organization must realize that putting more money into selection can significantly reduce the amount of money it must spend on training, especially if the increased commitment to selection allows the organization to hire a more capable work force.

SUMMARY

This chapter was designed to help you understand what is involved in making effective selection decisions. The basic objective of selection is to obtain the employees who are most likely to meet the organization's standards of performance and who will be satisfied and developed on the job.

To summarize the major points covered in this chapter:

1. Selection is influenced by environmental characteristics: whether the organization is public or private, labor market conditions and the selection ratio, union requirements, and legal restrictions on selection.
2. Reasonable criteria for the choice must be set prior to selection.
3. The selection process can include up to six steps:
    a. Preliminary screening interview.
    b. Completion of application blank/biodata form.
    c. Employment interview.
    d. Employment tests.
    e. Reference checks and recommendation letters.
    f. Physical examinations.
4. For more important positions (measured by higher pay and responsibility), the selection decision is more likely to be formalized and to use more selection techniques.
5. The effective organization prefers to select persons already in the organization over outside candidates.
6. More-effective selection decisions are made if both HR managers and the future supervisors of potential employees are involved in the selection decision.
7. Using a greater number of accepted methods to gather data for selection decisions increases the number of successful candidates selected.
8. Larger organizations are more likely to use sophisticated selection techniques.
9. For more-measurable jobs, tests can be used in the selection decision more effectively.
10. For jobs lower in the hierarchy, tests can be used more effectively in the selection decisions.
11. Even if the most able applicant is chosen, there is no guarantee of successful performance on the job.

Exhibit 8–13 summarizes the recommendations for use of the various selection methods in the model organizations (see Exhibit 1–8). While selection appears to be a universally used human resource activity, the techniques adopted are likely to be

EXHIBIT 8-13   Recommendations on Selection Methods for Model Organizations

Type of Organization	Screening Interview	Application Blank, Biodata	Employment Interview	Performance and Ability Tests*	Telephoned Background Reference Check†	Physical Exam
1. Large size, low complexity, high stability	X	X	X	X	X	Hospital
2. Medium size, low complexity, high stability	X	X	X	X	X	
3. Small size, low complexity, high stability	X	X				
4. Medium size, moderate complexity, moderate stability	X	X	X	X	X	
5. Large size, high complexity, low stability	X	X	X	X	X	Hospital
6. Medium size, high complexity, low stability	X	X	X			
7. Small size, high complexity, low stability	X	X	X			Hospital

* Usually for blue- and white-collar positions.
† Usually for white-collar and managerial positions.

based on the types of personnel selected rather than the types of organizations doing the selection.

Key Terms

QUESTIONS FOR REVIEW AND DISCUSSION

1. What are the goals of selection? What factors influence an organization's choice of selection methods?

2. What is a *selection ratio*? How does a selection ratio influence the effectiveness of selection?

4. What are the disadvantages associated with using an assessment center for manager selection?

5. What is the *utility* of a selection system? What are the major costs associated with a new selection system?

6. What are the three major types of employment interviews? What conditions must be met if an interview is going to be an effective selection technique?

7. What differences might exist between a selection system for a top executive and a selection system for an entry-level secretarial position?

8. What is the current status of drug testing in U.S. business? Do you think drug testing is justifiable? Why?

9. What is the Employee Polygraph Protection Act? What alteratives to polygraphs are organizations using? Are these alternatives effective?

10. What are the implications of the Americans with Disabilities Act for selection?

NOTES

[1] S. C. Gwynne (October 29, 1990), "The Right Stuff," *Time*, pp. 74–84.

[2] Scott T. Rickard (June 1981), "Effective Staff Selection," *Personnel Journal*, pp. 475–78.

[3] Gerard P. Panaro (1990), *Employment Law Manual* (Boston: Warren, Gorham, & Lamont), pp. 7–5.

[4] Nancy Asquith and Daniel E. Feld (1991 Supplement), *Employment Testing Manual* (Boston: Warren, Gorham, & Lamont), pp. 11–13.

[5] Ibid p. 9–5.

[6] Jum C. Nunnally (1978), *Psychometric Theory*, 2nd. ed. (New York: McGraw-Hill), p. 191.

[7] Wayne F. Cascio (1991), *Applied Psychology in Personnel Management*, 4th ed. (Englewood Cliffs, N.J.: Prentice-Hall), p. 151.

[8] Society for Industrial and Organizational Psychology (1987), *Principles for the Validation and Use of Personnel Selection Procedures*, 3rd ed. (College Park, Md.: Society for Industrial and Organizational Psychology).

[9] Robert H. Faley and Eric Sundstrom (August 1985), "Content Representativeness: An Empirical Method of Evaluation," *Journal of Applied Psychology*, pp. 567–71.

[10] Robert M. Guion (August 1978), "Scoring of Content Domain Samples: The Problem of Fairness," *Journal of Applied Psychology*, pp. 499–506.

[11] Society for Industrial and Organizational Psychology, Principles.

[12] James W. L. Cole (1980), *Statistical Proof of Discrimination* (New York: McGraw-Hill).

[13] T. G. Abram (August 1979), "Overview of Uniform Selection Guidelines: Pitfalls for the Unwary Employer," *Labor Law Journal*, pp. 495–502.

[14] Asquith and Feld, *Employment Testing Manual*, pp. 3-3–3-4.

[15] Barry Nathan and Ralph A. Alexander (Autumn 1988), "A Comparison of Criteria for Test Validation: A Meta-Analytic Investigation," *Personnel Psychology*, pp. 517–35.

[16] Gerald V. Barrett, James S. Phillips and Ralph A. Alexander (February 1981), "Concurrent and Predictive Validity Designs: A Critical Reanalysis," *Journal of Applied Psychology*, pp. 1–6.

[17] William Owens (1976), "Background Data," in *Handbook of Industrial and Organizational Psychology*, ed. Marvin D. Dunnette (Skokie, Ill.: Rand McNally), pp. 609–44.

[18] D. G. Lawrence, B. L. Salsburg, J. G. Dawson and Z.D. Fasman (March 1982), "Design and Use of Weighted Application Blanks," *Personnel Administrator*, pp. 47–53.

[19] Hannah R. Rothstein, Frank L. Schmidt, Frank W. Erwin, William A. Owens and Paul C. Sparks (April 1990), "Biographical Data in Employment Selection: Can Validities Be Made Generalizable?" *Journal of Applied Psychology*, pp. 175–84.

[20] Craig J. Russell, Joyce Mattson, Steven E. Devlin, and David Atwater (October 1990), "Predictive Validity of Biodata Items Generated from Retrospective Life Experience Essays," *Journal of Applied Psychology*, pp. 569–80.

[21] Bureau of National Affairs (May 5, 1983), *Employee Selection Procedures*, ASPA-BNA Survey No. 45 (Washington, D.C.).

[22] Rick Jacobs and Joseph E. Baratta (1989), "Tools for Staffing Decisions: What Can They Do? What Do They Cost?" in *Human Resource Planning Employment & Placement*, ed. Wayne F. Cascio (Washington, D.C.: Bureau of National Affairs), pp. 159–99.

[23] Bureau of National Affairs (September 1976), *Personnel Policies Forum*, Survey No. 114

[24] Gary P. Latham, Lise M. Saari, Elliot D. Pursell, and Michael A. Campion (August 1980), "The Situational Interview," *Journal of Applied Psychology*, pp. 422–27; Jeff A. Weekley and Joseph A. Gier (August 1987), "Reliability and Validity of the Situational Interview for a Sales Position," *Journal of Applied Psychology*, pp. 484–87.

[25] Richard A. Fear (1984), *The Evaluation Interview* (New York: McGraw-Hill).

[26] Richard Arvey and James Campion (Summer 1982), "The Employment Interview: A Summary and Review of Recent Research," *Personnel Psychology*, pp. 281–322.

[27] Angelo J. Kinicki, Chris A. Lockwood, Peter W. Hom, and Rodger W. Griffeth (October 1990), "Interviewer Predictions of Applicant Qualifications and Interviewer Validity: Aggregate and Individual Analyses," *Journal of Applied Psychology*, pp. 477–86.

[28] For a detailed discussion of interviewing errors, see Arvey and Campion, "The Employment Interview."

[29] Madeline E. Heilman and Melanie Stopeck (May 1985), "Attractiveness and Corporate Success: Different Causal Attributions for Males and Females," *Journal of Applied Psychology*, pp. 379–88.

[30] Michael M. Harris (Winter 1989), "Reconsidering the Employment Interview: A Review of Recent Literature and Suggestions for Future Research," *Personnel Psychology*, pp. 691–726.

[31] Buros Institute of Mental Measurements (1989), *Tenth Mental Measurements Yearbook*.

[32] Jacobs and Baratta, "Tools for Staffing Decisions," p. 173.

[33] Anne Anastasi (1982), *Psychological Testing* (New York: MacMillan).

[34] John R. Hollenbeck and Ellen M. Whitener (March 1988), "Reclaiming Personality Traits for Personnel Selection: Self-Esteem as an Illustrative Case," *Journal of Management*, pp. 81–92.

[35] Leatta M. Hough, Newell K. Eaton, Marvin D. Dunnette, John D. Kamp, and Rodney A. McCloy (October 1990), "Criterion Related Validities of Personality Constructs and the Effect of Response Distortion on Those Validities," *Journal of Applied Psychology*, pp. 581–95.

[36] H. Rorschach (1942), *Psychodiagnostics: A Diagnostic Test Based on Perception* (Berne, Switzerland: Huber).

[37] James A. Douglas, Daniel E. Feld, and Nancy Asquith (1989), *Employment Testing Manual* (Boston: Warren, Gorham & Lamont), p. 13–14.

[38] S. L. Jacobs (March 11, 1985), "Owners Who Ignore Security Make Worker Dishonesty Easy," *The Wall Street Journal*.

[39] Douglas, Feld, and Asquith, *Employment Testing Manual*, p. 13–11.

[40] Congress of the United States, Office of Technology Assessment (September 1990), "The Use of Integrity Tests for Pre-Employment Screening" (Washington, D.C.: U.S. Government Printing Office), OTA-SET-442.

[41] Paul R. Sackett and M. M. Harris (1984), "Honesty Testing for Personnel Selection: A Review and Critique," *Personnel Psychology*, pp. 221–45.

[42] *Myart v. Motorola* (1964), 110 Congressional Record 5662-64.

[43] (1982), *Ability Testing: Uses, Consequences, and Controversies*, Parts I and II (Washington, D.C.: National Academy Press).

[44] Dale Yoder and Paul D. Staudohar (February 1984), "Testing and EEO: Getting Down to Cases," *Personnel Administrator*, pp. 67–76.

[45] Anne Anastasi (Winter 1989), "Ability Testing in the 1980's and Beyond: Some Major Trends," *Public Personnel Management*, pp. 471–86.

[46] Carole Sewell (May 1981), "Pre-Employment Investigations: The Key to Security in Hiring," *Personnel Journal*, pp. 376–79

[47] Clemm C. Kessler III and Georgia J. Gibbs (January–February 1975), "Getting the Most from Application Blanks and References," *Personnel*, pp. 53–62.

[48] J. D. Rice (February 1978), "Privacy Legislation: Its Effect on Pre-Employment Reference Checking," *Personnel Administrator*, pp. 46–51.

[49] Robert Half (September 1985), "Tactics for Aggressive Reference Checking," *Personnel Journal*, p. 82.

[50] Richard Chase (November 1969), "Working Physiology," *Personnel Administrator*, pp. 47–53.

[51] Mitchell S. Novitt (January 1982), "Physical Examinations and Company Liability: A Legal Update," *Personnel Journal*, pp. 47–53.

[52] Asquith and Feld, *Employment Testing Manual*, p. 15–5.

[53] Jack Gordon (March 1987), "Drug Testing: As a Productivity Booster?" *Training*, pp. 22–34.

[54] On *Denenberg and Richard v. Denenberg*, see Tia Schneider (June 1987), "Employee Drug Testing and the Arbitrator: What Are the Issues?" *The Arbitrator Journal*, pp. 19–31.

[55] Asquith and Feld, *Employment Testing Manuals*, p. 12–8.

[56] J. Michael Crant and Thomas S. Bateman (April 1990), "An Experimental Test of the Impact of Drug-Testing Programs on Potential Job Applicants' Attitudes and Intentions," *Journal of Applied Psychology*, pp. 127–131.

[57] Kevin R. Murphy, George C. Thornton III, and D. H. Reynolds (Autumn 1990), "College Students' Attitudes toward Employee Drug Testing Programs," *Personnel Psychology*, pp. 615–31.

[58] Jacques Normand, Stephen D. Salyards and John J. Mahoney (December 1990), "An Evaluation of Preemployment Drug Testing," *Journal of Applied Psychology*, pp. 629-39.

[59] Panaro, *Employment Law Manual*, p. 4–28.

[60] Joan W. Hoffman and Ken Jennings (May 1987), "Will Drug Testing in Sports Play for Industry?" *Personnel Journal*, pp. 52–59.

[61] Anne Marie O'Keefe (June 1987), "The Case Against Drug Testing," *Psychology Today*, pp. 34–38.

[62] Bureau of National Affairs (February 4, 1987), "National Report on Substance Abuse," pp. 1–2.

[63] John P. Campbell, Marvin Dunnette, Edward E. Lawler III and Karl E. Weick (1970), *Managerial Behavior, Performance and Effectiveness* (New York: McGraw -Hill), p. 146.

[64] Paul R. Sackett (Spring 1987), "Assessment Centers and Content Validity: Some Neglected Issues," *Personnel Psychology*, pp. 13–25.

[65] (June 1987), "Assessment Centers," *Small Business Report*, pp. 22–24.

[66] Task Force on Assessment Center Guidelines (Winter 1989), "Guidelines and Ethical Considerations for Assessment Center Operations," *Public Personnel Management*, pp. 457–70.

[67] Douglas W. Bray and Donald L. Grant (1966), "The Assessment Center in the Measurement of Potential For Business Management," *Psychological Monographs* 80, no. 625, p. 25.

[68] Barbara B. Gaugler, Douglas B. Rosenthal, George C. Thornton III, and Cynthia Bentson (August, 1987), "Meta-Analysis of Assessment Center Validity," *Journal of Applied Psychology*, pp. 493–511.

[69] Joan E. Pynes and H. John Bernardin (October 1989), "Predictive Validity of an Entry Level Police Officer Assessment Center," *Journal of Applied Psychology*, pp. 831–33

[70] Peter J. Dowling and Randall S. Schuler (1989), *International Dimensions of Human Resource Management* (Boston: Kent Publishing), pp. 51–57.

[71] Nancy Adler (1990), *International Dimensions of Organizational Behavior*, 2nd ed. (Boston: Kent Publishing), p. 245.

[72] Cascio, *Applied Psychology in Personnel Management*, p. 298.

EXERCISE 8–1   Practicing the Selection Interview

· · · · ·

Objective: The exercise is designed to have students participate in structured and unstructured interviews involving selection decisions.

SET UP THE EXERCISE

1. The class or group is to be divided into equal numbers of 6, 8, 10, 12, or 14 people. The best number to work with is 10.

2. Suppose that 10 people are in the group (make adjustments based on size of group). Two individuals will play the role of the job applicant Nick Thomas. The autobiography of Nick should be read.

3. Two other group members are to play the role of interviewers using the unstructured format. They should review the unstructured interview material in Chapter 8, the job description for the position, and Nick's job application.

4. Two other group members should conduct interviews with a structured format. Consult Chapter 8 on the structured format. Also read the job description for the position, and Nick's job application (see page 287–88).

5. The remaining four members are to act as a panel of observers that will evaluate the structured versus the unstructured format. Read all materials — Chapter 8 on interviews, job description, autobiography, and application.

6. First, the unstructured interview should be conducted (take no more than six or seven minutes).

7. Second, conduct the structured interview (take no more than six or seven minutes).

8. Observers should rate the interviewers using these criteria:
   a. Which format yielded the most valuable information?
   b. Which format was easiest to conduct?
   c. Which format was able to probe the applicant's attitudes and feelings?

Job Application–Dante Foods

Name: Nick Thomas

Address: 1711 Western Avenue, Chicago, Ill. 60615

How Long at Present Address: 3 years

Date of Birth: March 18, 1970

Marital Status: Single

Number of Children:

U.S. Citizen: Yes

Do you have any physical defects? No If Yes, describe

Have you had any major illness in the past two years? No

If yes, describe

Please List Former Employers

Year	Name and address	Position	Reason for leaving
From 1986 to 1988 (Summers)	Gassmans 3514 E. 92 Street Chicago, Illinois	Clerk	College
From 1988 to Present	Safeway 10136 Commercial Chicago, Illinois	checker, assistant produce manager, and produce manager	
From to			
From to			

Hobbies: Fishing, Listening to Music, Exercise

Civic Organizations:

Professional Organizations:

Education	Date of Graduation	Major	Rank in Class and Grade Point Average
High School Bower	1988		65/275
College			3.1/4.0
University of Illinois at Chicago		Business	65 credits completed

When could you begin to work for Dante?

Next Week 7/20

A Learning Note

This exercise will illustrate that interviewing is a rather intricate task. One must be fully prepared to conduct any interview.

The Situation

Dante Foods is a chain of food stores operating in 20 locations in the Chicago area. The night manager of the Palmer Park store suddenly resigned, leaving a vacancy. The Palmer Park store has 40 full- and part-time employees. A brief job description of the night manager position was developed. Dante has a number of applicants and wants to fill the position as soon as possible. Nick Thomas seems a likely candidate for the vacancy.

Brief Job Description of Dante Night Manager

1. Reports directly to store manager.
2. Makes decisions concerning store tasks when on duty; usually from 6 P.M. to 12 midnight.
3. Supervises all night shift employees — full- and part-time.
4. Handles all emergencies and problems when on duty (for example, customers, deliveries, special food orders).
5. Closes books at end of shift and prepares morning orders for stockouts — canned goods, produce, and bakery products.

Nick Thomas Autobiography

I have lived in Chicago for the past 12 years. I was born in Washington, D.C., and lived in Arlington, Virginia, for 11 years. I enjoy school and really like to work with people.

My work experience ranges from delivering papers as a youngster to my present position of produce manager. I plan to become an executive in the food business working for a chain or even starting my own business.

My strongest trait is a dogged determination to do the job well. In anything I do, I work hard and always give my best effort. My weakest trait is that I sometimes become impatient with those people who do not do their best.

I enjoy fishing, listening to music, and staying in shape. Every year for the past three, I have spent at least two weeks fishing on Lake Baribou in Wisconsin. I actively work out with Nautilus equipment and weights at least four times a week.

I would like to finish my degree at the University of Illinois at Chicago within the next four or five years. I have to keep working to put myself through school. This is the only way that I can receive a college education.

APPLICATION CASE 8–1

· · · · ·

Bechtel Power Corporation's Use of Objective Welding Tests

Charles Ligons, a black man, was a welder at the Iowa Electric Light and Power, Duane Arnold Energy Center Construction site at Palo, Iowa. He worked at the site for Bechtel Power Corporation. Bechtel required that its welders be qualified in accordance with standards of the American Society of Mechanical Engineers Code. That code prescribes objective criteria for testing welders on various types of welding work and for placing them in two categories: (1) A-LH under which a welder qualifies to perform general welding jobs, and (2) AT-LH, involving more difficult welding procedures.

Prior to his arrival at the Palo site, Ligons passed a test that qualified him under AT-LH to perform heliarc welding. During his first week of employment, however, Ligons was required to report to the test shop for training and testing as a result of observations made by a welding engineer of a weld that Ligons had improperly prepared. Following a one-week training period, Ligons passed a simple plate welding test, but failed the same heliarc welding test he had passed before coming to Palo. Ligons spent several weeks on at least three separate occasions training for upgrading testing to improve his competence in heliarc welding.

On February 9, approximately 18 months after coming to the Palo site, Ligons was laid off with 58 other welders, all of whom were white. Ligons was informed that he was eligible for rehire when more welders were needed. The layoff was a result of a general reduction of the Palo work force.

Ligons was rehired in September. He required further training and testing for recertification. After about one month of training, he passed only the test qualifying him for the least difficult type of welding. About four months after being rehired, he was again laid off with five other welders.

Ligons believed that race was a motivating factor in the decision to lay him off. Bechtel claimed, however, that its testing procedures for upgrading a welder's qualifications had a relationship to the jobs for which they were used. They stated that the welding tests were based on objective welding standards set by the American Society of Mechanical Engineers. Bechtel was contractually bound to ensure that its welders were qualified and that all welding performed on the job complied with the American Society of Mechanical Engineers Code.

Discussion Questions

1. Do you believe that welding tests are necessary for the type of job Charles Ligons worked on?
2. Was the first layoff of Ligons legitimate?
3. Did the company make an attempt to help Ligons maintain and upgrade his welding competence?

PERFORMANCE EVALUATION
AND COMPENSATION

· · · · · · ·

*P*art Three discusses an extremely important part of a firm's overall HRM program: performance evaluation and compensation.

Chapter 9, Performance Evaluation, introduces the job of evaluating the performance of employees. This is an extremely difficult job that requires care in the development of measures to assess performance.

The subject of compensation and pay is introduced in Chapter 10, Compensation: An Overview. It discusses the potential impact of pay on employees and discusses pay level, pay structure, and individual pay determination. Chapter 11, Compensation: Methods and Policies, completes this discussion by focusing on incentives and pay programs, managerial compensation, and several significant policy issues regarding compensation.

Chapter 12, Employee Benefits and Services, covers benefits, services, and pensions. The potential impact of benefits and services that employers provide for employees are discussed.

9

PERFORMANCE EVALUATION

· · · · · · ·

LEARNING OBJECTIVES

—◦—

After studying this chapter, you should be able to:

· · ·

Define the term *performance evaluation*

· · ·

Discuss various types of rating errors that raters can make in performance evaluation programs

· · ·

Compare the advantages of various performance evaluation techniques

· · ·

Explain the role of a manager and his or her subordinate in a management by objectives program

· · ·

Describe the process of and skill required for a feedback review

CAREER CHALLENGE

*E*d Smart went to work in the maintenance department of Partridge Enterprises, a middle-sized firm, about a year ago. He enjoys working in maintenance, since he has always liked to work with his hands. His supervisor, Hector Garcia, is a good maintenance man who helps Ed when he doesn't understand a problem. But Ed has often wished he knew what Hector thinks of him on the job. Hector never tells Ed how he is doing. It seems that Hector chews him out about once a month. Ed wonders: Doesn't he think I am trying to do a good job? Doesn't he think I am a good maintenance man?

Knowing answers to these questions is important to Ed, because someday he'd like to move up. He hears that Joe is going to retire next year. Joe's job is better and pays more. Ed wonders if he has a chance to get the job. He also has heard that business at some branches is not good right now. People have been laid off. If the crunch hits the New York branch where Ed works, he might get laid off. He knows seniority is a factor in layoffs. But so is performance. He wishes he knew how he was doing so that he could improve himself, move up, and avoid getting laid off. Ed wants some kind of feedback from his boss.

T his chapter focuses on *performance evaluation* — the HRM activity designed to satisfy Ed's needs for performance feedback. Performance evaluation is the HRM activity that is used to determine the extent to which an employee is performing the job effectively. Other terms for performance evaluation include *performance review, personnel rating, merit rating, performance appraisal, employee appraisal,* or *employee evaluation.*

In many organizations, two evaluation systems exist side by side; the formal and the informal. Supervisors often think about how well employees are doing; this is the informal system. It is influenced by political and interpersonal processes so that employees who are liked better than others have an edge. On the other hand, a *formal performance evaluation* is a system set up by the organization to *regularly* and *systematically* evaluate employee performance. This chapter focuses only on formal performance evaluation systems.

A DIAGNOSTIC APPROACH TO PERFORMANCE EVALUATION

Exhibit 9–1 highlights the relevant factors from the diagnostic model that have significance for performance evaluation. One factor is the task. A white-collar or supervisory task is more likely to be formally evaluated than a blue-collar task. In addition, the performance evaluation technique used will differ with the task being evaluated. Other factors affecting performance evaluation are government requirements, regulations, and laws. Since the passage of antidiscrimination legislation, the government has investigated to determine if organizations discriminate against protected categories of employees in promotions, pay raises, and other rewards. Performance evaluation is the HRM method for allocating these rewards. By inducing organizations to keep better records to support their decisions, government action has indirectly encouraged better performance evaluation systems.

Other factors influencing performance evaluation are the attitudes and preferences of employees. For people such as Ed, whose values fit the work ethic, evaluations can be very important since they help people to determine how well they are performing. For employees with instrumental attitudes toward work, performance evaluations may be viewed differently, but they might be equally important to these persons. If they only want a job to earn money and pay is directly tied to performance, then evaluations will be important as well.

An important factor that can affect performance evaluation is the leader's (supervisor's) style. Supervisors can use the formal system in a number of ways: fairly or unfairly, in a supportive manner or punitively, positively or negatively. If the supervisor is punitive and negative with an employee who responds to positive reinforcement, performance evaluation can lead to the opposite of the results expected by the enterprise.

Finally, if there is a union present in the organization, performance evaluations might be affected. Some unions support while others oppose formal performance evaluations. Most oppose the use of unmeasurable, nonproduction-related factors in performance evaluation. They have good reason to doubt unclear factors such as "initiative" or "potential."

These are the major factors affecting the performance evaluation process. The next section will briefly examine the case for the use of formal performance evaluation.

EXHIBIT 9-1   Factors Affecting Performance Evaluation

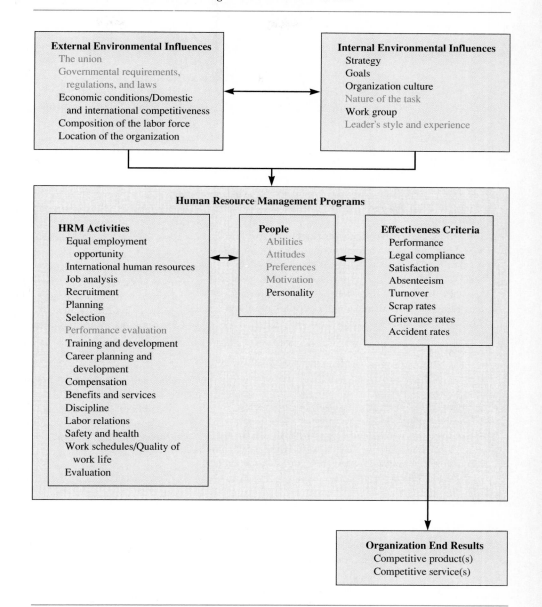

External Environmental Influences
The union
Governmental requirements,
   regulations, and laws
Economic conditions/Domestic
   and international competitiveness
Composition of the labor force
Location of the organization

Internal Environmental Influences
Strategy
Goals
Organization culture
Nature of the task
Work group
Leader's style and experience

Human Resource Management Programs

HRM Activities
Equal employment
   opportunity
International human resources
Job analysis
Recruitment
Planning
Selection
Performance evaluation
Training and development
Career planning and
   development
Compensation
Benefits and services
Discipline
Labor relations
Safety and health
Work schedules/Quality of
   work life
Evaluation

People
Abilities
Attitudes
Preferences
Motivation
Personality

Effectiveness Criteria
Performance
Legal compliance
Satisfaction
Absenteeism
Turnover
Scrap rates
Grievance rates
Accident rates

Organization End Results
Competitive product(s)
Competitive service(s)

CAREER CHALLENGE
(continued)

*T*he setting: Office of the executive vice president of Partridge Enterprises. Present are the executive vice president and the vice presidents of the corporation.

Tom Smith (executive vice president) As you know, we're here to make a recommendation to John (the president) on what if anything to do about Mary's suggestion. Mary, why don't you review the issue?

Mary Hartford (vice president, human resource management) You all received a copy of my memo to J.B. As you know, when I came here three years ago, I felt one of our top priorities in HRM would be to get an evaluation system really running online. I want this because performance evaluation is an outstanding motivation technique. After much thought and planning, the results are in my memo. I recommend we institute management by objectives–type evaluation systems for vice presidents through section heads, and a graphic rating scale for below that. The MBO would be done quarterly, the rating scale semiannually, and we'd tie rewards such as raises and promotions to the results of the evaluation.

The details are in the memo. We're too big and geographically dispersed now to continue using our informal system.

Tom Sounds good to me.

Dave Artem (vice president marketing) Me too.

Fred Fairfax (vice president, manufacturing) Well, it doesn't to me. We had one of these papermill forms systems here 10 years ago, and it was a waste of time. It just meant more paper work for us down on the firing line. You staff people sit up here dreaming up more for us to do. We're overburdened now. Besides, I called a few buddies in big firms who have P.E. They say it involves a lot of training of evaluators, and it makes half the employees mad when they don't get 100 percent scores on the ''grade report.'' It gets down to a lot of politics when it's all said and done.

If you recommend this, I'll send J.B. a counterproposal.

THE CASE FOR USING FORMAL EVALUATIONS

Should Ed be evaluated by his supervisor? In order to answer that question, think about Ed's situation in the Career Challenge above. Then consider the following potential purposes that can be served with the existence of a well designed, formal evaluation system:

Developmental purposes. It can determine which employees need more training and helps evaluate the results of training programs. It helps the subordinate-supervisor counseling relationship, and it encourages supervisors to observe subordinate behavior to help employees.

Reward purposes. It helps the organization decide who should receive pay raises and promotions. It can determine who will be laid off.

Motivational purposes. The presence of an evaluation program has a motivational effect: It encourages initiative, develops a sense of responsibility, and stimulates effort to perform better.

Legal compliance. It serves as a legally defensible reason for making promotion, transfer, reward, and discharge decisions.

Human resource and employment planning purposes. It serves as a valuable input to skills inventories and human resource planning.

Compensation. It provides information that can be used to determine what to pay and what will serve as an equitable monetary package.

Communications purposes. Evaluation is a basis for an ongoing discussion between superior and subordinate about job-related matters. Through interaction, the parties get to know each other better.

HRM research purposes. It can be used to validate selection tools, such as a testing program.

Research indicates that, of all these possible uses for performance evaluations, the most frequent include wage and salary administration, performance feedback, and helping the organization to identify individual employees' strengths and weaknesses.[1] It should also be evident that a formal performance evaluation system represents one of the most important HRM activities to an organization.

Of all of the relationships between performance evaluation and other HRM activities, none has recently been more critical to understand than the one between evaluations and equal employment opportunity, especially as it applies to promotions and terminations.

Performance Evaluation and the Law

As mentioned in Chapter 3, the Equal Employment Opportunity Commission is responsible for administering and enforcing the Civil Rights Act of 1964. The EEOC issued the *Uniform Guidelines on Employment Selection Procedures* in 1978, and these were intended to be applied to all human resource decisions. As such, these guidelines definitely have an effect on performance evaluation although the legal requirements for an appraisal system are less clearly defined by the guidelines; the guidelines focus heavily on validating selection procedures. Thus, it is actually more difficult to determine what makes a performance evaluation system legal.[2]

Most performance evaluation procedures rely to some extent on supervisors' judgments about an employee's behavior. These judgments are usually summarized by using one of several paper-and-pencil methods, each of which is designed to provide an accurate picture of the employee. Once employees' work-related behavior has been judged, the supervisors' ratings are used as input in making promotion, pay, transfer, and other human resource decisions.

Because supervisors' judgments have been used during the evaluation process, there is the potential for bias to exist in these decisions. This bias can be both intentional and unintentional. Many of the more common sources of bias in performance evaluations will be discussed later in this chapter.

A number of court rulings have focused on the responsibilities of management in developing and using a performance evaluation system in a legally defensible way. One of the most important early cases was *Brito v. Zia Company* (1973)[3] in which the company was found to be in violation of the law. The court ruled that the

---

EXHIBIT 9-2   Suggestions to Follow for Developing and Implementing Legally
Defensible Appraisal Systems

---

1. Procedures for personnel decisions must not differ as a function of the race, sex, national origin, religion, or age of those affected by such decisions.
2. Objective-type, nonrated, and uncontaminated data should be used whenever available.
3. A formal system of review or appeal should be available for appraisal disagreements.
4. More than one independent evaluator of performance should be used.
5. A formal, standardized system for the personnel decision should be used.
6. Evaluators should have ample opportunity to observe ratee performance (if ratings must be made).
7. Ratings on traits such as dependability, drive, aptitude, or attitude should be avoided.
8. Performance appraisal data should be empirically validated.
9. Specific performance standards should be communicated to employees.
10. Raters should be provided with written instructions on how to complete the performance evaluations.
11. Employees should be evaluated on specific work dimensions rather than a single overall or global measure.
12. Behavioral documentation should be required for extreme ratings (e.g., critical incidents).
13. The content of the appraisal form should be based on a job analysis.
14. Employees should be provided with an opportunity to review their appraisals.
15. Personnel decision makers should be trained on laws regarding discrimination.

Source: J. Bernardin and W. Cascio (1987), ''Performance Appraisal and the Law,'' in *Readings in Personnel and Human Resource Management*, 3d ed., R. S. Schuler, S. A. Youngblood, and V. Huber, eds. (St. Paul, Minn.: West Publishing).

company had not shown that its performance evaluation instrument was valid in the sense that it was related to important elements of work behavior in the jobs for which the employees were being evaluated. For example, some raters had little daily contact with the ratees.

Since the *Brito v. Zia Company* decision, there have been many other lawsuits concerned with the adequacy of performance evaluations. These have dealt with issues of sex, race, and age discrimination in termination, promotion, and layoff decisions. As mentioned previously, however, the courts' interpretations of what constitutes a legal performance evaluation system are not as straightforward as they are for selection systems. Recent analyses of court rulings have concluded that the actual validity of a performance evaluation system is less of an explicit issue than when a selection system has been challenged.[4]

While an organization should be concerned about the validity of its performance evaluations generally speaking, the way the system was developed and whether it is applied consistently seem currently to be more important from a legal perspective. In age discrimination cases, it also appears that the type of decision being challenged is important for determining how much proof a company will be required to produce.[5]

Despite this lack of clear guidelines, there are several important recommendations that should be followed before developing and using a performance evaluation system. These have been summarized in Exhibit 9–2.

FORMAL EVALUATION

To provide information that can serve the organization's goals and that complies with the law, a performance evaluation system must provide accurate and reliable data. The ability to generate accurate and reliable data is enhanced if a systematic process is followed. The following six steps can provide the basis for such a systematic process:

1. Establish performance standards for each position and the criteria for evaluation.
2. Establish performance evaluation policies on when to rate, how often to rate, and who should rate.
3. Have raters gather data on employee performance.
4. Have raters (and employees in some systems) evaluate employees' performance.
5. Discuss the evaluation with the employee.
6. Make decisions and file the evaluation.

Step 1 of this process is completed when an organization conducts a job analysis. Recall from Chapter 6 that one of the primary reasons for conducting job analysis is to write job descriptions, and an important part of a job description is a clear statement of the performance dimensions and standards expected from incumbents. In addition, the job analysis should have determined how these dimensions and standards are going to be measured.

The dimensions of performance upon which an employee is evaluated are called the *criteria of evaluation*. Examples include quality of work, quantity of work, and cost of work. One of the major problems with many performance evaluations is that they require supervisors to make *person evaluations* rather than *performance evaluations*. That is, the evaluation criterion in some systems is the personality of the incumbents rather than their levels of performance.

An effective criterion should possess the following characteristics:[6]

Relevance — A measure of performance must be as logically related to the actual output of an incumbent as possible.
Sensitivity — Any criterion must be able to reflect the difference between high and low performers. That is, high and low performers must receive criterion scores that accurately represent the difference in their performance.
Practicality — The criterion must be measurable and data collection cannot be inefficient or too disruptive.

The evidence is clear that single performance measures are ineffective because success is multifaceted. Most studies indicate that multiple criteria are necessary to measure performance completely. The multiple criteria are added together statistically or combined into a single multifaceted measure. The choice of criteria is not an easy process. One must be careful to evaluate both activities (for example, number of calls a salesperson makes) and results (for example, dollars of sales). A combination using results and activities as criteria is desirable.

How do you weigh the importance of multiple criteria? For example, if a salesperson is being evaluated on number of calls as well as sales dollars and is high on one and low on the other, what is the person's overall rating? Management must weigh these criteria.

A BNA study found that, for white-collar workers, performance factors such as the following were used by these percentages of organizations surveyed: quality of work (93 percent), quantity of work (90 percent), job knowledge (85 percent), and attendance (79 percent).[7] Personality factors used were initiative (87 percent), cooperation (87 percent), dependability (86 percent), and need for supervision (67 percent). The data for blue-collar workers were parallel: performance factors included quality of work (used by 91 percent), quantity of work (91 percent), attendance (79 percent).[7] Personality factors used were initiative (87 percent), cooperation (87 percent), dependability (86 percent), and need for supervision (67 percent). The data for blue-collar workers were parallel: performance factors included quality of work (used by 91 percent), quantity of work (91 percent), attendance (86 percent), and job knowledge (85 percent). Personality factors surveyed were dependability (86 percent), initiative (83 percent), cooperation (83 percent), and need for supervision (77 percent).

This study found that hard-to-measure personality traits are widely used. The key issue, however, is weighing the factors. The personality factors may be evaluated, but not weighed equally with performance.

Whether the evaluation should be based on actual or potential performance depends on the major purpose of the evaluation for the HRM function. In this respect, there are three principal purposes of performance evaluation:

- Improvement of performance.
- Promotion consideration.
- Salary and wage adjustments.

If the main purposes are improved performance or wage adjustment, the evaluation should be based on actual performance. If the main purpose is possible promotion, a different evaluation is needed, one that will assess potential performance on a new job. This situation is similar to the selection decision, in which past performance on one job must be projected to possible performance on a different one; it is easier to do if the employee has had experience that is relevant to the new job. But here the emphasis is different, and assessment of future potential on a different job is more difficult than actual assessment of past performance. Exhibit 9–3 presents a promotability form used at Armstrong.

Set Policies on When, How Often, and Who Evaluates

When Should Evaluation Be Done?   There are two basic decisions to be made regarding the timing of performance appraisal: One is when to do it, and the other is how often. In many organizations, performance evaluations are scheduled for arbitrary dates, such as the date the person was hired (anniversary date). Alternatively, every employee may be evaluated on or near a single calendar date. Although the single-day approach is convenient administratively, it probably is not a good idea. It requires raters to spend a lot of time conducting evaluation interviews and completing forms at one time, which may lead them to want to "get it over with" quickly. In addition, it may not be related to the normal task cycle of the employee; this factor can make it difficult for the manager to evaluate performance effectively.

It makes more sense to schedule the evaluation at the completion of a task cycle. For example, tax accountants see their year as April 16 to April 15. For professors and teachers, the year starts at the beginning of the fall term and terminates after the spring term. For others without a clear task cycle based on dates, one way to set the date is by goal setting. Goals can be established in such a way that the manager and employee agree on the task cycle, which terminates with an evaluation of the employee's performance during that cycle.

How Often Should Evaluation Be Done?   The second timing-related question is how often evaluation should be done. A BNA study found that 74

EXHIBIT 9-3   Sample Promotability Form

Armstrong

CONFIDENTIAL BUSINESS INFORMATION

PERSONNEL PROMOTABILITY

Name _____   Employee No. _____

Following the Personnel Performance and Development Review with the individual, complete as appropriate:

A. PROMOTABILITY WITHIN UNIT. It appears that this individual has the potential to advance beyond the present position in this organizational unit, as follows:

	Ready Now	Ready By (Date)
(Title)		
(Title)		

B. PROMOTABILTY INTO OTHER UNITS. This individual should be considered for opportunities outside this organizational unit. It is suggested that these recommendations be reviewed with appropriate unit (s) management, where practical.

_____

_____

_____

C. INDIVIDUAL IS NOT PROMOTABLE. It appears this individual is not promotable beyond the present position. (Mark (X) for appropriate reasons.)

☐ Own desire, unwilling to change work locations, or similar personal reasons.

☐ Capabilities are now fully utilized

☐ Other factors. (Specify) _____

_____

_____

_____

Evaluated by _____

Date evaluated _____

Reviewed by (Rater's Supervisor): _____

Please enclose the white copy of this form with Form 43289 and return to Director, Employee Relations, Lancaster. Retain buff copy.

percent of white-collar and 58 percent of blue-collar employees were evaluated annually, and 25 percent of white-collar and 30 percent of blue-collar employees were evaluated semiannually. About 10 percent of all employees were evaluated more than twice a year.[8]

Researchers have found that feedback on performance should be given frequently, and the closer the feedback to the action, the more effective it is. For example, it is more effective for a professor to correct an error on a computer program the first time the error appears and show the student how to change it than to wait and flunk the student at the end of the term.[9]

Why, then, do so few firms evaluate frequently? Generally speaking, it is because managers and employees have lots of other things to do. One way to reconcile the ideal with the reality in this respect is for the manager to give frequent feedback to employees informally, and then formally summarize performance at evaluation time. This, of course, is based on the assumption that employees value evaluation and feedback.

Another reason that some managers resist frequent subordinate evaluations is that they produce stress, especially if a rater has to use a system in which he or she has little faith or confidence. There is also the stress associated with having to inform another person that he or she is not performing at acceptable levels. Researchers have found that raters under stress tend to notice and recall negative information about those being evaluated. This recall, of course, is likely to result in the giving of less favorable evaluations.[10]

Despite the additional work that more-frequent appraisals require, there are a growing number of organizations that have begun to conduct quarterly reviews. More-frequent appraisals, such as quarterly ones, will probably have their greatest value to organizations in relatively unstable environments. When conditions affecting the organization's productivity change rapidly, it is desirable to make adjustments to individual performance more often than once a year. In addition, it is recommended that quarterly appraisals will be more valuable for newer, inexperienced workers.[11]

It is also important to keep in mind that effective performance evaluation is really an on-going process. That is, supervisors should be thinking about an employee's performance regularly during the evaluation cycle. Experiences from the Navy's Personnel Management Demonstration Project have indicated that using several progress update meetings during the evaluation cycle in addition to the formal evaluation at the end of the cycle enhance the overall effectiveness of the performance evaluation system.[12]

As Exhibit 9–4 shows, performance evaluation is another HRM activity that involves both line managers and HR specialists. For performance evaluation to be more than a yearly paperwork exercise, top management must encourage its use and use it to make reward decisions.

Who Should Evaluate the Employee?   Exhibit 9–4 indicates that the operating manager (the immediate supervisor) does the evaluation in a vast majority of cases. There are, however, other possibilities as well. Many corporations will use other raters to supplement the evaluations of the immediate supervisor:

Rating by a Committee of Several Superiors   The supervisors chosen are those most likely to come in contact with the employee. This approach has the advantages of offsetting bias on the part of one superior and adding additional information to the evaluation, especially if it follows a group meeting format.

EXHIBIT 9-4   Involvement of Human Resource and Operating Managers in Performance Evaluation

Performance Evaluation Function	Operating Manager	Human Resource Manager
Establish performance standards	Approves the standards	Calculated by HRM and engineers
Set policy on when performance evaluation takes place	Approves the policy	Recommends the policy
Set policy on who evaluates	Approves the policy	Recommends the policy
Set policy on criteria of evaluation	Approves the policy	Recommends the policy
Choose the evaluation system	Approves the system	Recommends the system
Train the raters		Done by HRM
Review employee performance	Done by OM	
Discuss the evaluation with the employee	Done by OM	
File the performance evaluation		Done by HRM

Rating by the Employee's Peers (Co-Workers)   In the peer evaluation system, the co-workers must know the level of performance of the employee being evaluated. For this system to work, it is preferable for the evaluating peers to trust one another and not be competitive for raises and promotions. This approach may be useful when the tasks of the work unit require frequent working contact among peers.

Rating by the Employee's Subordinates.   Exxon has used this system, and it is used in some universities (students evaluate faculty). It is used more for the developmental aspects of performance evaluation than are some of the other methods. Managers are less likely to accept being rated by subordinates if the information is going to be used for administrative purposes (for example, raises, promotions) than if it is used for development. This source of rating information is also more acceptable if the managers believe that the raters (subordinates) are familiar with the job. Also, subordinates' evaluations should probably be restricted to "people-oriented" issues such as leadership and delegation, rather than having them evaluate organizing, planning, and other less easily observed aspects of the manager's performance.[13]

Rating by Someone outside the Immediate Work Situation   Known as the field review technique, this method uses a specialized appraiser from outside the job setting, such as a human resource specialist, to rate the employee. This approach is often costly, so it is generally used only for exceptionally important jobs. It might be used for the entire work force if accusations of prejudice must be countered. A crucial consideration is that the outside evaluator is not likely to have as much data as evaluators in any of the other four approaches, and the use of an outside evaluator represents a somewhat atypical approach to appraising performance.

Self-Evaluation   In this case, the employee evaluates herself or himself with the techniques used by other evaluators. This approach seems to be used more often for the developmental (as opposed to evaluative) aspects of performance evaluation. It is also used to evaluate an employee who works in physical isolation.

Self-evaluations have often been met with skepticism by organizations because the self-interests of the employee could outweigh an objective evaluation. However, research has demonstrated that self-evaluations can correlate reasonably well with supervisors' ratings, especially if the employees have information about their peers' performance. In other words, with the help of information about their co-workers' performance, employees can provide accurate appraisals of their own performance.[14]

Rating by a Combination of Approaches   Finally, a combination of approaches can be used. For example, supervisors' ratings can be supplemented with self-evaluations or peer evaluations. Using self- and supervisor ratings together allows for meaningful discussions of past performance and areas in which improvement is needed. This kind of open, two-way communication forms the foundation for the effective use of performance evaluations as a major source of employee feedback.[15]

An example of the use of a combination program is the one at Glendale Federal Savings and Loan Association, Glendale, California.[16] The program has three critical elements:

1. Independent manager and employee completion of an evaluation instrument (see Exhibit 9–5 for employee's section, which is similar to manager's section).
2. Two-way (rater-ratee) communication of job performance, career goals, and additional job responsibilities.
3. High-level managerial review of the completed appraisal.

The multiple-approach program involving a number of managerial levels has been well received. Managers complete their evaluations on time, and key training and development data are extracted from the forms. Lincoln Electric, a company that has long been known as an innovator in HRM takes this multiple-level approach right to the top. That is, the president of the company personally reviews the performance assessments of each of the more than 2,000 employees in the company.[17]

Summary   Unlike the combination approaches at Glendale Federal and Lincoln Electric, evaluation by superiors only is the most frequently used method, as has been noted. Self-evaluation is used in about 5 percent of evaluations. Peer evaluation is sometimes used by the military and universities but is rarely used elsewhere.

It is probable that evaluation by superiors will continue to be the principal approach used. If the primary purpose of the evaluation is developmental, the organization might consider supplementing it with subordinate evaluations or self-evaluation. If the purpose of the process is reward, then the organization might consider adding peer evaluation to the superior's ratings. The field review approach would be used only in special cases.

The key to successful performance evaluation appears to be well-trained, carefully selected raters who are knowledgeable about the performance of those being evaluated.

EXHIBIT 9-5   Sample Evaluation Instrument: Employee's Section

SECTION I: EMPLOYEE'S COMMENTS   (To be completed by Employee)

MAJOR ACCOMPLISHMENTS: Briefly describe the major accomplishment you achieved in your position during the past appraisal period

SUPPORT NEEDED: What type of assistance, guidance or support do you need from your supervisor or Glendale Federal Savings to improve your job related performance in the future?

MAJOR AREA(S) OF RESPONSIBILITY: Indicate 1 or 2 major areas of responsibility in your job that you would like to focus on during the next appraisal period.

DEVELOPMENTAL ACTIVITIES: Describe any developmental activities you are presently engaged in or have completed this appraisal period–i.e., courses, workshops, work assignments.

PERFORMANCE FACTORS: In each category below indicate ONE area you would describe as one of your major strengths by checking the appropriate circle. If strength is not evident, leave catagory blank. NOTE: Select only those factors which are appropriate for this job.

COMMUNICATING
- ○ Writes clearly & concisely
- ○ Speaks clearly & concisely
- ○ Works well with peers
- ○ Works well with subordinates
- ○ Works well with superiors
- ○ Courteous & helpful to customers
- ○ Presents idea persuasively
- ○ _____

JOB SKILLS KNOWLEDGE
- ○ Completes work assignments
- ○ Knows major aspects of job
- ○ Needs little supervision
- ○ Makes few errors
- ○ Meets schedules
- ○ Keeps up to date on current developments in field
- ○ _____

PLANNING
- ○ Sets realistic goals
- ○ Analyzes needs acurately
- ○ Gets results
- ○ Develops a variety of solutions
- ○ Effectively identifies & solves problems
- ○ _____

ORGANIZING
- ○ Keeps files & resources up to date
- ○ Delegates tasks appropriately
- ○ Checks effectiveness of actions
- ○ Establishes work priorities
- ○ Uses time efficiently
- ○ _____

SUPERVISING
- ○ Accurately judges subordinates performance
- ○ Trains & prepares subordinates
- ○ Demonstrates effective leadership
- ○ Motivates subordinates
- ○ _____

CONTROLLING
- ○ Adheres to policies & procedures
- ○ Maintains acceptable quality standards
- ○ Keeps within expense limits
- ○ _____

OTHER
- ○ Knows where to find information
- ○ Develops creative ideas
- ○ Works well under pressure
- ○ Adjusts to change
- ○ Makes good decisions
- ○ _____

Indicate specific areas from the lists above you would like to improve upon. NOTE: Indicate only areas that are job related.

1. _____   2. _____   3. _____

CAREER INTEREST: If appropriate, indicate other areas of career interest or long-range career goals.

EMPLOYEE'S SIGNATURE _____ **DATE** _____

When you have completed SECTION I give this form to your supervisor

Gathering Data on Employees

With regard to gathering data on employees, the raters collect information by observation, analysis of data and records, and discussion with the employees. The data they gather are influenced by the criteria used to evaluate, the primary purpose of the evaluation, and the technique used to do the evaluation. Care should be exercised, however, to carefully document specific incidences of performance and the source of the information. Raters should also take care to not use "hearsay" information but restrict their evaluations to performance information that they have seen firsthand or have been able to verify through other sources.[18]

SELECTED EVALUATION TECHNIQUES

There are many different ways to evaluate employees, and some of the most common ones will be described here. Generally speaking, these methods can be divided into two broad categories. One category consists of methods that evaluate employees individually. In other words, the supervisor evaluates each employee without explicit, direct comparisons to other employees; the standards of performance are defined without reference to other employees.

The second category of methods depends on multiple-person evaluations. Multiple-person evaluations require the supervisor to directly and intentionally compare the performance of one employee with that of other employees. Thus, the standards of performance are relative: an employee's performance is defined as good or bad based on comparison with other employees' performance.

Individual Evaluation Methods

Graphic Rating Scale
There are several individual evaluation methods used in business today but the oldest and perhaps the most common one is the graphic rating scale. Using this technique, the rater is presented with a set of traits such as those shown in Exhibit 9–6 and asked to rate employees on each of the characteristics listed. The number of characteristics rated varies from a few to several dozen.

The ratings can be in a series of boxes as in the exhibit, or they can be on a continuous scale (0–9, or so). In the latter case, the rater places a check above descriptive words ranging from *none* to *maximum*. Typically, these ratings are then assigned points. For example, in Exhibit 9–6 *outstanding* may be assigned a score of 4 and *unsatisfactory* a score of 0. Total scores are then computed. In some plans, greater weight may be given to traits that are regarded as more important. Raters are often asked to explain each rating with a sentence or two.

To make the scale more effective, two modifications have been designed. One is the Mixed Standard Scale.[19] Instead of just rating a trait such as *initiative*, the rater is given three statements to describe the trait, such as:

She is a real self-starter. She always takes the initiative, and her superior never has to stimulate her. (Best description.)

While generally she shows initiative, occasionally her superior has to prod her to get her work done.

She has a tendency to sit around and wait for directions. (Poorest description.)

EXHIBIT 9-6   Typical Graphic Rating Scale

Name _____ Dept. _____ Date _____

	Out-standing	Good	Satis-factory	Fair	Unsatis-factory
Quantity of work Volume of acceptable work under normal conditions Comments:	☐	☐	☐	☐	☐
Quality of work Thoroughness, neatness, and accuracy of work Comments:	☐	☐	☐	☐	☐
Knowledge of job Clear understanding of the facts or factors pertinent to the job Comments:	☐	☐	☐	☐	☐
Personal qualities Personality, appearance, sociability, leadership, integrity Comments:	☐	☐	☐	☐	☐
Cooperation Ability and willingness to work with associates, supervisors, and subordinates toward common goals Comments:	☐	☐	☐	☐	☐
Dependability Conscientious, thorough, accurate, reliable with respect to attendance, lunch periods, reliefs, etc. Comments:	☐	☐	☐	☐	☐
Initiative Earnestness in seeking increased responsibilities. Self-starting, unafraid to proceed alone Comments:	☐	☐	☐	☐	☐

PROFESSIONAL PROFILE

Gary Thomas
Forest City Technologies, Inc.
Wellington, Ohio

Biography

Gary Thomas is director, employee relations, for Forest City Technologies, Inc., in Wellington, Ohio. Originally a journeyman tool & die maker, Mr. Thomas subsequently completed a B.A. in Psychology at Kent State University and did his graduate work at the University of Akron where he completed his M.A. in industrial/organizational psychology.

Mr. Thomas began his professional career as a plant training supervisor with P.P.G. Industries, Inc. He advanced through numerous "specialist" and "generalist" positions there as well as with Du Pont, Cain Chemical, and Occidental Petroleum Corp., prior to assuming his present position with Forest City Technologies, Inc. While at Cain Chemical, Inc., he was heavily involved in the early start-up of the employee relations function there, which was responsible for much of his current philosophy of employee relations management.

Job Description   As director, employee relations, Mr. Thomas is responsible for the conception and implementation of all human resources activities for his corporation. This includes compensation and benefits programs, employee training and development, staffing/recruiting, employee safety and health, performance appraisal programs, job evaluation systems, employee morale programs, and organizational/cultural development activities.

Performance Appraisal: A Viewpoint   Companies wishing to compete in today's global markets must have not only world-class technological, manufacturing, and quality systems, but more importantly, world-class employees, because it is employees that serve a company's customers. This challenge falls predominately to the employee relations profession, and the primary means of meeting it successfully lies in treating employees as partners in the business, as opposed to "cogs in the machine," as is so often the case in modern organizations. Only when employees perceive themselves as important "partners" in the organizational team will they contribute their fullest dedication, talents, loyalty, and creativity to the employment relationship.

The organizational systems and culture in our company are structured to create and maintain this form of environment, but more importantly, we communicate and reinforce it constantly in our interactions with employees. One primary mechanism for accomplishing this is through our "Joint Performance Appraisal System." This system is an innovative means for creating a partnership in what is traditionally a one-sided activity, that is, appraising employee performance.

Our performance appraisal system is an outgrowth of our carefully planned organizational growth and of our efforts to build systems for a small company that will continue to serve it well as it evolves into a much larger entity, which is what our future holds. As part of our development process, we held small-group brainstorming sessions with a sample of our employee population to arrive at what would be perceived as valid and fair dimensions of performance to be evaluated. This resulted in the identification of seven primary dimensions of performance reflective of our organizational culture for all manufacturing employees, with four additional factors applicable to supervisory employees. Descriptive anchors were developed for each of five levels of performance on each factor.

The partnership is created through our method of conducting the appraisals. We formally appraise performance twice yearly and use a highly participative approach to conducting the appraisals. Employees are given a blank copy of the appraisal by their supervisor

(continued on next page)

PROFESSIONAL PROFILE
(concluded)

well in advance of the appraisal date, along with instructions to appraise their own performance. The supervisor completes a form as well, and subsequently meets with each employee to compare ratings and the basis for the respective ratings, reinforce areas of strength, and develop plans for improving identified weaknesses. It is not unusual for supervisors to upgrade their ratings on one or more factors as a result of information brought out by the employees.

This joint appraisal approach results in considerable valuable information coming to light during the appraisal meetings, as much of the traditional defensiveness and fear have been removed from the appraisal environment. Appraisals are also more readily accepted by employees, as they have a large amount of input into their results. This process tremendously improves communications between employee and supervisor and enables them to work as a team even in a situation in which the more traditional approach tends to set them against each other.

Our plans are to continue this partnership approach and further extend it to a system we are developing to have employees appraise their supervisor's performance and have this information fed back to the supervisor in an anonymous form for developmental purposes.

After each description, the rater places a check mark (the employee fits the description), a plus sign (the employee is better than the statement), or a minus sign (the employee is poorer than the statement). The resulting seven-point scale is purported to be better than the graphic rating scale.

The second modification is to add operational and benchmark statements to describe different levels of performance. For example, if the employee is evaluated on job knowledge, the form gives a specific example: "What has the employee done to actually demonstrate depth, currency, or breadth of job knowledge in the performance of duties? Consider both quality and quantity of work." The performance descriptions are designed to guide the rater by giving examples of persons who deserve a particular rating (see Exhibit 9–7).

Forced Choice   Several potential problems with graphic rating scales led to the development of alternative rating methods. Graphic rating scales were thought to lead to many different errors of evaluation (to be discussed in a later section). Forced-choice methods were developed because graphic rating scales allowed supervisors to rate everyone high. As a result, there was no way to distinguish between good and poor performers. Recall that sensitivity is a necessary characteristic of a good criterion.

In a forced-choice format, the rater must choose from a set of descriptive statements about an employee. Typical sets of these statements are shown in Exhibit 9–8. Forced-choice items are usually prepared by an HR specialist, and then supervisors or others familiar with the ratees' performance evaluate how applicable each statement is. That is, they determine which statements describe effective or ineffective behavior.

Neutral statements are also sometimes included in forced-choice items. When the supervisors evaluate their employees, they check the statements that describe the employee or, if the items are like the ones shown in Exhibit 9–8, they rank the

---

EXHIBIT 9-7   Standards of Performance: Excerpts from Graphic Rating Scale

---

Far below standard rating:

1. Has serious gaps in technical-professional knowledge

   Knows only most rudimentary phases of job

   Lack of knowledge affects productivity

   Requires abnormal amount of checking

2. Reluctant to make decisions on his or her own

   Decisions are usually not reliable

   Declines to accept responsibility for decisions

3. Fails to plan ahead

   Disorganized and usually unprepared

   Objectives are not met on time

4. Wastes or misuses resources

   No system established for accounting of material

   Causes delay for others by mismanagement

EXHIBIT 9-8   Forced-Choice Items

Instructions: Rank from 1 to 4 the following sets of statements according to how they describe the manner in which _____ performs
                                              (name of employee)
the job. A rank of *1* should be used for the most descriptive statement, and a rank of *4* should be given for the least descriptive. No ties are allowed.

1. _____   Does not anticipate difficulties
   _____   Grasps explanations quickly
   _____   Rarely wastes time
   _____   Easy to talk to
2. _____   A leader in group activities
   _____   Wastes time on unimportant things
   _____   Cool and calm at all times
   _____   Hard worker

---

statements from most to least descriptive. The HR department then adds up the number of statements in each category (for example, effective behavior), and they are summed into an effectiveness index. Forced choice can be used by superiors, peers, subordinates, or a combination of these in evaluating employees.

Essay Evaluation   In the essay technique of evaluation, the rater is asked to describe the strong and weak aspects of the employee's behavior. In some organizations, the essay technique is the only one used; in others, the essay is combined with another form, such as a graphic rating scale. In this case, the essay summarizes the scale, elaborates on some of the ratings, or discusses additional dimensions that are not on the scale. In both of these approaches, the essay can be open-ended, but in most cases there are guidelines on the topics to be covered, the purpose of the essay, and so on. The essay method can be used by raters who are superiors, peers, or subordinates of the employee to be evaluated.

Critical Incident Technique   Simply stated, this technique requires raters to maintain a log of behavioral incidents that represent either effective or ineffective performance for each employee being rated. These incidents are **critical incidents.**

Because these incidents might not be directly comparable for different ratees, lists of standardized incidents can be prepared by the HR specialist in consultation with the operating managers. Then, the rating task becomes one of logging each time a subordinate engages in one of these behaviors.

An example of a *good* critical incident of a sales clerk is the following:

May 1 — Dan listened patiently to the customer's complaint, answered the woman's questions, and then took back the merchandise, giving the customer full credit for the returned product. He was polite, prompt, and interested in her problem.

On the other hand, a *bad* critical incident might read as follows:

August 12 — Dan stayed eight minutes over on his break during the busiest part of the day. He failed to answer three store manager's calls on the intercom to report to cash register 4 immediately.

Two factors make the critical incident technique successful. First, the supervisor has to be given enough time to observe each subordinate during the evaluation period. This is necessary so enough incidents are observed. Second, it is unreasonable to expect a supervisor to remember all of the incidents that were observed. Therefore, the supervisor must be willing to take the time to record the incidents that are seen in the log for each employee. Otherwise, many of the incidents might be forgotten. Diary keeping in the form of these employee logs has been shown to significantly improve the rating process.[20]

If the employee logs are used, the critical incidents that are recorded are valuable for performance evaluation interviews. If done properly, the logs can help to avoid many common rating errors and help facilitate discussions about how an employee's performance can be improved.

Checklists and Weighted Checklists

Another type of individual evaluation method is the checklist. In its simplest form, the *checklist* is a set of objectives or descriptive statements. If the rater believes that the employee possesses a trait listed, the rater checks the item; if not, the rater leaves it blank. A rating score from the checklist equals the number of checks.

A variation of the checklist is the *weighted checklist*. Supervisors and HR specialists familiar with the jobs to be evaluated prepare a large list of descriptive statements about effective and ineffective behavior on jobs, similar to the critical incident process. Judges who have observed behavior on the job sort the statements into piles describing behavior that is scaled from excellent to poor. When there is reasonable agreement on an item (for example, when the standard deviation is small), it is included in the weighted checklist. The weight is the average score of the raters prior to use of the checklist.

The supervisors or other raters receive the checklist without the scores and check the items that apply, as with an unweighted checklist. The employee's evaluation is the sum of the scores (weights) on the items checked. Checklists and weighted checklists can be used by evaluators who are superiors, peers, or subordinates, or by a combination.

Behaviorally Anchored Rating Scales

Smith and Kendall developed what is referred to as the **behaviorally anchored rating scale (BARS)** or the *behavioral expectation scale (BES)*.[21] The BARS approach relies on the use of critical incidents to serve as anchor statements on a scale. A BARS rating form usually contains 6 to 10 specifically defined performance dimensions, each with 5 or 6 critical incident

EXHIBIT 9-9   Sample BARS Dimension

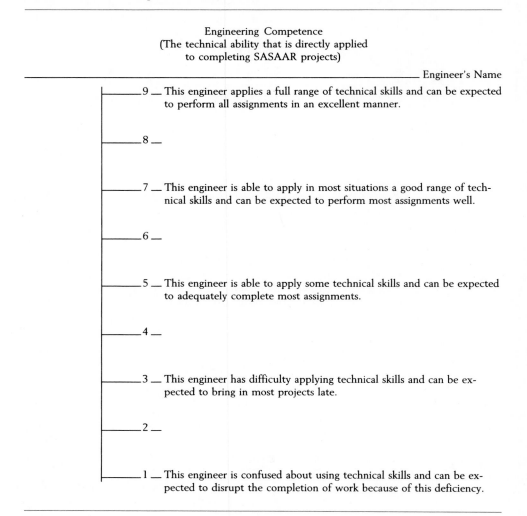

Engineering Competence
(The technical ability that is directly applied
to completing SASAAR projects)

_____ Engineer's Name

9 — This engineer applies a full range of technical skills and can be expected to perform all assignments in an excellent manner.

8 —

7 — This engineer is able to apply in most situations a good range of technical skills and can be expected to perform most assignments well.

6 —

5 — This engineer is able to apply some technical skills and can be expected to adequately complete most assignments.

4 —

3 — This engineer has difficulty applying technical skills and can be expected to bring in most projects late.

2 —

1 — This engineer is confused about using technical skills and can be expected to disrupt the completion of work because of this deficiency.

anchors. Exhibit 9–9 presents one performance dimension for engineering competence. The anchor statement for a rating of 9 is: "This engineer applies a full range of technical skills and can be expected to perform all assignments in an excellent manner." The rater would read the anchors and place an X at some point on the scale for the ratee.

A BARS usually contains the following features:

1. Six to 10 performance dimensions are identified and defined by raters and ratees (a group is selected to construct the form).
2. The dimensions are anchored with positive and negative critical incidents.
3. Each ratee is then rated on the dimensions.
4. Ratings are fed back using the terms displayed on the form.

The exact construction of a BARS is too complex for presentation here. However, it should be noted that usually two to four days are needed to develop a BARS.

EXHIBIT 9-10   Sample BOS Items for Supervisor

Is accurate in preparing cost reports for Johnson project crew.

| Almost Never | 1 | 2 | 3 | 4 | 5 | Almost Always |

Practices sound energy conservation in supervising project crews.

| Almost Never | 1 | 2 | 3 | 4 | 5 | Almost Always |

Is available for technical consultation when needed.

| Almost Never | 1 | 2 | 3 | 4 | 5 | Almost Always |

Develops fair and equitable work schedule.

| Almost Never | 1 | 2 | 3 | 4 | 5 | Almost Always |

The result of the developmental work is a jargon-free rating scale that is closely related to the requirements of a given job.

It is not clear, however, whether a BARS avoids many of the problems encountered with graphic rating scales. A BARS still seems to be susceptible to many kinds of rating errors.[22] However, there appear to be some important spin-offs from using a BARS program. It appears that subordinates involved with a BARS program are more committed, less tense, and more satisfied than counterparts using other programs.[23] Another possible benefit is that managers have feedback in the form of critical incident statements that are meaningful to subordinates. The incidents allow the supervisor to discuss specific instances of good and bad performance, and this tends to make the feedback more acceptable to subordinates than if the supervisor talked in vague generalities.[24]

Behavioral Observation Scales   Latham and associates developed the **behavioral observation scale (BOS)** performance evaluation approach.[25] Like BARS, the BOS uses the critical incident technique to identify a series of behaviors that cover the domain of the job. A major difference between BARS and BOS is that, instead of identifying those behaviors exhibited by the ratee during a rating period, the rater indicates on a scale how often the ratee was actually observed engaging in the specific behaviors identified in the BOS.

Exhibit 9–10 presents four behavior items that are used to appraise the performance of a first-line supervisor in a manufacturing plant. In this BOS appraisal form, 25 behavioral items are identified. The maximum score is 125 (25 × 5), and the minimum score is 25. Those supervisors with scores above 115 are considered excellent performers, while a score in the 25 to 34 range is considered extremely poor. Each firm using a BOS must determine the meaning and importance of the total score for their ratees.

As with BARS, there is no clear superiority of BOS over alternative rating scale formats. One very significant limitation of the BOS approach is the time and cost needed to develop it for actual use in ratings. Thus, although the technique seems to be an improvement over more traditional graphic rating scales, it may not be available to organizations with limited resources.[26]

Multiple-Person Evaluation Methods

By design, the methods of performance evaluation described so far are supposed to be used for evaluating employees one at a time — with no direct comparisons for an employee with another. In this section, three techniques that compare one employee's performance to that of one or more others will be discussed. While they differ in some ways, all three of these techniques yield similar kinds of information, namely, a list of employees ranked from best to worst.

Ranking

In their simplest form, rankings ask a supervisor to generate a list of subordinates in order on some overall criterion. This can be very difficult to do if the supervisor is asked to rank a large number of subordinates, for example, over 20. It is also much easier for the supervisor to rank the best and worst employees in a reliable way than it is to rank the average ones. Because of this difficulty, a variation of simple rankings is *alternative rankings*. In this approach, the evaluators pick the top employee first, then the bottom employee next. Then, the second best is chosen followed by the second worst. This process is followed until all persons have been ranked.

Paired Comparison

This approach can make the rankings easier for the supervisor and perhaps more reliable, especially when there are a large number of persons to rank. First, the names of the persons to be evaluated are placed on separate sheets (or cards) in a predetermined order, so that each person is paired with all others to be evaluated. The evaluator then checks the person that is the better performer within each set of two-person pairs. Typically, the criterion is again an overall measure of performance. The number of times that a person is chosen as the better employee is tallied, and results are indexed based on this number.

The scores derived from paired comparisons can be converted into standard scores by comparing the scores to the standard deviation and the average of all scores. This method can be used by superiors, peers, subordinates, or some combination of these groups.

There is, however, one potential limitation to paired comparisons. In order to guarantee that each employee is paired with every other employee, it requires $n(n-1)/2$ pairs where n equals the number of persons to be ranked. Thus, with only 10 subordinates, a supervisor will have to go through $10(10-1)/2$ or 45 pairs of names. This means that, with large numbers of subordinates, it can be a tedious assignment for the supervisor.

Forced Distribution

The forced-distribution system is similar to grading on a curve. The rater is asked to rate employees in some fixed distribution of categories, such as 10 percent in low, 20 percent in low average, 40 percent in average, 20 percent in high average, and 10 percent in high. One way to do this is to type each employee's name on a card and ask the evaluators to sort the cards into five piles corresponding to the ratings. This should be done twice for the two key criteria of job performance and promotability.

Exhibit 9–11 shows the results of forced-distribution evaluation of 20 employees. One reason forced distribution was developed was to try to alleviate such problems as inflated ratings and central tendency in the graphic rating scale.

A variation of forced distribution is the point allocation technique (PAT). In PAT, each rater is given a number of points per employee in the group to be

---

EXHIBIT 9-11   Forced-Distribution Evaluation of Employees in a Marketing
Research Unit

High 10 Percent	Next 20 Percent	Middle 40 Percent	Next 20 Percent	Low 10 Percent
Leslie Moore	Cinde Lanyon	Max Coggins	Art Willis	Wayne Allison
Tina Little	Sharon Feltman	Tina Holmes	Debbie Salter	Sherry Gruber
	Eddie Dorsey	Julis Jimenex	Tom Booth	
	Johnny Dyer	Lis Amendale	Lance Smith	
		Vince Gaillard		
		Missy Harrington		
		Bill King		
		Shelly Sweat		

---

evaluated, and the total points for all employees evaluated cannot exceed the number of points per employee times the number of employees evaluated. The points are allocated on a criterion basis. Forced distribution and PAT are most likely to be used by superiors, but could be used by peers or subordinates.

Management by Objectives

In most of the traditional performance evaluation systems, the raters judge past performance and attempt to report their judgments using one of the techniques described above. Because performance evaluation is used for making important decisions that affect employees, the rater is placed in a difficult and somewhat antagonistic role.

McGregor believed that, instead of creating antagonisms because of judgments, the superior should work with subordinates to set goals. This would enable subordinates to exercise self-control and management over their job performance behaviors. From the early beliefs of McGregor, Drucker, and Odiorne has emerged the management by objectives (MBO) approach.[27]

MBO is more than just an evaluation program and process. It is viewed as a philosophy of managerial practice, a method by which managers and subordinates plan, organize, control, communicate, and debate. By setting objectives through participation or by assignment from a superior, the subordinate is provided with a course to follow and a target to shoot for while performing the job. Usually, an MBO program follows a systematic process such as the following:

1. The superior and subordinate conduct meetings to define key tasks of the subordinate and to set a limited number of objectives (goals).
2. The participants set objectives that are realistic, challenging, clear, and comprehensive.
3. The superior, after consulting with the subordinate, establishes the criteria for assessing the accomplishment of the objectives.
4. Intermediate progress review dates are agreed upon and used.
5. The superior and subordinate make any required modifications in original objectives.
6. A final evaluation by the superior is made and a meeting is held with the subordinate in a counseling, encouragement session.

EXHIBIT 9–12   Examples of MBO Evaluation Form Objectives

Occupation in Organization	Type Organization	Objective Statement
Sales representative	Medium: Petrochemical firm	To contact six new clients in West AVA region and to sell to at least two of these new clients within the next semiannual cycle.
Product manager	Large: Food processing plant	To increase market share of creamy peanut butter by at least 3.5 percent before next objective meeting (nine months from today) without increasing costs by more than 2 percent.
Skilled machinist	Small: Job shop	To reduce flange rejects by 8 percent by August 15.
Accountant	Small: CPA firm	To attend two auditing seminars to improve and update audit knowledge by the end of summer (September 15).
Plant manager	Medium: Assembly-line plant	Decrease absenteeism of operating employees from 18.9 percent to under 10 percent by January 1.
Engineer	Large: Construction company	To complete power plant tower project within 30 days of government-specified target date of November 10.

7. Objectives for the next cycle are set by the subordinate after consulting with the superior, keeping in mind the previous cycle and future expectations.

MBO-type programs have been used in organizations throughout the world.[28] Approximately 200 of Fortune's 500 largest industrial firms report use of MBO-type programs. Various types of objectives have been set in these programs. A sample of some objectives taken from actual MBO evaluation forms is presented in Exhibit 9–12. Most of these objectives are stated in the language of the job or occupation. Some of them are routine, others are innovative, and some are personal, such as the accountant's objectives.

For MBO and other appraisal programs to be effective, these objectives must be clearly stated, measurable, and communicated to the subordinate in a timely fashion.[29] When objectives are stated clearly and they can be measured, it makes it easier for subordinates to attain the criteria of successful performance. This is especially important since subordinate acceptance of their objectives will lead to higher performance. To gain this acceptance, many firms have used participative goal setting for establishing MBO objectives.

An important feature of any MBO program is that discussions about performance evaluation center on results. The results hopefully are objective in nature and associated with certain work behaviors. The superior and subordinate dissect the objectives achieved and not achieved, and analysis serves to help subordinates improve in the next cycle of objective setting.

After three decades of interest, there is still cautious optimism about MBO among many practicing managers. First, MBO appeals to people because it doesn't require a superior to sit as judge. Second, MBO seems simple to implement. Nothing can be further from the truth. In fact, MBO requires patience, objective writing skills, interview skills, and overall trust between superiors and subordinates. These attributes are complex and difficult to maintain in MBO programs. Third, the literature cites example after example of MBO success stories. Unfortunately, many of the success stories are based on anecdotal statements of consultants who are in the business of selling MBO to clients. As reviews of the literature indicate, there are few rigorously designed field studies of MBO that find that it has a positive, long-lasting effect on performance.[30]

Not all MBO programs are identical, however. There are important differences between them. For example, the ways in which goals are determined can vary across programs. Some involve mutually set goals, while others involve only consultation with the employee — the supervisor actually maintains control over the goal that is established.

The differences that exist between MBO programs can be important for assessing their effectiveness. If an MBO program is established that is inconsistent with a supervisor's leadership style, then the program will not work as well as when the MBO characteristics complement the leader's style.[31]

A number of other pitfalls and problems with MBO have been identified. Some of these include:

. Too much paperwork.
. Too many objectives are set, and confusion occurs. (It appears to be more efficient to work with four, five, or six objectives.)
. MBO is forced into jobs where establishing objectives is extremely difficult.
. Failure to tie in MBO results with rewards. "Why are we doing this?" is an often-asked question.
. Too much emphasis on the short term.
. Failure to train superiors in the MBO process and the mechanics involved.
. Never modifying originally set objectives.
. Using MBO as a rigid control device that intimidates rather than motivates.

These and other problems need to be minimized or overcome if MBO is to have any chance for success.[32] MBO in some situations is very effective; in other cases, it is costly and disruptive. Just like the other evaluation techniques available, managers need to examine the purposes, costs, and benefits, and their preferences before selecting or discarding an MBO program.

Which Technique to Use

Perhaps you now feel overwhelmed by the large number of evaluation techniques. You should know that not all of them are used very often. It is generally recognized that the graphic rating scale is the most widely used technique. Studies indicate that the essay method is also widely used, usually as part of a graphic rating scale form. Checklists are also widely used. Studies show that other methods, such as forced choice, critical incident, BARS, BOS, field review, and MBO, *combined* are used by about 5 percent. Ranking and paired comparison are used by 10 to 13 percent of employers. MBO is most likely to be used for managerial, professional, and technical employees, not production and office personnel.[33]

Which technique should be used in a specific instance? The literature on the shortcomings, strengths, reliabilities, and validities of each of the techniques is vast. In essence, there are studies showing that each of the techniques is sometimes good, sometimes poor. The major problems are not with the techniques themselves, but *how they are used* and *by whom*. Untrained raters or those that have little talent or motivation to evaluate well can destroy or hamper *any* evaluation technique. The rater is more critical than the technique in developing effective evaluation systems.

Evaluation techniques can be judged on a series of criteria, such as costs and purposes. As noted in the discussion of the approaches to evaluation above, at least two major purposes are served by evaluation: counseling and personal development, and evaluation for rewards, such as an aid in promotion decisions. Some evaluation techniques serve one purpose better than others. Some systems cost more to develop and operate than others. Exhibit 9–13 scales the techniques on these criteria.

If the primary purpose of the evaluation is development, for example, the knowledgeable organization will use BARS, BOS, essay, critical incident, MBO, or field review tools. If the primary purpose of the evaluation is rewards, the organization might use graphic rating scales, field review, forced distribution, MBO, critical incident, BARS, or BOS. If the primary purpose of the evaluation is developmental, and costs are not a concern currently, then field review, MBO, or critical incident methods should be chosen. And if the primary purpose is development and costs are a consideration, the BARS or essay methods might be chosen.

POTENTIAL PROBLEMS WHEN CONDUCTING PERFORMANCE EVALUATIONS

Regardless of which technique or system is chosen, there are going to be many problems encountered trying to use it. None of the techniques is perfect; they all have limitations. Some of these limitations are common to all of the techniques, while others are more frequently encountered with certain ones.

Opposition to Evaluation

Most employees are wary of performance evaluation. Perhaps the most common fear is that of rater subjectivity. Introducing subjective bias and favoritism are real problems that create opposition to most performance evaluation systems. These fears are hidden, and other, more general arguments are provided. For example, those who oppose the use of formal performance evaluation systems argue that:

- They increase paperwork and bureaucracy without benefiting employees much. Operating managers do not use them in reward decisions (systems problems).
- Managers and employees dislike the evaluation process. Raters especially have problems with reaching decisions about the performance levels of employees.
- Employees who are not evaluated in the top performance category experience a reverse motivation effect: They slow down (employee problems).

System Design and Operating Problems

Performance evaluation systems break down because they are poorly designed. The design can be blamed if the criteria for evaluation are poor, the technique used is cumbersome, or the system is more form than substance. If the criteria used focus solely on activities rather than output results, or on personality traits rather than performance, the evaluation may not be well received. Some evaluation techniques

EXHIBIT 9-13 Selected Criteria for Choice of Performance Evaluation Techniques

Evaluative Base	Graphic Rating Scale	Forced Choice	MBO	Essay	Critical Incident	Weighted Checklist	BARS	BOS	Ranking	Paired Comparison	Forced Distribution	Performance Test	Field Review
Developmental cost	Moderate	High	Moderate	Low	Moderate	Moderate	High	High	Low	Low	Low	High	Moderate
Usage costs	Low	Low	High	High supervisory costs	High	Low	Low	Low	Low	Low	Low	High	High
Ease of use by rater	Easy	Moderately difficult	Moderate	Difficult	Difficult	Easy	Easy	Easy	Easy	Easy	Easy	Moderately difficult	Easy
Ease of understanding by those evaluated	Easy	Difficult	Moderate	Easy	Easy	Easy	Moderate	Moderate	Easy	Easy	Easy	Easy	Easy
Useful in promotion decisions	Yes	Yes	Yes	Not easily	Yes	Moderate	Yes	Yes	Yes	Yes	Yes	Yes	Yes
Useful in compensation and reward decisions	Yes	Moderate	Yes	Not easily	Yes	Moderate	Yes	Yes	Not easily	Not easily	Yes	Yes	Yes
Useful in counseling and development of employees	Moderate	Moderate	Yes	Yes	Yes	Moderate	Yes	Yes	No	No	No	Moderate	Yes

take a long time to carry out or require extensive written analysis, both of which many managers resist. If this is the problem, another technique can be chosen. Finally, some systems are not on-line and running. Some supervisors use the system, but others just haphazardly fill out the paperwork. Top management's support for performance evaluation can remedy this problem of ritualism.

Rater Problems

Even if the system is well designed, problems can arise if the raters (usually supervisors) are not cooperative and well trained. Supervisors may not be comfortable with the process of evaluation, or what Douglas McGregor called "playing God."[34] This is often because they have not been adequately trained or have not participated in the design of the program. Inadequate training of raters can lead to a series of problems in completing performance evaluations including:

Problems with the standards of evaluation.

Halo effect.

Leniency or harshness.

Central tendency error.

Recency of events error.

Contrast effects.

Personal bias (stereotyping; similar to me).

Standards of Evaluation
Problems with evaluation standards arise because of perceptual differences in the meaning of the words used to evaluate employees. Thus, *good*, *adequate*, *satisfactory*, and *excellent* may mean different things to different evaluators. Some teachers are "easy As," while others almost never give an A. *They* differ in their interpretation of *excellent*. If only one rater is used, the evaluation can be distorted. This difficulty arises most often in graphic rating scales but may also appear with essays, critical incidents, and checklists.

For example, Exhibit 9–14 presents a rating scale with unclear standards for four difficult-to-rate performance dimensions. What does "good" performance for quality of work mean? How does it differ from a "fair" rating? How would you interpret the quality or quantity of performance? This rating scale is ambiguous as it now stands. Perhaps defining the meaning of each dimension and training raters to apply the five ratings consistently could reduce the potential rating problem.

The Halo Effect
At one time, it was believed that halo errors in ratings were the major problem in performance evaluation. **Halo error** occurs when a rater assigns ratings on several dimensions of performance based on an overall, general impression of the ratee.

Halo error can either be a positive or a negative error, meaning that the initial impression can cause the ratings to either be too low or too high. Suppose that an information systems manager thought that one particular computer programmer was the best in the department at developing new software. If, on the basis of this impression, the programmer is given high ratings on decision making, getting along with peers, and leadership potential, then a halo error has occurred.

A problem with understanding and dealing with halo error is that the ratings only represent an error if they are not justified. That is, imagine that our computer programmer deserved high ratings on the three dimensions of performance other

EXHIBIT 9-14   A Rating Scale with Unclear Standards: A Graphic Rating Scale for Laboratory Scientists

Performance Dimension	Scale: Place an X for Rating of _____				
	Outstanding	Good	Fair	Below Accepted	Poor
Quality of technical reports					
Quantity of technical reports					
Creativeness					
Social interaction ability					

than programming. Even though the manager was basing the ratings on a general impression, they could represent an accurate evaluation. In other words, it is important to realize that there is a difference between *halo errors* and *true halo*, which occurs when uniformly high or low ratings across different aspects of performance are actually justified by the ratee's performance.

Interestingly, halo errors are not as common as once believed.[35] Raters do seem to be able to distinguish halo errors from true halo in many situations. When halo errors do occur, however, they can be very difficult to eliminate.[36] One procedure to reduce this type of error is to have the rater evaluate all subordinates on one dimension before proceeding to another dimension. The theory of this practice is that thinking in terms of one dimension at a time forces the rater to think in specific instead of overall terms when evaluating subordinates.

Leniency or Harshness Error   Performance evaluations require the rater to objectively reach a conclusion about performance. Being objective is difficult for everyone. Raters have their own rose-colored glasses with which they "objectively" view subordinates. Consequently, **leniency or harshness rating error** may occur in raters' evaluations of their subordinates. Some raters see everything good — these are lenient raters. Other raters see everything bad — these are harsh raters.

Exhibit 9–15 shows the distributions of lenient and harsh raters on a dimension called quality of work performance.[37] Suppose that Jack is an employee working for this particular rater. His ratings would be low if rated by the harsh rater and high if rated by the lenient rater.

Raters can assess their own harsh and lenient rating tendencies by examining ratings. This self-assessment is sometimes startling. Another method used to reduce harsh and lenient rating tendencies is to ask raters to distribute ratings — forcing a normal distribution (for example, 10 percent of the subordinates will be rated excellent, 20 percent rated good, 40 percent rated fair, 20 percent rated below fair, and 10 percent rated poor).

EXHIBIT 9-15   Distributions of Lenient and Harsh Raters

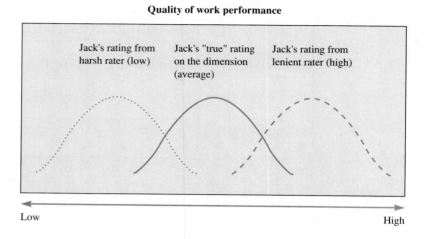

Quality of work performance

Jack's rating from harsh rater (low)

Jack's "true" rating on the dimension (average)

Jack's rating from lenient rater (high)

Low   High

Central Tendency Error

A **central tendency error** occurs when a rater avoids using high or low ratings and assigns average ratings. They resort to a philosophy that everyone is about average and rate subordinates around a 4 on a 1 to 7 scale or a 3 on a 1 to 5 scale. This type of "average" rating is almost useless. It fails to discriminate between subordinates. Thus, it offers little information for making HRM decisions regarding compensation, promotion, training needs, or what should be fed back to ratees. Raters must be made aware of the importance of discriminating across ratees and the use of evaluations. This sometimes stimulates raters to use less central (or average) ratings.

Recency of Events Error

One difficulty with many of the evaluation systems is the time frame of the behavior being evaluated. Raters forget more about past behavior than current behavior. Thus, many persons are evaluated more on the results of the past several weeks than on six months' average behavior. This is called a **recency of events rating error.**

Some employees are well aware of this difficulty. If they know the dates of the evaluation, they make it their business to be visible and noticed in many positive ways for several weeks in advance. Many evaluation systems suffer from this difficulty. It can be mitigated by using a technique such as critical incident or management by objectives (MBO) or by irregularly scheduled evaluations.

Contrast Effects

Recall that with the individual performance evaluation techniques each employee is supposed to be rated without regard to other employees' performance. There is some evidence, however, suggesting that supervisors have a very difficult time doing this. If a supervisor lets another employee's performance influence the ratings that are given to someone else, then a **contrast effect** has occurred.[38] For example, when the performance of an average employee is evaluated immediately after the performance of an outstanding employee has been evaluated, the supervisor might end up rating the average person as "below average" or "poor."

CAREER CHALLENGE

(continued)

*L*et's get back to Ed and his supervisor, Hector. Now that the vice presidents have had their meeting about performance evaluation, the tentative decision to start up Mary's plan has been passed on to the department heads.

Bob Woods (department head) I'm just reviewing your suggested pay and promotion recommendations for your unit, Hector. You know I try to delegate as much as I can. But I know some of the people you have set here for big raises and promotions, and I notice some surprising omissions. Since I'm responsible for the whole department, I'd like to review this with you. Understand, I'm not trying to undercut you, Hector.

Hector Garcia (supervisor) Oh, I understand, Bob. No problem! Where do you want to start?

Bob: Let me just highspot. I note that Mo Gibbs, who's always been in our high reward group, isn't here, nor is Ed Smart, a good worker. And you do have Joe Berlioz in your high reward group. In the past, he never appeared there. How did you make these recommendations?

Hector: I looked my people over and used my best judgment.

Bob: Well Hector, what facts did you use—did you look at the quarterly output printout, their personnel files, or what? How about performance evaluations? Partridge is thinking about a formal system to evaluate employees and help decide who should be promoted and get raises.

Hector: I believe I know my people best. I don't need to go through a lot of paperwork and files to come up with my recommendations.

Contrast effects can also occur when a supervisor unknowingly compares employees' present performance to their past performance and this comparison affects ratings. Someone who had been a poor performer in the past could get rated as "above average" if they improve their performance, even if the improvement actually only brings their performance up to "average."

Contrast effects are another rating problem that is difficult to eliminate. Fortunately, this type of error seems to dissipate over time and as more information about employees' performance is gathered.[39]

Personal Bias Error A **personal bias rating error** is an error related to a personal bias held by a supervisor that can occur in performance evaluations. There are several kinds of personal bias errors. Some can be conscious such as blatant discrimination against someone because of their sex or race. Or, in contrast, some supervisors might try to "play favorites" and rate people they like higher than people they don't like.[40]

Other personal bias errors are more subtle, and the supervisor might be totally unaware that they are being made. For example, there is an error that sometimes occurs when a rater gives a higher rating because the ratee has qualities or characteristics similar to his or her own. Likewise, giving a ratee a lower rating because of dissimilarities is another form of personal bias that can occur unconsciously.[41]

Personal bias errors have been detected in many studies of performance evaluation. On the other hand, several large-scale studies of actual performance evaluation systems have found that many of the potential errors are not as strong as once thought. For example, rating errors associated with ratees' sex and race do occur but the effect of these errors is very small in comparison to the effect that actual performance has on ratings.[42] Even small effects for characteristics such as sex and race are cause for concern, however. Thus, organizations that want to comply with equal employment opportunity legislation should attempt to eliminate such effects.

Eliminating Rater Errors   One method for dealing with the kinds of errors we have been discussing has been to change the format of the rating scales that supervisors are asked to complete. The trend has been to move from graphic rating scales with ambiguous anchors (fair, poor, excellent) to behaviorally oriented scales with well-defined anchors. After years of research, however, there is no clear superiority of newer rating formats.[43]

This lack of improvement in the accuracy of ratings by focusing on changing the format of rating scales has led researchers to concentrate more on the rating *process*. In other words, many attempts to improve the accuracy of performance evaluations are now focusing on the rater's ability to observe, recall, and report subordinate behavior. In this newer tradition, raters do seem more accurate when they are asked to evaluate specific aspects of an employee's performance in comparison to providing an overall evaluation.[44] In addition, diary keeping also seems to improve their rating accuracy.[45]

Rater Training   Another approach to improving performance evaluation has been to train raters to become more effective users of the organization's performance evaluation system. Training programs differ both in terms of their focus and in their cost and duration. The two most popular types are training programs designed to eliminate common rating errors such as halo error and training programs designed to improve the supervisor's observation and recording skills.

Programs dealing with errors do seem to eliminate many of these from ratings. In addition, even short, relatively inexpensive programs are effective at accomplishing this goal. However, there is much less evidence that this kind of training actually increases the accuracy of appraisals. Programs focused on observation and recording skills may offer greater improvements in accuracy than those that simply focus on errors.[46]

In either case, training alone will probably not solve the performance appraisal dilemma. Unless raters are motivated to use the system effectively and unless they are given the opportunity for observing their subordinates' performance, errors such as those that were discussed are likely to continue.

Employee Problems with Performance Evaluation

For the evaluation system to work well, the employees must understand it and feel that it is a fair way to evaluate performance. In addition, they must believe that the system is used correctly when making decisions concerning pay increases and promotions. Thus, for a performance evaluation system to work well, it should be as simple as possible — unnecessary complexity in rating forms or other evaluation procedures can lead to employee dissatisfaction.[47] The system should also be implemented in a way that fully informs employees about how it is going to be used.[48]

One way to help foster an understanding about the system is to allow employees to participate in its development. It can also be helpful if they are trained in performance evaluation methods so they can better understand how difficult the process can be. Self-evaluations can be a useful addition to an evaluation system, especially for purposes of facilitating performance evaluation discussions with a supervisor.

With regard to fairness, performance evaluation is in some ways like grading systems in schools. If you have received grades that you thought were unfair and inequitable and that were incorrectly computed or based on the "wrong things" (for example, always agreeing with the instructor), you know what your reactions were! Students will say "I got an A" for a course in which they worked hard and were fairly rewarded. They will say *He* (or she) gave me a D" if they feel it was unfair. Their reactions sometimes are to give up or to get angry. Similar responses can come from employees as well. If performance evaluation raters are incompetent or unfair, the employees may resist, sabotage, or ignore them.

THE FEEDBACK INTERVIEW

It is generally agreed that an effective performance evaluation system will involve two-way communication. That is, there must be active communication between the supervisor and the subordinate about performance. Evaluation should not be viewed simply as a once-a-year completion of rating forms. To the contrary, it is an on-going process.

To help with this communication, the supervisor should hold an evaluation interview with each subordinate in order to discuss his or her appraisal and to set objectives for the upcoming appraisal period. In addition, experts advise that employee development and salary action discussions should not occur in the same interview. However, this advice is not followed very often.[49] Thus, although 97 percent of organizations with formal evaluation systems give employees feedback,[50] many are not doing it in the best way possible.

Norman Maier describes three generally used approaches to these interview situations: tell and sell, tell and listen, and problem solving.[51] These are shown in Exhibit 9–16. Research on when each should be used indicates that the tell-and-sell approach is best for new and inexperienced employees, and that the problem-solving approach, which encourages employee participation, is useful for more-experienced employees, especially those with strong work ethic attitudes.

Although each of these interview types do differ in terms of the supervisor's behavior, effective evaluation feedback sessions share a number of characteristics. Annual discussions of performance should include:[52]

. Review of overall progress.
. Discussions of problems that were encountered.
. Agreement about how performance can be improved.
. Discussions of how current performance fits with long-range career goals.
. Specific action plans for the coming year; how to reach short- and long-term objectives.

At Metropolitan Property and Casualty Insurance Company, these kinds of recommendations have led to an entirely new focus in appraisal. After the company became dissatisfied with its traditional approach, it implemented a new program, called the "Focus on Achievement" program.[53] Rather than emphasizing evalua-

EXHIBIT 9-16   Three Types of Evaluation Interviews

	Tell and Sell	Tell and Listen	Problem Solving
Role of interviewer	Judge	Judge	Helper
Objective	To communicate evaluation To persuade employee to improve	To communicate evaluation To release defensive feelings	To stimulate growth and development in employee
Assumptions	Employee desires to correct weaknesses if he or she knows them Any person can improve who so chooses A superior is qualified to evaluate a subordinate	People will change if defensive feelings are removed	Growth can occur without correcting faults Discussing job problems leads to improved performance
Reactions	Defensive behavior suppressed Attempts to cover hostility	Defensive behavior expressed Employee feels accepted	Problem-solving behavior
Skills	Salesmanship Patience	Listening and reflecting feelings Summarizing	Listening and reflecting feelings Reflecting ideas Using exploratory questions Summarizing
Attitude	People profit from criticism and appreciate help	One can respect the feelings of others if one understands them	Discussion develops new ideas and mutual interests
Motivation	Use of positive or negative incentives or both (Extrinsic in that motivation is added to the job itself)	Resistance to change reduced Positive incentive (Extrinsic and some intrinsic motivation)	Increased freedom Increased responsibility (Intrinsic motivation in that interest is inherent in the task)
Gains	Success most probable when employee respects interviewer	Develops favorable attitude to superior, which increases probability of success	Almost assured of improvement in some respect
Risks	Loss of loyalty Inhibition of independent judgment Face-saving problems created	Need for change may not be developed	Employee may lack ideas Change may be other than what superior had in mind
Values	Perpetuates existing practices and values	Permits interviewer to change his or her views in the light of employee's responses Some upward communication	Both learn, since experience and views are pooled Change is facilitated

Source: Reproduced from Norman R. F. Maier (1976), *The Appraisal Interview; Three Basic Approaches* (La Jolla, Calif.: University Associates). Used with permission.

tions of past performance, this new perspective attempts to focus attention on future improvements in performance. The program is based on several key assumptions, all of which stress that the employee is responsible for his or her performance and that the supervisor's role in appraisal is primarily one of helping subordinates to achieve their own personal goals. A similar program was developed at Weyerhaeuser.[54] Both programs begin with the basic assumption that employees want to perform well and that appraisals should not be used as a way of controlling behavior, but rather as an important link in the feedback chain. Two-way communication is also critical to these new kinds of programs.

Following these suggestions is not always easy. There are obviously times when the supervisor must be a judge and not just a counselor. With appropriate interviewing skills, however, many of the problems with communicating performance to subordinates can be overcome. These skills include an ability to speak clearly, listen carefully, gather and analyze information thoroughly, and negotiate the availability and use of resources. A poor feedback interview occurs because of poor preparation, error and miscalculation about the purpose of the sessions, and failure of the rater and the ratee to achieve some accuracy in understanding each other. A rater should always realize that a ratee's perception is reality to him or her.[55]

A well-planned and well-conducted feedback interview will facilitate the sharing of information and perceptions between rater and ratee.[56] This doesn't mean that a rater should not criticize poor performance, or that some ratees will not become defensive. In fact, some ratees react to criticism in the form of feedback by becoming angry or sullen. However, taking the steps and practicing the skills discussed in this section should diminish the probability of an angry, unproductive feedback interview session. It can also be very helpful to let negative information flow naturally from the appraisal interview conversation.[57] In other words, rather than emphasizing the negative, it is easier for subordinates to accept criticism if discussions of shortcomings are seen as part of the larger topic of discussion, namely, ways of improving future performance. By focusing on job-related problems, involving the ratee in setting realistic performance goals, and providing useful information in a nonthreatening manner, a rater can effectively use the interview. The feedback interview is designed to accomplish goals such as: (1) recognizing and encouraging superior performance so that it will continue; (2) sustaining acceptable behaviors; and (3) changing the behavior of ratees whose peformance is not meeting organizational standards of acceptance.

Suggestions for Effective Evaluation Interviews: Steps and Skills

1. Raters and ratees should prepare for the meeting and be ready to discuss the employees's past performance against the objectives for the period.
2. The rater should put the employee at ease and stress that the interview is not a disciplinary session, but a time to review past work in order to improve the employee's future performance, satisfaction, and personal development.
3. The rater should budget the time so that the employee has approximately half the time to discuss the evaluation and his or her future behavior.
4. The rater should use facts, not opinions. Evidence must be available to document the claims and counterclaims.
5. The rater should structure the interview as follows:
   First, open with *specific positive remarks*. For example, if the employee's quantity of work is good, the superior might say, "John, your work output is excellent. You processed 10 percent more claims than was budgeted."
   Second, sandwich performance shortcomings between two positive result discussions. Be specific, and orient the discussion to *performance* comments, *not personal criticisms*. Stress that the purpose

CAREER CHALLENGE
(concluded)

*H*ector Garcia was not very happy about having to take time out from his supervisory duties to attend a training session about the new evaluation system. But he'd had some problems with his boss, Bob Woods, over pay and promotions. So even though it sounded like more paperwork and time, he decided to see what the trainers had to say.

The session began with some short lectures. But most of the session involved practice on how to complete the rating forms for several kinds of employees. The supervisors were encouraged to review their employees' files and to jot down notes about employees' good and bad performances. They also practiced the evaluation interviews on each other. Given the ratings, they completed interviews on a very good, average, and a poor employee. Other policies were also covered. They learned about the new MBO system and how it was going to work. Still, Hector was a bit skeptical.

Hector thought he'd better start the evaluations, since Bob had asked him how they were going. Hector decided to do Ed first. He still was a little worried about how it would go. Ed had been trained in what

to expect. "Hope they haven't built him up too high," Hector thought. In reviewing the files, his notes, and his observations, Hector realized he had overlooked how well Ed had come along. He had done an excellent job, and so Hector rated him high.

Hector called Ed in for the interview. Hector referred to his notes and started and ended the interview on a positive note. He talked just a little about the shortcoming he'd noticed and offered to help Ed improve. At the beginning of the interview, Ed had been nervous. But he beamed at the end.

Hector finished the interview by saying he was recommending Ed for a good raise at the earliest chance. Over the next few days, Ed seemed to be especially happy. Maybe it was Hector's imagination, but he seemed to be working a bit harder, too, although he was already a good worker.

The training, formal system, and well-prepared feedback interview seemed to pay off. (As shown in this chapter, there are specific requirements and skills associated with a well-designed performance appraisal system.)

of bringing the specific issues up is to alleviate the problems in the *future*, not to criticize the past. Probably no more than one or two important negative points should be brought up at one evaluation. It is difficult for many people to work toward improving more than two points. The handling of negative comments is critical. They should be phrased specifically and be related to *performance*, and it should be apparent to the employee that their purpose is not to criticize but to improve future performance. Many people become very defensive when criticized. Of course, the interviews should be private, between the employee and the evaluator. Third, conclude with *positive* comments and overall evaluation results.

6. The rater should guard against overwhelming the ratee with information. Too much information can be confusing, while too little information can be frustrating. The rater must balance the amount of information that is provided.

7. The rater should encourage ratee involvement and self-review and evaluation. Ask the ratee to do his or her own evaluation on a periodic basis.

8. The final aspect of the interview should focus on *future* objectives and how the superior can help the employee achieve enterprise and personal goals. Properly done, the interviews contribute importantly to the purposes of performance evaluation.

MAKE DECISIONS AND FILE THE EVALUATION

Once the employees and their supervisor have discussed the evaluation, the superior reviews the evaluation. BNA found that 80 percent of office employees and 76 percent of production employees surveyed had their evaluations reviewed in this manner. Next, the HR department reviews the evaluation and places it on file.[58]

If the employee is unhappy with the evaluation, BNA found that 68 percent of the production employees and 56 percent of the office employees surveyed could appeal it through the union (if they are unionized) or to the rater's superior. This is less common in nonbusiness organizations than businesses.

Performance reviews are designed to prevent situations such as Ed Smart's confusion and Hector Garcia's failure to give him positive feedback. If the evaluation has been properly done, the employee knows where he or she stands and has received positive feedback on accomplishments and help on shortcomings. This is the developmental aspect of performance evaluation. The reward aspect can include pay raises (see Chapters 10 and 11).

SUMMARY

Formal performance evaluation of employees is the HRM process by which the organization determines how effectively the employee is performing the job. It takes place primarily for white-collar, professional/technical, and managerial employees. It rarely is done for part-time employees, and only about half of all blue-collar employees experience it. Although the data are not entirely clear, it appears that, if properly done, performance evaluations and feedback can be useful for most organizations and most employees.

To summarize the major points covered in this chapter:

1. Factors in the diagnostic model that have significance for performance evaluation are:
   a. The task performed.
   b. The government.
   c. The attitudes and preferences of the employee.
   d. The leader's or supervisor's style.
   e. The union (if the employees are unionized).
2. The purposes that a formal performance evaluation can serve include:
   a. Developmental.
   b. Reward.
   c. Human resource planning.
   d. Compensation.
   e. Validation.
3. For a formal performance evaluation to be effective, five steps must be taken:
   a. Establish performance standards for each position.
   b. Establish performance evaluation policies on when and how often to evaluate, who should evaluate, the criteria for evaluation, and the evaluation tools to be used.
   c. Have raters gather data on employee performance.
   d. Discuss the evaluation with the employee.
   e. Make decisions and file the evaluation.
4. Performance evaluation systems have problems because of:
   a. Systems design and operating difficulties.

   b. Problems with the rater:
      1. Problems with standards of evaluation.
      2. The halo effect.
      3. Leniency or harshness rating error.
      4. Central tendency error.
      5. Recency of events rating error.
      6. Contrast effect.
      7. Personal biases.
   c. Employee problems with performance evaluation:
      1. Employees don't understand the system or its purpose.
      2. Employees are not work oriented.
      3. Evaluation may be below the employee's expectations.
5. Performance appraisal interviews that involve feeding back evaluation information are dreaded because of the arbitrariness of many evaluation programs. Selecting the best program for the employees and supervisors to use is an important HRM decision.
6. Properly performed, performance evaluation can contribute to organizational objectives and employee development and satisfaction.

Exhibit 9–17 provides recommendations for the use of evaluation tools in terms of the ability of the model organizations to use them. You can see from this exhibit that some tools are more universally applicable (essay, critical incident, graphic rating scale, MBO, ranking, forced distribution). Others have fewer applications (field review, forced choice), and still others are in the middle (assessment centers, BARS, BOS, weighted checklist).

KEY TERMS

QUESTIONS FOR REVIEW AND DISCUSSION

1. What advantages would a combination performance evaluation system (that is, the use of more than one technique) provide to managers responsible for evaluating subordinates?
2. Why would training in conducting performance evaluations be an important issue for organizations to consider?
3. Describe the major problems that can arise for the system, the rater, and the ratee in performance evaluation.
4. How often should formal performance evaluations take place? Informal ones? How often do they take place?
5. Who usually evaluates employees in organizations? Who should do so? Under what circumstances? What criteria should be used to evaluate employees? Which ones are used?

EXHIBIT 9-17   Recommendations on Evaluation Techniques for Model Organizations

Type of Organization	Graphic Rating Scale	Forced Choice	MBO	Essay	Critical Incident	Weighted Checklist	BARS	BOS	Ranking	Paired Comparison	Forced Distribution	Field Review
1. Large size, low complexity, high stability	X	X	X	X	X	X	X	X	X	X	X	X
2. Medium size, low complexity, high stability	X		X	X	X	X	X	X	X	X	X	
3. Small size, low complexity, high stability	X		X	X	X				X	X	X	
4. Medium size, moderate complexity, moderate stability	X		X	X	X	X			X	X	X	
5. Large size, high complexity, low complexity	X		X	X	X				X	X	X	X
6. Medium size, high complexity, low stability	X		X	X	X				X	X	X	
7. Small size, high complexity, low stability	X		X	X	X				X	X	X	

6. Compare graphic rating scales to BARS and BOS. What are the advantages of BARS and BOS over graphic rating scales? What are the limitations of each?

7. What are the characteristics of an effective appraisal interview? How should new and experienced employees be treated differently during the interview?

8. What should an organization do in order to help make sure that its performance evaluation system is legal? What is the role of job analysis in this process?

9. What is MBO? What advantages does it have over traditional performance evaluation methods? What are its weaknesses?

NOTES

[1] Jeanette N. Cleveland, Kevin R. Murphy, and Richard E. Williams (February 1989), "Multiple Uses of Performance Appraisal: Prevalence and Correlates," *Journal of Applied Psychology*, pp. 130–135.

[2] Gerald V. Barrett and Mary C. Kernan (Autumn 1987), "Performance Appraisal and Terminations: A Review of Court Decisions Since *Brito V. Zia* with Implications for Personnel Practices," *Personnel Psychology*, pp. 489–504.

[3] *Brito V. Zia Co.*, 478 F. 2d 1200 (10th. Cir., 1973).

[4] Christopher S. Miller, Joan A. Kaspin, and Michael H. Schuster (Autumn 1990), "The Impact of Performance Appraisal Methods on Age Discrimination in Employment Act Cases," *Personnel Psychology*, pp. 555–78.

[5] Ibid.

[6] Wayne F. Cascio (1991), *Applied Psychology in Personnel Management*, 4th ed. (Englewood Cliffs, N. J.: Prentice-Hall), pp. 64–65.

[7] Bureau of National Affairs (February 1975), "Employee Performance: Evaluation and Control," *Personnel Policies Forum*, Survey 108 (Washington, D.C.).

[8] Ibid.

[9] Daniel R. Ilgen and Jack M. Feldman (1983), "Performance Appraisal: A Process Focus," in *Research in Organizational Behavior*, eds. Barry M. Staw, and Larry L. Cummings (Greenwich, Conn.: JAI Press).

[10] Shanthi Srinivas and Stephen J. Motowidlo (May 1987), "Effects of Raters' Stress on the Dispersion and Favorability of Performance Ratings," *Journal of Applied Psychology*, pp. 247–51.

[11] George S. Odiorne (July–August 1990), "The Trend Toward the Quarterly Performance Review," *Business Horizons*, pp. 38–41.

[12] Robert M. Glen (Spring 1990), "Performance Appraisal: An Unnerving Yet Useful Process," *Public Personnel Management*, pp. 1–9.

[13] Glenn M. McEvoy (Summer 1990), "Public Sector Managers' Reactions to Appraisals by Subordinates," *Public Personnel Management*, pp. 201–12.

[14] Jiing-Lih Farh and Gregory H. Dobbins (August 1989), "Effects of Comparative Performance Information on the Accuracy of Self-Ratings and Agreement between Self- and Supervisor Ratings," *Journal of Applied Psychology*, pp. 606–10.

[15] McEvoy, "Public Sector Managers' Reactions," pp. 201–12.

[16] William J. Birch (June 1981), "Performance Appraisal: One Company's Experience," *Personnel Journal*, pp. 456–60.

[17] Toni A. Perry (November 1990), "Staying with the Basics," *HRMagazine*, pp. 73–76.

[18] Gerard Panaro (1990), *Employment Law Manual* (Boston: Warren, Gorham & Lamont), p. 2.06[1].

[19] Fritz Blanz, and Edwin Ghiselli (Summer 1972), "The Mixed Standard Scale: A New Rating System," *Personnel Psychology*, pp. 185–99.

[20] Angelo S. DeNisi, Tina Robbins, and Thomas P. Cafferty (February 1989), "Organization of Information Used for Performance Appraisals: Role of Diary Keeping," *Journal of Applied Psychology*, pp. 124–29.

[21] Patricia C. Smith and L. M. Kendall (April 1963), "Retranslation of Expectations: An Approach to the Construction of Unambiguous Anchors for Rating Scales," *Journal of Applied Psychology*, pp. 194–55.

[22] H. John Bernardin, and Richard W. Beatty (1984), *Performance Appraisal: Assessing Human Behavior at Work* (Boston: Kent Publishing).

[23] John M. Ivancevich (April 1980), "A Longitudinal Study of Behavioral Expectation Scales: Attitudes and Performance," *Journal of Applied Psychology*, pp. 139–46.

[24] Theodore J. Krein (May 1990), "Performance Reviews that Rate an 'A'," *Personnel*, pp. 38–40.

[25] Gary P. Latham, Charles H. Fay, and Lise M. Saari (Summer 1979), "The Development of Behavioral Observation Scales for Appraising the Performance of Foremen," *Personnel Psychology*, pp. 290–311.

[26] See the series of debates on the limitations of the BOS in H. John Bernardin, and Jeffrey S. Kane (Winter 1980), "A Second Look at Behavioral Observation Scales," *Personnel Psychology*, pp. 809–14; Gary P. Latham, Lise M. Saari, and Charles Fay (Winter 1980), "BOS, BES, and Baloney: Raising Kane with Bernardin," *Personnel Psychology*, pp. 815–21; and Kevin R. Murphy, C. Martin, and M. Garcia (October 1982), "Do Behavioral Observation Scales Measure Observation?" *Journal of Applied Psychology*, pp. 562–67.

[27] Douglas M. McGregor (1960), *The Human Side of Enterprise* (New York: McGraw-Hill); Peter F. Drucker (1954), *The Practice of Management* (New York: Harper & Row); and George S. Odiorne (1965), *Management by Objectives* (New York: Pitman Publishing).

[28] Steve Kaufman (January–February 1988), "Going for the Goods," *Success*, pp. 38–41; and Gary P. Latham, and Edwin A. Locke (Autumn 1979), "Goal Setting: A Motivational Technique that Works," *Organizational Dynamics*, pp. 68–80.

[29] Robert J. Sahl (October 1990), "Designing Effective Performance Appraisals," *Personnel Journal*, pp. 53–60.

[30] Jeffrey S. Kane and Kimberly A. Freeman (December 1986), "MBO Performance Appraisal: A Mixture That's Not a Solution," *Personnel*, pp. 26–36.

[31] Jan P. Muczyk and Bernard C. Reimann (May 1989), "MBO as a Complement to Effective Leadership," *Academy of Management Executive*, pp. 131–38.

[32] J. N. Kondrasuk (1981), "Studies in MBO Effectiveness," *Academy of Management Review*, pp. 419–30.

[33] Bureau of National Affairs, "Employee Performance."

[34] Douglas McGregor (May 1957), "An Uneasy Look at Performance Appraisal," *Harvard Business Review*.

[35] Kevin R. Murphy, and Douglas H. Reynolds (May 1988), "Does True Halo Affect Observed Halo?" *Journal of Applied Psychology*, pp. 235–38.

[36] Elaine Pulakos, Neal Schmitt, and C. Ostroff (February 1986), "A Warning about the Use of a Standard Deviation across Dimensions within Ratees to Measure Halo," *Journal of Applied Psychology*, pp. 29–32.

[37] Cascio, *Applied Psychology*, p. 83.

[38] Todd J. Maurer, and Ralph A. Alexander (February 1991), "Contrast Effects in Behavioral Measurement: An Investigation of Alternative Process Explanations," *Journal of Applied Psychology*, pp. 3–10.

[39] James W. Smither, Richard R. Reilly, and Richard Buda (August 1988), "Effect of Prior Performance Information on Ratings of Present Performance: Contrast versus Assimilation Revisited," *Journal of Applied Psychology*, pp. 487–96.

[40] Daniel J.B. Mitchell (1989), *Human Resource Management: An Economic Approach* (Boston: Kent Publishing), p. 78.

[41] Lawrence H. Peters, Edward J. O'Connor, Jeff Weekley, Abdullah Pooyan, Blake Frank, Bruce Erenkrantz (May 1984), "Sex Bias and Managerial Evaluations: Replication and Extension," *Journal of Applied Psychology*, pp. 349–52.

[42] Elaine D. Pulakos, Leonard A. White, Scott H.Oppler, and Walter C. Borman (October 1989), "Examination of Race and Sex Effects on Performance Ratings," *Journal of Applied Psychology*, pp. 770–80.

[43] Donald P. Schwab, Herbert G. Heneman III, and Thomas A. DeCotiis (Winter 1975), "Behaviorally Anchored Rating Scales: A Review of the Literature," *Personnel Psychology*, pp. 549–62.

[44] Robert A. Jako, and Kevin R. Murphy (October 1990), "Distributional Ratings, Judgment Decomposition, and Their Impact on Interrater Agreement and Rating Accuracy," *Journal of Applied Psychology*, pp. 500–05.

[45] DeNisi, Robbins, and Cafferty, "Organization of Information Used for Performance Appraisals," pp. 124–290.

[46] Jerry W. Hedge, and Michael J. Kavanagh (February 1988), "Improving the Accuracy of Performance Evaluations: Comparison of Three Methods of Performance Appraiser Training," *Journal of Applied Psychology*, pp. 68–73.

[47] William F. Giles, and Kevin W. Mossholder (August 1990), "Employee Reactions to Contextual and Session Components of Performance Appraisal," *Journal of Applied Psychology*, pp. 371–77.

[48] Sahl, "Designing Effective Performance Appraisals," pp. 53–60.

[49] Herbert H. Meyer (February 1991), "A Solution to the Performance Appraisal Feedback Enigma," *Academy of Management Executive*, pp. 68–76.

[50] Bureau of National Affairs, "Employee Performance."

[51] Norman Maier (1976), *The Appraisal Interview: Three Basic Approaches* (La Jolla, Calif: University Associates).

[52] Meyer, "A Solution to the Performance Appraisal Feedback Enigma," pp. 68–76.

[53] Joseph P. McCarthy (February 1991), "A New Focus on Achievement," *Personnel Journal*, pp. 74–76.

[54] Leslie F. Sorensen (July 1990), "Appraisal at Weyerhaeuser: Improving Staff Performance," *Management Accounting*, pp. 42–47.

[55] Richard Henderson (1984), *Performance Appraisal* (Reston, Va.: Reston Publishing), p. 267.

[56] Meyer, "A Solution to the Performance Appraisal Feedback Enigma," pp. 68–76.

[57] Krein, "Performance Interviews that Rate an 'A'," pp. 38–40.

[58] Bureau of National Affairs, "Employee Performance."

EXERCISE 9–1
. . . . .

The Selection and Appraisal of Administrative Assistants at Row Engineering

Objective The exercise is designed to have the student use knowledge about selection and performance appraisal to design an appraisal system.

Introduction

Row Engineering (name disguised) is a major engineering contractor, supplying aerospace firms, NASA, and the military with sophisticated equipment designs. Because of their rapidly expanding business, Row executives decided that a formal management information system (MIS) was needed. The MIS could be used to monitor progress on projects, limit employee access to classified information, reduce unnecessary duplication across similar projects, and generally increase efficiency by ensuring that the proper managers or engineers received timely and relevant information for decision making.

Row has four major design facilities scattered throughout the southern and eastern United States in areas where approximately 50 percent of all high school graduates are black. Engineers at the different facilities typically work on different projects. Thus, Row executives decided that one MIS department should be established for *each* of the four facilities. While these would be linked by computer, each MIS department would have a great deal of autonomy.

Each MIS department will be comprised of one administrator, seven administrative assistants, numerous technical personnel (for example, computer programmers) and clerical staff (for example, data entry personnel). The 28 administrative assistant positions will be key entry-level managerial positions. The administrative assistants will be responsible for securing and maintaining information for their assigned MIS area. Also, some may eventually be promoted to middle-level management positions in the future. Typical administrative assistant duties will include:

A. Determining appropriate information needs from various projects for the MIS database. To do so requires cooperation with project engineers and managers as well as personnel from other departments.

B. Working with other MIS administrative assistants to develop standardized information reporting procedures. Such procedures facilitate the aggregation and comparison of specific types of information from different projects.

C. Creating and distributing user-instruction manuals outlining correct information reporting and information acquisition procedures for various departments. Sometimes administrative assistants would provide orientation sessions for company personnel.

D. Ensuring that necessary and timely information is supplied by each project or department using standardized reporting procedures.

E. Supervising technical and clerical staff who are responsible for data input and retrieval.

F. Supervising technical staff who develop and purchase information-based software.

G. Maintaining project security. Illustrative duties include: documenting computer analyses, ensuring that only authorized personnel receive relevant information, supervising clerical staff, and preventing unauthorized photocopying of specific types of information.

H. Supplying information, as requested, to project managers, specific departments, and contract monitors.

I. Documenting and supplying information to the fiscal services department regarding monthly time and computer-use expenditures for various projects.

Fiscal services uses this information when comparing actual and estimated (budgeted) expenditures for various projects and departments.

J. Determining the MIS department's own budget needs.

About one year ago, the HR department conducted a formal job analysis of all existing administrative assistant positions throughout the corporation. From this analysis, a common job description was derived. This job description is reproduced below.

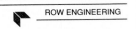 ROW ENGINEERING   **HOURLY JOB DESCRIPTION**

Job Title: Administrative Assistant   4-11-1193

I.   Function

        To provide adminstrative support to a company organization.

II.   Controls:

        Works under the direct supervision of a higher level administrator or technical manager but must exercise considerable judgment in the performance of assignments.

III.   Major Duties:

        A.   Utilizes a thorough knowledge of functions, activities, personnel, and organizations to perform various administrative duties incidental to the efficient operation of a company element.

        B.   Prepares charts and reports to reflect performance and overall efficiency of operations. Prepares, analyzes and evaluates data pertaining to cost and maintains systems for effective cost control.

        C.   Confers with operating managers to determine requirements for space, equipment, supplies, and other facilities. Provides co-ordination with Purchasing, Plant Services, and other company service organizations in meeting these requirements.

        D.   Conducts introductory non-technical interviews with job applicants, briefing them on general functions of the company element and obtaining pertinent information for use in subsequent technical interviews. Keeps management informed of interviews, schedules, job offers extended, rejections, acceptances, and anticipated starting dates.

        E.   Coordinates the introduction and indoctrination of new employees to the company element. Compiles materials for use in indoctrination lectures, welcomes new employees and arranges for tours of facilities. Ensures that all required paperwork is completed.

IV.   Requirements:

        Requires a high school education, with college level courses highly desirable, and approximately five (5) years administrative experience or a B.S. degree in Business Administration.

ROW FORM NO. 06206 ORIG.

Designing the Performance Appraisal System

Currently, all Row Engineering employees, including administrative assistants, are evaluated using a one-item, 10-point global rating scale. Ratings of either Unsatisfactory (1) or Superior (10) must be accompanied with written documentation. In addition to the rating supervisor, the department head and the evaluated employee must sign the form, indicating that they have read the evaluation.

ROW ENGINEERING		ROW ENGINEERING	
EMPLOYEE NAME	EMPLOYEE NO.	COST CENTER	DATE
RATING-SUPERVISOR-APPROVAL	DEPARTMENT HEAD-APPROVAL	EMPLOYEE	

CIRCLE APPROPRIATE RATING

UNSATISFACTORY 2   3   4   5   6   7   8   9   SUPERIOR

(WRITTEN DOCUMENTATION REQUIRED FOR RATINGS OF SUPERIOR OR UNSATISFACTORY AND FOR CLASSIFICATION CHANGES)

Recently, the HR manager has become concerned about the use of this type of rating scale. He has hired your human resource consulting firm to design a better performance appraisal system for the administrative assistant position with all the MIS departments.

Assignment: Write a three- to six-page report to this company describing and explaining your appraisal system. Your report should incorporate the following points:

A. A tactful explanation of the limitations of the present performance appraisal system.

B. An identification of the relevant dimensions (criteria) that should be measured in the new performance appraisal system. That is, how will the company distinguish the superior administrative assistants from those whose performance is merely adequate (or even inadequate)? Assume that the provided job description is correct.

C. How will *each* dimension be measured?

D. If you use some type of overall measure of performance, tell how you will measure it on a 100-point scale (100 = best). If you have several performance measures, tell how they will be combined into a composite criterion score. This composite score should be measured on a 100-point scale.

E. What weaknesses (if any) exist in your system? How will these be overcome?

A Learning Note

This exercise encourages the student to consider the uses, strengths, and weaknesses of a performance appraisal system.

This exercise was developed by Dr. William H. Ross, Jr., University of Wisconsin, La Crosse.

APPLICATION CASE 9-1   Performance Evaluation of Store Managers at
· · · · ·   Firestone Tire & Rubber

The Firestone Tire & Rubber Co. is the second largest tire company in the United States with about 18 percent of the market. Firestone manufactures and sells tires and related products for cars, trucks, buses, tractors, and airplanes. The tires are sold to automakers and consumers through 2,100 Firestone stores and many independent dealers, including Montgomery Ward. The stores are the vital link with the consumer.

A vital person in the link with consumers is the store manager. It is the store managers who are the key human resource in determining whether sales and profits will be sufficient. The following list is a description of the store managers' duties and a portion of the performance evaluation form used to appraise store managers. Each store manager is evaluated annually by his or her immediate supervisor.

EXHIBIT I   Setting Standards and Recording Results

Major Job Duties (Taken From Job Description)	Standard of Performance (Measure Or Criterion Of Success)	Employee's Performance (Percentage Of Time Standard is Met)			
		Less than 50%	50% to 75%	76% to 89%	90% or More
1.					
2.					
3.					
4.					
5.					
6.					

Instructions: This worksheet is to be used during the year for the purpose of providing supporting information for the annual employee assessment. First list the six most important job duties of the employee in decreasing order of importance. Establish standards for each major job duty. Record the employee's performance against the standard established (1, 2, 3, or 4). Refer to the employee's work results in the performance feedback or post-assessment interview.

EXHIBIT II   Work Review Comments

Instructions: Review the employee's performance against the standards established. Analyze the employee's performance in terms of quality (how good), quantity (how much), and work methods (how the employee went about getting work results). What job duties are being handled particularly well by the employee? What job standards are not being met? Complete this section before conducting the interview with the employee.

PERFORMANCE STRENGTHS ABOVE JOB STANDARDS: _____

_____

_____

_____

PERFORMANCE AREAS BELOW JOB STANDARDS: _____

_____

_____

_____

III. INTERVIEW RESULTS AND DEVELOPMENT PLAN

Instructions: The work counseling interview is an important part of any work results program. Section III should be completed after holding the interview. Comment on the employee's reaction to performance feedback and the plan you and the employee have developed for improving work results. Be specific in your description of the results of the interview and the developmental steps you and the employee have agreed upon.

EMPLOYEE REACTION TO PERFORMANCE FEEDBACK: _____

_____

_____

PLAN FOR IMPROVING WORK RESULTS: _____

_____

_____

_____

_____

_____

Employee's Signature

RATER TO PROCEED TO SECTION IV

Description of Store Manager Responsibilities

Summary of Duties   Has responsibility for securing maximum sales volume and maximum net profits. Supervises all phases of store operation — selling, merchandise display, service, pricing, inventories, credits and collections, operation, and maintenance. Responsible for the control of all store assets and prevention of merchandise shortages.

Interviews, selects, trains, and supervises all employees, following their progress and development. Conducts employee meetings and follows closely for satisfactory productivity.

Sets sales quotas for employees and follows for accomplishment. Works with salespeople and personally calls on commercial and dealer accounts.

Interprets and explains store operating policies and procedures to subordinates and follows for adherence. Investigates complaints and makes adjustments. Maintains store cleanliness.

A. *Human resource administration* – 30 percent
  1. Directly supervises pivotal employees and, through them, the other employees, directing activities, scheduling duties and hours of work, following for productivity and sales results. Instructs or directs the instruction of new and present employees in work procedure, results expected, sales quota program, product and price information, and so on, and follows for adherence to instructions. (Daily)
  2. Interviews applicants, obtains formal applications, determines qualifications (using employment questionnaires), and makes selection of best persons for open jobs or files applications for future consideration. (Weekly)
  3. Determines number of employees needed for profitable store operations, considering individual sales productivity, salary expense, anticipated human resource requirements, and so on. (Monthly)
  4. Prepares, plans for, and conducts employee meetings, instructing concerning new products and policies, developing sales enthusiasm, explaining incentive programs, holding sales demonstrations, and so on. (Semimonthly)
  5. Trains and directs the training of new employees, following established training programs for effective utilization, conducting on-the-job training, and supervising training activities for own employees and those being trained for other assignments. (Weekly)
B. *Selling and sales promotion* – 30 percent
  1. Breaks down store's sales into individual daily amounts for each employee, follows progress of employees in meeting quotas, determines and takes action necessary to help them reach the objective. (Daily)

  2. Works with salesperson in setting up sales objectives and reviewing accomplishments, using call and sales record sheets, and following to secure maximum sales effort and effective use of time. Makes calls with salespeople to determine effectiveness of contacts, reasons for lack of progress, and so on, giving help in closing sales, and securing additional business. (Daily)
  3. Contacts personally and by telephone, inactive accounts and prospective customers, promoting and soliciting sale of merchandise and services, and following to close the sales. Reviews prospect cards, assigns them to employees, and follows to secure sales from each. (Daily)
  4. Contacts selected commercial and dealer accounts for special sales promotion and solicitation, determining sales possibilities and requirements, selling merchandise and services and so on. (Daily)
  5. Prepares advertising copy, following merchandising program suggestions, and arranges for insertion of advertisements in local newspaper. Makes certain employees are alerted and store has merchandise to back up advertising. (Weekly)
  6. Maintains a firm retail, commercial, and wholesale pricing program according to established policies.
C. *Inventory sales and expense control* – 15 percent
  1. Reviews stock turnover records for overstock conditions, determines steps necessary to correct, and takes the appropriate action. Establishes stock levels and orders accordingly based on sales results as recorded in the stock ledgers for new tires and retreads. (Also major appliances)
  2. Prepares sales and expense budget covering projected sales and expenses for the period. (Monthly)
  3. Reviews expense control sheet, comparing actual expenses with budget figures, determines and takes action necessary to keep within the approved budget. (Daily)
  4. Is responsible for the completeness and accuracy of all inventories, accounting inventories, markup, markdown inventories, and so on.

D. *Checking* — 10 percent

1. Checks stock, automotive equipment, service floor, and so on, continually observing store activities, and determining that equipment is maintained in good operating condition. Makes inspection trips through all parts of the store, checking observance of safety and fire precautions, protection of company assets, and so on. Checks credit information secured for commercial and dealer accounts, and works with office and credit manager in setting up credit limits. (Weekly)

2. Is responsible for and investigates all cash shortages, open tickets, and missing tickets.

3. Investigates customer complaints, making adjustments or taking appropriate action for customer satisfaction. (Daily)

E. *Miscellaneous functions* — 15 percent

1. Reads and signs Store Operating Policy and Office Procedure Letters, analyzes and puts into operation new policies and procedures as received. (Weekly)

2. Prepares letter to district manager covering progress of the store, store plans, results se-

cured, market and special conditions, and so on. (Monthly)

3. Inspects tires and other merchandise in for adjustment, determines appropriate settlement, prepares claim forms, and issues credit, replaces, and so on. (Makes all policy adjustments.) (Daily)

4. Attends district sales and civic organization meetings, and takes part in civic affairs, community drives, and so on. (Weekly)

Discussion Questions

1. Do you consider the description of the Firestone store manager's responsibilities as important information that the raters of managers need to be knowledgeable about?

2. Does the portion of the performance evaluation form used at Firestone require any subjective judgments or considerations on the part of the rater?

3. Suppose that a Firestone manager received an outstanding performance evaluation. Does this mean that he or she is promotable? Why?

APPLICATION CASE 9–2   The Politics of Performance Appraisal

· · · · ·

Every Friday, Max Steadman, Jim Cobun, Lynne Sims, and Tom Hamilton meet at Charley's Food Place after work for refreshments. The four friends work as managers at Eckel Industries, a manufacturer of arc welding equipment in Minneapolis. The one-plant company employs about 2,000 people. The four managers work in the manufacturing division. Max, 35, manages the company's 25 quality control inspectors. Lynne, 33, works as a supervisor in inventory management. Jim, 34, is a first-line supervisor in the metal coating department. Tom, 28, supervises a team of assemblers. The four managers' tenures at Eckel Industries range from one year (Tom) to 12 years (Max).

The group is close-knit: Lynne, Jim, and Max's friendship stems from their years as undergraduate business students at the University of Minnesota. Tom, the newcomer, joined the group after meeting the three at an Eckel management seminar last year. Weekly get-togethers at Charley's have become a comfortable habit for the group and provide an opportunity to relax, exchange the latest gossip heard around the plant, and give and receive advice about problems encountered on the job.

This week's topic of discussion: performance appraisal, specifically the company's annual review process, which the plant's management conducted in the last week. Each of the four managers completed evaluation forms (graphic rating scale format) on each of his or her subordinates and met with each subordinate to discuss the appraisal.

Tom This was the first time I've appraised my people, and I dreaded it. For me, it's been the worst week of the year. Evaluating is difficult; it's highly subjective and inexact. Your emotions creep into the process. I got angry at one of my assembly workers last week, and I still felt the anger when I was filling out the evaluation forms. Don't tell me that my frustration with the guy didn't overly bias my appraisal. I think it did. And I think the technique is flawed. Tell me — what's the difference between a five and a six on "cooperation"?

Jim The scales are a problem. So is memory. Remember our course in human resource management in college? Philips said that, according to research, when we sit down to evaluate someone's performance in the past year, we will only be able to actively recall and use 15 percent of the performance we observed.

Lynne I think political considerations are always a part of the process. I know I consider many other factors besides a person's actual performance when I appraise him.

Tom Like what?

Lynne Like the appraisal will become part of the permanent written record that affects his career. Like the person I evaluate today, I have to work with tomorrow. Given that, the difference between a five and a six on cooperation isn't that relevant, because frankly, if a five makes him mad, and he's happy with a six.

Max Then you give him the six. Accuracy is important, but I'll admit it — accuracy isn't my primary objective when I evaluate my workers. My objective is to motivate and reward them so they'll perform better. I use the review process to do what's best for my people and my department. If that means fine-tuning the evaluations to do that, I will.

Tom What's an example of fine-tuning?

Max Jim, do you remember three years ago when the company lowered the ceiling on merit raises? The top merit increase that any employee could get was 4 percent. I boosted the ratings of my folks to get the best merit increases for them. The year before that, the ceiling was 8 percent. The best they could get was less than what most of them received the year before. I felt they deserved the 4 percent, so I gave the marks that got them what I felt they deserved.

Lynne: I've inflated ratings to encourage someone who is having personal problems but is normally a good employee. A couple of years ago, one of my better people was going through a painful di-

Written by Kim Stewart. Several of the perspectives presented here were drawn from an insightful study reported to Clinton O. Longenecker, Henry P. Sims, Jr., and Dennis A. Gioia (August 1987), "Behind the Mask: The Politics of Employee Appraisal," *The Academy of Management Executive*, pp. 183–91.

vorce, and it was showing in her work. I don't think it's fair to kick someone when they're down, even if their work is poor. I felt a good rating would speed her recovery.

Tom Or make her complacent.

Lynne No, I don't think so. I felt she realized her work was suffering. I wanted to give her encouragement; it was my way of telling her she had some support and that she wasn't in danger of losing her job.

Jim There's another situation where I think fine-tuning is merited — when someone's work has been mediocre or even poor for most of the year, but it improves substantially in the last two, three months or so. If I think the guy is really trying and is doing much better, I'd give him a rating that's higher than his work over the whole year deserves. It encourages him to keep improving. If I give him a mediocre rating, what does that tell him?

Tom What if he's really working hard, but not doing so great?

Jim If I think he has what it takes, I'd boost the rating to motivate him to keep trying until he gets there.

Max I know of one or two managers who've inflated ratings to get rid of a pain-in-the-neck, some young guy who's transferred in and thinks he'll be there a short time. He's not good, but thinks he is, and creates all sorts of problems. Or his performance is okay, but he just doesn't fit in with the rest of the department. A year or two of good ratings is a sure trick for getting rid of him.

Tom Yes, but you're passing the problem on to someone else.

Max True, but it's no longer my problem.

Tom All the examples you've talked about involve inflating evaluations. What about deflating them, giving someone less than you really think he deserves? Is that justified?

Lynne I'd hesitate to do that because it can create problems. It can backfire.

Max But it does happen. You can lower a guy's ratings to shock him, to jolt him into performing better. Sometimes, you can work with someone, coach them, try to help them improve, and it just doesn't work. A basement-level rating can tell him you mean business. You can say that isn't fair, and for the time being, it isn't. But what if you feel that if the guy doesn't shape up, he faces being fired in a year or two, and putting him in the cellar, ratings-wise, will solve his problem? It's fair in the long run if the effect is that he improves his work and keeps his job.

Jim Sometimes, you get someone who's a real rebel, who always questions you, sometimes even oversteps his bounds. I think deflating his evaluation is merited just to remind him who's the boss.

Lynne I'd consider lowering someone's true rating if they've had a long record of rather questionable performance, and I think the best alternative for the person is to consider another job with another company. A low appraisal sends him a message to consider quitting and start looking for another job.

Max What if you believe the situation is hopeless, and you've made up your mind that you're going to fire the guy as soon as you've found a suitable replacement. The courts have chipped away at management's right to fire. Today, when you fire someone, you must have a strong case. I think once a manager decides to fire, appraisals become very negative. Anything good that you say about the subordinate can be used later against you. Deflating the ratings protects yourself from being sued and sometimes speeds up the termination process.

Tom I understand your points, but I still believe that accuracy is the top priority in performance appraisal. Let me play devil's advocate for a minute. First, Jim, you complained about our memory limitations introducing a bias into appraisal. Doesn't introducing politics into the process further distort the truth by introducing yet another bias? Even more important, most would agree that one key to motivating people is providing true feedback — the facts about how they're doing so they know where they stand. Then you talk with them about how to improve their performance. When you distort an evaluation — however slightly — are you providing this kind of feedback?

Max I think you're overstating the degree of fine-tuning.

Tom Distortion, you mean.

Max No, fine-tuning. I'm not talking about giving a guy a seven when he deserves a two or vice versa. It's not that extreme. I'm talking about making slight changes in the ratings when you think that the change can make a big difference in terms of achieving what you think is best for the person and for your department.

Tom But when you fine-tune, you're manipulating your people. Why not give them the most accurate evaluation, and let the chips fall where they may? Give them the facts, and let them decide.

Max Because most of good managing is psychology, understanding people, their strengths and shortcomings. Knowing how to motivate, reward, and act to do what's in their and your department's best interest. And sometimes total accuracy is not the best path.

Jim All this discussion raises a question. What's the difference between fine-tuning and significant distortion? Where do you draw the line?

Lynne That's about as easy a question as what's the difference between a five and six. On the form, I mean.

Discussion Questions

1. In your opinion, and from an HRM perspective, what are the objectives of employee performance evaluation?

2. Based on these objectives, evaluate the perspectives about performance appraisal presented by the managers.

3. Assume you are the vice president of HRM at Eckel Industries and that you are aware that fine-tuning evaluations is a prevalent practice among Eckel managers. If you disagree with this perspective, what steps would you take to reduce the practice?

COMPENSATION OBJECTIVES

· · · · · · ·

LEARNING OBJECTIVES

After studying this chapter, you should be able to:

· · ·

Define compensation

· · ·

Understand how compensation systems help reach the goals of organizational effectiveness and employee satisfaction

· · ·

Explain how external and internal factors influence pay levels and pay structures

· · ·

Discuss how pay surveys help managers create efficient and equitable pay systems

· · ·

Understand the job evaluation process

CAREER CHALLENGE

Cardeson National Bank is a small firm that was founded in suburban Pittsburgh 14 years ago. For the first year and a half, it operated out of a prefabricated building on a small lot across from a shopping center. Then it built a nice building on the site. Later it added two branch offices in adjoining suburbs. CNB now employs about 150 persons.

The founder of the bank and still president is Joseph Paderewski, an entrepreneur who made his first career in construction and building. Joe is 55 years old. He has spent most of his energies building the bank by raising money from the original stockholders, developing a marketing plan to get enough depositors to use CNB, and finding good locations at which to build banks.

Joe does almost all the hiring. He also establishes the pay rates for each employee, based on experience, potential, and how much the employee needs to help support self and family. Recently, Guido Panelli, his executive vice president, started bringing Joe some problems he didn't have time for. Guido has mentioned something about salaries, but Joe hasn't given it much thought.

Joe has always had an open-door policy. Yesterday, a teller, Arte Jamison, came in to see him.

Arte Jamison Joe, you hired me five years ago. I came in to tell you that I'm quitting. I had to tell Mr. Panelli about this problem a couple of times and nothing happened. So I'm gone. I'm going to work for Pittsburgh National Bank for more money.

Joe Arte, don't quit for money. What do you need? I'll take care of it.

Arte That's not the point. You keep hiring in people with less experience than me at more pay. There's no future here with a situation like that. I quit.

Joe Sure sorry to see you go, Arte.

Poppa Joe sat in his office. He'd always liked Arte. What was happening? He called in Guido.

Joe Guido, what's happening around here? Arte Jamison just quit. He's a good man.

Guido Boss, I've tried to bring the subject up lots of times, and you're always too busy. We've got a poor pay system around here.

Joe What do you mean? I've always been fair.

Guido: You think you've been fair. But you're too busy to do all you've been doing. You hire some people at one pay level and others doing the same job at another. Some get behind and never get a raise. It's a mess.

I've asked one of our vice presidents, Mary Renfro, to take a course at the University of Pittsburgh's night MBA program on HRM, and look especially at compensation. She's done it. Now: Should I ask her to study the problem and talk to us about it?

Joe: O.K., let her do a study. But I'm not convinced we've got such a big problem because a few people quit.

Guido: Please boss, let's keep an open mind about this. Pay has an awfully important impact on employees.

INTRODUCTION

Compensation is the HRM function that deals with every type of reward that individuals receive in return for performing organizational tasks. It is basically an exchange relationship. Employees exchange their labor for financial and nonfinancial rewards. Financial compensation is both direct and indirect. Direct financial compensation consists of the pay an employee receives in the form of wages, salary, bonuses, and commissions. Direct financial compensation will be covered in this chapter and in Chapter 11. Indirect financial compensation is called *benefits* and consists of *all* financial rewards that are not included in direct financial compensation. Typical benefits include vacation, various kinds of insurance, and so on. Indirect financial compensation will be addressed in Chapter 12.

Nonfinancial rewards like praise, self-esteem, and recognition although not discussed in this text are also factors that affect employee satisfaction with the compensation system. Levels of employees' productivity can be related to nonfinancial rewards as well. A more comprehensive study of compensation would include a special section on nonfinancial rewards.

From the employee's point of view, pay is a necessity in life. The compensation received from work is one of the chief reasons people seek employment. Pay is the means by which they provide for their own and their family's needs. For people with instrumental attitudes toward work (as discussed in Chapter 2), compensation may be the only (or certainly a major) reason why they work. Others find compensation a contributing factor to their efforts. Pay can do more than provide for the physiological needs of employees, however. What a person is paid indicates his or her worth to an organization.

Compensation is one of the most important HRM functions for the employer, too. Compensation often equals 50 percent of the cash flow of an organization, and, for some service organizations, it is an even larger percentage. It may be the major method used to attract employees as well as a way to try to motivate employees towards more effective performance. Compensation is also significant to the economy. For the past 30 years, salaries and wages have equaled about 60 percent of the gross national product of the United States and Canada.

Historically, compensation systems including benefits management have been concerned with ensuring that people were equitably paid, that wage rates were competitively set, and that benefit plans were appropriately administered. Heisler et al. (1988) report that today the field of compensation and benefits management is increasingly complex and dynamic.[1] There are increased cost pressures and legal challenges. In order for U.S. business to become more competitive and survive in the global marketplace, many organizations seek ways to reduce costs of programs or activities that do not directly support revenue-generating operations. Since the cost of labor is so high, there is increased pressure to maximize the payoff from each dollar invested in employee compensation and benefits.

Objective of Compensation

The objective of the compensation function is to create a system of rewards that is equitble to the employer and employee alike. The desired outcome is an employee that is *attracted* to the work and *motivated* to do a good job for the employer. Patton suggests that in compensation policy there are seven criteria for effectiveness.[2] Compensation should be:

. *Adequate*. Minimum governmental, union, and managerial levels should be met.
. *Equitable*. Each person should be paid fairly, in line with his or her effort, abilities, and training.
. *Balanced*. Pay, benefits, and other rewards should provide a reasonable total reward package.
. *Cost-effective*. Pay should not be excessive, considering what the organization can afford to pay.
. *Secure*. Pay should be enough to help an employee feel secure and aid him or her in satisfying basic needs.
. *Incentive-providing*. Pay should motivate effective and productive work.
. *Acceptable to the employee*. The employee should understand the pay system and feel it is a reasonable system for the enterprise and himself or herself.

Do you think Cardeson National Bank's pay plan is achieving these objectives?

Compensation Decisions and Decision Makers

Pay can be determined absolutely or relatively. Some people have argued that a pay system set by a single criterion for a whole nation or the world (that is, the absolute control of pay) is the best procedure. Since absolute pay systems are not used, however, the pay for each individual is set *relative* to the pay of others. Pay for a particular position is set relative to three groups. These are:

. Employees working on similar jobs in other organizations (Group A).
. Employees working on different jobs within the organization (Group B).
. Employees working on the same job within the organization (Group C).

The decision to examine pay relative to Group A, that is, the **pay level,** is called the *pay-level decision*. The objective of the pay-level decision is to keep the organization competitive in the labor market. The major tool used in this decision is the pay survey, which will be discussed later in this chapter. The pay decision relative to Group B is called the *pay-structure decision*. The pay structure involves setting a value on each job within the organization relative to all other jobs. This uses an approach called *job evaluation*. The decision involving pay relative to Group C is called *individual pay determination*.

Consider Pete Johnson, custodian at Cardeson National Bank. Pete's pay is affected first by the pay-level policy of the bank — whether CNB is a pacesetter or a going-wage employer. Next, his pay is affected by how highly ranked *his* job is relative to other jobs within the bank, such as teller. Finally, his pay depends on how good a custodian he is, how long he has been with the enterprise, and other individual factors (individual pay determination).

Both general managers and HR specialists are involved in making compensation decisions. Top management makes the decisions that determine the total amount of the firm's budget that goes to pay, the pay form to be used (time pay versus incentive pay), and other pay policies. Top management also sets the pay strategy, that is setting the firm's compensation higher than, lower than, or equal to competition. In small firms, these decisions are often made by the owner. In medium-size and large firms, the HR department advises top management on all these issues. Managers at both the middle-management and supervisory levels also have an

PROFESSIONAL PROFILE

Biography

Lasha Dagg is salary administration manager, human resources, for British Columbia Telephone Company (B.C. Tel), Burnaby, British Columbia, Canada.

In her diverse career with B.C. Tel, Ms. Dagg has acquired an extensive knowledge of compensation issues. Because of the lack of formal training available to professionals in this area, she was a pioneer in her field.

In 1956, Ms. Dagg joined the company's customer service department. Like many female employees at that time, her career was postponed when she decided to start a family in 1959.

Before returning to B.C. Tel in 1969, Ms. Dagg continued in customer service — but this time in the retail field. Because of her background, B.C. Tel recruited her to help straighten out the fallout in customer service that resulted from a lengthy labor dispute.

In 1974, Ms. Dagg was promoted to her first management position and, in 1977, she transferred to human resources. Through self-development courses and company-sponsored education programs, she acquired valuable expertise. For three years, she specialized in employee benefits before becoming a salary administrator. Exploring another side of human resources, Ms. Dagg, five years later, moved into organizational planning for an 18-month stint. Then, an extraordinary opportunity presented itself — a 10-month project to learn and teach the quality-improvement process at Microtel, a subsidiary of the B.C. Tel group of companies. Ms. Dagg developed a complete quality training package and became a proficient trainer, instructing more than 280 managers and hourly workers.

In 1988, she returned to compensation to fill a newly created research and developmental position. Her mandate was to review compensation issues from a broad perspective, analyzing the impact of issues such as job-sharing, expatriate compensation, and sales incentive plans on the B.C. Tel Group of Companies.

Last year, Ms. Dagg was promoted to her current position.

Lasha Dagg
British Columbia Telephone
Company

Job Description   As salary administration manager, Lasha Dagg is responsible for a department of five compensation professionals and three clerical staff and directs an annual budget of Can. $1.5 million. As well as overseeing the job evaluations and salary program of B.C. Tel's management and exempt staff and developing strategic compensation plans, Ms. Dagg is responsible for expatriate compensation and the corporate incentive program.

One of her primary functions is to ensure that B.C. Tel's managers are paid equitably, from both an internal and an external viewpoint.

Variable compensation: A Viewpoint   Our challenge, as compensation practiners, is to think corporately. At B.C. Tel, we strive to tie compensation to customer and shareholder values. To accomplish this end, we are focusing on the five-year corporate strategic plan. Our first foray into this type of compensation was the management incentive compensation plan (MICP).

In fiscal year 1990, the MICP was put into place. It is the first concrete link between the strategic plan and compensation. Senior managers are given the opportunity to earn bonuses above and beyond their fixed salary, based on attainment of strategic plan objectives. At present, we are looking for approval to roll out the plan to the other management levels in 1991 or 1992. It is a dynamic process; it was designed to reflect each year's business plan.

Our initial design was modest. As more definitive measurements are established, the rewards will become more meaningful. Although it is still quite early to evaluate fully, in terms of motivation, the pilot project is a success. Senior managers are focusing their people on the bottom line. Furthermore, there is no risk for customers and shareholders with this plan, because, without tangible results at year end, there is no payout.

This is a very exciting time to be involved in compensation. Pay equity is a hot issue, especially in Canada, and global competition is on the horizon. To attract and retain top-notch employees, North American firms will be forced to examine variable compensation and other more creative and motivational forms of compensation.

impact on compensation decisions. Exhibit 10–1 details the decision responsibilities of operating managers and HR compensation specialists.

A DIAGNOSTIC APPROACH TO COMPENSATION

Perhaps you believe that pay is determined by a manager and an employee sitting down and talking it over, or that the government or unions should determine pay. In fact, pay is influenced by a series of internal and external factors. The diagnostic approach can be used to help you understand these factors better. Exhibit 10–2 highlights the diagnostic factors most important to compensation as an HRM activity. The nature of the task affects compensation primarily in the method of payment for the job, such as payment for time worked or incentive compensation. Individual pay determination including incentives and executive compensation, which differ in significant ways from other types of compensation, are discussed in Chapter 11.

EXHIBIT 10-1   The Roles of Operating and HR Managers in Making Pay Decisions

Pay Decision Factor	Operating Manager	HR Manager (HRM)
Compensation budgets	OM approves or adjust HRM preliminary budget	HRM prepares preliminary budget
Pay-level decisions: pay survey design and interpretation		HRM designs, implements, and makes decisions
Pay-structure decisions: job evaluation design and interpretation		HRM designs, implements, and makes decisions
Pay classes, rate ranges, and classification design and interpretation		HRM designs, implements, and makes decisions
Individual pay determination	Joint decision with HRM	Joint decision with OM
Pay policy decisions: method of payment	OM decides after advice of HRM	HRM advises OM
Pay secrecy	OM decides after advice of HRM	HRM advises OM
Pay security	OM decides after advice of HRM	HRM advises OM

EXHIBIT 10-2   Factors Affecting Compensation and Results

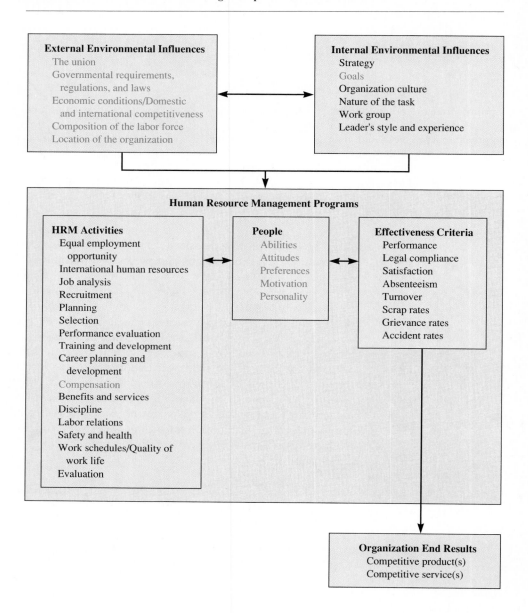

External Environmental Influences
The union
Governmental requirements,
   regulations, and laws
Economic conditions/Domestic
   and international competitiveness
Composition of the labor force
Location of the organization

Internal Environmental Influences
Strategy
Goals
Organization culture
Nature of the task
Work group
Leader's style and experience

Human Resource Management Programs

HRM Activities
Equal employment
   opportunity
International human resources
Job analysis
Recruitment
Planning
Selection
Performance evaluation
Training and development
Career planning and
   development
Compensation
Benefits and services
Discipline
Labor relations
Safety and health
Work schedules/Quality of
   work life
Evaluation

People
Abilities
Attitudes
Preferences
Motivation
Personality

Effectiveness Criteria
Performance
Legal compliance
Satisfaction
Absenteeism
Turnover
Scrap rates
Grievance rates
Accident rates

Organization End Results
Competitive product(s)
Competitive service(s)

One of the most significant factors affecting compensation systems is the nature of the individual employee. How employee attitudes and preferences directly affect performance is discussed in the following section. Employee attitudes and preferences also affect the pay structure.

Factors external to the organization — the government, unions, general economic conditions, and labor market conditions — all have an effect on pay or wage surveys.

Organizational factors include managerial goals and pay structure, labor budgets, and the size and age of the organization. Discussion of these factors in the sections that follow illustrates why employees and managers are paid the amounts they receive and which methods are used to pay people.

COMPENSATION AND MOTIVATION

Does a well-designed pay system motivate employees to greater performance, higher-quality performance, or greater employee satisfaction? The answer to this question has varied from the *yes* of Aristotle in ancient Greece and of scientific management in the early 1900s to the *no* of human relations theorists in the 1930s. Although most compensation experts believe that pay affects the motivation of employees, the controversy still rages. It is not possible to settle this age-old dispute here, but the various positions will be presented briefly.

Compensation and Employee Satisfaction

All would agree that effective compensation administration is desirable in efforts to increase employee satisfaction. And satisfaction with pay is important because, as many researchers have found, if pay satisfaction is low, job satisfaction is low.[3] A consequence of low job satisfaction is higher and more costly absenteeism and turnover.

Satisfaction is an evaluative term that describes an attitude of like or dislike.[4] *Pay satisfaction*, therefore, refers to an employee's like or dislike of the employer's compensation system. Unfortunately, research on pay or reward satisfaction is not very well developed. It is clear that it has many dimensions. You can reach that conclusion by just thinking about how many different rewards an organization offers its employees. For example, it is possible to be very happy with your salary but dissatisfied with your vacation or pension benefits. This makes measurement of pay satisfaction almost impossible.

Edward Lawler created a model that begins to explain the causes of pay satisfaction or dissatisfaction.[5] According to Lawler, the distinction between the amount employees receive and the amount they think others are receiving is the immediate cause of satisfaction or dissatisfaction with pay. If they believe these two amounts are equal, pay satisfaction results. Anticipation of pay satisfaction will influence an employee's decisions about how hard to work, and so on. The compensation system influences satisfaction and acts as feedback that allows employees to adjust subsequent behavior. If employees conclude that they are being paid too little, they may be absent or leave. If employees think they are being paid too much, they are bored or may overcompensate by working harder.

In sum, most people believe it is desirable to have a pay system that leads to pay satisfaction. However, research indicates that there is a relatively weak relationship between pay and pay satisfaction.[6] One reason that the relationship is not stronger is that people have different ideas about what their pay should be. Another reason for the weak relationship is that employees don't clearly understand how pay is determined. Therefore, nonjob factors such as being agreeable with the boss, having a pleasant personality, or making donations to the supervisor's favorite charity may be factors in the pay decision. Whether they are or not is sometimes not known to the employees.

Compensation and Employee Performance

Increasing payroll costs of the 1990s and competition in the global marketplace have caused managers throughout the United States to search for ways to increase productivity by linking compensation to employee performance.[7] High performance requires much more than employee motivation. Employee ability, adequate equipment, good physical working conditions, effective leadership and management, employee health, safety, and other conditions all help raise employee performance levels. But employees' motivation to work harder and better is obviously an important factor. A number of studies indicate that, if pay is tied to performance, the employee produces a higher quality and quantity of work.[8]

Not everyone agrees with this — some researchers argue that if you tie pay to performance, you will destroy the intrinsic rewards a person gets from doing the job well.[9] Intrinsic rewards are powerful motivators too, but the research on them has been limited to only a few studies. The importance of money to employees varies among individuals. If the organization claims to have an incentive pay system and in fact pays for seniority, the motivation effects of pay will be lost. The key to making compensation systems more effective is to be sure that they are directly connected to expected behaviors.[10]

In sum, theorists disagree over whether pay is a useful mechanism to increase performance. Because of individual differences in employees and jobs, it seems more fruitful to redirect this research to examine (1) the range of behaviors that pay can affect positively or negatively; (2) the amount of change pay can influence; (3) the kind of employees that pay influences positively and negatively; and (4) the environmental conditions that are present when pay leads to positive and negative results.

It can be said that performance-based compensation programs are viewed by organizations as anything from a miracle cost-reallocation process to a time-consuming waste of resources.[11] All of these views have merit. In order to implement such a program, it is paramount that managers keep in mind that the overall goal of a performance-based compensation system is to develop a productive, efficient, effective organization that enhances both employee performance and motivation.[12] The pay for performance program must, therefore, be driven by performance-oriented systems and processes rather than by the organization's compensation system and processes.

The point is that, although compensation in the form of pay for performance has intuitive appeal, it is extremely difficult to perfectly fit a pay for performance system together. A realistic and achievable performance-based compensation system can be implemented if it is based on a five-phase performance cycle.[13] The five phases are:

1. *Information sharing.* Development of an open communication between the supervisor and his or her employees.
2. *Performance contracting.* The goals of each broad area of job accountability and specific measures of performance must be discussed and mutually agreed upon. Performance measures must be relevant, specific, controllable, obtainable, and practical.
3. *Performance reinforcement.* The supervisor must periodically evaluate the employee's performance and give feedback so that behaviors can be adjusted before the annual performance evaluation.
4. *Periodic performance evaluation.* Actual achievement is compared with the goals set in phase 2 above. The performance evaluation should focus on actual

job performance, review of relevant accountabilities and performance measures, and actual achievement of these goals.
5. *Performance recognition*. Inform the employee immediately of the recognition (monetary and/or non-monetary) that results from the review of his or her performance during the last review cycle.

Developing a system that shows employees that pay is tied to performance requires a number of managerial skills. First, managers must be able to allocate pay on the basis of merit. Any merit pay increase must be meaningful, not a token, if it is to be motivational. Second, managers must be willing to specifically discriminate among subordinates, in terms of rating and rewarding performance. Third, the manager must communicate the pay system at the time of employment in terms of initial pay, expected long-term pay progressions, and pay adjustments.[14] This information should be communicated by the manager, who also informs the employee what performance levels are required to obtain the pay increases. Finally, managers must have the ability to discuss the pay for performance linkage with subordinates.

One reason why organizations have failed to tie pay to performance for their employees is that it requires quite a bit of effort and commitment by management.[15] Overcoming resistance to change is quite difficult.[16] A more simplified strategy is to conduct business as usual or not to work on creating a pay for performance perception among subordinates.

The first step in the direction of creating a pay for performance work culture is to develop performance evaluation systems that are considered equitable, meaningful, and comprehensive by both managers and employees. When pay rewards cannot be linked to measurable performance, management has a problem. That is, if performance measures are poorly developed, employees will have difficulty perceiving the connection between pay and performance. Thus, if compensation is to have any influence on motivation, it is extremely important to develop accurate measures of performance.

Linking pay to performance has become simpler than was originally thought due to computer technology.[17] Modern spreadsheet programs used on personal computers have made it possible to take performance evaluation ratings and directly transform them into projected pay increases. These pay increases can be costed out accurately and subsequently tied to the firm's overall financial strategy. Note, however, that this linkage is predicated on a performance evaluation system that is in place and is adequately communicated to and accepted by employees.

EXTERNAL INFLUENCES ON COMPENSATION

Besides being concerned about pay satisfaction and the pay for performance linkage, managers have to consider other influences when designing a compensation program. Among the factors that influence pay and compensation policies are those outside the organization: the government, unions, the economy, and the labor market.

Government Influences

The government directly affects compensation through wage controls and guidelines, which prohibit an increase in compensation for certain workers at certain times, and laws directed at the establishment of minimum wage rates, wage and hour regulations, and the prevention of discrimination directed at certain groups.

Wage Controls and Guidelines   Several times in the past the United States has established wage freezes and guidelines. President Harry Truman imposed a wage and price freeze from January 1951 to 1953, and President Richard Nixon imposed freezes from 1971 to 1974. *Wage freezes* are government orders that permit no wage increases. *Wage controls* limit the size of wage increases. *Wage guidelines* are similar to wage controls, but they are voluntary rather than legally required restrictions.

Economists and compensation specialists differ on the usefulness of wage and price freezes. Critics argue that controls are an administrative nightmare, which seriously disrupt the effective resource allocation market process and lead to frustration, strikes, and so on. Even the critics admit, however, that during times of perceived national emergency and for relatively brief periods, the controls might help slow (but not indefinitely postpone) inflation. Those favoring them believe that controls reduce inflation. The important point is that employers must adjust their compensation policies to any governmental wage guidelines and controls. Considerable data gathering is necessary when such programs are in effect, and the employer must be prepared to justify any proposed wage increases. Even when the controls have been lifted, there are frequently wage and price advisory groups — government or quasi-government groups that some politicians use to try to "jawbone" executives into keeping price increases lower. These bodies at times might influence prices, which in turn could limit the profits needed to give wage increases. One proposed solution is *TIP (tax-based income policy)*. Under a TIP, when employers give employees bigger raises than government standards, the employer receives a tax increase; when the raise is below standards, he or she receives a tax reduction.

Wage and Hour Regulations   The Fair Labor Standards Act of 1938 is the basic pay act in the United States. It has been amended many times and contains minimum wage, overtime pay, child labor, and equal pay provisions. Government agencies such as the Department of Labor's Wage and Hour Division enforce the wage and hour law. It has the right to examine employers' records and issue orders for back pay, get an injunction to prohibit future violations, and prosecute violators and send them to prison. For example, the department estimates that, in 1988, U.S. employers underpaid employees by $300 million, in violation of minimum wage and overtime regulations. In 1989, over 3.9 million U.S. workers were covered by the Fair Labor Standards Act.[18] The law includes the following provisions.

Minimum Wage   All employers covered by the law must pay an employee at least a **minimum wage** per hour. But many of the low-wage working poor work for small retail and service establishments that are not covered by the law.[19] These establishments make up part of the growing service sector of our economy and employ 76.1 percent of the low-wage working poor.

A brief history of the minimum wage rate is shown in Exhibit 10–3. In 1938, the minimum wage was 25 cents per hour. In 1984, the minimum was $3.35. In April 1991, the minimum wage rate was $4.25 per hour. As stated earlier, the minimum wage does not apply to all employees. For example, full-time students could be paid only $3.53 per hour for a period of up to one year. There are also other exceptions granted for apprentices, handicapped workers, and learners. A number of economists question the desirability of minimum wages, arguing that this law may price the marginal worker out of a job.

Overtime Pay   An employee covered by the law who works more than 40 hours per week must be paid one-and-one-half times the base wage. If bonuses are also

---

EXHIBIT 10-3   Historical Progression of the Minimum Wage Rate

Year	Rate per Hour
1938	$0.25
1939	0.30
1945	0.40
1956	1.00
1968	1.60
1974	2.00
1979	2.90
1981	3.35
1991	4.25

---

paid on a monthly or quarterly basis, the overtime pay equals one-and-one-half times the base pay and bonuses. Overtime pay tends to reduce the scheduling of longer hours of work.

The Fair Labor Standards Act provisions regarding minimum wage and overtime pay apply to employees classified as nonexempt, but does not apply to exempt employees.[20] An **exempt employee** is classifed to mean an executive employee, administrative employee, professional, or outside salesperson. An *executive employee* would be a manager who has authority over subordinates. An *administrative employee* would be a staff employee such as the president's assistant public relations coordinator. A *professional* is a person who has special knowledge acquired through education such as a company physician or lawyer. An *outside salesperson* sells goods or services to customers away from the organization.[21]

Nonexempt employees do not fit any of the above categories. Most noticeably, nonexempt employees are blue-collar workers, such as skilled and semiskilled manufacturing workers, truck drivers, and assembly-line workers. Nonexempt employees are covered by the minimum wage and overtime provisions of the law.

Child Labor Prohibition   The law prohibits employing persons between the ages of 16 and 18 in hazardous jobs such as meatpacking and logging. Persons under age 16 cannot be employed in jobs in interstate commerce except when they do nonhazardous work for a parent or guardian, and this requires a temporary work permit.

Equal Pay Act   Today, U.S. women working full-time earn only about 65 to 70 percent of what men earn.[22] Historically, it was felt that women worked sporadically to bring in money for luxuries. The Virginia Slims opinion poll of 1990 found that women and men work for the same primary reason.[23] Exhibit 10–4 reports the comparison between why women worked in 1980 and why they worked in 1990. Fully 55 percent of women work because they need the money to support their families. This is up from 46 percent 10 years ago. Thirty-two percent work to bring in extra money.

The Equal Pay Act (1963) amendment to the Fair Labor Standards Act is the first antidiscrimination law relating directly to females. The act applies to all employers and employees covered by the Fair Labor Standards Act, including executives, managers, and professionals. The Equal Pay Act requires **equal pay** for equal work

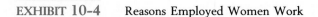

EXHIBIT 10-4   Reasons Employed Women Work

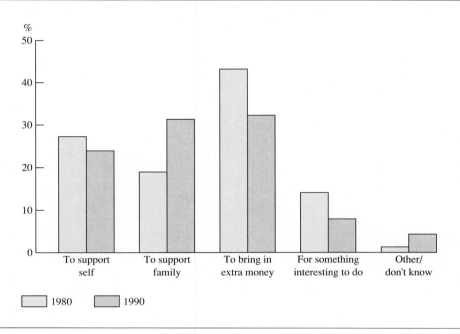

Source: Bickley Townsend and Kathleen O'Neil August 1990), "American Women Get Mad," *American Demographics*, p. 29.

for men and women. It defines equal work as work requiring equal skills, effort, and responsibility under similar working conditions.[24]

Under the Equal Pay Act, an employer can establish different wage rates on the basis of (1) seniority, (2) merit, (3) performance differences — quantity and quality, and (4) any factor other than sex. Shift work differentials are also permissible. All these exceptions, however, must apply equally to men and women. Since passage of the act, the female-male earnings gap narrowed significantly. And, between 1979 and 1987, the closing of the gap reflected increases in earnings per hour rather than in number of hours worked.[25] In an effort to close the remaining earnings gap, there has been a growing movement in the last few years to have the widely accepted concept of equal pay for equal jobs expanded to include equal pay for comparable jobs.

Comparable Worth   The doctrine of comparable worth (sometimes called *pay equity*) is not a position that provides that women and men be paid equally for performing equal work. **Comparable worth** is a concept that attempts to prove and remedy the allegation that employers systematically discriminate by paying women employees less than their work is intrinsically worth, relative to what they pay male employees who work in comparable professions. The term *comparable worth* means different things to different people. Comparable worth relates jobs that are dissimilar in their content (for example, nurse and plumber) and contends that individuals who perform jobs that require similar skill, effort, and responsibility under similar work conditions should be compensated equally.[26]

Advocates of comparable worth depend primarily upon two sets of statistics to demonstrate that women employees are discriminated against by employers. First,

EXHIBIT 10-5   Percentage Female of Traditional "Women's" Occupations, 1979 and 1986

Occupation	1979	1986
Secretaries	98.8	99.2
Registered nurses	94.6	92.7
Bank tellers	91.5	91.7
Phone operators	90.8	97.7
Child-care workers	88.9	97.7
Bookkeepers/auditing clerks	88.1	93.0
Waiters/waitresses	82.7	78.7
Cashiers	77.7	79.8
Health technicians	71.6	65.1
Elementary schoolteachers	60.9	81.9
Social workers	60.6	60.0

Source: U.S. Census Bureau (September 1987).

they point to statistics that show that women earn from 59 to 88 percent less than male employees overall.[27] For example, the U.S. Census Bureau found that in 1987 the median average income for females was $16,909, for males $26,008.[28] Second, women tend to be concentrated in lower-paying, predominately female jobs. In spite of the fact that more women are entering the work force, about one fourth of all women employed in 1988 worked in three job categories: secretarial/clerical, retail sales, and food preparation and service.[29] Exhibit 10–5 illustrates this distribution more fully.

The issue of comparable worth has been ruled on by the Supreme Court. In a five-to-four decision on June 9, 1984, the Supreme Court ruled that a sex discrimination suit can be brought under the 1964 Civil Rights Act on a basis other than discrimination based on "equal or substantially equal work."[30] The suit involved Washington County, Oregon, prison matrons claiming sex discrimination because male prison guards, whose jobs were somewhat different, received substantially higher pay. The county had evaluated the male's jobs as having 5 percent more job content than the female's jobs, and paid the males 35 percent more. On July 1, 1984, the state of Washington began wage adjustment payments to approximately 15,000 employees. For example, women in female-dominated jobs, now receive $4.17 more per week. This is the first of several adjustments aimed at eliminating state pay disparities between male and female jobs by 1993.[31]

Until the *Gunther v. Washington* county prison matron's case, the courts were split on the issue of comparable worth.[32] The ruling, although not mentioning the comparable worth concept, now permits women to bring suit on the grounds that they are paid less than men holding jobs of comparable, or less than comparable, worth — based on job content evaluation.

In another case involving the state of Washington, the *AFSCME* (American Federation of State, County, and Municipal Employees) *v. State of Washington*, the Court found that the state was guilty of direct, overt, and institutionalized pay discrimination. The Court found that jobs held predominantly by women had lower pay rates than jobs dominated by men, even when jobs were rated the same in job evaluation studies. The Court contended that the female job pay rates were incorrectly tied to market forces and not to job content. After all appeals are heard, it is possible that Washington state employees could be awarded as much as $500 million in salary adjustments and three years of back pay.[33]

In another important comparable worth case in San Jose, California, in 1981, several hundred women employees of the city walked off their jobs over the comparable worth issue. One eye-opening example in this situation was that senior librarians, typically female, earned 27 percent less than senior chemists, typically male, although the two jobs were rated comparably. The union and city reached a settlement on July 14, 1981, with the city agreeing to pay $1.45 million in raises for several hundred female employees to make their pay more equitable with men.

A few other pay equity cases have involved:[34]

1. Nurses working for the city of Denver, Colorado, starting at $1,000 per year less than painters, tree trimmers, and tire servicemen.
2. Jobs held primarily by females in a Westinghouse plant in Trenton, New Jersey, in general paying less than male jobs that were rated comparably by the company's job evaluation system.
3. Women handling health and beauty aids for a division of Super Valu Stores, Inc., in western Pennsylvania, eastern Ohio, and northern West Virginia, being paid $3,500 less annually than men handling perishable food.

In each of these cases and almost every instance of a case reaching the Court, the claim revolved around the job evaluation system (job evaluation will be discussed later in this chapter.)

HR specialists must be extremely careful about how job evaluation data are used in determining pay. They also must work at developing job evaluation systems that are valid and reliable. Comparable worth is an issue that requries a number of HR responses such as:

. Implementing a sound job evaluation system.
. Comparing pay across jobs on a regular basis. Are low-paying jobs being occupied by females and minorities? If so, look at this closely.
. Documenting the pay system.
. Clarifying and documenting the role that performance appraisal plays in pay.

The notion of value is extremely important when examining pay differentials between men and women. Most people would agree that water is more valuable than diamonds, but diamonds are much more expensive than water. This differential arises because the supply of water is abundant relative to demand. When secretaries, librarians, and cashiers are in short supply, what employers have to pay them will rise. Nurses are in short supply in the 1990s, and their wages have skyrocketed accordingly.

Comparable worth is being addressed in the public sector and increasingly in the private sector as firms try to react to labor supply and remain competitive. In order to do that, organizations should review their compensation systems by examining job descriptions, biased comparisons, and multiple pay plans to be sure women are not being discriminated against unfairly.[35] Comparable worth will continue to be a controversial issue as more court rulings are issued. It appears that HR departments will become more embroiled in the controversy. Special equity adjustments that have been required by the courts in comparable worth cases are going to have to be paid by someone. Both men and women are finding that comparable worth has been and will remain a costly issue.

Other Pay Legislation   The Civil Rights Act of 1964, and the Age Discrimination Act of 1967 are designed to assure that all persons of similar ability, seniority, and background receive the same pay for the same work. The Equal Employment Opportunity Commission enforces the Civil Rights Act, while the Wage and Hour Division enforces the Equal Pay Act and the Age Discrimination Act.

The Walsh-Healy Act of 1936 requires firms doing business with the federal government to pay wages at least equal to the industry minimum rather than the market area minimum. It parallels the Fair Labor Standards Act on child labor and requires time-and-a-half pay for any work performed after eight hours a day. It also exempts some industries. The Davis-Bacon Act of 1931 requires the payment of minimum prevailing wages of the locality to workers engaged in federally sponsored public works. The McNamara-O'Hara Service Contract Act requires employers who have contracts with the federal government of $2,500 per year or more, or who provide services to federal agencies as contractors or subcontractors, to pay prevailing wages and fringe benefits to their employees.

In addition to federal laws, 47 states have minimum wage laws covering intrastate employees and those not covered by federal laws. Some of these minimums are higher than the federal minimum. In such cases, the state minimums apply.

The government directly affects the amount of pay the employee takes home by requiring employers to deduct funds from employees' wages. Deductions include federal income taxes (withholding taxes), social security taxes, and possibly state and local income taxes. The federal government also has other laws governing pay deductions. The Copeland Act (1934) and Anti-Kickback Law (1948) are designed to protect the employee from unlawful or unauthorized deductions. The Federal Wage Garnishment Act (1970) is designed to limit the amount deducted from a person's pay to reduce debts. It also prohibits the employer from firing an employee if the employee goes in debt only once and has his pay garnished. The employer may deduct as much from the paycheck as required by court orders for alimony or child support, debts due for taxes, or bankruptcy court requirements.

Other Government Influences

In addition to the laws and regulations just discussed, the government influences compensation in many other ways. If the government is the employer, it can legislate pay levels by setting statutory rates. For example, the pay scale for teachers can be set by law or by edict of the school board, and pay depends on revenues from the current tax base. If taxes decline relative to organizations' revenue streams, no matter how much the organization may wish to pay higher wages, it cannot.

The government affects compensation through its employment-level policy too. One of the goals of the federal government is full employment of all citizens seeking work. The government may even create jobs for certain categories of workers, thus reducing the supply of workers available and affecting pay rates.

Union Influences

Another important external influence on an employer's compensation program is labor unionization. Unionized workers work longer hours and make more than non-unionized workers.[36] Unions have an effect whether or not the organization's employees are unionized if the organization is in an area where unionized enterprises exist. Unions have tended to be pacesetters in demands for pay, benefits, and improved working conditions. There is reasonable evidence that unions tend to increase pay levels, although this is more likely where an industry has been organized by strong unions. If the organization elects to stay in an area where unions are strong, its compensation policies will be affected.

There is a supportive interaction between unions and government influences on compensation. There are several federal laws that apply.[37] For example, the Davis Bacon Act and similar laws require employers with government contracts to pay prevailing wages. Prevailing wages for any locale are determined by the Department of Labor. In most instances, the prevailing wage is the union wage in that region. So unions help determine wages even for nonunionized employees.

When a union is trying to organize employees at a particular place of employment, the organizing campaign places constraints on the compensation manager.[38] The Taft-Hartley Act makes it illegal to change wage rates during the organizing campaign, so wages are effectively frozen for the duration. Refusal to bargain over wages is prohibited by this act. This means that the compensation manager is bound by the results of the collective bargaining process in setting wages. Unions reject merit increases and want all pay based on seniority, another limit to the flexibility of any compensation strategy. In fact, when an enterprise is unionized, it can expect to deal with union demands on every aspect of the wage and benefit package. Because of this, compensation packages in unionized firms often fail to achieve external, internal, or individual equity.

During hard economic times, union and non-union employees have made concessions in the form of wage cuts, wage freezes of previously negotiated increases, benefit reductions, work rules changes, and other forms of givebacks. Uniroyal, Inc.'s 16,000 employees gave up $27 million in compensation in 1980 and 1981. This savings was essential for Uniroyal to survive. At American Motors and Quality Aluminum Company, employees have given back millions of dollars. However, the union and management in these two firms reached agreement that all wage concessions were to be paid back under a plan based on improved company performance.[39] In 1990, the United Auto Workers and General Motors traded some job security for smaller wage increases.

A series of legal cases has requied employers to share compensation information with the unions if employees are unionized. For example, in *Shell Developmenet v. Association of Industrial Scientists — Professional Employees*, Shell was required to provide the union with a written explanation of salary curves and the merit system, as well as copies of current salary curve guides, merit ratings, and so on. In *Time Incorporated v. Newspaper Guild*, Time was required to provide the union with a list of salaries of employees. In *General Electric v. International Union of Electrical Workers*, GE was required to provide the union with the pay survey information it had gathered to form compensation decisions. Thus, employers would do well to communicate with and try to influence the union on compensation policy and levels.

Unions do try to bargain for higher pay and benefits, of course. The union is more likely to increase the compensation of its members when: the organization is financially and competitively strong; the union is financially strong enough to support a strike; the union has the support of other unions; and general economic and labor market conditions are such that unemployment is low and the economy is strong.[40]

Unions also bargain over working conditions and other policies that affect compensation. There is a tendency for unions to prefer fixed pay for each job category or rate ranges that are administered primarily to reflect seniority rather than merit increases. This is true in the private and other sectors. Unions press for time pay rather than merit pay when the amount of performance expected is tied to technology (such as the assembly line).

Economic Conditions and Compensation

Also affecting compensation as an external factor are the economic conditions of the industry, especially the degree of competitiveness, which affects the organization's ability to pay high wages. The more competitive the situation, the less able is the organization to pay higher wages. Ability to pay is also a consequence of the relative productivity of the organization, industry, or sector. If a firm is very productive, it can pay higher wages. Productivity can be increased by advanced technology, more-efficient operating methods, a harder-working and more-talented work force, or a combination of these factors.

One productivity index used by many organizations as a criterion in the determination of a general level of wages is the Bureau of Labor Statistics' "Output per Man-Hour in Manufacturing." This productivity index is published in each issue of the *Monthly Labor Review*. For about 70 years, productivity increased at an average annual rate of approximately 3 percent. The percentage increase in average weekly earnings in the United States is very closely related to the percentage change in productivity, plus the percentage change in the consumer price index. Unfortunately, in the 1970–90 period, productivity improvement in the United States had been less than 2 percent annually.

The degree of profitability and productivity is a significant factor in determining the ability of firms in the private and third sector to pay wages. In the public sector, the limitations of the budget determine the ability to pay. If tax rates are low or the tax base is low or declining, the public-sector employer may be unable to give pay increases even if they are deserved.

Nature of the Labor Market and Compensation

The final external factor affecting compensation to be discussed is the state of the labor market. Although many feel that human labor should not be regulated by forces such as supply and demand, it does in fact happen. In times of full employment, wages and salaries may have to be higher to attract and retain enough qualified employees; in depressions, the reverse is true. Pay may be higher if few skilled employees are available in the job market. This situation may occur because unions or accrediting associations limit the numbers certified to do the job. In certain locations, due to higher birthrates or a recent loss of a major employer, more persons may be seeking work. These factors lead to what is called *differential pay levels*. At any one time in a particular locale, unskilled labor rates seek a single level, and minimally skilled clerical work rates seek another. Research evidence from the labor economics field provides adequate support for the impact of labor market conditions on compensation.

Besides differences in pay levels by occupations in a locale, there are also differences between government and private employees and exempt and nonexempt employees, as well as international differences.

Two characteristics of the labor market deserve special emphasis regarding compensation decision making: (1) the aging of the labor force and (2) the global labor market.

Compensation and an Aging Labor Force   By the mid 1990s, many employers will be facing a shortage of entry-level employees. Potential employees in the 19–24 age category will decrease by 3.4 percent while employees in the 55+ category will increase by 3.4 percent. This critical shortage of entry-level personnel might be avoided if older employees could be encouraged to stay in or reenter the labor force.[41] In order to do this, federal retirement policies would need to be changed to both retain and attract seniors who possess needed skills.

The gap between job requirements and job skills is growing. Corporate policies that encourage early retirement through various buyout incentives only save compensation dollars in the short run. In the long run, companies will miss some of their most capable workers. Current government policies financially penalize retired workers who want to continue to work part-time and whose skills are still needed. Recommendations to fully utilize experienced seniors include removing the current earned income ceiling for Social Security payments for those 65 and older, restructuring corporate pensions (see Chapter 11), and designing innovative pay plans to retain and attract the older worker.

Compensation and an International Labor Force   Employers have been transporting cheap labor to work "on site" since the building of the pyramids.[42] Chinese railway builders were transported to the American West at the turn of the 19th century, and workers are now flown into Britain's Gatwick Airport from Ireland to work on the Channel Tunnel. Compensation specialists must base their plans on a competitive global marketplace. Issues that affect the compensation strategies of organizations competing in a global marketplace include:[43]

1. *Plant relocating.* For example, relocation to the sunbelt of Spain (good climate, cheap labor, Spanish-speaking) or Ireland's mist belt (poor climate, cheap labor, English-speaking).

2. *Body shopping.* Body shopping is the transmission of computer-related tasks by cable or satellite to a cheap, appropriately skilled labor force across the continent or the world. In 1981, Citicorp was one of the first firms to set up a processing site in South Dakota far from its New York City headquarters. Filipinos input medical records for U.S. firms at only $5,500 per year, only 20 percent of the U.S. salary for the same work ($22,000).

3. *Global wage differentials verging on the extreme.* For example, computer consultants in the United States are earning $75 an hour, and in India, consultants are working for the same firm for $5.00 an hour!

4. *Employing local (foreign) managers and workers.* A recent survey of *Forbes* 500 top managers said compensation of foreign nationals is a "hodgepodge" or a "nightmare." Providing pay packages for foreign nationals is much harder than for Americans abroad. Few foreign field offices have a compensation expert on staff. The result is low overhead at home and high frustration and inefficiency abroad.

5. *Moving U.S. employees to foreign locations.* Keeping employees and families at foreign sites costs three to five times the annual base pay at home.[44] Costs vary tremendously from country to country, for example, Mexico City to Tokyo. Compensation problems involve appropriate salary allowances, tax laws, travel and relocation funds, education for dependents, and emergency leaves.

ORGANIZATIONAL INFLUENCES ON COMPENSATION

In addition to the external influences on compensation already discussed, several internal factors affect pay levels: the size and age of the organization, the labor budget, and the goals of its controlling interests.

We don't know a great deal about the relationship between organization size and pay. Generally speaking, it appears that larger organizations tend to have higher pay levels. Little is known about age of the organizations and pay, but some theorists contend that newer enterprises tend to pay more than old ones.

The Labor Budget

The labor budget of an organization normally identifies the amount of money available for annual employee compensation. Every unit of the organization is influenced by the size of the budget.[45] A firm's budget normally does not state the exact amount of money to be allocated to each employee, but it does state how much is available to the unit. The discretion in allocating pay is then left to department heads and supervisors. These allocations form the basis of a manager's strategy.

The department heads and supervisors are in the best position to allocate the unit's labor budget dollars, assuming that they have the closest contact with and the best view of the employees. Theoretically, the contact and performance evaluation should permit a proper allocation of dollars. Thus, the department heads and supervisors take the budget amounts and, based on observation and evaluation, recommend who should get what amount of compensation. Exhibit 10–6 briefly describes some of the pay allocation decisions. Each of these decisions is significantly influenced and constrained by what amount is budgeted to a particular unit.

Goals of Controlling Interests and Managerial Pay Strategies

Another organizational influence on compensation is related to the goals of controlling interests and the specific pay strategy that managers select. The final authority in pay decisions, as shown in Exhibit 10–6, is top-level or senior management. These are the managers that make the overall strategic plan for the firm. Unfortu-

---

EXHIBIT 10-6   Allocation Decisions on Labor Budget

Position	Responsibility
Employees' immediate supervisor	Appraises performance; makes pay recommendation to supervisor.
Department head	Reviews each recommendation and initiates action based on budgeted amounts.
HRM: Compensation specialists	Review department head recommendations and consider equity, budget, objectives, and future plans. Consult with department heads on specialist's recommendations.
Senior or top-level management	Makes final decision on pay recommendations. Decision is based on labor budget and departmental allocations plus recommendations passed through various levels (supervisor, head, specialist).

CAREER CHALLENGE
(*continued*)

Guido Panelli went to Mary Renfro as he had promised Joe. He told her to go ahead and prepare a report that would point out the problems in HRM, especially in compensation, that CNB was facing. Mary remembered worrying about the situation at CNB after learning about the effect of pay on performance and satisfaction. At the bank, some employees seemed to be paid for seniority, others for family need. People doing the same job at about the same performance levels received different paychecks, and they knew it. This seemed to be a bomb about to go off.

She knew the bank was following the legal requirements of compensation with regard to minimum wage and overtime. But equal-pay requirements were another situation. Often single people were paid less than married people, and married people with several children were paid more than those who were childless or had only one child. Single females were paid the least.

At the time, the bank was not unionized: few banks were. The labor market was good for the bank right then. There always were more applicants than needed. This factor had helped CNB with its problem of high turnover, for there were many eager replacements. But what would happen if the labor market should change or if the inequities in the pay rates were not corrected?

nately, compensation is often an underutilized tool in supporting overall strategic objectives.[46] Therefore, many compensation plans have minimal impact on recruitment, motivation, and retention of employees. To be part of the strategic plan, the compensation system must be directly linked to the strategic goals of the organization, provide strong incentives, not support undesired behavior, offer valued rewards, and be communicated clearly.

The views of managers and supervisors about pay differ as much as the employees' views. For example, some managers and supervisors believe their employees should be compensated at high levels because they deserve it; they also accept or reject the idea that high pay or merit pay leads to greater performance or employee satisfaction: These attitudes are reflected in the pay-level strategy chosen by the managers of the organization. This is a major strategic choice top managers must make. Essentially, three pay-level strategies—high, low, or comparable—can be chosen by supervisors and managers. (The term *manager* will henceforth be used to reflect these two levels of compensation decision makers.)

The High Pay-Level Strategy   In this strategy, the managers choose to pay higher than average levels. The assumption behind this strategy is that you get what you pay for. These managers believe that paying higher wages and salaries will attract and hold the best employees, and this is the most effective long-range policy. Organizations that use this strategy are sometimes called *pacesetters*. The strategy may be influenced by pay criteria such as paying a living wage or paying on the basis of productivity.

The Low Pay-Level Strategy   At the opposite extreme is the low-pay strategy. In this case, the manager may chose to pay at the minimum level needed to hire enough employees. This strategy may be used because this is all the organization can pay — the ability to pay is restricted by other internal or external factors such as a limited labor budget or a forecasted decline in sales and profits.

The Comparable Pay-Level Strategy   The most frequently used strategy is to set the pay level at the going wage level. The wage criteria are comparable wages, perhaps modified by cost of living or purchasing power adjustments. For example, the Federal Pay Comparability Act of 1970 limits federal government compensation to the comparable wage paid in the private sector at the time. This going wage is determined from pay surveys. Thus, the policy of a manager following this strategy is to pay the current market rate in the community or industry, ± 5 percent or so.

These three strategies are usually set for the total organization, although the strategy might have to be modified for a few hard-to-fill jobs from time to time. The choice of strategy partially reflects the motivation and attitudes held by the manager. If the manager has a high need for recognition, the high-pay strategy might be chosen; otherwise, the low-pay strategy might be chosen. Another factor is the ethical and moral attitude of the manager. If the manager is ethically oriented, then a low-pay strategy is not likely to be chosen willingly.

THE PAY-LEVEL DECISION

The pay-level decision is made by managers who compare the pay of persons working inside the organization with those outside it. This decision is affected by multiple factors in interaction with one another that affect pay levels upward, downward, or laterally. These factors are shown in Exhibit 10–7. When factors such as managerial attitudes, the labor market, and competition change, the pressures on pay levels shift.[47] For example, in the decade of the 1990s, many companies may experience slow or little growth. Some will actually get smaller. This will put pressure on compensation in the downward direction.

But remember: The many external factors affecting the process, such as government and unions, are compounded by employees' job preferences, which include pay and nonpay aspects. And many employees do not have a sophisticated or comprehensive knowledge of all these factors. So you can see that the organization has a great deal of maneuvering room in the pay-level decision. To help make the pay-level decision, managers use a tool called a *pay* or *wage survey*.

PAY SURVEYS AND COMPARABLE PAY LEVELS

Pay surveys (also called *wage surveys)* are surveys of the compensation paid to employees by all employers in a geographic area, an industry, or an occupational group. Surveys must be carefully designed because their results are quoted and used in making compensation decisions. They are the principal tool used in the pay-level decision. These surveys help managers gauge the exact market rates for various

EXHIBIT 10-7   Factors Affecting the Pay-Level Decision

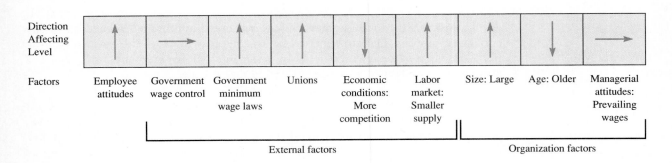

Direction Affecting Level	↑	→	↑	↑	↓	↑	↑	↓	→
Factors	Employee attitudes	Government wage control	Government minimum wage laws	Unions	Economic conditions: More competition	Labor market: Smaller supply	Size: Large	Age: Older	Managerial attitudes: Prevailing wages

| | External factors | Organization factors |

positions.[48] Obtaining valid, reliable pay surveys is critical to creating a compensation program that supports corporate financial goals.[49]

Who Conducts Pay Surveys?

Pay surveys are made by large employers, professional and consulting enterprises, trade associations, and the government. Some examples are described here.

Professional and Trade Association Surveys

The *American Management Association* (AMA) conducts surveys of professional and managerial compensation and provides about 12 reports on U.S. executives' salaries and 16 reports on foreign executives' salaries. The *Top Management Report* shows the salaries of 31,000 top executives in 75 top positions in 3,000 firms in 53 industries. The *Middle Management Report* covers 73 key exempt jobs between supervisor and top executives. The sample includes 460 firms with 15,000 middle-level executives. The *Administrative and Technical Report* covers jobs below the middle management level. The sample is 568 firms. The *Supervisory Management Report* provides national and regional data on salaries of 55 categories of foremen and staff supervisors in 700 companies.

Administrative Management Society

This group compiles records on the compensation of clerical and data processing employees. AMS surveys 7,132 firms with 621,000 clerical and data processing employees in 132 cities throughout the United States, Canada, and the West Indies. The data are gathered for 20 positions. A directory published every other year by cities and regions reports interquarterly ranges of salaries.

Society for Human Resource Management

The SHRM conducts salary surveys for personnel executives and others every second year.

Surveys by Other Organizations

Other organizations that do pay surveys include Pay Data Service (Chicago); Management Compensation Services; Bureau of National Affairs; Hay Associates; Abbott, Langer and Associates; and American Society of Corporate Securities. Many journals report on compensation, including *Compensation Review, Business Week, Dun's, Forbes, Fortune, Hospital Administration, Nation's Business* and *Monthly Labor Review*.

Government Surveys   U.S. government pay surveys include those by Federal Reserve banks, which survey private industry pay to set their employee's pay, and the Bureau of Labor Statistics (BLS). The BLS publishes three different surveys.

Area Wage Surveys   Annually, the BLS surveys about 200 areas (usually the Standard Metropolitan Statistical Areas) on the pay and benefits for white-collar and skilled blue-collar labor jobs. In alternate years, the pay and benefits for indirect manufacturing labor jobs are surveyed.

Industry Wage Surveys   The BLS surveys 50 manufacturing industries, 20 service industries, and public employees. Blue- and white-collar employees are covered. The surveys are done on one-, three-, and five-year cycles. Some industries are surveyed nationally (utilities, mining, manufacturing), and others by metropolitan area (finance, service, and trade).

Professional, Administrative, Technical, and Clerical (PATC) Surveys
BLS also annually surveys 80 occupational work-level positions on a nationwide basis. Occupations covered by the PATC survey include accountancy, legal services, engineering, drafting, clerical and chemistry. Although the BLS studies tend to follow the most sophisticated survey methods, they often do not relate to the area in which a firm is doing business.

How Pay Surveys Are Conducted and Used

How are these surveys done? One method is the personal interview, which develops the most accurate responses but is also expensive. Mailed questionnaires are probably the most frequently used method, and one of the cheapest. The jobs being surveyed by mail must be clearly defined, or the data may not be reliable. Telephone inquiries, as a follow-up to the mail questionnaires, are used to gather data. This procedure is quick, but it is also difficult to get detailed data over the phone.

There are a number of critical issues that determine the usefulness of surveys: the jobs to be covered, the employers to be contacted, and the method to be used to gather the data. Other employers cannot be expected to complete endless data requests for all the organization's jobs. However, a minimum of 30 percent of the jobs should be matched with market data to ensure an equitable evaluation of the firm's compensation system.[50] If the point method of job evaluation is used (described later in this chapter), the key jobs might be selected for surveying since they cover all pay ranges. The jobs that most employees hold should also be on the list (data entry clerks and underwriters for an insurance company, for example.)

The second issue concerns who will be surveyed. Most organizations tend to compare themselves with similar competitors in their industry. American Airlines might compare its pay rates to those of United Airlines, for example. However, it has been shown that employees might not compare their pay to that offered by competitors at all. Their basis of comparison might be friends' employers, or employers that they worked for previously. If the survey is to be useful, employees should be involved in choosing the organizations to be surveyed. The employers to be surveyed should include the most dominant ones in the area and a small sample of those suggested by employees.[51]

Government agencies use pay surveys of comparable private-sector jobs to set their pay levels. The evidence suggests that private-sector organizations use their own pay surveys rather than those provided by the government or other services.

These pay surveys are used primarily as general guidelines or as one of several factors considered in pay-level decisions. In fact, there is some evidence that organizations weigh job evaluation and individual pay determination more heavily than external pay comparisons. This makes sense, because pay surveys are not taken often (perhaps yearly) and are sometimes hard to interpret meaningfully.

Much care and thought must go into how the pay survey is conducted, and many factors, such as the source of data, must be considered.[52] An employer might not know if there is a pay differential between the job the firm offers and others. The difference might be due to difference in the job, fringe benefits provided, the time of the survey, or the pay level of the two areas. Remember too that there are many surveys an employer can use and many organizations and locales it can survey. This can give the employer a great deal of maneuvering room to handle problems such as relative ability or inability to pay certain wages or to deal with cost-of-living problems, and similar pay bargaining issues.

THE PAY-STRUCTURE DECISION

In addition to relating pay to pay levels paid for comparable jobs in other organizations, the enterprise must also determine **pay structures** for its employees having different jobs *within* the organization. Factors similar to those affecting pay levels affect these pay structures as well.

Managers can cope with the attempt to provide equal pay for positions of approximately equal worth by making arbitrary management decisions, engaging in collective bargaining, or using a special form of job analysis called **job evaluation.** If managers try to make these decisions without help from tools such as collective bargaining and job evaluation, unsystematic decision making is likely to lead to perceived inequities. Bargaining alone can lead to decisions based solely on the relative power of the employer and the union. Therefore, most compensation experts suggest that managerial decisions should be influenced by both the results of collective bargaining and job evaluation.

Job Evaluation

Job evaluation is intended to determine the relative worth of a job. A systematic comparison of the worth of one job to another eventually results in the creation of a wage or salary hierarchy. *Job evaluation* is the formal process by which the relative worth of various jobs in the organizations is determined for pay purposes. Essentially, it attempts to relate the amount of the employee's pay to the extent that her or his job contributes to organizational effectiveness.

It is not always easy to determine the worth of all jobs in an organization. The fact is that job evaluation involves making judgments that are subject to errors on the part of job evaluators.[53] It may be obvious that the effective physician will contribute more to the goals of patient care in the hospital than the nurse's aide. The point at issue is *how much* the differential is worth, and that means that a judgment must be made.

Since computing exactly how much a particular job contributes to organizational effectiveness is difficult, proxies for effectiveness are used. These proxies include skills required to do the job, amount and significance of responsibility involved, effort required, and working conditions. Compensation must vary with the differing demands of various jobs if employees are to be satisfied and if the organization is to be able to attract the personnel it wants.

Job evaluation is widely used. At least two thirds of all jobs have been evaluated. The following are among the reasons often cited for using a job evaluation program.[54]

- To establish a systematic and formal structure of jobs based on their worth to the organization.
- To justify an existing pay structure or to develop one that provides for internal equity.
- To provide a basis for negotiating pay rates when a firm bargains collectively with a union.
- To identify to employees a hierarchy of pay progression.
- To comply with equal-pay legislation.
- To develop a basis for a merit or pay for performance program.

Once an organization decides to use job evaluation, a series of decisions must be made to ensure its effectiveness. Part of the decision to use job evaluation, or the first step in using it effectively, is for management to involve employees (and, where appropriate, the union) in the system and its implementation. Most experts emphasize that job evaluation is a difficult task that is more likely to be successful if the employees whose jobs are being evaluated are involved in the process. Employees should be allowed to express their perceptions of the relative merits of their jobs compared to others. This participation affords an opportunity to explain the fairly complicated process of job evaluation to those most directly affected by it, and it will usually lead to better communication and improved employee understanding.

After the program is off to a cooperative start, usually a committee of about five members evaluates the jobs. Ideally, the committee includes employees, managers, and HR specialists. All members should be familiar with the jobs to be evaluated.

Job evaluation is usually performed by analyzing job descriptions and, occasionally, job specifications. Early in the process, it is imperative that job evaluators check the availability and accuracy of the job descriptions and specifications (see Chapter 6). It is usually suggested that job descriptions be split into several series, such as managerial, professional/technical, clerical, and operative. It makes sense in writing job descriptions to use words that are keyed to the job evaluation factors.

Another essential step in effective job evaluation is to select and weigh the criteria (compensable factors) used to evaluate the job. Although there is not a lot of research in this area, it appears that the results are the same whether all factors or just a few factors are considered, especially if the job evaluation is carefully designed and scaled. Typical of the most frequently used factors for job evaluation are education, experience, amount of responsibility, job knowledge, work hazards and working conditions. It is important that the factors used be accepted as valid for the job by those being evaluated.

Once the method of evaluating the job (to be discussed) is chosen, the evaluators do the job evaluations. Basically, those familiar with the jobs tend to rate them higher, especially if they supervise the jobs. It seems useful for each committee member to evaluate each job individually. Then the evaluators should discuss each job on which the ratings differ significantly, factor by factor, until agreement is reached.

EXHIBIT 10-8   Comparison Job Evaluation Systems

Comparison Basis	Nonquantitative Comparison (Job as Whole)	Quantitive Comparison (Parts of Factors of Jobs)
Job versus job	Job ranking	Factor comparison
Job versus scale	Job grading or classification	Point system

Job Evaluation Methods   The four most frequently used job evaluation methods are:

Job ranking
Factor comparison
Classification
The point system[55]

Job evaluation systems can be classified as shown in Exhibit 10–8.

Ranking of Jobs   The system used primarily in smaller, simpler organizations, is the **ranking of jobs.** Instead of analyzing the full complexity of jobs by evaluating parts of jobs, the job-ranking method has the evaluator rank-order *whole* jobs, from the simplest to the most challenging.

Sometimes, this is done by providing the evaluator with the information on cards. The evaluator sorts the jobs into ranks, allowing for the possibility of ties. If the list of jobs is large, the paired-comparison method, whereby each job is compared to every other job being evaluated, can be used. The evaluator counts the number of times a particular job is ranked above another, and the one with the largest number of first rankings is the highest ranked. There is no assurance that the ranking thus provided is composed of equal-interval ranks. The differential between the highest job and next highest job may not be exactly the same as that between the lowest and next lowest. If the system is used in an organization with many jobs, it is clumsy to use, and the reliability of the ratings is not good. Because of these problems, ranking is probably the least frequently used method of job evaluation.

Classification or Grading System   The **classification** or **grading system** groups a set of jobs together into a grade or classification. Then these sets of jobs are ranked on levels of difficulty or sophistication. It is a job-to-standard comparison, which solves many of the problems of simple job ranking. First, the job evaluator decides how many categories or classifications the job structure has to be broken into. Typically, there are around 8 with the number varying from 5 to 15.[56] The most publicized example of a classification system is the United States Office of Personnel Management General Schedule. It has 18 grades with 10 pay steps within the pay grades. This classification system is used for making compensation decisions for over 3 million federal employees.

The second step is to write definitions of each class. The definitions provide the production standards upon which the compensation system will be built. Exhibit 10–9 shows a five-level classification system with definitions for clerical workers.

EXHIBIT 10-9   Clerical Worker Classification System

Class I	Simple work, no supervisory responsibility, no public contact
Class II	Simple work, no supervisory responsibility, public contact
Class III	Work of medium complexity, no supervisory responsibility, public contact
Class IV	Work of medium complexity, supervisory responsibility, public contact
Class V	Complex work, supervisory responsibility, public contact

---

Source: Marc J. Wallance, Jr., and Charles H. Fay (1988) *Compensation Theory and Practice*, 2nd ed. (Boston: PWS-Kent Publishing).

Once the classes are defined, jobs to be evaluated are compared with the definitions and placed into the appropriate classification.

This method of job evaluation provides specific standards for compensation and accommodates any changes in the value of individual jobs. A job classification system can be constructed quickly, simply, and cheaply. It is easy to understand and easy to communicate to employees. Classification does have drawbacks, however. It is more detailed than job ranking, and it is assumed that there is a rigid relationship between job factors and value. As a result, especially in large firms, jobs are forced to fit into categories that are not entirely appropriate. Feelings of inequity can result. Deciding how many classifications there should be is also a problem. If there are too few classes, it will be difficult to differentiate job value and resulting wage levels. Too many classes make writing definitions almost impossible.

The Point System   The greatest number of job evaluation plans use the **point system.** It is the most frequently used because it is more sophisticated than ranking and classification systems and it is relatively easy to use.

Essentially, the point system requires evaluators to quantify the value of the elements of a job. On the basis of the job description or interviews with job occupants, points are assigned to the degree of various compensable factors required to do the job. For example, points are assigned based on skill required, physical and mental effort needed, degree of dangerous or unpleasant working conditions involved, and amount of responsibility involved in the job. When these are summed, the job has been evaluated.

Many point systems evaluate as many as 10 aspects or subaspects of each job. The aspects chosen should not overlap, should distinguish real differences between jobs, should be as objectively defined as possible, and should be understood by and acceptable to both management and employees. Because all aspects are not of equal importance in all jobs, different weights reflecting the relative importance of these aspects to a job must be set. These weights are assigned by summing the judgments of several independent but knowledgeable evaluators. Thus, a clerical job might result in the following weightings: education required, 50 percent; experience required, 25 percent; complexity of job, 12 percent; responsibility for relationships with others, 8 percent; working conditions and physical requirements, 5 percent.

Once the weights are agreed upon, reference to a point manual is appropriate. Experience required by jobs varies, as does education. A point manual carefully

EXHIBIT 10-10   Evaluation Points for Insurance Clerical Job (500-point system)

Factor	Weight	Degrees				
		1st	2nd	3rd	4th	5th
1. Education	50%	50	100	150	200	250
2. Experience	25	25	50	70	100	125
3. Complexity of job	12	12	24	36	48	60
4. Relationships with others	8	8	24	40		
5. Working conditions	5	10	15	20	25	

defines degrees of points from first (lowest) to fifth, for example. Experience might be defined in this way:

First degree, up to and including three months	25 points
Second degree, more than three months but less than six	50 points
Third degree, more than six months to one year	75 points
Fourth degree, more than one year and up to three years	100 points
Fifth degree, more than three years	125 points

These definitions must be clearly defined and measurable to ensure consistency in ratings of requirements from the job description to the job evaluation. The preliminary point manuals must be pretested prior to widespread use.

As displayed in Exhibit 10–10, factor 1, education, has five degrees, as do factors 2 and 3. On the other hand, factor 4 has three degrees, while factor 5 has four degrees. The maximum number of points is calculated by multiplying the points in the system by the assigned weights. For education, the maximum points would be 250 (50 percent weight multiplied by 500 maximum points).

An advantage of the point system is that it can be easily interpreted and explained to employees. On the other hand, it is a time-consuming process to develop a point system.

Factor Comparison   The **factor comparison method** was originated by Eugene Benge. Like the point system, it permits the job evaluation process to be done on a factor-by-factor basis. It differs from the point method in that jobs are evaluated or compared against a "benchmark" of key points. A factor comparison scale, instead of a point scale, is used. Five universal job factors used to compare jobs are:

. Responsibilities. The money, human resource, records, and supervisor responsibilities of the job.
. Skill. The facility in muscular coordination and training in the interpretation of sensory requirements.
. Physical effort. The sitting, standing, walking, lifting, moving, and so on.
. Mental efforts. The intelligence, problem solving, reasoning, and imagination.
. Working conditions. The environmental factors such as noise, ventilation, hours, heat, hazards, fumes, and cleanliness.

The evaluation committee follows six formal steps in examining jobs. First, the comparison factors are selected and defined. The five universal job factors will be used in working through an example. Factors, of course, could differ across execu-

---

EXHIBIT 10-11   Ranking Four Benchmark Jobs by Factors

	Factors				
Jobs	Responsibility	Skill	Physical Effort	Mental Effort	Working Conditions
Tool and die maker	2*	1	2	2	3
Shipping clerk	4	2	1	4	4
Systems analyst	1	4	4	1	2
Secretary	3	3	3	3	1

*1 is high, 4 is low. For working conditions, the higher the rating the poorer the conditions.

EXHIBIT 10-12   Apportionment of Wages to Benchmark Jobs

		Factors				
Jobs	Hourly Wage	= Responsibility +	Skill +	Physical Effort +	Mental Effort +	Working Conditions
Tool and die maker	$8.40	$2.00 (2)*	$2.50 (1)	$1.60 (2)	$1.50 (2)	$.80 (3)
Shipping clerk	5.80	.60 (4)	1.90 (2)	1.80 (1)	.60 (4)	.90 (4)
Systems analyst	7.10	2.30 (1)	1.10 (4)	1.20 (4)	1.90 (1)	.60 (2)
Secretary	5.00	1.00 (3)	1.50 (3)	1.30 (3)	1.00 (3)	.20 (1)

* The job ranking on each factor is shown in parentheses after the wage proportion.

---

tive, supervisory, and operating employee jobs. Second, the benchmark or key jobs are selected. These are common jobs found in the firm's labor market. Often a committee is used to select from 10 to 20 benchmark jobs. Third, the evaluators rank the key jobs on each of the compensation factors. The ranking is based on job descriptions and job specifications. Four benchmark jobs for the Moser Manufacturing Company of Tulsa, Oklahoma, are presented in Exhibit 10–11.

Fourth, job evaluators allocate a part of each key job's wage rate to each job factor. Moser Manufacturing's apportionment of wages to benchmark jobs is shown in Exhibit 10–12. The proportion of each wage assigned to the different critical factors depends on the importance of the factor. Each evaluator first makes an independent decision. Then the committee or group of evaluators meets to arrive at an apportionment consensus about assigning money values to the factors.

Fifth, the two sets of ratings (the ranking and assigned wage), are compared to determine the evaluator's consistency. Exhibit 10–13 displays this consistency of rating comparisons at Moser.

Sixth, a job comparison chart displays the benchmark jobs and the money values each job receives for each factor. The chart is used to rate other jobs as compared to the benchmark jobs. These jobs would be placed in an appropriate position in the chart. Exhibit 10–14 shows the Moser job comparison chart.

The factor comparison method has some advantages and disadvantages. One advantage is that it is a step-by-step formal method of evaluation. Furthermore, it permits you to see how the differences in factor rankings translate into dollars and

EXHIBIT 10-13   Rand versus Wage Comparisons

	Factors									
Jobs	Responsibility		Skill		Physical Effort		Mental Effort		Working Conditions*	
	R†	$‡	R	$	R	$	R	$	R	$
Tool and die maker	2	2	1	1	2	2	2	2	3	3
Shipping clerk	4	4	2	2	1	1	4	4	4	4
Tool and die maker	2	2	1	1	2	2	2	2	3	3
Systems analyst	1	1	4	4	4	4	1	1	2	2
Secretary	3	3	3	3	3	3	3	3	1	1

* Note that working conditions is reversed — poorer conditions receive more money.
† Rankings.
‡ Wage amounts.

EXHIBIT 10-14   Moser Job Comparison Chart

Money Amounts	Responsibility	Skill	Physical Effort	Mental Effort	Working Conditions
$2.50		Tool and die maker			
	Systems analyst				
2.00	Tool and die maker				
		Shipping clerk		Systems analyst	
			Shipping Tool and die maker		
1.50		Secretary		Tool and die maker	
			Secretary Systems analyst		
1.00	Secretary	Systems analyst		Secretary	
					Shipping clerk Tool and die maker
0.50	Shipping clerk			Shipping clerk	Systems analyst Secretary

cents. Probably the most negative aspect of the factor comparison method is its complexity. Although the method is easy to explain to subordinates, it is difficult to show them how such a system is developed. There is also the issue of subjectivity. Despite the systematic nature of the factor comparison method, it still relies on a committee or a group of evaluators' subjective judgment. Of course, subjectivity is also a problem with each of the other job evaluation methods.

Pay Classes, Rate Ranges, and Classifications

After completion of the job evaluation, the pay-structure process is completed by establishing pay classes, rate ranges, and job classifications.[57] A **pay class** (also called a **pay grade**) is a grouping of a variety of jobs that are similar in terms of work difficulty and responsibility. If an organization uses the factor comparison or point system of job evaluation, this is accomplished by use of pay-class graphs or point

---

EXHIBIT 10-15   Pay Classes and Pay Curve

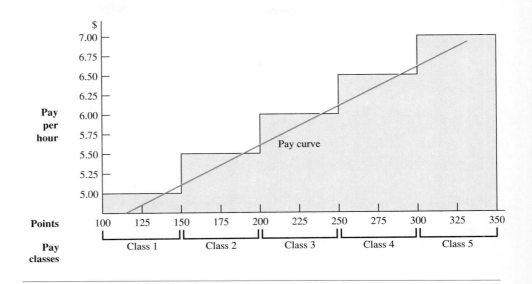

conversion tables. An example of a pay-class graph used by Dexter Electronics is given in Exhibit 10–15.

At intervals of say 50 points, a new pay class is marked off. The pay curve illustrated in Exhibit 10–15 is based on information obtained from wage and salary surveys and modified as necessary to reflect Dexter's policy to pay at, above, or below prevailing rates. This exhibit shows a single-rate pay system rather than a rate-range system in that all jobs within a given labor class will receive the same rate of pay. In this example, pay classes are determined by the point value that is determined through a point system method of job evaluation.

Exhibit 10–16, another pay-class graph, demonstrates how wage and salary survey data are combined with job evaluation information to determine the pay structure for an organization. A compensation trend line is derived by first establishing the general pay pattern, plotting the surveyed rates of key jobs against the point value of these jobs. The trend line can then be determined by a variety of methods, ranging from a simple eyeball estimate of the pay trend to a formalized statistical formulation of a regression line based on the sum of the least squares method. The appropriate pay rate for any job can then be ascertained by calculating the point value of the job and observing the pay level for that value as shown by the trend line. By taking a set percentage (example, 15 percent) above and below the trend line, minimum and maximum limit lines can be established. These limit lines can be used to help set the minimum and maximum rates if a pay range is used instead of a single rate for each job. The limit lines can also be used in place of the trend line for those organizations that wish to establish pay levels above market — the pay leaders — or those that want to pay slightly under the prevailing rates.

Although it is possible for a pay class to have a single pay rate (as in Exhibit 10–15), the more likely condition is a range of pays. These ranges can have the same spread, or the spread can be increased as the pay rate increases. An example of a pay structure with increasing rate ranges is given in Exhibit 10–16. The ranges are

EXHIBIT 10-16   Pay-Class Graph with Range of Pay

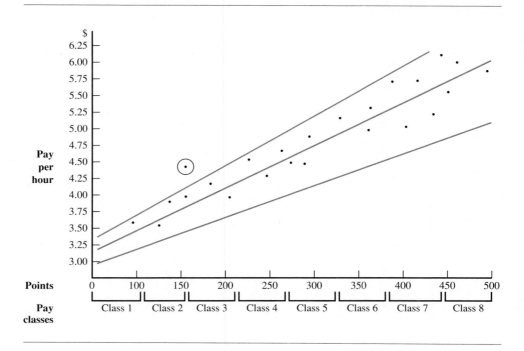

usually divided into a series of steps. Thus, within Class 4 (250–300 points), there might be four steps:

	Pay Range
Step 1	$4.20–4.40
Step 2	4.40–4.60
Step 3	4.60–4.85
Step 4	4.85–5.10

These steps in effect are money raises within a pay range to help take care of the needs of individual pay determination (to be discussed in Chapter 11). Similar ranges would ordinarily be determined for all other classes to illustrate the pay structure for all jobs in the pay plan. Within-grade increases are typically based upon seniority, merit, or a combination of both, as described in the next chapter.

The entire pay structure should be evaluated periodically and adjusted to reflect changes in labor market conditions, level of inflation, and other factors affecting pay. Although the typical structure is shown as linear, generally a more fair structure is curvilinear, with rates increasing exponentially as pay increases.

In Exhibit 10–16, the pay rate for a set of class 2 jobs is well above the maximum limit line, as shown by the ⊙ symbol. These jobs are paid too much relative to other jobs in the firm. These types of jobs are called **red circle** jobs or *overrated*.[58] Management has several methods that can be used with overpaid red circle jobs. One is to freeze the pay to individuals in jobs with the red circle rates until pay increases in the other jobs bring them in line. Second, transferring or promoting

CAREER CHALLENGE
(concluded)

Mary sat at her desk a few days later. She thought over the problems the bank was facing again. She had spent weeks learning about pay surveys, job evaluation, pay classifications, rate ranges — all the aspects of pay-level and pay-structure decisions. CNB had done nothing about any of these issues. How could they keep employees without much attention to pay practices?

As Mary wondered about these issues, she had the report she'd prepared for her HRM class before her. It compared the turnover rates and absenteeism at CNB to those of other banks like it in the Pittsburgh area. CNB was clearly in the worst shape.

She had interviewed supervisors and others who had talked with employees leaving CNB. A large number gave better pay as the reason for leaving. And even more often, fairness in treatment of pay was the reason given. She'd passed her report on to Guido. But would anything happen other than receiving a grade in class for her report?

Guido called Mary the next day to go over her findings. She decided to use her term report to illustrate possible solutions for CNB's dilemma.

Guido I've read your paper. I like the way it deals with the problems here at CNB. It was a good idea to calculate how much turnover costs the bank. This may have an impact on Joe. You've also prepared recommendations for changes in our pay program, as I asked you to do. Let me see if I understand your plan. Basically, you propose setting up a point system of job evaluation and establishing standardized pay classes and ranges that would allow for pay variations based on individual pay factors. You also recommend that we set up a pay policy according to going wages. In view of our profit picture, that seems reasonable. I'll present this plan to Poppa Joe tomorrow, with my endorsement.

Mary I'll be interested to see if it has any impact.

The next day Guido gave the report to Joe to read and comment on.

(This case will be continued in Chapter 11.)

---

employees in red circle jobs so that their rate of pay can be justified may be possible.[59] Third, the rate may have to be cut back to the maximum level for the job class. The pay-class graph can illustrate red circle jobs, but solving the problems associated with them is a challenging task for managers and compensation experts.

INDIVIDUAL PAY DETERMINATION

This chapter has begun the discussion of compensation. The objectives of compensation have been stated, and premises dealing with the multiple meanings of pay at work, external and internal factors influencing compensation, pay levels, pay surveys, and pay structures and their determination have been covered. At this point, the compensation analyst has information on comparable pay levels of competitors and the surrounding area and a system to evaluate jobs so that differentials between job descriptions can be established.

It is important to mention at this point that another decision must be made before the compensation analyst can complete the job of building an effective, efficient pay system. How does he or she determine what two people doing the same job, for example, computer programmer, should make? Should all computer programmers be paid the same? If not, on what basis should the differential in pay rest? The decision is called *individual pay determination*. These questions will be answered in Chapter 11.

SUMMARY

The major points covered in Chapter 10 are:

1. Compensation is the HRM function that deals with every type of reward that individuals receive in return for performing organizational tasks — wages, salaries, bonuses, commissions, benefits, and nonfinancial rewards like praise.
2. The objective of the compensation function is to create a system of rewards that is equitable to the employer and employee alike.
3. Compensation should be adequate, equitable, cost effective, secure, incentive-providing, and acceptable to the employee.
4. Compensation decisions are the joint responsibility of operating executives, supervisors, and HR specialists.
5. One of the most significant factors affecting compensation systems is the nature of the individual employee.
6. Effective compensation administration is desirable in efforts to increase employee satisfaction and employee productivity.
7. External influences on compensation systems include the government, unions, economic conditions, and the nature of the labor market.
8. Internal influences on compensation systems include the labor budget, goals of controlling interests, and managerial pay strategies (high, low, and comparable).
9. The pay-level decision involves comparing the firm's pay to multiple factors outside it. The pay survey is the tool used to help make this decision.
10. The pay-structure decision involves comparing jobs within the organization to each other to determine their relative worth.
11. Determining the worth of a job is difficult because it involves measurement and subjective decisions. Using systematic job evaluation procedures is recommended for determining a job's worth.
12. The four most widely used methods of job evaluation are job ranking, classification, the point method, and factor comparison.
13. Most managers group similar jobs into pay classes or rate ranges.
14. The wage curve (or line) illustrates the average target wage for each pay class.

KEY TERMS

QUESTIONS FOR REVIEW AND DISCUSSION

1. What is compensation? How can it be characterized as an exchange relationship?
2. What is the difference between direct and indirect financial compensation?
3. What are the objectives of the compensation function?
4. Pay for each individual in the United States is set relative to three groups. Name them and explain why each is important.
5. What is pay satisfaction? Why is it so difficult to measure and to relate it to a compensation system?
6. How would you go about creating a realistic, equitable performance-based pay system?
7. Discuss the major laws affecting compensation. How does each affect the compensation decisions?
8. What is the difference between equal pay and comparable worth? Why are these concepts so important?
9. Justify the need to consider the union as an external influence on pay for both unionized and nonunionized firms.
10. Name and explain briefly the international issues that affect compensation strategies.
11. Differentiate between the high, low, and comparable pay-level strategies.
12. Discuss sources of pay surveys and how they are conducted and used to make the pay-level decision.
13. Define the pay-structure decision. What is job evaluation and how does it help managers make the pay-structure decision?
14. Name and discuss four techniques of job evaluation. Include advantages and disadvantages of each.
15. Distinguish among and describe the interrelationships among pay classes, rate ranges, and pay classifications. What is a red circle job?

NOTES

[1] William J. Heisler, W. David Jones, and Philip O. Barnham, Jr. (1988), *Managing Human Resources Issues: Confronting Challenges and Choosing Options* (San Francisco: Jossey-Bass).

[2] Thomas Patton (1977), *Pay* (New York: Free Press).

[3] Graef S. Cyrstal (March 2, 1981), "Pay for Performance—Even If It's Just Luck," *The Wall Street Journal*, p. 16.

[4] Marc J. Wallace, Jr., and Charles H. Fay (1988), *Compensation Theory and Practice, 2nd ed.* (Boston: PWS-Kent Publishing).

[5] E. E. Lawler (1981), *Pay and Development* (Reading, Mass.: Addison-Wesley Publishing).

[6] George Milkovich and Jerry M. Newman (1990), *Compensation* (Plano, Tex.: Business Publications).

[7] James N. Finch (October 1988), "Computers Help Link Performance to Pay," *Personnel Journal*, pp. 120–26.

[8] Lawler, *Pay and Development*.

[9] Herbert Meyer (Winter 1975), "The Pay for Performance Dilemma," *Organizational Dynamics*, pp. 39–50.

[10] Andrew G. Spohn (Winter 1990), "The Relationship of Reward Systems and Employee Performance," *Compensation and Benefits Management* 6, pp. 128–32.

[11] Victoria A. Hoevemeyer (July 1989), "Performance-Based Compensation: Miracle or Waste?" *Personnel Journal*, pp. 64–68.

[12] Ibid.

[13] Ibid.

[14] Meyer, "The Pay for Performance Dilemma."

[15] William L. Milhal (October 1983), "More Research Is Needed: Goals May Motivate Better," *Personnel Administrator*, pp. 60–68.

[16] Robert P. Gandossy (October 1988), "Change Pay for Performance without Resistance," *Personnel Journal*, pp. 127–31.

[17] Finch, "Computers Help Link Performance to Pay."

[18] Steven E. Haugen and Earl F. Mellor (January 1990), "Estimating the Number of Minimum Wage Workers," *Monthly Labor Review* 113, no. 1, pp. 70–74.

[19] Ronald B. Mincy (July 1990), "Raising the Minimum Wage: Effects on Family Poverty," *Monthly Labor Review*, pp. 18–25.

[20] A Description of exemption is found in the U.S. Department of Labor (1973), Executive Administration, Professional and Outside Salesmen Exemption (Washington, D.C.: U.S. Government Printing Office).

[21] Robert M. Pattison (September 1987), "Fine Tuning Wage and Hour Practices," *Personnel Journal*, pp. 166–69.

[22] Michael W. Horrigan and James P. Markey (July 1990), "Recent Gains in Women's Earnings: Better Pay or Longer Hours?" *Monthly Labor Review*, pp. 11–17.

[23] Bickley Townsend and Kathleen O'Neil (August 1990), "American Women Get Mad," *American Demographics*, pp. 26–29, 32.

[24] Vida Gulbinas Scarpello and James Ledvinka (1988), *Personnel/Human Resource Management* (Boston: PWS-Kent Publishing, p. 363).

[25] Horrigan and Markey, "Recent Gains in Women's Earnings."

[26] Heisler et al., *Managing Human Resources Issues*.

[27] Barry Gerhart (April 1990), "Gender Differences in Current and Starting Salaries: The Role of Performance, College Major, and Job Title," *Industrial and Labor Relations Review* 43, pp. 418–33.

[28] Claudia E. Wayne (Winter 1990), "Pay Equity: An Issue Whose Time Has Come," *Compensation & Benefits Management* 6, pp. 117–20.

[29] Heisler et al., *Managing Human Resources Issues*, p. 77.

[30] Michael F. Carter (October 1981), "Comparable Worth: An Idea Whose Time Has Come?" *Personnel Journal*, pp. 792–94.

[31] Robert Buchele and Mark Aldrich (Summer 1985), "How Much Difference Would Comparable Worth Make?" *Industrial Relations pp. 222-33.*

[32] James T. Brinks (November 1981), "The Comparable Worth Issue: A Salary Administration Bombshell," *Personnel Administrator*, pp. 37–40; and Richard J. Schonberger and Harry W. Hennessey, Jr. (December 1981) "Is Equal Pay for Comparable Work Fair?" *Personnel Journal*, pp. 964–68.

[33] E. James Brennan (August 1984), "Why Laws Have Failed to End Pay Discrimination," *Personnel Journal*, p. 20.

[34] Benson Rosen, Sara Rynes, and Thomas A. Mahoney (July-August 1983), "Compensation, Jobs, and Gender," *Harvard Business Review*, p. 170; and Carter, "Comparable Worth," p. 793.

[35] Wayne, "Pay Equity"

[36] Sanford M. Jacoby and Daniel J. B. Mitchell (1988), "Measurement of Compensation: Union and Non-Union," *Industrial Relations* 27, no. 2, pp. 215–31.

[37] Wallace and Fay, *Compensation Theory and Practice*, pp. 148–50.

[38] Ibid., p. 150.

[39] Peter Cappeli (May 1984), "What Do Unions Get in Return for Concessions?" *Monthly Labor Review*, pp. 40–41

[40] William T. Dickens and Kevin Lang (April 1986), "Labor Market Segmentation and the Union Wage Premium," NBER Working Paper 1883 (Cambridge, Mass.).

[41] Frank Swoboda (September 9, 1990), "Smoothing the Way to Hiring Seniors," *Washington Post*, p. H3.

[42] John Parry and Mead Jennings (May 1990), "Hunting Heads in the Global Village," *International Management*, pp. 52–54.

[43] Spencer Hayden, (August 1990), "Our Foreign Legions Are Faltering," *Personnel*, pp. 40–44.

[44] Peter Van Pelt and Natalia Wolniansky (July 1990), "The High Cost of Expatriation," *Management Review* 79, no. 7, pp. 40–41.

[45] Milkovich and Newman, *Compensation*.

[46] William A. Schiemann (Winter 1990), "Do as I Pay, Not as I Say: Reaching Strategic Organizational and Employee Goals through Effective Compensation Policies," *Compensation & Benefits Management* 6, no. 2, pp. 121–27.

[47] Robert C. Ochsner (Winter 1990), "Strategic Compensation — Winning Strategies for the Nineties, Part I," *Compensation & Benefits Management*, 6, no. 2, pp. 172–73.

[48] Joseph E. McKendrick, Jr. (March-April 1990), "Salary Surveys: Roadmaps for the Volatile Employment Scene of the 1990s," *Management World* 19, no. 2, pp. 18–20.

[49] Margaret Dyekman (June 1990), "Take the Mystery out of Salary Surveys," *Personnel Journal* 69, no. 6, pp. 104–6.

[50] Dyekman, "Take the Mystery Out of Salary Surveys," p. 105.

[51] D. W. Belcher, N. Bruce Ferris and John O'Neill (September-October 1985), "How Wage Surveys Are Being Used," *Compensation and Benefits Review*, pp. 34–51.

[52] Gary D. Fisher (April 1985), "Salary Surveys — An Antitrust Perspective," *Personnel Administrator*, pp. 87–97, 154.

[53] Milkovich and Newman, *Compensation*, p. 161.

[54] Michael K. Mount and Rebecca A. Ellis (Spring 1987), "Investigations of In-Job Evaluation Ratings of Comparable Worth Study Participants," *Personnel Psychology*, pp. 85–96.

[55] John D. McMillan and Cynthia G. Brondi, (November 1986), "Job Evaluation" Generate the Numbers," *Personnel Journal*, pp. 56–63.

[56] Wallace and Fay, *Compensation Theory and Practice*, p. 206–7.

[57] Milkovich and Newman, *Compensation*.

[58] Jobs can also be underrated and underpaid. They would be red circled or, as found in the Dexter Company, they are green circled, which indicates an underrated level.

[59] Paul R. Reed and Mark J. Kroll (February 1987), "Red-Circle Employees: A Wage Scale Dilemma," *Personnel Journal*, pp. 92–95.

APPLICATION CASE 9–1   The Comparable Worth Debate

· · · · ·

Twin Oaks Hospital is a privately owned facility that serves Lexington, Colorado (population approximately 250,000). The 100-bed hospital has a staff of 350 employees, including over 200 nurses and 40 clerical and secretarial employees (an almost exclusively female group). In the last month, discontent concerning pay levels has been mounting among the hospital's nurses and secretarial/clerical employees. Discontent was spurred by recent developments at the Lexington Memorial Hospital, a public facility. There, the hospital administration agreed to demands by nurses and secretarial/clerical workers for a 5 percent pay increase. The administration further agreed to launch a job evaluation program that would evaluate the nursing and secretarial/clerical jobs on the basis of comparable worth. The administrators pledged that the study's findings would be used as the basis for any further pay adjustments.

The administration's moves came after demonstrations by nurses and clerical/secretarial workers and by a clear threat of unionization by the Union of American Nurses and the United Office Workers. Union organizers had held discussions with the nurses and office employees, and circulated the results of one comparable worth study to illustrate the extent of pay inequities (shown in Exhibit 1).

David Hardy, director of personnel at Twin Oaks, was acutely aware of the troubles brewing at his hospital. He knew that union organizers were meeting with employees and distributing the study flier. Overall, Twin Oaks' pay levels for its nurses and office staff were very similar to the levels at Lexington Memorial before the 5 percent increase. However, the levels were not competitive with compensation available in Denver, which is located about 100 miles north of Lexington. In the last week, Hardy had met with representatives of the two employee groups at their request. There, the spokeswomen made three requests: an immediate 5 percent pay increase, the establishment of a job evaluation program based on the concept of comparable worth, and a pledge to make wage adjustments based on study findings.

Hardy informed James Bledsoe, the hospital director, of the employees' requests; Bledsoe asked for a recommendation for action within three days. Before developing an action plan, Hardy met with his two top aides (Janet Sawyer and Charles Cooper) for an initial, informal discussion of the situation. In Hardy's view, the key question focused on whether to evaluate the jobs based on comparable worth.

"I favor launching the job evaluation program," said Janet Sawyer. "Nationwide, there is a disturbingly large gap between the pay levels of predominantly male and female jobs. Consider that there's no difference in the median education levels of men and women — about 12.6 years. Yet with the same median amount of education, women on the average earn 40.8 percent of a man's median pay. If we take a close look at our compensation levels across jobs from the perspective of comparable worth, we'd likely find some pretty disturbing gaps of our own.

"There's a growing precedent for comparable worth–based pay adjustments," she continued. "Over 30 states have comparable worth bills pending or commissions that are studying the issue. Minnesota has had comparable worth–based pay policies for its employees since 1983, and several city governments have implemented the concept."

"That's precedent in the public sector, not private industry," said Charles Cooper. "I would favor a pay increase, perhaps 5 percent, to keep us competitive with Lexington Memorial. However, agreeing to a job evaluation based on comparable worth is opening the door to a very questionable and costly concept.

"I'm troubled by the concept of comparable worth for three reasons," he continued. "First, if you implement comparable worth, you destroy our free market system. The market does discriminate but on the basis of supply and demand, which

Written by Kim Stewart. The situation, names, and characters are fictitious. Facts and some perspectives are drawn from: Peter B. Olney, Jr. (March-April 1987), "Meeting the Challenge of Comparable Worth: Part I," "*Compensation and Benefits Review*, pp. 34–44; Barbara R. Bergmann (May-June 1987), "Pay Equity — Surprising Answers to Hard Questions," *Challenge*, pp. 45–51; and Daniel Seligman (May 14, 1984), "Pay Equity is a Bad Idea," *Fortune*, pp. 133ff.

EXHIBIT 1   Findings from One Comparable Worth Study

	Head Nurse	Electrician	Clerk/Typist	Truck Driver
Knowledge and Skills	244 RN license; good judgment; people skills	122 Apprenticeship; technical know-how	106 High school diploma; type 60 wpm	61 Chauffeur's license
Mental Demands	106 Life-and death decisions; administer doctors' orders'; emotional stability	30 Troubleshooting; public safety	26 Always told what to do; pressure to get work done; monotony	10 Heavy traffic; speed limits
Responsibility	122 Supervise patient care; manage ward staff	30 Order supplies; safe wiring	35 Neat documents; manage small tasks	13 Truck maintenance; on-time deliveries
Working Conditions	11 Always on feet; constant demands; rotating shifts	15 Cramped quarters; strenuous assignments; fairly dangerous	0 Padded seat; constant interruptions; regular hours	13 Crazy schedule; tight space, long hours
Total Points	483	197	167	97
Monthly Salary	$2,390	$2,047	$1,264	$1,670

accurately reflects a job's worth. The market is blind to gender."

"I'm not so sure about its visual shortcomings in that regard," Janet said.

"I agree with Janet that a sizable wage gap does exist," Charles continued. "But according to some studies, much of that gap is not due to gender. For example, I've just reviewed a study by the U.S. Labor Department that found that over 50 percent of the gap between men's and women's pay is due to vocational training, the industries that women choose, and geographical location. The remaining gap could be due to sex discrimination, but frankly I'm not willing to destroy the free market system to find out.

"Second, there's the issue of implementation," Charles continued. "Here, comparable worth floats in a sea of subjectivity. If we conduct the evaluation, we must evaluate all jobs in the hospital, not just the nurses, secretaries, and clerical workers.

Doing so requires one evaluaton system with one set of job factors. Which factors do we use? How do we weigh the factors in calculating a job's worth? Few objective guidelines exist for us to use.

"And suppose we did implement comparable worth," he continued. "We might create internal pay equity across our jobs but it would not address our need to be externally competitive. For example, suppose we determine that two jobs are very similar in worth, almost identical. Using comparable worth as a basis, we provide the same pay for both jobs. However, marketwise we're paying far too much for one job and far too little for another. How do we attract people for the underpaid position? We end up with too many applicants for jobs already filled and not enough for jobs that go unfilled.

"Third, there's our primary concern — costs. We won't know how much comparable worth will cost us until we're into the evaluation program. However, given adjustments made in clerical and secretarial pay by government offices that have implemented comparable worth, the cost should be hefty. Look at the estimated price tag for implementing comparable worth nationwide — over $150 billion. Business and society would pay the bill via inflation and lowered productivity.''

"We could conduct an effective job evaluation program — other companies have,'' Janet countered. "General Electric has overhauled its job evaluation methods to reflect comparable worth concerns. BankAmerica has also made some changes; it's incorporated job factors into predominantly female jobs that weren't there before such as physical demands for computer VDT operators and bank tellers. We could also talk with Lexington Memorial about how they plan to conduct their job evaluation program.

"I'd suggest that we develop a job evaluation plan that's tailor-made for our hospital,'' Janet continued. "We could form a committee composed of 6 to 10 members with representatives from all functional areas. The committee would be charged with identifying the elements that should be considered in evaluating all jobs in the hospital. It would also determine the weights for all factors. For some factors such as knowledge and experience, accountability and judgment would be more difficult. But we could do it; others have.''

"What about costs?" David Hardy asked.

"Charles is right,'' Janet replied. "We won't really know until the evaluation task is complete. But as a very rough estimate, I'd say we would be raising the nursing and office workers' pay by at least 10 percent, probably more. However, we can phase in the increase over a number of years, a bit at a time.''

"What happens if the evaluation determines that some male-dominated jobs are overpaid?" asked Charles. "Do we reduce their pay while boosting the women's? Threat of unionization is a factor in regard to the nurses and clerical staff. What about the possibility of male employees unionizing because of pay cuts?''

"We'd have to address that question,'' Janet replied. "But given that most of our staff are women, overall our employees would be benefiting from comparable worth.''

"You know, I've heard a lot about women benefiting from comparable worth,'' said David Hardy. "But over the long term, I'm not so sure. It seems to me that if the concept is implemented nationwide, companies will have a higher wage bill with no increase in productivity. So they may pay the bill by reducing the number of jobs with the highest wage increases — jobs that women hold. Many women may find themselves out of work.''

"That might be,'' Janet said. "However, that hasn't happened in countries like Australia and Great Britain that have actively closed much of the gender-based wage gap in recent years.''

"Any other thoughts?" asked David.

"We should take a good look at a pay increase and perhaps even more than the 5 percent requested,'' Charles said. "But stay away from comparable worth. For private business, it is unchartered and dangerous territory.''

"This whole situation has raised questions in my mind about the fairness and validity of our pay structure,'' Janet said. "We may have problems. Let's look at it; and let's consider comparable worth. We may not be able to go the full 90 yards. How about a first few steps?''

Discussion Questions

1. In your view, is comparable worth a legitimate strategy for determining job compensation?

2. As the director of Twin Oaks' HR department, what recommendations would you make to James Bledsoe?

3. From an HRM perspective, what are the challenges of implementing comparable worth?

COMPENSATION: INDIVIDUAL PAY METHODS AND POLICIES

· · · · · · ·

LEARNING OBJECTIVES

———◦———

After studying this chapter, you should be able to:

· · ·

Understand how the individual pay determination decision is made

· · ·

Describe the distinct features of individual, group, and organizationwide incentive plans

· · ·

Define skill-based pay and contrast it to other pay techniques

· · ·

Understand on what basis executives in the United States and in the international marketplace are compensated

· · ·

Understand the pay administration issues of pay secrecy, pay compression, pay security, and two-tiered wage systems

CAREER CHALLENGE

*J*oe Paderewski sat in his big office in the rear of the Cardeson National Bank. Guido Panelli, his executive vice president, came in to drop off Mary Renfro's report on compensation, and to discuss other problems CNB was having with people and pay.

"For one thing, Joe, our executive turnover has been increasing. Mary is wondering if the executive compensation package is contributing to the problem. The employees who have quit have indicated a lack of adequate compensation, but we all know this is the most acceptable reason to give an employer for leaving. In any case, it's a problem, and we have to face it."

"CNB pays the going rate for salaries," Joe declared. "And there's our bonus system — when profits allow it."

"But some of those leaving said their new employers would have performance-share programs," Guido said.

Joe wondered what that meant, and he thought, "Maybe I should hire a consultant to advise us on the executive compensation program."

Meanwhile, over at Branch 1, Tom Nichols, the manager of the branch, was having a meeting with the tellers' supervisors to discuss pay. He hadn't wanted to attend the meeting; he didn't like meetings, and he knew this one would be bad. The tellers were never satisfied with their pay. Back in school, Tom had learned that pay was one thing that was never easily settled; people were always griping about it.

The meeting went like this:

Chet Tom, we're here because the troops are unhappy.

Tom The troops are always unhappy.

Chet Sure, but this time it's serious. My people are tired of punching time clocks and getting paid by the hour. Everyone else here at the bank gets salaries — 52 weeks a year. Why don't my tellers?

Tom Well, you know, it's always been done that way. Besides . . .

Chet Don't give me that "it's-always-been-done-that-way" stuff. You can do something about it. Talk to Joe. My people want the security of a regular paycheck and the dignity of no time clock. You know the union's been around. What are we going to do about it?

The other supervisors shook their heads, and Tom didn't know what to say.

Branch 2 was having its own problems. One day there was an incident involving two tellers and a supervisor. It all started when the following dialogue took place:

Martha Did you hear that Joanne makes $1.50 more an hour than me? I've been here longer than she has.

Sandra Why not go to June about it? She's the boss.

Martha (to June) How come Joanne makes $1.50 more than me? I've been here longer.

June How do you know that's true? We don't reveal salaries around here, and it's against company policy to discuss other people's pay.

Martha Never mind how I found out. And let's cut the company policy stuff. Why is Joanne paid more than I am?

It is now raise time again, and Joe is getting flak from all sides. He believes he can afford about 10 percent for raises. But who should get them?

After Guido left his office, Joe went over the situation in his mind. "Some deserve no raise, really," he thought. "Others deserve something; a few deserve a lot. But how should I divide the money? Should I really give no raise at all to some? With inflation what it is, that's like getting a pay cut, and they don't deserve *that*. And how much should the *average* employee get? The cost of living has gone up 7 percent. If I give them much more than that, there won't be enough to give big raises to the people who really deserve them, like Mary and Guido. And that says

(continued on next page)

389

CAREER CHALLENGE

(continued)

nothing about the people who deserve raises because, as Mary keeps saying, their base pay is too low, and what about the people who are being promoted? How am I going to allocate this raise money?''

After thinking it over, Joe decided to talk to Mary about the problems and her report. He asked her to come in and give him a brief summary of some of the major points about compensation she learned in the college course she had taken.

Joe Mary, I'm having problems with pay again, as you know. Will you give me a rundown on some of

the highlights of that course you took? I don't have a lot of time, though. That's why I'd rather have you tell me than read your report.

Mary I know you don't have much time. Let's cover some basics that we haven't discussed already.

With that, Mary briefed Joe on pay methods, executive compensation, and some key compensation issues raised in the incidents she and Guido had told him about.

L et's pick up where we ended in Chapter 10 and complete the discussion of the seven criteria for effective compensation introduced there. A compensation system that meets all these criteria will accomplish the objective of providing a system of rewards equitable to employer and employee alike, so that the employee's satisfaction and production are both heightened. As was discussed, an effective compensation system should be:

Adequate. Chapter 10 gave the legal definition of adequacy as set forth in minimum wage and other legislation. The managerial definition of adequacy, or pay-level policies designed to pay the going wage, was also described.

Equitable. Chapter 10 discussed job evaluation as one technique to be used to attain equity. The present chapter will touch upon the related policy issue of whether all employees should be paid salaries.

Incentive-providing. Chapter 10 discussed the theory behind the merit or incentive pay system. This chapter will discuss how incentive pay systems are designed and how raises are used as a form of incentive.

The other four criteria, which will be discussed primarily in this chapter, state that the compensation plan should be:

Secure. The extent to which the employee's pay seems adequate to satisfy basic needs.

Balanced. The extent to which pay is a reasonable part of the total reward package, which includes benefits, promotions, and so on. Chapter 12 discusses benefits.

Cost-effective. The extent to which the pay system is cost-effective for the organization

Acceptable to the employee. Whether employees think the pay system makes sense. Three aspects of this will be discussed: whether pay should be secret; compensation communication to achieve acceptability; and employee participation in pay decision making.

To the individual employee, the most important compensation decision is how much he or she will earn. This chapter presents various approaches to answering this question of *individual pay determination*. It also looks at the compensation of special groups such as executives and compensation administration issues such as pay secrecy.

INDIVIDUAL PAY DETERMINATION

Two issues need to be addressed to make the individual pay determination decision. First, the compensation specialist must answer these questions: How should one employee be paid relative to another when they both hold the same job in the organization? Should I pay all employees doing the same work at the same level the same? Secondly, if not, on what basis should I make the distinction — seniority or merit? Most employers do pay different rates to employees performing the same job.[1] Pay differentials are based on the following:

1. Individual differences in experience, skills, and performance.
2. Expectations that longer seniority and/or higher performance deserve higher pay.

Reasons for choosing to pay employees at different rates for the same job include:[2]

1. Pay differentials allow firms to recognize that different employees performing the same job make substantially different contributions to meeting organizational goals.
2. Differentials allow employers to communicate a changed emphasis on important job roles.
3. Differentials provide organizations with an important tool for emphasizing enterprise norms without having employees change jobs, that is, promotion.
4. Without differentials, the pay system violates the internal equity norms of most employees, reducing pay satisfaction and making attraction and retention of employees more difficult.
5. Pay differentials allow firms to recognize market changes between jobs in the same grade without requiring a major overhaul of the whole compensation system.

METHODS OF PAYMENT

Employees can be paid for the time they work, the output they produce, or a combination of these two factors.

Flat Rates[3]

In the unionized firm where wages are established by collective bargaining, single flat rates rather than different rates are often paid. For example, all Clerk Typist Is might make $6.50 per hour, regardless of seniority or performance. Flat rates correspond to some midpoint on a market survey for that job. Using a flat rate does not mean that seniority and experience do not differ. It means that employers and the union choose not to recognize these variations when setting wage rates. Unions insist on ignoring performance differentials for many reasons. They contend that performance measures are inequitable. Jobs need cooperative effort that could be destroyed by wage differentials. Sales organizations, for example, pay a flat rate for a job and add a bonus or incentive to recognize individual differences.

Choosing to pay a flat rate versus different rates for the same job depends on the objectives established by the compensation analyst. Recognizing individual differences makes the assumption that employees are not interchangeable or equally productive. By using pay differentials to recognize these differences, managers are trying to encourage an experienced, efficient, and satisfied work force.

Payment for Time Worked

Paying for time worked and establishing compensation systems based on time were the compensation methods discussed in Chapter 10. Pay surveys are used to establish competitive pay for the industry, and job evaluation is the principal method for setting time-pay schedules.[4] The majority of employees are paid for time worked in the form of wages or salaries. The difference between wage and salary is defined below:

Wage. Pay calculated at an hourly rate. Nonexempt employees who are covered by overtime and reporting provisions of the Fair Labor Standards Act are paid wages.[5]

Salary. Pay calculated at an annual or monthly rate rather than hourly. Those who are exempt from regulations of the Fair Labor Standards Act and do not receive overtime pay receive salaries.[6]

Pay ranges, pay classifications, and similar tools are developed for individual pay determination, the final step in a time-based pay system.

Salaries For Everyone?

One issue in the time-pay system is whether everyone should be paid a salary. (Tom Nichols' dilemma in dealing with hourly employees is an example.) Would you rather be paid strictly by the hour and not know your income week to week, month to month, or to be paid a salary so you could plan your budget? Or would you rather put in extra hours for no more pay? In general, most blue-collar employees are given hourly pay. However, an increasing number of employees are paid salaries, and there has been a movement to place *all* employees on salaries to give them the same benefits and working conditions others have. Firms such as IBM, Texas Instruments, Polaroid, and Avon have experimented with this plan.

One advantage claimed for this move is that blue-collar employees become more integrated into the organization, thus improving the climate of employee relations. No study claims that it improves productivity, and the report of its effects on absenteeism is mixed.[7] Some studies claim absenteeism decreases. Others have found that it increases, but management controls and peer pressure later bring it down to acceptable levels.[8]

Some individuals propose that, if all employees are paid salaries, it is possible that the long-run security of positions will be diminished. With hourly workers, if business is down, it is relatively easy for an organization to reduce the hours worked daily or weekly, save the labor costs, and adjust to the realities of the marketplace.

On the other hand, if everyone is on salary, management tends to look toward full layoffs or reduction in the labor force by attrition or terminations. *Providing salaries for everyone changes labor costs from variable to fixed with serious employment security implications.* The success of a total-salaries program requires stable, mature, responsible employees, a cooperative union, willing supervisors, and a work load that allows continuous employment.

Incentive Forms of Compensation

The methods for paying employees on the basis of output are usually referred to as incentive forms of compensation. **Incentive compensation** can be paid individually, to the work group, or on an enterprisewide basis. Incentive compensation assumes it is possible and useful to tie performance directly to pay, an issue discussed in detail in Chapter 10.

The wages and salaries of employees are typically adjusted at some point during the year. Historically, the adjustments have resulted in pay increases. Most employees expect to get at least one raise annually. When the general economy isn't healthy or in the case of increased foreign competition in some industries, employees have actually accepted decreases in pay. Employees at Ford, Uniroyal, Continental Airlines, and U.S. Steel (now USX) have given back some of their pay raises to help their firms compete and stay in business.

When pay is adjusted upward, it is usually based on four types of increases: (1) a general, across-the-board increase for all employees; (2) merit increases paid to employees based on some indicator of job performance; (3) a cost-of-living adjustment (COLA) based on the consumer price index (CPI); and (4) seniority. Typically, hourly employees in unionized firms are likely to receive general increases, whereas exempt salaried employees are more likely to receive merit pay increases.

Merit Incentives   Merit pay systems, which reward employees for past performance, have become an accepted method for rewarding good performance.[9] Traditionally, **merit pay** results in a higher base salary after the yearly performance evaluation and evenly spreads the merit increases throughout the subsequent year.[10] More than 80 percent of firms in the United States have some form of merit pay.[11] Exhibit 11–1 shows how a merit pay raise is related to performance rating at Rialto Manufacturing Company, a medium-sized firm located in Florida. The merit increase is also based on the individual's position in the salary classification. The lower the position in the range (first third), the larger the percentage of the merit increase.

EXHIBIT 11-1   Rialto Manufacturing Co. Position in Salary Classification (1989)

Employee's Performance	Bottom Third	Middle Third	Top Third
Outstanding	12–15%	9–11%	5–8%
Good	8–11	6–8	4–5
Average	4–7	4–5	2–3
Marginally satisfactory	1–3	3	1
Unsatisfactory	No increase	No increase	No increase

Merit pay advocates propose that it is the most valid type of pay increase, since it is tied directly to performance.[12] Rewarding performers, instead of marginal or nonperformers, is claimed to be a powerful motivator. However, there has been a constant decrease in the size of merit awards since 1982, causing firms to reevaluate methods of rewarding good performance.[13]

On the other hand, some individuals suggest that the validity of a merit pay system serving as an incentive rests on the quality of the performance evaluation system.[14] For example, the Civil Service Reform Act (CRSA) of 1978 was based on the premise that performance appraisals are completely valid as measures of quality. This premise was used to modify the federal merit system. However, the premise has two flawed assumptions: (1) that competence and incompetence are distributed in roughly the same percentages in a work group; and (2) that every supervisor is a competent evaluator. Merit awards in the civil service under CRSA were actually found to decrease morale.[15] Similar problems have occurred in the United Kingdom.[16] Many managers do not perform appraisals adequately and give undeserved rewards to avoid confrontation. If performance evaluation is biased, unreliable, or not well received by employees, the merit pay increase will be tainted and/or cause inflated evaluations. There is also the problem of receiving a small or no increase relative to others. Average and below-average performers can be demoralized for years.[17]

Some researchers claim that merit pay tends to tolerate, reward, and encourage mediocrity.[18] In practice, many merit pay systems fail to reward superior performance because of three problems:[19]

1. Employees fail to make the connection between pay and performance.
2. Secrecy of the reward is perceived by other employees as inequity.
3. Size of the merit award has little effect on performance.

Reduction in budgets and increased competition have also reduced the rewards available.[20]

Individual Incentives   Perhaps the oldest form of compensation is the individual incentive plan, in which the employee is paid for units produced. Today the individual incentive plan takes several forms: piecework, production bonuses; and commissions. These methods seek to achieve the incentive goal of compensation.[21]

Straight piecework usually works like this. An employee is guaranteed an hourly rate (probably the minimum wage) for performing an expected minimum output (the standard). For production over the standard, the employer pays so much per piece produced. This is probably the most frequently used incentive pay plan. The standard is set through work measurement studies, as modified by collective bargaining. The amount of the base rate and piece rates may emerge from data collected by pay surveys.

A variation of the straight piece rate is the differential piece rate. In this plan, the employer pays a smaller piece rate up to the standard and then a higher piece rate above the standard. Research indicates that the differential piece rate is more effective than the straight piece rate, although it is *much less* frequently used.[22]

Production bonus sytems pay an employee an hourly rate. Then a bonus is paid when the employee exceeds the standard, typically 50 percent of labor savings. This system is not widely used.

Commissions are paid to sales employees. Straight commission is the equivalent of straight piecework and is typically a percentage of the price of the item. A variation of the production bonus system for sales is to pay the salesperson a small salary and commission or bonus when she or he exceeds standards (the budgeted sales goal).

Individual incentives are used more frequently in some industries (clothing, steel, textiles) than others (lumber, beverage, bakery), and more in some jobs (sales, production) than others (maintenance, clerical). Individual incentives are possible only in situations where performance can be well specified in terms of output (sales dollars generated, number of items completed). In addition, employees must work independently of each other so that individual incentives can be applied equitably.

Are individual incentives effective? The research results are mixed.[23] Most studies indicate they do increase output. Although production increases, other performance criteria may suffer. For example, in sales, straight commission can lead to less attention being paid to servicing accounts. Working on hard-to-sell customers may be neglected because the salesperson will elect to sell to easy customers. There is also evidence that there are individual differences in the effect of incentives on performance.[24] Some employees are more inclined to perform better than others. This should not surprise you, since we know that people have varying motivations to work.

Incentive systems may be designed to affect outputs other than performance. For example, employers may use them to try to lower absenteeism and turnover. At least for some employees, incentive pay may lower satisfaction, however. Employees may be dissatisfied if they have to work harder or if they feel manipulated by the system.

For incentive plans to work, they must be well designed and administered. It appears that an individual incentive plan is likely to be more effective under certain circumstances.[25] These are when:

- The task is liked.
- The task is not boring.
- The supervisor reinforces and supports the system.
- The plan is acceptable to employees and managers and probably includes them in the plan's design.
- The incentive is financially sufficient to induce increased output.
- Quality of work is not especially important.
- Most delays in work are under the employees' control.

Ten to 20 percent of all large manufacturing corporations in the Untied States use some type of individual incentive system.[26] In Japan, all employees receive semiannual bonuses in December and June.[27] The amount of the bonus is related to the basic pay and expressed as a multiple of the monthly salary.

Group Incentives   Incentives can also be used to build a team culture, and rewards can be provided on a group basis.[28] Piecework, production bonuses, commissions and other individual incentives can also be paid to groups of individuals. This might be done when it is difficult to measure individual output, when cooperation is needed to complete a task or project, and when management feels this is a more appropriate measure on which to base incentives. Group incentive plans also reduce administrative costs. Most compensation professionals report that companies are increasingly interested in new group reward strategies, particularly small-group incentives.[29] Small-group incentive plans are one of the newest and fastest growing reward strategies.

There are a number of logical reasons why a group incentive plan is chosen. In some situations, jobs and work output are so interrelated that it is impossible to specifically pinpoint individual performance. In such a situation, a group incentive could be used. The Japanese have used group incentives to help foster group cohesiveness and reduce jeolousy. They assume that rewarding only one individual or a few workers will discourage a sense of teamwork.[30] In the United States, however, the American individual spirit and self-confidence is not fully supported by a teamwork or group approach. Thus, in the United States, there may be a clash between societal norms and group incentive systems.

In general, group incentives are appropriate if the following criteria can be met:[31] (1) There is a strong interdependence among individuals in a group. (2) It is hard to determine which individual is responsible for which level of achievement. (3) The company wants to reinforce group planning and problem solving. For small-group incentives to be effective, management must define its objectives carefully and then perform a situational analysis to select the most appropriate group incentive.

One example of an organization with a successful small-group incentive plan is Maid Bess Corporation, a small uniform manufacturer in Salem, Virginia. Intense foreign competition created the need for dramatic productivity increases. Management devised a contest strategy that involved measuring the productivity of all line employees. During the contest period, each small group's productivity was measured and fed back to the groups. At the end of the contest, cash prizes of $100 to $500 were awarded to employees in the groups with the highest increase in productivity. Contests are now run once a year, and productivity does not drop back to its previoius level after each round.[32]

In individual and group incentive systems, competition can result in withholding information or resources, political gamesmanship, not helping others, and even sabotaging the work of others. These behaviors can be costly to an organization that uses these types of incentive plans. In an attempt to minimize these problems of interindividual and intergroup competition, some organizations have elected to use organizationwide incentive plans.

Organizationwide Incentives   Payments shared by all members of the organization are a much more common incentive reward than individual or group incentives. These organizationwide payments are usually based on two performance concepts: a sharing of profits generated by the efforts of all employees altogether or a sharing of money saved as a result of employees' cost reduction efforts.[33] Three approaches to incentive plans are used at the organizationwide level: suggestion systems, company group incentive plans, and profit sharing.

Suggestion Systems   Corporate managers are realizing the benefits of soliciting opinions from employees regarding such critical competitive issues as cutting expenses, increasing revenues, and developing new lines of business.[34] Successful suggestion systems can be a profitable partnership between management and employees.[35] These suggestion systems are designed to encourage employee input for improvements in organization effectiveness. A recent survey by *Personnel* found that small and medium-size organizations are more likely to have such a system, but large manufacturers have used the system successfully as well.[36] The systems are frequently administered by human resource departments, and about half of them allow all company employees to submit suggestions. In Japan, suggestion systems are one of the main practical forms of worker participation schemes.[37]

Effective administration of the suggestion program is essential to its success. At Broan Manufacturing Company in Hartford, Wisconsin, employees get little furry stick-on bears or ducks for every suggestion they submit to the company's suggestion system. The program, called Broan's Fresh Ideas, named for the company's fresh air products, has generated more than $1.4 million worth of ideas in the last four years. For any idea that saves up to $200, employees receive one chance in a prize drawing. Ideas that result in greater savings receive additional chances. Every year at a banquet for successful suggesters, the drawings for a variety of prizes including money and extra vacation days are held. The program is successful because it involves employees on all levels, has management support, and uses in-house publicity.[38]

In general, suggestion systems seem to be useful incentive plans. But suggestion systems have often failed because there was no training or no sincere interest in the development of employees.[39] It is not enough to evaluate suggestions on the basis of savings alone. They must be evaluated in comparison with other suggestions. And employees may be motivated by a desire to be respected for their contributions, not, in the long-run, by prizes or wages. The system must be designed to fit the organization and its employees. For example, many Japanese companies require employees to make a certain number of suggestions per month, but this would be ill-advised in the United States.[40]

Gainsharing Incentive Plans

Gainsharing Incentive Plans   Gainsharing plans are companywide group incentive plans that are being used by organizations to unite diverse organizational elements behind the common pursuit of improved organizational effectiveness.[41] These are organizational systems for sharing benefits of improved productivity, cost reductions, or improvements in quality paid in the form of cash bonuses.[42] The gainsharing incentive system has proven to be exceptionally effective in enhancing organizationwide teamwork in hundreds of manufacturing and service organizations. Programs typically involve the entire organization in improvement efforts and provide that the resulting economic gains be shared by all employees. The gainsharing system is intended to improve overall organizational performance by allowing employees who contribute to performance results to share in the proceeds.[43] Gainsharing plans that use cash awards and have been in place for at least five years have shown productivity ratio improvements resulting in labor cost reductions of 29 percent.[44]

Lincoln Electric Plan: The most successful gainsharing or productivity sharing plan at a single company is the Lincoln Electric plan. Lincoln is a manufacturer of arc-welding machinery and electric motors with domestic sales of $441 million in 1989.[45] The company claims that its impressive profits stem from an inspired work force and entrepreneurial management ideas. Lincoln's gainsharing plan was developed by James F. Lincoln, who headed the company for 50 years and wrote the book, *Incentive Management*. With a work force of 2,500, the company has a mere 3 percent turnover ratio, including retirements. Employees are paid only for what they individually produce. There are no paid holidays and no unions. Promotions are based on merit, job reassignments must be accepted, and overtime is mandatory. The basic compensation system at Lincoln rests on the following principles: (1) All compensation is based on piecework. (2) There are no perquisites for managers. (3) After two years of employment, the worker cannot be laid off. (4) There is no mandatory retirement. An average Lincoln line employee makes $45,000 per year. In 1988, one employee earned $97,000!

An advisory board of several executives and about 30 employees reviews and makes suggestions for company improvements. The firm has a stock purchase plan in which about two thirds of the employees participate; they now own about one third of the total stock. The stock is privately traded and not sold on any exchange. Employees hire the replacements for vacancies in their work group. The company basically subcontracts the work to the work group, using past performance and time studies as standards of performance. When these standards are beaten, the employees share generously. This bonus is not used as a substitute for adequate wages and benefits, either. Needless to say, some individuals bid to go to work for Lincoln Electric.

Since 1983, more and more companies are implementing gainsharing plans using a formula that establishes a bonus based on improved productivity. Gainsharing rewards are normally distributed on a monthly or a quarterly basis.[46] The factors that dictate a gainsharing plan's success include (1) the size of the company, (2) the age of the plan, (3) the financial stability of the company, (4) unionization, (5) the company's technology, and (6) employee/manager attitudes. A gainsharing plan is expensive to administer, so projected benefits must be weighed against costs. While the Lincoln Electric model has become a classic, three other types of gainsharing plans are in use throughout the United States: the Scanlon Plan, the Rucker Plan, and Improshare. Exhibit 11–2 compares these three plans on 11 dimensions. Each of these plans will be discussed briefly below.

Scanlon Plan: The **Scanlon plan** is a combination suggestion, group incentive, and employee participation scheme that has been adopted by many small and medium-sized manufacturing firms.[47] In the late 1930s, Joe Scanlon, an unemployed steel worker, created a system of labor management relations that has now been adopted by over 2,000 companies of all sizes, union and nonunion, in all industries. To involve all employees in the problem-solving process and to improve overall productivity, Scanlon organized employees into productivity teams responsible for exploring any idea that would improve quality and output, eliminate waste, and save time. Scanlon realized that both white- and blue-collar employees must cooperate to make productivity improvements so the next step in the Scanlon plan is to organize a steering committee to (1) evaluate suggestions, (2) get budget approval, (3) establish priorities, and (4) report back to the employee teams. Gainsharing was used so that all employees would benefit financially from productivity improvements resulting from the suggestion system. The actual gainsharing formula is designed to suit the needs of the individual firm.[48]

The plan also involves a wage formula. Gains from increased productivity are paid in bonus form to all employees: operative workers, supervisors, indirect workers such as typists, and salespersons. Bonuses are received in proportion to shares. Management receives its share of productivity gains in increased profits. Advocates of the Scanlon plan contend that there are positive results for everyone. These include increased participation by all employees, better acceptance of change on everyone's part, greater efficiency for the company, and improved union/management relations. However, a number of Scanlon plans have failed. The plans have had more success when there are fewer than 1,000 participants and when employees fully understand the features of the plan. They can also work well in troubled companies, provided there are the necessary conditions of participation, communication, and identification.

Exhibit 11–3 shows how a company uses the Scanlon plan. A database year (1990 in this case) is used to calculate the Scanlon ratio of 30 percent. In 1992, sales increased to $1.2 million; according to the Scanlon ratio, the payroll costs should be $360,000. However, because of worker suggestions, improved efficiency, and better

EXHIBIT 11-2   Comparative Analysis of Three Gainsharing Plans

Program Dimension	Scanlon	Rucker	Improshare
Philosophy/theory	Original single unit; share improvements; people capable/willing to make suggestions, want to make ideas	Primarily economic incentive; some reliance on employee participation	Economic incentives increase performance
Primary goal	Productivity improvement	Productivity improvement	Productivity improvement
Subsidiary goals	Attitudes, communication, work behaviors, quality, cost reduction	Attitudes, communication, work behaviors, quality, cost reductions	Attitudes, work behaviors
Worker participation	Two levels of committees: screening (1) and production (many)	Screening committee and production committee (sometimes)	Bonus committee
Suggestion making	Formal system	Formal system	None
Role of supervisor	Chair of production committee	None	None
Role of managers	Direct participation in bonus committee assignments	Idea Coordinator: Evaluate suggestions, committee assignments	None
Bonus formula	$\dfrac{\text{Sales}}{\text{Payroll}}$	$\dfrac{\text{Bargaining-unit payroll}}{\text{Production value}}$	Engineering standard $\times$ BPF* Total hours worked
Frequency of payout	Monthly	Monthly	Weekly
Role of union	Negotiated provisions; screening committee membership	Negotiated provisions; screening committee membership	Negotiated provisions
Impact on management style	Substantial	Slight	None

* BPF = Base productivity factor.
Adapted from Christopher S. Miller and Michael H. Schuster (Summer 1987), "Gainsharing Plans: A Comparative Analysis," *Organizational Dynamics* 16, no. 1, p. 48.

EXHIBIT 11-3   A Company Scanlon Plan for 1988

1990 Database Year

Average sales value of production for 1990	=	$1,000,000
Average payroll costs for 1990	=	300,000
Scanlon ratio = $\dfrac{\$300,000}{\$1,000,000}$	=	30%

1992

Average sales value of production	=	$1,200,000
Allowable payroll cost	=	.30 ($1,200,000)
	=	360,000
Actual payroll cost	=	310,000
Savings available for bonus distribution	= $	50,000

work methods, the actual 1992 payroll costs were only $310,000. Thus, a savings of $50,000 was achieved. Workers typically would share in 75 percent of savings or $37,500. The remaining $12,500 would be given to the company. The $37,500 would then be distributed to employees based on their wage levels.

The philosophy of Rucker Plans falls between the humanistic orientation of Scanlon Plans and the ideal of an economically driven and rewarded employee of Improshare.

Rucker Plan: The **Rucker plan** has almost the same participatory elements as the Scanlon Plan but in smaller degrees.[49] However, the Rucker plan is less an employee-participation scheme than it is a practical realization that line workers have information that can help managers improve their skills. Rucker plans are based on employee involvement and suggestion systems. Some have two committees, production and screening, while others have only a screening committee. If there are two committees, the production committee has 10 to 15 hourly employees and an assortment of managers as members. It meets monthly and reviews suggestions and discusses production problems. The screening committee is comprised of hourly employees, the union leadership, and key management personnel. Its primary purpose is to administer the bonus program with less emphasis on immediate productivity or quality issues. It also may discuss production problems and long-range economic goals. One manager acts as the *idea coordinator* for processing all suggestions.[50] He or she directs suggestions to the appropriate managers for review and follows the idea through investigation to provide feedback to employees.

Rucker plans, like the Scanlon plans, relate bonus earnings to financial performance. The Rucker bonus formula is based on the relationship between production value and the payroll costs of production employees. Production value equals the selling price of a company's products minus defective goods returned minus the cost of materials, supplies, and services such as utilities. The firm's payroll is divided by the production value to determine the "standard" by which improvements in productivity are measured. This is a more sophisticated improvement measure than that used by the Scanlon plan. It includes not only labor costs but also materials, supplies, and services. Employees also get to share in any savings on these items. It is assumed that the employees will be more conservative in their use of materials, supplies, and services if they see the result in a bonus. *All* savings in labor costs are allocated to the employees in the Rucker plan.

It is important to note that reliance on "sales value" means the pricing policies of the firm or the marketplace can have a very real impact on the level of bonuses earned. A restrictive pricing policy, either internal or external as a result of market conditions, can reduce sales value and thus restrict resulting bonus payments. If this connection to outside forces is not fully communicated to the work force, failure to receive expected levels of bonus will result in dissatisfaction and *decreased productivity*.[51] This weakness can be successfully overcome. For example, a supplier to the auto industry sustained a recession and price squeeze with the plan intact by involving shop-floor employees in the long-range financial planning of the business. In 1984, Dixie Industries, a medium-size manufacturing company, implemented a Rucker plan. Within one year, profits increased and morale and teamwork improved.[52] In conclusion, Rucker plans are similar in procedure and results to the Scanlon plan and are used by about as many firms.

Improshare: **Improshare** was developed by Mitchell Fein. It supports consultative management practices.[53] It typically does not have any shop-floor participation. The basic underlying principle is raising the employees' motivation to work.[54] The philosophy of Improshare is to tie economic rewards to performance without any attempt at meaningful employee participation. Some firms do have a bonus committee to review the previous month's bonus calculations, however. Bonuses are determined by the calculation of a base productivity factor (BPF) involving engineered time standards, absorption of indirect hours, and actual hours worked. BPF equals total actual hours worked divided by total earned standard value hours. Earned standard value hours are computed by multiplying the time standard estimate per unit produced by total pieces produced during the measurement period. Actual hours worked includes all hours worked by both production and nonproduction employees involved in shipping, receiving, maintenance, and clerical operations.

Productivity equals the base value earned hours divided by total actual hours worked. To compute Improshare productivity, multiply earned standard value hours by the BPF and then divide the product by total actual hours worked. Productivity gains are represented by hours saved or gained. Gains are distributed on a 50 percent sharing basis between employees and the company. Each employee's bonus percentage is found by dividing total hours worked in the current period into labor hours gained allocated to employees.[55] Bonuses are calculated monthly and paid out weekly.

Both Rucker and Improshare plans are copyrighted programs. However, the plans can be duplicated without the aid of consultants. Various companies and unions have adapted the plans successfully to fit their own particular circumstances.

Spot Gainsharing Traditional gainsharing plans like the Scanlon plan are not designed to address many of the complex issues facing companies today. They fall short in three areas:[56] (1) They have a tendency to become institutionalized and thus fail to continue to vary pay with performance; (2) they are not flexible enough in terms of rewarding "star performers"; (3) service-sector firms are unable to isolate or measure productivity gains. (In particular, quality of service is amost impossible to measure.) Therefore, a new form of gainsharing, spot gainsharing, has been born.

Spot gainsharing focuses on a specific problem in a specific department rather than on performance improvements for the whole organization. Its goal is to produce peak performance from participants during a specified time period. It is generally short and focused on a specific solution to a specific production problem. For example, perhaps a company would like to eliminate work backlog. Savings associated with the solution of the problem, less the administrative costs of the spot gainsharing plan, are split between the company and its participating employees. When the problem is solved, the plan is terminated. Because employees know the plan will end once the problem is resolved, bonuses are perceived as a reward for the extra effort, not an extension of the wage structure as in the Scanlon, Rucker, and Improshare plans.

For spot gainsharing to be successful, the firm must identify a clear business need unrelated to any specific failure on the part of management or employees in the unit to be sure employees are not creating issues to trigger incentives. To identify real problems, managers should investigate the source of the problem, looking for conditions beyond employee control such as increased volume, high turnover, and reorganization.

The most critical factor in the success of *any* gainsharing plan is employee involvement.[57] Workers must be motivated to assume new and expanded roles because any plan will fail without employee enthusiasm, support, and trust. Surveys of employees can be used to obtain information to predict how the work force will respond to the gainsharing scheme. The firm will also have to address the dedication of cost-accounting support resources sufficient to assure accurate and challenging productivity targets.

Because gainsharing plans are proliferating, a new human resource professional is being created: productivity-gainsharing coordinator (PGC).[58] The PGC must be a true human resource generalist. Necessary skills include: good management and communication skills; accounting skills; technical knowledge of the firm's products and technology; and experience leading suggestion teams and other group discussions.

Profit-Sharing Plans   **Profit-sharing plans** distribute a fixed percentage of total organizational profit to employees in the form of cash bonuses or bonus amounts. These plans are typically found in three combinations: (1) Cash or current distribution plans provide full payment to participants soon after profits have been determined; this is usually quarterly or annually.[59] (2) Deferred plans credit a portion of current profits to employee accounts with cash payments made at the time of retirement, disability, severance, or death. (3) A combination of both incorporates aspects of current and deferred options. Eighty percent of the companies with some form of profit sharing use the deferred option. Almost 20 percent use the combination option. It is important to note that the incentive value of profit-sharing plans *declines* as the time between performance and payoff increases and as the size of the payoff declines relative to previous years. Therefore, the incentive value of working to increase the company's current profits when rewards are distributed much later is, at best, minimally effective.

Profit-sharing plans do offer two distinct advantages. They do not need elaborate cost-accounting systems to calculate rewards, and they are easily implemented by companies of any size. Smaller companies usually use the current distribution method, while larger organizations usually use the deferred option. Recent research on profit sharing suggests that about 20 percent of the private, nonfarm work force receives some kind of profit sharing.

Skill-Based Pay

One response of U.S. companies to increased foreign competition and technological innovation has been **skill-based** (or knowledge-based) **pay** plans.[60] The system is a new alternative to the traditional job-based compensation system; it does not reward the individual for the job they do or a particular job category.[61] Workers rotate among various tasks on a job until they learn them all.[62] Then they may rotate to another job and go through the same learning process. Knowledge-based pay systems reward workers for *acquiring* additional skills or knowledge within the same job category. This type of individually determined compensation provides a way to emphasize the importance of an employee's ideas, growth, and development. The rewards are based on acquisition and proficiency in new skills regardless of the employee's length of service.[63] Thus, another advantage of this system over traditional job-based pay is that it can be used to reward loyal employees when promotional opportunities may be scarce. This is particularly important as the work force ages and companies slim down because promotions become more scarce.

Skill-based pay has been implemented at a number of large manufacturing firms like General Motors and Honeywell. It is used with production workers only and must have the support of first-line supervisors.[64] It has been implemented most

successfully in new plants with participative management schemes. Known attributes of a skill-based pay system include (1) the need for high commitment to
training to achieve success; (2) the necessary use of job rotation; (3) the fact that the
choice of plan is tied to business needs; and (4) the fact that it is not for every
company.[65] The system identifies (1) tasks that need to be done, (2) skills necessary
to perform them, and (3) measures to be sure employees have learned and can use
these skills. Management support, organization structure, unionization, number of
departments, and employees' attitudes are all important in planning, developing,
implementing, and maintaining the system.[66] The movement towards skill-based
pay is still relatively new, but early evidence indicates that it provides workers with
greater job security and income by giving them the opportunity to increase their
skills in ways that make them more valuable to the organization. Advantages include
leaner staffing, lower rates of turnover and absenteeism, better problem-solving
skills, and more self-motivation.[67] Disadvantages are higher average hourly wages,
higher training costs, need for skills assessment, "topping out" of employees,
administrative complexity, and technological changes.

EXECUTIVE COMPENSATION

Americans are extremely fascinated by the earnings of senior executives in large
organizations.[68] Executive compensation is set on an individual basis because they
tend to be highly mobile. Therefore, boards of directors develop attractive compensation packages and individual employment contracts. In the private sector, executives receive salaries and many also receive incentive compensation such as bonuses.
Executives in the public and nonprofit sectors are normally compensated by salaries
alone. In addition, all executives receive benefits and special treatment that are
usually called *perquisites (perks)*.

A fundamental question in executive compensation is why business executives
should be paid incentives as well as salaries. A number of answers can be given. First,
it is argued that these incentives improve performance, and that is good for stockholders and employees. A second reason is that incentive compensation is a way of
retaining talented executives. Many have alternative employment opportunities
with other corporations or as entrepreneurs. The third reason is that business
executives are more likely to control their own compensation in the private sector
than in the public sector, where legislative bodies determine it, or in the third
sector, where boards, normally from outside the enterprise, have a great deal of
control. For these and other reasons, the compensation of business executives tends
to be lucrative and innovative enough to sidestep the everchanging tax laws.

Executive Salaries

Salaries of executives in the public sector are generally known to the public. Salaries
of executives in the nonprofit sector have not been widely studied. In general, the
highest salaries are paid in the private sector.[69] Many studies of private firms'
executive compensation have been done. In 1989, Craig McCaw was the highest
paid chief executive officer (CEO) in the United States with earnings of $54
million.[70] He earned $1 million in salary and bonuses and $53 million in stock gains.
Eight hundred top executives in the United States earned $712 million in salaries
and bonuses the same year. A total of 239 executives topped the $1 million a year
mark in salaries alone.[71] To give you some idea of salaries and bonuses of some top
executives in U.S. organizations you probably have done business with, look at some

EXHIBIT 11-4   The 25 Highest Paid Executives: 1989

Company	Chief Executive	Compensation				
		Salary and Bonus*	Percent Change	Other	Stock Gains	Total
McCaw Cellular	Craig O. McCaw	$ 289	−5%	—	$53,655	$53,944
LIN Broadcasting	Donald A. Pels	1,363	32	—	21,428	22,791
Lotus Development	Jim P. Manzi	991	NA	$ 49	15,372	16,412
Reebok International	Paul B. Fireman	14,606	28	—	—	14,606
BHC Communications	Herbert J. Siegel	13,687	NA	14	—	13,702
Freeport-McMoRan	James R. Moffett	1,359	−13	1,086	11,072	13,517
Torchmark	Ronald K. Richey	1,084	35	48	11,588	12,719
Great A&P Tea	James Wood	3,193	59	2,024	5,900	11,117
Coca-Cola	Roberto C. Goizueta	2,542	17	2,400	5,872	10,814
Walt Disney	Michael D. Eisner	9,589	28	6	—	9,595
Anheuser-Busch Cos.	August A. Busch III	1,464	−5	21	7,397	8,882
MCI Communications	William G. McGowan	1,325	−2	—	7,341	8,666
Ogden	Ralph E. Ablon	2,000	−3	284	5,015	7,299
Merck	P. Roy Vagelos	2,340	46	5	4,423	6,769
Wal-Mart Stores	David D. Glass	600	—		6,129	6,759†
Reliance Group	Saul P. Steinberg	6,265	39	281	—	6,546
Philip Morris Cos.	Hamish Maxwell	1,877	13	1,771	2,805	6,453
UST Inc.	Louis F. Bantle	2,126	23	22	3,635	5,783
Morgan Stanley	S. Parker Gilbert	5,475	24	20	—	5,495
Alexander & Baldwin	Robert J. Pfeiffer	1,473	11	509	3,476	5,459
Toys "R" Us	Charles Lazarus	5,277	19	16	—	5,293
ConAgra	Charles M. Harper	1,444	10	3,085	723	5,252
Interpublic Group	Philip H. Geier, Jr.	1,705	NA	3,320	—	5,025
Paramount Communications	Martin S. Davis	4,095	11	865	—	4,960
Ralston Purina	William P. Stiritz	1,064	3	53	3,790	4,907

n.a. = Not available.
* All dollar amounts in thousands.
† Prior-year data.
Source: Dana Wechsler (May 28, 1990), "Just Deserts," *Forbes* 145, no. 11, p. 208

of the 1989 data shown in Exhibit 11–4. Remember these figures are just for the salary and bonus portion of compensation.

Managers below top executives in medium-size and large enterprises have their salaries set by concepts similar to the ones used for hourly personnel. Compensation for lower-level managers is set using systems of job evaluation and external salary validations and tends to treat these managers as members of classes or grades.[72] A very popular salary survey that sets salaries for employees—managers included—in 200 *Fortune* 500 firms is the Hay System.

Smaller firms or those without a formal job evaluation system set salary relationships among managers on the basis of the "whole job" or job title rather than its component parts. Small firms may use a wage survey conducted by a trade association or local employers' groups as a standard. The typical small business executive in 1989 had a salary of $97,000 with a bonus of $35,000.[73] Most small firms have no formal compensation plan.

Some studies have been done on the relationship of the size and kind of business to salary amount. With regard to size, in general, as the firm increases in size, the top executive's salary increases. Several studies have examined the relative salaries of executives in different industries. For example, one study found that out of companies with sales larger than $10 billion, motor vehicle companies paid the highest, followed (in order) by conglomerates and firms in office machines and oil.[74] In the $5 billion category, the order was: motor vehicles, office machines, conglomerates, and oil.

Bonuses

A **bonus** is a compensation payment that supplements salary and can be paid in the present or in the future. In the latter case, it is called a *deferred bonus*. A majority of large and some small firms pay bonuses in the belief that doing so leads to better profitability and other advantages for organizations. Bonuses involve large expenditures of funds. They vary from 80 percent of top executives' salaries to 20 percent of the salaries of lowest-level participants. In spite of wide usage and high costs, there is little research support for their effectiveness. Unless more research does support the payment of bonuses, many may conclude they are an example of management's power to pay itself whatever it wants. This is an issue that can have an impact on the image the public holds about the ethics of corporate executives.

Bonus practices in large firms are typically based on percentage of net profits after deducting a reasonable earnings per share for the stockholders. In smaller firms, bonuses are based on attaining sales goals, as a percentage of sales or of net profits, or are totally discretionary. In fact, one study of small growing firms indicated that 81 percent of the firms used bonus compensation and that 51 percent of them based the bonus payment on a discretionary basis. Although some of the firms used fixed and annual formulas, most of them had no set formula or procedure.[75] This finding does lend support to the public image of chief executives paying themselves what they feel is fair.

Stock Options, Performance Shares, and Book-Value Devices

Another form of executive compensation used in the private sector is a set of devices tied to the firm's stock. The oldest form is the **stock option,** which gives executives the right to purchase company stock at a fixed price for a certain period of time. The option's price usually is close to the market price of the stock at the time the option is issued. The executive gains if the price rises above the option price during the option period enough to cover the capital gains tax on the stock should it be purchased.

The popularity of stock options has risen and fallen with the tax laws (especially the 1976, 1981, and 1986 laws), the level of interest rates, the state of the stock market, and the feelings of stockholders about them. At present, because of tax law changes and these other factors, the use of stock options as incentive compensation is decreasing.

Is this a great loss? Probably not. There was little research to indicate that stock options led to better performance; what evidence there was tended to indicate that they did not. But one implication of the research is that, as management's income from ownership-related sources (dividends and capital gains) increases, these instruments can serve to improve performance.

Innovative tax lawyers and tax accountants have worked up some new compensation forms to replace the stock option and still provide ownership and incentive compensation. Several variations are primarily incentive compensation oriented, others are ownership oriented, and still others are a mix of the two. The ownership-oriented devices are:

1. **Market Value Purchases.** The company lends the executive funds at low interest rates to buy company stock at current market value. The executive repays the loan by direct payment or receives credits on the loan payments for staying with the company and/or achieving a certain performance level.
2. **Book-Value Purchases.** The executive is offered a chance to buy the company stock at book value (or some similar nonmarket value measure) but can resell it to the company later, using the same formula price.
3. **Exercise Bonuses.** Payment to an executive when he or she exercises a stock option that is equal to or proportionate to the option gain is called an *exercise bonus*. This helps the executive keep the stock rather than sell it to pay the taxes on the gain.

One device that appears to be primarily a form of incentive compensation is *performance shares and performance units*, used by such companies as General Motors, Gulf, Texaco, Pepsico, and International Nickel. Performance shares grant stock units due the executive in the future (such as five years later) if performance targets are met. These units appreciate or depreciate as the company's stock does. Performance units are performance shares paid in cash instead of stock. The units are compensation unless they are to be used to buy stock. Both are viewed as compensation by the IRS.

Another device, *stock appreciation rights*, can be either compensation or ownership oriented. This device, attached to a stock option, allows the executive to accept appreciation in value in either stock or cash.

Most of these devices are fairly new and are still rarely used. All could have performance implications for the organization, but there is inadequate research at this stage to determine under what conditions they do so. The key to their success is the definition and identification of what constitutes performance.

Executive Perquisites

Executive perquisites or perks are rewards designed to satisfy several types of executive needs. A list of executive perks is presented in Exhibit 11–5. Some of these perks are also called *benefits* (as noted in the exhibit); these are discussed in Chapter 12. Research indicates that executives prefer the following perks the most: a corner office, financial counseling, a fitness club, and a company car.[76]

Since 1978, revenue acts have imposed tax penalties on perks and IRS policy has become more strict. In January 1988, the new permanent two-tier phase of the 1986 Tax Reform Act took affect. As a result, many executive perks have been curtailed or extended to other employees. Free use of a company car, maintenance of yachts and vacation retreats for personal use, and country club memberships that are not used at least 50 percent for business have almost been totally eliminated. Other perks like business travel expenses, business-related lunches, and business conferences at retreat locations must be justified as legitimate business expenses and provided not only to executives but also to other personnel. Free company cars and first-class air accommodations are permitted only for top executives.

EXHIBIT 11-5   Executive Perquisites: A Selected List

Company-provided car. The employee is able to use the car for both business and personal use. (According to the IRS, the employee must pay a flat monthly maintenance charge or a mileage charge for personal use.)

Parking. Special no-cost, readily accessible to work site parking services.

Chauffeured limousine. Normally provided only to the CEO or key officials. The chauffeur may also act as bodyguard.

Kidnap and ransom protection. A service of recent vintage aimed at protecting key officials who may be victims of such action.

Counseling service. Includes financial and legal services. Tax-related expenses are tax-deductible; cost of nonbusiness-related services is considered taxable income.

Attending professional meetings and conferences. Opportunity to enhance professional knowledge and enjoy activities at selected sites.

Spouse travel. The company pays for expenses incurred in taking a spouse to a convention or on a business trip.

Use of company plane and yacht. Opportunity to mix use of company plane and yacht for personal enjoyment and business purposes.

Home entertainment allowance. Executives who do considerable entertaining are frequently provided with a domestic staff or given a home servants allowance. The allowance may include cost of food and beverages and payment of utility bills.

Special living accommodations. Executives required to perform business activities at odd hours or at a considerable distance from home are provided with an apartment or permanent hotel accommodations.

Special dining rooms. The business provides special dining facilities for key officials and their business guests.

Special relocation allowance. A variety of relocation allowances is provided only to key officials. This includes low-interest loans to purchase a new home and complete coverage of all relocation expenses.

Use of company credit card. No waiting period for reimbursement of company-related charges and use of card for personal service and delay in repayment to the company.

Medical expense reimbursement. Coverage for all medical care.

College tuition reimbursement for children. Special programs that provide for college tuition.

Source: Richard I. Henderson (1985), *Compensation Management* (Reston, Va: Reston Publishing), pp. 655–56. Used with permission.

Executive Compensation Policy

How does an organization choose the compensation package for its executives? Effective executive compensation must meet the needs of both the organization and the individual executive. For the organization, the total compensation must be competitive with that of similar enterprises. Thus, it makes no sense to look at total compensation of executives, or averages. The effective firm determines the compensation of executives in similar-sized organizations in the same industry group with the same degree of competitiveness. Executive compensation must also be directly tied to the organization's strategy and objectives, so executive rewards will promote achievement of the organization's goals.

One way organizations try to satisfy the needs and desires of their executives is to adjust compensation methods to changing tax laws. This often leads to the use of more deferred compensation methods. Another way is to study the preferences and attitudes of executives toward the various compensation approaches. However, since each executive is different and has differing needs for compensation, studies of pay preferences are only partly indicative of what an enterprise should do.

In one study of the pay preferences of 300 executives in seven large companies, it was found that executives' compensation preferences vary widely.[77] One consistency was a preference for 75 percent of total compensation in cash and 25 percent in benefits and deferred items, which would mean a shift from the present 85/15 percent division to include more benefits. A way to deal with these differences is to set up a *cafeteria compensation system*. The cafeteria approach permits executives to determine the range of their compensation between present pay, deferred compensation, and benefits and services. This approach is described in more detail in Chapter 12, where the cafeteria approach to benefits is considered for all employees. It does not change the total compensation (that could lead to perceived inequities), but the mix of how the compensation is received. Although there are administrative hurdles to be overcome, this approach fits compensation theories and makes sense.

Other factors that influence executive pay are ownership and market concentration. One study found that in closely held firms, executive pay was correlated with profitability. Other studies agree with this, and it makes sense.[78] In firms where the owners can put on pressure, executives are likely to encourage higher profitability. In firms with no strong ownership interest, executives can set their salaries similar to those of executives in equal-size firms, regardless of profitability. Louis Brindisi of Booz, Allen, & Hamilton, Inc., argues that corporations should be tying executive pay more closely to shareholder gains in stock value and dividends. This is one method of measuring worth of contribution.[79]

Borden, Inc., is gradually phasing in a return on equity pay plan for its top 300 to 400 managers.[80] And at Libbey-Owens-Ford Company they are using monthly management reports that pinpoint the contribution to the creation of shareholder value each division makes. These companies along with Sears, Emhart, and Combustion Engineering are doing more than talking about tying pay to performance. They are phasing in specific pay for performance plans that are intended to motivate participants.

Labor unions are certainly one group that complains about the amount of salaries and bonus received by top executives. They believe that the total compensation paid to Lee Iacocca and others is obscene and unfair.[81] Compared to top executives, the pay of union leaders (usually in the $100,000 to $150,000 range) is pretty skimpy. Of course, the question one must ask is whether the pay differentials between top business managers and top union leaders are warranted. Do you think that business leaders are overpaid or that union leaders are underpaid?

International Executive Compensation

All over the world and in all sectors of the economy, executives receive perks. These tend to be larger in Europe and Asia than in the United States. For example, the European executive can receive free housing and other niceties in lieu of or in addition to higher salaries. A recent survey by the Japan Economic Institute found that while U.S. companies try to base an executive's compensation package (salary, bonus, perks) on his or her ability to produce profit or earn money for shareholders, most Japanese firms say that the differential in compensation between managers and nonmanagers is critical.[82] The Japanese work at not having too wide a gap in pay between managers and nonmanagers. In order to understand the differences between executive pay in the United States and in several of our major competitors, a comparison will be made among Great Britain, Germany, and Japan.[83]

Great Britain   Executives in Great Britain have been operating in a sluggish economy for many years. They must contend with a high marginal rate of taxation with a maximum rate of 83 percent levied on earned income. Therefore, large raises for British executives are highly inefficient. Raises are often flat-rate rather than percentage norms for pay increases so that highly paid executives could be seen as bearing their share of the burden of economic austerity. Nonpay rewards are not taxed as heavily. Therefore, British executives receive a wide range of perks: generous pensions, a company car, private health insurance, loans for housing and other purposes, tuition for children's schools, professional association fees, and generous expense accounts. Almost 63 percent of private-sector managers are provided with a company car. Cars and other fringe benefits have been awarded to junior executives since the 1970s.

Germany   The salary scale for managers in Germany ranges from 50,000 DM to 200,000 DM ($86,775 to $347,100) annually, with one third of managerial employees earning over 110,000 DM ($190,900) annually. Chief executives earn the highest amounts. Obligatory contributions to social security and tax rates that rise progressively with income in combination produce substantially reduced and greatly diversified net incomes. The portion of salaries that are dependent on profit sharing is decreasing, from 28 percent to 14 percent of base salary over the last five years. Bonuses and fringe benefits have become much more important than they used to be because of the high taxes and social security deductions. Ninety percent of managerial employees and members of executive boards have pensions. Managers at the executive level receive 50 to 55 percent of their pay as pensions.

Japan   The Japanese executive who earns over $335,000 would pay a national tax of 75 percent and municipal taxes of 14 percent. So, as in other foreign countries, executive salaries are comprised of innovative measures designed to compensate for this. Managerial compensation in Japan has four principal components: the basic salary, semiannual bonuses, a retirement allowance tied to the basic salary, and a monthly special allowance for entertaining clients. Peak compensation is reached when the executive is between 50 to 54 years of age. But as the age rises, the proportion of compensation based on seniority declines and the proportion based on merit increases. Executives also receive positional allowances and other supplementary payments related to their specific situation such as length of commute to work or number of children. These allowances compose 20 to 25 percent of monthly pay. Wage gaps between the levels of managerial employees are much smaller than in the United States, averaging at most 30 percent between executives of highest and lowest rank.

A wide range of social benefits are also received from company payments for social security and medical insurance to retirement bonuses and housing loans. These benefits account for at most 20 percent of total compensation. However, these benefits are not as expensive to provide in Japan as they are in the United States. Large, lump-sum payments are usual at retirement.

Understanding how compensation plans are developed abroad is increasingly important as many U.S. firms become multinational. If incentive compensation continues to prevail in the United States, companies will try to export these plans overseas to cover U.S. expatriates, third country nationals, and local nationals. Prior to implementing such a plan, firms need to answer questions that may arise because of foreign securities laws, foreign exchange control laws, income taxes for the employee, and income taxes for the employer.[84]

COMPENSATION ADMINISTRATION ISSUES

Managers must make policy decisions on four issues in compensation administration for employees and executives. These issues involve the extent to which (1) compensation will be secret, (2) compensation will be secure, (3) pay is compressed, and (4) compensation is two-tiered.

Pay Secrecy or Openness

The first compensation issue to be discussed is the extent to which the pay of employees is known by others in the enterprise. (This is the issue Martha raised in the Career Challenge at the beginning of the chapter.) How would you feel if your co-workers could find out what you make? Would you care? As with other issues, employees differ on this.

There are degrees of secretiveness and openness on pay information. In many institutions and organizations, pay ranges and even an individual's pay are open to the public and fellow employees. Examples are public-sector salaries (federal, state, and local governments), some universities, and unionized wage employees. This is called the *open system*.

The opposite is the *secret system*, in which pay is regarded as privileged information known only to the employee, her or his superior, and such staff employees as HRM and payroll. In the most secrecy-oriented organizations, employees are told they cannot discuss pay matters and, specifically, their own pay. The National Labor Relations Board has ruled that this is not a legitimate policy.

Corporate presidents differ in their preferences for full disclosure of employee compensation. For example, Robert Howell, TeleCheck Services, believes that an open pay system is a means of improving productivity. While Kenneth Porter of Can-Am Groups thinks open pay schemes just increase employee dissatisfaction.[85]

Which system is right? Research is mixed. Some findings favor the open system, others the secret system. Before an open system is tried, the individual's performance must be objectively measurable, and the measurable aspects of the jobs to be rewarded must be the significant ones. There should be little need for cooperation among jobs, and employees in the system should have a direct causal relationship on performance. The employees must also prefer the open system.

There is increasing recognition that some employees want a more open pay system. The opening up of a system and providing more information to employees certainly have costs and benefits. However, if an organization wishes to reduce the manipulative aura surrounding pay, actual or perceived, it is going to have to share additional pay information with employees. As more firms post job openings to make employees aware of opportunities, information on pay becomes a critical decision point.

As a step in deciding how much secrecy or how much openness is needed, managers first must clearly determine through observation (listening, talking, discussion in groups) what their employees want to know about pay. Then managers must decide if providing pay information will harm or benefit the firm. Finally, the

CAREER CHALLENGE
(*continued*)

Mary So you see, boss, we've really only scratched the surface on compensation at CNB. Our executive compensation system consists of salaries (and not high ones at that), and a few perks, like free club memberships. We haven't tried bonuses or stock options, performance shares, or anything else. Our executive turnover is probably related to our executive compensation system.

Joe Yeah, but high turnover also could be happening because we've hired a great group of executives.

Now we're a likely target for others to pirate executives from.

Mary I doubt it, boss.

Joe OK. What's left?

Mary What's left are some key compensation administration issues.

conditions cited above concerning the objective measuring of performance, degree of interdependence, and causal relationships on performance must be carefully weighed.

Pay Security

Current compensation can be a motivator of performance. But the belief that there will be future security in compensation may also affect it. Various plans for providing this security have been developed: the guaranteed annual wage, supplementary unemployment benefits, severance pay, seniority rules, and the employment contract.

A few companies provide a guaranteed annual wage (GAW) to employees who meet certain characteristics. For this type of plan to work, general employee-management relations must be good. And the demand for the product or service must be steady. The best known such plans are those of Procter & Gamble, Hormel Meats, and the Nunn-Bush Shoe Company. In one plan, the employer guarantees the employee a certain number of weeks of work at a certain wage after the worker has passed a probation period (say, two years). Morton Salt Company guarantees 80 percent of full-time work to all employees after one year of standard employment. Procter & Gamble has invoked its emergency clause only once since 1923 — in 1933 for a brief period at three plants. In the Hormel and Spiegel plans and others, a minimum income is guaranteed.[86]

In the supplementary unemployment benefits approach, the employer adds to unemployment compensation payments to help the employee achieve income security, if not job security (as in the GAW). The auto, steel, rubber, garment, and glass industries, among others, contribute to a fund from which laid-off employees

PROFESSIONAL PROFILE

Biography

Mary Kale is currently manager of compensation for Bethlehem Steel Corporation. She earned her B.S. degree in chemistry at Chatham College in Pittsburgh. She has held positions in metallurgy, recruiting, training, and employee benefits. Mary served as a Pew Fellow in the national leadership program in health policy at Boston University. She is a member of the executive council of the Conference Board, the American Compensation Association, and the American Association for the Advancement of Science. She serves on the boards of directors of Integrated Technologies Corporation and Community Services for Children.

Job Description   At Bethlehem Steel Corporation, the manager of compensation oversees corporate policy regarding pay and other reward and recognition mechanisms. Such issues as the appropriate base and incentive compensation by position, job evaluation and organization design, salary structures and compensation plans for each subsidiary and business unit, policy guidelines associated with pay for performance, the establishment and allocation of budgets, and periodic audits reside here. In addition, all aspects of executive compensation including stock-based awards, deferrals, and perquisites form a major part of the manager's responsibility.

Managing compensation for a large company requires a thorough knowledge of the organization, its plans and strategy for the future, tax law and its implications for pay and benefit delivery, as well as a fundamental knowledge of payroll systems and procedures. It also requires the ability to manage an internal staff of professionals and their interaction with administrators in the field.

Mary Kale
Bethlehem Steel

Pay for Performance: A Viewpoint   You have probably seen references to "pay for performance" and how companies make sure that such systems actually deliver what they suggest. At Bethlehem, we do this in two ways. First, like most organizations, we have a merit recognition system that provides for adjustments in an employee's base pay. In order to earn such an award, individuals must demonstrate a consistently high level of performance and initiative. A second form of recognition at Bethlehem is one that is team based and business results oriented. Awards under this program are made in recognition of achieving specific levels of operations performance in a given year. All nonunion employees participate in this program (union employees have their own separate profit-sharing plan).

Bethlehem implemented this dual approach in 1984, before such initiatives were common in large organizations. A recent effort to evaluate the effectiveness of the overall program concluded with the assessment that the system, with minor enhancements, will continue to be an important catalyst in the company's effort to achieve its strategic business goals.

are paid. During the 1973–74 recession, many of these funds in the auto industry went bankrupt. They provided less income security than was thought. Studies on plans in which unemployment was less severe than in autos show the system has helped in employment security.

In many organizations, the employer provides some income bridge from employment to unemployment and back to employment. This is *severance pay*. Typically, it amounts to one week's pay for each year of service. About 25 percent of union

CAREER CHALLENGE

(*continued*)

*I*n summing up what she had told Joe about compensation, Mary Renfro said, "Joe, that's it. We've discussed a lot of human resource management problems." Then she summarized the situation at Cardeson National Bank for him, as follows:

- You are making all the pay decisions. You hire people and pay them what you think they are worth, based on their experience (as you see it), their potential (as you see it), and their needs (as you see them). This has caused us a lot of inequity problems. Remember Arte Jamison? He was really underpaid and we lost him. You don't use pay surveys. You don't use job evaluation. You don't have pay classification — nothing. It's all in your head, and it varies with your feelings at the moment. You have ignored the equal-pay laws.

- You give raises similarly and throw in some factor for seniority — how, we don't know.

- Our turnover and absenteeism are high. I think that's largely because of pay problems. Turnover and absenteeism are complex factors, like profit. But you have been hearing a lot of complaints about pay lately, haven't you? Where there's smoke . . . . I've shown you the cost figures on turnover and absenteeism. It's a real cost. And that doesn't count morale problems directly — surly tellers, and so on.

- Executive turnover is high, too. It appears low pay and few incentives are one cause.

- There is pressure to put everyone on salary — as Tom Nichols knows.

- In spite of our pay secrecy policy, word about the differential pay situation is getting out. Remember Martha?

- We don't have a raise policy. We don't have a pay strategy.

- Should we continue time pay only, or go to an incentive plan, like a suggestion system or profit sharing?

While Joe is pondering these points, Guido stops by the office to help Mary make her points.

Guido Boss, Mary has some specific suggestions for you. They're all in her report that I've given you. I've discussed them with some of the other VPs and they generally agree . . . .

Joe Oh, they do, do they? I'll bet it'll all cost a lot of money. How can you build a bank like I'm trying to do and give away all the profits? I've been fair with everybody. And what do I get — complaints!

Well, Mary, show me where your specific suggestions for our personnel needs are in your report and I'll read them. I'll let you know.

Mary's report contained the following recommendations:

1. That one of the vice presidents be delegated to handle day-to-day HRM matters. Joe would deal only with policy decisions.

2. That a job evaluation point system be set up to determine proper pay. No person would have his or her pay lowered. But some people being paid below the suggested pay level should be raised as soon as possible. Those overpaid should be held at the same level until they are in the right category.

3. That area wage surveys be consulted in making pay decisions.

4. That a pay structure be set up.

5. That a pay strategy of paying going wages be approved.

6. That a systematic raise policy be established as soon as possible, fixing timing of, amount of, and criteria for raises.

7. That the pay secrecy policy be continued.

8. That current use of hourly pay and salaries be continued.

9. That the possibility of incentive pay for executives and other employees be investigated.

contracts require such severance pay. It doesn't guarantee a job, but it helps the employee when a job is lost.

In times of layoff, the basic security for most employees is their seniority. If an organization is unionized, the contract normally specifies how seniority is to be computed. Seniority guarantees the jobs (and thus the compensation) to employees with the longest continuous employment in the organization or work unit. Even in nonunionized situations, a strong seniority norm prevails, which gives some security to senior employees.

The United Auto Workers (UAW) and General Motors entered a job security agreement in 1984. It was decided that if jobs were eliminated by technological advances or because General Motors decided to buy more parts from cheaper sources rather than make them itself, those workers would be given other jobs within the company at the same pay—and retrained if necessary. Eligibility is determined by seniority; it is assumed that lifetime jobs are guaranteed for about 60 to 70 percent of the workers. This is roughly the same percentage of workers in major Japanese auto companies who have such pay and job security. A similar agreement was reached in 1990 negotiations.

General Motors, under the job security agreement, is allowed to eliminate as many as 100,000 jobs as it continues to install more robots on its assembly line and to farm out more parts orders to nonunion and foreign firms. How General Motors will absorb workers as they technologically move forward is still a problematic issue.[87]

Exhibit 11–6 traces some landmarks in pay, concessions, and pay–job-security issues involving management and labor. From 1948 with the annual cost-of-living adjustment (COLA) to the 1984 agreement on job security and pay, the auto workers and management have set precedents for other industries. One study reports that **COLA plans** are used in over 50 percent of the firms surveyed.[88]

EXHIBIT 11-6   From Paid Vacations to Quality Control Programs

1940	1948	1949	1955	1961
Establishment of 40 hours of annual paid vacation for employees with at least one year on the job.	An annual cost-of-living allowance {COLA} is written into Big Three contracts for the first time.	The Ford Motor Co. agrees to fund the auto industry's first blue-collar pension plan.	UAW president Walter Reuther vows to win a guaranteed annual wage—but settles for a supplemental unemployment benefit {SUB} fund.	The first profit-sharing plan is negotiated at tiny American Motors Corp.—but AMC did not make enough money that year to pay off.

1970	1980	1982	1984	1987
Pension plans are redrawn to allow retirement after 30 years' service.	UAW president Douglas Fraser is elected to the Chrysler Corp. board of directors.	Trapped in their worst peacetime sales slump since the 1930s, the Big Three wring an estimated $3.5 billion in wage concessions from the UAW.	UAW and General Motors agree to job and pay security plan for between 60 and 70% of firm's union members.	A moratorium on plant closings and union involvement in quality control.

Source: Adapted from (September 24, 1984), "Detroit Breaks New Ground," *Newsweek*, p. 49; Donald F. Ephlin (February 1988), "Evolution by Revolution: The Changing Relationship Between GM and the UAW," *Academy of Management Executive*, pp. 63–66; John Hillkirk (September 18, 1987), "Ford, UAW Reach Accord on Contract," *USA Today*, p. 1B.

CAREER CHALLENGE

(concluded)

A week later, Mary and Guido caught Joe in his office. He'd spent much of the time since their last meeting at the branch offices — very unusual behavior for him.

Guido Boss, are you free?

Joe I'm very busy. But come in for a moment.

Guido Mary and I have been wondering if you've had a chance to decide on those pay policy issues.

Joe Yes, I have. I believe we are a small bank. We don't need a lot of paperwork and bureaucracy. So I decided to chuck the whole report in the waste-basket.

Then I thought it over and decided I ought to compromise. So I accept suggestions 5, 7, and 8. I've already appointed John Bolts to investigate who is letting out the salary information around here. Now, I'm very busy. So please excuse me.

Six months later, Mary Renfro left the bank. Executive and employee turnover had continued to increase. Guido Panelli took a position with another company about six months after Mary left. The bank still has two branches and about the same number of employees. Profitability has declined some, but the bank is still profitable.

Pay Compression

Pay compression occurs when employees perceive that there is too narrow a difference between their own pay and that of their colleagues.[89] Many companies in the United States face a narrowing of the gap between senior and junior employees and between supervisors and subordinates.[90] Differentials of 10 percent or less are not unusual, and, in some instances, junior employees are brought in at salaries greater than those of their superiors. The resulting low morale can lead to decreasing productivity and higher absenteeism and turnover. One way to identify pay compression is to examine the relationship between salaries and incumbents' years of experience with the company.

Solutions for the pay compression problem include the following: (1) reexamining how many entry-level people are needed; (2) reassessing recruitment itself; (3) focusing on the job evaluation process, emphasizing performance instead of salary-grade assignment; (4) basing all raises on longevity; and (5) giving first-line supervisors and/or other managers the authority to recommend equity adjustments for selected incumbents who have been unfairly victimized by pay compression.

Two-Tiered Compensation Plans

Two-tiered compensation plans for nonmanagers date back to the 1930s. Today, however, they are growing in use in a number of industries.[91] The basic idea of **two-tiered compensation plans** is to protect the wages of workers hired before a certain date, but start new workers at a lower pay rate. Thus, older (in terms of company

---

EXHIBIT 11-7   Two-Tiered Wage Pay Plan

| Company | Workers Covered | Rate of Pay | | Difference |
		Older Workers	New Workers	
Boeing	26,000	$11.38/hour	$6.70/hour	$4.68
Giant Food	12,000	$5.96/hour	$5.00/hour	$1.95
American Airlines (pilots)	4,000	$36,000/year	$18,000/year	$18,000
Briggs & Stratton	8,000	$8.00/hour	$5.50/hour	$2.50
Dow Chemical	2,600	$7.08/hour	$6.90/hour	$0.18

Source: Adapted from Steven Flax (January 9, 1984), "Pay Cuts Before the Job Even Starts," *Fortune*, pp. 75–77.

---

tenure, not necessarily age) and new workers, although working side by side, would be paid differently. Management has supported two-tiered plans in order to lower labor costs.

Examples of the new worker differentials covered by labor contract agreements in various firms are presented in Exhibit 11–7. Under some two-tiered plans, new employees eventually attain the level of wages or salaries earned by older employees. Other plans are structured so that new workers will never attain the pay level of older workers. For example, newly hired employees at Kohler Company are frozen into a plan that pays them about 15 percent less than older employees.

There is some risk associated with two-tiered plans. The new workers may eventually question the equity of such a plan. There is also the possibility of legal liability. A union that agrees to such a plan may be liable for not representing all members equally under the duty of fair representation. However, when pay scales reach such levels that the costs are exorbitant or are noncompetitive, there may be few alternatives to job loss besides a two-tiered pay system.[92]

A recent research study examined perceptions of equity of nonunion workers in a permanent two-tier wage structure. The subjects were nonskilled production workers at a midwestern tool and die company. Low-tier employees were found to be more likely to perceive the wage structure as unfair, to have lower satisfaction with pay and lower organizational commitment, and to report poorer worker-management relations than high-tier employees.[93] Because of these attitudes, nonunion firms with two-tier pay systems may be more vulnerable to certification campaigns to bring in a union.

SUMMARY

Chapter 11 has continued the discussion of compensation by presenting some very important issues: individual pay determination, methods of payment, incentive forms of pay, executive compensation, and compensation administration issues. Chapter 12 will finish the discussion of the compensation system by covering all forms of benefits, both mandatory and voluntary.

1. The individual pay determination questions asks "How should one employee be paid relative to another doing the same job?"
2. Methods of payment are:
   a. Hourly wage.
   b. Salary.

3. Incentive forms of compensation include:
   a. Merit pay.
   b. Individual incentives.
   c. Group incentives.
   d. Organization-wide incentives.
4. Most employees are paid salaries; exceptions are blue-collar and some clerical employees.
5. Individual incentive plans are the most effective method to tie pay to performance; group incentive plans are the next most effective; organizationwide plans are the least effective.
6. Skill-based pay rewards employees for gaining new knowledge and skills and is not based on the traditional job evaluation system.
7. The least effective plans for tying pay to performance are across-the-board raises and seniority increases.
8. Executive compensation is set on an individual basis because executives tend to be highly mobile.
9. In the United States, executives receive attractive compensation packages including high salaries, incentive compensation such as bonuses, and perks.
10. Executives in Britain, Germany, and Japan usually receive lower salaries than their counterparts in the United States because taxes are so much higher. Most receive more perks, and some receive higher incentives than U.S. executives.
11. Pay secrecy is still practiced by a majority of firms, but it can decrease motivation in both union and nonunion employees.
12. Pay compression can have a demoralizing effect on employees. Some system of correcting inequities created by pay compression should be put into practice.

KEY TERMS

bonus	405	Rucker plan	400
COLA plans	414	salary	392
gainsharing plans	397	Scanlon plan	398
Improshare	400	skill-based pay	402
incentive compensation	393	spot gainsharing	401
merit pay	393	stock option	405
pay compression	415	two-tiered compensation plans	415
profit-sharing plans	402	wage	392

QUESTIONS FOR REVIEW AND DISCUSSION

1. What two issues need to be addressed to make the individual pay-determination decision?
2. When employers decide to pay individuals doing the same job different rates of pay, differentials are based on what three things?
3. How would an employer choosing to pay different rates to people on the same job justify that decision? Give at least three reasons.
4. What is the most typical payment method: time-based or output-based? Why?

5. Define incentive pay. Compare individual incentive pay to a group incentive pay system.
6. Compare and contrast positive and negative aspects of suggestion systems and profit-sharing plans.
7. What is the difference between merit pay and performance-based pay?
8. Are individual incentives effective in increasing productivity? Why or why not?
9. What does the term *gainsharing* mean? Use the gainsharing plan at Lincoln Electric to help explain the concept.
10. Compare and contrast the Scanlon, Rucker, and Improshare gainsharing plans. How does spot gainsharing differ from other gainsharing plans?
11. Defend the following statement: "Skill-based pay is a good way to cope with foreign competition."
12. How is executive pay in the United States, Great Britain, Japan, and Germany the same? How does it differ?
13. Should compensation be kept secret? Why or why not?
14. When does pay compression occur? How can it be avoided?
15. Why does management support using a two-tiered pay system?

NOTES

[1] George T. Milkovich and William F. Glueck (1985), *Personnel/Human Resource Management: A Diagnostic Approach* (Plano, Tex.: Business Publications).

[2] Marc J. Wallace, Jr., and Charles H. Fay (1988), *Compensation Theory and Practice*, 2nd ed. (Boston: PWS-Kent Publishing).

[3] Adapted from Milkovich and Glueck, *Personnel/Human Resource Management*, p. 542.

[4] Ellen Wojahn (August 1983), "How to Value Your Employee," *Inc.*, pp. 93–96.

[5] George T. Milkovich and Jerry M. Newman (1990), *Compensation*, 3rd ed. (Plano, Tex.: Business Publications), p. 5.

[6] Ibid.

[7] Edward E. Lawler III (1971), *Pay and Organizational Effectiveness: A Psychological View* (New York: McGraw-Hill).

[8] Ibid.

[9] Pamela A. Kaul (August 1988), "Motivation Is More Than Pay," *Association Management* 40, no. 8, pp. 16–20, 244.

[10] Suzanne L. Minken (June 1988), "Does Lump-Sum Pay Merit Attention?" *Personnel Journal* 67, no. 6, pp. 77–83.

[11] Frederick S. Hills, K. Dow Scott, Steven E. Markham, and Michael J. Vest (September 1987), "Merit Pay: Just or Unjust Desserts," *Personnel Administrator* 32, no. 9, pp. 52–59.

[12] Brigette W. Schay (Summer 1988), "Effects of Performance-Contingent Pay on Employee Attitutes," *Public Personnel Management* 17, no. 2, pp. 237–50.

[13] Minken, "Does Lump-Sum Pay Merit Attention," p. 80.

[14] John F. Sullivan (May/June 1988), "The Future of Merit Pay Programs," *Compensation and Benefits Review* 20, no. 3, pp. 22–30.

[15] Frederick C. Thayer (Spring 1987), "Performance Appraisal and Merit Pay Systems: The Disasters Multiply," *Review of Public Personnel Administration* 7, no. 2, pp. 36–53.

[16] David Drennan (March 1988), "Motivating the Majority," *Management Today*, pp. 88–92.

[17] Ibid.

[18] Charles L. Hughes (June 1986), "The Demerit of Merit," *Personnel Administrator* 31, no. 6, p. 40.

[19] Arthus Geis (January 1987), "Making Merit Pay Work," *Personnel* 64, no. 1, pp. 52–60.

[20] John F. Bache (May 1986), "Merit Increase Programs: Do We Really Pay for Performance?" *Supervision* 48, no. 5, pp. 14–17.

[21] Wallace and Fay, *Compensation Theory and Practice*, pp. 254–58.

[22] Carla O'Dell (1986), *People, Performance, and Pay: America Responds to the Competitiveness Challenge* (Scottsdale, Arizona: American Compensation Association).

[23] Milkovich and Newman, *Compensation*, pp. 303–7.

[24] Timothy L. Ross, Larry Hatcher, and Ruth Ann Ross (May 1989), "The Incentive Switch," *Management Review* 78, no. 5, pp. 22–26.

[25] Thomas Denton (Winter 1989), "Establishing a Rank and File Incentive System," *Topics in Health Care* 16, no. 2, pp. 72–79.

[26] Hermine Zagat Levine (July/August 1989), "The View from the Board: Where Are We Going? Part 2," *Compensation and Benefits Review* 21, no. 4, pp. 47–60.

[27] Myron J. Roomkin (1989), *Managers as Employees: An International Comparison* (New York: Oxford University Press), pp. 266–68.

[28] Ross et al., "The Incentive Switch," p. 22.

[29] James E. Nickel and Sandra O'Neal (March/April 1990), "Small-Group Incentives: Gain Sharing in the Microcosm," *Compensation and Benefits Review* 22, no. 2, pp. 22–29.

[30] Roomkin, *Managers as Employees*, p. 267.

[31] Nickel and O'Neal, *Small-Group Incentives*, p. 28.

[32] (June 1987), "Case History: Contests Can Improve Productivity," *Small Business Report* 12, no. 6, p. 98.

[33] Wallace and Fay, *Compensation Theory and Practice*, p. 257.

[34] Don Nichols (December 1989), "Bottom-Up Strategies: Asking the Employees for Advice," *Management Review* 78, no. 12, pp. 44–49.

[35] Michael Moore (November 1988), "Employee Suggestion Systems Can Work," *CMA Magazine* 62, no. 9, pp. 40–42.

[36] Maryellen Lo Bosco (October 1985), "Suggestions Systems," *Personnel* 62, no. 10, pp. 16–21.

[37] Koji Okubayashi (Spring 1989), "The Japanese Industrial Relations System," *Journal of General Management* 14, no. 3, pp. 67–88.

[38] (February 1989), "Suggestions Systems: A Fresh Idea", *Incentive* 163, no. 2, p. 56.

[39] John Allen (March 1987), "Suggestions Systems and Problem-Solving: One and the Same?" *Quality Circles Journal* 10, no. 1, pp. 2–5.

[40] Ibid.

[41] Charles W. DeBettingies (Summer 1989), "Improving Organization-Wide Teamwork Through Gainsharing," *National Productivity Review* 8, no. 3, pp. 287–94.

[42] Christopher S. Miller and Michael H. Schuster (Summer 1987), "Gainsharing Plans: A Comparative Analysis," *Organizational Dynamics* 16, no. 1, pp. 44–67.

[43] Jay R. Schuster and Patricia K. Zingheim (Spring 1989), "Improving Productivity Through Gainsharing: Can the Means be Justified in the End?" *Compensation and Benefits Management* 5, no. 3, pp. 207–10.

[44] Jerry McAdams (Winter 1990), "Alternative Rewards: What's Best for Your Organization?" *Compensation and Benefits Management* 6, no. 2, pp. 133–39.

[45] Gene Epstein (October 1989), "Inspire Your Team," *Success* 36, no. 8, p. 12.

[46] Theresa M. Welbourne and Luis R. Gomez-Mejia (July/August 1988), "Gainsharing Revisited," *Compensation and Benefits Review* 20, no. 4, pp. 19–28.

[47] R. J. Bullock and Edward E. Lawler III (Spring 1984), "Gainsharing: A Few Questions and Fewer Answers," *Human Resource Management*, pp. 18–20.

[48] Barrie T. Smith (February 1986), "The Scanlon Plan Revisited: A Way to a Competitive Tomorrow," *Production Engineering* 33, no. 2, pp. 28–31.

[49] Miller and Schuster, "Gainsharing Plans," p. 45.

[50] Ibid., p. 53.

[51] Miller and Schuster, "Gainsharing Plans," pp. 60–61.

[52] Zane Goggin (October 1986), "Two Sides of Gain Sharing," *Management Accounting* 68, no. 4, pp. 47–51.

[53] Miller and Schuster, "Gainsharing Plans," p. 62.

[54] Randolph J. Ford (August 1985), "New Approaches Improve White Collar Productivity," *Industrial Engineering* 17, no. 8, pp. 48–53.

[55] Ibid, p. 63.

[56] Kathryn A. DeCamp and Robin A. Ferracone (September 1989), "Spot Gainsharing Provides High-Impact Incentives," *Personnel Journal*, pp. 84–88.

[57] Jeffrey C. Ewing (January/February 1989), "Gainsharing Plans: Two Key Factors," *Compensation and Benefits Review* 21, no. 1, pp. 49–53.

[58] Steve Markham and Dow Scott, "A New Job for the 90's," *Personnel Administrator* 33, no. 8, pp. 36–40.

[59] Milkovich and Newman, *Compensation*, pp. 322–24.

[60] Nina Gupta, Timothy P. Schweizer, and Douglas Jenkins, Jr. (October 1987), "Pay-for-Knowledge Compensation Plans: Hypotheses and Survey Results," *Monthly Labor Review* 110, no. 10, pp. 40–43.

[61] Paul M. Schafer and Michael B. Jones (July/August 1989), "Skill-Based Approaches to Secretarial Pay," *Journal of Compensation and Benefits* 5, no. 1, pp. 42–45.

[62] Vida G. Scarpello and James Ledvinka (1988), *Personnel/Human Resource Management* (Boston: PWS-Kent Publishing), p. 203.

[63] Dale Feuer (May 1987), "Paying for Knowledge," *Training* 24, no. 5, pp. 57–66.

[64] Edward E. Lawler III and Gerald E. Ledford, Jr. (February 1987), "Skill-Based Pay: A Concept That's Catching On," *Management Review* 76, no. 2, pp. 46–51.

[65] Gupta et al., "Pay-for-Knowledge Compensation Plans," p. 42.

[66] Fred Luthans and Marilyn L. Fox (March 1989), "Update on Skill-Based Pay," *Personnel* 66, no. 3, pp. 26–31.

[67] Lawler and Ledford, "Skill-Based Pay," pp. 30–37.

[68] Roomkin, *Managers as Employees*, p. 79.

[69] (May 28, 1990), "Corporate America's Most Powerful People: The Pay," *Forbes* 145, no. 11, pp. 266–317.

[70] Dana Wechsler (May 28, 1990), "Just Deserts," *Forbes* 145, no. 11, p. 208.

[71] "Corporate America's Most Powerful People," p. 267.

[72] Roomkin, *Managers as Employees*, p. 80.

[73] Bruce G. Posner (September 1989), "Inc.'s Annual Survey: Executive Compensation 1989," *Inc.* 11, no. 9, pp. 74–88.

[74] Raymond F. Gorman (Spring 1986), "Executive Compensation and Firm Size: An Agency Perspective," *Studies in Economic Analysis* 10, no. 1, pp. 60–71.

[75] Ellen Wojahn (September 1984), "The Take at the Top," *Inc.*, pp. 44–56.

[76] (November/December 1986), "If You Could Take Your Pick of Perks, What Sort of Perks Would You Pick?" *Successful Executive* 1, no. 6, pp. 30–31.

[77] Wilbur Lewellen and Howard Lenser (September–October 1973), "Executive Pay Preferences," *Harvard Business Review*, pp. 115–220.

[78] Daniel Seligman (June 11, 1984), "Believe It or Not, Top-Executive Pay Makes Sense," *Fortune*, pp. 57–62.

[79] "Executive Pay: The Top Earners," *Business Week*, pp. 88–116.

[80] "Rewarding Executives for Taking the Long View," *Business Week*, pp. 99–100.

[81] (May 21, 1984), "Growing Furor over Pay of Top Executives," *U.S. News & World Report*.

[82] Lisa Miller Mesday (March 19, 1984), "Are You Underpaid?" *Fortune*, pp. 20–25.

[83] Roomkin, *Managers As Employees*, pp. 39–40.

[84] Michael J. Bishko (May/June 1990), "Compensating Your Overseas Executives, Part I: Strategies for the 1990s," *Compensation and Benefits Review* 22, no. 3, pp. 33–43.

[85] (January 1986), "The Pros and Cons of Open Pay Policies," *Small Business Report* 11, no. 1, pp. 30–31.

[86] Robert Zager (May-June 1978), "Managing Guaranteed Employment," *Harvard Business Review*, pp. 103–15.

[87] (September 24, 1984), "Detroit Breaks New Ground," *Newsweek*, pp. 48–49. Also see Dale D. Buss (April 18, 1983), "Lifetime Job Guarantees in Auto Contracts Arouse Second Thoughts among Workers," *The Wall Street Journal*, p. 27.

[88] In a COLA plan, the Bureau of Labor Statistics cost-of-living index is used to make wage and salary adjustments. The consumer price index (CPI) is used as a cost-of-living index. It is a measure of changes over time of a hypothetical basket of goods and services. The adjustment is not based on performance. See Milkovich and Glueck (1985), *Personnel/Human Resource Management*, pp. 442–48; C. R. Deitsch and D. A. Dilts (March 1982), "The COLA Clause: An Employee's Bargaining Weapon?" *Personnel Journal*, pp. 220–23; and (July 29, 1980), "Inflation's COLA Cure," *Time*, p. 57.

[89] Wendell C. Lawther (March 1989), "Ways to Monitor (And Solve) the Pay-Compression Problem," *Personnel* 66, no. 3, pp. 84–87.

[90] Andrews S. Richter (June 1989), "Compensation: Putting Some Sanity Back in Salaries," *Business Month* 133, pp. 89–90.

[91] Steven Flax (January 9, 1984), "Pay Cuts before the Job Starts," *Fortune*, pp. 75–77.

[92] (September 1984), "Two-Tier Wage Plans Can Help Control Wage Costs If Administered Properly," *Management Review*, p. 4.

[93] Dean B. McFarlin and Michael R. Frone (Winter 1990), "A Two-Tier Wage Structure in a Nonunion Firm," *Industrial Relations* 29, no. 1, pp. 145–54.

EXERCISE 11–1 Paying People for Work

· · · · ·

Objective The exercise encourages students to think about job conditions and occupations in terms of the most appropriate, if any, method of payment.

SET UP THE EXERCISE

1. Listed below are several job conditions. Decide whether payment should be made on the basis of time worked (hour, week, month), or on the basis of number of units produced or output (for instance, generators, cars painted, vouchers filed).

Job Condition	Time Payment	Output Payment
1. Quality is very important.	_____	_____
2. Quantity is difficult to measure.	_____	_____

Job Condition	Time Payment	Output Payment
3. Workers perceive little relationship between effort/performance and rewards.	_____	_____
4. Equipment is unreliable; thus, there are large chunks of downtime.	_____	_____
5. Management wants to create more competition between workers.	_____	_____
6. Incentive systems have been very successful.	_____	_____

Now examine the jobs listed here. Decide whether payment should be made on the basis of time or output.

Job	Time Payment	Output Payment
Police officer	_____	_____
Auto worker	_____	_____
Coal miner	_____	_____
College professor	_____	_____
Trucker	_____	_____
Neurosurgeon	_____	_____
Professional baseball player	_____	_____
Air traffic controller	_____	_____
Homemaker	_____	_____
Accountant	_____	_____
Judge (lawyer)	_____	_____
Carpenter	_____	_____
Nurse	_____	_____
Cashier at checkout	_____	_____

2. The instructor will form groups to discuss the individual ratings. What did each group find? Were there a lot of similarities or differences in opinions? Have a group spokesperson discuss the findings.

A Learning Note

This exercise encourages you to think about how payment for work decisions is made difficult by the characteristics of the job. It also raises issues concerning how individuals in various occupations are paid.

EXERCISE 11–2   Developing a Positive Reinforcement Sales Program

Objective   The exercise is designed to have students apply principles of motivation in designing a positive reinforcement program for sales personnel.

Set Up the Exercise

1. Please read the facts individually.

Palmay Cosmetics is a small firm with 15 salespeople in the New York City area. The salespeople put on demonstrations to sell a full line of women's cosmetics in the homes of customers. Each demonstration will have between 10 to 15 neighborhood women in attendance. The Palmay salesperson has a specific New York area territory. Usually the territories are the areas in which the salesperson lives. The salespeople receive commissions at the rate of 12 percent on gross sales. Bonuses are paid if sales exceed a previously set sales goal established jointly by the sales director and each salesperson. Pension and insurance benefits are paid by the company.

Two years ago, Palmay had four salespersons. Currently the company has 15 salespersons and plans to add 15 more in two years because of the growth in sales. Unfortunately, there has been some turnover (five women have left and been replaced) in the past nine months.

The president of Palmay, Sonja Kimslow, believes that applying behavior modification can improve performance, reduce turnover, and increase the morale of the sales force. She would like a skeleton plan that outlines what the company can do in terms of a positive reinforcement program to accomplish these objectives.

2. The class or group is to be divided into groups — six, seven, or eight persons are ideal. Each group is to develop a positive reinforcement program for Sonja's review. Think about the following points in developing the plans:
   a. What reinforcers should be used? How were they determined to be what was needed?
   b. How and when should the reinforcers be used?
   c. How should the consequences be assessed?
   d. Should punishment be included in any plan to improve performance at Palmay?
   e. What assumptions did the group make in putting their plan together?
3. A spokesperson for each group should present the group's plan to the class.

A Learning Note

This exercise should illustrate that there are some problems and difficulties associated with implementing a positive reinforcement program. The evaluation of such programs is one of these difficulties.

APPLICATION CASE 11–1   Parkside Textile

. . . . .

Organizational Background

Parkside Textile was opened in 1937 in the small town of Parkside, Maryland, on the lower Delmarva Peninsula. Over the course of the past 53 years, they have manufactured many different types of garments, ranging from children's wear to military apparel during World War II. The company has gone through several ownership changes and is presently owned by David Worth of Cherry Hill, New Jersey. Mr. Worth owns several other apparel factories in Pennsylvania and Virginia. At the present time, Parkside does contract work by making women's blouses for a major manufacturer in New York City. Ten different styles are produced, ranging from polyester camp shirts to knit pullovers.

The U.S. apparel industry has been in a financial decline over the past several years. Foreign competition, especially from Korea, China, and Japan, as well as other Southeast Asian countries, has put tremendous pressure on U.S. manufacturers to reduce labor costs in a highly labor-intensive industry. As a result, conflict can develop between employees and managers over lower-than-cost-of-living wages. Both the internal and external environments of Parkside are highly volatile as foreign competition steadily increases. The effects of foreign competition tend to produce a highly dynamic industry environment.

The organizational hierarchy at Parkside Textiles is fairly simple. Dick, the manager, holds the top post. There are five separate departments, each with a distinct set of functions. The first department is the cutting room, which employs 10 people and has one supervisor, Francie. The second department is the parts department, employing 40 people, called *operators*, who make the parts of the blouses. The parts department has one supervisor, Gertie. The third department employs 50 operators who sew the completed parts of the shirt together. They have a supervisor named Winnie. The fifth and final department is the shipping department, employing 12 people and one supervisor, Dan. Dick, the manager, has one assistant, Willie.

Case Description

Parkside Textile has very few performance standards and those that are in place are rarely, if ever, enforced. Inexperienced operators are hired, seated at a machine, and told to sew. Their work is never checked, and mistakes often go unnoticed. Older workers distrust management because the younger operators are not responsible for their work "like it used to be." Older operators take pride in their work; younger operators usually don't.

There aren't any formal rules either. People show up at work at "their" convenience and often accumulate many unexcused days. Regardless of the amount of time missed, nothing is ever said by supervisors or management. When an operator is late or absent, other operators must pick up the missed work along with trying to keep up with their own primary jobs. This means that employees that are on time and don't miss work often become discouraged

Ten years ago, operators were required to be competent at no more than two different operations. With increased foreign competition and its lower labor costs, managers are forcing operators to do as many as 10 separate jobs. Previously, an operator worked at one job all day. Now she may be responsible for 5 to 10 distinct operations per day. Therefore, there is no predictability to job structure and morale suffers again.

The piece-rate system of compensation also draws much criticism from the operators. They earn a specified rate per 100 shirts and are therefore compensated directly for their efforts. The system itself is based directly on Frederick Taylor's scientific management incentive pay system, where pay is tied directly to work. Work standards or piece rates are based on the amount of pieces the "best" operator can generate in an hour. The result is that this best operator becomes the performance standard for the other operators (both experienced and unexperienced). Often slower operators are never able to match the best time and are never able to earn the specified amount of money established by

Prepared by Paul L. Ewell, M.B.A. and Jean M. Hanebury, Assistant Professor of Management, Salisbury State University.

the standard. What this incentive pay system does not take into account is that some operators are naturally slower than others and that setting the standard by the fastest worker is not necessarily fair.

"Time study experts" calculate the piecework rates. They time the operators, pick the best, and set the standards. Often, employees feel that the time study expert does not objectively time operators. They might favor one operator over another or dislike an operator. The employees feel that this bias produces inaccurate rates.

Favoritism is apparent in another aspect of Parkside's operation. Because the plant is small and has been located in the same very small town for many years, many of the employees belong to only a few families. One floor employs three sisters with one sister being the supervisor. The cutting floor employs a father and son, and another son is the supervisor of shipping. Operators express the feeling that they don't belong to the "right" family; therefore, they don't get paid fairly. The manager's wife is also employed at the plant, and the head mechanic is married to another one of the supervisors. To further complicate matters, Dick, the manager, tries to supervise all of the employees of Parkside directly. He often goes directly to an individual employee rather than using his supervisors.

Discussion Questions

1. Evaluate Parkside's compensation system. What is good about it? What could be improved?

2. Is the operators' job appropriate for a skill-based system? How could you use the skill-based pay system to correct some of the inequities you have identified at Parkside?

3. At present, Parkside is using an individual incentive system, piecework. Would it be possible to use a group or gainsharing incentive system at this small plant? Which one would be most appropriate? Why?

4. Spot gainsharing could be used to help correct some of the problems at Parkside Textile. How would you use spot gainsharing to deal with the morale problem, the poor attendance problem, the feelings that the piece-rate system is unfair, and favoritism?

5. Since so many employees belong to the same family, is an open or closed pay system appropriate for Parkside? Why?

12

EMPLOYEE BENEFITS AND SERVICES

·······

LEARNING OBJECTIVES

⊖

After studying this chapter, you should be able to:

• • •

Define what is meant by the terms *benefits, services,* and *pensions*

• • •

Explain why organizations provide benefits and services to employees

• • •

Understand how to manage an effective benefits program

• • •

Illustrate the costs of benefits and services to employers in different industries

CAREER CHALLENGE

Carl Reems was the president of Coy Manufacturing of Whiting, Indiana. It was Carl's intention to keep his work force as satisfied and productive as possible. A number of problems concerning the Coy employee benefits and services package have come to a head over the past few months. Carl listened to a presentation that Pete Lakich, Coy's director of human resources, made to the firm's executive committee. In the presentation, Pete used some figures that seemed wrong to Carl. Pete claimed that, in manufacturing firms in the Whiting area (located just southeast of Chicago), the average fringe benefit and services costs per worker totaled $6,240. In fact, Pete gave a specific item-by-item breakdown of these costs to the committee.

After the meeting, Carl had this talk with Pete:

Carl Pete, where did you get those fringe benefit figures? They seem wrong.

Pete Carl, these are facts based on my program of monitoring costs and benefits of fringes.

Carl We must be paying the highest fringe benefits in the entire area!

Pete As a matter of fact, we are a little on the low end of the scale. Among similar firms in our area we are in the bottom one third in fringe benefit costs.

Carl Do you think this is one of the reasons we are not able to recruit and hold skilled employees?

Pete I'm not certain, but there is probably some connection. You know how employees exchange and compare wage, fringe, and service information.

Carl Let's look at the entire range of our fringe benefits and services and see what is needed to become more competitive. We would probably even improve production and morale by improving benefits and services.

Pete We do need to take a look, but we can't be so certain that more and better fringes and services can make productivity and morale jump up.

Carl Pete, you're just too conservative about the power of money. The carrot and the stick can always do the job, even in Whiting, Indiana.

Pete Don't jump to conclusions.

Do you agree with Carl or Pete about the motivational power of benefits and services?

INTRODUCTION

Indirect financial compensation is called *benefits and services*, which consists of *all* financial rewards that are not included in direct financial compensation. Unlike pay for performance programs and incentive plans, benefits and services are made available to employees as long as they are employed by an organization.

Employee benefits and services are a part of the rewards of employment that reinforce loyal service to the employer. Major benefits and services programs include pay for time not worked, insurance, pensions, and services like tuition reimbursement.

This definition of benefits and services can be applied to hundreds of programs. There is a lack of agreement on what is or is not to be included, the purposes to be served, responsibility for programs, the costs and values of the various elements, the units in which the costs and values are measured, and the criteria for decision making. Compensation decisions with respect to indirect compensation are more complex than those concerned with wages and salaries. This chapter will show that Pete's opinions about the impact of benefits and services is a valid position in most situations.

WHY DO EMPLOYERS OFFER BENEFITS AND SERVICES?

The programs offered in work organizations today are the product of efforts in this area for the past 60 years. Before World War II, employers offered a few pensions and services because they had the employees' welfare at heart, or they wanted to keep out the union. But most benefit programs began in earnest during the war, when wages were strictly regulated.

The unions pushed for nonwage compensation increases, and they got them. Court cases in the late 1940s confirmed the right of unions to bargain for benefits: *Inland Steel v. National Labor Relations Board* (1948) over pensions, and *W. W. Cross v. National Labor Relations Board* over insurance. The growth of these programs indicates the extent to which unions have used this right. In 1929, benefits cost the employer 3 percent of total wages and salaries; by 1949, the cost was up to 16 percent; and in the 1970s, it was nearly 30 percent. By 1990, costs of benefits and services totaled about 50 percent.[1]

Some employers provide these programs for labor market reasons; that is, to keep the organization competitive in recruiting and retaining employees in relation to other employers. Others provide them to keep a union out or because the union has won them during negotiations. Another reason often given for providing benefits and services is that they increase employee performance. Is this reason valid? In a study of benefits, it was found that none of these reasons explained the degree to which benefits and services were provided.[2] As organizations grow in size, they offer more benefits. The move to provide employee benefits and services is just another manifestation of bureaucracy.

Who Is Involved in Benefit Decisions?

HR executives often seek professional advice from specialists such as a member of the Society of Professional Benefit Administrators. These persons are independent consultants or are employed by benefit carriers like insurance companies. In very large organizations, the compensation department may have a specialist in benefits, usually called a *manager* or *director of employee benefits*, such as Ernest Griffes of Levi

---

EXHIBIT 12-1   The Role of Operating and HR Managers in Benefits and Services

Benefits and Services Function	Operating Manager (OM)	HR Manager (HRM)
Benefits and services budget	Preliminary budget approved or adjusted by top management	Preliminary budget developed by HRM
Voluntary benefits and services	Programs approved by OM (top management)	Programs recommended by HRM
Communication of benefits and services	OM cooperates with HRM	Primary duty of HRM
Evaluation of benefits and services		Done by HRM
Administration of benefits and services programs		Done by HRM

Strauss & Co. Exhibit 12–1 shows who is involved in benefit decisions within an organization. How the benefits and services decision is made is discussed later in the chapter. Many authorities argue that all organizations should have benefits and services, but there is little concrete evidence that they affect employee productivity or satisfaction.

A DIAGNOSTIC APPROACH TO BENEFITS AND SERVICES

Exhibit 12–2 highlights the most important factors in the diagnostic model of the HRM function that affect the administration of employee benefits and services. Unions have had a great impact on benefits. In the 1940s and 1950s, a major thrust of their bargaining was for increased or innovative benefits. Union pressure for additional holidays is being followed by demands for such benefits as group auto insurance, dental care, and prepaid legal fees. Union leaders have varied the strategy and tactics they use to get "more" The long-range goal is getting employers to perceive benefits not as compensation but as part of their own social responsibility.

Government requirements have affected the benefits area significantly. Three major benefits are legally required: workers' compensation, unemployment compensation, and social security. Progressive income taxes and the policy of the Internal Revenue Service to allow deductions of benefits costs as expenses have encouraged their development. In 1971, the federal government mandated four long holiday weekends. Passage of the Welfare Fund Disclosure Act requires descriptions and reports of benefits plans. The National Labor Relations Board and the courts have stringent rules on eligibility for benefits and the employer's ability to change an established benefits plan. Finally, the government's tax policy influences benefits. At present, benefits are tax free, though some agencies (in Canada, for example) appear interested in taxing benefits as income.

Economic and labor market conditions influence benefit decisions because in tight labor markets organizations seeking the best employees compete by offering better benefits and services packages, which are nontaxable income. In addition, the composition of the labor market has had an increasing impact on the type of benefits and services offered. For example, the number of women in the work force has

EXHIBIT 12-2   Factors Affecting Benefits, Services, Pensions, and Results

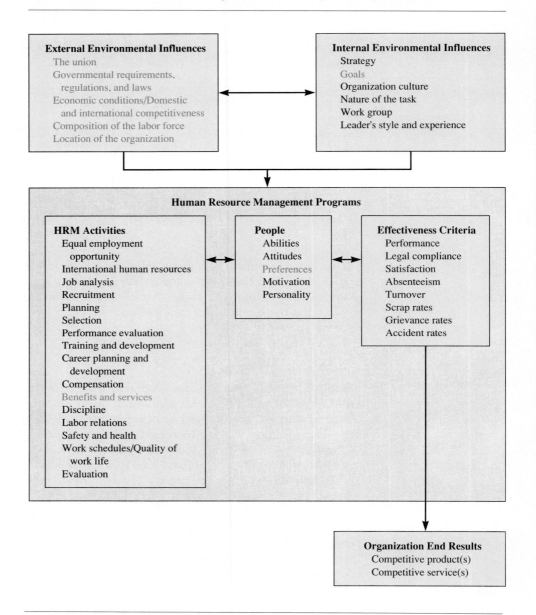

resulted in increasing pressure for longer maternity leaves, family leave benefits, child-care services, and elder-care services. The aging of the work force means that such services and benefits as preretirement planning, health insurance, and pensions are increasingly demanded.

The goals of managers and controlling interests affect the benefits-services package offered. Managers or owners may aim at employee satisfaction or may oppose unions. Also, other goals can influence whether a benefits program is set up and how generous it is.

Competition can induce an organization to add to or adjust its benefits-services plan. Certain companies are pacesetters in benefits; they introduce the newer benefits first. Examples of pacesetters in benefits are Apple Computer, Du Pont, Hewlett Packard, IBM, and Texas Instruments.[3] Let us look closely at the benefits offered by a sample company. Few companies can match the benefits that Time, Inc., employees receive. For example:

- If an employee works past 8 p.m. in New York, he or she not only receives $20 toward dinner, but also the right to take a cab all the way home (even if home is in New Jersey or Connecticut).
- The entire premium for medical and dental insurance for the whole family is paid by Time, Inc.
- The profit-sharing plan deposits into an employee's account 10 percent of his or her annual compensation, plus bonuses.
- The pension plan is completely paid into by the company.
- Education is paid if it's job-related, up to 100 percent of tuition.
- The company pays 50 percent of membership in an athletic club, provided the club has a cardiovascular fitness program.

Other leading employers follow the practices of pacesetters like Time, Inc. The benefits managers of the pacesetting companies regularly discuss benefits trends and read surveys of what the competition is offering.

In addition to observing and following pacesetters, many firms examine the preferences and attitudes of their employees toward them. For benefits to have an effect on employee satisfaction:

- Employees must know about their benefits.
- Employees must prefer the organization's benefits to those offered by other organizations.
- Employees must perceive the organization's benefits as satisfying more of their needs than competing employers' benefits would.

Presumably, if employees are satisfied with their benefits package, they will be absent less, be reluctant to quit, produce higher-quality products, and have fewer accidents. For benefits to have an affect on employee performance:

- Employees must see them as a strongly preferred end.
- Employees must perceive that by performing better they can increase their benefits.

Increases in the number of acquisitions and mergers during the 1970s and 1980s further complicated the benefits and services field as many successful takeover czars looted fat pension funds. International competition and the proliferation of the multinational corporation further affect the scope and type of benefits and services offered, especially to the expatriate employee.

MANDATED BENEFITS PROGRAMS

Three benefits programs offered by private and not-for-profit employers are mandated by federal and state governments. An employer has no choice about offering **mandated benefits programs** and cannot change them in any way without getting involved in the political process to change the existing laws. The three mandated programs are: unemployment insurance, social security, and workers' compensation.

Unemployment Insurance

In the 1930s, when unemployment was very high, the government was pressured to create programs to take care of people who were out of work through no fault of their own. **Unemployment insurance** (UI) was set up in the United States as part of the Social Security Act of 1935.

Unemployment insurance is designed to provide a subsistence payment to employees between jobs. The employer contributes to the UI fund (as do employees in Alabama, Alaska, and New Jersey). The base payment is increased if there is more than an average number of employees from an enterprise drawing from the fund (this is called the *experience rating*). Unemployment insurance and allied systems for railroad, federal government, and military employees cover about 65 million employees. Major groups excluded from UI are self-employed workers, employees of small firms with less than four employees, domestics, farm employees, state and local government employees, and nonprofit employers such as hospitals.

To be eligible for compensation, the employee must have worked a minimum number of weeks, be without a job, and be willing to accept a suitable position offered through a state Unemployment Compensation Commission. A Supreme Court decision granted unemployment insurance benefits to strikers after an eight-week strike period. The Court ruled that neither the Social Security Act nor the National Labor Relations Act specifically forbids making benefits payments to strikers. Each state decides on whether to permit or prohibit such payments.[4]

Federal unemployment tax for employers in all states accounts for .8 percent of payroll. The tax pays for administrative costs associated with unemployment compensation, provides a percentage of benefits paid under extended benefits programs during periods of high unemployment, and maintains a loan fund for use when a state lacks funds to pay benefits due for any month. Unemployment tax rates, eligibility requirements, weekly benefits, and duration of regular benefits vary from state to state.[5]

The employee receives compensation for a limited period. Typically, the maximum is 26 weeks, although a few states extend the term beyond this in emergency situations, such as when the number of insured unemployed reaches 6 percent.[6] The payment is intended to be about 50 percent of a typical wage and varies from a few dollars to over $200 a week in some states. Unemployment compensation averages about $109 a week nationally.

Before benefits are paid, the reason for being unemployed must be assessed.[7] An applicant can be disqualified for voluntarily quitting a job. On the other hand, a negotiated quit, that is, quitting to avoid discharge is a legitimate reason for collecting unemployment benefits. Some states penalize employers who report such quits as voluntary. Discharge from the job for work-related conduct usually means the applicant is disqualified. Proper documentation is an employer's best protection in unemployment hearings.

The unemployment insurance program is jointly run by the federal and state governments and is administered by the states. Federal guidelines indicate that presently the tax is 6.2 percent on the first $7,000 earned by each employee. Each state has its own set of interpretations and payments. Payments by employers and to employees vary with benefits paid, the experience ratings of organizations, and the efficiency of different states in administering the program. With the unemployment rate remaining relatively high, Alaska has enacted legislation that implements a job training program for persons receiving unemployment benefits. Nevada is conducting a feasibility study on the same type of program.[8]

PROFESSIONAL PROFILE

Paul J. Beddia
Lincoln Electric Company

Biography

Paul J. Beddia, a native of Dedham, Massachusetts, was graduated from Boston College and received his MBA from Fordham University.

He joined Lincoln Electric in 1956, working in Methods Engineering until 1964, when he transferred to the Boston office as a technical sales representative. Mr. Beddia moved to the Buffalo, New York, office in 1969, where he served as district sales manager. He returned to Cleveland in 1974 when he was promoted to assistant to the vice president of sales. On February 4, 1986, he was appointed to the position of sales manager. In July, 1989, he became vice president—Human Resources.

The Human Resource Function at Lincoln Electric Company The basic philosophy of the human resource function at the Lincoln Electric Company centers around the importance of people. The people we work with and the customers we serve deserve the very best we can offer at all times. Our main focus is on our employees — to encourage growth by involvement, participation, and teamwork.

While technology and capital are important in our efforts to improve quality, productivity, and profit, only *people* can make it happen! New technology, automation, and people skills must be constantly interfaced. Thus, we strive to create an environment where employees can achieve company and personal goals simultaneously.

We fully grasp and wholeheartedly accept the most essential fact of business life that the purpose of business is to make money. Profit is the resource which enables us to serve, grow, and prosper. Toward this end, we very aggressively try to do "nice things" to enhance our service. Most important, however, we are fully involved in the real business arena by being very profit-generating conscious. Our human resource function is part of a profit center. We concentrate and prioritize business opportunities, implement human resource business-oriented solutions, and measure the cost benefit of these solutions.

Our overall responsibilities include safety, employee relations, training and career development, recruiting and hiring, and benefits. The objective of each program is to positively impact quality, productivity, and profits.

Quality companies, products, or services are not the result of slogans, nor are they the outcome of management theories. Quality people are the key — those who are happy, in control, and motivated are the people who lead, manage, and work for successful companies. The challenge we face is to develop our "human" capital by enhancing all phases of an employee's life. Productivity and quality in the workplace are truly a function of the total human experience.

Unemployment compensation in both Canada and Europe differs from that provided in the United States.[9] For example, in Europe, employees who are placed on reduced work schedules (fewer hours per week) receive short-time unemployment compensation. Research has shown that the U.S. practice of paying unemployment only to those working zero hours can encourage the overuse of temporary layoffs. Canada, which has a much more liberal unemployment benefits program that includes both more liberal eligibility and faster delivery of benefits, has a much higher unemploymenet rate than the United States.

The availability of unemployment benefits affects when the covered employee returns to work.[10] Research using a large sample of unemployment insurance recipients found that both recalls of layoffs and new job acceptances increased sharply around the time of benefits exhaustion. Hard economic times seem to tempt more Americans to cheat on unemployment. Some individuals keep collecting and cashing unemployment checks after they find work. In 1982, it was estimated that approximately $3 billion a year may have been wasted through such fraud.[11] Based on this estimate, the government initiated a program to cut unemployment insurance fraud. The government is now using computers and extensive interviews to block costly fraudulent claims.

What can the employer do about UI cost increases? Responsible employers want to pay their fair share, but do not want to support abusers. They also do not want their experience ratings to increase costs. Much expert advice has been offered on how to cut costs of the program by stabilizing employment, keeping good records, challenging fraudulent claims, and issuing effective claim control procedures. Careful hiring and separation procedures, and claims verification and control can also cut costs. Effective managers try to control the costs of unemployment insurance just as much as inventory, advertising, or other costs.

Social Security

In 1935, the pension portion of the **social security** system was established under the Old-Age, Survivors and Disability Insurance (OASDI) program. (See Chapter 19 for disability and other provisions.) The goal of the pension portion was to provide *some* income to retired persons to *supplement* savings, private pensions, and part-time work. It was created at a time when the wealthy continued to live alone, the average person moved in with relatives, and the poor with no one to help them were put in a "poor house," or government-supported retirement home.

The program has a worthwhile objective. No one wants older peole to live out their last years in crushing poverty and with little or no dignity. Anyone whose grandparents had to live with their children because they could not survive any other way knows how hard this can be on everyone involved.

The basic concept was that the employee and employer were to pay taxes that would cover the retirement payments each employee would later receive in a self-funding insurance program. Initially, two goals were sought: adequate payments for all, and individual equity, which means that each employee was to receive what he or she and the employer had put into the fund. In the past 15 years, however, individual equity has lost out.

Social security taxes are paid by *both* employers and employees. Both pay a percentage of the employee's pay to the government. The percentage rose to 7.65 percent for both employee and employer in 1990. How much is paid by employee and employer is calculated on the average monthly wage (weighted toward the later years). Social security payments make up about one third of total federal outlays in the United States.[12]

Those receiving social security pensions can work part-time, up to a maximum amount that is increased each year to reflect inflation. The maximum a person aged 65 to 70 could earn before loss of social security benefits was $9,200 in 1990. Just about all employees except civilian federal government employees are eligible for social security coverage. Self-employed persons can join the system. They paid 10.75 percent in 1990, a tax of $4,579 for a person earning $42,600. Exhibit 12–3

EXHIBIT 12-3   Social Security Taxes, 1977–1990 and after

	Tax Rate for Employees and Employers (each)			Maximum Taxable Wage	Maximum Tax
Year	For Cash Benefits	For Hospitalization Insurance	Total		
1977	—	—	5.85%	$16,500	$ 965.25
1984	5.70%	1.30%	7.00	37,800	2,646.00
1985	5.70	1.35	7.05	39,600	2,791.80
1986	5.70	1.45	7.15	42,000	3,003.00
1987	5.70	1.30	7.15	*	*
1988–89	6.06	1.45	7.51	*	*
1990 and after	6.20	1.45	7.65	*	*

* The maximum will rise automatically as earnings levels increase.
Source: (January 1986), *Your Social Security* (Washington, D.C.: U.S. Government Printing Office), pp. 31–32.

shows that the tax rate paid by both employee and employer and the maximum taxable wage increased sharply between 1986 and 1990.

Employees become eligible to receive full benefits at age 65 or reduced benefits at age 62. Effective in 2027, an employee will not be able to retire with full benefits until age 67. If an employee dies, a family with children under 18 receives survivor benefits, regardless of the employee's age. An employee who is totally disabled before age 65 becomes eligible to receive insurance benefits. Under Medicare provisions of the social security system, eligible individuals aged 65 and older receive payments for doctor and hospital bills, as well as other related benefits and services.

The growth of international business has created another problem for companies dealing with social security payments.[13] The United States has international social security agreements with several countries. If such an agreement does not exist, social security law requires contributions to be paid on earnings of U.S. citizens or residents working for American employers *anywhere in the world.* As a result, U.S. citizens may have to make double contributions–once to the U.S. plan and once to the country in which they are employed. No contributions are necessary for those U.S. citizens employed by a foreign company, however.

In other countries, especially in Europe, more of the retirement burden is being transferred to the private sector by governments due to the financial strain created by aging populations.[14] Demographic projections in many countries show a consistent trend in the ratio of pensioners to social security contributors from the current 20 to 30 percent to nearer 40 to 50 percent over the next 40 years. Steps taken by foreign governments to meet this challenge include: (1) reducing the level of future benefits and (2) increasing social security taxes. More private retirement provisions are being made, particularly in Europe.

The same strong demographic trends are threatening the long-term financial security of Americans. These trends include longer life expectancy, an increasing risk of suffering long-term disability in older age, evolving work patterns, and new family norms. As a consequence, the elderly of the 21st century will need more money than previous generations did.[15] The most troublesome consequence of the aging baby boom's future is their potentially enormous need for long-term care. Several attempts to provide catastrophic health-care programs under social security have as yet proved unsuccessful. As an increasing number of workers hit retirement age, the ratio of active workers to social security recipients will decline alarmingly.[16] Therefore, the present pay-as-you-go scheme where current workers are taxed to provide the retirement income of current retirees will be threatened sometime after the year 2000.

Presidents Reagan and Carter called attention to some of the problems with the social security system. Specifically, they pointed out that the trust fund set up to pay the pensions was being rapidly depleted. This was happening for a number of reasons:

- Unrealistic inflation rate assumptions by the system's actuaries.
- Inaccurate assumptions of the birthrate.
- Unrealistic assumptions of the productivity increases by employees.
- Addition by Congress of beneficiaries who did not pay into the system fully.
- Withdrawal of many government employees from the system.

Another area of concern for the social security system is that many people continue to believe that social security is not just a supplement but should provide full support in retirement, at almost the same standard of living they had when they were working. Unfortunately, some voters reward congresspersons and senators who vote their way on a single issue. Social security is such an emotionally charged issue that voters listen very carefully to how a politician regards this benefit. The goal of providing full retirement support through social security benefits simply cannot be reached without a dramatic increase in taxes.

A number of changes in the social security system are being considered in an attempt to control future costs and benefits.[17] Probable changes include: (1) higher taxes on social security benefits; (2) participation of all state, local, and federal civil servants in the social security program; (3) beginning in the next three or four decades, employees will work longer and retire later; (4) dramatic changes in the social security, Medicare, and overall health-care systems; and (5) reduction in benefits. Probably the best way to save social security is to create a significant *communication* program to tell people the facts about retirement and social security. Everyone must understand these facts and comprehend how the facts apply to their own situations.

Women and Social Security   The social security system was designed around a model of the American family that is no longer valid. It was based on the traditional family structure in which the man worked outside the home and the woman stayed home to raise the children.[18] Under this system, married women usually earn *no more social security retirement benefits than if they'd never worked a day in their lives*. Most divorced women earn no more than half of their ex-spouse's benefit. Women widowed in their 50s who have no young children are not eligible to receive the benefits until they are 60. These inequities in the system, although acknowledged since the 1970s, have not been addressed because of the weakness of the system. Since the 1980s, when social security was put back on a sound footing, there have been two bills in Congress that seek to redress this inequity.

In 1989, the average monthly social security benefit for women was approximatly three-quarters of that paid to men ($488 compared to $639). By the year 2030, only one in three women over 65 will be married, further compounding the problem. Two other factors put women at a disadvantage. Women usually earn less than men, and they often stop working to care for children or elderly parents. The present system gives these women a difficult choice — base their social security benefits on their own earnings or get a check equal to 50 percent of their husband's, but not both. Divorced women must have been married at least 10 years to get spousal benefits. Since women live longer on average than men, more and more elderly women may be living in poverty in the future.

Workers' Compensation

Employees who incur expenses as a result of job-related illnesses or accidents receive a degree of financial protection from **workers' compensation** benefits. The workers' compensation programs are administered individually by the various states. Employers pay the entire cost of workers' compensation insurance. Premium expense is tied directly to each employer's past experience with job-related accidents and illnesses. The program should encourage employers to actively pursue safety and health programs — topics that will be covered in Chapter 19. Approximately 88.4 million workers were protected under workers' compensation insurance in 1987, and about $27.8 billion was paid to workers in benefits that year alone.[19]

BENEFITS AND RETIREMENT PLANS

In addition to the benefits required by the law, many employers also provide other kinds of benefits: compensation for time not worked, insurance protection, and retirement plans. There are many differences in employers' practices regarding these benefits. Exhibit 12–4 reports the percent of full-time employees in selected benefits programs in medium and large firms in 1989.

Compensation for Time Off

Can you imagine a life in which you went to work six days a week, 12 hours a day, 52 weeks a year for life? That's what life used to be like, although it has been shown that employees did not always work hard all that time. The concept of a paid holiday or vacation with pay did not exist. Now, most employers compensate for time that employees have not worked: break time, get-ready time, washup time, clothes-changing time, paid lunch and rest periods, coffee breaks, and so on. Employers also pay employees when they are not actually at work — holidays, vacations, sick leave, funeral leave, jury duty, and other personal leaves, such as to fulfill military obligations.

Studies of employees' preference indicate that work breaks are not strongly preferred; they are just expected.[20] Vacations are generally a highly preferred benefit. Preferences for holidays vary, and lower-paid and women employees have stronger preferences for sick leave. Unions have negotiated hard for added time off to give their members more leisure and to create jobs.

Let us take a closer look at some of the time off offered by employers.

Paid Holidays

Probably the most frequently offered of these times off with pay are paid holidays. At one time, every employee was paid only for actual holidays off with pay. The typical number of paid holidays has been increasing. Currently, 10 or more paid holidays are provided to full-time employees. The most typical holidays are: New Year's Day, Memorial Day, July 4, Labor Day, Thanksgiving Day, and Christmas. The new minivacation dates created by Congress through the federal

EXHIBIT 12-4 Percent of Full-Time Employees Participating in Selected Employee Benefits Program (Medium and Large Firms, 1989)[1]

Employee Benefits Program	All Employees	Professional and Administrative Employees	Technical and Clerical Employees	Production and Service Employees
Paid:				
Holidays	97%	97%	96%	97%
Vacations	97	98	99	95
Personal leave	22	28	30	14
Lunch period	10	4	4	16
Rest time	71	57	69	80
Funeral leave	84	87	86	80
Jury duty leave	90	95	92	87
Military leave	53	61	57	45
Sick leave	68	93	87	44
Maternity leave	3	4	2	3
Paternity leave	1	2	1	1
Unpaid:				
Maternity leave	37	39	37	35
Paternity leave	18	20	17	17
Sickness and accident insurance	43	29	29	58
Wholly employer financed	36	22	22	51
Partly employer financed	7	7	7	7
Long-term disability insurance	45	65	57	27
Wholly employer financed	35	50	43	23
Partly employer financed	9	15	14	4
Medical care	92	93	91	93
Employee coverage:				
Wholly employer financed	48	45	41	54
Partly employer financed	44	48	50	39
Family coverage:				
Wholly employer financed	31	28	25	37
Partly employer financed	60	64	66	54
Dental care	66	69	66	65
Employee coverage:				
Wholly employer financed	34	32	31	38
Partly employer financed	32	37	36	27
Family coverage:				
Wholly employer financed	25	23	21	28
Partly employer financed	42	46	46	37
Life insurance	94	95	94	93
Wholly employer financed	82	82	81	83
Partly employer financed	12	13	14	11
All retirement[2]	81	85	81	80
Defined benefit pension	63	64	63	63
Wholly employer financed	60	61	61	60
Partly employer financed	3	3	2	3
Defined contribution[3]	48	59	52	40
Uses of funds:				
Retirement[4]	36	43	39	31
Wholly employer financed[5]	14	15	14	12
Partly employer financed	22	28	24	18
Capital accumulation[6]	14	18	14	11
Wholly employer financed[5]	2	1	1	3
Partly employer financed	12	17	13	8

EXHIBIT 12-4   *(concluded)*

Employee Benefits Program	All Employees	Professional and Administrative Employees	Technical and Clerical Employees	Production and Service Employees
Types of plans:				
Savings and thrift	30	41	35	21
Deferred profit sharing	15	13	13	16
Employee stock ownership	3	4	3	3
Money purchase pension	5	8	6	3
Stock bonus	(7)	(7)	(7)	(7)
Stock option	(7)	(7)	(7)	(7)
Stock purchase	2	3	2	1
Cash only profit sharing	1	1	1	1
Flexible benefits plans	9	14	15	3
Reimbursement accounts	23	36	31	11

Note: Because of rounding, sums of individual items may not equal totals.

[1] Participants are workers covered by a paid time off, insurance, retirement, or capital accumulation plan. Workers eligible for paid or unpaid maternity and paternity leave are also covered. Employees subject to a minimu service requirement before they are eligible for benefit coverage are counted as participants even if they have not met the requirement at the time of the survey. If employees are required to pay part of the cost of a benefit, only those who elect the coverage and pay their share are counted as participants. Benefits for which the employee must pay the full premium are outside the scope of the survey. Only current employees are counted as participants; retirees are excluded.

[2] Includes defined benefit pension plans and defined contribution retirement plans. The total is less than the sum of the individual items because many employees participated in both types of plans.

[3] The total is less than the sum of the individual items because some employees participated in both retirement and capital accumulation plans, and in more than one type of plan.

[4] Plans were counted as retirement plans if employer contributions had to remain in the participant's account until retirement age, death, disability, separation from service, age 59½, or hardship.

[5] Employees participating in two or more plans were counted as participants in wholly employer-financed plans only if all plans were noncontributory.

[6] Includes plans in which employer contributions may be withdrawn from participant's account prior to retirement age, death, disability, separation from service, age 59½, or hardship.

[7] Less than 0.5 percent.

Source: U.S. Department of Labor (June 1990), *Employee Benefits in Medium and Large firms, 1989* (Washington, D.C.: Bureau of Labor Statistics), p. 4.

Monday-holiday law allow for three-day weekends in February for President's Day, in May for Memorial Day, in October for Columbus Day, and in November for Veteran's Day.

Paid Vacations   Another example of voluntary compensation offered for time not worked is paid vacations. This is the most expensive benefit for U.S. employers. Most organizations offer vacations with pay after a certain minimum period of service. The theory behind vacations is that they provide an opportunity for employees to rest and refresh themselves; when they return, hopefully, they will be more effective employees. Employees have pressed for more leisure to enjoy the fruit of their labors.

Government and military employees traditionally have been given 30 days' vacation. The typical vacation in the private sector is one week of paid vacation for an employee of less than a year's service, and two weeks for 1 to 10 years' service. Three-week vacations are offered annually to veterans of 10 to 20 years, and four weeks to the over-20-year tenured. In some firms, if employees don't take their vacations by the end of the year or a specified date, they forfeit the vacation days. Also, in some firms, if an employee is sick during a vacation, rescheduling the vacation is permitted. The trend in paid vacations for unionized employees is upward. It is predicted that by the year 2000 most people will receive about five weeks of paid vacation.[21] Vacations need to be well planned to allow the firm to continue to operate effectively.

International Vacation Benefits   U.S. employees earn higher real wages and have greater personal wealth than many foreign workers but they receive substantially less paid vacation than their international counterparts, especially in Western Europe. For example, workers in Western Europe get a guaranteed four or five weeks regardless of length of service.[22] In Japan, workers actually receive comparable vacation leave to the United States, but employees must often be forced to take time off. Research of vacation patterns in Europe has shown that unions were an important factor in determining longer vacations for all employees. If unions in the United States were allowed to be politically active as in Europe, vacation schemes here would be more comparable to the rest of the industrialized world.

Personal Time Off   Many employers pay employees for time off for funerals, medical/dental appointments, sickness in the family, religious observances, marriage, personal-choice holidays, and birthdays as holidays. If an organization uses flexitime scheduling (see Chapter 20), the need for time off is minimized. A BNA survey found that 9 out of 10 firms provide paid jury duty; 9 out of 10 provide paid leave for funerals of close relatives; and 7 out of 10 provide paid leave for military duty time. Typically, the pay is the difference between normal pay and military pay. Many policies apply to leaves for personal reasons, such as sickness in the family or marriage.

Sick Leave

Illness has a significant effect on the productivity of an organization. In most situations, organizations allow and pay for 1 sick day per month, or 12 per year. Employees often consider sick leave a continuation of salary, and thus the benefit is most often found among salaried workers. Accident and/or sickness insurance plans are more common with blue-collar employees.[23] A review of organization sick-leave programs shows some common characteristics.[24]

Sick-leave pay accrues over time (usually every pay period).

Upon termination of employment, no compensation is given for accrued sick leave. An exception to this policy is state and federal employees who can accrue sick leave and get paid upon termination.

Sick pay is granted when a worker is absent from work due to a short-term illness.

A written doctor's excuse is often necessary to return to work and get sick pay if the illness is longer than three days.[25] Sick-leave pay provides insurance to workers against loss of wages due to short-term illness.

A liberal sick-leave policy can cause *excessive* absenteeism.[26] It may communicate that the company does not value good attendance. Some firms are using what are called sick-leave banks to cut down on sick leave. Employees deposit a set portion of their earned sick-leave days into a company pool. Should an employee use all of his or her compensated sick leave, an application for withdrawal from the sick-leave bank can be made. However, these requests are carefully screened by a committee. The sick-leave bank has psychological benefits. Members become conservative in using banked days, using only what they need so that co-workers will have what they need in case of long-term illnesses or accidents.

The attitudes, expectations, and interest of society toward improved health, which characterized the 1980s, have found their way into organizations. Employees are placing a higher value and are more interested in maintaining good health. Consequently, there is now a growing interest in rewarding good health through organizational wellness programs.

For example, the Canadian Life Assurance Company implemented a fitness program that includes regular exercise and various health-education and lifestyle improvement classes.[27] Results have been impressive: Employees showed improvements in such measurements as body weight, body fat, flexibility, and cardiorespiratory fitness. Absenteeism was 22 percent lower than previously — estimated to be 2.5 days per person per year — which resulted in annual savings of $175,000 for the company.

Maternity and Parental Leave

The decline of the single income family has resulted in increased demand for another kind of benefit, maternity and/or parental leave.[28] The Pregnancy Discrimination Act of 1978, an amendment of Title VII of the Civil Rights Act, requires that pregnancy be treated just like any other temporary disability. Before the act, temporary disability benefits for pregnancy were paid in the form of either sick leave or disability insurance, if at all. Maternity leave and benefits are usually limited to six weeks, with or without pay. In addition to maternity leave, a few organizations provide paternity leave. For example, Bell Telephone gives fathers and mothers the option to take a six-month unpaid leave without the loss of benefits (for example, insurance) when a child is born. Mothers and fathers on Bell's plan are guaranteed the same job, or a similar one, at the same pay when they return to work.

The demands faced by expectant and working parents have created pressures to further accommodate employees' childbirth, adoption, and child-rearing responsibilities. The right of parents to stay home with their newborn child for a transition period without fear of losing their jobs and health insurance is still under argument at both the state and federal levels.[29] President Bush is said to support the idea of family leaves but does not believe they should be mandated by the federal government. In 1989, parental leave programs for either gender covered only 36% of full-time employees in medium- and large-size firms.[30] Paid maternity and parental leave was offered by 5 percent of employers in 1990.[31] Unpaid leave was offered by 42 percent of employers with the average length for most companies between 5 and 12 weeks. Less than 1 percent of the companies offered paid parental leave that averaged only three days.

The Family and Medical Leave Act, which has been considered in recent sessions of Congress, would require employers to give unpaid family leave to parents of newly born, newly adopted, or seriously ill children.[32] The General Accounting Office estimated that, if this law were passed, it would cost employers $236 million annually. However, employers, especially those with fewer than 100 employees, insist that this estimate does not include the cost of training employees to fill vacancies and lost productivity. Because of the increased political support for parental leave, organizations in the 90s may find that they have no choice but to provide time off for working parents.

Increased foreign competition and the growth of international business will also have an impact.[33] Parental leave policies are already established in Western Europe. For example, Germany has a complex set of special benefits including health and financial protection for pregnant women and young parents. Sweden has the most comprehensive and well-funded parental leave policy. The experience with family leave policies in Europe offers several lessons: A limited program of leave entitlements has a positive effect on productivity and creates few problems for employers; basic coverage should be established by law, giving employers the option to extend or embellish it; and basic parental leave benefits should carry some form of financial payment.

Employer-Purchased Insurance

The many risks encountered throughout life — illness (including drug dependency and AIDS), accident, and early death, among others — can be offset by buying insurance. Many employers can buy insurance cheaper than their employees can, and insurance is frequently offered as a benefit. The employer may provide it free to the employee or pay part of it. With the escalation in insurance costs during the 80s and 90s, the employee is being forced to participate by paying a share. Three major forms of insurance are involved: health, life, and disability/accident.

Health Insurance   Rising health-care costs have reached crisis proportions in the United States.[34] Health-care expenditures in 1988 totaled $500 billion and reached $600 billion in 1990. That is more than $1,500 for every U.S. citizen. In 1990, 11.4 percent of our gross national product (GNP) was spent on health care. On average, that translates into 11 cents for each dollar spent in the United States going for physician and hospital charges, prescription costs, and related health care needs like physical therapy. Employers bear a disproportionate amount of these escalating medical costs because 85 to 90 percent of all health insurance is purchased by employers as group plans.

Premiums on health plans increased 20 to 30 percent in 1989 and increases were approximately the same in 1990. Medical costs are increasing three times faster than the overall inflation rate. Every *Fortune* 500 firm spends over $100 million a year to provide health-care coverage with 13 percent of payroll dedicated to this purpose. Less than 10 years ago, only 5 percent of payroll went to health-care benefits.[35] Several factors help to continue this inflationary path: increasing health-care labor costs, an aging population, high cost of medical technology, rising malpractice insurance rates, oversupply of hospital beds, overutilization of and fee-for-service medicine, widespread transplants, AIDS treatment, and consumer belief that health coverage is an *entitlement*.

Health insurance can be purchased from Blue Cross (hospital expenses), Blue Shield (physician expenses), life insurance firms, or from a health maintenance organization (HMO). Blue Cross/Blue Shield runs its own HMO in addition to their traditional coverage. Studies indicate that employees prefer health insurance over most other benefits. Typically, health insurance includes hospitalization (room, board, and hospital service charges), surgical fees (actual surgical fees or maximum limits), and major medical fees (maximum benefits, typically $5,000 to $10,000 beyond hospitalization and surgical payments). Surveys report that almost all organizations have hospitalization plans, almost all non–blue-collar workers are provided with surgical and major medical plans, and about three fourths of blue-collar employees have major medical insurance.

Most employees get basic coverage. Beyond this, plans differ. Plans for salaried employees typically are of the major medical variety and provide "last-dollar coverage." This means that the employee must pay the first $200 of the cost or a similar deductible each year. Benefits may be based on either a specific cash allowance for various procedures or a service benefit that pays the full amount of all reasonable charges.[36]

Negotiated plans for time-pay workers generally have expanded coverage that provides specific benefits rather than comprehensive major medical coverage. This approach is preferred by union leaders because they feel individual benefits that can be clearly labeled will impress union members, and these benefits can be obtained with no deductible payments by employees. Also, until recently, coverage of some desired services was not available under major medical plans. Some of the more rapidly expanding benefits of the negotiated plans are prescription drugs, vision care, mental health services, and dental care. For example, typical dental coverage ranges from $1,000 to $2,000 yearly. About one employer in four provides this insurance.[37]

Health Maintenance Organizations (HMOs)
The Health Maintenance Organization Act of 1973 was intended to stimulate a prepaid health-care system. An **HMO** is a medical organization consisting of medical and health specialists (surgeons, internists, psychiatrists, nurses, physical therapists, and so on). HMOs offer outpatient services as well as hospital coverage for a fixed, monthly prepaid fee. Care is available 24 hours a day, seven days week. The emphasis of an HMO is on *preventative medicine* so that problems are caught in their early stages. Typically, the number of hospital days per 1,000 HMO members is about half the national average.[38] HMOs and other wellness programs will be discussed in more detail in Chapter 19.

Consolidated Omnibus Budget Reconciliation Act of 1985
Section 162(k) of the Consolidated Omnibus Budget Reconciliation Act of 1985 (COBRA) stipulates that employers with more than 20 employees are required to offer continuation of health-care coverage for 18 to 36 months after an employee termination.[39] COBRA has been amended three times since 1985. The act requires most employers to offer employees who leave the company the option of remaining members of the company's group health plans. Usually, employees who leave the company may extend coverage, at their own expense, for up to 18 months after termination.[40] For employees who were disabled when they left the company or who were working reduced hours, coverage can be extended to 29 months. COBRA explicitly states that spouses and children of covered employees can continue their coverage even if the employee dies or becomes eligible for Medicare. Disabled qualified beneficiaries can be charged up to 150 percent of the plan's applicable premiums since the passage of the Omnibus Budget Reconciliation Act of 1989 *(OBRA)*.

If an employer fails to comply with COBRA or OBRA regulations, the employer will not be allowed to deduct contributions made to that or any other group health plan. Employers complain that the legal details of COBRA will become a record-keeping nightmare. What triggers COBRA coverage is a qualifying event — death of a covered employee, divorce, legal separation, employee strikes, layoffs, and when a child ceases to be a dependent. Keeping track of qualifying events is causing anxiety and concern for HR managers who must comply.

Long-Term Care Legislation
The number of Americans older than 65 will double over the next 25 to 30 years.[41] This means that, unless the federal government becomes the major funding source for health- and custodial-care insurance,

the private insurance industry will need to provide policies to address these growing health-care concerns. Long-term care insurance products offered by employers under group plans are already growing in number.

Life Insurance

Group life insurance is one of the oldest and most widely available employee benefits. The employer purchases life insurance for each employee to benefit the employee's family. Group life insurance plans provide coverage to all employees without physical examinations with premiums based on the characteristics of the group as a whole.

Employee preference for group life insurance is not high. Surveys indicate that almost all employers offer group life insurance. In a typical program for a large company, the amount of insurance provided by the plan increases as salary increases, the typical amount being twice the salary in life insurance. But about a third of the companies surveyed have different plans for blue-collar employees, who usually get a flat amount (usually $5,000 to $10,000). Initially, the organization pays part of the premium, the employee the rest (contributory plan). The trend is moving toward noncontributory plans in which the company pays it all. But 34 percent of blue-collar, 38 percent of white-collar, and 40 percent of managerial plans are still contributory. In view of employee preferences, it probably should stay that way. Continued life insurance coverage after retirement, usually one third the coverage while working, is provided by 72 percent of large U.S. companies.[42]

Long-Term Sickness and Accident Disability Insurance

What happens to employees who have accidents at work that leave them unable to work, temporarily or permanently? Workers' compensation pays a very small part of these costs, since it was designed primarily to take care of short-term disability problems (see Chapter 19). Employer-funded, long-term disability insurance is designed to cover these cases, with payments supplementing benefits from workers' compensation, social security, and other agencies.

Some disability payments are very large. A roofer in Georgia who fell off a roof received over $5 million. About 75 percent of larger firms have this kind of insurance. Usually, blue-collar workers are covered by flat-amount coverage (usually $5,000 to $10,000). For other employees, coverage is tied to salary level. Usually, there is noncontributory coverage for all employees. The goal is to provide employees with at least half pay until pension time, but the primary recipients have been non–blue-collar employees.

The majority of long-term sickness and accident disability insurance plans provide benefits for up to 26 weeks. But about 20 percent provide these benefits for a year. About 75 percent of organizations provide such sickness and accident coverage.[43]

INCOME IN RETIREMENT

Retired employees can receive income from a number of sources: (1) savings and investments, (2) individual retirement accounts, (3) government pensions, and (4) employer pension plans.

Retirement Income from Savings and Work

An important source of retirement income is from savings. Studies find that persons save more (percentage-wise and absolutely) the higher their income, and those with private pensions are more likely to save money for retirement than those without them.[44]

Until the mid-1970s, little change in savings took place after social security started. As people were forced to pay social security taxes, their private savings for retirement tended to decline. But social security does not allow much work after retirement, and thanks to medical science and improved life style, people are living longer. So employees have seen the need to save more during their working years and have begun to do so. More persons will have to work to supplement social security payments in view of inflation, but if social security benefits increase substantially, people will save less during their work years.

IRAs and the 1986 Tax Reform Act

Under the 1981 law, any employee could make annual tax-excludable contributions of up to $2,000 to an individual retirement account **(IRA)** even if he or she was already enrolled in a company pension plan. If the employee contributed to a separate IRA for a nonworking spouse, they could make an overall annual contribution of $2,250. However, under the 1986 Tax Reform Act, no deductible IRA contributions can be made by active participants in an employer-sponsored retirement program, either for themselves or for their spouses, if their income is about the cutoff point of $50,000 of adjusted gross income on joint returns, or $35,000 on single. The term *active participant* is defined as one who participated, whether vested or not, in a private or public employer-sponsored retirement plan for any part of the plan year ending within the individual's taxable year.[45] Qualified voluntary employee contributions (QVECs), which allow an employee to contribute to a retirement plan and receive a tax benefit, are not permitted under the 1986 law.

Reducing deductibility for IRAs will discourage some individuals from saving for their retirement, which is not a desirable consequence. The final verdict on the impact of the 1986 law on retirement savings and conditions will not be apparent for a number of years.

An employee can have both a qualified voluntary employee contribution (QVEC) plan and an IRA.[46] A *qualified voluntary employee contribution* means that the employee pays, but the employer does not. The money is deposited with a qualified pension, profit-sharing, or similar plan. An employee who contributes, say, $1,000 to a QVEC can deposit only $1,000 in an IRA.

The employer has a number of alternatives under the 1981 law. The employer can add a QVEC provision to one or more of its existing plans or adopt a new plan offering employees a QVEC opportunity. Also, the employer can ignore QVECs altogether. Employees under the law will probably turn to the many IRAs offered by banks, insurance companies, and other financial institutions if they wish to accumulate tax-deductible contributions.[47] Some employers have decided to sponsor an IRA by arranging for withholding of employee pay and the transmittal of contributions to the employee-designated IRA agency. What management chooses, and how it affects its choice, is likely to have long-term implications for a company's benefits program and for its HRM policies overall.[48]

SEP-IRAs

Only 12 percent of small firms with fewer than 10 people are covered by a pension compared to 82 percent where payroll is 250 employees or more.[49] Small companies could implement simplified employee pension IRAs **(SEP-IRAs)** for each of their employees, however. What the company actually does is finance an individual retirement account for each employee. Maximum annual contribution to each account is $30,000 or up to 15 percent of compensation, whichever is less. Business contributions to the accounts are tax deductible and are not subject to social security or unemployment taxes. Funds are taxable when withdrawn upon retirement.

The 401(k) Plan

Internal Revenue Code Section 401(k) allows employees to save on a tax-deferred basis by entering into salary deferral agreements with their employer. The 1981 law permitted maximum salary deferral of $30,000 annually. The 1986 Tax Reform Act, however, reduced the salary deferral to $7,000 subject to slight increases as the cost of living increases. Deferrals to a **401(k) plan** must be coordinated with other salary deferrals if the individual participates in other plans. IRS pension regulations issued on May 14, 1990, modify regulations and allow employers to "restructure" 401(k) plans into components.[50]

The 401(k) plan helps employees save for retirement and encourages saving.[51] In some plans, employers match employee contributions. Most employees prefer 401(k)s to IRAs, and the number of firms offering such plans has risen dramatically in the last five years. The success of the 401(k) plan rests on identifying how much salary can be deferred to the plan, known as the *average actual deferral percentage* (ADP).[52] Nonprofit organizations cannot offer the plan at the present time, but Congress is considering lifting this restriction.[53]

Private Pensions

Most elderly Americans believe that security in the later years rests on a three-legged stool consisting of social security, savings, and private pensions. In 1989, an average retired couple had an income of about $15,200 per year of which 35 percent came from social security, 20 percent from private pensions, and the balance from savings, stocks, other assets, or employment after retirement. By the year 2010, social security and private pensions combined will provide no more than 40 percent of retirement income. More and more retirees will have to finance retirement by going back to work or remaining in the workplace longer. Combined with increasing longevity and inflation, the retiree of the 1990s will find it more and more difficult to maintain the same standard of living once retired.

All of the legs of the stool are wobbling. Personal savings are no longer considered a secure nest egg. There are problems with the stability of both the savings and loan and conventional banking system. Americans are noted for their anemic savings rates. Real estate investments no longer have a guaranteed payoff for the retiree with a paid-off-home. The health of social security is still at risk because of deficit spending, and many private pensions have been defunded. Therefore, it is important to examine the private pension system to see how it is changing.

Like many other benefits, private pensions are relatively new; the private pension plans in existence prior to 1950 covered less than one sixth of the nonagricultural work force. In the 1950s, many new plans were introduced and coverage was doubled. By 1960, about 15 million workers were covered. Coverage during the 1960s remained rather stable, and the percentage participating had also stabilized. Research by the Employee Benefit Research Institute shows that only 21 percent of self-employed workers are covered by some type of private pension plan, compared to 55 percent coverage among all workers.[54] In addition, the level of funding and number of private pension plans were eroded during the 1980s when acquisitions and mergers raided fat pension funds.

Studies found that the kinds of employees covered by private pensions vary greatly. Certain industries (mining; manufacturing, especially nondurable goods; construction; transportation; communication; and public utilities) tend to provide pensions more than others (retailing and services). Larger firms are more likely than smaller firms to have pensions. The higher the employee's income, the more probable it is that a pension exists. Unionized employees are more apt to be covered than nonunion employees. However, everyone working for employers with pension plans is not covered. Part-time employees, for example, are rarely included in pension plans.

With the increase in the existence of private pensions, there has been a dramatic reduction in the labor force participation rate of men aged 55 to 64.[55] By 1965, many private pension plans tended to change their rules toward the encouragement of earlier retirement. Combined with more generous social security benefits, these changes explain the tremendous increases in early retirement between 1965 and 1990. It is expected, however, that, as employees continue to react to pension uncertainty, fewer will opt for early retirement. The aging of the work force, the increase in longevity of the average American, and the tremendous increase in the level of pension liability have begun to change both the amount and type of private pensions being offered.[56]

Private employers are trying to make their retirement programs better to accomplish their corporate objectives. Defined benefits plans are on the decline in favor of defined contribution plans like the 401(k).[57] The reasons for this change include regulatory reductions in benefits for senior managers; increased administration costs; risk of severe sanctions for overfunded plans; and the increased likelihood of government scrutiny. Companies that are considering this change to defined contribution plans need to do several things. They should:

Clearly set corporate objectives.

Understand the advantages and disadvantages of each plan.

Measure the adequacy of expected benefits.

Carefully communicate the plan's benefits to employees.

Criticisms of Private Pensions   There is loud criticism of the private pension system. The criticisms center on mismanagement, misrepresentation of funds, and failure to keep up with inflation. For example, some people who thought they were covered were not because of complicated rules, insufficient funding, irresponsible financial management, and employer bankruptcies. Some pension funds, including both employer-managed and union-managed funds, have been accused of mismanagement, and others have required what the critics considered unusually long vesting periods. Over the years, therefore, pension regulation laws have been regularly debated. ERISA was passed in 1974 to respond to some of the criticisms.

Government Regulation of Private Pensions   The law regulating private pensions is the Employee Retirement Income Security Act **(ERISA)** of 1974. ERISA was designed to cover practically all employee benefit plans of private employers, including multi-employer plans. Basically, the legislation was developed to ensure that employees covered under pension plans would receive the benefits promised.

Existing regulations were tightened in ERISA, but the major impact of the law is in the minimum standards established, which all plans are required to meet. ERISA *does not require an employer to have a private pension plan*. Indeed, many existing private pension plans were terminated instead of meeting ERISA's requirements. The major provisions of the law are as follows:

Eligibility Requirements   Organizations were prohibited from establishing requirements of more than one year of service, or an age greater than 25, whichever is later. An employee hired before the age of 22 who continues unbroken service must at age 25 be given at least three years' service credit for vesting purposes (see explanation of vesting below). Employers who provide immediate 100 percent vesting are exempted in that they may require a three-year eligibility period.

Benefits Formula   A benefits formula is used to calculate the size of a pension payment. It expresses the relationship between wages and salaries earned while employed and the pension paid.

The first step in determining the formula is to indicate which earnings figure should be used as a base in this computation.[58] Some experts have noted a trend toward using the average of the final several years of employment as the base earnings figure. An earlier approach was to average career earnings, but this is not fair in an inflationary period.

Once average earnings are determined, by whichever formula approach is used, the actual pension benefit is determined by multiplying the average earnings times the number of years of service times the stipulated percentage, generally between 1 and 3 percent. Some firms offset this figure to some degree by social security benefits. This approach is generally designed to yield a monthly benefit, including social security; that is, approximately 50 percent of the individual's projected salary during the final year of employment.

Vesting Practices   **Vesting** is the right to participate in a pension plan. Pension plans state how long an employee must be employed before he or she has a right to a pension or a portion of it should the employee quit. When the employee has completed the minimum time after which he or she has a right to a pension, he or she is said to be *vested* in the pension.

The employer may choose from three vesting alternatives:

1. The 5-year service rule, whereby the employee receives 100 percent vesting after 5 years of service (note: employee contributions are fully vested *immediately)*.
2. The graded 15-year service rule, whereby the employee receives 25 percent vesting after 5 years of service, graded up to 100 percent after 15 years.
3. The rule of 45, which provides 50 percent vesting when age and service equal 45 (if the employee has at least five years of service), graded up to 100 percent vesting five years later.

The new vesting standards appear to provide a major advantage to employees. Previously, those who changed employment after 5 to 10 years of service did not receive benefits; now they will. Although small, the benefits received will increase the total income at retirement.

The vesting schedule used by a firm is often dictated by the demographic makeup of the workers.[59] An employer with a high-turnover situation may want to use the 100 percent vesting, 5-year scheduling. This means that any employee with fewer than 5 years service at the time he or she quits or is terminated receives no vested pension benefits.

Portability Practices   **Portability** is the right to transfer pension credits accrued from one employer to another. It becomes possible when several employers pool their pensions through reciprocal agreements.

From the employee's point of view, it is desirable for pensions to be transferable or portable. Employers, however, find portability an expensive provision. Under ERISA, portability becomes a voluntary option of the employee and his or her employer. If the employer agrees, a vested employee leaving a company is permitted to transfer (tax-free) the assets attributable to his or her vested pension benefits or vested profit-sharing or savings plan funds to an individual retirement account (IRA). The benefit to employees is in the opportunity to defer the payment of taxes on the funds.

Fiduciary Responsibility   **Fiduciaries** are persons responsible for pension trust funds. Because of the need to provide more effective safeguards for pension funds, the law has imposed new standards for fiduciaries and parties-in-interest such as trustees, officers or directors of the company, controlling shareholders, or attorneys. The "prudent man" rule is established as the standard for handling and investing pension plan funds.

A fiduciary is prohibited from engaging in certain activities. He or she may not: (1) deal with the fund for his own account; (2) receive personal consideration from any party dealing with the fund in connection with a transaction involving the fund; (3) make loans between the fund and a party-in-interest; and (4) invest more than 10 percent of the assets of the pension plans in securities of the employer.

Other Provisions   Some pension plans require employees to pay some of the costs of the pensions during employment *(contributory)*. Other employers pay all the pension costs *(noncontributory)*. Future payments of pensions can be set aside in special funds. These are called *funded* pension plans. *Nonfunded* or pay-as-you-go plans make pension payments out of current funds. Funded plans can be administered by insurance companies. Under the insured method, the payments made for each employee buy that worker an annuity for the retirement years. An unisured or trustee plan is usually administered by a bank or trust company. In these cases, the administrators invest the pension funds in securities, real estate, and so on, from which pension payments are generated.

ERISA provides for plan termination insurance to ensure vested pension benefits (similar to FDIC provisions at banks). The Pension Benefit Guaranty Corporation was set up to pay pensions to employees of firms whose pension plans become bankrupt.

Reporting and disclosure provisions of the law require the employer to provide employees with a comprehensive booklet describing major plan provisions, and to report detailed information concerning the operation and financing of the plan annually to the secretary of labor. The act also imposes limits on contributions and benefits and changes the tax rules related to lump-sum distributions to employees.

ERISA was changed by the Tax Reform Act of 1986 (TRA 86), but the Internal Revenue Service has delayed the deadline for plan amendments.[60] However, employers are not protected from liability to the Department of Labor. As a result, it is even more important for companies to conduct ERISA audits.

Public Pensions

Employees in the public sector also receive pensions. The Tax Foundation estimates pensions are almost universally available at the state and local levels. Federal employees are covered by civilian or military pension plans, and about two thirds of state and local government employees are also covered by social security. Typically, public pensions are contributory. The bulk of the cost is paid by the government and investment income. The employee usually contributes about 7 percent of wages or salary.

One study comparing private with public pensions found that the benefits levels of the latter are approximately *twice* the level of those in private industry.[61] Even adjusting for the portion paid for by the employees themselves, public pensions are still one third larger than those of private industry. The plans are not coordinated with social security. Since public pension and social security payments have been rising dramatically, a number of public servants now retire at greater net income than they had when working. Needless to say, this is a strong inducement to retire and has helped lead to a crisis in public pensions. The crisis is this: As public pensions rose (often because politicians gave public employees greater pensions than wage increases and left the bill for their successors to pay), funding did not. All the studies show a consistent pattern: a rising spread between funds and payouts.

There are only two ways to take care of this: raise taxes *dramatically* or lower pension checks. A third answer, to place the public plans under ERISA, is not helpful. A better solution is to reform the public pensions so that benefit payouts are coordinated with social security and total no more than private industry's payout of about 55 percent of final salary. The length of service required to receive full pensions should be more like that in private industry, too. Taxes must rise or benefits must fall, or the total government budget could be going to pensions. A large number of public pension plans have created new tiers with fewer benefits for new hires because some municipal governments found that they had bargained for overgenerous benefits, especially cost-of-living allowances.[62]

COMPULSORY OR FLEXIBLE RETIREMENT

Retirement has mixed meanings for people: Some look forward to it, others dread it. Various policies affect the way people will live in retirement. These include compulsory or flexible retirement policies.

A major issue regarding retirement has been whether it should be compulsory or flexible. There are advantages to both of these policies. Flexible retirement policies take account of individual differences, but can cause difficulty in administration, especially in regard to favoritism. Compulsory retirement assures a predictable turnover of older employees, opening up positions for younger ones, and equality of treatment for all employees. When new job openings come up, EEO requirements can be fulfilled more easily. However, those closest to retirement age favor flexible retirement policies, not compulsory ones.

Nevertheless, legislation that became effective January 1, 1979, stipulated that the third sector cannot have mandatory retirement policies that specify less than 70 years of age. Prior to this new legislation, federal employees could be forced to retire at age 70. There now is no maximum age limit for federal employment.

Early Retirement

The opposite of the movement to keep older employees working is early retirement. Some employees prefer not to work up until normal retirement age. In recent years, more than 90 percent of pension plans studied have made provision for early retirement.

Typically, the minimum age for early retirement is 55; others call for a minimum age of 60. Most early retirement plans require a minimum number of years of work (typically 10 or 15 years) before the employee is eligible for early retirement. As far as benefits are concerned, all plans will pay the actuarial equivalent of the normal retirement benefits, but 30 percent of the plans pay more than that. One study found that in a typical year an average of 10 percent of those eligible retire early, but this is related to the benefits paid. Only 5 percent of those with nonliberalized payments retire early, whereas 30 percent of those eligible for early retirement with liberalized benefits do so. The U.S. Census Bureau found that more men than women retire early.

Several studies have examined which employees take early retirement. They have found that black men have a lower propensity to retire early than white men. One study also found that employees are more likely to retire early if their pension benefits are higher, their dependents are fewer, their assets are higher, and their health is poorer. Blue-collar workers are more likely to retire early than white-collar workers. Executives are especially averse to early retirement. Government workers retire early more frequently than private-sector employees. But, in general, people are reluctant to retire early in times of inflation.

Employers Preretirement Programs

Because of the continued trend toward early retirement, companies are increasingly offering employees a preretirement planning program.[63] Preretirement programs may include seminars, booklets, other informational materials, and even retirement rehearsals or phased-retirement plans. More than 75 large corporations like Merck, Atlantic Richfield, and Alcoa have adopted the National Council on the Aging's retirement planning program. Basic topics included in most preretirement programs include health, money management, legal issues, and housing. The ideal program will be presented over a period of time with each session dealing in-depth with one particular issue.

A recommended comprehensive preretirement program includes these topics:

First meeting: Developing a healthy attitude for a happy retirement. This session emphasizes the positive steps society has taken to ease the financial burdens on senior citizens by reducing the costs of recreation, housing, and taxes. The potential retirees are encouraged to keep mentally and physially active, and programs designed to help, such as adult education, are discussed.

Second meeting: Leisure time converted to happiness. Potential retirees are acquainted with the variety of leisure time activities, and they are encouraged to choose specific goals and to take steps to develop plans that will bring them to fruition.

Third meeting: Is working in retirement for me? Retirees are given lectures on service projects and part-time job experiences that may provide variety in the retirement period.

Fourth meeting: Money matters. This session discusses the sources of funds available to retirees: social security, pensions, and supplementary jobs. Personal budgets can be developed for each retiree to help him or her adjust to the new income level more smoothly.

Fifth meeting: Relocation in retirement. The advantages and disadvantages of living in retirement communities, staying in present quarters (if possible), or moving in with children are discussed.

Sixth meeting: Other subjects. Rights under Medicare are discussed. Retirement publications such as *Harvest Years* and *Modern Maturity* are analyzed. The preparation of wills is encouraged. Social and marital adjustment problems during retirement are covered.

At present, the great majority of firms do the counseling when employees are 64 or 65 years old. About a third counsel employees between the ages of 60 to 65. Very few do so prior to age 60. Preretirement counseling is an inexpensive benefit that can help the employee a great deal.

EMPLOYEE SERVICES

Employee services is something of a catchall category of voluntary benefits. It includes all other benefits or services provided by employers. These are such varied programs as cafeterias; saunas and gyms; free parking lots; commuter vans; infirmaries; ability to purchase company products at a discount; and death, personal, and financial counseling. Several of the more frequently provided services will be discussed here.

Stock Ownership Plans

Many companies encourage employee purchase of company stock (often at advantageous prices), to increase employees' incentive to work, satisfaction, and work quality, and to reduce absenteeism and turnover. Purchase plans often allow for payroll deductions or company financing of the stock. Sometimes, the company will agree to buy the stock back at a guaranteed rate if it appears that the employee would take a significant loss. Companies use these plans for the same reasons as they do profit-sharing plans: When employees become partners in the business, they work harder.

Some of these plans (such as Procter & Gamble's) are very successful. In general, stock purchase plans have most of the disadvantages of profit sharing. It is hard for the truck driver to identify his or her working harder with an increase in the value of his stock. It is more difficult when the stock drops in price. Many stock ownership plans were terminated in the 1930s because of big drops in stock prices.

A major change in U.S. laws may have increased the usage of stock ownership plans. Congress authorized an establishment of an employee stock ownership plan **(ESOP)** through the mechanism of an employee stock ownership trust (ESOT). Firms have a number of incentives for setting up an ESOT. ERISA views an ESOT as an employee benefit plan. The Tax Reduction Act of 1975 allows firms with an ESOT to take an extra 1 percent investment tax credit in addition to the 10 percent investment tax credit.

ESOPs

Interest in employee stock ownership plans (ESOPs) has increased substantially in the past 10 years.[64] To establish an ESOP, the employer sets up a trust to hold the assets and typically makes contributions up to 25 percent of payroll for the eligible employees in the plan. Stock contributed to or purchased by the trust is allocated to the accounts of employees who have met the eligibility requirements of the ESOP. ESOPs are subject to vesting like private pensions. Plan enrollees are not taxed on the income earned by the plan, contributions to the plan, employer stock, or other amounts added to their accounts until the time of distribution.

Leveraged ESOP   In basic form, the leveraged ESOP is as follows:

- The ESOP trust obtains a loan to buy company stock.
- The company makes annual, tax-deductible contributions sufficient to repay the loan.
- The ESOP buys newly issued stock from the company, and the company uses the money to finance new capital.
- Each year, the ESOP uses the company's tax-deductible contributions to repay the loan.

The term *leveraged ESOP* is used because the trust borrows money to buy capital stock.

International ESOP   In the late 80s and early 90s, multinational firms have been offering stock ownership of the parent company to its worldwide employees. Extending the ESOP, with its favorable tax consequences, to non-U.S. employees is difficult because of the different tax laws in each country. A U.S. multinational generally is willing to extend such benefits only if it receives a direct or indirect U.S. tax benefit from its ESOP contributions.[65]

Education Programs

Many organizations provide off-the-job general education support for their employees. This varies from teaching basic skills such as reading to illiterate workers, to tuition-refund programs for managers, to scholarship and loan plans for employees' children.

Employees can receive up to $5,250 annually in tax-free educational assistance benefits from their employers under Section 127 of the Internal Revenue Code.[66] Reimbursements for graduate-level courses are taxable for employees. The nontaxable status of other tuition reimbursement plans is uncertain.[67] Despite this uncertainty, employers are still offering a broad range of educational benefits. The typical user of the program earns between $10,000 and $40,000 annually. About 71 percent of all reimbursements are for undergraduate courses. Eighty-five percent of employees who are eligible to participate do so. The two categories of employees who are most likely to participate are salaried full-time and nonunion hourly personnel.

Most companies are now limiting the amount of tuition they will pay, and they usually place some restrictions on the courses reimbursed. Courses must be relevant to the work being done, and a minimum grade level must be achieved. Reimbursements are also dependent on the employee finishing the course.

Child Care

Nearly 50 percent of today's workers are women and as many as 70 percent of these women have children under the age of six at home.[68] The Census Bureau reports that working mothers pay about $15.1 billion per year for child care while they work. The Labor Department estimates that, by 1995, more than 80 percent of the women between the ages of 25 and 44 will be working outside the home at least part-time. This fact suggests that corporate child care programs will become a necessity.

Regardless of these facts, only a small number of employers in the United States offer child care assistance to their employees.[69] Lack of child care keeps women from entering the work force and leads to higher turnover and absenteeism when they do.[70]

One company that offers child care assistance is Boehringer Ingelheim Corporation, a pharmaceutical firm with a highly trained, skilled work force of which 45 percent are women.[71] Their child care plan, begun in 1987, covers six different areas: (1) Up to eight weeks unpaid leave after the birth or adoption of a child; (2) an Internal Revenue Code Section 129 flexible spending account for child care expenses; (3) reimbursement of up to $1,000 for adoption fees; (4) a half-hour accommodation time for employees with preschool or school-age children; (5) provision of child care information; and (6) support of a child care consortium of employers.

These and many other options are available to any company who wishes to provide child care benefits: information and referral service within the company; child care payments; on-site child care; and adjustments to working life that give employees some flexibility in both time and place of work.[72] A well-planned child-care program can help businesses raise productivity and morale, cut absenteeism and turnover, and improve recruitment results.[73]

As more and more organizations investigate the benefits, there is likely to be more probing by employers of the attitudes of employees about child-care. Exhibit 12–5 is a questionnaire that can be used to investigate employee attitudes and feelings about child-care. With the threat of a federally mandated child-care benefit, information provided by such a survey could be used to help management decide what course to take in the child-care area.

Elder Care

People 65 or older will make up 23% of the U.S. population by 2050.[74] The ratio of the elderly to those of working age was approximately 20 per 100 in 1990 and will be 22 per 100 by 2010.[75] Recent research shows that at least 20 percent of all employees already provide assistance to one or more elderly relatives or friends. On average, these employees spend between 6 to 35 hours per week providing this care. At least 50 percent of these employees also have children at home. The burden falls more heavily on the working woman who traditionally took care of elderly relatives and did not work outside the home. The employee who is also a caregiver to seniors experiences the following problems: missed work (58 percent), loss of pay (47 percent), less energy to do their work well (15 percent). The employer of these individuals experiences problems as well: extensive telephone calls, tardiness, excessive absenteeism, unscheduled time off, and loss of concentration because of concern for the dependent person(s) welfare. The result is reduced productivity.

Elder care, including providing disability insurance for employees that covers nursing-home care for elderly relatives, is an emerging employee benefit. Employee services provided include referrals for day care for seniors, nursing home referrals, and training programs that deal with care giving. An example of an experimental comprehensive corporate elder care program is being implemented by the American Red Cross in Bethlehem, Pennsylvania.[76] Firms that are participating include Beth-

EXHIBIT 12-5   Child-Care Planning and Attitude Survey

Questionnaire

1. Would you be willing to give some time and your expertise to help organize (identify the program being proposed)?
   Many people, including some with no children, might volunteer to help organize or manage a program that is parent controlled.

2. Do you have dependent children under six years old living at home? If so, how are they cared for while you work?

3. How much do you pay for child-care services for each child using services?
   $ _____ for _____ hours per week for child _____ years old.
   The amount an employee presently pays may indicate what parents are willing to pay.

4. Would you be interested in enrolling a dependent child in a child-care center located close to where you work?
   The answer to this question, of course, does not constitute a commitment to enroll a child, but asking the question may avoid surprise that so many (or so few) are interested.

5. What is the age of the child (children) that you would be interested in enrolling in the child-care center?
   List ages, using age brackets, that determine teacher-child ratios for state licensing laws. Some centers have reported more demand for infant care (seldom available in the community) rather than preschool care.

6. What hours and days would you need child care?

7. Do any of the children that you're interested in enrolling have a handicap? If so, what is the child's condition?
   Planners may or may not be able to accommodate handicapped children, depending on the kind of handicap and the number of children affected.

8. What would you be willing to pay for care for one child in a child-care center near work?
   List alternative ranges of fees. Answers may be lower than parents are willing to pay once the center has opened. A better indicator of what employees will pay may be a comparison of family income with fees currently being paid at other centers.

9. What is your total gross family income?
   A rule of thumb often used is that a family can spend 10 percent of its gross income for child care. If planners are considering a sliding scale that will charge high-income families more, will there be enough high-income interest to balance enrollment by low-income families?

10. If all the following forms of child-care service were available to you, which would be your first choice?

11. Do you believe a service at the company (or non-profit organization) that supplied you with names of child-care providers in your community would help you in making your own child-care arrangements?

12. How would you describe your present child care arrangements.
    ■ Cost of care
    _____ too expensive
    _____ moderate
    _____ inexpensive
    ■ Location of care
    _____ close to home
    _____ close to work
    _____ inconvenient distance to travel
    _____ other: _____
    ■ Hours of care
    _____ available during times needed
    _____ not available as early as needed
    _____ not available as late as needed
    Other items could include evaluation of activities for children in present program, adequacy of staff, and so on.

13. Have you missed work during the past six months because (give number of days)
    _____ child was ill
    _____ sitter was ill
    _____ needed to find new care arrangements
    _____ other

14. Were you late for work during the past six months because of child-care problems?
    _____ No
    _____ Yes
    How many times? Describe problems: _____

15. Have you left work early during past six months because of child-care problems?
    _____ No
    _____ Yes
    How many times? Describe problems: _____

16. Do you ever waste time or make mistakes because you are worried about your child-care problems?
    _____ No
    _____ Some
    _____ A lot
    What problems bother you most? _____

Source: Commerce Clearing House (December 30, 1982), Ideas and Trends, p. 229.

lehem Steel and Binney & Smith. The elder care program will provide employee seminars, telephone information and referrals, counseling and case management, training for supervisors and management on elder care issues and support groups. A critical part of the program is training supervisors and other managers to understand and deal with employee care givers' dilemmas.

Financial Services

Some organizations give their employees help and encouragement to save funds through employee savings plans, credit unions, and thrift plans. Essentially, savings plans encourage employee thrift by matching all or part of an employee's contribution, up to, say 5 percent of the wage or salary. Credit unions help employees by providing loans at reasonable and market competitive rates of interest.

In the thrift plans, most funds are often invested for distribution at retirement. When companies have thrift plans, about 85 percent of employees participate.

Financial planning services are also being offered, especially to executives and professional personnel.[77]

Housing Help and Relocation Services

In the 1970s and 1980s, real estate prices skyrocketed. Because of that, the idea of employers assisting employees in obtaining affordable housing is gaining favor.[78] Scarce, affordable housing causes labor shortages, diminished productivity, unacceptable recruitment levels, retention and wage-cost distortions, and stagnant corporate real estate values.[79] As a result, some corporations are experimenting with a variety of employer-assisted housing schemes: (1) reducing the down-payment barrier; (2) assisting in post-purchase carrying costs; and (3) participating in programs to produce new or substantially rehabilitated housing units.

The average cost for transferring an employee in the United States is $37,000, which includes selling the old property and purchasing one in the new location.[80] Research by the Employee Relocation Council (ERC) has found that losses average $11,000 per house. To combat these losses, businesses are issuing formal compensation policies for transferred workers who lose money when they sell their homes. Companies are offering assistance in the areas of mortgages, prepurchase valuations, and cost-of-living differentials in response to appreciating or depreciating housing markets.

The 1986 Rax Reform Act has had an effect on how moving expense deductions are made. Thus, income tax preparatoin counseling and support is needed. For example, before 1987, employees deducted moving expenses from their gross income.[81] Beginning in 1987, transferred employees had to itemize deductions on their returns to include moving expenses that result from relocation. The changes in what is deductible, how reimbursed moving expenses are added to income, and other tax-related issues need to be addressed by individuals with income tax knowledge.

In addition to paying for moving expenses, granting cost-of-living allowances, providing assistance in selling homes, and dealing with taxes, organizations are now showing more concern about the spouse, family, and psychological aspects of relocation. A family that relocates experiences stress in spite of any financial benefits package. Relocation is stressful to some because it involves change and uprooting. Any time relocation occurs, there is anticipation, anxiety, and adjustment. Therefore, more and more firms, such as Baxter Travenol Laboratories, are providing personal and family counseling and assistance, in addition to financial benefits, to minimize the disruption, stress, and adjustment that inevitably is a part of relocation.[82]

Social and Recreational Programs

Today, more than 50,000 organizations provide recreation facilities for employees, on or off the job. According to Department of Labor statistics, about 28 percent of all employees in medium-size and large firms were eligible to use employer-subsidized recreation facilities in 1989.[83] Some experts foresee a growing trend to release employees from work time to participate in company-sponsored sports activities. These activities are intended to keep employees physically fit and tie them to their employers.

There are no available studies of the value, if any, of such benefits to the employer. These plans could be extensions of the paternalistic antiunion activities of some employers in the 1920s and later. Studies of the preferences of employees indicate that recreational services are the *least preferred* of all benefits and services offered by organizations.

FLEXIBILE BENEFITS PLANS AND REIMBURSEMENT ACCOUNTS

It is apparent from the previous discussion that employers have traditionally offered their workers benefit plans in a number of areas such as health care, life insurance, and retirement.[84] Typically, the only choice the employee has is a choice between one plan or another in any given area, that is, between a commercial health insurance plan and a health maintenance organization. With the continued escalation in the cost of benefits and the diversity of the labor force, two new approaches to offering benefits have attracted considerable attention — flexible benefits and reimbursement accounts. Exhibit 12–6 traces the increase in these plans since 1986.

When the Bureau of Labor Statistics first studied flexible and reimbursement accounts in 1986, only 5 percent of employees were eligible. By 1989, 7.8 million employees (24 percent) in medium-size and large firms were offered flexible benefits plans, reimbursement accounts, or both. A **flexible (cafeteria) benefits plan** allows employees to choose between two or more types of benefits. Most-common choices include health care, life insurance, disability insurance, and the option of receiving cash to spend on coverage in the open market. **Reimbursement accounts or flexible spending accounts** provide funds from which employees pay for expenses not covered by the regular benefits package. The accounts are usually pretax deductions so that the employee saves on federal taxes. Funds can be allocated for unreimbursed health care, child care, and care for elderly or disabled relatives.

Flexible benefits and reimbursement accounts can increase employee satisfaction and save employers from spending money on coverage that the employees don't want.[85] These plans provide for benefit trade-offs and cost sharing. It is important, however, that sufficient coverage must be provided in key benefits areas like health care, life insurance, and disability *regardless* of the choices made by the individual employee. Flexible plans that can easily self-adjust to changing circumstances and costs should also be designed.

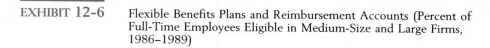

EXHIBIT 12-6   Flexible Benefits Plans and Reimbursement Accounts (Percent of
Full-Time Employees Eligible in Medium-Size and Large Firms,
1986–1989)

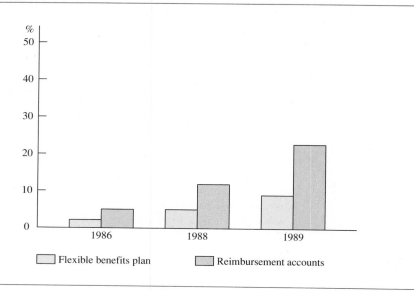

Source: U.S. Department of Labor (June 1990), *Employee Benefits in Medium and Large Firms, 1989* (Washington,
D.C.: Bureau of Labor Statistics), p. 122.

MANAGING AN EFFECTIVE BENEFITS PROGRAM

When top managers make benefits and services decisions, they must consider the
following facts:[86]

Mandated programs *must* be funded.

There is little evidence that benefits and services really motivate performance.
Nor do they necessarily increase satisfaction.

Most employees view benefits and services as *entitlements*.

Unions, competitors, and industry trends continue to pressure managers to
provide or increase voluntary benefits.

Costs of benefits and services continue to escalate dramatically.

To manage the benefits program effectively, certain steps are necessary. Four of
these are discussed below:

Step 1: Set Objectives and Strategy for Benefits

There are three strategies for benefits:

1. *Pacesetter strategy.* Be first with the newest benefits employees desire.
2. *Comparable benefits strategy.* Match the benefits programs similar organizations
   offer.
3. *Minimum benefits strategy.* Offer the mandatory benefits and those that are
   most desired and least costly to offer.

The decision about which strategy to use is made on the basis of management's goals. The third strategy may be chosen because of inability to pay more benefits, or because management believes the employees want more pay and fewer benefits. Before these costly benefits and services are offered, management must set objectives that fit its benefits strategy.

Step 2: Involve Participants and Unions in Benefits Decisions

Whatever strategy is chosen, it makes sense to find out what those involved desire in benefits and services. Yet, in most organizations, top managers alone judge which benefits the employees prefer. Without getting some employee-preference input, it is impossible to make these decisions intelligently. It is similar to a marketing manager trying to decide on consumer preferences with no market research input.

Therefore, it is wise to permit (and encourage) employee participation in decision making on benefits and services. When employees share in benefit decisions, they show more interest in them. One way for employees to participate in the decisions is to poll them with attitude surveys. Another is to set up employee benefits advisory commitees.

When the organization is unionized, it is vital that the union leadership be involved. Many times, the leadership knows what employees want in benefits. Sometimes, the leadership tries to maximize benefits without having determined what employees want. It is useful to involve the union leadership in preference studies so that all parties are seeking benefits desired by the employees.

Step 3: Communicate Benefits Effectively

Another method for improving the effectiveness of benefits and service is to develop an effective communication program. How can benefits and services affect the satisfaction and performance of employees if they do not know about the benefits or understand them? Yet most studies of employees and executives indicate they are unaware of the benefits or significantly undervalue their cost and usefulness.

It has always been desirable to improve benefits communications for this reason. But now there is another reason. For pensions, ERISA requires employers to communicate with employees by sending them an annual report on the pension plan and basic information on their pensions in language they can understand.

Many communication media can be used: employee handbooks, company newspaper, magazines, or newsletters; booklets; bulletin boards; annual reports; payroll stuffers; and employee reports. Other communication methods include filmstrips, cassettes, open houses and meetings with supervisors and employees. A problem of communication is retention of the message and learning it in its entirety. Most organizations handle these problems by using multiple media and sending the message many times. For example, Exhibit 12-7 is the chronology of a communications blitz used by Citicorp to explain their new plan. Citicorp had not changed its benefits plan for decades and they had recently acquired many new companies who had their own existing benefits plans. So employees were faced with a formidable amont of data to assimilate at one time. As part of their information blitz, Citicorp provided each employee with a printout of his or her benefits from the preceding year and a computer disk with an extensive workbook that included base salary so that employees could figure out-of-pocket expenses and tax implications of each benefit choice. About 1,000 human resource people received special training and traveled to different Citicorp sites to meet with employees and explain benefits.

EXHIBIT 12-7   Chronology of a Communications Blitz

February 1990: About 100 Citicorp employees, in focus groups, react to the first draft of a benefits workbook.

July 10: Citicorp chief John S. Reed sends letter to employees announcing new benefits plan; communications departments receive articles for use in newsletters.

July 11: Local managers tell their staffs how to get more information.

July 16: Brochures go out outlining the plan, giving thumbnail sketches of types of benefits.

July 30: Brochures on medical, dental, and flexible spending accounts go out.

Aug. 20: Disability insurance brochure goes out.

September: Phone lines staffed 20 hours a day, six days a week, with people trained to answer employee questions; video and interactive software distributed.

November 2: Deadline for choosing benefits.

Source: Claudia H. Deutsch (October 14, 1990), "Managing the Multimedia Benefits Kit," *New York Times*, section 3, part 2, p. 25.

In sum, organizations are spending billions on benefits and very little on benefits communications. To make these billions pay off, companies need to increase the quantity and improve the quality of their communications about the benefits they provide.

Step 4: Monitor the Costs Closely

In addition to considering costs in choice of benefits, it is vital that managers make sure the programs are administered correctly. Review of insurance claims is especially important. More-efficient administration procedures using computerized methods also can lead to greater savings and more satisfied employees.

Together, these four steps will make any benefits program more effective.

COST/BENEFIT ANALYSIS OF BENEFITS

Conrad Fiorello tells the story about a gunman who suddenly appeared at the paymaster's window at a large plant and demanded: "Never mind the payroll, Bud. Just hand over the welfare and pension funds, the group insurance premiums, and the withholding taxes." As indicated earlier, costs of benefits are going up twice as fast as pay.

When benefits costs increase the price of products and services, they are less competitive with other products, especially those from countries where the government pays for benefits. Higher benefits can reduce permanent employment, also, since it is cheaper to pay overtime or to hire part-time employees than to pay full-time wages and benefits. It may also reduce employee mobility, but most evidence thus far shows that it does not affect turnover at all.

It is rational for employees to want additional benefits since they constitute tax-free income. The costs of such benefits, however, have been rising substantially, and many organizations cannot afford to offer benefits and high wages as well. Just what does it cost employers to provide these benefits for their employees?

Various groups including the Department of Labor and the Bureau of Labor Statistics report on the costs of benefits. Exhibit 12–8 reports the costs of employee compensation *per hour worked* including total benefits broken down into paid leave, insurance, pension, savings, mandated benefits, and other benefits for the years

EXHIBIT 12-8 Employer Costs for Employee Compensation for Hour Worked (Private Industry, 1988 and 1989)

Compensation Component	1988, Total Cost (Dol.)	1989 Cost (Dollars)				
		Total	Goods Producing[1]	Service Producing[2]	Manufacturing	Nonmanufacturing
Total compensation	13.79	14.28	17.21	13.12	17.16	13.46
Wages and salaries	10.02	10.38	11.90	9.77	11.71	10.00
Total benefits	3.77	3.90	5.30	3.35	5.45	3.46
Paid leave	.97	1.00	1.20	.92	1.33	.91
Vacation	.48	.50	.62	.45	.68	.45
Holiday	.33	.34	.43	.30	.49	.30
Sick	.12	.12	.10	.13	.12	.13
Other	.04	.04	.04	.04	.04	.04
Supplemental pay	.33	.34	.60	.23	.65	.25
Premium pay	.17	.17	.37	.09	.40	.11
Nonproduction bonuses	.12	.12	.15	.10	.15	.11
Shift pay	.04	.05	.06	.03	.10	.03
Insurance	.78	.85	1.28	.68	1.40	.70
Pensions and savings	.45	.42	.57	.36	.54	.39
Pensions	.38	.34	.45	.30	.41	.32
Savings and thrift	.07	.06	.12	.06	.13	.07
Legally rquired[3]	1.22	1.27	1.61	1.14	1.48	1.21
Social Security	.61	.64	1.00	.77	1.00	.79
Federal unemployment	.03	.03	.03	.03	.03	.03
State unemployment	.12	.11	.16	.09	.15	.10
Workers' compensation	.24	.27	.41	.21	.29	.26
Other benefits[4]	.02	.02	.05	(z)	.05	(z)

Represents or rounds to zero. [1] Mining, construction, and manufacturing. [2] Transportation, communications, public utilities, wholesale trade, retail trade, finance, insurance, real estate, and services. [3] Includes railroad retirement, railroad unemployment, railroad supplemental unemployment, and other legally required benefits, not shown separately. [4] Includes severance pay, supplemental unemployment benefits, and for 1988, merchandise discounts in department stores.
Source: U.S. Bureau of Labor Statistics, *News, Employer Costs for Employee Compensation*, June 1988, USDL 89-295.

1988 and 1989. As you can see from this chart, almost 38 percent of total hourly compensation went for benefits in 1988 alone. That figure is continuing to rise. The most generous benefits are offered in the mining, construction, and manufacturing industries. Based on overall industry averages, the most costly benefits are paid leave ($1.00/hour), insurance ($.85/hour) and the mandated benefit of social security ($.84/hour).

In addition to the direct costs of benefits, there are added burdens, or indirect costs. One is the administration of these plans. They can become complicated, and paperwork proliferates. Because administrative costs at smaller organizations are especially high, some smaller organizations get together in joint benefits plans for their employees.

Financing benefits can also be complicated. Some companies have found that they can save money by creating tax-exempt trusts for benefits funds as disability pay: Examples include Westvaco, General Electric, TRW, and FMC Corporation.

An organization can compare its costs to those of other firms with the aid of data from an industry or professional group or published sources such as the United States Chamber of Commerce. Some other examples of such sources are the

CAREER CHALLENGE
(*concluded*)

After talking to other presidents and reading some literature that Pete gave him, Carl better understood Pete's conservatism about benefits and services. Carl reviewed what researchers have found and became convinced that pouring money into benefits and services doesn't mean that absenteeism will decrease, production will increase, and loyalty toward Coy Manufacturing will improve. "Employees have simply come to expect employers to provide competitive benefits and services," Carl thought, "I'm sure glad Pete brought this to my attention."

Conference Board, *Employee Benefit News*, Bureau of Labor Statistics, *Nation's Business*, and *Business Week*.

Cost of benefits can be calculated fairly easily:

1. Total cost of benefits annually for all employees.
2. Cost per employee per year — basis 1 divided by number of employee hours worked.
3. Percentage of payroll — basis 1 divided by annual payroll.
4. Cost per employee per hour — basis 2 divided by employee hours worked.

The benefits side of the equation is another issue, however. There has been little significant empirical research on the effects of benefits on productivity.

SUMMARY

Chapter 12 has described benefits and services as part of the rewards that reinforce loyal service to the employer. The chapter described mandated and voluntary employee benefits and some critical benefit decisions such as communication, administration, retirement benefits, child care, elder care, flexible benefit plans, reimbursement accounts, and employee participation.

To summarize the main points covered in this chapter:

1. Mandated benefit programs in the private and nonprofit sectors include unemployment insurance, social security, and workers' compensation.
2. To be eligible for unemployment insurance, an employee must have worked a minimum number of weeks, be without a job, and be willing to accept a position offered through a state Unemployment Compensation Commission.
3. Three kinds of benefits many employers provide voluntarily are:
   a. Compensation for time not worked (break time, coffee breaks, clothes-changing time, holidays, sick leave, vacations, and so on).
   b. Insurance protection (health, disability-accident, and life).

      c. Employee services (various benefits that can include cafeterias, gyms, free parking lots, discounts, and so forth).

4. Retirement income is received from three principal sources:
     a. Savings, investments, and part-time work.
     b. Private pension plans.
     c. Government program — social security.

5. The employee Retirement Income Security Act of 1974 is the law regulating private pensions.

6. To manage the benefit program effectively, follow these steps:
     a. Develop objectives and a benefit strategy.
     c. Communicate the benefits effectively.
     d. Monitor the costs closely.

7. To avoid administrative nightmares, employers should concentrate on fewer benefit plans and if possible implement those preferred by most employees.

The benefits plans recommended for the model organizations are given in Exhibit 12–9. Remember, for the benefits and services program to be effective, the operat-

---

EXHIBIT 12-9   Recommendations on Benefits and Services Programs for Model Organizations

Type of Organization	Benefits and Services							
	Legally Required Benefits	Vacation Plans	Paid Holidays	Group Life Insurance	Hospital-Medical Insurance	Accident-Disability Insurance	Employee Pension Program	Services
1. Large size, low complexity, high stability	X	*	*	*	X	X	X	*
2. Medium size, low complexity, high stability	X	*	*	*	X	X	X	*
3. Small size, low complexity, high stability	X	*	*	*	X	X	X	*
4. Medium size, moderate complexity, moderate stability	X	*	*	*	X	X	X	*
5. Large size, high complexity, low stability	X	*	*	*	X	X	X	*
6. Medium size, high complexity, low stability	X	*	*	*	X	X	X	*
7. Small size, high complexity, low stability	X	*	*	*	X	X		*

* Minimized.

ing manager and HR manager must work together. The operating manager helps the HR manager know what the employees prefer in benefits and asks for help in explaining the benefits and getting administrative problems cleared up. The HR manager helps the operating manager communicate the benefits to employees and administer the program.

KEY TERMS

QUESTIONS FOR REVIEW AND DISCUSSION

1. Describe government-mandated benefits and services. Should these programs exist? How can they be improved?
2. How does the social security system affect women retirees? Is it fair?
3. Compare vacations in the United States to those in Europe and Japan. How do we rate?
4. Define *maternity leave* and *parental leave*. How is the changing of the composition of the work force affecting these benefits?
5. What is meant when it is said that many employees view employee benefits and services as an entitlement? How can employers make employees realize that benefits must be earned?
6. What is an HMO? Compare an HMO health-care plan to the traditional health-care plan. Which one is most beneficial to the modern employer? Why?
7. How can a SEP-IRA help a small employer provide adequate retirement benefits for its employees?
8. How has the increase in the level of private pension benefits affected the work force participation of middle-aged men (55 to 64)?
9. Explain the major provisions of the Employee Retirement Income Security Act (ERISA) and how they affect private pensions.
10. Make a case for your employer's offering a flexible benefits plan and reimbursement account.

NOTES

1 James A. Curtis (August 1990), "Employee Benefits: The Next Generation," *CPA Journal* 60, pp. 8–10.
2 Betty A. Iseri and Robert R. Cangemi (March 1990), "Flexible Benefits: A Growing Option," *Personnel*, pp. 30–32.

[3] Cathy A. Cooley (June 1990), "1989 Employee Benefits Address Family Concern," *Monthly Labor Review* 113, no. 6, pp. 60–63.

[4] *New York Telephone, et al. v. New York Department of Labor et al.* (March 21, 1979), U.S. Supreme Court, No. 77–961.

[5] Catherine A. Shanklin (March 1990), "Unemployment Insurance: Survive the System," *Personnel Journal* 69, no. 3, pp. 84–89.

[6] C. Arthur Williams, John S. Turnbull, and Earl F. Cheit (1982), *Economic & Social Security* (New York: John Wiley & Sons).

[7] Shanklin, "Unemployment Insurance," pp. 84–89.

[8] Dianna Runner (January 1990), "Changes in Unemployment Insurance Legislation during 1989," *Monthly Labor Review* 113, no. 1, pp. 64–69.

[9] Kenneth Burdett and Randall Wright (December 1989), "Unemployment Insurance and Short-Term Compensation: The Effects on Layoffs, Hours per Worker and Wages," *Journal of Political Economy* 97, no. 6, pp. 1479–96; and Viven Moorthy (Winter 1989/1990), "Unemployment in Canada and the United States: The Role of Unemployment Insurance Benefits," *Federal Reserve Bank of New York Quarterly Review* 14, no. 4, pp. 48–61.

[10] Lawrence F. Katz and Bruce D. Meyer (February 1990), "The Impact of the Potential Duration of Unemployment Benefits on the Duration of Unemployment," *Journal of Public Economics* 41, no. 1, pp. 45–72.

[11] Joann S. Lublin (February 9, 1982), "Government Starts Cracking Down on Unemployment Insurance Fraud," *The Wall Street Journal*, p. 27.

[12] Ingemar Hansson and Charles Stuart (December 1989), "Social Security as Trade among Living Generations," *American Economic Review* 79, no. 5, pp. 1182–95.

[13] Bruce D. Schobel (April 1989), "Social Security Considerations in Transfers to or from the U.S.," *Benefis & Compensation International* 18, no. 10, pp. 18–24.

[14] Alfred G. Haggerty (April 1988), "Social Security: International Benefit Peril of the 90s?" *National Underwriter* 92, no. 14, pp. 32–33.

[15] Mathew Greenwald (February 1989), "Bad News for the Baby Boom," *American Demographics* 11, no. 2, pp. 34–37.

[16] Brian P. Smith (March 1990), "The Social Security System Threatens Personal Savings," *Savings Institutions* 111, no. 3, pp. 76–77.

[17] A. Haeworth Robertson (Winter 1988), "The Outlook for Social Security," *Topics in Total Compensation* 3, no. 2, pp. 123–29.

[18] (October 4, 1990), "There's a Renewed Interest in Making Social Security Fairer to Women," *Daily Times*, p. A-11.

[19] William J. Nelson, Jr. (April 1990), "Workers' Compensation: Coverage, Benefits, and Costs, 1987," *Social Security Bulletin* 53, no. 4, pp. 2–11.

[20] Robert C. Wender and Ronald L. Sladsky (December 1984), "Flexible Benefit Opportunities for the Small Employer," *Personnel Administrator*, pp. 111–18.

[21] Bill Keith (February 1, 1988), "Consumer Changes Tied to New Definition of Time," *Drug Topics* 132, no. 2, pp. 44, 47.

[22] Francis Green and Michael J. Potepan (Spring 1988), "Vacation Time and Unionism in the United States and Europe," *Industrial Relations* 27, no. 2, pp. 180–94; and Laurence Kelly (1985), "Paid Vacation Leave in Canada and Europe," *Worklife* 4, no. 5, pp. 1–2.

[23] James N. Houff and William J. Wiatrowski (June 1989), "Analyzing Short-Term Disability Benefits," *Monthly Labor Review* 112, no. 6, pp. 3–9.

[24] Barron H. Harvey, Judy A. Schultz, and Jerome F. Rogers (May 1983), *Personnel Administrator*, pp. 55–59.

[25] (1990), "Sick Leave or Sick-Out: The Reliability of Medical Certificates," *Worklife Report* 7, no. 4, pp. 10–11.

26 Mansour Sharifzadeh (October 1988), "Dealing with Your Absenteeism Problem," *Management Solutions* 33, no. 10, pp. 35–38.

27 Dennis Thompson (March 1990), "Wellness Programs Work for Small Employers, Too," *Personnel*, pp. 26–28.

28 Cynthia L. Reemers (1989), "Pregnancy Discrimination and Parental Leave," *Industrial Relations Law Journal* 11, no. 3, pp. 377–413.

29 Angela K. Calise (July 16, 1990), "Parents Push for Time Off After Childbirth," *National Underwriter* 94, 29, pp. 4, 14.

30 Joseph R. Meisenheimer, Jr. (October 1989), "Employer Provisions for Parental Leave," *Monthly Labor Review* 112, no. 10, pp. 20–24.

31 Calise, "Parents Push for Time Off," pp. 4, 14.

32 Kathleen Doherty (January 1990), "Parental Leave: Strategies for the 1990s," *Business & Health* 8, no. 1, pp. 21–23.

33 Susanne A. Stobier (Winter 1990), "Family Leave Entitlements in Europe: Lessons for the U.S.," *Compensation & Benefits Management* 6, no. 2, pp. 111–16.

34 Babara Ehrenreich (December 10, 1990), "Our Health-Care Disgrace," *Time* 136, no. 25, p. 112.

35 Fred Luthans and Elaine Davis (February 1990), "The Healthcare Cost Crisis: Causes and Containment," *Personnel*, pp. 24–30.

36 (March 1987), "A Report on Health Cost Strategies", *Employee Benefit News*, pp. 15–19.

37 (September 1987), "Free Program on Dental Reimbursement," *Employee Benefit News*.

38 Tamara M. Masters (May/June 1990), "Does Use of HMOs Result in Increased Health Care Costs?" *Journal of Compensation and Benefits* 5, no. 6, pp. 340–42.

39 Paul J. Roth and Reid A. Stiefel (May/June 1990), "Cost of COBRA Compliance Goes Up — Again," *Journal of Compensation and Benefits* 5, no. 6, pp. 325–29.

40 Robert J. Nobile (April 1990), "Wrestling with COBRA," *Personnel* 67, no. 4, pp. 6–14.

41 Hugh T. McCormick (Summer 1990), "Long-Term Care and Life Insurance Legislation," *Journal of Taxation of Investments* 7, no. 4, pp. 316–27.

42 Berkeley Rice (January 1985), "Why Am I in This Job?" *Psychology Today*, pp. 54–59.

43 Jerry S. Rosenblum and Victor G. Hallman (1981), *Employee Benefit Planning* (Englewood Cliffs, N.J.: Prentice-Hall).

44 Louis S. Richman (August 13, 1990), "The New Middle Class: How It Lives," *Fortune* 122, no. 4, pp. 104–13.

45 William M. Mercer-Meidinger (December 1986), "How Will Reform Tax Your Benefits," *Personnel Journal*, pp. 49–63.

46 Philip M. Alden, Jr. (December 1981), "New Tax Laws Voluntary Employee Contributions Forcing Management to Make Hard, Long-Term Choices," *Management Review*, pp. 21–23.

47 Mary Ann Pels (July 1990), "Breathe New Life into IRAs," *Credit Union Magazine* 56, no. 7, pp. 48–49.

48 Ibid.

49 (July 1990), "Simplified Employee Pensions: Good Choice for Small Business," *Profit-Building Strategies for Business Owners* 20, no. 7, pp. 3–4.

50 Jerry Geisel (July 19, 1990), "401(k) Rule Change May Raise Deferrals," *Business Insurance* 24, no. 28, pp. 1, 4.

51 Chuck Jones (June 1990), "401(k) Plan: A Hot Product and Getting Hotter," *Life Association News* 85, no. 6, pp. 57–59.

52 Geisel, "401(k) Rule Change May Raise Deferrals," pp. 1, 4.

53 Jones, "401(k) Plan," pp. 57–59.

[54] "Simplified Employee Pensions," pp. 3–4.

[55] Richard A. Ippolito (July 1990), "Toward Explaining Earlier Retirement after 1970," *Industrial and Labor Relations Review* 43, no. 5, pp. 556–69.

[56] Duane F. Hanf (July/August 1990), "Factors to Consider in Selecting a Retirement Plan," *Journal of Compensation and Benefits* 6, no. 1, pp. 43–47.

[57] Arnold J. Chassen (July 1990), "Whatever Happened to Defined Benefit Plans," *Management Accounting* 72, no. 1, pp. 18–19.

[58] Allen Stiteler (February 1987), "Finally Pension Plans Defined," *Personnel Journal*, pp. 44–53.

[59] George T. Milkovich and Jerry M. Newman (1987), *Compensation* (Plano, Tex.: BPI), p. 408.

[60] Jeffrey D. Mamorsky (March/April 1990), "ERISA Audits and the Attorney-Client Privilege," *Journal of Compensation and Benefits* 5, no. 5, pp. 312–15.

[61] (December 1989), "Public Plans Use Benefit Tiers to Reduce Costs," 44, no. 6, p. 66.

[62] Ibid.

[63] Catherine D. Fycock (July 1990), "Crafting Secure Retirements," *Human Resource Magazine* 35, no. 7, pp. 30–33.

[64] Ronald Farella and Barry M. Subhow (Spring 1990), "ESOPs Fables," *PA CPA Journal* 60, no. 4, pp. 42–45.

[65] Virginia L. Gibson and Edward D. Burmeister (July 1990), "America-Based ESOPs Get a Worldwide Look," *Pension World* 26, no. 7, pp. 22–23.

[66] Deborah Shalowitz (July 9, 1990), "Education Reimbursement Thriving Despite Uncertain Tax Status: Survey," *Business Insurance* 24, no. 28, p. 35

[67] (July 16, 1990), "Tuition Benefits Thrive," *National Underwriter* 94, no. 29, pp. 15, 20.

[68] Richard Levine (January 1989), "Childcare: Inching up the Corporate Agenda," *Management Review* 78, no. 1, pp. 43–47.

[69] Ibid.

[70] Judith Biscoff (January 1990), "Corporate-Sponsored Childcare: News from Abroad," *Employee Relations* 12, no. 1, pp. 13–16.

[71] (February 1989), "To Attract Employees, Companies Help with the Kids," *Employee Benefit Planning Review* 43, no. 8, pp. 68, 70.

[72] Biscoff, "Corporate-Sponsored Childcare," pp. 13–16.

[73] Raymond C. Collins and Renee Y. Magid (January 1989), "Taking the Myths out of ChildCare Planning," *Management Review* 11, no. 9, pp. 32–39.

[74] Karen Buglass (September 1989), "The Business of Eldercare," *American Demographics* 11, no. 9, pp. 32–39.

[75] Roy S. Azarnoff and Andrew E. Scharlach (September 1988), "Can Employees Carry the Eldercare Burden?" *Personnel Journal*, pp. 60–69.

[76] (May 1990), "American Red Cross Develops Corporate Eldercare Programs," *Employee Benefit Plan Review* 44, no. 11, pp. 26, 28.

[77] W. Barker French and Gary Warren (March 1990), "Planning for Financial Security," *Personnel*, pp. 34–36.

[78] Jane Moss Snow (May 1990), "Housing Help: The New Employee Benefit," *Mortgage Banking* 50, no. 8, pp. 55–60.

[79] David C. Schwartz and Daniel Hoffman (Spring 1990), "Employee-Assisted Housing: A Benefit of the 90s," *Employment Relations Today* 17, no. 1, pp. 21–29.

[80] Susan Galer (July 1990), "The Cost of Getting There from Here," *CFO* 6, no. 7, p. 12.

[81] (September 1987), "Runzheimer International," *Personnel Journal*, pp. 153–64.

[82] (September 1984), "Relocation," *Personnel Journal*, pp. 89–90.

[83] U.S. Department of Labor (June 1990), *Employee Benefits in Medium and Large Firms, 1989* (Washington, D.C.: Bureau of Labor Statistics).

[84] Ibid., p. 7

[85] John A. Haslinger and Donna M. Sheerin (July 1990), "Perspective on Benefits: Choice with Cost Control," *Pension World* 26, no. 7, pp. 41–42.

[86] Claudia H. Deutsch (October 14, 1990), "Managing the Multimedia Benefits Kit," *New York Times*, section 3, part 2, p. 25.

APPLICATION CASE 12–1   The Maternity/Paternity Leave Debate

· · · · ·

Since the early 1980s, an ongoing debate has emerged among businesses, government, and women concerning maternity leave for pregnant employees. The debate has centered on three issues: (1) the form and degree of maternity leave benefits provided by companies (especially whether the employee receives pay while on leave and is guaranteed her previous or comparable job upon return): (2) whether leave should be granted for fathers; and (3) whether leave benefits should be mandated by law or provided by companies on a voluntary basis.

Two factors have intensified interest in the issue. First, pregnant employees are increasingly common in the workplace because women are comprising a growing proportion of the work force. About 44 percent of the nation's employees are women, and women will comprise over two thirds of the new entrants into the work force through the early 1990s. Over 70 percent of these women will become pregnant sometime during their working years. In a work force increasingly characterized by expectant workers, the issue of maternity leave is of obvious interest.

Second, many assert that maternity leave is inadequate for most working women. The Pregnancy Discrimination Act mandates paid short-term maternity leave for employees of companies that provide disability insurance (usually six to eight weeks of paid leave), and five states (California, New York, New Jersey, Rhode Island, and Hawaii) require paid short-term maternity leave benefits by all companies. These state-mandated benefits usually amount to 50 to 66 percent of a woman's base pay for about 10 weeks. However, many small companies outside these five states aren't affected because they do not offer disability coverage. Thus, about 60 percent of America's working women don't receive any type of paid or job-protected maternity leave. According to a two-year study of 384 large companies by the Catalyst organization, too often a job-protected employee returning after taking leave "may lose out by having to return to a different job and essentially work her way back up."

Maternity leave advocates thus assert that most women are unjustly penalized financially and professionally for having children. Society also pays a price; because of financial need, many women return to work within a few weeks after delivery. Many pediatricians and psychologists assert that this early separation between mother and child threatens the child's cognitive and emotional growth because the separation hinders the development of a secure mother-child relationship, which is the foundation of a child's psychological growth. Many experts advise that a solid bonding requires four months of full-time parental attention. Said one advocate, "If society wants women to make economic contributions as well as nurture the next generation, some accommodations seem to be necessary. It is impossible for women to accomplish both work and family tasks without some support."

Congress is responding to these concerns with the Family and Medical Leave Bill. If passed, the law would require companies with 15 or more employees to provide up to 18 weeks of leave with job guarantees for the birth, adoption, or illness of a dependent. Both fathers and mothers would be eligible for leaves with protected seniority and pension credits and health benefits and could resume work on a gradual schedule. The leave is unpaid; however, the bill would also establish a commission to study the feasibility of a paid leave policy. The bill's supporters are quick to assert that the United States is the world's only industrialized nation without a national parental leave policy. Companies in Western Europe provide an average of six months' paid maternity leave. The European Economic Community has proposed a plan where all member countries require a parental leave of at least three months per employee per child to be used before the child is two years old.

Written by Kim Stewart and adapted from: Dana E. Friedman (March 1987), "Liberty, Equality, and Maternity!" *Across The Board*, pp. 10–17; Rosa Harris-Adler (March 1987), "Who Pays for Pregnancy?" *Report on Business*, pp. 60–63; Melissa A. Berman (March 1987), "What Do Women Get," *Across The Board*, pp. 18–20; Dana E. Friedman (August 1987), "Work vs Family: War of the Worlds, *Personnel Administrator*, pp. 36–38; Lesly Berger (February 1984), "The Corporate Scene," *Working Woman*, pp. 79–82; and Karen Krett (June 1985), "Maternity, Paternity, and Child Care Policies," *Personnel Administrator*, pp. 125–36.

Though endorsed by over 80 organizations, the Family and Medical Leave Bill is highly controversial and opposed by formidable critics. They include the U.S. Chamber of Commerce and CARE (Concerned Alliance of Responsible Employers), a 150-organization lobby that is working hard to defeat the bill. Critics present five reasons for opposing the bill:

1. *Economic impact:* The bill would cost the private sector $2.6 billion a year due to the costs of temporarily losing employees, hiring and training temporary employees, and the lowered productivity of newly trained employees.

2. *Small-business impact:* The financial burden of carrying nonworking employees and temporary substitutes and lowered productivity would bankrupt many small businesses. (Interestingly, the National Association of Women Business Owners opposes the bill due to concern about negative impact on small business.)

3. *Discrimination against women:* Because women employees would be viewed as more expensive, businesses would be less inclined to hire them.

4. *Voluntary benefits:* Parental leave benefits should be provided by companies voluntarily, with each company providing benefits geared to the company's and its employees' specific needs.

5. *Imbalance between the pregnant employees' rights and responsibilities:* If the law mandates maternity leave rights for employees, it should also mandate employee responsibilities. Employees should provide companies with more advance notice before taking leave. They should also provide several weeks' notice if, once on leave, they intend to quit. Failing to give adequate notice creates major problems in personnel planning and for employees temporarily hired or promoted to fill the gap. The bill does not mandate employee responsibilities.

Regardless of whether the Family and Medical Leave Bill becomes law, support for mandated maternity leave is gaining momentum in many states. In 1987, 28 states introduced legislation to provide some sort of maternity, paternity, and child-care leave, and more states are expected to consider parental leave bills. Although not required by law, a growing number of companies are implementing more generous parental leave policies. These companies are primarily large with pools of employees who can more easily assume the workload of a temporarily absent worker. For example, a 1984 survey of America's 1,500 largest companies found that 95 percent of the responding firms provide about five to eight weeks' maternity leave and most leaves are paid. About half of the companies provide job-protected leaves.

Many high-tech companies with highly skilled (and difficult-to-replace) employees and companies with many women in the management ranks (for example, companies in the banking, real estate, and insurance industries) also tend to have more progressive parental leave policies. For example:

1. Levi Strauss & Co provides up to 120 days of paid maternity leave with the employee's length of tenure determining the number of days paid at full salary. Employees with one or more years of service receive four weeks at full salary and the remaining weeks at 70 percent pay; those employed 11 years or more receive full pay for the full period. Employees can add sick days, vacation days at full pay, or an unpaid child-care leave to their disability period.

2. Johnson & Johnson Baby Products provides expecting employees full pay for up to 26 weeks after delivery and 90 days of unpaid leave for parents of natural or adopted children. J&J's "Baby Power" program also enables former J&J employees who left to raise families to fill jobs temporarily vacated by employees on leave.

3. Ameritrust Bank provides expectant mothers with up to two weeks of paid leave before delivery, six weeks of paid leave after delivery, and six months of unpaid leave with job protection. The employee's length of tenure determines the specific amount of leave provided. The company also maintains the "Perfectly Pregnant" program, which holds a meeting each month with pregnant employees to discuss company parental benefits and provide instruction in exercise and nutrition during pregnancy.

Although many companies are developing progressive policies for expecting mothers, few companies are offering leave for expectant fathers (14 percent according to a 1985 survey). Reports indicate that few fathers are taking paternity leave because they believe that their employer, while offering the leave, would not approve. According to the Catalyst study of 384 large companies, these employees' perceptions may be accurate. According to the study, over 40 percent of the companies providing paternity leave responded that they didn't view any paternity time off as reasonable. Catalyst researcher Phyllis Silverman concluded that many companies provide paternity leave only to protect themselves from possible discrimination suits.

Discussion Questions

1. Assume that you are the HR director for a manufacturing company that employs approximately 500 individuals (35 percent are

women) and that the Family and Medical Leave Bill is not law. Outline the provisions for a parental leave policy for the company. Be specific.

2. What are the key challenges facing management in implementing the policy?

3. Do you support a federally mandated, paid parental leave policy? Explain your position.

TRAINING AND DEVELOPMENT FOR BETTER PERFORMANCE

· · · · · · ·

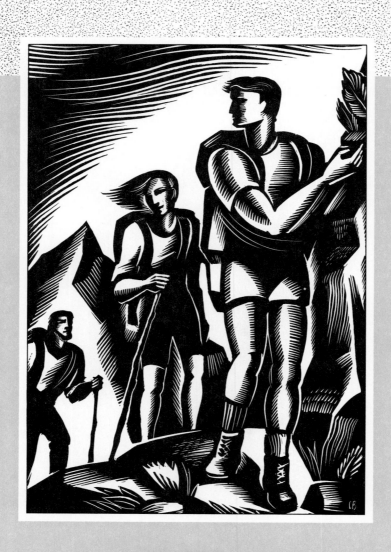

*P*art Four covers the training and development of employees. Chapter 13, Orientation and Training, discusses the orientation and training of employees. It focuses on improving the abilities and skills of employees. Chapter 14, Management and Organization Development, discusses the development of human resources with specific attention paid to managers. Chapter 15, Career Planning and Development, looks at career planning, an area of growing importance in organizations. In Chapter 16, Discipline and the Difficult Employee, positive discipline and punishment are examined in terms of where, when, and why each may be appropriate.

ORIENTATION AND TRAINING

·······

LEARNING OBJECTIVES

———◦———

After studying this chapter, you should be able to:

· · ·

Define what is meant by orientation, training, and learning

· · ·

Discuss the advantages of computer assisted instruction (CAI)

· · ·

Describe the characteristics of an orientation program

· · ·

Explain the role that a performance analysis can play in identifying employee training needs

· · ·

Compare on- and off-the-job training methods and approaches

· · ·

Illustrate the three phases in a training model used to define training more clearly

CAREER CHALLENGE

Harold Matthews was unhappy. He'd just had an unpleasant visit with his boss, William Custer. Harold is vice president of operations of Young Enterprises, a firm employing about 1,600 persons in the Los Angeles area. The firm manufactures parts for a large aircraft firm nearby.

Since Young Enterprises serves primarily one customer, costs are a major factor in their negotiations. Bill Custer told Harold that the new contract was not as good as the last one. Costs needed to be cut. Since labor costs are a high percentage of the total, Harold must begin to work on these. At the same time, purchasing was working on reducing materials costs and finance was trying to find ways to reduce the cost of capital.

Harold has decided to consult two groups of persons about the cost cutting: HRM specialists and his supervisors. First, he called a meeting of the department heads and key supervisors and prepared his figures. The facts are:

- Young Enterprises' labor costs are rising faster than their competitors' are, and faster than the cost of living.
- These costs are higher any way you measure them: number of employees per unit of output, cost per unit of output, and so on. What's more, the trend is worsening.

At the meeting, Harold explained the facts. Then he asked the supervisors for suggestions. He gave them strong "encouragement" to supervise each employee closely and to make sure that the firm gets a fair day's work for a fair day's pay. Harold took notes of the comments his supervisors made. Some of the better ones were:

Sally Feldman (supervisor) One of my problems is that the people HRM sends me are not producing at the output standards of the people I've lost through quits and retirement.

Art Jones (department head) Let's face it, when you look at the records, our recent output isn't up to what we expected when we installed the new machines.

Sam Jacobs (supervisor) The problem is our current crop of employees. They ain't what they used to be!

Harold wondered if they were just passing the buck–or if there was some truth to the complaints. He invited Gwen Meridith, the HRM vice president, in for help.

Harold Gwen, production costs are up and labor efficiency is down. The supervisors are blaming it on the employees. We put new machinery in to get production up. It's up, but not what it should be, given our investment. What do you think is going on?

Gwen I suspect that part of what they say has some truth to it. Lately, the job market is tight. Last week, I had 20 jobs to fill and only 20 applicants. About half really were somewhat marginal. And let's face it, we put the new machinery in with little preparation of the employees.

Harold What can we do? We have a serious cost problem.

Gwen The job market is still tight. I don't see any improvement in the near future. Sounds like we ought to gear up that training program I've been talking about.

Harold You prepare something for Bill. Then you and I will go to see him about it.

O rientation and training are processes that attempt to provide an employee with information, skills, and an understanding of the organization and its goals. Orientation involves starting the employee in the right direction, and training is designed to keep or to help a person continue to make positive contributions in the form of good performance.

Sam Lavalle reported to HRM as the notice of employment said to do. After about six of the new employees were there, orientation began. Miss Wentworth welcomed them to the company and then the "paper blitz" took place. In the next 30 minutes, she gave them a lot of paper — work rules, benefits booklets, pay forms to fill out, and so on. Sam's head was swimming. Then he got a slip telling him to report to his new supervisor, Andrew Villanueva, in Room 810. Andrew took Sam around the facility for three minutes, pointed out Sam's new workbench, and wished him good luck. Sam's case is an example of what most employees encounter: a formal orientation program that is brief and leaves a lot of questions unanswered. **Orientation** is the HRM activity that introduces new employees to the organization and to the employee's new tasks, managers, and work groups.

Walking into a new job is often a lonely and confusing event. The newcomer doesn't usually know what to say or whom to say it to, or even where he or she is supposed to be. Getting started is difficult for any new employee simply because the newness means not knowing what to expect, having to cope with a major life change (the job), and being unsure of the future. These ingredients suggest that newness anxiety will naturally be significant. It takes time to learn the ropes, and a good orientation program can help make this time be a positive experience. The first few days on the job are crucial in helping the employee get started in the right direction with a positive attitude and feeling.

Orientation has not been studied a great deal. Little scientific research has been done on whether orientation programs are adequate. Some experts view orientation as a kind of training.

There are different degrees of orientation needed depending on the experience, career path, and age of the person. A 50-year-old manager who is transferring to another department in the same company at the same job level may only need minimal orientation. However, a new, 20-year-old technician who is starting her first full-time job after attending a trade school may need a full-blown orientation. The orientation for any person is designed to make the person more comfortable, knowledgeable, and ready to work within the firm's culture, structures, and employee mix. Thus, examining the background of the employee is important in designing the proper type of orientation program.

THE PURPOSES OF ORIENTATION

Effectively done, orientation serves a number of purposes. In general, the orientation process is similar to what sociologists call *socialization*. Socialization occurs when a new employee learns the norms, values, work procedures, and patterns of behavior and dress that are expected in the organization. Some of the principal purposes of orientation are discussed in the next few sections.

To Reduce the Amount of Anxiety and Hazing a New Employee Experiences

Anxiety in this case means fear of failure on the job. It is a normal fear of the unknown focused on the ability to do the job. This anxiety can be made worse when old employees haze the new employee.

Hazing takes place when experienced employees "kid" the new employee. For example, experienced employees may ask the new worker, "How many toys are you producing per hour?" When she answers, she is told, "You'll never last. The last one who did that few wasn't here after two days."

Such hazing serves several purposes. It lets the recruit know he or she has a lot to learn and thus is dependent on the others for his or her job, and it is "fun" for the old-timers. But it can cause great anxiety for the recruit. Effective orientation alerts the new person to hazing and reduces anxiety.

To Reduce Employee Turnover

If employees perceive themselves as ineffective, unwanted, or unneeded, they may react to these feelings by quitting. Turnover is high during the break-in period, and effective orientation can reduce this costly reaction.

To Save Time for Supervisor and Co-Workers

Improperly oriented employees must still get the job done, and to do so they need help. The most likely people to provide this help are the co-workers and supervisors, who will have to spend time breaking in new employees. Good orientation programs save everyone time.

To Develop Realistic Job Expectations, Positive Attitudes toward the Employer, and Job Satisfaction

In what sociologists call the *older professions* (law, medicine) or *total institutions* (the church, prison, the army), job expectations are clear because they have been developed over long years of training and education. Society has built up a set of attitudes and behaviors that are considered proper for these jobs. For most of the world of work, however, this does not hold true. New employees must learn realistically what the organization expects of them, and their own expectations of the job must be neither too low nor too high.[1] Each worker must incorporate the job and its work values into his or her self-image.

Orientation helps this process. One way to illustrate how orientation serves these purposes is with the story in Exhibit 13–1 of how Texas Instruments developed its new orientation program.

WHO ORIENTS NEW EMPLOYEES?

Exhibit 13–2 describes how operating and HR managers run the orientation program in middle-sized and large organizations. In smaller organizations, the operating manager does all the orienting. In some unionized organizations, union officials are involved. HRM also helps train the operating manager for more effective orientation behavior.

An interesting way to orient employees is used at Hewlett Packard (H-P) in San Diego, California. At this H-P plant and also one in Waltham, Massachusetts, retired employees perform the orientation training. The response, according to Joe Costi, employee relations manager at the San Diego facility, has been fantastic. "Many newcomers comment this must be a good place to work, if retirees come back."[2]

EXHIBIT 13-1   Orientation at Texas Instruments

Texas Instruments knew that anxieties existing in the early period of work reduced competence and led to dissatisfaction and turnover. The anxiety resulted from awareness on the part of the female assemblers that they must reach the competence level they observed in the experienced employees around them. Many times they did not understand their supervisors' instructions but were afraid to ask further questions and appear stupid. Sometimes this anxiety was compounded by hazing.

Anxiety turned out to be a very important factor in the study at Texas Instruments, which investigated whether an orientation program designed to reduce anxiety would increase competence, heighten satisfaction, and lower turnover. The control group of new recruits were given the traditional orientation program: a typical two-hour briefing on the first day by the personnel department. This included the topics normally covered in orientation and the usual description of the minimum level of performance desired. Then they were introduced to the supervisor, who gave them a short job introduction, and they were off.

The experimental group was given the two-hour orientation the control group received and then six hours of social orientation. Four factors were stressed in the social orientation:

1. They were told that their opportunity to succeed was good. Those being oriented were given facts showing that over 99 percent of the employees achieved company standards. They were shown learning curves of how long it took to achieve various levels of competence. Five or six times during the day, it was stressed that all in the group would be successful.
2. They were told to disregard "hall talk." New employees were tipped off about typical hazing. It was suggested that they take it in good humor, but ignore it.
3. They were told to take the initiative in communication. It was explained that supervisors were busy and not likely to ask the new worker if she "needed help." Supervisors would be glad to help, but the worker must ask for it, and he or she would not appear stupid if he or she did so.
4. They were told to get to know their supervisor. The supervisor was described in important details — what he or she liked as hobbies, whether he or she was strict or not, quiet or boisterous, and so forth.

This social orientation had dramatic results. The experimental group had 50 percent less tardiness and absenteeism, and waste was reduced by 80 percent, product costs were cut 15 to 30 percent, training time was cut 50 percent, and training costs cut about 66 percent.

EXHIBIT 13-2   Relationship of Operating and HRM Managers
                    in Orientation

Orientation Function	Operating Manager (OM)	HR Manager (HRM)
Design the orientation program	OM should help in the design work	HRM is consultant with OM
Introduce the new employee to the organization and its history, personnel policies, working conditions, and rules. Complete paperwork.		HRM performs this
Explain the task and job expectations to employee	OM performs this	
Introduce employee to work group and new surroundings.	OM performs this	
Encourage employees to help new employee	OM performs this	

CHAPTER 13   Orientation and Training

HOW ORIENTATION PROGRAMS WORK

Orientation programs for new employees vary from quite informal, primarily verbal efforts, to formal schedules that supplement verbal presentations with written handouts. Formal orientations often include a tour of the facilities, or slides, charts, and pictures of them. Usually, they are used when a large number of employees must be oriented.

An example of areas that are covered in comprehensive orientation programs is presented in Exhibit 13–3. After an employee has received a general orientation of the organization, it is recommended that a more job-specific orientation be given. Exhibit 13–4 presents the areas that can be covered in a job-specific orientation program.

THE ORIENTATION INFORMATION OVERLOAD

As Exhibits 13–3 and 13–4 indicate, a new employee during orientation is provided with a great amount of information. The intent of providing the information is to present an understanding of how the organization and department operate. However, it is virtually impossible for any person to digest and learn the volume of orientation information that can be provided. Thus, the orientation should provide for the employee's receiving the information over more than a one-day or one-week period.

Developing an orientation program that takes place over a one-month period seems to be well suited for absorbing the volume of information needed by new employees. Unfortunately, too many organizations overload new employees with orientation information. They usually provide the information in a standard operating procedures manual and ask the employee to take a day or two to examine the material. Once this brief period is over, the employee is asked if there are any questions. When any questions are answered, the new employee begins to work.

Instead of a quick and information-overloaded orientation program, a more systematic and guided procedure is appropriate. A few guidelines for such a program are these:

1. Orientation should begin with the most relevant and immediate kinds of information and then proceed to more general policies of the organization. It should occur at a pace that the new employee is comfortable with.
2. The most significant part of orientation is the human side, giving new employees knowledge of what supervisors and co-workers are like, telling them how long it should take to reach standards of effective work, and encouraging them to seek help and advice when needed.
3. New employees should be "sponsored" or directed in the immediate environment by an experienced worker or supervisor who can respond to questions and keep in close touch during the early induction period.
4. New employees should be gradually introduced to the people with whom they will work, rather than given a superficial introduction to all of them on the first day. The object should be to help them to know their co-workers and supervisors.
5. New employees should be allowed sufficient time to get their feet on the ground before job demands on them are increased.

EXHIBIT 13-3   Areas Covered in a Comprehensive Orientation Program

1. **Overview of the company**
   - ☐ Welcoming speech
   - ☐ Founding, growth, trends, goals, priorities, and problems
   - ☐ Traditions, customs, norms, and standards
   - ☐ Current specific functions of the organization
   - ☐ Products/services and customers served
   - ☐ Steps in getting product/service to customers
   - ☐ Scope of diversity of activities
   - ☐ Organization, structure, and relationship of company and its branches
   - ☐ Facts on key managerial staff
   - ☐ Community relations, expectations, and activities

2. **Key policies and procedures review**

3. **Compensation**
   - ☐ Pay rates and ranges
   - ☐ Overtime
   - ☐ Holiday pay
   - ☐ Shift differential
   - ☐ How pay is received
   - ☐ Deductions; required and optional, with specific amounts
   - ☐ Option to buy damaged products and costs thereof
   - ☐ Discounts
   - ☐ Advances on pay
   - ☐ Loans from credit union
   - ☐ Reimbursement for job expenses
   - ☐ Tax shelter options

4. **Fringe benefits**
   - ☐ Insurance
   - ☐ Medical-dental
   - ☐ Life
   - ☐ Disability
   - ☐ Workers' compensation
   - ☐ Holidays and vacations (patriotic, religious, birthday)
   - ☐ Leave: personal illness, family illness, bereavement, maternity, military, jury duty, emergency, extended absence
   - ☐ Retirement plans and options
   - ☐ On-the-job training opportunities
   - ☐ Counseling services
   - ☐ Cafeteria
   - ☐ Recreation and social activities
   - ☐ Other company services to employees

5. **Safety and accident prevention**
   - ☐ Completion of emergency data card (if not done as part of employment process)
   - ☐ Health and first aid clinics
   - ☐ Exercise and recreation centers
   - ☐ Safety precautions
   - ☐ Reporting of hazards
   - ☐ Fire prevention and control
   - ☐ Accident procedures and reporting
   - ☐ OSHA requirements (review of key sections)
   - ☐ Physical exam requirements
   - ☐ Use of alcohol and drugs on the job

6. **Employee and union relations**
   - ☐ Terms and conditions of employment review
   - ☐ Assignment, reassignment, and promotion
   - ☐ Probationary period and expected on-the-job conduct
   - ☐ Reporting of sickness and lateness to work
   - ☐ Employee rights and responsibilities
   - ☐ Manager and supervisor rights
   - ☐ Relations with supervisors and shop stewards
   - ☐ Employee organizations and options
   - ☐ Union contract provisions and/or company policy
   - ☐ Supervision and evaluation of performance
   - ☐ Discipline and reprimands
   - ☐ Grievance procedures
   - ☐ Termination of employment (resignation, layoff, discharge, retirement)
   - ☐ Content and examination of personnel record
   - ☐ Communications: channels of communication — upward and downward — suggestion system, posting materials on bulletin board, sharing new ideas
   - ☐ Sanitation and cleanliness
   - ☐ Wearing of safety equipment, badges, and uniforms
   - ☐ Bringing things on and removing things from company grounds
   - ☐ On-site political activity
   - ☐ Gambling
   - ☐ Handling of rumors

7. **Physical facilities**
   - ☐ Tour of facilities
   - ☐ Food services and cafeteria
   - ☐ Restricted areas for eating
   - ☐ Employee entrances
   - ☐ Restricted areas (e.g., cars)
   - ☐ Parking
   - ☐ First aid
   - ☐ Rest rooms
   - ☐ Supplies and equipment

8. **Economic factors**
   - ☐ Costs of damage by select items with required sales to balance
   - ☐ Costs of theft with required sales to compensate
   - ☐ Profit margins
   - ☐ Labor costs
   - ☐ Cost of equipment
   - ☐ Costs of absenteeism, lateness, and accidents

Source: W. D. St. John (May 1980), "The Complete Employee Orientation Program," *Personnel Journal*, pp. 376–77. Reprinted with the permission of *Personnel Journal*, Costa Mesa, California; all rights reserved.

EXHIBIT 13-4   Areas Covered in Job-Specific Orientation Program

---

1. **Department functions**
   - ☐ Goals and current priorities
   - ☐ Organization and structure
   - ☐ Operational activities
   - ☐ Relationship of functions to other departments
   - ☐ Relationships of jobs within the department

2. **Job duties and responsibilities**
   - ☐ Detailed explanation of job based on current job description and expected results
   - ☐ Explanation of why the job is important, how the specific job relates to others in the department and company
   - ☐ Discussion of common problems and how to avoid and overcome them
   - ☐ Performance standards and basis of performance evaluation
   - ☐ Number of daily work hours and times
   - ☐ Overtime needs and requirements
   - ☐ Extra duty assignments (such as changing duties to cover for an absent worker)
   - ☐ Required records and reports
   - ☐ Checkout on equipment to be used
   - ☐ Explanation of where and how to get tools, have equipment maintained and repaired
   - ☐ Types of assistance available; when and how to ask for help
   - ☐ Relations with state and federal inspectors

3. **Policies, procedures, rules, and regulations**
   - ☐ Rules unique to the job and/or department
   - ☐ Handling emergencies
   - ☐ Safety precautions and accident prevention
   - ☐ Reporting of hazards and accidents
   - ☐ Cleanliness standards and sanitation (such as cleanup)
   - ☐ Security, theft problems and costs
   - ☐ Relations with outside people (e.g., drivers)
   - ☐ Eating, smoking, and chewing gum, etc., in department area
   - ☐ Removal of things from department
   - ☐ Damage control (e.g., smoking restrictions)
   - ☐ Time clock and time sheets
   - ☐ Breaks/rest periods
   - ☐ Lunch duration and time
   - ☐ Making and receiving personal telephone calls
   - ☐ Requisitioning supplies and equipment
   - ☐ Monitoring and evaluating of employee performance
   - ☐ Job bidding and requesting reassignment
   - ☐ Going to cars during work hours

4. **Tour of department**
   - ☐ Rest rooms and showers
   - ☐ Fire-alarm box and fire extinguisher stations
   - ☐ Time clocks
   - ☐ Lockers
   - ☐ Approved entrances and exits
   - ☐ Water fountains and eye wash systems
   - ☐ Supervisors' quarters
   - ☐ Supply room and maintenance department
   - ☐ Sanitation and security offices
   - ☐ Smoking areas
   - ☐ Locations of services to employees related to department
   - ☐ First aid kit

5. **Introduction to department employees**

Source: W. D. St. John (May 1980), "The Complete Employee Orientation Program," *Personnel Journal*, p. 377. Reprinted with permission of *Personnel Journal*, Costa Mesa, California; all rights reserved.

ASSIGNMENT, PLACEMENT, AND ORIENTATION FOLLOW-UP

The final phase of a well-designed and systematic orientation program is the assignment of the new employee to the job. At this point, the supervisor is supposed to take over and continue the orientation program. But, as the Texas Instruments study demonstrated, supervisors are busy people, and they can overlook some of the facts needed by the new employee to do a good job.

One way to ensure adequate orientation is to design a feedback system to control the program, or use the management by objectives technique. A form could be used to communicate this feedback from the trainee. The new employee could be instructed to: "Complete this checklist as well as you can. Then take it to your supervisor, who will go over it with you and give you any additional information you may need." The job information form is signed by employee and supervisor. An appointment set up with the orientation group in the first month on the job provides a follow-up opportunity to determine how well the employee is adjusting and permits evaluation of the orientation program. The form is designed not to test knowledge but to help improve the process of orientation.

INTRODUCTION TO TRAINING

Training is extremely important for new or present employees. Training is, in short, an attempt to improve current or future employee performance. The following specific points are important to know about training:

- **Training** is the systematic process of altering the behavior of employees in a direction to increase organization goals.
- A **formal training program** is an effort by the employer to provide opportunities for the employee to acquire job-related skills, attitudes, and knowledge.
- **Learning** is the act by which the individual acquires skills, knowledge, and abilities that result in a relatively permanent change in his or her behavior.
- Any behavior that has been learned is a skill. Therefore, skills improvement is what training will accomplish. Motor skills, cognitive skills, and interpersonal skills are targets of training programs.

One way to display the meaning and comprehensiveness of training and development is to present a graphic model. Exhibit 13–5 illustrates such a model. The needs assessment phase serves as the formulation for decisions that must be made at later phases. It is important for the needs assessment to be complete, timely, and accurate. After the needs assessment is completed, instructional objectives are needed. These objectives lead to the selection and design of instructional programs. If assessment and the selection and design of programs are done carefully, the evaluation of the training and development can be accomplished. As Exhibit 13–5 indicates, evaluation can provide information about when various training goals have been accomplished. Some important goals are:

- *Training validity.* Did the trainees learn skills, or acquire knowledge or abilities during the training?
- *Transfer validity.* Did the knowledge, skills, or abilities learned in training lead to improved performance on the job?
- *Intraorganizational validity.* Is the job performance of a new group of trainees in the same organization that developed the program comparable with the job performance of the original training group(s)?
- *Interorganizational validity.* Can a training program that has been validated in one organization be used successfully in another firm?

These questions (goals) result in different evaluation procedures being employed to examine what, if anything, training and development have accomplished.[3]

Learning Theory and Training

Since training is a form of education, some of the findings regarding learning theory logically might be applicable to training. These principles can be important in the design of both formal and informal training programs. The following is a brief summary of the way learning principles can be applied to job training.[4]

EXHIBIT 13-5   A General Systems Model of Training and Development

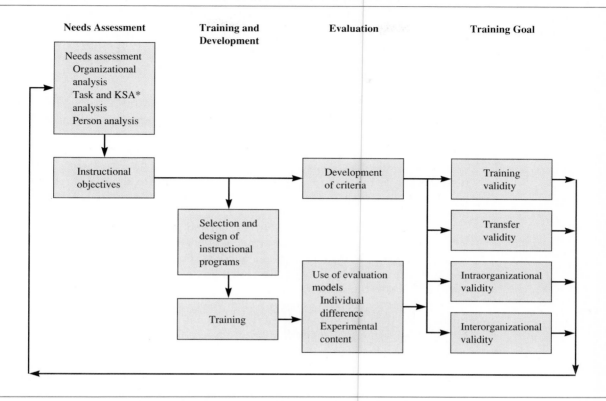

Source: From I. L. Goldstein (1986), *Training in Organizations: Needs Assessment, Development, and Evaluation*, 2nd ed. (Monterey, Calif.: Brooks/ Cole), p. 16. Reprinted by permission of the publisher.

The Trainee Must Be Motivated to Learn   In order to learn, a person must want to learn. In the context of training, motivation influences a person's enthusiasm for training, keeps attention focused on the training activities, and reinforces what is learned. Motivation is influenced by the belief and perceptions of the trainee. If a trainee is not motivated, little can be accomplished in a training program.

The Learning Must Be Reinforced   Behavioral psychologists have demonstrated that learners learn best with fairly immediate reinforcement of appropriate behavior. The learner must be rewarded for new behavior in ways that satisfy needs, such as pay, recognition, and promotion. Standards of performance should be set for the learner. Benchmarks for learning will provide goals and give a feeling of accomplishment when reached. These standards provide a measure for meaningful feedback.

The Training Must Provide for Practice of the Material   Learning requires time to assimilate what has been learned, to accept it, to internalize it, and to build confidence in what has been learned. This requires practice and repetition of the material.

The Material Presented Must Be Meaningful

Appropriate materials for sequential learning (cases, problems, discussion outlines, reading lists) must be provided. The trainer acts as an aid in an efficient learning process.

The learning methods used should be as varied as possible. It is boredom that destroys learning, not fatigue. Any method — whether old-fashioned lecture or programmed learning or a challenging computer game — will begin to bore some learners if overused.

The Material Presented Must Be Communicated Effectively

Communication must be done in a unified way, and over enough time to allow it to be absorbed.

The Material Taught Must Transfer to the Job Situation

The trainer must do her or his best to make the training as close to the reality of the job as possible. Thus, when the trainee returns to the job, the training can be applied immediately.[5]

As each aspect of training program design and implementation is discussed, you will see how these learning theory principles are applied. Training and management development are closely related to many HRM activities. For example, performance evaluation provides the data needed for training. Employment planning decisions may also dictate the need for added training.

Employee training is moderately well developed — a Stage III or possibly Stage IV function in HRM. But management development is a Stage II HRM function. Most people do it, but scientific evaluation of its results is rare.

A DIAGNOSTIC VIEW OF TRAINING

The most important determinants of training are the task to be done and the employees' abilities and attitudes. If the current employees have work ethic attitudes and the skills needed to do the jobs, training may not be too important for the organization. More often, because of conditions in the labor market, the organization is losing some employees to other enterprises that provide better rewards.

It is also unlikely that the task demands are stable. More frequently, because of volatile technology and market conditions, the jobs are changing, requiring more training so that employees can meet current effectiveness standards. For example, when computers are introduced or new production or operating techniques are instituted, employees must be retrained.[6]

The U.S. government also is becoming a vital influence on training. This has been happening in two ways. One is the pressure for equal employment opportunities and human rights. If, in an organization, minorities and women work only at the lowest-paid, least-skilled positions, pressure will be applied to upgrade the skills of those who have the potential for upward mobility, thus increasing the demand for training or retraining.

The second way government influences training is that it provides many training programs. These programs frequently have public policy purposes, such as reducing unemployment, upgrading the incomes of minority groups, or increasing the competitiveness of underdeveloped regions of the country.

In the United States, the federal government, through the Comprehensive Employment and Training Act (1974) and other work-force legislation, has allocated large sums of money for the training of potential workers for jobs.[7] The government reimburses training organizations (schools, business, unions) or trains the workers itself.

The California Employment Training Panel is a unique, state-sponsored program. The panel has provided $20 million in funds diverting unemployment insurance money to finance training that will reduce the states' jobless rolls.[8] The money helps companies hire and train unemployed workers, or retrain workers threatened with losing their jobs unless they learn new skills. The California program permits employers to pick their own trainees and choose whether they want to train in-house or use local colleges. It pays only for workers who complete the training course and succeed in holding jobs.

In an effort to expand the pool of entry-level job applicants, Congress has revised the Job Training Partnership Act (JTPA) to focus more attention on youth. The JTPA is the federal government's prime job training program to help the economically disadvantaged and long-term unemployed. Under the JTPA, the government pays up to half the costs associated with supervising and training full- or part-time employees.[9]

Government programs like the JTPA are needed since basic training among young people in reading and writing skills is lacking. According to a survey by the Society of Human Resource Management/Commerce Clearing House, a large number of unskilled people have been unknowingly employed. Out of 1,328 firms surveyed, 842 (more than 63 percent) employ people without basic skills, and of that number, only 258 (or 30 percent) provide some kind of literacy training. The training formats used include one-on-one tutoring, computer or video programs, and traditional in-class sessions.[10]

Some unions are also involved in employee training, especially in industries such as construction, in which the union is larger than the employer. In these cases, the union often does most or all of the training. A large proportion of this type of training occurs in apprenticeship programs.

The goals of management also affect training and development. For example, organization development programs are likely to be chosen by managers who feel that full development of employees is an appropriate enterprise goal.

The implications are that employee training is a major undertaking for employers. Almost all large organizations and most medium-sized ones run their own training programs. It is estimated that 39.5 million or about one third of the American work force received some kind of formal training in 1990. The trainees participated in about 1.3 billion hours of training.[11] The five most popular types of training are new orientation, performance appraisal, leadership, interpersonal skills, and new equipment orientation.

Training can be a costly endeavor. Exhibit 13–6 illustrates how an industrial firm could easily spend $100,000–$125,000 or more training just three or four salespeople. Whether an organization has management or professional development programs depends a great deal on its size. Smaller enterprises rarely run their own formal development program; the programs are informal at best. Larger organizations have elaborate formal programs combining on-the-job with off-the-job development.[12] Others, such as General Motors, the U.S. military, Exxon, and AT&T, have established large training and development centers for their managers. McDonald's runs Hamburger University in Oak Brook, Illinois, while Arthur Andersen trains accountants on an old college campus west of Chicago.[13] The Federal Executive Institute at Charlottesville, Virginia, is set up to develop federal government executives, as is the Executive Seminar Center in Berkeley, California, and the U.S. Post Office Center in Norman, Oklahoma. Aetna Insurance Institute was built at a cost of $42 million to handle over 31,000 Aetna Corporation students per year.[14] There has been tremendous growth in this area in the past 20 years, and the trend is expected to continue.

EXHIBIT 13-6   Average Costs of Training a Salesperson*

Type of Firm	1991
Industrial products (an engineering salesperson)	$35,129
Consumer products (a person selling food products to a grocery store)	$24,657
Services†	$26,112

* Includes salary, instructional materials, transportation, and living expenses incurred for training, instructional staff, outside seminars, and management time when it is part of training budget.
† Includes insurance, financial, utilities, transportation, and sales personnel.
Using data from *Sales & Marketing Management* magazine. Copyright February 16, 1987, p. 62 and these costs were developed by the authors.

The corporate classroom is now a growing business. Engineers can take classes that could lead to a master's degree. It is estimated that close to 100 companies — Eastman Kodak, Westinghouse Electric Co., and NCR among them — offer in-house course work that can lead to academically accredited degrees. National Technology University (NTU), based in Fort Collins, Colorado, is unique among corporate colleges with its electronic satellite network.[15] The university combines the resources of 22 member universities and several corporate sponsors to transmit advanced degree courses across the country. NTU students attend classes at their worksite, watch satellite transmissions, and talk with professors via telephones or electronic mail. After about 3½ years of study, they can earn various degrees.

HR executives and other managers now realize how important and large the commitment to training is becoming. The consensus accounting model reported by the American Society for Training & Development helps firms assess the costs and benefits of their training and development programs.[16] The consensus model consists of four steps:

1. Establish an organization-specific definition of training.
2. Determine all training cost categories.
3. Calculate training costs.
4. Code costs.

The economic costs of training need to be looked at, and training program evaluations must determine if the program has made a specific contribution to the organization's goals.

WHO IS INVOLVED IN TRAINING?

For training to be effective, top management must support it in an open manner. Employees must see that top management is supporting training personally and financially. As with other HRM activities, both operating and HR managers are involved in training. Exhibit 13–7 indicates how. Occasionally, more than these two groups are involved. For example, at General Telephone of Florida, the training, labor relations, and public affairs departments combined forces to prepare video training programs to train managers to handle grievances and arbitration. Community theater actors performed the roles to show participants how to perform while on the job.

In larger organizations, the HR manager most involved in the work described in Chapters 13 and 14 is called the *training director* or *training and development manager*.

EXHIBIT 13-7 The Role of Operating and HR Managers in Training

Training Activites	Operating Manager (OM)	HR Manager (HRM)
Determining training needs and objectives	Approved by OM	Done by HRM
Developing training criteria	Approved by OM	Done by HRM
Choosing trainer	Jointly chosen: nominated by OM	Jointly chosen: approved by HRM
Developing training materials	Approved by OM	Done by HRM
Planning and implementing the program		Done by HRM
Doing the training	Occasionally done by OM	Normally done by HRM
Evaluating the training	OM reviews the results	Done by HRM

MANAGING THE TRAINING PROGRAM
Determining Training Needs and Objectives

The first step in managing training is to determine training needs and set objectives for these needs. In effect, the trainers are preparing a training forecast (this is the assessment phase in Exhibit 13–5).

The needs assessment involves the analysis of the organization's needs; knowledge, skill, and ability needs to perform the job; and the person or jobholder's needs. The organizational needs assessment requires an examination of the long- and short-run objectives of the firm. The organization's financial, social, human resource, growth, and market objectives need to be matched with the firm's human talent, structure, climate, and efficiency. Where is the organization going and does it have the capability to get there? This is the important question that needs to be assessed. Typically, objectives, ratios, organization charts, historical records on absenteeism, quality of production, efficiency, and performance appraisals will be carefully reviewed.

The knowledge, skills, and abilities needed to perform the job are carefully considered. What are the tasks? What skills are needed to perform well? What does performing well mean? Data from current employees, supervisors, and experts need to be collected to complete this part of a needs assessment.

The employee's needs also must be considered. Asking the person what his or her needs are on the job and to perform the tasks can provide information and data. Examining the employee's performance against a standard or compared to that of co-workers can help identify strengths, weaknesses, and needs. Determining if a person can do the job is an important step in improving the firm's ability to match the person with the best job for him or her.

Each of these need assessment categories is important. However, focusing on the person's needs is especially important. It is at the individual and/or group level at which training is conducted.

There are four ways to determine employee training needs.[17]

1. Observe employees.
2. Listen to employees.

PROFESSIONAL PROFILE

Biography

Beverly A. Tarulli is manager of employee development for BellSouth Corporation, based in Atlanta, Georgia. She received her B.A. in psychology from Franklin and Marshall College, and her M.A. and Ph.D. degrees in industrial organizational psychology from the University of Akron.

Dr. Tarulli was previously manager of human resources research for BellSouth. Her responsibilities in that position included selection test development and validation, program development and evaluation, and human resources planning. Prior to joining BellSouth, she taught courses in personnel management and industrial/organizational psychology at the undergraduate and graduate levels.

Job Description   As manager of employee development, Dr. Tarulli is responsible for the design, development, and evaluation of employee development programs and supporting policies for both management and nonmanagement employees. In 1990, BellSouth introduced a comprehensive development program for its nonmanagement employees. The program offers workshops and courses through local community, junior, and technical colleges in the company's nine-state region. In 1991, BellSouth will trial an integrated management development program designed to allow managers to self-diagnose areas for improvement and target specific ways to self-develop.

Cost-Effective Development in the 90s: A Viewpoint   One of the challenges of the 90s for human resources professionals will be to ensure that the development of employees keeps pace with the rapidly changing skill needs of our jobs. At the same time, pressure to accomplish this in more cost-efficient ways will increase.

At BellSouth, we help employees to keep their skills current by identifying job-specific skill needs and communicating them to employees. Through organized development programs, employees can target their own development needs and receive direction for their development efforts. The company provides the resources, support, and opportunities for development, but individuals must supply the initiative, time, and effort. It is important not to ignore the impact that human resources policies and reward systems can have on fostering a corporate culture that encourages employee development. We have found that it is sometimes necessary to revise existing policies or introduce new ones to better support training and development efforts.

In most corporations, development has been synonymous with classroom training. BellSouth is shifting the focus of development away from total reliance on classroom training. In both our management and nonmanagement development programs, there is greater emphasis on development activities that occur outside of the classroom and on employees devoting some of their own time to development. We have also embarked on cooperative efforts with the educational community in the delivery of our skill-building, college-credit courses as well as our one-day workshops. In today's economic climate, it is more critical than ever to assess the costs and benefits of our development programs. Thus, training evaluation and assessing the degree of training is important.

Moving more employee development out of the classroom is an idea whose time has come. Particularly in a corporate environment where downsizing and cost efficiencies are the norm, we have not lost sight of the need for the continual development of our employees. We are just doing it smarter.

CAREER CHALLENGE

(continued)

Young Enterprises did not have a separate training department. So Gwen, with the assistance of Bob McGarrah, the director of training and development, began to think about a training program to help Harold Matthews reach his goal. The program might not have been needed if the job market weren't so tight. But since the applicants are so scarce, the training program was very important at this point.

Gwen Bob, what we need to determine is what training programs we should have right now. What do you suggest we do?

Bob The typical approach is to use organizational analysis, operational analysis, and person analysis. Besides, we need to do some sort of feasibility of cost/benefit analysis to see if the training is worth the effort. This will give us a set of training objectives for a program or set of programs. Then we design the program content and methods around these. After the program is run, we evaluate it.

Gwen At this point, let's set the objectives and design the program. Then we'll go back to Harold to see if he has any additional suggestions.

3. Ask supervisors about employees' training needs.
4. Examine the problems employees have.

In essence, any gaps between expected and actual results suggest training needs.[18] Active solicitation of suggestions from employees, supervisors, managers, and training committees can also provide training needs ideas.

By observation, asking, and listening, a manager or HR specialist is actually conducting a **performance analysis**.[19] There are a number of specific steps in using a performance analysis to determine training needs. Exhibit 13–8 outlines these steps.

Step 1: Behavioral Discrepancy   The first step is to appraise employees' performance. How are the employees doing now and how should they be doing? If a secretary is using a Wang word processor to prepare budgets and takes an average of 7.5 hours to complete the work, this record of performance can be used to assess her performance. This performance may be 2.0 hours over what is expected. Thus, there is a behavioral discrepancy — a difference between actual and expected.

Step 2: Cost/Value Analysis   Next, the manager must determine the cost and value of correcting the identified behavioral discrepancy. Is it worth the cost, time, and expense to have the secretary prepare the budgets in less than 7.5 hours?

Step 3: Is It a Can't Do or Won't Do Situation?   It is important to determine if the employee could do the expected job if he or she wanted to. Three questions need to be answered: (1) Does the person know what to do in terms of performance? (2) Could the person do the job if he or she wanted to? and (3) Does

EXHIBIT 13-8   Performance Analysis: Analyzing Training Needs

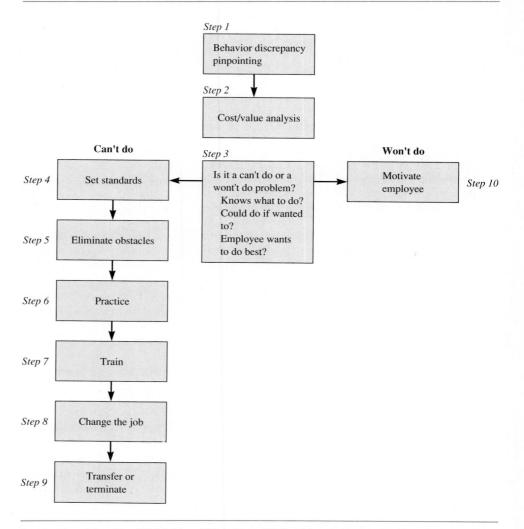

Source: Adapted from Donald Michalak and Edwin Yager (1979), *Making the Training Process Work* (New York: Harper & Row).

he or she want to do the job? Answering these questions requires observation, listening, and asking skills on the part of the person conducting the performance analysis.

Step 4: Set Standards   If a secretary doesn't know what the standard is, he or she may underperform. Establishing a standard and clearly communicating it can improve performance.

Step 5: Remove Obstacles   Not being able to complete budgets on time may be caused by frequent breakdowns of the equipment (the Wang system) or not receiving a job on time. Time, equipment, and people can be obstacles that result in behavior discrepancies.

Step 6: Practice   Practice, practice, practice may be one avenue to performing a job better. Does the manager permit the employee the needed practice time?

Step 7: Training   If the performance analysis indicates that behaviors need to be altered, training becomes a viable consideration before any training approaches can be weighed and considered as being best suited to correct the behavior discrepancy.

Step 8: Change the Job   Redesigning the job through job enrichment, job simplification, or job enlargement may be the best solution.

Step 9: Transfer or Terminate   If all else has failed, the employee may have to be transferred or terminated.

Step 10: Create a Motivational Climate   In some cases, a skilled and able employee may not want to perform the job as required, posing a motivational problem. A manager may then have to use a motivational approach that converts this undermotivated person into a motivated high performer. Rewards, punishment, discipline, or some combination may be needed to create a positive climate that results in the employee utilizing his or her skills optimally.

A performance analysis is a sound procedure that can provide insight into training needs and objectives. Such an analysis may illustrate that training is not the best solution to the behavior discrepancies identified. If this is the case, other solutions will surface as the performance analysis is conducted.[20]

If, however, the performance analysis identifies a training problem, then it is necessary to establish specific, measurable training objectives. Training objectives should be expressed in behavioral terms, if at all possible. The behavioral training objectives of a Bandell Manufacturing supervisory training program are:

- To improve supervisory understanding of laws pertaining to the use of the performance appraisal system.
- To improve listening and feedback skills for use in the performance appraisal program.
- To reduce by 20 percent for the year's program, the formal supervisor complaints that are filed with the HRM unit about the performance appraisal system.

By using behaviorally based objectives, the intent of the training program is identified. In some cases, it is difficult to specify behavioral objectives. For example, a new job may not have objectives because the manager is still attempting to clarify what behaviors are required. However, if behaviors can't be identified, one might be inclined to ask what the reason for the training is. A vague, ambiguous answer might suggest that the training purpose is not that important.

Choosing Trainers and Trainees

Great care must be exercised in choosing effective instructors or trainers. To some extent, the success of the training program depends on proper selection of the person who performs the training task.[21] Personal characteristics (the ability to speak well, to write convincingly, to organize the work of others, to be inventive, and to inspire others to greater achievements) are important factors in the selection of trainers. The process of needs analysis and training program development can be accomplished by company trainers. HR specialists or hired outside consultants who report to the HR manager or other top managers are used to perform a needs analysis and to conduct the training.[22]

Although much formal training is performed by professional trainers, often operating supervisors may be the best trainers technically, especially if the training manager helps them prepare the material. Using operating managers as trainers overcomes the frequent criticism that "Training is OK in the classroom, but it won't work on the shop floor or back on the job." The presence of *trained* trainers is a major factor in whether the training program is successful. It will help if these principles of learning are followed:

- Provide time for practice of the material.
- Require practice and repetition of the material.
- Communicate the material effectively.

Another planning factor is the selection of trainees who will participate in the programs. In some cases, this is obvious; the program may have been designed to train particular new employees in certain skills. In some cases, the training program is designed to help with EEO goals; in others, it is to help employees find better jobs elsewhere when layoffs are necessary or to retrain older employees. Techniques similar to selection procedures may be used to select trainees, especially when those who attend the program may be promoted or receive higher wages or salaries as a result.

The selection of trainees is not always limited to promising future leaders or newcomers who need to learn specific job-related skills. More and more companies now offer training programs for employees nearing retirement.[23] Some examples of such programs are:

- Chrysler has a seven-week training program relating to retirement issues, problems, and adjustments co-sponsored by the company and the United Auto Workers.
- AT&T sponsors a retiree group called the Telephone Pioneers of America. Pre-retirement and postretirement activities occur in meetings, discussions, and with personal counselors.
- Citicorp holds seminars with guest speakers and consultants who discuss health, aging, financial planning, and insurance.

The way a company treats its retirees is seen by all employees. The intent of pre- and postretirement training and educational programs is to provide accurate information and an open exchange of ideas about the experience of retiring.

TRAINING AND DEVELOPMENT PHASE

After needs and objectives have been determined and trainees and trainers have been selected, the program is run. This is the second phase shown in Exhibit 13–5. This phase includes selection of content and methods to be used and the actual training.

Selection of Training Content

From the analysis of the training needs and translating them into behavioral objectives, the training director derives the content of the training. Since there are well over 20,000 jobs listed in the *Dictionary of Occupational Titles*, the number of skills to be developed can be quite large. For example, communication, leadership, and budgeting skills are frequent subjects of training programs. But all kinds of skills can be taught.[24] The ones *to be* taught are derived from the training needs analysis. They can vary from typing skills improvement to learning a new computer language to effective use of a new machine.

Training Approaches for Employees

Both training for the unskilled and retraining for an employee follow one of four approaches, which combine elements of the *where* and *what* of training. The four principal types of training are apprenticeship, vestibule, on-the-job, and off-the-job training.

Apprentice Training
Apprentice training is a combination of on-the-job and off-the-job training. It requires the cooperation of the employer, trainers at the workplace and in schools (such as vocational schools), government agencies, and the skilled-trades unions.

Governments regulate apprentice training. In the United States, the major law is the Apprenticeship Act of 1937. Typically, the government also subsidizes these programs. The U.S. Department of Labor funds apprenticeship programs in the building trades, mining, auto repair, oil, and other fields. The department also issues standards and regulations governing these programs. About 30,000 persons are trained yearly by this method.

The apprentice commits to a period of training and learning that involves both formal classroom learning and practical on-the-job experience. These periods can vary from 2 years or so (barber, ironworker, foundry worker, baker, meat cutter, engraver) through 4 or 5 years (electrician, photoengraver, tool and die maker, plumber, job press worker), up to 10 years (steelplate engraver). During this period, the pay is less than that for the master workers. A weakness of apprenticeship training is that the amount of time a person serves as an apprentice is predetermined by members of the trade. The trade fails to take into consideration individual differences in learning time.

Germany has also supported apprenticeship-type programs. About half the children in Germany between 15 to 18 years old are enrolled in apprenticeship programs.[25] The Germans believe that a nation's competitiveness in global markets is significantly improved if the youth are properly trained.

Vestibule Training
In **vestibule training,** the trainee learns the job in an environment that simulates the real working environment as closely as possible. An example would be the simulated cockpit of a Boeing 767 used to train airline pilots in operating that specific aircraft.[26]

A machine operator trainee might run a machine under the supervision of a trainer until he or she learns how to use it properly. Only then is the trainee sent to the shop floor. This procedure can be quite expensive if the number of trainees supervised is not large, but it can be effective under certain circumstances. Some employees trained in the vestibule method have adjustment problems when they begin full-time work, since the vestibule area is safer and less hectic.

A form of vestibule training is now called "clinic training" at firms such as Wells Fargo Bank. For example, a Wells Fargo Bank branch manager may need to train tellers who can work the branches' busiest hours.[27] In a clinic, trainees work in peer groups to learn and practice new skills. They attend a short, instructional session presented during a staff meeting or at a central location.

They are taught, coached, and evaluated by a line employee, usually the manager. The typical Wells Fargo clinic is between 75 minutes and three hours long. In the clinic, the tellers are coached and observed as they practice the needed skills. The clinic requires few resources, and delivery of training costs stay low because travel, classroom, and instructor expenses are minimal.

On-the-Job Training   Probably the most widely used method of training (formal and informal) is on-the-job training. It is estimated that more than 60 percent of training occurs on the job. The employee is placed into the real work situation and shown the job and the tricks of the trade by an experienced employee or the supervisor.

Although this program is apparently simple and relatively less costly, if it is not handled properly the costs can be high in damaged machinery, unsatisfied customers, misfiled forms, and poorly taught workers. To prevent these problems, trainers must be carefully selected and trained. The trainee should be placed with a trainer who is similar in background and personality. The trainer should be motivated by training and rewarded for doing it well. The trainer should use effective training techniques in instructing the trainee.

One approach to systematic on-the-job training is the job instruction training (JIT) system developed during World War II.[28] In this system, the trainers first train the supervisors, who in turn train the employees. Exhibit 13–9 describes the steps of JIT training as given in the War Manpower Commission's bulletin, "Training within Industry Series in 1945." These are the instructions given to supervisors on how to train new or present employees.

Toll-free hotlines can help improve a firm's customer service. Training individuals to handle complaints and questions is done on the job in a number of firms. Toll-free numbers give customers an easy way to complain or ask questions. General Electric (GE) trains customer service operators on the job so that the realism of listening, thinking, and responding on the spot hits home.[29]

GE's answer center in Louisville, Kentucky, is open 24 hours a day. It employs 180 telephone representatives, 150 customer service reps, and 30 technicians. It handles 3 million calls from customers each year. Each rep is trained and is able to handle about 100 calls a day, each one lasting about 3.5 minutes. After learning about the firm's products, the rep is trained on the telephone. Communication and telephone skills are observed and critiqued. Other firms that use 800 numbers and on-the-job training include Armstrong Floors and Ceiling Building Products Division, J.C. Penney, and Ralston-Purina.

Mobil Oil uses an on-the-job training approach to achieve excellence among engineers in the exploration and producing division.[30] The objective at Mobil Oil is based on the premise that the most significant development of an engineer takes place on the job. Thus, task and competency mastering on the job is accomplished through:

EXHIBIT 13-9   Job Instruction Training (JIT) Methods

First, Here's what you *must do* to *get ready* to teach a job:
1. Decide what the learner must be taught in order to do the job efficiently, safely, economically, and intelligently.
2. Have the right tools, equipment, supplies, and material ready.
3. Have the workplace properly arranged, just as the worker will be expected to keep it.

Then, you should *instruct* the learner by the following *four basic steps:*

Step I — *Preparation* (of the learner)
1. Put the learner at *ease.*
2. Find out what he or she already knows about the job.
3. Get the learner interested and desirous of learning the job.

Step II — *Presentation* (of the operations and knowledge)
1. *Tell, show, illustrate,* and *question* in order to put over the new knowledge and operations.
2. Instruct slowly, clearly, completely, and patiently, one point at a time.
3. Check, question, and repeat.
4. Make sure the learner really knows.

Step III — *Performance tryout*
1. Test learner by having him or her perform the job.
2. Ask questions beginning with *why, how, when,* or *where.*
3. Observe performance, correct errors, and repeat instructions if necessary.
4. Continue until *you know learner knows.*

Step IV — *Follow-up*
1. Put the employee "on his or her own."
2. Check frequently to be sure learner follows instructions.
3. Taper off extra supervision and close follow-up until person is qualified to work with normal supervision.

Remember — if the learner hasn't learned, the teacher hasn't taught.

- Challenging assignments.
- Good role models
- Timely and comprehensive coaching.

These features are built into the Professional Development Progam (PDP). Assessments of the PDP are conducted so that comparisons can be made with a baseline of performance and a "benchmark," or goal of performance. Mobil affiliates in Canada, Nigeria, Norway, and Indonesia have adopted the PDP for on-the-job training and assessment. Mobil is pleased with the competency mastering displayed through assessment of their exploration and producing division engineers using the PDP. mated assembly line workers.[31] The retraining opportunity means that employees apply for a position in the program. The candidate's experience, performance, and education are used to decide who will be given the retraining opportunity. So far, IBM has about 10 candidates for each retraining slot. On-the-job retraining is important to a company like IBM, since having the best skill mix available to meet future changes and challenges is so vital for sustaining success in a rapidly changing field.

On-the-Job Training Experiences for Managers   There are three widely used approaches to on-the-job training. These programs are not mutually exclusive; often they are run simultaneously. On-the-job management training is the preferred type from many points of view, especially because of its relevance and immediate transferability to the job.

Coaching and Counseling   One of the best and most frequently used methods of training new managers is for effective managers to teach them.[32] The coach-superior sets a good example of what a manager does. He or she also answers questions and explains why things are done the way they are. It is the coach-superior's obligation to see to it that the manager-trainee makes the proper contacts so that the job can be learned easily and performed in an adequate way. In some ways, the coach-superior-manager-trainee relationship resembles the buddy system in employee training.

One technique the superior may use is to have decision-making meetings with the trainee. During these meetings, procedures are agreed upon. If the trainee is to learn, the superior must give him or her enough authority to make decisions and perhaps even make mistakes. This approach not only provides opportunities to learn, it requires effective delegation, which develops a feeling of mutual confidence. Appropriately chosen committee assignments can be used as a form of coaching and counseling.

Although most organizations use coaching and counseling as either a formal or an informal management development technique, it is not without its problems. Coaching and counseling fail when inadequate time is set aside for them, when the subordinate is allowed to make no mistakes, if rivaly develops, or if the dependency needs of the subordinate are not recognized or accepted by the superior.

More and more firms have been downsizing or laying off employees. They have cut back because of economic or strategic reasons. Managers after cutbacks need to serve as coaches and trainers to help alleviate the aftereffects of downsizing. The Work In America Institute has published a report, ''The Manager As Trainer, Coach, and Leader.''[33] The report includes five in-depth case studies of Eastman Kodak, Ford Motor Co., LTV Steel, Martin Marietta, and the New York State Developmental Disabilities Service Office. At a Louisville, Kentucky, Ford assembly plant, the program was designed to help subordinates adjust to the downsizing circumstances of a few employees. The coaching portion of the training employed the development of interpersonal skills to handle dissent and to encourage consensus. As coaches, the Ford managers helped the subordinates work through feelings of guilt and anger because of the downsizing.

In sum, many experts contend that coaching and counseling, when coupled with planned rotation through jobs and functions, are effective techniques. It can fit the manager's background and utilize the principle of learning by doing that has proven effective. Finally, the method involves the supervisors, which is essential to successful management development.

Transitory, Anticipatory Experiences   Another approach to management training is to provide transitory experiences. Once it has been determined that a person will be promoted to a specific job, provision is made for a short period before the promotion in which she or he learns the new job, performing some new duties while still performing most of the old ones. This intermediate position is labeled differently in various organizations as assistant-to, understudy, multiple management, or management apprenticeship.

The main characteristic of this type of program is that it gives partial prior experience to a person likely to hold a position in the future.[34] In some approaches, the trainee performs a part of the actual job; thus, an assistant does some parts of the job for the incumbent. In multiple management, several decision-making bodies make decisions about the same problem and compare them — a junior board or group's decisions are compared to those of senior management groups. Another variation is to provde trainees with a series of assignments that are part of the new job in order to train them and broaden their experiences.

To the extent that transitory experiences simulate the future job and are challenging, they seem to provide an eminently reasonable approach to management development. Little systematic study has been made of the effectiveness of this approach, however, and it appears to be used less often than coaching or counseling.

Transfers and Rotation   In another on-the-job approach, trainees are rotated through a series of jobs to broaden their managerial experience. Organizations often have developed programmed career plans that include a mix of functional and geographic transfers.

Advocates of rotation and transfer contend that this approach broadens the manager's background, accelerates the promotion of highly competent individuals, introduces more new ideas into the organization, and increases the effectiveness of the organization. But some research evidence questions these conclusions.[35] Individual differences affect whether or not the results will be positive, and generalists may not be the most effective managers in many specialized positions.

Geographic transfers are desirable when fundamentally different job situations exist at various places. They allow new ideas to be tried instead of meeting each situation with the comment, "We always do it that way here." As in many other types of development, trained supervisors can make this technique more effective.

In general, because of the perceived relevance of on-the-job experience, it should be provided in management development programs. Because of individual differences in development and rewards by organizations, however, off-the-job development programs should supplement them where expertise is not readily available inside the organization. Exclusively on-the-job programs lead to a narrow perspective and the inhibition of new ideas coming into the organization.

Off-the-Job Training

Other than apprenticeship, vestibule training, and on-the-job training, all other training is off-the-job training, whether it is done in organization classrooms, vocational schools, or elsewhere. Organizations with the biggest training programs often use off-the-job training. The majority of the 50,000 trainers in the United States and the $100 billion spent on training are in off-the-job training. A survey of training directors in *Fortune* 500 companies examined their views of which off-the-job training techniques were the most effective for specific objectives. The training directors indicated that if knowledge acquisition were the objective, it would be best to use programmed instruction. On the other hand, if the training was intended to improve the problem-solving skills of participants, then it would be better to use the case method of training (for example, having participants analyze job-related cases). Research suggests that the most popular methods of instruction for off-the-job training are lecture/discussion, programmed instruction, and computer-assisted instruction (CAI).[36]

Lecture/Discussion Approach   The most frequentnly used training method is for a trainer to give a lecture and involve the trainee in a discussion of the material to be learned. The effective classroom presentation supplements the verbal part with audiovisual aids such as blackboards, slides, and mock-ups. Frequently, these lectures are videotaped or audiotaped. The method allows the trainers' message to be given in many locations and to be repeated as often as needed for the benefit of the trainees. Videotape recording also allows for self-confrontation, which is especially useful in such programs as sales training and interpersonal relations.[37] The trainee's presentation can be taped and played back for analysis.

In 1990, the United States undertook the 21st decennial census. The Census Bureau hired about 565,000 staff to carry out the data collection. The temps had to be oriented and then trained.[38] The orientation and training involved the use of vestibule training, videotapes, and self-study. The videotapes were used to emphasize the history, quality aspects, and policies of the bureau. Demonstration videos were combined with on-the-job and classroom training to help the temps improve their census-taking skills. These census takers were all subjected to standardized training materials.

An interesting discussion approach to training is conducted at General Dynamics to teach ethics. All employees, from the top chairperson to operating employees, must attend training workshops.[39] The discussions at the workshops concentrate on resolving ethical conflicts. The trainees are also introduced to a toll-free ethics hotline. Employees who feel uncomfortable asking a ''boss'' questions about ethics are encouraged to use the hotline to get answers to ethics questions and dilemmas.

Programmed Instruction   A popular method used in organizational training is programmed instruction.[40] Material can be presented on teaching machines or in text form, and behaviorist learning principles are followed closely. Programmed instruction is a useful method for self-instruction when the development cost of the materials has been paid by another organization and the materials are available. It might also be a useful method if there are enough trainees to amortize the development cost, if the trainees are likely to be motivated enough to move ahead with this approach and if the material presented is suitable to the method. Programmed instruction has been described as follows:

> Programmed instruction is a technique for instructing without the presence or intervention of a human instructor. It is a learner-centered method of instruction, which presents subject-matter to the trainee in small steps or increments, requiring frequent responses from him and immediately informing him of the correctness of his responses. The trainee's responses may be written, oral, or manipulative. A response may be constructed, as in the completion type; it may be selected from among several alternatives, as in the multiple-choice type; or it may assume one or more of a variety of other styles.[41]

Features of programmed instruction are:

> Instruction is provided without the presence or intervention of a human instructor. The learner learns at his own rate (conventional group instruction, films, television, and other media and methods that do not allow learner control do not satisfy this criterion).
> Instruction is presented in small incremental steps requiring frequent responses by the learner; step size is a function of the subject matter and the characteristics of the learner population.
> There is a participative overt interaction, or two-way communication, between the learner and the instructional program.
> The learner receives immediate feedback informing him of his progress.
> Reinforcement is used to strengthen learning.
> The sequence of lessons is carefully controlled and consistent.
> The instructional program shapes and controls behavior.

Programmed instruction can have wide application in organizational training programs, especially for programs whose characteristics fit those discussed above. It can also be developed in computer-assisted forms.

CAREER CHALLENGE
(*concluded*)

After Bob and Gwen performed the training needs analysis, they isolated the skills training necessary. The supervisors and employees told him the key need was improved training in the use of the new equipment. He also identified other work-related skills that appeared to decrease employee efficiency.

Then Bob prepared a proposed training program. The training needs analysis had identified the employees who needed the training the most. For trainers, he decided to propose that the manufacturer of the new equipment should provide a trainer. This person would train Bob and several supervisors who appeared to have the greatest potential to run employee training programs. He also proposed that the manufacturer provide mock-ups of the machines to use in the training (if available). Lacking that, slides would be used. Then the firm would use several machines for training alone — a semivestibule approach. The cost would be minimal. The manufacturer would provide the training free.

Harold approved the plan, and the training sessions were conducted. Two months after the training was completed, however, there was little change in results. Gwen realized that they had not done as good a job in the cost feasibility study as they should have. No formal evaluation of the training had been planned or done.

Gwen and Bob went back to the supervisors to interview them on what had happened. Some of the comments were:

Sandy Feldman (supervisor) I told you people the problem was who you hired. Training clowns like I got won't help.

Sam Jacobs (supervisor) I thought that training would help. It did a little, for a while. But my problem has become discipline. They know how to do the job — they just don't seem to want to do it.

Harry Samson (supervisor) Maybe the problem was *how* the training was done — I don't know. I see few real results so far.

Bob and Gwen decided to do a formal evaluation of training on the next program. As for what to do now, performance evaluation time was coming up. Maybe the use of rewards for better employees would help. Maybe more and better training would have results. And maybe the labor market had opened up and some terminations and rehirings would be the answer. They'd just have to keep working on it until they could really help Harold and the company. (There will be more about this case in Chapter 14.)

Computer-Assisted Instruction   Many firms are now using *computer-assisted instruction (CAI)* to train employees. CAI permits self-paced learning and immediate feedback. A CAI system works as follows: A trainee sits at a terminal with a monitor. The computer is programmed with the training materials. The trainee communicates by programming or using the keyboard to input commands or requests. In one company, managers are able to learn how to use the inventory control system with CAI. They can make requests and assess how changes in their requests will influence their end-of-month budget statements.

Firms of all sizes are using computers. A survey of human resource directors indicated that 6.4 percent of organizations with 100 to 499 employees used computers for training, while 89 percent of large firms of 10,000 or more employees used computers for training. The distinctive advantages of CAI include availability, self-paced features, distribution and changeability, and work simulation.[42]

Control Data Corporation has developed a computer program called Plato. With Plato, an airline pilot uses the CAI and is able to reduce the vestibule training time spent in the jet simulator. The CAI provides a computer view of the instrument panel that is found in the simulator and the actual airplane.[43] However, instead of training in the simulator or the airplane, the pilot can become familiar with the instrument panel by using the computer. This form of corporation training results in more personal instruction and reduced training time.

Steelworkers are now being retrained in a state-funded program at the Pittsburgh Control Data Institutes, one of 26 Plato-equipped institutes in major cities. The eight-month course in computer technology is being attended by unemployed steelworkers. Because of industry's need for CAI, Plato is starting to have competitors. Digital Equipment Corporation now has a Plato-like system. Dozens of software houses are starting to emulate Plato programs, or training "courseware."[44]

Other examples of CAI can be found in such companies as Motorola, Detroit Edison, and the National Association of Security Dealers.[45] At Motorola, technicians and engineers are trained with courseware in basic electronics, microprocessors, and BASIC programming. Detroit Edison uses computers to train maintenance operators in uniform procedures to isolate and mark all equipment scheduled for maintenance with various colored tapes and tags. The National Association of Security Dealers uses computers to test more than 100,000 brokers annually.

The potential for computer-based training is limited only by the number of training needs. It is generally agreed that because of such advantages as self-pacing, privacy, immediate feedback, convenience, and adaptability CAI will become one of the most popular training approaches available.

No matter which training approach is used, it must be evaluated. This is the third phase of the model shown in Exhibit 13–5. Evaluation of training and development will be discussed in Chapter 14.

SUMMARY

To summarize the major points covered in this chapter:

1. The principal purposes of orientation include:
   a. To reduce start-up costs of a new employee.
   b. To reduce fear and anxiety of the new employee and hazing from other employees.
   c. To reduce turnover.
   d. To save time for supervisors and co-workers.
   e. To develop realistic job expectations, positive attitudes toward the employer, and job satisfaction.
2. In small enterprises, the operating manager does all the orienting; in middle-sized or larger enterprises, the operating and HR managers share this task.
3. Training is a form of education to which the following learning principles can be applied:
   a. The trainee must be motivated to learn.
   b. The learning must be reinforced.
   c. The training must provide for practice of the material.

    d. The material presented must be meaningful.

    e. The material taught must transfer to the job situation.

4. Purposes of training and development include:

    a. To improve the quantity of output.

    b. To improve the quality of output.

    c. To lower the costs of waste and equipment maintenance.

    d. To lower the number and costs of accidents.

    e. To lower turnover and absenteeism and increase employee job satisfaction.

    f. To prevent employee obsolescence.

5. When employee turnover is great, it is more important for the organization to provide formal technical training for employees.

6. Effective organizations design their training programs only after assessing the organization's and individual's training needs and setting training objectives.

7. Effective training programs select trainees on the basis of the trainees' needs as well as organizational objectives.

8. Effective training programs carefully select and develop trainers for the programs.

9. Training approaches for employees are:

    a. Apprenticeship.

    b. Vestibule.

    c. On-the-job training (for managers, these include coaching and counseling; transitory experiences; transfers and rotation).

    d. Off-the-job training (lecture/discussion; programmed instruction; computer-assisted instruction).

The recommendations on management training and development programs for model organizations are presented in Exhibit 13–10.

EXHIBIT 13-10   Recommendations on Management Training and Development Programs for Model Organizations

Type of Organization	Formal Program	Informal Program	On-the-Job Programs	Off-the-Job Programs
1. Large size, low complexity, high stability	X		X	X
2. Medium size, low complexity, high stability		X	X	
3. Small size, low complexity, high stability			X	X
4. Medium size, moderate complexity, moderate stability		X	X	X
5. Large size, high complexity, low stability	X		X	X
6. Medium size, high complexity, low stability		X	X	
7. Small size, high complexity, low stability			X	X

KEY TERMS

QUESTIONS FOR REVIEW AND DISCUSSION

1. What are the main purposes of orientation programs? What aspects of orientation seem to be the most neglected?
2. Describe the study of Texas Instruments' orientation program. What does it indicate to you about how to operate an orientation program?
3. Describe a typical orientation program. Which parts of it would you describe as important, very important, or less important? To the employee? To the employer?
4. Describe why a performance analysis may indicate that training is not what is needed to solve a particular problem.
5. Would different training techniques be used for temporary employees than what are used for full-time employees?
6. Why is training expensive? What are the costs involved?
7. Why would employees prefer to use corporate classrooms to earn various college-type degrees?
8. Who is involved in the planning and operating of formal training in organizations?
9. Why should analysis of an organization's training needs be performed before any formal training is initiated?
10. In the future, is training less or more likely to grow in importance in the strategic plans of an organization? Explain.

NOTES

[1] Walter D. St. John (May 1980), "The Complete Employee Orientation Program," *Personnel Journal*, pp. 373–78.
[2] (February 1982), "Companies Calling Retirees Back to the Workplace," *Management Review*, p. 29.
[3] I. L. Goldstein (1986), *Training in Organizations: Needs Assessment Development and Evaluation* (Monterey, Calif. Brooks/Cole).
[4] E. R. Hilgard and G. H. Bower (1966), *Theories of Learning* (New York: Appleton-Century-Crofts).
[5] Elaine I. Berke (February 1984), "Keeping Newly Trained Supervisors from Going Back to Old Ways," *Management Review*, pp. 14–16.
[6] Bradley R. Schiller (June 24, 1987), "Training Keeps the Job Machine Running," *The Wall Street Journal*, p. 24.
[7] William Mirengoff and Lester Rindler (1976), "The Comprehensive Employment and Training Act: Impact on People, Places, and Programs (Washington, D.C.: National Academy of Sciences).
[8] Michael Brody (June 8, 1987), "Helping Workers to Work Smarter," *Fortune*, pp. 86–88.
[9] (December 1990), "Congress Revises Job Training Program," *Personnel*, p. 6.

[10] (October 1990), "Not Enough Basic Training, *Personnel*, p. 14.

[11] (October 1990), "Who Gets Training," *Training*, p. 54.

[12] Constance Mitchell (September 28, 1987), "Corporate Classes: Firms Broaden Scope of their Education Programs," *The Wall Street Journal*, p. 27.

[13] Mary William Walsh (August 26, 1984), "Company Built Retreats Reflect Firms' Culture and Personalities," *The Wall Street Journal*, p. 25.

[14] Ibid.

[15] A. Vice Short (Winter 1987), "Are We Getting Our Money's Worth?" *New Management*, pp. 23–26.

[16] (December 1990), "Accounting Strategy," *Personnel*, p. 6.

[17] Donald Kirkpatrick (February 1977), "Determining Training Needs," *Training and Development Journal*, pp. 22–25.

[18] Vicki S. Kaman and John P. Mohr (October 1984), "Training Needs Assessment in the Eighties: Five Guideposts," *Personnel Administrator*, pp. 47–53.

[19] Donald Michalak and Edwin Yager (1979), *Making the Training Process Work* (New York: Harper & Row).

[20] Carol Haig (October 1984), "A Line Manager's Guide to Training," *Personnel Journal*, pp. 42–45.

[21] Larry E. Greiner (Winter 1987), "Confessions of an Executive Educator," *New Management*, pp. 35–38.

[22] Stephen B. Wehrenberg (July 1984), "Inside or Outside Resources: Which Are Best for Training?" *Personnel Journal*, pp. 23–24.

[23] Stephen B. Wehrenberg (September 1984), "Preparing to Retire: Educational Programs that Help Employees," *Personnel Journal*, pp. 41–42.

[24] William J. Rothwell (November 1983), "Curriculum Design in Training: An Overview," *Personnel Administrator*, pp. 53–57.

[25] (February 9, 1991), "Job Training: Missing Bridge," *The Economist*, pp. 30–31.

[26] Shelby Hodge (August 9, 1981), "Flights of Fancy Qualify Pilots on the Ground," *Houston Chronicle*, p. 3AA.

[27] Carol Harg (September 1987), "Clinics Fill the Training Niche," *Personnel Journal*, pp. 134–39.

[28] Fred Wickert (February 1974), "The Famous JIT Card: A Basic Way to Improve It," *Training and Development Journal*, pp. 6–9.

[29] Chris Lee (August 1990), "1-800-Training," *Training*, pp. 39–45.

[30] Jeremy Cobb and John Gibbs (Fall 1990), "A New, Competency-Based, On-The-Job Program for Developing Professional Excellence in Engineering," *The Journal of Management Development*, pp. 60–72.

[31] Hastings H. Huggins, Jr. (August 1983), "IBM's Retraining Success Based on Long-Term Manpower Planning," *Management Review*, pp. 29–30.

[32] Walter Mahler and William Wrightnour (1973), *Executive Continuity* (Homewood, Ill.: Richard D. Irwin), chapters 6 and 7.

[33] (April 1991), "Downsizing After-Shocks Demand Coaching, Training, and Leading," *Personnel*, p. 16.

[34] Roger O'Meara (1972), "Off the Job Assignments for Key Employees," in *Manpower Planning and Programming*, eds. Elmer Burack and James Walker (Boston: Allyn & Bacon), pp. 339–46.

[35] Robert Pitts (May 1977), "Unshackle Your 'Comers,'" *Harvard Business Review*, pp. 127–36.

[36] Ibid.

[37] Willard Thomas (December 1980), "Shoot the Works with Videobased Training," *Training and Development Journal*, pp. 83–87.

[38] Catharine Burt and Joan March (April 1990), "How To Train and Manage 500,000 Temps," *Management Review*, pp. 40–45.

[39] (September 1990), "Ethics Training: In Tune with Corporate Culture," *Conference Board*, p. 12.

[40] A. N. Nash, Jan P. Muczyk, and F. L. Vettori (Autumn 1971), "The Role and Practical Effectiveness of Programmed Instruction," *Personnel Psychology*, pp. 397–418.

[41] Leonard Silvern (1970), "Training: Man-Man and Man-Machine Communications," in *Systems Psychology*, ed. K. yon De Greene (New York: McGraw-Hill), pp. 383–405.

[42] Ralph E. Granger (September 1990), "Computer-Based Training Works," *Personnel Journal*, pp. 85–91.

[43] Gary Dessler (1984), *Personnel Management* (Reston, VA: Reston Publishing), p. 247.

[44] (March 28, 1983), "Computerized Training May Finally Be About to Take Off," *Business Week*, p. 88.

[45] William A. Hultyen (October 1984), "An Introduction to Computerized Training," *Personnel Journal*, pp. 22–23.

APPLICATION CASE 13-1

. . . . .

Dunkin' Donuts and Domino's Pizza:
Training for Quality and Hustle

Dunkin' Donuts and Domino's Pizza share the same requirement for business success: Provide a high-quality product at impressive speed. Domino's guarantees a hot, tasty pizza delivered to your doorstep within 30 minutes (a considerable challenge given that 80 percent of a day's orders at a Domino's franchise are typically received during three hours of a 12-hour day). Dunkin' Donuts promises fresh donuts every four hours and fresh coffee every 18 minutes.

To meet this requirement, both fast-food companies face the same training challenge: Train a very young (typically aged 18 to 21) and inexperienced work force to meet rigorous performance standards. Both companies must train in an industry where turnover averages 300 to 400 percent yearly and where company locations are widely dispersed. Domino's operates 3,800 stores throughout the United States and seven foreign countries; Dunkin' Donuts' 1,400 shops span the United States and 12 foreign countries.

The two companies approach this training challenge with a highly decentralized training function. At Domino's Pizza, 85 percent of a nonsupervisory employee's training occurs on the job and is provided by the store manager or franchise owner. Each employee is usually trained to fill most of the shop's five hourly jobs (order taker, pizza maker, oven tender, router, and driver), which helps during rush hours when a crew member doesn't appear for work. Performance standards are demanding; the order taker must answer a call within three rings and take the order within 45 seconds. The pizza maker must make the pizza and place it in the oven within one minute. The oven tender must take one pizza out while putting another one in within five seconds and cut and box the pizza by the count of 15. Domino's encourages dedication to speed by keeping tabs on the fastest service and delivery times reported by its stores and publishing them as "box scores" in *The Pepperoni Press*, the company newspaper.

Although the bulk of training is on the job far away from corporate headquarters, Domino's corporate training staff maintains some control over training by providing a variety of training aids. The staff makes available to shop management 14 video tapes (with instructor's manuals) on such tasks as delivery, dough management, image, and pizza making. Each shop is equipped with a VCR. The videos are upbeat, fast-moving, and musical (MTV-styled) with a heavy dose of comedy geared to its high school and college-aged audience. Young Domino's employees play the roles in the videos.

Each shop also displays corporate-produced training posters on job hints/reminders throughout the work area. Above the production line, for example, are large color picturess of how a pizza should look at each step of the production process. Two popular posters: a glossy color picture of "The Perfect Pepperoni" pizza, and a picture of a pizza cursed with the 10 common flaws (for example, scorched vegetables, air bubbles). The training materials communicate many key points with Donimo's-styled lingo, "Dominese." For example, getting "blown away" means missing the "TMS" which stands for Domino's infamous 30-minute delivery guarantee. How to avoid this costly mistake? Sharp "PRP," prerush preparation.

Store managers (aged 21–25) are trained by means of a six-course, typically six-month MIT program that includes coursework in pizza dough management, people management, cost management, and in how to conduct-on-the-job training of hourly employees. Manager trainees progress through five levels of training with higher performance requirements and more responsibilities added at each level. On-the-job training is an important part of the training program.

Many franchise owners (and all company-owned stores) send management trainees to the regional training center for classes taught by corporate trainers; however, management training often is decentralized with franchise owners conducting the MIT courses themselves. Franchise owners must be certified to conduct the formal courses for their manager trainees. The certification process requires that the owner complete the "Training Dynamics" course on how to teach manager trainees, observe certified teachers training the MIT series of courses,

Written by Kim Stewart and adapted from: Dale Feuer (July 1987), "Training for Fast Times," *Training*, pp. 25–30; and Dale Feuer (July 1985), "Training at Dunkin' Donuts: Taking It to the Stores," *Training*, pp. 55, 59–61.

and then co-teach the series with a regional trainer who must approve the franchisee's performance. The quality of training provided by franchise owners is enhanced by the owners' substantial in-store management experience. Only Domino's store managers may apply for franchise ownership.

Domino's corporate training staff is also involved in developing franchise owners by means of a rigorous training program for all prospective owners. The training includes a series of courses on contracts, site selection, store construction, and marketing, with an early, heavy emphasis on the nitty-gritty aspects of ownership to discourage those who are less than totally committed.

Like Domino's Pizza, Dunkin' Donuts' corporate training staff conducts a demanding training program for its franchise owners. Prospective franchisees undergo six weeks of training at the Dunkin' Donuts University in Braintree, Massachusetts. There, they spend four weeks in production training, learning how to make donuts, coffee, soup, and other products, and how to operate and maintain the production equipment. Performance standards are rigorous; the final production test requires that a trainee make 140 donuts within eight hours (enough to fill a shop's donut case). Each batch of donuts is weighed and measured for length and height. If a batch of six cake donuts is one ounce too light or heavy, for example, the batch fails the test.

Franchisees spend the last two weeks focusing on financial aspects of the business and on developing employee management skills (for example, supervising, performance appraisal, interpersonal communication). The 12-member training staff conducting the program are all former store managers or district sales managers with about 10 years experience with the company.

Training of hourly employees is totally decentralized. Franchise owners serve as trainers and receive how-to instruction for this task. Like Domino's Pizza, Dunkin' Donuts' corporate training staff also provides training video cassettes for owners to use. Quarterly clinics on quality control are also conducted by the company's district managers and technical advisers.

Dunkin' Donuts uses a different and decentralized approach to training its store managers who are not franchise owners. Rather than have franchise owners conduct the training, the company selects experienced store managers and trains them as store manager trainers. Their trainers train new managers using a program and materials developed by the corporate staff. This decentralized approach is relatively new for Dunkin' Donuts and was adopted after the company dropped its 12-week training program conducted totally at corporate headquarters. With the centralized approach, new manager turnover was 50 percent during training. Under the new decentralized, on-site approach, turnover during training is about .5 percent, and annual training costs have decreased from $418,000 to $172,000.

People-related management skills are emphasized in training both franchise owners and store managers. Dunkin' Donuts credits this emphasis as a major reason why its annual turnover rate for hourly workers (80 percent) is considerably less than the industry average.

Discussion Questions

1. What are the strengths and shortcomings of a decentralized approach to training managers and hourly employee's? Discuss.

2. Develop a plan for determining the training needs of the hourly paid staff of a Domino's Pizza franchise.

3. In your opinion, why was the turnover rate among management trainees in Dunkin's Donuts' centralized program so high?

14

MANAGEMENT AND ORGANIZATION DEVELOPMENT

· · · · · · ·

LEARNING OBJECTIVES

⊖

After studying this chapter, you should be able to:

• • •

Define the meaning of organization development (OD)

• • •

Discuss the differences among OD programs that are targeted for individuals, for groups, or for the total organization

• • •

Explain the importance of evaluation training and OD and how it can be done in an organization

• • •

Illustrate how the diagnosis portion of OD is conducted

• • •

Compare the distinct characteristics of sensitivity training, transactional analysis, and team building

• • •

Describe the six phases of a Grid OD program

CAREER CHALLENGE

(*continued*)

Later the same year, Gwen Meridith, Young Enterprise's HR vice president was faced with another problem. She received the results of Young's third annual attitude survey from the firm's consultant. (An *attitude survey* is an instrument to measure employees feelings about their employer.)

Bob McGarrah, the director of training and development, was called in to discuss them.

Gwen Bob, look at the results of the items on training and development. Even though we have not had the desired results on our new training program, Item 17 indicates that the blue-and white-collar employees are very satisfied with our technical training program. So are the managers. Now look at the questions on development. There seems to be serious dissatisfaction there on the part of the employees and managers. With regard to the employee dissatisfaction, this may be related to Item 27. There is a fair amount of dissatisfaction with their supervisors' management styles. Maybe that is

why our training program has not given us the desired results! What do you think?

Bob Well, Gwen, we haven't done much on nontechnical training here at Young. We have not tried to run off-the-job development programs. We don't do career development. Nor have we ever considered organizational development programs. How do you feel about them?

Gwen As you know, Bob, my background is labor relations. I have kept up in other areas such as EEO, OSHA, and compensation. But I'm asking for your help on this. I'm not too familiar with these programs. Why don't you get together a report to tell me what's happening in development these days.

Bob prepared a summary of the current trends and happenings in development for managers and employees. The next section covers many of the points Gwen wanted to know about development programs.

INTRODUCTION TO MANAGEMENT DEVELOPMENT

This chapter completes the two-chapter unit on training and development of employees. Chapter 13 focused primarily on the training of employees to improve their abilities. In addition, an organization must be concerned about the development of the management team — supervisors, middle-level managers, and top-level executives. Management development focuses on developing in a systematic manner the knowledge base, attitudes basic skills, interpersonal skills, and technical skills of the managerial cadre.[1]

Since managers are such a vital cog in the success of any organization, an entire chapter is devoted specifically to the development of managers. Technical or operating employees must also be trained and developed, but it is very important to have a managerial cadre that possesses knowledge, skills, and motivation.

APPROACHES FOR DEVELOPING MANAGERS

There are numerous management development approaches available. Brochures, testimonials, books, and articles extol the virtues of the management development approach. The programs offer a number of advantages as expressed by consultants, managers, or others familiar with the particular approach. Unfortunately, few of the approaches have been scientifically evaluated, and there is relatively little known about where to use a particular approach and what kind of managers (personality type, experience, education) is able to derive the most benefit from a particular approach.[2]

Management development and training is an important element as organizations attempt to gain a competitive advantage.[3] Data suggest that U.S. corporations spent over $30 billion in 1988 to provide some 17.6 million training courses.[4] A University of Michigan study and a Hay Associates study found that the most profitable companies (based on the PIMS database) showed the greatest commitment to management and executive development.[5] A study of 300 *Fortune* service 500, and the top 100 *Fortune* international 500 companies also provided some interesting data. Of the 153 survey respondents, 64 percent representated *Fortune* 500 industrial companies, 25 percent represented service 100 companies, and 11 percent represented international 100 companies. The 1988 study was designed to trace trends in management development. The content of the in-company executive programs reported by respondents is presented in Exhibit 14–1.

The perceived benefits of in-company programs as reported by respondents are shown in Exhibit 14–2. The most often cited benefits were those of specificity and relevance to the corporation, cost and economic issues, and team building/culture development.

Over 91 percent of the respondents reported their company had sponsored executives in university-based development programs of at least two weeks' duration. The perceived benefits of university-based programs are presented in Exhibit 14–3.

The earliest management programs designed to affect managerial attitudes, called *human relations programs*, were oriented toward individual development. Human relations programs were an outgrowth of the human relations movement, which fostered consideration of the individual in the operation of industry from the 1930s to the 1950s. The rationale of the movement from the organization's point of view was that an employee-centered liberal supervisory style would lead to more satisfied employees. This, in turn, would reduce absenteeism, employee turnover, and

EXHIBIT 14-1   In-Company Programs Offered by Respondents

Topic	Response Frequency (%)
Leadership/motivation/communication	78%
General management	64
Human resource management	60
Organizational change and development	60
Corporate/business strategy development	58
Finance	58
Marketing	55
Strategy implementation	48
Executive decision making	47
Sales management	44
Global business environment	38
Production/operations management	37
Information/decision support systems	34
Accounting	32
Executive computer skills	31
Business-government relations	23
World trade and economics	20
International finance	16
Mergers/acquisitions and divestitures	15
Logistics management	14
Research & development management	14
Humanities/liberal arts	6

Source: Adapted from Albert A. Vicere and Virginia T. Freeman (1990), "Executive Education in Major Corporations: An International Survey," *Journal of Management Development*, p. 10.

EXHIBIT 14-2   Perceived Benefits of In-Company Programs

Benefit	Response Frequency (%)
Programs more specific to organization and its needs	58%
Savings in both time and money	28
Help develop an organizational culture, build teams, implement change	27
Better availability of resources; scheduling efficiency	20
Complementary to external programs: use both internal and external programs	19
Provide a discussion forum or idea exchange; opportunity for people to meet; internal networking	13
Better control of content, faculty, and participants	6
Provide interaction with top management	4

Note: Respondents could indicate more than one benefit.
Source: Adapted from Albert A. Vicere and Virginia T. Freeman (1990), "Executive Education in Major Corporations: An International Survey," *Journal of Management Development*, p. 11.

EXHIBIT 14-3   Perceived Benefits of University Programs

Benefit	Response Frequency (%)
Provide outside perspective, exposure to other viewpoints, networking	59%
Generalize specialists and broaden their vision	39
Expose executives to a variety of programs that cannot be delivered as economically or effectively in-company	38
Expose executives to faculty experts and latest management information in a high-quality academic setting	37
Allow executives to reflect on, and gain insight into, career, work role, personal style, and effectiveness; encourage renewal; insulate from work	13
In-company and university programs complementary	4
Provide rewards and contribute to self-esteem	4
Gain specific skill or functional expertise	3

Note: Respondents could indicate more than one benefit.
Source: Adapted from Albert A. Vicere and Virginia T. Freeman (1990), "Executive Education in Major Corporations: An International Survey," *Journal of Management Development*, p. 13.

strikes. Sometimes, the style also increased performance. But, as was discussed in Chapter 2, effective performance has multiple causes, and supervisory attitudes and behavior are only one factor influencing it.

The effectiveness of these general human relations programs was measured by direct improvement in objectively measured results, such as a reduction in turnover. The programs were also called *effective* if they changed the attitudes of the managers in the direction desired or if the managers participating said the programs were worthwhile. In reviewing the evidence on the effectiveness of human relations programs, it has been determined that 80 percent of the programs evaluated had significant positive results, as measured by attitudes and opinions about these programs.[6]

Such positive results have encouraged organizations to continue to conduct interpersonal skills and attitude-change programs. A number of the in-class training techniques are used in interpersonal skills and attitude-change development programs.

The Case Method

One widely used technique is the **case method**. A case is a written description of a real decision-making situation in the organization or a situation that occurred in another organization. Managers are asked to study the case to determine the problems, analyze the problems for their significance, propose solutions, choose the best solution, and implement it. More learning takes place if there is interaction between the managers and instructor. The instructor's role is that of a catalyst and facilitator. A good instructor is able to get everyone involved in solving the problem.

The case method lends itself more to some kinds of material (for example, business policy analysis) than to well-structured material. It is easier to listen to a lecture and be given a formula than to tease the formula out of a case, for example. With good instructors and good cases, the case method is a very effective device for improving and clarifying rational decision making.[7]

The instructor using the case method must guard against (1) dominating the discussion, (2) permitting a few people to dominate the discussion, or (3) leading the discussion toward his or her preferred solution. As a catalyst, the instructor should encourage divergent viewpoints, initiate discussion on points the managers are missing, and be thoroughly prepared.[8]

Variations on the Case Method

One variation of the case method is the *incident method*. In the incident method, just the bare outlines of a problem are given initially, and the students are assigned a role in which to view the incident. Additional data are available if the students ask the right questions. Each student "solves" the case, and groups based on similarity of solutions are formed. Each group then formulates a strong statement of position, and the groups debate or role-play their solutions. The instructor may describe what actually happened in the case and the consequences, and then everyone compares their solutions with the results. The final step is for participants to try to apply this knowledge to their own job situations.

Role Playing

Role playing is a cross between the case method and an attitude development program. Each person is assigned a role in a situation (such as a case) and asked to play the role and to react to other players' role playing. The player is asked to pretend to be a focal person in the situation and to react to the stimuli as that person would. The players are provided with background information on the situation and the players. There is usually a brief script provided to the participant. Sometimes, the role plays are videotaped and reanalyzed as part of the development situation. Often, role playing is done in small groups of a dozen or so persons. The success of this method depends on the ability of the players to play the assigned roles believably. If done well, role playing can help a manager become more aware of and sensitive to the feelings of others.

Although role playing is a cross between the two, comparison of the general forms of role playing and the case method suggest a few differences between the two.[9]

Case Study	Role Playing
1. Presents a problem of analysis and discussion.	1. Places the problem in a real-life situation.
2. Uses problems that have already occurred in the company or elsewhere.	2. Uses problems that are now current or are happening on the job.
3. Deals with problems involving others.	3. Deals with problems in which participants themselves are involved.
4. Deals with emotional and attitudinal aspects in an intellectual frame of reference.	4. Deals with emotional and attitudinal aspects in an experimental frame of reference.
5. Emphasis is on using facts and making assumptions.	5. Emphasis is on feelings.
6. Trains in the exercise of judgments.	6. Trains in emotional control.
7. Furnishes practice in analysis of problems.	7. Provides practice in interpersonal skills.

The In-Basket Technique

Another method used to develop managerial decision-making abilities is the in-basket technique. The participant is given materials (typically memos or descriptions of things to do) that include typical items from a specific manager's mail and a telephone list. Important and pressing matters, such as out-of-stock positions, customer complaints or the demand for a report from a superior, are mixed in with routine business matters, such as a request to speak at a dinner or a decision on the date of the company picnic four weeks hence. The trainee is analyzed and critiqued on the number of decisions made in the time period allotted, the quality of decisions, and the priorities chosen for making them. In order to generate interest, the in-basket materials must be realistic, job-related, and not impossible to make decisions on.

Management Games

Essentially, management games describe the operating characteristics of a company, industry, or enterprise. These descriptions take the form of equations that are manipulated after decisions have been made.

In a typical computerized management game procedure, teams of players are asked to make a series of operating (or top-management) decisions. In one game, for example, the players are asked to decide on such matters as the price of the product, purchase of materials, production scheduling, funds borrowing, marketing, and R&D expenditures. When each player on the team has made a decision, the interactions of these decisions are computed (manually or by computer) in accordance with the model. For example, if price is linearly related to volume, a decrease in price of X percent will affect the volume, subject to general price levels. Players on the team first reconcile their individual decisions with those of the other team members prior to making a final decision. Then each team's decision is compared with those of the other teams. The result of that team's profit, market share, and so forth is compared, and a winner or best team performance is determined.

Looking Glass is a management game that is used to permit individuals to operate or participate as managers in the simulation of a hypothetical glass manufacturing company with 4,000 employees and $200 million in annual sales.[10] Executives from IBM, AT&T, Monsanto, and Union Carbide have used Looking Glass to provide a picture to participants of their management style. Looking Glass was developed at the Center for Creative Leadership, a non-profit think tank in Greensboro, North Carolina.

Another management game used to develop managers is Simmons Simulator, Inc., a make-believe high-technology multinational firm with $3 billion in annual sales. It is used to train top managers at IBM in the company's corporate planning process. Financial Services Industry is a game that simulates a business day in which managers grapple with planning decisions that are influenced by technological change and government deregulation of the financial industry. Management games emphasize problem-solving skill development.

Hard evaluation evidence is scarce on whether Looking Glass, Simmons Simulator, or Financial Services accomplish the desired outcomes. A major concern is to rigorously assess whether participation in management games means that the manager is a better performer back on the job.

Advantages of games include the integration of several interacting decisions, the ability to experiment with decisions, the provision of feedback experiences on decisions, and the requirement that decisions be made with inadequate data, which usually simulates reality. The main criticisms of most games concern their limitation of novelty or reactivity in decision making, the cost of development and administration, the unreality of some of the models, and the disturbing tendency of many participants to look for the key to win the game instead of concentrating on making good decisions. Many participants seem to feel the games are rigged, so that a few factors or even a single factor may be the key to winning.

Behavior Modeling

A development approach for improving interpersonal skills is **behavior modeling,** which is also called *interaction management* or *imitating models*.[11] The key to behavior modeling is learning through observation or imagination. Thus, modeling is a "vicarious process" that emphasizes observation.

One behavior modeling approach begins by identifying 19 interpersonal problems that employees, especially managers, face. Typical problems are: gaining acceptance as a new supervisor, handling discrimination complaints, delegating responsibility, improving attendance, effective discipline, overcoming resistance to change, setting performance goals, motivating average performance, handling emotional situations, reducing tardiness, and taking corrective action.[12]

There are four steps in the process:

1. Modeling of effective behavior — often by use of films.
2. Role playing.
3. Social reinforcement — trainees and trainers praise effective role plays.
4. Transfer of training to the job.

Behavior modeling has been introduced into such organizations as AT&T, General Electric, IBM, RCA, Boise Cascade, Kaiser Corporation, Olin, and B.F. Goodrich. The research evidence is generally positive. In a series of studies, the groups trained in behavior modeling have outperformed those who received no training or traditional management development training.[13]

One interesting program using behavior modeling was reported in a study conducted in the manufacturing operation of a major forest products company.[14] The program was divided into seven weekly workshop sessions, each lasting about six hours. The sessions focused on a particular problem-solving situation, such as dealing with a performance problem or motivating a subordinate.

The specific parts to the behavior modeling approaches used were:

1. A conceptual lecture.
2. A videotape demonstration of the skills being taught.
3. A rehearsal period for practicing the behaviors.
4. A feedback and reinforcement period for refining the behaviors.
5. Participants entered into contracts and committed themselves to the newly acquired skills on the job.
6. A follow-up discussion on how things were going on the job.

These six phases were built into each workshop session. Each session covered critical incidents selected from a survey of all first-line supervisors in the company. The supervisors had been asked to identify the most difficult problems they faced in managing their subordinates.

The second phase of each session involved a modeled demonstration. The supervisors in the training program observed a videotape that depicted a company supervisor successfully employing skills to solve the problem. The videotaped model performed each step in solving the problem. As participants watched, they were asked to identify the steps being taken and make comments in their notebooks for future reference. After observing the models, the participants rehearsed the skill in the classroom.[15]

Improved supervisory behavior in dealing with 10 difficult problems led to improved performance on the job. Average daily production of trained supervisors versus controls increased. Furthermore, grievance rates decreased and absenteeism steadily declined. This behavior modeling program, then, has the kind of positive impact organizations desire.

Behavior modeling offers a number of promising possibilities in organizations.[16] One especially important need in organizations is to develop effective leaders. Modeling appears to offer some promise for leadership skills development, if used in conjunction with videotape methods.[17] The participants can view their style, behaviors, strengths, and weaknesses and learn from this personal, first-hand view. A person who sees herself or himself in action has a vivid reminder that she or he can benefit from practice.

Outdoor-Oriented Programs

Cases, games, modeling, and role plays are still popular, but an increasingly popular form of development are the outdoor or real-life action-oriented programs. Leadership, teamwork, and risk-taking are top-priority items in the outdoor-oriented programs. The programs conducted in remote areas combine outdoor skills with classroom seminars.[18] Most of the programs have taken their cues from Outward Bound programs originated in the early 1960s. River rafting, mountain climbing, night searching, team competition, boat races, rope climbing, and problem-solving exercises are popular types of outdoor training.

One example of an action-oriented exercise is the "zip line" cable portion. A cable stretches from a cliff high above a river and ends in a field on the other side. The individual grabs a handle, jumps off the cliff, and rockets down the cable to the field, usually twisting, yelling, and holding on for dear life.

Teamwork and trust are objectives that outdoor programs attempt to achieve. Do these outdoor programs work? When a participant returns to the office, is he or she more team-oriented? To date, there is no set of studies available that indicate that these programs are effective.[19] There is also the issue of whether an organization has a right to send or encourage a person to participate in a program that requires some athletic ability, the enjoyment of the outdoors, or risk-oriented exercises.

Which Development Approach Should Be Used?

Deciding on the development approach or combination of approaches must be done on the basis of weighing various criteria. The choice can be made on the basis of the number of managers to be developed, the relative costs per manager for each method, the availability of development materials in various forms (including the instructor's capabilities), and the employees' relative efficiency in learning. In general, it is true that the more active the manager, the greater the motivation to learn. The probability of success is higher in that instance. If there are only a few instructors, individualized programmed instruction may be considered. If none of the managers is capable of giving certain instructions, outside instructors may be contacted, or movies or videotapes might be used. Finally, the method used should reflect the degree of active participation desired for the program.

Inevitably, the question as to the effectiveness of each form of development or training must be answered. There are studies to support the effectiveness of all

EXHIBIT 14-4   Learning Objectives of Three Approaches to Learning

Learning Objective	Techniques		
	Humanist	**Cognitivist**	**Behaviorist**
Knowledge			
Transmit information	Inductive discussion Inductive game Debrief experience Relevance discussion Active elaboration	Lecture/film Graphic illustration Panel/interview SME Class presentation Reading Question and answer Review	Multiple choice Memorization Association
Verify information	Confirmatory discussion	Test	Question with answer
Skill			
Induce response	Discuss action Visualize action Inductive case study	List steps Demonstration Success stories	Behavioral model Behavioral samples Prompting/cueing
Strengthen response (practice)	Mental rehearsal Project	Case study	Worksheets Skill drill (game) Simulation Role play
Apply the skill	Action plan Planning guide Elaboration (skit) Contract	Coaching/feedback	Realistic practice Job aid prompts On-job reinforcement
Attitude			
	Self-assessment Encounter experience Discussion of beliefs Reverse role play Guided reflection Group decision	Authority statement Vicarious experience Debate Testimony	Assessment Pleasant experience Reinforcement

Source: Adapted from Tom Kramlinger and Tom Huberty (December 1990), "Behaviorism versus Humanism," *Training & Development Journal*, p. 43.

methods; if a method is appropriate for the particular program in question, it should be used.

The classic debate continues about which development approach or technique is best. There are those who favor a combination of approaches, while others prefer a humanist or behaviorist array of techniques.[20] The techniques of behaviorism include behavioral modeling, role play, positive reinforcement, and simulations. The preferred techniques of the Carl Rogers humanist approach to development include self-assessment, visualization, and guided reflection. There are also advocates of cognitive approaches who believe that lectures, discussion, readings, and debates are the best approach to use.

Exhibit 14–4 presents the learning objectives offered by the three approaches to learning. The objectives can involve knowledge, skill or attitude. To accomplish these objectives, an array of humanist, cognitivist, and behaviorist techniques are available. Based on theory and research, it appears that simpler tasks, like word processing or filing, are learned efficiently by behaviorist techniques. On the other hand, more complex tasks such as learning how to be an effective leader of employees often requires cognitive and humanistic approaches. Also, the ability of the learner needs to be considered. More-sophisticated learners usually require more-cognitive approaches and a chance to discuss their viewpoint.

ORGANIZATION DEVELOPMENT: AN OVERVIEW

Organizations and their environments are dynamic and constantly changing. New technologies are developed, competitors enter and leave markets, inflation increases, and productivity fluctuates. These are the kinds of changes that managers in general and specifically HR managers face. *Organizational development* (OD) is a process of change that involves the continuing development of human resources. It is a newly emerging area of study directed toward using behavioral science knowledge to deal with problems of change.[21] There is still no definition of *organization development* that is universally accepted. Perhaps the most quoted definition of OD is that it is:

an effort *(a)* planned, *(b)* organizationwide, *(c)* managed from the top, to *(d)* increase organizational effectiveness, and health through *(e)* planned intervention in the organization's "processes" using behavioral science knowledge.[22]

According to this definition, OD is planned, since it requires systematic diagnosis, development of a program, and the mobilization of resources (trainers, participants, teaching aids). It involves either the entire system or an entire unit. It must have top-management commitment if it is to be a success. The definition also suggests that OD is not a specific technique such as behavior modeling, transactional analysis, or sensitivity training. These techniques and others often are part of an OD effort, but they are used only after their relevance and utility are demonstrated by a careful diagnosis.

Exhibit 14–5 lists a variety of OD approaches that are available to managers. There is no one best approach. The crucial point to consider is what does the diagnosis shows.

The Importance of Diagnosis: OD's Base

An important characteristic of any OD intervention is that it should follow diagnosis.[23] A manager's perception of a problem is not a sufficient reason to implement a technique such as behavior modeling. Only after data are collected in a scientific way through interviews, observations, questionnaires, and/or checks of records should a planned OD intervention be considered and selected. Exhibit 14–6 presents the diagnosis phase of OD in a schematic diagram.

The collection of diagnostic data is considered to be a part of the action research orientation of OD.[24] Action research involves seven main steps:

1. Problem identification.
2. Consultation among experts. This could involve hired consultants, HR specialists, and senior executives.
3. Data collection and diagnosis.
4. Feedback of findings to key people.

EXHIBIT 14-5   Thirteen Major "Families" of Organizational Development (OD)
Interventions

Organizational development activities come in a variety of forms. All share the organizational development focus on improving the effectiveness of an organization's self-diagnosis and problem-solving abilities, rather than solving any particular organizational problem.

1. *Diagnostic Activities:* fact-finding activities designed to ascertain the state of the system, the status of a problem, the "way things are." Traditional data-collection methods — including interviews, questionnaires, and meetings — are commonly used.
2. *Team-Building Activities:* activities designed to enhance the effective operation of system teams.
3. *Intergroup Activities:* activities designed to improve effectiveness of interdependent groups. The focus is on joint activities.
4. *Survey Feedback Activities:* activities involving analyzing data produced by a survey and designing action plans on these data. Survey feedback activities are a major component of the diagnostic activities category, but they are important enough to be considered a separate category as well.
5. *Education and Training Activities:* activities designed to improve skills, abilities, and knowledge of individuals. There is a wide range of possible approaches, from T-group and sensitivity training, to structured experiencial exercises, to lecturing, and concentrating on technical, interpersonal, or other competencies.
6. *Technostructural or Structural Activities:* activities designed to improve the effectiveness of the technical or structural inputs and constraints affecting individuals or groups. Examples would include job enrichment, matrix structures, management by objectives, and physical settings interventions.
7. *Process Consultation Activities:* activities on the part of the consultant that help managers understand and act on human processes in organizations. This includes teaching skills in diagnosing and managing communications, leadership, cooperation and conflict, and other aspects of interpersonal functioning.
8. *Grid Organization Development Activities:* activities developed by Robert Blake and Jane Mouton, constituting a six-phase change model involving the entire organization. The phases include upgrading individual managers' leadership abilities, team improvement activities, intergroup relations, corporate planning, development of implementation tactics, and evaluation of change and future directions.
9. *Third-Party Peacemaking Activities:* activities designed to manage conflict between two parties, and conducted by some third party, typically a skilled consultant.
10. *Coaching and Counseling Activities:* activities that entail working with individuals to better enable them to define learning goals, learn how others see their behavior, explore alternative behaviors, and learn new behaviors.
11. *Life- and Career-Planning Activities:* activities that help individuals identify life and career objectives, capabilities, areas of strength and deficiency, and strategies for achieving objectives.
12. *Planning and Goal-Setting Activities:* activities that include theory and experience in planning and goal setting. They may be conducted at the level of the individual, group, and total organization.
13. *Strategic Management Activities:* activities that help key policymakers identify their organization's basic mission and goals; ascertain environmental demands, threats, and opportunities; and engage in long-range action planning.

Source: W. French and C. Bell, *Organizational Development: Behavioral Science Interventions for Organization Improvement*, 3/e (Englewood Cliffs, N. J.: Prentice-Hall, 1983), pp. 126–28. Adapted by permission.

5. Group discussion of the diagnostic data and findings.
6. Action. The adoption of techniques such as sensitivity training, transactional analysis, and team building.
7. Evaluation of the action steps taken in Step 6.

EXHIBIT 14-6 Diagnosis Steps in OD Programs

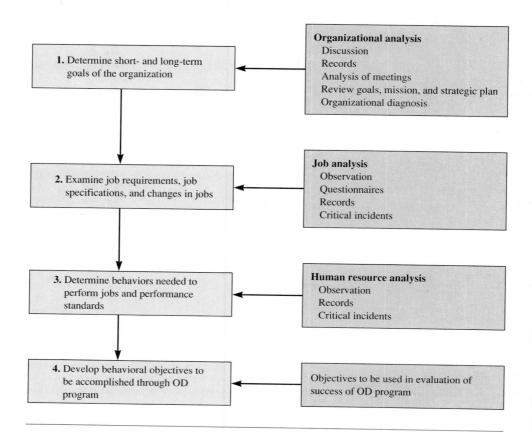

The HR department of specialists may be involved in any or all of these seven action research steps. For the purposes of this book, the action step is extremely important for developing human resources; it involves determining which planned interventions or techniques are available for use as part of OD programs.

OD: INDIVIDUAL AND INTERPERSONAL TECHNIQUES

One way to classify OD techniques is on the basis of the target area they are intended to affect. There are four target areas: Individual, interpersonal, group, and organizational. Sensitivity training is designed to improve the awareness of individuals. Transactional analysis is supposed to help people understand the principles of transactions with others so that more meaningful interpersonal interactions occur. Sensitivity training and transactional analysis will be discussed next. Then, team building, which focuses on the group, and the grid, which addresses the organization as a target, will be covered.

PROFESSIONAL PROFILE

Biography

Roger M. Blakeney is director of the Center for Executive Development in the College of Business Administration at the University of Houston. After interrupting his education to serve two and a half years in the airborne infantry of the U.S. Army, he returned to Texas A&M University to complete his B.S. Following a summer of selling Bibles door-to-door, he entered graduate school at the University of Houston where he earned his M.A. and Ph.D. in industrial/organizational psychology. Upon completion of his internship at EXXON, U.S.A., he joined the faculty of the University of Houston College of Business Administration as an instructor and now also is an associate professor of management as well as being a licensed psychologist.

Roger N. Blakeney
University of Houston

Dr. Blakeney has worked with over 65 companies and organizations as a consultant, trainer, and researcher including several major oil/petrochemical, health-care, retail, and financial firms, plus NASA and the U.S. Air Force.

Job Description As director, Roger Blakeney is responsible for the overall operation of the center including ensuring that the revenues from the programs it conducts at least cover the expenses of running it. Especially important is the identification and development of the programs that the center offers and the quality of service it provides to support them. Though the center makes extensive use of information technology, its operation is still labor intensive; thus, the selection, training, and supervision of its personnel are a critical element in its success.

The Global Economy and the Changing Nature of the Work Force: A Viewpoint At a time when U.S. corporations are coming to grips with the need to become much more competitive in the global economy, they are also faced with having to learn to utilize a work force that is rapidly becoming diverse. When the Hudson Institute published its landmark study in 1987, *Workforce 2000*, it quantified a phenomenon that

business and other leaders had sensed for years—the American work force doesn't look, or act, like it used to. Today, *Workforce 2000* has become the buzzword for a labor force that is quickly being transformed by the entry of increasing numbers of women and ethnic minorities including many immigrants.

The new work force will be comprised of more women, more minorities, more older workers, fewer high-potential young employees, more dual-career families, more single parents, more disadvantaged or disabled workers, and more workers who change jobs more often. Already, valuable employees leave or drop out, claiming disillusionment with the system and frustration with the ability to reach their career goals. Attrition, absenteeism, inadequate performance, and underutilization of employees' abilities and potential are costing U.S. business billions of dollars in competing in the demanding global economy.

The dual revolutions of the global economy and *Workforce 2000* require a dramatic change in the way we manage and a redefinition of the corporation. Add to these things the need to work and manage cross-culturally, and human resource professionals will need a depth of knowledge and skill that is unprecedented in the history of the field. Yet, they will have the opportunity to help their organizations respond to these twin revolutions of the end of the 20th century and help determine their role in the 21st century.

Sensitivity Training

The first sensitivity training course was held in 1946 in New Britain, Connecticut. Since this beginning, it has been used by psychotherapists, counselors, trainers, and HR specialists.[25] Overall, **sensitivity training** (also referred to as *T-Group*, *process group*, and *encounter group*) focuses on:

- Making participants aware of and sensitive to the emotional reactions and expressions in themselves and others.
- Increasing the ability of participants to perceive, and to learn from, the consequences of their actions through increased attention to their own and other's feelings.

The Group　The sensitivity group process varies from trainer to trainer. However, a typical meeting involves a group of 10 to 12 people, meeting away from the job.[26] The emphasis is on: "How do you feel right now?" "What do you feel about others in the group?" "What will it take to make you feel better?" There is little structure imposed by the trainer on the group. Each group member is encouraged to say what he or she is thinking and how each sees others in the group.

Because of its nature, the sensitivity training group is a controversial OD technique. Some believe that it is unethical, impractical, and dangerous.[27] However, some research suggests that sensitivity training can change participant behavior. Participants can increase their sensitivity when working with other people. Furthermore, a few studies indicate that sensitivity training can improve organizational performance. It has, however, been shown that sensitivity training can increase the anxiety levels of some participants.[28]

A survey of personnel directors of large firms found that about twice as many of the respondents indicated a negative response toward the use of sensitivity training as those who said they would recommend it.[29] These directors may be listening more closely to the critics than to some of the supportive research results. Two things are certain about sensitivity training: Only qualified trainers should be used, and only employees who volunteer to participate should attend this type of training program.

A form of sensitivity training is practiced in Japanese management training camps. Kanrisha training camp offers a 13-day experience in self-analysis and development. A typical day at the camp begins at 5 A.M. and ends at 9 P.M.[30] It starts with similarly dressed (white exercise clothes) managers doing a round of calisthenics. The exercises are timed by observant instructors. The managers wear on their clothes ribbons of shame that indicate their personal shortcomings — speech, relating to people, writing ability.

The camp instructors push each manager every day in calisthenics, classroom teachings, skill development exercises, personal self-assessment exercises, group discussion meetings, and speech making. Most of the participants have been hand-picked because they are considered to be highly promotable by their firms. The camp is intended to put pressure on the participants so that they must use every skill, amount of energy, and knowledge that they possess to survive. Survival means that the self must overcome the pressures, the screaming instructors, and the long, tiring days. The Japanese refer to the experience as *Hell Camps*.

Transactional Analysis

Transactional analysis (TA) is not really accepted by most OD experts as a full-fledged technique to use in developing human resources. Instead, TA is considered a useful tool or technique to help people better understand themselves. Organizations such as Polaroid, Texas Instruments, American Airlines, and Bank of America use TA.

Eric Berne is usually credited with starting the interest in TA with his book, *Games People Play*.[31] TA remains popular because it is based on the psychoanalytic theories of Freud.[32] Three important ego states are used in TA: child, adult, and parent.

Child State

This is the state where a person acts as an impulsive child. Immature behavior is displayed. An example would be an employee who, when reprimanded by a boss after doing a job, throws a temper tantrum and shouts, cusses, and screams about the unfairness of the system.

Adult State

In this state, the person acts like a mature adult. The adult state person is fair, objective, and careful in what he or she does. An example would be a manager who, in reviewing the production record of a subordinate, states, "Well, output is down a little, but we can look at it together and see what went wrong — was it equipment, not enough help, or poor quality parts?"

Parent State

In this state, people act like domineering, nagging parents. They are critical and all-knowing in their interactions, often talking down to others. A manager who states, "You shouldn't horse around because we are paying you to put in a fair day's work, not to play and hold down performance."

Generally, people exhibit all three ego states, but one often dominates the other two. The emphasis in TA development training seminars is on encouraging participants to engage in *adult state behaviors*. It is this state that leads to effective interpersonal relations. A TA training program emphasizes the analysis of the transactions between people. It is these interactions of ego states that can significantly influence behavior.

Exhibit 14–7 shows effective interaction between an HR manager and a subordinate. The two ego states involved are adult to adult. The two parties are communicating at the same ego state.

A different kind of interaction is displayed in Exhibit 14–8. The HR manager speaks as an adult, but the specialist replies as a child, thus weakening the communication between the two.

In Exhibit 14–9, there is a breakdown in interaction. The adult HR manager speaks to the adult in the specialist. However, the child in the specialist replies to the parent in the HR manager.

Two other concepts in TA are strokes and games. *Strokes* means that people need cuddling, affection, recognition, and praise. Strokes can be viewed as reinforcers. A "Good morning," a "Hello," or a "How are you doing?" from a boss may be a positive stroke that helps interactions.[33]

When used as an OD technique, TA is designed to develop more adult states in people so that effective interactions occur. To date, few studies have been reported on the scientific analysis of TA interventions.[34] Instead, testimony of TA consultants dominates the literature supporting this approach.[35] Until more-rigorous

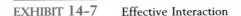

EXHIBIT 14-7   Effective Interaction

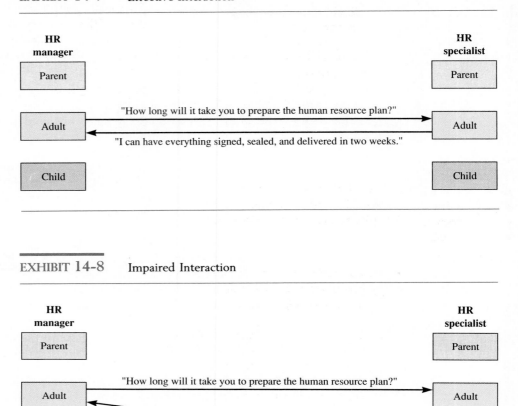

EXHIBIT 14-8   Impaired Interaction

EXHIBIT 14-9   A Breakdown in Interaction

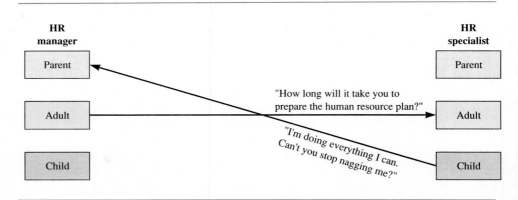

research is conducted on the effectiveness of TA as an OD tool, HR managers and specialists must cautiously consider its relative value for their situation or problem.

OD: A GROUP TECHNIQUE

There are numerous OD techniques that focus on improving the effectiveness of groups (the target), such as process consultation, survey feedback, and team building. In order to understand more fully these types of techniques, team building is presented.

Team Building

Team building is a development process that helps or prepares organizational members to work more efficiently or effectively in groups. It is designed to enhance the problem-solving, communication, and sensitivity-to-others skills of individual team members.[36]

Any organization depends on the cooperation of a number of people if it is to be successful. Consequently, teams of people have to work on a temporary or permanent basis in harmony.[37] Task forces, committees, project teams, or interdepartmental groups are the kinds of teams that are frequently brought together.

In one organization, team building followed this pattern:[38]

1. A *team skills workshop*. Production teams in the firm went through a 2½-day workshop working on various experiential exercises.
2. *Data collected*. Attitude and job data were collected from all teams (individual members).
3. *Data confrontation*. Consultants presented data to teams. It was discussed and problem areas sorted out. Priorities were also established by each team.
4. *Action planning*. Teams developed their own tentative plans to solve problems.
5. *Team building*. The teams finalized plans to solve all the problems identified in Step 4 and to consider barriers to overcome.
6. *Intergroup team building*. The groups that were interdependent met for two days to establish a mutually acceptable plan.

When team building is successful, participation is encouraged and sustained. There also can be improved communication and problem solving within and between teams. Team building has proven to be most successful when the technique is tailored to fit the needs and problems of the groups involved.[39]

How far can organizations go with team building? Some believe that "teams," or what some refer to as *high-performance teams*, are the wave of the future. At Corning, there are 3,000 teams that management recognizes that are empowered to complete their tasks as they determine how best to do the job.[40] The teams typically consist of 3 to 30 workers, sometimes blue-collar, sometimes white-collar, and sometimes both.

A number of firms that have encouraged and rewarded teams are receiving a lot of attention.

• At a General Mills cereal plant in Lodi, California, teams schedule, operate, and maintain machinery so efficiently that the factory runs with no managers present during the night shift.

- A team of Chaparral steel mill workers traveled around the world to observe and evaluate production machinery. The team selected and installed the plant's machinery.
- After organizing its home office operations into teams, Aetna Life & Casualty reduced the ratio of middle managers to workers from 1 to 7 down to 1 to 30 while at the same time improving customer service.[41]

Federal Express has been particularly successful using teams in its back-office operations in Memphis. As part of a companywide push to convert to teams, Fedex organized its 1,000 clerical workers into superteams of 5 to 10 people. Company efficiency and accuracy have improved significantly.

OD: AN ORGANIZATIONWIDE TECHNIQUE

By *organizationwide*, OD experts mean the total system involved or that a clearly identifiable unit, department, or plant is the target. The independence of the identifiable system or subsystem is extremely important when using an organizationwide technique.

Grid OD

One of the most publicized programs in OD was first introduced and researched by Blake and Mouton and is called the *Managerial Grid*.®[42] It consists of six phases directed toward enhancing organizational performance. The completion of the six-phase Grid program would cover a period of three to five years.

The **Grid OD** program is built upon a framework for understanding leadership styles of managers, as presented in Exhibit 14–10. The Grid depicts five different patterns of leadership, although 81 cells represent the two leadership concerns, production and people. Each person completes a questionnaire resulting in a determination of their leadership style. Blake and Mouton propose that the best way to lead is to be a 9, 9 — which typifies high concern for both production and people.

The specific objectives of a Grid OD program are to:

- Study the organization as an interacting system and apply techniques of analysis in diagnosing problems.
- Understand the rationale of systematic change.
- Gain insight into the strategies of Grid OD for increasing performance.
- Examine the documents and forms used in different phases and simulate their application to the participant's own situation.
- Evaluate the styles of leadership and techniques of participation most likely to produce high-quality results.
- Assess the effort and expense required and risks involved relative to the potential of increased profit and human effectiveness.[43]

These objectives are accomplished, according to Blake and Mouton, by following the six-phase program.[44]

Phase I: *Study of the Grid*. Concepts about the various leadership styles are taught. The participants' styles are evaluated and reviewed. Fifty hours of problem-solving tasks and exercises are completed.

EXHIBIT 14-10   Managerial Grid

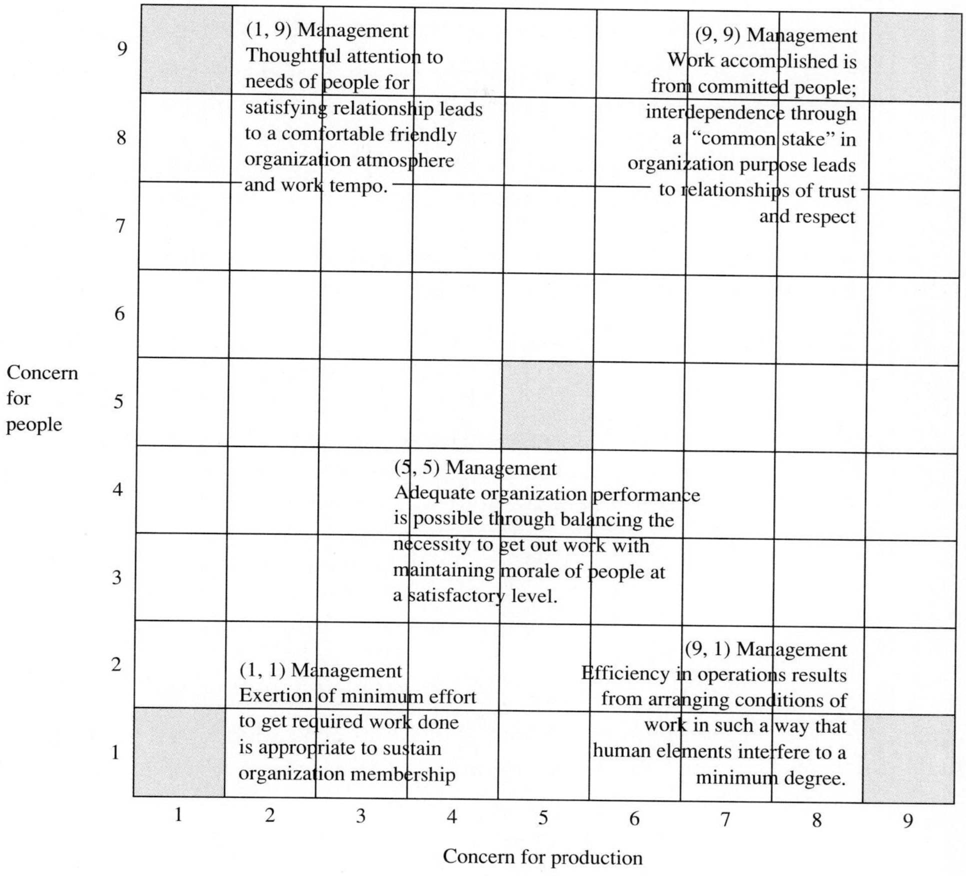

A grid with "Concern for people" on the vertical axis (1–9) and "Concern for production" on the horizontal axis (1–9).

(1, 9) Management
Thoughtful attention to needs of people for satisfying relationship leads to a comfortable friendly organization atmosphere and work tempo.

(9, 9) Management
Work accomplished is from committed people; interdependence through a "common stake" in organization purpose leads to relationships of trust and respect

(5, 5) Management
Adequate organization performance is possible through balancing the necessity to get out work with maintaining morale of people at a satisfactory level.

(1, 1) Management
Exertion of minimum effort to get required work done is appropriate to sustain organization membership

(9, 1) Management
Efficiency in operations results from arranging conditions of work in such a way that human elements interfere to a minimum degree.

Source: Robert R. Blake and Jane S. Mouton (1964), *The Managerial Grid* (Houston: Gulf Publishing), p. 10.

Phase II: *Team Development.* Participants spend time analyzing their leadership styles and group skills. The key objective in the first two phases is to build trust and respect within the teams.

Phase III. *Intergroup Development.* Emphasis is on intergroup relationships. Joint problem solving is used in simulated situations.

Phase IV. *Developing an Organization Model.* The emphasis is on the importance of strategic planning and bringing together top- and lower-management groups. Linking the top and lower levels by establishing a framework is one result of this phase.

Phase V. *Implementing the Model.* Groups are given tasks to implement the Phase IV–developed model. Structural, process, and personnel plans are established to use the model.

Phase VI: *Evaluation*. The evaluation of the overall Grid is part of this phase. Modifications are made, and a critique of the program is also part of this final phase. A standardized 100-item questionnaire is part of the evaluation in order to examine such areas as individual behavior, teamwork, intergroup relations, problem solving, and corporate strategy.

The Grid has been adopted totally, or in part, by thousands of organizations and hundreds of individuals. A large amount of the support for Grid OD comes from its founders, Blake and Mouton.[45] However, a comprehensive review of OD does give some support to Blake and Mouton's claims.[46] It has been found to have a positive impact on intergroup relationships and teamwork, as well as on performance and satisfaction. But, as is true with most training and development techniques, Grid OD needs to be researched more. HR managers considering the use of Grid OD must cautiously weigh the potential costs and benefits of this extremely popular technique.

OD: An Organizationwide Approach to Internationalization

The importance of internationalization has been emphasized through major changes in the world: the crumbling of the Berlin Wall, the raising of the Iron Curtain, and the privatization of many industries in Mexico and Latin America. Fiat (an automobile manufacturer in Italy) asked itself if its managers were ready to meet the challenges of change throughout the world. The result of this questioning was the development of the internationalization of management project at Fiat.[47] First, the firm conducted a self-study of the degree of international knowledge possessed by Fiat managers. Interviews were conducted with Fiat opinion leaders.

The results led to the creation of five work teams that focused on:

- Organization for internationalization.
- Quality of resources.
- Education and training.
- Communication.
- Recruitment of internationally qualified managers.

Each of these groups made recommendations to top management about how to internationalize Fiat in terms of the group's selected area. The education and training group recommended courses, revision of current programs, and visitations to other international locations to learn more about international practices. Courses were also designed for non-Italian managers of Fiat companies around the world. Language and cultural sensitivity competency were improved in all Fiat programs.

Fiat management has concluded that, since the internationalization project has been implemented, there is a higher integration and respect between Italian and non-Italian managers, better communication between departments and plants, and more successful recruitment of young managers. There is also much more sensitivity within Fiat about its international role and how to operate in a changing world.

EVALUATION OF TRAINING AND DEVELOPMENT

In Chapter 13, the problem Gwen Meridith and Harold Matthews faced was deciding whether the training offered was effective. They had not designed a formal evaluation of the training program. This section focuses on the evaluation.

The evaluation step is the final phase of the training and development program. Cost/benefit analysis generally is more feasible for training and development than for many other HRM functions. Costs are relatively easy to compute: They equal direct costs of training (trainer cost, materials costs, and lost productivity, if training is done on company time) and indirect costs (a fair share of administrative overhead of the HR department).[48]

Essentially, the evaluation should be made by comparing the results (the benefits) with the objectives of the training and development program that were set in the assessment phase. It is easier to evaluate the results of some programs (for example, typing) than others (for example, Outward Bound training and leadership).[49] The criteria used to evaluate training and development depend on the objectives of the program and who sets the criteria: management, the trainers, or the trainees. For example, one study found that trainees who were asked to develop their own evaluative criteria chose standards that varied from knowledge of the subject to the amount of socializing allowed during training sessions.[50]

Criteria for Evaluation

There are three types of criteria for evaluating training: internal, external, and participant reaction. *Internal criteria* are directly associated with the content of the program — for example, whether the employee learned the facts or guidelines covered in the program. *External criteria* are related more to the ultimate purpose of the program — for example, improving the effectiveness of the employee. Possible external criteria include job performance rating, the degree of learning transferred from training and development sessions to on-the-job situations and increases in sales volume, or decreases in turnover. *Participant reaction*, or how the subjects feel about the benefits of a specific training or development experience, is commonly used as an internal criterion.

Most experts argue that it is more effective to use multiple criteria to evaluate training.[51] Others contend that a single criterion, such as the extent of transfer of training to on-the-job performance or other aspects of performance, is a satisfactory evaluation approach.

One view of a multiple-criterion evaluation system was developed by Kirkpatrick.[52] He suggests measuring the following:

Participant reaction. Whether subjects like or dislike the program. The participant indicates his or her satisfaction with the program.

Learning. The extent to which the subjects have assimilated the knowledge offered and skills practiced in the training program. Does the participant score higher on skill demonstration tests after the training or development than before?

Behavior. An external measure of changes or lack of changes in job behavior. The ratings a participant received on the performance appraisal (comparison of before and after appraisal ratings).

Results. The effect of the program on organizational dimensions such as employee turnover, productivity, volume of sales, or error-free letters typed.

At present, many firms assess reaction, but very few measure behavioral results. Travelers is one firm that stresses evaluation at the behavioral level. Travelers believes that it's more relevant to examine management behavior, supervisory style, and strategic planning before and after training.[53] Travelers has identified management competencies for supervisors, managers, and directors and has developed a continuum of 27 training programs for each managerial level. Analysis of these competencies shaped training and evaluation programs. Travelers is interested in finding out if these competencies are being used more effectively after training. Rigorous, statistically perfect evaluation is not that important to Travelers. The issue of whether managers after training are using their competencies is the focus of evaluation at Travelers.

A number of evaluation instruments and methods can be used to measure results of training and development (see the table listing evaluation methods). Data that can be used for evaluation include information on the trainee in the program; the trainee's immediate superiors and superiors above immediate supervisors; the trainee's subordinates (where applicable); and nonparticipants from the work setting, including the subject's peers, company records, and nonparticipants from outside the work setting who might be affected by the program (for example, clients).

Evaluation Methods for Training and Development Programs

Company Records.   Either exiting records or those devised for the evaluation of training or development, used to measure production turnover, grievances, absenteeism, and so on.

Observational Techniques.   Interviewing, field observation, and other methods to evaluate skills, ability, communication, and productivity.

Critical Incidents.   Using crucial incidents that occur on the job.

Ratings.   Judgments of ability, performance, or ratings of satisfaction with various factors.

Questionnaires.   A variety of types to measure decision making, problem solving, attitudes, values, personality, perceptions, and so on.

Tests.   Written examinations or performance tests to measure changes in ability or knowledge.

A Matrix Guide

One useful device to address the evaluation issue is to work with a systematic evaluation matrix. A matrix, because of its organization, can help those involved with training and development programs to systematically review relevant issues or questions. Exhibit 14–11 presents such a matrix, which could be used as a guideline for evaluating any of the programs and techniques covered in Chapters 13 and 14.

The relevant issues, skill improvement, training and development materials, costs, and long-term effects are crucial questions that can be answered by use of evaluation. It is important to understand that the issues and questions provide only the direction that evaluation can take. The actual design and data collection of the evaluation phase of training and development require following the scientific method as used by behavioral scientists. Simply asking participants if they liked the program after attending a sensitivity group or a behavioral modeling session is not very scientific. What would you expect to be the answer? Certainly, most of us like new experiences, new ideas. However, this does not mean that a program is good or beneficial for improving performance or increasing interpersonal skills on the job. Perhaps the most pressing question is whether what is learned in training transfers to the job. Another crucial issue is what strategies management can use to facilitate positive transfer of learning the job.[54]

Someone in authority (usually someone above the HR specialist involved in the training or development, such as a director of human resources or vice president of operations) must hold those who train and develop employees accountable. The efficient use of people, dollars, and facilities must be clearly shown. This can only be

EXHIBIT 14-11   An Evaluation Matrix: Issues to Consider

The Relevant Issues to Cover and Evaluate	Examples of What to Measure	What to Examine for Answers	How to Collect Data to Answer Issue Questions
1. Are the participants learning, changing attitudes, and/or improving skills?	Participants' attitudes and/or skills before and after (even during training or development sessions)	Comments Method of participation Co-workers Superiors	Interview Questionnaires Records Observation
2. Are the training or development materials used on the job?	Participants' on-the-job performance, behavior, and style	Subordinate performance, attitudes, and style	Records Interview Questionnaires Critical incidents Observation
3. What are the costs of training and development programs and techniques?	The fixed and variable costs of conducting the training or development	Cost of trainers Participant time Travel expenses Consultant fees Training aids Rent Utilities	Budget records
4. How long does the training or development have an effect on participants?	Participants' on-the-job performance, behavior, and style over an extended period of time.	Subordinate performance, attitudes, and style	Records Interview Questionnaires Critical incidents Observation (collected a number of times)

done if the evaluation phase is completed and sound research designs are used. Evaluation is certainly not easy, but it is a necessary and often glossed-over part of training and development.[55]

In sum, formal training and development have been shown to be more effective than informal or no training and development. However, the results tends to be assumed rather than evaluated for most training and development programs.

Research Designs

There are numerous research designs that can be used to assess the effectiveness of training and development. The more rigorous the design, the more confidence that can be placed on the principle that changes in learning, behavior, or results are due to the program.[56]

A simple design is shown in Exhibit 14–12. One group of participants in the program is assessed before and after the experience. The differences in the measures, baseline versus after design, may be due to the training or development or there may be a "Hawthorne Effect" — that is, the employees conclude that they are being studied, so they work harder than usual. There is also the probability that over time employees gain experience and acquire ways to do the job better. Self-development may have nothing to do with the training or development program. The baseline/after one-group design doesn't address the Hawthorne or natural job experience improvement issues.

EXHIBIT 14-12   One Group: Baseline/After Design

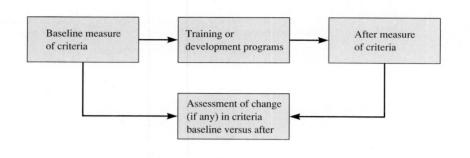

EXHIBIT 14-13   Two Groups: After Design

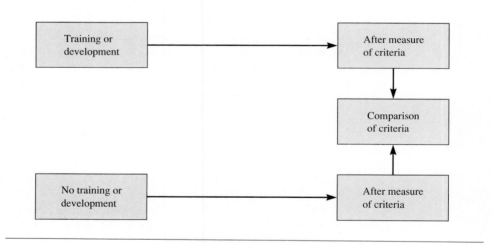

A research design that is used to address the Hawthorne and the job experience issues is shown in Exhibit 14–13. This is a two-group design. One group receives the training or development program, while the other group receives no training.

This design is an improvement over the one-group design, but we don't know if the groups were comparable to begin with. Perhaps the no-training or development group was initially significantly better performers. Since no baseline measures were taken, the conclusions drawn are somewhat debatable.

Exhibit 14–14 shows a two-group design that uses baseline measures. This is a better design than the one-group or the no-baseline, two-group design. It permits the researcher to conclude with some confidence that differences in the criteria (learning, behavior, results) may be attributable to the training or development program.

EXHIBIT 14-14   Two Groups: Baseline/After Design

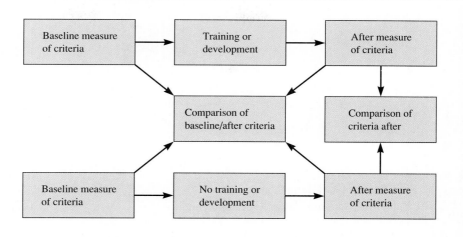

Arthur Andersen uses a two-group evaluation design since showing improvement is considered important in making future expenditures on training. For example, Arthur Andersen compared an accelerated learning technique to a traditional instructional design to determine which method was most economical. Participants were randomly asked to participate in either an experimental (accelerated learning) or control (traditional) group.[57] The traditional group was evaluated, soon after training, as superior to the accelerated learning group in terms of participants' knowledge gains and reactions. However, a follow-up four months after training revealed that behavior improvements on the job were higher for the accelerated learning group than for the control group. This two-group, longitudinal design led to further study of the economic value of accelerated learning techniques at Arthur Andersen.

Other much more sophisticated two-, three-, and multiple-group research designs are available. The manager must decide which design will be used. It is recommended that, in most cases, some type of design be used to evaluate training or development programs to determine their value, if any, to the organization.[58]

The important point to note is that in *most* cases evaluation is in order. There may be programs that cannot demonstrate quantitative improvements, using a rigorous evaluation design, that are beneficial to employees. One such program is Outward Bound experiences for managers. Outward Bound has been used in the United States since 1962.[59] It is designed to develop character, self-confidence, and leadership. Most Outward Bound programs consist of a series of perceived high-risk activities that require teamwork and problem-solving skills. Interspersed with the activities are debriefing sessions in which participants analyze their feelings and experiences. Lectures and discussions on management skills are also included.

Are these programs successful? Qualitative statements from participants are positive. However, the transferability of skills back to the job are hard to quantify. Evaluation studies have not proven or disproven the value of Outward Bound.

CAREER CHALLENGE
(concluded)

*A*fter absorbing the material Bob has brought her, Gwen approaches Lester Young, Young Enterprise's president, on an informal basis.

Gwen You know, Les, our last attitude survey indicated major dissatisfaction with our development program at Young. We've been doing some research in our shop about development programs. I'm sure I couldn't work it into this year's budget. But we're only six weeks away from the new budget time. I feel the program is very important at this time. As you know, we were not completely satisfied with the training program on the new machinery. In addition, one or two of our supervisors have come in to complain about the lack of any organization development program for them. How would you like us to proceed?

Lester I have heard some talk about OD at a recent American Manufacturers Association meeting. I hear it's quite costly. We may have some problems in this area, but we're in no position to make a major investment in development at the present time in view of our earnings situation. Why not work up a modest program for presentation to the budget and goals meeting six weeks from now—no more than 5 percent of your current budget as an increment.

Gwen Will do, Les.

Gwen and Bob put together a proposal that they viewed as Phase 1. They proposed a supervisory development program with some help from the HR department for one half of 1 percent of current budget.

After investigating the potential costs of an OD consultant, they felt they should begin to move in the development area. They proposed some beginning funds for planning an OD program, the first phase of which would involve initial diagnosis and small sample data collection. They proposed to set up an experiment using a behavior-modeling program in one unit for supervisory style, with a control group. Evaluation procedures were to be formal. They specified desired outputs: better readings from the attitude survey, some improvements in turnover and absenteeism, and some results in the productivity problem.

Lester and the budget and goals committee accepted the proposal. Phase 1 began, and it was successful. Little by little, the company accepted a development program.

SUMMARY

This chapter has introduced the important areas of the development of human resources and the evaluation of training and development programs.

To summarize the major points covered in this chapter:

1. Management development is the process by which managers gain the experience, skills, and attitudes to become or remain successful leaders in their organization.

2. Management and professional development is designed to reduce obsolescence and to increase employee satisfaction and productivity.

3. Methods used to modify employee and managerial attitudes and interpersonal skills include behavior modeling, sensitivity training, transactional analysis, and team building.

EXHIBIT **14-15**   Recommendations for Use of OD in Model Organizations

Type of Organization	Types of OD				
	Behavior Modeling	**Sensitivity Training**	**Transactional Analysis**	**Team Building**	**Grid OD**
1. Large size, low complexity, high stability		X	X		
2. Medium size, low complexity, high stability		X	X		
3. Small size, low complexity, high stability			X		
4. Medium size, moderate complexity, moderate stability	X	X	X	X	X
5. Large size, high complexity, low stability	X	X	X	X	X
6. Medium size, high complexity, low stability	X	X	X	X	X
7. Small size, high complexity, low stability	X		X	X	

4. A popular organizationwide OD program is the Managerial Grid, which was first introduced by Blake and Mouton.

5. Organization development programs, such as the Grid, overlap the other methods. The Grid seeks to change attitudes, values, organization structure, and managerial practices to improve performance.

6. The final phase of any training and development program is evaluation. It is, unfortunately, often bypassed by organizations. There are some cases, however, where rigorous evaluation may not illustrate qualitative improvements.

Exhibit 14–15 provides some recommendations for the use of various OD programs and techniques for the model organization.

KEY TERMS

behavior modeling	515	sensitivity training	522
case method	512	team building	525
Grid OD	526	transactional analysis	523
role playing	513		

QUESTIONS FOR REVIEW AND DISCUSSION

1. How can you describe the characteristics of a few OD programs designed to improve interpersonal skills and attitudes?

2. What would be some of the possible consequences of not being involved in state-of-the-art management development programs for employees?

3. What are the advantages and disadvantages associated with using university-based training programs?

4. How could a person's expectations about training influence what they learn in a formal training program?

5. Why do you think many organizations fail to evaluate their training and development programs?

6. Why would a research study not be able to capture what are referred to as *qualitative reactions* to a training program?

7. What costs would be involved in implementing a full-fledged Grid OD program?

8. Present a research design that could be used to evaluate the effectiveness of a team-building development program.

9. Should management be concerned about what amount of training transfers to the actual job? Why?

10. The predecessors to current development programs were called *human relations programs*. What was the major emphasis on these programs, and how effective were they?

NOTES

[1] Jay Lorsch, ed. *Handbook of Organizational Behavior* (Englewood Cliffs, N.J. Prentice-Hall, (1987); and Alan Mumford, ed. (1986), *Handbook of Management Development* (Brookfield, Vt.: Gower).

[2] Robert Townsend (1984), *Further Up the Organization* (New York: Alfred A. Knopf).

[3] "Six Lessons from the Corporate Classroom," *Harvard Business Review*, H. Bernhard and C. Ingolls (September–October 1988), p. 40.

[4] R. Fulmer (1988), "Corporate Management Development: The State of the Art," *The Journal of Management Development* 7, no. 2, p. 57.

[5] Albert A. Vicere and Virginia T. Freeman (1990), "Executive Education in Major Corporations: An International Survey," *Journal of Management Development*, pp. 5–16.

[6] John P. Campbell, Marvin D. Dunnette, Edward E. Lawler III, and Karl E. Weick, Jr. (1970), *Managerial Behavior, Performance and Effectiveness* (New York: McGraw-Hill).

[7] Kenneth N. Wexley and Gary P. Latham (1981), *Developing and Training Human Resources in Organizations* (Glenview, Ill.: Scott, Foresman), p. 193.

[8] Chris Argyris (April 1980), "Some Limitations of the Case Method: Experiences in a Management Development Program," *Academy of Management Review*, pp. 291–98.

[9] A. R. Solem (September–October 1960), "Human Relations Training: Comparison of Case Study and Role Playing," *Personnel Administrator*, pp. 27–37.

[10] Peter Petre (October 29, 1984), "Games That Teach You to Manage," *Fortune*, pp. 65–72.

[11] See Allen Kraut (Autumn 1976), "Developing Managerial Skills via Modeling Techniques: Some Positive Research Findings — A Symposium" (other articles in this series cover modeling), *Personnel Psychology*, pp. 325–61; and Gary Latham and Lise Saari (June 1979), "Application of Social Learning Theory of Training Supervisors through Behavior Modeling," *Journal of Applied Psychology*, pp. 239–46.

[12] D. Johnson and M. Socher (1987) "Behavior Modeling Training: Why, How, and What Results," *Journal of European Training* 76, no. 2, pp. 62–72.

[13] Charles C. Manz and Henry P. Sims, Jr. (January 1981), "Vicarious Learning: The Influence of Modeling on Organizational Behavior," *Academy of Management Review*,

pp. 105–14; and B. L. Rosenbaum (July 1978), "New Uses of Behavior Modeling," *Personnel Administrator*, pp. 27–28.

[14] Jerry Porras and P. O. Berg (April 1978), "The Impact of Organizational Development," *Academy of Management Review*, pp. 259–60.

[15] P. J. Decker and B. R. Nathan (1985), *Behavior Modeling Training Principles and Applications* (New York: Praeger Publishers).

[16] James C. Robinson (1982), *Developing Managers through Behavior Modeling* (San Diego: University Associates), Chapter 2.

[17] Henry P. Sims, Jr., and Charles C. Manz (January 1982), "Modeling Influences on Employee Behavior," *Personnel Journal*, pp. 58–65.

[18] Betty Wisendanger (October 1990), "Take Me to the River," *Sales & Marketing Management*, pp. 62–67.

[19] Kurt Eichenwald (June 24, 1990), "Wall Street in Search of Itself on the Yampa," *New York Times*, pp. 4–5F.

[20] Tom Kramlinger and Tom Huberty (December 1990), "Behaviorism versus Humanism," *Training and Development Journal*, pp. 41–45.

[21] Robert L. Smith (January 1984), "OD Can Be a Discipline," *Training and Development Journal*, pp. 102–4.

[22] This definition was originally developed by R. Beckhard (1969), *Organization Development: Strategies and Models* (Reading, Mass.: Addison-Wesley Publishing), p. 16.

[23] David Nadler (1977), *Feedback and Organization Development: Using Data-Based Methods* (Reading, Mass.: Addison-Wesley Publishing), pp. 34–40.

[24] Peter A. Clark (1972), *Action Research and Organizational Change* (New York: Harper & Row).

[25] Leland Bradford, Jack R. Gibbs, and Kenneth Bene, eds. (1964), *T-Group Theory and Laboratory Method* (New York: John Wiley & Sons).

[26] K. Back (1972), *Beyond Words: The Story of Sensitivity Training and the Encounter Movement* (New York: Russell Sage Foundation).

[27] George Odiorne (October 1973), "The Trouble with Sensitivity Training," *Training Directors Journal*, pp. 19–37.

[28] Robert J. House (December 1969), "T-Group Training: Good or Bad?" *Business Horizons*, pp. 69–77.

[29] William J. Kearney and Desmond D. Martin (December 1974), "Sensitivity Training: An Established Management Development Tool?" *Academy of Management Journal*, pp. 755–60.

[30] Richard Phalon (June 18, 1984), "Hell Camp," *Forbes*, pp. 56–58.

[31] Eric Berne (1964), *Games People Play* (New York: Ballantine Books).

[32] Sigmund Freud (1960), "Psychopathology of Everyday Life," in *The Standard Edition of the Complete Psychology Works of Sigmund Freud*, ed. J. Strackey (London: Hogarth Press).

[33] Dorothy Jonerward and Philip Seyen (1978), *Choosing Success* (New York: John Wiley & Sons).

[34] Donald D. Bowen and Rayhu Nath (January 1978), "Transactional Analysis in OD: Applications within the NTL Model," *Academy of Management Review*, pp. 86–87.

[35] Wexley and Latham, *Developing and Training Human Resources*, p. 188.

[36] Malcolm Shaw (1985), "Work Team Development Training," in *Human Resources Management and Development Handbook*, ed. William R. Tracey (New York: AMACOM), pp. 1113–24.

[37] W. G. Dyer (1977), *Team Building: Issues and Alternatives* (Reading, Mass.: Addison-Wesley Publishing).

[38] Warren R. Nielsen and John R. Kimberly (1973), "The Impact of Organizational De-

velopment on the Quality of Organizational Output," *Academy of Management Proceedings*, pp. 528–29.

[39] Robert R. Blake, Jane Srygley Mouton, and Robert L. Allen (1987), *Spectacular Teamwork* (New York: John Wiley & Sons).

[40] Briane Dumaine (May 7, 1990), "Who Needs a Boss?" *Fortune*, pp. 52–60.

[41] Thomas F. O'Boyle (June 4, 1990), "From Pyramid to Pancake," *The Wall Street Journal*, pp. R37–38.

[42] Robert R. Blake and Jane S. Mouton (1978), *The New Management Grid* (Houston: Gulf Publishing).

[43] Brochure from Scientific Methods, Inc., Austin, Texas.

[44] A summary is provided in Robert R. Blake and Jane S. Mouton (May 1975), "An Overview of the Grid," *Training and Development Journal*, pp. 29–37.

[45] Fred Luthans (1981), *Organizational Behavior* (New York: McGraw-Hill), p. 618.

[46] Jerry Porras and P. O. Berg (April 1978), "The Impact of Organizational Development," *Academy of Management Review*, pp. 259–60.

[47] Enrico Auteri and Vittoria Tesio (Winter 1990), "The Internationalization of Management at Fiat," *The Journal of Management Development*, pp. 6–16.

[48] Robert O. Brinkerhoff (1987), *Achieving Results from Training* (San Francisco: Jossey-Bass).

[49] Harold E. Fisher (January 1988), "Make Training Accountable: Assess Its Impact," *Personnel Journal*, pp. 73–75.

[50] R. A. Guzzo, R. D. Jette, and R. A. Katzell (Spring 1985), "The Effects of Psychologically Based Intervention Programs on Work Productivity: A Meta-Analysis," *Personnel Psychology*, pp. 275–92.

[51] Darlene F. Russ-Eft and John H. Zenger (April 1985), "Common Mistakes in Evaluating Training Effectiveness," *Personnel Administrator*, pp. 57–62.

[52] Donald L. Kirpatrick (November 1983), "Four Steps To Measuring Training Effectiveness," *Personal Administrator*, pp. 19–25.

[53] (July 1990), "Evaluation Framework, Design, and Reports," *Training & Development Journal* (Supplement), pp. 5–28.

[54] Kenneth N. Wexley and Timothy T. Baldwin (September 1986), "Posttraining Strategies for Facilitating Positive Transfer: An Empirical Exploration," *Academy of Management Journal*, pp. 503–20.

[55] For an interesting view of one of the pioneers of OD, see (April 1981), "A Dialogue with Warren Bennis," *Training and Development Journal*, pp. 19–26.

[56] Donald L. Kirkpatrick (November 1983), "Four Steps to Measuring Training Effectiveness," *Personnel Administrator*, pp. 19–25.

[57] (July 1990), "Evaluation Practices," *Training & Development Journal* (Supplement), pp. 526–27.

[58] William D. Hicks and Richard J. Klimoski (September 1987), "Entry into Training Programs and Its Effects on Training Outcomes: A Field Experiment," *Academy of Management Journal*, pp. 532–42.

[59] Glenn M. McEvoy and Paul F. Buller (August 1990), "Five Uneasy Pieces in the Training Evaluation Puzzle," *Training & Development Journal*, pp. 39–42.

EXERCISE 14–1   Making Responses

* * * * *

Objective   The exercise is designed to have students apply the three ego states of transactional analysis — child, adult, parent.

SET UP THE EXERCISE

1. Divide the class into groups of four or five.
2. Individually complete the transactional analysis response form.
3. Discuss in the group the individual responses. Consult Chapter 14 to review the child, adult, and parent states.

Transactional Analysis Response Form

Make a child, adult, and parent response to each of the following statements:

A. Is HRM an important function in organizations?
   Child:

   Adult:

   Parent:

B. Eating nutritional food is good for your health.
   Child:

   Adult:

   Parent:

C. Are your a good driver?
   Child:

   Adult:

   Parent:

D. Do you litter the highways?
   Child:

   Adult:

   Parent:

E. Jim (Anne) is a good student in this course (program).
   Child:

   Adult:

   Parent:

F. You always force your views on other people.
   Child:

Adult:

Parent:

4. Which of these states is the dominant one for you?

A Learning Note

This exercise will illustrate clearly the differences in the three ego states. It will also illustrate that the adult state is much more relevant and effective when answering any kind of question or issue.

APPLICATION CASE 14–1
·····

A Windfall or a Headache — The New Budget Dilemma

Rick Battista always seemed to be asking for more resources from his boss and the firm. He wanted new personal computers for his staff. He wanted additional money to support training for all his department's employees. Rick wanted his people to be the best trained, in all aspects of human resource management programs. Rick's subordinates were responsible for all company programs — compensation, performance appraisal, job analysis, collective bargaining, recruitment, selection, and safety. In addition, Rick was responsible for all development programs for the entire management cadre of Alief Casting Corporation. Thus, his 10 subordinates and over 125 managers were considered Rick's development domain.

Over the past three years, Rick has been asking Don Alief, the CEO, for sufficient funds to mount a solid companywide OD program. Rick's diagnosis of Alief Corporation's OD needs has been ongoing for three years. He has reviewed company records, conducted interviews, talked to individuals who have left Alief for other firms, administered surveys, and examined performance appraisal data. All of this diagnostic work has resulted in a solid conclusion that Alief managers do not possess the skills and competencies to support the firm's plans to expand into international markets. Managers do not understand international transactions, they lack negotiating skills, they are not developing subordinates for advancement, and they lack communication skills. In addition to these managerial deficiencies, Rick has determined that his immediate subordinates are not trained to conduct job analysis, to implement reward and incentive programs, or to properly utilize human resource infor-

mation systems. He believed that everything was being operated with no plan for the future.

Rick was surprised when Don called him to his office. Don informed Rick that he finally agreed that management development had to be supported. Don proceeded to inform Rick that, on his orders, $1 million was deposited in Rick's budget for the next 12 months to do the devleopment job. All Don wanted was some tangible results that he could use with the board of directors. Don emphasized that development had to show results that he could take to the board to justify the $1 million commitment.

Rick was so astonished that he mumbled a few unintelligible comments and thanked Don for his support and the financial backing. Rick knew that Don was serious about tangible results and knew that he had to spend the money very carefully. However, when reality set in, Rick kept asking himself what Don meant by the term *tangible results*. What does Don really want Rick to do with the money?

Discussion Questions

1. What does Rick have to do in terms of budgeting his OD funds?
2. Is it realistic to expect tangible OD-initiated results in a one-year period?
3. How should Rick divide the OD funds in terms of his unit and the company's managers?
4. How should Rick proceed after this initial meeting with Don?

CAREER PLANNING AND DEVELOPMENT

· · · · · · ·

LEARNING OBJECTIVES

———◯———

After studying this chapter, you should be able to:

· · ·

Define the term *career*

· · ·

Describe the potential organizational benefits that can result from mentoring relationships

· · ·

Explain why organizations need to be concerned about dual careers

· · ·

Discuss how career pathing can be used within an organization

· · ·

State how career planning is done in organizations

CAREER CHALLENGE

Jim Lucio was a 50-year-old executive with Neal Engineering Construction Company in Mesa, Arizona, a suburb of Phoenix. Despite his professional engineering training, and his good position with the company, Jim had an identity problem. This conversation between Jim and Norbert Wislinski, his boss, indicates a midcareer concern.

Norb Jim, you're really moving on the Salt River Project. Costs are under control and you've been able to control Tony (the chief engineer).

Jim To be honest, Norb, I'm sick of the project, Tony, and everything about the job. I can't sleep, eat, or relax.

Norb I'm sorry to hear that. Do you need some time off?

Jim No. I need to rethink my whole career. I've just lost my intensity. It hasn't been sudden. It's been growing over the last year.

Norb You know I'll do anything I can to help you. You're what made this company a success.

Jim Thanks. But I have to really do some soul searching. I've always wanted to own my own business, be my own boss. I just haven't been brave enough to take the plunge.

Norb Jim, you know I'm selfish. I need you here at Neal, but if you make the break, I'll help you any way I can.

Jim Thanks again, Norb. I have to think more about this. It is a whole career change. Serious business for a 50-year-old engineer.

Jim Lucio has changed and now he is trying to cope with his thoughts and feelings. This is a difficult time in Jim's life. He seems to have it all, but something is missing. He is not satisfied. Norb is an understanding manager who also seems to realize that Jim Lucio is at a midcareer point in life and wants to make a change.

B ecause of organizational change and growth, managers must pay attention to developing people and placing them in key positions. Organizational growth through expansion, mergers, and acquisitions creates new management positions and changes the responsibilities of existing positions. Capable people must be available to fill the new and bigger jobs. Moreover, the contemporary concern for developing the full potential of all employees through job opportunities that provide responsibility, advancement, and challenging work reinforces such efforts. Even organizations facing a stable or a contracting future recognize that a key to performance is the development of human resources.

As organizations change, so do their employees. For example, a recently hired HR manager has different needs and aspirations than does the midcareer or the preretirement HR manager. All of us move through a fairly uniform pattern of phases during our careers. The different phases produce different opportunities and stresses that affect job performance. Effective managers comprehend these implications and facilitate the efforts of employees who wish to confront and deal with their career and life needs.

Finally, it should be noted that managers should be concerned with their own career development. By their nature, managers are likely to be concerned with their career goals and with the paths that are most likely to lead to those goals. Yet managers often lack the ability and the information needed to develop their career plans in systematic and explicit ways. But we see more and more evidence of growing interest in providing individuals with information that will help them to identify their goals and to understand what they should do to reach them.

In this chapter, we will review a number of programs that organizations and managers can use to plan and develop careers. Some of these programs have been used in management for many years to identify and select promising managerial talent. For example, assessment centers and performance appraisal programs have long been used to develop managers, though the traditional emphasis of these programs has been placed on the satisfaction of organizational needs. More recently, the programs have been revised to include the consideration of employee needs as well.

A DIAGNOSTIC APPROACH TO CAREER PLANNING AND DEVELOPMENT

Exhibit 15–1 highlights the diagnostic factors most important to career planning and development as an HRM activity. People have always had careers, but only recently has serious HRM attention been directed to the way careers develop and the type of planning that is needed to achieve career satisfaction. The key to the diagnostic factors influencing careers is not in the person, the external environmental influences, or the internal influences themselves, but rather the ways in which these major factors interact.

Certainly, careers do not just happen in isolation from environmental and personal factors. Every person's career goes through a series of stages. Each of these stages may or may not be influenced by attitudes, motivation, the nature of the task, economic conditions, and so forth. The HRM employee must be sensitive to the ''career cycle'' and the role that different influences such as those shown in Exhibit 15–1 can play at different points.

An adequate matching of individual needs, abilities, preferences, motivation, and organizational opportunities will not just happen. Individuals, organizations, and experts in areas such as HRM all must take responsibility for things they can control.

EXHIBIT 15-1   Factors Affecting Career Planning and Development

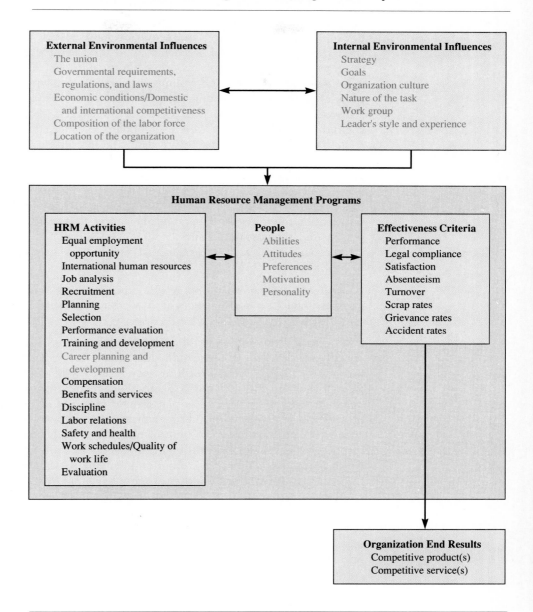

For example, organizations and HR employees must realize the needs of employees. On the other hand, employees must have a clear picture of the opportunities available now and anticipated in the future. Organizations should not guess or assume some set of career needs. Likewise, employees should not have to guess how career development occurs in the organization. A sharing of information, an understanding of the "career stage," and concern about the kind of forces highlighted in Exhibit 15–1 must be established as part of an ongoing career planning and development effort. Anything less will probably result in the inefficient use of human resources.

THE CONCEPT OF CAREER

The concept **career** has many meanings. The popular meaning is probably reflected in the idea of moving upward in one's chosen line of work — making more money; having more responsibility; and acquiring more status, prestige, and power. Although typically restricted to lines of work that involve gainful employment, the concept of career can apply to other life pursuits. For example, we can think of homemakers, mothers, and volunteer workers as having careers. For they too advance in the sense that their talents and abilities to handle larger responsibilities grow with time and experience. A mother of teenagers plays a far different role than she did when the children were preschoolers.

Perhaps, the most concise, up-to-date, and interesting view of careers, job hunting, and career changing is the annual guide written ty Richard Bolles, *The 1991 What Color Is Your Parachute?*. Since 1970, he has updated his book, which addresses careers and what they mean to people. The practical advice proposed by Bolles applies to almost any career or job one could imagine. He also offers career information resources, by geographical location, that can prove valuable in helping a person understand career issues.[1]

A concise definition of *career* that emphasizes its importance is offered by Greenhaus:

> A career is the pattern of work-related experiences (e.g., job positions, job duties, decisions, and subjective interpretations about work-related events) and activities over the span of the person's work life.[2]

This definition emphasizes that the term *career* does not imply success or failure except in the judgment of the individual, that a career consists of both attitudes and behavior, and that it is an ongoing sequence of work-related activities. Yet, even though the concept of career is clearly work-related, it must be understood that a person's nonwork life and roles play a significant part in a career. For example, the attitudes of a 50-year-old midcareer manager (*midcareer* means at about the midpoint of a person's working tenure) about a job advancement involving greater responsibilities can be quite different from those of a manager nearing retirement. A single person's reaction to a promotion involving relocation is likely to be different from that of a father or a mother of school-age children.

The values of society change over time, and, consequently, how a person reacts to a career may be modified. Today, a growing number of people who are in managerial and professional careers seem less obsessed with advancement, continual success, and salary progression. Family needs and spending time off the job with loved ones are becoming topics that individuals are discussing and considering more completely.[3] Judy Pesin, who once worked 12-hour days as a vice president of Citicorp accepted a part-time job after the birth of her child four years ago. She stated, "Unless I'm inventing a cure for AIDS, unless I'm really making a major social contribution, it's not worth missing my daughter growing up." Flexibility in scheduling, part-time employment, and working at home are all being considered very important for more individuals who are softening their career-driven personalities.

Now that you have started to think about the notion of careers, it would be useful to consider your own career aspirations. The exercise that follows will enable you to think about a career and its meaning. Although you can do the exercise without input from others, it would be helpful to share and compare the results. The exercise is presented in a step-by-step format, and it can be completed on a separate sheet of paper.

1. Draw a horizontal line that depicts the past, present, and future of your *career*. On that line, mark an *X* to show where you are now.

2. To the left of the *X*, that part of the line that represents your *past*, identify the events in your life that gave you genuine feelings of fulfillment and satisfaction.

3. Examine these historical milestones, and determine the specific factors that seem to have caused those feelings. Does a pattern emerge? Did the events occur when you were alone or when you were with other people? Did you accomplish some objective alone or with other people? Write down as much as you can about the events and your reactions to them.

4. That part of the line to the right of the *X* represents your *future*. Identify the career-related events from which you expect to realize genuine fulfillment and satisfaction. You should describe these events as explicitly as possible. If you are only able to write such statements as "get my first job" or "get my first raise," you probably have ill-defined career expecations.

5. After you have identified these future career-related events, rank them from high to low in terms of how much fulfillment and satisfaction you expect to derive from them.

6. Now go back to Step 3 and rank the historical events from high to low in terms of the actual fulfillment and satisfaction you derived from them. Compare your two sets of ranked events. Are they consistent? Are you expecting the future to be the same as or different from the past? If you expect the future to be considerably different from the past, are you being realistic about the fulfillment and satisfaction that you think the future events will provide?

7. Discuss your results with your classmates and your instructor. How do you compare with your classmates in terms of your self-understanding and your understanding of the role of a career in providing personal fulfillment and satisfaction?

Career Stages

Most working people prepare for their occupation by undergoing some form of organized education in high school, trade school, vocational school, or college. They then take a first job, but the chances are that they will move to other jobs in the same organization or in other organizations. Eventually, over the course of their career, they settle into a position in which they remain until retirement. The duration of each stage varies among individuals, but most working people go through all of these stages.

Studies of career stages have found that needs and expectations change as the individual moves through the stages.[4] Managers in American Telephone and Telegraph (AT&T) expressed considerable concern for safety needs during the initial years on their jobs. This phase, termed the *establishment phase*, ordinarily lasted during the first five years of employment. Following the establishment phase is the *advancement phase*, which lasts approximately from age 30 to age 45. During this period, the AT&T managers expressed considerably less concern for the satisfaction of safety needs and more concern for achievement, esteem, and autonomy.

The *maintenance phase* follows the advancement phase. This period is marked by efforts to stabilize the gains of the past. Although no new gains are made, the maintenance phase can be a period of creativity, since the individual has satisfied many of the psychological and financial needs associated with earlier phases. Al-

EXHIBIT 15-2   Career Stages and Important Needs

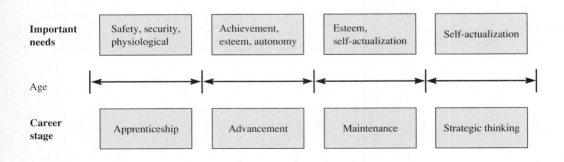

Important needs	Safety, security, physiological	Achievement, esteem, autonomy	Esteem, self-actualization	Self-actualization
Age	←——————→	←——————→	←——————→	←——————→
Career stage	Apprenticeship	Advancement	Maintenance	Strategic thinking

though each individual and each career will be different, it is reasonable to assume that esteem and self-actualization would be the most important needs in the maintenance phase. But, as we will see, many people experience what is termed the *midcareer crisis* during the maintenance phase. Such people are not achieving satisfaction from their work, and, consequently, they may experience psychological discomfort.

The maintenance phase is followed by the *retirement phase*. The individual has, in effect, completed one career, and he or she may move on to another one. During this phase, the individual may have opportunities to experience self-actualization through activities that it was impossible to pursue while working. Painting, gardening, volunteer service, and quiet reflection are some of the many positive avenues that have been followed by retirees. But the individual's financial and health status may make it necessary to spend the retirement years in satisfying safety and physiological needs. Exhibit 15–2 summarizes the relationship between career stages and needs.

The fact that individuals pass through different stages during their careers is evident. It is also understandable that individual needs and motives are different from one stage to the next. But managing the careers of others requires a more complete description of what happens to individuals during these stages. One group of individuals whose careers are of special significance to the performance of modern organizations are the *professionals*. Knowledge workers—such as professional accountants, scientists, and engineers—are one of the fastest growing segments of the work force. This segment constitutes 32 percent of the work force at present (blue-collar workers make up 33 percent).[5] Many professionals spend their careers in large, complex organizations after having spent several years obtaining advance training and degrees. The organizations that employ them expect them to provide the innovativeness and creativity for organizational survival in dynamic and competitive environments. Obviously, the performance levels of professional employees must be of the utmost concern for the organizations' leaders.

Stage I   Young professionals enter an organization with technical knowledge, but often without an understanding of the organization's demands and expectations. Consequently, they must work fairly closely with more-experienced persons. The relationship that develops between the young professionals and their supervisors is an *apprenticeship*. The central activities in which apprentices are expected to show competence include *learning* and *following directions*. To move successfully and effectively through Stage I, one must be able to accept the *psychological state of dependence*. And some professionals cannot cope with being placed in a situation similar to that which they experienced while in school. They find that they are still being directed by an authority figure, just as they were in school, whereas they had anticipated that their first job would provide considerably more freedom.

Stage II   Once through the dependent relationship of Stage I, the professional employee moves into Stage II, which calls for working independently. Passage to this stage depends on the employee having demonstrated competence in some specific technical area. The technical expertise may be in a content area, such as taxation, product testing, or quality assurance, or it may be in a skill area, such as computer applications. The professional's primary activity in Stage II is to be an *independent contributor* of ideas in the chosen area. The professional is expected to rely much less on direction from others. The *psychological state of independence* may pose some problems because it is in such stark contrast to the state of dependence required in Stage I. Stage II is extremely important for the professional's future career growth. However, those who fail at this stage do so because they do not have the necessary self-confidence.

   In the case at the beginning of this chapter, there is an indication that Jim Lucio is at Stage II in his career development. As the opening Career Challenge stated, Jim really values his independence. He wants to be his own boss and run his own business. Independence is a high priority for him as it is for most professionals at Stage II.

Stage III   Professionals who enter Stage III are expected to become the mentors of those in Stage I. They also tend to broaden their interests and to deal more and more with people outside the organization. Thus, the central activities of professionals at this stage are *training* and *interaction* with others. Stage III professionals assume *responsibility for the work of others*, and this characteristic of the stage can cause considerable psychological stress. In previous stages, the professional was responsible only for his or her own work. But now it is the work of others that is of primary concern. Individuals who cannot cope with this new requirement may decide to shift back to Stage II. Individuals who derive satisfaction from seeing other people move on to bigger and better jobs will be content to remain in Stage III until retirement.

   In the *Change Masters*, Kanter argued that all companies that want to achieve excellence should encourage managers to become mentors to their employees.[6] Kotter agreed that mentors, sponsors, coaches, and role models can be especially important in helping others in their careers. He stated, "Virtually all of the successful and effective executives I have known have had two or more of these kinds of relationships in their careers."[7]

   The relationship between individuals who share knowledge and viewpoints is referred to as *mentoring*. Mentoring in an organization can contribute to employee instruction, job performannce, and retention rate.[8] There is also the transmission of corporate culture that could benefit the mentor and mentee, as well as the organization.

   As defined by Kram, a **mentoring relationship** is a relationship between a junior and senior colleague that is viewed by the junior as contributing positively to his or her development.[9] The junior person is developed by a range of career advancement activities (coaching, exposure and visibility, and protection) that the senior person facilitates. Also, the mentoring relationship provides the junior person with support that helps him or her acquire a sense of personal identity. The person in Stage III serving as a mentor can derive tremendous satisfaction from the growth, development, and advancement of a protégé.[10] In some organizations, such as J.C. Penney, Sears, and IBM, Stage III professionals will not be promoted until they can demonstrate an ability to prepare junior subordinates for promotion and more job responsibilities.[11]

Mentoring relationships have been hard to form for women and minority workers.[12] Researchers have suggested that some men hesitate to act as mentors for female protégés because of the sexual innuendos that often accompany such relationships. Some firms are attempting to overcome barriers of race and sex by assigning mentors to promising young executives. At BankAmerica Corporation, a senior manager may be asked to serve as a coach and mentor to three or four juniors for a year at a time.

Stage IV   Some professional employees remain in Stage III; for these professionals, Stage III is the career maintenance phase. Other professionals progress to yet another stage. This stage is not experienced by all professionals, because its fundamental characteristic involves *shaping the direction of the organization itself*. Although we usually think of such activity as being undertaken by only one individual in an organization — its chief executive — in fact, it may be undertaken by many others. For example, key personnel in product development, process manufacturing, or technological research may be Stage IV types. As a consequence of their performance in Stage III of their careers, Stage IV professionals direct their attention to long-range strategic planning. In doing so, they play the roles of manager, entrepreneur, and idea generator. Their primary job relationships are to *identify* and *sponsor* the careers of their successors and to interact with key people outside the organization. The most significant shift for a person in Stage IV is to accept the decisions of subordinates without second-guessing them. Stage IV professionals must learn to influence; that is, practice leadership through such indirect means as idea planting, personnel selection, and organizational design. These shifts can be difficult for an individual who has relied on direct supervision in the past.

The concept of career stages is fundamental for understanding and managing career development. It is necessary to comprehend *life stages* as well. Individuals go through career stages as they go through life stages, but the interaction between career stages and life stages is not easy to understand.

CAREER CHOICES

Perhaps the most important decision a person makes is what career he or she should pursue. At some point, you will likely make a career decision and ask yourself career questions such as: What do I want to be when I grow up? What are my strengths and weaknesses? Why can't I sell more products?

John L. Holland, a career counseling expert, has proposed and researched a theory of career (vocational) choice.[13] Holland suggests that the choice of a career is an expression of personality and not a random event, though chance can play a role. He also believes that what a person accomplishes and derives from a career depends on the congruence between his or her personality and the job environment.[14]

Holland contends that each individual to some extent resembles one of six personality types:

- *Realistic.* This individual prefers activities involving the manipulation of machinery or tools — a machinist.
- *Investigative.* This individual prefers to be analytical, curious, methodical, and precise — a research scientist.
- *Artistic.* This person is expressive, nonconforming, original, and introspective — an interior decorator.
- *Social.* This person enjoys working with and helping others and purposefully avoids systematic activities involving tools and machinery — a school counselor.
- *Enterprising.* This person enjoys activities that permit him or her to influence others to accomplish goals — a lawyer.
- *Conventional.* This individual enjoys the systematic manipulation of data, filing records, or reproducing materials — an accountant.

The more one resembles any given type, the more likely one is to display some of the behaviors and traits associated with that type.

Holland suggests that, whereas one personality type predominates, individuals use a wide range of strategies for coping with their environment and that many strategies fall within the boundaries of two or more types.[15] Holland uses a hexagon to illustrate the closeness and distance between the six personality types. Exhibit 15–3 (page 552), illustrates Holland's hexagon analysis. He has determined by research that the closer two orientations are in the hexagon arrangement, the more similar are the personality types. Therefore, he claims that the adjacent types, for example, realistic-investigative and social-enterprising, are similar, while nonadjacent types, for example, realistic-social and artistic-conventional, are dissimilar.[16] Using Holland's analysis and logic, one would conclude that if a person's predominant and secondary orientations are similar, he or she will have a relatively easy time selecting a career. On the other hand, dissimilar orientations (predominant and secondary) may result in difficulty choosing a career.

Various quantitative instruments have been used to assess a person's resemblance to the six personality types.[17] The Vocational Preference Inventory asks a person to indicate the vocations that appeal to him or her from a list of 84 occupational titles (14 titles for each of the six scales). The person's responses are scored and profiled. The higher a person's score on a scale, the greater the resemblance to the type that scale represents.

The Strong Vocational Interest Blank has been used to assess a person's resemblance to each personality type by selecting six Strong scales to represent each type. The Vocational Exploration and Insight Kit (VEIK) is used to help individuals who are concerned about their career future. The VEIK requires each person to sort 84 cards to generate a measure of the interest the individual has in an occupation. The individual is then asked a series of questions about how he or she sorted (ranked) the occupations. The person is also asked to indicate what skills he or she possesses. An action plan for seeking additional information about preferred occupations is worked out.

Examining Your Skills

Determining what skills one has is extremely important in making career choices. Holland's work on career choice suggests that simply preferring one career or occupation over another is not enough. A person must have or be able to develop the skills required to perform the job. A person may have an investigative orienta-

EXHIBIT 15-3   Choosing an Occupational Orientation (Holland hexagon)

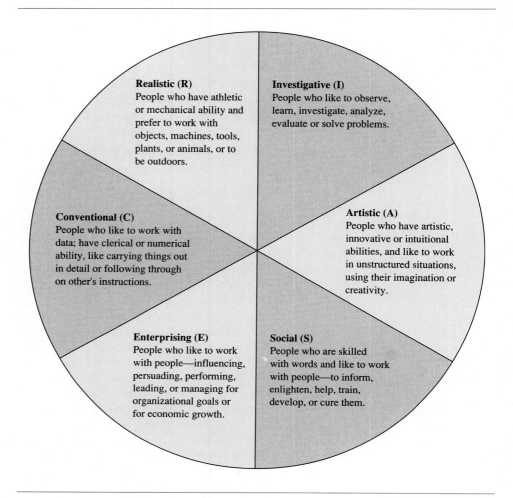

Realistic (R)
People who have athletic or mechanical ability and prefer to work with objects, machines, tools, plants, or animals, or to be outdoors.

Investigative (I)
People who like to observe, learn, investigate, analyze, evaluate or solve problems.

Conventional (C)
People who like to work with data; have clerical or numerical ability, like carrying things out in detail or following through on other's instructions.

Artistic (A)
People who have artistic, innovative or intuitional abilities, and like to work in unstructured situations, using their imagination or creativity.

Enterprising (E)
People who like to work with people—influencing, persuading, performing, leading, or managing for organizational goals or for economic growth.

Social (S)
People who are skilled with words and like to work with people—to inform, enlighten, help, train, develop, or cure them.

Source: Richard Bolles (1979), *The Quick Job Hunting Map* (Berkeley, Calif.: Ten Speed Press), p. 5.

tion, but whether he or she has the skills to be a research scientist, physician, or biologist will play a significant part in which specific occupation is selected.[18]

The *Dictionary of Occupational Titles (DOT)*, published by the U.S. Government Printing Office, provides information on the skills required for over 20,000 jobs. As discussed in Chapter 6, the DOT illustrates skills in three areas — data, people, and things. Exhibit 15–4 presents the three basic skill categories in a hierarchical form. For example, under people skills, taking instruction, helping, and serving is a low-key skill, while mentoring is the highest skill level.

Using the skill categories shown in Exhibit 15–4, identify which skills you enjoy and can use effectively. This self-assessment will initiate some consideration of the skills you possess or think can be developed. Now go back to the Holland hexagon in Exhibit 15–3 and determine where your preferred style is. This is not a scientific assessment, since Holland's Vocational Preference Inventory or VEIK would provide a more precise view.

EXHIBIT 15-4   The Three Basic Skill Categories

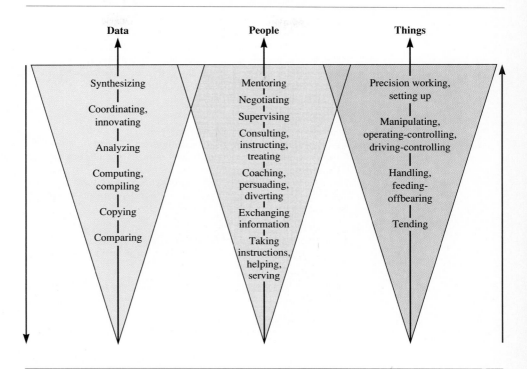

Source: Richard Bolles (1976), *What Color Is Your Parachute?* (Berkeley, Calif.: Ten Speed Press), p. 73.

By weighing your skills and your personality orientation, you are creating a better understanding of career choices and career compatibility. However, this is often not enough to ensure a successful career, and more and more organizations are playing a significant role in helping employees reach their potential. As a result, more HRM resources are being devoted to career development programs.

CAREER DEVELOPMENT: A COMMITMENT

When an organization understands the importance of career development, it typically offers numerous opportunities to employees.[19] These opportunities can involve simply a tuition reimbursement program or a detailed counseling service for developing individual career path plans. An example of the type of career development programs available in various organizations and industries is presented in Exhibit 15–5 (page 554).

The programs presented in Exhibit 15–5 are most valuable when they are: (1) regularly offered, (2) open for all employees, and (3) modified when evaluation indicates that change is necessary. The overall objective of these programs is to match employee needs and goals with current or future career opportunities in the organization. Thus, a well-designed career development effort will assist employees in determining their own career needs, develop and publicize available career opportunities in the organization, and match employee needs and goals with the

EXHIBIT 15-5   Career Development Programs

Career counseling:
    Career counseling during the employment interview
    Career counseling during the performance appraisal session
    Psychological assessment and career alternative planning
    Career counseling as part of the day-to-day supervisor/subordinate relationship
    Special career counseling for high-potential employees
    Counseling for downward transfers

Career pathing:
    Planned job progression for new employees
    Career pathing to help managers acquire the necessary experience for future jobs
    Committee performs an annual review of management personnel's strengths and weaknesses and
    then develops a five-year career plan for each
    Plan job moves for high-potential employees to place them in a particular target job
    Rotate first-level supervisors through various departments to prepare them for upper-management
    positions

Human resources:
    Computerized inventory of backgrounds and skills to help identify replacements
    Succession planning or replacement charts at all levels of management

Career information systems:
    Job posting for all nonofficer positions; individual can bid to be considered
    Job posting for hourly employees and career counseling for salaried employees

Management or supervisory development:
    Special program for those moving from hourly employment to management
    Responsibility of the department head to develop managers
    Management development committee to look after the career development of management groups
    In-house advanced management program

Training:
    In-house supervisory training
    Technical skills training for lower levels
    Outside management seminars
    Formalized job rotation programs
    Intern programs
    Responsibility of manager for on-the-job training
    Tuition reimbursement program

Special groups:
    Outplacement programs
    Minority indoctrination training program
    Career management seminar for women
    Preretirement counseling
    Career counseling and job rotation for women and minorities
    Refresher courses for midcareer managers
    Presupervisory training program for women and minorities

Source: Reprinted, by permission of the publisher, from "Career Development Strategies in Industry: Where Are We and Where Should We Be?" M. A. Morgan, (March–April 1979), *Personnel*, © 1979 by AMACOM, a division of American Management Associations, p. 16. All rights reserved.

organization. This commitment to career development can delay the obsolescence of human resources that is so costly to an organization.

At Owens-Illinois, Inc., for example, a formal career opportunity program is used. It is the firm's policy to promote persons from within the company whenever possible. The career opportunity program provides several services to employees:

1. It makes available a broad range of information about available jobs and the qualifications needed to fill them.
2. It provides a system through which qualified employees may apply for these positions.
3. It helps employees establish career goals.
4. It encourages a meaningful dialogue between employees and supervisors about the employees' career goals.

Exhibit 15–6 presents one of the career opportunity response forms that is completed by employees and managerial personnel. The supervisor who makes the hiring decision explains why he or she made the decision that was reached. No matter who is selected for the job, the form is returned to the employee who submitted it for consideration.

Dow Jones & Company, Inc., publishes *The Wall Street Journal* and *Barron's*. Until a few years ago, the company had no formal career development program for its approximately 4,500 employees. Now, Dow Jones has a formal career development program that employees like Kevin Letz appreciate.[20] Kevin was a night-time delivery driver for *The Wall Street Journal* in Naperville, Illinois. He worked in that capacity for five years while earning college credits during the day. He finally received an M.B.A. and a C.P.A. certificate. He informed his boss that he wanted to enter the firm's new "Druthers" program. It is called this since it suggests that the person would "druther" be working elsewhere in the firm.

Kevin was able to present his educational records and skills as indicators of his interest to move from the position of driver to accountant. He was chosen to fill an accountant position in the firm's South Brunswick, New Jersey, office.

The Druthers program requires that employees show the initiative needed to make a job change. Qualified candidates for openings are interviewed. Their current managers are asked questions about performance, attendance, and potential. In the past few years, 411 interdepartmental druthers requests have been submitted. The company has placed 131 employees in new positions, and another 61 employees are under consideration for appropriate vacancies as they arise.

Three points in the careers of individuals are particularly crucial for career development. The *recent hiree* begins his or her career with a particular job and position. Experiences on this first job can have considerable positive and negative effects on future performance. The *midcareer* person is subject to pressures and responsibilities different from those of the recent hiree, but he or she is also at a critical point. The *preretirement* person is uncertain and anxious about the future. The following sections describe some career development problems of recent hirees, midcareer managers, and preretirement employees.

CAREER DEVELOPMENT FOR RECENT HIREES

Recently hired employees face many anxious moments. They have selected their positions on the basis of expectations regarding the demands that the organization will make of them and what they will receive in exchange for meeting those demands.[21] Young managers, particularly those with college training, expect opportunities to utilize their training in ways that lead to recognition and advancement. In too many instances, recently hired managers are soon disappointed with their initial career decisions. Although the specific causes of early career disappointments vary from person to person, some general causes have been identified.

EXHIBIT 15-6   Career Opportunity Response Form — Owens-Illinois

Form 5287-R6

Owens-Illinois Career Opportunity Program Response Form

Section 1

Name	Soc. Sec. No.		Home Phone	O4 Ext.	O4 Mail Location
Present Job Title	Div.	Department			☐ Hourly ☐ Salary
Present Supervisor		Supervisor's Signature			
Is your supervisor aware that you have responded to this Career Opportunity Program? ☐ Yes ☐ No				Number of months on current position	

Job You Are Responding to

Job Title	Div.	Department	Rate Group/Points	Location
Divisional Personnel Coordinator	Posting Dates	HRS Requisition No.	Date Form Completed	

To Apply

1. Compare your experience, education, and skills against the selection criteria stated on the posting

2. Complete Sections 1 and 2 of this form and the Career Summary Form and forward to
   Career Opportunity Program - 2, OIB, Human Resource Systems

3. Please do not keep any pages of this form. A copy of this form will be returned to you by the Divisional Personnel Coordinator.

* **Supervisor Approval**

4. Your supervisor must approve your responding to a job under the following policies.

   • Non-exempt and hourly -
     ıf you have been on the job less than 12 months.

   • Exempt through 129 points -
     if you have been on the job less than 18 months.

   • Greater than 130 points -
     if you have been on the job less than 24 months.

   • All personnel responding -
     before you may receive an interview

Human Resource Use Only

Date Received

(White and Canary copies - Return to Employee, Pink copy - Retained by Division)

EXHIBIT 15-6 *(concluded)*

Form 5287-R6

Owens-Illinois Career Opportunity Program Response Form

Section 1

Name	Soc. Sec. No.		Home Phone	O4 Ext.	O4 Mail Location
Present Job Title	Div.	Department			☐ Hourly ☐ Salary
Present Supervisor		Supervisor's Signature			
Is your supervisor aware that you have responded to this Career Opportunity Program? ☐ Yes ☐ No				Number of months on current position	

Job You Are Responding to

Job Title	Div.	Department	Rate Group/Points	Location
Divisional Personnel Coordinator	Posting Dates	HRS Requisition No.	Date Form Completed	

Section 2

Candidate
State how your qualifications meet posted criteria

Section 3

Divisional Personnel Director
1. Review all responses.   2. Turn down, interview or forward files to Selecting Supervisor.
3. If turned down, state reason why candidate is not being considered further and return Response Form and Career Summary Form to candidate.

Section 4

Selecting Supervisor
1. Review all responses
2. If no further consideration is given, indicate reason why and return Response Form and Career Summary Form to Division Personnel Coordinator.
3. If you wish to interview, schedule interviews through your Division Personnel Coordinator.
4. If candidate is not offered position after the interview, state reason and return Response and Career Summary Forms to Div. Personnel Coordinator.

Date	Signed

Section 5

Divisional Personnel Director
1. Complete Referral Summary Form indicating status of candidates and return form to HR Systems.
2. Return Resource and Career Summary Forms to candidate.

Date	Signed

(White and Canary copies - Return to Employee, Pink copy - Retained by Division)

Causes of Early Career Difficulties

Studies of the early career problems of young managers typically find that those who experience frustration are victims of "reality shock." These young managers perceive a mismatch between what they thought the organization was and what it actually is. Several factors contribute to reality shock, and it is important for young managers and their managers to be aware of them.

The Initial Job Challenge

The first jobs of young managers often demand far less of them than they are capable of delivering. Consequently, young managers believe that they are unable to demonstrate their full capabilities and that, in a sense, they are being stifled. This particular cause is especially damaging if the recruiter has been overly enthusiastic in "selling" the organization to the managers when they were recruited.

Some young managers are able to *create* challenging jobs even when their assignments are fairly routine. They do this by thinking of ways to do their jobs differently and better. They may also be able to persuade their managers to give them more leeway and more to do. Unfortunately, many young managers are unable to create challenge. Their previous experiences in school were typically experiences in which challenge had been given to them by their teachers. The challenge had been created for them, not by them.

Initial Job Satisfaction

Recently hired managers with college training often believe they can perform at levels beyond those of their initial assignments. After all, they have been exposed to the latest managerial theories and techniques, and in their minds, at least, they are ready to run the company. Disappointment and dissatisfaction are the sure outcomes, however, when they discover that their self-evaluations are not shared by others in the organization. The consequences of unrealistic aspirations and routine initial assignments are low job satisfaction, in particular, and low satisfaction of growth and self-actualization needs, in general.

Initial Job Performance Evaluation

Feedback on performance is an important managerial responsibility. Yet many managers are inadequately trained to meet this responsibility. They simply do not know how to evaluate the performance of their subordinates. This management deficiency is especially damaging to new managers. They have not been in the organization long enough to be socialized by their peers and other employees. They are not yet sure of what they are expected to believe, what values to hold, or what behaviors are expected of them. They naturally look to their own managers to guide them through this early phase. But when their managers fail to evaluate their performance accurately, they remain ignorant and confused as to whether they are achieving what the organization expects of them.

Not all young managers experience problems associated with their initial assignments. But those who do and who leave the organization as a consequence of their frustrations represent a waste of talent and money. One estimate placed the cost of replacing a manager (including recruiting costs, training expenses, and subpar performance during the early phases) at $50,000 in the first year alone.[22] Thus, the cost of losing capable young managers outweighs the cost of efforts and programs designed to counteract initial job problems.

Programs and Practices to Counteract Early Career Problems

Managers who wish to improve the retention and development of young management talent have several alternatives.

Realistic Job Previews

One way to counteract the unrealistic expectations of new recruits is to provide realistic information during the recruiting process. As was discussed in Chapter 7, this practice is based on the idea that a recruit should know both the bad and the good things to expect from a job and the organization. Through realistic job previews (RJPs), recruits are given opportunities to learn not only the benefits that they may expect, but also the drawbacks. Studies have shown that the recruitment rate is the same for those who receive RJPs as for those who do not.[23] More importantly, those who receive RJPs are more likely to remain on the job and to be satisfied with it than are those who have been selected without using RJPs. The practice of "telling it like it is" is used by a number of organizations, including the Prudential Insurance Company, Texas Instruments, and the U.S. Military Academy.

A Challenging Initial Assignment

Managers of newly hired people should be encouraged to slot them into the most demanding of the available jobs. Successful implementation of this policy requires managers to take some risks, because managers are accountable for the performance of their subordinates. If the assignments are too far beyond the ability of the subordinates, both the managers and the subordinates share the cost of failure. Thus, most managers prefer to bring their subordinates along slowly by giving them progressively more difficult and challenging jobs, but only *after the subordinates have demonstrated their ability*. Newly hired managers have *potential for performance*, but have not *demonstrated performance*. Thus, it is risky to assign an individual to a task for which there is a high probability of failure. But studies have indicated that managers who experienced initial job challenge were more effective in their later years.[24]

An Enriched Initial Assignment

Job enrichment is an established practice for motivating employees with strong growth and achievement needs. If the nature of the job to be assigned is not intrinsically challenging, the newly hired manager's superior can enrich the assignment. The usual ways to enrich a job include giving the new manager more authority and responsibility, permitting the new manager to interact directly with customers and clients, and enabling the new manager to implement his or her own ideas (rather than merely recommending them to the boss).

Demanding Bosses

A practice that seems to have considerable promise for increasing the retention rate of young managers is to assign them initially to demanding supervisors. In this context, *demanding* should not be interpreted as "autocratic." Rather, the type of boss most likely to get new hires off in the right direction is one who has high but achievable expectations for their performance. Such a boss instills in the young managers the understanding that high performance is expected and rewarded and, equally important, that the boss is always ready to assist them through coaching and counseling.

The programs and practices that are intended to retain and develop young managers — particularly recent hires with college training — can be used separately or in combination. In all cases, a manager should seek to establish policies that would retain those recent hirees who have the highest potential to perform effectively. Although such practices are not perfect, they are helpful not only in retaining young managers, but also in avoiding the problems that can arise during the middle phase of a manager's career.

CAREER DEVELOPMENT FOR MIDCAREER MANAGERS

Managers in the midstages of their careers are ordinarily key people in their organizations. They have established a place for themselves in society, as well as at work. They occupy important positions in the community, often engage in civic affairs, and are looked upon as model achievers in our achievement-oriented culture. Yet popular and scholarly articles and books appear yearly that discuss the "midcareer ciris," "middle-aged dropout," and "midlife transition." These kinds of pressures cause executives to disappear from their jobs, drink heavily, or, at worst, drop out totally. A person at midcareer is attempting to deal with the job, bodily decline, the realization of mortality, and aging. Such lost talent is expensive to replace, and more and more organizations are initiating practices to deal with the problems of the midcareer manager.

One important approach used to develop midcareer managers is training.[25] Making available training to improve skills, improve knowledge, and help employees grow intellectually sends a signal to the trainees that they are valued. The mere fact that the company shows an interest introduces the Hawthorne effect. It is a signal that the trainees are needed, valued, and still attractive to the firm. It is especially important at the midcareer juncture to receive signals from the organization.

The Midcareer Plateau

Managers face the **midcareer plateau** during the adult stage of life and the maintenance phase of careers. At this point, the likelihood of additional upward promotion is usually quite low. Two reasons account for the plateau. First, there are simply fewer jobs at the top of the organization, and even though the manager has the ability to perform at that level, no opening exists. Second, openings may exist, but the manager may lack either the *ability* or the *desire* to fill them.[26]

Managers who find themselves stifled in their present jobs tend to cope with the problems in fairly consistent ways. They suffer from depression, poor health, and fear and hostility toward their subordinates. Eventually, they "retire" on the job or leave the organization physically and permanently. Any one of these ways of coping results in lowered job performance and, of course, lowered organizational performance.[27]

The midcareer, middle-age crisis has been depicted in novels, movies, dramas, and psychological studies. Although each individual's story is different and unique, the scenario has many common features. Each story and research indicates that the midcareer crisis is real and has psychological and often physical effects that can become dangerous if not properly handled. Jim Lucio, for example, has insomnia, loss of appetite, and is on edge because of his midcareer crisis.

Of course, not all managers respond to their situations in the same ways. Some, perhaps most, cope constructively. A few examples of some inidividuals who coped effectively are the following:

- John W. Culligan, 70, currently chairperson of the executive committee at American Home Products, was 64 and had been a fixture in the company for 42 years, when he was promoted.
- Thomas S. Derek retired from a 30-year career as a life insurance agent and decided to start the Ugly Duckling Rent-A-Car agency in Tucson. Today, he is 74 and owns a business that has 600 outlets and gross annual rentals of $84.5 million.
- Joyce Fox got her first job at 41 and is now a senior vice president in charge of international loans at American Express Bank.

There are many other stories of individuals who just play along and seem to be plateaued or never recognized.[28] However, some event or person triggers a series of changes and opportunities. John Culligan waited patiently after reaching a plateau; Thomas Derek changed careers; Joyce Fox decided that her age was not a detriment and entered the labor force exuding confidence, wisdom, and maturity. Each of these individuals used their own tailor-made career plateau–coping strategy.

Programs and Practices to Counteract Midcareer Problems

Counteracting the problems that managers face at midcareer involves providing *counseling* and *alternatives*.

Midcareer Counseling
Organizations such as Du Pont, Alcoa, and Western Electric employ full-time staff psychiatrists to assist employees in dealing with career, health, and family problems.[29] In the context of such counseling, midcareer managers are provided with professional help in dealing with the depression and stress they may experience. Since midcareer managers are usually well-educated and articulate, they often only need someone to talk to, someone skilled in the art of listening. The process of verbalizing their problems to an objective listener is often enough to enable midcareer managers to recognize their problems and to cope with them constructively.

Midcareer Alternatives
Effective resolution of the problems of midcareer crises requires the existence of acceptable alternatives. The organization cannot be expected to go beyond counseling on personal and family problems. But when the crisis is precipitated primarily by career-related factors, the organization can be an important source of alternatives. In many instances, the organization simply needs to accept career moves that are usually viewed as unacceptable. Three career moves that have potential for counteracting the problems of midcareer managers are lateral transfers, downward transfers, and fallback positions.[30]

Lateral transfers involve moves at the same organizational level from one department to another. A manager who has plateaued in production could be transferred to a similar level in sales, engineering, or some other area. The move would require the manager to learn quickly the technical demands of the new position, and there would be a period of reduced performance as this learning occurred. But, once qualified, the manager would bring the perspectives of both areas to bear on decisions.

Downward transfers are associated with failure in our society; an effective manager simply does not consider a move downward to be a respectable alternative. Yet downward transfers are, in many instances, not only respectable alternatives, but entirely acceptable alternatives, particularly when one or more of the following conditions exist:

The manager values the quality of life afforded by a specific geographic area and may desire a downward transfer if required in order to stay in or move to that area.

The manager views the downard transfer as a way to establish a base for future promotions.

The manager is faced with the alternative of dismissal or a downward move.

The manager desires to pursue autonomy and self-actualization in nonjob-related activities — such as religious, civic, or policital activities — and for that reason may welcome the reduced responsibility (and demands) of a lower-level position.

The use of *fallback positions* is a relatively new way to reduce the risk of lateral and downward transfers. The practice involves identifying in advance a position to which the transferred manager can return if the new position does not work out. By identifying the fallback position in advance, the organization informs everyone who is affected that some risk is involved but that the organization is willing to accept some of the responsibility for it and that returning to the fallback job will not be viewed as "failure." Companies such as Heublein, Procter & Gamble, Continental Can, and Lehman Brothers have used fallback positions to remove some of the risk of lateral and upward moves. The practice apppears to have considerable promise for protecting the careers of highly specialized technicians and professionals who make their first move into general management positions.

The suggestion that organizations initiate practices and programs to assist managers through midcareer crises does not excuse managers from taking responsibility for themselves. Individuals who deal honestly and constructively with their lives and careers will early on take steps to minimize the risk of becoming *obsolete* or redundant. At the outset of their management careers, they can begin to formulate their *career plans and paths*. Often, they will be assisted in this process by the organization that employs them.

CAREER DEVELOPMENT FOR PRERETIREMENT

Even with laws protecting against age discimination, do people still want to retire at an earlier age than 70? What is the organization's responsibility in preparing employees for retirement? Will dissatisfied workers and those with good pension plans retire early?

Too many organizations are ill-prepared to deal with the effects of the legislation, have few programs that cope with the preretirement employee, and are unable to answer the questions raised above.[31] Management needs to consider in much more depth the following issues:

- When do employees plan to retire?
- Who is attracted to early retirement?
- What do employees plan to do during retirement? Can the organization help them prepare for these activities?
- Do retirees plan a second career? Can the organization assist in this preparation?
- Which retirees can still be consulted by the organization to help new employees?

Programs and Practices to Minimize Retirement Adjustment Problems

These and other similar questions can be addressed through counseling and education programs for preretirees. Retirement is feared by some and anticipated by others. Counseling and education programs can make the transition from being employed to retirement much smoother.

In most cases, the retired person must learn to accept a reduced role, to manage a less-structured life, and to make new accommodations to family and community. Educational workshops and seminars and counseling sessions are invaluable for the preretirement person to make the transition from work to retirement. These activities can be initiated by HR departments.

IBM is one organization that has attempted to aid in this transition by offering tuition rebates for courses on any topic within three years of retirement. Many IBM preretirees have taken advantage of this program to prepare for second careers (learning new skills, professions, and small business management).[32]

Those HR departments that are truly dedicated to the development of human resources will become more involved with the preretiree's problems, fears, and uncertainties in the 1990s. Perhaps a new measure of concern for human resources will be the degree of organizational commitment in the form of preretirement preparation for those who have devoted themselves to their careers.

CAREER PLANNING AND PATHING

Many of us sit and think about where we will be in 10 years careerwise. We also wonder how we are going to get there. This is a form of career thinking that can be brought into sharper focus by career planning.[33] Individuals and organizations are beginning to learn how important career planning is from a motivational perspective.

The practice of organizational *career planning* involves matching an individual's career aspirations with the opportunities available in an organization. **Career pathing** is the sequencing of the specific jobs that are associated with those opportunities. The two processes are intertwined. Planning a career involves the identification of the means for achieving desired ends; and in the context of career plans, career paths are the means for achieving goals. Although career planning is not entirely new — as early as 1920, General Electric and Western Electric has such programs — many organizations are just now beginning to use it as a way to proact rather than react to the problems associated with early career and midcareer crises.[34]

The career planning and career pathing process is depicted in Exhibit 15–7. Its successful employment places equal responsibility on the individual and the organization. The individual must identify his or her aspirations and abilities and, through counseling, recognize what training and development are required for a particular career path. The organization must identify its needs and opportunities and, through work-force planning, provide the necessary career information and training to its employees. Such companies as Weyerhaeuser, Nabisco, Gulf Oil, Exxon, and Eaton use career development programs to identify a broad pool of talent available for promotion and transfer opportunities. Companies often restrict career counseling to managerial and professional staff, but IBM, GE, and TRW provide career counseling for both blue-collar and managerial personnel.

Human resource information systems (HRIS) are becoming more prominent in career planning and pathing decision making. The HRIS is used to collect, store,

---

EXHIBIT 15-7   A Career Planning Process

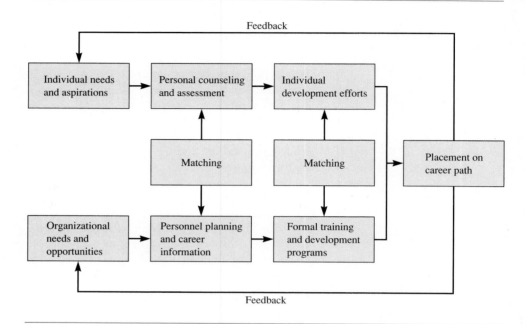

Source: Based on John C. Alpin and Darlene K. Gerster (March-April 1978), "Career Development: An Integration of Individual and Organizational Needs," *Personnel*, p. 25.

analyze, and report information on employees, their jobs, and personnel costs. Various databases are linked to provide a description of the type of information shown in Exhibit 15–7. In other words, what are the:

- Organization's needs?
- Individual's skills and experience?
- Training and development requirements?

Matching the data (organizational and individual) provides output to line managers, HR specialists, and others requesting information. Mainframes and microcomputers are capable of providing HRIS data to help make career decisions.

A microcomputer-based HRIS provides information on age, gender, position, experience, performance appraisal, and compensation,[35] as well as statistical presentations of what employees cost and whether compliance with affirmative action is adhered to when a person is placed in a particular career path.

The career database can be continually updated when an HRIS is available. For example, suppose Mary is sent to an executive development program in June and her last performance appraisal in August indicated that she was ready to take on more job responsibility. Mary has also asked her supervisor for more challenging work. The computerized output report could reflect the most recent changes in Mary's job skills, training program attendant, and expressed needs.

IBM is a firm that uses an HRIS to closely examine its needs for future human resources and the internal talent availabale to fulfill these future needs. IBM attempts to integrate employees' career needs and goals with its own needs and goals. The firm works to provide the individual employee with the kind of career path opportunities that will be individually rewarding. In situations where there is growth and expansion of jobs, matching individual and organizational needs and goals is possible. However, in downsizing or poor growth situations, the matching, even with an accurate HRIS, becomes difficult.

Career Planning

Individual and organizational needs and opportunities can be matched in a variety of ways. According to an American Management Association (AMA) survey, the most widely used approaches are (1) informal counseling by the personnel staff and (2) career counseling by supervisors. These approaches are often quite informal. Somewhat more formal and less widely, although increasingly, used practices involve workshops, seminars, and self-assessment centers.

Informal Counseling   The HR staffs of organizations often include counseling services for employees who wish to assess their abilities and interests. The counseling process can also move into personal concerns; and this is proper, since, as we have already seen, life concerns are important factors in determining career aspirations. In this context, career counseling is viewed by the organization as a service to its employees, but not as a primary service.

Career counseling by supervisors is usually included in performance evaluations. The question of where the employee is going in the organization arises quite naturally in this setting. In fact, the inclusion of career information in performance appraisal has created the current interest in career planning. A characteristic of effective performance evaluation is to let the employee know now only how well he or she has done, but also what the future holds. Thus, supervisors must be able to counsel the employee in terms of organizational needs and opportunities not only within the specific department, but throughout the organization. Since supervisors usually have limited information about the total organization, it is often necessary to adopt more formal and systematic counseling approaches.

Formal Counseling   Workshops, assessment centers, and career development centers are being used increasingly in organizations. Typically, such formal practices are designed to serve specific employee groups. Management trainees and "high-potential" or "fast-track" management candidates have received most of the attention to date. However, women employees and minority employees have been given increased attention. Career development programs for women and minority employees are viewed as indications of an organization's commitment to affirmative action.

One example of a formal organizational career planning system is Syntex Corporation's Career Development Center. The center was the result of the realization that the managers in Syntex were unable to counsel their subordinates because they (the managers) were too caught up in their own jobs. The center's staff first identifies the individual's strengths and weaknesses in eight skill areas that Syntex believes to be related to effective management. These eight areas are: (1) problem analysis; (2) communication; (3) goal setting; (4) decision making and conflict handling; (5) selecting, training, and motivating employees; (6) controlling employees; (7) interpersonal competence; and (8) the use of time. On the basis of scores in the eight areas, each manager sets career and personal goals. The center's staff assists the manager to set realistic goals that reflect his or her strengths and weaknesses in the eight areas.

The highlight of each manager's career planning effort is attendance at a week-long seminar. Usually attended by 24 managers at a time, the seminar places each participant in simulated management situations that require applications of the eight skill areas. Subsequently, each candidate reviews his or her own career plan, a plan that includes career goals, timetables, and required personal development. The purpose of the seminar is to encourage realistic self-appraisal. Following the seminar, participants meet with their immediate supervisors to set up their career development plans.

Organizations can use a variety of practices to facilitate their employees' career plans. One of the oldest and most widely used practices is some form of *tuition aid program*. Employees can take advantage of educational and training opportunities available at nearby schools, and the organization pays some or all of the tuition. J. I. Case, a Tenneco company with corporate offices in Racine, Wisconsin, is but one of many organizations that provide in-house courses and seminars as well as tuition reimbursement for courses related to the individual's job.

Another practice is *job posting;* that is, the organization publicizes job openings as they occur. The employees are thus made aware of the opportunities. Effective job posting requires more than simply placing a notice on the company bulletin board. At a minimum, job posting should meet the following conditions:

1. It should include promotions and transfers, as well as permanent vacancies.
2. The available jobs should be posted at least three to six weeks prior to external recruiting.
3. The eligibility rules should be explicit and straightforward.
4. The standards for selection and the bidding instructions should be stated clearly.
5. Vacationing employees should be given the opportunity to apply ahead of time.
6. Employees who apply but are rejected should be notified of the reason in writing, and a record of the reason should be placed in their personnel files.

Whatever approach is used, the crucial measure of its success will be the extent to which individual and organizational needs are satisfied.

Career Pathing

The result of career planning is the placement of an individual into a job that is the first of a sequential series of jobs. From the perspective of the organization, career paths are important inputs into work-force planning. An organization's future work force depends on the projected passage of individuals through the ranks. From the perspective of the individual, a career path is the sequence of jobs that he or she desires to undertake in order to achieve personal and career goals. Although it is virtually impossible to completely integrate the organizational and individual needs in the design of career paths, systematic career planning has the potential for closing the gap between the needs of the individual and the needs of the organization.[36]

Traditional career paths have emphasized upward mobility in a single occupation or functional area. When recruiting personnel, the organization's representative will speak of engineers', accountants', or salespersons' career paths. In these contexts, the recruiter will describe the different jobs that typical individuals will hold as they work progressively upward in an organization. Each job, or "rung," is reached when the individual has accumulated the necessary experience and ability and has demonstrated that he or she is ready for promotion. Implicit in such career paths is the attitude that failure has occurred whenever an individual does not move on up after a certain amount of time has elapsed. Such attitudes make it difficult to use lateral and downward transfers as alternatives for managers who no longer wish to pay the price of upward promotion.

An alternative to traditional career pathing is to base career paths on real-world experiences and individualized preferences. Paths of this kind would have several characteristics:

1. They would include lateral and downward possibilities, as well as upward possibilities, and they would not be tied to "normal" rates of progress.
2. They would be tentative and responsive to changes in organizational needs.
3. They would be flexible enough to take into account the qualities of individuals.
4. Each job along the paths would be specified in terms of *acquirable* skills, knowledge, and other specific attributes, not merely in terms of educational credentials, age, or work experience.[37]

Realistic career paths, rather than traditional ones, are necessary for effective employee counseling. In the absence of such information, the employee can only guess at what is available.

An example of a career path for general management in a telephone company is depicted in Exhibit 15–8. According to the path, the average duration of a manager's assignment in first-level management is four years—2½ years as a staff assistant in the home office and 1½ years as the manager of a district office in a small

---

EXHIBIT 15-8   Career Path for General Management in a Telephone Company

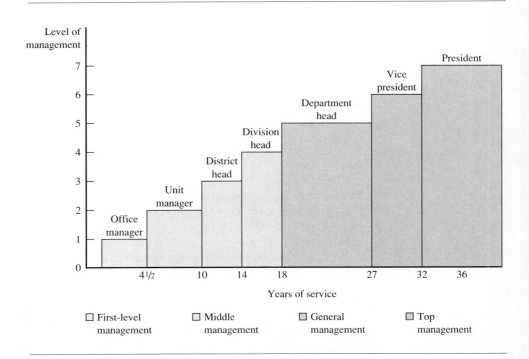

city. By the 14th year, the average manager should have reached the fourth level of management. The assignment at this level might be that of division manager of commerical sales and operations division. Obviously, not all managers reach the fifth level, much less the seventh (president). As one nears the top of the organization, the number of openings declines and the number of candidates increases.

CAREER DEVELOPMENT PROBLEMS AND ISSUES

Organizations that undertake career development programs are certain to encounter some difficult issues along the way.[38] The following problems are based on the actual experiences of some organizations.

Integrating Career Development and Work-Force Planning

The relationship between career development and work-force planning is obvious. Career development provides a *supply* of talents and abilities; work-force planning projects the *demand* for talents and abilities. It would seem that organizations that undertake one of these activities would undertake the other. Surely it makes little sense to develop people and then have no place to put them; or to project needs for people, but have no program to supply them. In fact, some organizations do have one or the other but not both.

Even companies that make use of both career development programs and work-force planning have difficulty in integrating the efforts of the two. One reason is that each is done by different specialists. Career development is often done by psychologists, and work-force planning is the job of economists and systems analysts. Practitioners of these two disciplines have difficulty in communicating with each other. Their training and backgrounds create promotional barriers to effective communication.

A second reason for failure to integrate the efforts of career development and work-force planning is related to the *organizational structure*. Career development is usually the function of *personnel departments*. Work-force planning is the function of *planning staffs*. The two activities are carried out in two organizationally distinct units. The manager who is responsible for both units may be the chief executive officer or a group executive.

Managing Dual Careers

As more and more women enter the working world and pursue careers, managers will increasingly confront the problems of **dual careers.** The problem arises because the careers of husbands and wives may lead them in different directions. There may be problems because each person works different shifts, one at night and one during the day.[39] There are a growing number of dual-career couples working on the same job as police officers, fire fighters, professors, accountants, lawyers, machinists, and even managers.[40]

A more obvious problem can arise when the organization offers the husband or wife a transfer (involving a promotion) but it is rejected because the required relocation is incompatible with the spouse's career plans. One study reports that one in three executives cannot, or will not, relocate because this would interfere with the career of the spouse.[41] Thus, organizations *and* individuals lose flexibility as a consequence of dual careers.

PROFESSIONAL PROFILE

Biography

Jan T. Gillespie is vice president of human resources for Randall's Food Markets, Inc., of Houston, Texas. Jan graduated from the University of Georgia with a B.B.A. Degree in business management. Jan started in the supermarket industry at the age of 14 as a part-time sacker. During his high school and college years, he worked in various capacities in retail store operations. After graduating from college, he spent three years on active duty in the U.S. Navy as a person-nelman. Upon discharge from the Navy, he returned to the supermarket chain he had previously worked for as assistant director of store operations. From this position, he progressed to director of store operations with the responsibility for 120 store locations. In January of 1982, he became the director of human resources and progressed to the position of vice president of human resources and a member of the board of directors of this billion-dollar corporation. For a short period of time, he worked for a contingency recruiting firm in the southeast before joining Randall's Food Markets in September of 1987 in the position of director of human resources. In January of 1989, he was promoted to the position of vice president of human resources.

Job Description   As vice president of human resources, Jan is responsible for the employee relations of the organization. This entails handling numerous matters regarding consultations with employees to ensure open lines of communication and job satisfaction. He is also responsible for the very important task of maintaining accurate and complete personnel records for 10,500 employees. He is also responsible for the training of all employees, which includes programs for all entry-level employees as well as extensive management development programs for the exempt staff members of the organization.

As is the case in all successful human resource departments, Jan is fortunate to be supported by a strong and experienced human resource staff. This consists of an assistant personnel manager, manager of employee training, manager of employee records, and

Jan T. Gillespie
Randall's Food Markets, Inc.

an employment specialist. Along with this exempt staff, Randall's human resource department has exempt positions of audio visual specialist, four district trainers, and various nonexempt support staff.

Open-Door Policy: A Viewpoint   Jan believes there is no question that the greatest resource Randall's has as a corporation is its employees. Randall's is fortunate to have beautiful facilities and a commitment to excellence, which is fostered by Randall's executives, but it is the individual employees that make the success of Randall's. At Randall's, employees like to say they are "a member of the Randall's family."

To ensure this feeling of being a part of the Randall's family or a part of the Randall's team, Jan feels it is critical that Randall's or any other organization have a true open-door policy. At Randall's, the open-door policy basically means that, if an employee has a problem or concern, they should feel comfortable talking with any member of management to obtain the feeling of satisfaction that they are seeking. Employees are always encouraged to follow the normal chain of command in talking with their immediate supervisor, but, if at any time this communication process breaks down, the employee is encouraged to go to the next superior of that individual to resolve their problem or concern.

Randall's trains and coaches its managers to realize that at times employees may want to talk with some-
(continued on next page)

PROFESSIONAL PROFILE
(concluded)

one else and that no manager should feel hurt if this happens. Maybe they should evaluate their rapport with that employee so that the next time the employee has a concern they will feel more comfortable coming to them instead of the other individual.

An interesting part of Randall's open-door policy is a program called "Open Line." Posted in each store in the employee break room area is a small bulletin board with a supply of Open Line forms. These forms are a means whereby an employee can write, on a confidential basis, about a concern, problem, or sometimes a suggestion they may have for improving the company. These forms require no postage, and go to the "director of Open Line" who is Jan Gillespie, the vice president of human resources.

Jan reads each of these open lines and personally follows up to ensure that either himself or a member of management handles their concerns. There are times when an employee's concern cannot be resolved in the manner they are requesting, but they are given the professional courtesy of a personal response with the end result being that they know they are appreci-

ated and that the communication lines are always open.

An additional program Randall's human resource department is involved in to ensure that Randall's open-door policy is working is a program called "Employee Circle." This program is a very simple process whereby employees are selected at random from one particular store location or support facility. This group of employees, which usually consists of 15 to 20 people, are invited to attend an "employee circle" where Jan Gillespie and a member of his staff have a very open discussion with these employees. There are no members of direct line supervision at this meeting, so the employees can feel free to talk and discuss anything that is on their minds.

They are asked to bring forward any suggestions they have on improving their department, individual location, or any other areas of the Randall's organization. Their comments are extremely confidential. Only the items that are a consensus of the group are written on a flip chart and sent to the appropriate members of management.

The issue of paternity leaves has dual-career overtones. Cray Research, Inc., offers family leave for fathers who want to take time off after their new baby is born.[42] Many of these eligible males have wives that work. However, how many of the 4,000 eligible Cary employees have taken paternity leave in the past year? No more than four. The notion of taking six months off is assumed to be fatal to a person's career. Peer pressure helps perpetuate the belief that paternity leaves unfairly burden co-workers with extra assignments.

At Campbell Soup Co.'s headquarters in Camden, New Jersey, not a single employee has taken paternity leave in the three years since the firm began offering a three-month unpaid benefit. Dow Jones & Co. has offered a six-month unpaid leave for three years. But only 10 men have taken the leave. Some couples have adopted a compromise on paternity leave by having the husband work at home while the wife recovers. Again, compromises or not taking the leave are the rule because of assumed career consequences.

At present, more than 53 million employed men and women are two-career couples. There is no reason to believe that the number will decrease with time; in fact, the reasonable assumption to make is that both the number and the proportion of dual-career couples will increase.[43] The problems associated with this phenomenon are relatively new, but those who have studied these problems offer the following advice:

1. An organization should conduct an employee survey that gathers statistics and information regarding the incidence of dual careers in its *present* and *projected* work force. The survey should determine (*a*) how many employees are at present part of a two-career situation, (*b*) how many people interviewed for positions are part of a dual-career situation, (*c*) where and at what level in the organization the dual-career employees are, (*d*) what conflicts these employees now have, and (*e*) whether dual-career employees perceive company policy and practices to be helpful to their careers and careers of their spouses.

2. Recruiters should devise methods that present realistic previews of what the company offers dual-career couples. Orientation sessions conducted by HR departments should include information that helps such couples identifiy potential problems.

3. Career development and transfer policies must be revised. Since the usual policies are based on the traditional one-career family, they are inapplicable to dual-career situations. The key is to provide more flexibility.

4. The company should consider providing career couples with special assistance in career management. Couples are typically ill-prepared to cope with the problems posed by two careers. When wives earn more than their husbands, marriages often face strain and the need for adjustments.[44]

5. The organization can establish cooperative arrangements with other organizations. When one organization desires to relocate one dual-career partner, cooperative organizations can be sources of employment for the other partner.[45]

6. The most important immediate step is to establish flexible working hours. Allowing couples the privilege of arranging their work schedules so that these will be compatible with family demands is an effective way to meet some of the problems of managing dual-career couples.[46]

It would be a mistake to believe that dual-career problems exist only for managerial and professional personnel. Nonmanagerial personnel are also members of dual-career families. Managers will confront problems in scheduling overtime for these people and in transferring them to different shifts.

General Electric has set up a network with other firms to share information about job opportunities for dual-career couples. At Economics Laboratory, Inc., in St. Paul, companies in the area are advised of the availability of the spouses of relocated employees.[47]

Middle-Aged Women Looking for a Career

After 20 years of raising children, being a good wife, and doing her bit for the community, 43-year-old Ruth Sugerman, of Lawrenceville, New Jersey, wanted a job. But those 20 years had left a big gap in her résumé. To help fill the void, she became an intern. The intern program is run by Creative Alternatives for Women.[48]

The program Ruth joined offers women a chance to develop confidence in their abilities to succeed in business by involving them in courses, workshops, and seminars designed to help women identify their work interests.

After completing the classroom work, the women receive the internships. They are salaried and usually work for three to six months. The jobs include market research, public relations, data processing, and banking.

Ruth Sugerman interned with Educational Testing Service, Inc., as a researcher. Now she is a full-time senior research assistant on the same project. The career reentry program restored Ruth's confidence and permitted her to retool while being paid. This, however, is a point of contention. Some HR experts believe that interns shouldn't be paid since they are hired as unknown quantities. What do you think? Should interns, men or women, be paid?

The Japanese society still believes that women are not better off having careers.[49] Although the Japanese government passed an equal opportunity law for women in 1986, the majority of Japanese believe that the middle-aged women shouldn't be working full-time. Adequate care of the family can't be accomplished if a person has a career. This feeling certainly doesn't apply to a majority of Americans. U.S. society has changed with regard to women in the work force in general and having middle-aged women returning to the workforce after raising children. It is not likely that the Japanese view about careers for women will become the dominant viewpoint in the United States.

Dealing with EEO Problems

The initial thrust of affirmative action programs is to recruit and place women and minority employees into managerial and professional positions. Many organizations have been successful in that effort, but their success has created additional problems. For example, the career development needs of women and minority employees require nontraditional methods.

A study by Van Glinow and Morrison provides some disappointing data about women and minority advancement to executive-level positions. They found that:

- In *Fortune* 500 corporations, only 3.6 percent of board directorships and 1.7 percent of corporate officerships are held by women.
- In the federal government, only 2 percent of the jobs with grade G.S.1 and above were filled by women.
- Only one black headed a *Fortune* 1000 company.[50]

They suggest that a **glass ceiling** blocking upward career advancement is still a reality. The researchers suggest that there are still people who believe that women and minorities do not have the abilities, style, or background to be effective managers. This reluctance to admit that some women and minorities do have managerial abilities is discouraging. Thus, women and minorities feeling resistance, in many cases, decide to leave the corporate work force. This results in an unfortunate drain of needed corporate and managerial talent.

There is a limited amount of information about minority participation in major corporations. In a 1985 survey of 1,362 senior executives in *Fortune* 1000 companies, there were 4 blacks, 6 Asians, 3 Hispanics, and 29 women. This survey data suggests that women and minorities hold few of the top-level, decision-making positions in America's largest companies.[51]

In the midst of EEO and affirmative action concerns, the employees most likely to feel threatened are white males of average competence. Above-average white males will usually progress; below-average performers will always lag behind. The threat is most keenly felt when the economy slows down and what few promotions are available go to women and minority employees. White males are not much comforted to be told that such practices are temporary and are intended to correct past injustices. So what can managers do to help?

No company practice can guarantee that average-performing white male employees will go along with affirmative action programs. But some practices offer promise. First, the company should provide open and complete information about promotions. Instead of being secretive about promotions (in the hope that if white males aren't told they are being passed over for promotion, they won't notice it), the organization should provide information that permits white males to see precisely where they stand. If given such information, they will be less likely to overestimate their relative disadvantage and will be able to assess their position in the organization more accurately.

A second practice that seems promising is to make sure that white males receive as much career development assistance as other groups. White males may also need information about occupational opportunities *outside the company*. Since their upward mobility may be temporarily stifled by the company's affirmative action efforts, the average white male should be given the opportunity to seek career mobility elsewhere. In summary, the management that is sincerely pursuing affirmative action through career development must not expect all employees to go along with and support the effort. Vested interests are at stake when one group progresses at the expense of another.

Job Layoffs and Loss

Business and farm bankruptcies, layoffs in manufacturing and service industries, permanent closing of obsolete plants, and other similar events have altered the lives of millions of workers and their familites.[52] As of late 1991, about 6.7 percent (9.0 million) of the United States' labor force (including only those actively seeking work) was unemployed.

A **job layoff** exists when three conditions occur: (1) there is no work available at the time and the employee is sent home; (2) management expects the no-work situation to be temporary; and (3) management intends to recall the employee. **Job loss,** on the other hand, means that the employee has permanently lost his or her job.[53] In layoff and job loss situations, there is inevitably a halt to any career development and progression.[54] No company is immune to eliminating jobs. Some of the pillars of the business world such as AT&T, Monsanto, American Airlines, Inc., Sears Roebuck & Co., and ITT have laid people off.[55]

Research has shown that job loss produces dangerous increases in personal stress. For instance, the work of sociologist Harvey Brenner provides convincing evidence on the effects of job loss. He shows that higher levels of job loss (unemployment) have been associated with higher levels of social disorders, mental hospital first admissions, and suicide.[56] Such associations raise a number of important questions. Who is most vulnerable to the stress caused by job loss, and why? Do short-term layoffs have different effects than permanent job loss? How important are such factors as support from family and friends in conditioning the impact of job loss?

Cobb and Kasl conducted a two-and-a-half-year study of the effects of job loss on 100 employees prior to job loss and after losing their jobs.[57] They found that:

. Job loss is stressful and requires several months for a person to adjust.

. Job loss is associated with depression, anomie, and suspicion.

. Self-reports of illness and drug use were high during the anticipation phase, dropped at termination, and rose again at six months.

- Those who were unemployed longer and had less social support experienced more stress.

Although the Cobb and Kasl study is well designed, it has a number of limitations. The sample size was only 100. Also, the sample was predominantly composed of white, middle-aged males. The Cobb and Kasl research and other similar studies have resulted in a number of tentative conclusions:[58]

- Denial or disbelief is a typical initial response to rumors of job loss.
- As rumors circulate and as individuals lose their jobs, there is a high level of anxiety among job stayers.
- Several weeks after job loss, there is a period of relaxation and relief, of optimism, and vigorous efforts to find a new job.
- Friends and family can play a major support role.
- Four or more months after job loss, those workers still unemployed go through a period of doubt — in which some people experience panic, rage, and erratic behavior.

The likelihood that a person will experience all of these stages depends on the duration of unemployment (how long his or her career is halted). Differences of personality and circumstances (such as age and degree of financial security) influence the timing and the intensity of job loss effects.

Managerial Responses to Career Halt

Consistently strong performance is one effective approach to guard against the need to use job layoffs or job loss approaches.[59] An efficient performance appraisal system can help management pinpoint poor performance and initiate corrective steps. Even when managers use performance appraisal systems, there may be other uncontrollable events such as a cutback in market demand, reduced resources availability, and competitive forces that require some form of labor force cutback.

The best time to prepare for job layoff and job loss is when business is good. Establishment of *layoff criteria* is an important step. Typically, seniority is the most used criterion in determining who will be laid off. However, if a valued and reliable performance appraisal system is in place, it could be used to make decisions. Some firms use a panel of managers from outside the work unit being cut back to decide who will be laid off and who will stay.

The creation of an *outplacement services* unit within the HRM unit or hiring an outplacement consultant is another valuable step in preparing for possible job layoff and job loss.[60] **Outplacement** consists of a variety of job placement services that an organization offers to people who are being asked to leave.[61] These services may include résumé writing, use of company telephones for calling potential employers, letters of introduction, reference letters, payment of placement fees, and career counseling. In some cases, a company may pay for retraining as a person learns the skills necessary to begin the career again elsewhere or to enter a new career.[62] Outplaced employees sometimes form support groups so that they can exchange information about job opening and feelings.

In addition to outplacement services, organizations can provide payments so that individuals have some financial resources to draw upon during the transition between jobs. The most common is *severance pay*, based on the age of the employee and his or her years of services.

Since job layoffs and job loss are expected to be problems that will continue into the foreseeable future, management must continue to study the problems and

CAREER CHALLENGE
(*concluded*)

After thinking about his goals, present position, and the future he saw at Neal, Jim Lucio made the decision to leave the company. It wasn't easy, and he had some fears, but Jim really felt that a second career was best for him. He didn't make a hasty decision; he knew all about the idea of a midcareer crisis. Jim decided to go after the thing he always wanted, his own business. He now is a partner in a database management system company in Hamilton, Ohio. He felt good, slept well, and jumped into his second career with enthusiasm. Norb and everyone at Neal wished him well. His co-workers even had a party for Jim to show him that they really cared and wanted him to be happy in his new career as a business owner in the computer field.

experiment with solutions.[63] There are still many gaps in our understanding of what happens to people when their careers are halted temporarily or permanently. We need more information on:

- Women's and minority workers' reactions to job layoffs and loss.
- The longer-range effects of job loss.
- How personality predisposes reactions to job loss.
- The effectiveness of outplacement services.

Much work and managerial action need to be done on the effects of career halt. As stated by Harry Maurer,

Work, if the longing of the unemployed is any indication, remains a fundamental need — even in the crushing form it has increasingly assumed in the modern world. It provides not simply a livelihood, but an essential passage into the human community. It makes us less alone.[64]

SUMMARY

This chapter has been designed to discuss the importance of career planning and development.

To summarize the major points covered in this chapter:

1. A career is an ongoing sequence of work-related activities. It is not something that occurs in isolation, but is work-related.
2. Individuals go through four career stages — prework, initial work stage, the stable stage, and the retirement stage.
3. Mentoring can be extremely important to a junior employee in terms of personal development.

4. In selecting a career, individuals are expressing a part of their personality.

5. Three points in careers are of particularly crucial importance for career development — when a person is just hired, at midcareer, and at preretirement.

6. Programs to combat problems of the new hiree include realistic job previews, challenging initial assignments, and demanding bosses.

7. Programs to combat midcareer problems include counseling to illustrate and develop midcareer alternatives (transfers, retraining).

8. Programs to combat preretirement problems include counseling, workshops and seminars on what to expect, alternative careers, and coping with change.

9. Career pathing can inform people about the sequence of job opportunities in the organization.

10. Career planning involves matching a person's aspirations with opportunities. Some commonly used practices involve counseling, seminars, and even self-assessment centers.

11. A growing issue of importance is the dual-career couple. Organizations need to become more active in finding ways to minimize problems of dual-career couples.

12. Career progress and development can halt because of a temporary cutback in the work force or a permanent reduction in the work force. The layoff or job loss situations can create psychological and behavioral problems for individuals and families that are affected.

KEY TERMS

career	546	job layoff	573
career pathing	563	job loss	573
career stages	547	mentoring relationship	549
dual careers	568	midcareer plateau	560
glass ceilings	572	outplacement	574

QUESTIONS FOR REVIEW AND DISCUSSION

1. Do you believe that it is possible to ask people to serve as mentors or mentees? Why?

2. Why do recently retired people need to be prepared for the differences between work and retirement?

3. Find a person who has been laid off from his or her job and ask that person why he or she was laid off. What did you find out?

4. What is the meaning of the term *career success* to an individual?

5. Why are some people satisfied with what is identified as a midcareer plateau?

6. Should organizations be concerned about dual-career issues such as career conflict, job relocation, and salary differences? Why?

7. In John Holland's system, skills are divided into six clusters or families. Which cluster best describes you? Does your skill cluster match up well with the kind of career you will pursue?

8. Have you made a career choice? What is it and do you have the skills and personality for the particular career? How do you determine this?

9. Women seem to have to face what is called a *glass ceiling*. Why would individuals hinder or block the advancement of women up the management ladder?

10. How could a manager evaluate the effectiveness (or lack of) of the outplacement services used in her or his firm?

NOTES

[1] Richard N. Bolles (1991), *The 1991 What Color Is Your Parachute?* (Berkeley, Calif.: Ten Speed Press).

[2] Jeffrey H. Greenhaus (1987), *Career Management* (Hinsdale, Ill.: Dryden Press), pp. 6–7.

[3] Cathy Trust and Carol Hymorvitz (June 18, 1990), "Careers Start Giving in to Family Needs," *The Wall Street Journal*, pp. B1 and B5.

[4] Douglas T. Hall and Khalil Nougain (1968), "An Examination of Maslow's Need Hierarchy in an Organizational Setting," *Organizational Performance and Human Behavior*, pp. 12–35.

[5] Phillip R. Harris (June 1985), "Future Work," *Personnel Journal*, pp. 52–58.

[6] Rosabeth Kanter (1984), *The Change Masters* (New York: Simon & Schuster).

[7] John Kotter (1985), *Power and Influence* (New York: Free Press).

[8] James A. Wilson and Nancy S. Elman (November 1990), "Organizational Benefits of Mentoring," *Academy of Management Executive*, pp. 88–94.

[9] K. E. Kram (1984), *Mentoring at Work* (Glenview, Ill.: Scott, Foresman).

[10] Robert D. Bretz, Jr., and George F. Dreher (1987), "Sponsored versus Contest Mobility: The Role of Mentoring in Managerial Careers," in *Readings in Personnel and Human Resource Management*, ed. R. S. Schuler, S. A. Youngblood, and V. L. Herbert (St. Paul, Minn.: West Publishing), pp. 311–19.

[11] Charles D. Orth, Harry E. Wilkinson, and Robert C. Benfari (Spring 1987), "The Manager's Role as Coach and Mentor," *Organizational Dynamics*, pp. 66–74.

[12] Sebywyn Fernstein (November 10, 1987), "Women and Minority Workers in Business Find a Mentor Can Be a Rare Commodity," *The Wall Street Journal*, p. 31.

[13] John L. Holland (1983), *Holland's Vocational Preference Inventory* (Palo Alto, Calif.: Consulting Psychologists Press).

[14] John L. Holland (1973), *Making Vocational Choices: A Theory of Careers* (Englewood Cliffs, N.J.: Prentice-Hall).

[15] John L. Holland, D. C. Darger, and P. G. Power (1980), *My Vocational Situation* (Palo Alto, Calif: Consulting Psychologists Press).

[16] Gary Dessler (1984), *Personnel Management* (Reston, Va: Reston Publishing), p. 500.

[17] Stephen G. Weinrach (1984), "Determinants of Vocational Choice: Holland's Theory," in *Career Choice and Development*, ed. Ursula Delworth and Gary R. Hanson (San Francisco: Jossey-Bass), pp. 61–93.

[18] Donald E. Super (May 1983), "Assessment in Career Guidance: Toward Truly Developmental Counseling," *Personnel and Guidance Journal*, pp. 555–62.

[19] Manuel London and Stephen A. Stumpf (1982), *Managing Careers* (Reading, Mass.: Addison-Wesley Publishing), p. 4.

[20] Richard K. Broszeit (October 1986), "If I Had My Druthers . . . A Career Development Program," *Personnel Journal*, pp. 84–90.

[21] Arnon E. Reichers (April 1987), "An Interactionist Perspective on Newcomer Socialization Rates," *Academy of Management Review*, pp. 278–79.

[22] (March 1981), "What Does It Cost to Train New People?" *Training/HRD*, p. 16.

[23] John P. Wanous (1980), *Organizational Entry* (Reading, Mass.: Addison-Wesley Publishing), pp. 51–79.

[24] Hall, *Careers in Organizations*, p. 67.

[25] Joe Fitz-enz (August 1990), "Getting and Keeping Good Employees," *Personnel*, pp. 25–28.

[26] Thomas P. Ference, James A. F. Stoner, and E. Kirby Warren (October 1977), "Managing the Career Plateau," *Academy of Management Review*, p. 604.

[27] C. V. Entrekin and J. G. Everett (August 1981), "Age and Midcareer Crisis: An Empirical Study of Academics," *Journal of Vocational Behavior*, pp. 84–97.

[28] Fay Rice (August 31, 1987), "Lessons from Late Bloomers," *Fortune*, pp. 87–91.

[29] Manfred F. R. Kets de Vries (Autumn 1978), "The Midcareer Conundrum," *Organizational Dynamics*, p. 58.

[30] Douglas T. Hall and Francine S. Hall (Summer 1976), "What's New in Career Management," *Organizational Dynamics*, pp. 21–27.

[31] Sydney P. Freedberg (October 13, 1987), "Forced Exits? Companies Confront Wave of Age-Discrimination Suits," *The Wall Street Journal*.

[32] Jeffrey Sonnenfeld (November/December 1978), "Dealing with the Aging Work Force," *Harvard Business Review*, pp. 81–92.

[33] Walter Kiechel III (June 27, 1983), "The Neglected Art of Career Planning," *Fortune*, pp. 153–55.

[34] Linda Brooks (1984), "Career Planning Programs in the Workplace," in *Career Choice and Development*, ed. Ursula Delworth and Gary Hanson (San Francisco: Jossey-Bass), pp. 388–405.

[35] Wayne F. Cascio (1991), *Applied Psychology in Personnel Management* (Englewood Cliffs, N.J.: Prentice-Hall), pp. 236–43.

[36] John D. Gridley (May 1986), "Who Will Be Where When?" *Personnel Journal*, pp. 50–58.

[37] James W. Walker (Fall 1976), "Let's Get Realistic about Career Paths," *Human Resource Management*, pp. 2–7.

[38] This section is based on Hall and Hall, "What's New in Career Management," pp. 27–30.

[39] Joanne S. Lublin (March 8, 1984), "Couples Working Different Shifts Take on New Duties and Pressures," *The Wall Street Journal*, p. 27.

[40] Glenn Slay (November 15, 1987), "Spouses in Blue," *Houston Chronicle*, pp. 1, 13.

[41] Francine S. Hall and Douglas T. Hall (Spring 1978), "Dual Careers — How Do Couples and Companies Cope with the Problem?" *Organizational Dynamics*, p. 58.

[42] Suzanne Alexander (August 24, 1990), "Fears for Careers Curb Paternity Leaves," *The Wall Street Journal*, pp. B1, B8.

[43] (November 16, 1987), "A Job for the Trading Spouse, Too," *Business Week*, p. 239.

[44] Laurie Hays (June 15, 1987), "Pay Problems: How Couples React When Wives Out-Earn Husbands," *The Wall Street Journal*, p. 19.

[45] Gail Benson and Jane Holston (1987), *Smart Moves* (Houston, Tex.: River Forest Publishing).

[46] E. J. Smith (October 1981), "The Working Mother: A Critique of the Research," *Journal of Vocational Behavior*, pp. 191–211.

[47] Maria H. Sekas (April 1984), "Dual-Career Couples — A Corporate Challenge," *Personnel Administrator*, p. 74.

[48] Erik Larson (September 2, 1981), "Firms Providing Business Internships Lure Middle-Aged Women Looking for Work," *The Wall Street Journal*, p. 21.

[49] Jenny C. McCune (November 1990), "Sayonara to Womb-to-Tomb?" *Personnel*, pp. 11–12.

[50] (December 1990), "The Unbreakable Glass Ceiling," *Personnel*, p. 17.

[51] Edward W. Jones, Jr. (May-June 1986), "Black Managers: The Dream Deferred," *Harvard Business Review*, pp. 84–93.

[52] Barbara Rhine (May 1984), "Business Closings and Their Effects on Employees: The Need for New Remedies," *Labor Law Journal*, pp. 268–80.

[53] Dessler, *Personnel Management*, p. 512.

[54] Terry F. Buss and F. Stevens Redburn (1983), *Mass Unemployment* (Beverly Hills, Calif.: Sage Publications).

[55] (March 23, 1987), "You're Fired," *U.S. News and World Report*, pp. 50–54.

[56] M. H. Brenner (1973), *Mental Illness and the Economy* (Cambridge, Mass.: Harvard University Press).

[57] S. Cobb and S. V. Kasl (1977), *Termination: The Consequences of Job Loss* (Cincinnati: Department of Health, Education, and Welfare).

[58] R. Catalano and C. D. Dooley (March 1983), "Health Effects of Economic Instability: A Test of Economic Stress Hypothesis," *Journal of Health and Social Behavior*, pp. 46–60.

[59] Gene L. Morton (September 1983), "Helping Managers and Employees Cope with Work-Force Cutbacks," *Training and Developmental Journal*, pp. 50–54.

[60] Loretta D. Foxman and Walter L. Polsky (September 1984), "How to Select a Good Outplacement Firm," *Personnel Journal*, pp. 94–97.

[61] William J. Morin and Lyle York (1982), *Outplacement Techniques* (New York: AMACOM), pp. 101–31.

[62] Nadeem Shahzel (June 1984), "Outplacement Services at Interfaith Medical Center," *Personnel Administrator*, pp. 56–63.

[63] H. G. Kaufman (1982), *Professionals in Search of Work* (New York: John Wiley & Sons).

[64] (June 1982), "The Stress of Job Loss," *Occupational Health and Safety*, p. 26.

EXERCISE 15–1   Career: A Self-Assessment

· · · · ·

Objective   This exercise is designed to encourage students to think about themselves in terms of a career. It also requires students to engage in the development of a personal career plan of action.

SET UP THE EXERCISE

1. Individually complete the self-assessment career exercise. Take your time, give each section serious thought, and after careful thought make any necessary changes.
2. The instructor will set up groups of four or five to discuss any aspect of the self-assessment that individuals want to talk about. Each individual should discuss at least *one* part or issue of his or her career assessment.
3. After the discussion, each individual is to complete the action plan form.

Career Self-Assessment Form

A. *What is the ideal* career?
   Describe briefly what appears to you to be the ideal career. This is not necessarily the career you want or are in, but what you feel is ideal.

B. What Skills do I have?
    List the three most obvious skills that you possess.
    1.

    2.

    3.

C. List the job experience that you have had.
D. Rate each of the outcomes you want from a job.

	Extremely Important						Not Really Important
1. Job Security	7	6	5	4	3	2	1
2. Pay	7	6	5	4	3	2	1
3. Advancement opportunity	7	6	5	4	3	2	1
4. Social interaction	7	6	5	4	3	2	1
5. Challenge	7	6	5	4	3	2	1
6. Travel	7	6	5	4	3	2	1
7. Respect of colleagues	7	6	5	4	3	2	1
8. Feedback	7	6	5	4	3	2	1
9. Variety	7	6	5	4	3	2	1
10. Autonomy	7	6	5	4	3	2	1
11. Power	7	6	5	4	3	2	1
12. Recognition	7	6	5	4	3	2	1

E. Describe how often you think about your ideal career. What kind of things do you usually think about?

Career Action Plan

Now that you have thought about a career and have discussed it in a group, it is time to consider preparing your own career action plan. State the kind of actions that you really plan to do. Also, seriously consider the potential obstacles in your path. Only work on *two* specific career planning goals.

Action for Goal	When Will I Do it	Obstacles	How Obstacles Can Be Overcome
Action for Goal I Description:			
Action for Goal II Description:			

Now describe how you will determine whether your two action plans were successful. That is, how will you evaluate the progress being made?

Evaluation Description

Action Plan I

Action Plan II

A Learning Note

The difficulty of career progress evaluation will be highlighted. It will also help students compare an ideal career with their own career plans, experience, and preferred outcomes.

APPLICATION CASE 15–1   The Dual-Career Couple

· · · · ·

America's work force has been largely comprised of the heads of traditional families — the husbands who work as the employed breadwinners while the wives remain home to raise the children. However, today the "traditional family" comprises less than 10 percent of all households. Increasingly, both spouses are launching careers and earning incomes. These dual-career couples now account for 40 percent of the work force (over 47 million employees) and their numbers will substantially increase.

The advent of the dual-career couple poses challenges for the working spouses and for business. According to one recent survey of over 800 dual-career couples by Catalyst, couples experience a myriad of problems, most notably difficulties with allocating time (the top-ranked complaint), finances, poor communication, and conflicts over housework. For couples with children, meeting the demands of career and family usually becomes the top concern. Recent studies indicate that dual-career families need: (1) benefits plans that enable couples to have children without jeopardizing careers; (2) more-flexible work arrangements to help balance family-career demand; (3) freedom from anxieties about child care while at work; and (4) employer assistance in finding spouse employment when the employee relocates (a need of both parents and childless couples).

For businesses, the challenge lies in helping to ease the problems of dual-career couples, especially those with children. According to a study commissioned by *Fortune* magazine, organizations are losing productivity and employees due to the demands of family life. The study found that, among the 400 working parents surveyed, problems with child care were the most significant predictors of absenteeism and low productivity. For example, 41 percent of those surveyed took at least one day in the three months preceding the survey to handle family matters; 10 percent took from three to five days. (These figures on a national scale amount to hundreds of millions of dollars in lost productivity.) About 60

percent of the parents polled expressed concerns about time and attention given to their children, and these anxieties were linked to lower productivity. Overall, many experts advise that companies that ignore the problems of dual-career couples (and working parents per se) stand to lose output and even valued employees.

Companies are beginning to respond to these needs in a number of ways. A growing number of organizations are:

1. **Hiring Spouses of Employees or Helping Them Find Jobs**   Studies indicate that more employees are refusing relocation assignments if their working spouses cannot find acceptable jobs. In 1990, about 75 percent of all corporate moves involved dual-career couples. In response, many companies have recently begun to offer services for "trailing spouses." These services include arranging interviews with prospective employers, providing instruction in résumé writing, interviewing, and contract negotiation, and even paying plane fares for job-hunting trips. Some companies (General Mills, 3M, American Express) use outside placement services to find jobs for trailing spouses. Over 150 northern New Jersey companies created and use a job bank that provides leads for job-hunting spouses.

A small and growing number of companies (Chase Manhattan Bank; O'Melveny & Myers, one of the nation's largest law firms) are breaking tradition and hiring two-career couples. Martin Marietta maintains an affirmative hire-a-couple policy and hires about 100 couples a year in its Denver division. Proponents assert that couples who work for the same company share the same goals, are often more committed to the company, and are more willing to work longer hours. Hiring couples helps attract and keep top employees, and reloca-

Written by Kim Stewart and adapted from: Veronica J. Schmidt and Norman A. Scott (August 1987), "Work and Family Life: A Delicate Balance," *Personnel Administrator*, pp. 40–46; Fern Schumer Chapman (February 16, 1987), "Executive Guilt: Who's Taking Care of the Children?" *Fortune*, pp. 30–37; Anastasia Toufexis (November 16, 1987), "Dual Careers, Doleful Dilemmas," *Time*, p. 90; Irene Pave (December 16, 1985), "Move Me, Move My Spouse," *Business Week*, pp. 57, 60; Ronald F. Ribaric (August 1987), "Mission Possible: Meeting Family Demands," *Personnel Administrator*, pp. 70–79; and Lawrence Rout (May 28, 1980), "Pleasures and Problems Face Married Couples Hired by Same Firms", *The Wall Street Journal*, pp. 1, 28.

tions are also easier for the couple and the company.

However, many companies still shun the practice, asserting that problems outweigh advantages. Often-cited problems include the consequences of unequal performance — one spouse being promoted faster than the other resulting in jealousy, or difficulties in firing one spouse while retaining the other. Forced competition can also be problematic: "You always . . . have a built-in tension with couples comparing job assignments, salary levels, and so forth," said one personnel manager of Price Waterhouse & Co., which opposes the practice. "Pillow talk" (couples exchanging confidential information) and problems inherent in the marriage going sour are also potential liabilities. A number of companies with polices of hiring couples forbid spouses supervising each other.

2. **Providing Day-Care Assistance**   Over 3,000 companies now provide day-care services and financial assistance or referral services for child care (a 50 percent increase in company participation since 1984).

About 150 companies currently operate on-site, or near-site, day-care centers. For example, American Savings and Loan Association established the Little Mavericks School of Learning in 1983 for 150 children of employees on a site within walking distance of several of its satellite branch locations. Established as a non-profit subsidiary and with a staff of 35, the center's services include regular day care, holiday care, sick-child care, Boy and Girl Scout programs, a kindergarten program, and afterschool classes. Service fees range from $135 to $235 a month depending on the type of service, and parents pay via payroll deductions. Company officials report that the center has substantially reduced employee absenteeism and personal phone calls and has been a substantial boon to recruitment and retention. However, as many companies have found, limited openings prohibit serving all parent employees, and some employees get preferential treatment, sometimes those who can afford external day-care services.

Many companies contract outside day-care services run by professional groups, thus relieving the company of the headaches of running a center. For example, IBM contracted the Work/Family Directions child-care consulting group to establish 16,000 home-based family centers and to open 3,000 day-care centers for IBM employees and other families throughout the United States. About 80 companies have created programs to help parents of sick children. If a child of an employee of First Bank System (Minneapolis) becomes ill, the company will pay 75 percent of the bill for the child's stay at Chicken Soup, a sick-child day-care center. The policy enables parents to still work and saves the company money. A growing number of companies arrange to send trained nurses to the sick child's home.

Other companies are providing partial reimbursement for child-care services per se. Zayre Corporation pays up to $20 a week for day-care services for employees who work at corporate headquarters. A growing number of cafeteria fringe benefits programs enable employees to allocate a portion of fringe benefits to pay for day-care services. Chemical Bank pays these benefits quarterly in pretax dollars.

3. **Providing Flexible Time Off**   A number of companies are combining vacation and sick leave to increase the amount of time off for family life. At Hewlett Packard, for example, employees receive their regular vacation days plus five additional days of unused sick leave. Employees can take the time off in any increments at any time. Employees can carry a number of unused days over to the next year (the number is determined by tenure), and employees who leave the company receive cash value for their unused days (at current salary level).

4. **Providing Job Sharing**   This program enables two people to share the same job on a part-time basis and is a major boon to spouses who want to continue their careers while raising children. The program was first established by Steelcase, Inc., in Grand Rapids, Michigan, where company officials assert the program has reduced turnover and absenteeism, boosted morale, and helped achieve the company's affirmative action objectives. However, job sharing can be difficult to implement as the

program requires that a job be divided into two related but separate assignments, that job sharers are compatible, and that the supervisor can provide task continuity between the two job sharers.

Discussion Questions

1. What are the advantages and potential liabilities of hiring two-career couples beyond those noted in the case?
2. Many of the services for dual-career couples and parent employees are provided by large corporations that have far greater financial resouces than smaller companies. Identify and discuss potential ways in which a small company's HRM function can alleviate the challenges facing parent employees and employees with working spouses.
3. Suppose a dual-career couple involves spouses who are each in a different career stage. Does this situation pose problems for the couple? For the organization(s) that employ(s) them? Discuss.

DISCIPLINE AND THE DIFFICULT EMPLOYEE

· · · · · · ·

CAREER CHALLENGE

Managers supervise a variety of types of employees as part of their work. Most employees perform effectively most of the time. But any management development session eventually comes around to a discussion of employees like Al, Susan, Joyce, or Tom. These four employees are employed by a small conglomerate in the Boston area, Judge Incorporated. Judge owns manufacturing and retailing units.

- Al is the salesperson who had the largest sales increases of any of the sales force just after he was hired. Later, his sales dropped off. When his supervisor checked, Al was found to be making just enough sales calls to reach his quota.

- Susan is often a good worker. Then there are days when all the forms she types have serious errors on them. These are the days Susan is drinking.

- Joyce seems to do good work. She is courteous to the customers. She puts the stock up quickly and marks the prices accurately. But Joyce takes more than her paycheck home every week.

- Tom is a pretty good employee. But John, his supervisor, is driven up the wall by him. Tom just can't seem to follow the company rules. And when John tries to talk to him about it, Tom gives him a hard time and may even seem to threaten him if he tries to do anything about the problem.

At present, Judge Incorporated has no well-organized discipline system.

*T*hese examples illustrate a time-consuming and worrisome aspect of the HRM job: dealing fairly with the difficult employee. The seriousness of the problem is reinforced by the fact that the largest number of cases going to arbitration involves disciplinary matters. Unionized organizations have ways of dealing with these incidents, but most employees do not work in a unionized situation.

This chapter is concerned with the characteristics of difficult employees and some of the reasons for their problems. It also considers systems of discipline and appropriate means for rehabilitating difficult employees. Too often, discipline has been oriented toward punishment for past misdeeds. This is required in Joyce's case, but more important for the others is behavioral change to improve employee productivity.

The emphasis of the chapter will be *on-the-job behavior*. Organizations such as the military have tried to control the total behavior of the employee; the military often will court-martial and punish soldiers for civilian offenses, such as speeding, whether or not civilian authorities prosecute. The work organization, however, should be concerned with off-the-job behavior only when it affects work behavior. Thus, if Susan drinks before work so that she cannot do her job, this is of concern to her employer. If she has a few drinks after work and this in no way affects her job, it is none of her employer's business, even if the boss happens to be a teetotaler.

Generally, the operating supervisor is the person primarily involved in disciplining employees. HR specialists may be involved as advisers if they are asked to do so by the operating manager. Sometimes, the HR manager serves as a second step in investigation and appeal of a disciplinary case. Or, when the union is involved, the HR manager may advise the operating manager on contract interpretation for a specific case.

Discipline is a Stage III HRM activity as defined in Exhibit 1–7 (Chapter 1). Some studies have been performed on the topic, but there is a wide divergence in the disciplinary practices applied in various organizations.

A DIAGNOSTIC APPROACH TO DISCIPLINE

Exhibit 16–1 highlights the factors affecting the discipline process in an organization. As we have seen, an employee's attitude toward work is a crucial factor in productivity or performance, and discipline may play an important part in this attitude. (The kind of discipline system used is normally related to the organization.) It will be more formal in larger organizations, especially those that are unionized. It is quite informal in small organizations.

How strict discipline is depends on the nature of the prevailing labor markets. In times of high unemployment, for example, it can be quite strict. It is also related to the supportiveness of the work group (if the work group "covers" for the employee and feels the issue is unimportant, management's ability to discipline will be limited), and to the nature of the leader or supervisor (an autocratic leader's approach to discipline will be quite different from a participative leader's). The government and the legal system may provide support for employer or employee.

The effective operating or HR manager will try to diagnose each of these factors in the discipline situation. For example, the supervisor may try to diagnose the difficult employee's motivation, with a view to improving performance. This is not always easy to do. If the manager does not know the employee well, it may be virtually impossible. Discipline is one of the most challenging areas in the HRM

EXHIBIT 16-1   Factors Affecting the Discipline of Personnel

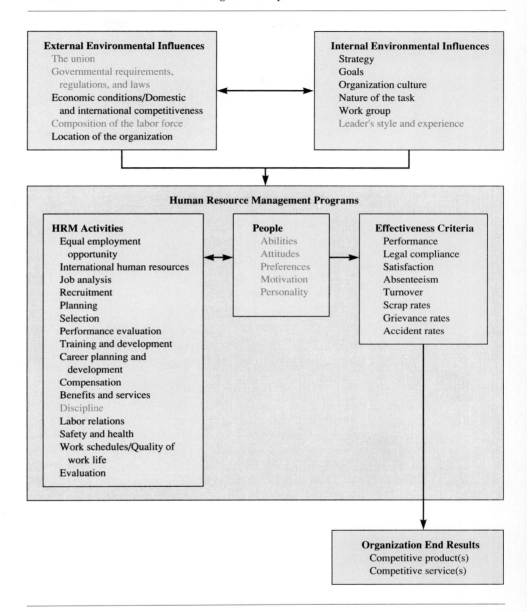

function. The diagnostic approach has many advantages over the "give him a fair trial before you hang him" approach in dealing with the difficult employee.

CATEGORIES OF DIFFICULT EMPLOYEES

Employees whose behavior can be described as difficult can be classified into one of four categories:

Category 1.   Those whose quality or quantity of work is unsatisfactory due to lack of abilities, training, or job motivation. (Al is an example.)

Category 2.   Those whose personal problems off the job begin to affect job productivity. These problems can include alcoholism, drugs, or family relationships. (Susan is an example.)

Category 3.   Those who violate laws while on the job by such behavior as stealing from the organization or its employees or physical abuse of employees or property. (Joyce is an example.)

Category 4.   Those who consistently break company rules and do not respond to supervisory reactions. (Tom is an example.)

The difficulty of determining the causes of any human behavior pattern was noted in Chapter 2. It is especially difficult to assess the causes of undesired behavior, but Miner has devised a scheme for analyzing deficient behavior that provides a checklist of possible causes.[1]

1. Problems of intelligence and job knowledge.
2. Emotional problems.
3. Motivational problems.
4. Physical problems.
5. Family problems.
6. Problems caused by the work group.
7. Problems originating in company policies.
8. Problems stemming from society and its values.
9. Problems from the work context (for example, economic forces) and the work itself.

Many of these causes can influence deficient behavior, which can result from behavior of the employee alone, behavior of the employer alone, or interaction of the employee and employer. Al's behavior (Category 1), which is directly related to the work situation, could be caused by emotional, motivational, or organizational problems. If Susan is drinking (Category 2) because of family problems, then the primary cause of her behavior is outside the control of the employer. Frequently, difficult behavior is caused by personal and employment conditions that feed one another. Joyce's behavior — theft and other illegal activities (Category 3) — is normally dealt with by security departments and usually results in termination and possibly prosecution of the employee. Tom's behavior (Category 4) is often caused by motivational, job, or emotional problems.

Category 1: The Ineffective Employee

Employees whose performance is due to factors directly related to work are theoretically the easiest to work with and to adjust. Chapter 13 introduced a systematic approach for investigating performance discrepancies. The approach is applicable not only for training but also for coping with ineffective, poor-performing employees. Recall that the approach indicates that there are some key issues that managers must consider. For example, the employee is not performing well; the manager thinks there is a training problem. There are three general follow-up questions a manager might use to analyze the problem:

1. *What is the performance discrepancy?* Why do I think there is a training problem? What is the difference between what is being done and what is supposed to be done? What is the event that causes me to say that things aren't right? Why am I dissatisfied?

2. *Is it important?* Why is the discrepancy important? What would happen if I left the discrepancy alone? Could doing something to resolve the discrepancy have any worthwhile result?

3. *Is it a skill deficiency?* Could he do it if he really had to? Could he do it if his life depended on it? Are his present skills adequate for the desired performance?

If there is a skill deficiency, then it must be corrected. On the other hand, if the problem is not a skill deficiency, then the performance problem must be addressed in terms of removing obstacles, creating a more positive motivational climate, or by bringing about some type of job change.

In summary, ineffective performance may be the result of skill, job, or motivational climate factors. Each of these factors must be carefully weighed in considering Al's sales drop-off described in the opening Career Challenge.

Category 2: Alcoholic and Drug-Abusing Employees

The Alcoholic Employee

Americans have had a love-hate relationship with alcohol. Its social use in moderation is associated with ceremonies and sociability.[2] At the same time, many believe that alcohol is a source of crime and deviant behavior. Since substance abuse is believed to affect 12 percent of the work force, alcohol use is an important topic of concern. Substance abuse has an adverse impact on work attendance, productivity, safety, and health-care cost.

The greatest incidence of alcoholism is in people aged 35 to 55 who have been employed at the same enterprise 14 to 20 years. The direct cost to industry of substance abuse is estimated to be about $100 billion per year in lost productivity and allied expenses.[3] This estimate may be low because alcoholics and other abusers often are sent home as "sick" rather than as drunk.

Of course, alcoholic consumption does not affect all employees the same at work, nor does it affect performance of tasks equally. Studies indicate that alcoholic intake tends to reduce some performance levels (for example, cognitive and perceptual-sensory skills) more than others (psychomotor skills).[4] For many persons, it takes about an hour for the alcohol to affect performance negatively. Also, compared to workers who are not alcohol abusers, problem drinkers take two-and-a-half times more absences of eight days or more, receive three times as much sick leave and accident benefits, and make five times as many workers' compensation claims.[5] About a third of America's largest employers have set up alcoholism control programs. Many medical plans now cover the costs of treatment for alcoholism.

Employees assistance programs (EAPs) began appearing in the United States around 1950 when alcohol abuse was first addressed as a major problem. Under these programs, "constructive confrontation" became the standard procedure.[6] The employee was given an ultimatum to correct the problem or leave.

Today's EAPs have a broader, more comprehensive approach. The programs offer counseling and referral services to employees regardless of the causes of their problems. The new philosophy is that the firm has no right to interfere with the private lives of its workers, but it does have a right to impose standards of work behavior and performance. Also, EAPs now are not confined to alcoholism. Some EAPs include coverage for drug abuse, personal emotional problems, financial difficulties, AIDS, elder care, and other problems that impair work performance.[7]

EAPs have become accepted as a proactive procedure to help employees at or off the worksite. Most EAPs share the following characteristics.

- Employees needing assistance are identified and referred to the program.
- The employee is introduced into the program and his or her problem is evaluated. The employee receives counseling and may be given a referral for treatment.
- Employees receive professional diagnosis and treatment. These are usually provided by outside agencies.

General Motors has one of the largest EAPs. To date, over 500,000 employees have participated. Each year, about 100,000 employees use the program for alcohol and drug abuse problems. It has a written policy, clear procedures, and endorsement by both top management and union leaders.

At most organizations with EAPs, managers are trained to follow specific procedures when they become aware that an employee's performance is declining. The manager is trained to discuss the problem with the employee. The manager attempts only to encourage the employee to improve his or her behavior. The manager does not provide rehabilitative counseling. If the problem is not corrected, the employee is told about counseling services. The EAP is given a confidential option. Managers serve to only identify the performance decline and then refer employees to the EAP.

How effective EAPs are is still a hotly debated topic. A spokesperson for Marsh & McLennan companies, a consulting firm, said, "There are still many unanswered — and a number of unasked — questions about EAPs' effectiveness and their impact on reducing the direct and indirect costs of substance abuse."[8] He pointed out that much of the data on effectiveness is subjective.

A Marsh & McLennan survey of *Fortune* 1,000 CEOs found that the majority view EAPs as the most important workplace activity for dealing with substance abuse. The obstacles to specific objective data include thet lack of clinical outcome measures and the confidentiality of data. To date, a perfect and rigorous study of EAP effectiveness has not been conducted. However, it is likely that this lack of scientific data will not slow down or detract from the interest in an application of EAPs.

The Drug-Abusing Employee

Employers are also finding more employees abusing drugs, such as cocaine and heroin, on the job. Drug abuse manifests itself in ways similar to alcoholism. Counselors at the Cocaine National Helpline polled callers of the 800-COCAINE hotline and found that 75 percent admitted to occasional cocaine use while at work, and 69 percent said they regularly worked while under the influence of the drug. The problems may be less well known to employers because of laws against possession and use of drugs, which cause employees to hide their abuse.

One *Fortune* 500 company released profiles of the typical drug abuser that indicate, compared with the norm for a working unit, the drug user:

- Functions at about 67 percent of his or her potential.
- Is 3.6 times more likely to be involved in an accident.

- Receives three times the average level of sick benefits.
- Is five times more likely to file a workers' compensation claim.
- Is repeatedly involved in grievance procedures.
- Misses 10 or more times as many work days.[9]

In some industries, drug- and alcohol-influenced mistakes cost lives. From 1975 to 1986, approximately 50 train accidents were attributed to workers under the influence of drugs or alcohol: 37 people were killed, 80 injured, and property valued at $34 million was destroyed.[10]

An increasing number of firms believe that some absenteeism, turnover, accidents, industrial espionage, and lower productivity are caused by drug addiction, and that some thefts are caused by drug users trying to support their habits. What has been done about it?

The Drug-Free Workplace Act of 1988 requires contractors and grantees of federal agencies to provide drug-free workplaces. The act gave drug testing a legal imprimatur. The American Management Association (AMA) has discovered a trend in companies engaged in antidrug initiatives. In 1990, 51.5 percent of the firms responding to an AMA survey performed drug testing, and there was an increase in education and awareness programs since the 1989 survey.[11] Companies seem to have learned that education on the dangers of drugs is important for employees. Exhibit 16–2 shows the workplace initiatives to combat drug abuse.

Random drug testing of current employees is still rare: Only 3.4 percent of all respondents (9.1 percent of those that test current employees) use random selection as a basis for drug testing. There are 13 companies that test at random; of 1,055 employees so tested, 7.3 percent had positive results.

Drug testing is relatively new to the U.S. workplace. U.S. Department of Transportation regulations that went into effect in December 1989 require that 4 million

EXHIBIT 16-2   Workplace Initiatives to Combat Drug Abuse: The Four-Year Trend

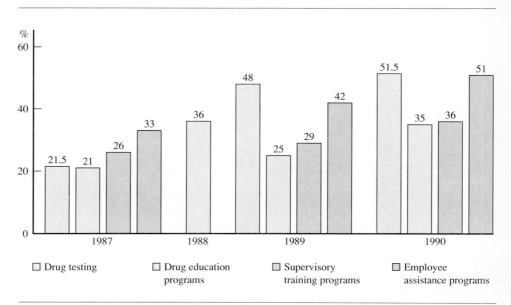

Source: Eric Rolfe Greenberg (July 1990), "Workplace Testing," *Personnel*, p. 29.

workers in the private sector of the transportation industry are required to undergo random testing for drug abuse. The rationale is that, in the transportation industry and other hazardous facilities, safety is crucial. Thus, a drug-free work force is needed to assure the public safety.[12] There are, however, worker doubts about the accuracy of testing. Many employees approve of tests for new employees and for current employees whose on-the-job behavior suggests the influence of drugs. But they are opposed to postaccident, periodic, and random drug testing. Employees ask why in a postaccident situation should random testing be conducted when the cause lies elsewhere, such as in equipment failure? A crash of two airplanes on a runway at the Los Angeles International Airport on February 1, 1991, brought out this concern. One airplane was landing and the second airplane was taking off when both pilots were instructed to use runway 24. Despite this obvious air traffic control error, the pilot of the landing plane was subjected to a random substance-abuse screen.

Intrusion upon a person's privacy is a serious issue and so is a train, truck, or airplane crash that results in injuries and death.[13] Random drug testing law is still an underdeveloped area. However, employees need to have a substance abuse program that includes a testing component. Schachter and Geidt listed 10 drug-policy guidelines that seems reasonable and defensible in court.[14]

1. Address the problem of drug abuse squarely.
2. Establish clear rules and enforce them consistently.
3. Conduct proper investigations of suspected violations.
4. Follow appropriate disciplinary guidelines.
5. Train supervisors and educate employees.
6. Develop a policy on rehabilitation or employee assistance.
7. Be sensitive to employees' rights to privacy.
8. Take reasonable steps to protect employees and others from harm caused by substance abusers.
9. Know the applicable statutes and regulations.
10. Practice good employee relations.

Following these 10 guidelines shows that a firm is attempting to deal with substance abuse proactively and fairly.

Better-Bilt Aluminum Co., Inc., in Prescott Valley, Arizona, implemented a drug and alcohol abuse policy about 18 months ago. Since then, accidents have dropped from 51 percent two years prior to the new policy and 44 percent one year prior to the new policy to less than 10 percent. The Better-Bilt program is based on education, the use of an EAP, and signing a letter of understanding the firm's program, and drug-testing policies. It was management's goal to have a clear, well-defined, and enforced program.[15]

Companies follow similar control programs for drugs as they do for alcohol, although drug treatment methods vary more than alcohol treatment methods. Drug usage is illegal, and public attitudes toward drug use are much more negative than those toward alcohol use. In industry, the company health department can try to rehabilitate drug users. Often, however, the ultimate decision is discharge and discipline, although this may lead to arbitration.

Arbitrators have discharged drug-using employees if their habit ruins a firm's reputation or causes it to lose business. They are more likely to uphold discharges for drug usage after conviction than after arrest alone, and they discipline drug pushers more severely than drug users. In general, arbitrators tend to urge employers to give drug-using employees a second chance, if they agree to participate in rehabilitation programs.

Catetory 3: Participants in Theft, Crime, and Illegal Acts

Employers often have to deal with employees who engage in various illegal acts. Employees may steal (remember Joyce), misuse company facilities or property, disclose trade secrets, embezzle, or kidnap executives for terrorism purposes. They may sabotage products, or use company telephones and credit cards for personal use, or pirate company materials or labor to repair their own homes. One source estimates that 75 percent of stolen goods are taken by employees and suppliers. Yet some arbitrators have recently ruled that employee property (such as their cars in the parking lot) cannot be searched without a warrant. Organizations try to deal with employee theft, which is estimated to cost over $25 billion annually, and similar problems in a number of ways.[16] One is to try to screen out likely thieves. For example, a weighted application blank has been developed to help with this. Exhibit 16–3 lists other ways to prevent employee theft.

A method organizations can use to oversee theft and criminal prevention is to set up a security department or program. Often, this responsibility is assigned to the HR department. Typically, the protection program is called *industrial security* and includes security education, employment screening, physical security, theft and fraud control, and fire prevention.

Most companies engage in at least minimal industrial security operations, such as identification or "badge" systems, prior employment screening, special safeguards for or destruction of sensitive documents, and escort services for visitors. There is

---

EXHIBIT 16-3   Ways to Minimize Employee Theft

1. The employee should be made to feel that the job is worth keeping, and it would not be easy to earn more elsewhere.
2. Normal good housekeeping practices — no piles of rubbish or rejects or boxes, no unused machines with tarpaulins on them, and no unlocked, empty drawers — will help ensure that there are no places where stolen goods can be hidden. The first act of the thief is to divert merchandise from the normal traffic flow.
3. Paperwork must be carefully examined and checked at all stages so invoices cannot be stolen or altered.
4. Employees' cars should not be parked close to their places of work. There should be no usable cover between the plant doors and the cars.
5. Do not allow employees to make sales to themselves, their friends, or their family members.
6. Whether the plant is open or closed at night, bright lights should blaze all around the perimeter, so no one can enter or leave without being seen.
7. There should be adequate measures to control issuance of keys. There have been cases where a manager or supervisor would come back at night for a tryst with a girlfriend or a boyfriend and give her an armload of merchandise to take home with her. Key control is very important.
8. As far as possible, everyone entering or leaving should have an identification card.
9. Unused doors should be kept locked. If only two must be open to handle the normal flow of traffic, the rest should be bolted.
10. Everything of value that thieves could possibly remove, not just obvious items, must be safeguarded.

research available that suggests that the larger the organization, the greater the likelihood that theft prevention and security observation programs will be used.[17] Most organizations also attempt at least some industrial security planning in selecting sites and designs for remodeling or construction of facilities. Security vulnerabilities are assessed, and structural barriers such as fences, lighting, and the building itself are designed to reduce security hazards.

Since Congress banned the use of polygraph tests to gauge the honesty of current and prospective employees in 1988, many firms have begun using "integrity tests."[18] These tests are particularly popular with retailers who are concerned with theft. They are used by 28 percent of wholesale and retail companies that responded to the annual American Management Association survey.

Evidence on the validity and reliability of integrity tests is sketchy. Studies show that about 30 to 60 percent of the people taking the test fail. Thus, publishers of the tests warn employees to use other evidence when determining a candidate's integrity. Whether integrity tests can help a firm screen out candidates who have stolen property or have a tendency to steal has serious legal implications. To date, the integrity test approach seems no better or more accurate than the banned polygraph test.

Category 4: The Rule Violators

Difficult employees of the fourth category consistently violate company rules, such as those prohibiting sleeping on the job, having weapons at work, fighting at work, coming in late, or abusing the supervisor. An especially difficult issue is verbal and physical abuse of supervisors. Recall Tom in the opening Career Challenge. It is useful (though not necessary) for the organization to have an established rule prohibiting verbal and physical abuse. Disputes charging abuse often go to arbitration. In general, arbitrators take the position that the decisions of supervisors deserve respect. Their rulings have been influenced by several facets of the cases:

The nature of the verbal abuse. If the shop talk is usually obscene, unless the employee personally applies the obscenities to the supervisor, arbitrators are not likely to uphold disciplinary measures for the use of obscene words.

The nature of the threat. Discipline will be upheld if an employee *personally* threatens a supervisor, but not if the employee talks vaguely about threats.

The facts in physical abuse cases. If the employee directly attacks the supervisor personally *and if* the employee was not provoked, the disciplinary decision will be upheld by arbitrators.

Arbitrators have treated altercations between supervisors and union stewards differently from those between supervisors and other employees. They view the supervisor and steward as equal and feel the steward need not be as "respectful" as other employees.

It is more difficult to establish rules about other infractions. Many organizations prohibit gambling on company grounds to avoid lowering productivity and losing time from work because of fights over gambling losses. Yet few work very hard to prohibit nickel-dime poker at lunch.

Organizations usually have rules prohibiting employees from making decisions when there is a conflict of interest (such as a purchasing agent who has an interest in a supplier) or when the employee is indebted to others. Many organizations prohibit their employees from accepting gifts over some nominal value or from being guests at lavish parties. Conflict-of-interest dealings are usually specifically prohibited.

THE DISCIPLINE PROCESS

Exhibit 16–4 is a model of the discipline process. The employer establishes goals and rules and communicates them to employees. Employee behavior is then assessed, and modification may be found desirable. This process is an attempt to prevent difficulties and is positive in nature. It is designed to help employees succeed.

The first element in the process is the establishment of *work and behavior rules*. Work goals and standards were discussed as part of performance evaluation (Chapter 9). Through whatever method is used (time and motion study, examination of past performance or performances by others, management by objectives), a set of minimally acceptable work goals is established. Behavior rules cover many facets of on-the-job behavior. They can be categorized as concerning behavior that is directly or indirectly related to work productivity. Both types are often negatively described as prohibited behavior. Exhibit 16–5 lists some examples of employee behavior rules.

The second important element in the disciplinary process is the *communication* of the rules to all employees. Unless employees are aware of the rules, they can hardly be expected to follow them. Closely related are a willingness to accept the rules and their enforceability. If employees or their representatives participate in the formation of the rules, their cooperation is more likely to be ensured. Employees must be convinced that the rule is *fair and related to job effectiveness*.

It is useful for management to seek employee advice on periodic revision of rules. The objective is to reduce the number of rules to the minimum and enforce those that are important. Customs and conditions change. Rules, like laws, need regular updating to achieve the respect and acceptance necessary for order in the workplace.

The third element of the disciplinary process is an *assessment mechanism*. In most organizations, performance evaluation is the mechanism for assessing work behavior deficiency. Rule-breaking behavior usually comes to the attention of management when it is observed or when difficulties arise and investigation reveals certain behavior as the cause.

EXHIBIT 16-4   Elements in a Disciplinary System

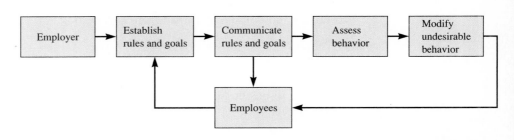

EXHIBIT 16-5   Examples of Employee Behavior Rules

I. Rules Directly Related to Productivity
   A. Time rules
      1. Starting and late times.
      2. Quitting time.
      3. Maximum break and lunch times.
      4. Maximum absenteeism.
   B. Prohibited-behavior rules
      1. No sleeping on the job.
      2. No leaving workplace without permission.
      3. No drinking on the job.
      4. No drug taking on the job.
      5. Limited nonemployer activities during work hours.
   C. Insubordination rules
      1. Penalties for refusal to obey supervisors.
      2. Rules against slowdowns and sit-downs.
   D. Rules emphasizing laws
      1. Theft rules.
      2. Falsification rules.
   E. Safety rules
      1. No smoking rules.
      2. Safety regulations.
      3. Sanitation requirements.
      4. Rules prohibiting fighting.
      5. Rules prohibiting dangerous weapons.
II. Rules Indirectly Related to Productivity
   A. Prevention of moonlighting.
   B. Prohibition of gambling.
   C. Prohibition of selling or soliciting at work.
   D. Clothing and uniform regulations.
   E. Rules about fraternization with other employees at work or off the job.

Finally, the disciplinary process concludes with a system of *administering punishment or motivating change.* This varies from supervisory administration of discipline to formal systems somewhat like courts or grievance procedures.

APPROACHES TO DISCIPLINE

Discipline for each of the categories of employee behavior just discussed can be applied in various ways. A negative approach is to emphasize the punitive effects on undesirable behavior. A more positive approach emphasizes what can be done to prevent the undesirable behavior from reoccurring.

Hot Stove Rule

One view of discipline is referred to as the **hot stove rule.** This approach to discipline is discussed in terms of what happens when a person touches a hot stove. The consequences are:

1. *A warning system.* A good manager has, before any behavior has occurred, communicated what are the consequences for the undesirable behavior.

EXHIBIT 16-6   Hudson Manufacturing's Progressive Discipline
                      for Unexcused Absences

An unexcused absence is defined in the labor-management agreement Sec. 7, paragraph 12, pp. 9–181 as any absence not approved by the immediate manager of the employee. Hudson permits absence for personal illness, jury duty, vacation, and death in the family according to Sec. 7, paragraph 15, pp. 9–184 specifications. In each case the supervisor must be consulted. Other absences must be approved before they occur. Failure to comply with the unexcused absence guidelines will be subject to the following:

- First violation will result in an oral warning within 48 hours of return to work and a written record of the act being placed in the employee's file.
- Second violation will result in a written warning being placed in the employee's file within 48 hours of return to work.
- Third violation will result in a two-day layoff without pay and a statement of the layoff being placed in the employee's file.
- Fourth violation will result in a two-week layoff without pay and a statement of the layoff being placed in the employee's file.
- Fifth violation will result in the immediate and permanent dismissal of the employee.
- The record of unexcused absence will begin anew after three years. All unexcused absences on the record will be eliminated and a new file will begin every three years.

---

2. *An immediate burn.* If discipline is required, it must occur immediately after the undesirable act is observed. The person must see the connection between the act and the discipline.
3. *Consistency.* There are no favorites — stoves burn everyone the same. Any employee who performs the same undesirable act will be disciplined similarly.
4. *Impersonality.* Disciplinary action is not pointed toward a person; it is meant to eliminate undesirable behaviors.

The hot stove rule assumes that the discipline being applied will be impersonal. However, a serious question arises on whether every employee is equal. Is a newly hired employee with only a few weeks on the job and unfamiliar with company rules and programs the same as an employee with 20 years of job tenure? People, situations, and the undesirable behaviors differ, and the hot stove rule, if followed to the letter, fails to recognize individual and situational differences.

Progressive Discipline

The **progressive pattern of discipline** is an approach in which a sequence of penalties is administered, each one slightly more severe than the previous one. The goal is to build a discipline program that progresses from less severe to more severe in terms of punishment. One example of a progressive discipline approach applied to unexcused absences is the program used at Hudson Manufacturing. The progressive steps are outlined in Exhibit 16–6.

Hudson's progressive approach becomes especially harsh after three unexcused absence violations. It is important in any disciplinary system to formally record what the policy is and what and when action was taken. The Hudson approach does this. The courts are especially sensitive to the quality of records kept by management in using a progressive discipline approach.

Positive Discipline

Hot stove rules and progressive discipline focus on past behavior. There is also the possibility that employees who are disciplined in a punitive way will rarely build time commitment into their jobs or feel better about the job or company as a result. In contrast to punitive discipline approaches, positive discipline is another approach. The advocates of this approach view it as future-oriented, as working with employees to solve problems so that problems do not occur again.

General Electric (GE) Meter Business Department in Somersworth, New Hampshire, uses a positive discipline approach.[19] In General Electric's system, there are written reminders about behaviors and no warnings. There is provision for what is called a decision-making leave as the final disciplinary step instead of suspension or termination. If the employee, after the leave, fails to commit to the rules and policies of the firm, she or he is then discharged.

A cross section of supervisors and line managers implemented the GE positive discipline approach. The team developed a 12-phase communication program that included meetings, slide/tape presentations, brochures, and training to explain the program and its features to employees. In the first two years of the program, there has been a significant reduction in the number of formal disciplinary steps taken compared to the previous period, when punitive discipline was used. In the second year of the program, 3,295 counseling sessions were conducted by supervisors to discuss a specific need for improvement and to gain the employee's agreement to make necessary corrections. The effectiveness of these meetings is demonstrated by the fact that only 65 oral reminders were issued. Seven employees were placed on decision-making leave; all seven returned without any need to discharge them.

Some of the employee comments on the GE positive discipline program are:

- "I think whenever a company will treat us like adults, as individuals, it's a good thing."
- "It certainly is an improvement. . . . Now when you do something wrong . . . they talk with you rather than talk down to you. You feel like an adult."
- "The decision-making leave with pay makes you feel guilty. I'd feel like a heel!"

The positive discipline approach is a program that recognizes that people make mistakes. It is a discipline program that deemphasizes punitive action by management. Yet, it is still a discipline program that uses the most punishing consequence of all, being discharged.

ADMINISTRATION OF DISCIPLINE

The hot stove rule, progressive discipline, and positive discipline approaches are each applied in a formal manner. Likewise, in unionized organizations, the employee has a formalized procedure that provides adequate protection: the grievance procedure discussed in Chapter 18. In nonunionized situations, the hierarchical system is the most prevalent. However, management today is no longer free in any situation, union or nonunion, to administer discipline without concern for potential legal challenges.

Hierarchical Discipline Systems

Discipline is administered to most nonunion employees by the supervisor, who also evaluates the employee. If the employee is in need of discipline, the supervisor decides what is to be done. In this hierarchical system, the conditions allow a supervisor who might be arbitrary, wrong, or ineffective to be police officer, judge, and jury over the employee. In many of our courts, a person accused of a crime such as speeding can have counsel, the judge is not the arresting officer, and the penalty may be a $50 fine. In the employment situation, where the employee has none of these safeguards, the penalty for an infraction of work rules may be his or her job or salary. Even if convicted of speeding, the employee can appeal to a higher court. What can the employee do if he/she is unfairly fired by the supervisor? There is, of course, the *open-door policy:* The employee could appeal to the supervisor's superior. But this is usually no help at all. The whole value system of the hierarchy is based on support among supervisors to build a good management team. The informal open-door policy can lead to a quasi-legal form of justice such as that developed by IBM, in which the employee's case is recorded and systematically reviewed at several levels. A strictly hierarchical justice system is more prevalent in businesses than in other work organizations.

A feeling of helplessness and lack of due process for employees can become a *powerful* force leading to the unionization of enterprises. To work at all, hierarchical systems must be considered fair by employees. There must be adequate proof of any deviance. Employees will support discipline only if they feel that the disciplined employee was treated fairly and consistently compared to other past offenders. Mitigating circumstances must be considered if disciplinary procedures are taken. The minimal safeguard to prevent serious injustice in the hierarchical system is the mandated right to job transfer in disputes with less than overwhelming evidence against the employee.

If hierarchical systems are to be effective and fair, operating and HR managers must administer discipline equitably. There have been a few studies of the extent to which this is so. One study on the subject found that, even in companies with a well-developed discipline system, discipline was unevenly administered.[20]

If discipline is called for, the manager can apply a series of sanctions to improve future performance or behavior. These vary from a brief parental-type chat to discharging the employee. A typical discipline system follows a progressive pattern of steps. Each step in the progression proves more severe for the disciplined employee.

The first step in a progressive pattern involves what is called *counseling* or a *verbal discussion* or *warning*. This is the most frequent method of disciplinary action. The supervisor determines if, in fact, a violation took place, explains to the employee why the violation significantly affects productivity, and suggests that it should not happen again. Sometimes, the supervisor pushes counseling to the "chewing out" stage.

If a second or more serious violation takes place, the supervisor again counsels the employee, this time noting that the incident will be entered in the employee's personnel file. This is actually called the *written warning step* in a progressive pattern of discipline. If the violation was sufficiently serious, the employee may also be given an oral or written warning of the consequences of a future reoccurrence. An example of an employee warning report from Dailey Oil Tools, Inc., is presented in Exhibit 16–7. This report is placed in the employee's file.

EXHIBIT 16-7   Employee Warning Report

DAILEY OIL TOOLS, INC.
HOME OF THE
L. I Drilling Jars
IN OPERATION SINCE 1900

EMPLOYEE WARNING REPORT

Employee's Name _____   Date of
Clock or   Warning _____   Dept. _____   Shift _____
Payroll No. _____

Type of Violation	☐ Attendance ☐ Safety ☐ Other _____	☐ Carelessness ☐ Tardiness	☐ Disobedience ☐ Work Quality	**W A R N I N G**

W A R N I N G   Violation Date _____

Violation Time _____ a.m. p.m.

Place Violation Occurred _____

Company Statement	Employee Statement
	Check Proper Box ☐ I concur with the Company's statement ☐ I disagree with the Company's statement for the following reasons: I have entered my statement of the above matter. Employee's Signature _____ Date _____

Warning Decision

Approved By _____
               Name   Title   Date

List All Previous Warnings Below When Warned And By Whom	
Previous Warning: **1st Warning** Date _____ Verbal _____ Written _____	I have read this "warning decision" and understand it. Employee's Signature _____ Date _____
Previous Warning: **2nd Warning** Date _____ Verbal _____ Written _____	Signature of person who prepared warning Title Date
Previous Warning: **3rd Warning** Date _____ Verbal _____ Written _____	Supervisor's Signature _____ Date _____

Copy Distribution

☐ Employee   ☐ Supervisor   ☐ Foreman
☐ Industrial Relations   ☐   ☐ Union Rep.

If the incident concerns decreasing productivity, the employees may request transfer or be asked to transfer to another job. The employee may have been placed in the wrong job, there may be a personality conflict between the employee and the supervisor, or more training might help. In some rare cases, demotions or downward transfers are used.

If counseling and warnings do not result in changed behavior, and if a transfer is not appropriate, the next progressive step is normally a *disciplinary layoff*. If any damage resulted from the deviant behavior, the deductions can be made from the employee's pay over a period of time. Most disciplinary action will not require such a severe step. The layoff is usually of short duration, perhaps a few days or up to a week.

The ultimate progressive discipline step is discharge or termination of employment. To many inexperienced managers, discharge is the solution to any problem with a difficult employee. Often, discharge is not possible, because of seniority rules, union rules, too few replacements in the labor market, or a number of other reasons.

Discharge has many costs, both direct and indirect. Directly, it leads to a loss of all the human resource investments already made, for recruiting, selection, evaluation, and training; many organizations also pay severance pay. Then, these same investments must be made again for the replacement, and frequently there is a period during which the new employee is not as productive as the former employee. The indirect costs are the effect on other employees of firing one of their numbers. If it is a blatant case of severe inability or deviant behavior, there is not much of a problem with peer group resentment. But too often, the facts are not clear, and other employees may feel the employer acted arbitrarily. Some employees may seek employment elsewhere to prevent an arbitrary action happening to them. Others may reduce productivity in protest.

Thus, discharge is the *last alternative* — when all else fails or in very serious cases, such as discovery of fraud or massive theft. One subtle reason restrains many supervisors from suggesting discharges. If the supervisor has had the employee for a long time, management may begin to ask: "If the employee is so bad, why wasn't he or she downgraded sooner? Why didn't the supervisor get rid of the employee sooner? Why did he or she hire him or her in the first place? Do you think she or he's a good judge of employees? Is she or he really supervisory timber?" Many discharges are reversed by arbitrators. For these reasons, actual discharges are rare and, when they occur, a record is made of the reasons. Exhibit 16–8 represents the documentation used at Dailey Oil Tools for terminated or discharged employees.

Termination at Will

Each year, U.S. employers in the private sector fire about 3 million employees for noneconomic reasons.[21] Such terminations are called *discharge for cause*. Protection against unjust discharge is provided to a minority of all employees through collective bargaining, antidiscrimination laws, civil service, and teacher tenure laws.[22] All other employees are subject to the **termination-at-will** doctrine. As one court put it 100 years ago: "Employment relationships of an indefinite duration may be terminated at any time without notice for good cause, for no cause, or even for cause morally wrong.[23]

There were in 1990 about 25,000 wrongful-discharge cases pending compared to 200 in 1980. The average jury award to employees wrongfully discharged is + $602,000. And the average defense attorney's fee in a wrongful-discharge lawsuit

EXHIBIT 16-8   Termination Report

DAILEY OIL TOOLS, INC.
HOME OF THE
L I Drilling Jars
IN OPERATION SINCE 1960

TERMINATION REPORT

PROFILE DATA (To Be Completed By Employee's Immediate Manager)

EMPLOYEE NAME	SOCIAL SECURITY NUMBER
ADDRESS	MANAGER/SUPERVISOR
POSITION	

☐ EXEMPT   ☐ NON-EXEMPT   ☐ FULL-TIME   ☐ PART-TIME   ☐ TEMPORARY

AGE	HIRE DATE	SALARY

LAST PERFORMANCE RATING

NOTICE GIVEN?   ☐ NO   ☐ YES, _____ DAYS   ☐ VERBAL   ☐ WRITTEN

REASONS FOR TERMINATION (Check Appropriate Reason(s) and Explain Fully).

VOLUNTARY

__ Personal Reasons
__ Medical Reasons
__ Domestics Reasons
__ Another Position
__ Dissatisfied (Wgs., Hrs., Wk.)
__ Transportation Difficulties
__ Marriage
__ Leaving Area
__ Attend School
__ Military
__ Deceased
__ Retirement
__ Other (Specify)

INVOLUNTARY

__ Unadaptable or Unsatisfactory
__ Unsatisfactory Attendance
__ Attitude Unsatisfactory
__ Excessive Tardiness
__ Violation of Company Rules
__ Refused to do Assigned Work
__ Extensive Absence due to illness
__ Lack of Work
__ Other (Specify)

IMPACT ON COMPANY

Do the Circumstances of this Termination Qualify the Employee for Unemployment Benefits Taxable to the Company?
☐ YES   ☐ NO   ☐ QUESTIONABLE

EVALUATION (Check One and Explain Below)
☐ SIGNIFICANT LOSS (Key Employee)   ☐ LOSS   ☐ NO IMPACT   ☐ ADVANTAGE

WOULD YOU RECOMMEND REHIRE?   ☐ NO   ☐ YES   ☐ SIMILAR JOB   ☐ DIFFERENT JOB

INTERNAL CORRECTIVE ACTION INDICATED?   ☐ NO   ☐ YES

COMMENTS

EVALUATION BY:	DATE

DOT-726 (R 4/61)

PROFESSIONAL PROFILE

Kenneth W. Tynes
Cessna Aircraft Company

Biography

Kenneth W. Tynes is manager of professional employment for Cessna Aircraft Company.

Mr. Tynes, a native of Monroe, Louisiana, holds a
master's degree from Webster University with a
human resources management major and a bachelor's
degree in administrative management from Brigham
Young University. He is also an accredited personnel
manager.

Mr. Tynes's experience has included personnel as-
sigments in both the public and private sectors. He
served as a personnel assistant, safety coordinator, and
employee relations manager prior to joining Cessna in
1979. Previous assignments within the Cessna organization have included serving as wage and salary manager for the marketing divisions and as personnel and
training manager for the finance subsidiaries.

A Performance Problem: How It Was Handled at
Cessna   Human resource problems often provide the
opportunity to affect people's lives while benefiting
the company. One such example involved an older,
minority employee with 30 years' seniority in the
company and a satisfactory performance record until
recently. The employee (who is called John here)
developed performance, attendance, tardiness, and attitude problems. Kenneth Tynes became involved
when John's supervisor contacted him regarding possible disciplinary actions that could be taken against
John.

This meeting yielded some interesting facts. John's
performance was extremely poor, he was operating
material-loading equipment in a hazardous manner,
and he was no longer reliable. The supervisor wanted
to terminate John's employment. However, John had
performed well for 30 years, with problems occurring
only recently. Kenneth discussed with the supervisor
the possibility that John's actions were symptoms of

the problem rather than the problem itself. They
agreed to investigate the matter before forming any
conclusions.

The pattern created by John's behavior caused
Kenneth to suspect a problem with alcohol. The supervisor and Kenneth met with John regarding his
situation. They spoke candidly with him about the
safety problems, the liability exposure, and the need
for performance improvement. John expressed concern for his job. Once he felt comfortable with their
motives, he opened up and really talked. Alcohol
abuse was the main problem.

They explained the company's employee assistance
program to John and made sure that he understood
how the company could help if he desired to participate. John elected to enter the rehabilitation program
at a local hospital. Six weeks later, John finished the
program and returned to work.

The course pursued allowed John to regain his
previous performance level in the company. In addition, John did not become another turnover statistic or
worse — a discrimination claimant against the company. Cessna also demonstrated their commitment to
their employees through this effort.

---

exceeds $125,000 — win or lose.[24] The three theories that have been advanced in
support of wrongful-discharge suits are based on claim of violation of public policy,
the existence of an implied contract, and the covenant of good faith and fair
dealing.[25]

Public Policy Exception   This view argues that an employer cannot fire an employee for reasons that violate public policy. Today, 20 states have recognized this exception in cases in which an employee was fired for refusing to commit an unlawful act, for performing an important public obligation, or for exercising a statutory right or privilege. In general, cases involve refusing to give false testimony, reporting illegal conduct by an employer (called "whistle blowing"), or refusing to violate a professional code of ethics.[26]

In one of the earliest cases, the California Court of Appeals ruled in 1959 that it was against public policy for the Teamsters' Union to fire a business agent for refusing to give false testimony before a legislative committee.[27]

In an Illinois case, an employee alleged that he was fired for offering information to the police about possible criminal behavior on the job by another co-worker and for agreeing to help in the investigation.[28] The court held that there is a clear public policy favoring investigation and prosecution of criminal offenses.

Implied Contract Exception   The implied contract exception as recognized in 13 states has found an implied promise of job tenure for employees with satisfactory performance records, in employee handbooks, in personnel manuals, or in oral statements that an employee would not be discharged without just cause.

The California Court of Appeals found that evidence supported the claim that an implied promise was made to an employee based on the 32-year duration of his employment, his promotions and commendation, assurances he received, and the employer's personnel policies.[29] The employee claimed that he was discharged for refusing to participate in negotiations with a union because of a purported "sweetheart agreement" that enabled the company to pay women lower wages than male employees.

In a New York case, an employee signed an application stating that employment would be subject to the company's handbook, which said that dismissal would occur only for just and sufficient cause.[30] He also received from his supervisor oral assurances of job security. The New York Court of Appeals held that there was sufficient evidence of a contract and a breach of contract to sustain a cause of action.

The Good Faith and Fair Dealing Exception   In three states, California, Massachusetts, and Montana, it is held that no matter what an employer says or does to make it clear that termination is at will and that an employee may be dismissed without cause, the employer must deal with the employee fairly and in good faith.

In Massachusetts, the Appellate Court ignored an explicit written contract that reserved to the employer the right to fire an employee for any reason.[31] The employee, a 61-year-old salesperson with 40 years of service, claimed that he was fired to avoid paying him sales commissions on a multimillion dollar order. The court held it was for a jury to decide, which the jury did, if the employer's motive in firing him was suspect.

In 1983, the Montana Supreme Court approved a jury award of $50,000 to a cashier who alleged that she was discharged without warning and was forced to sign a letter of resignation.[32] The employer claimed that she was fired for carelessness, incompetency, and insubordination. The court said that there was sufficient evidence for the jury to find fraud, oppression, or malice and held that an employer's breach of good faith and fair dealing is a reason for which damages may be recovered.

The principles and decision just presented may not appear surprising or unreasonable to nonlawyers. They merely support what is considered fair and decent employer behavior. However, in some jurisdictions, the courts' rulings are based on narrow interpretations of the law, public policy, implied contract, and good faith and fair dealing. For example, the District of Columbia Court of Appeals rejected a public exception claim when one employee stated that his employer had required that he testify in an administrative proceeding and then fired him in retaliation for testifying against the employer's interest.[33] Also, in New York, a court ruled that a bank employee, who alleged that he had been discharged because he had uncovered evidence of illegal foreign currency manipulation was terminated at will because he had no written employment contract.[34]

Even under the most liberal interpretation of the termination-at-will doctrine, the National Labor Relations Act, and Title VII of the Civil Rights Act, the recognized exceptions still only apply to a small percentage of the 3 million employees discharged each year. The overwhelming majority of discharged employees are fired for such acts as excessive absenteeism, dishonesty, theft, insubordination, possession or use of intoxicants or illegal drugs, refusal to accept a job assignment, and falsifying company records or application forms.[35]

Current State   Since the 1970s, state courts increasingly have restricted the at-will doctrine. There is much variation from state to state. However, employees have been found to have a right to take legal action against their employer when their termination violated "public policy"; refusing to commit an unlawful act (for example, perjury or price fixing); performing a public obligation (for example, absent because of jury duty); exercising the rights of shareholders (for example, refusing to support a merger); and whistle-blowing (for example, reporting alleged employer violations of the law).[36]

Japan, Great Britain, France, Germany, and Canada all require an employer to show just cause in terminating an employee. U.S. employers still are allowed more power than found in these other industrialized nations in at-will firings. Using the power unfairly is not likely to result in a cooperative and committed work force. Arbitrary discharge seems to not make much sense as image, goodwill, and fairness become beacons in the new era facing employers. The new era is one that suggests that shortages of qualified and skilled human resources are becoming acute. Terminating at-will is not likely to result in more applicants being attracted to a firm.

Other Discipline and Appeal Systems

Although the progressive discipline and grievance system is *by far* the most used in industry, other employing organizations use different models more often. A few business organizations have also taken steps to design systems that may protect the employee from arbitrary supervisory action more effectively than the hierarchical model does. The alternatives to the hierarchical models are peer, quasi-judicial, and modified hierarchical approaches. In the *peer system*, a jury of peers evaluates and punishes. The *quasi-judicial approach* uses an independent arbitrator or ombudsman to resolve disputes. *Modified hierarchical systems* are regular appeals channels *inside* the organization, but including someone other than the supervisor's superior. One mechanism is to have all disputed dismissals or behavior modification plans submitted to specified management executive or executives far removed from the scene, who hear the facts, and judge whether proper action was taken.

Nonhierarchical systems are used by such varied organizations as unions like the United Auto Workers, the Civil Service Commission in the U.S. government, and the U.S. military. The private sector almost never uses nonhierarchical systems.

It must be noted that there is little or no empirical evidence that providing nonhierarchical systems necessarily provides fairer treatment of emloyees. But a study of the history of justice under various systems in the public domain would indicate justice is much more likely under systems that provide for independent assessment of evidence and judgments than one in which the superior is prosecutor, judge, and jury.

THE DISCIPLINARY INTERVIEW: A CONSTRUCTIVE APPROACH

As previously mentioned, managers in some cases must tell an employee in clear terms that his or her behavior or job performance is below par. Suppose that this is accomplished through a discussion of poor performance, which is in essence a disciplinary interview.[37] There are several guidelines that can help the manager accomplish a constructive discussion with the ineffective performer.

1. *Root Out the Causes.* The manager needs to determine if personal problems are playing a role in the poor performance (for example, fatigue, alcohol, insomnia). This can be done by listening to the employee and to his or her co-workers, and by observation of the employee on the job.

2. *Analyze Other Reasons for Poor Performance.* If personal problems are not the main cause of poor performance, examine such factors as:
   a. Lack of skill and training to do the job.
   b. Low effort.
   c. Situational circumstances beyond the employee's control.

3. *Prepare for the Disciplinary Interview.* After analyzing possible causes and reasons for poor performance, prepare for the interview. Check the employee's previous record and even talk to previous supervisors about the employee.

4. *Conduct the Interview with Care and Professionalism.*
   a. Keep it private — public criticism is too stark and often negative.
   b. Criticize selectively — emphasize job-related performance causes. Tell the employee what you think and try to avoid being aggressive. Stay calm and be polite at all times.
   c. Let the employee speak — be a good listener; don't rush the meeting. Allow the employee to give his or her side of the story. A good rule is to show that you are listening by asking questions that indicate you are receiving the message being delivered.
   d. Take one point at a time — don't confuse points. Focus on one problem at a time.
   e. Attack the problem and not the person — in focusing on each point, remember to attack the act and not the self-concept.

5. *Issuing the Discipline.* Don't make a joke of having to discipline the employee. There really is nothing funny about being disciplined for poor performance or inappropriate behavior. Prescribe the disciplinary steps to be taken in specific terms and with a specific timetable. Do not end the disciplinary interview until you are certain that the employee understands the discipline and what is expected. Also, assure the employee his or her future performance will be judged without considering past ineffective performance problems.

6. *Don't Expect to Win a Popularity Contest.* A person who administers discipline in an equitable and firm manner will not win popularity contests. However, this person will be respected, and a manager who is respected is invaluable to

CAREER CHALLENGE
(*concluded*)

*J*eremy Schultz, the HR vice president at Judge Incorporated, is reflecting on the results of his interviews with four supervisors this week. These supervisors are responsible for Al, Susan, Joyce, and Tom.

Because of these four and many similar employees, Jeremy decides to set up a formal disciplinary system. In consultation with supervisors and selected employees, he sets up in written form the rules of working at Judge. The performance evaluation system is strengthened to make the goals clearer.

Jeremy runs some training sessions and communicates the new system to the employees. The new discipline system sets up a step-by-step process and a set of "costs":

   1st violation or problem: Counseling by supervisor.

   2nd violation or problem: Counseling by supervisor and recording in personnel file.

   3rd violation or problem: Disciplinary layoff.

   4th violation or problem: Discharge.

For alcohol or drug problems, mandatory counseling at counseling centers is required, or discharge will result. Legal violations result in discharge and prosecution.

In all cases of disciplinary layoff, the employee will receive counseling from HRM. If there appear to be problems between supervisor and employee, Jeremy will serve as an ombudsman.

With regard to Al, Susan, Joyce, and Tom, Jeremy recommends the following actions:

Al. Transfer him to a new supervisor. There appeared to be a personality conflict between Al and his supervisor. (The transfer did not help. Eventually Al received a disciplinary layoff and was terminated, in spite of much counseling.)

Susan. Ask her to join Alcoholics Anonymous. (She did, and got her drinking problem under control.)

Joyce. Watch for evidence that she is stealing. (When the evidence was clear, she was terminated and prosecuted. The judge gave her a suspended sentence.)

Tom. Give him counseling about his behavior. (The supervisor reported later that Tom was a better employee.)

All in all, Jeremy felt the new disciplinary system was working rather well.

---

an organization. The disciplinary interview is a serious part of the management job that unfortunately must be conducted regularly.

These few guidelines are designed to correct a problem or modify ineffective behaviors and are not intended to embarrass or publicly ridicule an employee. A constructive disciplinary interview can play an instrumental role in converting an ineffective performer into a productive member of the organization.

SUMMARY

Some of the most difficult human resource management problems involve handling difficult or ineffective employees. Guidelines for assessing the causes and how to deal with these situations follow:

1. Most deviant or difficult employees' problems probably have multiple causes. Some of these are listed below:
   a. Problems of intelligence and job knowledge.
   b. Emotional problems.
   c. Motivational problems.
   d. Physical problems.
   e. Family problems.
   f. Problems caused by the work group.
   g. Problems originating in company policies.
   h. Problems stemming from society and its values.
   i. Problems from the work context (for example, economic forces) and the work itself.
2. Categories of employees that cause discipline problems include:
   a. The ineffective employee.
   b. Alcoholic and drug-abusing employees.
   c. Participants in theft, crime, and illegal acts.
   d. The rule violators.
3. The discipline process involves:
   a. Employer establishing rules and goals.
   b. These rules and goals being communicated to the employees.
   c. Employee behavior being assessed.
   d. Undesirable behavior being modified, punished, and so on.
   e. Depending on the behavior, its severity, and the number of offenses, continued violation might result in termination.
4. Employers should concentrate on trying to modify the effects and advise rehabilitation and counseling for such problems as alcoholism and drug addiction.
5. For discipline systems to be effective, the disciplinary review must take place as soon after the action as possible. It must be applied consistently and impersonally.

Exhibit 16–9 gives recommendations for the use of different kinds of justice systems in the model organizations defined in Chapter 1.

It is important to remember that discipline is an area in which help is needed from many areas: supervisors, HRM, the work group, arbitrators, and top management. Each has a crucial role to play if the discipline system is to be effective.

KEY TERMS

hot stove rule 598
progressive pattern of discipline 599

termination-at-will 603

QUESTIONS FOR REVIEW AND DISCUSSION

1. In developing an EAP, what factors regarding the role of managers need to be considered?
2. Why is termination at will a concept whose time probably has passed?
3. Would a union support a discipline program within an organization? Why?
4. What are limitations of applying the hot stove rule to all employees?

EXHIBIT 16-9   Recommendations for Model Organizations on Difficult Employees and Discipline

Type of Organization	Reinforce Hierarchical Justice Systems with			
	Hierarchical Justice Systems	Peer Committees	Ombudsmen	Outside Committees
1. Large size, low complexity, high stability	X		X	X
2. Medium size, low complexity, high stability	X		X	
3. Small size, low complexity, high stability	X	X		
4. Medium size, moderate complexity, moderate stability	X		X	
5. Large size, high complexity, low stability	X		X	X
6. Medium size, high complexity, low stablity				
7. Small size, high complexity, low stability	X	X		

5. How serious a problem is the alcoholic employee at work? How should the alcoholic employee be handled?

6. Why is random drug testing a controversial issue in organizations?

7. How serious is the problem of an employee who violates criminal laws? How should the employee be dealt with?

8. Describe the key elements in the discipline process.

9. What are the arguments against the use of ''integrity tests''?

10. How would a union attempting to organize workers use termination at will in its organizing campaign?

NOTES

[1] John Miner (1975), *The Challenge of Managing* (Philadelphia: W. B. Saunders).

[2] Larry A. Pace and Stanley J. Smits (April 1989), ''Workplace Substance Abuse: A Proactive Approach,'' *Personnel Journal*, pp. 84–88.

[3] Jerry Beilenson (January 1991), ''Are EAPs the Answer,'' *Personnel (HR Focus)*, p. 3.

[4] Jerrold Levine, Gloria G. Kramer, and Ellen N. Levine (June 1975), "Effects of Alcohol on Human Performance: An Integration of Research Findings Based on an Abilities Classification," *Journal of Applied Psychology*, pp. 285–93.

[5] Joseph F. Madonia (June 1984), "Managerial Responses to Alcohol and Drug Abuse among Employees," *Personnel Administrator*, pp. 134–39.

[6] Stephen H. Applelbaum and Barbara T. Shapiro (July 1989), "The ABCs and EAPs," *Personnel*, pp. 39–46.

[7] Gary C. Brice and Mitchell R. Alegre (July-August 1989), "Eldercare as an EAP Concern," *EAP Digest*, pp. 31–35.

[8] (August 1990), "Jury Still Out on EAPs," *Personnel (HR Focus)*, p. 3.

[9] J. Castro (March 17, 1986), "Battling the Enemy within," *Time*, p. 53.

[10] Ibid.

[11] Eric R. Greenberg (July 1990), "The 1990 AMA Survey: Part 2," *Personnel*, pp. 26–29.

[12] James R. Rediker and Jonathan A. Segal (June 1989), "Profits Low? Your Employees May Be High!" *Personnel*, pp. 72–78.

[13] Alan Hanson (July 1990), "What Employees Say about Drug Testing," *Personnel*, pp. 32–36.

[14] V. Schachter and T. E. Geidt (November 1985), "Cracking Down on Drugs," *Across the Board*, pp. 28–37.

[15] Cheryl Theime (August 1990), "Better-Bilt Builds a Substance Abuse Program That Works," *Personnel Journal*, pp. 52–58.

[16] Larry Reynolds (January 1991), "Truth or Consequences," *Personnel (HR Focus)*, p. 5.

[17] Philip Puysiner (1984), *Security and Loss Prevention* (Boxton: Butterworth).

[18] Jerry Bekenson (December 1990), "Under Surveillance," *Personnel (HR Focus)*, pp. 3–4.

[19] Allan W. Bryant (February 1984), "Replacing Punitive Discipline with a Positive Approach," *Personnel Administrator*, pp. 79–87.

[20] Edward L. Harrison (February 1982), "Legal Restrictions on the Employer's Authority to Discipline," *Personnel Journal*, pp. 136–41.

[21] Jack Stieber (1987), "Employment-At-Will: An Issue for the 1980s," in *Personnel and Human Resources Management*, ed. Randall S. Schuler, Stuart A. Youngblood, and Vandra L. Huber (St. Paul, Minn.: West Publishing), pp. 379–86.

[22] David W. Ewing (1983), *Do It My Way or You're Fired* (New York: John Wiley & Sons).

[23] *Payne v. Western Atlanta R.R.*, 81 Tenn. 507–20 (1984).

[24] James G. Frierson (September 1990), "How to Fire without Getting Burned," *Personnel*, pp. 44–48.

[25] (1982), *The Employment-At-Will Issue, a BNA Special Report* (Washington, D.C.: Bureau of National Affairs).

[26] J. P. Near and M. P. Miceli (February 1986), "Retaliation against Whistleblowers: Predictions and Effects," *Journal of Applied Psychology*, pp. 137–45.

[27] *Peterman v. International Brotherhood of Teamsters, Local 396*, 174 C.A. 2d 1984, 344, P. 2d 25, 1959.

[28] *Palmeteer v. International Harvestor Co.*, 85 Ill. 2d 124, 421 N.E.

[29] *Pugh v. See Candies, Inc.*, 116 Cal. App. 3d 311, 171 Cal. rept. 917, 1981.

[30] *Weiner v. McGraw-Hill*, 83 A.D. 2d 810, 442, N.Y.S.2d 11 (1st Dept. 1981).

[31] *Fortune v. National Cash Register*, 373 Mass. 96, 364 N.E.2d 1251, 1977.

[32] *Gates v. Life of Montana Insurance Co.*, Mont. Sup. Ct. No. 83-468, August 5, 1983.

[33] *Ivy v. Army Times Publishing Co.*, 428 A.2d 831 (D.C. 1981).

[34] *Edwards v. Citibank*, 100 Misc. 2d 59, 418 N.Y.S. 269 (Supr. Ct. N.Y., 1979).

[35] F. Elkouri (1973), *How Arbitration Works*, 3rd ed. (Washington, D.C.: Bureau of National Affairs), pp. 652–66.

[36] William E. Fulmer and Ann W. Casey (May 1990), "Employment at Will: Options for Managers," *Academy of Management Executive*, pp. 102–7.

[37] David N. Campbell, R. L. Fleming, and Richard C. Grote (July-August 1985), "Discipline without Punishment — at Last," *Harvard Business Review*, pp. 174–78; and Guvene G. Alpander (March 1980), "Training First-Line Supervisors to Criticize Constructively," *Personnel Journal*, pp. 218–21.

EXERCISE 16–1   Making Difficult Decisions

· · · · ·

Objective   To permit individuals to consider and decide whether the actions taken by management are fair, equitable, and legally defensible under the termination-at-will concept.

SET UP THE EXERCISE

1. Groups of four, six, or eight will form to discuss each of the following situations.
2. Prepare a brief group statement explaining the group decision.
3. Review with the entire class each of the group decisions.

John Rogorski

John Rogorski was employed as a department manager in a retail store for three years. He maintained that during the initial job interview he was told that the firm expected to expand operations. The firm, because of slow growth, had to terminate John after three years of employment. The company maintained that John was given no guarantee of employment and was fired under the at-will doctrine.

Was John's firing justified under the termination-at-will concept?

Peter Rybark

Peter Rybark was an untenured assistant professor at a private college in Oregon. He was sent a memo this past May stating that his annual academic year salary from September to May would be $40,000. He signed a statement about his salary and sent it to the college personnel director. In December, after the fall semester, Peter was informed that his services were no longer needed. He argued that he had an annual contract and was unfairly fired. The college informed him that it had the right to terminate an untenured professor whenever it chose to do so.

Was Peter's firing acceptable under the termination-at-will concept?

Dirk Mansfield

Dirk Mansfield was a technician in the machine shop of Millfield Corporation. He was meeting at lunchtime, during breaks, and after work with employees attempting to convince them to start and support a union. After six months of meetings, Dirk was informed by his supervisor that he was fired. He was told that he had violated union-organizing procedures and was using the company premises without permission to organize a union. Therefore, because of union-organizing rules violations, he was terminated.

Was Dirk's firing justifiable under the termination-at-will concept?

Learning Note

This exercise illustrates that, in making termination decisions, consideration must be given to the law.

APPLICATION CASE 16–1   The Case For and Against Drug Testing

• • • • •

In two short months, top management at Castulon Corporation realized that the company had an employee who might have a drug abuse problem. In October, an electronics engineer was found at his desk clearly stoned ("He literally fell off his chair," the engineer's supervisor said). In November, a security guard discovered two employees in the company parking lot during the lunch hour, snorting cocaine in a car. All three employees were fired. Bob McRary, CEO of Castulon Corp., was particularly disturbed by these incidents. Castulon manufactures electronic systems that monitor and control the levels of hazardous chemicals in industrial plants. Any mistakes made by drug-dependent employees in the design/production of a system could provide disastrous results for system users.

McRary assigned Michael O'Brien, vice president of personnel, the task of developing a written proposal for a drug testing program for Castulon's job applicants and 600 employees. The proposal would recommend procedures for establishing a program and propose the program's content. The proposal would also present a comprehensive coverage of the pros and cons of establishing drug testing at Castulon. Undecided, McRary wanted to review all sides of the question before making a decision.

Michael O'Brien sought the help of Normal Sterling, director of employee relations, and Beverly Shaver, director of employee recruitment and selection, in preparing the proposal. As he often did when handling difficult issues, O'Brien asked each director to assume one position — either for or against mandatory drug testing — and to prepare a 10-page position paper presenting their views based on research and a thorough consideration of the issues at hand. O'Brien would use the papers as input for the final proposal.

Today, Norman Sterling (who chose the advocate position) and Beverly Shaver (who selected the opponent's view) submitted their papers to O'Brien. Now, in his office and at O'Brien's request, the two managers are discussing their positions.

"I accepted this assignment initially supporting a drug testing program, and after considering the issues, I'm more convinced we need one, for three primary reasons," Norman Sterling asserted.

"First, we have a responsibility for providing a safe workplace for our employees, and any drug use on the job compromises safety," he continued. "There's no question that drug use results in more accidents on the job. One study which compared employees who use drugs with nonusers found that an employee who uses drugs is almost four times more likely to be involved in a job-related accident.

"If you want more evidence, look at the transportation industry," Sterling continued, thumbing through his report to read a passage. "In the train industry alone, about 50 accidents since 1975 have been attributed to mistakes made by drug- or alcohol-impaired employees. Those accidents cost 37 lives, injured 80 others, and destroyed over $34 million in property. In our company, we should be very concerned because our manufacturing people work with heavy equipment. A drug user may not only hurt himself but injure other workers.

"Second, we have a responsibility to produce safe products for our customers. We manufacture electronic systems that monitor and control the levels of hazardous chemicals in plants. That's our business; we've installed thousands of systems worldwide. If a mistake is made in the design or manufacture of a system, toxic chemicals can overflow in a facility, and a tragedy the size of Bhopal, India, could occur. Drug use increases the risk.

"Then there are the costs our company pays because of drug use," Sterling continued. "We have the costs of higher absenteeism. The study I mentioned also found that drug-using employees are absent 10 times or more as many days as nonusers. We bear the costs of higher insurance premiums given that drug-using employees receive three times the average level of sick benefits and are five

Written by Kim Stewart. Facts and several perspectives were drawn from: Janice Castro (March 17, 1986), "Battling the Enemy within," *Time*, pp. 52ff; Lewis L. Maltb (June 1987), "Why Drug Testing Is a Bad Idea," *Inc.*, pp. 152–53; Ian A. Miners, Nick Nykodym, and Diand M. Samerdyke-Traband (August 1987), "Put Drug Detection to the Test," *Personnel Journal*, pp. 90–97; and Anne Marie O'Keefe (June 1987), "The Case against Drug Testing," *Psychology Today*, pp. 34–36, 38.

times more likely to file a workers' compensation claim. There are the costs of lower productivity, impaired decision making, and employee theft from the company. Stories abound in the media of addicted employees stealing from their employers to support their drug habits. In one such reported case, a high-level advertising executive billed clients for work never performed and used the revenues to support a $2,000-a-week habit.''

"I think you've raised some legitimate concerns, but I think we should first question whether we have a drug problem the size of which merits such a major action as mandatory drug testing," Beverly Shaver replied. "We've had two incidents, but only two. The high quality of our products and low accident and absenteeism record don't indicate widespread drug use among our employees.

"Since we're quoting studies, I found one that's very interesting," she continued. "Although the media paints a picture of a massive drug use problem nationwide, a recent study by the National Institute on Drug Abuse found that for all drugs except cocaine, current use levels are well below 1979, which was the peak year for drug use in the United States. Do we really have a problem?''

"All it takes is one impaired employee who makes one design or manufacturing mistake and thousands of people could be killed," Sterling replied. "Also, we may not have a problem now, but we may very well have one soon. The figures are startling on young people now entering the work force. One study says that about two-thirds of these new workers have taken illegal drugs and 44 percent have done so in the last year. Another survey among companies using preemployment drug test screening among applicants found that 20 to 50 percent of applicants 18 to 25 years old tested positive. Some of these folks are our future employees.''

Michael O'Brien interjected, "Let's assume for a moment that we have a drug problem. Is drug testing the way to solve it?''

"No. I think it creates more problems than it solves," Shaver asserted. "First is the inaccuracy problem. Suppose we tested using the EMIT test, which is the most widely used procedure. It boasts a 97 percent accuracy rate under ideal conditions. But conditions are rarely if ever ideal. Samples are contaminated by employees or mishandled by labs or the test just fails. The figures are scary; the Centers for Disease Control re-analyzed urine sam-

ples from 13 labs chosen at random to test the accuracy rate. They found that the results of 66 percent of the lab tests were wrong—false positives. Other studies have found similar results.

"It's no wonder given that many over-the-counter drugs, and even foods test positive as illegal drugs," Shaver continued. "Cough syrups can test positive as cocaine. Datril, Advil, and Nuprine can test positive as marijuana, and even poppy seeds on hamburger buns can test positive as morphine. I wonder, given this high false-positive rate, how many jobs have been unjustly lost and careers ruined?''

"We can solve the inaccuracy problem by performing second and even third tests when an initial positive finding is obtained," Sterling countered. "We could use a different and more-thorough procedure and a different laboratory to reduce the chances of sample mishandling.''

"We could, but costs are a big factor," Shaver replied. "The EMIT costs about $18 per test. We can expect a lot of false positives from what I've read. Given the high false-positive rates, I wouldn't trust a second or even third follow-up EMIT test. We could use the most reliable test—the gas chromatography/mass spectroscopy test. It costs $60 per test. With 600 employees and a few hundred applicants each year, costs could get out of hand.''

"What are the other issues?" O'Brien asked.

"There's the issue of individual rights," Shaver asserted. "Mandatory drug testing essentially involves searching the contents of an individual's most valued possession—his body, and searching without probable cause. Doesn't the 14th Amendment to the Constitution guarantee an individual's right to be secure against unreasonable searches without probable cause?''

"The 14th Amendment doesn't apply to most dealings between a private company and its employees, including drug testing," Sterling asserted. "We're on sure footing with a drug testing program as long as it is fairly and consistently administered and thoroughly documented, and as long as we don't reveal test results to a third party.''

"Technically, the 14th Amendment doesn't apply, but the spirit of the amendment should," Shaver said. "Here's my most serious concern. When we implement mandatory drug testing, we are presuming that our employees are guilty, not innocent. That's what we're communicating to them. It's an act of distrust, and it violates the spirit of mutual trust we've maintained with our employees.

"We have the best employees in the industry," she continued. "They're highly committed to Castulon; they often go the extra mile on their own without being asked. I think that's the case because we've stayed out of their private lives but have been supportive. There's a deep, mutual trust here. Mandatory drug testing violates that trust, and I think it will undermine our relationship with employees."

"Yes, we could make our people feel like criminals if the program is badly handled," Sterling responded. "But it wouldn't be. No trust is violated if we explain the potential costs of drug use, and make employees feel as if they're cooperating to resolve a troublesome problem, not as if they're potential criminals."

"Norman, I'll quote Lewis Maltby, vice president of Drexel Engineering, who's written widely on why his company will not implement drug testing," Shaver said. "When you say to an employee, 'You're doing a great job, just the same, I want you to pee in this jar and I'm sending someone to watch you,' you've undermined that trust.'"

"Folks, I feel like I'm moderating a debate," O'Brien said. "So, any closing remarks? Beverly?"

"Again, I'm disturbed about the effect that a drug testing program will have on our employees. And the issue of privacy. I wonder if we have the right to information that test results would give us — information about whether an employee is being treated for asthma, heart disease, diabetes, depression, or a host of other illnesses. But essentially, I feel that if we do have a drug problem, we can more effectively deal with it in other ways. As a preventive strategy, we can be very selective in our

hiring by thoroughly evaluating job candidates, especially their past work record. We can train managers to identify employees who are possibly drug dependent. There are other strategies that don't have the potentially explosive results a testing program will have."

"If approached carefully, I don't think employees will be offended by the program," Sterling said. "As for more-selective hiring, we are already very selective, and as far as drug use is concerned, our careful selection procedure has failed in at least three cases. We need a program that definitely works, and drug testing fits the bill."

Michael O'Brien rose from his desk. "Thank you both for your input," he said. "I'll send you a copy of the proposal once I submit it to Bob later this week. He says he'll make a decision soon after reviewing the proposal. I'll let you know."

Discussion Questions

1. Should Castulon Corporation establish a drug testing program? If so, recommend a specific policy for the program that includes disciplinary procedures for dealing with employees who test positive for drug use.

2. What are the most difficult challenges facing an organization in establishing a drug testing program? Discuss.

3. Some observers assert that, since alcohol abuse is more prevalent in the workplace and its effects just as costly, companies should also test for alcohol use. Do you agree? Explain.

LABOR RELATIONS

· · · · · · ·

*T*wo chapters make up Part 5. Chapter 17, Labor Unions: History, Laws, and Issues, covers the history, laws and some current issues facing labor unions, including unemployment, the quality of work life, membership, resistance to unions, and international unions. Chapter 18, Organizing and Collective Bargaining, focuses on organizing campaign issues and strategies and collective bargaining. The rights of employees in nonunionized situations are also covered in this chapter. The future of unions is also covered.

17

LABOR UNIONS: HISTORY, LAWS, AND ISSUES

· · · · · · ·

LEARNING OBJECTIVES

—⊖—

After studying this chapter, you should be able to:

· · ·

Understand the history of the labor movement in the United States

· · ·

Describe the role that unions play in the lives of unionized employees

· · ·

Explain why employees join unions

· · ·

Explore the role that federal labor law and the National Labor Relations Board play in labor-management relations

· · ·

Discuss the decline of labor unionism in the United States

· · ·

Contrast labor unionism in Europe, Asia, and Latin America with that in America

· · ·

Forecast the future of labor unions in the 1990s

CAREER CHALLENGE

*H*ardisty Manufacturing Company (HMC) is a fairly new firm that has grown substantially in its short history. Hardisty is located in the Boston area and manufactures consumer goods. It has a volatile technology and employs about 750 persons.

The president of the company is Tom Hardisty. He used to work for the largest firm in the industry, until he had a fight with his boss, quit, and went into competition with his former employer. Several of the key executives of Hardisty were recruited from the same firm.

The last year or two have seen increases in sales for HMC. But because of extreme competitive pressures, profits have been low or nonexistent. At times, HMC has had to lay off employees. And pay and benefit increases have not kept up with inflation. Tom has been too busy trying to keep sales up and financing available to notice the lack of positive change in his own paycheck. That isn't necessarily true for all the others at HMC. Stan Goebel, the HRM VP, has tried to bring this up with Tom from time to time. But Tom always seems to be too busy to talk about the problem.

Then one day, Stan came rushing into Tom's office.

Stan Tom, there are union organizers on the parking lot trying to get our employees to sign authorization cards.

Tom Authorization cards? What are they? We engineers don't know much about unions and don't like them much either.

Stan An authorization card is the form the organizers use to get enough people to sign up to hold an election that can unionize us.

Tom Stan, calm down. You're shaking! We have nothing to worry about. It's one happy family here. Our employees won't join a union.

Stan Oh yeah? Then why are many of them signing the cards?

Tom You saw some signing?

Stan Yeah. Lots of them.

There was a pause while Tom thought for awhile.

Tom What can we do?

Stan Well, for one thing, we can't throw them off the parking lot. We allowed charities to solicit there. Remember, I warned you!

Tom No. I meant, what should we do to keep the union out?

Stan The union must get 30 percent of the employees to sign the cards. . . .

Tom They'll never get that many. The few malcontents will sign and the rest. . . .

Stan I've talked to enough HRM people who've been through this. You can't assume that. You gotta do something.

Tom Let's talk about unions and labor relations and decide what we should do. . . .

Stan then discussed some facts of life with Tom: About labor relations, unions, contracts, law, grievances, and similar issues affecting Hardisty Manufacturing Company.

T his chapter is about a political and economic force in our society — the labor union. It discusses the union in the context of *labor relations*. **Labor relations** is a continuous relationship between a defined group of employees (represented by a union or association) and an employer. The relationship includes the negotiation of a written contract concerning pay, hours, and other conditions of employment and the interpretation and administration of this contract over its period of coverage.

Labor relations is a much-discussed HRM activity. Few employers or employees get as emotionally involved over recruiting methods or career development plans, for example, as they do over labor-management relations.[1] The reason is that collective bargaining goes to the heart of employee relations problems: power. Whoever has the power to fire an employee has power over whether that employee and his or her family can survive. Whoever has the power to discipline an employee because of poor performance has the power to affect significant human needs negatively, as noted in Chapter 2. Underlying the concept of leadership in management is the need for power.

Most employers and unions have used their power fairly. The majority of employers have hired employees, given them reasonable jobs, compensated them well, respected their dignity, and retired them after rewarding careers. However, some employers have not dealt with their employees as well. They have exploited them economically and wielded many a blow to their human dignity.

Likewise most unions and associations have represented the membership well. They have fought hard and fair for improved working conditions, better wages, human dignity, and a sharing of the fruits of labor. Some, however, have been corrupt, violent, and an embarrassment to the membership. In the United States, work conditions considered unfair or exploitative have led to the development of the collective bargaining process. Employees have joined together so that, as individuals, they do not have to stand alone against the power of a General Electric, a Department of Defense, a Yale Univeristy, or a Barnes Hospital.

In considering collective bargaining, one focus is the big picture: national and international unions all locked in major struggles with industry or in Congress. As interesting as this is, the focus of this chapter is primarily on the effects of labor relations activities on the HRM function of the employer. National contracts, and especially national contracts for a multiunit organization, are the business of a few top managers, a few top union officials, some staff lawyers and support persons, and a few government officials. Very few individuals are involved in these interactions. This chapter is concerned with how the collective bargaining process affects the *day-to-day operations* of an employer and its employees.

A DIAGNOSTIC APPROACH TO LABOR RELATIONS

Exhibit 17–1 highlights the diagnostic factors that are important in labor relations. The attitudes of employees toward unions influence whether they will join or support a union in the workplace.[2] Managerial attitudes toward unions in general and the union officials they deal with in particular also affect labor relations.

The goals of the controlling interests influence managerial attitudes and behavior toward labor relations. If management is very antiunion, the negotiation and administrative process will not proceed smoothly. The union is the other focal organization in effective collective bargaining relationships. Union officials and management interact daily and at contract time. Union and managerial attitudes toward each other affect the degree of peace and effectiveness that can exist in labor-management relations.

EXHIBIT 17-1   Factors Affecting Labor Relations

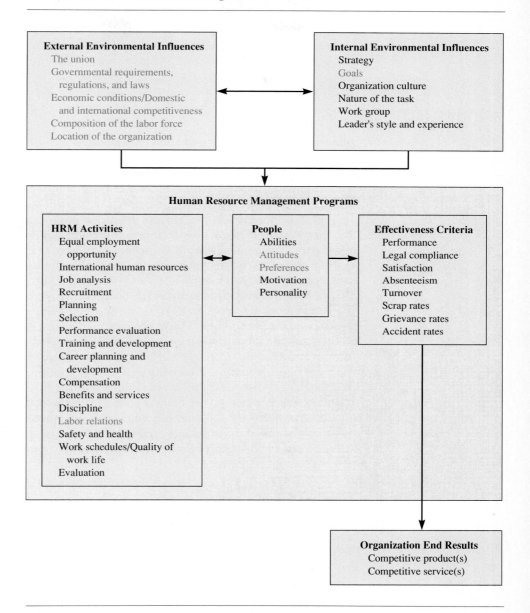

In addition to union requirements, two other environmental factors influence the nature of collective bargaining. Labor market conditions influence both management and the unions in their relationships. If the labor market has a surplus and the demand for goods is soft, management has an advantage. It can sustain a strike, and perhaps even benefit economically from one. Under those conditions, union members are less likely to vote for a strike. When the labor market is tight and the demand for goods strong, the union has the advantage. The other factor is government, which creates the legal environment within which labor relations take place.

Government boards rule on legal differences in the system, and government mediators and conciliators often help settle disputes.

Labor relations vary by the sector in which the organization operates. As will be described shortly, unions relate to managers in the business world (private sector), in government settings (public sector), and in other settings such as health, education, and voluntary organizations (third sector). Differing labor relations among the sectors are due to institutional and legal differences.

A BRIEF HISTORY OF AMERICAN LABOR UNIONS

Unions have a long history in the United States. Even before the Declaration of Independence, skilled artisans joined together to provide members' families with financial aid in the event of illness or death.[3] Today, many blue- and white-collar employees have joined together in unions. Their philosophy is the same: In joining together, there is strength. In fact, a **union** is a group of employees who have joined together to achieve present and future goals that deal with employment conditions.

The power of employees joined together is evident at the bargaining table, where union and management meet to discuss numerous issues. Many of the HRM decisions discussed in this book were influenced by union-management bargaining agreements. Employers in unionized organizations must often consult with union officials before taking actions that affect union members. In addition, many non-unionized companies have a workers' committee or council that managers consult before taking action. Their HRM policies and practices may affect employees' interest in unionizing. Thus, managers should be concerned with unions; they may either negotiate with union representatives at the bargaining table or face employees who want to form a union. Union objectives, organization, leadership, and attitudes are important for managers to know about.

Unions have existed in the United States since the colonial era. They originally functioned as fraternal societies providing help for members. Today, most unions are part of national organizations, many affiliated with the AFL–CIO (American Federation of Labor–Congress of Industrial Organizations).

Early Unions

Employers successfully resisted the earliest efforts to organize unions. In 1806, a court ruling made it a "conspiracy in restraint of trade" for workers to combine or exert pressure on management. In effect, unions were illegal until 1842, when the Massachusetts Supreme Court, in *Commonwealth v. Hunt*, decided that *criminal conspiracy* did not exist if unions did not use illegal tactics to achieve goals.

Even then, employers still resisted by discharging employees who joined unions. It was also easy for employers to have employees sign **yellow-dog contracts,** which promised that a prospective employee (job applicant) would not form or join a union. Employers also obtained court injunctions against strikers.

Early unions promoted social reform and free public education. Some of the more militant groups — such as the secret society of anthracite miners called the Molly Maguires from the Pennsylvania coal mines — were considered socialist or anarchist. They were involved in a series of widely publicized murders, riots, and bloodshed initiated by both the employers in the coal regions of Pennsylvania and the Molly Maguires themselves.

Union Federation: Craft versus Industrial Unions

The turbulent 1870s and 1880s brought growing recognition of the labor union approach to social and economic problems. These experiences helped solidify the union movement and encouraged the development of a nationwide organization.[4]

The first union federation to achieve significant size and influence was the Knights of Labor, formed around 1869. This group attracted employees and local unions from all crafts and occupational areas. In general, there are two types of unions: industrial and craft. **Industrial union** members are all employees in a company or industry, regardless of occupation. **Craft union** members belong to one craft or to a closely related group of occupations. The strength of the Knights was diluted because it failed to integrate the needs and interests of skilled and unskilled, industrial and craft members.

A group of national craft unions cut their relationship with the Knights of Labor around 1886 to form the **American Federation of Labor (AFL).** They elected Samuel Gompers of the Cigar Makers' Union president. At first, the AFL restricted membership to skilled tradespeople, such as machinists, bricklayer, and carpenters.

Growth in the union movement from 1886 to 1935 was slow. The government's attitude toward union organizing was neutral, indifferent, or negative. But, with the passage of federal laws in the 1920s and 1930s protecting the union organizing process, union membership began to grow. (More will be said about organizing in Chapter 18.) Thus, formal laws helped unions grow during their formative years.

In 1935, the **Congress of Industrial Organizations (CIO)** was formed by John L. Lewis, president of the United Mine Workers, in cooperation with a number of presidents of unions expelled from the AFL. The CIO was formed to organize employees in industrial and mass-production jobs. The CIO wanted to organize craft and unskilled employees within an industry, such as assembly-line workers, machinists, and assemblers. Soon the AFL began to offer membership to unskilled workers too. Competition for new union members led to bitter conflicts between the AFL and CIO, but in 1955 they merged.

LABOR LEGISLATION

The union-management pattern of interaction is governed by state and federal laws.[5] These laws have evolved through common law and through rulings by the National Labor Relations Board (NLRB) and the courts. Figuratively speaking, these laws swing back and forth like a pendulum, at times favoring management and at times favoring unions.

Early Labor Law

The first government legislation affecting unions and management was the Arbitration Act of 1888. This act encouraged the voluntary settlement of labor disputes in the railroad industry. In 1926, the Railway Labor Act was passed by Congress. It provided railroad employees with the right to organize and bargain collectively with management.

In the 1930s, the federal government became involved in labor disputes outside the railroad industry. The Norris-LaGuardia Act, also called the Anti-Injunction Act, was passed in 1932. The act limited the powers of federal courts to stop union picketing, boycotts, and strikes. *Injunctions*, court decrees to stop union activities, had provided employers with an easy way to hinder union activities. The Norris-LaGuardia Act also made the yellow-dog contracts unenforceable.

The National Labor Relations Act (Wagner Act)

The *National Labor Relations Act*, better known as the **Wagner Act,** was passed in 1935. The stated purpose of the act was to encourage the growth of trade unions and restrain management from interfering with this growth. As originally drafted, it included seven topics:

1. The recognition of employees' rights to bargain collectively.
2. Limitations on collective bargaining.
3. Representation.
4. Certification/decertification elections.
5. Terms of collective bargaining agreements.
6. Problem of company unions.
7. The right to strike.[6]

This act made the government take an active role in union-management relationships by restricting the activities of management. Five unfair labor practices specified in the Wagner Act are summarized in Exhibit 17–2. Justification of the Wagner Act was based on the fact that an individual employee has unequal bargaining power when compared to the position of the employer.[7]

The power to implement the Wagner Act was given to a five-person **National Labor Relations Board** (NRLB) and a staff of lawyers and other personnel responsible to the board. The board sets up elections, on request, to determine if a given group of workers wishes to have a union as a bargaining representative. The board also investigates complaints of unfair labor practices. If an unfair labor charge is filed with the NLRB and the investigation is initiated, the NLRB has an array of alternatives, as presented in Exhibit 17–3, that can be used to resolve the complaint.

EXHIBIT 17-2   Employer Unfair Labor Practices

- *To interfere with, restrain, or coerce employees in the exercise of their rights to organize* (threaten employees with loss of job if they vote for a union, grant wage increases deliberately timed to discourage employees from joining a union).

- *To dominate or interfere with the affairs of a union* (take an active part in the affairs of a union, such as a supervisor actively participating in a union, show favoritism to one union over another in an organization attempt).

- *To discriminate in regard to hiring, tenure, or any employment condition for the purpose of encouraging or discouraging membership in any union organization* (discharge an employee if he or she urges others to join a union, demote an employee for union activity).

- *To discriminate against or discharge an employee because he or she has filed charges or given testimony under the Wagner Act* (discriminate against, fire, or demote an employee because he or she gave testimony to NLRB officials or filed charges against the employer with the NLRB).

- *To refuse to bargain collectively with representatives of the employees; that is, bargain in good faith* (refuse to provide financial data, if requested by the union, when the organization pleads losses; refuse to bargain about a mandatory subject, such as hours and wages; refuse to meet with union representatives duly appointed by a certified bargaining unit).

EXHIBIT 17-3   NLRB Alternatives for Handling Unfair Labor Practice Charges

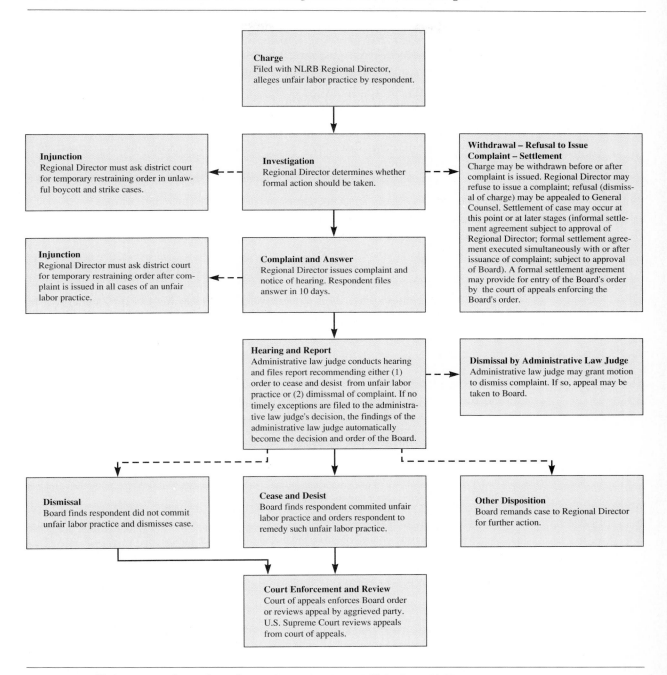

Source: Bruce Feldacker (1980), *Labor Guide to Labor Law* (Reston, Va.: Reston Publishing), pp. 14–15.

The Taft-Hartley Act

The Wagner Act was considered prolabor. In order to swing the pendulum back toward management, Congress in 1947 passed the **Taft-Hartley Act** (also called the *Labor-Management Relations Act*), which amended and supplemented the Wagner Act. The Taft-Hartley Act guaranteed employee bargaining rights and specifically forbade the five unfair employer labor practices first established in the Wagner Act. But the act also specified unfair union labor practices. The union was restrained from such practices as those shown in Exhibit 17–4.

Union membership increased significantly after the Wagner Act was passed. Under aggressive union leadership, members were recruited, and the union cause became so popular that from 1935 to 1947 the membership rolls increased from 3 million to 15 million.

The other major effects of the Taft-Hartley Act include the following:

. It denied supervisors legal protection in organizing their own unions.
. It provided the president of the United States, through the attorney general, the right to seek an 80-day court injunction against strikes or lockouts that could affect the nation's health.
. The union was forbidden to deduct union dues from members' paychecks without prior written permission.
. Employers could express their views against unions as long as they made no attempt to threaten or bribe employees.

EXHIBIT 17–4   Union Unfair Labor Practices

• *To restrain or coerce employees in the exercise of their right to join or not to join a union, except when an agreement is made by the employer and union that a condition of employment will be joining the union, called* a union security clause *authorizing a union shop* (picket as a mass and physically bar other employees from entering a company facility, act violently toward nonunion employees, threaten employees for not supporting union activities).

• *To cause an employer to discriminate against an employee other than for nonpayment of dues or initiation fees* (cause an employer to discriminate against an employee for antiunion activity, force the employer to hire only workers satisfactory to the union).

• *To refuse to bargain with an employer in good faith* (insist on negotiating illegal provisions such as the administration's prerogative to appoint supervisors, refuse to meet with the employer's representative, terminate an existing contract or strike without the appropriate notice).

• *To engage, induce, encourage, threaten, or coerce any individual to engage in strikes, refusal to work, or boycott where the objective is to:*
     Force or require any employer or self-employed person to recognize or join any labor organization or employer organization.
     Force or require an employer or self-employed person to cease using the products of or doing business with another person, or force any other employer to recognize or bargain with the union unless it has been certified by the NLRB.
     Force an employer to apply pressure to another employer to recognize a union.
Examples are: picketing a hospital so that it will apply pressure on a subcontractor (food service, maintenance, emergency department) to recognize a union; or forcing an employer to do only business with others, such as suppliers, who have a union, or picketing by another union for recognition when a different one is already certified.

• *To charge excessive or discriminatory membership fees* (charge a higher initiation fee to employees who did not join the union until after a union-security agreement is in force).

• *To cause an employer to give payment for services not performed (featherbedding)* (force an employer to add people to the payroll when they are not needed, force payment to employees who provide no services).

Soon after the Taft-Hartley Act was put into practice, a number of corrupt practices in the union movement were disclosed. Investigations uncovered union leaders who had misused and stolen union membership fees and funds. It was also determined that some union leaders were involved with organized crime. The AFL expelled the entire International Brotherhood of Teamsters when the leaders failed to correct a criminal act uncovered in Senate hearings.

In 1974, Congress extended the coverage of the Taft-Hartley Act to private nonprofit hospitals and nursing homes. The extension was a major matter. Approximately 2 million employees working in about 3,300 nonprofit hospitals were affected. Before 1974, the NLRB assumed jurisdiction over health-care institutions. However, until the 1974 amendment, the NLRB was not authorized to handle cases in the nonprofit sector because the original law expressly exluded it from doing so.

Recognizing that hospitals supply a critical public service, the 1974 amendment established a special set of dispute-settling procedures. Unions representing hospital employees must give a 90 days' notice before terminating a labor agreement, 30 days more than Taft-Hartley requires in other industries. In addition, a hospital union cannot strike or picket unless it gives 10 days' notice. This notice requirement, not found in other industries, provides hospital management with the opportunity to make arrangements for the continuity of patient care.[8] There are other provisions of the 1974 amendment that apply to hospitals.

One of the most important elements of the Taft-Hartley Act is section 146, involving *right-to-work requirements*. Section 146 provided that, should any state wish to pass legislation more restrictive of union security than the union shop (that is, to outlaw labor contracts that made union membership a condition of retaining employment), the state was free to do so. Exhibit 17–5 presents a map that shows

EXHIBIT 17-5   Right-to-Work States

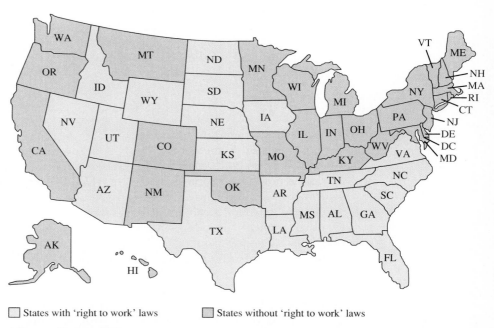

☐ States with 'right to work' laws   ☐ States without 'right to work' laws

* Data as of January 1988.

the states (21) that have enacted **right-to-work laws.** These states ban any form of compulsory union membership.

The Landrum-Griffin Act

In the 1950s, Congressional investigations uncovered a number of illegal practices on the part of unions. At this time, Congress assumed that the individual union members were still not protected enough by the labor laws in existence. In 1959, Congress passed the **Landrum-Griffin Act,** which is officially designated the *Labor-Management Reporting and Disclosure Act*. It was designed to regulate the internal affairs of unions.

This act, referred to as the *bill of rights of union members*, gave every union member the right to (1) nominate candidates for union office, (2) vote in union elections, and (3) attend union meetings. Union members also had the right to examine union accounts and records. In addition, the union was required to submit an annual financial report to the secretary of labor. Employers had to report any payments or loans made to unions, the officers, or members. This portion of the act was to eliminate what are called *sweetheart contracts*, under which the union leaders and management agree to terms that work to their mutual benefit, but maintain poor working conditions for other employees.

In general, labor unions were opposed to the passage of the Landrum-Griffin Act because it restricted union control over their organizations. The AFL–CIO believed it could handle any abuses through good internal management. However, the Senate Select Committee on Improper Activities in Labor and Management, headed by Senator McClellan, uncovered numerous abuses inside the union in the late 1950s. This Senate investigation weakened the prestige of unions and made it easier to pass the Landrum-Griffin Act.

As the shifts in labor legislation indicate, there have been noticeable shifts in public policy toward labor unions. It has moved in this century from encouragement and support to modified support with regulation, to specific regulations of union affairs. The U.S. public is now, with television and other media, able to acquire an up-close look at union-management relationships and behavior. The future public policy toward these relationships and behaviors will depend largely upon what the U.S. public sees and wants.

GOVERNMENT-EMPLOYEE LEGISLATION

An increasingly important factor in U.S. labor relations is the growth of unions in the public sector. Federal, state, and local governments employed 17.6 million workers in 1989, with most of the growth at the state and local levels. Public employees now account for 25 percent of AFL–CIO membership, an increase of 10 percent since 1976. There are three separate sectors with their own labor relations policies in the federal government alone: the executive branch, postal workers, and 19 other agencies including the Tennessee Valley Authority.[9] The American Federation of State, County, and Municipal Employees (AFSME) increased its membership by 443,000, an increase of 68 percent in just 15 years. With a total membership of more than 1 million, AFSME is now one of the largest unions affiliated with the AFL–CIO. The American Federation of Government Employees (AFGE) now represents 675,465 federal employees. About 89.5 percent (644,000) of all postal workers are unionized. In 1989, public-sector unions represented about 7.6 million or approximately 44 percent of all government employees.[10]

EXHIBIT 17-6   State and Local Government Bargaining Agreements 1986 to 1988

				Units with —					
				1,000 to 4,999 workers			5,000 or more workers		
	Total								
Item	1986	1987	1988	1986	1987	1988	1986	1987	1988
Workers covered, total (1,000):									
All settlements	873	1,291	1,061	450	538	497	423	754	564
State government	313	462	404	89	115	97	224	347	306
Local government	560	830	658	361	422	400	199	407	258
Average wage adjustment (percent):									
First year of contract:									
All settlements	5.7	4.9	5.1	5.2	4.7	5.0	6.2	5.0	5.2
State government	6.3	4.1	5.3	5.0	4.2	5.3	6.8	4.1	5.3
Local government	5.3	5.3	5.0	5.1	4.9	4.9	5.6	5.8	5.2
Over the life of contract									
All settlements	5.7	5.1	5.3	5.4	4.8	5.1	6.0	5.3	5.5
State government	6.0	4.2	5.0	6.0	4.3	4.7	6.0	4.2	5.1
Local government	5.6	5.6	5.5	5.4	4.9	5.2	6.0	6.2	6.0
Total effective wage adjustments (percent):	5.5	4.9	4.7	n.a.	4.6	4.6	n.a.	5.2	4.7
Source:									
Current settlements	2.4	2.7	2.3	n.a.	2.6	2.4	n.a.	2.7	2.2
Prior settlements	3.0	2.2	2.4	n.a.	1.9	2.2	n.a.	2.5	2.5
Cost-of-living adjustments	n.a.	n.a.	n.a.	n.a.	(z)	(z)	n.a.	(z)	(z)
State government	5.6	4.3	4.1	n.a.	3.9	4.4	n.a.	4.5	4.0
Local government	5.4	5.3	5.1	n.a.	4.8	4.7	n.a.	6.0	5.5

n.a. = Not available.
Source: Adapted from U.S. Bureau of Labor Statistics (March 1990), *Current Wage Developments* (Washington, D.C.).

Laws that are favorable to the growth of public-sector unions increase the probability that government workers will organize. Labor relations throughout the public sector are governed by policies, statutes, executive orders, and ordinances.[11] The Civil Service Reform Act covers employee relations at the federal level while the Postal Reorganization Act of 1970 covers postal workers. States located in the Northeast, North, Midwest, on the West Coast, and Alaska and Hawaii have laws that favor public-sector bargaining. Sun belt states except the state of Florida and Southwest and lower Rocky Mountain states do not have such legislation. Altogether 38 states and the District of Columbia have statutes or executive orders that support collective bargaining for at least some public employees.[12]

There are major differences between labor law and regulation in the private and public sectors.[13] In the private sector, the law tries to encourage management and labor to bargain as equals. In the public sector, the government defines itself as the superior through the use of the sovereignty doctrine, which has weakened in recent years. The *sovereignty doctrine* holds that the federal and state governments represent the sovereign power of the people. Consequently, only the government can delegate by legislation to various organizations or by voluntarily delegating authority to them in certain areas. In addition, responsibility for negotiating with employees is complicated by the separation of powers doctrine. Some managerial responsibility lies with the executive branch, some with the legislative.

Public-sector collective bargaining is relatively new in the United States and has not been developed definitively. There is more clarity for federal employees than others. In the public sector, federal labor relations are regulated by executive orders issued by the president alone. Each new order rescinds previous orders on the same topic. In 1962, President John Kennedy issued Executive Order 10988, designed to parallel federal bargaining to private bargaining. It included a strong management-rights clause and banned strikes and the union shop. This was the first recognition ever on the part of the government that its employees could join unions and bargain collectively.

Executive Order 11491, issued by President Richard Nixon in 1969 to update 10988, was designed to bring public bargaining even closer to that in the private sector. Under this order, the secretary of labor has the authority to determine bargaining units, to supervise procedures for union recognition, and to examine standards for unfair labor practices and rule on them.

Executive Order 11491 also created the Federal Labor Relations Council (FLRC), which reviews decisions of the secretary of labor, chairman of the Civil Service Commission, and director of the Office of Management and Budget. The FLRC supervises the Federal Service Impasses Panel, comprised of seven neutral members appointed by the president from outside the federal service to settle labor disputes in that sector. Executive Order 11491 also required a simple majority of employees to choose an exclusive representative union and stipulated criteria for determining the bargaining unit.

Executive Order 11838, issued by President Gerald Ford in 1975, required federal agencies to bargain with their employees on all issues unless the agency could show *compelling need* not to negotiate. All HRM policies became subject to negotiation. The FLRC was appointed the final arbitrator on these issues and on what constitutes compelling need. Subjects for grievances were also broadened. But this order still bans union-agency shops and has a strong management-rights clause.

Labor relations regulations for public employees at state and local levels are diverse and complicated. For example, 12 states have no applicable labor laws at all for public employees. Another 20 states have such laws, and the other 18 have laws that cover certain aspects of labor relations for these employees.

For a time, it was thought the answer to this confusion might be a federal law applicable to state and local employees, but the Supreme Court and other federal courts have made it clear that the federal government cannot interfere with state and local employees. These rulings have also held that these governments do not have to bargain with their employees. So the degree of public bargaining practiced and the methods used vary from state to state and city to city.

In January 1979, the Executive Orders were supplemented by what is called the *Federal Service Labor-Management Relations Statute*. The act applies to employees in federal agencies except the Postal Service (covered by the Taft-Hartley Act), the FBI, the General Accounting Office, the National Security Agency, the CIA, and agencies dealing with federal employee labor relations. Employees of the legislative and judicial branches were also excluded.

The Federal Labor Relations Authority is charged with overseeing the act in a manner similar to the National Labor Relations Board. Bargaining rights are limited under the statute. Federal employees may not bargain over wages and benefits, hiring or promotion, or classification of positions. The labor organization may not advocate a strike, and unauthorized strikes may lead to decertification (the union is no longer the representative of the employee) and discipline of individual members. These steps were taken by the government under this statute when the Professional Air Traffic Controllers (PATCO) union was decertified in 1981.

In addition to federal law, the states have passed labor laws affecting certain aspects of labor relations. Normally, these laws affect strikes, picketing, boycotts, and collective bargaining by public employees. These laws vary across states and between employee groups within states.

For collective bargaining to be successful, many people believe that labor must have the *right to strike*. As previously mentioned, most public-sector legislation prohibits strikes or limits the circumstances under which they can be used and their length. Public services are considered to be *essential* and, of course, are provided with taxpayers' money.

In addition to government employees, there are also an estimated 3 million public employees who belong to professional and civil service associations that are not counted as labor unions. However, in many cases, they are very much like labor unions. For example, the National Education Association has 2 million members, many of whom are covered by collective bargaining agreements.[14]

THE STRUCTURE AND MANAGEMENT OF UNIONS

Union structure in the United States consists of four levels: the federation of unions (AFL–CIO), intermediate, national, and local. Each will be discussed briefly.

Federation of Unions

The majority of national and international labor unions now belong to the AFL–CIO, although a number of unions, representing over 3 million members, are unaffiliated. However, in 1987, one of the most powerful unions, the Teamsters, became reaffiliated with the AFL–CIO. The structure of the present AFL–CIO is shown in Exhibit 17–7.

How does the AFL–CIO work? Its chief governing body is the biennial convention, which sets policy. Between conventions, the executive officers, assisted by the executive council and the general board, run the AFL–CIO. Executive officers are the *president*, who interprets the constitution between meetings of the executive council and heads the union staff, and the *secretary-treasurer*, who is responsible for financial affairs. The executive council also has 33 vice presidents. It meets three times a year and sets policy between conventions. The general board consists of the executive council and the head of each affiliated national union and department.

National headquarters provides many services to subsidiary union bodies: training for regional and local union leaders, organizing help, strike funds, and data to be used in negotiating contracts. Specialists available for consultation include lawyers, public relations specialists, and research personnel.

Very large unions that are members of the AFL–CIO are those of the steelworkers, electrical workers, carpenters, machinists, hotel and restaurant workers, and state, county, and local government employees. However, no national union is required to affiliate with the AFL–CIO. For example, the United Mine Workers, a once very powerful union, is not affiliated with AFL–CIO.

Intermediate Union Bodies

Intermediate organizing bodies interface with the AFL–CIO, national, and local units.[15] Intermediate units include regional or district offices, trade conferences, conference boards, and joint councils. They are usually affiliated with a national union and provide services to a given geographic area. The purpose of these

EXHIBIT 17-7   Structural Organization of the American Federation of Labor and Congress of Industrial Organization

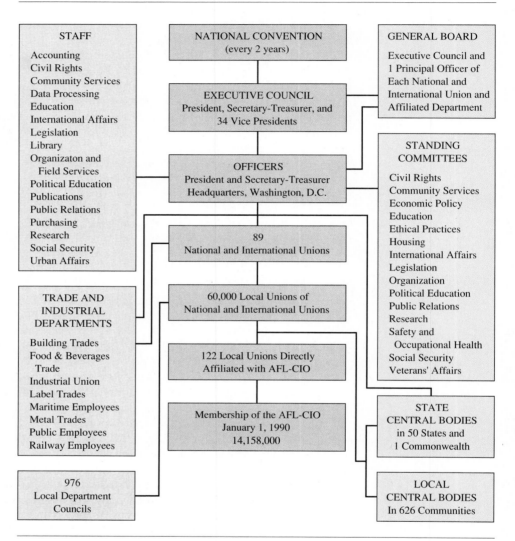

Source: AFL–CIO.

intermediate bodies is to help coordinate union membership, organize discussions of issues pertaining to the relationships between labor and management, and join together local unions with similar goals. They may provide office space and other facilities for local unions.

The National Union

The constitution of the national union establishes the rules, policies, and procedures under which the local unions may be chartered and become members. Each national union exercises some control over the local unions. These controls usually deal with the collection of dues, the admission of new members by the local, and the use of union funds. The national also provides the local unions with support for organizing campaigns and the administration of contracts. There are approximately 100 national union organizations ranging in size from 1 million plus members — Teamsters and AFSME unions — to just 18 members — a unit in the printing trade.

The Local Union

The grassroots of labor organizations in the United States is the local craft or industrial union. Members of a craft union have the same skills, for example, carpentry, bricklaying, and electrical installation. Members of an industrial union have different skills, ranging from unskilled laborers to highly skilled technicians, but they all work in the same industry — auto, rubber, mines, and so on. There are about 60,000 local unions. Locals have direct influence over the membership. Through the local, members exercise their complaints and pay the dues that support the national union.

The activities of locals are conducted by officials elected by the members. The elected officials include a president, vice president, secretary-treasurer, business representative, and committee chairperson. Elected officials of local unions often have full-time jobs in addition to their regular union duties.

In many local unions, the **business representative** is the dominant person. The major responsibilities of the business representative are to negotiate and administer the labor agreement and to settle problems that may arise in connection with the contract. The business representative also collects dues, recruits new members, coordinates social activities, and arranges union meetings.

The **union steward** represents the interests of local union members in their relations with managers on the job. In the auto industry, the steward (called a *committee person*) devotes full time to solving disputes that arise in connection with the union-management labor contract.

The role of a district commiteeman (union steward) named Charlie Bragg, who worked in a Ford Motor Company plant, was described as follows:

He might be called, in fact, the fixer — the man to whom workers can turn in times of trouble. . . . Unofficially, Mr. Bragg is the union to his people and often the only representative they deal with. . . .

The main function of a committeeman is to settle problems right on the floor. Mr. Bragg says, "I'm a mediator, a foot-soldier out here. Without the committeeman, Ford couldn't run this plant."

It is Charlie Bragg and the men like him who are fighting disciplinary actions, getting supply racks fixed, arranging days off, getting bathrooms cleaned and drinking fountains unclogged. (On the average day, Mr. Bragg handles about 20 individual problems.)

His prime goal, he says, is keeping his constituents happy. But, he also must remain on working terms with their supervisors, who, he feels must regard him as tough, but flexible.[16]

In United Steelworkers Union 1010 in East Chicago, Indiana, the union steward is called a *griever*. Alan Moseley is the busy, overworked, and highly stressed griever who is paid approximately $350 per month by the union and who also is paid $16 per hour by Inland Steel for his regular work as a quality inspector.[17] Alan works a full job and is also the union steward. He blames the stress of handling hundreds of grievances and complaints a year for his 50-pound weight gain, sleepless nights, and little time off to be with his family.

Charlie Bragg and Alan Moseley are the union's direct link to management. They are the front-line representatives who must work for the workers they represent. They try hard to keep the lines of communication, trust, and respect open between union members and management.

Managing the Union

The job of managing a union at the national or local level is challenging and time consuming. Union officials need to be dedicated, willing to work long hours, able to counsel members on personal problems, and skilled in influencing people. This combination of skills and abilities must also be obvious to members; tenure in office, especially at the local level, depends on projecting a favorable impression. Officers must run periodically for reelection. Some of the managerial problems facing union officials are member apathy, financial control, and recruitment of new members.

It is common knowledge that the majority of union members are apathetic about attending union meetings and voting on contracts on strike decisions. Thus, it is difficult for union officials to encourage members to take their union responsibilities more seriously.

Unions are financed through dues, fines, and initiation fees collected at the local level. However, union members resist high assessments. Union officials must convince members that, unless the union has a sound financial base, it won't have the power to secure favorable labor agreements.

The drive to organize more employees always faces union officials. Without new members, unions don't have the strength to carry out tactics to satisfy the needs, preferences, and interests of the membership. Developing effective organizing drives is the responsibility of local and national unions alike. Organizing will be discussed in more detail in Chapter 18.

WHY JOIN A UNION?

One important function of a union is to negotiate and administer the contract with the employer, which covers wages, hours, and the conditions of employment. The contract designates the formal terms of the union-management agreement in very specific language. It usually covers about two or three years. More details on contracts will be presented in Chapter 18. In addition to having a specific contract, there are many other attractive features of union membership, and these appeal to different segments of the work force. There is no single answer to the question of why employees join a union. It is generally correct to state that employees join unions to satisfy needs that are important to them.[18] Certainly, needs and what is important differ among individuals.

First, many employees want some *assurance that their jobs will exist* in the future. They do not want to be fired or arbitrarily laid off because of a personality clash with a manager, an economic recession, or because of automation caused by the introduction of new technology. Unions, through collective bargaining, continually discuss and debate the issue of job security.

For 300 employees at the Bethlehem Steel plant in Johnstown, Pennsylvania, having a job for life is a reality. Since July 1983, mechanical workers in the bar, rod, and wire divisions have been protected from any type of layoff. It is estimated that fewer than 100 of the major employers in the United States have worked out plans to provide job security. IBM, a nonunion firm, was one organization that provided job security. But, with the increasing success of Japanese and other competition, IBM was forced to use some layoffs for the first time in 40 years.

Second, people *need to socialize* and be part of a group. Unions meet these needs by bringing together people with similar interests and goals. Through meetings, social events, educational programs, and common projects, unions can build a strong bond of friendship and team spirit.

Third, a *safe and healthy place to work* is important to employees. Unions in the United States and Canada have pushed hard for good working conditions. This well-publicized emphasis on improved working conditions appeals to employees who are considering a union.

Perhaps one of the strongest motives for joining a union is that it provides employees with a *communication link* to management. This link enables them to express dissatisfactions and disagreements about the job, management, and other issues. One such link is the grievance procedure detailed in the union-management contract.

Finally, compensation is an important reason for working. Employees want to receive a *fair day's pay for a fair day's work* and *good fringe benefits*. They are very concerned with receiving pay and fringe benefits that are competitive in the community.

UNION SECURITY

Labor unions have, since their beginning, stressed the importance of *union security* or preservation of membership. Labor legislation also addresses the issue of union security. Unions want to increase their security by requiring all employees to join the union once it is elected as the organization's legitimate bargaining agent. This is especially true if the union is voted in by a slim margin. In such cases, some employees obviously don't want to join the union. Different types of union "shops" have developed as a result, and they represent various degrees of union security.[19]

Restricted Shop

When management tries to keep a union out without violating any labor laws, a **restricted shop** exists. A restricted shop is an attitude rather than a formal arrangement. Management may try to provide wages and fringe benefits that make the union and what it can offer unattractive. This is a legal effort to make the union's organizing ineffective.[20]

It is illegal to create a restricted shop by dismissing employees who want to unionize; trying to influence employees who are thinking about starting a union; or promising rewards if the union is voted down. These activities could result in legal action against management.

Open Shop

An **open shop** is one in which there is neither a union present nor a management effort to keep the union out. The employees have total freedom to decide whether or not they want a union. This type of shop is a prime target for union organizing efforts.

Agency Shop

In the **agency shop,** all employees pay union dues whether or not they are members of the union. This means that no employee is a "free rider," someone who does not belong to a union or pay dues but turns to the union for help and enjoys the higher wages and other benefits that the union provides. *Everyone* pays dues for the services of an organized union even though some employees are not members. Unions in the public-sector workplace are increasingly seeking agency shop agreements.[21]

Preferential Shop

In the **preferential shop,** the union is recognized, and union members are given preference in some areas. For example, when hiring new employees, union members are given preference over nonunion members. This type of preference may also be given in such areas as promotion and layoff. Many of these preferential decisions are in violation of the Taft-Hartley Act. If there is an excessive amount of preferential treatment, a closed shop may exist, which is also prohibited by the Taft-Hartley Act.

The Union Shop

The **union shop** requires the employee to join a union after being hired. An employer may hire any person, but, within a period of time, that employee must join the union or lose the job. Under the Taft-Hartley Act, this period of time can be shorter than 30 days. But, under the Landrum-Griffin Act, this period can be shortened to seven days in the construction industry only. Most union-management labor contracts provide for the union shop.

The Taft-Hartley Act allows states to forbid union shops by passing what are called *right-to-work laws*. Under these laws, two persons doing the same job must be paid the same wages, whether or not they belong to the union. The union believes this is unfair, because the nonunionized employees pay no dues but share in the benefits won by the union. Twenty-one states, located primarily in the South, the Great Plains, and the Southwest have right-to-work laws. Some of the larger states with these laws are Texas, Florida, Georgia, and Arizona.

Closed Shop

The **closed shop** requires that a new employee be a union member when hired. The union itself provides labor to the organization. Although this type of shop is illegal, modified closed shops are found in the construction, printing, and maritime industries. For rexample, an ironworkers' union hall sends out union members to construction sites on request. A nonunion member has little chance to be sent from a union hall to a job, because the union's business agent makes the assignment. Union members elect the business agent, while the nonunion members have no vote.

In the United Kingdom, 25 percent of all union members and 10 percent of all other employees work in a closed shop. Employers in the United Kingdom feel that this closed-shop arrangement stops fragmented bargaining and may lead to more loyal employees. However, the Prime Minister is threatening legislation to outlaw the closed shop there. In the United States, powerful construction unions have hurried their own demise with costly strikes and major wage and benefit increases. The result was that more and more industries turned to open-shop contractors.[22]

Maintenance of Membership

Another technique unions use to guarantee membership is called *maintenance of membership*. When this clause is inserted into a contract, union members cannot resign from the union during the life of a contract. There is an escape period before the new contract takes effect when employees can resign from the union without penalty, however.

LABOR-MANAGEMENT RELATIONS

The role of a labor relations manager is a very important one on the HR team. Surveys indicate that labor relations is the most important issue to be faced in unionized firms. Both HR and operating managers are involved in labor relations. *HR managers or specialists* are, of necessity, technical experts on labor relations who train and advise operating managers on the contract provisions. They also bargain with the union on the contract and serve as a step in the grievance process. But *operating managers* are the persons who implement the contract. They advise HRM on problem areas in the contract so they can try to improve them during the next negotiations, and they face grievances first. An overall, vital influence in labor relations is exerted by *top management*. Top managers' attitudes toward unions strongly influence the attitudes of HR and operating managers and help determine whether union-management relations will be amiable or combative. Top managers also strongly influence the negotiating process. The bargaining philosophy and strategy they assume at the time of negotiations will help determine whether and how soon a contract will be signed, or whether a strike, lockout, and arbitration or other processes will occur.

Labor-Management Stereotypes

There have been a number of studies of the attitudes of how labor and management view each other. In general, they show the unflattering, dysfunctional stereotypes they have developed of one another. These stereotypes can distort the data presented during discussions about working conditions, pay, and so on. One union stereotype of a labor relations manager is a "pretty boy," snobbish, country-club type, fawning over his boss, who could not find his way to the bathroom with a map and never worked a real day's work in his life. His job is only to cheat honest workers out of a few cents an hour to get a big bonus. Some labor relations managers, on the other hand, stereotype the union official as a loudmouth, uneducated goon who probably is stealing pension funds and no doubt beats up uncooperative workers. He will ruin the company because he does not understand the dog-eat-dog marketplace.

These differences in perceptions between the two groups are compounded by major differences in such factors as age, education, and social class background. Furthermore, the employer organizations are hierarchical: The labor relations manager has a boss to report to. The union is peer-oriented: The agreement must be approved by a vote of the members. The union leader has to be reelected to remain in office.

In sum, one of the challenges of labor relations is that on the union side of the table the representatives have more conflicts and less structure than those on the employer's side. There are conflicts within the management side, too, but usually there is an official, such as the president of the organization, who can settle these conflicts by a decision. This is not so on the union side.

Government Officials and Others

The role players in labor relations are the employees, union officers, and labor relations executives. But others also do have an impact. The first are the government regulatory bodies that administer the labor laws. In the United States, the National

Labor Relations Board administers the laws and regulations in the private and not-for-profit sectors. Many states also have state boards to administer state labor laws.

Labor relations administrators have two major duties:

To supervise representation elections and certify unions as bargaining agents.

To hear appeals of alleged violations of the laws.

Most experts believe the boards do a satisfactory job with elections. Some contend they are too slow in processing violation appeals. However, they receive a large number of complaints, and it is not an easy job. For example, in a typical month, over 4,000 new cases are filed with the NLRB. Some who favor the union side contend that these delays benefit management, and management deliberately takes its time and regularly appeals violation decisions. For example, cases where management is charged with firing prounion employees might take two years (with appeals and delays) to decide. By then the fired employees have other jobs or are tired of the process. Management disputes this, and the NLRB and other boards have attempted to expedite these cases.[23]

Others with a possible impact on labor relations include customers and the general public. Customers and clients of the organization may mobilize to move the negotiation process along faster. Customers who need goods or services may exert pressure on the employer directly to settle or lose the business. They also do this indirectly by buying elsewhere and letting the home office know it.

The general public tends to be neutral or uninterested in most labor-management incidents. Both sides try to mobilize public support through the media, however, because, if the public is denied service, it can bring political or other pressure to bear on the settlement. This normally happens when the public is severely affected by the loss of the goods or services.

ISSUES FACING UNIONS

Labor unions began struggling in the 1980s to stop serious erosion of their membership base. To attract and retain members, unions have concentrated their efforts on issues that employees are concerned about: job security, rising health-care costs, child care, comparable worth, foreign competition, unemployment, and recruiting new members. These issues are an important part of the motivational forces influencing employees to unionize.[24]

In October 1989, the 18th constitutional convention of the AFL–CIO solidified labor's position:

This country needs a labor law which assures the right of self-organization in fact as well as in theory to all workers — public as well as private, professional as well as non-professional, part-time as well as full-time, temporary as well as permanent, ''managerial'' employees and guards as well as production and service workers.[25]

Decline of Unions

The 1990s is a critical time for unions in the United States. Membership has decreased by half since the early 1950s to less than 17 percent of the work force. Only 20 percent of union members work in the manufacturing sector, and this base continues to erode. Unions are in real danger of becoming marginally relevant to the U.S. workplace.[26] Five key issues facing unions in this volatile environment include:[27]

1. The switch from a manufacturing to a service-based economy.
2. Increasingly cut-throat foreign competition with lower labor costs.
3. Dramatic demographic changes in the work force — more women, Hispanics, and illegal immigrants.
4. Antiunion management attitudes.
5. Continued shift in employment and job creation from *Fortune* 500 firms to small, entrepreneurial businesses.

The general public's confidence in unions shows real decline, from a public approval rating of 76 percent in 1957 to 55 percent in 1988.[28] The manufacturing sector of the economy will generate almost no new jobs in the next 13 years, and its contribution to the gross national product will be less than 17 percent by the year 2000.[29]

The climate on the management side of labor relations is more adversarial than 10 years ago since the launching of a union-free environment program by the National Association of Manufacturers.[30] President Reagan's decertification of the air traffic controllers and the lack of a neutral and effective National Labor Relations Board have escalated labor's decline.[31] To take advantage of lower labor costs, many employers are subcontracting or outsourcing much of their assembly and production work to Third World nations and right-to-work states.

Industry has been closing plants all across the country, but especially hard hit is the union heartland of the Northeast and Midwest. Takeovers, mergers, and acquisitions have put marginal employers out of business. Recent contract negotiations are characterized by wage concessions and givebacks as unions try to provide members with job security. The only segment in which unions are making some gains is the public sector. However, cutbacks in government spending could mean fewer new jobs and fewer workers to organize.

If any successful organizing gains are accomplished in the 1990s, they will be with new groups that are beginning to dominate the work force — engineers, programmers, and technical workers. Union organizing efforts in these areas will be different from the traditional ones. Instead of simply passing out handbills at a plant gate informing workers about the benefits of unionization, there will be a greater "Madison Avenue" touch. Television, newspaper, and carefully prepared pamphlets will be used by the unions. These campaigns will be resisted by equally "slick" and professional antiunion management campaigns. Management will emphasize more of the individual spirit and skill theme that they claim will be dampened if a person joins a union that emphasizes collectivism and group solidarity.

It remains to be seen whether the sharp decline in union membership can be stopped and reversed.[32] Perhaps the most important starting point should focus on the public's image of unions.

Labor Unions and the Public Image

If labor unions are to remain strong political and social forces, they must stem their recent decline and negative public image. Still, the majority of Americans believe that unions do more good than harm. Most people feel that strong unions provide the only way for many workers to get a fair piece of the economic pie. The union is also viewed as a legitimate representative for workers to voice complaints and grievances.

Perhaps some of the public's growing disapproval of labor unions is directed toward the behavior of labor union leaders rather than the union's objectives. Many people still believe that labor leaders are less likely than business leaders to act in the national interest. In fact, today the public shows a greater disdain for labor leaders than they do business leaders. It is evident that corrupt and autocratic labor leader behavior is given more media publicity than corrupt and autocratic business leader behavior. However, as long as union leader corruption is publicized, the image of the union movement will remain more negative. Hopefully, union leaders who are aware of the problems poor image can cause will encourage and promote improved union leader behavior. Unless unions can improve their image, their efforts to remain a major force in society will fail.

Unemployment

Many organizations have searched for and found technological advances that resulted in increased productivity. American Telephone & Telegraph Company has cut some 120,000 jobs from its payroll because of automation. The U.S. Treasury Department has replaced workers by using computers. The steel industry (heavily unionized) has had to cut its work force from about 500,000 to slightly more than 200,000 because of technological changes. In many instances, these advances were necessary in order for the organization to remain competitive. In some cases, the technology has displaced workers, many of whom belonged to unions. For years, unions resisted technological changes that displaced labor. However, as it became apparent that improvements in productivity were the only way to increase compensation, many unions changed their attitude about technology. Some unions now support technological improvement and work with management representatives to minimize the displacement of workers. They bargain for compensation for displaced workers, retraining, and relocation assistance for laid-off employees.

In 1990, there were approximately 6.5 million unemployed Americans. Hardest hit by the recent jobless spiral were blue-collar workers, blacks, and teenagers. The heaviest concentration of unemployment in the late 1980s was in the auto, steel, and construction industries, clustered in factory towns in the Midwest and the industrial Northeast. These are union industries and union geographic regions.[33] Five states alone — California, Illinois, New York, Ohio, and Pennsylvania — account for about half of all union members.

Even if the economy reverses, there are experts who believe that in some industries employment will never fully rebound. Industries seem to be searching for ways to expand the use of computers and robots to improve quality and reduce labor costs.[34] If this trend continues, the union will have fewer blue-collar workers to attract into the membership. Fewer members could mean less political power for the union.

Social Dilemmas

Labor unions support the principle of equal rights for all people regardless of race, sex, creed, or national origin. Furthermore, like employers, unions must comply with the provisions of the 1964 Civil Rights Act. In the West and Southwest, equal opportunity for Hispanic migratory workers has been a rallying point for union organizing efforts. Unions recognize that the changing labor force means that supporting women's issues will help attract new members. Therefore, organized labor advocates a national family leave policy that would help working parents cope with their family and job responsibilities.[35] Because women make up fully two thirds of the new entrants to the labor force and single parents are becoming the typical family group, unions are also lobbying in Congress for a national child-care policy.

Literacy is another social problem that unions are trying to address. Increasing numbers of high school graduates cannot read and write at a sixth-grade level. Immigrants, especially Hispanics and inner-city youth, appear to be severely under-educated. There is a growing pool of untrained workers who are ill-equipped for jobs in high-skills occupations. Thus, the union must push for both training programs teaching basic (reading, math, and so on) and sophisticated technical skills. Both unions and management face the fact that in an unhealthy economy with a huge federal deficit finding enough jobs for those who are capable and willing to work will not be easy.

Membership

Union membership significantly increased from 1933 to 1947. In 1933, there were only 3 million union members, accounting for about 7 percent of the total labor force; by 1947, there were 15 million union members.

The number of union members continued to increase until 1956, declined until 1963, and started to grow slowly until it reached 22 million workers in 1980, or about 23 percent of the total labor force and 28 percent of nonagricultural employees.[36] However, since 1980, there has been a decline in union membership. By December 1990, union members constituted less than 17 percent of the labor force. Labor officials claim that corporate cost cutting, massive layoffs, deregulation, and plant closings will lead to more appeal among workers to join unions. However, since this text was revised, there has been further erosion in membership. Exhibit 17–8 lists membership for AFL–CIO unions for the period 1979 to 1989. Exhibit 17–9 details the characteristics of union members for 1983 and 1988. The largest number of members fall within the age category of 25 to 34. Men outnumber women slightly. Government employees are a close second to members from the manufacturing sector.

The organizational and recruiting efforts of unions have varied according to changes in economic, social, and political conditions. New membership drives are taking place in the public sector, which includes military personnel, police, and fire fighters; among professionals, including teachers, medical personnel, athletes, and lawyers; and among employees in service industries.

Another area that unions are attempting to unionize is agriculture. Organizing efforts are especially intense in the grape, lettuce, citrus, and cotton regions of California.

In addition to these new organizing efforts in industries and professions, unions are also attempting to attract white-collar, female, and black employees. In the past, white-collar employees identified more with management practices and antiunion ideals and philosophy. But now, because of boredom and frustration in many white-collar jobs, some employees have considered unionizing.

The proportion of working men who are members of labor unions is declining. However, the number of female union members is increasing to approximately 5.2 million. The Coalition of Labor Union Women, an alliance of blue-collar working women, was formed in 1974 to end sex discrimination in wages and hiring. It also is attempting to elect more women as union officials. With more women officials, other women might believe that unions welcome them and need their abilities and skills.

EXHIBIT 17-8   U.S. Membership in AFL–CIO Unions by Selected Union, 1979 to 1989

Labor Organization	1979	1985	1987	1989	Labor Organization	1979	1985	1987	1989
Total	13,621	13,109	12,702	14,100	Hotel Employees and Restaurant Employees	373	327	293	278
Actors and Artists	75	100	95	97	Ironworkers	146	140	122	111
Automobile, Aerospace, and Agriculture (UAW)	(x)	974	998	917	Laborers	475	383	371	406
Bakery, Confectionery and Tobacco	131	115	109	103	Letter Carriers (NALC)	151	186	200	201
Boiler Makers, Iron Shipbuilders	129	110	90	75	Machinists and Aerospace (IAM)[2]	688	537	521	517
Bricklayers	106	95	84	84	Office and Professional Employees	83	90	86	84
Carpenters	626	616	617	613	Oil, Chemical, Atomic Workers (OCAW)	146	108	96	71
Clothing and Textile Workers (ACTWU)	308	228	195	180	Painters	160	133	128	128
Communication Workers (CWA)	485	524	515	492	Paperworkers Int'l	262	232	221	210
Electrical Workers (IBEW)	825	791	765	744	Plumbing and Pipefitting	228	226	220	220
Electronic, Electrical and Salaries	243	198	185	171	Postal Workers	245	232	230	213
Operating Engineers	313	330	330	330	Retail, Wholesale Department Store	122	106	140	137
Fire Fighters	150	142	142	142	Rubber, Cork, Linoleum, Plastic	158	106	97	92
Food and Commercial Workers (UFCW)	1,123	989	1,000	999	Seafarers	84	80	80	80
Garment Workers (ILGWU)	314	210	173	153	Service Employees (SEIU)	537	688	762	762
Glass, Molders, Pottery and Plastics	50	104	97	86	Sheet Metal Workers	120	108	108	108
Government, American Federation (AFGE)	236	199	157	156	State, County, Municipal (AFSCME)	889	997	1,032	1,090
Graphic Communications	171	141	136	124	Steelworkers	964	572	494	481
					Teachers (AFT)	423	470	499	544
					Teamsters	n.a.	n.a.	n.a.	1,161
					Transit Union	94	94	94	96
					Transport Workers	85	85	85	85
					Transportation/ Communications Int'l	127	102	113	86

Source: American Federation of Labor and Congress of Industrial Organizations (1990), Report of the AFL–CIO Executive Council (Washington, D.C.: AFL–CIO).

Black employees are another fast-growing segment and a target of union organizers. In 1988, there were approximately 2.8 million black trade unionists. However, blacks have not been represented in union management in proportion to their membership. Furthermore, several unions have been found guilty of discriminating against blacks. Both blacks and women are demanding more say in union decisions and will certainly acquire additional power as unions attempt to increase their membership.

Resistance to Unions

Despite well-planned and systematic organizing efforts, about 83 percent of the total labor force, or 91 million workers, still are not unionized. One reason is that many people distrust unions. Some people believe that unions stand against individualism and free enterprise. They feel that people should get ahead on their own skills and merits. They resent the union's position in favor of collectivism and the use of seniority in personnel decisions involving promotions, layoffs, and pay increases.

EXHIBIT 17-9 Union Members, by Selected Characteristics: 1983 and 1988

Characteristic	Total (1,000s) 1983	Total (1,000s) 1988	Union Members[1] (1,000s) 1983	Union Members[1] (1,000s) 1988	Represented by Unions[2] (1,000s) 1983	Represented by Unions[2] (1,000s) 1988	Percent Union Members 1983	Percent Union Members 1988	Percent Represented by Union 1983	Percent Represented by Union 1988	Total (earnings)[a] 1983	Total (earnings)[a] 1988	Union Members[1] 1983	Union Members[1] 1988	Represented by Unions[a] 1983	Represented by Unions[a] 1988	Not Represented by Unions 1983	Not Represented by Unions 1988
Total	88,290	101,407	17,717	17,002	20,532	19,241	20.1%	16.8%	23.3%	19.0%	351	444	366	469	381	465	316	397
16–24 years	19,305	19,469	1,749	1,206	2,145	1,457	9.1	6.2	11.1	7.5	210	249	281	312	275	309	203	242
25–34 years	25,978	30,688	5,097	4,578	5,990	5,223	19.6	14.9	23.1	17.0	321	363	382	453	376	447	304	365
35–44 years	18,722	24,382	4,648	5,178	5,362	5,858	24.8	21.2	28.6	24.0	369	449	411	504	407	501	339	419
45–54 years	13,150	15,468	3,554	3,706	4,014	4,107	27.0	24.0	30.5	26.6	366	452	404	507	402	505	335	415
55–64 years	9,201	9,237	2,474	2,139	2,788	2,371	26.9	23.2	30.2	25.7	346	419	392	479	390	479	316	394
65 years and over	1,934	2,162	196	194	234	225	10.1	9.0	12.1	10.4	260	323	336	451	330	437	236	298
Men	47,856	53,912	11,809	11,019	13,270	12,132	24.7	20.4	27.7	22.5	378	449	416	508	414	505	349	416
Women	40,433	47,495	5,908	5,982	7,262	7,109	14.6	12.6	18.0	15.0	252	315	309	403	307	399	237	300
White	77,046	87,176	14,844	13,932	17,182	15,759	19.3	16.0	22.3	16.1	319	394	398	498	391	484	295	398
Men	42,168	46,783	10,134	9,294	11,364	10,210	24.0	19.9	26.9	21.8	387	465	423	513	421	512	362	432
Women	34,877	40,393	4,710	4,638	5,818	5,549	13.5	11.5	16.7	13.7	254	318	314	410	313	406	240	305
Black	8,979	11,176	2,440	2,559	2,850	2,896	27.2	22.0	31.7	25.9	261	314	331	417	324	413	222	279
Men	4,477	5,502	1,420	1,438	1,615	1,601	31.7	26.1	36.1	29.1	293	347	366	458	360	455	244	298
Women	4,502	5,674	1,020	1,121	1,235	1,297	22.7	19.8	27.4	22.9	231	288	292	374	287	369	209	263
Hispanic[4]	n.a.	7,623	n.a.	1,220	n.a.	1,353	n.a.	16.0	n.a.	17.7	n.a.	290	n.a.	400	n.a.	397	n.a.	270
Men	n.a.	4,535	n.a.	837	n.a.	913	n.a.	18.5	n.a.	20.1	n.a.	307	n.a.	431	n.a.	430	n.a.	283
Women	n.a.	3,088	n.a.	384	n.a.	440	n.a.	12.4	n.a.	14.3	n.a.	260	n.a.	328	n.a.	325	n.a.	249
Full-time workers	70,976	92,692	16,271	15,773	18,745	17,753	22.9	19.1	26.4	21.5	313	365	388	480	383	476	288	358
Part-time workers	17,314	18,716	1,446	1,229	1,787	1,488	8.4	6.6	10.3	8.0	(x)	(x)	(x)	(x)	(x)	(x)	(x)	(x)
Managerial and professional specialty	19,657	24,369	3,354	3,644	4,307	4,470	17.1	15.0	21.9	18.3	437	552	423	559	421	550	446	552
Technical, sales, and administrative support	26,024	32,271	3,377	3,312	4,199	3,976	12.1	10.3	15.0	12.3	281	347	350	424	341	417	270	333
Service occupations	12,875	14,178	1,971	1,989	2,306	2,225	15.3	14.0	17.9	15.7	205	245	305	369	299	384	182	218
Precision, production, craft, and repair	10,542	11,766	3,466	3,164	3,760	3,374	32.9	26.9	35.7	28.7	377	430	456	536	450	531	322	368
Operators, fabricators, and laborers	15,416	17,010	5,452	4,815	5,839	5,105	35.4	28.3	37.9	30.0	275	313	366	436	361	429	226	273
Farming, forestry, and fishing	1,775	1,813	96	77	122	91	5.5	4.2	6.9	5.0	196	229	292	358	287	357	190	222
Agricultural wage and salary workers	1,446	1,492	49	30	55	35	3.4	2.0	3.6	2.4	196	230	(s)	(s)	(s)	(s)	196	236
Private nonagricultural wage and salary workers	71,225	82,741	11,933	10,674	13,369	11,723	16.8	12.9	18.8	14.2	307	375	369	474	385	466	286	363
Mining	869	711	180	133	201	146	20.7	18.7	23.1	20.5	481	525	470	528	470	523	486	526
Construction	4,109	5,193	1,131	1,096	1,207	1,151	27.5	21.1	29.4	22.2	348	405	516	603	510	596	296	359
Manufacturing	19,066	20,430	5,303	4,516	5,812	4,854	27.8	22.1	30.5	23.8	335	402	370	443	366	440	315	395
Transportation and public utilities	5,142	6,053	2,182	2,001	2,376	2,144	42.4	33.1	46.2	35.4	417	489	449	530	445	525	366	446
Wholesale and retail trade, total	18,061	20,597	1,568	1,386	1,775	1,559	8.7	6.7	9.8	7.6	252	301	353	405	348	401	242	294
Finance, insurance, and real estate	5,559	6,812	160	178	228	238	2.9	2.6	4.1	3.5	296	391	264	390	265	384	297	391
Services	18,400	22,944	1,410	1,365	1,770	1,631	7.7	5.9	9.6	7.1	272	340	303	369	303	366	266	335
Government	15,618	17,175	5,736	6,296	7,109	7,483	36.7	36.7	45.5	43.6	351	444	366	469	381	465	316	397

Note: This data is annual averages of monthly data. It covers employed wage and salary workers 16 years old and over. Excludes self-employed workers whose businesses are incorporated although they technically qualify as wage and salary workers.
B = Data not shown where base is less than 50,000.
n.a. = Not available.
x = Not applicable.
[1] Members of a labor union or an employee association similar to a labor union.
[2] Members of a labor union or an employee association similar to a union as well as workers who report no union affiliation but whose jobs are covered by a union or an employee association contract.
[3] For full-time employed wage and salary workers, 1983 revised since originally published.
[4] Hispanic persons may be of any race.

Source: U.S. Bureau of Labor Statistics (January 1983 and January 1988), *Employment and Earnings*.

Many professionals resist unions because they view them as dominated by blue-collar employees. Doctors, lawyers, and professors assume that they should not be associated with blue-collar tactics and behavior. This attitude is somewhat contrary to some of the actions of such professional associations as the American Medical Association. (The major difference between an association and a union is that the association believes payment is a matter between the individual performing the service and the customer.)

Some employees resist unions because they choose to identify with management values and practices. Management typically does not support union tactics. These nonmanagers may consider their aspirations to be a part of management when they resist union organizing efforts.

The reasons for resisting union organizing efforts may also be based on historical impressions and beliefs. Some well-known union leaders have been associated with illegal acts. One report found that about 450 union officers had been convicted of serious labor-related crimes from 1973 to 1980.[37] There has also been some union-incited violence during organizing campaigns, although such violence may have received more publicity than management-provoked violence. An accurate check of unbiased history books finds that company "thugs" were just as plentiful as union "thugs."[38]

FOREIGN UNIONS AND UNIONS IN MULTINATIONAL CORPORATIONS[39]

Between 1989 and 1990, many political and economic changes took place in the global marketplace. Perhaps the most important of these is the demolition of the Berlin Wall and the democratic experiment undertaken in the Soviet Union. The uniting of the European Common Market countries slated for 1992 and the return of Hong Kong to mainland China in 1997 are two more challenges to the ever-changing global economy. With these developments, it is increasingly important for the student of labor relations to be familiar with unions in foreign countries and multinational corporations.

The labor relations system of the United States is unique in the world. It rests on the premise of business unionism that focuses on economic not political pressure to force management to give in to demands. Other countries' unions differ most from their United States counterparts in that in many countries labor unions are actually political parties that run candidates for office, for example, Solidarity in Poland and the Labour Party in Great Britain. Canadian unions are most similar to those in the United States.[40] Western and Eastern European unions are politicized. Unions in Japan are organized at the enterprise level, and many unions in the developing countries of Latin America are radically militant.

The United States has the lowest percentage of unionized workers in the developed world, approximately 17 percent. The most unionized countries are Finland and Sweden where approximately 80 to 90 percent of all employees belong to unions.

Canada

In the period during and after World War II, labor leaders, employers, and governments in both Canada and the United States reached an agreement called the *Labor Accord*. They substantially supported the collective bargaining system of labor relations. Because of Canada's size and the geographic dispersion of its populated

CAREER CHALLENGE
(concluded)

*T*om Hardisty and Stan Goebel had lunch after their discussion about labor relations. After lunch, Stan said: "We could follow a strategy of fighting the union to keep it out. Or we could let nature take its course and live with it."

Tom replied, "That's what you think! I'm *not* running a unionized place. I'll sell out first! You need to figure out how to keep that #*&%$ union out of HMC!"

Stan then presented a communication program and proposed increases in pay and benefits as part of the "keep the union out" strategy. He costed out the proposed changes in pay and benefits and took these to Tom.

---

regions, collective bargaining is more decentralized. The single-firm unions are the most predominant bargaining unit. Industrywide bargaining occurs in railways, communications, airlines, and broadcasting.[41] Membership in unions is about 37.5 percent of the nonagricultural work force.

Labor unions in Canada have not been as flexible as those in the United States in the 1980s and 1990s. They have stuck to "job control" unionism and shied away from union-management cooperation. Also, the Canadian labor movement is a viable partisan political strategy as in Great Britain.[42]

Great Britain and the European Community

There are more than three times as many labor unions in Great Britain as there are in the United States with each manufacturing firm typically negotiating with about seven different unions. There is little formal labor law so there are many ways of engaging in collective bargaining. The unions are closely tied to the Labour Party and support state pensions and nationalized health service. Wildcat strikes, which are illegal in the United States, are the most frequent form of labor protest in Great Britain. The grievance system and arbitration have been virtually rejected. Union membership is on the decline going from 54 percent in 1979 to approximately 40 percent in 1990.

The heads of state of the European Community other than Great Britain voted for a social charter of worker rights in late 1989. Many rights were guaranteed to all workers in these countries: right to organize, to participate in company decisions, to work in a safe environment, to be paid equitable wages, to have access to vocational training, to have equal opportunities for women, and for children, seniors, and the disabled to be protected. Some of these rights have been legislated here in the United States while others are still being decided. It is still unclear how these rights will be guaranteed after 1992 when the barriers between European countries are removed.

Central and South America

The union movement is still young in the developing countries of Central and South America. Even though Mexico, Venezuela, and Argentina have higher percentages of the work force as union members than the United States, the right to collective bargaining is not guaranteed. These are developing countries with the problems that come with growing industries, cheap labor, and exploitation. The most common feature of unions in Central and South America is their connection to political parties. In Mexico, unions constitute a large proportion of the ruling political class. In some countries, like Peru, labor unions are quite radical and even have been noted for terrorist activities.[43]

Japan

In Japan most firms have a single union. This phenomenon is called *enterprise unionism* with both factory and clerical workers up to section chief in the same union.[44] There is no strict division between labor and management. University graduates often begin their working career as ordinary workers and remain members of the union until they are promoted to the top. There is no federation similar to the AFL–CIO, but a series of federations based on industry membership. All bargaining is done by the central organization at the same time each spring, the "spring offensive." Details of the contracts are then worked out at the individual firms. This is a wage-equalizing mechanism.

Japanese people have a cultural aversion to official confrontation-type talks. For example, 46 percent of firms with labor unions do not hold talks with the union before introducing new technology. Talks are more likely in larger firms, but the importance of collective bargaining is almost nonexistent. They prefer informal talks on the shop floor, and dissatisfied workers are more likely to remain silent and not to complain.

Multinationals

The emergence of the global economy means that many large firms operate in more than one country at the same time. Companies based in the United States have holdings around the world. Companies from Great Britain, Germany, Japan, and many other nations hold property and operate in the United States. Unions have viewed multinational corporations more as enemies than as opportunities. Transplanting local labor relations to foreign soil has not been very fruitful except as an exception to the rule. At this point, union relations within multinationals and at the transnational level are only an information-sharing process.

Union leaders have tried to use both collective bargaining and lobbying for new legislation to interact with multinationals with mixed results. "Guidelines for MNCs" have been developed by the Organization for Economic Cooperation and Development in Paris, which is an attempt to guarantee the same social rights for workers around the world as those guaranteed to the members of the European Community. Many barriers remain, including:

1. Differences in labor laws.
2. Absence of a central union decision-making authority.
3. Cultural differences.
4. Lack of coordination of activities.

5. Differing national priorities.
6. Employer resistance.

SUMMARY

This chapter has introduced you to labor relations, a sometimes emotionally charged HRM activity. It has discussed the history of labor unions, why unions appeal to some employees, some major issues facing unions, the structure and management of unions, and major labor legislation. It has also discussed foreign labor unions.

To summarize the major points covered in this chapter:

1. A union is a group of employees who have joined together to achieve present and future goals that deal with employee conditions.
2. Three major laws affecting labor-management relations in the United States are the Wagner Act (1935), the Taft-Hartley Act (1947) (which amended the Wagner Act), and the Landrum-Griffin Act of 1959.
3. The National Labor Relations Board (NLRB) administers the laws and regulations in the private and not-for-profit sector (health care and universities).
4. The second largest group of unionized employees is 3 million employees in the public sector. In the public sector, federal labor relations are regulated by executive orders issued by the president of the United States and the Federal Service Labor-Management Relations Statute.
5. The contact point for the membership is the local union. Through the local, members voice their complaints. The union steward or commiteeperson or griever is the member with on-the-job contract. If a union member has a complaint that deals with the labor-management contract, the steward is contacted.
6. Unions appeal to workers for various reasons. Some of the cited reasons are job security, strength in numbers, protection against unfair management action, and the communication link to management.
7. Some of the issues that unions must face today and in the future are declining membership, creating a more positive public image, unemployment, equal rights for all people, attracting additional members, and some hard-core resistance to unions.
8. The global economy has made a knowledge of foreign labor relations important. The complications that exist when dealing with a multinational corporation have just started to be explored.

KEY TERMS

QUESTIONS FOR REVIEW AND DISCUSSION

1. Why would merging two small unions into one be an important strategy for the AFL–CIO to promote and support?
2. Why do some individuals decide to join a union?
3. What will unions have to do to attract more blacks, women, and white-collar members?
4. Compare and contrast labor unions in the rest of the world to those in the United States. How are they the same? How are they different?
5. What kind of image do you now have of unions and the union movement?
6. Explain the impact of the Wagner Act on the growth of trade unions.
7. Why is it so difficult for unions to be effective when operating in a multinational company?
8. The union steward is considered a key communication link between labor and management. Why?
9. Can federal employees unionize? Explain.
10. A person was heard to comment, "Unions do not have to exist. Look at IBM and Delta Airlines. They have been doing fine without them." What is your opinion of this comment?

NOTES

[1] John A. Fossum (1989), *Labor Relations*, 4th ed. (Homewood, Ill.: BPI/Irwin).

[2] Arthur A. Sloane and Fred Witney (1988), *Labor Relations* (Englewood Cliffs, N.J.: Prentice-Hall).

[3] U.S. Department of Labor (1976), "Brief History of the American Labor Movement," Bulletin 1,000 (Washington, D.C.: U.S. Government Printing Office), pp. 1–104.

[4] A. H. Raskin (December 1981), "From Sitdowns to Solidarity: Passage in the Life of American Labor," *Across the Board*, pp. 12–32.

[5] Thomas A. Kochan, Harry C. Katz, and Nancy R. Mower (1984), *Worker Participation and American Unions* (Kalamazoo, Mich.: W. E. Upjohn Institute for Employee Research).

[6] Kenneth Casebeer (1989), "Drafts of the Wagner Act," *Industrial Relations Law Journal* 11, no. 1, pp. 73–131.

[7] Bruce E. Kaufman (Summer 1989), "Labor's Inequality of Bargaining Power: Changes Over Time and Implications for Public Policy," *Journal of Labor Research* 10, no. 3, pp. 286–98.

[8] James B. Lewis (Winter 1989), "The Health Care Challenge for Labor and Jointly Managed Funds," *Compensation & Benefits Management* 5, no. 2, pp. 121–24.

[9] Charles J. Coleman (1989), "Federal Sector Labor Relations: A Reevaluation of the Policies," *Journal of Collective Negotiations in the Public Sector* 16, no. 1, pp. 37–40.

[10] William H. Holley, Jr., and Kenneth M. Jennings (1991), *The Labor Relations Process*, 4th ed. (Hinsdale, Ill.: Dryden Press), pp. 433–35.

[11] Ibid.

[12] Ibid.

[13] John A. Fossum, *Labor Relations*, pp. 51–53.

[14] E. Edward Herman, Alfred Kuhn, and Ronald L. Siefer (1987), *Collective Bargaining and Labor Relations* (Englewood Cliffs, N.J.: Prentice-Hall), pp. 405–15.

[15] Adapted from Holley and Jennings, *The Labor Relations Process*, pp. 114–15.

[16] Walter S. Mossberg (July 26, 1973), "On the Line: A Union Man at Ford, Charlie Bragg, Deals in Problems," *The Wall Street Journal*, p. 1.

[17] Alex Kotlowitz (April 1, 1987), "Job of Shop Steward Has Frustrations in Era of Payroll Cuts," *The Wall Street Journal*, pp. 1, 19.

[18] Michael A. Curme, Barry T. Hirsch, and David M. Macpherson (October 1990), "Union Membership and Contract Coverage in the United States, 1983–1988," *Industrial & Labor Relaltions Review* 44, no. 1, pp. 5–33.

[19] Edward Brankley and Mel E. Schanake (June 1988), "Labor Relations: Exceptions to Compulsory Union Membership," *Personnel Journal* 67, no. 6, pp. 114–22.

[20] Jeff B. Lyskal (March 2, 1981), "Beating the UAW—Three Times," *Forbes*, pp. 37–39.

[21] R. Douglas Collins (Summer 1986), "Agency Shop in Public Employment," *Public Personnel Management* 15, no. 2, pp. 171–79.

[22] Herbert Metcalf (September 1989), "Can the Closed Shop Ban Open Doors for Unions?" *Personnel Management* 21, no. 9, pp. 32–36.

[23] (July 28, 1989) "NLRB Reports Case Backlog at Lowest Level Since 1978," *Daily Labor Report*, p. A-4.

[24] Rod Willis (February 1988), "Can American Unions Transform Themselves?" *Management Review*, pp. 14–21.

[25] American Federation of Labor and Congress of Industrial Organization (November 1989), *AFL-CIO Policy Resolutions, Eighteenth Constitutional Convention* (Washington, D.C.: AFL-CIO), p. 1.

[26] Willis, "Can American Unions Transform Themselves?" pp. 14–21.

[27] Peter J. Sheridan (October 1985), "Can Unions Accommodate the Forces of Change?" *Occupational Hazards* 47, no. 10, pp. 153–60.

[28] Willis, "Can American Unions Transform Themselves?" p. 15.

[29] Ibid.

[30] Jerome Rosow (February 1988), "Positive, Gradual Change," *Management Review*, pp. 16–17.

[31] Ibid.

[32] Richard B. Freeman (Winter 1986), "Unionization in Troubled Times," *New Management*, pp. 8–10.

[33] Bill Shaporito (February 2, 1987), "The Smokestacks Won't Tumble," *Fortune*, pp. 30–32.

[34] Michael McFadden (May 11, 1987), "Protectionism Can't Protect Jobs," *Fortune*, pp. 121–28.

[35] AFL-CIO, *AFL-CIO Policy Resolutions*, pp. 12–13.

[36] Sloane and Witney, *Labor Relations*, p. 34.

[37] (September 8, 1980) "Union Corruption: Worse Than Ever," *U.S. News & World Report*, p. 33.

[38] Raskin, "From Sitdowns to Solidarity," pp. 12–32.

[39] This section is based on Holley and Jennings, *The Labor Relations Process*, pp. 469–93.

[40] Roy J. Adams (1989), "North American Industrial Relations: Divergent Trends in Canada and the U.S." *International Labour Review* 128, no. 1, pp. 47–64.

[41] Holley and Jennings, *The Labor Relations Process*, p. 480.

[42] Adams, "North American Industrial Relations," p. 470.

[43] Holley and Jennings, *The Labor Relations Process*, pp. 484–85.

[44] Naota Sasaki (1990), *Management and Industrial Structure in Japan* (Oxford: Pergammon Press), pp. 38, 52, 55–58, 99+.

EXERCISE 17–1   Pro-, Neutral, and Antiunion?

. . . . .

Objective: To examine the reader's feelings, emotions, and attitudes about the union movement and joining a union.

SET UP THE EXERCISE

By the time you are enrolled in the present course, you have developed an opinion about unions. Friends, parents, and the media have helped shape your opinion. Are your opinions logical or are they emotional? Would you ever become a spokesperson for the union? How do your opinions compare to others in the course?

Each person is asked to complete the following 15-item scale. There are no right or wrong answers. Circle the letter that best describes your opinion for each of the items. Your instructor will tell you how to score your responses and will ask you to discuss your score with others in the classroom. What does your score tell you about your attitudes toward unions, their goals, and their impact on society?

1. *a.* Unions are needed to keep management interested in and responsive to rights.
   b. Unions have served their purpose and are no longer needed.
2. *a.* Unions are too concerned with job security.
   b. Unions want their members to be highly productive members of an organization.
3. *a.* Unions push hard for the autonomy of all members.
   b. Unions are overly protective of the autonomy of too many nonproductive employees.
4. *a.* Unions use their strike powers too frequently.
   b. Unions only strike when they have to gain benefits for members.
5. *a.* Unions are more democratically operated than management committees or councils.
   b. Democracy and unionism are contradictory terms.
6. *a.* Public employees should have every right to strike.
   b. It is not in the best interest of society to permit public union members to strike.
7. *a.* The union movement is the primary reason why Americans have a good standard of living.
   b. Management has been the driving force behind technological advancement, which has resulted in our high standard of living.
8. *a.* Unions are too close to socialism for most Americans.
   b. Unions in the United States are not political forces or a power like they are in European nations.
9. *a.* Without unions, more Americans would have become unemployed in the late 1980s.
   b. The unions' resistance to improvements, retraining, and change has resulted in a large number of plant closings and business failures.
10. *a.* Union leaders are corrupt.
    b. Union leaders are no more corrupt or unethical than managers.
11. *a.* Unions advocate promotions based on merit.
    b. Union politics dictate a posture that seniority is more important than merit in reward decisions.

12. *a.* Union violence is a thing of the past.
    b. Unions still beat and intimidate those opposed to their viewpoints.
13. *a.* Managers would fire at will workers who opposed their orders.
    b. Managers need the respect of workers and will only fire those who break clearly stated rules.
14. *a.* Unions are for the blue-collar, minimally educated person who can't stand up to management.
    b. Unions can, with their strength and prestige, represent any employee — blue-collar or white-collar.
15. *a.* Unions are responsible for the growth of the human resource management field.
    b. Management supported, encouraged, and implemented the human resource department to support their mission and goals.

APPLICATION CASE 17–1   Modern Management, Inc.: Union Busters with
. . . . .   Briefcases

In the old days, they used billy clubs and brass knuckles. However, today's union busters go by the name "labor relations consultants" — but they're still out to stop unions from organizing employees. Union busters give private counseling on specific company policies, advising management how to circumvent union organizing efforts.

Herbert Melnick operates Modern Management, Inc., of Bannockburn, Illinois. His firm has 70 consultants engaged in helping firms avoid unionization. The consultants are paid over $700 plus expenses per day. The firm has had a 93 percent success rate. Today, there are about 1,000 firms like Modern Management and another 1,500 independent practitioners in the union-busting business. Critics call their specialization psychological manipulation of the workers' attitudes in the workplace.

Nonunion companies want to prevent unionization. Management of a unionized shop wants to decertify the union. These goals are within the purview of Modern Management and other union busters. Are they successful? In the NLRB representation elections lost by unions, over 90 percent involve labor relations consultants.

The House Subcommittee on Labor Management Relations issued a report on labor relations consultants. A key recommendation was that the Department of Labor should be more diligent in enforcing the reporting requirements for consultants under the Landrum-Griffin Act. "Virtually every union is required to and does report its activities under the provisions of the Act," the report says. "It is inequitable that the Department does not require consultants, even in instances when they are clearly running management's antiunion campaign, to disclose their involvement."

Some of the situations that led to the call for tighter controls involved PPG Industries, St. Francis Hospital (Milwaukee, Wisconsin), and Humana Corporation. Following are brief descriptions of these situations.

PPG Industries

The law firm representing PPG Industries' Lexington, North Carolina plant reportedly trumped up an alienation of affection suit against Teamsters'

organizer Pat Suporta filed in May 1979, seeking to discredit her. Suporta had helped win an election at the plant in July 1978. Even after the suit was withdrawn in June 1979, PPG attempted (but failed) to use it as new evidence to get the NLRB to overturn IBT certification. The company's law firm is Hogg, Allen, Ryce, Norton & Blue in Coral Gables, Florida. In a separate incident, PPG fired employee Terri Drake in March 1979, four days after she was identified as a union supporter. She and many others on the in-plant committee were blacklisted and couldn't get jobs in the Lexington area. The company also was found to have bugged an employees' cafeteria.

St. Francis Hospital

In the first NLRB complaint directly against a labor consultant, the board charges that Modern Management, Inc., "independently violated the National Labor Relations Act by its having complete control and use of supervisory personnel at St. Francis Hospital in a systematic and antiunion campaign." The tactics included, the complaint says, "illegal interrogations, promises of benefits, promises of improved conditions of employment and threats of reprisal against employees for engaging in union activities." The St. Francis Federation of Nurses and Health Professionals, American Federation of Teachers, lost an October 1979 election by a vote of 100 to 95. NLRB set aside the election in July 1980.

Humana Corp.

Lloyd Laudermilch, a member of Operating Engineers Local 501 in Las Vegas, Nevada, was coached by management at Sunrise Hospital, its parent company, Humana Corp., and its consultants, West Coast Industrial Relations, on how to initiate, gather support for, and file a decertification petition with NLRB. This is a clear violation of the law, which forbids an employer from discussing a decertification petition with employees. Laudermilch was asked — but refused — to sign an affidavit saying that he had never talked to any management people about filing the petition. For his efforts, Laudermilch was promised a better job: busting unions at other hospitals owned by Humana. He kept the union informed of his activities, and the decertification effort failed.

Discussion Questions

1. Should union busters like Modern Management be permitted to stop union organizing efforts?

2. Why would union busting be a popular tactic among organizations?

3. Are union busters like Modern Management worth $700 a day plus expenses for each labor relations consultant? Why?

ORGANIZING AND COLLECTIVE BARGAINING

· · · · · · ·

LEARNING OBJECTIVES

After studying this chapter, you should be able to:

· · ·

Define *collective bargaining*

· · ·

Outline the steps in the union organizing campaign

· · ·

Discuss the role of the National Labor Relations Board (NLRB) in an organizing campaign

· · ·

Describe what is meant by the term *organizing a bargaining unit.*

· · ·

Explain *what is meant by a grievance system and the steps taken before a grievance reaches the point of going to arbitration*

· · ·

Differentiate between *mediation* and *arbitration*

CAREER CHALLENGE

*T*om and Stan met to discuss the organizing situation and the communications programs. Here is a part of the conversation.

Tom The communications program looks good, Stan. We'll have personal visits with the employees to talk about the union problem. The supervisors will run some of the meetings. You and I will split up and attend as many as we can. You'll train the supervisors on why the employees shouldn't join the union. But we can't afford to add these pay and benefit increases at this time.

Stan You know the union will exploit that. Our money situation, together with the lack of security because of layoffs, puts us at a big disadvantage.

Tom I know it. But it's your job to keep the union out.

In the next days and weeks, Stan did his best. Lots of meetings were held. He also mailed letters to the employees' homes.

W hen employees are significantly dissatisfied with their situation in the workplace, union organizing is a possible outcome. The elements of the workplace that are most likely to trigger union organizing include lack of security, low wages, and supervisory practices that are hostile to the individual employee.[1] The AFL–CIO describes *organizing* as "the labor movement's lifeblood and the most critical element in the pursuit of our historic goal of helping working people secure justice, dignity, and a voice in the workplace and throughout society."[2]

Organizing efforts at Hardisty Manufacturing (HMC) are what Tom and Stan are concerned about. The efforts at HMC are typical of thousands of others that involve a face-off between union and management. More about the details of organizing will be presented in this chapter.

The organizing campaign determines who will represent or speak for whom in the collective bargaining process. **Collective bargaining** is a process by which the representatives of the organization (the employer) meet and attempt to work out a contract with representatives of the workers (the employees).[3] The employees' representative can be a union or a group of unions. In the private, public, and not-for-profit sectors of society, employees have the right to self-organization in order to collectively bargain through a *unit* of their choosing. A *bargaining unit* is a group of two or more employees who share common employment interests and conditions and may reasonably be grouped together.[4] In determining whether a proposed bargaining unit is appropriate, the following points are considered: (1) the history of collective bargaining in the organization and (2) the desires of the employees in the proposed unit.

This chapter will first discuss how unions organize in firms and how management responds to the organizing campaign. Next, we will turn to the collective bargaining process and administration of the labor-management contract. Finally, the current public image of labor unions and the future of labor unionism will be discussed.

THE BARGAINING UNIT: THE WORKERS' CHOICE

A union can exist only if workers prefer to be unionized. Someone at Hardisty Manufacturing, or perhaps a group of employees, has called a union representative to come to the plant to "talk union" with the workers. The union considers the employees at Hardisty a viable unit that the union will attempt to win over. The employees who make up the bargaining unit can be decided upon jointly by labor and management, or by one or the other, but it is an important determination. Often, union and management will disagree as to which employees or groups of employees are eligible for inclusion in a particular proposed unit. Obviously, both union and management want as much bargaining power as possible. Management may examine the makeup of the proposed unit to determine if required exclusions (for example, supervisors, security guards) have been made. If the union's proposed unit is not suitable, management may challenge the proposal and present its own proposed unit. In general, the union will seek as large a unit as possible, while management will attempt to restrict a unit's size.

The final determination by labor sector of the appropriate bargaining unit is in the hands of the following agencies and/or individual(s):

Private sector (for example, General Motors, Xerox, USX) — The National Labor Relations Board (NLRB).

Railway and airline sector (for example, Illinois Central, TWA) — The National Mediation Board.

EXHIBIT 18-1   Sequence of Organizing Events

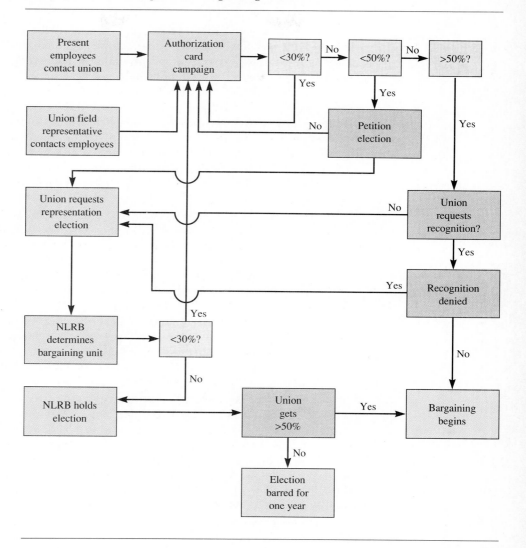

Postal sector — The National Labor Relations Board (NLRB).

Federal sector (for example, air traffic controllers) — Assistant Secretary of Labor for Labor-Management Relations.

Public sector (for example, California Highway Patrol, New York Sanitation Department) — Varies in accordance with state and local statutes.

Exhibit 18–1 represents a concise model that summarizes the union organizing and representation election process. The exhibit only applies to sectors in which the NLRB has jurisdiction. As shown, the organizing process leads to an *authorization* card campaign. This is what Tom and Stan are suddenly confronted with. It is the union's way of finding out how many workers are for unionization. The card, when signed by an employee, authorizes the union to represent that employee during negotiations. At least 30 percent of the employees in the unit must sign before the NLRB will set up an actual election. If over 50 percent of the unit employees sign up, the union can directly demand to be recognized as the representative of the unit.

There are three ways that a union can be certified. If the union can demonstrate that it represents a majority of the firm's employees, management can recognize the union as the exclusive bargaining representative *voluntarily*. This outcome is not very typical, however. Most unions achieve recognition through petitioning the National Labor Relations Board for a **representation election** after the authorization cards demonstrate employee interest.[5] The NLRB will conduct a secret-ballot election. Certification elections are usually held within 45 days of the initial request. If the union receives a simple majority (50 percent plus one vote), the NLRB *certifies* the union as the exclusive bargaining representative and collective bargaining begins. If they fail to get the majority of votes cast, they cannot represent the employees. No new representation election can be held for that bargaining unit for a period of one year.

The third way that a union can be recognized is for the NLRB to *direct* the employer to recognize the union without an election.[6] This happens when the employer engages in serious unfair labor practices during the union organizing campaign. The conclusion here is that it would be impossible to hold a fair, impartial election because of the employer's previous unethical, antiunion practices. The NLRB has actually ordered collective bargaining rights in about 1 percent of all cases.

Occasionally, the NLRB conducts a **decertification election.** A decertification election is just the opposite of the certification election. If employees decide they no longer need a union either between contracts or when the union fails to negotiate an initial contract during that first 12-month period, decertification elections can be held. A simple majority ($^{50}\!/_{50}$ split) is decided in favor of management, and the union is no longer the official bargaining representative. Decertification elections increased in frequency in the 1980s and unions lost them more frequently. For example, in 1986, over 1,000 decertification elections were conducted by the NLRB, and the union only won approximately 30 percent.[7]

Antiunion consultants, or union busters, have had significant success in keeping unions out and helping management encourage employees to decertify unions. The AFL–CIO has identified 520 consulting and law firms that assist companies in warding off unions. The union feeling about these consultants is that they prevent employees from exercising their rights. Management, however, feels that they are important in helping organizations use legal means to remain union-free or to decertify unions.[8]

REPRESENTATION CAMPAIGNS: THE UNIONS

The laws and executive orders covering labor relations require an employer to bargain with the representatives selected by the employees. The union's intention is to convince employees that being a member will lead to important outcomes — better wages, fairer treatment from management, job security, and better working conditions. Unions attempt to stress issues that are meaningful, current, and obvious to employees.

In the 1990s, union organizers are finding a new kind of employee who is more difficult to organize. This employee accepts less, trusts less, and wants more.[9] New organizing issues are being addressed by unions.[10] Insecurity is the most important

CAREER CHALLENGE

(continued)

Stan sat in his office and went over his program. So far, the efforts of Hardisty's management to squelch the union through communication had not been as effective as Stan had hoped. He kept hearing more and more talk about the union — in fact, his communication program seemed to have backfired in some instances, having forced many employees to think seriously about unionization for the first time. Stan himself was beginning to feel that the union was inevitable.

He got out a pencil and paper and began to write down all the reasons he could think of for remaining nonunionized. (One reason he neglected to write down, of course, was the lecture he'd get from Tom if the union ever succeeded at Hardisty.)

issue facing nonunionized firms.[11] Job retraining and advance notice of plant closings are pertinent organizing issues. Traditional issues of grievance procedures, job security, improved benefits, and higher pay are still the most commonly stressed issues in organizing campaigns, however. Lack of sensitivity regarding employee complaints, inept supervision, and poor communication are the most serious mistakes management can make that help pave the way for successful organizing campaigns.[12]

The scope of the organizing campaign is changing.[13] Unions are now trying to organize new bargaining units outside their traditional industries. The concept of *jurisdiction* is what is important here. *Union jurisdiction* refers to the territory within which a union organizes and engages in collective bargaining.[14] In the past, a union stuck to organizing a single industry or individual job type(s). With the decline of heavy industry, this type of union organizing is no longer productive. In the 1990s, it will not be unusual for unions to recruit new members from industries other than those defined as their primary jurisdictions. One researcher found that in the period 1976 to 1985 about half of total certification elections occurred outside of the primary jurisdictions of unions.[15] Union mergers have also expanded jurisdictions.

Some unions have even changed their names to reflect their broader organizing base. In 1983, the Laundry, Dry Cleaning and Dye House Workers became the Textile Processors, Service Trades, Health Care, Professional and Technical Employees International Union. The International Union of Electrical, Radio, and Machine Workers became the International Union of Electronic, Electrical, Technical, Salaried and Machine Workers. The Brotherhood of Railway, Airline and Steamship Clerks became the Transportation-Communications International Union in 1987.[16] Even the United Auto Workers has begun organizing campaigns among public sector, bank, health-care, and child-care employees.

REPRESENTATION CAMPAIGNS: MANAGEMENT

Research has shown that union organizing campaigns are often associated with significant declines in firm profitability.[17] Therefore, most organizations prepare some type of campaign to oppose the union's move to organize workers. It is important to know that the NLRB forbids management actions to suppress the union and to intimidate employees considering unionization. These are considered unfair management practices. For example, firing a union supporter or disciplining a worker that is involved in organizing efforts may be considered an unfair labor practice. If these actions are not supported with facts and are related to organizing efforts, management can become involved in lawsuits.

Normally, the HR department is responsible for presenting management's side of the story. As previously discussed, outside consultants or antiunion experts trained in preventing organizing often are used. One popular management approach is to emphasize that a union is run by outsiders. The outsider is pictured as being uninformed, uninterested, and unqualified.[18] Management attempts to communicate clearly and forcefully to the employees about the advantages of remaining nonunionized. Speeches, question-and-answer sessions, bulletin board posters, personal letters to employees, and articles in the company newspaper are used to promote the nonunion advantages.

Three basic forms of union opposition have been identified: (1) positive labor relations without a union, (2) legal campaigns, and (3) breaking the law.[19] Organizations that have higher wages, better working conditions, more equitable supervisory practices, and generous benefits are less likely to commit unfair labor practices than firms with lower wages and less favorable working conditions.[20] Strong management opposition is an important contributing factor to the continuing decline in unionization.

THE ROLE OF THE NLRB: WATCHING THE CAMPAIGN

The NLRB is responsible for conducting the election and certifying the results of organizing efforts in the private and public sectors. Often, the NLRB is faced with preelection charges of one group against the other about unfair practices. The NLRB has to decide whether a specific management or union tactic was fair under the guidelines of the law.

The NLRB is a watchdog. Unfair labor practices charges can be filed by an employee, an employer, the union, or any person. A formal charge requires the NLRB to officially review the claim. It is the NLRB in the private and postal sectors that guards against and prevents any interference in the lawful procedures to select the bargaining representative. If the interference is considered significant, an election can be set aside and rerun.

The NLRB pays particular attention to the following areas:

Concerning the Employer

1. The NLRB makes sure that the questioning of employees about union membership is done in a fair and nonintimidating manner.
2. The NLRB checks to see if the union information provided to employees is truthful.
3. The NLRB does not allow any final presentations within 24 hours preceding the election.

Concerning the Union

1. The NLRB makes sure that no threats or intimidation are used to gain votes.
2. The NLRB guards the employees against the union's promises of special treatment for votes if the union wins.
3. No final presentations are allowed within 24 hours preceding the election.

If a union legally wins an organizing election, it is recognized as the exclusive bargaining representative of a unit. The NLRB requires that both the elected union and management bargain in good faith. This requirement is spelled out in the Taft-Hartley Act as follows:

> For the purposes of this section, to bargain collectively is the performance of the mutual obligation of the employer and representative of the employees to meet at reasonable times and confer in good faith with respect to wages, hours, and other terms and conditions of employment, or the negotiation of an agreement, or any question arising thereunder, and the execution of a written contract incorporating any agreement reached if requested by either party, but such obligation does not compel either party to agree to a proposal or require the making of a concession.

If either party does not bargain in good faith, unfair labor practices can be charged. The costs, publicity, and hostility associated with not bargaining in good faith are usually too significant to disregard. Of course, good faith doesn't mean that the union or management must agree with each other about issues. This is the essence of collective bargaining — disagreement and negotiation. An absence of good faith would include:

1. An unwillingness to make counterproposals.
2. Constantly changing positions.
3. The use of delaying tactics.
4. Withdrawing concessions after they have been made.
5. Refusal to provide necessary data for negotiations.

COLLECTIVE BARGAINING

As stated at the beginning of the chapter, *collective bargaining* is a process by which the representatives of the organization meet and attempt to work out a contract with the employees' representative — the union. *Collective* means only that representatives are attempting to negotiate an agreement. *Bargaining* is the process of cajoling, debating, discussing, and threatening in order to bring about a favorable agreement for those being represented.

The collective bargaining process and the final agreement reached are influenced by many variables.[21] Exhibit 18–2 graphically identifies some of the variables influencing the union and management representatives. For example, the state of the economy affects collective bargaining. In a tight economy, a union push for higher wages is less likely to succeed, because it would be inflationary. The firm's representative must also consider whether the company can pay an increased wage based on current and expected economic conditions.

There are three basic types of collective bargaining: distributive bargaining, integrative bargaining, and concession bargaining.[22] *Distributive bargaining* occurs when labor and management are in conflict on an issue and when the outcome is a win/lose situation.[23] For example, if the union wins a 40-cent-an-hour increase,

---

EXHIBIT 18-2   The Forces Influencing the Bargaining Process

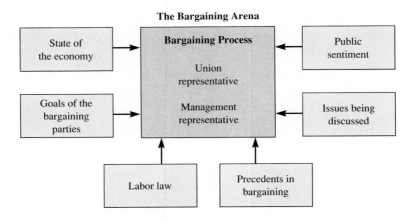

management has lost some of its profit. *Integrative bargaining* occurs when the two sides face a common problem, for example, high employee absenteeism. Both parties can attack the problem and seek a solution that provides for a win/win outcome. Integrative bargaining can result in accommodation of both sides' needs without cost or through a simultaneous gain.

Concession bargaining exists when there is something of importance given back to management. Concessions can consist of wage cuts, wage freezes of previously negotiated increases, benefits, reductions, work-rule changes that result in increased management flexibility, and other similar actions. An analysis by two labor relations researchers estimated that 30 to 50 percent of all unionized workers in major industries (for example, machinery, air transportaiton, apparel, metal) had granted concessions.[24] However, some unions have fought back and have traded concessions for power and stock. For example, in 1986, members of the United Steelworkers gained stock from LTV, Bethlehem Steel, Kaiser Aluminum, and Wheeling–Pittsburgh Steel.[25]

Each of the forces shown in Exhibit 18–2 involves a union and a management response. Each side of the collective bargaining table will be influenced by such factors as the economy and the environment. Unions and management are now painfully aware of how inflation, foreign competition, and the mood of a society can affect the issues being discussed at the bargaining table.

The actual process of collective bargaining involves a number of steps, such as: (1) prenegotiation; (2) selecting negotiators; (3) developing a bargaining strategy; (4) using the best tactics; and (5) reaching a formal contractual agreement.

Prenegotiation

In collective bargaining, both sides attempt to receive concessions that will help them achieve their objectives. As soon as a contract is signed by union and management, both parties begin preparing for the next collective bargaining sessions. Even with no union, that is useful. Thus, the importance of careful prenegotiation preparation cannot be overemphasized.

EXHIBIT 18-3   Bargaining Data for Negotiators

Internal to the Firm	External to the Firm
Number of workers in each job classification	Comparative industry wage rates
Compensation per worker	Comparative occupational wage rates
Minimum and maximum pay in each job classification	Comparative fringe benefits
Overtime pay per hour and number of annual overtime hours worked by job classification	Consumer price index
	Patterns of relevant bargaining settlements
Number of employees, by categories, who work on each shift	
Cost of shift differential premiums	
History of recent negotiations	
Cost of fringe benefits	
Cost-of-living increases	
Vacation costs by years of service of employees	
Demographic data on the bargaining unit — members by sex, age, and seniority	
Cost and duration of lunch breaks and rest periods	
An outline of incentive, progresson, evaluation, training, safety, and promotion plans	
Grievance and arbitration awards	

Data of all types are maintained by both unions and management. Exhibit 18–3 presents examples of data that are useful to both management and unions. In addition to the internal and external data, it is also important to check the background of the union negotiators. This will allow management to interpret the style and personality of the negotiators.

The computer has now become a valuable tool for both the union and management in prenegotiation and actual negotiations.[26] The computer can store data, help negotiators prepare various economic scenarios, and interface with various database sources. One result of computer technology is that union and management negotiators have at their disposal in a short period detailed information that can be used or altered to fit their particular strategy. For example, a union negotiator requested information on the company's financial status and salaries paid to officers. Within 90 seconds, this information was made available from a database.

Selecting the Negotiators

Bargaining team members on both sides are called *negotiators* and usually represent areas of particular interest in the contract and/or they have expertise in specific negotiated areas. Each side is led by a person designated the *chief negotiator*. On the management side, the chief negotiator is usually the top HRM or labor relations executive of the organization. Management will also include at least one line manager, usually the plant manager. This person can answer issues related to the day-to-day administration of the contract and answer questions related to negotiating issues. The team of negotiators typically consists of an HR expert, a lawyer, a

CAREER CHALLENGE

(*continued*)

Stan wanted to know more about the union. The vote had still not been taken, but he knew from talk around the plant that the union already had an edge. He called his researchers together to see if they could find out a little about the union's past history — particularly its success or failure at the bargaining table. Jim Rogers, Stan's assistant, came to Stan with the information.

Jim It looks pretty grim for our side, Stan, if the union wins the election. They've got a very successful team of negotiators, starting with the local union president. They've won four out of six of their negotiations so far.

Stan And with our money problems, we can't offer our people as much as the union can. What's this local president like?

Jim He's a young guy, 35 years old; college man. His strategy in the past has been to let management do the talking first, then he comes up with points for the union's side. And he's always armed with a lot of statistics and facts to back him up.

Stan Well, we know his main argument will center around our refusal to increase pay and the threat of layoffs due to our financial situation.

Jim He's got us there.

Two hours later, it was announced that Hardisty would be laying off 20 percent of its workers. Stan ran into Tom's office.

Stan Tom, we can't lay these people off now, right in the middle of the union's campaign! We're practically handing ourselves over to the union if we do this!

Tom Pipe down, Stan. It's your job to beat the union, but I've got to keep our heads above water, too.

Stan I think this is the wrong move to make, Tom.

Tom Too late now . . . it's done. Now what has your department found out about this union?

---

manager, or vice president with knowledge of the entire business organization and various experts (for example, employee benefits manager).

The union also uses the team approach. The union team generally consists of business agents, shop stewards, the local union president (chief negotiator) and, when the negotiation is very important, representatives from the national union headquarters. The union team is often elected by the union members, and the chief negotiator may have little input into the selection process.[27] One or more rank-and-file members will be on the team. They come from various operating departments to be sure that concerns of different departments are equally represented.

The negotiating teams (union and management) meet independently before the actual bargaining sessions and plan the best strategy to use. This preparation identifies the chief spokesperson and the roles of each member of the team. Specific roles that are performed include:

Leader (chief negotiator), usually the most senior team member.

Summarizer, the person who summarizes the negotiations to date.

Recorder, the person who both keeps notes on various agreements and observes the opposition team.[28]

Developing a Bargaining Strategy

Because the labor agreement must be used for a long period of time, it is important
to develop a winning strategy and tactics. The *strategy* is considered to be the plan
and policies that will be pursued at the bargaining table. *Tactics* are the specific
actions taken in the bargaining sessions. It is important to spell out the strategy and
tactics because bargaining is a give-and-take process with the characteristics of a
poker game, a political campaign, or a heated debate.[29]

An imporant issue in mapping out a strategy involves the maximum concessions
that will be granted. By shifting a position during the bargaining, the other side may
build up expectations that are difficult to change. By granting too much, one side
may be viewed as weak. How far management or the union will go before it risks a
work stoppage or lockout is considered before the sessions begin and is a part of the
strategic plan.

Another part of management's strategic plan is to develop the total cost profile of
the maximum concession package. This is, what these concessions will cost the
company today and in the future? Will HRM policies or production procedures
have to be changed if these concessions are granted? This form of future planning
helps management determine how willing it is to take a strike. Planning for a strike is
certainly difficult, but the issue should be included in strategy planning.

Using the Best Tactics

Tactics are calculated actions used by both parties. Occasionally, tactics are used to
mislead the other party. But they are also used to secure an agreement that is
favorable to either management or the unions.

A number of popular tactics have been used by both the union and management
to secure a favorable agreement.[30] These tactics are:

1. *Conflict-Based.* Each party is uncompromising, takes a hard line, and resists
   any overtures for compromise or agreement. Typically, what happens is that
   one party mirrors the other party's actions.
2. *Armed Truce.* Each party views the other as an adversary. Although they are
   adversaries, it is recognized that an agreement must be worked out under the
   guidelines specified by the law. In fact, the law is literally followed to the letter to reach agreement.
3. *Power Bargaining.* Each party accepts the other party with the knowledge that
   a balance of power exists. It would be nonproductive to pursue a strategy of
   trying to eliminate the other party in the relationship.
4. *Accommodation.* Both parties adjust to each other. Compromise, flexibility,
   and tolerance in positive forms are used in favor of emotion and raw power. It
   is claimed that most managers and union leaders have engaged in accommodation for the bulk of union-management bargaining issues.
5. *Cooperation.* Each side accepts the other as a full partner. This means that
   management and the union work together not only on everyday matters but
   in such difficult areas as technological change, quality of work life improvements, and business decision making.

These five tactics are only some of the many tactics that exist.

For example, General Electric used a tactic called *Boulwarism* (named after Lemuel Boulware, General Electric's vice president of public and employee relations who developed it). GE's management worked out an offer that was final and presented it to the union. No matter how heated or long negotiations became, the offer was final. The National Labor Relations Board ruled that the Boulware tactic was a failure to bargain in good faith.[31] GE appealed this decision and won in the lower courts. However, the Supreme Court informed GE that it could not give one best offer, but had to start lower in order to permit the union to obtain benefits and save face with the membership.

By 1969, Boulwarism was starting to become an ineffective tactic. The long-competitive factions within the GE unions began to coordinate their bargaining efforts. There was also the attrition of GE managers who had worked with Boulwarism for years. A long and bitter strike in 1969, along with these other factors, resulted in adjustments in GE's negotiation procedures. Instead of making one — and only one — offer, there were modifications as negotiations occurred. Thus, Boulwarism as practiced in its heyday has become a historical reference point at GE.

The highly skilled and effective negotiator on either side must be in complete control of his or her emotions and be somewhat of an actor. There are times when a "performance" is given to make an effective point. In order to give these performances, the person must be in control of the situation. Threats, abusive language, and tirades are considered weak tactics by both parties. Logical presentations, good manners, and calmness seem to be more effective than threatening tactics.

Reaching a Formal Contractual Agreement

The union-management contract designates the formal terms of agreement. The average contract is designed to be in effect for two or three years, and it varies from a few typewritten pages to more than a hundred pages, depending on the issues covered, the size of the organization, and the union.

One of the continuing problems of union-management contracts is their readability. A study of 196 collective bargaining agreements from the Bureau of Labor Statistics analyzed contracts using readability indexes such as the Flesch, Farr-Jenkins-Patterson, and Gunning formulas.[32] The analyses indicated that contracts are difficult to read and that some sections are, in fact, incomprehensible. It is ironic that many of the contract sections that deal with seniority, discipline, and grievance procedures are not understandable to a rank-and-file employee who is most affected. Perhaps lawyers can understand what is presented, but stewards, union members, and other nonlawyers generally cannot make sense of the contract. Unfortunately, studies conducted over 30 years ago showed the same kind of results.[33]

The typical labor contract is divided into sections and appendixes. The standard sections that can be covered in some labor agreements are shown in Exhibit 18–4. The exhibit shows that a major part of the contract is concerned with such employment issues as wages, hours, fringe benefits, and overtime.

In general, the contract spells out the authority and responsibility of both union and management. *Management rights* appear in one of two forms. The first involves a statement that the control and operation of the business are the right of management except in cases specified in the contract. The second is a list of all management activities that are not subject to sharing with the union. Included are such topics as planning and scheduling production, purchasing equipment, and making final hiring decisions.

EXHIBIT 18-4 Content of a Labor Agreement

Purpose and intent of the parties	Vacations
Scope of the agreement	Seniority
Management	Safety and health
Responsibilities of the parties	Military service
Union membership and checkoff	Severance allowance
Adjustment of grievance	Savings and vacation plan
Arbitration	Supplemental unemployment benefits program
Suspension and discharge cases	S.U.B. and insurance grievances
Rates of pay	Prior agreements
Hours of work	Termination date
Overtime and holidays	

Source: Adapted from USX Corporation and the United Steelworkers Union, "Labor Agreement."

The *union rights* spelled out in the contract involve such issues as the role the union will play in laying off members or in such areas as promotion and transfer. The union stresses *seniority* as a means of reducing the tendency for discrimination and favoritisim in HRM decision making.

ADMINISTERING THE CONTRACT

Day-to-day compliance with the contract's provisions is an important responsibility of the supervisor or first-line manager. This individual is the management representative who works most closely with union members. As the representative of management, the supervisor must discipline workers, handle grievances, and prepare for such actions as strikes.

Discipline

Most contracts agree that management in a unionized firm has a right to discipline workers, providing all discipline follows legal due process.[34] If an employee challenges a disciplinary action, the burden of proof rests with the company. It is important that when an employee breaks rules or performs below standard, the supervisor act immediately by calling a meeting with the employee. A formal discipline interview should be scheduled. Discipline should not be used if the supervisor has failed to make workplace rules clear or to warn the employee in advance.

Many union-management contracts specify the types of discipline and the offenses for which corrective action will be taken. Some of the infractions that are typically spelled out are:

- *Incompetence.* Failure to perform the assigned job.
- *Misconduct.* Insubordination, dishonesty, or violating a rule, such as smoking in a restricted area.
- *Violations of the contract.* Initiating a strike when there is a no-strike clause, for example.

The contract should list penalties for such infractions.[35] Inconsistent application of discipline is sometimes a problem as the discussion in Chapter 16 illustrated.

EXHIBIT 18-5   A Grievance Procedure: A Unionized Situation

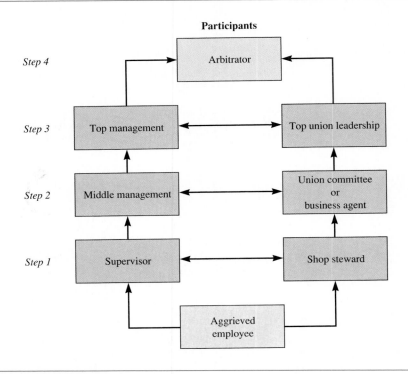

Grievances

A **grievance** is a complaint about an organizational policy, procedure, or managerial practice that creates dissatisfaction or discomfort, whether it is valid or not.[36] The complaint may be made by an individual or by the union.

Grievance procedures are usually followed in unionized companies, but they are also important channels of communication in nonunionized organizations. In the unionized organization, the contract contains a clause covering the steps to be followed and how the grievance will be handled. The number of steps varies from contract to contract. But a labor union is not essential for establishing a procedure.

Exhibit 18–5 illustrates a four-step grievance procedure used in a unionized company.

1. The employee meets with the supervisor and the union steward and presents the grievance. Most grievances are settled at this point.
2. If the grievance is not settled at step 1, there is a conference between middle management and union officials (a business agent or union committee).
3. At this point, a top-management representative and top union officials (for example, the union president) attempt to settle the grievance.
4. Both parties (union and management) turn the grievance over to an arbitrator who makes a decision. Arbitration is usually handled by a mutually agreed-upon single individual or a panel of an odd number.[37]

Although most grievances are handled at step 1, there are a number of important principles for managers to follow. They should (1) take every grievance seriously; (2) work with the union representative; (3) gather all information available on the grievance; (4) after weighing all the facts, provide an answer to the employee voicing the grievance; and (5) after the grievance is settled, attempt to move on to other matters.

Even though the grievance procedure shown in Exhibit 18–5 is typically used in large unionized firms (for example, AT&T, Proctor & Gamble, and Republic Steel), such a procedure is also needed in nonunion firms. In nonunion firms, a number of grievance approaches — open-door policy, ombudsman, juries of peers, hearing officers, and outside arbitration — have been used with some success.[38] The lack of any grievance procedure causes frustration, antagonism, and anxiety among many employees. These feelings and attitudes are not healthy for good employee-management relations. They also can spark an interest to organize a formal bargaining representative.

An example of a nonunionized employer with a formal grievance procedure is that of Duke University in Durham, North Carolina. Duke employs over 15,000 people of which two thirds work in the university's medical center.[39] In the current system, as displayed in Exhibit 18–6, a grieving employee is allowed to choose an advocate (second-year M.B.A. students are selected as employee advocates) only from within the Duke community. The final step is a jointly selected internal hearing panel or, in the case of termination, one of a panel of five professional arbitrators.

Interestingly, the main purpose of using M.B.A. student advocates to resolve grievances was to avoid using legal counsel, which usually led to long, drawn-out hearings. The students gain valuable real-world experience from their hands-on experience in requesting and debating employee rights. The program has been successful for over three years. It is likely that a program similar to Duke's could work in other organizations if (1) there were an accepted grievance procedure in place, (2) a college or university interested in developing hands-on applications of grievance resolution were available, and (3) management and employees were interested in grievance resolution instead of long, drawn-out, legal-oriented debates and political maneuvering.

In the unionized setting, an important determinant of the outcome of any grievance is the climate of labor relations.[40] Grievances are more likely to be settled favorably when the labor relations climate is positive. When the union-management climate is cooperative and harmonious, the chances of grievances being granted or partially granted at lower levels in the process are increased tremendously. However, when the relationship is distant or hostile, more grievances are denied or withdrawn.

Mediation

Mediation is the process in which a neutral third party helps labor and management reach agreement.[41] It is an inexpensive alternative to strikes when faced with an impasse during negotiations. The Federal Mediation and Conciliation Service (FMCS) was created as an independent agency by the Taft-Hartley Act in 1947. The FMCS maintains offices in major cities such as New York, Chicago, St. Louis, and San Francisco. It employs approximately 300 mediators, who perform their services without charge to participants. The FMCS mediates about 15,000 labor disagreements a year.

EXHIBIT 18-6   Duke University's Grievance Process for Nonunion Employees

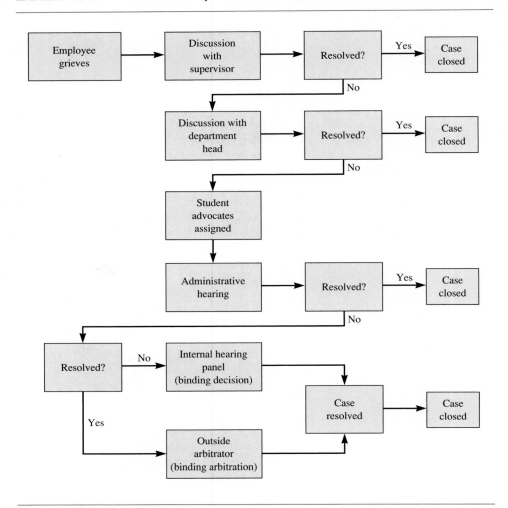

Source: Edmund M. Diaz, John W. Minton, and David M. Saunders (April 1987), "A Fair Nonunion Grievance Procedure," *Personnel Journal*, p. 14.

A *mediator* is a reviewer of facts, a creative facilitator, and a professional lis-tener.[42] He or she relies on the power of persuasion to get both parties to settle a dispute. A successful mediator possesses the following characteristics: impartiality, sincerity, communications skills, persistence, self-control, expertise, creativity, and general acceptability as a neutral party.[43] These attributes are essential in order to have management and labor reconcile their differences. The mediators make sug-gestions that may be accepted or rejected by both parties or either party.[44]

Arbitration

The grievance procedure does not always result in an acceptable solution. When a deadlock occurs, most contracts (about 96 percent) call for arbitration. **Arbitration** is a quasi-judicial process in which the parties agree to submit an unresolvable dispute to a neutral third party for binding settlement. Both parties submit their positions, and the arbitrator makes a decision.

The contract typically specifies how a dispute goes to arbitration. Normally, the case would have gone through the first three steps in the grievance procedure (Exhibit 18–5). At the last step, for instance, if management denies the grievance or fails to modify its position sufficiently to satisfy the union, the union can request arbitration.

Procedures for selection of an arbitrator are usually written into the contract. The most typical arrangement is to use a single impartial arbitrator who hears the evidence and renders an award, or to have a tripartite board consisting of a management representative, a union representative, and an impartial chairperson.

The arbitrators generally come from three major sources. The first group consists of attorneys who are full-time arbitrators. The second group is made up of academics who are experts in labor law, human resources management, and labor economics. The third group includes respected members of the community, such as teachers and ministers.

The *award* is the decision reached by the arbitrator. It conveys the decision, a summary of the evidence, and the rationale for the decision. In preparing the award, the arbitrator must examine a number of issues:

1. Can the dispute be arbitrated?
2. Did the grievance allege an actual violation of the contract?
3. Were the grievance procedures followed in a timely manner?

If these criteria are met, the arbitrator then investigates the dispute.

The arbitrator works hard to ensure that the award draws from the framework and intent of the contract. Most contracts prohibit arbitrators from adding to or subtracting from the intent of the contract. The arbitrator must clearly show how the award fits the meaning of the contract.

Arbitration is criticized because of time delays and expense. Research found that the length of time from request for arbitration to the arbitrator's award averages between 200 to 263 days.[45] The time delay is often caused by a shortage of qualified and experienced arbitrators. It is also true that either labor or management may delay the process waiting for a favorite arbitrator to hear the case.[46]

Part of the cost of arbitration is due to the time delays. The fees charged by arbitrators also are a major expense. The normal daily fee is between $400 and $500 plus travel and study time. Both sides usually engage an attorney, which is quite expensive. Also, employees involved in the complaint from both the labor and management side must be paid their regular wages during the arbitration process. Costs are divided equally between management and the union. These costs of arbitration may cause problems, especially for some unions. A financially unstable union is sometimes reluctant to become involved in arbitration at all. This reluctance can undermine union members' respect and image of the union.

In order to expedite cases and maintain some cost control, some union and management officials use *expedited arbitration procedures*. An example of such a procedure is the one used by the major steel producers and the United Steel Workers of America. Relatively inexperienced arbitrators are used to decide routine grievances within 10 days of the original complaint. Abbreviated decisions (one- or two-pages) are made within one or two days of the hearing.[47] Cases are presented by local management and union representatives instead of "pros" from the union or management. The fee for expedited arbitration hearings is $50 to $100 from each party and only for the hearing day.

Strikes

A **strike** is an effort to withhold employee services so that the employer will make greater concessions at the bargaining table. The strike, or a potential strike, is a major bargaining weapon used by the union. But before a union strikes, it needs to consider the legality of striking, the members' willingness to endure the hardships of a long strike, and the employer's ability to operate the organization without union members. The greater the employer's ability to operate the organization, the less chance the union will have of gaining the demands it makes.

There are a number of different types of strikes, including:

- *Economic strike.* Based on a demand for better wages or fringe benefits than the employer wants to provide.
- *Jurisdictional strike.* Exists when two unions argue over who has the right to perform a job. For example, bricklayers and ironworkers may both want to install steel rods in doorways. The rods are made a part of the brickwork and are needed to hold up heavy steel doors. If either group strikes to force the employer to grant the work to its members, a jurisdictional strike occurs. This type of strike is illegal under the Taft-Hartley Act.
- *Wildcat strike.* An unapproved strike that suddenly occurs because one union subgroup has not been satisfied by a grievance decision or by some managerial action. The union leaders do not sanction this type of strike.
- *Sitdown strike.* When employees strike but remain in the plant. Such strikes are illegal because they are an invasion of private property.

When any strike occurs, management must be able to function during the work stoppage, and the company property must be protected from strike sabotage.

Management generally views strikes with a mixture of fear and loathing. Even the threat of a strike can force concessions from management at the bargaining table, and any strike usually leaves an aftertaste that poisons labor relations for years.

Strikes are more frequent but shorter when the economy is booming. Costs of the strike for both sides are determined differently. The level of unemployment must be considered carefully by the union. When unemployment is high, the employer may easily hire replacement workers and strikers cannot find alternative employment. The health of the product market determines the cost of the strike for the employer. If there is stiff competition and alternative products available, the employer is at greater risk of losing market share permanently.

Only 10 to 15 percent of contract negotiations end in a strike. There was a downward trend in the number of strikes in the United States until 1989. Between 1970 and 1979, 1 to 3 million workers were involved in 4,000 to 6,000 strikes each year.[48] The total amount of working time lost was low between 1974 and 1980. In 1980, 33,000 labor days (workdays) were lost to strikes, versus 48,000 labor days in 1974.[49] Strikes over noneconomic issues have been drastically reduced. In 1976, there were 1,950 strikes during the course of disputes over working conditions and union jurisdiction. In 1984, there were just 389 strikes. Time lost to strikes was at its lowest between 1983 and 1988, with the latter setting a record low.[50] However, in 1989, the downward trend changed with a significant increase in the number and duration of strikes. Labor disputes covered many industries, including airlines, buses, telephone companies, and the mining industry.[51] Work stoppages in 1989 included:

- The Eastern Airlines strike by 8,500 members of the International Association of Machinists, joined by 3,500 members of the Air Line Pilots Association, and 6,000 flight attendants of the Transport Workers Union.
- 60,000 striking NYNEX employees, members of Communications Workers of America and the International Brotherhood of Electrical Workers.
- United Mine Workers (1,700) striking in the coal fields of Virginia, West Virginia, and Kentucky against the Pittston Corporation.
- A seven-state strike against the Boeing Company by 57,000 members of the International Association of Machinists.

The government reduced the power of the strike weapon with the Omnibus Budget Reconciliation Act of 1981. Effective October 1, 1981, striking workers and their families were no longer eligible for food stamps. But the decline in the number of strikes doesn't mean that the strike is not a powerful weapon available to unions. Strikes will still be used even in rough economic times despite workers' desires, unstable economics, and increased technological changes that have weakened unions' willingness and ability to mount them.

If and when a union mounts a strike, it usually resorts to *picketing* procedures. The union hopes to shut down the company during a strike, so it places members at plant entrances to advertise the dispute and discourage persons from entering or leaving the buildings. Peaceful persuasion through the formation of a picket line is legal, but violence is not. Picketing may also take place, without a strike, to publicize union viewpoints about an employer.

Another type of union pressure is the **boycott.** In a primary boycott, union members do not patronize the boycotted firm. This type of boycott is legal. A secondary boycott occurs when a supplier of a boycotted firm is threatened with a union strike unless it stops business with the boycotted company. This type of boycott is generally illegal under the Taft-Hartley Act. A special type of boycott is the **hot cargo agreement.** Under this agreement, the employer permits union members to avoid working with materials that come from employers who have been struck by a union. This type of boycott is illegal according to the Labor-Management Disclosure Act, except in the construction and clothing industries.

Management's response to these union pressures may be to continue operations with a skeleton crew of managerial personnel, to shut down the plant, or to lock the employees out. The **lockout** is an effort to force the union to stop harassing the employer or to accept the conditions set by management. Lockouts are also used to prevent union work slowdowns, damage to property, or violence related to a labor dispute. Many states allow locked-out employees to draw unemployment benefits, thereby weakening the lockout. In practice, the lockout is more of a threat than a widely practiced weapon of management.

In 1987, the 28 owners of the National Football League teams discovered that, during the players' strike, the organizations were much more profitable.[52] The players' strike showed that a football team is a peculiar labor force. It is organized labor by definition, yet its members are both more and less cohesive than many workers. There is an enormous disparity in wages. There is also no strike fund to bolster players in time of need. Thus, the owners were able to take a strong stand for three weeks, and the players gave in and came back to play.

The team owners used players who crossed the picket lines and played for significantly less money than the regular players. The lower salary expenses per week ($854,000 for regulars versus $230,000 for replacement players) meant higher profits for management.[53] Therefore, although attendance decreased during the strike, the profits earned were higher. The owners, by locking out the regulars and using replacement players, could earn a profit. The 1987 National Football League strike is an example of what one party can do to the other when they have the resources, a united front, and a plan.

Some experts believe that too much attention is paid to money and benefits issues before, during, and after a strike. In fact, one study of unionized strike and unionized nonstrike companies suggests that workers vote for a strike only when they are frustrated because their needs, wants, and ideas go unheard or unanswered. In such situations, management becomes the enemy, an adversary to be punished by a strike. Instead of waiting for a strike to happen, it has been suggested that management needs to be more aggressive in finding out about employee sentiments and needs.

There are some companies that are aggressively attempting to uncover employee needs and wants before they lead to a strike. At Sears, Roebuck, a program of regular managerial visits with employees, discussion sessions, and attitude surveys are used. Kraft, Inc., uses outside help to determine employee sentiment. A team of experts, headed up by the vice president of personnel, visits each production and retail facility to conduct interviews and to hold feedback sessions. Corrective action is taken as quickly as possible. Rockwell International uses a program headed by the vice president of personnel that involves holding regular discussion meetings with engineers. The meetings cover engineers' concerns about computer needs, materials, educational opportunities, and access to libraries. These meetings, according to the management of Rockwell, have led to a more stable and constructive relationship between employees and managers.

Strikes in the Public Sector

Strikes by public-sector employees are prohibited by most states, and legislation provides injunction and penalty provisions if strikes occur.[54] Some public employees in Alaska, Hawaii, Idaho, Minnesota, Montana, Oregon, Pennsylvania, Vermont, and Wisconsin have been granted the right to strike, however. Even with the legal prohibitions against strikes in the public sector, they are quite common, particularly at the local level. In the recent past, school employees have been involved in long and costly labor disputes across the United States. Most strikes in the public sector are aimed at increasing the employees' bargaining power.

Strikes in the public sector by government workers are troublesome for unions, management, and the government. The issue of "government sovereignty" is raised to argue against such strikes. Of course, the public employee unions like the Professional Air Traffic Controllers (PATCO) argue against this claim of the government.[55] The union argues that taking away the strike weapon reduces public employee unions to a second-class type of power.

In the summer of 1981, 12,000 air traffic controllers went on strike. President Reagan claimed that the strike violated the oath taken by the controllers not to strike. The typical and usually followed practice by which a strike by public employees is "glossed over" was replaced by the president's decision to fire every striking air traffic controller. The action by President Reagan to hold public employees to the no-strike provisions of the contract has served notice to other unionized employees in the U.S. Postal Service and in state and local governments.[56] Most observers believe that PATCO leaders such as the president, Robert Poli, totally miscalculated public reaction. The strike by air traffic controllers, with average annual salaries of $35,000, didn't generate a groundswell of public support.[57] The PATCO strike was a setback for organized labor in government employment — which is the union's main target for growth.

UNION-MANAGEMENT COOPERATION

The traditional relationship between labor and management in the United States has been adversarial. Organized labor believes that management *never* has the needs of the worker in mind. Management believes that labor is always out to grasp for more and more concessions. Collective bargaining rests on this premise, with the two sides facing off across a table.

On closer examination, it is apparent that both sides must cooperate to some extent in order to remain strong. Labor needs jobs, good working conditions, and fair wages and benefits. Management wants to maximize profits while supplying quality products. Labor is strongest when the economy is strong. Then management can pass along the desired outcomes and recoup them with higher prices. So both labor and management benefit from a strong economy and a healthy, profitable organization. As more management and labor leaders realize this and as foreign competition intensifies, there is a groundswell movement in the United States toward better labor-management cooperation.

Unions are becoming almost as interested as management in finding innovative methods to give more say about how they work. Programs like quality circles and quality of work life systems that solicit ideas are becoming more popular.[58] Union leaders who once worried about being "management's lackey" have been surprised to find that cooperating with management has raised their standing with members.

The United Auto Workers, the United Steelworkers of America, the Communications Workers of America, the International Brotherhood of Electrical Workers, and the Telecommunications International Union — together representing about a fifth of the nation's organized workers — have signed national labor agreements committing themselves to plans for a better employee work life. Unions have convinced managers that many workers want to take their jobs seriously and want to be treated fairly.

During the early 1970s, the major steel companies and the United Steelworkers agreed upon a bold plan to fight the growing threat of imported steel. Joint labor-management committees sat down together to analyze and offer solutions to the problem. Lloyd McBride, the now-deceased United Steelworker's president said about the first of these meetings:

> The management guys came in and said, "Well, we want to talk about the productivity of this operation. Down in this department we could eliminate this job." The union sat there and then one representative said, "Well, that would create some problems for us. But the problems would not be so great if we could get rid of your brother-in-law down there who's not doing much. . . ."

Confrontation, war, and adversarial relations were hard to change, according to McBride. The early 1970s effort came to a halt because both parties were so locked in their previous styles of fighting against each other.[59]

At about the same time, the United Auto Workers were attempting to work with General Motors (GM) to solve productivity problems. GM had become more concerned about the lagging productivity per worker. The GM managers were aware that the traditional solutions from the top down were only somewhat successful when workers came in late or failed to report to work at all. Irving Bluestone, then director of the UAW's GM department, saw an opportunity to advance his belief that unions could cooperate with management to advance the workers' responsibilities and stature. He pushed his idea hard, and, in the 1973 contract negotiations, GM and the UAW signed the first national quality of work-life agreement in the United States.

The agreement has become the model of labor-management cooperation.[60] Nowhere in it did the word *productivity* appear. Management would seek its rewards from work improvements in higher product quality and lower absenteeism. All the quality of work life programs would be strictly voluntary, and none would be used unilaterally to raise production rates or reduce human resource requirements. Labor-management work improvement committees that have been working at GM have given workers more job control and opened up communication between workers and supervisors.

Many union leaders initially feared that labor-management cooperation would undermine the collective bargaining process. After all, nothing could be further from the spirit of "us versus them" than mutually identifying and solving problems. Some unionists worried that management would use cooperative programs such as quality of work life improvements to chip away at benefits won through bargaining.

In practice, the lines between cooperation and conflict have been relatively clear.[61] Few managers or labor leaders have tried to abuse the cooperation problem-solving activities. GM and Ford are pressing the UAW wage concessions, and the UAW is pushing them for more wages, more job security, and more benefits.

The 1987 United Auto Workers' contract with Ford and GM are considered to be important in labor's effort to gain secure employment.[62] Previously, job-protection insurers applied only when the UAW could show that a laid-off worker was covered. The new agreement reverses the burden of proof. It guarantees the jobs of current workers under all circumstances except for falling sales. In return, the UAW agreed to set up joint labor-management committees at each plant. These cooperative committees develop plans for boosting productivity and quality.[63]

Former Secretary of Labor William Brock III stated that labor-management cooperation is simply the thing to do because it is both the right thing to do and a matter for survival.[64] He cited as an example of what labor-management cooperation could do the case of the GM plant in California where the plant folded because both the union and management would not give in to the other's demands. This same plant is now a joint Toyota/GM operation with much more flexible work rules. The same United Auto Workers who forced the plant out of existence several years ago now operate on the "team approach." Absenteeism is down from 20 percent to 2 percent. Team members are cross-trained to do each other's jobs. And the UAW members organized and threatened to picket USX because they were supplying poor quality steel. Labor at the Toyota/GM plant contended they could not make a good quality car without quality steel.

Labor-management cooperation can make management more effective and unions more cost-conscious.[65] One way to promote labor-management cooperation is to create joint union-management committees.[66] These committees allow labor and management to work out joint solutions to employee problems. The main obstacle to the growth of such committees and other labor-management cooperation techniques is suspicion.[67] Both sides still do not trust each other. In addition, a new form of industrial relations is being fostered by some managers. It is called the

PROFESSIONAL PROFILE

Biography

Gregory M. Watts, APM, is a personnel director for Chicago Switch, Inc., a division of Illinois Tool Works, Inc.

Mr. Watts, a native of Chicago, is a graduate of Southern Illinois University in Carbondale, Illinois.

Mr. Watts is a member of the following professional groups: American Society for Personnel Administration, Midwest Industrial Management Association, and the Electronics Personnel Administration.

The Union Contract and Arbitration: A Viewpoint. Recently, management made a decision to discontinue the operation of a tool and die department due to a sales slump.

Twenty-four union employees lost their jobs, and two were kept on until operations were completely severed. Under the firm's severance pay policy, each received a severance allowance under the following plan:

1–5 years of service	2 weeks
6–10 years of service	4 weeks
11–15 years of service	6 weeks
Over 15 years of service	8 weeks

Gregory Watts
Chicago Switch, Inc.

Soon a vacancy developed among the two who were kept on, and the company hired someone from the outside to fill the job. One of the "severees" complained to the union, stating "the job should have been filled according to the seniority of those who got severance. After all, when there is a layoff, workers are recalled according to their length of service."

The company did not see it that way and maintained that once a worker receives severance pay, he or she loses former rights.

The case eventually went to arbitration, and the company won. The arbitrator stated that "employees who accept severance pay are not entitled to claim any other benefits, because, by accepting severance pay, they have released any rights they may have had under the contract. Since seniority is a right under the contract, it cannot be used as a way to recall by those who received severance allowances."

new industrial relations (NIR) and contains the union-free doctrine.[68] A union-free environment can be achieved through any of three processes: (1) union attrition; (2) union avoidance; and (3) union-management cooperation. A union-free strategy gets rid of the union but not its function, which is to deal equitably with the workers.

Given the current economic and competitive climate, unions, as well as managers, cannot afford to overlook the possibility of more labor-management cooperation. The long-run survival of many organizations and unions may depend somewhat on the degree of cooperation achieved.

THE RIGHTS OF EMPLOYEES IN NONUNIONIZED SITUATIONS

The rights of union members are spelled out in labor contracts. However, most employees — *about 83 percent* — do not belong to unions. Do these nonunionized employees have safe working conditions, the right to privacy, fair wages, and other workplace rights? The answer varies from industry to industry and company to company.

During the formative years of the U.S. republic, the rights of people who worked for others were not a high priority issue.[69] With the birth of the Industrial Revolution, the rights of workers began to take on an importance of their own. Since then, employee rights have evolved through several phases. The first right concerned the abolition of slavery. Then, intolerable working conditions in factories became the primary issue. Protecting children in the workplace came next. With the growth of labor unions, various new rights were added: the right to strike, immunity from lawsuits under breach of contract, and the right to bargain collectively. Nonunion employees also want to have some say in their work destiny. In the decades since the social legislation of the 1960s, there has been an increasing emphasis among nonunionized workers on the other rights of employment — employment discrimination, health in the workplace, adequate pension plans, privacy, and the right to a job. The traditional view that "top management knows best" is being challenged more and more.

Privacy

The right to privacy is a part of constitutional law. However, nonunion organizations in most states give managers the right to monitor employees' conversations on company telephones without notifying the employees. Other invasions of privacy occur when an employer collects data about a worker — psychological tests, attitude surveys, and medical records. The privacy may be invaded again when the information collected is put to use. Management may use the information to make promotion decisions and answer inquiries from credit bureaus, insurance companies, and social agencies.

IBM, the most publicized nonunion organization in the United States, makes a major issue about employee rights and especially privacy.[70] At IBM:

1. Management can collect and keep in its personnel files only those facts about employees that are required by law or that are necessary to manage operations. IBM's job application forms no longer request previous addresses or information on whether the employee has relatives in the firm. Nor does it ask about prior mental problems, convictions dating back more than five years, or more recent criminal charges that have not resulted in conviction.

2. Performance evaluations more than three years old must be weeded from an employee's personnel file.

3. Employees are entitled to know how filed information about them is being used.

4. An employee is entitled to see most of the information on file about him or her. Management may withhold some information, such as a confidential discussion of an opportunity for promotion that was never given.

5. Personality and general intelligence tests are not permissible information for employee records.

IBM believes that, by being open and concerned about employee privacy, workers are happier. It is proud of the employees' continuing eagerness to reject unions. IBM wants its employees to feel that unions are not necessary, and protecting their privacy seems to help.

Firing Nonunion Workers

The right of employers in private industry to fire workers not protected by a union contract is coming under close scrutiny, as discussed earlier in Chapter 16.[71] The trend in many states today is away from the doctrine of employment at will.[72] This term is defined as the right of the employee to quit when they choose balanced by the right of the employer to fire an employee without giving a reason.[73] Movement is toward the idea that employment involves a contract between the two parties that the employer can break for *"just cause."* This trend may result in unprecedented *job security* for nonunionized workers.

Estimates indicate that companies in private industry discharge about 1 million permanent employees each year without a "fair hearing." It was estimated that, between 1988 and 1990, over 400,000 mid- and upper-level managers with three or more years of experience would be laid off permanently.[74] A slowing economy in 1990 overshot that estimate.

The idea of a contractual employment relationship has left employers open to lawsuits by employees who claim they were terminated wrongfully.[75] Court decisions in several states have awarded large settlements to employees who were judged to be fired capriciously.[76] Courts in Washington and Michigan have upheld claims by nonunion workers that promises made in employee handbooks — and even orally — constituted a job contract that precluded dismissal except for just cause. Workers in California have also won the right to seek punitive damages on top of lost wages in dismissal cases.[77]

A frequently cited case involved the Shriner's Hospital for Crippled Children, which fired registered nurse, Juanita Vorhees. One evening, she playfully tossed a few drops of water at a patient. The patient tossed some back. Ms. Vorhees wiped up the water and everyone laughed, except her supervisor who reported the incident to the hospital's administrator. Ms. Vorhees was fired for gross violation of her duties. She sued the hospital claiming that "just cause" for dismissal was not supported. The Superior Court of Seattle ruled that the hospital failed to demonstrate this in dismissing Vorhees; her award — her job and back wages.

Capricious dismissal is not a thing of the past. Unfair discharge suits in nonunion firms will probably continue to increase in number in the future as companies merge, retrench, economize, and try to combat foreign competition. Recently, the author of this chapter was contacted by a friend at 7 A.M. one morning. The woman was calling from her office where she had been locked in by her supervisor until she signed both a letter of resignation and a guarantee that she would not sue for unjust dismissal. While she was speaking on the phone, an angry supervisor could be heard pounding on the door and urging her to get it over with. The company had recently changed hands, and old employees were being fired without reason to make room for new appointees. Out of fear, she complied.

However, there is a growing feeling among legal observers that a manager in a nonunion firm *or* a union firm is not entitled to penalize an employee unfairly. To avoid claims of wrongful discharge, employers should follow an HRM procedure that gives employees a chance to improve and that meets more stringent legal

CAREER CHALLENGE

(concluded)

The ballots of the union-versus-management vote were counted at Hardisty Manufacturing Company. The union had gotten 30 percent of the employees to sign authorization cards. And the NLRB had stepped in to schedule the unionization election. Shortly after the NLRB examiner left, Tom called Stan into his office.

Tom How could we lose this election? Why do I have an HR manager if he can't beat the union?

Stan It's not over yet. They still have to get a majority. But Tom, we've got to start thinking about a strategy . . . the tactics we'll use . . . this problem isn't going to just "go away" . . . we've got to face it. I've been in touch with some professional negotiators who've agreed to speak for us, in case the union wins.

Tom Is that necessary?

Stan I think it is. There's a lot going against us. We were really hurt by the pay item. You told me we had to lay people off to cut costs, but the layoffs came in the middle of the union's organizing campaign. A lot of people felt threatened. When people get threatened, they join unions.

Tom I'm tired of excuses. Just do your job and shut out that union! Hire whoever you have to. And I promise you, we'll have no more layoffs. We just had to keep our heads above water, that's all, so we had to lay off some workers. But no more. I'll help you in any way I can. By the way, how's that communication program coming along?

Between then and the election, both sides campaigned, but Stan felt that the management's efforts weren't as organized or as effective as the union's. At the last minute, Tom called back the workers who had been laid off; the votes looked close. But when the representative votes were counted, the union had won. HMC challenged the votes of several persons, but in the end, the NLRB declared the union as the bargaining agent, and negotiation began.

One week later, Stan quit. Tom had refused to talk to him since the election. After the experience, both men felt hostile toward unions, but Stan blamed Tom more than anything. He felt that Hardisty's whole antiunion campaign had been mismanaged from the start.

requirements.[78] Courts have developed a two-part test that can be used to determine "just cause":

1. Certain inappropriate conduct is grounds for immediate dismissal.
2. Discharged employees must have received fair warning, expressed or implied, that their conduct was grounds for termination.

The Future of Unions in the United States

A famous management theorist, Peter Drucker, predicts that by the year 2010 industrial workers will make up only 5 to 10 percent of the work force in developed non-Communist countries.[79] That means that the early base of unionism will be almost completely eroded. In 1990, unions all over the world were losing members and along with them power, but the leader of a powerful union, Solidarity, Lech Walensa, was elected to lead Poland's new government. Since 1974, U.S. unions have lost two fifths of their membership, however. Adding pressure on unions is the fact that much of what unions traditionally stood for had already been enacted into law.

The above erosion of union power rests on three factors:

1. The shift in the work force from blue-collar manufacturing workers to better-educated, service/knowledge workers.
2. Increased product market competitiveness is a global market.
3. A decrease in the demand by nonunionized employees for union representation.[80]

However, new tactics are being used to organize new kinds of workers.[81] Unions are providing members access to credit cards, prepaid legal care, term life insurance, and travel clubs. They are aggressively recruiting women and minorities. Unions are consolidating via mergers to reduce expenses. They are encouraging older employees to remain in the work force and advocating programs for them. And unions are becoming more effective in organizing both the service and public employment sectors of the economy.

The future of U.S. unions and the key to them remaining an important part of our economy will depend on the following critical factors:[82]

1. The quality of union leadership.
2. Willingness to experiment with innovative organizing techniques.
3. Frequent involvement with the rank-and-file employee.
4. The ability to appeal to better-educated professional, service/knowledge workers.
5. Genuine cooperation with management.

SUMMARY

This chapter has focused on union organizing campaigns and management resistance to them. In addition, the collective bargaining process was spelled out. Employee rights in the nonunionized work force were explored briefly. And, the future of unions was examined.

To summarize the major points covered in this chapter:

1. A union can exist only if workers vote to become unionized. If a union doesn't receive at least 50 percent plus 1 vote of the votes cast in a representation election, it can't serve as the employee's exclusive bargaining representative.
2. Management and union face off and campaign against each other. Each presents its view of the situation.
3. The union organizing campaign and management resistance to organizing in the private sector are watched over closely by the National Labor Relations Board to prevent unfair labor practices.
4. *Collective bargaining* is a process by which the representatives of the organi-

zation meet with the employees' representative — the union — to try to work out a contract.

5. The steps in the collective bargaining process include:
   a. Prenegotiation.
   b. Selecting negotiators.
   c. Developing a bargaining strategy.
   d. Using the best bargaining tactics.
   e. Reaching a formal contractual agreement.

6. The day-to-day compliance with union-management contract provisions is an important responsibility of the first-line supervisor and the shop steward. They are both involved in such contract-related issues as discipline, grievance procedures, and strikes.

7. A *grievance* is a complaint about an organizational policy, procedure, or managerial practice that creates dissatisfaction or discomfort, whether it is valid or not. It can be filed by an individual employee or the union.

8. The grievance procedure does not always result in an acceptable solution. *Mediation* is the process by which a third party helps labor and management reach an agreement. *Arbitration* is a quasi-judicial process in which the parties agree to submit an unresolvable dispute to a neutral third party for binding settlement.

9. A *strike* is an effort to withhold employee services so the employer will make greater concessions at the bargaining table. There appears to be a distinct trend toward fewer strikes. Strikes in the public sector are prohibited in most states.

10. A *primary boycott* occurs when striking union members do not patronize the boycotted firm. It is another legal way for the union to exert pressure on the organization. Threats to the firm's suppliers, called a *secondary boycott*, are illegal.

11. The *lockout* is the managerial equivalent of a strike. Management can continue operating with a skeleton crew of managers, shutdown the plant, or lock employees out.

12. The traditional adversarial union-management relationship has been giving way to union-management cooperation. Adverse economic times, foreign competition, and technological advancements have created more interest in both union and management to look for ways to cooperate.

13. The rights of nonunionized employees are being upheld by the courts. Courts are becoming more involved in the areas of privacy and dismissal.

14. Unions are reviving membership by using new tactics to organize new kinds of workers.

KEY TERMS

QUESTIONS FOR REVIEW AND DISCUSSION

1. Outline the union organizing process. How can employees get the National Labor Relations Board to conduct a representation election?
2. Why should the NLRB, a federal government agency, be needed to supervise and oversee representation elections?
3. What stages does each side go through during collective bargaining? Do negotiators at a bargaining table need to possess some acting abilities? Explain.
4. What skills should a person possess to be a successful and respected mediator?
5. Name and define the various types of strike. How does a strike differ from a lockout?
6. Should public employees, such as air traffic controllers, police officers, and postal workers, be permitted to strike? Why or why not?
7. How would the economic situation in the country influence the type of labor-management cooperation that is pursued by both parties?
8. What is needed in a nonunionized situation before a grievance process such as that used by Duke University can have a fair chance of succeeding?
9. Why would professionals such as nurses, engineers, and educators want to join unions since unions have been traditionally associated with blue-collar industrial workers?
10. What will unions have to do to guarantee their place in the U.S. economy of the future?

NOTES

[1] John A. Fossum (1989), *Labor Realtions*, 4th ed. (Homewood, Ill: BPI/Irwin).

[2] American Federation of Labor and Congress of Industrial Organizations (November 1989), *AFL–CIO Policy Resolutions, Eighteenth Constitutional Convention* (Washington, D.C.: AFL–CIO), Publication No. 3-0290-18, p. 4.

[3] Fossum, *Labor Relations*, p. 6.

[4] Benjamin Taylor and Fred Witney (1987), *Labor Relations Law* (Englewood Cliffs, N.J.: Prentice-Hall), p. 11.

[5] William H. Holley, Jr., and Kenneth M. Jennings (1991), *The Labor Relations Process*, 4th ed. (Chicago: Dryden Press), p. 134.

[6] Ibid., p. 135.

[7] Arthur A. Sloane and Fred Whitney (1988), *Labor Relations* (Englewood Cliffs, N.J.: Prentice-Hall), p. 109.

[8] Kim Moody (1988), *An Injury to All* (London: Verso), pp. 10, 101 +.

[9] Norman Metzger (May 1990), "Addressing Employee Needs in the 1990s," *Hospital Material Management Quarterly*, 11, no. 4, pp. 49–56.

[10] Monty L. Lynn and Jozell Brister (Winter 1989), "Trends in Union Organizing Issues and Tactics," *Industrial Relations* 28, no. 1, pp. 104–13.

[11] Jerry Jakulovics (February 1988), "Subtler Approaches to Organizing Foreseen," *Management Review* 77, no. 2, p. 24.

[12] Matthew Goodfellow (October 1989), "Unions: Is It Time?" *Best's Review* 89, no. 6, pp. 19–27.

[13] Gary N. Chaison and Dileep G. Dhavale (Summer 1990), "The Changing Scope of Union Organizing," *Journal of Labor Research* XI, no. 3, pp. 307–22.

14 Jack Barbash (1956), *The Practice of Unionism* (New York: Harper & Row), p. 87.

15 Gary N. Chaison (1987), *"The Recent Expansion of Union Organizing Jurisdictions,"* Working Paper No. 87–102, Graduate School of Management, Clark University, Worcester, Massachusetts.

16 Chaison and Dhavale, "The Changing Scope of Union Organizing," p. 309.

17 Stephen G. Bronars and Donald R. Deere (Winter 1990), "Union Representation Elections and Firm Profitability," *Industrial Relations* 29, no. 1, pp. 15–37.

18 James F. Rand (June 1980), "Preventive Maintenance Techniques for Staying Union-Free." *Personnel Journal*, pp. 497–99.

19 Metzger, "Addressing Employee Needs in the 1990s," p. 54.

20 Richard B. Freeman and Morris M. Kleiner (April 1990), "Employer Behavior in the Face of Union Organizing Drives," *Industrial & Labor Relations Review* 43 no. 4, pp. 351–65.

21 Reed Richardson (1985), *Collective Bargaining by Objectives* (Englewood, N.J.: Prentice-Hall).

22 J. Y. Cousins and J. B. McCall (1986), "The Professional Approach to Collective Bargaining," *Management Decision* 24, no. 6, pp. 41–44.

23 Richard E. Walton and Robert B. McKersie (1965), *A Behavioral Theory of Labor Negotiations* (New York: McGraw-Hill), pp. 3–4.

24 Peter Capelli and Robert B. McKersie (1985), "Labor and the Crisis in Collective Bargaining," in *Challenges and Choices Facing American Labor*, ed. Thomas A. Kochan (Cambridge, Mass.: MIT Press).

25 Aaron Bernstein (December 14, 1987), "Move Over, Boone, Carl and Ira — Here Comes Labor," *Business Week*, pp. 124–25.

26 Deborah O. Cantrell (September 1984), "Computers Come to the Bargaining Table," *Personnel Journal*, pp. 27–30.

27 Fossum, *Labor Relations*, pp. 169–70.

28 Ibid., p. 171.

29 G. Edward Herman, Alfred Kuhn, and Ronald L. Seeber (1987), *Collective Bargaining and Labor Relations* (Englewood Cliffs, N.J.: Prentice-Hall), pp. 243–47.

30 Sloane and Witney, *Labor Relations*, p. 223.

31 Herbert R. Northrup (1964), *Boulwarism* (Ann Arbor, Mich.: Bureau of Industrial Relations, University of Michigan).

32 James Buchan and Clyde Scott (November 1984), "Readability Levels of Collective Bargaining Agreements," *Personnel Administrator*, pp. 73–80.

33 Jeanne Lauer and D. G. Patterson (January 1951), "Readability of Union Contracts," *Personnel*, pp. 36–40.

34 Robert N. Lussier (August 1990), "A Discipline Model for Increasing Performance," *Supervisory Management* 35, no. 8, pp. 6–7.

35 Richard Avery and John M. Ivancevich (January 1980), "Punishment in Organizations: A Review, Propositions, and Research Suggestions," *Academy of Management Review*, pp. 123–32.

36 Paul F. Salipante and Rene Bouwen (1990), "Behavioral Analysis of Grievances: Conflict Sources, Complexity and Transformation," *Employee Relations* 12, no. 3, pp. 17–22.

37 Peter Feuille and Michael LeRoy (March 1990), "Grievance Arbitration Appeals in the Federal Courts: Facts and Figures," *Arbitration Journal* 45, no. 1, pp. 35–47.

38 Alan Balfour (March-April 1984), "Five Types of Non-Union Grievance Systems," *Personnel*, pp. 69–76.

[39] Edmund D. Diaz, John W. Minton, and David M. Saunders (April 1987), "A Fair Nonunion Grievance Procedure," *Personnel Journal*, pp. 13–18.

[40] Ali Dastmalchian and Ignance Ng (Spring 1990), "Industrial Relations Climate and Grievance Outcomes," *Industrial Relations* 45, no. 2, pp. 311–24.

[41] Steven Briggs and Daniel J. Koys (1990), "An Empirical Investigation of Public Sector Mediator Effectiveness," *Journal of Collective Negotiations in the Public Sector* 19, no. 2, pp. 121–28.

[42] David A. Dilts and Ahmad Karim (Winter 1990), "The Effect of Mediators' Qualities and Strategies on Mediation Outcomes," *Industrial Relations* 45, no. 1, pp. 22–37.

[43] Ibid.

[44] Steven Briggs (1987), "Labor/Management Conflict and the Role of the Neutral," in *Personnel and Human Resource Management*, ed. R. S. Schuler, S. A. Youngblood and V. L. Huber (St. Paul, Minn.: West Publishing), pp. 418–24.

[45] (May 14, 1983), "Labor Arbitration Seen in Need of Improvement," *Daily Labor Report*, p. 1.

[46] Holley and Jennings, *The Labor Relations Process*, p. 282.

[47] Ibid.

[48] Robert J. Flanagan, Lawrence M. Kahn, Robert S. Smith, and Ronald G. Ehrenberg (1989), *Economics of the Employment Relationship* (Glenview, Ill.: Scott, Foresman), p. 452.

[49] Herbert E. Meyer (November 2, 1981), "The Decline of Strikes," *Fortune*, pp. 66–70.

[50] Holley and Jennings, *The Labor Relations Process*, p. 209.

[51] AFL–CIO, *AFL-CIO Policy Resolutions*, pp. 2–3.

[52] Robert Johnson (October 14, 1987), "Team Owners Discover the Strike Brings a Big Benefit: An Improved Bottom Line," *The Wall Street Journal*, p. 33.

[53] Bill Saporito (October 26, 1987), "The Life of a $725,000 Scab," *Fortune*, pp. 91–94.

[54] Fossum, *Labor Relations*, pp. 454–55.

[55] Peter Gall and John Hoerr (August 24, 1981), "How Labor Loses from the PATCO Strike," *Business Week*, p. 35.

[56] Ibid.

[57] Ben Burdetsky and Marvin S. Katzman (July 1984), "Is the Strike Iron Still Hot?" *Personnel Journal*, pp. 48–52.

[58] James W. Thacker and Mitchell W. Fields (Winter 1987), "Union Involvement in Quality-of-Worklife Efforts: A Longitudinal Investigation," *Personnel Psychology*, pp. 97–111.

[59] Irving H. Siegel and Edgar Weinberg (1982), *Labor-Management Cooperation: The American Experience* (Kalamazoo, Mich.: W. E. Upjohn Institute).

[60] Ibid.

[61] Robert E. Steiner (May 1981), "The Labor-Management Cooperation Act," *Personnel Journal*, pp. 344–45.

[62] John Hillkirk (September 18, 1987), "UAW Reach Accord on Contract," *USA Today*, p. 1.

[63] Aaron Bernstein (January 11, 1988), "A Demanding Year for Labor," *Business Week*, p. 1; and Jacob M. Schlesinger (October 9, 1987), "GM, UAW Reach Tentative Pact: Officials Say It's Similar to Ford's," *The Wall Street Journal*, p. 2.

[64] William Brock III (Summer 1990), "The Importance of Labor Management Cooperation," *Journal of Labor Research* XI, no. 3, pp. 225–30.

[65] Mark Rosenbaum (Autumn 1989), "Partners in Productivity: An Emerging Consensus in Labor-Management Relations," *Productivity Review* 8, no. 4, pp. 357–64.

66 Paula B. Voos (Winter 1989), "The Influence of Cooperative Programs on Union-Management Relations, Flexibility, and Other Labor Relations Outcomes," *Journal of Labor Relations* 10, no. 1, pp. 103–17.

67 Beverely Geber (August 1987), "Teaming Up with Unions," *Training* 24, no. 8, pp. 24–31.

68 Jack Barbash (Winter 1987), "Like Nature, Industrial Relations Abhors a Vacuum: The Case of the Union-Free Strategy," *Industrial Relations* 42, no. 1, pp. 168–78.

69 James Fraze and Martha T. Finney (1990), "Employee Rights between Our Shores," *Personnel Administrator* 33, no. 3, pp. 50–54, 79.

70 Interview with Frank Cary (September-October 1976), "IBM's Guidelines to Employee Privacy," *Harvard Business Review*, pp. 82–90.

71 Gary S. Marx (July 1990), "Protection Worth Demanding," *Bobbin* 31, no. 11, pp. 102, 104.

72 Jeffery L. Pellissier (May 1990), "Avoiding the Wrongful Termination Pitfall," *Cornell Hotel & Restaurant Administration Quarterly* 31, no. 1, pp. 118–23.

73 William E. Fulmer and Ann Wallace Casey (May 1990), "Employment at Will: Options for Managers," *Academy of Management Executive* 4, no. 2, pp. 102–7.

74 Robert J. McCaffery (1988), *Employee Benefit Programs* (Boston: PWS-Kent), p. 87.

75 Pellissier, "Avoiding the Wrongful Termination Pitfall," p. 120.

76 (April 6, 1981), "The Growing Cost of Firing Nonunion Workers," *Business Week*, pp. 95–98.

77 David W. Ewing (1983), *Do It My Way or You're Fired* (New York: John Wiley & Sons).

78 Pellissier, "Avoiding the Wrongful Termination Pitfall," p. 122.

79 Peter F. Drucker (March 20, 1990), "Peter Drucker Asks: Will Unions Ever Again Be Useful Organs of Society?" *Industry Week* 238, no. 6, pp. 16–22.

80 Henry S. Farber (January 1990), "The Decline of Unionization in the U.S.: What Can Be Learned from Recent Experience?" part 2, *Journal of Labor Economics* 8, no. 1, pp. S75–S105.

81 Don Nichols (February 1988), "Today's Unions: A Mixed Bag," *Management Review* 77, no. 2, pp. 43–44.

82 Rod Willis (February 1988), "Can American Unions Transform Themselves?" *Management Review* 77, no. 2, 14–29.

EXERCISE 18–1   Union-Management Contract Negotiations

Objective   To permit individuals to become involved in labor-management contract negotiations in a role-playing session.

SET UP THE EXERCISE

1. Groups (even number of groups) of four to eight people will form. Half of the groups will be union teams and the other half will be management teams.

2. Read the description of the Dana Lou Corporation of Hamilton, Ohio.

3. Review and discuss in groups the four bargaining issues and the data collected on competitors (15 minutes).

4. The instructor will provide the union team(s), the "union negotiators" instructions; and the management teams(s), the "management negotiations" instructions.

5. Groups face off against each other (one management team versus one union team). The negotiator represents the team's position.
6. Individuals should answer the exercise questions after the negotiations — Step 2 of the negotiations.

Dana Lou Corporation

Dana Lou Corporation is a medium-sized company with about 1,100 employees in Hamilton, Ohio, a suburb of Cincinnati. It competes in the electronic repair parts industry and is slightly larger than most of its main competitors. The firm's success (profitability and growth) has been attributed to a dedicated work force that takes great pride in their work.

In 1964, the Communications Workers of America (CWA) organized the plant. Since then, labor-management relations have been good, and there were only two days lost to a strike in 1972. Labor and management both feel that the cooperation between them is much better than that found in other firms of the same size in the area.

The current labor-management contract expires in three weeks. Representatives from the union and management have been negotiating a number of bargaining issues for the last three days, but there seems to be little agreement.

The Bargaining Issues

1. Republic National Medical and Dental Insurance Protection
   a. Present contract: Dana Lou pays 50 percent of premiums for all full-time employees.
   b. New contract issues: The CWA wants Dana Lou to pay the full premium; management wants to hold the line.
   In terms of costs, the data look like this:

Percent of Premium Paid	Dana Lou Contribution	
0	-0-	
25	$ 55,000	
50	110,000	Present Contribution
75	$165,000	
100	220,000	

2. Preventive health director, staff, and participation
   a. Present contract: Dana Lou has two part-time physicians and two full-time nurses (cost is $66,000 per year).
   b. New contract issues: The CWA wants a full-time fitness director, a full-time physician, counselors for alcohol and drug abuse problems, and partial payment for employee use of YMCA and YWCA exercise facilities (estimated increase over present arrangements, $108,000).

3. Vacation benefits
   a. Present contract: One-week full pay for the first year, two weeks for employees with 2 to 10 years of service, and three weeks for employees with over 10 years.
   b. New contract issues: CWA wants all employees with 15 or more years of service to have four weeks of full-paid vacation. Management wants no change in present program.

4. Wage increases for skilled quality inspectors
   a. Present contract: Inspectors' rate is $5.95 per hour; inspector apprentices, $4.30.
   b. New contract issues: CWA wants an increase of $0.50 per hour for the plant's 95 inspectors and a $0.40 per hour increase for the plant's 25 inspector apprentices. Management wants to hold the line on salary increases because they believe that layoffs will have to occur. Union's proposal would cost Dana Lou 95 × $0.05 = $47.50 and 25 × $0.40 = $10.00 or $57.50 total per hour.

Competitor Data (Hamilton, Ohio, Survey)

	Blue Fox Corp.	Wintex, Inc.	Lafley Mfg.
Company contribution to medical and dental insurance	100%	50%	50%
Preventive health director	No	No	No
Payment of physical fitness fees for employees	Yes	No	Yes
Vacation benefits	1 week in first year; 3 weeks all employees after 1 year	2 weeks all employees until 10 years of service and then 3 weeks	2 weeks all employees for first 5 years and then 3 weeks
Wage rate inspectors	$5.80	$5.97	$5.93
Inspector apprentices	$4.45	$4.50	$4.20

The Negotiations

1. One member from each of the two groups facing each other will negotiate the four issues. The rest of the group must remain *totally* quiet during the negotiations. The negotiators should role-play for exactly 20 minutes. At the end of this time, they should record the agreement points reached.

Final Agreements

Medical and dental protection _____

_____

_____

Preventive health director/Staff and participation _____

_____

_____

Vacation benefits _____

_____

_____

Wage increases _____

_____

_____

2. Each individual is to analyze the negotiations:

How successful were the negotiators? _____

Would you have negotiated differently? How? _____

_____

Were the negotiations prepared? _____

A Learning Note

This exercise will illustrate how difficult discussing issues can be when people have a fixed attitude or position.

6

EMPLOYEE SAFETY, HEALTH, WORK LIFE, AND EVALUATION

. . . . . .

T he safety and health of employees, customers, and the environment are important matters for HR personnel. Chapter 19 covers safety and the government's role regarding safe and healthy work conditions. The issue of AIDS in the workplace is carefully examined. A person's work schedule can impact his or her work behavior and performance, as well as affect activities outside of work. The importance of properly scheduling work and the quality of work life is emphasized in Chapter 20. Work scheduling, flexitime, part-time, job-sharing, and compressed workweek schedules are analyzed in terms of employee reactions. Where, why, and how these types of schedules are used is covered. Quality circles and other worker participation programs are discussed in terms of benefits, costs, and limitations. In Chapter 21, Evaluating the HRM Function, the methods required to examine the impact of the HRM function are examined. Measurement of the costs and benefits of the HRM function is an important practice occurring in an increasing number of organizations. This final chapter takes another look at HR managers as they perform their important jobs in organizations of all sizes.

19

EMPLOYEE SAFETY AND HEALTH

· · · · · · ·

LEARNING OBJECTIVES

───○───

After studying this chapter, you should be able to:

· · ·

Define *safety hazards, health hazards, health,* and *stress*

· · ·

Describe why an increasing number of firms are attempting to control and prevent smoking in the workplace

· · ·

Explain how environmental and person stressors interact to cause stress

· · ·

Discuss why preventive health and AIDS programs are likely to grow in popularity

· · ·

Illustrate when OSHA requires an organization to report and record an illness, injury, or death

CAREER CHALLENGE

*T*he ambulance had just pulled away from Lysander Manufacturing. It was headed for a Denver hospital, carrying Dale Silas. Dale had been badly hurt; there was already talk that he might be disabled for the rest of his life.

Clint Woodley, the plant manager, wondered what he could have done to prevent Dale's injury. It was not the first injury this year at Lysander. Clint decided to visit his friend, Bob Undine, who operated a similar plant in a nearby town. He called Bob and arranged to have lunch the next day.

At lunch, Clint explained how upset he was about Dale's injury. Dale had been with Lysander for 15 years — longer than Clint had been. He had a wife and five children to support. The word from the hospital was not very good.

Bob Well, Clint, sometimes accidents happen. You know our business is dangerous. And sometimes the men are not following the safety rules. What is your safety record over the last few years?

Clint I don't really know. We've only got records since OSHA (Occupational Safety ahd Health Act) came in. But the HRM guy, Otto Richmond, handles that paperwork. When our people are hired, we tell them to be careful. The supervisors are supposed to handle that.

Bob You mean you don't have a safety unit?

Clint No.

Bob Then you probably don't do accident research, safety design and prevention, safety inspections, or safety training either, do you?

Clint No. We do fill out the OSHA paperwork. Luckily, we've never been inspected by OSHA.

Bob Well, then, maybe you ought to be upset about Dale. You aren't doing all you could to protect your employees. And if you don't do it, OSHA will make you.

Clint I don't want that. Can I come back with you and see how you operate safety programs at your plant?

Bob Sure.

*T*his chapter covers the important HRM topics of workplace safety and health. Historically the manufacturer's workplace, the factory, was filled with safety and health risks hazards like dangerous machinery and poor lighting. The modern service industry's workplace is also just as hazardous with high levels of stress and repetitive motion disorders such as carpal tunnel syndrome.

Safety hazards are those aspects of the work environment that have the potential of immediate and sometimes violent harm to an employee. Examples of injuries are loss of hearing, eyesight, or body parts; cuts, sprains, bruises, broken bones; burns and electric shock.

Health hazards are those aspects of the work environment that slowly and cumulatively (and often irreversibly) lead to deterioration of an employee's health. Examples are cancer, poisoning, and respiratory diseases, as well as depression, loss of temper, and other psychological disorders. Typical causes include physical and biological hazards, toxic and cancer-causing dusts and chemicals, and stressful working conditions.

Safety violations have been the cause of some of the most tragic accidents that have taken lives. In 1979, the Three Mile Island nuclear power plant had an accident leading to the near meltdown of the plant's reactor core. In the Kemery Commission Report (named after the president's commission chairman), it was stated that human error in terms of inadequate operator training was the main cause of the accident. This error endangered the entire population of the Pennsylvania community in which the plant was located.[1]

In December 1984, the worst industrial accident in history occurred. Poisonous methyl isocyanate gas leaked from a storage tank at a Union Carbide plant in Bhopal, India, killing 3,000 people and injuring another 300,000.[2] The accident was the result of operating errors, design flaws, maintenance failures, and training deficiencies.

Union Carbide was sued for billions of dollars; compensation settlements are still occurring and are likely to be over $1 billion. In many of the lawsuits, Union Carbide's own 1982 safety report on the plant has been used since it stated "a higher potential for a serious accident or more serious consequences if an accident should occur." Another comment stated:

> That report "strongly" recommended among other things, the installation of a larger system that would supplement or replace one of the plant's main safety devices, a water spray designed to contain a chemical leak. That change was never made, plant employees said, and [when the leak happened] that spray was not high enough to reach the escaping gas.[3]

In January 1986, America's space program was stopped cold by the loss of the shuttle Challenger and its seven-person astronaut flight crew. After 25 aborted countdowns for the flight, the routine monitoring with inboard computers of 2,000 vital functions missed the critical rocket joints and O-ring tolerances. Despite technological sophistication, cost constraints, tight schedules, and human errors contributed to this tragic loss of lives.

These three highly publicized accidents and their tragic losses indicate that safety and health issues need to be given a high priority in decision-making circles. Accidents are costly not only in terms of human lives, but also in terms of disabling injuries, the loss of public image, and insurance premiums.

According to the AFL–CIO, work in the United States continues to be dangerous. Job hazards span all levels of the economy. "Trench cave-ins, toxic chemicals, infectious diseases, video display terminals, and job design problems put

EXHIBIT 19-1   Reported Occupational Injury and Illness Incidence Rates* per 100 Full-Time Workers, Private Sector, 1972–1988

Year	Total Recordable Cases	Lost Workday Cases	Nonfatal Cases without Lost Workdays	Lost Workdays
1972	10.9	3.3	7.6	47.9
1973	11.0	3.4	7.5	53.3
1974	10.4	3.5	6.9	54.6
1975	9.1	3.3	5.8	56.1
1976	9.2	3.5	5.7	60.5
1977	9.3	3.8	5.5	61.6
1978†	9.4	4.1	5.3	63.5
1979†	9.5	4.3	5.2	67.7
1980	8.7	4.0	4.7	65.2
1981	8.3	3.8	4.5	61.7
1982	7.7	3.5	4.2	58.7
1983†	7.6	3.4	4.2	58.5
1984†	8.0	3.7	4.3	63.4
1985	7.9	3.6	4.3	64.9
1986	7.9	3.6	4.3	65.8
1987	8.3	3.8	4.4	69.9
1988	8.6	4.0	4.6	76.1

Note: Data for 1972 exclude estimates for agricultural production, railroads, and most of mining. Data for 1975–88 exclude farms with fewer than 11 employees.
* The incidence rates represent the number of injuries and illnesses or lost workdays per 100 full time-workers.
† In 1978, 1979, 1983, and 1984, small nonfarm employers in low-risk industries were not surveyed. To maintain comparability with the other data, a statistical method was developed to provide estimates for those employers.

millions of workers at risk of injuries and illnesses."[4] On average, *one employee in eight* is killed or injured at work *each year*.[5] But some occupations (such as construction) have many more injuries per year than others (such as file clerks), so the odds for some workers are worse than one in eight each year.

Statistics on safety and health hazards are debated. Government statistics for 1988 reported 6.4 million occupational injuries and illnesses.[6] The incidence of injuries in 1988 was significantly higher than for the previous few years, but it was unclear how much of the increase was due to an increase in health and safety hazards and how much was due to improved employer record-keeping.

Exhibit 19–1 reports the occupational injury and illness incident rates per 100 full-time workers in the private sector between 1972 and 1988. All sources do not report the same death and accident figures for the same period. Note the use of the word *report*. A number of studies indicate that perhaps as few as half of all occupational accidents are reported.

There were 3,400 fatalities in 1987 and 3,270 in 1988 as shown in Exhibit 19–2.[7] Causes of these fatalities are detailed in Exhibit 19–3. There were 6.2 million job-related illnesses reported in the private sector for 1988 and approximately 241,000 occupational illnesses in the same time period.

Accidents and illnesses are not evenly distributed among occupations in the United States. Employees facing serious health and safety dangers include fire fighters, miners, construction and transportation workers, roofing and sheet metal

EXHIBIT 19-2   Employment and Reported Occupational Injury and Illness Fatalities for Employers with 11 Employees or More by Industry Division, 1987 and 1988

| | Annual Average Employment | | | | Fatalities | | | |
| | 1987 | | 1988 | | 1987 | | 1988 | |
Industry Division	Number (1000s)	Percent	Number (1000s)	Percent	Number	Percent	Number	Percent
Private sector*	73,924	100%	76,320	100%	3,400	100%	3,270	100%
Agriculture, forestry, and fishing	911	1	938	1	80	2	110	3
Mining	627	1	627	1	150	4	220	7
Construction	3,798	5	3,847	5	820	24	850	26
Manufacturing	18,427	25	18,757	25	790	23	660	20
Transportation and public utilities	4,971	7	5,116	7	580	17	650	20
Wholesale and retail trade	20,062	27	20,782	27	460	14	540	16
Finance, insurance, and real estate	5,513	7	5,568	7	140	4	—	—
Services	19,616	27	20,684	27	380	11	—	—

Note: Because of rounding, components may not add to totals. Dashes indicate no data reported or data that do not meet publication guidelines.
* Employment data are derived primarily from the BLS–State Current Employment Statistics program. Employment and fatality estimates have been adjusted to exclude establishments with fewer than 11 employees as obtained from the Annual Survey of Occupational Injuries and Illnesses.
Source: U.S. Department of Labor (August 1990), *Occupational Injuries and Illnesses in the U.S. by Industry, 1988* (Washington, D.C.: Bureau of Labor Statistics), p. 49.

workers, recreational vehicle manufacturers, lumber and woodworkers, and blue-collar and first-line supervisors in manufacturing and agriculture. A few white-collar jobholders face relative danger: dentists and hospital operating room personnel, beauticians, and X-ray technicians.

All accidents and diseases are tragic to the employees involved, of course. There is pain at the time of the accident, and there can be psychological problems later. In addition to pain, suffering, and death, there are also direct measurable costs to both employee and employer. About 54 million workdays were lost in 1988 due to sickness and/or injury.[8] Lost workday rates varied from 16.3 per 100 full-time workers in finance, insurance, and real estate to 150.3 in mining. Exhibit 19–4 charts occupational injury incident rates for lost workdays by industry division for 1987 and 1988. Occupational health and safety issues are responsible for the direct costs of workers' compensation and indirect costs of lost productivity for the enterprise. The average company's workers' compensation for disability payments is 1.5 percent of payroll, and the indirect costs are estimated to be at least five times greater. Indirect costs include cost of wages paid to the injured employee, damage to plant and equipment, costs of replacement employees, and time costs for supervisors and human resource staff investigating and reporting the accident or illness. Both because of the humanitarian desire of management to reduce suffering and because of the huge direct and indirect costs of accidents, deaths, and illnesses, the effective enterprise tried hard to create safe and healthy conditions at work.

An unsafe or unhealthy work environment can also affect an employee's ability and motivation to work. As noted in Chapter 2, security/preservation is one of the most fundamental needs people have. Poor safety and health conditions are likely to endanger fulfillment of the security needs of employees.

EXHIBIT 19-3

Distribution of Fatalities by Cause: Reported Occupational Injury and Illness Fatalities for Employers with 11 Employees or More, 1987–1988 Average (in percent)*

Cause†	Total Private Sector‡	Agriculture, Forestry, and Fishing	Mining—Oil and Gas Extraction Only	Construction	Manufacturing	Transportation and Public Utilities§	Wholesale and Retail Trade	Finance, Insurance, and Real Estate	Services
Total, all causes	100	100	100	100	100	100	100	100	100
Highway vehicles	28	31	23	18	19	42	26	64	51
Falls	12	5	3	21	9	2	19	0	11
Electrocutions	9	5	4	15	5	14	5	0	5
Industrial vehicles or equipment	9	21	18	11	10	6	10	1	4
Heart attacks	8	5	8	9	10	8	3	23	11
Stuck by objects other than vehicles or equipment	8	9	32	6	13	3	7	0	2
Assaults	5	6	0	=	1	1	21	8	8
Aircraft crashes	4	4	0	1	5	15	1	1	3
Caught in, under, or between objects other than vehicles or equipment	4	2	0	10	4	1	1	0	=
Explosions	3	0	3	3	4	1	3	0	1
Gas inhalation	3	8	4	2	5	3	2	2	=
Fires	2	0	1	2	3	1	1	0	1
Plant machinery operations	2	1	1	1	9	0	1	1	0
All other#	3	4	2	2	3	3	1	0	3

Note: Because of rounding, components may not add to totals.
* Results are the average of the two years because sampling errors for data by cause of fatality are too large to provide reliable annual estimates at the industry division level.
† Cause is defined as the object or event associated with the fatality.
‡ Exlcudes coal, metal, and nonmetal mining and railroads, for which data are not available.
§ Excludes railroads.
‖ Between 0.1 and 0.5 percent.
The "All other" category includes, for example, contact with carcinogenic or toxic substances, drowning, train accidents, and various occupational illnesses.
Source: U.S. Department of Labor (August 1990), Occupational Injuries and Illnesses in the U.S. by Industry, 1988 (Washington, D.C.: Bureau of Labor Statistics), p. 49.

EXHIBIT 19-4   Reported Occupational Injury Incident Rates for Lost Workdays by Industry Division, Private Sector, 1987 and 1988

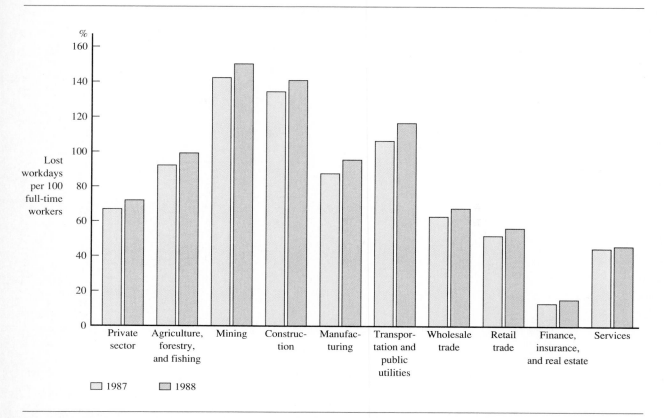

Source: U.S. Department of Labor (August 1990), *Occupational Injuries and Illnesses in the U.S. by Industry, 1988* (Washington, D.C.: Bureau of Labor Statistics), p. 4

Until recently, the typical response to concern about health and safety was to compensate the victims of job-related accidents with workers' compensation and similar insurance payments. This chapter will discuss various compensation approaches and organizational programs designed to *prevent* accidents, health hazards, and deaths at work.

A DIAGNOSTIC APPROACH TO SAFETY AND HEALTH

The environmental factors important to health and safety are highlighted in Exhibit 19–5. Probably the most crucial factor is the *nature of the task*, especially as it is affected by the technology and working conditions of the organizational environment. For instance, health and safety problems are a lot more serious for coal miners — whose working conditions require them to breathe coal dust in the air — than for typists. An X-ray technician has a much greater chance of getting cancer as a result of working conditions than does an elementary school teacher. Some examples of potential job hazards are presented in Exhibit 19–6.

EXHIBIT 19-5   Factors Affecting Safety and Health

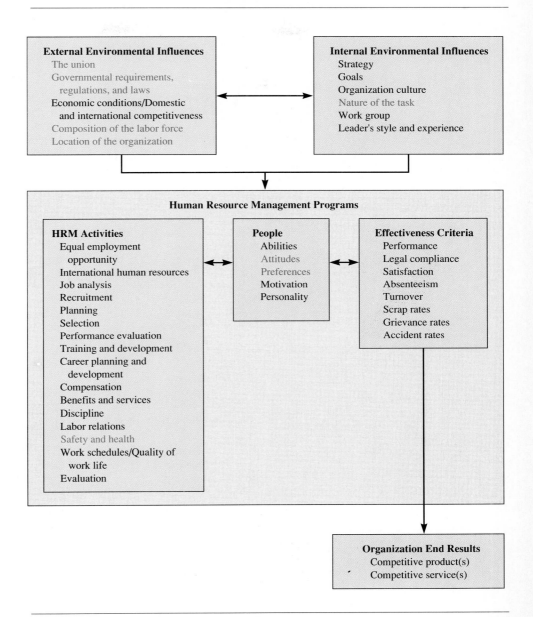

Charles Farley considered himself lucky to land a job at a Monsanto Co. plant in 1946.[9] Today, the ex-chemical worker is retired (at 55 years old) and is suffering from pain in his shoulder and legs. In 1982, he had a heart attack, and in February 1983 he underwent quadruple heart-bypass surgery. He attributes his premature health problems to long-term exposure to toxic chemicals. He is one of 172 former and current Monsanto workers and spouses suing the company. They are seeking more than $700 million in damages.

EXHIBIT 19-6   Examples of Job and Safety Hazards

Occupation	Potential Hazard	Possible Outcome
Textile workers	Cotton dust	Brown lung or byssinosis (a debilitating lung disease)
	Noise	Temporary or permanent hearing loss
	Chemical exposures	
	Aniline-based dyes	Bladder cancer and liver damage
	Formaldehyde	Dermatitis, allergic lung disease, possibly cancer
	Furfuraldehyde	Dermatitis, respiratory irritation, fatigue, headache, tremors, numbness of the tongue
	Moving machine parts without barriers	Loss of fingers or hands
Hospital workers	Infectious diseases	
	Hepatitis	Liver damage
	Herpes simplex virus	Painful skin lesions
	Chemical exposures	
	Anesthetic gases	Spontaneous abortions
	Metallic mercury	Poisoning of nervous system and kidneys
	Inorganic acids and alkalis	Irritation to respiratory tract and skin
	Physical hazards	
	Ionizing radiation	Burns, birth defects, cancer
	Microwave radiation	Sterility, harm to eyes, possible increased risk of cataracts
	UV light	Burning or sensitization of skin, skin cancer, cataracts
	Safety hazards	
	Lifting or carrying	Back pain or permanent back injury
	Puncture wounds from syringes	Infections
Welders	Infrared and visible light radiation	Burns, headache, fatigue, eye damage
	UV radiation	Burns, skin tumors, eye damage
	Chemical exposures	
	Carbon monoxide	Cardiovascular disease
	Acetylene	Asphyxiation, fire, explosion
	Metallic oxides	Contact dermatitis, eye irritation, respiratory irritation, metal fume fever (symptoms similar to the flu), possible kidney damage
	Phosphine	Lethal at even low doses: irritating to eyes, nose, skin; acts as anesthetic
Clerical workers	Improperly designed chairs and workstations; lack of movement	Backache, aggravation of hemorrhoids, varicose veins, and other blood-circulation conditions, eyestrain
	Noise	Hearing impairment, stress reactions
	Chemical exposures	
	Ozone from copy machines	Irritation of eyes, nose, throat; respiratory damage
	Benzene and toluene in rubber cement and "cleaners"	Benzene is associated with several blood diseases (including leukemia), and toluene may cause intoxication
	Methanol and ammonia in duplicating machine solvents	Irritation to eyes, nose, and throat

Monsanto has faced legal action before. The company was one of eight that settled for $180 million with Vietnam veterans charging contamination from Agent Orange, a defoliant used in the Vietnam War. In 1982, the company paid millions to settle suits by railroad workers after a rail car spilled chemicals made by the company.

A second vital factor is *employee attitudes* toward health and safety; they can vary from concern for safety and cooperation regarding safety programs, to apathy. If employees are apathetic, the best employer or safety program and the most stringent safety inspection by the government or the safety specialists in the HR department will not be successful in improving safety and health conditions.

A third factor affecting health and safety on the job is *government*. Federal and state governments have attempted to legislate conditions to improve safety and health for some years.[10] Some government programs currently in operation will be discussed later. However, perhaps the most publicity about government involvement has been the accident that closed down the Three Mile Island nuclear plant in 1979. This accident led to the discovery of dangers at other nuclear plants.[11] As a result, the Nuclear Regulatory Commission identified dozens of improvements — ranging from new equipment to better operator training — for the country's 72 operating nuclear reactors.

A fourth factor is the *trade unions*. Many unions have been very concerned about the safety and health of their employees and have pressured employers in collective bargaining for better programs. Some unions have taken extraordinary steps to protect their members' health and safety. For example, the Teamsters' Union hired a nationally known occupational health expert to investigate unexplained illnesses at the Robert Shaw Controls Company plant in Ohio. The United Rubber Workers' contract calls for a study of effects of benzene on employees. The Oil, Chemical and Atomic Workers Union has been subsidizing medical interns and residents to study occupational health conditions in plants where their members work. Unions also have used their political power to get legislation passed to improve the safety and health of members.

A fifth factor is *management's goals*. Some socially responsible managers and owners had active safety programs long before the laws required them. They made safety and health an important strategic goal and implemented it with significant safety consideration designed into the enterprise's layout. The safety program included safety statistics, contests, and training sessions. Other managers, not so safety conscious, did little other than what was required by law. Thus, managerial attitudes play a large part in the significance of the health and safety program of the enterprise.

The final factor affecting health and safety programs is *economic conditions*. We would accept the worst possible assumptions about human nature if we believed that any employer *knowingly* would choose to provide dangerous working conditions or would refuse to provide reasonable safeguards for employees. But there is a lack of knowledge about the consequences of some dangerous working conditions, and even when there is such knowledge, economic conditions can prevent employers from doing all they might wish. The risks of being a uranium miner are well known: 10 to 11 percent will die of cancer within 10 years. As long as there are no alternative methods and as long as there is a need for uranium, some employees will be risking shorter lives in these jobs. Engineers and scientists are constantly at work to determine the danger and to prevent or mitigate the consequences. But the costs of some of the prevention programs are such that the enterprise may find them prohibitive and may consider the programs economically infeasible.

WHO IS INVOLVED WITH SAFETY AND HEALTH?

As with other HRM functions, the success of a safety and health program requires the support and cooperation of operating and HR managers. But it is more complicated than that. In some organizations, safety is a separate function, though both operating managers and staff still have their parts to play to protect employees.

Top management must support safety and health with an adequate budget. Managers must give it their personal support by talking about safety and health with everyone in the firm. Acting on safety reports is another way top managers can be involved in these efforts. Without this support, the safety and health effort is hampered. Some organizations have responded to the environmental problems that can increase accidents, deaths, and disabilities by placing the responsibility for employee health and safety with the chief executive officer of the organization: the hospital administrator, the agency administrator, the company president. This is the approach taken by most smaller organizations that are concerned about health and safety.

Operating managers are also responsible, since accidents and injuries will take place and health hazards will exist in the work unit. They must be aware of health and safety considerations and cooperate with the specialists who can help them reduce accidents and occupational illnesses. In larger and some medium-sized organizations, there is a safety unit in the HR department. This chapter will illustrate what a safety and health specialist does.

The success of the safety program rests primarily on how well employees and supervisors cooperate with safety rules and regulations. Often, this relationship is formalized in the creation of a safety committee consisting of the safety specialist, representative employees, and managers.

Usually, there are two levels of safety committees. At the policy level is the committee made up of major division heads; this committee sets safety policy and rules, investigates major hazards, and has budget responsibility. At the departmental level, both supervisors and managers are members. Safety committees are concerned with the organization's entire safety program: inspection, design, record-keeping, training, and motivation programs. The more people who can be involved through the committees, the more likely is the program to be successful. Finally, the government inspector plays a role in keeping the organization on its toes regarding the safety of the employees.

CAUSES OF WORK ACCIDENTS AND WORK-RELATED ILLNESSES

Work accidents and work-related illnesses have many causes. The major causes of occupational accidents are:

- The task to be done.
- The working conditions.
- The nature of the employees.

Some examples of causes in the task and working conditions area include poorly designed or inadequately repaired machines, lack of protective equipment, and the presence of dangerous chemicals or gases. Other working conditions that contribute to accidents include excessive work hours leading to employee fatigue, noise, lack of proper lighting, boredom, horseplay and fighting at work. The National Institute for Occupational Safety and Health (NIOSH) is charged with finding out more about the causes of accidents and occupational health hazards.

There are data to indicate that some employees have more accidents than the average. Such a person is said to be an *accident repeater*. These studies indicate that employees who (1) are under 30 years of age, (2) lack psychomotor and perceptual skills, (3) are impulsive, and (4) are easily bored are more likely to have accidents than others.[12] Although some believe accident proneness can be measured by a set of attitude or motivational instruments, most experts who have examined the data carefully do not believe that attitudinal-motivational "causes" of accidents are a significant influence on accident rates. We need to know much more about accident proneness before such serious actions as attempting to screen out the accident-prone person are implemented.

ORGANIZATION RESPONSES TO SAFETY AND HEALTH

The safety department or unit and the safety committee can take three approaches to improving the safety of working conditions:

. Prevention and design.
. Inspection and research.
. Training and motivation.

Bob Undine's plant, mentioned at the beginning of this chapter, has taken all three approaches.

Safety Design and Preventive Approaches

Numerous preventive measures have been adopted by organizations in attempts to improve their safety records. One is to design more safety into the workplace through safety engineering. Engineers have helped through the study of human-factors engineering, which seeks to make jobs more comfortable, less confusing, and less fatiguing. This can keep employees more alert and less open to accidents.

Safety engineers design safety into the workplace with the analytical design approach. This total design approach analyzes all factors involved in the job. Included are such factors as speed of the assembly line, stresses in the work, and job design. On the basis of this analysis, steps are taken to improve safety precautions. Protective guards are designed for machinery and equipment. Color coding warns of dangerous areas. Standard safety colors, which should be taught in safety classes, include gray for machinery and red where the area presents danger of fire. Other dangers may be highlighted by bright orange paint.

Protective clothing and devices are also supplied for employees working in hazardous job situations. These can include:

Head protection, principally with helmets.
Eye and face protection, with goggles, face shields, and spectacles.
Hearing protection, with muffs and inserts.
Respiratory protection, with air-purifying devices such as filter respirators and gas masks, and air-supplying devices.
Hand protection, with gloves.
Foot and leg protection, with safety shoes, boots, guards, and leggings.
Body protection, with garments such as suits, aprons, jackets, and coveralls.
Belts and lifelines to prevent those working in high places from falling.

The few studies on the effectiveness of these preventive design measures indicate that they do reduce accidents.[13]

Well-designed rest periods increase safety and productivity, as do clearly understood rules and regulations. These rules should be developed from analysis of equipment and conditions, such as flammability. No-smoking areas and hard hat areas where safety helmets are required for all employees and visitors are examples.

The U.S. Surgeon General would like to see a "smoke-free" society by the year 2000.[14] The sales charts of the tobacco industry show that smoking in the United States is declining rapidly.[15] The Smoking Policy Institute (SPI) is an organization that monitors smoking demographics.[16] It reported in March 1990 that 60 percent of all U.S. businesses now have antismoking policies and restrictions that are becoming more stringent all the time. About 14 percent of those companies that do not as yet have a no smoking policy plan to institute one in the near future. There is also increased pressure in the United Kingdom to restrict or exclude smoking from the workplace.[17] Since the EPA released its report on secondary smoke as a carcinogen like asbestos, an education campaign has helped reduce resistance to a smoke-free workplace in the United States.

For example, at the beginning of 1986, Blue Cross/Blue Shield of Maryland decided to create a smoke-free workplace. As of the end of 1986, the firm considered the program a success. The firm reviewed the medical histories of its 900 employees. The review indicated that 36 percent of the employees were smokers. It was estimated that costs due to illnesses, accidents, and absenteeism of smokers averaged about $185,000 a year. A three-phase program was installed:

Phase I: All smoking was banned in meeting, conferences, and training sessions.

Phase II: Nine months after Phase I, all work areas were declared smokefree. Smoking areas were established, but all cigarette vending machines were removed.

Phase III: Three months after Phase II, smoking was prohibited on all company premises. Employees who failed to comply faced the full range of disciplinary action: from warning to suspension and finally termination.

Now that the Blue Cross/Blue Shield no smoking program is in place, employees do not smoke on company premises. Admittedly, one reason for such perfect compliance is that employees were warned about losing their jobs.

What is your opinion on a no smoking ban?

Some smokers and nonsmokers contend that a smoke-free workplace is just a smoke screen to cover the fact that many U.S. places of business have high levels of indoor pollution.[18] This has come to be called the *sick building syndrome* (SBS). Let's look at an example of the sick building syndrome. New carpeting was installed in an office in Washington, D.C., in 1987, and employees immediately complained of dizziness and burning in the lungs.[19] Within two months, 700 employees were -affected. They picketed the building and had the carpeting removed.

The Clean Air Act passed by Congress 20 years ago is now moving indoors as the public becomes increasingly aware of the various indoor pollution hazards like smoking and the carpeting above. Sometimes, contamination is caused by a single airborne contaminant. Sometimes, chemicals and poor ventilation combine to cause the hazard. It is estimated that SBS costs U.S. industry 10s of billions of dollars each year in absenteeism and medical bills. SBS can be attacked by using low-toxicity building materials and new environmentally safe paints and carpeting now available at a premium of 10 percent to 30 percent above the cost of the old hazardous products. It is a *new* health and safety challenge being raised with more vigor each year by affected employees.

Inspection, Reporting, and Accident Research

A second activity of safety departments or specialists is to inspect the workplace with the goal of reducing accidents and illnesses. The safety specialist is looking for a number of things, including answers to these questions:

Are safety rules being observed? How many near misses were there?

Are safety guards, protective equipment, and so on being used?

Are there potential hazards in the workplace that safety redesign could improve?

Are there potential occupational health hazards?

A related activity is to investigate accidents or "close calls" to determine the facts for insurance purposes. More important, such investigations also can determine preventive measures that should be taken in the future. Following an accident requiring more than first aid treatment, the safety specialist, HR specialist, or manager must *investigate* and report the facts to the government and insurance companies. These data are also used to analyze the causes of accidents, with a view to preventing possible recurrences.

Reporting of accidents and occupational illnesses is an important part of the safety specialist's job. Usually, the report is filled out by the injured employee's supervisor and checked by the safety specialist. The supervisor compiles the report because he or she usually is present when the accident occurs. And doing so requires the supervisor to think about safety in the unit and what can be done to prevent similar accidents.

At regular intervals during the work year, safety and personnel specialists carry out **accident research;** that is, systematic evaluation of the evidence concerning accidents and health hazards. Data for this research should be gathered from both external and internal sources. Safety and health journals point out recent findings that should stimulate the safety specialist to look for hazardous conditions at the workplace. Reports from the National Institute of Occupational Safety and Health, a research organization created by OSHA legislation, also provide important data inputs for research. Data developed at the workplace included accident reports, inspection reports by the government and the organization's safety specialists, and recommendations of the safety committees.

Accident research often involves computation of organizational accident rates. These are compared to industry and national figures to determine the organization's relative safety performance. Several statistics are computed. Accident frequency rate is computed per million labor hours of work, as follows:

$$\text{Frequency rate} = \frac{\text{Number of accidents} \times 1{,}000{,}000}{\text{Number of work hours in the period}}$$

The accidents used in this computation are those causing the worker to lose work time.

The second statistic is the accident severity rate. This is computed as follows:

$$\text{Accident severity rate} = \frac{\text{Number of workdays lost} \times 1{,}000{,}000}{\text{Number of work hours in the period}}$$

OSHA suggests reporting accidents as number of injuries per 100 full-time employees per year, as a simpler approach. The formula is:

$$\frac{\text{Number of illnesses and injuries}}{\text{Total hours worked by all employees for the year}} \times 200,000$$

The base equals the number of workers employed (100 full-time equivalent) working full-time (for example, 40 hours per week and for 50 weeks if vacation is 2 weeks). OSHA visits workplaces in high-hazard industries and conducts inspections in firms with above-average lost-workday injury rates. The 1988 rate for manufacturing was 3.8 per 100 workers.

The organization's statistics should be compared with the industry's statistics and government statistics (from the Department of Labor and OSHA). Most studies find that although effective accident research should be very complex, in reality it is unsophisticated and unscientific.

Safety Training and Motivation Programs

The third approach organizations take to safety is training and motivation programs. Safety training usually is part of the orientation program. It also takes place during the employee's career. This training is usually voluntary, but some is required by government agencies. Studies of the effectiveness of such training are mixed. Some studies indicate that some methods, such as job instruction training (JIT) and accident simulations, are more effective than others. Others contend that the employees' perception that management really believes in safety training accounts for its success.[20] A few studies find that the programs make employees more *aware* of safety, but not necessarily safer in their behavior. Nevertheless, effectively developed safety training programs can help provide a safer environment for all employees.

Safety specialists have also tried to improve safety conditions and accident statistics by various motivation devices, such as contests and communication programs. These are intended to reinforce safety training. One device is to place posters around the workplace with slogans such as "A Safe Worker Is a Happy Worker." Posters are available from the National Safety Council or can be prepared for the enterprise. Communication programs also include items in company publications and safety booklets and billboards. The billboard in front of Bob Undine's plant, for example, reads:

Welcome to American Manufacturing Company

A Good Place to Work
A Safe Place to Work

We have had no accidents for
<u>182</u> days

Sometimes, safety communications are tied into a safety contest. If lower accidents result over a period, an award is given. The little research that has been done on safety communications and contests is mixed. Some believe they are useful. Others contend they have no effect or produce undesirable side effects, such as failure to report accidents or a large number of accidents once the contest is over or has been lost.[21]

In general, too little is known scientifically at this point to recommend use or reduction of safety motivation programs. One example of the needed research is a study that examined the conditions under which safety motivation and education programs were effective in a shelving manufacturing company. It found that:

. There are safety-conscious people and others who are unaware of safety. The safety-conscious people were influenced by safety posters.
. Safety booklets were influential to the safety-conscious employees when their work group was also safety-conscious.
. Five-minute safety talks by supervisors were effective when the work group was safety-conscious and when the supervisor was safety-conscious.
. Safety training was effective for the safety-conscious employee when the supervisor and top management were safety-conscious.
. Safety inspections were effective when the work group and supervisor were safety-conscious.

GOVERNMENT RESPONSES TO SAFETY AND HEALTH PROBLEMS

Although many organizations (such as Bob Undine's) have done a good job of safeguarding the safety and health of their employees, with little or no supervision from government sources, others (such as Clint Woodley's) have not. This has led governments to become involved in holding the organization responsible for prevention of accidents, disabilities, illnesses, and deaths related to the tasks workers perform and the conditions under which they work.

Prior to passage of the **Occupational Safety and Health Act** in 1970, the feeling was that private organizations had not done enough to assure safe and healthy working conditions. In 1936 alone, there were 35,000 workplace deaths reported. In 1970, the year in which OSHA became law, an estimated 14,200 workers died, 2.2 million suffered disabilities, and another 300,000 to 500,000 suffered from occupationally induced illnesses.[22] The federal law in effect, the Walsh-Healy Act, was thought to be too weak or inadequately enforced, and state programs were incomplete, diverse, and lacked authority. The basic requirements of OSHA are presented in Exhibit 19–7.

Lobbying by unions and employees led to the passage of several federal laws related to specific occupations, such as the Coal Mine Health and Safety Act of 1969 and the related Black Lung Benefits Act of 1972. The movement for federal supervision of health and safety programs culminated in passage of the Occupational Safety and Health Act administered by the **Occupational Safety and Health Administration (OSHA)** of the Department of Labor. To conduct research and develop safety and health standards, the act created the National Institute of Occupational Safety and Health (NIOSH).

OSHA, the product of three years of bitter legislative lobbying, was designed to remedy safety problems on the job. The compromise law that was enacted initially received wide support. Its purpose was to provide employment "free from recognized hazards" to employees. OSHA provisions originally applied to 4.1 million businesses and 57 million employees in almost every organization engaged in interstate commerce.[23]

OSHA has been enforced by federal inspectors or in partnership with state safety and health agencies. It encourages the states to assume responsibility for developing and administering occupational safety and health laws and carrying out their own statistical programs. Before being granted full authority for its programs, a state must go through three steps. First, the state plan must have the preliminary approval of OSHA. Second, the state promises to take "developmental steps" to do

---

EXHIBIT 19-7 Job Safety and Health Protection Requirements per OSHA

The Occupational Safety and Health Act of 1970 provides job safety and health protection for workers through the promotion of safe and healthful working conditions throughout the nation. Requirements of the act include the following:

Employers:

Each employer must furnish to each of his employees employment and a place of employment free from recognized hazards that are causing or are likely to cause death or serious harm to his employees; and shall comply with occupational safety and health standards issued under the Act.

Employees:

Each employee shall comply with all occupational safety and health standards, rules, regulations, and orders issued under the Act that apply to his own actions and conduct on the job. The Occupational Safety and Health Administration (OSHA) of the Department of Labor has the primary responsibility for administering the Act. OSHA issues occupational safety and health standards, and its Compliance Safety and Health Officers conduct jobsite inspections to ensure compliance with the Act.

Inspection:

The Act requires that a representative of the employer and a representative authorized by the employees be given an opportunity to accompany the OSHA inspector for the purpose of aiding the inspection. Where there is no authorized employee representative, the OSHA Compliance Officer must consult with a reasonable number of employees concerning safety and health conditions in the workplace.

Complaint:

Employees or their representatives have the right to file a complaint with the nearest OSHA office requesting an inspection if they believe unsafe or unhealthful conditions exist in their workplace. OSHA will withhold, on request, names of employees complaining. The Act provides that employees may not be discharged or discriminated against in any way for filing safety and health complaints or otherwise exercising their rights under the Act. An employee who believes he has been discriminated against may file a complaint with the nearest OSHA office within 30 days of the alleged discrimination.

Citation:

If upon inspection OSHA believes an employer has violated the Act, a citation alleging such violations will be issued to the employer. Each citation will specify a time period within which the alleged violation must be corrected. The OSHA citation must be prominently displayed at or near the place of alleged violation for three days, or until it is corrected, whichever is later, to warn employees of dangers that may exist there.

Proposed Penalty:

The Act provides for mandatory penalties against employers of up to $1,000 for each serious violation and for optional penalties of up to $1,000 for each nonserious violation. Penalties of up to $1,000 per day may be proposed for failure to correct violations within the proposed time period. Also, any employer who willfully or repeatedly violates the Act may be assessed penalties of up to $10,000 for each such violation. Criminal penalties are also provided in the Act. Any willful violation resulting in death of an employee, upon conviction, is punishable by a fine of no more than $10,000, or by imprisonment for not more than six months, or by both. Conviction of an employer after a first conviction doubles these maximum penalties.

Voluntary Activity:

While providing penalties for violations, the Act also encourages efforts by labor and management, before an OSHA inspection, to reduce injuries and illnesses arising out of employment. The Department of Labor encourages employers and employees to reduce workplace hazards voluntarily and to develop and improve safety and health programs in all workplaces and industries. Such cooperative action would initially focus on the identification and elimination of hazards that could cause death, injury, or illness to employees and supervisors. There are many public and private organizations that can provide information and assistance in this effort, if requested.

Source: OSHA Bulletin.

certain things at certain times, such as adjusting legislation, hiring inspectors, and providing for an industrial hygiene laboratory. OSHA monitors the state plan for three years, and if the state fulfills these obligations, the third step is a trial period at full-enforcement levels for at least a year. At the end of this intensive evaluation period, a final decision is made by OSHA on the qualifications of the state program.

If OSHA and the employer fail to provide safe working conditions, employees as individuals or their unions can seek injunctions against the employer to force it to do so or submit to an inspection of the workplace. The employer cannot discriminate against an employee who takes these actions. OSHA has many requirements, but the three that most directly affect most employers are:

Meeting safety standards set by OSHA

Submitting to OSHA inspections.

Keeping records and reporting accidents and illnesses.

OSHA Safety Standards

OSHA has established safety standards, defined as those "practices, means, operations, or processes, reasonably necessary to provide safe . . . employment." The standards can affect any aspect of the workplace; new standards were established or proposed, for example, for such factors as lead, mercury, silica, benzene, talc dust, cotton dust, and general health hazards. The standards may be industrywide or apply only to a specific enterprise.

The assistant secretary of labor revises, modifies, or revokes existing standards or creates new ones on his or her own initiative or on the basis of petitions from interested parties (employees or unions). The National Institute of Occupational Safety and Health in the Department of Health and Human Services (HHS) is responsible for doing research from which standards are developed and for training those involved to implement them. Federal or national standards (such as those of the National Fire Protection Association) have also become OSHA standards. And temporary emergency standards can be created for imminent danger. Employers may be granted temporary variances by showing inability to comply with a standard within the time allowed, if they have a plan to protect employees against the hazard.

The employer is responsible for knowing what these standards are and abiding by them. This is not easy. The *initial* standards were published in *The Federal Register* in 350 pages of small print, and interpretations of the standards are issued yearly *by volume*. One recent annual volume was 780 pages long! OSHA officers work with compliance operations manuals two inches think. Even the *checklist* that summarizes the general industry standards is 11 pages long and lists 80 items. The responsible manager is subject to thousands of pages of such standards. If they are not met, an organization can be shut down, and the responsible manager can be fined or jailed for not meeting OSHA's standards.

OSHA Inspections

To make sure the law is obeyed, OSHA inspectors visit places of employment, on their own schedules or on invitation of an employer, union, or employee. An employee who requests an inspection need not be identified to the employer. If the employer is found guilty of a violation, the penalties includes (1) for willful or repeated violations, $10,000 per violation; (2) for citation for serious violation,

$1,000 each; (3) for citation for less serious violation, up to $1,000 discretionary; (4) for failure to correct cited violation, $1,000 per day; (5) for willful violation causing death, up to $10,000 or up to six months in jail; (6) for falsification of statements or records, up to $10,000 and/or six months in jail.

A Supreme Court decision ruled that employers can bar OSHA job safety inspectors from their workplaces if the inspectors don't have a search warrant.[24] But these warrants have been made easier to obtain. They can be issued by a court in advance without notifying the employer, so the surprise element of the inspection can be maintained.

OSHA inspectors examine the premises for compliance and the records for accuracy. They categorize a violation as *imminent danger* (in which cause they can close the business), *serious* (which calls for a major fine), *nonserious* (fine up to $1,000), or *de minimum* (small — notification is given, but no fine). The employer has the right to appeal fines or citations within OSHA (up to the level of the OSHA Review Commission) or in the courts.

OSHA Record-Keeping and Reporting

The third major OSHA requirement is that the employer keep standardized records of illnesses and injuries and calculate accident ratios. These are shown to OSHA compliance officers who ask to see them. The form used is illustrated in Exhibit 19–8. Accidents and illnesses that must be reported are those that result in deaths, disabilities that cause the employee to miss work, and medical care injuries that require treatment by a physician.

An OSHA guide to when to report and record an illness, injury, or death is shown in Exhibit 19–9. Injuries or illnesses that require only first aid and involve no loss of work time need not be reported. Employers go to great lengths to categorize incidents as "minor injuries," trying to treat them through first aid and keeping the employee on the job (even a make-work job), to avoid reporting them. To do so might lead to an OSHA inspection or raise their workers' compensation insurance rates. The employer must also report accident frequency and severity rates. The firm must also post OSHA Form 102 — a summary of the injuries and illnesses report — in a prominent place at work.

During the years when Ronald Reagan was president, OSHA's budget was cut by 25 percent and enforcement of its principals was nearly nonexistent.[25] But under President Bush's new Assistant Secretary of Labor, Gerard F. Scannell, the agency has begun to put health and safety issues back on the front burner. For example, Scanell noted that 36 percent of all employee deaths happen on the road, so he has proposed new rules for those who drive on the job. He has issued new safety guidelines for those whose work involves repetitive movements. And he has begun the practice of requiring violators to institute companywide hazard-reduction even if only one plant is cited. Between January 1989 and August 1990, a tougher OSHA:

- Wrote a proposal that would require workers to wear seat belts if they drive as part of their jobs.
- Set guidelines to prevent repetitive-motion disorders.
- Enacted a new rule to protect health-care workers from exposure to AIDS and hepatitis B.
- Used large fines to punish companies for breaking OSHA guidelines.

EXHIBIT 19-8   OSHA Injury and Illness Reporting Form

VIII Injury and Illness Summary (covering calendar year 1990)

Instructions:
- This section may be completed by copying data from OSHA Form No. 102 "Summary, Occupational Injuries and Illnesses," which you are required to complete and post in your establishment.
- Leave Section VIII blank if there were no recordable injuries or illnesses during 1977
- Code 30 – Add all occupational illnesses (Code 21 + 22 + 23 + 24 + 25 + 26 + 29) and enter on this line for each column (3) through (8).
- Code 31 – Add occupational injuries (Code 10) and the sum of all occupational illnesses (Code 30) and enter on this line for each column (3) thriugh (8).

Code (1)	Category (2)		Fatalities (deaths) (3)	Lost workday cases			Nonfatal cases without lost workdays*	
				Number of cases (4)	Number of cases involving permanent transfer to another job or termination of employment (5)	Number of lost cases (6)	Number of cases (7)	Number of cases involving transfer to another job or termination of employment (8)
10	Occupational injuries							
21	Occupational illnesses	Occupational skin diseases or disorders						
22		Dust diseases of the lungs (pneumoconioses)						
23		Respiratory conditions due to toxic agents						
24		Poisoning (systematic effects of toxic materials						
25		Disorders due to physical agents (other than toxic materials)						
26		Disorders due to repeated trauma						
29		All other occupational illnesses						
30		Sum of all occupational illnesses (Add Codes 21 through 29)						
31	Total of all occupational injuries and illnesses (Add Codes 10 + 30)							

* Nonfatal cases without lost workdays - Cases resulting in Medical treatment beyond first aid, diagnosis of occupational illness, loss of consciousness, restriction of work or motion, or transfer to another job (without lost workdays).

Comments _____

_____

IX   Report prepared by _____ Date _____

     Title _____ Area code and phone _____

EXHIBIT 19-9   Guide for Reporting and Recording Accidents, Illnesses, and Deaths

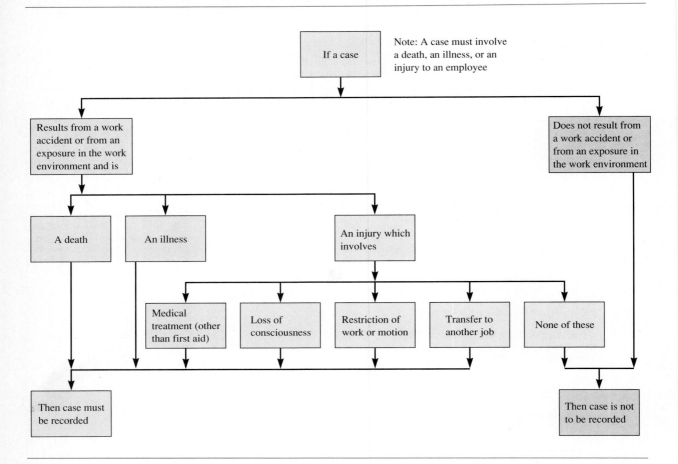

In October 1990, Scannell formalized an OSHA policy that now counts each separate infraction of the law as a *separate violation.*[26] If 200 machines guards are missing from the same type of machine, that is now counted as 200 violations instead of 1. Although the maximum fine that OSHA can impose is still $10,000, fines in the millions could be imposed with the new counting procedure. He is also seeking more criminal convictions of offending companies' managers. A stricter OSHA has begun to raise the hopes of employees and change managers' view on compliance.

Some Consequences of OSHA: Mangement's View

Many managers level serious criticisms at OSHA, some of which we discuss below.

Safety Standards   The general conclusion of most managers is that the agency's standards, more than 20 years after the law was passed, are still unreadable, arbitrary, overly specific, too trivial, too costly to implement, and unworkable. An example of the trivia in the OSHA standards appears in a publication on ranch safety.

It suggests to ranchers that, "since dangerous gases come from manure pits, you should be careful not to fall into manure pits." We don't suppose many ranchers willingly fall into them, with or without OSHA guidelines on dangerous gases.

A more critical condition than the poor quality of the standards is the fact that originally many of them were not in written form. OSHA has enough difficulty writing standards for existing technology, and it *really* has problems with new technologies where no standards exist. It is very difficult to adjust old standards to new technologies. In standards already set, the readability should be improved.

Managers feel all standards should not have equal emphasis. More importantly, the agency should categorize the subparts of the standards into categories based on the likelihood of accident or illness. These categories might be:

Most important. To be enforced at once and fully.

Of *average importance.* To be enforced later and in the spirit, not the letter, of the regulation.

Desirable. To be enforced when the most important standards and those of average importance are in full compliance.

If the standards were publicized to highlight these weights, employers could live with OSHA a bit more easily.

OSHA Inspections   OSHA does not inspect each industry with equal frequency. Initially, they set up five target industries to be inspected often because of their high rates of accidents: roof work; sheet metal work; meatpacking; miscellaneous transportation (mobile homes); and lumber and wood products. Later, foundries and casting and metal-stamping industries were added to the target industries list. Target health hazard industries are those involving asbestos, carbon monoxide, cotton dust, lead, and silica.

Appealing Violations   An employer who wishes to appeal a violation citation can do so within OSHA, through the Occupational Safety and Health Review Commission, or through the federal courts. Generally speaking, neither management nor labor has been happy with the inspections, one side claiming too few, the other too many. The Supreme Court decision regarding the need for search warrants is a result. Because of a shortage of inspectors and this Court ruling and because OSHA recognizes that it cannot enforce the law without the employer's help, the agency has begun to emphasize *voluntary compliance*. This consists of educational programs and "dry run" inspections in which the employer is advised of hazards but is given a chance to correct them before a citation is issued.

Consequences of Record-Keeping and Reporting   Few managers would quarrel with the need to keep adequate records on accidents and health and to calculate accident ratios. It seems reasonable for them to be recorded and reported in a standarized way, for ease in summarizing. But OSHA has been severely criticized by managers for the amount of paperwork required and the frequent changes in it.

Worker's Responsibility   Management feels that an important factor is not presently covered in OSHA's approach: the worker's responsibility for his or her own health and safety. All the responsibility is placed on *management*. For example, if employees wish to skip medical tests to determine if they are developing an occupational disease, OSHA has ruled they can. If an employee refuses to cooperate in safety matters and an OSHA inspector finds a violation, the *company* is held responsible. For example, there are many instances of employees refusing to wear the safety equipment recommended by OSHA. If the inspector sees this, OSHA *fines the company*. All the company can do is discipline (or possibly fire) the employee.

Some Consequences of OSHA: Union's View

As would be expected, the union's view of OSHA is more favorable than management's. The union believes that the passage of OSHA and its history clearly demonstrate the need for a federal role in safety and health.[27] The identification of hazard is a task of such proportion that it can only be accomplished with the resources and authority of the federal government.

The union believes that OSHA has clearly made great strides despite managerial resistance. Fatalities have decreased 10 percent since OSHA, meaning that the lives of thousands of workers have been saved. Similarly, thousands of workers have been spared serious injuries, with a 15 percent overall decline in total injuries during OSHA's lifetime.

OSHA Regulations and Worker Involvement

OSHA has provided workers access to the employer's records of illnesses and injuries. Consequently, many employers have encouraged the participation of workers in the enforcement process. Where effective, local union safety and health committees have been established to deal with problems at the plant level. Armed with training and education, and backed by their international unions, these local committees are having an impact on making the workplace safer and healthier. Health and safety are now the fastest growing among union programs. Each year, under OSHA's New Directions program, more than 20,000 workers are trained in recognition and control of hazards, more than half through union programs.

Justice Is Too Slow

Every time a major standard to improve safety and health is proposed, management resists. They use every political and legal avenue to block standards. Management consultants are hired to argue against the standard's validity. Who suffers? The workers, say the unions. Their argument is that the courts take too long to make rulings.

The estimated time of standards development for changes in safety and health conditions is two and one half to three years. Judicial stays may add one or more years' delay. For example, the Coke Oven standard, subject of a United Steelworkers union petition for regulation in 1971, was still pending in 1982 before the U.S. Supreme Court.

OSHA Enforcement Differences

The OSHA staff is still too small to do the job. A major purpose of the law was to achieve a nationwide, uniform, strong enforcement program. Despite the intent, enforcement is still somewhat unsystematic. There are differences in enforcement aggressiveness from area to area in the country. The union would like to see more aggressive enforcement across the country.

During the cutbacks of the Reagan years, there was a return to more severe, more frequent, and more costly accidents and illnesses. Even the Bush administration has exempted meatpacking from the OSHA inspections if they put in place ergonomic programs to deal with repetitive-motion injuries like carpal tunnel syndrome.[28]

Some Jobs Are Still Not Covered or Covered Inadequately   There are
still extremely dangerous jobs not covered by OSHA standards. Grain elevator and
mill workers are not covered by a specific OSHA standard. Grain handlers face the
threat of sudden death in an explosion each day or the eventual development of an
incapacitating illness arising from their chronic exposures to grain dust and
pesticides. More and more workers spend their days in front of video display
terminals (VDTs) on personal computers. Although research and tests conducted in
the United States and Canada have failed to find any radiation hazards from VDTs,
they do cause some problems such as poor posture, eyestrain, skeletal-muscular
aches, and general fatigue.

Another area not well-covered by standards involves cases of robots injuring
employees. Since more and more robots are being introduced into the workplace,
there is likely to be a higher rate of people-robot accidents unless precautions are
taken.[29] There have already been a few safety guidelines developed such as:

- Sharp edges and corners should be eliminated in the design of robots.
- Points of people-robot contact should be padded on the robot.
- Robots should be built with shear pins and breakaway sections to absorb the
  impact of collisions with people.[30]

Obviously, more safety rules, procedures, and laws will be introduced as the
number of robots increases significantly in the next decade.

In policy resolutions of the AFL–CIO adopted in 1989, it was noted that "greater
attention to problems like *ergonomics* (the impact of design and task structure on
employees) and video display terminals and hazards in the construction and service
sectors" are needed.[31] The report also cited the need for research into the effects of
chemicals and work processes on older and younger workers, with the results being
developed into effective safety standards. "Improved standards on methylene chlo-
ride, cadmium, infectious diseases, and confined space entry procedures and generic
standards for medical surveillance and environmental monitoring" should be top
priorities for OSHA in the 1990s.[32]

Unions believe that OSHA has resulted in better-informed employees, increased
union involvement in safety and health, and better working conditions. These are all
positive contributions. However, unions are still not satisfied that OSHA has
achieved everything that it should. Workers are still needlessly being killed and
subjected to work situations that are detrimental to their quality of life.

OSHA: The 1990s[33]

It appears that OSHA will be as important as environmental law in the workplace of
the 1990s. More employees are likely to exercise their rights concerning business
hazards including:

- The right to request an OSHA inspection.
- The right to be present during the inspection.
- The right to protection from reprisal for reporting the company to OSHA.
- The right to access to his or her company medical records.
- The right to refuse to work if there is a real danger of death or serious injury or
  illness from job hazards.

In addition, since 1988, OSHA has adopted a hazard communication standard
that applies to all employers that states that an employer must develop a written
hazard communication program for employees that covers all hazardous chemicals

in their workplace. A continual training program must also be in effect so that employees are up-to-date on workplace risks. Employers are not yet fully complying with this standard either by failing to provide training or to address the basic requirements of the standard. It appears that the 1990s will be an era in which employers will be compelled to address health and safety hazards in the workplace more consistently in order to escape increased punitive action from OSHA.

What can the operating manager or HR specialist do to help keep the enterprise in compliance with OSHA? The HR specialist should know the standards that apply to the organization and check to see that they are being met. HRM is also responsible for keeping OSHA records up-to-date and filing them on time. The operating manager must know the standards that apply to his or her unit or department and see that the unit meets the standards. As citizens, all managers should see to it that OSHA is effective at the organization. But they can also write their congressional representatives to improve it so that:

Standards are understandable and focus on important items.

Advisory inspections are permitted.

Records and reports are minimized, efficient, and correct.

Ultimately, whether OSHA succeeds or fails depends on a decrease in the number and severity of accidents and the incidence of occupational disease in the working population.[34] OSHA's annual reports are phrased in bureaucratic "success" terms such as increases in numbers of inspections, pamphlets printed, and dollars spent on research. Until it can show that the *costs* of enforcement are exceeded by the *benefits* in terms of reduced accidents, fewer fatalities, and fewer occupational disease victims, we shall have to wait to see whether the program should be called a success or a bureaucratic nightmare.

HEALTH PROGRAMS

Health care cost Americans $542 billion in 1989.[35] Large companies like those in the *Fortune* 500 now spend over $100 million each year to provide employee health-care benefits. That means that the average employer was paying 13 percent of payroll for medical benefits in 1989 as compared to 5 percent just 10 years ago.

One way of defining *health* is to say that it is the absence of disease. You will remember from the beginning of this chapter that health hazards like physical and biological hazards, toxic and cancer-causing dusts and chemicals, and stressful working conditions put employees at risk at work. So the work environment itself can cause disease. This is in addition to the other health risks that the average employee meets in his or her daily life outside the workplace. A more informative definition of **health** is "a state of physical, mental, and social wellbeing."[36] This definition points to the relationships among body, mind, and social patterns. An employee's health can be harmed through disease, accident, or stress.[37] Managers now realize that they must be concerned about the general health of employees including their psychological well-being. An otherwise competent employee who is depressed and has low self-esteem is as nonproductive as one who is injured and hospitalized.

A number of factors are contributing to the sharp rise in the cost of health benefits.[38] These include:

1. The aging of the work force. Older employees have more chronic illnesses.
2. Competition among health-care carriers that raises instead of lowers the cost of care.

3. Shifting of cost from the government to the private sector.
4. Inefficiency of health-care providers.
5. Increasing malpractice litigation.
6. Failure of employers to respond to these changing patterns.

As a result, more and more companies are switching from the traditional health-care scheme of insuring against health crises as they occur to a preventive or wellness approach to health-care management.

Preventive Health Care: A Wellness Approach

The preventive or wellness approach to employer health-care plans includes spending thousands of dollars to develop facilities that help employees take better care of themselves.[39] The **preventive** or wellness approach encourages employees to make lifestyle changes now through better nutrition, regular exercise programs, abstinence from smoking and alcohol use, stress counseling, and annual physical examinations.

One large company that has adopted the preventive approach to health care successfully is the Adolph Coors Company in Golden, Colorado.[40] Over the last 10 years since the program was first instituted, Coors estimates a savings of approximately $1.99 million annually from decreasing medical claims, decreased absenteeism, and increased productivity. Each $1 spent on the wellness program provides a $6.15 payback. During the same 10-year period, comparable-sized organizations saw health-care costs rise 18 percent while Coors' only rose 5 percent.

Chairman and CEO William Coors says that wellness has become part of the corporate culture. The first step in the program was the opening of a 25,000-square-foot wellness facility, a completely equipped gym that all Coors employees were encouraged to use. Various new programs were also instituted including stress management, weight loss, smoke cessation, nutritional counseling, health risk assessment, and orthopedic rehabilitation. Both employees and spouses were encouraged to take advantage of free mammography and blood pressure screenings, employee and family counseling, and pre- and postnatal education offered on-site.

The Coors wellness program is based on a six-step model of behavioral change: awareness, education, incentives, programs, self-action, and follow-up and support. Each employee is made aware through a health hazard appraisal (HHA), which is a statistical evaluation of that person's individual health risks. The HHA includes suggestions for lowering the risk and changing behavior to live a longer, healthier life. Incentives include refunding the cost of weight loss programs that an employee undertakes if the loss is maintained for a full 12 months. Various programs like the gym and nutritional counseling are offered on-site as support.

Coors has identified what they believe are the 12 key elements of a successful wellness program:

1. CEO support and direction.
2. Wellness as a stated priority in the company's policy statement.
3. Inclusion of family members as well as the employee.
4. Accessibility of the program to the whole family.
5. Employee input into programs offered, times, and so on.
6. Needs assessment before each phase of the program is instituted.
7. Periodic in-house evaluation to be sure objectives are being met.
8. Ongoing communication of program's goals and components.

9. HRM monitoring of related issues like AIDS, cancer, and so on.
10. Community involvement.
11. Staffing with qualified health-care specialists.
12. Establishment of a separate budget for the wellness program.

Many other companies employing thousands of employees report exceptional paybacks from adopting the wellness approach. The Prudential Insurance Company reported that its Houston office reduced disability days by 20 percent and obtained a $1.93 savings for every dollar invested in its in-house exercise program. Its major medical costs dropped from $574 to $302 per employee in just two years.[41] A fitness program including regular exercise and various health-education and lifestyle improvement classes was started at the Canadian Life Assuance Company resulting in a 22 percent drop in absenteeism. Johnson & Johnson uses a wellness approach called "Live for Life," which includes nutrition, stress management, smoking cessation, and fitness. They compared 5,000 employees who enrolled in the program to 3,000 who did not and found that hospital costs per person for participants were 34 percent lower than for nonparticipants! Nonparticipants averaged 76 hours of absence each year while participants averaged 56 hours (20 hours less).

Mid-sized and small employers can offer scaled-down versions of the corporate giants while still reaping the same benefits. It is important that the same 12 steps detailed by Coors be followed regardless of the company's size, however. The wellness approach can also be successfully integrated with a retiree health benefit plan.[42] An ongoing research program in California is monitoring the impact of Senior Healthtrac, a program designed to improve retirees' health and lower medical costs. The plan has been offered to 250,000 older Americans, many of whom were employees of BankAmerica and Blue Shield of California. After just a year, about $133 per year in direct medical-cost savings for each participant was recorded.

The wellness or preventive approach is not foolproof, particularly if the approach is adopted without fully understanding the necessity of manager commitment and manager-employee communication.[43] Almost 80 percent of corporations offering a wellness program continue without any quantifiable proof that the program is saving them money or increasing productivity. Promised reductions in health-care premiums from insurers are not always delivered and are minimal, at best. Employees who need the help most may not participate. Note, therefore, that the immediate benefits of a preventive approach to health care are minimal and that the ultimate payback is in the long term.

The preventive health move into organizations has brought with it some potential legal problms. Sentry Life Insurance has a $1.5 million fitness center at corporate headquarters in Stevens Point, Wisconsin.[44] Who is liable if an employee injures himself or herself in the center? This question was put to the test when an overweight man in his late 40s collapsed of a heart attack in the center. The man had reduced his weight from 270 to 180 pounds too fast and ignored the training regimen prescribed by the company. However, the firm continued to permit his use of the center. Fortunately for Sentry, a lawsuit based on a negligence claim was not filed.

To minimize legal risk, many corporations abide by guidelines established by the College of Sports Medicine. The guidelines recommend a series of tests to determine risks to program participants and prescribe training regimens. A health history and series of physical tests are used. Also a stationary bike stress test to determine heart rate and blood pressure is administered. The test results help establish the safe parameters of a training program tailored to fit the person.

Stress Management

Stress is a common experience that is a part of life.[45] However, the concept of stress is a very difficult one to pin down in specific terms. There are experts who think of stress as the pressures in the world that produce emotional discomfort. Others feel that emotional discomfort is the stress that is caused by pressure or conditions that are called *stressors*. Still others view stress in terms of physiological or body reactions: blood pressure, heart rate, or hormone levels.[46] We will define **stress** as a person's physical, chemical, and mental reactions to stressors or stimuli in the environment. Stress occurs whenever environmental forces (stimuli) throw the bodily and mental functions of a person out of equilibrium.

Stress has typically been cast in terms of negative reactions. Of course, it can also be good for a person. Stress is what helps a person complete a report on time or generate a good, quick problem-solving procedure. This chapter acknowledges the positive aspects of stress — but our main attention will be on the negative aspects of stress.

Stress and Disease

Job-related stress has been associated with a vast array of diseases such as coronary heart disease, hypertension, peptic ulcers, colitis, and various psychological problems such as anxiety and depression. Research has shown that stress affects the endocrine system, the cardiovascular system, the muscular system, and the emotions directly.[47] It also has a general arousal influence on the entire body.

Stress and disease linkage continues to be studied and is of interest to managers. A person who is emotionally troubled and depressed because of stress is often unable to function on the job and may even create problems for other workers if he or she attempts to work. In general, psychological job stress reactions are not severe psychoses. They are, however, frustrating; they do reduce a person's desire to work; they do cause feelings of fatigue. Thus, although many experts are concerned about the stress-coronary heart disease association, there is also the possible stress-psychological reaction association.

Stressors can be negative or positive, like getting a divorce or getting married. Both positive and negative stressors can inhibit bodily functions. Some stressors are traumatic, happening in crisis situations, for example, the death of a parent. Other stressors occur daily, like the drive to work on a freeway. Buildups of daily stressors can be just as deadly as a trauma. And we can experience stress consciously or unconsciously. As a result, some people are unaware of the stress that is affecting their daily lives.[48]

The Person/Environment Fit

Changes in the work and personal environment are inevitable. Too often, managers underestimate how changes can throw a person off kilter. A person who does not feel comfortable with his or her work environment is in what psychologists refer to as a *state of disequilibrium*. The person's skills, abilities, goals does not fit with the work environment (boss, coworkers, compensation system). The costs of the lack of fit in person/environment can be many: subjective (feeling fatigued), behavioral (accident prone), cognitive (a mental block), physiological (elevated blood pressure), and/or organizational (higher absence rate).[49]

Research studies point out that these five levels of stress caused by disequilibrium of lack of fit are costly. The costs to an organization are found in premature deaths of employees, higher rates of accidents, performance inefficiencies, increased turnover, increased disability payments, and many other areas.[50]

One way to attack the stress cost problem is to identify the stressors that contribute to it. Exhibit 19–10 is presented to show some of the major person and environmental stressors that lead to stress and dysfunctional consequences. This managerial model illustrated that stress is caused by the interaction of people with their environment. It is a person's perception of a work situation that can make a stressor stressful. This is what is portrayed in Exhibit 19–10. Covering each deatil of Exhibit 19–10 is beyond the scope of this book. Consequently, only a few of the stressors will be examined.

Workload   A person's workload can cause stress. Workload can relate to the quantity of the work (quantitative) or the quality (qualitative) of the activity to be completed (mental requirements). Underload can create problems as well as overload. Overload can cause a person to work long hours to stay even, which can result in fatigue and more accidents. On the other hand, boredom can set in if a person is underloaded. A bored worker often avoids work by staying at home more frequently. The worker who is bored and stays at home often mopes around, which results in a lack of adequate exercise to maintain a healthy body.[51] It is a vicious circle.

Role Conflict   How a person behaves in a given job depends on many factors. A combination of the expectations and demands an employee places upon him- or herself and those of co-workers results in a set of forces called *role pressures*. When a situation arises in which two or more role pressures are in conflict with one another, role conflict exists. Role conflict exists whenever compliance with one set of pressures makes compliance with another set difficult, objectionable, or impossible.

Researchers have found that conflict is associated with job dissatisfaction and anxiety.[52] It has also been linked to heart disease, elevated blood pressure, and excessive eating. Role conflict seems to undermine a peaceful work state and leads to physiological and psychological changes.

Life Events   Holmes and Rahe have studied how life events can contribute to a stressful life.[53] A **life event** is a significant personal experience, for example changing jobs, which can have both positive or negative consequences for the individual. Based on their research, they developed a numerical value for each life event, ranking the events in order of magnitude. After developing the scoring system, the medical histories and life events scores of patients were reviewed. It was found that patients who had a high score on what the researchers called the Social Readjustment Rating Scale (SRRS) were more likely to contract illness following the events. The SRRS is presented in Exhibit 19–11. People with scores of over 300 were very likely to contract some form of stress-related illness, such as ulcers, migraine headaches, colitis, and heart disease, in the near future.

The work of Holmes and Rahe with the SRRS points out the connection between life changes (stressors) and a lowered resistance to fight illness. This connection is illustrated by information such as: 10 times as many widows and widowers die during the first year after the death of a spouse as nonwidowed individuals in a similar age-group. Also, the illness rate for divorced persons during the first year after the divorce is 12 times higher than for married persons.

A Person Stressor: Type A Behavior Pattern   In the 1950s, two cardiologists, Friedman and Rosenman, began to look at the way a person's behavior pattern can be used to predict the incident of coronary heart disease.[54] What they discovered was called the **Type A behavior pattern.** It is defined as:

EXHIBIT 19-10   A Managerial Model for Examining Job Stress

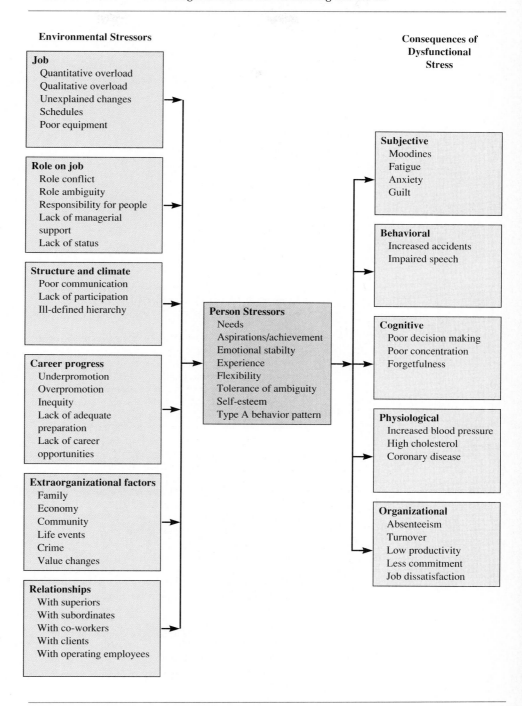

Environmental Stressors

**Consequences of
Dysfunctional
Stress**

Job
Quantitative overload
Qualitative overload
Unexplained changes
Schedules
Poor equipment

Role on job
Role conflict
Role ambiguity
Responsibility for people
Lack of managerial
support
Lack of status

Structure and climate
Poor communication
Lack of participation
Ill-defined hierarchy

Person Stressors
Needs
Aspirations/achievement
Emotional stabilty
Experience
Flexibility
Tolerance of ambiguity
Self-esteem
Type A behavior pattern

Career progress
Underpromotion
Overpromotion
Inequity
Lack of adequate
preparation
Lack of career
opportunities

Extraorganizational factors
Family
Economy
Community
Life events
Crime
Value changes

Relationships
With superiors
With subordinates
With co-workers
With clients
With operating employees

Subjective
Moodines
Fatigue
Anxiety
Guilt

Behavioral
Increased accidents
Impaired speech

Cognitive
Poor decision making
Poor concentration
Forgetfulness

Physiological
Increased blood pressure
High cholesterol
Coronary disease

Organizational
Absenteeism
Turnover
Low productivity
Less commitment
Job dissatisfaction

EXHIBIT 19-11   The Social Readjustment Rating Scale

Instructions: Check off each of these life events that has happened to you during the previous year. Total the associated points. A score of 150 or less means a relatively low amount of life change and a low susceptibility to stress-induced health breakdown. A score of 150 to 300 points implies about a 50 percent chance of a major health breakdown in the next two years. A score above 300 raises the odds to about 80 percent, according to the Holmes-Rahe statistical prediction model.

Life Events	Mean Value
1. Death of spouse	100
2. Divorce	73
3. Marital separation from mate	65
4. Detention in jail or other institution	63
5. Death of a close family member	63
6. Major personal injury or illness	53
7. Marriage	50
8. Being fired at work	47
9. Marital reconciliation with mate	45
10. Retirement from work	45
11. Major change in the health or behavior of a family member	44
12. Pregnancy	40
13. Sexual difficulties	39
14. Gaining a new family member (e.g., through birth, adoption, oldster moving in, etc.)	39
15. Major business readjustment (e.g., merger, reorganization, bankruptcy, etc.)	39
16. Major change in financial state (e.g., a lot worse off or a lot better off than usual)	38
17. Death of a close friend	37
18. Changing to a different line of work	36
19. Major change in the number of arguments with spouse (e.g., either a lot more or a lot less than usual regarding child rearing, personal habits, etc.)	35
20. Taking on a mortgage greater than $10,000 (e.g., purchasing a home, business, etc.)	31
21. Foreclosure on a mortgage or loan	30
22. Major change in responsibilities at work (e.g., promotion, demotion, lateral transfer)	29
23. Son or daughter leaving home (e.g., marriage, attending college, etc.)	29
24. In-law troubles	29
25. Outstanding personal achievement	28
26. Wife beginning or ceasing work outside the home	26
27. Beginning or ceasing formal schooling	26
28. Major change in living conditions (e.g., building a new home, remodeling, deterioration of home or neighborhood)	25
29. Revision of personal habits (dress, manners, associations, etc.)	24
30. Troubles with the boss	23
31. Major change in working hours or conditions	20
32. Change in residence	20
33. Changing to a new school	20
34. Major change in usual type and/or amount of recreation	19
35. Major change in church activities (e.g., a lot more or a lot less than usual)	19
36. Major change in social activities (e.g., clubs, dancing, movies, visiting, etc.)	18

EXHIBIT 19-11   *(concluded)*

Life Events	Mean Value
37. Taking on a mortgage or loan less than $10,000 (e.g., purchasing a car, TV, freezer, etc.)	17
38. Major change in sleeping habits (a lot more or a lot less sleep, or change in part of day when asleep)	16
39. Major change in number of family get-togethers (e.g., a lot more or a lot less than usual)	15
40. Major change in eating habits (a lot more or a lot less food intake, or very different meal hours or surroundings)	15
41. Vacation	13
42. Christmas	12
43. Minor violations of the law (e.g., traffic tickets, jaywalking, disturbing the peace, etc.)	11

Note: Today, item numbers 26 and 37 would have to be adjusted upward.
Source: Reprinted with permission from *Journal of Psychosomatic Research* 11, no. 2, T. H. Holmes and R. H. Rahe, "The Social Readjustment Rating Scale," pp. 213–18. Copyright 1967, Pergamon Press, Ltd.

an action-emotion complex that can be observed in any person who is aggressively involved in a chronic, incessant struggle to achieve more and more in less and less time, and if required to do so, against the opposing efforts of other things or other persons.

The hard-core Type A person is hard-driving, is competitive, has a sense of time urgency, and is chronically impatient with delays. (The opposite of the Type A is the Type B person.) Research has linked the Type A personality with coronary heart disease. Type A men have been found to experience 6½ times the incidence of heart disease than Type B men.[55] Also, the Type A person has higher blood pressure than the Type B.

There is little doubt that Type A behavior is associated in some ways to a number of diseases. The precise role it plays, however, is not clear. It is incorrect to definitely associate Type A with stress. Yet, there is likely to be more stress experienced by Type As. Type As tend to create stress for themselves by constantly exposing themselves to stressors that the Type B avoid, like work overload, handling too many projects, and always rushing to finish one job just to start a new job. The Type A person seems to be in a constant struggle with time and with other people. This behavior results in hyperaggressiveness that manifests itself as free-floating hostility.[56]

Pinpointing Worker Stress   There are a number of methods available to managers for identifying stress within themselves and employees. The precise identification of negative stress should be left to the professional. A well-trained behavioral scientist, physician, or counselor can use psychological tests, in-depth interviews, or medical history forms and medical tests to uncover stress problems.

The nonprofessional involved in pinpointing stress problems at work is the manager. He or she can also do some diagnosis. First, the manager should look for sudden, unexplained changes in mood, tensions, and loss-of-temper episodes. Second, when an efficient worker becomes sloppy or when a prompt worker becomes late, this signifies changes in behavior. This can be a signal that the person is experiencing stress.

Coping with Stress   Stress in life is inevitable. However, when it hurts the person, co-workers, or the organization, it must be addressed. There are two ways to cope with stress. The first is to eliminate the source of the stressor(s) that is causing the stress by changing policies, the structure, the work requirements, or whatever is necessary. The second approach is to deal with the stress individually or oganizationally.

Individual stress-coping programs include meditation, biofeedback, training, exercise, diet, and even prayer. These programs work for some people. They help the person feel better, relax, and regenerate energy. A few coping programs are briefly mentioned in Exhibit 19–12.

There are also organizational stress-coping programs. Experts in organizations can use their knowledge about stress and employee health to develop and implement organization-sponsored stress-coping workshops and seminars.[57] In addition, these experts can recommend structural, job, and policy changes that can eventually improve the well-being of employees.

Levi Strauss & Co. has had an ongoing stress management program in which 1,500 employees have participated in an all-day seminar. Relaxation techniques and self-motivation procedures are taught, and the examination of life goals, identification of harmful personality traits, and behavior modification techniques are part of the program.[58]

EXHIBIT 19-12   Stress Coping Methods: A Few Samples

Planning: Much stress in personal and work life can be managed by planning. Take some time to assess your personal and career goals. At work, set aside some time to plan tomorrow's activities. How do they relate to your goals or your company's goals?

Physical exercise: Regular exercise can contribute to the physical health of the individual, and it can also help the person overcome stress, both as an outlet and as physical conditioning. Of course, you should consult a physician before embarking on a strenuous exercise program.

Diet: Prolonged stress can deplete your body's supply of infection-fighting vitamins, leaving you susceptible to disease. Also, eating habits change under stress. The manager, up against a deadline, might well work through lunch or arrive late at dinner and unwind by downing a double scotch. During stressful periods, maintaining a good diet is essential.

Biofeedback: This therapeutic technique is used in the treatment of migraine headaches, high blood pressure, muscle tension, and other stress-related problems. It involves the monitoring of one or more body functions with electronic devices that signal the user with tones, clicks, or lights. For example, people can learn to control brain waves, pulse rate, blood pressure, and the temperature in their hands and feet.

Meditation or relaxation: Emerging from Far Eastern philosophies, these techniques include meditation, transcendental meditation, yoga, and Zen. The Americanization of meditation, which was popularized in Herbert Bensen's book, *The Relaxation Response,* has a person sit in a comfortable chair in a quiet area with subdued lighting. The person closes his or her eyes, takes a deep breath, and exhales. Each time the person exhales, he or she repeats a single word or mantra. Repeating this single word helps to eliminate distracting thoughts. This process takes approximately 20 minutes, although some individuals can achieve refreshing relaxation in just a few moments.

Variations include tensing and relaxing muscles until relaxation of the entire body is reached. Others recommend thinking of a favorite vacation spot — a deserted beach or a calm lake — recalling all the sights and sounds.

Psychotherapy: A wide variety of interpersonal techniques are used that usually involve intensive one-to-one work with a professional therapist.

Psychoanalysis: This is a form of psychotherapy during which the therapist takes the patient into the depths of his or her personality to examine the root of abnormal behavior.

At Employees Mutual Life Insurance Co. in Des Moines, Iowa, the stress coping program focuses on identifying individual stressors. Participants log a personal concerns inventory in which they rate the importance of 58 areas of concern for 21 days. It is assumed that just the identification of stressors is beneficial for helping individuals cope with stress.[59]

The HR department has a role to play in stress-coping programs. It can provide specialists, facilities, monitoring or evaluation, and other important resources. Organizations such as IBM, Tenneco, Control Data, Shell, and Prudential already have HR employees performing such duties as setting up exercise classes, initiating fitness programs, and providing diet counseling. More and more organizations have become concerned about and involved in stress management in the 1990s. Stress management programs are even being developed in Japan where white-collar employees are paying a high price for success in alcoholism, mental breakdowns, and suicide.[60]

During the past 20 years, many stress management programs have met with variable success.[61] It is not enough to inform employees about the risks of stress. Even pointing out behaviors that cause or enhance stress does not mean that the employee will change his or her negative behavior. The desire to change behavior may not be enough. Therefore, guidelines to follow when instituting a stress management program must include knowledgeable presenters and programs that are relevant and specific to each individual and to each work environment.

AIDS IN THE WORKPLACE

Acquired immune deficiency syndrome **(AIDS)** was first reported in the United States in 1981. Each of the letters in AIDS stands for a word:

Acquired. The disease is passed from one person to another.

Immune. It attacks the immune system the body's defense mechanism, which normally protects the body from disease.

Deficiency. The defense system is not working.

Syndrome. A group of symptoms that, when they occur together, mean a person has a particular disease or condition.

In 1981, there were over 100,000 cases in the United States. And by 1991, it was estimated that between 270,000 and 365,000 Americans had developed the disease, with 2,000,000 being exposed to the virus.[62] AIDS is an infectious disease in which the body's immune system is damaged in varying, usually progressive, degrees of severity. There is increasing evidence that a vast majority of those exposed to HIV (human immunodeficiency virus) will eventually develop full-blown AIDS.

The Center for Disease Control announced in 1990 that between 1 and 1.5 million Americans were already infected with HIV. Those infected include a growing percentage of drug abusers, babies of drug abusers, and children between the ages of 13 to 19. Homosexuals, bisexuals, drug abusers, and the black and Hispanic population are disproportionately represented in those who had already developed full-blown AIDS in the United States.[63] AIDS has become an epidemic that has resulted in escalating health-case insurance and disability costs, rising disability, a loss of important employees, and other work-force disruptions. AIDS had now been found in every state and in almost every foreign country. While ongoing research attempts to find both treatment and cure, no cure has yet been found — and the prognosis is that there may be no AIDS vaccine for 25 or more years. Today, a person with AIDS will incur between $70,000 and $141,000 in medical bills from diagnosis to death.[64]

Fear of AIDS at Work

A case of AIDS at work is a serious issue for both the victim and that person's fellow employees. Self-disclosure about AIDS raises the potential for retaliation from working peers, supervisors, and other employees in general.[65] At New England Telephone & Telegraph Company, an employee named Paul told his supervisor that he had AIDS. The supervisor allegedly passed the information along to Paul's co-workers. Some of the co-workers began to threaten Paul and he was terminated. The AIDS victim sued his employers, charging handicap discrimination, breach of privacy, and other violations of Massachusetts state law. The case was settled out of court, and Paul was reinstated. When Paul returned to work, his co-workers walked off the job. Medical experts were called in to discuss AIDS and how it is transmitted before the employees returned to work.

Legal Battles about AIDS

AIDS is a debilitating disease with a potential for affecting job performance. Consequently, employers must consider the legal factors regarding AIDS victims as employees.[66] The American Civil Liberties Union (ACLU) recently gathered 6,000 reports of discrimination against AIDS sufferers including discrimination in housing, insurance, and government services as well as at the workplace.[67] The ACLU concluded that 34 percent of AIDS patients have experienced discrimination on the job or while seeking employment. The result is a growing number of lawsuits involving AIDS. For example, an employee with AIDS charged that his company, H&H Music Company, and their insurer denied him $1 million in potential health benefits. His suit alleged that both this employer and their insurer switched all employees from a group medical plan to a self-insured plan to avoid liability. The patient has sued for reinstatement of $995,000 in lost medical benefits and $4 million in punitive damages.

Developing and Implementing an AIDS Policy

A poll conducted in 1987 of 600 senior HR managers by Louis Harris and Associates, inc., found that 89 percent of the respondents had no specific policy to deal with employees with AIDS.[68] Eighty-five percent of those polled have no information program about AIDS for their employees, and 72 percent of those have no intention of implementing one. By July 1990, a new survey found that many businesses were still unprepared for the impact of AIDS.[69] Clearly, employers and the courts are slowly beginning to face the realities of AIDS in the workplace.

Before developing any policy, there are a number of practical problems employers must be aware of regarding AIDS:

1. *Asking applicants if they have AIDS.* This is not an acceptable question. Asking whether a person is handicapped in such a way to inhibit him or her is acceptable. If the person volunteers that he or she has AIDS, an employer must determine if the disability will affect performance.

2. *Requiring job applicants to be tested for AIDS.* Some states prohibit employers from doing this test. Check the law and ask how the results will be used.

3. *If applicants' test positive for AIDS, can they be denied a job?* They can be denied employment only if it is determined that the applicant cannot perform the job.
4. *Can an employee with AIDS be disciplined, terminated, or placed on leave?* Again, as long as the job can be performed, he or she cannot be disciplined or terminated or placed on leave.
5. *Must an employer keep knowledge about an employee having AIDS or testing positive confidential?* Yes, there should be no medical information passed on to co-workers.
6. *Can an employer be held liable by employees who claim to have contracted AIDS on the job?* This is a difficult dilemma. The current state of medical knowledge indicates that AIDS cannot be transmitted through normal workplace interaction. Thus, it is questionable that the employer could be found guilty.

A company can choose one of three approaches when confronting the AIDS challenge:[70]

1. Categorizing AIDS under a comprehensive life-threatening illness policy.
2. Forming an AIDS-specific policy.
3. No policy.

BankAmerica uses the first approach, identifying all resources available through the company's HR department for any employees facing a life-threatening illness. The policy also includes 10 guidelines for managers of stricken employees. Morrison and Foerster, a law firm, has a six-point AIDS-specific policy. If the no policy approach is chosen, the work force must be kept informed about AIDS and told that AIDS victims are *entitled* to remain employed.

With the threat of over 2 million infected Americans by 1991, an AIDS policy may be too late for those already ill or carrying the virus.[71] A federal law prohibiting discrimination was still in the formative stage at this writing, but many courts have already ruled that asymptomatic-infected people are protected from discrimination under the Vocational Rehabilitation Act. Most states have some form of handicap laws and some, such as Florida, Maine, Massachusetts, New Jersey, and New York, have already acted to protect AIDS victims from discrimination based on their handicap statuses. California and Wisconsin also protect AIDS victims from employment discrimination.

Testing is prohibited under federal law unless it is job-related. Hotlines, job flexibility, part-time work, flexible hours, or working at home are other approaches to keep the infected employee gainfully employed. In addition, the federal government is suggesting that employers take steps to establish guidelines on handling accidents involving blood or other body fluids to control the spread of the infection.

New evidence suggests that AIDS-infected health-care workers, doctors, dentists, and so on pose a risk after the Center for Disease Control confirmed infection of more than five patients by a dentist in Florida who has since died of AIDS.[72] Guidelines for health professionals have not as yet been implemented, however.

AIDS–HIV is a disease syndrome that remains almost 100 percent fatal.[73] Its treatment will cost U.S. businesses and individual citizens 10s of billions of dollars each year. The stress of the AIDS epidemic has pointed out the weak points of our American health-care system: lack of preventive medicine, a shortage of hospitals ready to deal with the chronically ill, and no universal access to health insurance. Business leaders like Lee Iacocca and other top leaders have begun to lobby for legislation that would socialize medicine because the plight of the AIDS patients and its challenge to business are just a shadow of the health-care burden that the aging population will soon present.

EMPLOYEE ASSISTANCE PROGRAMS (EAPs)

The 1980s was a decade when addiction to alcohol and other drugs and depression and other stressors reached epidemic levels in the work force.[74] It was estimated by the Alcohol, Drug Abuse, and Mental Health Administration (ADAMHA) that annual productivity losses of almost $100 billion could be attributed to drug and alcohol abuse in 1986 alone.[75] The figure is expected to double in the early 90s. Instead of having separate preventive health, alcohol abuse, and drug abuse programs, some organizations have developed a total, all-encompassing approach called an **employee assistance program** or *EAP*.

EAPs can help troubled employees obtain counseling and referrals before their problems become overwhelming. They are not therapy programs. They focus on minor problems as they occur or refer employees to an accredited professional if the problem is more pronounced. In most EAPs, the cornerstone is voluntary participation. Posters, fliers, pay-envelope inserts, and bulletin boards are used to inform employees how to use the program. A common theme is the confidential nature of the EAP.

McDonnell Douglas Corporation commissioned a study of its EAP program in 1988 that revealed the program saved $4 for every $1 spent in reduced health claims and lower absenteeism rates for EAP "graduates."[76] McDonnell's program combines medical treatment with in-house and off-site counseling. It is designed to deal with a wide range of psychological stressors including family, marital, or financial problems. Similar findings are reported by other firms. However, it is important to note that EAPs have limitations, especially where the treatment of alcohol or drug addiction is concerned. Permanent cures of these conditions do not exist, with return to addiction or a new addiction always a possible outcome. Businesses must decide when to stop investing in those employees' rehabilitation and when it is too risky to reinstate addicted employees into high-risk positions.

WORKERS' COMPENSATION AND DISABILITY PROGRAMS

Disability programs are designed to help workers who are ill or injured and cannot work (see Chapter 12). Employees show little preference for them. Although before his accident Dale Silias in the opening Career Challenge was probably not too interested in workers' compensation, he is now. He's also interested in Lysander's health insurance plan.

There are three programs in the United States for private-and not-for-profit-sector employees. One is federal. The social security system is called OASDI, and the "DI" stands for disability insurance. A person who is totally disabled and unable to work can receive a small payment, perhaps $60 a week, from social security until age 65. As with other social security programs, this is financed by employer and employee payroll contributions.

The second program is the state-run workers' compensation, financed by employer payments. It pays for permanent partial, total partial, or total disability arising from employment. Requirements, payments, and procedures vary somewhat from state to state. Workers' compensation systems are compulsory in most states. For federal government employees, the Federal Employees Compensation Act of

1949 (last amended in 1974) provides for payments for accidents and injuries paralleling workers' compensation.

The compensation comes in two forms: monetary reimbursement and payment of medical expenses. The amount of compensation is based on fixed schedules of minimum and maximum payments. Disability payments are often based on formulas of the employees' earnings, modified by economic conditions and the number of dependents. There is usually a week's waiting period prior to the payment of the compensation and fixed compensation for permanent losses.

The employee receives workers' compensation no matter whose fault an accident is. Payment is made for physical impairments and for neuroses that may result from a physical loss. The employer must also pay compensation for diseases that result from occupations (such as black lung disease in mining) and for the results of undue stress laid on employees, such as hernias resulting from lifting heavy materials. Both workers' compensation laws and OSHA require the employer to keep detailed accident and death records.

The employer pays the entire cost of workers' compensation, usually by participating in private insurance plans or state-run systems or by self-insurance. The improvement of safety conditions at the work site can lead to lower insurance costs if accidents decline as a result.

The cost of workers' compensation and disability payments varies by industry and type of work. It can be divided between short-term disability protection (sick leave, and sickness and accident insurance) and long-term disability insurance. Long-term disability usually pays between 50 and 60 percent of earnings and is provided to about 45 percent of all U.S. employees. Payments do not usually begin until the person has been disabled six monhts or more.[77] Benefits may last a specified number of months or until retirement, depending on the employee's age at the time of disability. Employees in New York and New Jersey are covered by mandatory temporary disability insurance plans that pay weekly benefits for 26 weeks ($170 in New York and $241 in New Jersey). Maximum payments for these plans range from between $4,001 to $10,000, with the average in 1989 being $5,627. About 90 percent of white-collar and 71 percent of blue-collar employees are covered by long-term disability plans.

Criticism of workers' compensation programs centers on the fact that the systems were designed to prevent hardship but not to discourage return to work or rehabilitation of the injured worker. The National Commission on State Workers' Compensation was very critical of state workers' compensation plans. It found that the benefits are too low and too many employers have inadequate accident prevention programs. The commission made 80 specific recommendations to the states that, if not actuated, should be legislated by Congress.

The third program under which employees receive workers' compensation is private disability insurance provided by employers. About two-thirds of the companies surveyed provide accident and sickness insurance to their employees (usually for blue-collar workers). A variation for white-collar workers is sick pay–salary continuance insurance. About 85 percent of the companies surveyed have this. These plans pay wages or salaries to employees with short-term disabilities. Generally, they supplement workers' compensation. Long-term disability pay or pensions for employees was also being offered by 74 percent of companies surveyed for managers, 62 percent for white-collar employees, and 28 percent for blue-collar workers. This insurance is designed to supplement government programs and bring total compensation up to a more livable level. Luckily for Dale Silas, Lysander does have disability coverage.

CAREER CHALLENGE
(*concluded*)

After the visit to Bob's plant, Clint returned to his own. He did not feel good, thinking that maybe a safety unit could have prevented Dale's accident. That night, he drove to Denver to visit Dale in the hospital. There was good news: Dale would not be totally disabled. He would be handicapped, but he would be able to work about half the time after his recuperation.

Clint had taken the time to check with Otto Richmond of the HR department about the company's disability plan and workers' compensation. He could tell Dale that, between the two plans, his compensation would be kept up at its normal level.

Clint I feel very upset though, Dale. Maybe, just maybe, your accident needn't have happened. So

I'm hiring a safety specialist as soon as possible to try to avoid similar accidents in the future.

Dale I'm glad you are. But it was my fault too. I've been at Lysander a long time. I know I shouldn't have done that with the machine. I just got sloppy.

Clint The best news I've gotten in a long time is that you'll be back. Will you help me with the safety program?

Dale I'm a living witness of what can happen if you're not safety-conscious. You can bet I'll be behind the safety program.

In the years that followed, Lysander's safety record improved. The improvement was at least partly due to the new safety program Clint installed.

EVALUATION OF SAFETY AND HEALTH PROGRAMS

Health and (especially) safety programs have begun to receive more attention in recent years. The consequences of inadequate programs are measurable: increased workers' compensation payments, an increased number of lawsuits, larger insurance costs, fines from OSHA, and union pressures. A safety management program requires these steps:

1. Establishment of indicator systems (for example, accident statistics).
2. Development of effective reporting systems.
3. Development of rules and procedures.
4. Rewarding supervisors for effective management of the safety function.

Top-management support is needed, and the proper design of jobs and worker-machine interactions is necessary, but probably the key is participation by employees.

A health and safety program can be evaluated fairly directly in a cost/benefit sense. The costs of safety specialists, new safety devices, and other measures can be calculated. Reductions in accidents, lowered insurance costs, and lowered fines can be weighed against these costs. Programs can be judged by other measurable criteria like improvements in job performance, decreases in sick leave, and reductions in disciplinary actions and in grievances.[78] Records of claims and referrals must also be kept. At the same time, managers must realize that cause-and-effect relationships may be complex and benefits of a health and safety program both tangible and intangible. The most cost-effective safety programs need *not* be the most expensive. Programs that combine a number of safety approaches — safety rules, off-the-job safety, safety training, safety meetings, medical facilities, and strong top-management participation — work when the emphasis is on the engineering aspects of safety. Cost/benefit studies for health and safety programs can be very helpful in analyzing and improving them.

SUMMARY

1. Safety hazards are those aspects of the work environment that have the potential of immediate and sometimes violent harm to an employee.

2. Health hazards are those aspects of the work environment that slowly and cumulatively lead to deterioration of an employee's health.

3. Some tragic safety and health problems have been highly publicized such as the Bhopal, India, gas leak, the Three Mile Island nuclear accident, and the NASA Challenger loss.

4. On average, one employee in eight is killed or injured at work each year in the United States.

5. The major causes of occupational accidents are the task to be done, the working conditions, and the employee.

6. Organizational responses to health and safety challenges include:
   a. Safety design and preventive approaches.
   b. Inspection, reporting, and accident research.
   c. Safety training and motivation programs.
   d. Auditing safety programs.
   e. Health programs for employees.

7. A growing number of firms are attempting to control or prohibit smoking at work.

8. The Occupational Safety and Health Act is the culmination of the movement for federal supervision of health safety programs. It has requirements such as:
   a. Meeting safety standards set by OSHA.
   b. Submitting to OSHA inspections.
   c. Keeping records and reporting accidents and illnesses.

9. Stress can play a major role in the health of employees. Thus, more firms are now concerned about understanding and managing stress. Individual- and organization-based stress management programs are being used.

10. The preventive or wellness approach to health care encourages employees to make lifestyle changes now through better nutrition, regular exercise, abstinence from smoking and alcohol use, stress counseling, and annual physical examinations.

11. AIDS is a devastating disease that has become a problem that managers must address. Some firms are attempting to educate the work force so that misconceptions and fear do not create a nonproductive work environment.

12. An employee assistance program (EAP) is a total, all-encompassing approach to dealing with escalating alcohol and drug abuse problems, which cost U.S. businesses over $100 billion in 1986.

EXHIBIT 19-13   Recommendations on Health and Safety for Model Organizations

Type of Organization	Formal Safety Department	Safety as Duty of HR Specialist	Formal Health Department	Arrangement with Health Team	Preventive Health Programs	Stress Management Programs (Organizations)	AIDS Program
1. Large size, low complexity, high stability	X		X			X	X
2. Medium size, low complexity, high stability	X			X		X	X
3. Small size, low complexity, high stability		X		X			
4. Medium size, moderate complexity, moderate stability	X			X	X	X	X
5. Large size, high complexity, low stability	X		X		X	X	X
6. Medium size, high complexity, low stability	X			X	X	X	X
7. Small size, high complexity, low stability				X	X		

13. Workers' compensation and disability programs are designed to help workers who are ill or injured and cannot work.

14. A health and safety program should be periodically evaluated to be sure it is providing both service to employees and payback to the company's bottom line.

Exhibit 19–13 provides recommendations on health and safety for the model organizations described in Exhibit 1–7 (Chapter 1).

KEY TERMS

QUESTIONS FOR REVIEW AND DISCUSSION

1. How do top managers, operating executives, employees, union officials, safety committees, and safety specialists interact to make the workplace healthy and safe?
2. Why would an EAP that involves AIDS education and support be needed in a highly productive and successful company?
3. What is the meaning of the *person/environment fit* concept?
4. Why should organizations be concerned about the consequences of occupational stress?
5. Are smokers' rights being violated by nonsmoking policies?
6. What are some major causes of accidents and work-related illnesses?
7. Describe some of the programs organizations used to prevent accidents and illnesses. Which are the most effective? Least effective?
8. Why is there some resistance in organizations regarding the development of an AIDS policy and program?
9. Why did the U.S. government legislate in the occupational safety and health area?
10. What legal requirements must an organization follow in the health and safety area?

NOTES

1 Steven Fink (1986), *Crisis Management* (New York: AMACOM).
2 Ian Mitross, Paul Shrivastava, and Firdaus E. Udivactra (November 1987), *Effective Crisis Management*, pp. 283–91.
3 (January 28, 1985), "Bhopal," *New York Times*, p. 24.
4 American Federation of Labor and Congress of Industrial Organization (November 1989), *AFL-CIO Policy Resolutions, Eighteenth Constitutional Convention* (Washington, D.C.: AFL–CIO), p. 73.
5 U.S. Department of Labor (August 1990), *Occupational Injuries and Illnesses in the U.S. by Industry, 1988* (Washington, D.C.: Bureau of Labor Statistics), p. 1.
6 Ibid.
7 Ibid.
8 Ibid., p. 3.
9 John Curley (June 20, 1984), "Monsanto and 172 Employees Go to Court over Allegations of Dioxin Contamination," *The Wall Street Journal*, pp. 31, 45.
10 Robert E. Harvey (October 14, 1981), "Industry Faces Costly Remedies for Occupational Illness," *Iron Age*, pp. 21–67.
11 John R. Emshwiller (February 26, 1982), "Many Nuclear Plant Perils Remain Three Years after Three Mile Island," *The Wall Street Journal*, p. 23.
12 Bureau of Labor Statistics (1978), *Injury Rates by Industry* (Washington, D.C.: U.S. Government Printing Office).
13 Morton E. Grossman (August 1990), "The $5.2 Billion Investment in Safety," *Personnel Journal*, pp. 54–55.
14 Tracy E. Benson (May 7, 1990), "Smoke Signals Get Mixed Reviews," *Industry Week*, 239, no. 9, pp. 18–19.
15 Diane Dimond (September 1990), "The Butt Stops Here," *Insurance Review* 51, no. 9, pp. 55–58.

[16] Laura Stanley (March 1990), "The Butt Stops Here," *Across the Board*, 27, no. 3, pp. 57–58.

[17] Richard W. Painter (1990), "Smoking Policies: The Legal Implications," *Employee Relations* 12, no. 4, pp. 17–21.

[18] Benson, "Smoke Signals Get Mixed Reviews," p. 19.

[19] Faye Rice (June 2, 1990), "Do You Work in a Sick Building?" *Fortune* 122, no. 1, pp. 86–88.

[20] Martin E. Personick and Katherine Taylor-Shirley (January 1989), "Profiles in Safety and Health: Occupational Hazards of Meatpacking," *Monthly Labor Review*, pp. 3–12.

[21] Thomas A. Stewart (October 22, 1990), "Do You Push Your People Too Hard?" *Fortune* 122, no. 10, pp. 121–24, 128.

[22] D. S. Thelam, D. Ledgerwood, and C. F. Walters (Ocotber 1985), "Health and Safety in the Workplace: A New Challenge for Business Schools," *Personnel Administrator*, pp. 37–38.

[23] (April 1980), "Will Reform Be the Death of OSHA?" *Nation's Business*, pp. 55–58.

[24] (April 19, 1977), "Justices to Hear Test of Job Unit's Safety Checks," *The Wall Street Journal*, p. 14.

[25] (August 20, 1990), "A New Chief Has OSHA Growling Again," *Business Week*, p. 57.

[26] Michael A. Verspej (November 5, 1990), "Stability at OSHA," *Industry Week*, p. 56.

[27] "A New Chief Has OSHA Growling Again," p. 57.

[28] Verspej, "Stability at OSHA," p. 56.

[29] Donald N. Smith and Richard C. Wilson (1982), *Industrial Robots: A Delphi Forecast of Markets and Technology* (Dearborn, Mich.: Society of Manufacturers Engineers).

[30] Vincent M. Altamoro (July 1983), "Working Safety with the Iron-Collar Worker," *National Safety News*, pp. 33–37.

[31] AFL–CIO, *AFL-CIO Policy Resolutions*, pp. 73–74.

[32] Ibid.

[33] This section is based on R. Henry Moore (June 1990), "OSHA: What's Ahead for the 1990s," *Personnel*, pp. 66–69.

[34] Adrienne C. Locke (January 15, 1990), "Goals of New OSHA Leader: Fair, Firm, and Consistent," *Business Insurance* 24, no. 3, pp. 1, 35–36.

[35] Fred Luthans and Elaine Davis (February 1990), "The Healthcare Cost Crisis: Causes and Containments," *Personnel*, pp. 24–30.

[36] Gloria C. Gordon and Mary Sue Henifin (1981), "Health and Safety, Job Stress, and Shift Work," in *Making Organizations Human and Productive*, ed. H. Meltzer and Walter R. Nord (New York: John Wiley & Sons), p. 322.

[37] John M. Ivancevich and Michael T. Matteson (Autumn 1980), "Optimizing Human Resources: A Case for Preventive Health and Stress Management," *Organizational Dynamics*, pp. 4–25.

[38] William J. Heisler, W. David Jones, and Phillip O. Benham, Jr. (1988), *Managing Human Resource Issues: Confronting Challenges and Choosing Options* (San Francisco: Jossey-Bass), pp. 55–60.

[39] Dennis Thompson (March 1990), "Wellness Programs Work for Small Employers Too," *Personnel*, pp. 26–28.

[40] Shari Caudron and Michael Rozek (July 1990), "The Wellness Payoff," *Personnel Journal* 69, no. 7, pp. 54–62.

[41] Thompson, "Wellness Programs Work for Small Employers Too," p. 27.

[42] Harry Harrington and Nancy Richardson (August 1990), "Retiree Wellness Plan Cuts Health Costs," *Personnel Journal*, pp. 60, 62.

[43] Caudron and Rozek, "The Wellness Payoff," pp. 54–62.

[44] Jonathan Miller (December–January 1984), "Are You Liable to Be Liable?" *Corporate Fitness & Recreation*, pp. 23–30.

[45] Michael E. Cavanagh (July 1988), "What You Don't Know About Stress," *Personnel Journal*, pp. 53–59.

[46] For various interpretations of stress, see L. Kevin Hamberger and Jeffrey M. Lohr (1984), *Stress and Stress Management* (New York: Springer Publishing Co.); Tom Cox (1978), *Stress* (Baltimore: University Park Press); Hans Selve (1976), *The Stress of Life* (New York: McGraw-Hill); and K. Albrecht (1979), *Stress and Manager* (Englewood Cliffs, N.J.: Prentice- Hall).

[47] David S. Allen (January 1990), "Less Stress, Less Litigation," *Personnel*, pp. 32–35.

[48] Cavanagh, "What You Don't Know about Stress," pp. 54–55.

[49] Eric H. Marcus (August 1990), "The Cost of Mental Distress," *Personnel Journal*, pp. 66–68.

[50] Ibid., p. 66.

[51] Lawrence Kelly (1990), "Understanding Absenteeism," *Worklife Report* 8, no. 4, pp. 7–9.

[52] Helen L. Richardson (June 1990), "De-Stress," *Transportation and Distribution* 31, no. 6, pp. 22–25.

[53] T. H. Holmes and R. H. Rahe (1967), "The Social Readjustment Rating Scale," *Journal of Psychosomatic Medicine*, pp. 213–18.

[54] Meyer Friedman and Diane Ulmer (1984), *Treating Type A Behavior and Your Heart* (New York: Alfred A. Knopf); and Meyer Friedman and R. Rosenman (1974), *Type A Behavior and Your Heart* (New York: Alfred A. Knopf).

[55] James C. Quick, Debra L. Nelson, and Jonathan D. Quick (1990), *Stress and Challenge at the Top: The Paradox of the Successful Executive* (New York: John Wiley & Sons), p. 33.

[56] Ibid., p. 34.

[57] Michael T. Matteson and John M. Ivancevich (1982), *Managing Job Stress and Health* (New York: Free Press).

[58] Susan Chase (August–September 1983), "Putting the Stress on Control," *Corporate Fitness and Recreation*, pp. 25–30.

[59] Ibid.

[60] (August 7, 1986), "The High Price Japanese Pay for Success," *Business Week*, pp. 52–54.

[61] Neil Niven and David Johnson (November 1989), "Does Stress Management Work?" *Management Services* 33, no. 11, pp. 18–21.

[62] Martha McDonald (July 1990), "How to Deal with AIDS in the Workplace," *Business & Health* 8, no. 7, pp. 12–22.

[63] Ibid.

[64] Brad Edmonson (March 1990), "AIDS and Aging," *American Demographics*, pp. 28–34.

[65] (April 1990), "Conspiracy Against AIDS Patient? Human Resource Focus," *Human Resources Magazine*, pp. 3–4.

[66] Marilyn Chase (May 18, 1987), "In Lives and Dollars, the Epidemic's Toll Is Growing Inexorably," *The Wall Street Journal*, pp. 1, 8.

[67] "Conspiracy Against AIDS Patient?" p. 4.

[68] Thomas J. Coates et al. (Spring 1987), "A Psychosocial Research Agenda," *Annals of Behavioral Medicine*, pp. 21–28.

[69] Joseph Feldschuh (December 18, 1989), "AIDS and Ostriches: Business Is Not Facing Up to the Scourge," *Barron's* 69, no. 51, pp. 16–17, 26.

[70] Alan Emery (June 1989), "AIDS Strategies That Work," *Business & Health* 7, no. 6, pp. 43–46.

[71] James S. Redeker and Jonathan A. Segal (Spring 1988), "The Legal Ramifications of AIDS Discrimination," *Business & Society Review* 65, pp. 18–24.

[72] McDonald, "How to Deal with AIDS in the Workplace," p. 13.

[73] Edmonson, "AIDS and Aging," p. 30.

[74] Tom Pope (August 1990), "EAPs: Good Idea, But What's the Cost?" *Management Review* 79, no. 8, pp. 50–53.

[75] Cheryl Thieme (August 1990), "Better-Bilt Builds a Substance Abuse Program That Works," *Personnel Journal*, pp. 52–58.

[76] Linda Stern (May 1990), "Why EAPs Are Worth the Investment," *Business & Health* 8, no. 5, pp. 14–19.

[77] Bureau of Labor Statistics (June 1990), *Employee Benefits in Medium and Large Firms, 1989* (Washington, D.C.: U.S. Department of Labor), pp. 18–21.

[78] Douglas C. Harper (September 1988), "Why Health Care Costs So Much," *Personnel Journal* 67, no. 9, pp. 44–51.

APPLICATION CASE 19–1   Campus Foods Systems

. . . . .

As part of a master's program in food-services management, Cindy Breen has just begun her internship with Campus Food Systems (CFS). CFS is a self-operated university food-service department at Cindy's alma mater, Gulfport State College. As a department, CFS reports directly to the vice president of administration, the office generally responsible for nonacademic matters co-funded by the school. Self-operated food-service programs try to minimize loss rather than maximize profit. They are operated by employees of the institution, as opposed to contract operations run by professional management companies like Marriott Corporation and ARA Services, profit-making enterprises.

CFS employs about 60 full-time employees. In addition, the staff is supplemented by almost 100 students who provide part-time labor. Thus approximately 160 employees, largely part-time, are responsible for providing three distinct dining services to the Gulfport campus: Watkins Dining Hall (traditional cafeteria service for residents); Sea Breeze Cafe (fast-food service for students, faculty, staff, and guests); and Catering (a full range of catering services offered both on and off campus). A fourth function, Stores, orders, receives, inventories, and disburses food and nonfood supplies to the other three operations.

Cindy knows that most self-operated food-service programs are located at much larger universities. A small operation like CFS is always vulnerable to a takeover threat from large contractors like Marriot. Smaller schools are easy targets. Also, turnover in the administration makes the takeover threat stronger since Gulfport just changed presidents. President Sheila Dawes comes from a large university that used ARA to administer dining-room operations. Cindy's supervisor, Jake Platt, has told her that she must help him assure the new college president that CFS should remain self-operated.

Cindy has only been working at CFS for two weeks and Jake has just assigned her to manage the student help. Her responsibilities include interviewing, selecting, training, scheduling, and disciplining about 100 part-time employees. She also has been charged with preparing a report of Work Accidents in the Food Service Areas for the previous calendar year. This report will be sent to President Dawes and the Human Resource Department and forwarded to both state and OSHA agencies to comply with state and federal safety and health legislation. Jake has told her to minimize the severity of the occupational illness and accident report. He says that CFS can't afford to "inflate" these statistics. They might attract President Dawes's attention. Jake also hinted to Cindy that both her grade in the internship and a favorable job recommendation rested on how she handled the accident report. Some of the accidents Jake has asked her to minimize include the following:

- Bill Black, part-time employee, fractured and cut right hand when spring-loaded piston on food cart snapped back and caught his hand between the cart and a heavy loading cart door. Cindy has learned that Bill's injury has resulted in a permanent partial disability of two fingers.
- Leslie Campbell, Ophrah Moses, Cici Potts, Winne Chung and George Wilson all cut their hands on the same meat slicer at different times. Each accident was caused when another employee failed to replace the knife guard after cleaning it.
- Winston Knapp received burns on his face, chest, legs, and stomach when hot water splashed out of the steamer into which he had lowered a tray of hot food.

Jake also asked her to omit any accidents for which reports were not made to Human Resources at the time of the incident. So far, Cindy has documented 46 such incidents, ranging from a box falling on a student's head to severe cuts from broken glass and knives. But, Jake said not to worry. They were all student-employees who used their parents' health insurance to cover medical expenses.

Cindy is distressed by the number of accidents that have occurred during the previous calendar year at CFS. She has just reviewed Bureau of Labor Statistics for 1990 in her Restaurant Management

Written by Jean M. Hanebury, assistant professor of management, Perdue School of Business, Salisbury State University, Salisbury, Maryland.

class. Cindy knows that working in food service can be quite dangerous, but the number of accidents at CFS during the last year is about 20 percent more than other comparable small food-service operations. In addition she found many accidents had never been reported to the state.

Another problem with the incident reports Jake has supplied Cindy to compile her report is the fact that they fail to mention Rick James, the student-employee who contracted a severe case of salmonella poisoning from handling diseased seafood. Rich has just returned from a three-month hospital stay. He had been so ill that he had become paralyzed and at first was not expected to live. He missed almost a whole semester of school. Since Rick's illness, CFS has forbidden student-employees to handle raw seafood, but that rule has been frequently violated due to high absenteeism and turnover of full-time personnel.

Cindy sits contemplating what her sense of values tells her to do next. She has jotted down her alternatives:

1. Prepare the report as Jake has asked, with omissions.
2. Prepare the report, but include the incident reports.
3. Prepare the report including all incident reports, previously unreported accidents, and Rick's serious illness.
4. Go to Fred White, CFS Director and Fred's supervisor, and give him a complete report.
5. Send the complete report directly to President Dawes.
6. Call OSHA and ask them to come inspect UFS.
7. Leak the story to the student newspaper and the local press.

Discussion Question

What should Cindy do and why? Frame your answer in terms of a safe and healthy workplace.

20

WORK SCHEDULING
AND QUALITY OF WORK LIFE

· · · · · · ·

LEARNING OBJECTIVES

————⊖————

After studying this chapter, you should be able to:

· · ·

Define the traditional workweek, flexitime, permanent part-time employment, job-sharing, and the compressed workweek

· · ·

Describe why quality of work life programs are considered to be important for achieving organizational goals

· · ·

Explain why fatigue may be an especially troublesome problem with the compressed workweek

· · ·

Discuss some of the employee benefits derived from flexitime, part-time, and job-sharing schedules

· · ·

Distinguish between quality of work life and productivity

CAREER CHALLENGE

*T*he turnover of registered nurses at La Grange Community Hospital in La Grange, Illinois, had become epidemic. The hospital, located in a suburb of Chicago, employed over 450 nurses. Amanda Wilson was hired about six months ago as the hospital administrator. She noticed that the turnover at La Grange Community was higher than any other hospital of similar size in the area. Amanda assigned Jack Quenton, an in-house (hospital-employed) HR researcher, to examine the problem. Jack worked on the problem for about three months.

Last week, Jack submitted a report to Amanda. The report was based on a review of the hospital's HRM programs, what other hospitals in the area were doing in terms of HR programs, and exit interviews Jack had conducted with 30 nurses who had quit La Grange Community recently. As Amanda worked her way through the thorough report, she was especially astonished by the exit interview data. It showed that most of the ''leavers'' — the nurses who had quit — wanted a more flexible working schedule. They had objected to the standard eight-hour shifts.

The report recommended that La Grange Community immediately undertake a pilot experiment of instituting a flexitime working schedule in the medical-surgical wards. The experiment would run for one year, and then decisions about schedules in other units such as maternity, emergency, operating room, and intensive care would be made.

Amanda asked Jack to provide her with more details on nontraditional work schedules like flexitime. She wanted to see what others had done and whether flexitime could be used in nursing. The details Jack presented to Amanda are similar to the material covered in this chapter.

D espite a growing number of experiments to change the length and arrangement of the five-day, 40-hour workweek, it has remained a fixture in industry for over 40 years. Since 1940, the workweek has been relatively stable, despite a growing feeling that many people would derive more satisfaction from an increase in leisure time. The traditional work schedule remains: (1) five 8-hour days; (2) from 9 A.M. to 5 P.M.; (3) Monday to Friday; and (4) with a standard lunch hour and a few coffee breaks daily. During the past two decades, however, industry, government, education, and health-care institutions have become interested in new kinds of work schedules.

This chapter will examine a few of the newer schedules, namely flexitime (in which employees vary their starting and stopping time), part-time, work sharing (in which two workers share the job; for example, one works the morning, the other works the afternoon), and compressed workweeks (working less than five days, for instance, a four-day, 10-hour day schedule). HR departments are naturally involved in the decision making that goes into work scheduling. Specifically, HR specialists aid management in examining, implementing, and evaluating alternative work schedules. These HRM activities are extremely important in devising work schedules that contribute to improved morale, increased productivity, and enhanced leisure time gratification.

Breaking the traditional patterns of work scheduling for the sake of change is not the reason why newer work schedules are being considered by more and more organizations. They are being given serious consideration because in a number of experiments and settings they have been associated with improved end results — satisfaction, performance, and morale. This chapter will examine not only work scheduling, but also the kind of impact it is having on people and organizations. About 10 years ago, modified work schedules were a German import — foreign, different, and of questionable value. There are now about 9.5 million full-time workers in the United States using flexible work schedules and compressed workweeks, and an additional 11.8 million workers hold voluntary, permanent part-time jobs.[1] This constitutes about 20 percent of the entire labor force in the United States.

A survey of 521 of the largest U.S. corporations found that 93 percent offered some kind of alternative work schedule. The most common arrangement was part-time work; the second most common was flexitime. One fifth of the firms offer job-sharing, and a growing percentage — about 7 percent — offer work at home. About 33 percent of the companies offer compressed workweeks — a 40-hour week worked in fewer than 5 days.[2]

THE CHANGING WORK ENVIRONMENT

Changes and questions about work schedules are occurring at an accelerated rate in organizations. In this chapter, our focus is on work scheduling changes and questions that have been raised about scheduling practices. A few of these questions are:

- The standard five-day, 40-hour-a-week work schedule offers organizations consistency, ease of administration, and predictability. What does it offer the worker?
- Many workers report dissatisfaction with their jobs. Is a major contributing cause the lockstep work schedules they have?
- Most workers pour into cities and towns to their jobs, lemminglike, at the same time every morning, and then leave together every evening. The result is

clogged roads, jammed public transportation, and frayed nerves. Is there any way this type of clogging and jamming can be reduced?[3]

These facts of everyday living pose interesting challenges to HR specialists. The challenges and questions raised will be addressed by examining actual company use of new work schedules. Their answers will indicate that today's work environment is demanding changes in the traditional work schedules. The changes of expectations place a premium on improved management of organizational time and resources.

Worker's expectations about the job, the organization, and the family unit are different from those of a generation ago. Today, many workers are requesting jobs that have security, provide an acceptable level of earnings and fringe benefits, but also provide more autonomy, responsibility, and opportunity for self-development. The work ethic still exists, but there is now a request for increased self-dignity.

More and more workers claim that they would like to exchange some work time for more personal time. By personal time, they mean time for leisure, family, household tasks, and education. Time to develop hobbies and to enjoy the fruits of hard work.[4]

Family structures have changed dramatically in the past 10 years. The "traditional family" of husband (breadwinner), wife (homemaker), and two children has all but vanished. Only 7 percent of all family units fit this model.[5] In many families, both husband and wife work; there are also more single-parent families, and a large number of single people. Many of these trends create the potential for conflict between work (the job) and home (the family, leisure time).

Productivity pressures, increased competition, and a concern about treating people more fairly have also encouraged many employers to examine new work schedules. The concept of viewing workers as assets in accounting terms is gaining acceptance in more organizations.

Energy consumption and conservation are now regular agenda issues discussed by organizations. Ways to contain costs of heating, cooling, lighting, and operating offices and plants are constantly being examined. This examination includes paying attention to the impact of work schedules on energy costs.

A DIAGNOSTIC APPROACH TO WORK SCHEDULING

Exhibit 20–1 examines how work scheduling is affected by various factors in the environment. Work-scheduling decision makers must pay attention to external environment influences. The union in some cases has resisted changes in work scheduling. Unions have a disdain for tampering with overtime laws. It took the union time, patience, argument, and lobbying to gain the 8-hour day and the 40-hour week. Overtime work at a premium pay is something the union is fearful of losing with the move toward more part-time employment and compressed work-weeks.

Government legislation affects work schedules. In fact, the Walsh-Healy Public Contracts Act of 1936 and the Fair Labor Standards Act of 1938 were passed to reduce hours of work and encourage the spreading of work among unemployed people.

Economic conditions also play a role in work scheduling. Downturns, stagflation, and other conditions have resulted in an increase in part-timers and a decrease in the number of hours worked by full-time employees.

The goals of management also play a major role in work scheduling. Management may feel that work schedules can affect morale, satisfaction, and productivity; and,

EXHIBIT 20-1   Factors Affecting the Work-Scheduling Decisions

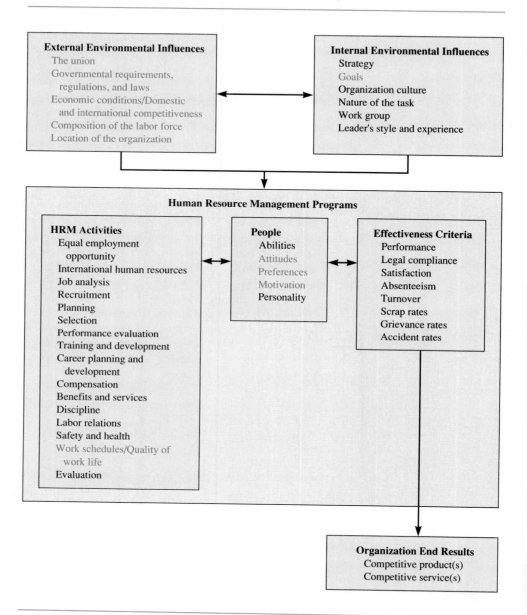

if so, managers would be inclined to experiment with scheduling. On the other hand, management may want a schedule that is easy to administer; in that case, it is best to stay with the traditional one. However, other workers may not prefer a nontraditional work schedule. Determining these preferences, attitudes, and motivations about work schedules is the responsibility of line managers and HR specialists. Implementing a changed work schedule without diagnosing what workers want and think is likely to be a costly, frustrating mistake.

EXHIBIT 20-2   Distribution of Men and Women Using Various Work Schedules

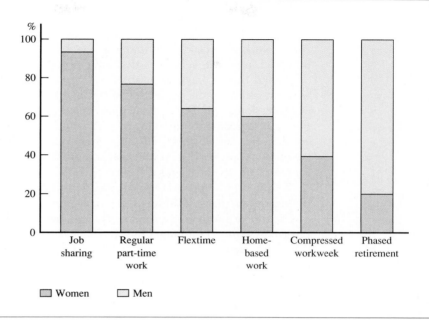

Source: Kathleen Christensen (July–August 1990), "Here We Go into the 'High-Flex' Era," *Across the Board*, p. 23.

Apparently, management needs to think about why women seem to be more enthusiastic about alternative work schedules than men. With the exception of the compressed workweek (working 40 hours in less than five days) and phased retirement, the alternative work schedules are pursued more by women.[6] Perhaps men still fear that some of these schedules might harm their image within the firm. Exhibit 20–2 shows the distribution of men and women using various forms of work scheduling in 1990.

LEGISLATION: THE GOVERNMENT

The union wants to protect its members from the exploitation that is possible through some of the modified work schedules. Most collective bargaining agreements require premium pay (usually time and a half) after eight hours of work in a day. In fact, the Fair Labor Standards Act requires overtime pay after 40 hours a week for employees in interstate commerce and public administration.

Many compressed workweek schedules call for 9, 10, 11, or 12 hours of work a day. It would be uneconomical for employers to pay overtime rates for those extra hours. Flexitime with fixed workdays of eight hours or less are no problem with labor unions. But when the flexitime schedule permits variable length days (8½, 9, 10 hours), the union often raises the issue of exploitation and the law.

HR specialists must consult and be knowledgeable about four federal statutes when considering changes in work schedules. The Fair Labor Standards Act of 1938 has already been presented. The Walsh-Healy Public Contracts Act requires overtime pay after eight hours a day for employees working on federal contracts of more than $10,000.[7] The Contract Work Hours and Safety Standards Act requires overtime pay after eight hours on federal construction contracts. The Federal Pay Act is applied to all nonexempt federal construction contracts. The Federal Pay Act is applied to all nonexempt federal workers. It requires overtime pay after 8 hours a day or 40 hours a week. These laws exempt many supervisory and professional employees who have been able to be placed on new work schedules. Many blue-collar workers would like to have the same scheduling opportunities, but are hemmed in by the very laws that have protected them for years.

Several unions have been able to accept changes in traditional work schedules without giving up the protection of the law. Local 21 of the International Federation of Professional and Technical Employees, at the request of its members, negotiated flexitime agreements in California. About 1,000 union members, all white-collar employees, were covered. The agreement was that: (1) the contract contain explicit language about workers' protection and provide an appropriate grievance procedure for overtime disputes, and (2) the employees must be held accountable for meeting their time requirements. One contract with Almeda County set up an 80-hour pay period rather than a 40-hour week or 8-hour day.[8]

Of course, even in situations that are nonunion, the laws must be followed regarding work scheduling. One challenge is to increase the flexibility of new work-scheduling alternatives without violating the law. Building in such flexibility will require more cooperation and agreement between labor and management. Agreement can only occur if the details and specifics of each work scheduling alternative are clearly understood.

FLEXITIME

Flexible work time (*flexitime* for short) is a schedule where employees are able to select their starting and quitting times within limits set by management.[9] A flexible schedule can differ in a number of ways: (1) daily versus periodic choice of starting and quitting time; (2) variable versus constant length of workday (crediting and debiting hours is allowed); and (3) core time — the management-imposed requirement of hours when all employees must be on the job. The different types of flexitime going from the least to the most flexible are:

Flexitour. Requires employees to select specific starting and quitting times, and work on the schedule for a specific period like a week or month. The work period is usually eight hours.

Gliding time. Variation in starting and quitting times is permitted, but work-day total is usually eight hours.

Variable day. Credit and debit of work hours are permitted (such as working 10 hours one day and 6 hours on another day), as long as the total hours worked are even at the end of the week (40) or month (160).

Maniflex. Credit and debit hours are permitted, and a core time is not required on all days. The core may be 10 A.M. until 2 P.M., Monday and Friday only.

Flexiplace. An employee can change the location of work as well as the hours — working at home, at satellite locations, and so on, are examples.

There are also many professionals, sales personnel, professors, and managers who set their own work hours informally who are not counted in the flexitime statistics.

Many types of jobs have converted to flexitime: they include bank tellers, accounting departments, engineers, keypunch operators, laboratory technicians,

EXHIBIT 20-3   Verser Engineering and Construction Company Flexitime Schedule
(Total for Workday Must Be Eight Hours)

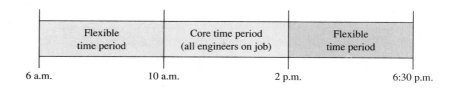

Flexible time period	Core time period (all engineers on job)	Flexible time period

6 a.m.   10 a.m.   2 p.m.   6:30 p.m.

nurses, data processors, nonexempt production workers, insurance clerks, and claim examiners. A directory of the users of flexitime has even been published.[10]

Flexitime is difficult to implement in production units with assembly lines and multiple shifts. In such units, it is impossible to have workers coming and going since work pace is largely machine controlled. Also, it is difficult to arrange flexitime for receptionists, retail sales clerks, bus drivers, or nurses (for example, operating room or intensive care units). In these cases, the job must be continuously covered, thus limiting the type of work scheduling.

In flexitime systems, there are two major time periods — **core work time** and flexible work time. During the core time period, all employees in a unit or group must be at work. The flexible time period is the hours within which the employee is free to choose whether or not to be on the job. There is, of course, the requirement that during a day a required number of hours must be worked. A typical flexitime schedule is shown in Exhibit 20–3 for Verser Engineering and Construction Co., a medium-sized firm that has used this schedule for over 14 years.

Some Benefits of Flexitime

The reported success rates of flexitime programs are impressive. Half or more of all user firms report economic improvements. Increased productivity, lower unit labor costs, and improved morale have been attributed to flexitime.[11] There are also benefits in less paid absence and idle time, increased morale, and less overtime pay (because of less absence and higher productivity).[12]

One study of a flexitime schedule found that the most dramatic improvement was the increase of satisfaction with the work schedule. Satisfaction with interactions and friends also increased for those employees in a utility company, management and nonmanagement, who were on a flexitime schedule.[13]

One might ask why there are productivity gains. Flexitime apparently increases the effective quantity of labor input. For example, if a car breaks down on the way to work, the worker can stay later to make up the lost time. The firm gets more hours of work and, therefore, more productivity for the same cost. Also, because many workers like flexitime, an employer may have an easier time recruiting workers that prefer this type of work schedule. Again, because of the match between work schedule and worker preference, there is likely to be less absenteeism and turnover, reducing costs and increasing productivity.

There is another potential benefit of flexitime in that the schedule could be matched with the person's biological clock. Some of us are morning people — we are more productive in the A.M. Others are afternoon or early evening people. Flexitime permits employers in many cases to set up work schedules that optimize worker productivity and take advantage of the workers' biological clocks.

Some Problems of Flexitime

Productivity gains, morale improvements, cost containment — it sounds so attractive that we may wonder why every organization doesn't have flexitime work schedules. The reason is that flexitime can cause some major problems. Supervisors have to change their procedures and even work harder at the outset to implement flexitime schedules. Consequently, many supervisors drag their feet and resist flexitime.

There is also the increased cost in some organizations of heating and cooling buildings for longer workdays. The regular day is from 9 A.M. to 5 P.M. A flexitime schedule may require the building or plant to be open from 6:00 A.M. to 7:30 P.M. The result is more energy expenses.

There is also the problem of using flexitime in only some jobs. While some workers are on flexitime, there are employees who are not able to have this kind of work schedule. What can happen is antagonism and jealousy across occupations between the "haves" and the "have-nots."

The publicity given flexitime in the popular press and management literature has been positive; yet, some workers do not prefer flexitime. How can they say *no* when everyone around them is saying *yes*? This is a question that is not easy to answer. However, it points out that the assumption that everyone wants to go on a flexitime schedule may not be correct. What is a benefit to one worker may be a threat or inconvenience to another.

Managing Flexitime

There are a number of guidelines for successfully managing flexitime work schedules. Top-management support is essential. Flexitime transfers some control over work from managers to workers. The top-management team must actively support this shifting of control. A climate of trust in the judgment of workers about their schedules is important. For example, if an honor system for checking in is used before flexitime is implemented, it would be a display of lack of trust if a formal sign-in, sign-out system is used after flexitime has been implemented. Top management has to encourage all levels of management to be supportive and trusting with flexitime schedules.

Another important guideline is to help the first-line supervisor. The job of this level supervisor gets more difficult with flexitime because he or she must: (1) still generate results, (2) balance the work schedules, (3) provide workers with some scheduling flexibility, and (4) plan further into the future. Thus, the first-line supervisor has fewer decisions to make about individual schedules, but still has responsibility to do the job. This responsibility is especially crucial in planning and coordinating activities.

A third management guideline is that supervisors should be trained to meet their new responsibilities and problems. The training should focus on what flexitime is, the supervisors' responsibilities, what research indicates about flexitime schedules, and some of the pitfalls to avoid. The supervisors need to understand a few important points that can be presented in training. They are:

Work schedule choices, responsibility, and authority need to be clearly communicated to workers.

. The design of flexitime schedules must be understood — core hours (when everyone must be present), day length, timekeeping methods, disciplinary procedures.

. Jobs may have to be redesigned in order for flexitime to work. Training could cover job redesign approaches.

The fourth management guideline is that flexitime, like other work scheduling programs, should be evaluated. The schedule should be evaluated in terms of productivity, morale, energy costs, and the overall climate of the organization. A cost/benefit framework can be used to examine the effects of flexitime. It may also be worthwhile from a public goodwill standpoint to include in the evaluation an analysis of flexitime's impact on transportation efficiency.

In Ottawa, the number of federal employees who started work during the heavy 30-minute peak rush-hour period dropped from 78 to 40 percent after flexitime was implemented. In Toronto, after a year of citywide flexitime, almost half of the downtown employees on flexitime schedules elected to travel outside the peak rush hour in the morning.[14]

Including a transportation analysis as part of the flexitime analysis can be important not only for city governments, but also for organizations. Those firms that take into consideration the impact of flexitime on transportation patterns and congestion can derive public relations benefits. For example, they could, by using flexitime where possible, help the entire city or area run more smoothly. In the future, citizens could associate social responsibility and flexitime scheduling when considering what an organization is doing for the community.

PART-TIME EMPLOYMENT

Part-time work includes all work demanding less than full time. The U.S. government counts people who work less than 35 hours a week as part-timers. For federal employees, 32 hours a week is the dividing line between full- and part-time work. Today, about 30 million workers are considered part-timers, or about 25 percent of the U.S. labor force.[15] Part-time jobs appear to be increasing 40 to 50 percent faster than full-time jobs.[16]

Two thirds of all part-timers are adult women. The next largest component, 25 percent, consists of teenagers. Part-time employment is especially prevalent in the fast-food industry, insurance, and banks. For example, 90 percent of the 250,000 employees of McDonald's fast-food restaurants are part-timers.[17] There are several kinds of part-time employees:

Permanent part-time employment. The job and the workers are expected to be part-time for a long time on a regular basis.

Job-sharing. Two or more part-timers share one job. The workers are part-time, but the job is full-time.

Working at home. Individuals decide that because of family responsibilities, personal preference, or lifestyle needs working out of the home is preferable to traveling everyday to an office. Information technology has enabled more and more individuals to stay connected with a firm via the computer. This kind of work arrangement can be part- or full-time.

Work sharing. A temporary reduction in working hours chosen by a group of employees during economic hard times. This is an alternative to being laid off.[18]

Temporary part-time employment. The worker is on a job only a short time (organizations such as Kelly Girls).

Phased retirement. Part-time employment selected by employees who are gradually changing from full-time to retired status.

Permanent part-time employment is quite common in wholesale and retail trade industries as well as in service industries. Although it is common, it is still largely unnoticed. Part-time employment works especially well where there are specific jobs to complete, independent projects such as insurance claims, and where the workload has a predictable cycle such as in banking traffic. On the other hand, part-time employment is not well suited for managerial jobs or where the work flow requires a worker to be continuously available.

An example of staffing an organization with a part-time work force is found at Control Data Corporation. The company wanted to allow mothers needing supplemental income the opportunity to work. A part-time work schedule was established. Control Data opened a bindery that would collate, bind, and mail computer manuals and documents to customers.[19]

The bindery runs from 6 A.M. to 10 P.M. with employees, mostly minority women from an economically depressed area of St. Paul, Minnesota, choosing a three-, four-, or six-hour shift. The choices were designed to fit the workers' needs. The plant employs female heads of households, handicapped people who cannot work full-time, and students. Workers are compensated the same hourly rate as full-time workers in comparable jobs at other Control Data plants, and fringe benefits are prorated proportionate to hours worked.

Supervisors work standard eight-hour shifts. However, it should be mentioned that almost all of the supervisors started as part-timers. As their home situations and career plans changed, they expressed interest and converted to full-time work when it was available.

The productivity per capita in this part-time staffed plant is much higher than at other plants of the firm. Profits are up, and employees appear to be committed and dedicated. Management also believes that there is less worker fatigue because of the shorter shifts.

Provident Bank of Cincinnati introduced an interesting solution to the need for part-time help.[20] The bank has time during the week when only two or three tellers, instead of five or six, are needed. The bank created a pay program that would make working part-time on Fridays and other peak times unusually attractive.

Provident insituted a peak-time workers program. These employees are those who do not want to work full-time and can afford to be without employer-provided benefits plans. A peak-time teller may be hired to work five hours per day for three days a week. However, his or her schedule may be five hours on Monday, three on Thursday, and seven on Friday.

One of the objectives of the Provident Bank peak-time pay programs is to reduce administrative expenses. Also, this type of program assumes that the part-time employees attracted to this type of system value their descretionary time and high take-home pay more than a holiday or permanent job.

Another example of part-time work involves what is being called the *flexible approach.* This is an available pool of people who are paid for working on a scheduled part-time basis.[21] The employees are paid either on a retainer basis or for work actually performed. The flexiforce can fill in the needs and respond to personnel needs on short notice. Retained older, experienced, and knowledgeable employees can serve as a firm's flexiforce.

Some Benefits of Permanent Part-Time Employment and Job-Sharing

Permanent part-time employment succeeds when it is used for a specific operating purpose. For example, when Occidental Life Insurance Company's business grew, management decided that it needed more than a single eight-hour shift of claims examiners, keypunch operators, and record clerks to process business. There was not enough work for a whole eight-hour second shift. The answer was to establish a part-time minishift that worked from 5 P.M. until 10 P.M.[22]

When Massachusetts Mutual Life Insurance Company had trouble recruiting full-time office employees, they established job-sharing. One employee worked from 9 A.M. to 2 P.M. (usually a mother with children in school), and the other worker came in from 2 P.M. to 5 P.M. (usually a student from a local college).

There may also be a more favorable attitude formed by part-timers toward the organization and its policies than found among full-time employees. One study examined the attitudes of part-time versus full-time employees toward various aspects of organizations: structure, trust, power, and job satisfaction.[23] The researchers found that full-time and part-time employees differed in their attitudes. Part-time employees had more favorable attitudes toward the organization and the distribution of power in the organization. Part-timers also reported higher levels of overall job satisfaction.

Since this is a study based on employees in only one organization and there are some methodological problems associated with it, such as low reliabilities, the results must be treated cautiously. There is a growing need for more full-time versus part-time employment research to determine empirically the benefits, costs, and problems associated with part-time scheduling.[24]

The main employer benefits of part-time and job-sharing scheduling are reduced labor cost, including less overtime. In addition, productivity is often higher, absenteeism and tardiness are lower, and (except for students), turnover is lower.[25] There is also the possibility that with part-timers there is less job fatigue caused by working on tedious, repetitive jobs. Thus, performance is better because workers complete jobs in shorter time spans.[26]

Some Problems with Part-Time Scheduling

A number of problems are associated with part-time employment. Management in some cases must examine and work out a plan to balance fringe benefits paid to part- and full-time employees. Not all fringe benefits can be prorated to time actually worked. This results in feelings of inequity by both part- and full-timers.

Although most part-timers have paid vacations, only about half get any group health or life insurance or pension plans. A major stumbling block is the health insurance (vacations and pensions can be more easily prorated). Companies are faced with paying $1,000 to $2,000 annually for health insurance for part-timers. Prorating health insurance premiums payments means that the insurance company agreement has to fit part- and full-time employees. It is extremely difficult to work out an equitable prorated basis.

One solution to the health insurance problem is to allow employees to select their mix of fringe benefits. As cited earlier in this text, this is called a *cafeteria benefit program*. Full- and part-time employees could choose from among the fringe benefits. The company's contribution to the cafeteria selection could be based on time worked (full or part). Another solution is the one described earlier used by Provident Bank in which peak pay is used to preclude paying any fringe benefits.

Labor unions pose another problem in part-time scheduling. Permanent part-time employment has been referred to as, "Another piece of bread in this dry sandwich of alternative work schedules."[27] Unions are reluctant to support part-time employment because it increases the competition for jobs during periods of high unemployment. The full-time employee more than the part-timer is a union member. Thus, union opposition is largely based on protecting the interests of its members.

There is also the belief that part-time workers are not interested in advancement opportunities. This is a stereotype that comes from part-time employment's association with low-level jobs, and the fact that women and students hold most part-time jobs. There are also some who feel that part-time work is not worthy or masculine. Among all permanent part-time workers, 70 percent are women. These stereotypes are difficult to overcome. The work ethic for decades has encouraged people to work full-time. This cultural barrier and the stereotype are slowly being overcome by the positive contributions made by part-time employees. Only through part-time or job-sharing schedules can many people work, earn an income, and make productive inputs into society. This message is slowly beginning to find its way to society.

Managing Part-Time Employment and Job-Sharing

A managerial concern of part-time employment and job-sharing is their potentially high labor costs. Some labor costs are fixed per employee. Since part-time employees work fewer hours than full-time employees, their hourly cost can be higher. Managers with the aid and guidance of HR specialists must develop a fringe benefit program that is fair to part-time and job-sharing employees. Unless this is done, the stereotypes and negative reactions directed toward part-time employment and job-sharing will continue.

Effectively managing various HR activities is also important in controlling costs for part-time and job-sharing work scheduling. Recruitment costs can be high for part-time employment because more people have to be recruited and regular recruitment methods are not suited to finding part-timers and job sharers is attractive enough to retain them as employees. There are also specialized part-time and job-sharing placement companies that may be able to provide services to the organization.

Supervision of part-timers can be costly. The part-time employee is not on the job as much as the full-time employee. Thus, if self-starting, self-motivated part-timers can be attracted, the costs of supervision can be reduced or at least controlled within acceptable limits.

It also makes sense in terms of HRM to treat part-time and job-sharing employees as important human resources. Fair treatment, equitable compensation, and opportunities for job-involved decision making are important steps in making part-time and job-sharing acceptable and attractive types of work schedules.

Job-sharing presents a number of special kinds of management problems: (1) matching the workers as partners and then with the job; (2) encouraging and rewarding cooperative work efforts; (3) deciding the specific work schedule; and (4) encouraging communication between partners. If employers initiate job-sharing, it is very important for the organization to thoroughly analyze the jobs and the prospective partners. The employer's role and involvement are especially important in determining work schedules and creating a supportive atmosphere for the job sharers to work as a team. Even when job-sharing arrangements are initiated by workers, there is a distinct need to maintain open communication and cooperation. Instead of balancing the needs and preferences of a single employee and the job, management must balance the needs and preferences of two employees and the job.

COMPRESSED WORKWEEKS

The **compressed workweek (CWW)** is a work schedule in which a trade is made between the number of hours worked per day, and the number of days worked per week, in order to work the standard number of hours.[28] The CWW can be: (1) four days of 10 hours each — 4/40; (2) three-day workweeks often about 12 hours each day — 3/36; (3) four-and-one-half-day workweeks with four 9-hour periods and one 4-hour day; and (4) a work weekend of two 12-hour days, paid at premium rates.

Some Benefits of Compressed Workweeks

The regular utilization of facilities is a benefit of the CWW. There are fewer start-ups if a four- or three-day schedule is used. However, if a business plant, office, or facility must be open at least five days, the CWW causes some job coverage problems.[29] In situations where employers are able to cut utility and overhead costs by closing on the fifth day, the CWW offers cost savings.

There have been a few research studies that indicate that the morale of CWW workers is higher and paid absences lower than workers under standard work schedules.[30] In a quasi-experimental study in a manufacturing facility, a 25-month investigation was conducted. The study examined satisfaction, absenteeism, and performance of 4/40 workers versus 5/40 workers. At the end of the 13-month period of the study, workers on the 4/40 work schedule were more satisfied with job conditions, experienced less anxiety-stress, and performed better than did the comparison 5/40 workers. However, these benefits were not found at the 25-month data point.[31] It was concluded that the 4/40 may have a short-term impact, but that long-term benefits must be questioned and examined more closely.

The Utah State Office of Education undertook an experimental implementation of the compressed workweek,[32] in which the plan was made available at the discretion of employees. Entire divisions elected to remain on standard schedules, while others made a number of optional schedules available on an individual preference basis. The most popular optional schedule was a 4/40. The most improvement among employees in terms of increased morale and productivity were found among those individuals who elected to work the 4/40 schedule. Unfortunately, the productivity improvements were based solely on self-ratings and should be accepted cautiously.

The traditional 5/40 workweek has been under attack in the nursing profession. Because nursing care of hospitalized patients is a seven-day, 24-hour responsibility, nursing has not been one area of CWW popularity. This lack of popularity seems to be changing. The list of hospitals using CWWs is increasing yearly. The CWW schedules for nurses include a 7/70 at Valley Medical Center in Fresno, California, a

7/56 at Baptist Medical Center-Montclair in Birmingham, Alabama, a 2/16 week-end plan at Women's Hospital in Houston, and a 4/40 at University Hospital in Seattle.[33]

The evaluation of these nurse work-scheduling programs has been conducted by in-house researchers. The results suggest lower staff turnover, reduced overtime, less absenteeism, and improved job satisfaction. There are a number of critics who remain unconvinced about the impact of the CWW. Some feel that nurses on flexitime schedules tend to stand out as an elite group, and this will eventually decrease morale. There is also the issue of fatigue. Nurses working more than eight hours are prone to more errors. An error in nursing can be a life or death matter.[34]

Some Problems with Compressed Workweeks

Labor laws and union contracts often specifically address the issue of working more than eight hours a day. Overtime rates usually have to be paid for a more than eight-hour workday. Collective bargaining has to specifically cover this issue.

One union agreed to a 3/36 plan for 400 full-time employees of the Meredith Corporation printing plant in Des Moines, Iowa. It was decided in labor-management discussions that the printing presses cannot be run on the basis of five-day workweeks. They had to be operated all seven days, but this would be too demanding on employees and their families. The solution was to assign a fourth crew where there were previously three. The company also created two 12-hour shifts per day. This allowed the continuous operation of the presses. One crew works Monday to Wednesay, and the other works Thursday to Saturday. Sunday work is alternatively divided between the crews. The Sunday work is paid at double time. This system is given credit for production improvement and absenteeism decreases.[35]

A problem with CWWs is that fatigue often affects performance. Working 10-, 11-, or 12-hour days in any job can be very tiring. Not only can performance suffer, but there is the probability of increased accident frequency. A tired worker often inadvertently becomes more lax with regard to health and safety practices. A mistake of a machine operator can cause injury, while an error by a nurse can cause life-threatening problems.

The CWW does not have the flexibility of a flexitime work schedule. The person who must work a compressed schedule may find that his or her life and personal time become more complicated. Those workers with child-rearing obligations may have a special set of problems working a 3/36 or 4/40 schedule. They may have to be away from home during times that their children are not in school.

Unlike flexitime and part-time employment, the CWW does not give workers any more freedom of choice. Preferring the CWW schedule in order to stay away from work in larger blocks of time is not a positive vote for this type of schedule. It is more of a job avoidance vote.

Managing Compressed Workweeks

An important part of implementing the CWW is the matching of workers' schedules with the necessary operating schedule. Customers, clients, and others dealing with an organization expect timely service. When a person goes to the store to purchase a product at midday, on, say, a Friday, she expects the store to be open for business. Management needs to carefully work out a coverage plan when using CWW schedules.

There is also the need to pay close managerial attention to the fatigue associated with longer workdays. Fatigue is a serious problem as each study reporting on the impact of the CWW has shown.[36] Not only can fatigue result in a decrease in effectiveness, it can be harmful to the tired worker, co-workers, and even commuters who will be on the road with the worker. It is management's responsibility to examine more closely the consequences of the longer workday on fatigue. There may well be an increase in legal action brought by workers who claim that the CWW and especially the fatigue caused by it precipitated family, personal, and job-related problems. Certainly, management would be implicated in such cases.

QUALITY OF WORK LIFE

An important concern of managers is the **quality of work life (QWL)** of employees. Specifically, they are concerned with how the QWL affects the productivity of organizations, the morale and well-being of employees, and how it can be improved to help accomplish meaningful organizational and individual goals. The meaning of the QWL is elusive since different interpretations have been offered.[37] To some, *QWL* refers to industrial democracy or increased worker participation in decision making. To some, the term is employee involvement or labor-management "jointness" as it is called in the auto industry.[38] To others, *QWL* refers to a set of interventions intended to improve productivity. There are also some who believe that *QWL* means the application of methods to humanize the work of employees.

A comprehensive interpretation of the meaning of *QWL* was developed by Walton.[39] He suggested eight categories that when examined in total indicate what is meant by *QWL*. The categories are:

1. Adequate and fair compensation for hard working, performing employees.
2. A safe and healthy work environment.
3. A job that permits an individual to develop his or her skills and knowledge.
4. Opportunities to grow and develop on the job, while also having job security.
5. A sense of feeling like a team that is helpful and encouraging to one's self-esteem.
6. A work environment that distributes rewards equitably, permits personal privacy, and tolerates dissent.
7. A job that encourages a person to schedule and take personal time for family and leisure activities.
8. An organization that is socially responsible and one that the employee is proud to be working for.

Each interpretation of QWL focuses on the individual employee. Therefore, *QWL* is defined here as the degree to which employees are able to satisfy their needs, goals, and aspirations while performing their jobs and working with colleagues.

A unique interpretation of quality of work life is provided by Marriott Corporation. The firm conducted a number of internal surveys to determine how important family services were to employees. The results indicated that they were extremely important. Thus, Marriott created a work and family life department.[40] By helping

PROFESSIONAL PROFILE

Betty Bessler
Mary Kay Cosmetics

Biography

Betty Bessler, vice president of human resources, joined Mary Kay Cosmetics, Inc., in 1975 to establish a personnel function in the manufacturing division of Mary Kay. Prior to joining Mary Kay, she was personnel manager of Liquid Paper Corporation, where she established the corporate personnel function.

Ms. Bessler earned a bachelor's degree from the University of Dallas and has done graduate work in business at the University of Dallas and Southern Methodist University. She also attended Harvard University's executive development program in human resource management. She is a member of SHRM, Dallas Human Resource Management Association, and the Dallas Human Resources Roundtable. She currently serves on the board of Girls Incorporated of Metropolitan Dallas, and was one of 50 women selected for the 1983 Leadership Texas program.

Job Description   Ms. Bessler has responsibility for employment, employee relations, compensation and benefits, management and employee training and development, and security. She supervises a staff of 50. She serves on the executive committee, the operating committee, the profit sharing committee, the compensation committee, and the customer service steering committee of Mary Kay.

Employee Involvement: A Viewpoint   Employee involvement and participation are critical to survival in the 90s. Creative action teams, or CATs as they are called at Mary Kay, bring employees together from different work areas and levels to solve problems, create solutions, and develop new products and programs. Currently, over 60 CATs are working throughout the company on everything from glamour shade-name brainstorming to a more environment-friendly packing material. One CAT that Ms. Bessler is personally working with is a group of parents of preschool children working on ways Mary Kay Cosmetics can better meet the needs of working parents. From the recommendations made by this group, the company will be implementing a parental leave policy, a reduced waiting period for STD, a latch-key children's message center, an allowance for time off for children's medical appointments, and an internal child-care referral network. The human resources division will also be working with supervisors on allowing more flexibility to help families and single parents meet the challenges that result from combining career and family responsibilities. Having not only the input from this task force but allowing them to make presentations to key executives has won the support for and approval of these "working family" benefits enhancements throughout the company. Employee involvement works because people support what they help create.

employees manage their lives, Mariott was convinced it would lead to better customer service, a better-managed business, and long-term employee loyalty. The new department has been responsible for an on-site day-care center for employees at its Washington, D.C., headquarters, a child-care discount program, a family seminar series, a pretax family care spending account, a home work program, and a newsletter.

Quality of Work Life and Productivity

Quality of work life and productivity are independent. Management can improve the QWL by reducing the demands made on employees, by slowing down assembly lines, and by increasing the amount of paid time off given to employees. The result would, in most cases, be reduced productivity.[41]

Why isn't it always possible to improve QWL and productivity at the same time? The answer is that some misunderstandings about work and people exist. First, there is an assumption that improving QWL results in immediate productivity gains. Simply permitting or asking workers to participate in decision making is not always interpreted accurately. An employee who has never participated before is reluctant to change his or her behavior.[42]

Second, there is an assumption about a simple cause/effect linkage. That is, improvements in the QWL lead to higher productivity. Whether improvements occur are contingent on a whole list of factors — the employer's attitudes, how the group perceives the improvements, how the improvements are introduced, and how patient management is in waiting for results.

Third, managers often forget about how the technology, employees, and rituals of a firm interact. Again, the complexities and realities of organizational life result in uncertainty, anxiety, and barriers for the successful introduction of QWL improvements.

QWL improvements may take a long time to show productivity gains. The use of QWL improvements should not be viewed as a ''quick fix.'' Any QWL improvements used must be linked to the overall strategic plan of the company and given sufficient time to yield results. It is the patience of managers that is rigidly tested by most QWL programs. Meager productivity gains are often the incentive for discarding or minimizing the QWL effort.

Quality of Work Life Programs

There are a wide array of QWL programs that have been offered, implemented, and evaluated in organizational settings. There are worker participation programs, job design programs, alternative work schedule programs, and employee security programs. The job design approach is covered in Chapter 6, the alternative work schedule programs are covered in the present chapter, and employment security programs are covered in Chapters 15 and 19. Thus, only worker participation programs will be developed at this point.

Worker Participation Programs

Such prominent behavioralists as Argyris, Bennis, and Likert have encouraged managers to permit more worker participation in decision making.[43] Sashkin claims that employee participation is not only effective but that its use is an ethical imperative.[44] Instead of considering worker participation as an ethical imperative it seems more realistic to examine how it is used and where it is successful.

Rocco, Inc., is a privately held poultry company headquartered in Harrisburg, Virginia. The company's corporate mission emphasizes that employee participation will be emphasized in conducting all aspects of the business.[45] This was interpreted by Human Resource Manager Barbara Ward to mean helping each employee to fully participate. Unfortunately, Ms. Ward and other Rocco managers concluded that too many employees couldn't participate because their literacy skills were inadequate.

Unless employees' reading and writing skills were improved, they couldn't fully participate and would be held back in promotions. First, Rocco hired tutors to provide instruction. Because of the distance between each of the Rocco plants, a system that would work in all locations was needed. Hiring tutors, finding appropriate classrooms, and other obstacles slowed down the literacy improvement project. A committee of Rocco employees and James Madison University professors prepared an application for a U.S. Department of Education grant. The funds were used to hire a director, teachers, and a curriculum specialist and to purchase instructional material. A mobile learning center was constructed. Memos, videos, and communication letters about the program were sent to employees. The video helped bring the literacy problem into the open.

To date, 60 Rocco employees have been in the program; 46 people are either in the program or have graduated. A total of 16 participants have passed the GED examination, which is required in lieu of a high school diploma. The Rocco literacy improvement program is an example of one firm that wants its employees to participate in all phases of management. The company is committed to the improvement of the quality of life of its employees on and off the job.

Joint Union Management   QWL efforts have been used with some success. Unions have power to influence various company decisions through contract negotiations and grievance handling. Joint union-management QWL programs can be used to address concerns and problems not spelled out in the collective bargaining agreement. A study in a large midwestern utility examined the impact of a joint union-management QWL program. Three different teams were established.[46] In Team A, a steering committee of managers and union representatives was established. Team B was a team of functional managers and the union steward. The third, Team C, was a problem-solving group of the supervisor and union steward along with volunteers from rank-and-file employees.

All three teams received training in group-process skills and problem-solving skills. Each team addressed problems faced by employees (such as workflow, work schedule, redesign of the job and work area). Each team addressed issues that they considered to be a problem.

Results indicated a significant increase within all three QWL groups in perceptions of the union rank-and-file contribution in improving the job. The rank and file believed that they have more influence and say about their jobs. The majority of union members, no matter what team represented them, were favorably predisposed toward union involvement in joint QWL efforts. Whether these same results can be replicated in other organizations, unionized and nonunionized, needs to be further examined.

Quality Circles   **Quality circles** (QCs) have been used in QWL programs. A quality circle is a small group of employees and their supervisor from the same work area, who voluntarily meet on a regular basis to study quality control and productivity problems. The group attempts to identify problems, to solve them, and to monitor the implementation of their solutions.[47]

Quality circles are popular in U.S. and Japanese firms. QCs in Japan give specific attention to statistical quality control issues and often meet on their own rather than on company time. A bonus for improvements of QCs in Japan is based on the performance of the entire organization.

QCs in the United States create a parallel organizational structure.[48] They operate independently from the existing organizational structure. Lawler and

EXHIBIT 20-4   Phases of a Quality Circle's Life

Phase	Activity	Destructive forces
Start-up	Publicize	Low volunteer rate
	Obtain funds and volunteers	Inadequate funding
	Train	Inability to learn group-process and problem-solving skills
Initial problem solving	Identify and solve problem	Disagreement on problems
		Lack of knowledge of operations
Approval of initial suggestions	Present and have initial suggestions accepted	Resistance by staff groups and middle management
		Poor presentation and suggestions because of limited knowledge
Implementation	Relevant groups act on suggestions	Prohibitive costs
		Resistance by groups that implement
Expansion of problem solving	Form new groups	Member-nonmember conflict
	Old groups continue	Raised aspirations
		Lack of problems
		Expense of parallel organization
		Savings not realized
		Rewards wanted
Decline	Fewer groups meet	Cynicism about program
		Burnout

Source: Edward E. Lawler III and Susan A. Mohrman (January–February 1985), ''Quality Circles after the Fad,'' *Harvard Business Review*, p. 67.

Mohrman identified six stages in the growth and decline of quality circles. Exhibit 20–4 presents these stages.

Some organizations assign major responsibilities to QCs. Toyota, for example, assigns over 90 percent of customer complaints to its circle for problem-solving solutions. At the Western Electric Plant in Shreveport, Louisiana, suggestions made by one QC about work scheduling are reported to have saved over $500,000.[49]

Lockheed and Honeywell were among the early adopters of QCs in the United States. Lockheed adopted them in the 1970s for use in missile manufacturing projects. Honeywell also adopted them in the 1970s and is still using them as a major example of an organizational change toward embracing participative management.

Critics of quality circles caution managers about simply adopting them without weighing some possible problems.[50] Lawler and Mohrman report that QCs have life cycles that must be understood. The initial enthusiasm carries the group for some time. However, there are issues such as false expectations, cynicism about the QC's impact on the QWL, and burnout about meeting every week that need to be considered. QCs appear to, at least initially, make employees feel better about their job. This, in turn, apparently leads to improved attendance and less turnover for QC participants. However, what about the nonparticipants? Individuals not in QCs may resent the fact that participants are meeting four times a month and being paid, while the nonparticipants are still working. Considering the potential benefits and costs of implementing a QC program is an important consideration for managers.[51]

Employee-Centered Work Redesign   Without abandoning the successful team methods in QCs and traditional management-directed work redesign, the employee-centered approach involves the individual worker in creative decision making.[52] Employee-centered work redesign emphasizes total accountability. In redesigning the job, the employee must be able to justify how the changes will improve quality and support the organization's mission. Employees also must be able to justify how their job redesigns will give them greater job satisfaction and an opportunity for personal growth.

Employee-centered work redesign was first introduced at several southern California community hospitals. Since this introduction, surveys indicate that it has been effective in reducing turnover, improving morale, and improving quality of work. Exhibit 20–5 illustrates some of the employee and organizational benefits associated with employee-centered work redesign.

New Design Plants   **New design plants** have been constructed by such firms as H.J. Heinz, Rockwell, Mead, and Cummins Engine.[53] These plants reflect interest in worker participation in the form of an organizational effort to increase the employees' say about work, rewards, knowledge exchange, and power sharing. In the design and construction of these facilities, employees participate in the decisions made about the layout of machinery, equipment, and the recreational areas of the plant. There is also an attempt to have employees help develop jobs that are challenging, motivating, and satisfying. It is because of this type of worker participation that these plants are referred as *new design plants*.

The equality of employees is stressed in many new plants. General Motors carefully planned the constitution of a plant in Troy, Michigan.

At General Motors Corporation's new Saturn headquarters in Troy, Michigan, everybody will be equal. But the office design firm GM hired to furnish the new building didn't quite believe that.

Saturn managers told the firm, which GM won't name, that the furniture and carpeting in every office had to be exactly the same grade and quality — no special treatment for the executives. But the design company ordered special furniture and decoration for Saturn's eight top officials anyway. "More expensive desks, credenzas, lamps, ashtrays, the whole shot," says a GM employee.

EXHIBIT 20-5   Employee-Centered Work Redesign

Critical Factors	Employee Benefits	Organizational Benefits

• Strong commitment from management to the program to ensure success.
 • Teamwork between employees and their managers to redesign work functions.
 • Organizational benefit in one or more of the following areas:
   1. Work productivity.
   2. Work quality.
   3. Cost containment.
 • Demonstrate positive impact on staff and existing systems.
 • Hands-on problem-solving format.
	• Career and professional growth opportunities realized within the organization.
	 • Increased employee job satisfaction.
	 • Employees gain insights into the organization.
	 • Opportunity to contribute to organizational goals.
	 • Employees learn to communicate their needs, concerns, and interests.
	 • Broaden organization prospective.
	 • Promote career growth opportunities.
	 • Access to information.
	 • Identify critical skills.
		• Greater use of employees.
		 • Tap into employee skills, knowledge, and creativity.
		 • Increased productivity and improved quality.
		 • Reduced employee turnover.
		 • Employees become stakeholders, not jobholders, in the organization.
		 • Increased accountability leads to cost-effective behavior.
		 • Promote positive work attitude to discourage employee grievances.
		 • Support cooperative teamwork between employees and management.

Source: Stephen L. Perlman (November 1990), "Employees Redesign Their Jobs," *Personnel Journal*, p. 38.

Saturn officials stuck to their principles: They cancelled that part of the order. Not taking the "executive" furniture saved the company more than $1 million.[54]

The HR department is usually much more important in new design plants than in traditional ones. Many of the typical HRM tasks such as selection and pay administration are assigned to participative work teams. The HRM unit doesn't ignore these tasks but works to help the teams accomplish the various activities. Although the HRM unit works less on traditional tasks, they are more involved than usual on job design issues.

An important reason for the effectiveness of the new design plants is the central role played by the plant's self-managing work teams.[55] These work teams are given the responsibility for such areas as quality, selection, inventory, and production scheduling. Building effective self-managing teams appears to take years. The teams need constant monitoring, reviewing, and, in many cases, renewing. Exactly how to build effective teams is an inexact science. The necessary training, the amount of autonomy, the size, and the role managers are to play with the teams are not exactly known. Thus, experimentation continues in attempting to locate the right or the best mix so that effective self-managing work teams become excellent in all phases of accountability, creative problem solving, and productivity.[56]

The benefits of the four worker participation programs just covered—joint union-management committees, quality circles, employee-centered work redesign, and new design plants—may not only be economic ones. In some cases, improved self-esteem, job satisfaction, and organizational commitment are important results. In general, worker participation programs are initially positively perceived by participants. However, the benefits of such enthusiasm may be short-term, if management holds false expectations and attempts to impose participation on a skeptical,

CAREER CHALLENGE

(concluded)

Amanda finished her reading on the subject of new work schedules and was interested in flexitime. She believed that it could work in some units, but was still skeptical about the use in other units. For example, in intensive care, full-time coverage is important and vital. She also wondered whether providing scheduling alternatives for some nurses and not others would increase the turnover rate even more. Despite these concerns, she was willing to experiment with flexitime on a limited basis. She called Jack Quenton, the HR manager, the supervisor of nursing, and two nursing supervisors to start the process of setting up the experiment.

untrained, and undermotivated work force. The worker participation QWL programs like the other attempts at improving the life and experiences of participating employees can be successful in improving productivity and morale. However, there is simply not enough evidence available to declare QWL programs as always being successful. In some cases, successes can be documented while, in other cases, pinpointing production, attitudinal, or other improvements are not possible.

SUMMARY

A major change occurring in the workplace is the willingness of union leaders, managers, and workers to experiment with various work schedules and to work toward the improvement in the quality of work life. Today, the traditional five-day, 40-hour workweek is followed by most people. However, this chapter shows that HR specialists and managers are becoming more and more involved with nontraditional work schedules. There is also interest in taking steps to help employees satisfy their needs and goals while working on the job.

To summarize the major points covered in this chapter:

1. The work environment, workers' scheduling preferences and expectations, and demographics are changing. Now, people are beginning to question the economic, social, and personal value of working a five-day, 40-hour, Monday to Friday schedule. These questions and many experiments indicate that there are alternatives.

2. Part-time work is the most popular alternative to the traditional work schedule, and flexitime is the second most popular alternative.

3. Part-time employment means working less than 35 hours a week in private industry and less than 32 hours a week in the federal government. Twenty-two million Americans, mostly women and teenagers, are part-time employees.

4. Flexitime schedules can differ on many dimensions — for example, variable versus constant length of workday, when the worker must be present, and even the location of where the work takes place.

5. Data indicate that about 11.9 percent of all full-time wage and salary workers are on flexible schedules.

6. Job-sharing is a form of part-time employment in which two or more part-timers share a full-time job. This is especially convenient for employees with special personal challenges, such as child rearing or going to school while working.

7. The compressed workweek (CWW) is a schedule in which a trade is made between the number of hours worked per day and the number of days worked per week. Thus, instead of a five-day, 40-hour (5/40) schedule, people may work 4/40, 3/36, 7/70, and so forth.

8. There are numerous interpretations of what the quality of work life is. It is defined here as the degree to which employees are able to satisfy their needs, goal, and aspirations while performing their jobs.

9. Quality of work life efforts include job design programs, worker participation programs, alternative work-scheduling arrangements, and employee security programs.

10. Worker participation programs have appeared in the form of joint union-management teams, quality circles, employee-centered work redesign, and new plant designs. Some of the research suggests that these programs can improve morale and productivity.

KEY TERMS

compressed workweek (CWW)	755	job sharing	751
core work time	749	new design plants	762
flexible work time	748	quality circles	760
flexible work time	749	quality of work life (QWL)	757

QUESTIONS FOR REVIEW AND DISCUSSION

1. Would job-sharing be a solution to problems of layoffs in the steel and automobile industry? Why?

2. What is the difference between employee-centered work redesign and management-directed work redesign?

3. Why would a young worker prefer to work part-time?

4. Does working part-time pose a threat to the cultural tradition of being employed full-time? Explain.

5. Why is job-sharing significantly more popular among women than among men?

6. Why does the traditional five-day, 40-hour workweek still remain the predominant work schedule in the United States and Canada?

7. Why would managerial support be so important at the start of using flexitime scheduling?

8. What are some potential limitations and problems associated with quality circles?

9. It is stated that quality of work life and productivity are independent. What does this mean?

10. Can the new plant designs be used in nonmanufacturing situations? Explain.

NOTES

[1] Amy Saltzman (1991), *"Downshifting, Reinventing Success on A Slower Track* (New York: Harper Collins), p. 83.

[2] Kathleen Christensen (July–August 1990), "Here We Go into the 'High-Flex' Era," *Across the Board*, p. 22.

[3] Stanley D. Nollen (April 1980), "What Is Happening to Flexitime, Flexihour, Gliding Time, the Variable Day, Permanent Part-Time Employment, and the Four-Day Week?" *Across the Board*, p. 6.

[4] Paul Blyton (1985), *Changes in Working Time: An International Review* (New York: St. Martin's Press).

[5] Jennifer McEnroe (February 1991), "Split-Shift Parenting," *American Demographics*, pp. 50–52.

[6] David A. Ralston (August 1990), "How Flexitime Eases Work/Family Tensions," *Personnel*, pp. 45–48.

[7] Richard I. Henderson (1985), *Compensation Management* (Reston, Va.: Reston Publishing), p. 68

[8] Stanley Nollen and Virginia Hider Marten (1978), *Alternative Work Schedules* (New York: AMACOM).

[9] Many interesting examples of flexitime scheduling can be found in Stanley Nollen (1981), *New Work Schedules in Practice: Managing Time in a Changing Society* (New York: Van Nostrand Reinhold).

[10] (1978), *Alternative Work Schedule Directory* (Washington, D.C.: National Council on Alternative Work Patterns).

[11] David A. Ralston, William P. Anthony, and David J. Gustafson (May 1985), "Employees May Love Flexitime, But What Does It Do to the Organization's Productivity?" *Journal of Applied Psychology*, pp. 272–79, and Stanley D. Nollen (September 1979), "Does Flexitime Improve Productivity?" *Harvard Business Review*, pp. 12, 16–18, 22.

[12] C. W. Proehl, Jr. (October 1978), "A Survey of the Empirical Literature on Flexible Work Hours: Character and Consequences of a Major Innovation," *Academy of Management Review*, pp. 837–53.

[13] Randall B. Dunham and John L. Pierce (April 1983), "The Design and Evaluation of Alternative Work Schedules," *Personnel Administrator*, pp. 67–75.

[14] Nollen, *New Work Schedules in Practice*, p. 23.

[15] Daniel Forbes (October 1987), "Part-Time Work Force," *Business Month*, pp. 45–47.

[16] Richard S. Belous (March 1989), "How Human Resource Systems Adjust to the Shift toward Contingent Workers," *Monthly Labor Review*, pp. 7–12.

[17] Judith L. Ennis (March 1985), "Temporaries," *Personnel Journal*, pp. 97–99.

[18] Fred Best (1980), *Work Sharing: Policy Options and Assessments* (Kalamazoo, Mich.: Upjohn Institute for Employment Research).

[19] A.R. Cohen and H. Gadon (1979), *Alternative Work Schedules: Integrating Individual and Organizational Needs* (Reading, Mass.: Addison-Wesley Publishing), pp. 100–101.

[20] Stuart J. Maklin and Julie Charles (November 1984), "Peak-Time Pay for Part-Time Work," *Personnel Journal*, pp. 60–65.

21 Robert C. Ford and Ken Jennings (December 1984), "The Case for Flexiforce," *Personnel Journal*, p. 80.

22 Nollen, "What Is Happening?" p. 14

23 Bruce J. Eberhardt and Abraham B. Shani (December 1984), "Full-Time versus Part-Time Employment Status on Attitudes toward Specific Organizational Characteristics and Overall Job Satisfaction," *Academy of Management Journal*, pp. 893–900.

24 Nancy L. Rotchford and Karlene H. Roberts (April 1982), "Part-Time Workers as Missing Persons in Organizational Research," *Academy of Management Review*, pp. 228–34.

25 Kim Watford (April 14, 1986), "Shorter Workweeks: An Alternative to Layoff," *Business Week*, pp. 77–78.

26 Ethel B. Jones and James E. Long (Fall 1979), "Part-Week Work and Human Capital Investment by Married Women," *Journal of Human Resources*, p. 18.

27 John Zalusky (Summer 1977), "Alternative Work Schedules: A Labor Union View," *Journal of the College and University Personnel Association*, p. 42.

28 Simcha Ronen and Sophia B. Primps (January 1981), "The Compressed Work Week as Organizational Change: Behavioral and Attitudinal Outcomes," *Academy of Management Journal*, p. 61.

29 Richard E. Kopelman (Spring 1986), "Alternative Work Schedules and Productivity: A Review of the Evidence," *National Productivity Review*, pp. 150–65.

30 L. W. Foster, J. C. Latack, and L. J. Reindl (1979), "Effects and Promises of the Shortened Work Week," paper presented at the 39th annual meeting of the Academy of Management, Atlanta, Georgia.

31 For the 13-month study, see John M. Ivancevich (1974), "Effects of the Shorter Workweek on Selected Satisfaction and Performance Measures," *Journal of Applied Psychology*, pp. 717–21; for the 25-month study, see John M. Ivancevich and Herbert L. Lyon (February 1977), "The Shortened Workweek: A Field Experiment," *Journal of Applied Psychology*, pp. 34–37.

32 David E. Nelson (June 1983), "Employee Control Is an Important Option in Variable Work Schedules," *Personnel Administrator*, pp. 118–23.

33 Elmina M. Price (June 1981), "Seven Days On and Seven Days Off," *American Journal of Nursing*, pp. 1, 142–43; and (June 1981), "The Demise of the Traditional 5/40 Workweek?" *American Journal of Nursing*, pp. 1138–41.

34 Suzanne LaViolette (March 1981), "Shortage Spurs Flurry of Flexitime Experiments," *Modern Health Care*, p. 42.

35 (January 1981), "Union Agreement Gives Workers 3-day Week, 4-day Weekends," *Management Review*, p. 31.

36 Phillip J. Hubek and Donald J. Petersen (March 1985), "Arbitration and the Shortened Work Week: No Easy Answers," *Personnel*, pp. 8–10.

37 John Nirenberg (June 1986), "The Quality of Work Life Issue: The Corporation as the Next Political Frontier," *International Journal of Manpower*, pp. 27–36.

38 John Hoerr (July 10, 1989), "The Payoff from Teamwork," *Business Week*, pp. 56–62.

39 R. W. Walton (Fall 1973), "Quality of Working Life: What Is It?" *Sloan Management Review*, pp. 11–21.

40 (January 1991), "Quality of Life," *Personnel Journal*, p. 50.

41 J. Lloyd Suttle (1977), "Improving Life at Work — Problems and Prospects," in *Improving Life at Work*, ed. J. Richard Hackman and J. Lloyd Suttle (Santa Monica, Calif.: Goodyear Publishing), p. 9.

42 Barry A. Stein (1983), *Quality of Work Life in Action* (New York: American Management Association).

[43] Edwin A. Locke, David M. Schweiger, and Gary P. Latham (Winter 1986), "Participation in Decision Making: When Should It Be Used?" *Organizational Dynamics*, pp. 65–79.

[44] Marshall Sashkin (Spring 1984), "Participative Management Is an Ethical Imperative," *Organizational Dynamics*, pp. 4–22.

[45] Patricia L. May (October 1990), "Back To Basics," *Personnel Journal*, pp. 63–69.

[46] James W. Thacker and Mitchell W. Fields (1987), "Union Involvement in Quality-of-Worklife Efforts: A Longitudinal Investigation," *Personnel Psychology*, pp. 97–111.

[47] Phillip C. Thompson (1982), *Quality Circles* (New York: American Management Association).

[48] Keith Bradley and Stephan Hill (Winter 1987), "Quality Circles and Managerial Interests," *Industrial Relations*, pp. 68–82.

[49] (1985), "The Changing American Workplace: Work Alternatives in The 80's," *An AMA Survey Report* (New York: American Management Association).

[50] Edward E. Lawler III and Susan A. Mohrman (Spring 1987), "Quality Circles: After the Honeymoon," *Organizational Dynamics*, pp. 42–54.

[51] Edward E. Lawler III (1986), *High Involvement Management* (San Francisco: Jossey-Bass).

[52] Stephen L. Perlman (November 1990), "Employees Redesign Their Jobs," *Personnel Journal*, pp. 37–40.

[53] Ibid., p. 170.

[54] (August 2, 1985), "Saturn's New Plant," *The Wall Street Journal*, p. 1.

[55] Edward E. Lawler III (Fall, 1990), "The New Plant Revolution Revisited," *Organizational Dynamics*, pp. 5–14.

[56] J. Richard Hackman, ed. (1990), *Groups That Work* (San Francisco, Jossey-Bass), p. 5.

APPLICATION CASE 20–1   Toyota: One Firm's Concept of Quality of Work Life
. . . . .

At a management conference in Houston, a Japanese executive told a large U.S. audience that the Japanese auto industry is so far ahead of the Americans that the United States will never catch up. The emphasis was on the word *never*. Firms like Toyota and Honda use all their skills to keep getting better and better. Although the Japanese are noted for improving production and inventory procedures, it is the area of quality of life for all employees that they are working extra hard. In fact, the concept of *kaizen*, which means continuous improvement, applies to all aspects of Toyota's strategy, plan, and objectives.

In 1926, Sakichi Toyoda established the Toyoda Automatic Loom Works in central Japan to produce a loom he invented. Prior to his death in 1930, he sold the rights to his invention and gave the proceeds to his son, Kiichero Toyoda, to begin an auto business. In 1933, Toyoda opened an automotive department within the loom works and began copying U.S. engine designs. When protectionist legislation (1936) improved prospects for Japanese automakers, Toyoda split off the car department, and, for clarity in spoken Japanese, changed its name to Toyota. Today, Toyota has 40 percent of Japan's domestic market and is the second largest non-U.S. company and the world's third-largest maker of motor vehicles behind General Motors and Ford.

Toyota has eliminated layers of management, reduced staff, reorganized product development, and is talking more and more about the quality of work life of Toyota employees. Toyota is also pushing for more global outreach. Toyota is number 1 in Southeast Asia, is now making inroads in Latin America, and is getting ready to charge into Europe. Toyota has opened up its plants to outsiders. The new aggressiveness and openness are intended to humanize Toyota more than it ever has in the past.

The management of new Toyota models is now headed up by a chief engineer who has a broad range of responsibilities. The chief is in charge of everything associated with the car: The physical dimensions, the engineering and production, the suppliers, and the marketing decisions are all under the control of the engineer. Now, the chief engineer position is considered one with a wide power base and almost unlimited decision-making latitude.

Teamwork is emphasized in Toyota plants. The teamwork begins in the work of the chief engineer with the product and manufacturing engineers. The emphasis is on building the very best car and giving the customers what they want. Each worker on the line serves as the customer for the process just before his or hers. He or she becomes a quality control inspector. If a piece or assembly is not exactly right, it is not accepted. The team backs each person's decision to not accept poor quality work.

Toyota, like all employers in Japan, faces a shortage of skilled labor because of slowing population growth and a national reluctance to import workers. Thus, Toyota is attempting to enrich all jobs by making work a creative endeavor. Workers and managers work together to eliminate the three D's of automobile manufacturing: dangerous, dirty, and demanding work. Toyota is also investing $770 million over the next four years to improve worker housing, add dining halls, and build new recreational facilities. About 24,000 Toyota employees in Japan live in company-subsidized housing.

Toyota employees are being retrained to work with less supervision, accept more responsibility, and advance prospects along more quickly. New training, a new emphasis on quality of work life, and a new concern about how employees make decisions are what Toyota means by improving the culture and effectiveness of employees.

Discussion Questions

1. Does the Toyota quality of work life philosophy focus on the individual employee? Explain.

2. What in Toyota's changes appears to be an attempt to humanize the work of employees?

3. How can Toyota evaluate whether their quality of work life efforts have been successful?

Sources: Alex Taylor III (November 19, 1990), "Why Toyota Keeps Getting Better and Better and Better," *Fortune*, pp. 66–79; Gary Hoover, Alta Campbell and Patrick J. Spain (1990), *Profiles of Over 500 Major Corporations* (Emeryville, Calif.: Reference Press), p. 537.

EVALUATING THE HRM FUNCTION

· · · · · · ·

LEARNING OBJECTIVES

After studying this chapter, you should be able to:

· · ·

Define the evaluation of the HRM function

· · ·

Describe the difference between functional and dysfunctional turnover

· · ·

Explain why HR managers must have diagnostic skills

· · ·

Discuss the purposes served by evaluating the activities and programs of the HRM unit

The setting is a massive conference room. The top managers of General Products, a large manufacturing company in Seattle, are participating in the annual planning meeting. Each functional vice president presents the department's budget for next year, after a review of the past year's accomplishments.

After Emily Park, vice president for marketing, completes her budget request, her advertising budget for the next year is cut, with the explanation that "profits are down at the plant."

Denton Major, vice president for HRM and organization planning, speaks next.

Denton Well, folks, I'm not going to take much of your time. It's been a long day. You know what we do for the company. We hire, train, and pay the employees, provide benefits, counsel, help with discipline, EEO, and so on.

HRM is not asking for any major increases. My budget is simply last year's budget adjusted upward 6 percent for inflation. Any questions?

Emily Wait a minute, Denton. My budget just got cut. Here you come asking for 6 percent more than last year. I suppose we have to have an HR department. But why shouldn't my advertising budget be increased and your budget cut? After all, advertising brings in customers and helps us make money. What *specifically* does HRM do for our profit and loss statement? How *specifically* does HRM help us reach our goals of growth and profitability?

Emily has unknowingly pointed out what purpose a personnel audit serves. If Denton had been systematically evaluating the HR department, he would have some answers ready. And it looks like he will need some good ones, or the HRM budget and activities could well be cut.

$\boxed{T}$ here is an old motto in HRM that, if you can't measure it, forget it. The premise of this saying is that, if you can't show what contribution you are making, there is little hope that anyone will pay attention to your requests. Therefore, measurement in terms of evaluation is a high priority need in any HRM unit. For that matter, showing a contribution in any unit in an enterprise should be a top priority.

Evaluation of the HRM function, the human resource management audit, is defined as a systematic, formal experience designed to measure the costs and benefits of the total HRM program and to compare its efficiency and effectiveness with the organization's past performance, the performance of comparable effective enterprises, and the enterprise's objective. Evaluation of the activities and programs of the HRM unit is performed for these purposes:

- To justify HRM's existence and budget.
- To improve the HRM function by providing a means to decide when to drop activities and when to add them.
- To provide feedback from employees and operating managers on HRM effectiveness.
- To help HRM make a significant contribution to the organization's objectives.

Top management's part in the HRM audit is to insist that all aspects of the organization be evaluated and to establish the general philosophy of evaluation. The HR department is often involved in designing the audit. In part, the data for the audit arise from the cost/benefit studies of the HRM activities as described in Chapters 3 to 20. A variety of methods can be used to conduct audits, including interviews, questionnaires, observations, or a combination of these.[1] The operating manager's role is to help gather the data and to help evaluate the HRM function in the same way it evaluates other functions and users of resources in the organization. An evaluation program can be useful in improving the quality of the programs and services provided by an HRM unit.[2]

Evaluation of the HRM function is a Stage II activity—many researchers have advocated its implementation, but only a few good empirical studies of effective and ineffective ways of evaluating or auditing HRM activity have been done.

In one study, a panel of experts drawn from management, unions, human resource managers, and employees was asked to determine the most important HR department activities.[3] Exhibit 21–1 presents the results of the study.

This study also identified the criteria that were considered to be the best indicators of an HRM unit's efforts in an organization. The list of criteria suggest that the satisfaction of the managers and people using HRM services and programs is extremely important. See Exhibit 21–2.

The results from this and other studies point to the need for an HRM unit to pay attention to the needs and interests of multiple constituents.[4] In fact, Tsui—in conducting the research—refers to her study as a multiple constituency approach. Managers, employees, and executives are constituencies that the HR department is serving.

A DIAGNOSTIC APPROACH TO EVALUATION OF THE HRM FUNCTION

As emphasized in each chapter, a diagnostic approach to HRM practices is considered to be a feasible and informative method. This approach actually encourages the evaluation of the HRM unit and its activities. Exhibit 21–3 shows the factors in the

---

EXHIBIT 21-1   Selected Important HRM Department Activities

1. Provide advice and counsel to management on individual employee problem identification and solution (e.g., deal with adverse or difficult personnel situations such as absenteeism).
2. Communicate to management the philosophy, legal implications, and strategy relating to employee relations.
3. Ensure consistent and equitable treatment of all employees.
4. Administer grievance procedure according to policy (identify and analyze problems, review deviations and exceptions, resolve problems).
5. Provide advice and counsel to management on staffing policy and related problems.
6. Coordinate the hiring procedure (establish starting salaries, send offer letters, follow up to obtain acceptance, administer medical questionnaires).
7. Communicate compensation/benefits programs to management (interpret/explain compensation policies and procedures, inform management of legal implications of compensation practices).
8. Process benefits claims (health, workers' compensation, pension, unusual or unique claims).
9. Assist management in resolving salary problems involving individual employees (salary equity issues).
10. Ensure compliance with federal and state fair employment practices.
11. Communicate sexual harassment policy and other communications of general EEO philosophy and objectives.
12. Keep up with HR programs developed at the corporate or central HR departments.

EXHIBIT 21-2   Twelve Most Meaningful Criteria for Evaluating the Effectiveness of the HR Department

Subjective criteria.

1. Level of cooperation from HR department.
2. Line managers' opinion of personnel department effectiveness.
3. Degree to which the department is open and available to all employees to deal with problems or explain company policies.
4. Employees' trust and confidence in the personnel department.
5. Quickness and effectiveness of responses to each question brought to the HRM department.
6. Rating of quality of service provided by the personnel department to other departments.
7. Rating of quality of information and advice provided to top management.
8. Satisfaction and dissatisfaction of clients—managers and employees.

Objective criteria.

9. Degree to which the department has a strategy to support local management business plans in relation to human resources.
10. Affirmative action goal attainment.
11. Average time taken to fill requisitions.
12. Efficiency—personnel department budget/population served.

---

diagnostic model that affect evaluation of the HRM function in an organization. A major factor in determining whether evaluation takes place is the orientation or attitudes of the controlling interest—the top-level executives—toward evaluation and the organization's style.

EXHIBIT 21-3   Factors Affecting the Evaluation of the HRM Function

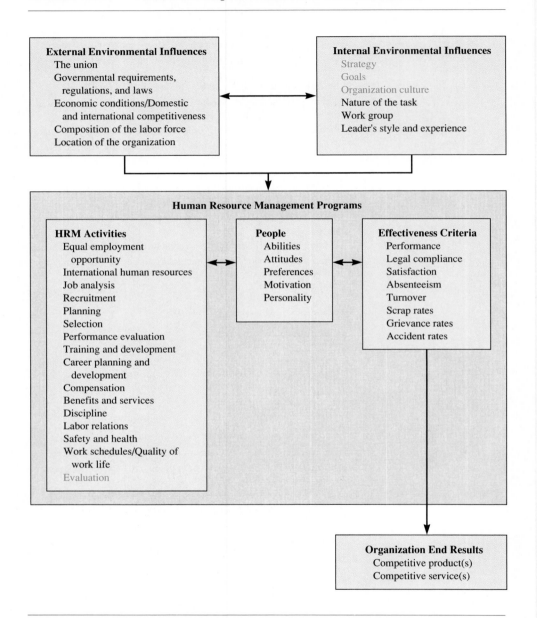

Some managers and HR researchers believe that formal evaluations of such human resource criteria as output measures, lost time, turnover, and ratings of performance are very useful. Others do not favor them.[5] Formal evaluations of the function are more likely to be conducted in some types of organizations than others. Larger organizations that are labor intensive and geographically dispersed probably have some type of evaluation for most functional departments, including HRM. Such programs are also more likely when economic conditions are bad, particularly for profit-oriented organizations, because they can establish the cost effectiveness of such functions.

The evaluation of the effectiveness of HRM programs is needed to determine how healthy the overall organization is in accomplishing its mission and goals. Evaluation serves as a unifying force in that it focuses attention on crucial factors such as performance, satisfaction, turnover, and absenteeism. Without an evaluation philosophy and theme, the various HRM programs are treated in a fragmented fashion. Staffing experts focus on securing the best new hires. The compensation specialist's concern is having a competitive pay system. The training expert works to create a learning and development atmosphere. Each of these areas is important for the well-being of the organization, but there is often little effort at integrating the various activities. The attempt to evaluate each of the HRM programs separately and together as a collective set of what the HR department is doing fosters a unifying spirit. The success or failure of HRM is considered in terms of the unit, not as an individual phenomenon.[6]

APPROACHES TO EVALUATION OF THE HRM FUNCTION

Once it has been decided that it is useful to evaluate the effectiveness of the HRM function and the organization's use of human resources, the next issue is how it should be done and what measures or criteria of effectiveness should be used. The criteria can be grouped as follows:

1. Performance measures.
   a. Overall HRM performance. For example, the unit labor costs per unit of output.
   b. HR department costs and performance — the cost per employee of HRM programs.
2. Compliance measures.
   a. Compliance with legal requirements such as minimum wages, privacy, termination at will, workers' compensation, EEOC, and OSHA.
3. Employee satisfaction measures.
   a. Employees' satisfaction with their jobs.
   b. Employees' satisfaction with HRM activities such as training programs, pay, benefits administration, and career development communication programs.
4. Indirect measures of employee performance.
   a. Employee turnover — rate of quits as a percentage of the labor force and by units over time.
   b. Absenteeism — rate of voluntary absences of the labor force and by units over time.
   c. Scrap rates (poor quality output that must be scrapped).
   d. Other measures of quality.
   e. Rates of employee requests for transfer.
   f. Number of grievances per unit and in total labor force over time.
   g. Safety and accident rates.
   h. Number of improvement suggestions per employee over time.

Each of these measures — or some combination of them — expresses the efficiency and/or effectiveness of the HRM effort. To make HRM worthwhile, it is necessary for the organization to measure its achievements against specific goals, such as:

Reduce labor costs by 3 percent this year.

Reduce absenteeism by 2 percent this year.

Increase the satisfaction index by 5 percent compared to last year's attitude survey results.

These goals are set relative to past trends, current achievements of other relevant organizations, or higher aspiration level of today's managers.

Once these criteria are set, the next decision is to determine which of the approaches to evaluation is to be used. In this chapter, we will examine some of the more frequently used approaches to evaluation of the HRM function. A full examination is beyond the scope of this text.[7]

EVALUATION BY CHECKLIST

One approach is to review and analyze the practices of organizations that are considered to be effective in terms of HRM policies and practices. This is usually implemented by developing a checklist of the model organization's HRM activities. Checklists are also used by consultants to analyze an organization's HRM function.

In the checklist approach to evaluation, the HR department or a consultant prepares a list of important HRM activities to be performed. The checklist usually requires the analyst to check yes or no columns beside the listed activity. The checklist may also include items designed to determine if exising HRM policies are being followed. The items on the checklist are usually grouped by HRM activity area, such as employment planning or safety and health. Exhibit 21–4 presents a sample of checklist items that would stimulate discussion and debate among managers about HRM activities.

Although a checklist is better than a totally informal approach, it still is a rather simple approach to evaluation. And even though checklists provide a format that is relatively easy to record and prepare, scoring interpretation is quite difficult. Three *no*s in one group of items may not equal three others. Some of the policies are more important than others. Ignoring EEOC or OSHA rules is a lot more negative than the absence of a winter holiday party, for example.

STATISTICAL APPROACHES TO EVALUATION

The most frequently used formal evaluation methods are those that examine the work organization's employment statistics and analyze them. The statistical approach can be much more sophisticaed than checklists. The statistics gathered are compared to the unit's own past performance or to some other yardstick of measurement. Of course, quantitative factors alone never explain or evaluate anything by themselves. The *reasons* for the statistics are the important thing; statistics only indicate where to begin to look for evaluation problems.

The raw data of such reports are interesting themselves, and they can provide some input to evaluation. Most organizations that perform evaluation, however, analyze these data by the use of ratios and similar comparative methods. Exhibit 21–5 provides a list of such ratios and similar analytical methods. Once these and similar ratios are computed for an organization, they can be compared to similar organizations' ratios.[8]

The statistical approaches used most frequently consider turnover, absenteeism, grievances, attitude surveys and other measures of effectiveness, and statistical analysis of the HR department itself. Because of the widespread organizational review of these statistics, they were selected for inclusion in this chapter.

EXHIBIT 21-4   HRM Audit: An Illustration
(An Interview with the Operating Manager)

---

1. What would you say are the objectives of your plant?
2. As you see it, what are the major responsibilities of managers?
3. Have there been any important changes in these over the last few years in the plant?
4. Are there any personnel responsibilities on which you think many managers need to do a better job?
5. What are some of the *good* things about employee relations in this plant?
6. Do you feel there are any important problems or difficulties in the plant? Causes? How widespread? Corrective measures?
7. Do you have any personnel goals for the year?
8. Overall, how well do you feel the personnel department does its job? Changes the department should make?

Community relations
9. What are managers expected to do about community relations? Is there plant pressure? Reaction to pressures?
10. What have you done about community relations? Do you encourage subordinates to participate in them? What are your personal activities?

Safety and medical
11. Who is responsible for safety in your area? Role of group leaders and lead men?
12. What things do you do about safety? Regular actions? Results achieved?
13. Do you have any important safety problems in your operation? Causes? Cures? How widespread?
14. What does the specialist do? How helpful are his activities? Other things he should do?
15. Are there any other comments or suggestions about safety you would like to make?
16. Have you any comments about the dispensary? Employee time involved? Types of service offered? Courtesy?

Communication
17. How do you keep your people informed? What are your regular communication activities? Particular problems?
18. How do you go about finding out information from employees? Channels and methods? How regularly are such channels used? How much information is passed on to employee superiors? How much interest do supervisors show? Does personnel provide information?
19. Has the personnel department helped improve communication in the plant? What assistance is needed? Nature of assistance provided?
20. Has the personnel department helped you with your own communication activities?

Communication channels available
21. What improvement is needed in these?
22. Are there any other comments about communication you'd like to make? Any changes or improvements you'd especially like to see?

Manpower planning
23. What kind of plans do you have for meeting the future manpower needs of your own component? Indicate plans for hourly, nonexempt. How far do plans extend into the future?
24. What does your manager do about planning for future manpower needs? How is this planning related to your own planning?
25. What part does the personnel department play in planning for the future manpower needs of your component? Of the plant as a whole?

Human resource development
26. How is the training of employees handled in your group? (on-the-job training) Who does? Procedures followed?
27. What changes or improvements do you think should be made in the training of employees? (on-the-job training) Why?
28. What changes or improvements do you feel are needed in the amount or kind of classroom training given here? Why?
29. Have you worked with your subordinates on improving their current job performance? Inside or outside regular appraisal? Procedure? Employee reaction? Results? Improvements needed?
30. Have you worked with subordinates on plans for preparing for future job responsibilities? Inside or outside regular appraisal? Procedure? Employee reaction? Results? Improvements needed?
31. What does personnel do to help you with your training and development problems?
32. Do you have any other comments on personnel development or training?

EXHIBIT 21-4   *(concluded)*

Personnel practices

33. How are employees added to your work group? New employees for example. (*Probe:* Specify exempt, nonexempt, hourly. Procedure followed? How are decisions made? Contribution of personnel? Changes needed and reasons? Transfers?)

34. How is bumping or downgrading handled? (*Probe:* Specify nonexempt or hourly. Procedure followed? How are decisions made? Contribution of personnel? Changes needed and reasons?)

35. How are promotions into or out of your group handled? (*Probe:* Specify exempt, nonexempt, hourly. Procedure followed? How are decisions made? Contribution of personnel? Changes needed and reasons?)

36. Do you have any problems with layoffs? (*Probe:* Nature of problems? Possible solutions? Contribution of personnel?)

37. How do you handle "probationary" periods? (*Probe:* Specify hourly, nonexempt, exempt. Length of period? Union attitude? How handled?)

38. How are inefficient people handled? (*Probe:* Specify hourly, nonexempt, exempt. How do you handle? How do other supervisors handle? Frequency?)

Salary administration — Exempt

39. What is your responsibility for exempt salary administration? (*Probe:* Position evaluation? Determining increases? Degree of authority?)

40. How do you go about deciding on salary increases? (*Probe:* Procedure? Weight given to merit? Informing employees? Timing?)

41. What are your major problems in salary administration? (*Probe:* Employee-centered? Self-centered? Plan-centered?)

42. Has the personnel department assisted you with your salary administration problems? How? (*Probe:* Administrator's role? Nature of assistance? Additional assistance needed and reasons?)

Salary administration — Nonexempt

43. What is your responsibility for nonexempt salary administration? (*Probe:* Nature of plan? Position evaluation? Changes needed and reasons?)

44. How has the personnel department helped in nonexempt salary administration? (*Probe:* Specify personnel or other salary administrators. Nature of assistance? Additional assistance needed and reasons?)

Source: Reprinted by permission from "Auditing PAIR," by Walter R. Mahler, in *ASPA Handbook of Personnel and Industrial Relations*, ed. D. Yoder and H. Heneman, pp. 2–103. Copyright © 1979 by The Bureau of National Affairs, Inc., Washington, D.C. 20037.

Evaluation of Turnover

Turnover is the net result of the exit of some employees and entrance of others to the work organization. Turnover can be quite costly to an employer. One estimate is that it costs U.S. industry $11 billion a year.[9] The costs of turnover include: increased costs for social security and unemployment compensation; terminal vacations; severance pay; underutilized facilities until the replacement is hired; employment costs, such as recruiting ads and expenses, interview time, test costs, computer record costs, and moving expenses; and administration costs of notification and payroll changes. Obviously, there is also a loss of productivity until the new employee reaches the performance level of the one who left the job.

Average monthly turnover rates for the 1990 period presented were 1.0 percent of the work force in the Bureau of National Affairs' survey. The bar graphs in Exhibit 21–6 show turnover averages by size of firm or industry, and region of the country.[10]

All turnover is not a net loss, however. Employees who are not contributing to organizational effectiveness should be retrained or dehired. The employer has no

---
EXHIBIT 21-5   HRM Evaluation Ratios

Effectiveness Ratios
   Ratio of number of employees to total output — in general.
   Sales in dollars per employee for the whole company or by organizational unit (business).
   Output in units per employee hour worked for the entire organizational unit.
   Scrap loss per unit of the organization.
   Payroll costs by unit per employee grade.
Accident Ratios
   Frequency of accident rate for the organization as a whole or by unit.
   Number of lost-time accidents.
   Compensation paid per 1,000 hours worked for accidents.
   Accidents by type.
   Accidents classified by type of injury to each part of the body.
   Average cost of accident by part of the body involved.
Organizational Labor Relations Ratios
   Number of grievances filed.
   Number of arbitration awards lost.
Turnover and Absenteeism Ratios
   Attendance, tardiness, and overtime comparisons by organizational unit as a measure of how well
   an operation is handling employees.
   Employee turnover by unit and for the organization.
Employment Ratios
   Vacations granted as a percentage of employees eligible.
   Sick-leave days granted as a percentage of labor-days worked.
   Military leaves granted per 100 employees.
   Jury duty leaves granted per 100 employees.
   Maternity leaves granted per 100 employees.
   Educational leaves granted per 100 employees.
   Personal leaves granted per 100 employees.
   Employment distribution by chronological age.
   Employment distribution by length of service with organization.
   Employment distribution by sex, race, national origin, religion.
   Managerial distribution by chronological age, sex, race, national origin, religion.
   Average age of work force.
   Average age of managerial work force.

---

control over some types of turnover. A student's husband or wife, for example, may work until graduation and then move away.

There are several quantitative methods for computing turnover. Some of the traditional formulas are:

$$\text{Separation rate} = \frac{\text{Number of separations during the month}}{\text{Total number of employees at midmonth}} \times 100 \qquad (1)$$

$$\text{Quit rate} = \frac{\text{Total quits}}{\text{Average working force}} \times 100 \qquad (2)$$

$$\text{Avoidable turnover} = \frac{\text{Total separations} - \text{Unavoidables}}{\text{Average work force}} \times 100 \qquad (3)$$

Formula 1 is the most general and is the one recommended by the Department of Labor. Formula 2 tries to isolate a difficult type of turnover. Formula 3 is the most refined; it eliminates quits by unavoidables, those groups that can be expected to leave: part-timers and women leaving for maternity reasons. These data can be

---

EXHIBIT 21-6   1990 Turnover Rates: 12-Month Average

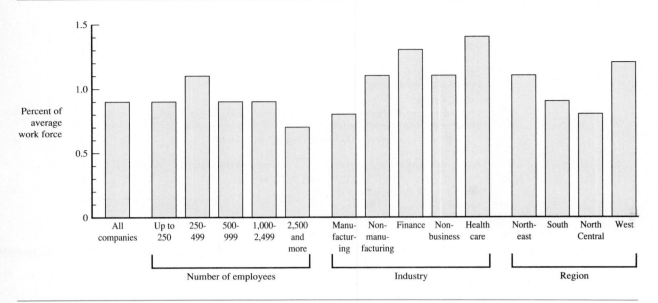

Source: *BNA's Quarterly Report on Job Absence and Turnover, 4th Quarter, 1990* (1991), (Bureau of National Affairs).

refined further by computing turnover per 100 employees by length of employment, by job classification, by job category, and by each organizational unit.

One BNA study found that 57 percent of the organizations surveyed computed the data in such a way as to analyze turnover by department or division. This is more likely to be done in large businesses and nonmanufacturing firms than in other types of organizations. Organizations that include all employees in the calculation (67 percent) could determine the differences in turnover by employee groups. In one recent year, the average turnover was 4.2 percent, but the rate in one organization was as high as 38 percent.[11]

One way employers analyze the turnover rate is to compare the organization's rate with those of other organizations. Various sources publish average turnover rates quarterly or yearly. These include agencies such as the government labor departments, the Administrative Management Society, and the Bureau of National Affairs, who publishes quarterly reports on turnover and absenteeism. Another approach is to analyze the enterprise's turnover by comparing the differences in rates by employee classifications or departments.

Most theories of turnover maintain that employees leave their jobs when their needs are not being satisfied at their present place of work *and* an alternative job becomes available that the employees believe will satisfy more of their needs. An excellent and informative effort at explaining and discussing the turnover process is that offered by Mobley and Mobley, Griffeth, and Meglino.[12] They suggested, empirically tested, and supported the view that job attitudes are extremely important in the decision to leave an organization. The research work indicates that the intention to quit is a significant predictor of actual quitting behavior. Mobley's theory of the importance of job attitudes has been tested and cross-validated with workers in various occupations — clerical, nursing, and manufacturing.[13]

CAREER CHALLENGE

(*continued*)

Denton applied some quantitative formulas to acquire a better picture of the General Products turnover situation. Here is what he found:

$$\text{Separation rate} = \frac{\text{Average for last six months}}{\text{Total number of employees at midmonth}} \times 100$$

$$= \frac{397}{9{,}000} \times 100$$

$$= \underline{4.4\%}$$

$$\text{Quit rate} = \frac{\text{Total quits}}{\text{Average working force}} \times 100$$

$$= \frac{318}{8{,}750} \times 100$$

$$= \underline{3.6\%}$$

$$\text{Avoidable turnover} = \frac{\text{Total separations} - \text{Unavoidables}}{\text{Average work force}} \times 100$$

$$= \frac{397 - 94}{8{,}750} \times 100$$

$$= \underline{3.5\%}$$

He looked at these figures and compared them to figures that he had on two of the main competitors in the Seattle area. He found that General Products' rates were significantly lower than those of the competitors. This data would help him build a case for HRM's contribution to General Products the next time he had to fight for budget dollars.

One organizational researcher has suggested that levels of turnover are often overstated.[14] He suggests that some turnover is beneficial or functional. This is the case when a person wants to leave the organization and the management is unconcerned about the loss. This lack of concern may be due to the poor evaluation of the person's performance or a lack of ability. If researchers add this type of turnover to what is called *dysfunctional turnover*, the number of leavers is overstated. Dysfunctional turnover occurs when a person leaves an organization and the firm wants to retain the person.

Dalton contends that the traditional analysis of turnover (especially Formulas 1 and 2 in this chapter) disregards the organizational benefits of functional turnover. Even with functional turnover there are some costs — recruitment, training, and a portion of the administrative overhead.[15] Consequently, HR researchers should consider separating dysfunctional and functional turnover.

Analysis of a large number of studies examining the interrelationships between turnover and absenteeism shows that, in general, these factors are interrelated.[16] That is, if turnover is high, absenteeism is also likely to be high. These studies also found that both were caused by the same factors. In general, employees first exhibited high absenteeism, which led to high turnover. Thus, absenteeism and turnover are not alternative methods of showing dissatisfaction. Rather, high absenteeism is a sign that high turnover is likely in the future.

Overall, organizations try to reduce turnover by a number of methods: better employee selection, orientation, communication, supervisor training, incentive awards, and data analyses. In addition, many organizations have tried to determine why their turnover takes place. One method is to interview employees just before they leave the enterprise to try to determine why they are leaving. This is called an *exit interview*. Some find exit interviews unreliable and not useful. Others contend that, properly done, they are reliable enough for these purposes. Problems can arise when exiting employees give partial reasons for leaving because they need references from the employer or might want to be reemployed at a future date. A sample of a UNISYS Corporation exit interview data collection form is presented in Exhibit 21–7.

Other methods that have been tried to reduce turnover, besides exit interviews, include telephone or in-person interviews a few weeks after termination. These would seem to have the same flaws as exit interviews, but little data are available on the reliability of these methods. Another approach is to give employees a questionnaire as they are exiting and ask them to complete it and mail it back a month or so later. This gives the employee some protection and would appear to be a much better approach than the others. Organizations using this method find a rather low percentage of employees complete the questionnaires, however. No reliability data appear to be available on these questionnaires.

In summary, turnover needs to be examined and monitored since it involves the most important resource of an organization. The firm needs to know who is leaving, why they are leaving, and whether any effort on their part can slow turnover. These are questions that can be answered if a thorough evaluation of a turnover program is implemented.[17]

Evaluation of Absences

A second measure used to evaluate the HRM function is absenteeism rates. **Absenteeism** is the failure of employees to report for work when they are scheduled to work. *Tardiness* is partial absenteeism, employees reporting late to work.

Absenteeism is undesirable because of its cost and the operating problems it causes.[18] Absenteeism's costs to the organization include the costs of benefits, which continue even when workers are absent, so benefit costs are higher per unit of output. Overtime pay also may be necessary for the worker who is doing the job for the missing worker. Facilities may be underutilized and productivity may drop because of reduced output due to understaffing. There also may be increased costs for replacements, substandard production, the need for more help from supervisors and peers, and increased inspection costs.

It is estimated that 400 million workdays are lost per year in the United States because of absenteeism. This is about 5.1 days per employee.[19] In many industries, absenteeism runs as high as 10 to 20 percent of the work force on any given day. Combining the average number of workdays lost per year (over 400 million) with an estimate of the daily cost of nonmanagerial absenteeism per worker, $66 including wages, fringe benefits, and loss in productivity, yields an annual cost of about $26.4 billion.[20]

How is absenteeism computed? The standard formula used by over 70 percent of those who compute absenteeism is:[21]

$$\frac{\text{Number of employee days lost through job absence in the period}}{\text{Average number of employees} \times \text{Number of work days}} \times 100.$$

EXHIBIT 21-7   UNISYS Corporation Exit Interview Data Collection Form

---

EFFECTIVE DATE CURRENT POSITION	CORPORATE UNIT/DEPARTMENT		

FIRST NAME MIDDLE INITIAL LAST NAME	EMPLOYMENT DATE		COST CENTER

CLASSIFICATION TITLE

STATUS:
EXEMPT ☐   NON-EXEMPT ☐   HOURLY ☐

TYPE OF ACTION (SHOULD BE SAME AS CHECKED ON PERSONNEL ACTION NOTICE):

VOLUNTARY QUIT ☐   (COMPLETE ALL REMAINING SECTIONS OF FORM)

     RELEASE ☐   DISCHARGE   ☐   RETIREMENT ☐

     LAYOFF ☐   LEAVE OF ABSENCE ☐   OTHER (EXPLAIN IN REMARKS SECTION)

☐ **A. BENEFITS DISCUSSED**
- MEDICAL, DENTAL EXTENSIONS–GROUP
- LIMITED COVERAGE–INDIVIDUAL

☐ **B. ELIGIBILITY/ENROLLMENT FORM PRESENTED**
- INSTRUCTIONS
- EXPLANATORY LETTER
- PRICE SHEETS

☐ **C. BEST FINAL DISTRIBUTION FORM SIGNED**

☐ **D. CONFIDENTIAL INFORMATION FORM SIGNED**

☐ **E. PACKAGE INSPECTION INFORMATION DISTRIBUTED**

☐ **F. RETURN OF COMPANY PROPERTY**
- ID CARD
- HEALTH ID CARD
- AMERICAN EXPRESS CARD/
  BALANCE OUTSTANDING
- TELEPHONE CREDIT CARD
- KEYS
- MANUALS/DOCUMENTS
- OFFICE EQUIPMENT: B20, OFISWRITER,
  TYPEWRITER, ETC.

☐ **G. UNUSED VACATION DAYS**

☐ **H. PERSONAL PROFILE RETRIEVED**

☐ **I. FORWARDING ADDRESS AND PHONE NO.**

_____

_____

_____

INTERVIEWER'S COMMENTS AND EVALUATION OF REASONS FOR TERMINATION:

_____

_____

_____

_____

_____

_____

_____

_____

_____

_____

_____

_____

_____   _____

    INTERVIEWER'S NAME/POSITION   DATE OF INTERVIEW

Most others use a variation of this formula, such as

$$\frac{\text{Total hours of absence}}{\text{Total hours worked (or scheduled)}} \times 100$$

Of 136 enterprises surveyed by the BNA, about 40 percent calculated absenteeism rates, usually for all employees, and most often monthly (54 percent) or annually (40 percent). Of those calculating absenteeism, 70 percent did so by department or division. Most also separated out long-term absences from short-term ones.

Current research raises questions about the use of absence rates, especially aggregate measures of absenteeism, to evaluate the HRM function. Some observers suggest abandoning the measure. It appears that it is more useful to pursue research designed to identify absence-prone persons, work groups, working conditions, and communities with a view to designing strategies to reduce absenteeism.

One example is a study by Behrend and Pocock of 1,200 employees of a General Motors plant in Scotland. One of the major conclusions of this study was that overall absence ratios, although of some use, are open to serious misinterpretation.[22] For example, the "average" employee in their study experienced three absences per year, totaling about 18 days. But the range was from employees who were not absent 1 day in six years to several who were absent 600 days over the six-year period. The authors convincingly demonstrate that it makes much more sense to classify employees into categories of absence proneness. When this approach is used, management can focus on workers with higher absence rates. Remedial action can then be taken to improve health if the cause appears to be illness, or by counseling, discipline, and so on, if health is not a factor.

Evaluation of Complaints and Grievances

A *complaint* is a statement (in written or oral form) of dissatisfaction or criticism by an employee to a manager. A *grievance* is a complaint that has been presented formally and in writing to a management or union official. Chapter 18 discussed what grievances are and how they are processed. The complaint-grievance rate and the severity of the grievances are another way to evaluate the HRM function. Of course, not all complaints or grievances relate to HRM issues. They can be about equipment, machinery, and other matters, too. And the grievance rate can be related to the militancy of the union or the imminence to contract negotiations. Nevertheless, an increase in the rate and severity of complaints and grievances can indicate dissatisfaction, which in turn might lead to increases in absenteeism and turnover. Both factors indicate how successful the HR department is in securing productivity and satisfaction for the employee. Statistical analyses of complaints and grievances have not been done as scientifically as for turnover and absenteeism.

Evaluation Using Attitude and Opinion Surveys

Another way to assess employee and managerial attitudes about the HRM program is through the use of attitude or opinion surveys. An **attitude** or **opinion survey** is a set of written instruments completed by employees (usually anonymously) expressing their reactions to employer policies, practices, and job characteristics.

Effective attitude surveys are designed with precise goals in mind. The questions and items used are designed professionally and are tested on a sample of employees for reliability and validity prior to administration. Several other administrative factors may affect the validity. One is whether the employees feel that the employer is sincerely interested in knowing the truth and will act wherever possible to follow up on their suggestions.

The survey may include many HRM activities, job satisfaction, and other aspects of the organization's operations. Usually, after the results of the survey are in, they are analyzed and fed back to the employee units. Organizations use attitude surveys to help evaluate the effectiveness of the total HRM program, or parts of it, such as pay, benefits, or training.

About 30 percent of organizations (mostly the larger and medium-sized ones) conduct regular attitude surveys. They are usually conducted on a yearly basis.[23] The organization itself can design the surveys, but approaches developed by consultants and similar services are also available. The survey develops a "snapshot view" of employee attitudes by unit and total organization. Typical attitudes surveyed are given in Exhibit 21–8.

One vital factor in the usefulness of attitude surveys is maintaining confidentiality of the data provided by employees. To assure reliability and validity of the data as far as possible, it has become typical to assure anonymity by questioning groups of employees together. Often, the information is gathered by an outside consultant, such as a university professor.

A typical survey is handled as follows. The HR department contacts a consultant to administer the survey. The consultant first works with HRM in developing the data-gathering approach. Design of these questionnaires or interview schedules is an important technical project. It should be done by professionals in HRM or with expertise in surveying. Typically, the consultant works with the HR department and a sample of operating managers and employees in developing the survey. Finally, the consultant gathers the data and processes it or sends it to a computer service center for processing. No one from the employing organization sees the actual data or questionnaires completed by the employees.

In preparation for the attitude survey, employees receive a letter explaining the purpose of the study (such as to improve working conditions). The letter also

---

EXHIBIT 21-8   Attitude Covered in Surveys

Attitudes about Working Conditions on the Job	Compensation and Rewards	Attitudes about the Supervisor	Attitudes about the Employer
Physical working conditions	Salaries	Communication abilities	HRM policies
Work scheduling and planning	Benefits	Qualifications and abilities	Communications
Work assignments and worker abilities	Promotions	Supervisory style	General reputation in community
Job demands	Status and recognition		Reputation nationally
Job security	Promotion opportunities		Attitudes toward future unionization
Hours of work			
Safety on the job			
Interpersonal relations at work			
Adequacy of training by employer			

PROFESSIONAL PROFILE

Biography

A 23-year veteran manager of Dr Pepper/Seven-Up Companies, Inc., Quigley was elected a corporate vice president in April 1981 and corporate vice president, administration in 1988.

Career Summary   After a four-year stint as assistant director of personnel of Dallas-based Morton Foods, Inc., division of General Mills, Quigley joined Dr Pepper Company in March 1967 as director of personnel and training. He was named director of personnel two years later. In June 1980, the firm's personnel function was expanded and reorganized as the human resources department. Quigley was elected a corporate vice president of Dr Pepper Company in 1981. In 1988, his role broadened by a promotion to vice president, administration of Dr Pepper/Seven-Up Companies, Inc., and the assumption of additional duties.

His responsibilities include managing purchasing, human resources, travel services, training, facilities, office services, security, and transportation. He reports to executive vice president Ira M. Rosenstein.

Professional Activities   Quigley has been involved in many professional societies including the American Society for Training and Development (ASTD) and the American Society for Personnel Administration (ASPA). He has served in the national leadership ranks of ASPA from district director of North Texas to chairman of the board of ASPA in 1982 to a member of the executive committee. He has served as a member of the board of the Personnel Accreditation Institute, the ASPA Foundation, and CLEAR (Council on Legislation, Education, and Research).

John L. Quigley, Jr.
Dr Pepper/Seven-Up Companies,
Inc.

Quigley recently served as a distinguished visiting executive at Texas A & M University in addition to serving on the HRM advisory board in the Department of Management in the College of Business at the university. Presently, he is serving on the board of directors at the Dallas Child Guidance Clinic, Junior Achievement, and I Have A Dream Foundation. He also serves on the advisory council for the new master's degree program at the University of Dallas Graduate School of Management. Quigley is also involved with the Juvenile Diabetes Foundation, United Way of Dallas, and Rotary Club of Dallas, and serves on the Rotary International Committee.

explains the safeguards for the employees that will be provided, such as the use of consultants. If a questionnaire is used, the employees complete them in homogenous groups (exempt or nonexempt, for example).

The two principal methods used to gather data are interviews and questionnaires. Sometimes, both are used by an organization. Surveys indicate that almost two thirds of the employers use questionnaires alone, less than 10 percent use only interviews, and the rest use a combination of both.[24] Studies suggest that information is more reliable and complete if interviews are used. Usually, the interviews follow the structured approach. If questionnaires are used, three approaches are followed: *yes, no,* or *don't know* answers; open-ended essay questions; or structured questions with multiple-choice answers. An example of the latter is given in Exhibit 21–9.

EXHIBIT 21-9   Attitude Survey (Partial Sample)

INSTRUCTIONS

This is a survey of the ideas and opinions of Baker Company salaried employees. WHAT YOU SAY IN THIS QUESTIONNAIRE IS COMPLETELY CONFIDENTIAL. We do not want to know who you are. We do want to know, however, how employees with different interests, experience, and doing different kinds of work, feel about their jobs and Baker.

This is not a test. There are no right or wrong answers. Whether the results of this survey give a true picture of the Baker Company depends on whether each of you answers each of the questions in the way you really feel. The usefulness of this survey in making Baker a better place to work depends on the honesty and care with which you answer the questions.

Your answers will be compiled with many others and summarized to prepare a *report* for Baker. Your identity will always be protected. We do not need your name, only your impressions. Your written comments will be put in typewritten form so that your handwriting will not even be seen by anyone at Baker.

Please complete each of the six parts of the survey so that all of your impressions can be recorded. Remember your honest impressions are all that we are asking for.

PART I: THE JOB AND CONDITIONS

The statements below are related to certain aspects of your job at Baker. Please circle the response number that best describes how you feel about the statement.

1 = Strongly disagree   2 = Disagree   3 = Undecided   4 = Agree   5 = Strongly agree

Pay	Strongly Disagree	Disagree	Undecided	Agree	Strongly Agree
My pay is all right for the kind of work I do	1	2	3	4	5
I make as much money as most of my friends	1	2	3	4	5
My pay allows me to keep up with the cost of living	1	2	3	4	5
I am satisfied with the pay I receive for my job	1	2	3	4	5
Most employees at Baker get paid at least what they deserve	1	2	3	4	5
I understand how my salary is determined	1	2	3	4	5

What changes, if any, should be made with the Baker pay system?_____

_____

Fringe Benefits					
Our major fringe benefit plan provides excellent coverage	1	2	3	4	5
I understand what our fringe benefits at Baker are	1	2	3	4	5
I am satisfied with our fringe benefit plan	1	2	3	4	5

What, if anything, should be done with the Baker fringe benefit plans?_____

_____

_____

After the data are gathered, they are analyzed. Present responses are compared to past ones to see if the trends are positive or negative. Responses from different subunits are compared to see if some are more favorable than others.

Overall indications lead to management actions of one type or another. Policies are revised, enforced, or created, and the results are communicated to the employees. The attitude survey tends to generate expectations on the part of employees. Thus, management needs to be sure that some feedback and action follow the survey. Failure to do something often results in future resistance to surveys and to a feeling that any survey is ritualistic and not useful, as both managers and researchers have found.[25]

HRM EVALUATION RESEARCH: FINAL COMMENTS

The purposes of HRM evaluation research are to find solutions for human resources problems, to aid in evaluation of the HRM function, and to extend the knowledge of human resources to all those concerned. This activity is performed by universities, consultants, independent research institutes, and/or employers. The growing list of employers who perform their HRM research include AT&T, IBM, and General Electric. Sometimes, HRM research is attached to units other than HR departments, such as research and development groups. One study asked HR researchers to estimate how they spent their time. They reported that they spent 20 percent consulting with line managers, 15 percent running their department, 9 percent on self-development, and 55 percent on research. Of the time spent on research, 13 percent was spent analyzing HRM statistics, 15 percent on studying improved means of employment, 16 percent on improving the organization climate, and 11 percent on studying training and development.[26]

In 1934, Cohen and Nagel suggested that there were four basic ways of knowing. These are tenacity, intuition, authority, and science. Managers and HRM researchers use all these techniques. Managers use *tenacity* when they form a belief about an HRM issue (such as, if a worker is paid more, productivity will increase). This belief continues to be held even if research shows it to be incorrect. Managers use *intuition* on HRM matters when they feel an answer to be obvious or when they have a hunch on how to solve a problem. *Authority* is used when managers seek answers or methods or programs from an expert or consultant. Asking a performance appraisal expert to implement what he or she feels is best is using authority.

Science in HRM as presented in this book is used to solve, diagnose, and evaluate problems. In contrast to tenacity, intuition, and authority, science aims at obtaining answers, charting the way by using information and knowledge that are objective. The meaning of *objectivity* in this sense is that the knowledge about absenteeism, turnover, or safety and health ratios is certifiable, independent of individual opinion. It means that the research data were obtained by the use of the scientific method of inquiry. In other words, the scientific approach to HRM evaluation research involves using some rigorous standards of science in an attempt to minimize subjectivity and maximize objectivity.

The use of the scientific approach to HRM evaluation research consists of four stages: (1) observation of the situation in the real world; (2) formulation of explanations of the situation using induction; (3) generation of predictions about the situation using deduction; and (4) verification of the predictions using scientific methods. This approach to HRM research is shown in Exhibit 21–10. If there is anything that will enhance the prestige and influence of the HRM function in

EXHIBIT 21-10   Four Stages of the Scientific Approach to HRM Research

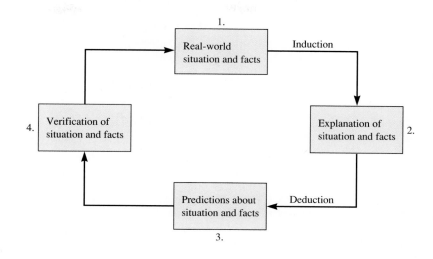

organizations, it is the use of more science and rigorous research to study and understand the kinds of HRM programs covered in Chapters 3 to 20. By using more HRM evaluation research, managers can reduce the risks of relying too heavily on opinions or prejudices about people, programs, environmental forces, and the future.

THE HR MANAGER: A LAST LOOK

This book has been designed to help you view the HRM function in action and to see the full range of activities and programs conducted by employees in this function. Some readers may already work in HRM or will work in such a department in the future. Certainly, most readers will be involved in their careers with human resource issues, problems, and challenges.

Each manager in an organization must be kept up to speed about HRM issues, programs, and techniques. We have attempted always to be realistic and to show HRM in all its glory and power, as well as in a condition of being overworked and even uncertain. There is nothing unique to the HR department being overworked, understaffed, and uncertain. We all experience these conditions occasionally. In viewing the HR professional and the activities he or she conducts, the book relied on a number of mechanisms.

The Diagnostic Approach

It was shown that the effective HR manager is a diagnostician who observes the various aspects of the organization's environment. She or he considers the size, structure, goals, and style of the organization, and the nature of employees, the tasks, the work groups, and the leaders. The diagnostic manager realizes that the HRM policies of the organization must be congruent with all these factors — and others — if HRM is to do its part to contribute to organization effectiveness.

CAREER CHALLENGE
(concluded)

The setting is again the conference room at General Products. The time is the next annual planning meeting. Last year, because Denton Major was not in a position to justify his budget for HRM, he was not awarded the 6 percent increase he asked for. In fact, HRM was cut by the same percentage figure as the marketing department was. If he could help it, that wouldn't happen again. In the past year, he had examined HRM audit approaches.

In evaluation, use of a checklist or copying other organizations appeared useful and easy. Compliance methods appeared useful, as did attitude surveys. Statistical approaches, especially evaluation of turnover, also appeared to be helpful.

As Denton waited, he was confident of the results of his budget request this year. Eventually, his time came to present his request.

Denton The HR department has a report that is included in your packet of materials. You'll note that we have the results of our compliance audit. The company is substantially in compliance with government regulations. This was not true a year ago. But we set that as an objective and reached it.

From the checklist, attitude survey, and compliance items, we came up with qualitative and quantitative targets for our HRM program. Our major targets were to reduce costly turnover and improve the cost effectiveness of our compensation program.

Next year's objectives are given on page 10 of the report. You'll also note our cost/benefit studies justify the shift of funds among our HRM programs and the justification for an 8 percent increase in our budget.

Henry The budget for HRM is well-documented and appears reasonable.

Emily A big improvement from last year's presentation, Denton.

Denton's budget was approved.

The myth that the work of HRM units and specialists is too subjective and complex to properly evaluate is not accepted. If this myth is accepted, then HRM is set apart from the rest of the organization. The diagnostic approach searches for ways to evaluate the impact, if any, of a specific HRM activity or program. It refuses to accept the notion that the effectiveness of the work done by the HRM unit and specialists can't be measured. The success of any HRM unit depends on management's ability to take measures of performance. There is no escaping the need to measure, evaluate, and monitor HRM. Without measures of effectiveness, owners, managers, and employees within the unit itself would have no idea of what contributions HRM is making to the organization. As HRM proves its worth to firms, it becomes an active participant in the overall strategic planning of the firm.[27]

A diagnostic HR manager wants other managers and people to know how well his or her unit is performing. That is, the manager wants to report accomplishments. By using a diagnostic approach and collecting evaluation indicators of performance, the HR manager will not only inform, but will also be able to persuade others about the unit's worth. The need to persuade others is specially important when managers must present their case and attempt to secure limited resources and funds for their unit.

Model Organizations

This mechanism was used in many chapters to focus attention specifically on how HRM activities are performed differently in different types of organizations. This is certainly true of the many different kinds of organizations in the private, public, and not-for-profit sectors.

The Role of the Top Manager and Operating Manager

Top managers and operating managers have important parts to play in the HRM process. Successful HR managers know how to relate to these persons and to present HRM programs to them in the language and thought processes of operating and top managers. These managers have responsibilities for human resources that HR managers can help them fulfill. How is this done?

THE HR MANAGER IN ACTION

The HR manager portrayed in this book manages by objectives and works at showing others how HRM contributes to organizational goals. Few organizations exist solely to hire and develop people. They exist to reach goals such as producing goods to satisfy customers while achieving a profit, or curing patients at reasonable cost, or improving the education of teenage children in a community.

The HR manager today must not only be a diagnostician, but a researcher and futurist as well. As this chapter and the diagnostic theme of the book illustrates, research of HRM programs is essential. Without adequate research, important human resource planning, performance evaluation, training and development, and industrial relations, HRM programs will have to be run on the basis of hunches and intuition.

Many of the measurement and methodological problems associated with HRM research still need to be improved.[28] Improvement is likely to be brought about by more thorough and careful research studies being conducted and reported.

As a futurist, the HR manager must develop a profile of the people in society. In the United States and Canada, a wealth of statistics are available to help develop future recruitment, selection, development, and employment growth plans. Some of the statistics that are used and scrutinized are birth rates, changing family patterns, education levels, and age patterns. These statistics need to be consulted so that organizations can better cope with the people available for employment. Today, we know that lifestyles are changing, and the average U.S. and Canadian citizen is better educated than previous generations of workers. The so-called baby boom generation (25 to 44 years old) is growing older.

Tomorrow's work force will be more diverse in terms of gender and race, marked by intense competition for jobs and promotions, and less unionized.[29] By the year 2000, the labor force participation of women is projected to reach 67 percent, as compared with 74 percent for men.[30] This kind of information will be critical in determining what kind of HRM programs will be needed. Most of the decisions made about the programs will emanate from top managers, since they are the strategic decision makers.

The HR manager is part of the team that makes the key decisions, the strategic decisions, such as: What type of person do we need to hire or retain to accomplish our mission? Are we going to grow? In what direction are we going to grow? Are we going to merge with another organization? What type of reward system will be needed to continue being viewed as an attractive firm?

Each of these strategic decisions have important implications for HR managers. And the HR department can provide important counsel about the human resources affecting these decisions. HRM can only have the impact it should have if its leadership is well-trained to do the job and if it can convey to top management a goal-oriented attitude when seeking additional funds to do its job.

The HR manager who is part of the top-management team will be reporting what programs have been phased out, with appropriate savings, and what programs have been kept, and the savings and improvements resulting from them. Specific budget justifications will be made for proposed additions, and specific measureable results that will help the enterprise reach its goals will be proposed. Further, the HR manager will be able to show how to achieve these results. Managers who are used to making decisions this way will know that this executive team makes the *real* decisions that affect personnel.

In the small organization, the executive responsible for HRM and other functions should begin to consider HRM decisions in the same hard-nosed way he or she does other decisions. Resources are scarce, and human resources are the most precious to conserve and develop. The failure of small-organization owners to pay attention to HRM is often a step toward legal suits, loss of key personnel, and lost profits.[31]

Many explanations for economic and productivity woes in the United States and developed Western nations have been advanced. In the United States, the culprits include inadequate investment in new plants, overregulation from the government, and excessive taxation. No doubt these are contributors to many problems. Perhaps a closer look at HRM activities and programs also is needed to get to the core of the nation's problems — inflation, lagging productivity, and the unfavorable trade balance. HR experts can help attack problems involving human attitudes and behavior. This is the overriding challenge of HRM as a field of study and research.

An interesting survey of opinion leaders, corporate officers, consultants, editors, journalists, and academics in the HRM area looked at the future in terms of managing human resources. Several suggestions were offered that seemed worthy of consideration. The HRM function was encouraged in the future to:

. Treat employees as important assets.
. Encourage more worker participation in decision making.
. Provide better training for managers and employees.
. Offer better career development opportunities.
. Tie more rewards and recognition to performance.
. Develop better labor-management relations.
. Increase the HRM input in strategic planning and business decisions.[32]

The implications of changing values in society, an aging population, technological change, the emphasis on equality and cultural diversity, and resistance to authority are being recognized by HRM practitioners. They are aware that a single plan or program (selection, training, performance appraisal) will not work every time, for all workers, in all organizations. Also, they know that managing workers now requires plans and programs appropriate for today's and tomorrow's work force. The traditional methods to pay workers, schedule work, evaluate performance, select employees, compensate workers, enforce discipline, improve workers' safety and health, and so forth are changing drastically. These and other changes will require proactive HRM programs that are difficult to initiate, sustain, and evaluate. Yet, the heart of HRM is people: Only in this century have we seen the awakening of organizations to this most important asset. In effect, the HRM manager of the future will play an even greater role than is played today in the dynamic, increasingly fast-paced world. Such a set of challenges is not for the faint-hearted. We happen to believe that there are many HR specialists and general managers interested in HRM who are willing to accept such a set of challenges.

SUMMARY

Any function as important as the effective use of human resources needs to be evaluated. The difficulty in evaluating the results of the HRM function is that effectiveness has multiple causes, and it is difficult to separate out how much of the effectiveness results from each cause. Here is a list of some of the major statements in the evaluation section of Chapter 21 to use as a guideline.

1. Evaluation of the HRM function is a systematic, formal experience designed to measure the costs and benefits of the total HRM program and to compare its efficiency and effectiveness with the enterprise's past performance, the performance of comparable effective organizations, and the firm's objectives.
2. This evaluation is performed to
   a. Justify HRM existence and budget.
   b. Improve the HRM function by providing a means to decide when to drop activities and when to add them.
   c. Provide feedback from employees and operating managers on HRM's effectiveness.
   d. Help HRM to do its part to achieve the objectives of the organization.
3. Evaluation of the HRM function can be done by one or a combination of the following means:
   a. Checklist.
   b. Statistical approaches, including evaluation of turnover, absenteeism, and complaints and grievances, and the use of attitude and opinion surveys.
   c. Compliance methods of evaluation.

Exhibit 21–11 provides recommendations for the model organizations on HRM audits and evaluation and research.

KEY TERMS

absenteeism	782
attitude or opinion survey	784

QUESTIONS FOR REVIEW AND DISCUSSION

1. Since HRM evaluation research can be so informative, why isn't it conducted in most firms?
2. What ethical issues should an HR specialist be concerned about in conducting an attitude survey?
3. What kind of research on women in the work force will be needed to help HR managers better utilize their skills, talents, and expertise?
4. Why is it important for an HRM unit to clearly display to other units how well it is performing?
5. Why do some experts feel that the level of turnover in organizations has been overstated?

EXHIBIT 21-11   Recommendations for Model Organizations on Research and Evaluation of the HRM Function

Type of Organization	Checklist	Statistical	Compliance	Performed by			
				Organization	Consultant	Organization and Consultant	HRM Research Department
1. Large size, low complexity, high stability			X	X			X
2. Medium size, low complexity, high stability		X	X			X	
3. Small size, low complexity, high stability	X				X		
4. Medium size, moderate complexity, moderate stability		X	X			X	
5. Large size, high complexity, low stability			X	X			X
6. Medium size, high complexity, low stablity	X					X	
7. Small size, high complexity, low stability							

6. Compare and contrast the statistical indicators of HRM evaluation. Which are the best indicators? How are they measured?

7. Why must an HR manager be a diagnostician and also look into the future?

8. What costs are involved in evaluating turnover?

9. Why are perfectly accurate or precise measures of HRM activities and programs an ideal that is not likely to be achieved?

10. As the work force becomes more culturally diverse, what kinds of considerations in designing HRM evaluation studies will have to occur?

NOTES

[1] Wayne F. Cascio (1987), *Costing Human Resources: The Financial Impact of Behavior in Organizations* (Boston: Kent Publishing).

[2] Clay Carr (September 1987), "Injecting Quality into Personnel Management," *Personnel Journal*, pp. 43–51.

[3] Anne S. Tsui (1984), "Personnel Department Effectiveness: A Tripartite Approach," *Industrial Relations*, pp. 184–87.

[4] Anne S. Tsui (1988), ''Activities and Effectiveness of the Human Resource Department: A Multiple Constituency Approach,'' in *Personnel and Human Resource Management*, ed. R. S. Schuler, S. A. Youngblood, and V. L. Huber (St. Paul, Minn.: West Publishing), pp. 465–83.

[5] Wayne F. Cascio (1991), *Applied Psychology In Personnel Management* (Englewood Cliffs, N.J. Prentice-Hall), p. 52.

[6] Jac Fitz-Enz (1984), *How to Measure Human Resources Management* (New York: McGraw-Hill), p. 23.

[7] A more complete treatment of HRM evaluation can be found in Michael W. Mercer (1989), *Turning Your Human Resource Department into a Profit Center* (New York: AMACOM).

[8] Joel Lapointe (January 1988), ''How to Calculate the Cost of Human Resources,'' *Personnel Journal*, pp. 34–45.

[9] (June 1987), ''Employment Turnover: Measurement and Control,'' *Compensation and Benefits Review*, pp. 64–74.

[10] The BNA data is based on BNA's *Report on Job Absence and Turnover, 3rd Quarter, 1985.*

[11] (May 1974) Bureau of National affairs, *Employee Absenteeism and Turnover*, Personnel Policies Forum, Survey 106 (Washington, D.C.: U.S. Government Printing Office).

[12] William Mobley (April 1977), ''Intermediate Linkages in the Relationship between Job Satisfaction and Employee Turnover,'' *Journal of Applied Psychology*, pp. 237–40; and W. Mobley, R. Griffeth, H. Hand, and B. Meglino (May 1979), ''Review and Conceptual Analysis of the Turnover Process,'' *Psychological Bulletin*, pp. 408–14.

[13] Richard T. Mowday, Christine Koberg, and Angeline McArthur (March 1984), ''The Psychology of the Withdrawal Process: A Cross-Validation Test of Mobley's Intermediate Linkages Model of Turnover in Two Samples,'' *Academy of Management Journal*, pp. 79–94.

[14] D. R. Dalton (1981), ''Turnover and Absenteeism: Measures of Personnel Effectiveness,'' in *Applied Readings in Personnel and Human Resource Management*, ed. R. J. Schuler, J. M. McFillen, and D. R. Dalton (St. Paul, Minn.: West Publishing).

[15] D. R. Dalton, D. M. Krackhardt, and L. W. Porter (December 1981), ''Functional Turnover: An Empirical Assessment,'' *Journal of Applied Psychology*, pp. 716–21.

[16] R. M. Steers and S. R. Rhodes (November-December 1980), ''A New Look at Absenteeism,'' *Personnel*, pp. 60–65; and Dalton, ''Turnover and Absenteeism.''

[17] Jeanne M. Carsten and Paul E. Spector (August 1987), ''Unemployment, Job Satisfaction, and Employee Turnover: A Meta-Analytic Test of the Muchinsky Model,'' *Journal of Applied Psychology*, pp. 374–81.

[18] P. M. Muchinsky and P. C. Morrow (December 1980), ''A Multidisciplinary Model of Voluntary Employee Turnover,'' *Journal of Vocational Behavior*, pp. 263–90.

[19] Rick D. Hacket and Robert M. Guion (June 1985), ''A Reevaluation of The Absenteeism-Job Behavior Satisfaction Relationship,'' *Organizational Behavior and Human Decision Processes*, pp. 340–81; and S. F. Yolles, D. A. Carone, and L. W. Krinsky (1975), *Absenteeism in Industry* (Springfield, Ill.: Charles C. Thomas, 1975).

[20] R. M. Steers and S. R. Rhodes (August 1978), ''Major Influences on Attendance: A Process Model,'' *Journal of Applied Psychology*, p. 391.

[21] Bureau of National Affairs, *Employee Absenteeism and Turnover*, p. 15.

[22] Hilde Behrend and Stuart Pocock (November-December 1976), ''Absence and the Individual: A Six-Year Study in One Organization,'' *International Labour Review*, pp. 311–27.

[23] (March 22, 1979), ''Personnel Policies: Research and Evaluation,: ASPA–BNA Survey No. 37, *Bulletin to Management*, p. 6.

[24] David R. York (May 1985), "Attitude Surveying," *Personnel Journal*, pp. 70–73.

[25] R. B. Dunham and F. J. Smith (1979), *Organization Surveys* (Glenview, Ill.: Scott, Foresman); and Paul R. Lees-Haley and Cheryl E. Lees-Haley (October 1982), "Attitude Survey Norms: A Dangerous Ally," *Personnel Administrator*, pp. 51–56.

[26] John Hinrichs (August 1969), "Characteristic of the Personnel Research Functions," *Personnel Journal*, pp. 597–604.

[27] Julie Cohen (October 1990), "The New HR Agenda Takes Shape," *Personnel (HR Focus)*, pp. 1, 2.

[28] Marc J. Wallace, Jr. (January 1983), "Methodology, Research Practice, and Progress in Personnel and Industrial Relations," *Academy of Management Review*, pp. 6–13.

[29] Thomasine Rendero (August 1990), "HR Panel Take a Look Ahead," *Personnel*, pp. 14–24.

[30] (1990), *Statistical Abstract of the United States* (Washington, D.C.: U.S. Department of Commerce), p. 389.

[31] Eric G. Flamholz, Yvonne Randle, and Sonja Sackmann, (June 1987), "Personnel Management: The Tenor of Today," *Personnel Journal*, pp. 60–70.

[32] S. William Alper and Russell E. Mandel (November 1984), "What Policies and Practices Characterize the Most Effective HR Departments?," *Personnel Administrator*, p. 124.

MEASURING THE HUMAN RESOURCE ACTIVITIES

· · · · · · ·

Traditionally, the HR department has been evaluated in vague, subjective terms. This has occurred for basically two reasons: first, the wrong questions were being asked; second, management bought the claim that it was not possible to apply quantitative methods to a function that was viewed principally from a qualitative standpoint.

The staff and management of what has now come to be called the *human resources department* allowed that misperception to perpetuate itself. From the inception of the first HR department until modern times, few people seemed to be concerned about the performance of the department. There was no formal career path into or through HRM, and the few institutions of higher learning that taught HRM did not bother to teach measurement techniques. As a result, people did not know how to evaluate their work objectively. For some, the application of cold numbers to a function whose apparent mission was to "help employees with their problems" and to "improve morale" seemed to be a conflict of values. Others did not want to take on the extra work of collecting data and performing the calculations because they saw no use for it. Senior management had not asked for it. In time, a hidden fear developed. The department was often maligned by others within the larger organization. Many HR people developed the attitude that their job was not too important, and that if they were to go to the trouble of quantitatively measuring and reporting their work, the numbers would confirm the perception that they were not doing well. This attitude still exists in the minds of many today.

Every human resource manager must understand why a company is in business. The purpose of business is to earn a profit. This is the harsh reality of the real world. Being nice to people is fine. Supporting the development of people is a worthy endeavor. Helping workers improve their skills and confidence is an excellent undertaking. But the core of businesses is to make money. If a firm doesn't make money, how can it survive? Who will subsidize the firm? Do you think that a not-for-profit firm can survive without making money? If the human resource department is to be considered an essential unit, it must measure its value and its contributions to the firm.

As a result of not proving their value to the organization in objective terms, the human resources department is not considered part of the mainstream of organizational management. It is viewed as a cost center and reactive maintenance activity. In order to turn that outmoded attitude around, it is necessary for human resources management to learn to speak the language of business, which is numbers. A mathematical methodology

Originally prepared by Jac Fitz-enz, president, Saratoga Institute. Adapted and updated by author of text.

needs to be applied as a system that serves both as a day-to-day monitoring instrument and as a model for doing cost justification and cost/benefit analyses of specific projects or programs.

Two of the foremost management authorities, Peter Drucker and W. Edwards Deming, have come out strongly for the development of measurement skill as an indigenous capability of a manager.

BASIC PRINCIPLES

The application of quantitative methods to human resources management has generated a set of basic principles that are critical to the success of the measurement system. These are based on the experience of managers in many types and sizes of organizations.

1. *The productivity and effectiveness of any function can be measured by some combination of cost, time, quantity, or quality indexes.* In some cases, psychological measures of attitudes and morale are also useful and possible.
2. *A measurement system promotes productivity by focusing attention on the important issues, tasks, and objectives.* A quantitative system not only helps to clarify what is to be accomplished, but also how well it should be done.
3. *Professional and knowledge workers are best measured as a group.* In order to be optimally effective, a professional group needs to work together. Measuring the work of individuals in relationship to each other promotes divisiveness and counterproductive competition.
4. *Managers can be measured by the efficiency and effectiveness of the units they manage.* The nature of managerial work is to get things done through other people. Therefore, it follows that the output of the group is an indication of the skill of the manager. There are obvious exceptions to this, but the rule applies nevertheless.
5. *The ultimate measurement is not efficiency, but effectiveness.* The objective of an organization is not only to create the most output with the least input. More important is to create the most appropriate outcome at any given point in time.

BUILDING BLOCKS OF A MEASUREMENT SYSTEM

The first problem that people face when they set out to build a measurement system is the apparent multitude of activities that are taking place and the seemingly impossible task of differentiating, isolating, and labeling of quantifiable variables. It is somewhat analogous to looking at a 1,000-pound steer and wondering how you can get a hamburger out of it. The solution is relatively simple.

There are only four classes of variables that can be subjected to a quantitative system. They are:

1. *People* (as described by their organizational roles, such as receptionist, clerk, recruiter, trainer, compensation analyst, or manager).
2. *Things* (physical objects such as equipment, files, application forms, facilities, and supplies).
3. *Processes* (people doing something with a thing or with another person such as interviewing, filing, training, scheduling, and counseling).
4. *Results* (the outcomes of the interactions of people, things, and processes).

Everything within the department or related to the department's activity, whether it be inside the larger organization or outside it (such as a job applicant), can be classified into one of these four categories.

The next step is to list all the variables within each category that one might want to measure in some way. Then, the variables can be compared one at a time to each other until a relationship that can be expressed in terms of cost, time, quantity (volume or frequency), or quality becomes evident. This outcome is the *dependent variable*.

Examples of some typical dependent variables, often called *measures* by human resource managers, are: interviews per hire, absenteeism rate, hours per trainee, average hire cost, counseling hours per topic, records processed per clerk, or the ratio of benefit costs to payroll cost.

Once the dependent variables are chosen for inclusion in the measurement system, an equation must be created to complete the measure. These are often self-evident. Some examples are:

$$\text{Average hire cost} = \frac{\text{Selection costs}}{\text{Number hired}}$$

Absenteeism rate

$$= \frac{\text{Number of absent days}}{\text{Number of workdays available}}$$

Average health-care cost

$$= \frac{\text{Total cost of health benefits}}{\text{Total number of employees}}$$

Cost per trainee hour

$$= \frac{\text{Total cost of training}}{\text{Number trained} \times \text{Hours trained}}$$

HOW TO QUANTIFY QUALITY

One refuge that opponents of measurement have sought is the issue of quality. They argue that the work of the human resources function is highly qualitative and therefore inherently not susceptible to quantification. The quality issue is not the sole province of the human resource department. Products must be manufactured to quality specifications. Salespeople must sell only to accounts that pay their bills. Although it is clear that quality is everyone's criterion, that does not solve the problem of how to quantify it.

The solution lies in the creation of a composite measure. For example, if the issue is recruiter effectiveness, one must first decide what constitutes effectiveness. Clearly, it is a function of more than one measure. If effectiveness could be defined by one objective term, it would not be subjective. A recruiter's effectiveness may be defined as a combination of how fast hires are accomplished, how cheaply they are achieved, how many are completed, and the quality of the people hired. And therein lies another potential problem. Hire quality is a subjective issue itself. In order to use it in the effectiveness measure, it must first be quantified. So, a composite of hire quality needs to be constructed, the quality objectified, and that quantitative value plugged into the recruiter effectiveness formula. The end result might look like this.

Recruiter Effectiveness =

$$\frac{\text{CH} + \text{TFJ} + \text{QH} + (\text{Other chosen indexes})}{\text{Number of indexes used}}$$

where,

Cost of hire (CH) = $450 (average)
Time to fill jobs (TFJ) = 15 days (on average)
Quality of hires (QH) = 90 percent
(per quality measure)

Plus others. . . .

Dollars, days, and percent can be normalized by comparing them to a preset goal and calculating percent of goal achievement for each. Each issue can also be weighted by importance. A simple illustration (omitting "other" undefined variables) is:

Measure	Result	Goal	Goal Achievement Percent × Weighting Factors	
Cost of hire	$450	$500	11% × 4 =	444
Time to fill	15	12	80% × 3 =	240
Quality	90%	85%	106% × 5 =	530
				1,214

$$1{,}214 \div 12 = 101\%$$

SUMMARY

In order for the human resources function to take its place as an integral part of the organization, it must learn to use the language of business, which is numbers. This applies whether the organization is profit or not-for-profit. There are a number of personal, departmental, and organizational values to be derived from maintaining a quantitative performance measurement system. Personally, the people in the department are able to see how well they are doing. They are able to identify problems in early stages and find the source of the solution. They have data to build cost justification proposals that will help them obtain needed resources. They will be able to prove their contribution to the productivity and profitability of the larger organization. As a result of all this, they will gain the respect and position they desire.

SOURCES OF HUMAN RESOURCE MANAGEMENT INFORMATION: WHERE TO FIND FACTS AND FIGURES

· · · · · · ·

This appendix is divided into three main parts: periodicals, publishers, and organizations specializing in providing information in a variety of areas of HRM. While the listings are not intended to be exhaustive, they do provide a good cross section of major sources of facts and figures.

The listings contain the names of national organizations. You might consult your local chamber of commerce, college or university, and personnel association chapter for information and resources as well.

I. Periodicals.

A. General business journals that often contain HRM material.
   Academy of Management Executive
   Advanced Management Journal
   Business Horizons
   California Management Review
   Harvard Business Review
   Organizational Dynamics
   Sloan Management Review

B. Specialized journals. The HRM specialist can advance his or her knowledge of the field by reading specialized journals. These include:
   Administrative Management
   American Federationist
   Arbitration Journal
   BNAC Communication (quarterly)
   Bulletin on Training (monthly)
   Compensation and Benefits Review (quarterly)
   Employment Benefit Plan Review

Paul N. Keaton, University of Wisconsin, LaCrosse.

Employee Benefits Journal (quarterly)
Employee Relations Law Journal
Human Resource Management
Human Resource Planning
Industrial Relations (triannual)
Industrial Relations News (weekly)
Labor Law Journal (monthly)
Monthly Labor Review (monthly)
National Productivity
Personnel (bimonthly)
Personnel Journal (monthly)
Personnel Management (monthly)
Personnel Management Abstracts (quarterly)
Public Personnel Management (bimonthly)
Training and Development Journal (monthly)

C. Scholarly journals. The following is a list of publications written primarily for scholars and executives interested in HR management. Reading these requires more technical training than the journals listed above.

Academy of Management Journal
Academy of Management Review
Human Organization
Human Relations
Human Resource Management
Industrial and Labor Relations Review
Industrial Relations
Journal of Applied Behavoral Science
Journal of Applied Psychology
Journal of Human Resources
Journal of Labor Research
Journal of Vocational Behavior
Organizational Behavior and Human Decision Processes
Personnel Psychology
Training: Journal of Human Resource Development

II. Specialized HRM Publishers.

Bureau of Law and Business, Inc.
64 Wall Street
Madison, CT 06443

Capitol Publications
1300 North 17th Street
Arlington, VA 22209

Commerce Clearing House, Inc.
4025 West Peterson Avenue
Chicago, IL 60646
(312) 583-8500

Executive Enterprises Publications Co., Inc.
22 West 21st Street
New York, NY 10010-6904
(212) 645-7800

Federal Publications, Inc.
1120 20th Street, N.W.
Washington, DC 20036
(202) 337-7000

National Association for Management
1617 Murray
Wichita, KS 67212
(316) 721-4684

Personnel Policy Service, Inc.
P.O. Box 7697
Louisville, KY 40257-0697
(502) 897-6782

Research Institute of America, Inc.
90 Fifth Avenue
New York, NY 10011
(212) 645-4800

III. Organizations[1]

A. Private.

American Arbitration Association (AAA)
140 West 51 Street
New York, NY 10020
(212) 484-4000

American Association for Counseling and Development (AACD)
(formerly American Personnel and Guidance Association (APGA)
5999 Stevenson Avenue
Alexandria, VA 22304
(703) 823-9800

American Compensation Association (ACA)
P.O. Box 29312
Phoenix, AZ 85038-9312
(602) 951-9191

American Management Associations (AMA)
135 West 50th Street
New York, NY 10020
(212) 586-8100

American Psychological Association (APA)
1200 17th Street, N.W.
Washington, DC 20036
(202) 955-7600

[1] Deborah M. Burek, ed. (1991), *Encyclopedia of Associations*, 25th ed. (Detroit: Gale Research Company).

American Society for Hospital Personnel Administration (ASHPA)
840 North Lake Shore Drive
Chicago, IL 60611
(312) 280-6358

American Society for Training and Development (ASTD)
600 Maryland Avenue, S.W., Suite 305
Washington, DC 20024
(202) 484-2390

Association of Private Pension and Welfare Plans (APPWP)
1725 K Street, N.W., Suite 801
Washington, DC 20006
(202) 659-8274

Bureau of Labor Statistics (BLS) Department of Labor
441 G. Street, N.W.
Washington, D.C. 20212
(202) 523-1590

College and University Personnel Association (CUPA)
11 Dupont Circle, Suite 120
Washington, D.C. 20036
(202) 462-1038

Human Resource Planning Society
228 East 45th Street
New York, NY 10017
(212) 490-6387

Industrial Relations Research Association
7226 Social Science Building
University of Wisconsin
Madison, WI 53760
(608) 262-2762

International Association for Personnel Women (IAPW)
5820 Wilshire Boulevard
Suite 500
Los Angeles, CA 90036
(213) 937-9000

International Association of Pupil Personnel Workers (IAPPW)
c/o William E. Myer
P.O. Box 36
Barnesville, MD 20838
(301) 340-7501

National Association of Educational Office Personnel (NAEOP)
1902 Association Drive
Reston, VA 22091
(703) 860-2888

National Association of Manufacturers (NAM)
1776 F Street
Washington, DC 20006
(202) 626-3700

National Association of Para-Legals Personnel (NAPLP)
c/o Howard W. Ross
9431 North Leamington
Skokie, IL 60077
(312) 676-9263

National Association of Personnel Consultants (NAPC)
3133 Mt. Vernon Avenue
Alexandria, VA 22305
(703) 684-0180

National Association of Pupil Personnel Administrators (NAPPA)
225 North Washington Street
Alexandria, VA 22314
(703) 549-9117

National Association of Student Personnel Administrators (NASPA)
160 Rightmire Hall
1060 Cermaek Road
Columbus, OH 43210
(614) 422-4445

National Labor-Management Foundation (NLMF)
1901 L Street, N.W., Suite 711
Washington, DC 20036
(202) 296-8577

Newspaper Personnel Relations Association (NPRA)
11600 Sunrise Valley Drive
Reston, VA 22091
(703) 648-1000

Prentice-Hall Personnel Service
Prentice-Hall, Inc.
Sylvan Avenue
Englewood Cliffs, NJ 07632

Society for Human Resource Management (SHRM)
606 North Washington Street
Alexandria, VA 22314
(703) 548-3440

Special Interest Group for Computer Personnel Research (SIGCPR)
5776 Stoneridge Mall Road
Atrium, Suite 350
Pleasonton, CA 94566
(415) 463-2800

U.S. Chamber of Commerce
1615 H Street, N.W.
Washington, DC 20062

B. Government.

1. Federal.

Bureau of Labor Statistics (BLS)
Department of Labor
3rd Street and Constitution Avenue, N.W.
Washington, DC 20210

Department of Labor
3rd Street and Constitution Avenue, N.W.
Washington, DC 20210

Equal Employment Opportunity Commission (EEOC)
2401 E Street, N.W.
Washington, DC 20506

Federal Mediation and Conciliation Service
Washington, DC 20427

Occupational Safety and Health Administration (OSHA)
200 Constitution Avenue, N.W.
Washington, DC 20210

Office of Federal Contract Compliance (OFCC)
200 Constitution Avenue, N.W.
Washington, DC 20210

2. State Offices of Labor and Industrial Relations

Alabama:	Industrial Relations Office 649 Monroe Street Montgomery, AL 36104
Alaska:	Department of Labor Employment Security Building 416 Harris Street (P.O. Box 1149) Juneau, AK 99811
Arizona:	Labor Department Industrial Commission Commerce Building 1601 West Jefferson Street Phoenix, AZ 85007
Arkansas:	Department of Labor Capital Hill Building 4th & High Streets Little Rock, AR 72201
California:	Department of Industrial Relations State Building Annex 455 Golden Gate Avenue (P.O. Box 603, 94101) San Francisco, CA 94102
Colorado:	Division of Labor Department of Labor and Employment 1313 Sherman Street Denver, CO 80203
Connecticut:	Department of Labor 200 Folly Brook Boulevard Withersfield, CT 06109
Delaware:	Department of Labor 801 West Street Wilmington, DE 19801

Florida:

Division of Labor
Department of Labor and Employment Security
200 Ashley Building
1321 Executive Center Drive East
Tallahassee, FL 32301

Georgia:

Department of Labor
288 Labor Building
254 Washington Street, S.W.
Atlanta, GA 30334

Hawaii:

Department of Labor and Industrial Relations
Keelikolani Building
825 Mililani Street
Hononlulu, HI 96813

Idaho:

Department of Labor and Industrial Services
400 Industrial Administration Building
317 Main Street
Boise, ID 83702

Illinois:

Department of Labor
100 North 1st Street
Springfield, IL 62702

Indiana:

Division of Labor
1013 State Office Building
108 North Senate Avenue
Indianapolis, IN 46204

Iowa:

Bureau of Labor
307 East 7th Street
Des Moines, IA 50309

Kansas:

Employment Division
Department of Human Resources
401 Topeka Avenue
Topeka, KS 66603

Kentucky:

Bureau for Manpower Services
Department of Human Services
275 East Main Street
Frankfort, KY 40601

Louisiana:

Department of Labor
1001 North 23rd Street
Baton Rouge, LA 70802

Maine:

Bureau of Labor
Department of Manpower Affairs
State Office Building
Augusta, ME 04330

Maryland:

Division of Employment Services
Department of Human Resources
1100 North Eutaw Street
Baltimore, MD 21201

Massachusetts:

Department of Labor and Industries
Leverett Saltonstall State Office Building
100 Cambridge Street
Boston, MA 02202

Michigan:	Department of Labor 300 East Michigan Avenue Lansing, MI 48926
Minnesota:	Department of Labor and Industry Space Center Building 444 Lafayette Road St. Paul, MN 55101
Mississippi:	Employment Security Commission 1520 West Capitol Street Jackson, MS 39209
Missouri:	Department of Labor and Industrial Relations 421 East Dunklin Street Jefferson City, MO 65101
Montana:	Department of Labor and Industry 35 South Last Chance Gulch Helena, MT 59601
Nebraska:	Department of Labor 550 South 16th Street (P.O. Box 94600) Lincoln, NE 68509
Nevada:	Office of the Labor Commissioner 601 Kinkead Building 505 East King Street Capitol Complex Carson City, NV 89701
New Hampshire:	Department of Labor 1 Pillsbury Street Concord, NH 03301
New Jersey:	Public Employment Relations Commission Labor and Industry Building John Fitch Plaza Trenton, NJ 08625
New Mexico:	Labor and Industrial Commission 509 Camino de los Marquez Santa Fe, NM 87501
New York:	Department of Labor State Campus, Building 12 1220 Washington Avenue Albany, NY 12240
North Carolina:	Department of Labor Labor Building West Edenton Street (P.O. Box 27407) Raleigh, NC 27611
North Dakota:	Department of Labor State Capitol Bismarck, ND 58505
Ohio:	Department of Industrial Relations 2323 West 5th Avenue Columbus, OH 43204

Oklahoma: Department of Labor
                    118 State Capitol
                    Lincoln Blvd.
                    Oklahoma City, OK 73105

Oregon: Bureau of Labor and Industries
                    State Office Building
                    1400 S.W. 5th Avenue
                    Portland, OR 97201

Pennsylvania: Department of Labor and Industry
                    1700 Labor and Industry Building
                    Harrisburg, PA 17120

Rhode Island: Department of Labor
                    CIC Complex
                    220 Elmwood Avenue
                    Providence, RI 02908

South Carolina: Labor Department
                    Landmark Center
                    3600 Forest Drive
                    (P.O. Box 11329)
                    Columbia, SC 29211

South Dakota: Department of Labor
                    425 Joe Foss Building
                    Pierre, SD 57501

Tennessee: Department of Labor
                    501 Union Street
                    Nashville, TN 37219

Texas: Department of Labor and Standards
                    Sam Houston State Office Building
                    201 East 14th Street
                    (P.O. Box 12157, Capitol Station)
                    Austin, TX 78711

Utah: Division of Labor
                    Industrial Commission
                    350 East 500 Street, South
                    Salt Lake City, UT 84111

Vermont: Department of Labor and Industry
                    State Office Building
                    120 State Street
                    Montpelier, VT 05602

Virginia: Department of Labor and Industry
                    4th Street Office Building
                    205 North 4th Street
                    (P.O. Box 12064)
                    Richmond, VA 23241

Washington: Department of Labor and Industries
                    334 General Administration Building
                    Olympia, WA 98504

West Virginia: Department of Labor
                        B-451 State Office Building 6
                        1900 Washington Street, E.
                        Charleston, WV 25305

Wisconsin: Department of Industry, Labor and Human Rela-
                        tions
                        401 General Executive Facility 1
                        201 East Washington Avenue
                        (P.O. Box 7398)
                        Madison, WI 53707

Wyoming: Department of Labor and Statistics
                        Barrett Building
                        2301 Central Avenue
                        Cheyenne, WY 82002

District of   Department of Employment Services
  Columbia: 600 Employment Security Building
                        500 C Street, N.W.
                        Washington, DC 20001

C. Addresses of a sample of labor unions in the United States, listed
alphabetically by trade with membership figures and national affiliation.

AFL–CIO
815 16th Street, N.W.
Washington, DC 20006   *14,100,000*

Air Line Pilots Association, International (ALPA)
1625 Massachusetts Avenue, N.W.
Washington, DC 20036   *44,000*

International Union, United Automobile, Aerospace and Agricultural
  Implement Workers of America (UAW)
8000 West Jefferson
Detroit, MI 48214   *1,197,000*   *AFL-CIO*

United Brotherhood of Carpenters and Joiners of America (UBC)
101 Constitution Avenue, NW
Washington, DC 20001   *700,000*   *AFL-CIO*

Amalgamated Clothing and Textile Workers Union (ACTWU)
15 Union Square
New York, NY 10003   *272,669*   *AFL-CIO, CLC*

Communications Workers of America (CWA)
1925 K Street, N.W.
Washington, DC 20006   *650,000*   *AFL-CIO*

United Food and Commercial Workers International Union (UFCWIU)
Suffridge Building
1775 K Street, N.W.
Washington, DC 20006   *1,300,000*   *AFL-CIO*

American Federation of State, County and Municipal Employees
  (AFSCME)
1625 L Street, NW
Washington, DC 20036   *1,200,000*   *AFL-CIO*

International Association of Machinists and Aerospace Workers (IAM)
1300 Connecticut Avenue
Washington, DC 20036   *800,000*   *AFL-CIO*

International Union, United Mine Workers of America (UMWA)
900 15th Street, N.W.
Washington, DC 20005   *240,000*

Oil, Chemical and Atomic Workers International Union (OCAW)
P.O. Box 2812
Denver, CO 80201   *120,000*   *AFL-CIO*

American Postal Workers Union (APWU)
1300 L Street, N.W.
Washington, D.C. 20005   *320,000*   *AFL-CIO*

United Steel Workers of America (USWA)
Five Gateway Center
Pittsburgh, PA 15222   *750,000*   *AFL-CIO*

American Federation of Teachers (AFT)
555 New Jersey Avenue, N.W.
Washington, D.C. 20001   *715,000*   *AFL-CIO*

National Education Association (NEA)
1201 16th Street, N.W.
Washington, DC 20036   *1,600,800*

International Brotherhood of Teamsters, Chauffeurs, Warehousemen
   and Helpers of America (IBT)
25 Louisiana Avenue, N.W.
Washington, DC 20001   *2,000,000*

CAREER PLANNING

· · · · · · ·

Career planning is an individualized process. Each of us has a unique set of values, interests, and work and personal experiences. Understanding how this unique set of factors blends is an important part of career planning. But it is also necessary to understand the requirements of various jobs so that your own personality and intellectual abilities can be matched with the job. Your career decisions will shape your lifestyle.

College students eventually have to find out how they fit into the spectrum of career choices available. The purpose of this appendix is to provide:

1. A few career basics and hints on self-assessment.
2. Information on the mechanics of getting a job.

CAREER BASICS AND SELF-ANALYSIS

First, before thinking about specific career areas, sit back and spend some time mulling over those things that you want from a career. Here are a few questions to consider:

- Do you want a job or a career? Do you want it to be personally satisfying, or are the financial rewards enough? How important is career advancement?
- Are the status and prestige associated with a career important to you?
- What about financial rewards?

- Do you have geographical preferences? What about living in a large versus a small city?
- What size employer would you prefer? Might this preference change later on?

Now, think about yourself for a minute.

- What education, experience, and skills do you have to offer?
- Are you quantitatively ("thing") oriented or qualitatively ("people") oriented, or do you enjoy both? There is a place for both types in organizations.
- What are your weak and strong points? How will they relate to your performance on the job?
- What kind of work is interesting to you?
- What kind of work do you like?
- What kind of work will make you feel worthwhile?

A personal evaluation of these and similar questions is a worthwhile exercise. These questions may help you develop a job or career identity.

Professional Help for Self-Assessment

Professional counselors can help you decide which career path to take. Most high schools and colleges provide free counseling services, where trained professionals help a person perform a realistic self-assessment.

Vocational tests are often used to verify one's self-analysis and to reveal any hidden personal characteristics. This test information is then explained and interpreted by professional counselors. No one test or battery of tests can make a career choice for you. But tests can supplement the information you are reviewing as you mull over career opportunities and personal characteristics. Your college placement office has counselors who can recommend which tests are most appropriate.

In addition, the counselor can help you with your self-assessment by providing publications discussing career opportunities. Some widely publicized and frequently used publications include:

- *College Placement Annual*, College Placement Council, Inc., 62 Highland Avenue, Bethlehem, PA 18017 (215) 868-1421. Published annually. Provides information on current job openings in companies, as well as suggestions on preparing résumès and interviewing for jobs.
- *Occupational Outlook Handbook*, U.S. Department of Labor, Government Printing Office, Washington, D.C. (202) 783-3238. Published annually. Lists all major companies, with a brief description of job requirements, opportunities available, and future job prospects.

Self-assessment, help from a professional counselor, and career publications can provide the necessary background information to properly plan your career. But in the final analysis, you alone must make the career decision and seek appropriate job opportunities. A counselor, parent, or friend cannot make a career decision for you.

THE JOB SEARCH: A PLAN

In school, you prepare for examinations by organizing your notes and planning. In searching for a job, you also need to organize and plan. The first job after college can affect your entire career, so a plan is a must. Without a plan, you will lose valuable time and experience unnecessary frustration. There is no single best job-search plan, but there are some basic principles. Because your time is limited, you should use a systematic procedure to narrow the number of job possibilities.

When evaluating any particular career, there are some specific issues that you should consider. As you think over the broad career options available, examine them with the following areas in mind:

- What are the qualifications for the job? Will you need more education, more experience?
- What is the financial situation? Is the salary reasonable? How are the benefits? What salary is likely in three to five years? Is there going to be a conflict between the value you place on money and your returns from this job?
- What are the opportunities for advancement? Do these appear to jibe with your aspirations?
- What is the present supply and demand status for this field and what might it be in the future?
- Will the job involve much travel? Is that desirable or undesirable? How mobile are you?
- What is the atmosphere associated with the job? Is it pressure-filled, demanding, cooperative, tranquil, or creative?
- Is this job something that you will be proud of? Does it fit your self-image?
- Is it work that you will enjoy? Is it in line with your goals and ethics? Will you be happy?

Within any given career choice, one faces a number of prospective employers. Each company offers different conditions, opportunities, and rewards to its employees. Here are some important questions to ask about the firms you are considering:

- Does the company have opportunities for a person with my skills, aptitudes, and goals?
- What are the promotion opportunities in the company?
- Does the company usually promote from within?
- What type of professional development is available for new employees?
- What kind of working environment exists within the company?
- What is the future growth potential for the company and the industry?

Answers to these kinds of questions will enable you to narrow the available job opportunities. Answers can be found in such sources as company annual reports, *Standard and Poor's Corporation Records*, and *Dun and Bradstreet's Reference Book of*

Manufacturers. Another source is the company's employees. If you know some employees, ask them for first-hand information.

Most companies furnish brochures on career opportunities. These sources are impressive, but they often give a totally positive picture of the company. Consult your school's placement officer to learn more about each company and to determine the accuracy of the brochures.

There are two other sources you should consult — newspapers and professional magazines. The classified ads, especially in the Sunday or weekend editions, provide a lot of job information. These advertisements usually provide information about job vacancies, the type of people the company is looking for, and the person or post office box to contact if you are interested. An outstanding listing of job opportunities appears in *The Wall Street Journal.* It lists jobs at the highest level as well as openings at the supervisory level.

Professional magazines, such as *Personnel Journal, Training and Industry, Human Resource Management,* and *Nation's Business,* often list vacancies. These advertisements are for recent graduates or people with work experience. If you are interested in a particular occupation, consulting the professional magazines in that functional area can be helpful. Specialized trade journals are also good sources for job leads. Even the Yellow Pages in phone directories are a helpful guide to companies operating in a particular area. Talk to family, friends, faculty members, and others who may know of job leads or people with pertinent information.

PERSONALIZING THROUGH A RÈSUMÈ

After personal and professional self-assessments and a job search via newspapers, professional magazines, and employment agencies, the next step is to personalize your campaign. You must communicate to others who you are. The basic devices used to communicate are the rèsumè, letters, the telephone, and personal interviews.

A *rèsumè* is a written summary of who you are. It is a concise picture of you and your credentials for a job. A rèsumè should highlight your qualifications, achievements, and career objectives. It should be designed to present you as an attractive candidate for a job.

There is no generally accepted format for a rèsumè. Its purpose is to introduce you to the employer and to get you an interview. Few, if any, employers hire college graduates solely on the contents of a rèsumè. In most cases, you can attract attention with a one-page rèsumè. Longer rèsumès are for people who have had extensive professional experience.

Employees like rèsumès that read well and look attractive. Rèsumès read well if they are concise, grammatically correct, and easy to follow. Rèsumès look more inviting if they are reproduced on an offset press on high-quality paper. There are companies that prepare professional rèsumès for a fee. The Yellow Pages in the telephone directory can provide names of firms that sell this service.

Other elements found in good rèsumès are job objectives, educational background, college activities, work experiences, and references. The arrangment of these elements is a personal decision. But keep the rèsumè uncluttered and neatly blocked, to create an attractive and informative rèsumè with eye appeal. Exhibit 1 presents an example of an effective rèsumè.

It may be necessary to prepare a different rèsumè for each employer, so that your credentials can be slanted for the job openings. Whether you think a different rèsumè for each company can do the job is a decision that only you can make.

Just as important as the point to include are some points to avoid in preparing your rèsumè. *Don't:*

- State what salary you want.
- Send a rèsumè with false information.
- Send a rèsumè that is sloppy and contains typographical or grammatical errors.
- Clutter your rèsumè with unnecessary information.
- Inform employers that you will accept only a certain kind of position.
- Use fancy colors or gimmicks to sell yourself.

A cover letter should accompany the rèsumè. The objective of the cover letter is to introduce you. It can also encourage the employer to read your rèsumè and meet with you. The cover letter should

EXHIBIT 1   Sample Rèsumè

JILL M. MURPHY
4896 CRELING DRIVE
NEW YORK, NY 10011
(212) 431-0019

OBJECTIVE

A challenging position in marketing, utilizing analytical and problem-solving skills.

EDUCATION

Sept. 1985
May 1990

NEW YORK UNIVERSITY
School of Business Administration
Major: Marketing and Finance
G.P.A. 3.9; Dean's List; NYU Tuition scholarship

School of Social Sciences
G.P.A. 3.9; Dean's List; concentration in mathematics and psychology.

Sept. 1982
June 1985

NOTRE DAME HIGH SCHOOL
G.P.A. 3.9
Class Honors; Phi Beta Kappa; National Honor Society; State Champion, Women's Extemporaneous Speaking, 1979; Major Delegation Award at National Model United Nations in Washington, D.C., 1978, 1979.

EXPERIENCE

May 1990
present

Assistant Marketing Manager, PepsiCo.
Responsibilities included the coordination of planning, implementing and evaluating the Pepsi Challenge Program in New York City. This required close liaison with PepsiCo's marketing and sales activities as well as its advertising agency and the media. Achieved increase of over 100% in program participants, totaling over 60,000 people.

Planned and implemented a Mountain Dew sampling program.

On own initiative, developed a Coordinator's Handbook which PepsiCo plans to distribute nationwide.

Sept. 1987
May 1988

Vice President, Alpha Kappa Gamma Sorority
Responsible for housing policies, human resource planning, and discipline.

Sept. 1986
Sept. 1987

Assistant Treasurer, Alpha Kappa Gamma Sorority
Responsible for funds to finance all sorority events. Included collection, recording and billing for sixty-five individual accounts.

Summer 1986

Salesperson, Revlon, Inc.

Summer 1985

Information Manager, Summer Concert Series at New York University

ACTIVITIES

Project Director, Marketing Club at New York University; Seminar for Republican Campaign Coordinators, Washington, D.C.; New York University Campus Orchestra; NYC Symphony Youth Orchestra.

REFERENCES

Available on request

not duplicate the more detailed rèsumè. Instead, it should add to what is presented in the rèsumè and show that you are really interested in working for the company. The cover letter also reveals how well you can communicate. This clue is often used by employers to put prospective employees into one of two categories: a good communicator or a poor communicator.

Employers receive cover letters and rèsumès from many more job applicants than they could ever hire or even interview. Therefore, they screen whatever letters and rèsumès they receive. Screening is often accomplished rather quickly, so it is better to present your story and objectives concisely and neatly.

The number of letters and rèsumès you send depends on your strategy. Some people narrow down their list of organizations to the ones they really would like to work for and prepare a personal cover letter to accompany the rèsumè. Other candidates use a "shotgun" approach. They mail numerous letters and rèsumès to any company with an opening in a particular area of interest. The newspapers, professional magazines, listings in the placement office, telephone directories, directories or organizations, and tips from friends are used to develop a potential list. Then perhaps as many as 200 letters and rèsumès are sent out.

THE INTERVIEW STRATEGY

An outstanding cover letter, rèsumè, and job-search strategy are not enough to get you the job you want. You must also perform well at the interview. The interview is an oral presentation with a representative of a company. A good recruiter is interested in how a job candidate expresses himself or herself. The interviewer is both an information source and an information prober. As an information source, the interviewer provides you with knowledge about careers in the organization and the company in general. As a prober, the interviewer wants to determine what makes you tick and what kind of person you are.

An Interview Plan

In searching for job openings, it is necessary to have a plan. This is also the case in having a successful interview. In order to do a good job at the interview, you must be thoroughly prepared. Of course, you must know yourself and what type of career you want. The interviewer will probe into the areas you covered in your self-assessment and in developing a career objective. During the interview, you must make it clear why a person with your strengths and objectives should be hired by the company.

The preparation for answering the question "Why you?" involves some homework. You should gather facts about the employer. Annual reports, opinions from employees of the firm, brochures, up-to-date financial data from *The Wall Street Journal*, and recent newspaper articles can be used. Exhibit 2 identifies some of the information that can be used to prepare for the interview. Whether the initial interview is on the campus or in the office of the president of the company, prior preparation will impress the interviewer. This prepared-

---

EXHIBIT 2   Homework Information for the Interview

Location of headquarters, offices, plants
Officers of the organization
Future growth plans of the company
Product lines
Sales, profit, and dividend picture
Price of stock (if available)
Competitors of the company
Organizational structure
Kind of entry-level positions available
Career paths followed by graduates
Union situation
Type of programs available for employees (stock option, medical, educational)

ness will allow you to explore other important areas about the company that you don't know about. It will also allow the interviewer to probe into such areas as your grades, motivation, maturity, ability to communicate, and work experience. This information is important for the company in making a decision whether to have you visit for a second, more in-depth interview.

Interview preparation also involves your personal appearance and motivational state. There isn't enough space here to focus extensively on dress, hair, and value codes. The next best advice is to be yourself and to come prepared to meet with a representative of the organization. If you are to work as an accountant for some firm, then you must comply with standards of performance as well as dress and appearance codes. Use your own judgment, but be realistic: Employers don't like shoulder-length hair on a male salesperson or barefooted production supervisors. These biases will not be corrected in an interview, so don't be a crusader for a cause. The interview is not the best place to project a personal distaste for or discomfort with dress or hair-length standards.

Interviewing makes most people slightly nervous. But if you are well-prepared and really motivated to talk to the representative, the interview will probably go well. Consider the interview as a challenge you can meet because you are interested in succeeding. An alert candidate with modest confidence has a good chance of impressing the interviewer.

The Actual Interview

The interview has been called a conversation with a purpose. During the interview, the company representative and the candidate both attempt to determine if a match exists. Are you the right person for the job? The attempt to match person and job follows a question-and-answer routine. The ability to answer questions quickly, honestly, and intelligently is important. The best way to provide a good set of answers is to be prepared.

Exhibit 3 provides a list of some commonly asked questions. The way you answer these and similar questions is what the interviewer evaluates. Remember that the interviewer is trying to get to know you better by watching and listening.

One effective way to prepare for the interview session is to practice answering the questions in Exhibit 3 before attending the actual interview. This does not mean to develop "pat" or formal answers, but to be ready to intelligently respond. The sincerity of the response and the intelligent organization of an answer must come through in the interview.

Most interviewers eventually get around to asking about your career plans. The purpose of asking these kinds of questions is to determine your reasonableness, maturity, motivation, and goals. The important point is to illustrate by your response that you have given serious thought to your career plans. An unrealistic, disorganized, or unprepared

---

EXHIBIT 3   Some Questions Frequently Asked by Interviewers

Why do you want to work for our company?

What kind of career do you have planned?

What have you learned in school to prepare for a career?

What are some of the things you are looking for in a company?

How has your previous job experience prepared you for a career?

What are your strengths? Weaknesses?

Why did you attend this school?

What do you consider to be a worthwhile achievement of yours?

Are you a leader? Explain.

How do you plan to continue developing yourself?

Why did you select your major?

What can I tell you about my company?

career plan is one way to fail in the interview. Interviewers consider a candidate immature if he or she seems to be still searching and basically confused.

At various points in the interview, it may be appropriate to ask questions. These questions should be important and should not be asked just to appear intelligent. If something is important in evaluating the company, ask the question. It is also valuable if you can ask a question that displays meaningfulness. But don't ask so many questions that the interviewer is answering one after the other. Some frequently asked questions are summarized in Exhibit 4.

The majority of interviews last between 20 and 30 minutes. It is best to close on a positive and concise note. Summarize your interests, and express whether you are still interested in the company. Interviewers will close by stating that you will hear from the company. You may want to ask if he or she can give you an approximate idea of how long it will be before you hear from them. Typically, an organization will contact a candidate within four or five weeks after the interview.

One valuable practice to follow after the actual interview is to write down some of the points covered. List the interviewer's name, when the company will contact you, and your overall impression of the company. These notes can be useful if you are called for a later interview. Any person talking to 10 or more companies usually has some trouble recalling the conversation if no notes are available.

One issue that may or may not come up during the interview is salary. Most companies pay a competitive starting wage. Therefore, it is really not that important to ask what your starting salary will be. Individuals with similar education, experience, and background are normally paid the same. Instead of asking about salary in the initial interview, do some checking in the placement office at your school or with friends working in similar jobs.

Should you send a thank you letter after the interview? This seems to be a good way to refresh the interviewer's memory. The follow-up letter should be short. Expressing your appreciation for the interview shows sincerity. It also provides an opportunity to state that you are still interested in the company.

Interviewers are important processors of information for the company, so it is important to impress them at the interview. Unfortunately, not every candidate can win (winning means that the candidate will be asked to visit the company or to undergo further interviewing). "Why was I rejected?" is a question everyone has to ask at some point. Exhibit 5 lists some of the reasons why candidates are not successful in an interview.

VISITING THE COMPANY AND THE JOB OFFER

If you are fortunate enough to be invited for a company visit, consider yourself successful. The letter of invitation or telephone message will specify

---

EXHIBIT 4   Some Questions Frequently Asked by Job Candidates

How is performance evaluated?

How much transfer from one location to another is there?

What is the company's promotion policy?

Does the company have development programs?

How much responsibility is a new employee given? Can you provide me with some examples?

What preferences are given to applicants with graduate degrees?

What type of image does the company have in the community?

What schools provide the bulk of managerial talent in the company?

What are the company's policies for paying for graduate study?

What social obligations would I have?

What community service obligations would I have?

EXHIBIT 5   Some Reasons for Not Winning

Disorganized and not prepared
Sloppy appearance
Abrasive and overbearing
Unrealistic goals or image of oneself
Inability to communicate effectively
No interest shown in the type of company interviewed
Not alert
Poor grades
Only interested in money
Provided contradictory answers to questions

---

some available dates. If you are still interested in the company, you must send a formal acceptance. Even if you are not interested in visiting, a short note thanking the company displays your courtesy.

In some cases, your visit will be coordinated by the interviewer you already met. However, it may be the personnel department or management development officer who handles the details. The important point is not who will be coordinating but that you must again prepare for a series of interviews. During this series, you should be asking specific questions about job duties, performance expectations, salary, fringe benefits, and career paths. It is at this phase of the career and employment decision process that you need this kind of information.

One of the main reasons for inviting candidates to visit the company is to introduce them to managers and the organization. These introductions will be brief, but they are important. It is reasonable to expect to meet five or more individuals during the company visit. In some cases, you will be given a tour of the plant, office, or laboratory. A wide array of people will be asked to comment on your employability after you leave. So consider every interview important, and remember to act alert, organized, and interested. You may be bored because many questions are repeated by different managers, but remember that sincerity and interest are variables that these managers will each be asked to comment on.

During the company visit, you will probably not be given a job offer. In most situations, a week to two weeks may pass before the company contacts you. If you are successful, you will receive a formal job offer. After receiving the offer, make an immediate acknowledgment. Thank the employer and indicate an approximate date when you will furnish a decision.

A CONCLUDING NOTE

This appendix has focused on planning. Self-assessment, seeking professional help, the job search, personalizing your job campaign, interviewing, and visiting companies all involve prior planning. The person who plans his or her campaign to find a worthwhile and satisfying job will be more successful than the disorganized person. Thus, the most important principle in finding the best job for you is to work hard at planning each stage. Good luck!

Additional Reference on Business Careers

Bolles, Richard N., *What Color Is Your Parachute?* 1991.

GLOSSARY

· · · · · · ·

Chapter 1

human resource management (HRM) A function performed in organizations which facilitates the most effective use of people (employees) to achieve organizational and individual goals. Terms used interchangeably with HRM include *personnel, human resource management,* and *employee development.*

HRM objectives Objectives are the ends a department such as HRM is attempting to accomplish. Some of the specific HRM objectives are: (1) to provide the organization with well-trained and well-motivated employees; (2) to communicate HRM policies to all employees; and (3) to employ the skills and abilities of the work force efficiently.

HRM policy A general guide to decision making in important decision areas.

HRM procedure A specific direction to action. It tells a person how to do a particular activity.

Chapter 2

external HRM influences The environmental forces outside the organization, such as unions, government, and economic conditions.

internal HRM influences Those internal (inside the organization) environmental forces, such as goals, organizational style, tasks, work group, and the leader's style of influencing.

motivation The attitudes that predispose a person to act in a specific goal-directed way. It is an internal state that directs a person's behaviors.

personality The characteristic way a person thinks and behaves in adjusting to his or her environment. It includes the person's traits, values, motives, genetic blueprint, attitudes, abilities, and behavior patterns.

productivity The output of goods and services per unit of input of resources used in a production process.

strategy What an organization's key executives hope to accomplish in the long run.

work group Two or more people who work together to accomplish a goal and who communicate and interact with each other.

Chapter 3

adverse impact A situation in which a significantly higher percentage of members of a protected group (women, blacks, Hispanics) in the available population are being rejected for employment, placement, or promotion.

affirmative action Gives preferential treatment in hiring, recruitment, promotion, and development to groups that have been discriminated against.

Age Discrimination Act of 1967 (amended 1978) Protects workers between the ages of 40 and 70 against job discrimination.

Americans with Disabilities Act 1990 A comprehensive, anti-discrimination law aimed at integrating the disabled into the workplace. It prohibits all employers from discriminating against disabled employees or job applicants when making employment decisions.

Civil Rights Act, Title VII 1964 An important law that prohibits employers, unions, employment agencies, and joint labor-management committees controlling apprenticeship or training programs from discriminating on the basis of race, color, religion, sex, or national origin.

Equal Employment Opportunity Commission (EEOC) The Civil Rights Act, Title VII, 1964 gave the EEOC limited powers of resolving charges of discrimination and interpreting the meaning of Title VII. Later in 1972, Congress gave EEOC the power to bring lawsuits aginst employers in the federal courts.

equal employment opportunity programs (EEO) Programs implemented by employers to prevent employment discrimination in the workplace or to take remedial action to offset past employment discrimination.

Pregnancy Discrimination Act of 1978 This law makes it unlawful to discriminate on the basis of pregnancy, childbirth, or related medical conditions in employment-type decisions.

Rehabilitation Act of 1973 An act that is enforced by the Office of Federal Contract Compliance Programs (OFCCP), requires that all employers with government contracts of $2,500 or more must set up affirmative action programs for the handicapped.

sexual harassment Unwelcome sexual attention that causes the recipient distress and results in an inability on the part of the recipient to effectively perform the job requirements.

The 4/5ths rule Discrimination is likely to occur if the selection rate for a protected group is less than 4/5ths of the selection rate for a majority group.

Chapter 4

culture shock The feelings of frustration and confusion that result from being constantly subjected to strange and unfamiliar cues about what to do and how to get it done when trying to live in a new culture.

ethnocentric HRM perspective A view of HRM where an organization thinks that the way of doing things in the parent country is the best way, no matter where business is being done.

expatriate manager A manager who is on assignment in a country other than the parent country of the organization. This person is also called a *parent country national* (PCN).

Foreign Corrupt Practices Act of 1977 A law that makes it illegal for a U.S. organization to pay bribes to foreign officials for the purpose of getting a competitive advantage in doing business

host country national An employee of an international organization who is from the local work force rather than being from the parent country of the organization

multinational corporation An international organization with operations that are defined by national boundaries to a greater extent than in a global corporation.

parent country national A manager from the corporation's home country who is on assignment in another country. Usually called an expatriate.

repatriation The process of being reintegrated back into domestic operations after being on an international assignment outside of the United States.

geocentric HRM perspective A view of HRM where nationality is ignored and managers are hired on the basis of qualifications, not on their nationality.

global corporation A corporation with a geocentric HRM perspective. National boundaries are ignored and HRM is viewed as a way of integrating operations all over the world.

third country national A manager working for an international organization who is from a country other than the parent country of the organization or from the host country in which the assignment is located.

Chapter 5

executive information system (EIS) A specialized information system used by top level executives in HR planning.

human resource information system (HRIS) The method used by an organization to collect, store, analyze, report, and evaluate information and data on people, jobs and costs.

human resource planning The process that helps to provide adequate human resources to achieve future organizational objectives. It includes forecasting future needs for employees of various types, comparing these needs with the present work force, and determining the numbers or types of employees to be recruited or phased out of the organization's employment group.

replacement chart A display or chart usually of technical, professional, and managerial employees. It includes name, title, age, length of service, and other relevant information on present employees.

skills inventory A list of the names, personal characteristics, and skills of the people working for the organization. It provides a way to acquire these data and makes them available where needed in an efficient manner.

strategic planning In simple terms, the process of determining what an organization's mission is and how it plans to achieve the goals that are associated with the mission.

Chapter 6

autonomy The degree to which the job provides substantial freedom, independence, and discretion to the individual in scheduling the work and in determining the procedures to be used in carrying it out.

feedback The degree to which carrying out the work activities required by the job results in the individual's obtaining direct and clear information about the effectiveness of his or her performance.

functional job analysis (FJA) A job analysis method that attempts to identify what a worker does in performing a job in terms of data, people, and things.

Job. A group of positions that are similar in their duties, such as a computer programmer or compensation specialist.

job analysis The process of gathering, analyzing, and synthesizing information about jobs.

job analysis information format A questionnaire that provides the core information about a job, job duties, and job requirements.

job characteristics model A mode of job design that is based on the view that three psychological states toward a job affect a person's motivation and satisfaction level. These states are experienced meaningfulness, experienced responsibility, and knowledge of results. A job's skill variety, identity, and task significance contribute to meaningfulness; autonomy is related to responsibility; and feedback is related to knowledge of results.

job description The job analysis provides information about the job that results in a description of what the job entails.

job enlargement A method of designing jobs that increases the number of tasks performed by a job incumbent without increasing the level of responsibility. It is sometimes called horizontal job change.

job enrichment A method of designing a job so that employees can satisfy needs while performing the job. The job characteristics model is used in establishing a job enrichment strategy.

job family A group of two or more jobs that have similar job duties.

job specification A second product of job analysis. It is a written explanation of the knowledge, skills, abilities, traits, and other characteristics necessary for effective job performance.

Management Position Description Questionnaire (MPDQ) A checklist of 208 items related to concerns and responsibilities of managers.

position The responsibilities and duties performed by an individual. There are as many positions as there are employees.

Position Analysis Questionnaire (PAQ) A structured questionnaire of 194 items used to quantitatively assess jobs. It assesses information input, mental processes, work output, relationships, job contracts, and various other characteristics.

process chart A chart that displays how jobs are linked or related to each other.

skill variety The degree to which the job requires a variety of different activities in carrying out the work, which involves the use of a number of an individual's skills and talents.

strategic job analysis A form of job analysis that tries to predict what a job will look like in the future.

task A coordinated and aggregated series of work elements used to produce an output (units of production or service to a client).

task identity The degree to which the job requires completion of a "whole" and identifiable piece of work — that is, doing a job from beginning to end with a visible outcome.

task significance The degree to which the job has a substantial impact on the lives or work of other people — whether in the immediate organization or the external environment.

Chapter 7

applicant tracking system Computer programs that generate job requisition information and cross reference applicant qualifications with job openings.

employee leasing Paying a leasing firm to provide the organization with a ready-made pool of human resources.

executive search firm A "head hunting" firm that specializes in upper level executive recruitment. Executive search firms are usually on retainer and charge higher fees than regular employment agencies.

Immigration Reform and Control Act of 1986 All employers are required to screen every job applicants' eligibility for lawful employment. Thus, the employer has a major responsibility for not permitting illegal immigrants to be or remain employed.

job posting A listing of job openings that includes job specifications, appearing on a bulletin board or in company publications.

job search The set of activities a person (job candidate) initiates to seek and find a position that will be comfortable and rewarding.

realistic job preview A briefing that provides a job candidate with accurate and clear information about the attractive and unattractive features of a job. Being realistic so that expectations are accurate is the objective of a realistic job preview.

recruitment The set of activities an organization uses to attract job candidates who have the abilities and attitudes needed to help the organization achieve its objectives.

Chapter 8

assessment center A selection technique that uses simulations, tests, interviews, and observations to obtain information about candidates.

content validity The degree to which a test, interview, or performance evaluation measures skill, knowledge, or ability to perform.

construct validity A demonstrated relationship between underlying traits inferred from behavior and a set of test measures related to those traits.

criterion-related validity The extent to which a selection technique is predictive of or correlated with important elements of job behavior.

genetic screening The use of blood and urine samples to determine whether a job applicant carries genetic traits that could predispose him or her to adverse health effects when exposed to certain chemicals or job-related toxins.

reliability Refers to a selection technique's freedom from systematic errors of measurement or its consistency under different conditions.

selection The process by which an organization chooses from a list of applicants the person or persons who best meet the selection criteria for the position available, considering current environmental conditions.

structured interview Interview that follows a prepared pattern of questions that were structured before the interview was conducted.

utility When the use of a selection technique improves the quality of the persons hired. It is assessed using cost/benefit analysis.

weighted application blank An application form designed to be scored and used in making selection decisions.

Chapter 9

Behaviorally Anchored Rating Scale (BARS) A rating scale that uses critical incidents as anchor statements placed along a scale. Typically 6 to 10 performance dimensions, each with 5 to 6 critical incident anchors, are rated per employee.

Behavioral Observation Scale (BOS) A method similar to the BARS that uses the critical incident technique to identify a series of behaviors that describe the job. A 1 (Almost Never) to 5 (Almost Always) format is used to rate the behaviors.

central tendency error A rating tendency to give ratees an average rating on each criteria. That is, on a 1 to 7 scale, circling all 4s, or on a 1 to 5 scale, selecting all 3s.

contrast effect A rating error that occurs when a rater allows an individual's prior performance or other recently evaluated individuals to affect the ratings given to an employee.

criteria relevance A good measure of performance must be reliable, valid, and closely related to an employee's actual level of productivity.

criteria sensitivity A good measure of performance should reflect actual differences between high and low performers.

critical incident rating The system of selecting very effective and ineffective examples of job behavior and rating whether an employee displays the type of behaviors specified in the critical incidents.

forced-choice ratings A type of individually-oriented rating format where the rater must choose which of several statements about work behavior is most descriptive of an employee.

forced distribution A method of ranking similar to grading on a curve. Only certain percentages of employees can be ranked high, average, or low.

halo error A rating error that occurs when a rater assigns ratings on the basis of an overall impression (positive or negative) of the person being rated.

harshness rating error The tendency to rate everyone low on the criteria being evaluated.

leniency rating error The tendency to rate everyone on every criteria high or excellent.

management by objectives A managerial practice where managers and subordinates jointly plan, organize, control, communicate, and debate the subordinate's job and performance. As a performance evaluation technique, it focuses on establishing and measuring specific objectives.

paired-comparison rankings A method of ranking where subordinates are placed in all possible pairs and the supervisor must choose which of the two in each pair is the better performer.

performance evaluation The HRM activity that is used to determine the extent to which an employee is performing the job effectively.

personal bias rating error The bias that a rater has about individual characteristics, attitudes, backgrounds, and so on influence a rating more than performance.

recency of event rating error A rating tendency to use the most recent events to evaluate a ratee's performance instead of using a longer, more complete time frame.

Chapter 10

classification or grading system A job evaluation method that groups jobs together into a grade or classification.

comparable worth An issue that has been raised by women and the courts in recent years. It means that the concept of equal pay for equal jobs should be expanded to the notion of equal pay for comparable jobs. If a job is comparable to other jobs as determined by job content analysis, that job should be comparable.

compensation Compensation is the P/HRM function which deals with every type of reward that individuals receive in return for performing organizational tasks.

equal pay Equal pay for equal work for men and women. Equal work is defined as work requiring equal skills, effort, and responsibility under similar working conditions.

exempt employee A person working in a job that is not subject to the provisions of the Fair Labor Standards Act (1938) with respect to minimum wage and over-time pay. Most professional, executives, administrators, and outside salespersons are classified as exempt.

factor comparison method A job evaluation method that uses a factor-by-factor comparison. A factor comparison scale, instead of a point scale, is used. Five universal job factors used to compare jobs are; responsibilities, skills, physical effort, mental effort, and working conditions.

job evaluation The formal process by which the relative worth of various jobs in the organization is determined for pay purposes.

minimum wage The Fair Labor Standards Act of 1938, as amended, states that all employers covered by the law must pay an employee at least a minimum wage. In 1992 the minimum was $4.25 per hour.

nonexempt employee A person working in a job that is subject to the minimum wage and overtime pay provisions of the Fair Labor Standards Act. Blue-collar and clerical workers are two major groups of nonexempt employees.

pay class A convenient grouping of a variety of jobs that are similar in their work difficulty and responsibility requirements.

pay surveys Surveys of the compensation paid to employees by all employers in a geographic area, an industry, or an occupational group.

point system The most widely used job evaluation method. It requires evaluators to quantify the value of the elements of a job. On the basis of the job description or interviews with job occupants, points are assigned to the degree of various factors required to do the job.

ranking of jobs A job evaluation method often used in smaller organizations, in which the evaluator ranks jobs from the simplest to the most challenging—for example, clerk to research scientist.

red circle rates A pay rate above a wage or salary level that is considered maximum for the job class. This means that the job is overpaid and overrated.

Chapter 11

bonus A compensation payment that supplements salary and can be paid in the present or in the future.

COLA plans The adjustment of pay by automatic cost-of-living adjustment (COLA). In COLA plans, when the Bureau of Labor Statistic's Cost of Living In-

dex increases by a rounded percentage, the wages and salaries are automatically increased by that percentage.

gainsharing plans An organizational-based plan such as the Scanlon Plan designed to permit employer-employee sharing in the benefits resulting from improved productivity, cost reductions, or quality improvements.

improshare plan An industrial engineering-based productivity measurement and sharing plan developed in the mid-1970s by Mitchell Fein. In this plan there is an equal sharing among participating employees in all productivity gains.

incentive compensation Paying employees on the basis of output.

merit pay A reward that recognizes employees for superior past performance.

pay compression Occurs when employees perceive that there is too narrow a difference between their own pay and that of their colleagues.

profit-sharing plan A compensation plan in which payment of a regular share of company profits to employees is made as a supplement to their normal compensation.

Rucker plan A form of gainsharing plan based on employee involvement and suggestion systems which relate bonus earnings to financial performance.

salary Pay calculated at an annual or monthly rate rather than hourly.

Scanlon plan A combination group incentive, suggestion and employees participation plan developed by Joseph Scanlon. Gains from increased productivity are paid in bonus form to all employees.

skill-based pay A new alternative to the traditional job-based compensation system which rewards the individual for acquiring additional skills or knowledge.

spot gainsharing A short-term gainsharing scheme which focuses on a particular problem and specific department. Savings associated with the problem's solution less administrative costs are split between the company and its participating employees.

stock option Provides employees with the right to purchase company stock at a fixed price for a certain period of time.

two-tiered pay plans A pay structure in which the top pay for new employees is substantially lower than that for old (tenured) employees.

wage Pay calculated at an hourly rate.

Chapter 12

COBRA The Consolidated Omnibus Budget Reconciliation Act of 1985 requires that employers with more than 20 employees must offer continuation of health care coverage for 18 to 36 months after an employe is fired, quits, or is laid off.

ERISA Employment Retirement Income Security Act of 1974. ERISA is the law designed to cover practically all employee benefit plans of private employers, including multiemployer plans.

ESOP An employee stock ownership plan authorized by Congress and funded through the mechanism of an employee stock ownership trust (ESOT).

fiduciary A fiduciary is a person responsible for pension trust funds.

flexible (cafeteria) benefits plan A benefits plan which allows employees to choose between two or more types of benefits.

HMO A health maintenance organization is a medical organization consisting of medical and health specialists which stresses preventive medicine.

indirect financial compensation All financial rewards (benefits and services) which are not included in direct financial compensation.

IRA An individual retirement account.

mandated benefit Three types of benefits which an employer must provide employees because of state and federal regulations: unemployment insurance, social security, and workers compensation.

OBRA Omnibus Budget Reconciliation Act of 1989. Amendment which modifies coverage under COBRA.

portability The right to transfer pension credits accrued from one employer to another.

reimbursement account An account into which employees can place tax-deferred funds which can be used to pay for expenses not covered by the regular benefits package.

SEP-IRA Simplified employee pension-IRAs which can be implemented by small employers to help employees finance their retirements.

social security The federally mandated pension fund which was designed to provide *some* income to retired persons to *supplement* savings, private pensions and part-time work.

unemployment insurance A state mandated insurance benefit designed to provide a subsistence payment to employees between jobs.

vesting The right of employees to participate in a pension plan.

workers' compensation Disability and death benefits mandated and administered by the states.

401(k) The section of the Internal Revenue Code which allows employees to save on a tax-deferred basis by entering into salary deferral agreements with an employer.

Chapter 13

apprentice training A combination of on-the-job and off-the-job training. The apprentice, while learning the job, is paid less than the master worker. Some of the jobs in which one serves as an apprentice include electrician, barber, tool and die maker, and plumber.

learning The act by which a person acquires skills, knowledge, and abilities that result in a relatively permanent change in his or her behavior.

management development The process by which managers gain the experience, skills, and attitudes to become or remain successful leaders in their organizations.

orientation The HRM activity that introduces new employees to the organization and the employee's new tasks, superiors, and work groups.

performance analysis A systematic procedure that is used to determine if training is needed to correct behavior deficiencies.

training The systematic process of altering the behavior of employees in a direction to increase organizational goals.

vestibule training A trainee learns a job in an environment that closely resembles the actual work environment. For example, pilots at United Airlines train (vestibule) in a jet simulation cockpit.

Chapter 14

behavior modeling Participants learn by observing a role model behavior. The fundamental characteristic of modeling is that learning takes place by observation or imagination of another individual's experience.

case method A training technique in which a description (a case) of a real situation is analyzed by participants. The interaction of the participants and trainer is valuable in improving the degree of learning that occurs.

grid OD A program that involves six phases designed to improve organizational performance. The phases include determining the participants' leadership styles, team building, intergroup development, and evaluation.

role playing The acting out of a role by participants. Participants play act a role that others in the training session observe. Participants play an active part in role plays.

sensitivity training A training technique that was first used in 1946. In it small groups of participants focus on emotions and how they feel about themselves and the group. Usually little structure is imposed by the trainer. The group members are encouraged to say or do what they feel.

team building A development method that attempts to improve the cooperation between teams.

transactional analysis A training technique designed to help the people participating better understand their own ego states and those of others; to understand the principles behind transactions; and to interact with others in a more comfortable way.

Chapter 15

career Individually perceived sequences of attitudes and behaviors associated with work-related experiences and activities over the span of an individual's work life.

career path A sequence of positions through which an organization moves an employee.

career stages The distinct stages that individuals go through in their careers, typically: prework, initial work, stable work, and retirement.

dual-career couples A situation in which a husband and wife have careers.

glass ceiling A hypothetical barrier used to describe a barrier that seems to face minorities and women in advancing up the management hierarchy.

job layoff A condition that exists when no work is available and the employee is sent home, management views the no-work situation as temporary, and management intends to recall the employee.

job loss A condition in which there is no work and the individual is sent home permanently.

midcareer plateau A point reached during the adult stage of life where a person feels stifled and not progressing as he or she had planned or would like.

mentoring relationship A relationship between a junior and senior colleague that is considered by the junior person to be helpful in his or her personal development.

outplacement Service provided by some firms to individuals who are permanently asked to leave. The services may include resume preparation help, counseling, and training.

Chapter 16

hot stove rule A discipline program that is described in terms of touching a hot stove. There is an immediate burn, a warning system, consistency, and impersonal application of discipline.

progressive pattern of discipline A discipline program that proceeds from less severe disciplinary actions (a discussion) to a very severe action (being discharged). Each step in the progression becomes more severe.

termination-at-will A condition under which an employer is free to terminate the employment relationship, either for some specific reason, or even no reason at all. In a growing number of courts, the employer's right to terminate at will is being challenged.

Chapter 17

AFL-CIO A group of union members consisting of individuals that merged membership in 1955 from the American Federation of Labor and the Congress of Industrial Organizations.

agency shop A situation in which all employees pay union dues whether or not they are union members.

American Federation of Labor (AFL) A union group devoted to improving economic and working conditions for craft employees.

business representative The local union's representative who is responsible for negotiating and administering the labor agreement and for settling problems in connection with the contract.

closed shop A situation in which a new employee must be a union member when hired. Popular in the construction, maritime, and printing industries.

Congress of Industrial Organizations (CIO) A union formed by John L. Lewis, president of the United Mine Workers. It was formed to organize industrial and mass-production workers and was devoted to improving economic and working conditions.

craft union A group of individuals who belong to one craft or closely related group of occupations (e.g., carpenters, bricklayers).

guaranteed annual wages An agreement that guarantees regular employees a certain amount of money or hours of work. Its purpose is to provide some degree of economic security.

labor relations The continuous relationship between a defined group of employees (e.g., a union or association) and an employer.

Landrum-Griffin Act A labor law passed in 1959 that is referred to as the bill of rights of union members. It was designed to regulate and audit the internal affairs of unions.

Nation Labor Relations Board A government regulatory body that administers labor laws and regulations in the private and third sectors.

open shop A work situation in which neither a union is present nor is there a management effort to keep the union out.

preferential shop The union is recognized and union members are given preference in some areas. These preferences are in violation of the Taft-Hartley Act.

restricted shop A practice initiated by management to keep a union out without violating labor laws. A restricted shop is an attitude rather than a formal arrangement.

right-to-work laws A law that specifies that two persons doing the same job must be paid the same wages, whether or not they are union members. Nineteen states have right-to-work laws.

Taft-Hartley Act A labor amendment of the Wagner Act, passed in 1947, that guaranteed employees' bargaining rights and also specified unfair labor union practices that would not be permitted.

union A group of employees who have joined together to achieve present and future goals that deal with employment conditions.

union shop A situation in which an employee is required to join a union after being hired.

union steward A union representative who works at the job site to solve disputes that arise in connection with the labor-management labor contract.

Wagner Act A labor law passed in 1935 that was designed to encourage the growth of trade unions and restrain management from interfering with the growth.

yellow-dog contracts A contract (now illegal) that required that a person (such as a job applicant) would not join or form a union.

Chapter 18

arbitration A quasi-judicial process in which the parties agree to submit the unresolvable dispute to a neutral third party for binding settlement.

boycott A primary boycott finds union members not patronizing the boycotted firm. In a secondary boycott a supplier of a boycotted firm is threatened with a union strike unless it stops doing business with the firm. This type of boycott is illegal under the Taft-Hartley Act.

collective bargaining The process by which the representatives of the organization meet and attempt to work out a contract with representatives of the union.

decertification election An election in which employees who are represented by a union vote to drop the union.

grievance A complaint about a job that creates dissatisfaction or discomfort for the worker.

hot cargo agreement The employer permits union members to avoid working with materials that come from employers who have been struck by a union. This type of boycott is illegal.

lockout A management response to union pressures in which a skeleton crew of managerial personnel is used to maintain a workplace and the total plant is basically closed to employees.

mediation A process in which a neutral third party helps through persuasion to bring together labor and management. The dispute is settled because of the skills and suggestions of a mediator.

representation election A vote to determine if a particular group will represent the workers in collective bargaining.

strike An effort by employees to withhold their services from an employer in order to get greater concessions at the collective bargaining table.

Chapter 19

accident research The systematic evaluation of the evidence concerning accidents and health hazards.

AIDS Acquired Immune Deficiency Syndrome is an infectious disease in which the body's immune system is damaged. Thus, AIDS victims are susceptive to many diseases.

employee assistance programs (EAP) A program designed to help employees with personal, family, and work problems. Although these programs are voluntary, managers are instructed on how to confront the problems when they occur.

health The state of physical, mental, and social well-being.

health hazards Those aspects of the work environment which slowly and cumulatively (and often irreversibly) lead to deterioration of an employee's health.

life events The changes in a person's life that can contribute to stress.

Occupational Safety and Health Act (1970) An act designed to protect the safety and health of employees. According to this act, employers are responsible for providing workplaces free from hazards to safety and health.

Occupational Safety and Health Administration (OSHA) The government agency resonsible for carrying out and administering the Occupational Safety and Health Act.

preventive (wellness) programs A program instituted within an organization to achieve a high level of employee wellness and to decrease health impairment costs. Programs typically involve health screening exams, stress testing, and physician recommendations.

safety hazards Those aspects of the work environment that have the potential of immediate and sometimes violent harm to an employee.

stress A person's physical, chemical, and mental reactions to stressors or stimuli in the environment — the boss, co-workers, P/HRM policies, and so on.

type A behavior pattern An action-emotion complex

that can be observed in a person who is aggressive, in a struggle against time, competitive, and chronically impatient.

Chapter 20

compressed workweek (CWW) A work schedule in which a trade is made between the number of hours worked per day, and the number of days worked per week, in order to work the standard length hours — four days, 10 hours each day or three days, 12 hours each day are examples of the CWW schedule.

core work time A period of time in a flexitime work schedule in which all employees in a particular unit or group must be at work.

employee-centered work redesign The individual employee is permitted to redesign his or her job and set of job tasks. The employee, however, is held accountable for any creative changes made in changing the job.

flexitime work schedules A work schedule in which the employee is able to select his or her starting and quitting time within limits set by management.

flexible work time A period of time in a flexitime work schedule in which the employee is free to choose whether or not to be on the job.

job sharing A situation in which two or more part-timers share one job. The workers are part time, but the job is full time.

new design plants A plant that is constructed and laid out with inputs made by employees.

part-time employment A job in which a person works less than 25 hours a week. For federal employees, 32 hours a week is the dividing line between full- and part-time work.

quality circles A 4- to 15-person work group that usually meets once a week to solve work-related problems.

quality of work life The degree to which employees are able to satisfy their needs, goals, and aspirations while performing their jobs and working with colleagues.

Chapter 21

absenteeism The failure of employees to report to work when they are scheduled to do so.

attitude survey A set of written instruments completed by employees expressing their reactions to employer policies and practices.

Name Index

. . . .

COMPANY INDEX

· · · · · · ·

SUBJECT INDEX

• • • • • • •